CONTENTS

KU-071-199

Index   532

Maps

ON THE ROAD WITH FODOR'S

WE'RE ALWAYS THRILLED to get letters from readers, especially one like this:

It took us an hour to decide what book to buy and we now know we picked the best one. Your book was wonderful, easy to follow, very accurate, and good on pointing out eating places, informal as well as formal. When we saw other people using your book, we would look at each other and smile.

Our editors and writers are deeply committed to making every Fodor's guide "the best one"—not only accurate but always charming, brimming with sound recommendations and solid ideas, right on the mark in describing restaurants and hotels, and full of fascinating facts that make you view what you've traveled to see in a rich new light.

About Our Writers

Our success in achieving our goals—and in helping to make your trip the best of all possible vacations—is a credit to the hard work of our extraordinary contributors.

Dianne Aaronson, who revised the Mojave Desert and Death Valley chapter, is a long-time Californian, a fitness trainer and massage therapist who writes health and fitness articles for San Francisco Bay Area and other publications. Dianne "enjoyed the chance to share with readers what I've discovered on past trips to the desert—it's a grand, austere paradise with limitless potential for revelation." She has contributed to other Fodor's guides, including *San Francisco '96* and *'97* and *California's Best Bed & Breakfasts.*

Colleen Dunn Bates, who revised the Central Coast chapter, has southern California roots that go back to the mid-19th century—her great-great-great-grandfather was the first white settler in Ventura County. Like many California natives, Colleen is a lifelong surfer, "Though as the mother of two young daughters I don't get in the water as much these days," she says. On shore, Bates is the author of *The Eclectic Gourmet Guide to Los Angeles* and writes for several publications, among

them *Shape, Westways, Travel and Leisure,* and *Cooking Light.*

Deke Castleman, who updated the Lake Tahoe chapter, grew up in New York and Boston but fled the East Coast for the wide-open spaces of the American West. He discovered the region's many wonders while engaged in a variety of occupations—door-to-door vacuum-cleaner salesman in central California, tour guide at Alaska's Denali National Park, and locksmith on Lake Tahoe's north shore. Deke recently moved to Las Vegas, where he is senior editor of Huntington Press, a gambling publishing company.

Claudia Gioseffi, who updated the Wine Country, Sierra National Parks, and Monterey Bay chapters, brings an art, food, and wine background to *California '97.* The author of an ongoing series of artist profiles for Caldwell Snyder Galleries of New York and San Francisco, Claudia's travel writings have appeared in *Country Bed & Breakfast Inns.* A food writer and the former editor of the *Epicurean Rendezvous* guides, the San Francisco resident managed to cover every important restaurant in California, Florida, and New York—without gaining an ounce.

Jane E. Lasky, who updated the Los Angeles chapter, is a syndicated newspaper columnist, television producer, and author of several travel books. She also publishes articles in many national magazines such as *Vogue, Connoisseur, Los Angeles, Travel and Leisure,* and *Esquire.* She writes a monthly travel column for *Buzz* magazine.

Marty Olmstead, who revised the North Coast and Far North chapters, is the former travel editor of *San Francisco Focus* magazine, for which she crisscrossed the state many times. Accounts of her voyages around the globe have appeared in *Travel and Leisure,* the *Los Angeles Times, Geo, Glamour,* and the *San Francisco Chronicle.* Since 1989 she has lived in Sonoma County, which she "appreciates for its role in California's history and its proximity to grapes—the North Coast's most famous (legal) crop."

Bobbi Zane, who revised the Palm Springs chapter and wrote the Gold Country chapter, has been visiting the state's southern desert region since her grandfather, a Hollywood producer, took her on weekend getaways to La Quinta Resort. She became intrigued with the "haunting history to be discovered at every turn" in the Gold Country while working for a Sacramento television station in the 1960s. She returns to the area yearly. Bobbi's byline has appeared in the *Los Angeles Times, Los Angeles Daily News, Orange County Register,* and *San Jose Mercury News*. She has contributed to *California's Best Bed & Breakfasts* and *San Diego '97* among many other Fodor's titles. With her husband, Gregg, she publishes *Yellow Brick Road,* a monthly newsletter about bed-and-breakfast inns.

Daniel Mangin, the editor of *California '97,* recently moved to New York to work as a full-time editor at Fodor's after spending 20 years in the Golden State, most of them in San Francisco. He first traversed California as the stage manager and lighting director of two '70s punk rock bands, one of which, he reminisces with nary a trace of regret, "hit just short of the big time. One year we stayed at low-budget motels, the next year it was four-star hotels with private butlers and antique furniture (we were well-behaved rockers). The experience taught me what travelers of all budgets need and expect." Daniel writes about the arts for Bay Area and national publications, and for Fodor's has co-authored *Sunday in San Francisco* and edited *California's Best Bed & Breakfasts* and *San Diego '97.*

New This Year

This year we've reformatted our guides to make them easier to use. Each chapter of *California '97* begins with brand-new recommended itineraries or neighborhood walks to help you decide what to see in the time you have; a section following them points out the optimal time of day, day of the week, and season for your journey. You may also notice our fresh graphics. More readable and more helpful than ever? We think so—and we hope you do, too.

Also check out Fodor's Web site (http://www.fodors.com/), where you'll find travel information on major destinations around the world and an ever-changing array of travel-savvy interactive features.

How to Use This Book

Organization

Up front is the **Gold Guide.** Its first section, **Important Contacts A to Z,** gives addresses and telephone numbers of organizations and companies that offer destination-related services and detailed information and publications. **Smart Travel Tips A to Z,** the Gold Guide's second section, gives specific information on how to accomplish what you need to in California as well as tips on savvy traveling. Both sections are in alphabetical order by topic.

Each city chapter in *California '97* begins with an Exploring section, which is subdivided by neighborhood; each subsection recommends a walking or driving tour and lists sights in alphabetical order. Each regional chapter is divided by geographical area; within each area, towns are covered in logical geographical order, and attractive stretches of road and minor points of interest between them are indicated by the designation *En Route*. Throughout, Off the Beaten Path sights appear after the places from which they are most easily accessible. And within town sections, all restaurants and lodgings are grouped together.

To help you decide what to visit in the time you have, all the regional chapters begin with recommended itineraries; you can mix and match those from several chapters and the city tours to create a complete vacation. The A to Z section that ends all chapters covers getting there, getting around, and helpful contacts and resources.

At the end of the book you'll find Portraits, essays about California, followed by suggestions for pretrip reading, both fiction and nonfiction, and movies on tape with California as a backdrop.

Icons and Symbols

★ Our special recommendations

✕ Restaurant

🏠 Lodging establishment

✕🏠 Lodging establishment whose restaurant warrants a detour

⚠ Campground

☾ Rubber duckie (good for kids)

☞ Sends you to another section of the guide for more info

✉ Address

☎ Telephone number

☉ Opening and closing times

💳 Admission prices (those we give apply only to adults; substantially reduced fees are almost always available for children, students, and senior citizens)

Numbers in white and black circles—② and ❷, for example—that appear on the maps, in the margins, and within the tours correspond to one another.

Dining and Lodging

The restaurants and lodgings we list are the cream of the crop in each price range. Price charts appear in the Pleasures and Pastimes section that follows each chapter introduction.

Hotel Facilities

We always list the facilities that are available—but we don't specify whether they cost extra: When pricing accommodations, always ask what's included.

Restaurant Reservations and Dress Codes

Reservations are always a good idea; we note only when they're essential or when they are not accepted. Book as far ahead as you can, and reconfirm when you get to town. Unless otherwise noted, the restaurants listed are open daily for lunch and dinner. We mention dress only when men are required to wear a jacket or a jacket and tie. Look for an overview of local dining in the Pleasures and Pastimes section that follows each regional chapter's introduction.

Credit Cards

The following abbreviations are used: **AE**, American Express; **D**, Discover; **DC**, Diners Club; **MC**, MasterCard; and **V**, Visa.

Please Write to Us

You can use this book in the confidence that all prices and opening times are based on information supplied to us at press time; Fodor's cannot accept responsibility for any errors. Time inevitably brings changes, so always confirm information when it matters—especially if you're making a detour to visit a specific place. In addition, when making reservations be sure to mention if you have a disability or are traveling with children, if you prefer a private bath or a certain type of bed, or if you have specific dietary needs or any other concerns.

Were the restaurants we recommended as described? Did our hotel picks exceed your expectations? Did you find a museum we recommended a waste of time? If you have complaints, we'll look into them and revise our entries when the facts warrant it. If you've discovered a special place that we haven't included, we'll pass the information along to our correspondents and have them check it out. So send your feedback, positive and negative, to the *California '97* Editor at 201 East 50th Street, New York, New York 10022—and have a wonderful trip!

Karen Cure

Karen Cure
Editorial Director

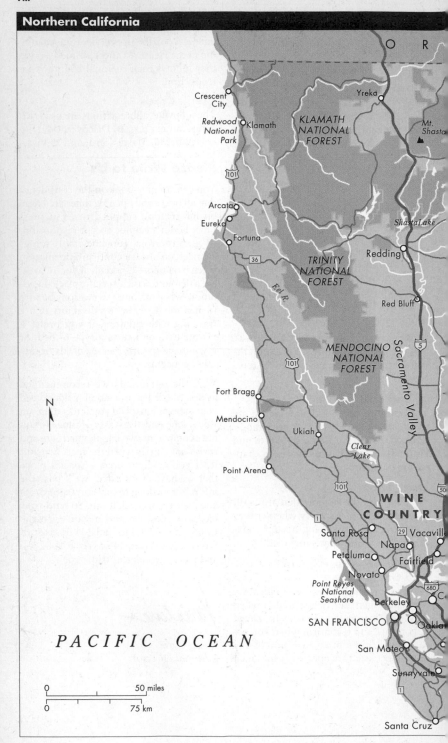

O R

Crescent
City

Yreka

Redwood
National
Park

Klamath

KLAMATH
NATIONAL
FOREST

Mt.
Shasta

▲

101

Arcata

Eureka

Fortuna

Shasta Lake

36

Redding

Eel R.

TRINITY
NATIONAL
FOREST

Red Bluff

5

101

MENDOCINO
NATIONAL
FOREST

Sacramento Valley

Fort Bragg

Mendocino

Ukiah

Clear
Lake

Point Arena

101

50

WINE
COUNTRY

1

Santa Rosa

29 Vacaville

Napa

Petaluma

Fairfield

Novato

680

Point Reyes
National
Seashore

Berkeley

C

SAN FRANCISCO

Oakla

San Mateo

Sunnyvale

PACIFIC OCEAN

1

N

0   50 miles

0   75 km

Santa Cruz

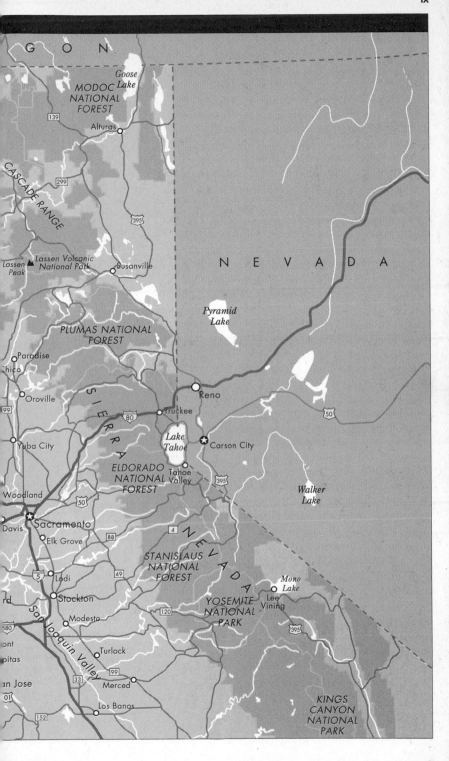

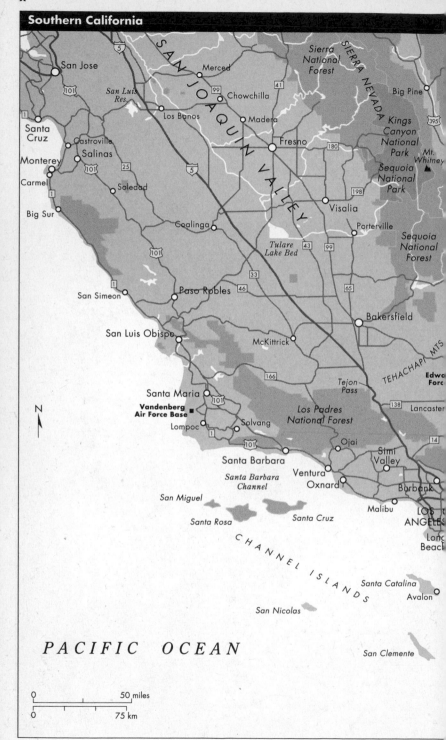

San Jose

San Luis
Res.

Merced

Chowchilla

Madera

Los Banos

Fresno

Santa
Cruz

Castroville

Salinas

Monterey

Carmel

Soledad

Big Sur

Coalinga

San Simeon

Paso Robles

San Luis Obispo

McKittrick

Santa Maria

**Vandenberg
Air Force Base** ■

Lompoc

Solvang

Santa Barbara

*Santa Barbara
Channel*

San Miguel

Santa Rosa

Ventura

Oxnard

Ojai

Simi
Valley

Burbank

Malibu

Santa Cruz

LOS
ANGELES

Long
Beach

Sierra
National
Forest

SIERRA NEVADA

SAN JOAQUIN VALLEY

Big Pine

Kings
Canyon
National
Park

Mt.
Whitney ▲

Sequoia
National
Park

Visalia

Porterville

Sequoia
National
Forest

*Tulare
Lake Bed*

Bakersfield

TEHACHAPI MTS

*Tejon
Pass*

Edwa
Forc

Lancaster

Los Padres
National Forest

N

CHANNEL ISLANDS

Santa Catalina

Avalon

San Nicolas

PACIFIC   OCEAN

San Clemente

0   50 miles

0   75 km

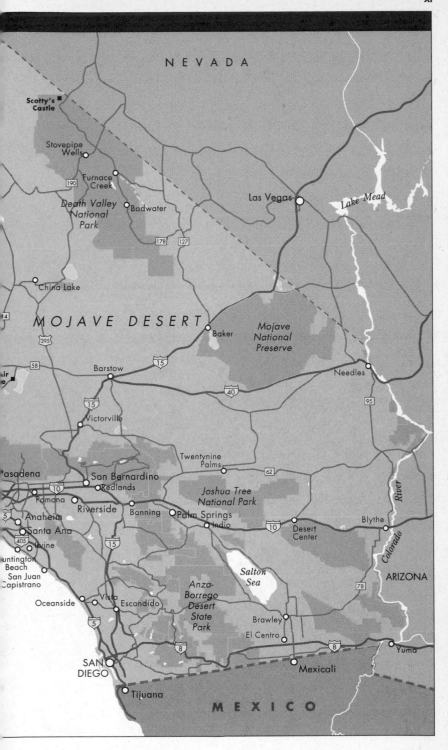

The United States

CANADA

BRITISH COLUMBIA
ALBERTA
SASKATCHEWAN
MANITOBA

Vancouver
Victoria
Seattle
Olympia
WASHINGTON
Portland
Salem
OREGON
Calgary
Regina
Winnipeg
Trans-Canada Hwy.
Great Falls
Missouri R.
Columbia R.
Spokane
MONTANA
Helena
NORTH DAKOTA
Fargo
Bismarck
IDAHO
Billings
Boise
Snake R.
SOUTH DAKOTA
Pierre
Missouri R.
WYOMING
Cheyenne
NEBRASKA
Lincoln
Carson City
Sacramento
San Francisco
NEVADA
Salt Lake City
UTAH
Denver
Colorado Springs
COLORADO
KANSAS
Fresno
Las Vegas
Colorado R.
CALIFORNIA
Santa Barbara
Los Angeles
San Diego
Flagstaff
ARIZONA
Phoenix
Tucson
Santa Fe
Albuquerque
NEW MEXICO
Amarillo
OKLAHOMA
Oklahoma City
PACIFIC OCEAN
BAJA CALIFORNIA
SONORA
El Paso
CHIHUAHUA
Rio Grande
TEXAS
Austin
San Antonio
Dallas
MEXICO
COAHUILA
NUEVO LEON
TAMAULIPAS

RUSSIA
ARCTIC OCEAN
Bering Strait
Nome
Bering Sea
ALASKA
Fairbanks
CANADA
Anchorage
Juneau
ALEUTIAN ISLANDS
PACIFIC OCEAN

0   400 miles
0   400 km
N

Honolulu
Oahu
Maui
HAWAII
Hawaii
PACIFIC OCEAN

World Time Zones

International Date Line

MONDAY
SUNDAY

+12 +13

-9

-10

-11

+11

+12

-10

-10

+11

+12

+11 +12 - -11 -10 -9 -8 -7 -6 -5 -4 -3 -2

-4

-3

-7

-5 -4

-5 -4

-3:30

-7

-6

-4

-5

-4 -3

-4

-3

-3

Numbers below vertical bands relate each zone to Greenwich Mean Time (0 hrs.).
Local times frequently differ from these general indications,
as indicated by light-face numbers on map.

Algiers, **29**	Berlin, **34**	Delhi, **48**	Istanbul, **40**
Anchorage, **3**	Bogotá, **19**	Denver, **8**	Jerusalem, **42**
Athens, **41**	Budapest, **37**	Djakarta, **53**	Johannesburg, **44**
Auckland, **1**	Buenos Aires, **24**	Dublin, **26**	Lima, **20**
Baghdad, **46**	Caracas, **22**	Edmonton, **7**	Lisbon, **28**
Bangkok, **50**	Chicago, **9**	Hong Kong, **56**	London
Beijing, **54**	Copenhagen, **33**	Honolulu, **2**	(Greenwich), **27**
	Dallas, **10**		Los Angeles, **6**
			Madrid, **38**
			Manila, **57**

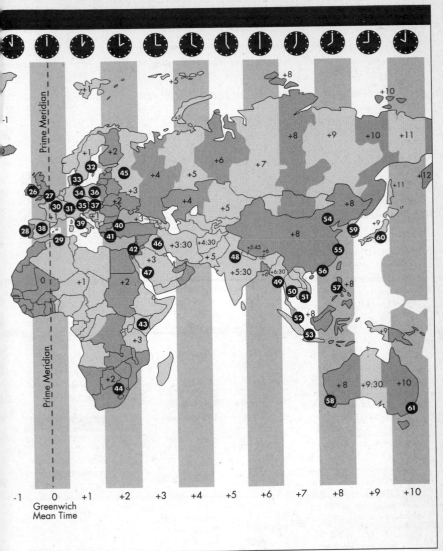

IMPORTANT CONTACTS A TO Z

An Alphabetical Listing of Publications, Organizations, and Companies that Will Help You Before, During, and After Your Trip

A

AIR TRAVEL

The major gateways to California include San Francisco International Airport (SFO) and Los Angeles International Airport (LAX). Flying time is roughly six hours from New York and four hours from Chicago. Flying between San Francisco and Los Angeles takes one hour.

CARRIERS

Carriers serving California include **Air Canada** (☎ 800/776–3000), **Alaska** (☎ 800/426–0333), **America West/America West Express** (☎ 800/235–9292), **American/American Eagle** (☎ 800/433–7300), **British Airways** (☎ 800/247–9297), **Continental** (☎ 800/525–0280), **Delta** (☎ 800/221–1212), **Japan Air Lines** (☎ 800/525–3663), **Midwest Express** (☎ 800/452–2022), **Northwest** (☎ 800/225–2525), **Reno Air** (☎ 800/736–6247), **SkyWest** (☎ 800/453–9417), **Southwest Airlines** (☎ 800/435–9792), **TWA** (☎ 800/221–2000), **United** (☎ 800/241–6522), and **USAir** (☎ 800/428–4322).

From the United Kingdom, carriers serving California include **American** (☎ 0345/789–789), **British Airways** (☎ 0181/897–4000; outside London, 0345/222–111), **Delta** (☎ 0800/414–767), **United** (☎ 0800/888–555), and **Virgin Atlantic** (☎ 01293/747–747).

COMPLAINTS

To register complaints about charter and scheduled airlines, contact the U.S. Department of Transportation's **Aviation Consumer Protection Division** (✉ C-75, Washington, DC 20590, ☎ 202/366–2220). Complaints about lost baggage or ticketing problems and safety concerns may also be logged with the **Federal Aviation Administration (FAA) Consumer Hotline** (☎ 800/322–7873).

PUBLICATIONS

For general information about charter carriers, ask for the Department of Transportation's free brochure **"Plane Talk: Public Charter Flights"** (✉ Aviation Consumer Protection Division, C-75, Washington, DC 20590, ☎ 202/366–2220). The Department of Transportation also publishes a 58-page booklet, **"Fly Rights,"** available from the Consumer Information Center (✉ Supt. of Documents, Dept. 136C, Pueblo, CO 81009; $1.75).

For other tips and hints, consult the Consumers Union's monthly **"Consumer Reports Travel Letter"** (✉ Box 53629, Boulder, CO 80322, ☎ 800/234–1970; $39 1st yr).

B

BETTER BUSINESS BUREAU

For local contacts, consult the **Council of Better Business Bureaus** (✉ 4200 Wilson Blvd., Suite 800, Arlington, VA 22203, ☎ 703/276–0100, FAX 703/525–8277).

BUS TRAVEL

Greyhound (☎ 800/231–2222) provides service to and throughout California.

C

CAR RENTAL

The major car-rental companies represented in California are **Alamo** (☎ 800/327–9633; in the U.K., 0800/272–2000), **Avis** (☎ 800/331–1212; in Canada, 800/879–2847), **Budget** (☎ 800/527–0700; in the U.K., 0800/181181), **Dollar** (☎ 800/800–4000; in the U.K., 0990/565656, where it is known as Eurodollar), **Hertz** (☎ 800/654–3131; in Canada, 800/263–0600; in the U.K., 01345/555888), and **National InterRent** (☎ 800/227–7368; in the U.K., where National is known as Europcar InterRent, 01345/222525). In Los Angeles, rates for an economy car with unlimited mileage begin at

$31 a day and $150 a week. This does not include tax on car rentals, which is 8¾%. In San Diego, rates for an economy car with unlimited mileage begin at $28 a day and $150 a week. This does not include tax on car rentals, which is 7%. In San Francisco, rates begin at $33 a day and $143 a week. This does not include tax on car rentals, which is 8¼%.

RENTAL WHOLESALERS

Contact **Auto Europe** (☎ 207/828–2525 or 800/223–5555).

CHILDREN & TRAVEL

FLYING

Look into **"Flying with Baby"** (✉ Third Street Press, Box 261250, Littleton, CO 80163, ☎ 303/595–5959; $4.95 includes shipping), cowritten by a flight attendant. **"Kids and Teens in Flight,"** free from the U.S. Department of Transportation's Aviation Consumer Protection Division (✉ C-75, Washington, DC 20590, ☎ 202/366–2220), offers tips on children flying alone. Every two years the February issue of **Family Travel Times** (☞ Know-How, *below*) details children's services on three dozen airlines. **"Flying Alone, Handy Advice for Kids Traveling Solo"** is available free from the American Automobile Association (AAA) (✉ Send legal-size SASE: Flying Alone, Mail Stop 800, 1000 AAA Dr., Heathrow, FL 32746).

KNOW-HOW

Family Travel Times, published quarterly by Travel with Your Children (✉ TWYCH, 40 5th Ave., New York, NY 10011, ☎ 212/477–5524; $40 per yr), covers destinations, types of vacations, and modes of travel.

LOCAL INFORMATION

Consult Fodor's lively by-parents, for-parents **Where Should We Take the Kids? California** (available in bookstores, or ☎ 800/533–6478; $17).

Helpful city guides include **The Parents' Guide to L.A.,** ($19.95 plus $4–$5 shipping; Mani Flattery Publications, c/o SCB Distributors, ✉ 15612 South New Century Dr., Gardena, CA 90248, ☎ 310/532-9400), which includes discount coupons for area attractions; **Sacramento with Kids,** by Dierdre Honnold ($11.95 plus $2 shipping and 7¾% sales tax for CA residents; Wordrights International, ✉ Box 1941, Carmichael, CA 95609, ☎ 916/483–4961); and **San Jose with Kids** ($11.95 plus $2 shipping and 7¾% sales tax for CA residents; also from Wordrights).

San Francisco/Peninsula Parent (✉ Box 1280, Millbrae 94030, ☎ 415/342–9203), **Parents Press** (✉ 1454 6th St., Berkeley 94710, ☎ 510/524–1602), **Parents Monthly** (✉ 8611 Folsom Blvd., Suite A, Sacramento 95826, ☎ 916/383–7012), **L.A. Parent** (✉ Box 3204, Burbank

91504, ☎ 818/846–0400), and **San Diego Family Press** (✉ Box 23960, San Diego 92193, ☎ 619/685–6970) are monthly newspapers that list activities for children. These free papers can be found in racks at many libraries and some supermarkets; they are available by mail for a small fee.

TOUR OPERATORS

Contact **Grandtravel** (✉ 6900 Wisconsin Ave., Suite 706, Chevy Chase, MD 20815, ☎ 301/986–0790 or 800/247–7651), which has tours for people traveling with grandchildren ages 7–17.

Rascals in Paradise (✉ 650 5th St., Suite 505, San Francisco, CA 94107, ☎ 415/978–9800 or 800/872–7225) arranges family trips to several California resorts and ranches with children's programs. Child care—if desired—is included.

Travelling With Children (✉ 2313 Valley St., Berkeley, CA 94702, ☎ 510/848–0929; in CA, 800/499–0929; FAX 510/848–0935) offers consultation services and makes reservations for California guest ranches, house rentals, rafting trips, Disneyland packages, and other family vacations.

CUSTOMS

CANADIANS

Contact **Revenue Canada** (✉ 2265 St. Laurent Blvd. S, Ottawa, Ontario K1G 4K3, ☎ 613/993–0534) for a copy of the free brochure **"I Declare/**

THE GOLD GUIDE / IMPORTANT CONTACTS

Je Déclare" and for details on duty-free limits. For recorded information (within Canada only), call 800/461–9999.

U.K. CITIZENS

HM Customs and Excise (⊠ Dorset House, Stamford St., London SE1 9NG, ☎ 0171/202–4227) can answer questions about U.K. customs regulations and publishes a free pamphlet, **"A Guide for Travellers,"** detailing standard procedures and import rules.

D

DISABILITIES & ACCESSIBILITY

COMPLAINTS

To register complaints under the provisions of the Americans with Disabilities Act, contact the U.S. Department of Justice's **Disability Rights Section** (⊠ Box 66738, Washington, DC 20035, ☎ 202/514–0301 or 800/514–0301, FAX 202/307–1198, TTY 202/514–0383 or 800/514–0383). For airline-related problems, contact the U.S. Department of Transportation's **Aviation Consumer Protection Division** (☞ Air Travel, *above*). For complaints about surface transportation, contact the Department of Transportation's **Civil Rights Office** (☎ 202/366–4648).

DISCOUNT PASSES

The **National Park Service** (⊠ Box 37127, Washington, DC 20013-7127) provides a Golden Access Passport free to those who are medically blind or have a permanent disability; the

passport covers the entry fee for the holder and anyone accompanying the holder in the same private vehicle and a 50% discount on camping and some other user fees. Apply for the passport in person at a national recreation facility that charges an entrance fee; proof of disability is required.

LOCAL INFORMATION

"Around the Town with Ease" gives accessibility ratings to the 109 most visited Los Angeles sites. Send $2 to the Junior League of Los Angeles (⊠ 630 N. Larchmont Blvd., Los Angeles 90004, ☎ 213/957–4280). Accessible San Diego (⊠ 2466 Bartel St., San Diego 92123, ☎ 619/279–0704) publishes the 45-page **"Access in San Diego Guide"** (cost: $5).

San Francisco Convention and Visitors Bureau (⊠ Box 429097, San Francisco 94142-9097, ☎ 415/391-2000, TTY 415/392–0328) has free pamphlets and booklets with information about public transportation and the accessibility of various attractions. These include the dated but still helpful **"Guide to San Francisco for the Person Who Is Disabled."** The California State Coastal Conservancy (Publications Dept., ⊠ 1330 Broadway, Suite 1100, Oakland 94612, ☎ 510/286–1015) publishes the free booklet **"Wheelchair Riders Guide to San Francisco Bay and Nearby Shorelines."**

ORGANIZATIONS

TRAVELERS WITH HEARING IMPAIRMENTS➤ The **American Academy of Otolaryngology** (⊠ 1 Prince St., Alexandria, VA 22314, ☎ 703/836–4444, FAX 703/683–5100, TTY 703/519–1585) publishes a brochure, "Travel Tips for Hearing Impaired People."

TRAVELERS WITH MOBILITY PROBLEMS➤ Contact the **Information Center for Individuals with Disabilities** (⊠ Box 256, Boston, MA 02117, ☎ 617/450–9888; in MA, 800/462–5015; TTY 617/424–6855); **Mobility International USA** (⊠ Box 10767, Eugene, OR 97440, ☎ and TTY 541/343–1284, FAX 541/343–6812), the U.S. branch of a Belgium-based organization (☞ *below*) with affiliates in 30 countries; **Moss-Rehab Hospital Travel Information Service** (☎ 215/456–9600, TTY 215/456–9602), a telephone information resource for travelers with physical disabilities; the **Society for the Advancement of Travel for the Handicapped** (⊠ 347 5th Ave., Suite 610, New York, NY 10016, ☎ 212/447–7284, FAX 212/725–8253; membership $45); and **Travelin' Talk** (⊠ Box 3534, Clarksville, TN 37043, ☎ 615/552–6670, FAX 615/552–1182), which provides local contacts worldwide for travelers with disabilities.

TRAVELERS WITH VISION IMPAIRMENTS➤ Contact the **American Council of the Blind** (⊠ 1155 15th St. NW, Suite 720, Washington, DC 20005,

☎ 202/467–5081, FAX 202/467–5085) for a list of travelers' resources or the **American Foundation for the Blind** (✉ 11 Penn Plaza, Suite 300, New York, NY 10001, ☎ 212/502–7600 or 800/232–5463, TTY 212/502–7662), which provides general advice.

IN THE U.K.

Contact the **Royal Association for Disability and Rehabilitation** (✉ RADAR, 12 City Forum, 250 City Rd., London EC1V 8AF, ☎ 0171/250–3222) or **Mobility International** (✉ rue de Manchester 25, B-1080 Brussels, Belgium, ☎ 00–322–410–6297, FAX 00–322–410–6874), an international travel-information clearing-house for people with disabilities.

PUBLICATIONS

Several publications for travelers with disabilities are available from the **Consumer Information Center** (✉ Box 100, Pueblo, CO 81009, ☎ 719/948–3334). Call or write for its free catalog of current titles. The Society for the Advancement of Travel for the Handicapped (☞ Organizations, *above*) publishes the quarterly magazine *"Access to Travel"* ($13 for 1-yr subscription).

Fodor's *Great American Vacations for Travelers with Disabilities* (available in bookstores, or ☎ 800/533–6478; $18) details accessible attractions, restaurants, and hotels in U.S. destinations. The 500-page *Travelin' Talk Directory* (✉ Box 3534, Clarksville, TN 37043, ☎ 615/552–6670, FAX 615/552–1182; $35) lists people and organizations who help travelers with disabilities. For travel agents worldwide, consult the *Directory of Travel Agencies for the Disabled* (✉ Twin Peaks Press, Box 129, Vancouver, WA 98666, ☎ 360/694–2462 or 800/637–2256, FAX 360/696–3210; $19.95 plus $3 shipping). The Sierra Club publishes *Easy Access to National Parks* (✉ Sierra Club Store, 85 2nd St., San Francisco, CA 94105, ☎ 415/977–5630 or 800/935–1056, FAX 415/977–5795; $16 plus $3 shipping).

TRAVEL AGENCIES & TOUR OPERATORS

The Americans with Disabilities Act requires that all travel firms serve the needs of all travelers. That said, you should note that some agencies and operators specialize in making travel arrangements for individuals and groups with disabilities, among them **Access Adventures** (✉ 206 Chestnut Ridge Rd., Rochester, NY 14624, ☎ 716/889–9096), run by a former physical-rehab counselor.

TRAVELERS WITH MOBILITY PROBLEMS➤ Contact **Hinsdale Travel Service** (✉ 201 E. Ogden Ave., Suite 100, Hinsdale, IL 60521, ☎ 708/325–1335), a travel agency that benefits from the advice of wheelchair traveler Janice Perkins; and

Wheelchair Journeys (✉ 16979 Redmond Way, Redmond, WA 98052, ☎ 206/885–2210 or 800/313–4751), which can handle arrangements worldwide.

TRAVELERS WITH DEVELOPMENTAL DISABILITIES➤ Contact the nonprofit **New Directions** (✉ 5276 Hollister Ave., Suite 207, Santa Barbara, CA 93111, ☎ 805/967–2841) and **Sprout** (✉ 893 Amsterdam Ave., New York, NY 10025, ☎ 212/222–9575), which specializes in custom-designed itineraries for groups but also books vacations for individual travelers.

TRAVEL GEAR

The **Magellan's** catalog (☎ 800/962–4943, FAX 805/568–5406), includes a range of products designed for travelers with disabilities.

DISCOUNTS & DEALS

AIRFARES

For the lowest airfares to California, call 800/FLY–4–LESS. Also try 800/FLY–ASAP.

CLUBS

Contact **Entertainment Travel Editions** (✉ Box 1068, Trumbull, CT 06611, ☎ 800/445–4137; $28–$53, depending on destination), **Great American Traveler** (✉ Box 27965, Salt Lake City, UT 84127, ☎ 800/548–2812; $49.95 per yr), **Moment's Notice Discount Travel Club** (✉ 7301 New Utrecht Ave., Brooklyn, NY 11204, ☎ 718/234–6295; $25 per yr, single or family),

Privilege Card (✉ 3391 Peachtree Rd. NE, Suite 110, Atlanta, GA 30326, ☎ 404/262–0222 or 800/236–9732; $74.95 per yr), **Travelers Advantage** (✉ CUC Travel Service, 49 Music Sq. W, Nashville, TN 37203, ☎ 800/548–1116 or 800/648–4037; $49 per yr, single or family), or **Worldwide Discount Travel Club** (✉ 1674 Meridian Ave., Miami Beach, FL 33139, ☎ 305/534–2082; $50 per yr for family, $40 single).

HOTEL ROOMS

For discounts on hotel rates, contact the **Hotel Reservations Network** (☎ 800/964–6835) or **Quickbook** (☎ 800/789–9887).

PUBLICATIONS

Consult *The Frugal Globetrotter,* by Bruce Northam (✉ Fulcrum Publishing, 350 Indiana St., Suite 350, Golden, CO 80401, ☎ 800/992–2908; $15.95). For publications that tell how to find the lowest prices on plane tickets, *see* Air Travel, *above.*

G

GAY & LESBIAN TRAVEL

ORGANIZATIONS

The **International Gay Travel Association** (✉ Box 4974, Key West, FL 33041, ☎ 800/448–8550, FAX 305/296–6633), a consortium of more than 1,000 travel companies, can supply names of gay-friendly travel agents, tour operators, and accommodations.

LOCAL INFORMATION

Many California cities large and small have lesbian and gay publications available in sidewalk racks and at bars and other social spaces; most have extensive events and information listings. The papers include *San Francisco Bay Times* (✉ 288 7th St., San Francisco 94103, ☎ 415/227–0800), *Mom Guess What Newspaper* (✉ 1725 L St., Sacramento 95814, ☎ 916/441–6397), *Edge* (✉ 6434 Santa Monica Blvd., Los Angeles 90038, ☎ 213/962–6994), *Bottom Line* (✉ 1243 N. Gene Autry Trail, Palm Springs 92262, ☎ 619/323–0552), and *Gay & Lesbian Times* (✉ 3911 Normal St., San Diego, 92103, ☎ 619/299–6397).

PUBLICATIONS

Most local gay publications and several national magazines such as *Out* and the *Advocate* include travel ads and listings and run occasional travel-related features. The 16-page **"Out & About"** (☎ 212/645–6922 or 800/929–2268, FAX 800/929–2215), a newsletter that publishes 10 issues per year ($49), reports on resorts, hotels, guest houses, cruise lines, and airlines. Its editors pioneered a rating system to assess travel industry policies and programs as they affect gay and lesbian travelers. The gay travel magazine, *Our World* (☎ 904/441–5367, FAX 904/441–5604), covers many destinations in 10 issues ($35) per year.

Several California destinations are profiled in *Fodor's Gay Guide to the USA* (available in bookstores or contact Fodor's Travel Publications, ☎ 800/533–6478; $19.50).

SWITCHBOARDS & HOT LINES

For general information, contact the **Gay and Lesbian Community Services Center** (✉ 1625 N. Schrader Blvd., Los Angeles 90028, ☎ 213/993–7400), the **Lambda Community Center** (✉ 1931 L St., Sacramento 95814, ☎ 916/442–0185), **Lesbian and Gay Men's Community Center** (✉ 3916 Normal St., San Diego 92103, ☎ 619/692–4297), or, in the San Francisco Bay Area, the **Pacific Center Lesbian, Gay and Bisexual Switchboard** (☎ 510/841–6224).

TOUR OPERATORS

Toto Tours (✉ 1326 W. Albion Ave., Suite 3W, Chicago, IL 60626, ☎ 312/274–8686 or 800/565–1241, FAX 312/274–8695) offers group tours to worldwide destinations.

TRAVEL AGENCIES

The largest agencies serving gay women and men are **Advance Travel** (✉ 10700 Northwest Fwy., Suite 160, Houston, TX 77092, ☎ 713/682–2002 or 800/292–0500), **Club Travel** (✉ 18739 Santa Monica Blvd., W. Hollywood, CA 90069, ☎ 310/358–2200 or 800/429–8747), **Islanders/ Kennedy Travel** (✉ 183 W. 10th St., New York, NY 10014, ☎ 212/242–3222 or 800/988–1181), **Sky**

Link Women's Travel (✉ 2460 W. 3rd St., Suite 215, Santa Rosa, CA 90405 ☎ 707/570–0105 or 800/225–5759), and **Now Voyager** (✉ 4406 18th St., San Francisco, CA 94114, ☎ 415/626–1169 or 800/255–6951).

I
INSURANCE

IN CANADA

Contact **Mutual of Omaha** (✉ Travel Division, 500 University Ave., Toronto, Ontario M5G 1V8, ☎ 416/598–4083; in Canada, 800/465–0267).

IN THE U.S.

Travel insurance covering baggage, health, and trip cancellation or interruptions is available from **Access America** (✉ 6600 W. Broad St., Richmond, VA 23230, ☎ 804/285–3300 or 800/334–7525), **Carefree Travel Insurance** (✉ Box 9366, 100 Garden City Plaza, Garden City, NY 11530, ☎ 516/294–0220 or 800/323–3149), **Near Travel Services** (✉ Box 1339, Calumet City, IL 60409, ☎ 708/868–6700 or 800/654–6700), **Tele-Trip** (✉ Mutual of Omaha Plaza, Box 31716, Omaha, NE 68131, ☎ 800/228–9792), **Travel Guard International** (✉ 1145 Clark St., Stevens Point, WI 54481, ☎ 715/345–0505 or 800/826–1300), **Travel Insured International** (✉ Box 280568, East Hartford, CT 06128, ☎ 203/528–7663 or 800/243–3174), and

Wallach & Company (✉ 107 W. Federal St., Box 480, Middleburg, VA 22117, ☎ 540/687–3166 or 800/237–6615).

IN THE U.K.

The **Association of British Insurers** (✉ 51 Gresham St., London EC2V 7HQ, ☎ 0171/600–3333) gives advice by phone and publishes the free pamphlet **"Holiday Insurance,"** which sets out typical policy provisions and costs.

L
LODGING

For information on hotel consolidators, *see* Discounts, *above.*

APARTMENT & VILLA RENTAL

Among the companies to contact are **Property Rentals International** (✉ 1008 Mansfield Crossing Rd., Richmond, VA 23236, ☎ 804/378–6054 or 800/220–3332, FAX 804/379–2073), **Rent-a-Home International** (✉ 7200 34th Ave. NW, Seattle, WA 98117, ☎ 206/789–9377 or 800/488–7368, FAX 206/789–9379), and **Vacation Home Rentals Worldwide** (✉ 235 Kensington Ave., Norwood, NJ 07648, ☎ 201/767–9393 or 800/633–3284, FAX 201/767–5510). Members of the travel club **Hideaways International** (✉ 767 Islington St., Portsmouth, NH 03801, ☎ 603/430–4433 or 800/843–4433, FAX 603/430–4444; $99 per yr) receive two annual guides plus quarterly newsletters and arrange rentals among themselves.

CAMPING

Destinet (✉ 9450 Carroll Park Dr., San Diego, CA 92121) handles camping reservations, which in many cases are required, in California's national (☎ 800/365–2267) and state (☎ 800/444–7275) parks.

The *California RV and Camping Guide,* available free from the **California Travel Parks Association** (✉ Box 5648, Auburn, CA 95604, ☎ 916/823–1076, FAX 916/823–6331), has information about nearly 400 private parks and campgrounds throughout the state and bordering areas of Oregon and Nevada.

HOME EXCHANGE

Some of the principal clearinghouses are **HomeLink International/Vacation Exchange Club** (✉ Box 650, Key West, FL 33041, ☎ 305/294–1448 or 800/638–3841, FAX 305/294–1148; $70 per yr), which sends members three annual directories, with a listing in one, plus updates; and **Intervac International** (✉ Box 590504, San Francisco, CA 94159, ☎ 415/435–3497, FAX 415/435–7440; $65 per yr), which publishes four annual directories.

M
MONEY MATTERS

ATMS

For specific **Cirrus** locations in the United States and Canada, call 800/424–7787. For U.S. **Plus** locations, call 800/843–7587 and enter the area code and first three digits of the number from which you're calling (or of the calling area in which you want to locate an ATM).

P
PARKS

NATIONAL PARKS

A variety of passes is available for senior citizens, travelers with disabilities, and frequent visitors. The passes can be purchased at any park that charges admission or obtained by mail from the **National Park Service** (⊠ Dept. of the Interior, Washington, DC 20240).

STATE PARKS

For information on state parks, beaches, and recreation areas, contact the **California State Park System** (⊠ Dept. of Parks and Recreation, Box 942896, Sacramento 94296, ☎ 916/653–6995). For campsite reservation numbers, *see* Lodging, *above*.

PASSPORTS & VISAS

U.K. CITIZENS

For fees, documentation requirements, and to request an emergency passport, call the **London Passport Office** (☎ 0990/210410). For U.S. visa information, call the **U.S. Embassy Visa Information Line** (☎ 01891/200–290; calls cost 49p per minute or 39p per minute cheap rate) or send a self-addressed, stamped envelope to the **U.S. Embassy Visa Branch** (⊠ 5 Upper Grosvenor St., London W1A 2JB). If you live in Northern Ireland, write to the

U.S. Consulate General (⊠ Queen's House, Queen St., Belfast BTI 6EO).

PHOTO HELP

The **Kodak Information Center** (☎ 800/242–2424) answers consumer questions about film and photography. The ***Kodak Guide to Shooting Great Travel Pictures*** (available in bookstores; or contact Fodor's Travel Publications, ☎ 800/533–6478; $16.50) explains how to take expert travel photographs.

S
SAFETY

"Trouble-Free Travel," from the AAA, is a booklet of tips for protecting yourself and your belongings when away from home. Send a stamped, self-addressed, legal-size envelope to Flying Alone (⊠ Mail Stop 75, 1000 AAA Dr., Heathrow, FL 32746).

SENIOR CITIZENS

EDUCATIONAL TRAVEL

The nonprofit **Elderhostel** (⊠ 75 Federal St., 3rd floor, Boston, MA 02110, ☎ 617/426–7788), for people 60 and older, has offered inexpensive study programs since 1975. Courses cover everything from marine science to Greek mythology and cowboy poetry. Fees for programs in the United States and Canada, which usually last one week, run about $300, not including transportation.

ORGANIZATIONS

Contact the **American Association of Retired**

Persons (⊠ AARP, 601 E St. NW, Washington, DC 20049, ☎ 202/434–2277; annual dues $8 per person or couple). Its Purchase Privilege Program secures discounts for members on lodging, car rentals, and sightseeing, and the AARP Motoring Plan (☎ 800/334–3300) furnishes domestic triprouting information and emergency roadservice aid for an annual fee of $39.95 ($59.95 for a premium version). Senior citizen travelers can also join the AAA for emergency road service and other travel benefits (☞ Driving, *above,* and Discounts & Deals *in* Smart Travel Tips A to Z, *below*).

Additional sources for discounts on lodgings, car rentals, and other travel expenses, as well as helpful magazines and newsletters, are the **National Council of Senior Citizens** (⊠ 1331 F St. NW, Washington, DC 20004, ☎ 202/347–8800; annual membership $12) and Sears's **Mature Outlook** (⊠ Box 10448, Des Moines, IA 50306, ☎ 800/336–6330; annual membership $9.95).

SPORTS

FISHING

California has abundant fishing options: deep-sea fishing expeditions, surf fishing from the shore, and freshwater fishing in streams, rivers, lakes, and reservoirs. You'll need a California fishing license. State residents pay $25.70 ($4 for senior citizens and those on limited income), but nonresidents must fork over $69.55 for a one-year license. Both residents and nonresidents can purchase a one-day license for $9.20. For information, contact the **Department of Fish and Game** (✉ 3211 S St., Sacramento 95816, ☎ 916/227–2244). The department can also advise you on hunting licenses and regulations.

STUDENTS

GROUPS

One major tour operators specializing in student travel is **Contiki Holidays** (✉ 300 Plaza Alicante, Suite 900, Garden Grove, CA 92640, ☎ 714/740–0808 or 800/266–8454).

HOSTELING

In the United States, contact **Hostelling International–American Youth Hostels** (✉ 733 15th St. NW, Suite 840, Washington, DC 20005, ☎ 202/783–6161 or 800/444–6111 for reservations at selected hostels, FAX 202/783–6171); in Canada, **Hostelling International–Canada** (✉ 205 Catherine St., Suite 400, Ottawa, Ontario K2P 1C3, ☎ 613/237–7884); and in the United Kingdom, the **Youth Hostel Association of England and Wales** (✉ Trevelyan House, 8 St. Stephen's Hill, St. Albans, Hertfordshire AL1 2DY, ☎ 01727/855215 or 01727/845047). Membership (in the U.S., $25; in Canada, C$26.75; in the U.K., £9.30) gives you access to 5,000 hostels in 77 countries that charge $5–$30 per person per night.

ORGANIZATIONS

A major contact is the **Council on International Educational Exchange** (Mail orders only: ✉ CIEE, 205 E. 42nd St., 16th floor, New York, NY 10017, ☎ 212/822–2600). The **Educational Travel Centre** (✉ 438 N. Frances St., Madison, WI 53703, ☎ 608/256–5551 or 800/747–5551, FAX 608/256–2042) offers rail passes and low-cost airline tickets, mostly for flights that depart from Chicago.

In Canada, also contact **Travel Cuts** (✉ 187 College St., Toronto, Ontario M5T 1P7, ☎ 416/979–2406 or 800/667–2887).

PUBLICATIONS

Check out the *Berkeley Guide to California* (available in bookstores; or contact Fodor's Travel Publications, ☎ 800/533–6478; $17.50).

T
TOUR OPERATORS

Among the companies that sell tours and packages to California, the following are nationally known, have a proven reputation, and offer plenty of options.

GROUP TOURS

DELUXE➤ **Globus** (✉ 5301 S. Federal Circle, Littleton, CO 80123, ☎ 303/797–2800 or 800/221–0090, FAX 303/795–0962), **Maupintour** (✉ Box 807, 1515 St. Andrews Dr., Lawrence, KS 66047, ☎ 913/843–1211 or 800/255–4266, FAX 913/843–8351), and **Tauck Tours** (✉ Box 5027, 276 Post Rd. W, Westport, CT 06881, ☎

203/226–6911 or 800/468–2825, FAX 203/221–6828).

FIRST CLASS➤ **Brendan Tours** (✉ 15137 Califa St., Van Nuys, CA 91411, ☎ 818/785–9696 or 800/421–8446, FAX 818/902–9876), **Caravan Tours** (✉ 401 N. Michigan Ave., Chicago, IL 60611, ☎ 312/321–9800 or 800/227–2826), **Collette Tours** (✉ 162 Middle St., Pawtucket, RI 02860, ☎ 401/728–3805 or 800/832–4656, FAX 401/728–1380), **Gadabout Tours** (✉ 700 E. Tahquitz Canyon Way, Palm Springs, CA 92262, ☎ 619/325–5556 or 800/952–5068), and **Mayflower Tours** (✉ Box 490, 1225 Warren Ave., Downers Grove, IL 60515, ☎ 708/960–3793 or 800/323–7604, FAX 708/960–3575).

BUDGET➤ **Cosmos** (☞ Globus, *above*).

PACKAGES

Independent vacation packages are available from major tour operators and airlines. Contact **Adventure Vacations** (✉ 10612 Beaver Dam Rd., Hunt Valley, MD 21030-2205, ☎ 410/785–3500 or 800/638–9040, FAX 410/584–2771), **American Airlines Fly AAway Vacations** (☎ 800/321–2121), **Continental Vacations** (☎ 800/634–5555), **Delta Dream Vacations** (☎ 800/872–7786), **SuperCities** (✉ 139 Main St., Cambridge, MA 02142, ☎ 617/621–0099 or 800/333–1234), **TWA Getaway Vacations** (☎ 800/438–2929), **United Vacations** (☎ 800/328–6877), and **USAir Vacations**

(☎ 800/455–0123). **Gogo Tours,** based in Ramsey, New Jersey, and **Kingdom Tours,** based in Plains, Pennsylvania, sell packages to California only through travel agents. For rail packages that combine air, hotel, and tour options, contact **Amtrak's Great American Vacations** (☎ 800/321–8684).

Also contact **Amtrak**'s Great American Vacations (☎ 800/321–8684). For independent self-drive itineraries, contact **Budget World-Class Drive** (☎ 800/527–0700; in the U.K., 0800/181181).

FROM THE U.K.

Tour operators offering packages to San Francisco include **British Airways Holidays** (✉ Astral Towers, Betts Way, London Rd., Crawley, West Sussex RH10 2XA, ☎ 01293/723–121), **Jetsave** (✉ Sussex House, London Rd., East Grinstead, West Sussex RH19 1LD, ☎ 01342/312–033), **Key to America** (✉ 1–3 Station Rd., Ashford, Middlesex TW15 2UW, ☎ 01784/248–777), **Kuoni Travel Ltd.** (✉ Kuoni House, Dorking, Surrey RH5 4AZ, ☎ 01306/742–222), and **Premier Holidays** (✉ Premier Travel Center, Westbrook, Milton Rd., Cambridge CB4 1YG, ☎ 01223/516–688).

Travel agencies that offer cheap fares to California include **Trailfinders** (✉ 42–50 Earl's Court Rd., London W8 6FT, ☎ 0171/937–5400), **Travel Cuts** (✉ 295A Regent St., London W1R 7YA,

☎ 0171/637–3161; ☞ Students, *above*), and **Flightfile** (✉ 49 Tottenham Court Rd., London W1P 9RE, ☎ 0171/700–2722).

THEME TRIPS

ADVENTURE➤ For biking, hiking, climbing, kayaking, and camping adventures, contact **Trek America** (✉ Box 189, Rockaway, NJ 07866, ☎ 201/983–1144 or 800/221-0596, FAX 201/983–8551) and **Mountain Travel-Sobek** (✉ 6420 Fairmount Ave., El Cerrito, CA 94530, ☎ 510/527–8100 or 800/227–2384, FAX 510/525–7710). For fishing, horseback riding, and camping in northern California's Marble Mountain wilderness area, contact **Access to Adventure** (✉ Box 92520 Hwy 96, Somes Bar, CA 95560, ☎ 916/469–3322 or 800/552–6284, FAX 916/469–3357).

BALLOONING➤ Champagne balloon trips out of San Francisco and the Napa Valley area are run by **Above the West Hot Air Ballooning** (✉ Box 2290, 6744 Washington St., Yountville, CA 94599, ☎ 707/944–8638 or 800/627–2759) and **Bonaventura Balloon Company** (✉ 133 Wall Rd., Napa, CA 94558, ☎ 707/944–2822 or 800/359–6272, FAX 707/944–2220).

BICYCLING➤ Affordable weeklong California cycling vacations are sold by **Cycle America** (✉ Box 485, Cannon Falls, MN 55009, ☎ 507/263–2665 or 800/245–3263). For road and mountain biking tours that include stays

in inns or at campsites, contact **Backroads** (✉ 1516 5th St., Berkeley, CA 94710-1740, ☎ 510/527–1555 or 800/462–2848, FAX 510/527–1444). Mountain and road biking in northern California is available from **Bicycle Adventures** (✉ Box 7875, Olympia, WA 98507, ☎ 360/786–0989 or 800/443–6060, FAX 360/786–9661) and **Timberline** (✉ 7975 E. Harvard, #J, Denver, CO 80231, ☎ 303/759–3804 or 800/417–2453, FAX 303/368–1651). For a variety of innovative California cycling tours try **Imagine Tours** (✉ Box 475, Davis, CA 95617, ☎ 800/228–7041). For deluxe cycling trips, contact **Butterfield & Robinson** (✉ 70 Bond St., Toronto, Ontario, Canada M5B 1X3, ☎ 416/864–1354 or 800/387–1147).

CROSS-COUNTRY SKIING➤ **Backroads** (☞ *above*).

FOOD & WINE➤ ☞ Chapter 5.

FISHING➤ **Anglers Travel** (✉ 3100 Mill St., #206, Reno, NV 89502, ☎ 702/324–0580 or 800/624–8429, FAX 702/324–0583), **Fishing International** (✉ Box 2132, Santa Rosa, CA 95405, ☎ 800/950–4242), and **Rod & Reel Adventures** (✉ 3507 Tully Rd., #B6, Modesto, CA 95356-1052, ☎ 209/524–7775 or 800/356–6982, FAX 209/524–1220).

GOLF➤ Packages including accommodations, confirmed tee times, and golfing fees and lessons are offered by **Stine's Golftrips**

(✉ Box 2314, Winter Haven, FL 33883-2314, ☎ 941/324-1300 or 800/428-1940, FAX 941/325-0384).

HEALTH➤ **Spa-Finders** (✉ 91 5th Ave., #301, New York, NY 10003-3039, ☎ 212/924-6800 or 800/255-7727) represents many spas in California.

HIKING➤ Hiking and walking tours are offered by **American Wilderness Experience** (✉ Box 1486, Boulder, CO 80306, ☎ 303/444-2622 or 800/444-3833, FAX 303/444-3999). **Backroads** (☞ Bicycling, *above*) offers hiking and walking tours for a range of fitness levels.

HORSEBACK RIDING➤ Riding trips including deluxe camping or lodge accommodations are offered by **American Wilderness Experience** (☞ Hiking, *above*). **FITS Equestrian** (✉ 685 Lateen Rd., Solvang, CA 93463, ☎ 805/688-9494 or 800/666-3487, FAX 805/688-2943) has several California programs.

KAYAKING➤ Kayaking trips in the Grand Canyon are sold by **Orange Torpedo Trips** (✉ Box 1111, Grants Pass, OR 97526-0294, ☎ 541/479-5061 or 800/635-2925, FAX 541/471-0995).

LEARNING➤ **Earthwatch** (✉ Box 403, 680 Mount Auburn St., Watertown, MA 02272, ☎ 617/926-8200 or 800/776-0188, FAX 617/926-8532) recruits volunteers to serve in its EarthCorps as short-term assistants to scientists on research

expeditions. **Oceanic Society Expeditions** (✉ Fort Mason Center, Bldg. E, San Francisco, CA 94123-1394, ☎ 415/441-1106 or 800/326-7491, FAX 415/474-3395) runs natural-history, whale-watching, and dolphin-research expeditions. **Smithsonian Study Tours and Seminars** (✉ 1100 Jefferson Dr. SW, Room 3045, MRC 702, Washington, DC 20560, ☎ 202/357-4700, FAX 202/633-9250) operates natural-history tours.

MOTORCYCLING➤ **Western States Motorcycle Tours** (✉ 1823 W. Seldon La., Phoenix, AZ 85021, ☎ FAX 602/943-9030) includes California in its tours of the wild, wild West.

MUSIC➤ **Dailey-Thorp Travel** (✉ 330 W. 58th St., #610, New York, NY 10019-1817, ☎ 212/307-1555 or 800/998-4677, FAX 212/974-1420) has San Francisco opera packages that include hotel stays, dining at fine restaurants, and sightseeing.

RIVER RAFTING➤ California river trips are available from **Access to Adventure** (☞ Adventure, *above*) and **Action Whitewater Adventures** (✉ Box 1634, Provo UT 84603, ☎ 800/453-1482, FAX 801/375-4175). **OARS** (✉ Box 67, Angels Camp, CA 95222, ☎ 209/736-4677 or 800/346-6277, FAX 209/736-2902) has trips on the Tuolumne, Merced, Kern, Cal Salmon, and Klamath rivers. **Whitewater Voyages** (✉ Box 20400, El Sobrante, CA 94820-0400, ☎ 510/222-

5994 or 800/488-7238, FAX 510/758-7238) has voyages on rivers throughout California.

SAILING➤ Whale watching and yachting in northern California are the specialties of **Adventure Sailing International** (✉ 3020 Bridgeway, #271, Sausalito, CA 94965, ☎ 415/381-9503 or 800/762-6287).

SPORTS➤ Rose Bowl packages including accommodations and transportation are available from **Spectacular Sport Specials** (✉ 5813 Citrus Blvd., New Orleans, LA 70123-5810, ☎ 504/734-9511 or 800/451-5772, FAX 504/734-7075) and **Dan Chavez's Sports Empire** (✉ Box 6169, Lakewood, CA 90714-6169, ☎ 310/920-2350 or 800/255-5258). **Championship Tennis Tours** (✉ 7350 E. Stetson Dr., #106, Scottsdale, AZ 85251, ☎ 602/990-8760 or 800/468-3664, FAX 602/990-8744) arranges packages to the Newsweek Champions Cup.

TRAIL RUNNING➤ **Backroads** (☞ *above*) offers trips along California's northern coast for trail-running enthusiasts.

WHALE WATCHING➤ **Pacific Sea Fari Tours** (✉ 2803 Emerson St., San Diego, CA 92106, ☎ 619/226-8224) sails out of San Diego to the Sea of Cortez and San Ignacio Lagoon in search of gray and blue whales.

YACHT CHARTERS➤ Contact **Ocean Voyages** (✉ 1709 Bridgeway, Sausalito, CA 94965, ☎ 415/332-4681, FAX

THE GOLD GUIDE / IMPORTANT CONTACTS

415/332–7460) for adventures off the California coast.

ORGANIZATIONS

The **National Tour Association** (NTA, ✉ 546 E. Main St., Lexington, KY 40508, ☎ 606/226–4444 or 800/755–8687) and the **United States Tour Operators Association** (USTOA, ✉ 211 E. 51st St., Suite 12B, New York, NY 10022, ☎ 212/750–7371) can provide lists of members and information on booking tours.

PUBLICATIONS

Contact the USTOA (☞ Organizations, *above*) for its **"Smart Traveler's Planning Kit."** Pamphlets in the kit include the "Worldwide Tour and Vacation Package Finder," "How to Select a Tour or Vacation Package," and information on the organization's consumer protection plan. Also get copy of the Better Business Bureau's **"Tips on Travel Packages"** (✉ Publication 24-195, 4200 Wilson Blvd., Arlington, VA 22203; $2). The National Tour Association will send you **"On Tour,"** a listing of its member operators, and a personalized package

of information on group travel in North America.

TRAIN TRAVEL

Amtrak (☎ 800/872–7245) trains (the *Zephyr,* from Chicago via Denver, and the *Coast Starlight,* traveling between Los Angeles and Seattle) stop in Oakland (✉ Jack London Sq., 245 2nd St.) and Emeryville (✉ 5885 Landregan St.); shuttle buses connect the Emeryville station and the Ferry Building on the Embarcadero at the foot of Market Street in San Francisco and Cal-Train's depot at 4th and Townsend streets.

TRAVEL AGENCIES

For names of reputable agencies in your area, contact the **American Society of Travel Agents** (ASTA, ✉ 1101 King St., Suite 200, Alexandria, VA 22314, ☎ 703/739–2782), the **Association of Canadian Travel Agents** (✉ 1729 Bank St., Suite 201, Ottawa, Ontario K1V 7Z5, ☎ 613/521–0474, FAX 613/521–0805), or the **Association of British Travel Agents** (✉ 55-57 Newman St., London W1P 4AH, ☎ 0171/637–2444, FAX 0171/637–0713).

TRAVEL GEAR

For travel apparel, appliances, personal-care items, and other travel necessities, get a free catalog from **Magellan's** (☎ 800/962–4943, FAX 805/568–5406), **Orvis Travel** (☎ 800/541–3541, FAX 703/343–7053), or **TravelSmith** (☎ 800/950–1600, FAX 415/455–0554).

V

VISITOR
INFORMATION

Contact the **California Division of Tourism** (✉ 801 K St., Suite 1600, Sacramento, CA 95814, ☎ 916/322–2881 or 800/462–2543, FAX 916/322–3402) for a packet with information about the state's attractions. The office will send a packet to U.K. visitors who call or fax the 916 numbers.

W

WEATHER

For current conditions and forecasts, plus the local time and helpful travel tips, call the **Weather Channel Connection** (☎ 900/932–8437; 95¢ per minute) from a Touch-Tone phone.

SMART TRAVEL TIPS A TO Z

Basic Information on Traveling in California and
Savvy Tips to Make Your Trip a Breeze

A

AIR TRAVEL

If time is an issue, **always look for nonstop flights,** which require no change of plane. If possible, **avoid connecting flights,** which stop at least once and can involve a change of plane, even though the flight number remains the same; if the first leg is late, the second waits.

For better service, **fly smaller or regional carriers,** which often have higher passenger satisfaction ratings. Sometimes they have such in-flight amenities as leather seats or greater legroom, and they often have better food.

CUTTING COSTS

The Sunday travel section of most newspapers is a good place to look for deals.

MAJOR AIRLINES➤ The least-expensive airfares from the major airlines are priced for round-trip travel and are subject to restrictions. Usually, you must **book in advance and buy the ticket within 24 hours** to get cheaper fares, and you may have to **stay over a Saturday night.** The lowest fare is subject to availability, and only a small percentage of the plane's total seats is sold at that price. It's smart to **call a number of airlines, and when you are quoted a good price, book it on**
the spot—the same fare may not be available on the same flight the next day. Airlines generally allow you to change your return date for a $25 to $50 fee. If you don't use your ticket, you can apply the cost toward the purchase of a new ticket, again for a small charge. However, most low-fare tickets are nonrefundable. To get the lowest airfare, **check different routings.** If your destination has more than one gateway, **compare prices to different airports.**

FROM THE U.K.➤ To save money on flights, **look into an APEX or Super-Pex ticket.** APEX tickets must be booked in advance and have certain restrictions. Super-Pex tickets can be purchased right at the airport.

ALOFT

AIRLINE FOOD➤ If you hate airline food, **ask for special meals when booking.** These can be vegetarian, low-cholesterol, or kosher, for example; commonly prepared to order in smaller quantities than standard fare, they can be tastier.

SMOKING➤ Smoking is not allowed on flights of six hours or less within the continental United States. Smoking is also prohibited on flights within Canada. For U.S. flights longer than six hours or international flights, **contact your carrier regarding**
its smoking policy. Some carriers have prohibited smoking throughout their system; others allow smoking only on certain routes or even certain departures of that route.

C

CAMERAS, CAMCORDERS, & COMPUTERS

IN TRANSIT

Always **keep your film, tape, or disks out of the sun;** never put these on the dashboard of a car. Carry an extra supply of batteries, and **be prepared to turn on your camera, camcorder, or laptop computer for security personnel** to prove that it's real.

X-RAYS

Always **ask for hand inspection at security.** Such requests are virtually always honored at U.S. airports. Photographic film becomes clouded after successive exposure to airport X-ray machines. Videotape and computer disks are not harmed by X-rays, but **keep your tapes and disks away from metal detectors.**

CAR RENTAL

CUTTING COSTS

To get the best deal, **book through a travel agent who is willing to shop around.** When pricing cars, **ask where the rental lot is located.** Some off-airport locations offer lower rates—even though their lots are only minutes away from the terminal via complimentary shuttle. You also may want to **price local car-rental companies,** whose rates may be lower still, although service and maintenance standards may not be as high as those of a national firm. Ask your agent to **look for fly-drive packages,** which also save you money, and **ask if local taxes are included** in the rental or fly-drive price. These can be as high as 20% in some destinations. Don't forget to find out about required deposits, cancellation penalties, drop-off charges, and the cost of any required insurance coverage.

Also **ask your travel agent about a company's customer-service record.** How has it responded to late plane arrivals and vehicle mishaps? Are there often lines at the rental counter, and—if you're traveling during a holiday period—does a confirmed reservation guarantee you a car?

INSURANCE

When driving a rented car, you are generally responsible for any damage to or loss of the rental vehicle, as well as any property damage or personal injury that you cause. Before you rent, **see what coverage you already have** under the terms of your personal auto insurance policy and credit cards.

For about $14 a day, rental companies sell protection, known as a collision- or loss-damage waiver (CDW or LDW), that eliminates your liability for damage to the car; it's always optional and should never be automatically added to your bill. Some states, including California, have capped the price of CDW and LDW.

In most states, the renter's personal auto insurance or other liability insurance covers damage to third parties. Only when the damage exceeds the renter's own insurance coverage does the car-rental company pay. In California, car-rental companies are not automatically responsible when the renter causes personal injury or property damage. If you do not have auto insurance or an umbrella insurance policy that covers damage to third parties, purchasing CDW or LDW is highly recommended.

U.K. CITIZENS

In the United States you must be 21 to rent a car; rates may be higher if you're under 25. You'll pay extra for child seats (about $3 per day), compulsory for children under five, and for additional drivers (about $2 per day). To pick up your reserved car you will need the reservation voucher, a passport, a U.K. driver's license, and a travel policy that covers each driver.

SURCHARGES

Before you pick up a car in one city and leave it in another, **ask about drop-off charges or one-way service fees,** which can be substantial. Note, too, that some rental agencies charge extra if you return the car before the time specified on your contract. To avoid a hefty refueling fee, **fill the tank just before you turn in the car**—but be aware that gas stations near the rental outlet may overcharge.

CHILDREN & TRAVEL

In many ways California is made to order for traveling with children: Kids love Disneyland, the San Diego Zoo, the Monterey Aquarium, the San Francisco cable cars, the city-owned gold mine in Placerville, and the caverns at Lake Shasta.

When traveling with children, **plan ahead** and **involve your youngsters** as you outline your trip. When packing, **include a supply of things to keep them busy** en route (☞ Children & Travel *in* Important Contacts A to Z, *above*). On sightseeing days, try to **schedule activities of special interest to your children,** like a trip to a zoo or a playground. If you **plan your itinerary around seasonal festivals,** you'll never lack for things to do. In addition, **check local newspapers for special events** mounted by public libraries, museums, and parks.

BABY-SITTING

For recommended local sitters, **check with your hotel desk.**

DRIVING

If you are renting a car, don't forget to **arrange**

for a car seat when you reserve. Sometimes they're free.

FLYING

On domestic flights, children under two not occupying a seat travel free, and older children are charged at the lowest applicable adult rate.

BAGGAGE➤ In general, the adult baggage allowance applies to children paying half or more of the adult fare.

SAFETY SEATS➤ According to the FAA, it's a good idea to **use safety seats aloft** for children weighing less than 40 pounds. Airline policies vary. U.S. carriers allow FAA-approved models but usually require that you buy a ticket, even if your child would otherwise ride free, since the seats must be strapped into regular seats.

FACILITIES➤ When making your reservation, **request children's meals or freestanding bassinets** if you need them; the latter are available only to those seated at the bulkhead, where there's enough legroom. If you don't need a bassinet, **think twice before requesting bulkhead seats**—the only storage space for in-flight necessities is in inconveniently distant overhead bins.

GAMES

In local toy stores, look for travel versions of popular games such as Trouble, Sorry, and Monopoly ($5–$8).

LODGING

Most hotels allow children under a certain age to stay in their parents' room at no extra charge; others charge them as extra adults. Be sure to **ask about the cutoff age.**

CUSTOMS & DUTIES

To speed your clearance through customs, **keep receipts for all your purchases abroad.** If you feel that you've been incorrectly or unfairly charged a duty, you can **appeal assessments in dispute.** First ask to see a supervisor. If you are still unsatisfied, **write to the port director** at your point of entry, sending your customs receipt and any other appropriate documentation. The address will be listed on your receipt. If you still don't get satisfaction, you can take your case to customs headquarters in Washington.

IN CALIFORNIA

British visitors aged 21 or over may import the following into the United States: 200 cigarettes or 50 cigars or 2 kilograms of tobacco; 1 U.S. liter of alcohol; gifts to the value of $100. Restricted items include meat products, seeds, plants, and fruits. Never carry illegal drugs.

IN CANADA

If you've been out of Canada for at least seven days, you may bring in C$500 worth of goods duty-free. If you've been away for fewer than seven days but for more than 48 hours, the duty-free allowance drops to C$200; if your trip lasts between 24 and 48 hours, the allowance is C$50. You cannot pool allowances with family members. Goods claimed under the C$500 exemption may follow you by mail; those claimed under the lesser exemptions must accompany you.

Alcohol and tobacco products may be included in the seven-day and 48-hour exemptions but not in the 24-hour exemption. If you meet the age requirements of the province or territory through which you reenter Canada, you may bring in, duty-free, 1.14 liters (40 imperial ounces) of wine or liquor *or* 24 12-ounce cans or bottles of beer or ale. If you are 16 or older, you may bring in, duty-free, 200 cigarettes, 50 cigars or cigarillos, and 400 tobacco sticks or 400 grams of manufactured tobacco. Alcohol and tobacco must accompany you on your return.

An unlimited number of gifts with a value of up to C$60 each may be mailed to Canada duty-free. These do not affect your duty-free allowance on your return. Label the package "Unsolicited Gift— Value Under $60." Alcohol and tobacco are excluded.

IN THE U.K.

From countries outside the European Union, including the United States, you may import, duty-free, 200 cigarettes, 100 cigarillos, 50 cigars, or 250 grams of tobacco; 1 liter of spirits or 2 liters of fortified or sparkling wine or liqueurs; 2 liters of still table wine; 60 milliliters of perfume; 250 milliliters of toilet water; plus £136 worth of other goods, including gifts and souvenirs.

D

DISABILITIES & ACCESSIBILITY

California is a national leader in making attractions and facilities accessible to people with disabilities. Since 1982 the state building code has required that all areas for public use be made accessible. State laws more than a decade old provide special privileges, such as license plates allowing special parking spaces, unlimited parking in time-limited spaces, and free parking in metered spaces. Insignia from states other than California are honored.

When discussing accessibility with an operator or reservationist, **ask hard questions.** Are there any stairs, inside *or* out? Are there grab bars next to the toilet *and* in the shower/tub? How wide is the doorway to the room? To the bathroom? For the most extensive facilities, meeting the latest legal specifications, **opt for newer accommodations,** which more often have been designed with access in mind. Older properties or ships must usually be retrofitted and may offer more limited facilities as a result. Be sure to **discuss your needs before booking.**

DISCOUNTS & DEALS

You shouldn't have to pay for a discount. In fact, you may already be eligible for all kinds of savings. Here are some time-honored strategies for getting the best deal.

LOOK IN YOUR WALLET

When you **use your credit card to make travel purchases,** you may get free travel-accident insurance, collision damage insurance, medical or legal assistance, depending on the card and bank that issued it. Visa and MasterCard provide one or more of these services, so **get a copy of your card's travel benefits.** If you are a member of the AAA or an oil-company-sponsored road-assistance plan, always **ask hotel or car-rental reservationists for auto-club discounts.** Some clubs offer additional discounts on tours, cruises, or admission to attractions. And don't forget that auto-club membership entitles you to free maps and trip-planning services.

JOIN A CLUB?

Discount clubs can be a legitimate source of savings, but you must use the participating hotels and visit the participating attractions in order to realize any benefits. Remember, too, that you have to pay a fee to join, so **determine if you'll save enough to warrant your membership fee.**

DIVERS' ALERT

Scuba divers take note: **Do not fly within 24 hours of scuba diving.**

G

GAY AND LESBIAN TRAVEL

San Francisco, Los Angeles, West Hollywood, San Diego, and Palm Springs are among the California cities with visible lesbian and gay communities (*see* Gay and Lesbian Travel *in* Important Contacts A to Z, *above,* for a list of local publications and switchboards).

I

INSURANCE

Travel insurance can protect your monetary investment, replace your luggage and its contents, or provide for medical coverage should you fall ill during your trip. Most tour operators, travel agents, and insurance agents sell specialized health-and-accident, flight, trip-cancellation, and luggage insurance as well as comprehensive policies with some or all of these coverages. Comprehensive policies may also reimburse you for delays due to weather—an important consideration if you're traveling during the winter months. Some health-insurance policies do not cover preexisting conditions, but waivers may be available in specific cases. Coverage is sold by the companies listed in Important Contacts A to Z; these companies act as the policy's administrators. The actual insurance is usually underwritten by a well-known name, such as The Travelers or Continental Insurance.

Before you make any purchase, **review your existing health and home-owner policies** to find out whether they cover expenses incurred while traveling.

BAGGAGE

Airline liability for baggage is limited to $1,250 per person on domestic flights. On international flights, it amounts to $9.07 per pound or $20 per kilogram for checked baggage (roughly $640 per 70-pound bag) and $400 per passenger for unchecked baggage. Insurance for losses exceeding the terms of your airline ticket can be bought directly from the airline at check-in for about $10 per $1,000 of coverage; note that it excludes a rather extensive list of items, shown on your airline ticket.

COMPREHENSIVE

Comprehensive insurance policies include all the coverages described above plus some that may not be available in more specific policies. If you have purchased an expensive vacation, especially one that involves travel abroad, comprehensive insurance is a must; **look for policies that include trip delay insurance,** which will protect you in the event that weather problems cause you to miss your flight, tour, or cruise. A few insurers will also sell you a waiver for preexisting medical conditions. Some of the companies that offer both these features are Access America, Carefree Travel, Travel Insured International, and

TravelGuard (☞ Insurance *in* Important Contacts A to Z, *above*).

FLIGHT

You should **think twice before buying flight insurance.** A supplement to the airlines' coverage, it's expensive and basically unnecessary. Charging a ticket to a major credit card often automatically provides you with coverage that may also extend to travel by bus, train, and ship.

U.K. TRAVELERS

According to the Association of British Insurers, a trade association representing 450 insurance companies, it's wise to **buy extra medical coverage when you visit the United States.** You can buy an annual travel insurance policy valid for most vacations during the year in which it's purchased. If you are pregnant or have a preexisting medical condition make sure you're covered before buying such a policy.

TRIP

Without insurance, you will lose all or most of your money if you cancel your trip regardless of the reason. Especially if your airline ticket, cruise, or package tour is nonrefundable and cannot be changed, it's essential that you **buy trip-cancellation-and-interruption insurance.** When considering how much coverage you need, look for a policy that will cover the cost of your trip plus the nondiscounted price of a one-way airline ticket should you need to return home early. Read the fine print carefully,

especially sections that define "family member" and "preexisting medical conditions." Also **consider default or bankruptcy insurance,** which protects you against a supplier's failure to deliver. Be aware, however, that if you buy such a policy from a travel agency, tour operator, airline, or cruise line, it may not cover default by the firm in question.

L

LODGING

Hotels in cities may or may not provide parking facilities, and there is usually a charge if they do. Motels, which are more common along the highways and outside cities, have parking space but may not have some of the amenities that hotels typically have—on-site restaurants, lounges, and room service.

Bed-and-breakfasts and inns have become extremely popular in California. These are not usually economy lodgings—their prices are often at the top of the scale. Most typically they are large, older homes, renovated and charmingly decorated with antiques, with a half-dozen guest rooms. Sometimes the inn is a renovated hotel from the last century with a dozen or more rooms. The price usually includes breakfast, which may be a Continental breakfast—juice, coffee, and some simple pastries—or a four-course feast. Baths may be private or shared. Few B&Bs allow smoking; virtually none take pets.

APARTMENT & VILLA RENTAL

If you want a home base that's roomy enough for a family and comes with cooking facilities, **consider taking a furnished rental.** This can also save you money, but not always—some rentals are luxury properties (economical only when your party is large). Home-exchange directories list rentals—often second homes owned by prospective house swappers—and some services search for a house or apartment for you (even a castle if that's your fancy) and handle the paperwork. Some send an illustrated catalog; others send photographs only of specific properties, sometimes at a charge; up-front registration fees may apply.

HOME EXCHANGE

If you would like to find a house, an apartment, or some other type of vacation property to exchange for your own while on holiday, **become a member of a home-exchange organization,** which will send you its updated listings of available exchanges for a year and will include your own listing in at least one of them. Arrangements for the actual exchange are made by the two parties involved, not by the organization.

M
MONEY & EXPENSES

CASH ADVANCES

Before leaving home, **make sure that your credit cards have been programmed for ATM use.** Local bank cards often do not work overseas either; **ask your bank about a Global Access debit card,** which works like a bank card but can be used at any ATM displaying a Visa logo.

N
NATIONAL PARKS

If you are a frequent visitor, senior citizen, or traveler with a disability, you can **save money on park entrance fees** by getting a discount pass. The Golden Eagle Pass can be a good deal if you plan to visit several parks during your travels. Priced at $25, it entitles you and your companions to free admission to *all* parks for a year. It does not cover additional park fees such as those for camping or parking. Both the Golden Age Passport, for U.S. citizens or permanent residents 62 or older, and the Golden Access Passport, for travelers with disabilities, entitle holders to free entry to all national parks plus 50% off fees for the use of all park facilities and services except those run by private concessionaires. Both passports are free; you must show proof of age and U.S. citizenship or permanent residency (such as a U.S. passport, driver's license, or birth certificate) or proof of disability. All three passes are available at all national park entrances.

P
PACKING FOR CALIFORNIA

The most important single rule to bear in mind in packing for a California vacation is to **prepare for changes in temperature.** An hour's drive can take you up or down many degrees, and the variation from daytime to nighttime in a single location is often marked. Take along sweaters, jackets, and clothes for layering as your best insurance for coping with variations in temperature. Include shorts or cool cottons unless you are packing for a midwinter ski trip. Always tuck in a bathing suit; most lodgings have a pool, spa, and sauna.

While casual dressing is a hallmark of the California lifestyle, in the evening men will need a jacket and tie for many good restaurants, and women will be more comfortable in something dressier than regulation sightseeing garb.

Considerations of formality aside, bear in mind that **San Francisco and other coastal towns can be chilly** at any time of the year, especially in summer, when the fog is apt to descend and stay.

Bring an extra pair of eyeglasses or contact lenses in your carry-on luggage, and if you have a health problem, **pack enough medication** to last the trip. It's important that you **don't put prescription drugs or valuables in luggage to** be checked, for it could go astray.

LUGGAGE

Airline baggage allowances depend on the airline, the route, and the class of your ticket; ask in advance. In general, on domestic flights you are entitled to check two bags. A third piece may be brought on board, but it must fit easily under the seat in front of you or in the overhead compartment. In the United States, the FAA gives airlines broad latitude regarding carry-on allowances, and they tend to tailor them to different aircraft and operational conditions. Charges for excess, oversize, or overweight pieces vary.

SAFEGUARDING YOUR LUGGAGE➤ Before leaving home, **itemize your bags' contents** and their worth, and label them with your name, address, and phone number. (If you use your home address, cover it so that potential thieves can't see it readily.) Inside each bag, **pack a copy of your itinerary.** At check-in, **make sure that each bag is correctly tagged** with the destination airport's three-letter code. If your bags arrive damaged—or fail to arrive at all—file a written report with the airline before leaving the airport.

PASSPORTS & VISAS

CANADIANS

No passport is necessary to enter the United States.

U.K. CITIZENS

British citizens need a valid passport to enter the United States. If you are staying for fewer than 90 days and traveling on a vacation, with a return or onward ticket, you probably will not need a visa. However, you will need to fill out the Visa Waiver Form, 1-94W, supplied by the airline.

It is advisable that you **leave one photocopy of your passport's data page** with someone at home and keep another with you, separated from your passport, while traveling. If you lose your passport, promptly call the nearest embassy or consulate and the local police; having the data page information can speed replacement.

SENIOR-CITIZEN DISCOUNTS

To qualify for age-related discounts, **mention your senior-citizen status up front** when booking hotel reservations, not when checking out, and before you're seated in restaurants, not when paying the bill. Note that discounts may be limited to certain menus, days, or hours. When renting a car, **ask about promotional car-rental discounts**—they can net even lower costs than your senior-citizen discount.

STUDENTS ON THE ROAD

To save money, **look into deals available through student-oriented travel agencies.**

To qualify, you'll need to have a bona fide student ID card. Members of international student groups are also eligible (☞ Students *in* Important Contacts A to Z, *above*).

T

TELEPHONES

LONG-DISTANCE

The long-distance services of AT&T, MCI, and Sprint make calling home relatively convenient and let you avoid hotel surcharges; typically, you dial an 800 number in the United States.

TIPPING

At restaurants, a 15% tip is standard for waiters; up to 20% may be expected at more expensive establishments. The same goes for taxi drivers, bartenders, and hairdressers. Coat-check operators usually expect $1; bellhops and porters should get 50¢ to $1 per bag; hotel maids in upscale hotels should get about $1 per day of your stay. On package tours, conductors and drivers usually get $10 per day from the group as a whole; check whether this has already been figured into your cost. For local sightseeing tours, you may individually tip the driver-guide $1 if he or she has been helpful or informative. Ushers in theaters do not expect tips.

TOUR OPERATORS

A package or tour to California can make your vacation less expensive and more hassle-free. Firms that

THE GOLD GUIDE / SMART TRAVEL TIPS

sell tours and packages reserve airline seats, hotel rooms, and rental cars in bulk and pass some of the savings on to you. In addition, the best operators have local representatives available to help you at your destination.

A GOOD DEAL?

The more your package or tour includes, the better you can predict the ultimate cost of your vacation. Make sure you know exactly what is covered, and **beware of hidden costs.** Are taxes, tips, and service charges included? Transfers and baggage handling? Entertainment and excursions? These can add up.

Most packages and tours are rated deluxe, first-class superior, first class, tourist, or budget. The key difference is usually accommodations. If the package or tour you are considering is priced lower than in your wildest dreams, **be skeptical.** Also, **make sure your travel agent knows the accommodations** and other services. Ask about the hotel's location, room size, beds, and whether it has a pool, room service, or programs for children, if you care about these. Has your agent been there in person or sent others you can contact?

BUYER BEWARE

Each year a number of consumers are stranded or lose their money when operators—even very large ones with excellent reputations— go out of business. To avoid becoming one of

them, take the time to **check out the operator**—find out how long the company has been in business and ask several agents about its reputation. Next, **don't book unless the firm has a consumer-protection program.** Members of the USTOA and the NTA are required to set aside funds for the sole purpose of covering your payments and travel arrangements in case of default. Nonmember operators may instead carry insurance; look for the details in the operator's brochure— and for the name of an underwriter with a solid reputation. Note: When it comes to tour operators, **don't trust escrow accounts.** Although there are laws governing those of charter-flight operators, no governmental body prevents tour operators from raiding the till.

Next, **contact your local Better Business Bureau and the attorney general's offices** in both your own state and the operator's; have any complaints been filed? Finally, **pay with a major credit card.** Then you can cancel payment, provided that you can document your complaint. Always **consider trip-cancellation insurance** (☞ Insurance, *above*).

Big vs. Small➤ Operators that handle several hundred thousand travelers per year can use their purchasing power to give you a good price. Their high volume may also indicate financial stability. But some small companies provide more

personalized service; because they tend to specialize, they may also be more knowledgeable about a given area.

USING AN AGENT

Travel agents are excellent resources. In fact, large operators accept bookings made only through travel agents. But it's good to **collect brochures from several agencies** because some agents' suggestions may be skewed by promotional relationships with tour and package firms that reward them for volume sales. If you have a special interest, **find an agent with expertise in that area**; ASTA can provide leads in the United States. (Don't rely solely on your agent, though; agents may be unaware of small-niche operators, and some special-interest travel companies only sell direct.)

SINGLE TRAVELERS

Prices are usually quoted per person, based on two sharing a room. If traveling solo, you may be required to pay the full double-occupancy rate. Some operators eliminate this surcharge if you agree to be matched up with a roommate of the same sex, even if one is not found by departure time.

W
WHEN TO GO

Any time of the year is the right time to go to California. There won't be skiable snow in the mountains between Easter and Thanksgiving; there will usually be rain in December, January, and February in the lowlands, if that bothers you; it will be much too hot to enjoy Palm Springs or Death Valley in the summer. But San Francisco, Los Angeles, and San Diego are delightful year-round; the Wine Country's seasonal variables are enticing; and the coastal areas are almost always cool.

The climate varies amazingly in California, not only over distances of several hundred miles but occasionally within an hour's drive. A foggy, cool August day in San Francisco makes you grateful for a sweater, tweed jacket, or light wool coat. Head north 50 miles to the Napa Valley to check out the Wine Country, and you'll probably wear shirt sleeves and thin cottons.

Daytime and nighttime temperatures may also swing widely apart. Take Sacramento, a city that is at sea level but in California's Central Valley. In the summer, afternoons can be very warm indeed, in the 90s and occasionally over 100°. But the nights cool down, often dropping 40°.

It's hard to generalize much about the weather in this varied state. Rain comes in the winter, with snow at higher elevations. Summers are dry everywhere. As a rule, compared to the coastal areas, which are cool year-round, inland regions are warmer in summer and cooler in winter. As you climb into the mountains, there are more distinct variations with the seasons: Winter brings snow, autumn is crisp, spring is variable, and summer is clear and warm.

CLIMATE

The following are average daily maximum and minimum temperatures for the major California cities.

Climate in California

LOS ANGELES

Jan.	64F	18C	May	72F	22C	Sept.	81F	27C
	44	7		53	12		60	16
Feb.	64F	18C	June	76F	24C	Oct.	76F	24C
	46	8		57	14		55	13
Mar.	66F	19C	July	81F	27C	Nov.	71F	22C
	48	9		60	16		48	9
Apr.	70F	21C	Aug.	82F	28C	Dec.	66F	19C
	51	11		62	17		46	8

SAN DIEGO

Jan.	62F	17C	May	66F	19C	Sept.	73F	23C
	46	8		55	13		62	17
Feb.	62F	17C	June	69F	21C	Oct.	71F	22C
	48	9		59	15		57	14
Mar.	64F	18C	July	73F	23C	Nov.	69F	21C
	50	10		62	17		51	11
Apr.	66F	19C	Aug.	73F	23C	Dec.	64F	18C
	53	12		64	18		48	9

SAN FRANCISCO

Jan.	55F	13C	May	66F	19C	Sept.	73F	23C
	41	5		48	9		51	11
Feb.	59F	15C	June	69F	21C	Oct.	69F	21C
	42	6		51	11		50	10
Mar.	60F	16C	July	69F	21C	Nov.	64F	18C
	44	7		51	11		44	7
Apr.	62F	17C	Aug.	69F	21C	Dec.	57F	14C
	46	8		53	12		42	6

1 Destination: California

RESTLESS NIRVANA

COASTAL CALIFORNIA began its migration from somewhere far to the south millions of years ago. It's still moving north along the San Andreas Fault, but you have plenty of time for a visit before Santa Monica hits the Arctic Circle. If you've heard predictions that some of the state may fall into the Pacific, take the long view and consider that much of California has been in and out of the ocean throughout its history. The forces that raised its mountains and formed the Central Valley are still at work.

Upheaval has always been a fact of life in California—below ground and above. Floods, earthquakes, racial strife, immigration woes, high unemployment, and Orange County's scandal-ridden bankruptcy are but a few of the high-profile traumas—not to mention that famous celebrity murder case—that have tarnished California's image in recent years. Things got so bad in the early 1990s that U-Haul declared a shortage of trucks because so many residents were abandoning the Golden State. This was just fine with the many natives whose "Welcome to California: Now Go Home" bumper stickers had greeted several decades of arrivals—few states have grown as rapidly as California, which had a population of approximately 7 million as World War II came to a close and now is home to more than 32 million.

From the outside looking in, it may have seemed that, along with its AAA bond rating, California might lose its appeal as a travel destination. But even before its stunning economic turnaround, the Golden State had too many "positives" to be written off: dramatic coastline; rugged desert and mountain regions; Hollywood glitz and Palm Springs glamour; a potpourri of Pacific Rim, European, and Latin American influences; and a fabled history as a conduit for fame and fortune, hope and renewal.

California has always been a place where initiative—as opposed to class, family, or other connections—is honored above all else. The state has lured assertive types who metaphorically or otherwise have come seeking "gold"—in the Sacramento foothills, in Hollywood, and, more recently, in the Silicon Valley. To be sure, not everyone achieves the mythical California dream, but neither is it totally an illusion. The sense of infinite possibility, as much a by-product of the state's varied and striking land forms as media hype, is what most tourists notice on their first trip. It's why so many return—sometimes forever.

More so than most of its residents are willing to admit, California is a land of contradiction, where "reality" is a matter of opinion—which is why the cinema, an enterprise based wholly on the manipulation of reality, is the perfect signature industry for the state. Take for instance two volumes in many local libraries about the historic chain of 21 California missions established by Spanish Catholic priests, most notably Father Junípero Serra. One book is titled *California's Missions: Their Romance and Beauty*. Its author details Serra's strategy "to convert and civilize the Indians" who resided in late-18th-century California. The other tome, *The Missions of California: A Legacy of Genocide*, disputes the contentions of "mission apologists" and illustrates how on levels physical and spiritual the mission system "was the first disaster for the Indian population of California."

The truth? It's likely somewhere in between (though recent scholarship has tended to show Serra and other missionaries in a less than favorable light). The treatment of other groups over the years has been equally problematic, and the scapegoating of "foreigners"—often by first-generation Californians with no sense of the irony of their protestations—is a cyclical blot on the state's conscience. California's move to the forefront of the controversy over affirmative action gave many across the nation the impression that its residents wish only to roll back the clock. But the circumstances here are more complex than they appear on the surface because the state has a more diverse population than most others in the Union. California may very well play an integral role in the formulation of more equitable and up-to-date antidiscrimination policies. In any case, as with the debate over immigration and the previous "taxpayer revolts" of the 1970s and 1980s, the state's residents have forced discussion of an issue that citizens elsewhere have brooded over but not confronted.

California is a restless nirvana. The sun shines and all is beautiful; then the earth shakes and all is shattered. It's time to rebuild. And the state bounces back—San Francisco from the 1906 and 1989 quakes, Los Angeles from ones in 1971 and 1994. Billions are made during the Cold War defense boom; then communism collapses, bases close, and unemployment skyrockets. It's time to diversify. And the state does, making new overtures to Asia and Latin America.

And to tourists, who find that although California isn't perfect—what place is?—it's a source of endless diversion, natural and man-made. "Wow!" is a word one hears often here—at Half Dome in Yosemite, during the "Backdraft: 10,000 Degrees of Excitement" experience at Universal Studios, in the pleasingly symmetrical courtyard of the J. Paul Getty Museum, or among the redwoods of Humboldt County. If Texans like things "big" and New Yorkers like a little style, what delights Californians most is drama—indoors or out.

There is no way to take in this "show" in one trip, so don't try. Seventy-five percent of California's visitors return at least once, an impressive quotient of satisfied customers. As you travel through California's various regions you will get a sense of the great diversity of cultures, the ongoing pull between preservation and development, and the state's unique place in the landscapes of geography and the imagination.

WHAT'S WHERE

Keep in mind the very long distances. If you drive between San Francisco and Los Angeles on Highway 1, remember that it is not only more than 400 miles but also a difficult road to drive. Scenic routes, such as Highway 1 along the coast, Highway 49 in the Gold Country, and Highways 50 and 120 across the Sierra Nevada, require attention to driving and enough time for frequent stops.

The Central Coast

Highway 1 between Big Sur and Santa Barbara is a spectacular stretch of terrain. The road demands an unhurried pace, but even if it didn't, you'd find yourself stopping often to take in the scenery. Don't expect much in the way of dining, lodging, or even history until you arrive at Hearst Castle, publisher William Randolph Hearst's testament to his own fabulousness. Sunny, well-scrubbed Santa Barbara's Spanish-Mexican heritage is reflected in the architectural style of its courthouse and mission.

The Far North

Soaring mountain peaks, wild rivers brimming with fish, and almost infinite recreational possibilities make the Far North a sports lover's paradise. Hot nightspots and cultural enclaves do not abound, but you will find some of the best hiking, fishing, and hunting in the state. Some Bay Area families return to this region year after year. Many enjoy the outdoors from their own piece of paradise—a private houseboat. Keep in mind that much of the Far North can be very hot in summer.

Lake Tahoe

The largest alpine lake in North America is famous for its clarity, deep blue water, and snowcapped peaks. Though Lake Tahoe possesses abundant natural beauty and accessible wilderness, nearby towns are highly developed and the roads around it often congested. Summertime is generally cooler here than in the foothills, and the clean mountain air bracingly crisp. When it gets hot, the plentiful beaches and brisk water are only minutes away.

Los Angeles

In certain lights Los Angeles displays its Spanish heritage, but much more evident is its participation in the Pacific Rim cultural and economic boom. Hollywood, the beaches, and Disneyland are all within an hour's drive. Also here are freeways (lots of them), important examples of 20th-century domestic architecture, and Beverly Hills, noted for its shops and mansions. Despite the city's reputation for a laid-back lifestyle, a visit here can be fairly over-whelming because of the size and variety of the region. Careful planning will help.

The Mojave Desert and Death Valley

When most people assemble their "must-see" list of California attractions, the desert isn't often among the top con-tenders. What with its heat and vast, sparsely populated tracts of land, the desert is no Disneyland. But that's precisely why it deserves a closer look. The natu-ral riches here stagger: rolling waves of sand dunes, black cinder cones thrusting up hundreds of feet into the air from a blis-tered desert floor, riotous sheets of wild-flowers, bizarrely shaped Joshua trees basking in an orange glow at sunset, and an abundant silence that is both dramatic and startling.

Monterey Bay

The Monterey Peninsula is steeped in his-tory. The town of Monterey was Cali-fornia's first capital, the Carmel Mission headquarters for California's entire 18th-century mission system. The peninsula also has a rich literary past. John Stein-beck's novels immortalize the area, and Robert Lewis Stevenson strolled its streets for inspiration for *Treasure Island*. The present is equally illustrious. Blessed with a natural splendor undiminished by time or commerce, the peninsula is home to vi-sionary marine habitats and luxurious re-sorts and golf courses.

The North Coast

The North Coast can only be summed up in superlatives. Migrating whales and other sea mammals swim past the dramatic bluffs that make the 400 miles of shore-line north of San Francisco to the Oregon border among the most photographed landscapes in the country. Along cypress-and redwood-studded Highway 1 you will find many small inns, uncrowded state beaches and parks, art galleries, and restaurants serving imaginative dishes that showcase locally produced ingredi-ents.

Palm Springs Desert Resorts

Palm Springs and its neighbors—Palm Desert, Rancho Mirage, Indian Wells—are among the fastest-growing and wealthi-est communities in the nation. The desert

lures visitors and residents for the same reasons: striking scenery and the therapeutic benefits of a warm, arid climate. Resort hotel complexes contain championship golf courses, tennis stadiums, and sparkling swimming pools—lushly landscaped oases, towering palms, natural waterfalls, and hot mineral springs round out the picture.

Sacramento and the Gold Country

The gold-mining region of the Sierra Nevada foothills is a less expensive, if also less sophisticated, region of Califor-nia but not without its pleasures, natural and man-made. Spring brings wildflow-ers, and in fall the hills are colored by bright-red berries and changing leaves. The hills are golden in the summer—and hot. Din-ing has improved remarkably in recent years, and many fine bed-and-breakfast inns have sprung up. The Gold Country has a mix of indoor and outdoor activi-ties, one of the many reasons it's a great place to take the kids.

San Diego

To visitors, the city and county of San Diego may seem like a conglomeration of theme parks: Old Town and the Gaslamp Quar-ter historically oriented ones, the wharf area a maritime-heritage playground, La Jolla a genteel throwback to southern California elegance, Balboa Park a con-vergence of the town's cerebral and action-oriented personae. There are, of course, real theme parks—Sea World and the zoo and Wild Animal Park—but the great outdoors, in the form of forests, land-scaped urban areas, and a string of sandy beaches, forms the biggest of them all.

San Francisco

San Francisco is a sophisticated city with world-class hotels and the greatest con-centration of excellent restaurants in the state. The town has an undeserved repu-tation as the kook capital of the United States, yet it's the country's number one tourist destination. Why? To use the ver-nacular, the vibe here is cool, from North Beach coffeehouses to Chinatown tea em-poriums, Golden Gate Park, and Haight Street's head shops (yes, they're still around). People in San Francisco know how to have a good time; the high spirits can't help but rub off on visitors.

The Sierra National Parks

The highlight for many California travelers is a visit to one of the national parks in the Sierra Nevada mountain range. Yosemite is the state's most famous park and every bit as sublime as one expects. Its Yosemite-type or U-shape valleys were formed by the action of glaciers during recent ice ages. Other examples are found in Kings Canyon and Sequoia national parks, which are adjacent to each other and usually visited together. All the Sierra National Parks contain fine, tall groves of *Sequoiadendron gigantea* trees.

The Wine Country

The Wine Country is one of California's most popular tourist regions. Many Sonoma and Napa Valley wineries are perfect sites for meals, picnics, or tastings, and there are top-notch bed-and-breakfasts and restaurants in the area. There are many ways to explore the region: hiking and bicycling for the active set and going on balloon, train, and glider rides for those seeking a less strenuous overview. People here know how to pamper themselves: in Calistoga and other towns are resorts and health spas with mud baths, massages, sulfur whirlpool baths, and other rejuvenating treatments.

PLEASURES AND PASTIMES

Beaches

With 1,264 miles of coastline, California is well supplied with beaches. They are endlessly fascinating: you can walk on them, lie and sun on them, watch seabirds and hunt for shells, dig clams, or spot seals and sea otters at play. From December through March you can witness the migrations of the gray whales. What you can't always do at these beaches is swim. From San Francisco northward, the water is simply too cold for all but extremely hardy souls. Even along the southern half of the coast, some beaches are too dangerous for swimming because of the undertow. Look for signs and postings and take them seriously.

Access to beaches in California is generally excellent. The state park system includes many fine beaches, and oceanside communities have their own public beaches. Through the work of the California Coastal Commission, many stretches of private property that would otherwise seal off a beach from outsiders have public-access paths and trails.

Dining

California's name has come to signify a certain type of modern, healthful, sophisticated cuisine, using local ingredients, creatively combined and served in often stunning presentations. San Francisco and Los Angeles have scores of top-notch restaurants—an expensive meal at one of these gourmet shrines is often the high point of a trip to California. The Wine Country, just north of San Francisco, and Santa Barbara are also known for superb restaurants. In coastal areas, most restaurants' menus usually include some seafood, fresh off the boat. Don't neglect the culinary bounty of California's mixed ethnic population—notably Mexican and Chinese, but also Japanese, Scandinavian, Italian, French, Belgian, English, Thai, and German restaurants.

Fishing

California has abundant fishing options: deep-sea fishing expeditions, surf fishing from the shore, and freshwater fishing in streams, rivers, lakes, and reservoirs. You'll need a California fishing license (☞ Sports *in* Important Contacts A to Z).

Golf

Golf is a year-round sport in California. Though its most famous courses are in the Pebble Beach and Palm Springs desert resorts areas, there are championship courses all over the state (☞ Outdoor Activities and Sports in each chapter for listings of courses).

Hot-Air Ballooning

Large, colorful balloons drift across the valleys of the Wine Country, where the air drafts are particularly friendly to this pastime, as well as in San Diego, the Palm Springs area, and the Gold Country. Hot-air ballooning is not cheap, however: a ride costs in excess of $100 (☞ Theme Trips *in* Important Contacts A to Z).

Parks

NATIONAL PARKS➤ There are eight national parks in California: Death Valley,

Joshua Tree, Lassen Volcanic, Redwood, Sequoia, Kings Canyon, Yosemite, and the Channel Islands. National monuments include Cabrillo, in San Diego, and Muir Woods, north of San Francisco.

California has three national recreation areas: Golden Gate, with 87,000 acres both north and south of the Golden Gate Bridge in San Francisco; the Santa Monica Mountains, with 150,000 acres from Griffith Park in Los Angeles to Point Mugu in Ventura County; and Whiskeytown-Shasta-Trinity, with 240,000 acres, including four major lakes, in the Far North. Point Reyes National Seashore is on a peninsula north of San Francisco.

STATE PARKS➤ California's state-park system includes more than 200 sites; many are recreational and scenic, others historic or scientific. Among the popular sites are Angel Island in San Francisco Bay, reached by ferry from San Francisco or Tiburon; Anza-Borrego Desert, 600,000 acres of the Colorado Desert northeast of San Diego; Humboldt Redwoods, with its tall trees; Empire Mine, one of the richest mines in the Mother Lode, in Grass Valley; Hearst Castle at San Simeon; and Leo Carrillo Beach, north of Malibu, with lively tidal pools and numerous secret coves. Most state parks are open year-round.

Shopping

If you are shopping for something unique to California, look at the output of its many resident artists and craftspeople. You can find their creations—paintings, drawings, sculpture, wood carvings, pottery, jewelry, handwoven fabrics, handmade baskets—from one end of the state to the other at city galleries, neighborhood shops, out-of-the-way mountain studios, roadside stands, and county fairs. San Francisco and Los Angeles are centers of clothing manufacture; if you're a bargain hunter, you'll want to explore the factory outlets in both cities.

Skiing

Snow skiing in the Lake Tahoe area and elsewhere is generally limited to the period between Thanksgiving and late April, though in years of heavy snowfall skiers can still hit some trails as late as July. Other ski options include Mt. Shasta and Lassen Volcanic National Park in the Far North, and Mammoth Lake and the San

Bernardino Mountains in southern California.

Water Sports

Swimming and surfing, scuba diving, and skin diving in the Pacific Ocean are favorite year-round California pleasures in the southern part of the state, although these become seasonal sports on the coast from San Francisco northward. Sailboats are available for rent in many places along the coast and inland. River rafting—whitewater and otherwise—canoeing, and kayaking are popular, especially in the northern part of the state, where there are many rivers.

Wine Tasting

You can visit wineries in many parts of the state, not only in the Wine Country north of San Francisco. Vintners associations in the Gold Country, Santa Barbara, Santa Cruz, and other wine-growing areas provide brochures (see individual chapters for details) with lists of wineries that open for tastings. Wineries and good wine stores will package your purchases for safe travel or shipping.

NEW AND NOTEWORTHY

San Francisco

San Franciscans are talking about a "whole new era" these days, what with the 1996 inauguration of flashy mayor Willie Brown, voter approval for a new downtown baseball stadium (scheduled for completion in time for the 2000 baseball season), and new construction or renovation of some major cultural facilities. The ball got rolling in 1995 with the opening of the $62 million **San Francisco Museum of Modern Art.** The building, designed by internationally celebrated Mario Botta and an instant hit, gave the city's collection of 20th-century art a world-class setting for the first time. The museum and nearby Yerba Buena Gardens arts complex, with its inviting grass esplanade, continue to attract cultural institutions to the surrounding blocks. The **California Historical Society**'s library and gallery moved here in late 1995, and the Mexican Museum plans to arrive before the end of the century.

Performing-arts organizations remain at temporary locations this year, primarily because of seismic upgrades of their permanent homes. The **War Memorial Opera House** will be closed through September 1997, making nomads out of San Francisco's opera and ballet. The **American Conservatory Theater,** the city's leading nonprofit theater company, returned to its stunningly restored home, the historic **Geary Theater,** which had been damaged by the 1989 Loma Prieta earthquake. The new, state-of-the-art **San Francisco Public Library,** designed to meld with the Civic Center's stately collection of classical beauties, holds twice the number of books as its predecessor; its interior features a five-story skylit atrium, a café, many special-collection rooms, and a rooftop garden and terrace. On the northwestern edge of the city, the **California Palace of the Legion of Honor,** which specializes in European painting, drawings, and sculpture, reopened to great acclaim in the fall of 1995.

The long-delayed **Underwater World** at **Pier 39** finally opened in 1996, affording visitors a glimpse, from a transparent tunnel, of 2,000 marine species in a 700,000-gallon aquarium. Another recent attraction at Pier 39 is *San Francisco: The Movie,* a 35-minute, 70mm travelogue projected onto an oversize screen.

Along the Embarcadero, which has been undergoing face-lift after face-lift since the Loma Prieta earthquake, the **Promenade Ribbon**—a 5-foot-wide, 2½-mile-long glass-and-concrete strip billed as the "longest art form in the nation"—is the waterfront's yellow-brick road. Due for completion in 1997, it will run from Telegraph Hill down to South Beach.

Union Square continues its transformation from a shopping district serving San Francisco's old guard to a livelier neighborhood. **Nike Town,** expected to open early in 1997, will be a retail theater of athletic wear and video entertainment.

Los Angeles

Angel's Flight, the world's shortest funicular ride, was erected in 1901 and taken out of service in 1969. After a restoration project, two orange-and-black Victorian trolleys are once again grappling with steep Bunker Hill, making their way up a 45-degree angle to California Plaza, home of the Museum of Contemporary Art. Another back-to-the-future attraction, the novel **Museum of Neon Art,** moved to the city center following a brief stint at Universal City Walk. The museum contains illuminating exhibitions by local artists, as well as vintage advertising signs made of the electrified gaseous material.

The $360 million **J. Paul Getty Center** is expected to open in 1997 in the Santa Monica Mountains, high above Brentwood. The entire Getty collection, with the exception of the benefactor's antiquities, which will remain housed in the J. Paul Getty Museum in Malibu, will be exhibited in the new setting.

The **Hollywood Entertainment Museum** has scheduled a fall 1997 move into the former Max Factor Museum building in the heart of Hollywood. Visitors will get to know Tinseltown through artifacts, films, and early recordings. The **Aquarium of the Pacific** is set to open in 1997 as Queensway Bay's new centerpiece attraction, in San Pedro near the *Queen Mary.* At **Disneyland,** the big news is a revamping of **Tomorrowland** that will begin in 1997 prior to a 1998 debut. Rides like the **Astro Orbiter** and **Rocket Rods** should send everyone spinning. A new 3-D film *Honey, I Shrunk the Audience,* will replace Michael Jackson's *Captain E-O.*

Los Angeles may have lost both of its pro-football teams, but the city does have a new major-league soccer club, the **Los Angeles Galaxy,** which plays at the Rose Bowl.

San Diego

Balboa Park, one of the nation's great cultural and recreational centers, saw the completion of several renovation projects in 1996. The **Mingei International Museum,** one of only a handful of facilities in the world devoted to the subject of folk art, moved into a new Spanish–style building that blends well with the older park architecture. Two of Balboa Park's most important gardens underwent major alterations. Landscapers added 11 acres to the **Japanese Friendship Garden,** and a tea pavilion was slated for completion before the end of the year. Park horticulturists also recaptured the graceful lines of the Alcazar Garden during the California Pacific International Exposition of 1935–36. The site was modeled after the gardens surrounding the Alcazar Castle in Seville.

The main facility of the **Museum of Contemporary Art, San Diego** reopened in La Jolla after a two-year, $8.3 million expansion and remodeling directed by renowned architect Robert Venturi and his colleagues at Venturi, Scott Brown, and Associates. The museum's setting rivals the art: patrons can look out from the top of a grand stairway onto a garden that contains rare 100-year-old California plant specimens and, beyond that, to the Pacific Ocean.

San Diego remains an auto-oriented city, but it's easier than ever to see its historic Old Town section now that the trolley line has expanded east. Another transit addition: the *Coaster,* a new light rail line that runs from Oceanside into the downtown area.

On the shopping front, longtime southern California retailer The Broadway went out of business. Before too many tears could be shed, though, renowned retailer Macy's stepped into the void, making a splashy San Diego debut.

Sacramento

As the gateway to the Gold Country, Sacramento is gearing up for the three-year-long **California Gold Discovery to Statehood Sesquicentennial** celebration, set to run throughout the Golden State from 1998 to 2000.

Preservation remains a priority in the state's capital. Looking to the past for inspiration, Sacramento has facilitated the rehabilitation of street after tree-shaded street of **Victorian and Edwardian mansions** and smaller homes surrounding the Capitol building.

Three decades in the making, refurbished **Old Sacramento** now successfully recaptures the feeling of riverfront life during the gold rush. Shops lining gaslit cobblestone streets fulfill the same functions they did a century and a half ago, purveying merchandise needed by visitors passing through. The centerpiece of the area remains the **California State Railroad Mu-**

seum, the largest and most comprehensive collection of its kind in the area.

FODOR'S CHOICE

No two people will agree on what makes a perfect vacation, but it can be helpful to know what others think. Below is a list of Fodor's Choices. We hope you'll have a chance to experience some of them yourself while visiting California. We have tried to include something for everyone and from every price category. For more detailed information about each entry, refer to the appropriate chapters within this guidebook.

Lodging

★**Château du Sureau, Oakhurst.** This romantic inn is a fairy-tale castle. With Erna's Elderberry House restaurant, one of California's best, right on the premises, you may find it hard to tear yourself away to visit nearby Yosemite National Park. *$$$$*

★**Hotel Bel-Air, Los Angeles.** This secluded celebrity mecca's extensive exotic gardens and creek (complete with swans) make for a resortlike ambience right in the city. *$$$$*

★**Ritz-Carton Hotel, Laguna Niguel.** The classiest hotel along the coast, the Ritz draws guests from around the world with its sweeping oceanside views, gleaming marble, and stunning antiques. *$$$$*

★**Post Ranch Inn, Big Sur.** This luxurious retreat is the ultimate in environmentally conscious architecture. Each unit has its own hot tub, stereo system, private deck, and massage table. *$$$$*

★**Hotel Majestic, San Francisco.** One of San Francisco's original grand hotels, this five-story yellow-and-white Edwardian looks like a wedding cake. *$$$*

★**The Lodge at Torrey Pines, La Jolla.** This inn commands a view of miles and miles of coastline. It's adjacent to a public golf course, a state beach, and a nature reserve. *$$*

★**San Simeon Pines Motel, Cambria.** Set amid 9 acres of pines and cypresses, this motel-style resort near Hearst Castle has its own golf course and is directly across from Leffingwell's Landing, a state picnic area on the rocky beach. $–$$

Scenic Drives

★**17-Mile Drive, Carmel.** The wonders are both man-made and natural as this road winds its way through Carmel and Pebble Beach.

★**Highway 1 from Big Sur to San Simeon.** The twisting section of coastal highway affords some breathtaking ocean vistas before arriving at Hearst Castle.

★**Highway 49, the Gold Country.** California's pioneer past comes to life in the many towns along this 325-mile highway at the base of the Sierra foothills.

★**Kings Canyon Highway.** During the summer, the stretch of Highway 180 in Kings Canyon National Park from Grant Grove to Cedar Grove is spectacular.

★**Mulholland Drive, Los Angeles.** One of the most famous thoroughfares in Los Angeles winds through the Hollywood Hills, across the spine of the Santa Monica Mountains, stopping just short of the Pacific Ocean.

Historic Buildings

★**Coit Tower, San Francisco.** The WPA-era murals are as striking as the view at this monument to its city's volunteer firefighters.

★**Lachryma Montis (General Vallejo's Home), Sonoma.** The last Mexican governor of California built this large Victorian Gothic house with a white marble fireplace in every room.

★**Griffith Park Observatory and Planetarium, Los Angeles.** One of the largest telescopes in the world is open to the public for free viewing every clear night. In the planetarium—immortalized in *Rebel Without a Cause*—dazzling daily shows duplicate the starry sky.

★**Hearst Castle, San Simeon.** In its heyday a playground for the rich and famous, this renowned attraction sits in solitary splendor on the 127 acres that were the heart of newspaper magnate William Randolph Hearst's 250,000-acre ranch.

★**Hotel Del Coronado, San Diego.** Coronado Island's most prominent landmark was the world's first electrically lighted hotel.

★**Mann's Chinese Theater, Hollywood.** The architecture of the former "Grauman's Chinese" is a fantasy of pagodas and temples. Its courtyard is open for browsing of celebrity cement hand- and footprints.

★**Mission Santa Barbara.** The "queen" of the chain of 21 Spanish missions established in California is still active as a Catholic church.

★**California State Capitol, Sacramento.** The lacy plasterwork of the rotunda of this 1869 structure has all the complexity and color of a Fabergé egg. Outside, the 40-acre Capitol Park is one of the oldest gardens in the state.

Lovely Sights

★**El Capitan and Half Dome, Yosemite National Park.** Yosemite's two most famous peaks are also its most photographed.

★**View from Emerald Bay Lookout, Lake Tahoe.** This aquatic cul-de-sac is famed for its jewel-like shape and colors.

★**Golden Gate Bridge Vista Point and Marin Headlands, Marin County.** On a clear day, San Francisco glistens from this vantage point at the bridge's north end.

★**Huntington Library, Art Gallery, and Gardens, Pasadena.** The botanical splendors here include the 12-acre Desert Garden and 1,500 varieties of camellias.

★**La Jolla Cove at sunset.** It's beautiful any time of day, but as the sun goes down over the cove and its towering palms, the view is a postcard come to life.

Restaurants with Fabulous Atmosphere

★**Stars, San Francisco.** Jeremiah Tower's eatery is a must on every traveling gourmet's itinerary. The dining room has a clublike ambience, and the food ranges from grills to ragouts to sautés. $$$

★**George's at the Cove, La Jolla.** A wall-length window in the elegant main dining room, renowned for its fresh seafood specials, overlooks the cove. There's also an informal café and outdoor terrace, both with sweeping views of the coast. $$–$$$

★**Granita, Malibu.** Wolfgang Puck's coastal outpost has striking interior details and a menu that favors seafood, along with the chef's signature California-inspired dishes. *$$–$$$*

★**Greens at Fort Mason, San Francisco.** The expansive bay views alone would be worth a visit to this airy restaurant. The bonus: a wide, eclectic, and creative spectrum of meatless cooking. The homemade breads promise nirvana. *$$–$$$*

★**Café Beaujolais, Mendocino.** All the rustic charm of peaceful, backwoods Mendocino is here, with great country cook-

ing to boot. The ever-evolving dinner menu is cross-cultural. *$$*

★**Montrio, Monterey.** *Esquire* named this Restaurant of the Year in 1995, declaring that it "sums up in every way what is best about California restaurants." The magazine's right. *$$*

★**Samoa Cookhouse, Samoa (near Eureka).** Get a feel for dining during the heyday of the North Coast logging industry at this lumberman's hangout, which dates back to the late 19th century. *$*

FESTIVALS AND SEASONAL EVENTS

WINTER

JANUARY➤ Palo Alto's annual **East-West Shrine All-Star Football Classic** (☎ 415/661–0291) is America's oldest all-star sports event. In Pasadena, the annual **Tournament of Roses Parade and Football Game** (☎ 818/449–7673) takes place on New Year's Day, with lavish flower-decked floats, marching bands, and equestrian teams, followed by the Rose Bowl game.

FEBRUARY➤ The legendary **AT&T Pebble Beach National Pro-Am** golf tournament (☎ 408/649–1533) begins in late January and ends in early February. In San Francisco, home of the largest concentration of Chinese-Americans in the country, the climax to the annual **Chinese New Year Celebration** is the Golden Dragon Parade (☎ 415/982–3000). This year is the Year of the Ox. Los Angeles also has a Chinese New Year Parade (☎ 213/617–0396). Indio's **Riverside County Fair and National Date Festival** (☎ 619/863–8247) is an exotic county fair with an Arabian Nights theme; camel and ostrich races, date exhibits, and tastings are among the events.

SPRING

MARCH➤ **Snowfest** in North Lake Tahoe (☎ 916/583–7625) is the largest winter carnival in the West, with skiing, food, fireworks, parades, and live music. The finest female golfers in the world compete for the richest purse on the LPGA circuit at the **Nabisco Dinah Shore Golf Tournament** in Rancho Mirage (☎ 619/324–4546). The **Mendocino/Fort Bragg Whale Festival** (☎ 707/961–6300) includes whale-watching excursions, marine art exhibits, wine and beer tastings, crafts displays, and a chowder contest.

APRIL➤ A large cast presents the **Ramona Pageant,** a love story based on the novel by Helen Hunt Jackson, on weekends in late April and early May on a mountainside outdoor stage (☎ 909/658–3111). More than 1,200 costumed revelers re-create a springtime 16th-century country fair at the popular **Renaissance Pleasure Faire** (☎ 800/523–2473), from late April to mid-June in the foothills of the San Bernardino Mountains.

MAY➤ The **Music at the Wineries** festival in the Gold Country boosts spirits with a world-class jazz session in Plymouth (☎ 209/267–0211). Inspired by Mark Twain's story "The Notorious Jumping Frog of Calav-

eras County," the **Jumping Frog Jubilee** in Angels Camp (☎ 209/736–2561) is for frogs and trainers who take their competition seriously. Sacramento hosts the four-day **Dixieland Jazz Jubilee** (☎ 916/372–5277) usually on Memorial Day weekend or on one of the last two weekends in May; it's the world's largest Dixieland festival, with 125 bands from around the world. In Monterey, the squirmy squid is the main attraction for the Memorial Day weekend **Great Monterey Squid Festival** (☎ 408/649–6544). You'll see squid cleaning and cooking demonstrations, taste treats, and enjoy the usual festival fare: entertainment, arts and crafts, and educational exhibits.

SUMMER

JUNE➤ Starting in late May and running into early June is a national ceramics competition and exhibition called **Feats of Clay** in the Gold Country (☎ 916/645–9713). During the first weekend in June, Pasadena City Hall Plaza hosts the **Chalk It Up Festival.** Artists use the pavement as their canvas to create masterpieces that wash away when festivities have come to a close. There are also musical performances and exotic dining kiosks. The proceeds benefit arts and homeless organizations of the Light-Bringer Project (☎ 818/449–3689). A wine event for serious sippers, the **Napa Valley Wine Auction** in St. Helena features open houses, a wine tasting, and an auction. Preregistration by April 1 is required (☎ 707/963–5246). Each year on Father's Day is the **Tour of Nevada City Bicycle Classic** (☎ 916/265–2692 or 800/655–6569).

JULY➤ During the **Carmel Bach Festival,** the works of Johann Sebastian Bach and 18th-century contemporaries are performed for three weeks; events include concerts, recitals, and seminars (✉ Box 575, Carmel 93921, ☎ 408/624–1521). During the last weekend in July, Gilroy, the self-styled Garlic Capital of the World, celebrates its smelly but delicious product with the **Gilroy Garlic Festival** (☎ 408/842–1625), featuring such unusual concoctions as garlic ice cream.

AUGUST➤ The **California State Fair** (☎ 916/263–3000) showcases the state's agricultural side, with high-tech exhibits, rodeo, horse racing, carnival, and big-name entertainment. It runs 18 days from August to Labor Day in Sacramento. Santa Barbara's **Old Spanish Days' Fiesta** (☎ 805/962–8101) is the nation's largest all-equestrian parade. The citywide celebration includes two parades, two Mexican marketplaces, free variety shows with costumed dancers and singers, a carnival, and a rodeo.

The northern California **Renaissance Pleasure Faire** (☎ 800/523–2473) is held from late August to mid-October (at press time its location was undetermined).

AUTUMN

SEPTEMBER➤ In Guerneville, jazz fans and musicians jam at Johnson's Beach for the **Russian River Jazz Festival** (☎ 707/869–3940). The **San Francisco Blues Festival** (☎ 415/826–6837) is held at Fort Mason in late September. The **Los Angeles County Fair** in Pomona (☎ 909/623–3111) is the largest county fair in the world. It hosts entertainment, exhibits, livestock, horse racing, food, and more.

OCTOBER➤ The **Grand National Rodeo, Horse, and Stock Show** (☎ 415/469–6057) at San Francisco's Cow Palace is a 10-day, world-class competition, with 3,000 top livestock and horses. In Carmel, speakers and poets gather for readings on the beach, seminars, a banquet, and a book signing at the **Tor House Poetry Festival** (☎ 408/624–1813), which honors the poet Robinson Jeffers, an area resident for many years.

NOVEMBER➤ The **Death Valley '49er Encampment,** at Furnace Creek, commemorates the historic crossing of Death Valley in 1849, with a fiddlers' contest and an art show (☎ 619/786–2331). Pasadena's **Doo Dah Parade,** a fun-filled spoof of the annual Rose Parade, features the Lounge Lizards, who dress as reptiles and lip-sync to Frank Sinatra favorites, and West Hollywood cheerleaders in drag (☎ 818/449–3689).

DECEMBER➤ For the **Newport Harbor Christmas Boat Parade** in Newport Beach (☎ 714/729–4400), more than 200 festooned boats glide through the harbor nightly December 17–23. In Columbia in early December, the **Miner's Christmas Celebration** features costumed carolers and children's piñatas. Related events include a Victorian Christmas feast at the City Hotel, lamplight tours, and Las Posados Nativity Procession (☎ 209/536–1672). The internationally acclaimed El Teatro Campesino (☎ 408/623–2444) annually stages its nativity play *La Virgen Del Tepeyac* in the Mission San Juan Bautista.

2 The North Coast

*From Muir Beach
to Crescent City*

*The North Coast can only be summed
up in superlatives. Migrating whales
and other sea mammals swim past the
dramatic bluffs that make the 400
miles of shoreline north of San
Francisco to the Oregon border among
the most photographed landscapes in
the country. Along cypress- and
redwood-studded Highway 1 you will
find many small inns, uncrowded state
beaches and parks, art galleries, and
restaurants serving imaginative dishes
that showcase locally produced
ingredients.*

By Marty
Olmstead

BETWEEN SAN FRANCISCO BAY and the Oregon border lies the aptly named Redwood Empire, where national, state, and local parks welcome visitors year-round. The shoreline's natural attributes are self-evident, but the area is also rich in human history, having been the successive domain of Native American Miwoks and Pomos, Russian traders, Hispanic settlers, and more contemporary fishing folk and lumberjacks. All have left visible legacies. This region is sparsely populated, with only 10 towns of more than 700 inhabitants.

Pleasures and Pastimes

Beaches

The waters of the Pacific along the North Coast are fine for seals, but most humans find the temperatures downright arctic. When it comes to spectacular cliffs and seascapes, though, the North Coast beaches are second to none. Explore tidal pools, watch for sea life, or dive for abalone. Don't worry about crowds: On many of these beaches you will have the sands largely to yourself.

Bicycling

Hardy riders take to Highway 1 year-round to experience the full beauty of the North Coast by mountain or racing bike. If you've trained sufficiently, biking all or a portion of the coast can be exhilarating. Bike-rental facilities are included in the Outdoor Activities and Sports listings for some of the towns covered in this chapter).

Dining

Despite its small population, the North Coast lays claim to several well-regarded restaurants that reflect the state's position on the culinary cutting edge. Seafood is abundant, of course, as are locally grown vegetables and herbs. In general, there is more of a dining variety near the coast than inland. Dress is usually informal, though dressy casual is the norm at some of the pricier establishments listed below.

CATEGORY	COST*
$$$$	over $50
$$$	$30–$50
$$	$20–$30
$	under $20

per person for a three-course meal, excluding drinks, service, and 7¼% tax

Fishing

Depending on the season (and whether it's a good year in general for fishing), you can fish for rockfish, salmon, and steelhead in the rivers. Charters leave from Fort Bragg, Eureka, and elsewhere for ocean fishing. There's particularly good abalone diving around Jenner, Fort Ross, Point Arena, Westport, and Trinidad.

Lodging

Restored Victorians, rustic lodges, country inns, small hotels, and chic new structures contribute to the exceptional range of accommodations along the North Coast. In several cases there are only one or two places to spend the night in a particular town; some of these are destinations in themselves. The best bed-and-breakfasts along the coast are often sold out on weekends months in advance, so reserve early.

CATEGORY	COST*
$$$$	over $175
$$$	$120–$175
$$	$80–$120
$	under $80

All prices are for a standard double room, excluding 8% tax.

Nightlife and the Arts

Eureka, Ferndale, and Mendocino have long-standing repertory theater companies that perform contemporary and classic American plays. As for nightlife, if you're after a swinging, raucous time, the North Coast may not be the place for you, though almost every town of any size has a watering hole, often with good live music.

Whale Watching

From any number of excellent observation points along the coast, you can watch gray whales during their annual winter migration season or, in the summer and fall, blue or humpback whales. Another option is a whale-watching cruise (☞ Guided Tours *in* Contacts and Resources, *below*).

Exploring the North Coast

Exploring the northern California coast is easiest by car. Highway 1 is a beautiful, if sometimes slow and nerve-racking, drive. You'll want to stop frequently to appreciate the views, and there are many portions of the highway along which you won't drive faster than 20–40 mph. You can still have a fine trip even if you don't have much time, but be realistic and don't plan to drive too far in one day. The itineraries below proceed north from San Francisco.

Great Itineraries

Numbers in the text correspond to numbers in the margin and on the North Coast maps.

IF YOU HAVE 3 DAYS

Some of the finest redwoods in California reside less than 20 miles north of San Francisco in **Muir Woods National Monument** ①. After walking through the woods, stop for an early lunch in **Inverness** or continue on to **Fort Ross** ⑦, a reconstructed 19th-century Russian settlement. If you haven't eaten lunch, a deli-grocery store nearby sells picnic ingredients. Catch the sunset at quiet ▦ **Gualala.** On the morning of day two, drive to ▦ **Mendocino** ⑨. Spend the rest of your time in the North Coast browsing the many galleries, shops, historic sites, and beaches and parks of this cliffside enclave. Return to San Francisco via Highway 1, or the quicker route of Highway 128 east to U.S. 101 south.

IF YOU HAVE 7 DAYS

Early on your first day, walk through **Muir Woods** ①. Then visit windswept **Stinson Beach** ② for a walk on the shore and lunch. In springtime and early summer, head north on Highway 1 to Bolinas Lagoon, where you can see bird nestings at **Audubon Canyon Ranch** ③, a 1,000-acre wildlife sanctuary. At other times of the year, continue north on Highway 1. One-third of a mile beyond **Olema,** look for a sign marking the turnoff for the **Bear Valley Visitor Center** ⑤, the gateway to the **Point Reyes National Seashore.** Tour a reconstructed Miwok Indian Village just a short walk from the visitor center. Spend the night in nearby ▦ **Inverness** or one of the other coastal Marin towns. The next day, stop at **Goat Rock State Beach** and **Fort Ross** ⑦ on the way to ▦ **Mendocino** ⑨. Explore the town and make a side trip to **Fort Bragg** for a visit to **Mendocino Coast Botanical Gardens** and possibly a trip on the *Skunk Train.* If you're in the mood to splurge, late on your third af-

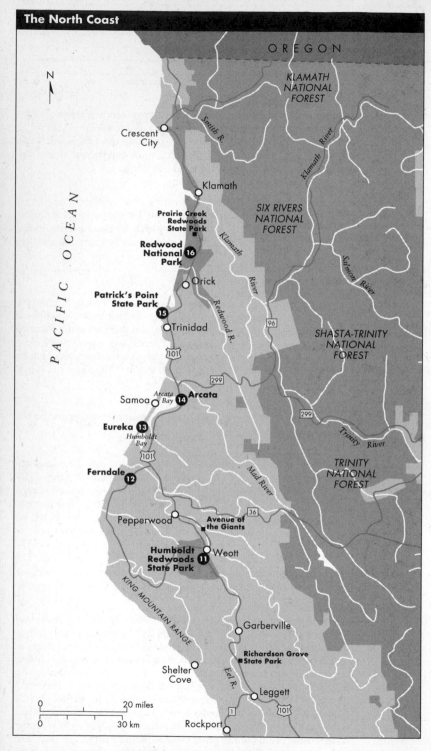

16

O R E G O N

KLAMATH
NATIONAL
FOREST

Smith R.

Crescent
City

Klamath River

Klamath

SIX RIVERS
NATIONAL
FOREST

Prairie Creek
Redwoods
State Park

Redwood
National
Park **16**

Klamath River

Salmon River

Orick

PACIFIC OCEAN

Patrick's Point
State Park **15**

Trinidad

Redwood R.

96

SHASTA-TRINITY
NATIONAL
FOREST

101

299

Samoa

Arcata
Bay **14** **Arcata**

299

Eureka **13**

Humboldt
Bay

Trinity River

101

Ferndale **12**

Mad River

TRINITY
NATIONAL
FOREST

Pepperwood

36

Avenue of
the Giants

Humboldt
Redwoods
State Park **11**

Weott

KING MOUNTAIN RANGE

Garberville

Richardson Grove
State Park

Shelter
Cove

Eel R.

Leggett

0   20 miles

0   30 km

1

101

Rockport

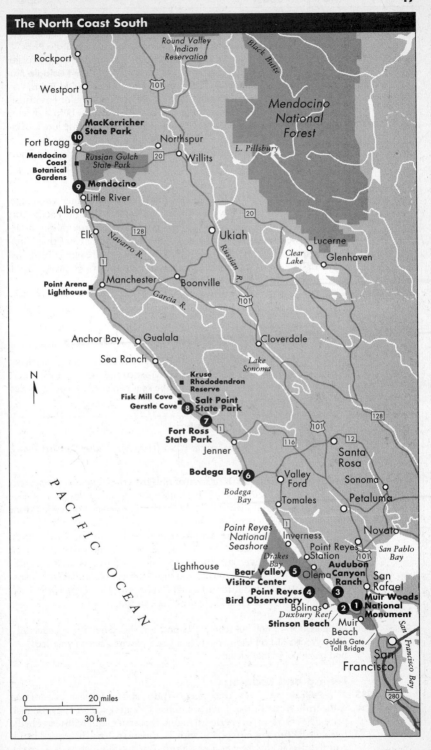

ternoon drive inland and spend the night at the Benbow Inn in 🏨 **Garberville.** Otherwise, linger in the Mendocino area. Either way, on your
fourth day drive through parts of **Humboldt Redwoods State Park** ⑪,
including the **Avenue of the Giants.** Stop for the night in the Victorian
village of 🏨 **Ferndale** ⑫ and visit the cemetery and the **Ferndale Museum.** On day five, drive to 🏨 **Eureka** ⑬. Have lunch in **Old Town,** visit
the shops, and get a feel for local marine life on a Humboldt Bay cruise.
Begin day six with breakfast at the **Samoa Cookhouse** before driving
about an hour to **Patrick's Point State Park** ⑮. Have a late lunch overlooking the harbor in **Trinidad** before returning to Eureka for the night.
Return to San Francisco on day seven. The drive back takes six hours
on U.S. 101; it's nearly twice as long if you take Highway 1.

When to Tour the North Coast

The North Coast is a year-round destination, though when you go de-
termines what attraction you will see. The migration of the Pacific gray
whales, for instance, is a wintertime phenomenon, roughly mid-December to early April. Winter days are usually more clear than summer days, particularly July and August, when views are often obstructed
by fog. The coastal climate is quite similar to San Francisco's, although winter nights are colder than in the city.

SOUTHERN MARIN COUNTY

Muir Woods, Stinson Beach, and Bolinas

Much of the Marin County coastline is less than an hour away from
San Francisco, but the pace is slower. Most of the sights below, which
afford experiences of the forest and the sea, can easily be done as day
trips from the city.

Muir Woods National Monument

❶ *17 mi north of San Francisco on U.S. 101 to Mill Valley/Stinson Beach
exit (Hwy. 1).*

The world's most popular grove of old-growth *Sequoia sempervirens*
was one of the country's first national monuments. A number of easy
hikes can be accomplished in an hour; there's even a short valley-floor
trek, accessible to travelers with disabilities, that takes only 10 minutes to walk. The coast redwoods that grow here are mostly between
500 and 800 years old and as tall as 236 feet. Along Redwood Creek
are other trees—live oak, madrone, and buckeye, as well as wildflowers (even in winter), ferns, and mushrooms. Note: Parking is easier before 10 AM and after 4 PM. ⊠ *Panoramic Hwy., off Hwy. 1,* ☎
415/388–2595. 🎫 *Free.* ☉ *Daily 8 AM–sunset.*

OFF THE   **MUIR BEACH** – Small but scenic, this patch of shoreline, 3 miles south of
BEATEN PATH   Muir Woods just off Highway 1, is a good place to stretch your legs
             and gaze out at the Pacific.

Dining and Lodging

$$$$ ✗🏨 **Pelican Inn.** This atmospheric Tudor-style B&B is a five-minute
★   walk from Muir Beach. Each room has Oriental scatter rugs, English
prints, heavy velvet draperies, hanging tapestries, and half-tester beds.
Even the bathrooms are special, with Victorian-style hardware and hand-
painted tiles in the shower. Locals and tourists compete at darts in the
ground-floor pub, which has a wide selection of brews, sherries, and
ports. The Pelican's restaurant (closed Mon.; $$–$$$) serves sturdy En-
glish fare, from fish-and-chips to prime rib and Yorkshire pudding. Room

rates include full English breakfast. ⊠ *10 Pacific Way at Hwy. 1, 94965,* ☎ *415/383–6000. 7 rooms. Restaurant. MC, V.*

Stinson Beach

❷ *8 mi from Muir Woods via Panoramic Hwy., 25 mi from San Francisco, U.S. 101 to Hwy. 1.*

Stinson Beach has the most expansive sands (4,500 feet) in Marin County; it's as close as you'll get to the stereotypical feel of a southern California beach (when the fog hasn't rolled in). On any hot summer weekend, every road to Stinson Beach is jam-packed, so factor this into your plans.

Dining

$–$$$ ✕ **Stinson Beach Grill.** A great selection of beer and wine, art on the
★ walls, and outdoor seating are among the draws here, but the food is memorable, too. Seafood and several types of oysters are served at lunch and dinner; the evening menu includes pasta, lamb, chicken, or other hearty dishes. ⊠ *3465 Hwy. 1,* ☎ *415/868–2002. AE, MC, V.*

$–$$ ✕ **Sand Dollar.** This pleasant pub serves great hamburgers and other sandwiches for lunch and decent seafood for dinner; there's an outdoor dining deck. ⊠ *Hwy. 1,* ☎ *415/868–0434. MC, V.*

Bolinas

❸ The **Audubon Canyon Ranch,** a 1,000-acre wildlife sanctuary along the Bolinas Lagoon, is open for courting and mating season, mid-March through mid-July. Great blue herons and egrets are among the 60 species that call this home. The egrets nest in the redwood trees in Schwarz Grove. Telescopes and bird-hide observation posts allow for easier viewing. A small museum surveys the geology and natural history of the region. A bookstore and a picnic area are also on-site. ⊠ *4900 Hwy. 1, along Bolinas Lagoon,* ☎ *415/868–9244.* ▱ *Donation requested.* ⊙ *Mid-Mar.–mid-July, weekends and holidays 10–4.*

If you're looking for abuse, at the northern edge of Bolinas Lagoon, a couple of miles beyond the Audubon Canyon Ranch, take the unmarked road running west from Highway 1. It leads to the sleepy town of **Bolinas.** Don't expect a warm welcome: Some residents of Bolinas are so wary of tourism that whenever the state tries to post signs, they tear them down.

Nightlife

Smiley's Schooner Saloon. Virtually the *only* nightlife in Bolinas, this congenial bar (assuming you haven't come in with a camera around your neck) hosts live music on Friday and Saturday nights. ⊠ *41 Wharf Rd.,* ☎ *415/868–1311.*

POINT REYES NATIONAL SEASHORE

Duxbury Reef, Olema, and Inverness

The Point Reyes National Seashore, which borders the northern reaches of the Golden Gate National Recreation Area (☞ Chapter 5), is a great place for hiking to secluded beaches, viewing wildlife, and driving through rugged, rolling grasslands. Highlights here include the half-mile Earthquake Trail, which passes by what is believed to be the epicenter of the 1906 quake that destroyed much of San Francisco, and the late-19th-century Point Reyes Lighthouse, a good spot to watch for whales. Horses and mountain bikes are permitted on some trails. The towns of Olema, Point Reyes Station, Inverness, and Tomales, all in or near the national seashore, have dining, lodging, and recreational facilities.

Duxbury Reef Area

2 mi northwest of Bolinas off Mesa Rd.

❹ Birders love the **Point Reyes Bird Observatory,** a sanctuary and research center within the Point Reyes National Seashore but more easily accessible from Bolinas. The area harbors nearly 225 species of bird life; banding occurs daily May through November as well as weekends and Wednesdays December through April, weather permitting. ⊠ *West on Mesa Rd., off Olema–Bolinas Rd.,* ☎ *415/868–0655.* ☎ *Free.* ☉ *Visitor center daily 8–6.*

Mile-long **Duxbury Reef,** a nature preserve, is the largest shale intertidal reef in North America. Check a tide table if you plan to explore the reef, which is accessible only at low tide. Look for starfish, barnacles, sea anemones, purple urchins, limpets, sea mussels, and the occasional red and black abalone. ⊠ *From Bolinas, take Mesa Rd. off Olema–Bolinas Rd.; make a left on Overlook Dr. and a right on Elm Ave. to the beach parking lot.*

Olema

9 mi from Bolinas on Hwy. 1.

★ **❺** The Point Reyes National Seashore's **Bear Valley Visitor Center** has exhibits of park wildlife as well as rangers with advice about beaches, the Point Reyes Lighthouse, whale watching, hiking trails, and camping. A reconstructed Miwok Indian Village is a short walk from the visitor center. It provides insight into the daily lives of the first human inhabitants of this region. ⊠ *Bear Valley Rd. west of Hwy. 1,* ☎ *415/663–1092.* ☎ *Free.* ☉ *Weekdays 9–5, weekends 8–5.*

Outdoor Activities and Sports

Many of the beaches in Point Reyes National Seashore are accessible off Bear Valley Road. **Limantour Beach** (⊠ End of Limantour Beach Rd.) is one of the most beautiful of Point Reyes sands; trails lead to other beaches north and south of here.

Five Brooks Stables (⊠ 8001 Hwy. 1, ☎ 415/663–1570), rents horses and equipment; from the stables, horseback trails wind through the Point Reyes woods and along the beaches.

Trailhead Rentals (⊠ 88 Bear Valley Rd. at Hwy. 1, ☎ 415/663–1958) supplies bicycles and binoculars.

Point Reyes Station

2 mi from Olema on Hwy. 1.

Point Reyes Station, a stop on the North Pacific Coast Narrow-Gauge Railroad until 1933, has a number of false-front buildings, including the popular Western Saloon. The busiest place in town is Toby's Feed Barn, which sells offbeat gifts (many festooned with cows) as well as serious feed and grain to local farmers. There's a market on Main Street for picking up picnic supplies en route to Point Reyes.

Lodging

$ 🏠 **Point Reyes Hostel.** These dorm-style lodgings in an old clapboard ranch house within are a good deal for budget travelers. The family room is limited to families with children five and under and must be reserved well in advance. ⊠ *Off Limantour Rd., Box 247, 94956,* ☎

415/663–8811. Send $12 per adult per night, $6 per child, with reservation request; state your gender. Shared kitchen. MC, V.

Shopping
Gallery Route One, a nonprofit cooperative, exhibits area artists in all media. ⊠ *11101 Hwy. 1,* ☎ *415/663–1347.*

Inverness

4 mi from Point Reyes Station on Sir Francis Drake Blvd., northwest from Hwy. 1.

Inverness boomed after the 1906 earthquake when wealthy San Franciscans built summer homes in its hills. Today, many of the structures serve as full-time residences or small bed-and-breakfast inns. A deli, grocery store, restaurants, and shops are all located along Sir Francis Drake Boulevard.

★ The **Point Reyes Lighthouse Visitors Center** is a 45-minute drive from Inverness, across rolling hills that resemble Scottish heath. On busy weekends during the season, parking near the lighthouse is difficult. The view alone persuades most people to make the effort of walking down—and then back up—the hundreds of steps from the clifftops to the lighthouse below. If you choose to skip the descent, you can still see the whales from the cliff. ⊠ *Western end of Sir Francis Drake Blvd.,* ☎ *415/669–1534.* ☉ *Thurs.–Sun. 10–5 (steps close at 4:30).*

Dining and Lodging
$ ✕ **Grey Whale.** This casual place is a good stop for pizza, salad, pastries, and espresso. ⊠ *12781 Sir Francis Drake Blvd.,* ☎ *415/669–1244. MC, V.*

$$$ ✕🏨 **Manka's.** Three intimate, wood-paneled dining rooms, glowing with candlelight and piano music, provide the setting for creative American-regional cuisine. Specialties include caribou, pheasant, and other unusual game grilled in the fireplace, line-caught fish, and homemade desserts. Two of the four smallish guest rooms above the restaurant (closed Tuesday and Wednesday year-round, Sunday–Thursday in January; no lunch) have private decks that look onto Tomales Bay. Rooms in the Redwood Annex and two cabins are also available. ⊠ *30 Calendar Way,* ☎ *415/669–1034. 14 rooms. Restaurant. AE, MC, V.*

$$$–$$$$ 🏨 **Blackthorne Inn.** An adult-size fantasy tree house, this imaginative structure is highlighted by a 3,500-square-foot deck with stairways to higher decks. The solarium was made with timbers from San Francisco wharves; the outer walls are salvaged doors from a railway station. A glass-sheathed, octagonal tower called the Eagle's Nest crowns the inn. Buffet breakfast is included. ⊠ *266 Vallejo Ave., Box 712, Inverness Park 94937,* ☎ *415/663–8621. 5 rooms, 2 with shared bath. Hot tub. MC, V.*

$$$ 🏨 **Ten Inverness Way.** The comfortable living room of this low-key inn has a classic stone fireplace and a player piano; cozy rooms are highlighted by such homespun touches as patchwork quilts, lived-in-looking antiques, and skylighted dormer ceilings. Full breakfast is included. ⊠ *Inverness Way, Box 63, 94937,* ☎ *415/669–1648. 5 rooms. Hot tub. MC, V.*

Shopping
Shaker Shops West has an exceptional array of reproduction Shaker furniture and gift items, each with a fine, turn-of-the-century sensibility. ⊠ *5 Inverness Way,* ☎ *415/669–7256.*

Tomales

16 mi from Point Reyes Station on Hwy. 1.

Lodging

$$　▦ **Tomales Country Inn.** Secluded by trees—pine, fir, and acacia—this Queen Anne house, built entirely of redwood, is decorated with original art, some of it local. One of the nicer rooms has an Eastlake walnut bed and a view of a small park. The very private third-floor room looks out over the inn's gardens, a local church, and surrounding hills and pastures. Room rates include Continental breakfast. ⊠ *25 Valley St., Box 376, 94791,* ☎ 𝔽𝔸𝕏 *707/878–2041. 5 rooms, 3 with shared bath. No credit cards. Closed Tues.–Wed. and Dec. 20–28.*

Valley Ford

7 mi north of Tomales on Hwy. 1.

Lodging

$$　▦ **Inn at Valley Ford.** The rooms at this small B&B, a Victorian farmhouse built in the late 1860s, are named after literary figures, characters, or periods—books commemorating each chamber's theme grace its bookshelves. Bird-watching is a favorite pastime here: blue herons, egrets, hawks, and owls make Valley Ford their home. Room rates include a full gourmet breakfast, which comes with the inn's specialty, old-fashioned cream scones. ⊠ *14395 Hwy. 1, Box 439, 94972,* ☎ *707/876–3182. 4 rooms with 2 shared baths, 1 cottage suite with private bath. DC, MC, V.*

OFF THE　　　　**OSMOSIS ENZYME BATHS –** The tiny town of Freestone, 4 miles north of
BEATEN PATH　　Tomales, has a few good shops, such as Pastorale, a women's clothing boutique, but the real reason to detour inland from Highway 1 is Osmosis Enzyme Baths. This spa, in a two-story clapboard house on extensive grounds, specializes in several treatments, including a detoxifying "dry" bath in a blend of enzymes and fragrant wood shavings. After 20 minutes in the tub, opt for a 75-minute massage in one of the freestanding Japanese-style pagodas near the creek that runs through the property. ⊠ *209 Bohemian Hwy., Freestone,* ☎ *707/823–8231.*

SONOMA AND MENDOCINO

Bodega Bay to Fort Bragg

The gently rolling countryside of coastal Marin gives way to more dramatic scenery north of Bodega Bay. Cattle cling for their lives (or so it seems) to steep inclines alongside the increasingly curvy highway, now traveling right along the coast. Past Jenner, the road twists and turns; by the time it reaches Sea Ranch, hairpin curves and stunning vistas compete for drivers' attention.

Bodega Bay

❻ *8 mi from Valley Ford on Hwy. 1, 65 mi north of San Francisco via U.S. 101 and Hwy. 1.*

Bodega Bay is one of the busiest harbors on the Sonoma County coast. Dozens of commercial boats pursue a variety of ocean fish as well as the famed Dungeness crabs. Galleries and T-shirt shops line either side of Highway 1; a short drive around the harbor leads to the Pacific. This is the last stop, townwise, before Gualala, and a good spot for stretching the legs and taking in the salt air. For a closer look, visit the **Bodega**

Marine Laboratory (☎ 707/875–2211 for directions), on a 326-acre reserve on nearby Bodega Head. The lab gives free tours and peeks at intertidal invertebrates, such as sea stars and sea anemones, on Fridays from 2 to 4 PM.

Dining and Lodging

$$$ ✕⊡ **Inn at the Tides.** This complex of condominium-style buildings has spacious rooms with high, peaked ceilings and uncluttered decor. All rooms have a view of the harbor, and some have fireplaces. Continental breakfast is included. The inn's two restaurants serve both old-style and more adventurous seafood dishes; in season, you can by a slab of salmon or live or cooked crab at a seafood stand on the premises. ⊠ *800 Hwy. 1, Box 640, 94923, ☎ 707/875–2751 or 800/541–7788,* FAX *707/875–2669. 86 rooms. 2 restaurants, refrigerators, room service, pool, hot tub, sauna, coin laundry. AE, MC, V.*

Outdoor Activities and Sports

The operators of the 700-acre **Chanslor Guest Ranch** lead guided horseback rides along the coastal wetlands and into Salmon Creek canyon. ⊠ *2660 Hwy. 1,* ☎ *707/875–2721.*

Bodega Bay Sportfishing charters ocean-fishing boats and rents equipment. ⊠ *Bay Flat Rd.,* ☎ *707/875–3344.*

Shopping

The **Ren Brown Gallery** on the north end of town is renowned for its selection of Asian arts, crafts, furnishings, and design books. This two-floor gallery also represents a number of local artists worth checking out. ⊠ *1781 Hwy. 1,* ☎ *707/875–2922.*

Jenner

10 mi north of Bodega Bay on Hwy. 1.

The Russian River empties into the Pacific Ocean at Jenner. The town has a couple of good restaurants and some shops. Just south of the river is windy **Goat Rock State Beach,** where a colony of sea lions (walk north from the parking lot) resides most of the year. The beach is open daily from 8 AM to sunset; there's no day-use fee.

Dining

$$–$$$ ✕ **River's End.** At the right time of year, diners at this rustic restaurant ★ can view sea lions lazing on the beach below. The creative fare is eclectic/German—seafood, venison, and duck dishes. Brunches here are exceptional. ⊠ *Hwy. 1, north end of Jenner,* ☎ *707/865–2484. MC, V. Closed Jan.–Feb. 13.*

Fort Ross State Park

❼ *9 mi north of Jenner on Hwy. 1.*

Fort Ross, completed in 1821, became Russia's major fur-trading outpost in California. The Russians brought Aleut sea-otter hunters down from their Alaskan bailiwicks to hunt pelts for the czar. In 1841, the area depleted of seal and otter, the Russians sold their post to John Sutter, later of gold-rush fame. After a local Anglo rebellion against the Mexicans, the land fell under U.S. domain, becoming part of California in 1850. The state park service has reconstructed Fort Ross, including its Russian Orthodox chapel, a redwood stockade, officers' barracks, and a blockhouse. The excellent museum here documents the fort's history and some of the North Coast's. ☎ *707/847–3286.* ⊠ *$5 per vehicle (day use).* ⊙ *Daily 10–4:30. Closed Dec. 25, Jan. 1. No dogs allowed past parking lot.*

Lodging

$$$$ ⊞ **Timberhill Ranch.** The winding country road just south of Fort Ross
★   that leads east from Highway 1 to the Timberhill Ranch gives visitors
      just enough time to ease into the restful pace of this secluded resort.
      Simple and serene, Timberhill has 15 cabins decorated with quilts and
      fresh flowers. Each has a fireplace and private patio where guests can
      enjoy the breakfast brought to them on a golf cart—perhaps sharing
      croissants with the resident ducks and geese that waddle up from the
      ranch's huge pond. Timberhill's inspired six-course dinners (included,
      with breakfast, in the room rates) take place by candlelight. ⊠ *35755
      Hauser Bridge Rd. (Timber Cove Post Office), 95421, ☎ 707/847–
      3258, ℻ 707/847–3342. 15 cottages. Minibars, refrigerators, pool,
      outdoor hot tub, tennis courts, hiking. AE, MC, V.*

$$–$$$$ ⊞ **Fort Ross Lodge.** The lodge, about 1½ miles north of the same-named
      Russian fort, is somewhat dated and wind-bitten, but all but four of
      its rooms have fireplaces and spectacular views of the Sonoma shore-
      line; some have a private hot tub on a back patio. Seven hill suites have
      sauna, hot tub, and fireplace. ⊠ *20705 Hwy. 1, 95450, ☎ 707/847–
      3333. 22 rooms. Refrigerators. AE, MC, V.*

Salt Point State Park

❽ *11 mi north of Jenner on Hwy. 1.*

Salt Point State Park yields a glimpse of nature virtually untouched by
humans. At the 6,000-acre park's **Gerstle Cove** you'll probably catch
sight of seals sunning themselves on the beach's rocks and deer roam-
ing in the meadowlands. The unusual formations in the sandstone are
called tafoni and are the product of hundreds of years of erosion. A
very short drive leads to Fisk Mill Cove. A five-minute walk uphill brings
you to a bench from which there is a dramatic overview of Sentinel
Rock and the pounding surf below. ⊠ *Hwy. 1, ☎ 707/847–3221. ☜
$5 per vehicle (day use). Camping $14 peak season, $12 off-season (☎
800/444–7275). ☉ Daily sunrise–sunset.*

Kruse Rhododendron Reserve, a peaceful, 317-acre forested park, has
thousands of rhododendrons that bloom in light shade in the late
spring. ⊠ *Hwy. 1, just north of Fisk Mill Cove. ☜ Free.*

Lodging

$ ⊞ **Stillwater Cove Ranch.** Sixteen miles north of Jenner, overlooking
      Stillwater Cove, this former boys' school has been transformed into
      a pleasant, if spartan, place to lodge. ⊠ *22555 Hwy. 1, 95450, ☎
      707/847–3227. 7 rooms. No credit cards.*

Sea Ranch

18 mi from Fort Ross on Hwy. 1.

Sea Ranch is a development of stylish second homes, on 5,000 acres
overlooking the Pacific. To appease critics, Sea Ranch built public
beach-access trails off Highway 1 south of Gualala. Even some mili-
tant environmentalists deem architects William Turnbull and Charles
Moore's housing reasonably congruent with the surroundings; others
find the weathered wood buildings beautiful.

Dining and Lodging

$$$–$$$$ ✕⊞ **Sea Ranch Lodge.** The lodge, close to beaches, trails, and golf, is
      set high on a bluff with ocean views. Some rooms have fireplaces, and
      some have hot tubs. Handcrafted wood furnishings and quilts create
      an earthy, contemporary look. The restaurant, which overlooks the Pa-
      cific, serves good seafood and homemade desserts. Guests receive a com-

plimentary wine and fruit basket upon arrival. ⊠ *60 Sea Walk Dr., Box 44, 95497,* ☎ *707/785–2371 or 800/732–7262,* FAX *707/785–2243. 20 rooms. Restaurant. AE, MC, V.*

$$–$$$ 🖼 **Sea Ranch Escape.** The Sea Ranch houses, sparsely scattered on a grass meadow fronting a stretch of ocean, are a striking sight from Highway 1. Groups or families can rent fully furnished houses for two nights (minimum) or more. Linen, housekeeping, and catering services are available for a fee. You can dine at superb nearby restaurants or stock up on provisions from one of the markets in Gualala and make use of the full kitchens. All houses have TVs and VCRs; some have hot tubs and some take pets. Rates are most expensive next to the surf; prices recede with distance from the beach, although all the houses have views of the surrounding meadows and forest. ⊠ *60 Sea Walk Dr., Box 238, 95497,* ☎ *707/785–2426 or 800/732–7262,* FAX *707/785–2124. 55 houses. MC, V.*

Gualala

11 mi north of Sea Ranch on Hwy. 1.

This former lumber port remains a sleepy drive-through except for the several ocean-view motels that serve as headquarters for visitors exploring the coast. It lies just north of the Gualala River (a good spot for fishing), which serves as the county line for Mendocino. On the river's Sonoma side, **Gualala Point Regional Park** (⊠ Hwy. 1, ☎ 707/785–2377), open daily from 8 AM until sunset, is an excellent whale-watching spot. The park has picnicking—the day use fee is $3—and camping for $14 per night.

Dining and Lodging

$$–$$$$ ✕🖼 **St. Orres.** One of the North Coast's most eye-catching inns, St. Orres reflects the area's Russian influence. The main house is crowned by two onion-domed towers. The exterior is further accented by balconies, stained-glass windows, and wood-inlaid towers. Two rooms overlook the sea, and the other six are set over the garden or forest; all the rooms in the main house share baths. The tranquil woods behind the house hold 11 rustic cottages; eight have woodstoves or fireplaces. Those traveling with children are placed in the cottages. Room rates include a full breakfast. For dinner, the inn's restaurant (closed Wed. in winter) is so popular that even patrons with reservations are sometimes kept waiting. It serves dinner only, a fixed-price meal ($$$–$$$$) with a choice of five entrées (meat or fish) plus soup and salad. ⊠ *Hwy. 1, 2 mi north of Gualala, Box 523, 95445,* ☎ *707/884–3303,* FAX *707/884–3903. 8 rooms, 11 cottages. Restaurant, hot tub, sauna, beach. MC, V.*

$$$–$$$$ 🖼 **Whale Watch Inn.** This fine inn lives up to its name—most rooms here claim views (through cypress trees) down the coast, where whales often come close to shore on their northern migration in early spring. Year-round, the scent of pine and salt-sea air fills the rooms, all of which have fireplaces and small decks; some have whirlpool baths or kitchens. A 132-step stairway leads down to a small, virtually private beach. Set amid 2½ acres, the Whale Watch maintains well-kept gardens that bloom even in winter. A full breakfast is brought to guests in their rooms. ⊠ *35100 Hwy. 1, 95445,* ☎ *707/884–3667 or 800/942–5342,* FAX *707/884–4815. 12 rooms, 6 suites. AE, MC, V.*

$$–$$$ 🖼 **Old Milano Hotel.** Overlooking the spectacular coast just north of
★ Gualala and set amid English gardens, the Old Milano is one of California's premier bed-and-breakfasts. The 1905 mansion is listed on the National Register of Historic Places. Rooms are appointed with

exceptional antiques; five of the upstairs rooms have ocean views, and another overlooks the gardens. All upstairs rooms share bathrooms. The downstairs master suite has a private sitting room and a picture window framing the sea. Those in search of something different might consider the caboose with a wood-burning stove. Breakfast is included, and dinners are offered on a different schedule, depending on the season, but usually Wednesday through Sunday. ⊠ *38300 Hwy. 1, 95445,* ☎ *707/884–3256. 9 rooms. Hot tub. MC, V. No smoking.*

En Route   For a dramatic view of the surf, take the marked road off Highway 1 north of the fishing village of Point Arena to the **Point Arena Lighthouse** (☎ 707/882–2777). First constructed in 1870, the lighthouse was destroyed by the 1906 earthquake that also devastated San Francisco. Rebuilt in 1907, it towers 115 feet from its base, 50 feet above the sea. The lighthouse is open for tours daily from 11 until 2:30, one hour later in summer and on some holidays; admission is $2.50. As you continue north on Highway 1 toward Mendocino there are several beaches, most notably **Manchester State Beach,** 3 miles north of Point Arena.

Elk

39 mi north of Gualala on Hwy. 1.

Dining and Lodging

$$$–$$$$ ✕🔝 **Harbor House.** Constructed in 1916 by a timber company to entertain its guests, this redwood ranch-style house has a dining room with a view of the Pacific. Five of the six rooms in the main house have fireplaces, and some are furnished with antiques original to the house. There are also four smallish cottages with fireplaces and decks. Room rates include breakfast and dinner. The restaurant (reservations essential), which serves California cuisine, is highly recommended; there's limited seating for those not spending the night. ⊠ *5600 S. Hwy. 1, 95432,* ☎ *707/877–3203. 10 rooms. Restaurant. No credit cards.*

$$–$$$$ 🔝 **Elk Cove Inn.** Private, romantic cottages are perched on a bluff above the pounding surf. One room's shower has a full-length window that shares this magnificent view of the Pacific. Skylights, wood-burning stoves in some rooms, and hand-embroidered cloths are just some of the amenities. An 1883 Victorian home has four rooms with spacious dormer windows and window seats, a parlor, and an ocean-view deck. A full gourmet breakfast is included. ⊠ *6300 S. Hwy. 1, Box 367, 95432,* ☎ *707/877–3321. 10 rooms. Beach. AE, MC, V.*

NEED A   If you're driving directly to Mendocino from points south and just want
BREAK?   to grab a quick lunch or a good cup of coffee, visit the café at the
Greenwood Pier Inn, on Highway 1 in Elk.

Albion

4 mi north of Elk on Hwy. 1.

Dining and Lodging

$$$ ✕ **Ledford House.** The menu at this restaurant on a bluff is divided into hearty bistro dishes—mainly stews and pastas—and equally large-portioned examples of California cuisine: ahi tuna, grilled meats, and the like. ⊠ *3000 N. Hwy. 1,* ☎ *707/937–0282. AE, MC, V. Closed Mon. in summer, Mon.–Tues. in winter. No lunch.*

$$$–$$$$ ✕🔝 **Albion River Inn.** Modern, two-room cabins at this inn overlook
★   the dramatic bridge and seascape where the Albion River empties into

the Pacific. All but two have decks facing the ocean. Six have a hot tub for two, and eight have double bath tubs. The decor ranges from antique furnishings to wide-back willow chairs. A full breakfast is included. In the glassed-in dining room, which serves grilled dishes and fresh seafood, the views are as spectacular as the food. ⊠ *3790 N. Hwy. 1, Box 100, 95410,* ☎ *707/937–1919; from northern CA, 800/479– 7944;* FAX *707/937–2604. 20 rooms. Restaurant. AE, MC, V.*

Little River

3 mi north of Albion on Hwy. 1.

Dining and Lodging

$$ ✕ **Little River Restaurant.** Despite its modest appearance, this tiny place across from the Little River Inn serves some of the best dinners in the Mendocino area. Steak and fresh seafood are the specialties. ⊠ *Hwy. 1,* ☎ *707/937–4945. No credit cards. Closed Tues.–Thurs. and Dec. No lunch.*

$$$$ ✕🏠 **Heritage House.** The cottages at this resort have stunning ocean views. The dining room, also with a Pacific panorama, serves breakfast and dinner, which are included with the room rate for guests; others should make reservations in advance. Each room's decor is unique, but all are appointed with plush furnishings, and many have private decks, fireplaces, and whirlpool tubs. ⊠ *Hwy. 1, 95456,* ☎ *707/937–5885,* FAX *707/937–0318. 72 rooms. Restaurant. MC, V. Closed Jan.–mid-Feb.*

$$–$$$$ 🏠 **Glendeven.** The New England–style main house of this tranquil inn
★ has five rooms, all with private bath, three with fireplace. The converted barn holds a two-bedroom suite with kitchen and an art gallery. The 1986 Stevenscroft building has a high-peaked, gabled roof and weathered barnlike siding. The four rooms within all have fireplaces. The owners, both designers, have decorated the guest rooms with antiques, contemporary art, and ceramics. Room rates include breakfast. ⊠ *8221 N. Hwy. 1, 95456,* ☎ *707/937–0083,* FAX *707/937–6108. 9 rooms, 1 suite. AE, MC, V.*

Mendocino

❾ *2 mi north of Little River on Hwy. 1, 138 mi north of San Francisco on U.S. 101 to Hwy. 128 to Hwy. 1.*

This 19th-century town may look familiar to fans of the television series *Murder, She Wrote.* Mendocino played the role of Cabot Cove, Maine. The subterfuge worked because so many of the original settlers here came from the Northeast and built houses in the New England style. By the 1950s, artists and craftspeople began flocking here, finding the setting inspirational and less suburban than places like Sausalito. In their wake came other adventuresome souls, several of whom opened small inns in large older homes. Others established restaurants and cafés. There is still a bit of the old town to be seen in dives like Dick's Place, a bar near the Mendocino Hotel. The rest of the small downtown area is devoted almost exclusively to shops and restaurants.

The area arts scene is flourishing. The **Mendocino Art Center** (⊠ 45200 Little Lake St., ☎ 707/937–5818) has exhibits, art classes, a gallery, and a theater. The **Kelley House Museum** (⊠ 45007 Albion St., ☎ 707/937–5791) is a refurbished 1861 structure displaying historical photographs of Mendocino's logging days, antique cameras, Victorian-era clothing, furniture, and artifacts. Admission is $1; the museum is open June–September, daily 1–4, and October–May, Friday–Monday

1–4. The green and red **Chinese Joss Temple** on Albion Street dates to 1882.

The restored **Ford House,** built in 1854, serves as the visitor center for Mendocino Headlands State Park. The house has a scale model of Mendocino as it looked in 1890, when the town had 34 water towers and a 12-seat outhouse. History walks leave from the house Saturdays at 1 PM. The park itself consists of the cliffs that border the town; access is free. ⊠ *Ford House, Main St.,* ☎ *707/937–5397.* 🎟 *Free.* ☉ *Daily 11–4, with possible temporary midweek closings in winter.*

★ The **Mendocino Coast Botanical Gardens** were established as a private preserve in 1962, with additional acreage added over the years. Along 2 miles of coastal trails, with ocean views and observation points for whale watching, is a splendid array of flowers; the rhododendrons are at their peak from April to June, and fuchsias, heather, and azaleas are resplendent. This is a fine place to stop for a picnic. ⊠ *18220 N. Hwy. 1, between Mendocino and Fort Bragg,* ☎ *707/964–4352.* 🎟 *$5.* ☉ *Mar.–Oct., daily 9–5; Nov.–Feb., daily 9–4.*

Dining and Lodging

$$ × **Cafe Beaujolais.** All the rustic charm of peaceful, backwoods Men-
★ docino is here, with great country cooking to boot. The ever-evolving dinner menu is cross-cultural and includes such delicacies as Yucate-can Thai crab cakes and a barbecued rock-shrimp-filled corn crepe with avocado and blood-orange pico de gallo. Owner Margaret Fox runs the mail-order Cafe Beaujolais bakery—be sure to take home a pack-age or two of her irresistible *panforte,* a dense cake made with almonds, hazelnuts, or macadamia nuts. ⊠ *961 Ukiah St.,* ☎ *707/937–5614. No credit cards.*

$$ × **955 Ukiah St.** The interior of this smart restaurant beside Cafe Beaujolais is woodsy and the California cuisine creative. Specialties in-clude pastas topped with original sauces and fresh fish, such as Pacific red snapper, wrapped in phyllo dough and topped with pesto and lemon sauce. ⊠ *955 Ukiah St.,* ☎ *707/937–1955. MC, V. Closed Mon.–Tues. July–Nov., Mon.–Wed. Dec.–June. No lunch.*

$$–$$$$ ×🏠 **MacCallum House.** With the most meticulously restored Victorian exterior in Mendocino, this 1882 inn, complete with gingerbread trim, transports patrons back to another era before they've even entered. Com-fortable furnishings and antiques enhance the period feel. In addition to the main house, there are individual cottages and barn suites around a garden with a gazebo. The menu at the firelit, redwood-paneled restau-rant (reservations essential) changes quarterly. The focus is on fresh local seafood. ⊠ *45020 Albion St., Box 206, 95460,* ☎ *707/937–0289. 21 rooms. Restaurant, bar. MC, V.*

$$–$$$$ ×🏠 **Mendocino Hotel.** From the outside, this hotel looks like something out of the Wild West, with a period facade and balcony that overhangs the raised sidewalk. Inside, an elegant atmosphere is achieved by stained-glass lamps, Remington paintings, polished wood, and Persian carpets. All but 14 of the rooms have private baths, and the 19th-century decor is appealing. Deluxe garden rooms have fireplaces and TVs. The wood-paneled dining room, fronted by a glassed-in solarium, serves fine fish dishes and the best deep-dish ollalieberry pies in California. ⊠ *45080 Main St., Box 587, 95460,* ☎ *707/937–0511 or 800/548–0513,* 📠 *707/937–0513. 51 rooms. Restaurant, bar, room service. AE, MC, V.*

$$$–$$$$ 🏠 **Headlands Inn.** All rooms at this magnificently restored 1868 Cape
★ Cod–style building have private baths, feather beds, and fireplaces; some overlook a garden and the pounding surf, and others have village

views. There is also a private cottage on the premises. Gourmet breakfast is served in your room, and afternoon tea is served in an upstairs sitting room. ⊠ *Howard and Albion Sts., Box 132, 95460,* ☎ *707/937–4431. 5 rooms. AE, MC, V.*

$$$–$$$$ 🏠 **Stanford Inn by the Sea.** The comfortable wood-paneled rooms at this two-story lodge have decks with ocean views, traditional furnishings with four-poster or sleigh beds, fireplaces or woodstoves, and an appealing selection of paintings by local artists. Complimentary buffet breakfast is served in the sitting room downstairs. ⊠ *Just south of Mendocino, east on Comptche–Ukiah Rd. (off Hwy. 1), Box 487, 95460,* ☎ *707/937–5615 or 800/331–8884,* ℻ *707/937–0305. 24 rooms. Refrigerators, indoor pool, hot tub, sauna, bicycles. AE, D, DC, MC, V.*

$$–$$$ 🏠 **Brewery Gulch Inn.** This 1860s farmhouse bed-and-breakfast, a short drive from town, has retained its old-fashioned rural character, complete with chickens, which supply the eggs for breakfast. Antiques, wood floors, and hand-sewn quilts enhance cozy rooms, two with fireplaces. ⊠ *9350 N. Hwy. 1, 94560,* ☎ *707/937–4752. 5 rooms, 2 with shared bath. MC, V.*

$$–$$$ 🏠 **Joshua Grindle Inn.** Mendocino's oldest B&B stands on a 2-acre hilltop near the Highway 1 turnoff into town. The original farmhouse has five guest rooms, a parlor, and a dining room. Two outbuildings, the Watertower (an upper room has windows on all four sides) and the Cottage, have five additional rooms. Furnishings throughout the inn are simple but comfortable American antiques: Salem rockers, wing chairs, steamer-trunk tables, painted pine beds. Full breakfast is included. ⊠ *44800 Little Lake Rd., 95460,* ☎ *707/937–4143. 10 rooms. MC, V.*

$–$$ 🏠 **Mendocino Village Inn.** This 1882 Queen Anne Victorian inn has been refurbished in a potpourri of styles, with one room providing a southwestern motif, another reminiscent of a whaling captain's quarters, and a third with California Mission–style furnishings. There also is a two-story water-tower suite. Eight of the rooms have fireplaces or woodstoves, some have ocean views, and others look out on the garden. Breakfast is included. ⊠ *44860 Main St., Box 626, 95460,* ☎ *707/937–0246; in CA, 800/882–7029. 13 rooms, 2 with shared bath. No credit cards.*

Nightlife and the Arts

Mendocino Theatre Company. This community theater has been around for two decades. Its repertoire ranges from classics like *Uncle Vanya* to more recent works like *Other People's Money.* ⊠ *Mendocino Arts Center, 45200 Little Lake St.,* ☎ *707/937–4477.*

Patterson's Pub. This Irish-style watering hole is a friendly gathering place day or night, though it does become boisterous as the evening wears on. ⊠ *10485 Lansing St.,* ☎ *707/935–4782.*

Outdoor Activities and Sports

Catch-a-Canoe and Bicycles Too (⊠ Stanford Inn by the Sea, Mendocino, ☎ 707/937–0273) has daily and hourly rentals.

Shopping

Many fine artists exhibit their wares in Mendocino, and the streets of this compact town are so easily walkable that you're sure to find a gallery with something that strikes your fancy. You might start at the **Mendocino Art Center** (☞ *above*). The **Mendocino Hat Company** has a selection of caps, berets, Panama hats, and virtually any other kind of headcovering. **Old Gold** is a good place to look for locally designed and crafted jewelry.

Fort Bragg

10 mi north of Mendocino on Hwy. 1.

Fort Bragg has changed more than any other coastal town in the last few years. The decline in what was the top industry, timber, is being offset in part by a boom in charter-boat excursions and other tourist pursuits. The city is also attracting many artists—even luring some from nearby Mendocino, where the cost of living is higher and available space more expensive. This basically blue-collar town is the commercial center of Mendocino County.

The **Skunk Train,** a remnant of the region's logging days, dates from 1885 and travels a route, through redwood forests inaccessible to automobiles, from Fort Bragg to the town of Willits, 40 miles inland. A fume-spewing, self-propelled train car that shuttled passengers along the railroad got nicknamed the *Skunk Train,* and the entire line has been called that ever since. Excursions are now given on historic trains and replicas of the *Skunk Train* motorcar that are more aromatic than the original. In summer you have a choice of going partway to North-spur, a three-hour round-trip, or making the full seven-hour journey to Willits and back. ⊠ *Foot of Laurel St., Fort Bragg,* ☎ *707/964–6371. Fort Bragg–Willits: departs daily 9:20* AM. ▨ *$26. Fort Bragg–Northspur: departs mid-June–early Sept., daily 9:20* AM *and 1:40* PM; *early Sept.–mid-June 10* AM *and 2* PM. ▨ *$21.*

★ ❿ **MacKerricher State Park** includes 10 miles of sandy beach and several square miles of dunes. Fishing (at two freshwater lakes, one stocked with trout), canoeing, hiking, jogging, bicycling, camping (143 sites available), and harbor-seal watching at Laguna Point are among the popular activities—many of which are accessible to travelers with disabilities. Whales can often be spotted December through mid-April from the nearby headland. Rangers lead nature hikes throughout the year. ⊠ *3 mi north of Fort Bragg on Hwy. 1,* ☎ *707/937–5804.* ▨ *Free.*

Dining and Lodging

$$ ✕ **The Restaurant.** The name may be generic, but this place isn't. California cuisine is served in a dining room that doubles as an art gallery. There is a jazz brunch on Sunday. ⊠ *418 N. Main St.,* ☎ *707/964–9800. MC, V. Closed Wed. No lunch Sat., Mon., Tues.*

$$$–$$$$ ▥ **Grey Whale Inn.** Each room at this former hospital is decorated with floral spreads or handcrafted quilts. Three rooms have fireplaces, four have an ocean view, and a deluxe room has a private, two-person whirlpool tub and sundeck. Rooms off Main Street are quieter. Room rates include a generous buffet breakfast. ⊠ *615 N. Main St., 95437,* ☎ *707/964–0640 or 800/382–7244,* ℻ *707/964–4408. 14 rooms. Billiards. AE, D, MC, V.*

Outdoor Activities and Sports

Ricochet Ridge Ranch (⊠ 24201 N. Hwy. 1, ☎ 707/964–7669) conducts guided trail rides to the Mendocino–Ft. Bragg beaches.

En Route   North on Highway 1 from Fort Bragg, past the coastal mill town of Westport, the road cuts inland around the **King Range,** a stretch of mountain so rugged that it was impossible to build the intended major highway through it. Highway 1 joins the larger U.S. 101 at the town of Leggett. **Richardson Grove State Park,** north of Leggett along U.S. 101, marks your first encounter with the truly giant redwoods, but there are even more magnificent stands farther north in Humboldt and Del Norte counties.

REDWOOD COUNTRY
Garberville to Crescent City

The majestic redwoods that grace California's coast become more plentiful as you head north. Their towering ancient presence defines the landscape.

Garberville

70 mi from Fort Bragg on Hwy. 1 to U.S. 101, 197 mi north of San Francisco on U.S. 101.

Although it's the largest town in the vicinity of Humboldt Redwoods State Park, Garberville hasn't changed a whole lot since timber was king. There's still no traffic light, and only a couple of stop signs, along its six-block main drag, but the town is a pleasant place to stop for lunch, pick up picnic provisions, or poke through arts-and-crafts stores. A few miles below Garberville, perched along Eel River, is an elegant Tudor resort, the **Benbow Inn** (☞ Dining and Lodging, *below*), which is listed on the National Register of Historic Places. Even if you are not staying here, stop in for a drink or meal and a look at the architecture and gardens.

Dining and Lodging

$ ✕ **Woodrose Cafe.** This unpretentious eatery, a local favorite, serves basic breakfast items and healthy lunches. Dishes include chicken, pasta, and vegetarian specials. ⊠ *911 Redwood Dr., ☎ 707/923–3191. No credit cards. Closed weekends. No dinner.*

$$$$ ✕🖽 **Benbow Inn.** Set alongside the Eel River one highway exit south
★ of Garberville, this three-story Tudor-style manor resort is the equal of any in the region. The most luxurious of the antiques-filled rooms are on the terrace, with fine views of the Eel River; some have fireplaces, and 18 have TV with VCR. Guests have canoeing, tennis, golf, and pool privileges at an adjacent property. The wood-paneled dining room ($$–$$$) serves American cuisine, with the focus on fresh salmon and trout dishes. ⊠ *445 Lake Benbow Dr., 95442, ☎ 707/923–2124 or 800/355–3301. 55 rooms. Restaurant, lobby lounge, refrigerators, lake. AE, D, MC, V. Closed early Jan.–mid-Mar.*

Humboldt Redwoods State Park

⓫ *15 mi north of Garberville on U.S. 101.*

The **Avenue of the Giants** begins north of Garberville. Along this stretch of two-lane blacktop, you will find yourself enveloped by some of the tallest trees on the planet. The road cuts through part of the Humboldt Redwoods State Park, 51,222 acres of redwoods and waterways, and follows the south fork of the Eel River. The visitor center near Weott (☎ 707/946–2263) is open in the spring and summer and can provide information on the region's recreational opportunities and flora and fauna. Founders Grove contains some of the tallest trees in the park.

Ferndale

⓬ *30 mi north of Weott via U.S. 101 to Hwy. 211.*

The stately town of Ferndale maintains some of the most sumptuous Victorian homes in California, many of them built by 19th-century timber barons and Scandinavian dairy farmers. The queen of them all is the **Gingerbread Mansion,** a bed-and-breakfast (☞ Lodging, *below*).

A beautiful, sloped graveyard sits on Ocean Avenue west of Main Street. Numerous shops carry a map for self-guided tours of this lovingly preserved town.

The **Ferndale Museum** is a storehouse of antiques from the turn of the century. ⊠ *515 Shaw Ave.,* ☎ *707/786–4466.* ⊡ *$1.* ☉ *Oct.–June 1, Wed.–Sat. 11–4, Sun. 1–4; also Tues. 11–4 in summer.*

Lodging

$$–$$$$ 🛏 **Gingerbread Mansion.** The exterior of this classic Victorian bed-and-breakfast has the most playful paint job on the North Coast. The mansion's carved friezes set off its gables, and turrets dazzle the eye. Inside, comfortable parlors and spacious bedrooms are laid out in flowery Victorian splendor. Some have views of the mansion's elegant English garden, and one has side-by-side bathtubs. In 1995, innkeeper Ken Tolbert transformed the top floor into a suite that is so deluxe it would be suitable for a top San Francisco hotel—a vision in marble, with black and gold accents, it holds a claw-foot tub and a shower that could fit six. Ask about off-season discounts. Room rates include full breakfast. ⊠ *400 Berding St., off Brown St., Box 40, 95536,* ☎ *707/786–4000. 9 rooms. Bicycles. AE, MC, V.*

$$–$$$ 🛏 **Victorian Inn.** This hostelry occupies the second floor of a beautifully renovated Victorian building on Ferndale's perfectly preserved Main Street. Rooms are decorated in muted colors and have antique armoires, feather comforters, original moldings, and some claw-foot tubs. Downstairs are the inn's casual bar and restaurant. ⊠ *400 Ocean Ave., at Main St.,* ☎ *707/786–4949 or 800/576–5949,* 𝖥𝖠𝖷 *707/786–4648. 12 rooms. AE, D, MC, V.*

Outdoor Activities and Sports

Eel River Delta Tours (⊠ 285 Morgan Slough Rd., Ferndale, 95536, ☎ 707/786–4187) conducts a two-hour boat trip that emphasizes the wildlife and history of the Eel River's estuary and salt marsh.

Shopping

Ferndale's shops are all lined up along Main Street. **Golden Gait Mercantile** seems to be lost in a time warp, what with Burma Shave products and old-fashioned long johns as well as penny candy. For gifts, you can't do better than **Withywindle,** which sells local stoneware, porcelain, jewelry, and wearable art. The shopkeepers also specialize in gift baskets crammed with various gourmet products from the shelves.

Eureka

⑬ *10 mi north of Ferndale, 269 mi north of San Francisco on U.S. 101.*

Eureka, population 28,500, is the North Coast's largest city. It has gone through cycles of boom and bust, first with mining and later with timber and fishing. There are nearly 100 Victorian buildings here, many of them well preserved. The most splendid (and most photographed in the state) is the **Carson Mansion** (⊠ M and 2nd Sts.), built in 1885 by the Newsom brothers for timber baron William Carson. The house is now occupied by a private men's club. Across the street is another Newsom extravaganza popularly known as the **Pink Lady.**

For proof that contemporary architects still have the skills to design lovely Victoriana, have a look at the **Carter House** B&B inn (⊠ 3rd and L Sts.; ☞ Dining and Lodging, *below*) and keep in mind that it was built in the 1980s, not the 1880s.

The **Chamber of Commerce** has maps for self-guided driving tours of Eureka's architecture and information on how to join organized tours.

✉ *2112 Broadway,* ☎ *707/442–3738 or 800/356–6381.* ☉ *Weekdays 9–5.*

The **Clarke Museum** has an extraordinary collection of northwestern California Native American basketry and artifacts of Eureka's Victorian, logging, and maritime eras. ✉ *240 E. St.,* ☎ *707/443–1947.* ✑ *Donations accepted.* ☉ *Feb.–Dec., Tues.–Sat. and July 4 noon–4.*

NEED A BREAK? **Ramone's** (✉ 209 E St., ☎ 707/442–6082), a casual bakery café that also serves light sandwiches, has been voted Eureka's best place to grab a cup of coffee for the past few years running.

The structure that gave **Fort Humboldt State Historic Park** its name once guarded white settlers against the Indians. Ulysses S. Grant was posted here in 1854. The old fort is no longer around, but on its grounds are re-creations of the logging industry's early days, including a logging museum, some ancient steam engines (they rev them up the third Saturday of the month), and a logger's cabin. It's a good place for a picnic. ✉ *3431 Fort Ave.,* ☎ *707/445–6567.* ✑ *Free.* ☉ *Daily 9–4.*

To explore the waters around Eureka, take a **Humboldt Bay Harbor Cruise.** You can observe some of the region's bird life while sailing past fishing boats, oyster beds, and decaying timber mills. ✉ *Pier at C St.,* ☎ *707/445–1910 or 707/444–9440.* ✑ *$8.50. Departs May–Sept., daily 1, 2:30, and 4. Cocktail-cruise fare $5.50. Departs daily 5:30.*

Dining and Lodging

$$$ ✕ **Restaurant 301.** Mark and Christi Carter, owners of Eureka's fanciest hotels, also run one of the town's best restaurants. Most of the vegetables and herbs used in the food are grown at the hotel's greenhouse and nearby ranch, to provide the kitchen with the freshest possible ingredients. Try the superbly presented fish or duck, and don't skip the appetizers—especially the warm goat cheese and pâté. ✉ *301 L St.,* ☎ *707/444–8062. AE, D, DC, MC, V. Closed Tues.–Wed. No lunch.*

$ ✕ **Cafe Waterfront.** This small eatery across from the marina has a long bar with TV. Sandwiches and affordable seafood dishes are the menu mainstays. ✉ *102 F St.,* ☎ *707/443–9190. MC, V.*

$ ✕ **Samoa Cookhouse.** The recommendation here is more for atmosphere, ★ of which there is plenty: this is a longtime lumberman's hangout. The Samoa's cooks serve three substantial meals family-style at long wooden tables. Meat dishes dominate the menu. Save room (if possible) for dessert. ✉ *Cookhouse Rd. (from U.S. 101, cross Samoa Bridge, turn left onto Samoa Rd., then left 1 block later onto Cookhouse),* ☎ *707/442–1659. AE, D, MC, V.*

$$$–$$$$ ▥ **Carter House, Hotel Carter, and Cottage.** The Carter family runs three ★ properties in downtown Eureka. The Carter House, built in 1982 following the floor plan of a San Francisco mansion, has an antiques-laden sitting area and gorgeous rooms with heirloom furniture. Two doors down, the Cottage, an original Victorian, contains three rooms and a big sitting area with contemporary southwestern decorations. The hotel, catercorner to the Carter House, has an airy, elegant lobby and suites. Handsome brocaded spreads cover the beds; some rooms have fireplaces and whirlpool tubs. A large breakfast, served in the hotel's sunny dining room, is included with a night's stay in any of the three buildings. *Hotel:* ✉ *301 L St., 95501,* ☎ FAX *707/444–8062; 23 rooms. Carter House:* ✉ *1033 3rd St.,* ☎ *707/445–1390; 5 rooms. Cottage:* ✉ *3rd St.,* ☎ *707/445–1390; 3 rooms. AE, D, DC, MC, V.*

$$–$$$ 🏠 **An Elegant Victorian Mansion.** This restored Eastlake mansion in a residential neighborhood east of the Old Town lives up to its name. Each room is decked out in period furnishings and wall coverings, down to the carved-wood beds, fringed lamp shades, and pull-chain commodes. The innkeepers may even greet you in vintage clothing and surprise you with old-fashioned ice-cream sodas in the afternoon. They'll lure you further into their time warp with silent movies on tape, old records played on the windup Victrola, croquet on the rose-encircled lawn, and guided tours of local Victoriana in their antique automobile. The Victorian flower garden holds more than 100 rosebushes. Gourmet breakfast is included. *☒ 14th and C Sts., 95501, ☎ 707/444–3144 or 800/386–1888. 4 rooms with 4 shared baths. Massage, sauna, croquet, bicycles, laundry service. MC, V.*

Nightlife

Lost Coast Brewery & Cafe. This bustling microbrewery is the best place in town to relax with a pint of strong ale or porter. It also serves soups, salads, and light meals for lunch and dinner. *☒ 617 4th St., ☎ 707/445–4480.*

Outdoor Activities and Sports

Hum-Boats (*☒ 2 F St., ☎ 707/443–5157*) provides sailing rides, sailboat rentals, guided kayak tours, and sea kayak rentals and lessons. The company also runs a water-taxi service on Humboldt Bay.

Shopping

Eureka has several art galleries in the district running from C to I streets between 2nd and 3rd streets. Specialty shops in Old Town include the original **Restoration Hardware** (*☒ 417 2nd St., ☎ 707/443–3152*), a good place to find stylish yet functional home and garden accessories and clever polishing and cleaning products. The **Irish Shop** (*☒ 334 2nd St., ☎ 707/443–8343*) carries imports from the Emerald Isle, mostly fine woolens.

Arcata

🔟④ *9 mi north of Eureka on U.S. 101.*

The home of Humboldt State University is one of the few California burgs to retain a town square. Like Eureka to the south, Arcata has some restored Victorian buildings. A farmers' market takes place in the town square on Saturday mornings May through November. For a self-guided tour of Arcata, pick up a map from the **Chamber of Commerce** (*☒ 1062 G St., ☎ 707/822–3619*). It's open weekdays from 10 to 4.

Dining and Lodging

$$ ✕ **Abruzzi.** Salads and hefty pasta dishes take up most of the menu at this upscale Italian restaurant just off the town square. Abruzzi serves *panini* (Italian sandwiches) at lunch and pastas (such as linguine *pescara*, with a spicy seafood-and-tomato sauce) for lunch and dinner. *☒ 791 8th St., at corner of H St. (entrance on H St.), ☎ 707/826–2345. No lunch Sat.–Wed. AE, D, MC, V.*

$ ✕ **Crosswinds.** This restaurant serves good Continental cuisine in a casual, sunny Victorian setting, to the tune of live, classical music. *☒ 10th and I Sts., ☎ 707/826–2133. MC, V. Closed Mon. No dinner.*

$$ 🏠 **Hotel Arcata.** Flowered bedspreads and claw-foot bathtubs lend character to the rooms of this historic landmark overlooking the town square. Rates include use of a nearby health club as well as (on weekdays) Continental breakfast. *☒ 708 9th St., 95521, ☎ 707/826–0217 or 800/344–1221, FAX 707/826–1737. 32 rooms. Restaurant. AE, D, DC, MC, V.*

Shopping

For its size, Arcata has an impressive selection of shops, especially near its town square. Fabrics, clothing, housewares, and books are the best bets. **Plaza Design** (⊠ 808 G St., ☎ 707/822–7732) specializes in gifts, papers, and innovative furnishings.

Trinidad

14 mi north of Arcata on U.S. 101.

First visited by a Portuguese expedition in 1595, the waters here are now sailed by fishing boats trolling for salmon. Picturesque Trinidad Bay's harbor cove and rock formations look both raw and tranquil.

Dining and Lodging

$$–$$$ ✕ **Larrupin' Cafe.** This restaurant has earned widespread fame for its
★ Cajun ribs and fresh fish dishes, served in a bright yellow, two-story house on a quiet country road 2 miles north of Trinidad. ⊠ *1658 Patrick's Point Dr.,* ☎ *707/677–0230. Reservations essential. No credit cards. Closed Mon.–Wed. No lunch.*

$–$$ ✕ **Merryman's Dinner House.** Fresh fish and a romantic oceanfront setting make this a perfect spot for hungry lovers. ⊠ *100 Moonstone Beach,* ☎ *707/677–3111. No credit cards. No lunch; no dinner weekdays Oct.–Mar.*

$–$$ ✕ **Seascape.** With its glassed-in main room and a deck for alfresco dining, this is an ideal place to take in the splendor of Trinidad Bay. The breakfasts are great, the lunches are substantial, and the dinners feature good seafood. ⊠ *At pier,* ☎ *707/677–3762. MC, V.*

$$$ ▥ **Trinidad Bed and Breakfast.** Overlooking Trinidad Bay, this Cape Cod–style shingle house has an unforgettable ocean view. The innkeepers provide a wealth of information about the nearby wilderness, beach, and fishing habitats. The living room is warmed by a crackling fireplace. Room rates include breakfast. ⊠ *560 Edwards St., Box 849, 95570,* ☎ *707/677–0840. 2 rooms and 2 suites (1 with fireplace). Reservations essential. D, MC, V.*

Patrick's Point State Park

⑮ *5 mi north of Trinidad, 25 mi north of Eureka on U.S. 101.*

This park is a "sleeper" that relatively few people know about, but those who do return again and again. Set on a forested plateau almost 200 feet above the surf, it has stunning views of the Pacific (good for whale and sea-lion watching), picnic areas, bike trails, and hiking trails through old-growth forest. There are also tidal pools at Agate Beach and a small museum with natural-history exhibits. ☎ *707/677–3570.* ▦ *$5 per vehicle (day use). Camping $14 per vehicle.*

Redwood National Park

⑯ *22 mi north (Orick entrance) of Trinidad on U.S. 101.*

After 115 years of intensive logging, this 113,200-acre parcel of tall trees came under government protection in 1968, marking the California environmentalists' greatest victory over the timber industry. The park encompasses three state parks (Prairie Creek Redwoods, Del Norte Coast Redwoods, and Jedediah Smith Redwoods) and is more than 40 miles long.

For detailed information about Redwood National Park, stop at the **Redwood Information Center** (☎ 707/488–3461) between the park entrance and the town of Orick. There you can also get a free permit to drive up the steep, 17-mile road (the last 6 miles are gravel) to reach the Tall Trees Grove, where a 3-mile round-trip hiking trail leads to the world's first-, third- and fifth-tallest redwoods. Whale watchers will find the deck of the visitor center an excellent observation point, and birders will enjoy the nearby Freshwater Lagoon, a popular layover for migrating waterfowl.

Within Lady Bird Johnson Grove, just off Bald Hill Road, is a short circular trail to resplendent redwoods. This section of the park was dedicated by, and named for, the former first lady. For additional spectacular scenery, take Davison Road along a stunning seascape to Fern Canyon. This gravel road winds through 4 miles of second-growth redwoods, then hugs a bluff 100 feet above the pounding Pacific surf for another 4 miles.

To reach the entrance to Redwood's Prairie Creek Redwoods State Park, take the Elk Prairie Parkway exit off the U.S. 101 bypass. Extra space has been paved alongside the parklands, providing fine vantage points from which to observe an imposing herd of Roosevelt elk grazing in the adjoining meadow. Revelation Trail in Prairie Creek is fully accessible to visitors with disabilities.

Klamath

20 mi north of Orick on U.S. 101.

Lodging

$ Hostelling International—Redwood National Park. This turn-of-the-century inn is a stone's throw from the ocean; hiking begins just beyond its doors. Lodging is dormitory style. ⊠ *14480 U.S. 101 at Wilson Creek Rd., 95548,* ☎ ℻ *707/482–8265. No credit cards.*

Crescent City

20 mi north of Klamath on U.S. 101.

If you're in Del Norte County's largest town on President's Day weekend, don't miss the annual World Championship Crab Races, one of the town's most popular events. Crescent City is named for the shape of its harbor; during the 1800s this was an important steamship stop.

Dining and Lodging

$ ✕ Harbor View Grotto. This glassed-in dining hall overlooking the Pacific prides itself on its fresh fish entrées. ⊠ *155 Citizen's Dock Rd.,* ☎ *707/464–3815. No lunch. MC, V.*

$ ▥ Curly Redwood Lodge. This lodge was built from a single redwood tree, which produced 57,000 board feet of lumber. The decor in the guest rooms also makes the most of that tree, with paneling, platform beds, and dressers built into the walls. The rooms are a decent size, and there is a fireplace in the lobby. ⊠ *701 Redwood Hwy. S, 95531,* ☎ *707/464–2137,* ℻ *707/464–1655. 36 rooms. AE, DC, MC, V.*

En Route   Travelers continuing north to the Smith River near the Oregon border will find fine trout and salmon fishing as well as a profusion of flowers. Ninety percent of America's lily bulbs are grown in this area.

NORTH COAST A TO Z

Arriving and Departing

By Car

Highway 1 and U.S. 101 are the main north–south coastal routes. Highway 1 is often curvy and difficult (though always visually pleasing) all along the coast. Driving directly to Mendocino from San Francisco is quicker by taking U.S. 101 to Highway 128 to Highway 1 instead of driving up the coast. U.S. 101 itself becomes as twisty as Highway 1 as it winds its way to the northernmost corner of the state. (For information about renting a car in San Francisco, *see* San Francisco A to Z *in* Chapter 5.) **Hertz** (☎ 800/654–3131) rents cars at the Eureka-Arcata airport (no phone) in McKinleyville.

By Plane

United Express (☎ 800/241–6522) has regular nonstop flights from San Francisco to Eureka/Arcata. This is the fastest and most direct way to reach the redwood country.

Getting Around

By Car

Although there are excellent services along Highway 1 and U.S. 101, gas stations and mechanics are few and far between on the smaller roads.

Contacts and Resources

Emergencies

Ambulance (☎ 911). **Police** (☎ 911).

Guided Tours

Oceanic Society Expeditions (✉ Fort Mason, San Francisco, ☎ 415/474–3385) conducts whale-watching and other nature cruises north and west of San Francisco throughout much of the year. **New Sea Angler and Jaws** (✉ Bodega Bay, ☎ 707/875–3495) runs cruises on weekends December–April.

Visitor Information

Eureka/Humboldt County Convention and Visitors Bureau (✉ 1034 2nd St., Eureka, CA 95501, ☎ 800/346–3482; in CA, 800/338–7352). **Fort Bragg–Mendocino Coast Chamber of Commerce** (✉ Box 1141, Fort Bragg, CA 95437, ☎ 800/726–2780). **Redwood Empire Association** (✉ Cannery, 2801 Leavenworth St., 2nd floor, San Francisco, CA 94133, ☎ 415/543–8334, ℻ 415/543–8337). **West Marin Chamber of Commerce** (✉ Box 1045, Point Reyes Station, CA 94956, ☎ 415/663–9232).

3 The Far North

Including Mt. Shasta, Lake Shasta, and Lassen Volcanic National Park

Soaring mountain peaks, wild rivers brimming with fish, and almost infinite recreational possibilities make the Far North a sports lover's paradise. Hot nightspots and cultural enclaves do not abound, but you will find some of the best hiking, fishing, and hunting in the state. Some Bay Area families return to this region year after year. Many enjoy the outdoors from their own piece of paradise—a private houseboat. Keep in mind that much of the Far North can be very hot in summer.

By Marty
Olmstead

THE FAR NORTH LANDSCAPE has been writ large by ancient volcanic activity. The scenery is best symbolized by Mt. Shasta, a 14,162-foot-high mountain that can be seen for 100 miles around. Less dramatic but more extensive is Lassen Volcanic National Park at the southern end of the Cascade Range. The geology here is interesting, not merely for evidence of past but also current geothermal activity. The 10,457-foot Mt. Lassen and 50 wilderness lakes are the park's centerpieces. The Far North's natural and artificially created wonders include the sulfur vents and bubbling mud pots of Lassen Volcanic National Park and immense Shasta Dam. Plentiful access to the wilderness, without crowding, is the Far North's hallmark. There are few towns and fewer cities. Natural history dwarfs the footsteps of mankind in this grand gymnasium for body and soul.

Pleasures and Pastimes

Camping
You'll find everything from the well-outfitted campgrounds in McArthur-Burney Falls Memorial State Park, which have hot water, showers, and flush toilets, to isolated campsites on Lake Shasta that can be reached only by boat. There are seven campgrounds within Lassen Volcanic National Park. Reservations are not accepted; it's first come, first served. For campground and other information, contact Lassen Volcanic National Park or the Shasta Cascade Wonderland Association (☞ Contacts and Resources *in* The Far North A to Z, *below*).

Dining
Redding, the urban center of the Far North, has the greatest selection of restaurants. In the smaller towns, cafés and simple restaurants are the rule, though there is the occasional culinary surprise. Dress is always informal in the Far North.

CATEGORY	COST*
$$$$	over $50
$$$	$30–$50
$$	$20–$30
$	under $20

per person for a three-course meal, excluding drinks, service, and 7¼% tax

Lodging
Beyond the large chain hotels and motels in the Redding area, accommodations are a blend of rusticity, simplicity, and coziness. Most visitors to rural areas spend much of their time in the outdoors and prefer informal camps and motels. Wilderness resorts close in fall and reopen only after the snow season ends in May.

CATEGORY	COST*
$$$$	over $175
$$$	$120–$175
$$	$80–$120
$	under $80

All prices are for a standard double room, excluding 8% tax.

Outdoor Activities and Sports
Fishing, houseboating, and animal-pack trips are popular Far North diversions. Cascading rivers, mammoth lakes, and bountiful streams draw sportfishers. Hikers, backpackers, hunters, skiers, and other outdoor enthusiasts enjoy idyllic conditions for most of the year. Castle Crags State Park and Lassen Volcanic National Park have abundant

hiking and walking trails. In winter, the slopes of Mt. Shasta contain challenging ski runs, but crowds are few and far between.

Exploring the Far North

The Far North encompasses three vast counties (Tehama, Shasta, and Trinity), land that stretches from the valleys east of the Coast Range to the Nevada border and from the almond and olive orchards north of Sacramento to the Oregon border.

Great Itineraries

The tri-county area's most scenic parts lie along the two-lane roads that crisscross the region, which is bisected by I–5. East of I–5 are dramatic mountain peaks, to the west heavily forested areas and interesting small towns.

Numbers in the text correspond to numbers in the margin and on the Far North map.

IF YOU HAVE 3 DAYS

From I–5 above Redding, head northeast on Highways 299 and 89 to **McArthur-Burney Falls Memorial State Park** ⑥. To appreciate the falls, take the short stroll to an overlook or hike down for an even closer view. Continue north on Highway 89. Long before you arrive in the town of ⊞ **Mt. Shasta,** you will spy the conical peak for which it is named. This is a great photographic opportunity, particularly late in the day, when low-lying clouds often cast a pink glow on the mountain. The central **Mt. Shasta** ⑦ exit east leads out of town along the **Everett Memorial Highway.** Take this scenic drive, which climbs to almost 8,000 feet. The views of the mountain and the valley below are extraordinary. Stay overnight in town. On the second day, head south on I–5 toward the **Lake Shasta Caverns** ⑧ and the **Shasta Dam** ⑨. **Lake Shasta** is visible on both sides of the highway as it crosses the water near the dam, which is on the west side of I–5. Overnight either in ⊞ **Redding** ⑪ or ⊞ **Weaverville** ⑩. Near Redding, Highway 299 leads west toward the **Whiskeytown-Shasta-Trinity National Recreation Area.** Visit Weaverville on your third day—be sure to take the **Joss House** tour—and have lunch in town before returning to Redding.

IF YOU HAVE 5 OR 6 DAYS

Get a glimpse of the Far North's heritage in **Red Bluff** ① at the **Kelly-Griggs House Museum** and **William B. Ide Adobe State Historic Park** ②. Head north on I–5 and settle in for the night in the town of ⊞ **Mt. Shasta.** The next day, check on trail conditions on **Mt. Shasta** ⑦ and pick up maps at the Forest Service Ranger Station. Pack a picnic lunch before taking the **Everett Memorial Highway** up the mountain and hiking around. Spend the night a few miles south in ⊞ **Dunsmuir** at the **Railroad Car Resort,** where all the accommodations are old cabooses. On your third day, take an early-morning hike in nearby **Castle Crags State Park,** whose 225-million-year-old crags tower over the Sacramento River at heights up to 6,000 feet. Continue south on I–5 and tour **Shasta Dam** ⑨. Spend the night camping in the area or in ⊞ **Redding** ⑪. On your fourth morning, head west on Highway 299 to **Shasta,** a gold-mining town that's a shadow of its former, prosperous self. Continue west on 299 to ⊞ **Weaverville** ⑩ and stay the night there or back in Redding. If you will be leaving the area on your fifth day but have a little time, zip north and visit **Lake Shasta Caverns** ⑧. If you're remaining and it's between late May and early October, spend the next day and a half exploring **Lassen Volcanic National Park.** Highway 44 heads east from Redding into the park, entering near **Chaos Jumbles** ⑤, created by a rock avalanche. Also on Lassen Park Road are **Hot Rock** ④, a huge

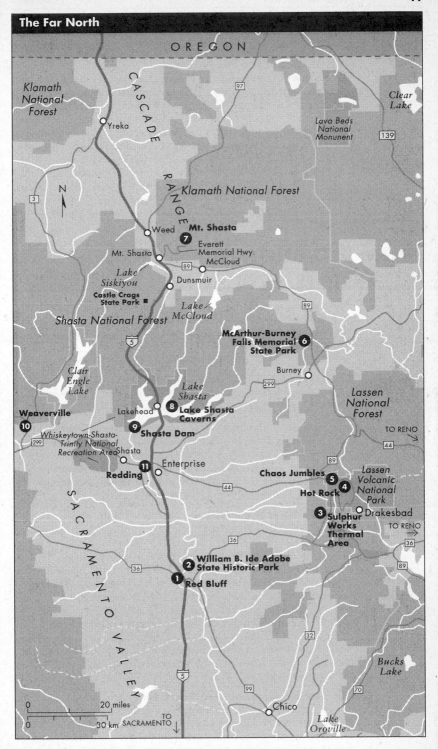

The Far North

boulder that tumbled onto its current site during volcanic activity earlier this century, and the **Sulphur Works Thermal Area** ③, where you can have a stinky good time viewing the steam vents.

When to Tour the Far North

This region attracts the greatest number of tourists during the summer, when the fishing is easy and the camping is comfortable. Summers can be dry and scorching; families flock to the lakes for swimming and motorboating. The valley around Redding is mild in the winter, but cooler temperatures prevail at the higher elevations to the east and north. In winter, Mt. Shasta is a good downhill ski area. Otherwise, much of the area is too cold for outdoor pleasures, and roads to the region's most awesome sights, including much of Lassen Volcanic National Park, are closed from October until late May because of hazardous driving conditions. Be aware that many restaurants and museums here have limited hours and sometimes close for stretches of the off-season.

FROM RED BLUFF TO MT. SHASTA

Lassen, Mt. Shasta, Weaverville, and Redding

The sights below are arranged in a loop that begins in the south at I–5 in Red Bluff and swings around to the northeast on state highways, through Lassen Volcanic National Park and then north to Mt. Shasta. The remaining attractions are off I–5 heading south toward Redding, with a jog to the west to the towns of Shasta and Weaverville.

Red Bluff

❶ *179 mi north of San Francisco, I–80 to I–505 to I–5.*

Named for both the color of the soil and the town's location above the Sacramento River, Red Bluff was established in the mid-19th century, just before Victorian architecture became the style of choice. Historic structures of two types remain: The streets west of the town's main drag hold a number of gracefully restored Victorian structures; downtown looks like a stage set for a western movie.

The **Kelly-Griggs House Museum,** a restored 1880s Victorian home, holds an impressive collection of antique furniture, housewares, and clothing arranged as though a refined Victorian family were still in residence: An engraved silver tea server waits at the end table; a "Self Instructor in Penmanship" sits on a desk; and costumed mannequins seem frozen in conversation in the upstairs parlor. The museum's collection includes carved china cabinets and Native American basketry. In the Ishi Room is an exhibit about the "last wild Indian." *Persephone*, the painting over the fireplace, is by Sarah Brown, daughter of abolitionist John Brown, whose family settled in Red Bluff after his execution. The Brown home is part of the self-guided tour of Red Bluff Victoriana; maps are available here. ⊠ *311 Washington St.,* ☎ *916/527–1129.* 🎫 *Donation suggested.* ☉ *Thurs.–Sun. 1–4.*

❷ The **William B. Ide Adobe State Historic Park** is a memorial to the first and only president of the short-lived California Republic of 1846. The Bear Flag Party proclaimed California a sovereign nation, no longer under the dominion of Mexico, and the republic existed for 25 days before it was occupied by the United States. The flag concocted for the republic has survived, with only minor refinements, as California's state flag. What is thought to be Ide's adobe home was built in the 1850s and now displays period furnishings and artifacts of the era. ⊠ *21659*

*Adobe Rd., ☎ 916/529–8599. ⊟ $3 donation requested per vehicle.
⊙ Park and picnic facilities 8 AM–sunset year-round; home 11–4 in
summer (in winter, look for ranger to unlock the house).*

Dining

$$ ✕ **Snack Box.** A renovated Victorian cottage is cheerfully decorated
with unabashedly corny pictures and knickknacks, all rural and many
featuring cattle and sheep. The food need make no apologies, however.
Soups, omelets, blue-plate specials, and even simple items such as
grilled-cheese sandwiches are perfectly executed. ⊠ *257 Main St., 1
block from Kelly-Griggs Museum,* ☎ *916/529–0227. No credit cards.
No dinner.*

Lassen Volcanic National Park

45 mi east of Redding on Hwy. 44, 48 mi east of Red Bluff on Hwy. 36.

Lassen Volcanic National Park provides a look at three sides of the
world's largest plug volcano. Except for the Nordic ski area, the park
is largely inaccessible from late October to late May because of snow.
The Lassen Park Road (the continuation of Highway 89 within the park)
is closed to cars in winter but open to intrepid cross-country skiers,
conditions permitting. Even in the best of weather, services are sparse.
In the southwest corner of the park, a café and a gift shop are open
during the summer. At the Manzanita Lake campground another store,
also open only in summer, has gas and fast food. The *Lassen Park Guide,*
available for a nominal fee at the visitor center and park entrance, de-
tails these and other facilities. ⊠ *Headquarters and visitor center:
38050 Hwy. 36 East, Mineral 96063,* ☎ *916/595–4444.* ⊟ *$5 per
vehicle in summer, free in winter.* ⊙ *Visitor center weekdays 8–4:30
year-round, summer weekends 8–4:30; hrs sometimes vary.*

In 1914 the 10,457-foot Mt. Lassen began a series of 300 eruptions
that went on for seven years. Molten rock overflowed the crater, and
the mountain emitted clouds of smoke and hailstorms of rocks and vol-
canic cinders. Proof of the volcano's volatility becomes evident shortly

❸ after you enter the park at the **Sulphur Works Thermal Area.** Board-
walks take you over bubbling mud and hot springs and through the
nauseating sulfur stink of steam vents. ⊠ *Lassen Park Rd., south end
of park.*

Bumpass Hell Trail, a 3-mile round-trip hike to the park's most inter-
esting thermal-spring area, allows visitors to view hot and boiling
springs, steam vents, and mud pots up close. The trail climbs and de-
scends several hundred feet. Be sure to stay on trails and boardwalks
near the thermal areas. What may appear to be firm ground may be
only a thin crust over scalding mud. ⊠ *Off Lassen Park Rd., 5 mi north
of Sulphur Works Thermal Area.*

❹ **Hot Rock,** a 400-ton boulder, tumbled down from the summit during
the volcano's active period and was still hot to the touch when locals
found it. Although cool now, it's still an impressive sight. ⊠ *Lassen
Park Rd., north end of park.*

❺ **Chaos Jumbles** was created 300 years ago when an avalanche from the
Chaos Crags lava domes spread hundreds of thousands of rocks 2 to
3 feet in diameter over 2 square miles. ⊠ *Lassen Park Rd., north end
of park.*

Dining and Lodging

$$$$ ✕▥ **Drakesbad Guest Ranch.** The 100-year-old guest ranch at Drakes-
bad, at elevation 5,700 feet near Lassen Volcanic National Park's
southern border on Lake Almanor, is isolated from most of the rest of

the park. Rooms in the lodge, bungalows, and cabins don't have electricity; they're lighted by kerosene lamps. But the accommodations are clean and comfortable and include furnace heat and either half or full bath. Reservations should be made well in advance (the waiting list can be up to two years long); all meals are included. ⊠ *Chester–Warner Valley Rd. north from Hwy. 36 (booking office: 2150 N. Main St., Suite 5, Red Bluff 96080),* ☎ *916/529–1512,* FAX *916/529–4511. 19 rooms. Dining room, pool, badminton, horseback riding, horseshoes, Ping-Pong, volleyball, fishing. MC, V. Closed early Oct.–early June.*

$ ✕🏨 **Lassen Mineral Lodge.** Reserve rooms at this motel-style property as far in advance as possible. You can rent cross-country skis at the lodge's ski shop; there's also a general store. ⊠ *Hwy. 36, Mineral 96063,* ☎ *916/595–4422. 20 rooms. Restaurant, bar, pool, tennis courts. MC, V.*

Outdoor Activities and Sports

SNOWSHOE TOURS

National Park Service rangers conduct snowshoe tours at **Mt. Lassen Ski Park.** Various natural history topics are covered. ☎ *916/595–4444 for directions. No reservations.* ⊠ *$1 donation for upkeep of snowshoes.* ☉ *Jan.–Apr., Sat. 1:30* PM.

McArthur-Burney Falls Memorial State Park

❻ *30 mi north of Lassen Volcanic National Park on Hwy. 89.*

Just inside the southern boundary of this state park, Burney Creek wells up from the ground and divides into two cascades that fall over a 129-foot cliff and into a pool below. The thundering water creates a mist at the base of the falls, often highlighted by a rainbow. Countless ribbonlike falls stream from hidden moss-covered crevices—an ethereal backdrop to the main cascades. Each day, 100 million gallons of water rush over these falls; Theodore Roosevelt proclaimed them "the eighth wonder of the world." A self-guided nature trail descends to the foot of the falls. There is a lake and beach for swimming. A campground, picnic sites, trails, and other facilities are available. The camp store is open Memorial Day–Labor Day. ⊠ *24898 Hwy. 89, Burney 96013,* ☎ *916/335–2777.* ⊠ *$5 per vehicle (day use). Camping: May–Sept., $14 per night; Oct.–Apr., $12 per night. Campground reservations (necessary in summer) are made through Destinet,* ☎ *800/444–7275.*

Mt. Shasta

❼ *52 mi from McArthur-Burney Falls Memorial State Park on Hwy. 89, 61 mi north of Redding on I–5.*

Mt. Shasta—the mountain and the town—made headlines in 1987, when participants in the worldwide Harmonic Convergence converged on the region because they believed the mountain held special powers. They weren't the first: Legends of eerie phenomena and mythical animals have surrounded the mountain, a 16-million-year-old dormant volcano, for decades. Part of its lure, no doubt, is that few people make it to the perennially ice-packed summit. An automobile road travels only as high as the timberland, and the final 6,000 feet are a tough climb of rubble, ice, and snow. The crowning jewel of the 2.5 million-acre Shasta–Trinity National Forest, Mt. Shasta is popular with day hikers, especially in spring, when flowers like the fragrant Shasta lily adorn the rocky slopes. As for the town of Mt. Shasta, it is not so much a destination as a place to eat and sleep. There is not much to do or see, even on the main thoroughfare.

Dining and Lodging

$$–$$$ ✕ **Michael's Restaurant.** Wood paneling, candlelight, and wildlife prints by local artists create an unpretentious setting for such Italian specialties as stuffed calamari, filet mignon scaloppine, linguine pesto, and other Continental dishes. ⊠ *313 N. Mt. Shasta Blvd.,* ☎ *916/926–5288. AE, D, MC, V. Closed Sun.–Mon.*

$$ ✕ **Lily's.** This restaurant in a light-filled, white clapboard home—complete with picket fence—serves pasta with jalapeño, grilled chicken, and a Mediterranean variation with sun-dried tomatoes and artichoke hearts. Among the unusual salads are a spicy shrimp-and-chicken dish and the Jalisco, steak and greens with tomatoes. ⊠ *1013 S. Mt. Shasta Blvd.,* ☎ *916/926–3372. MC, V.*

$–$$ ▥ **Tree House Best Western.** The clean, standard rooms at this motel, a half-mile from downtown Mt. Shasta, are decorated with natural-wood furnishings. ⊠ *111 Morgan Way at I–5 and Lake St., Box 236, 96067,* ☎ *916/926–3101 or 800/528–1234,* ᴲᴬˣ *916/926–3542. 95 rooms. Restaurant, lounge, indoor pool. AE, D, DC, MC, V.*

$–$$ ▥ **Wagon Creek Inn.** This lodgepole-pine log home in a quiet residential neighborhood 2 miles outside town is one of the area's most affordable inns, with crisp, country decor; a living room with fireplace, television, and VCR; and laid-back hospitality. Continental breakfast is included. ⊠ *1239 Woodland Park Dr., 96067,* ☎ *916/926–0838 or 800/995–9260. 3 rooms, 2 with shared bath. MC, V.*

Outdoor Activities and Sports

HIKING

The **Forest Service Ranger Station** (☎ 916/926–4511) provides constantly updated information on trail conditions. The **Fifth Season Mountaineering Shop** (☎ 916/926–3606) operates a recorded 24-hour climber-skier report, (☎ 916/926–5555).

MOUNTAIN CLIMBING

Shasta Mountain Guides (☎ 916/926–3117) leads hiking and ski-touring groups to the summit of Mt. Shasta.

SKIING

Mt. Shasta Ski Park. On the southeast flank of Mt. Shasta are three lifts on 300 skiable acres. The terrain is 20% beginner, 60% intermediate, 20% advanced. Top elevation is 6,600 feet; its base, 5,500 feet; its vertical drop, 1,100 feet. The longest run is 1.2 miles. Night skiing goes until 10 PM Wednesday–Saturday. There is a ski school with a beginner's special: lifts, rentals, lessons. The "Powder Pups" program is for ages four–seven. Lodge facilities include food and beverages, ski shop, and rentals. ⊠ *Hwy. 89 exit east from I–5, just south of Mt. Shasta,* ☎ *916/926–8610. Snow information:* ☎ *916/926–8686.*

Dunsmuir

10 mi south of Mt. Shasta on I–5.

This tiny town fell on hard times with the disappearance of the railroad and the decline of logging. Named for a 19th-century coal baron, Dunsmuir is surrounded by **Crags Creek State Park.** The town's other major attraction, especially for kids, is the nearby **Railroad Park Resort,** whose patrons spend the night in restored rail cars.

Castle Crags State Park is a hiker's paradise. Granite spires created millions of years ago still poke the skies at altitudes of more than 4,000 feet. There are excellent trails at lower altitudes in this 6,000-acre park, which also has picnic areas, rest rooms, showers, and, for $12 a night, plenty of campsites. ⊠ *Off I–5, 6 mi south of Dunsmuir,* ☎ *916/235–2684.* ◻ *$5 per vehicle (day use).*

Lodging

$–$$ 🏨 **Railroad Park Resort.** At this railroad buff's delight, antique cabooses have been converted into cozy, wood-paneled motel rooms in honor of Dunsmuir's railroad legacy. Set in its own little park, the resort has a modestly *Orient Express*–style dining room and a lounge fashioned from vintage rail cars. The landscaped grounds contain a huge logging steam engine and a restored water tower. ⊠ *100 Railroad Park Rd., 96025,* ☎ *916/235–4440 or 800/974–7245,* FAX *916/235–4470. 24 cabooses, 4 cabins. Pool, hot tub. AE, D, MC, V.*

Lake Shasta Area

34 mi south of Mt. Shasta (to town of Lakehead) on I–5, 12 mi north of Redding on I–5.

The many Shastas—mountain, lake, river, town, dam, and forest—derive from the name of the Indians who inhabited parts of the region in the 19th century (variously, Shatasla and Sastise). The Indian pronunciation for the river was *tschasta,* which evolved into modern-day speech.

❽ Stalagmites, stalactites, odd flowstone deposits, and crystals entice visitors of all ages to the **Lake Shasta Caverns.** A two-hour tour includes a catamaran ride across the McCloud arm of Lake Shasta and a bus ride up Grey Rock Mountain to the cavern entrance. The caverns are a constant 58°F year-round, making them an appealingly cool retreat on a hot summer day. All cavern rooms are well lit, and the crowning jewel is the spectacular cathedral room. The guides are friendly, enthusiastic, and informative. ⊠ *Shasta Caverns Rd. exit from I–5,* ☎ *916/238–2341 or 800/795–2283.* ◻ *$12.* ⊙ *Daily 9–4; tours May–Sept. on the hr, Oct.–Apr. at 10, noon, and 2.*

★ **Lake Shasta** has 370 miles of shoreline and 21 varieties of fish. You can rent fishing boats, ski boats, sailboats, canoes, paddleboats, Jet Skis, and Windsurfer boards at one of the many marinas and resorts along the shore. Lake Shasta is known as the houseboat capital of the world (☞ Outdoor Activities and Sports, *below,* for information about rentals).

★ ❾ **Shasta Dam** is the second-largest and the fourth-tallest concrete dam in the United States. At twilight the sight is magical, with Mt. Shasta gleaming above the not-quite-dark water and deer frolicking on the hillside beside the dam. The dam is lit after dark, but there is no access from 10 PM to 6 AM. The dam's visitor center has fact sheets and photographic and historic displays. ⊠ *Shasta Dam Blvd.,* ☎ *916/275–4463.* ⊙ *Dam 6 AM–10 PM; visitor center weekdays 8–5 (tours at 10, noon, 2 year-round, more often in summer), weekends 9–5 (tours 10, noon, 2 year-round, on the hr 9–4 in summer).*

Dining

$$ ✕ **Tail O' the Whale.** This restaurant overlooking Lake Shasta is distinguished by its nautical decor. Seafood, prime rib, poultry, and Cajun pepper shrimp are the specialties. ⊠ *10300 Bridge Bay Rd., Bridge Bay exit from I–5,* ☎ *916/275–3021. D, MC, V.*

Outdoor Activities and Sports

FISHING

The Fishin' Hole (⊠ 3844 Shasta Dam Blvd., Central Valley 96019, ☎ 916/275–4123) carries supplies and provides information about conditions, licenses, and fishing packages.

HOUSEBOATING

Houseboats come in all sizes except small. As a rule these moving homes come with cooking utensils, dishes, and most of the equipment you'll need—you supply food and linens. Renters are given a short course in how to maneuver the boats before they set out on cruises; it's not difficult, as the houseboats are slow moving. You can fish, swim, sunbathe on the flat roof, or just sit on the deck and watch the world go by. The shoreline of Lake Shasta is beautifully ragged, with countless inlets; it's not hard to find privacy. Expect to spend a minimum of $200 a day for a craft that sleeps six. There is usually a three-night minimum in peak season. **Shasta Cascade Wonderland Association** (☞ Contacts and Resources *in* Far North A to Z, *below*) has more information.

Shasta

7 mi west of Redding on Hwy. 299.

The ruins of the once-prosperous gold-mining town of Shasta, now a 13-acre **state historic park** with a few restored buildings, afford the opportunity to see how prospectors lived a century ago. A museum in the old courthouse has an eclectic array of California paintings, memorabilia, and a *Prairie Traveler* guidebook with advice on encounters with Indians. Continue down to the basement to see the iron-bar jail cells, and step outside for a look at the scaffold where murderers were hanged. ⊠ *Hwy. 299,* ☎ *916/243–8194.* ☞ *$2.* ☉ *Mar.–Oct., Wed.–Sun. 10–5; Nov.–Feb., Fri.–Sun. 10–5.*

Weaverville

🔟 *40 mi west of Shasta on Hwy. 299 (called Main St. in town).*

This old mountain town of nearly 5,000 is one of the Far North's most charming. Although the city includes rows of car dealers and the like, downtown blocks maintain their historic gold-rush ambience. Weaverville is a popular headquarters for family vacations and biking, hiking, fishing, hunting, and gold-panning excursions.

John Weaver was one of three men who built the first cabin, in 1850, in the town that would later be named for him. By 1851, Weaverville was the Trinity County seat and included neighboring communities such as Frenchtown, Englishtown, Germantown, Irishtown, and a sizable Chinatown.

The most visible legacy of the Chinese presence is the **Weaverville Joss House,** a Taoist temple built in 1874. Called Won Lim Miao, the "Temple Amongst the Forest Beneath the Clouds," by Chinese miners, it attracts worshipers from around the world. With its golden altar, carved wooden canopies, and intriguing artifacts, the Joss House is a piece of California history that can best be appreciated in the company of a guide. The original temple building and many of its furnishings—some of which had come from China—were burned in 1873, but members of the local Chinese community soon rebuilt it. An ornate wooden gate leads to the porch of this bright-blue building. ⊠ *Oregon and Main Sts.,* ☎ *916/623–5284.* ☞ *Nominal charge for 40-min guided tours, on the hr 10–4.* ☉ *Summer daily 10–5, rest of yr Thurs.–Mon. 10–5.*

Fires destroyed many parts of Weaverville; surviving buildings are mostly brick. Since the upper floor was often owned by a different person than the lower floor of many old downtown buildings, outdoor spiral staircases were constructed to permit each owner a private entrance. Three such buildings remain visible in the downtown Historic District.

The **Trinity County Courthouse** (✉ Court and Main Sts.), built in 1857 as a store, office building, and hotel, was converted to county use in 1865. The Apollo Saloon in the basement became the county jail. **Trinity County Historical Park** (✉ 408 Main St., ☎ 916/623–5211) is home to the Jake Jackson Memorial Museum, which has a blacksmith shop, a replica stampmill, and the original jail cells of the Trinity County Courthouse.

Dining and Lodging

$$ ✕ **La Grange.** This diner-esque eatery is one of the few places in Weaverville open for lunch and dinner six days a week. Stick to basics like chicken and pasta; the kitchen is still learning how to cook trout. On the plus side, La Grange serves plenty of vegetables and sells beer and wine. ✉ *315 N. Main St., ☎ 916/623–5325. MC, V.*

$ ✕ **La Casita.** Weaverville's only real Mexican restaurant serves the standard regimen—all the quesadillas (including one with roasted chili peppers), tostadas, enchiladas, tacos, and tamales you could want, many of them available in a vegetarian version. This casual spot is open from late morning through early evening, so it's a great for a mid-afternoon snack. ✉ *254 Main St., ☎ 916/623–5797. No credit cards.*

$ ✕ **Mustard Seed.** This is the place for breakfast in Weaverville. Try the Belgian waffles or some hippie fare like granola and multigrain breads. Deli fare, quesadillas, fruit plates, and other items round out the menu. The cozy restaurant, which is indeed painted mustard yellow, has one of the few espresso machines in town. ✉ *254 Main St., above La Casita restaurant, ☎ 916/623–2922. No credit cards.*

$ 🏠 **Red Hill Motel.** Housekeeping cabins make this the best choice among Weaverville motels. A two-bedroom cabin with a full kitchen is popular with families. ✉ *Box 234, Red Hill Rd., 96093, ☎ 916/623–4331. 14 rooms, 10 of them cabins with carports. D, DC, MC, V.*

Outdoor Activities and Sports

FISHING

Just below the Lewiston Dam, east of Weaverville on Highway 299, is the **Fly Stretch** of the Trinity River, a world-class flyfishing area. The **Pine Cove Boat Ramp** provides quality fishing access for visitors with disabilities—decks here are built over prime trout-fishing water. Open all year, Pine Cove is best for fishing from April through October.

HIKING

Several trails offer different levels of day hikes close to Weaverville as well as multiday hikes within the Trinity Alps Wilderness. Contact the **Weaverville Ranger Station** (☎ 916/623–2121) for maps and information.

Shopping

All the good shopping is right downtown. To dress the part of the Wild West explorer, check out the **Western Shop** (✉ 226 Main St., ☎ 916/623–6494) for outdoor gear, bolo ties, cowboy hats, and much more. To get your bearings, try the extraordinary selection of books on the natural history, attractions, and interesting sights of the Far North at **Hays Bookstore** (✉ 106 Main St., ☎ 916/623–2516).

OFF THE
BEATEN PATH
TRINITY HERITAGE SCENIC BYWAY – This road, on maps as Highway 3, runs north from Weaverville for 120 miles up to the intersection with I–5, just before Yreka in the town of Edgewood. Natural attractions are visible all along this beautiful, forest-lined road, which is often closed during the winter months. A major portion of the route follows the path established by early miners and settlers as it climbs from 2,000 to 6,500 feet.

Redding

⓫ *218 mi from San Francisco on I–80 to I–505 to I–5 north, 12 miles south of Lake Shasta on I–5.*

With a population of approximately 70,000, Redding is the hub of the Far North, by far its biggest city. Though not of much interest itself, it serves as a useful headquarters for exploring the surrounding countryside.

Dining and Lodging

$$ ✕ **Hatch Cover.** This establishment's dark-wood paneling and views of the adjacent Sacramento River give diners a shipboard feel. The menu emphasizes seafood, but you can also get steaks and combination plates. The appetizer menu is extensive, a good excuse for enjoying the outside deck in nice weather. Check out the exotic after-dinner drinks. ⊠ *202 Hemsted Dr.,* ☏ *916/223–5606. From the Cypress Ave. exit off I–5, turn left, then right on Bechelli La., and left on Hemsted Dr. AE, D, MC, V. No lunch weekends.*

$$ ✕ **Jack's Grill.** Although it looks like a dive from the outside, this steak house and bar is immensely popular with residents throughout the territory, who come in for 16-ounce steaks. The place is usually jam-packed and noisy. ⊠ *1743 California St.,* ☏ *916/241–9705. AE, MC, V. Closed Sun. No lunch.*

$$$ 🏨 **Red Lion Motor Inn.** Landscaped grounds and a large patio area with outdoor food service are the highlights here. Rooms are spacious and comfortable. Misty's, the lobby's fancy restaurant ($$$), is popular among locals for its steak Diane. Pets are allowed with advance notice. ⊠ *1830 Hilltop Dr., Hwy. 44/299 exit east from I–5, 96002,* ☏ *916/221–8700 or 800/547–8010,* FAX *916/221–0324. 194 rooms with bath. Restaurant, bar, coffee shop, room service, pool, wading pool, hot tub, putting green. AE, D, MC, V.*

$$ 🏨 **La Quinta.** Recently remodeled rooms here are done in pastels and have dark-wood furniture; the spotless, white-tile bathrooms have full-length mirrors. The spacious lobby has a cozy sitting area. ⊠ *2180 Hilltop Dr.,* ☏ *916/221–8200 or 800/531–5900. 145 rooms. Restaurant, pool, hot tub. AE, D, DC, MC, V.*

Outdoor Activities and Sports

The **Fly Shop** (⊠ 4140 Churn Creek Rd., ☏ 916/222–3555) has information about licenses, current fishing conditions, guides, and special fishing packages.

Park Marina Watersports (⊠ 2515 Park Marina Dr., ☏ 916/246–8388) rents rafts and canoes for outings on the Sacramento River, May–September.

THE FAR NORTH A TO Z

Arriving and Departing

By Bus

Greyhound Lines (☏ 800/231–2222) buses travel I–5, serving Red Bluff, Redding, Dunsmuir, and Mt. Shasta City.

By Car

I–5, an excellent four-lane divided highway, runs up the center of California through Red Bluff and Redding and continues north to Oregon. Lassen Park can be reached by Highway 36 from Red Bluff or, except in winter, Highway 44 from Redding; Highway 299 leads from Redding to McArthur-Burney Falls Memorial State Park. These are very good two-lane roads that are kept open year-round. If you are travel-ing through this area in winter, however, always carry snow chains in your car.

By Plane

Redding Municipal Airport (✉ Airport Rd., ☎ 916/224–4321) is served by **United Express** (☎ 800/241–6522).

By Train

Amtrak (☎ 800/872–7245) has stations in Redding (✉ 1620 Yuba St.) and Dunsmuir (✉ 5750 Sacramento Ave.).

Getting Around

By Bus

In Redding, a city bus system, **"The Ride"** (☎ 916/241–2877), serves the local area daily except Sunday.

By Car

An automobile is virtually essential to tour the Far North unless you arrive by bus, plane, or train and intend to travel the region entirely by foot or bicycle.

Contacts and Resources

Car Rentals

Avis (✉ Redding Municipal Airport, ☎ 916/221–2855 or 800/331–1212). **Enterprise** (✉ 361 E. Cypress Ave., Redding, ☎ 916/223–0700 or 800/325–8007). **Enterprise** (✉ 570 Antelope Blvd., Red Bluff, ☎ 916/529–0177 or 800/325–8007). **Hertz** (✉ Redding Municipal Airport, ☎ 916/221–4620 or 800/654–3131). For agencies in San Fran-cisco, *see* San Francisco A to Z *in* Chapter 5.

Emergencies

Ambulance (☎ 911). **Police** (☎ 911).

Visitor Information

Lassen Volcanic National Park (✉ 38050 Hwy. 36 East, Mineral 96063, ☎ 916/595–4444). **Mt. Shasta Convention and Visitors Bureau** (✉ 300 Pine St., Mt. Shasta 96067, ☎ 916/926–4865 or 800/926–4865). **North-ern Buttes District Office, State of California Department of Parks and Recreation** (✉ 400 Glen Dr., Oroville 95966, ☎ 916/538–2200). **Red Bluff–Tehama County Chamber of Commerce** (✉ 100 Main St., Red Bluff 96080, ☎ 916/527–6220 or 800/655–6225). **Redding Convention and Visitors Bureau** (✉ 777 Auditorium Dr., Redding 96001, ☎ 916/225–4100 or 800/874–7562). **Shasta Cascade Wonderland As-sociation** (✉ 14250 Holiday Rd., Redding 96003, ☎ 916/275–5555 or 800/326–6944). **Siskiyou County Visitors Bureau** (✉ 808 W. Lennox St., Yreka 96097, ☎ 916/842–7857 or 800/446–7475). **Trinity County Chamber of Commerce** (✉ 317 Main St., Weaverville 96093, ☎ 916/623–6101).

4 The Wine Country

You don't have to be a wine enthusiast to appreciate the mellow beauty of Napa and Sonoma counties, whose rolling hills and verdant vineyards resemble those of Tuscany and Provence. Here, among state-of-the-art wineries, restaurants whose cuisine is as serious as their wine, and luxury hotels where mud baths and massage are daily guest rituals, you just might discover that life need have no nobler purpose than enjoying the fruits of the earth.

I**N 1862,** after an extensive tour of the wine-producing areas of Europe, Count Agoston Haraszthy de Mokcsa reported a promising prognosis to his adopted California: "Of all the countries through which I passed, not one possessed the same advantages that are to be found in California. . . . California can produce as noble and generous a wine as any in Europe; more in quantity to the acre, and without repeated failures through frosts, summer rains, hailstorms, or other causes."

Updated by
Claudia
Gioseffi

The "dormant resources" that the father of California's viticulture saw in the balmy days and cool nights of the temperate Napa and Sonoma valleys are in full fruition today. While the wines produced here are praised and savored by connoisseurs throughout the world, the area continues to be a fermenting vat of experimentation, a proving ground for the latest techniques of grape growing and wine making.

For many, wine making is a second career. Many say making wine is a good way to turn a large fortune into a small one, but that hasn't deterred the doctors, former college professors, publishing tycoons, and airline pilots who come to try their hands at it.

In 1975 Napa Valley had no more than 20 wineries; today there are almost 10 times that number. In Sonoma County, where the web of vineyards is looser, there are more than 100 wineries, and development is now claiming the cool Carneros region at the head of the San Francisco Bay, deemed ideal for growing the chardonnay grape.

In addition to state-of-the-art viticulture and dining, the Wine Country is steeped in California history. The town of Sonoma is filled with remnants of Mexican California and the solid, ivy-covered, brick wineries built by Haraszthy and his disciples. Calistoga is a virtual museum of Steamboat Gothic architecture, replete with the fretwork and clapboard beloved of gold-rush prospectors and late-19th-century spa goers. St. Helena is home to a later architectural fantasy, the beautiful Art Nouveau mansion of the Beringer brothers. The latter-day postmodern extravaganza of Clos Pegase is in Calistoga.

Tourism's growth has produced tensions, and some residents look askance at projects like the Wine Train between Napa and St. Helena. Still, the area's natural beauty will always draw tourists—from the spring, when the vineyards bloom yellow with mustard flowers, to the fall, when fruit is ripening. Haraszthy was right: This is a chosen place.

Pleasures and Pastimes

Dining

Over the past decade, many star chefs from San Francisco's top restaurants and other urban areas of the United States have migrated to the Napa Valley and contributed to the emergence of what has come to be known as Wine Country Cuisine. This style of cooking revolves around the area's locally grown produce and other ingredients, wines that rival any in France or Italy, and a casual, elegant lifestyle enjoyed outdoors in the warmth of the sun. Other influences include California and Mediterranean cuisines and an eclectic range of American-regional fare—as well as the culinary heritage of early settlers from Italy, France, and Mexico. As a result, food now rivals wine as the principal attraction in the region.

Those on a budget will find an appealing range of reasonably priced eateries. Gourmet delis offer superb picnic fare, and brunch is a cost-effective strategy at high-end restaurants. With few exceptions (which are noted within individual restaurant listings), dress is informal. Where reservations are indicated to be essential, you may need to reserve a week or more ahead; during the summer and early fall harvest seasons you may need to book several months ahead.

CATEGORY	COST*
$$$$	over $50
$$$	$30–$50
$$	$20–$30
$	under $20

*per person for a three-course meal, excluding drinks, service, and 7½% sales tax

Hot-Air Ballooning

Day after day, large, colorful balloons fill the morning sky high above the Wine Country's valleys. To aficionados, peering down at the vineyards from the vantage point of the clouds is the ultimate California experience. Many hotels arrange excursions, and most flights take place soon after sunrise, when the calmest, coolest time of day offers maximum lift and soft landings. Prices depend on the duration of the flight, number of passengers, and services (some companies provide extras such as pickup at your lodging or champagne brunch after the flight). Expect to spend about $165 per person.

Lodging

In a region where first-class restaurants and wineries attract connoisseurs from afar, it's no surprise that a legion of elegant lodgings has sprung up to accommodate them. Ranging from quaint to elegant to utterly luxurious, the area's many inns, hotels, and spas are usually exquisitely appointed. Most local bed-and-breakfasts have historic Victorian and Spanish architecture and serve a full country breakfast highlighting local produce and specialties. The newer hotels and spas are often state-of-the-art buildings offering comforts such as massage treatments or spring water–fed pools; many house world-class restaurants or are just a short car ride away from gastronomic bliss.

Not surprisingly, staying in the Wine Country is expensive. Since Santa Rosa is the largest population center in the area, it has the largest selection of rooms, many at moderate rates. Try there if you've failed to reserve in advance or have a limited budget. Keep in mind that many B&Bs are fully booked long in advance of the summer season. For all accommodations in the area, rates are lower on weeknights and about 20% less in the winter.

CATEGORY	COST*
$$$$	over $175
$$$	$120–$175
$$	$80–$120
$	under $80

*All prices are for a standard double room, excluding 12% tax.

Wine Tasting

Wine tasting can be an educational, fascinating, and even mysterious ritual. The sight of impeccably polished glasses and uniquely labeled bottles lined up in a row, the tour guide's commentary on the character of each wine, the decadent mood of the vineyards with their full-to-bursting grapes—all combine to create an anticipation that's gratified with the first sip of wine. Learning about the origin of the grapes, the terraces on which they're grown, the weather that produced them, and the methods by which they are transformed into wine will give you a new understanding and appreciation of wine—and a great afternoon (or all-day) diversion. Unless otherwise noted within individual listings, visits to the wineries are free.

Exploring the Wine Country

Two main areas comprise the Wine Country, the Napa Valley and the Sonoma Valley. Five major paths cut through the valleys: U.S. 101, Highways 12, and 121 through Sonoma County, and Highway 29 and the Silverado Trail north through the Napa Valley from the town of Napa.

Great Itineraries

Because there are more than 400 wineries in and around the Napa and Sonoma valleys, it pays to be selective when planning your visit. Better to mix up the wineries with other sights and diversions—a picnic, a trip to the village museum, a ride in a hot-air balloon—than to try to visit them all in one day.

Numbers in the text correspond to numbers in the margin and on the Wine Country map.

IF YOU HAVE 1 DAY

Begin your tour where northern California winemaking got its start, at **Buena Vista Carneros Winery** ⑬, east of Sonoma's town plaza on East Napa Street to Old Winery Road north. From there, proceed north on Highway 12 and east on Trinity Road, Dry Creek Road, and the Oakville Grade (the last two have some twisty patches) to Highway 29, the main route through the Napa Valley. Slip north to **St. Helena** for a tour of the museum and library at the Culinary Institute of America. Have lunch here or drive the short distance south to downtown St. Helena. After lunch, visit the **Silverado Museum** (from Main Street, head east on Adams Street past the railroad tracks and right on Library Lane) before driving north to **Calistoga.** Turn right onto Dunaweal Lane (it's right before you get to Calistoga proper) and ride the gondola to **Sterling Vineyards** ⑨. If you have time, explore Calistoga and dine there.

IF YOU HAVE 3 DAYS

Visit **Buena Vista Carneros Winery** ⑬ or the **Gloria Ferrer Champagne Caves** ⑮ on the morning of day one, and have lunch in **Sonoma** or **Glen Ellen.** Explore **Jack London State Park** in the early afternoon. East from Highway 12, take Trinity Road, Dry Creek Road, and the Oakville Grade to Highway 29, and then head north to Rutherford for a late-afternoon tour of the **Robert Mondavi** ④ winery. Overnight in ☒ **St. Helena** or ☒ **Calistoga.** On the morning of day two, take a Napa Valley balloon ride—or visit one of Calistoga's spas, where you can have a mud bath, steam, or massage (or all three). In the afternoon take Highway 29 to just south of Calistoga, turning east onto Dunaweal Lane to visit **Sterling Vineyards** ⑨. After you've tasted wine and descended Sterling's gondola, head across Dunaweal a bit to the east to **Clos Pegase** ⑩, a postmodern gem of a winery. Start day three with an early-morning stroll through the grounds of **Chateau Montelena** ⑫ winery (north on Highway 29 to Tubbs Lane), then drive south on 29 for lunch at Tra Vigne or the Culinary Institute of America in **St. Helena.** From there, head west toward Santa Rosa on Petrified Forest Road and Calistoga Road, which runs into Highway 12. Continue west on 12 and then north on Santa Rosa Avenue to get to the **Luther Burbank Home and Gardens.** You should have time to slip south on Highway 12 and Highway 121/12 to **Domaine Carneros** ⑭ (head south on Duhig Road) for a late-afternoon tour of their champagne-making facilities.

IF YOU HAVE 7 DAYS

Begin with the historic town of **Sonoma,** whose colorful plaza and mission evoke early California's Spanish past. Afterward, head north to

⌂ **Glen Ellen** and the Valley of the Moon. Picnic and explore the grounds at Jack London State Historic Park. Next morning, visit **Kenwood Vineyards** ⑱ before leaving for **Santa Rosa,** the Wine Country's largest town, and **Healdsburg,** where a host of "hidden" wineries—including **Piper Sonoma** ⑲—lie nestled in the woods along the roads. Spend the night in ⌂ **Healdsburg.** On the third day, head into the Napa Valley and spend the day in ⌂ **Calistoga,** noted for its mud baths and mineral springs. Wake up early on the fourth day for a balloon ride, then slip over to **Cuvaison** ⑪ or nearby **Clos Pegase** ⑩, both in Calistoga. Spend the night in Calistoga or ⌂ **St. Helena.** On day five, visit the galleries, shops, and eateries of St. Helena before heading to the Oakville Grocery, a must-see landmark. Spend the night in ⌂ **Rutherford.** Explore nearby **Yountville** on day five before heading for the **Hess Collection** ① on Mount Veeder, where a brilliant art collection and excellent wines may keep you occupied for hours. Spend the night in ⌂ **Yountville.** On your last day, return to the town of Sonoma via the Carneros Highway, stopping at **Gloria Ferrer Champagne Caves** ⑮, the landmark **Buena Vista Carneros Winery** ⑬, and the **Carneros Alambic Distillery**—the first alambic brandy producer in California.

When to Tour the Wine Country

When grapes are harvested during the crush, usually in September, the Wine Country celebrates with street fairs and festivals that vary from year to year. Oktoberfest is an annual celebration in Sonoma, and in both valleys golf tournaments, wine auctions, and art and food fairs occur.

In season (April–October) the Napa Valley draws crowds of tourists, and traffic along Highway 29 from St. Helena to Calistoga is often backed up on weekends. The Sonoma Valley, Santa Rosa, and Healdsburg are a bit less crowded. To avoid crowds, visit the Wine Country during the week and get an early start in the morning. Pack a sun hat, since summer is usually very hot and dry, and autumn (Indian Summer) can be even hotter. Although winter in the Wine Country lacks the bright yellows and greens of spring and the brilliant gold and reds of autumn, the quiet, stark beauty this season bestows upon the landscape is appealing in its own way.

Most wineries are open daily from at least 10–4 (and as late as 5 or 6 in the summer), though some close Monday or Monday and Tuesday. Some require advance reservations for tours.

THE NAPA VALLEY

Napa

46 mi from San Francisco, I–80 north to Hwy. 37 west to Hwy. 29 north.

Although the town of Napa doesn't offer much in the way of attractions, it leads conveniently to most sites in both the Napa and Sonoma valleys, especially if you're entering the region from east of San Francisco.

❶ On the steep slopes of Mt. Veeder 9 miles northwest of Napa, the **Hess Collection Winery and Vineyards** is one of the best-kept secrets of the valley (don't give up; the road leading to the winery is long and winding). Located on the property that was the original Napa Valley home of the Christian Brothers, the simple, rustic limestone structure, circa 1903, has been transformed into a modern winery and museum. Swiss owner Donald Hess's personal collection includes works by contem-

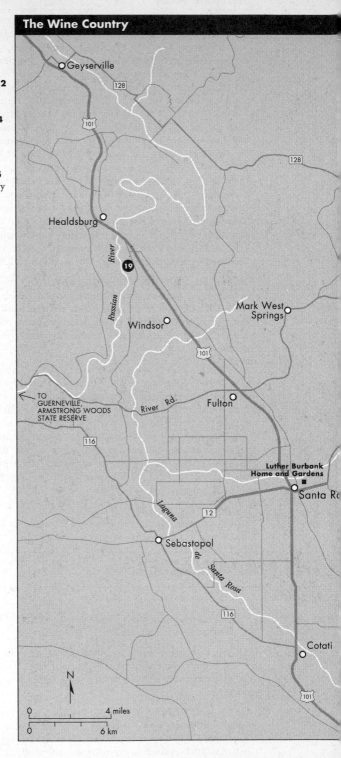

The Wine Country

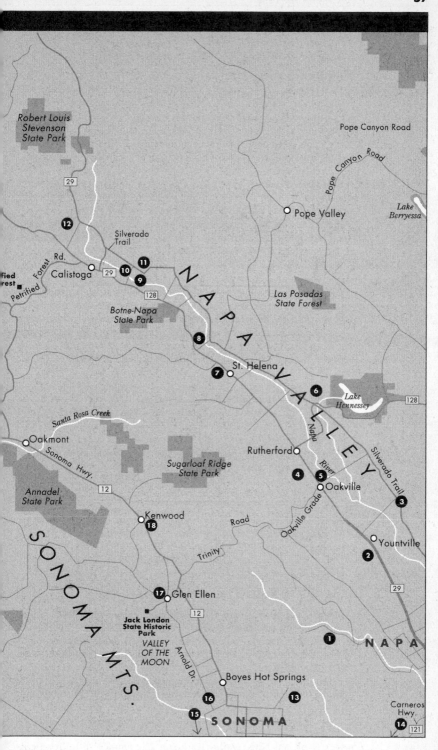

Robert Louis
Stevenson
State Park

Pope Canyon Road

Pope Canyon Road

Pope Valley

Lake
Berryessa

29

12

Silverado
Trail

Forest Rd.

Petrified
rest

Calistoga

29

10

11

9

128

Botne-Napa
State Park

Las Posadas
State Forest

NAPA

8

St. Helena

7

6

Lake
Hennessey

128

Santa Rosa Creek

VALLEY

Oakmont

Sonoma Hwy.

Sugarloaf Ridge
State Park

Rutherford

Napa

Silverado Trail

Annadel
State Park

12

4

5

Oakville

3

River

Kenwood

18

Road

Oakville Grade

Yountville

2

Trinity

29

SONOMA

17

Glen Ellen

12

Jack London
State Historic
Park

1

N A P A

VALLEY
OF THE
MOON

Arnold Dr.

Boyes Hot Springs

MTS.

16

13

Carneros
Hwy.

15

S O N O M A

14

121

porary European and American artists such as Robert Motherwell, Francis Bacon, and Frank Stella. Cabernet sauvignon is the real strength of the winery, though it also produces some fine chardonnays. ⊠ *4411 Redwood Rd.,* ☎ *707/255–1144.* ⊙ *Daily 10–4.*

Dining and Lodging

$$–$$$ ✕ **La Boucane.** Chef-owner Jacques Mokrani has created a gorgeous little gem of a restaurant in a restored 1885 Victorian decorated with period antiques. Classic French cuisine (rack of lamb, champagne-crisp duck) is delivered with style in a candle-lit dining room enhanced by silver, linen, and a red rose on each table. ⊠ *1778 2nd St. (at Jefferson St. in downtown Napa),* ☎ *707/253–1177. MC, V. Closed Sun. and Jan. No lunch.*

$–$$ ✕ **Bistro Don Giovanni.** The ambience here is casual Mediterranean, with terra-cotta tile floors, high ceilings, and a spacious outdoor patio with an expansive view of the valley. Winning items include the pastas and grilled entrées such as pork chops with garlic-infused mashed potatoes. Don't miss the delectable fruit-crisp dessert, which changes daily. ⊠ *4110 St. Helena Hwy. 29,* ☎ *707/224–3300. AE, DC, MC, V.*

$ ✕ **Jonesy's Famous Steak House.** This spacious and informal local favorite with a children's menu has attracted aviation buffs, steak lovers, and kids of all ages since 1946. One entire wall has an expanse of windows with a prime view of the Napa County Airport landing strip. Inside, prime steaks, weighted down with Sacramento River rocks to keep juices in, are seared over a dry grill. Roasted chicken, homemade soups, and fresh fish round out the fare. ⊠ *2044 Airport Rd., halfway between Napa and Vallejo, off Hwy. 29,* ☎ *707/255–2003. AE, D, DC, MC, V. Closed Mon. and 1 wk at Christmas.*

$$$$ ✕🏨 **Silverado Country Club.** This luxurious 1,200-acre resort in the hills east of the town of Napa has cottages, kitchen apartments, and one- to three-bedroom efficiencies, many with fireplaces. With golfing, tennis, and eight pools, it's a place for serious sports enthusiasts and anyone who enjoys the conveniences of a full-scale resort. Dinner only—Pacific Rim cuisine—is served at the elegant Vintner's Court restaurant. The Royal Oak serves steak and seafood nightly. A bar and grill is open for breakfast and lunch; in the summer lunch includes an outdoor barbecue. ⊠ *1600 Atlas Peak Rd., 94558 (6 mi east of Napa via Hwy. 121),* ☎ *707/257–0200 or 800/532–0500,* ℻ *707/257–2867. 277 condo units (300 sleeping rooms). 3 restaurants, bar, 8 pools, 2 18-hole golf courses, 22 tennis courts, bicycles. D, DC, MC, V.*

Yountville

13 mi north of Napa on Hwy. 29.

Yountville at first glance looks like a slightly backwater town because of its small size and bungalow-style houses, but after a second look, its restaurants, stores, and vineyards reveal Yountville's own brand of Wine Country savoir faire. The town's main attraction is **Vintage 1870** (⊠ 6525 Washington St., ☎ 707/944–2451), a 26-acre complex of boutiques, restaurants, and gourmet stores. The vine-covered brick buildings were built in 1870 and housed a winery, livery stable, and distillery. The original mansion of the property is now the popular Mexican-style Compadres Bar and Grill; adjacent to that is the Red Rock Cafe, housed in the train depot Samuel Brannan built in 1868 for his privately owned Napa Valley Railroad. The remodeled railroad cars are now on the property of the Napa Valley Lodge (☞ Dining and Lodging, *below*) for the touring pleasure of guests.

② **Domaine Chandon** is owned by the French champagne producer Moet-Hennessy and Louis Vuitton. Tours of the sleek modern facilities on this beautifully maintained property include sample flutes of the méthode champenoise sparkling wine. Champagne is $3–$4 per glass, hors d'oeuvres are complimentary, and an elegant restaurant beckons gourmets. ✉ *California Dr., off Hwy. 29,* ☎ *707/944–2280.* ☉ *Tours daily 11–5, except Mon. and Tues. Nov.–Apr.*

③ In 1993 the World Wine Championships gave **Stag's Leap Wine Cellars** a platinum award for their 1990 Reserve Chardonnay, designating it the highest-ranked premium chardonnay in the world. Their proprietary red table wine, Cask 23, consistently earns accolades from *Connoisseur* and *The Wine Spectator.* ✉ *5766 Silverado Trail (from Hwy. 29 take Yountville Cross Rd. east to Silverado Trail south),* ☎ *707/944–2020.* ☕ *Tasting fee $3.* ☉ *Daily 10–4; tours by appointment; closed major holidays.*

Dining and Lodging

$$$$ ✕ **Domaine Chandon.** Part of the world-renowned winery, this large, formal dining room caters to wine and food aficionados with a daily-changing menu of expertly prepared, French-inspired California cuisine. Sonoma duck breast is served with polenta and green-olive sage juice; quail are nested on a bed of risotto. Desserts are a must: Try the warm chocolate cake with double-vanilla ice cream, or one of the daily-made sorbets. The cavernous room looks out over miles of vineyards and native oaks. There is also outdoor service on a tree-shaded patio. ✉ *California Dr. (Yountville exit off Hwy. 29, toward Veterans' Home),* ☎ *707/944–2892. Reservations essential. Jacket required. AE, D, DC, MC, V. Closed Mon. and Tues. Nov.–Apr. No dinner Mon. and Tues. May–Oct.*

$$$$ ✕ **French Laundry.** Though it dates back to 1977, this intimate, cottage-style restaurant only entered Wine Country stardom when chef Thomas Keller assumed ownership in the mid-'90s. Inside an old converted brick building surrounded by lush gardens, fresh flowers and gentle lighting make patrons feel like well-tended houseguests being treated to an exquisite meal. The prix-fixe menus, which include four or five courses, feature canapés such as "bacon and eggs"—quail eggs paired with bacon and served atop tiny silver spoons; entrées such as pan-roasted Virginia striped bass with sweet peppers and black olives, or thyme-scented eggplant with potato gnocchi; and for dessert, "coffee and doughnuts" (cinnamon sugared doughnuts with cappuccino ice cream), or warm chocolate truffle cake with caramel cream. ✉ *6640 Washington St.,* ☎ *707/944–2380. Reservations essential. AE, MC, V. Closed Mon. and 1st 2 wks in Jan. No lunch Sun., Tues.*

$$ ✕ **Mustards Grill.** Grilled fish, steak, local fresh produce, and an impressive wine list are served in a boisterous, noisy bistro with a black-and-white marble floor and upbeat artwork. The thin, crisp, golden onion rings are addictive. Expect to encounter a crowd, since this is a wine maker's hangout. ✉ *7399 St. Helena Hwy., (Hwy. 29, 1 mi north of Yountville),* ☎ *707/944–2424. Reservations essential. D, DC, MC, V.*

$$ ✕ **Ristorante Piatti.** A small, stylish trattoria with a pizza oven and open kitchen, this cheery place is full of good smells and happy people. Its authentic regional Italian cooking is the perfect cure for a jaded appetite. Homemade pastas are the best bet. ✉ *6480 Washington St.,* ☎ *707/944–2070. AE, MC, V.*

$ ✕ **The Diner.** One of the best-known and most-appreciated stop-offs in the Napa Valley, this breakfast-centric eatery has local sausages and house potatoes that are not to be missed. Healthful versions of Mexican and American classics are served for dinner. ⊠ *6476 Washington St., ☎ 707/944–2626. No credit cards. Closed Mon.*

$$$$ 🏨 **La Residence.** Even though it's within feet of the St. Helena Highway, "La Res" is secluded and romantic enough to make you feel as if you've flown to France, or at least New Orleans. It's housed in two buildings—The Mansion, a renovated 1870s Gothic Revival manor house built by a riverboat captain from New Orleans; and Cabernet Hall, a newer, French-style barn. Both buildings overlook a pool, a manicured garden, and towering oak trees that bathe the entire property in shade. The innkeepers, David Jackson and Craig Claussen, are hospitable—welcoming all guests with wine, cheese, and hors d'oeuvres—but never intrusive. Rooms are spacious and comfortable, with period antiques, fireplaces, and double French doors opening onto verandas or patios. ⊠ *4066 St. Helena Highway, Napa Valley 94558, ☎ 707/253–0337, FAX 707/253–0382. 20 rooms. Dining room, pool, hot tub, business services. D, DC, MC, V.*

$$$$ 🏨 **Napa Valley Lodge.** Spacious rooms overlook the vineyards and the valley at this hacienda-style lodge; a tile roof, covered walkways, balconies, patios, and colorful gardens add to the Mediterranean mood. Freshly brewed coffee is provided to guests, along with a Continental breakfast and the morning paper. Some rooms have fireplaces, others have wet bars. ⊠ *2230 Madison St. at Hwy. 29, 94599, ☎ 707/944–2468 or 800/368–2468, FAX 707/944–9362. 55 rooms. Refrigerators, pool, hot tub, sauna, exercise room. D, DC, MC, V.*

$$$$ 🏨 **Vintage Inn.** All the rooms at this luxurious inn have fireplaces, whirlpool baths, refrigerators, private verandas or patios, hand-painted fabrics, window seats, and shuttered windows. A welcome bottle of wine, Continental breakfast with champagne, and afternoon tea are all complimentary. ⊠ *6541 Washington St., 94599, ☎ 707/944–1112 or 800/351–1133, FAX 707/944–1617. 80 rooms with bath. Refrigerators, pool, spa, tennis court, bicycles. D, DC, MC, V.*

Hot-Air Ballooning

Napa Valley Balloons (☎ 707/944–0228 or 800/253–2224 in CA) in Yountville operates rides over the valley. The **Vintage Inn** (☞ *above*) also arranges rides.

Oakville

2 mi north of Yountville on Hwy. 29

There are three reasons to visit the town of Oakville: its grocery store, its scenic mountain grade, and Opus One, its magnificent, highly exclusive winery. The **Oakville Grocery** (⊠ 7856 St. Helena Hwy., also known as Hwy. 29), built in the late 1880s to serve as a grocery store and Wells Fargo Pony Express Stop, now carries a bounty of gourmet foods that cater to an international clientele.

❹ At **Robert Mondavi,** tasters are encouraged to take the 60-minute production tour with complimentary tasting before trying the reserve wines ($1–$5 per glass). In-depth, three- to four-hour tours and gourmet lunch tours are also popular. Afterward, visit the art gallery, and look for the summer concerts that are held on the grounds. ⊠ *7801 St. Helena Hwy., ☎ 707/259–9463. ☺ May–Oct., daily 9–5:30; Nov.–Apr., daily 9:30–4:30; closed major holidays.*

❺ **Opus One,** the combined venture of famed California wine maker Robert Mondavi and the French Baron Philippe Rothschild, is famed for its vast semicircular barrel cellar, which holds 1,000 barrels side-by-side. When you approach Opus One from the parking lot, it looks

Surfing contest, Malibu Beach, California
Photo © 1996 Catherine Karnow

like a giant spaceship landed on a bucolic hill. Up close, the futuristic building, created by the same architects who gave San Francisco its Transamerica "pyramid" skyline, reveals distinctly classical lines; inside, it's an elegant blend of classic 18th-century France and casual California Wine Country. The state-of-the-art facilities produce about 20,000 cases (a relatively small quantity) of ultrapremium, Bordeaux-style, red wine from grapes grown in the estate's own vineyards and in the surrounding Oakville appellation. ⊠ *7900 St. Helena Hwy.*, ☎ *707/963–1979.* ⌑ *Tasting fees vary.* ☉ *Daily 10–4:30; tours by appointment.*

Rutherford

1 mi north of Oakville on Hwy. 29.

❻ The wine at **Rutherford Hill Winery** is aged in French oak barrels stacked in more than 30,000 square feet of caves—the largest such caves in the nation. Tours of the caves can be followed by a picnic in the orchards: choose among oak, olive, or madrone. ⊠ *200 Rutherford Hill Rd. (from Hwy. 29, take Rutherford Cross Rd. east to the Silverado Trail north),* ☎ *707/963–7194.* ☉ *Weekdays 10–4:30, weekends 10–5. Tour times vary seasonally; call for detailed information.*

Dining and Lodging

$$$$ ⛺ **Rancho Caymus Inn.** California-Spanish in style, this inn has well-maintained gardens and large suites with kitchens and whirlpool baths. Well-chosen details include decorative handicrafts, beehive fireplaces, tile murals, stoneware basins, and llama-hair blankets. ⊠ *1140 Rutherford Rd., 94573 (junction of Hwys. 29 and 128),* ☎ *707/963–1777 or 800/845–1777,* ℻ *707/963–5387. 26 rooms. DC, MC, V. 2-night minimum Apr.–Nov.*

$$–$$$$ ✕⛺ **Auberge du Soleil.** As you sit on a wisteria-draped deck sipping
★ a late-afternoon glass of wine, with acres of terraced olive groves and rolling vineyards at your feet, you'll swear you're in Tuscany. The Mediterranean spell lingers inside, where Santa Fe accents create an atmosphere of irresistible indolence. The hotel's renowned restaurant is a symphony of earth tones and wood beams, with an outdoor deck that looks out on the valley. The frequently changing menu emphasizes local produce and also includes unusual specialties such as roasted lobster sausage and rosemary-roasted rack of lamb. A moderately priced bar menu offers slow-roasted garlic with homemade pretzels and pan-seared salmon sandwiches. ⊠ *180 Rutherford Hill Rd., 94573 (off Silverado Trail just north of Rte. 128),* ☎ *707/963–1211 or 800/348–5406,* ℻ *707/963–8764. 50 rooms. Pool, hot tub, massage, steam room, 3 tennis courts, exercise room. D, MC, V.*

St. Helena

2 mi north of Rutherford on Hwy. 29.

St. Helena offers visitors a glimpse of country beauty, epitomized by the overgrown, arching Sycamore trees that bow across Main Street to touch each other as you near Calistoga. But the main reason people come here is for the abundant selection of wineries—many of which lie along the route from Yountville to St. Helena—and restaurants, including the newly opened West Coast campus of the Culinary Institute of America.

❼ **Beringer Vineyards** has been operating since 1876. Tastings are held in the Rhine House mansion, where hand-carved oak and walnut furniture and stained-glass windows feature Belgian Art Nouveau at its most opulent. The Beringer brothers, Frederick and Jacob, built the mansion in 1883 for the princely sum of $30,000. Tours are given every 30 minutes, and include a visit to the deep limestone tunnels in which the wines mature. ⊠ *2000 Main St.,* ☎ *707/963–4812.* ☼ *Daily 9:30–4; summer hrs sometimes extended to 5; closed major holidays.*

❽ **Freemark Abbey Winery** was founded in the 1880s by Josephine Tychson, the first woman to establish a winery in California. ⊠ *3022 St. Helena Hwy. N,* ☎ *707/963–9694.* ☼ *Mar.–Dec., daily 10–4:30; Jan.–Feb., Thurs.–Sun. 10–4:30. Tour daily at 2.*

For some nonalcoholic sightseeing, visit the **Silverado Museum,** in a pristine Victorian building. Its Robert Louis Stevenson memorabilia consists of more than 8,000 artifacts, including first editions, manuscripts, and photographs. ⊠ *1490 Library La., at Adams St.,* ☎ *707/963–3757.* 🎟 *Free.* ☼ *Tues.–Sun. noon–4; closed major holidays.*

The Culinary Institute of America set up its West Coast headquarters in the century-old Greystone Winery—the former site of the Christian Brothers Winery and a national historic landmark—in late 1995. The CIA campus consists of 30 acres of lush herb and vegetable gardens, a 15-acre merlot vineyard, and a Mediterranean-inspired restaurant with student-assisted, professional chefs at the helm. Also on the property are a well-stocked culinary store, a quirky yet interesting corkscrew and winepress museum, and a culinary library. ⊠ *2555 Main St.,* ☎ *800/333–9242,* 🆇 *707/967–1113.*

Dining and Lodging

$$$$ ✗ **Terra.** The twosome who own this unpretentious restaurant housed in a century-old stone foundry learned their culinary skills at the side of chef Wolfgang Puck. Hiro Sone was head chef at L.A.'s Spago, and Lissa Doumani was the pastry chef. Southern French and northern Italian favorites include a pear and goat cheese salad with warm pancetta and sherry vinaigrette, and a duck breast in an intriguing cherry sauce. Save room for Lissa's desserts. ⊠ *1345 Railroad Ave.,* ☎ *707/963–8931. Weekend reservations essential. MC, V. Closed Tues. No lunch.*

$$$ ✗ **Trilogy.** Chef-owner Diane Pariseau pairs one of the best and most extensive contemporary wine lists in the valley with superb renditions of California-French cuisine on a daily changing prix-fixe menu. Pariseau deftly juxtaposes flavors and textures; her all-star entrées—grilled chicken breast on a nest of sautéed apples and green peppercorns, grilled tuna steak with olive oil and sweet red pepper purée—are artfully presented. ⊠ *1234 Main St.,* ☎ *707/963–5507. Reservations essential. MC, V. Closed Mon. and 3 wks in Dec. No lunch weekends.*

$$$ ✗ **Wine Spectator Greystone Restaurant.** The restaurant of the Culinary Institute of America draws part of its staff from the cooking school, although professional chefs, not students, command the large open kitchen. The menu has a Mediterranean spirit and emphasizes small plates such as roasted peppers and eggplant, beets and fennel with Parmesan, and chicken terrine with aioli. Main dishes range from leg of lamb with white beans to poussin with lemon risotto. Though food and service can be unpredictable, the property is exquisite. ⊠ *2555 Main St.,* ☎ *707/967–1010. AE, DC, MC, V. Closed Tues.*

$$–$$$ ✗ **Showley's.** In a building that dates from 1860, this homey, family-run restaurant has two dining rooms, the smaller of which has a bar. The seasonal menu reflects the owner-chef's interest in international flavors as well as local products (there's a fig tree out back that inspired an annual fig menu in late summer). Fresh fish and meats are noteworthy, especially the garlic chicken, tenderloin of pork, and roast monkfish with garlic-mashed potatoes. Desserts to try are the famous chocolate phyllo pastry "hoo hoo" layered with Valrhona chocolate pastry cream and fresh raspberries, or the homemade ice creams. ⊠ *1327 Railroad Ave.,* ☎ *707/963–1200. AE, D, MC, V.*

$$ ✗ Brava Terrace. Vegetables plucked straight from the restaurant's own garden are used to enliven chef-owner Fred Halpert's trademark pasta, risotto, and cassoulet dishes; chocolate-chip crème brûlée provides a grand finale. Brava has a comfortably casual ambience with a full bar, a large stone fireplace, a romantic outdoor terrace overlooking a shady brook, and a heated deck with views of the valley floor and Howell Mountain. ⊠ *3010 St. Helena Hwy. (Hwy. 29, ½ mi north of St. Helena),* ☎ *707/963–9300. Reservations essential on weekends. AE, D, DC, MC, V. Closed Wed. Nov.–Apr. and last 2 wks of Jan.*

$$ ✗ Tra Vigne. This Napa Valley fieldstone building has been transformed
★ into a striking, extremely popular trattoria with a huge wood bar, impossibly high ceilings, and plush banquettes. Homemade mozzarella, olive oil, and vinegar, and house-cured pancetta and prosciutto contribute to a one-of-a-kind tour of Tuscan cuisine. Although getting a table without a reservation is sometimes difficult, drops-ins can sit at the bar. The outdoor courtyard in summer is a sun-splashed Mediterranean vision of striped umbrellas and awnings, crowded café tables, and rustic pots overflowing with flowers. The Cantinetta delicatessen in the corner of the courtyard offers wine by the glass and gourmet picnic fare. ⊠ *1050 Charter Oak Ave. (off Hwy. 29),* ☎ *707/963–4444. Reservations essential in dining room. D, DC, MC, V.*

$$$–$$$$ ✗🖬 Meadowood Resort. This sprawling, 256-acre resort looks like a scene from an F. Scott Fitzgerald novel, complete with croquet lawns, a golf course, and hiking trails. Stay in the rambling, country lodge or one of the separate bungalow suites clustered on the hillside. For the popular weekend brunch (nonguests welcome), refined French cuisine with a California twist is served as part of a prix fixe menu in either a dining room with a cathedral ceiling, a fireplace, and lush greenery, or outdoors on a terrace overlooking the golf course. A lighter menu of pizzas and spa food can be had at breakfast and lunch (and early dinners Friday and Saturday) at a second, less formal and less expensive Meadowood restaurant, the Grill. ⊠ *900 Meadowood La., 94574,* ☎ *707/963–3646 or 800/458–8080,* 🖷 *707/963–3532. Restaurant reservations essential. 85 rooms with bath. 2 restaurants, bar, room service, 2 pools, hot tub, massage, sauna, steam room, 9-hole golf course, 7 tennis courts, croquet, health club. D, DC, MC, V.*

$$$$ 🖬 Harvest Inn. This Tudor-style inn with 47 fireplaces overlooks a 14-acre vineyard and the hills beyond. Although the property is set close to a main highway, the lush landscaping and award-winning brick and stonework create an illusion of remoteness. Most rooms have wet bars, refrigerators, antique furnishings, and fireplaces. Pets are allowed in certain rooms for a $20 fee. Complimentary breakfast is served in the breakfast room and on the patio overlooking the vineyards. ⊠ *1 Main St., 94574,* ☎ *707/963–9463 or 800/950–8466,* 🖷 *707/963–4402. 55 rooms. Refrigerators, 2 pools, 2 hot tubs. D, MC, V.*

$$$$ 🖬 Wine Country Inn. Surrounded by a pastoral landscape of vine-
★ yards and hills dotted with old barns and stone bridges, this is a peaceful New England–style retreat. Rural antiques fill all of the rooms, most of which overlook the vineyards with either a balcony, patio, or deck. Most rooms have fireplaces, and some have private hot tubs. A hearty country breakfast is served buffet-style in the sun-splashed common room, and wine tastings are scheduled in the afternoons. ⊠ *1152 Lodi La., 94574,* ☎ *707/963–7077,* 🖷 *707/963–9018. 24 rooms with bath. Pool, hot tubs. MC, V.*

$$$–$$$$ ⊞ **Hotel St. Helena.** This restored 1881 hostelry provides Old World comfort. Antique furniture fills the rooms, which are colored in rich, appealing tones of burgundy. Complimentary Continental breakfast is included. Smoking is discouraged—the only evidence of the New World. ⊠ *1309 Main St., 94574,* ☎ *707/963–4388,* ⅎ *707/963–5402. 14 rooms with bath, 4 rooms with shared bath. DC, MC, V.*

Calistoga

3 mi north of St. Helena on Hwy. 29.

In addition to its wineries, Calistoga is noted for its mineral water, hot mineral springs, mud baths, steam baths, and massages. The Calistoga Hot Springs Resort was founded in 1859 by maverick entrepreneur Sam Brannan, whose ambition was to found "the Saratoga of California." He tripped up the pronunciation of the phrase at a formal banquet— it came out "Calistoga"—and the name stuck.

One of Sam Brannan's cottages, preserved as the **Sharpsteen Museum,** has a magnificent diorama of the Calistoga Hot Springs Resort in its heyday. ⊠ *1311 Washington St.,* ☎ *707/942–5911.* ⊡ *Donations accepted.* ☉ *May–Oct., daily 10–4; Nov.–Apr., daily noon–4.*

At **Indian Springs,** $90 entitles enthusiasts to a mud bath, mineral-water shower, and mineral-water bath, plus time in the steam room, a blanket wrap, and a 25-minute massage. The cost without massage is $55. The spa has 16 cottages with studio or one-bedroom units and a larger structure with three bedrooms. Reservations are recommended for spa treatments. ⊠ *1712 Lincoln Ave.,* ☎ *707/942–4913.* ☉ *Daily 9–7.*

❾ **Sterling Vineyards** sits on a hilltop overlooking Calistoga, its pristine white Mediterranean-style buildings reached by an enclosed gondola from the valley floor. The view from the tasting room is superb, and the gift shop is one of the best in the valley. ⊠ *1111 Dunaweal La.,* ☎ *707/942–3300.* ⊡ *$6.* ☉ *Daily 10:30–4:30; closed major holidays.*

❿ Neoclassical art adorns the walls of **Clos Pegase,** a winery designed by architect Michael Graves, the exemplar of postmodernism, and commissioned by Jan Schrem, a publisher and art collector. The wines produced here are equally acclaimed. ⊠ *1060 Dunaweal La.,* ☎ *707/ 942–4981.* ☉ *Daily 10:30–5; closed major holidays.*

⓫ Swiss-owned **Cuvaison** specializes in chardonnay, merlot, and cabernet sauvignon for the export market. Two small picnic areas on the grounds look out over Napa Valley. ⊠ *4550 Silverado Trail,* ☎ *707/ 942–6266.* ☉ *Daily 10–5; tours by appointment.*

⓬ **Chateau Montelena** is a vine-covered 1882 building set amid Chinese-inspired gardens, complete with a lake, red pavilions, and arched bridges. The gardens are great for romantic picnics, but be sure to reserve in advance. ⊠ *1429 Tubbs La. (off Hwy. 29 north of Calistoga),* ☎ *707/942–5105 or 800/222–7288, outside Bay Area.* ☉ *Daily 10– 4; tours at 11 and 2, by appointment only.*

☾ Many families bring children to Calistoga to see **Old Faithful Geyser of California** blast its 60-foot tower of steam and vapor about every 40 minutes (the pattern is disrupted if there's an earthquake in the offing). One of just three regularly erupting geysers in the world, it is fed by an underground river that heats to 350°F. The spout lasts three minutes. Picnic facilities are available. ⊠ *1299 Tubbs La., 1 mi north of Calistoga,* ☎ *707/942–6463.* ⊡ *$5.* ☉ *Daily 9–6 during daylight savings time, 9–5 in winter. Call ahead if you're traveling a long distance to make sure the geyser will be active when you arrive.*

⚙ The **Petrified Forest** contains the remains of the volcanic eruptions of Mount St. Helena 3.4 million years ago. The force of the explosion uprooted the gigantic redwoods, covered them with volcanic ash, and infiltrated the trees with silica and minerals, causing petrification. Explore the museum, then picnic on the grounds. ⊠ *4100 Petrified Forest Rd., 5 mi west of Calistoga off Hwy. 128,* ☎ *707/942–6667.* ⊠ *$3.* ☉ *Summer, daily 10–6; winter, daily 10–4:30.*

⚙ **Robert Louis Stevenson State Park** encompasses the summit of Mount St. Helena. It was here, in an abandoned bunkhouse of the Silverado Mine, that Stevenson and his bride, Fanny Osbourne, spent their honeymoon in the summer of 1880. The stay inspired Stevenson's "The Silverado Squatters," and Spyglass Hill in *Treasure Island* is thought to be a portrait of Mount St. Helena. The park's 3,000 acres are undeveloped except for a fire trail leading to the site of the bunkhouse—which is marked with a marble tablet—and to the summit beyond. ⊠ *Hwy. 29, 3 mi north of Calistoga.*

Dining and Lodging

$$–$$$ ✕ **All Seasons Cafe.** Bistro cuisine has a California spin in this sun-
★ filled setting with marble tables and a black-and-white checkerboard floor. The seasonal menu includes organic greens, wild mushrooms, local game birds, and house-smoked beef and salmon, as well as homemade breads, desserts, and ice cream from an on-site ice-cream plant. There's also a superb list of wines, all at bargain prices. For lunch there's a tempting selection of pizza, pasta, and sandwiches. ⊠ *1400 Lincoln Ave.,* ☎ *707/942–9111. MC, V. Brunch Fri.–Sun. Closed Wed.*

$$ ✕ **Catahoula Restaurant and Saloon.** Inside the Mount View Hotel and
★ Spa, this homey restaurant, named after Louisiana's state dog, is the brainchild of chef Jan Birnbaum, whose credentials include stints at the Quilted Giraffe in New York and Campton Place in San Francisco. Using a large wood-burning oven as a stove, Birnbaum churns out California-Cajun dishes such as spicy gumbo with andouille sausage, oven-braised lamb shank with red beans, whole roasted fish, and duck confit salad with tangerines. Save room for tantalizing desserts such as chocolate-sour cherry bread pudding, buttermilk amber pie, or a wood-fired chocolate s'more that will bring you back to the campfire. Sit at the counter and watch the chef cook—it's the best entertainment in town. ⊠ *1457 Lincoln Ave.* ☎ *707/942–2275. Reservations essential. MC, V. Closed Tues. and Jan.*

$ ✕ **Boskos Ristorante.** Set in a restored sandstone building that dates back to the 1800s, this family-style eatery dishes up homemade pasta, pizza, and garden-fresh salads. *Glorioso* (pasta shells with garlic, mushrooms, and red chilies) is a favorite entrée. Leave room for the homemade chocolate cheesecake. ⊠ *1364 Lincoln Ave.,* ☎ *707/942–9088. Reservations not accepted. No credit cards.*

$$$–$$$$ ▥ **Brannan Cottage Inn.** This exquisite Victorian cottage with lacy white fretwork, large windows, and a shady porch is the only one of Sam Brannan's 1860 resort cottages still standing on its original site. Rooms have their own private entrances, and elegant stenciled friezes of stylized wildflowers cover the walls. Full breakfast is included. ⊠ *109 Wapoo Ave., 94515,* ☎ *707/942–4200. 6 rooms with bath. Breakfast room. MC, V.*

$$$–$$$$ ▥ **Mount View Hotel.** A full-service European spa delivers state-of-the-art pampering, and three cottages are each equipped with private redwood deck, Jacuzzi, and wet bar. Catahoula's, the popular restaurant and saloon, serves southern-inspired American cuisine. ⊠ *1457 Lincoln Ave., 94515,* ☎ *707/942–6877,* ℻ *707/942–6904. 33 rooms with bath. Restaurant, pool, spa. MC, V.*

$$ ⊞ **Mountain Home Ranch.** This rustic ranch, established in 1913, is set on 300 wooded acres, with hiking trails, a creek, and a fishing lake. The seven cabins spread over the grounds are ideal for families; each has a full kitchen and bath, and the majority have wood-burning fireplaces. There is just one TV, in the dining room, and no phones. In summer, the modified American plan (full breakfast and dinner) is used; otherwise, Continental breakfast is included. Special children's rates are available. ⊠ *3400 Mountain Home Ranch Rd., 94515 (north of town on Hwy. 128, left on Petrified Forest Rd., right on Mountain Home Ranch Rd., to end; 3 mi from Hwy. 128),* ☎ *707/942–6616,* FAX *707/942–9091. 6 rooms with bath in main lodge, 11 cabins. 2 pools, tennis court. MC, V. Closed Dec.–Jan.*

Hot-Air Ballooning and Gliding

American Balloon Adventures operates flights out of Calistoga. A deluxe flight includes a catered brunch finale at the Silverado Country Club. ⊠ *Box 795, Calistoga 94515,* ☎ *707/942–6546 or 800/333– 4359.* ☉ *Year-round, weather permitting; morning flights only; hrs vary with seasons.*

Calistoga Gliders gives participants a bird's-eye view of the entire valley. On clear days, visibility on a glider extends to the San Francisco skyline, the snowcapped Sierra peaks, and the Pacific Ocean. ⊠ *1546 Lincoln Ave.,* ☎ *707/942–5000.* ☞ *$110–$150 for 2 passengers, depending on length of ride.* ☉ *Daily 9 AM–sunset (weather permitting); closed Thanksgiving, Dec. 25.*

THE SONOMA VALLEY

While the Napa Valley is upscale and elegant, Sonoma Valley is over-alls-and-corduroy, with an air of countrified innocence—yet its Alexander, Dry Creek, and Russian River valleys are no less productive of award-winning vintages. Here, family-run wineries treat visitors like personal friends, and tastings are usually free.

Sonoma

45 mi from San Francisco, north on U.S. 101, east on Hwy. 37, and north on Hwys. 121 and 12.

Sonoma is the site of the last and the northernmost of the 21 missions established by the Franciscan order of Father Junípero Serra; its central plaza includes the largest group of old adobes north of Monterey. The **Mission San Francisco Solano,** whose chapel and school were used to bring Christianity to the Indians, is now a museum with a fine collection of 19th-century watercolors. ⊠ *114 Spain St. E,* ☎ *707/938– 1519.* ☞ *$2, includes the Sonoma Barracks on the central plaza and General Vallejo's home, Lachryma Montis.* ☉ *Daily 10–5; closed major holidays.*

⓭ The landmark **Buena Vista Carneros Winery** (follow signs east from Sonoma Plaza), set among towering trees and fountains, is a must-see. It was here, in 1857, that Count Agoston Haraszthy de Mokcsa laid the basis for modern California wine making, bucking the conventional wisdom that vines should be planted on well-watered ground by instead planting on well-drained hillsides. Chinese laborers dug tunnels 100 feet into the hillside, and the limestone they extracted was used to build the main house. Although their wines are produced elsewhere in the Carneros region today, the winery offers tours, a gourmet shop, an art gallery, and great picnic spots. ⊠ *18000 Old Winery Rd.,* ☎ *707/938–1266.* ☉ *Daily 10:30–4:30.*

A tree-lined approach leads to **Lachryma Montis,** which General Mariano Vallejo, the last Mexican governor of California, built for his large family in 1851. The Victorian Gothic house is secluded amid beautiful gardens; opulent Victorian furnishings include a white marble fireplace in every room. ⊠ *3rd St. and Spain St. W,* ☎ *707/938–1519.* ⊠ *$2.* ⊙ *Daily 10–5; closed major holidays.*

Dining and Lodging

$$ ✕ **Eastside Oyster Bar & Grill.** Chef-owner Charles Saunders has received rave reviews for his creative culinary flair and health-conscious approach. The California fare here is made from fresh and local ingredients only—even the fish, meat, and poultry are local—and the produce comes from an organic garden. Specialties include a delicate hangtown fry (plump oysters on a bed of greens and beets with Sonoma mustard vinaigrette), creative renditions of roast chicken or Sonoma lamb, and stellar salads and vegetarian dishes. Inside, the intimate dining room has a marble fireplace and a cozy bistro atmosphere; outside there's a wisteria-draped terrace where diners enjoy a picture-window view into the pastry kitchen. ⊠ *133 E. Napa St. (just off downtown plaza square),* ☎ *707/939–1266. AE, DC, MC, V. Sun. brunch.*

$$ ✕ **Ristorante Piatti.** On the ground floor of the remodeled El Dorado Hotel, a 19th-century landmark building, this is the Sonoma cousin of the Ristorante Piatti in Yountville. Pizza from the wood-burning oven and northern Italian specials (spit-roasted chicken, ravioli with lemon cream) are served in a rustic Italian setting with an open kitchen and bright wall murals, or on the outdoor terrace. ⊠ *El Dorado Hotel, 405 1st St. W (facing the plaza),* ☎ *707/996–2351. AE, MC, V.*

$ ✕ **The Cafe.** The atmosphere is informal at this bistro with overstuffed booths, ceiling fans, and an open kitchen. Country breakfasts, pizza from the wood-burning oven, and tasty California renditions of northern Italian cuisine are the specialties. ⊠ *Sonoma Mission Inn, 18140 Sonoma Hwy. (2 mi north of Sonoma on Hwy. 12 at Boyes Blvd.),* ☎ *707/938–9000. AE, DC, MC, V. Weekday brunch.*

$ ✕ **La Casa.** Whitewashed stucco, red tile, and serapes adorn this restaurant near Sonoma Plaza. There's bar seating, a patio out back, and an extensive menu of traditional Mexican food: chimichangas and snapper Veracruz for entrées, sangria to drink, and flan for dessert. The food is not the world's best, but locals love the casual atmosphere. ⊠ *121 E. Spain St.,* ☎ *707/996–3406. AE, DC, MC, V.*

$$$–$$$$ ✕⌷ **Sonoma Mission Inn & Spa.** This classy 1920s resort blends Mediterranean and old-California architecture for a look that's early Hollywood: Gloria Swanson would fit right in. Despite its unlikely location off the main street of tiny, down-home Boyes Hot Springs, guests come from afar to use the hotel's extensive spa facilities and treatments—including a pool that's heated by warm mineral water pumped from underground wells—and also for the classic spa food. Rooms in the newer buildings of the resort are much larger and more attractive than the smallish standard rooms in the main building. ⊠ *18140 Hwy. 12 (2 mi north of Sonoma at Boyes Blvd.), Box 1447, 95476,* ☎ *707/938–9000 or 800/358–9022; in CA, 800/862–4945;* ⅋ℵ *707/996–5358. 170 rooms with bath. 2 restaurants, 2 bars, coffee shop, 2 pools, 2 hot tubs, sauna, steam room, 2 tennis courts, health club. DC, MC, V.*

$$$$ ⌷ **Thistle Dew Inn.** A half-block from Sonoma Plaza, this turn-of-the-century Victorian home is filled with collector-quality arts-and-crafts furnishings. Owners Larry and Norma Barnett live on the premises, and Larry prepares creative, sumptuous breakfasts and hors d'oeuvres in the evenings. Four of the six rooms have private entrances and

decks, and all have queen-size beds with antique quilts, private baths, and air-conditioning. Welcome bonuses include a hot tub and free use of the inn's bicycles. ✉ *171 Spain St. W, 95476,* ☎ *707/938–2909 or 800/382–7895 in CA. 6 rooms with bath. MC, V.*

$$$–$$$$ ⊞ **El Dorado Hotel.** Claude Rouas, the owner of Napa's acclaimed
★   Auberge du Soleil, opened this small hotel in a building that dates to 1843. Rooms reflect Sonoma's mission era, with Mexican-tile floors and white walls. The best rooms are numbers 3 and 4, which have big balconies overlooking Sonoma Plaza. Only four of the rooms—the ones in the courtyard by the pool—have bathtubs; the rest have showers only. ✉ *405 1st St. W (on Sonoma Plaza),* ☎ *707/996–3030 or 800/289–3031,* ⅋ *707/996–3148. 27 rooms. Restaurant, pool. MC, V.*

$$–$$$ ⊞ **Vineyard Inn.** Built as a roadside motor court in 1941, this inn with red-tile roofs brings a touch of Mexican village charm to an otherwise lackluster location—at the junction of two main highways. Set in the heart of Sonoma's Carneros region, across from two vineyards, it's the closest lodging to Sears Point Raceway. Rooms have queen-size beds. Continental breakfast is included. ✉ *23000 Arnold Dr. (at junction of Hwys. 116 and 121), 95476,* ☎ *707/938–2350 or 800/359–4667. 9 rooms with bath, 4 suites. Breakfast room. MC, V.*

Shopping

Several stores in four-block **Sonoma Plaza** attract gourmets from miles around. Within the plaza, the **Sonoma French Bakery** (✉ 466 1st St. E, ☎ 707/996–2691) is famous for its sourdough bread and cream puffs. The **Sonoma Cheese Factory** (✉ 2 Spain St., ☎ 707/996–1000), run by the same family for four generations, makes Sonoma jack cheese and a tangy Sonoma Teleme. Great swirling baths of milk and curds are visible through the windows, along with flat-pressed wheels of cheese.

Carneros

9 mi southeast of Sonoma, Hwy. 12 to Hwy. 121/12.

One of the most important viticultural areas in the Wine Country, the Carneros region, between the towns of Sonoma and Napa, has a long, cool growing season tempered by maritime breezes and fogs off the San Pablo Bay—optimum conditions for growing pinot noir and chardonnay grapes. This is an open and scenic area of the wine country, where endless terraced vineyards stretch uninterrupted toward the horizon.

⑭ **Domaine Carneros** lies within a 138-acre estate dominated by a classic château that was inspired by Champagne Taittinger's historic Château de la Marquetterie in France. Carved into the hillside beneath the winery, Domaine Carneros's cellars produce sparkling wines reminiscent of the Taittinger style and using only Carneros grapes. At night the château is an oasis of light and beauty against the dark, terraced horizon. By day, activity buzzes throughout the visitors center, the touring and tasting rooms, and the kitchen and dining room, where private luncheons and dinners emphasize food-and-wine pairings. ✉ *1240 Duhig Rd., off Carneros Hwy. across Napa County line,* ☎ *707/257–0101.* ☯ *Daily 10:30–6. Tours hourly in summer; at 11, 1, and 3 in winter. No appointment necessary, except for group tours.*

OFF THE   **CARNEROS ALAMBIC DISTILLERY** – Here you'll learn the history and folk-
BEATEN PATH   lore of the rare alambic brandy. Tours include an explanation of the dou-
ble-distillation process, which eliminates all but the finest spirits for aging; a view of the French-built alambic pot stills that resemble Al-addin's lamp; a trip to the atmospheric oak barrel house, where taped

angels' chants set the mood; and a sensory evaluation of various vintage brandies (no tasting allowed, by law). ⊠ *1250 Cuttings Wharf Rd. (from Domaine Carneros, head 1 mi east on Carneros Hwy. 121/12 almost to town of Napa),* ☎ *707/253-9055,* ℻ *707/253-0116.*

⑮ The vintners at **Gloria Ferrer Champagne Caves** age their wines in a "cava," or cellar, where several feet of earth maintain a constant temperature—an increasingly popular alternative to temperature-controlled warehouses. ⊠ *23555 Carneros Hwy. 121,* ☎ *707/996-7256.* ▨ *Tasting fees by the glass and type of champagne.* ☉ *Daily 10:30–5:30; tours every hr 11–4.*

⑯ A son of the famous Sebastiani family decided to strike out on his own and opened **Viansa.** The winery's ocher-color building is surrounded by olive trees and overlooks the valley. Inside is an Italian food and gift market. ⊠ *25200 Arnold Dr.,* ☎ *707/935–4700.* ☉ *Daily 10–5.*

Glen Ellen

7 mi north of Sonoma on Hwy. 12.

Writer Jack London lived in the Sonoma Valley for many years; the towns of Glen Ellen and Kenwood commemorate him with place names. A bookstore in **Jack London Village** (⊠ 14301 Arnold Dr., ☎ 707/935–1240) is filled with London's books and memorabilia. Century-old **Jack London Saloon** (⊠ 13740 Arnold Dr., ☎ 707/996–3100) has a nostalgic appeal.

In the hills above Glen Ellen—known as the Valley of the Moon—lies **Jack London State Historic Park.** London's collection of South Seas artifacts can be seen at The House of Happy Walls, a museum of London's effects. The ruins of Wolf House, which London designed and which mysteriously burned down just before he was to move in, are close to the House of Happy Walls. London is buried on the property. ⊠ *2400 London Ranch Rd.,* ☎ *707/938–5216.* ▨ *Parking $5 per car.* ☉ *Park daily 9:30–sunset, museum daily 10–5; museum closed major holidays.*

⑰ Some 2 million cases of wine are bottled annually in this area. As you drive along Highway 12, you'll see orchards and rows of vineyards flanked by oak-covered mountain ranges. One of the best-known local wineries is **Benziger Family Winery,** which specializes in premium estate and Sonoma County wines. Their Imagery Series is a low-volume release of unusual red and white wines distributed in bottles with art labels by well-known artists. ⊠ *1883 London Ranch Rd.,* ☎ *707/935–3000. Complimentary tasting of Sonoma County wines; tasting fees vary.* ☉ *Daily 10–4:30.*

Lodging

$$$$ ▥ **Gaige House Inn.** Ardath Rouas, one of the originators of Auberge du Soleil in the Napa Valley, owns and runs this inn, which was built in the 19th century as a personal residence. A large pool surrounded by a green lawn, striped awnings, white umbrellas, and magnolias conjures up a manicured Hamptonslike glamour. Inside, abstract art contrasts well with the inn's antiques and traditional furnishings. The chef's gourmet first-rate country breakfast is served in a bright dining room downstairs or outside on the terrace. Three garden rooms on the ground floor in back (numbers 6, 7, and 8) have private entrances, and the Gaige Suite is spectacular. ⊠ *13540 Arnold Dr., 95442,* ☎ *707/935–0237 or 800/935–0237,* ℻ *707/935–6411. 9 rooms. Breakfast room, pool, jogging. D, MC, V.*

$$$–$$$$ 🏠 **Beltane Ranch.** On a slope of the Mayacamas range on the eastern side of the Sonoma Valley lies this 100-year-old house built by a retired San Francisco madam. Part of a working cattle and grape-growing ranch—the nearby Kenwood Winery has a chardonnay made from the ranch's grapes—the Beltane is surrounded by miles of trails through oak-studded hills. Innkeeper Rosemary Woods and her family, who have lived on the premises for 50 years, have stocked the comfortable living room with dozens of books on the area. The rooms, all with private baths and antique furniture, open onto the building's wraparound porch. ✉ *11775 Sonoma Hwy. (Hwy. 12), 95442,* ☎ *707/996–6501. 4 rooms. Tennis court, hiking, horseshoes. No credit cards.*

$$$–$$$$ 🏠 **Glenelly Inn.** Just outside Glen Ellen, this sunny little establishment, built as an inn in 1916, has all the comforts of home. Mother and daughter innkeepers Ingrid and Kristi Hallamore serve breakfast in front of the common room's cobblestone fireplace and local delicacies in the afternoons. On sunny mornings, guests may eat outside under the shady oak trees. ✉ *5131 Warm Springs Rd., 95442,* ☎ *707/996–6720. 8 rooms. Breakfast room, outdoor hot tub. MC, V.*

Kenwood

3 mi north of Glen Ellen on Hwy. 12.

Kenwood has a historic train depot and several restaurants and shops that specialize in locally produced gourmet products.

⑱   The rustic grounds at **Kenwood Vineyards** complement the attractive tasting room and artistic bottle labels. Kenwood produces all premium varietals, but is best known for its signature Jack London Vineyard reds—pinot noir, zinfandel, merlot, and a unique Artist Series Cabernet. ✉ *9592 Sonoma Hwy.,* ☎ *707/833–5891.* 🍷 *Free tasting.* ☉ *Daily 10–4:30; no tours.*

Dining

$$ ✕ **Kenwood Restaurant & Bar.** This is where Napa and Sonoma chefs eat on their nights off. Indulge in California country cuisine in the sunny, southern France–style dining room, or head through the French doors to the patio for a memorable view of the vineyards. ✉ *9900 Hwy. 12,* ☎ *707/833–6326. MC, V. Closed Mon.*

Santa Rosa

8 mi northwest of Kenwood on Hwy. 12.

Santa Rosa is the Wine Country's largest city and a good bet for moderately priced hotel rooms, especially for those who have not reserved in advance.

The **Luther Burbank Home and Gardens** commemorate the great botanist (1849–1926) who lived and worked on these grounds for 50 years, single-handedly developing the modern techniques of hybridization. Arriving as a young man from New England, he wrote: "I firmly believe . . . that this is the chosen spot of all the earth, as far as nature is concerned." The Santa Rosa plum, Shasta daisy, and lily of the Nile agapanthus are among the 800 or so plants he developed or improved. ✉ *Santa Rosa and Sonoma Aves.,* ☎ *707/524–5445.* 🍷 *Gardens free; guided tours of house and greenhouse $2.* ☉ *Gardens Nov.–Mar., daily 8–5; Apr.–Oct., daily 8–7; tours Apr.–Oct., Wed.–Sun. 10–4.*

Dining and Lodging

$$$ ✕ **Cafe Lolo.** Consistently praised by Bay Area publications, this is a casual but elegant gourmet spot. Chef-owner Michael Quigley serves fresh seafood, daily changing risotto and pasta dishes, free-range chicken, rabbit, and lots of goat cheese and local produce on his lunch and dinner menus. Don't pass up the chocolate kiss, an individual warm, very chocolatey cake with a wonderfully soft, rich center. ⊠ *620 5th St.,* ☎ *707/576–7822. AE, MC, V. Closed Sun. No lunch Sat.*

$$$ ✕ **John Ash & Co.** The thoroughly regional cuisine here emphasizes beauty, innovation, and the seasonal availability of food products grown in Sonoma County and in the restaurant's organic garden. In spring, local lamb is roasted with hazelnuts and honey; in fall, farm pork is roasted with fresh figs and Gravenstein apples. Desserts are delicious and the wine list extensive. With patio seating outside and a cozy fireplace indoors, the slightly formal restaurant looks like a Spanish villa amid the vineyards and is a favorite spot for Sunday brunch. A café menu offers bites between meals. ⊠ *4330 Barnes Rd. (River Rd. exit west from Hwy. 101),* ☎ *707/527–7687. Weekend reservations essential. AE, MC, V. No lunch Mon.*

$–$$ ✕ **Lisa Hemenway's.** A shopping center seems an unlikely location for a restaurant find, but this eatery is light and airy, with soft wine-country colors and a garden view from the patio. The fare represents American and international cuisine, from grilled sea bass with Singapore curry to red chili crepes and tapas. The adjacent café, Tote Cuisine, has a vast selection of tempting takeout selections for picnickers. ⊠ *714 Village Ct. Mall (east on Hwy. 12, at Farmer's La. and Sonoma Ave.),* ☎ *707/526–5111. AE, MC, V. Sun. brunch.*

$ ✕ **Mixx.** Great service and an eclectic "mix" of dishes define this small restaurant with large windows, booth and table seating, high ceilings, and French blown-glass chandeliers. Nightly homemade pasta and seafood dishes are served, along with regional specialties such as grilled Cajun prawns and New Mexican stuffed chilies—all based on locally grown ingredients and served with Napa Valley wine. ⊠ *135 4th St. (at Davis behind the mall on Railroad Sq.),* ☎ *707/573–1344. AE, MC, V. No lunch weekends.*

$$$$ ▥ **Vintner's Inn.** Set on 50 acres of vineyards, this French provincial inn has large rooms, many with wood-burning fireplaces, and a trellised sun deck. Breakfast is complimentary, guests are entitled to discounted passes to an affiliated health club nearby, and VCRs can be rented for a small fee. ⊠ *4350 Barnes Rd., 95403 (River Rd. exit west from U.S. 101),* ☎ *707/575–7350 or 800/421–2584,* ℻ *707/575–1426. 44 rooms. Restaurant, hot tub. DC, MC, V.*

$$$ ▥ **Fountaingrove Inn.** A redwood sculpture and a wall of cascading
★ water distinguish the lobby at this elegant, comfortable inn in the heart of the Sonoma Valley. Rooms have work spaces with modem jacks. Buffet breakfast is complimentary, and there's also an elegant restaurant with a piano player and a stellar menu. Guests have access to a nearby 18-hole golf course, a tennis court, and a health club nearby, for a fee. Golf packages are available, as are discounts for senior citizens. ⊠ *101 Fountaingrove Pkwy. (near U.S. 101), 95403,* ☎ *707/578–6101 or 800/222–6101,* ℻ *707/544–3126. 85 rooms. Restaurant, room service, pool, hot tub, meeting rooms. D, DC, MC, V.*

$$–$$$ ▥ **Los Robles Lodge.** This pleasant, relaxed motel overlooks a pool that's
★ set into a grassy landscape. Rooms are available for people with disabilities and for nonsmokers. Pets are allowed, except in executive rooms, which have whirlpools. ⊠ *1985 Cleveland Ave., 95401 (Steele La. exit west from Hwy. 101),* ☎ *707/545–6330 or 800/255–6330,* ℻ *707/575–5826. 104 rooms. Restaurant, coffee shop, pool, outdoor hot tub, nightclub, coin laundry. D, DC, MC, V.*

Nightlife and the Arts

The **Luther Burbank Performing Arts Center** presents a full events calendar of concerts, plays, and other performances by locally and internationally known artists. Send away for the calendar in advance if you're planning a trip. ⊠ *50 Mark West Springs Rd.,* ☎ *707/546–3600.* ⊙ *Box office Mon.–Sat. noon–6 and approximately 1 hr before most events.*

For symphony, ballet, and other live theater performances throughout the year, call the **Spreckels Performing Arts Center** (☎ 707/584–1700 or 707/586–0936; box office Tues.–Sat. noon–5) in Rohnert Park. Wineries often schedule concerts and music festivals during the summer.

OFF THE
BEATEN PATH

KORBEL CHAMPAGNE CELLARS – Photographic documents of the North West Railway are displayed in a former train stop, providing a historical overview of the Russian River area. And of course, there's champagne too. ⊠ *13250 River Rd., west off U.S. 101, Guerneville,* ☎ *707/887-2294.* ⊙ *Oct.–Apr., daily 9–4:30; May–Sept., daily 9–5; tours on the hr 10–3.*

Healdsburg

17 mi north of Santa Rosa on U.S. 101.

Healdsburg remains undeveloped and relatively untrafficked. The wineries in this area, discreetly located along winding roads, are not always visible to the casual observer. Many vineyards lie along the Russian River west of U.S. 101 (☎ 707/433–6782 for a map).

⑲ State-of-the-art **Piper Sonoma** specializes in méthode champenoise sparkling wines. ⊠ *11447 Old Redwood Hwy.,* ☎ *707/433–8843.* ⊙ *Daily 10–5.*

Dining and Lodging

$–$$ ✗ **Bistro Ralph.** The bistro's small, frequently changing, California-style menu includes dishes such as Szechuan pepper calamari and braised lamb shanks with mint essence. The stark industrial setting is tempered by a couple of trees perched incongruously on the bar and a friendly wait staff. ⊠ *109 Plaza St.,* ☎ *707/433–1380. Reservations essential on weekends. MC, V. No lunch weekends.*

$$$–$$$$ ✗🏠 **Madrona Manor.** This 1881 Victorian mansion, surrounded by 8 acres of wooded and landscaped grounds, provides a storybook setting for a candlelight dinner or brunch on the outdoor deck. Those who stay the night can stay either in the three-story mansion, the carriage house, or one of two separate cottages. Mansion rooms are recommended: All nine have fireplaces, and five contain the antique furniture of the original owner. Though breakfast is served to guests only, others can sample great food from the brick oven, smokehouse, orchard, and kitchen garden in the evening. Chef Todd Muir turns out dishes fit for a wine baron: smoked lamb salad, smoked scallops with onion confit, and Dungeness crab mousse. The seasonal menu is à la carte. ⊠ *1001 Westside Rd. (take central Healdsburg exit from Hwy. 101, turn left on Mill St.), Box 818, 95448,* ☎ *707/433–4231 or 800/258-4003,* 𝖥𝖠𝖷 *707/433–0703. 21 rooms with bath. Restaurant, pool. D, DC, MC, V.*

$$$$ 🏠 **Healdsburg Inn on the Plaza.** This 1900 brick building has a bright solarium and a roof garden. The rooms, most with fireplaces, are spacious, with quilts and pillows piled high on antique beds. In the bath-

rooms, claw-foot tubs are outfitted with rubber ducks. Full breakfast, afternoon coffee and cookies, and early evening wine and popcorn are included. ⊠ *110 Matheson St., 95448,* ☎ *707/433–6991. 10 rooms. Breakfast room. MC, V.*

$$ 🖭 **Best Western Dry Creek Inn.** Continental breakfast and a bottle of wine are complimentary at this three-story Spanish Mission–style motel, and there's also a coffee shop next door. Midweek discounts are available, and direct bus service from San Francisco's airport can be arranged. ⊠ *198 Dry Creek Rd., 95448,* ☎ *707/433–0300 or 800/528–1234; in CA, 800/222–5784;* ℻ *707/433–1129. 102 rooms with bath. Pool, hot tub, coin laundry. AE, D, DC, MC, V.*

THE WINE COUNTRY A TO Z

Arriving and Departing

By Bus
Greyhound (☎ 800/231–2222) runs buses from the Transbay Terminal at 1st and Mission streets in San Francisco to Sonoma and Santa Rosa.

By Car
From San Francisco, cross the Golden Gate and go north on U.S. 101, east on Highway 37, and north on Highway 121 and Highway 12 into Sonoma. To drive to Napa wineries, continue east on Highway 121/12 to Highway 29 and proceed north from that junction.

From east of San Francisco, take I–80 north to Highway 37 west to Highway 29, which heads north through the town of Napa and the rest of the Napa Valley. If you're going to Sonoma County, head northwest at Highway 29's junction with Highway 12. When coming from north of the Wine Country, take U.S. 101 south. Exit at Geyserville and follow Highway 128 southeast into the Napa Valley, or continue south on U.S. 101 to Healdsburg or to Highway 12 for other Sonoma County wineries.

By Plane
The closest major airports are in San Francisco and Oakland.

Getting Around

By Bus
Sonoma County Area Transit (☎ 707/585–7516) maintains a frequent and reliable bus schedule. **Napa Valley Transit** (☎ 707/255–7631) provides daily public transportation.

By Car
Although traffic on the two-lane country roads can be heavy, the best way to get around the sprawling Wine Country is by private car. Rentals are available at the airports and in San Francisco, Oakland, Santa Rosa, and Napa.

The **Rider's Guide** (⊠ 484 Lake Park Ave., Suite 255, Oakland 94610, ☎ 510/653–2553) produces tapes about the history, landmarks, and wineries of the Sonoma and Napa valleys that you can play in your car (maps also provided). The tapes are available at some local bookstores and can also be ordered directly from Rider's Guide for $12.95 (Napa tape) and $11.95 (Sonoma tape), plus $2 postage.

Contacts and Resources

B&B Reservation Agencies

Bed & Breakfast Exchange (☎ 707/942–5900), for Napa County. **Wine Country Inns of Sonoma County** (☎ 707/433–4667). **Wine Country Reservations** (☎ 707/257–7757, FAX 707/257–7844).

Emergencies

Ambulance (☎ 911). **Police** (☎ 911).

Guided Tours

Full-day guided tours of the Wine Country usually include lunch and cost about $50. The guides, some of whom are winery owners themselves, know the area well and may show you some lesser-known cellars. Reservations are usually required.

Gray Line (⊠ 350 8th St., San Francisco 94103, ☎ 415/558–9400) has bright-red double-decker buses that tour the Wine Country.

Great Pacific Tour Co. (⊠ 518 Octavia St., San Francisco 94102, ☎ 415/626–4499) operates full-day tours of Napa and Sonoma, including a summer picnic lunch and a winter restaurant lunch, in passenger vans that seat 14.

HMS Tours (⊠ 707 4th St., Santa Rosa 95404, ☎ 707/526–2922 or 800/367–5348) fashions customized tours of the Wine Country for four or more people, by appointment only.

Napa Valley Wine Train (⊠ 1275 McKinstry St., Napa 94559, ☎ 707/253–2111 or 800/427–4124) serves lunch, dinner, or a weekend brunch on one of several restored 1915 Pullman railroad cars that run between Napa and St. Helena. Round-trip fare costs $22 during dinner and $30 during brunch and lunch; meals of three to five courses cost between $26 and $47.50. In winter, service is sometimes limited to Thursday through Sunday; call ahead. There is a special "Deli" car for families with children on weekend brunch trips and weekday lunch trips.

Wine Country Wagons (⊠ Box 1069, Kenwood 95452, ☎ 707/833–2724, FAX 707/833–1041) conducts four-hour horse-drawn wagon tours that include three wineries and end at a private ranch, where a lavish buffet lunch is served. Tours depart daily at 10 AM, May through October; advance reservations are required.

Visitor Information

Calistoga Chamber of Commerce (⊠ 1458 Lincoln Ave., Calistoga 94515, ☎ 707/942–6333). **Healdsburg Chamber of Commerce** (⊠ 217 Healdsburg Ave., Healdsburg 95448, ☎ 707/433–6935 or 800/648–9922 in CA). **Napa Valley Conference and Visitors Bureau** (⊠ 1310 Napa Town Center, Napa 94559, ☎ 707/226–7459). **Russian River Wine Road** (⊠ Box 46, Healdsburg 95448, ☎ 707/433–6782). **St. Helena Chamber of Commerce** (⊠ 1080 Main St., Box 124, St. Helena 94574, ☎ 707/963–4456 or 800/799–6456, FAX 707/963–5396). **Sonoma County Convention and Visitors Bureau** (⊠ 5000 Roberts Lake Rd., Rohnert Park 94928, ☎ 707/586–8100 or 800/326–7666, FAX 707/586–8111).

5 San Francisco

With Side Trips to Marin County, the East Bay, and the Peninsula

San Francisco is a sophisticated city with world-class hotels and the greatest concentration of excellent restaurants in the state. The town has an undeserved reputation as the kook capital of the United States, yet it's the country's number one tourist destination. Why? To use the vernacular, the vibe here is cool, from North Beach coffeehouses to Chinatown tea emporiums, Golden Gate Park, and Haight Street's head shops (yes, they're still around). People in San Francisco know how to have a good time; the high spirits can't help but rub off on visitors.

IN ITS FIRST LIFE, SAN FRANCISCO was little more than a small, well-situated settlement. Founded by Spaniards in 1776, it was prized for its natural harbor, so commodious that "all the navies of the world might fit inside it," as one visitor wrote. The 1848 discovery of gold at John Sutter's sawmill in the nearby Sierra foothills transformed the sleepy little settlement into a city of 30,000. As millions of dollars' worth of gold was panned and blasted out of the hills, a "western Wall Street" sprang up. Just as gold production began to taper off, prospectors turned up a rich vein of silver in Virginia City, Nevada, and surrounding areas. San Francisco, the nearest financial center, prospered again. The city remains a financial hub, though nowadays its attentions are as much transoceanic as transcontinental. San Francisco prides itself on its role as a Pacific Rim capital, and overseas investment has become a vital part of its economic life. In terms of both geography and culture, San Francisco is about as close as you can get to Asia in the United States.

Loose, tolerant, and even licentious are words that are used to describe San Francisco; bohemian communities thrive here. As early as the 1860s, the "Barbary Coast"—a collection of taverns, whorehouses, and gambling joints on or near Pacific Avenue close to the waterfront—was famous, or infamous. North Beach, the city's Little Italy, became the home of the Beat Movement in the 1950s. The Haight-Ashbury district became synonymous with hippiedom, giving rise to such legendary bands as Jefferson Airplane, Big Brother and the Holding Company (fronted by Janis Joplin), and the Grateful Dead in the 1960s. And, as most of the world knows, lesbians and gay men have found the town hospitable.

The Gay and Lesbian Freedom Day Parade, each June, vies with the Chinese New Year Parade, in February, as the city's most elaborate. They both get competition from Japantown's Cherry Blossom Festival, in April; the Columbus Day and St. Patrick's Day parades; Carnaval in the Hispanic Mission District, in May; and the May Day march, a labor celebration in a labor town. The mix of ethnic, economic, social, and sexual groups can be bewildering, but the city's residents—whatever their origin—face it with aplomb and even gratitude. Everybody in San Francisco has an opinion about where to get the best burrito or the hottest Szechuan eggplant or the strongest cappuccino, and even the most staid citizens have learned how to appreciate good camp.

Technically speaking, San Francisco is only California's fourth-largest city, behind Los Angeles, San Diego, and nearby San Jose. But that statistic is misleading: The Bay Area, which stretches from the bedroom communities north of Oakland and Berkeley south through Silicon Valley (the Peninsula cities that have become the center of America's computer industry) and San Jose, is really one continuous megacity, with San Francisco as its heart.

EXPLORING SAN FRANCISCO

By Toni Chapman

Updated by Chris Borris

San Francisco is a relatively small city, with just over 750,000 residents nested on a 46½-square-mile tip of land between San Francisco Bay and the Pacific Ocean. San Franciscans cherish the city's colorful past, and many older buildings have been spared from demolition and nostalgically converted into modern offices and shops. Longtime locals rue the sites that got away—spectacular railroad and mining-boom-era residences lost in the '06 earthquake and subsequent fire (which actually did more damage than the quake), the elegant Fox Theater, Playland at the Beach.

But despite acts of God, the indifference of developers, and the mixed record of the city's Planning Commission, much of architectural and historical interest remains. Bernard Maybeck, Julia Morgan, Willis Polk, and Arthur Brown Jr. are among the noted architects whose designs still remain in the city's downtown and neighborhoods.

San Francisco neighborhoods are self-aware, and they retain strong cultural, political, and ethnic identities. Locals know this pluralism is the real life of the city. Experiencing San Francisco means visiting the neighborhoods: the colorful Mission District, gay Castro, countercultural Haight Street, serene Pacific Heights, bustling Chinatown, and still-bohemian North Beach.

Exploring involves navigating a maze of one-way streets and restricted parking zones. Public parking garages or lots tend to be expensive, as are hotel parking spaces. The famed 40-plus hills can be a problem for drivers who are new to the terrain. Cable cars, buses, and trolleys can take you to or near many of the area's attractions.

Union Square

Since 1850 Union Square has been the heart of San Francisco's downtown. Its name derives from a series of violent pro-union demonstrations staged here just prior to the Civil War. This is where you will find the city's finest department stores and its most exclusive boutiques. There are 40 hotels within three blocks of the square, and the city's leading art galleries and downtown theater district are nearby.

The square itself is a 2½-acre oasis planted with palms, boxwood, and seasonal flowers, and peopled with a kaleidoscope of characters: office workers sunning and brown-bagging, street musicians, several very vocal preachers, and a fair share of homeless people. Events throughout the year include fashion shows, free noontime concerts, ethnic celebrations, and noisy demonstrations. Auto and bus traffic is often gridlocked on the four bordering streets. Post, Stockton, and Geary are one-way, while Powell runs in both directions until it crosses Geary, where it becomes one-way south to Market Street. Union Square covers a convenient but costly four-story underground garage; close to 3,000 cars use it on busy holiday shopping and strolling days. For cheaper parking, try the nearby Sutter-Stockton Garage.

A Good Walk
Numbers in the text correspond to numbers in the margin and on the Downtown San Francisco map.

The **San Francisco Visitors Information Center** ① is on the lower level of Hallidie Plaza at Powell and Market streets. For a true San Francisco treat, head up the stairs to the **cable-car terminus** ②. Heading north from the cable-car terminus along bustling Powell Street, it's three blocks to **Union Square** ③. The stately and historic **Westin St. Francis Hotel** ④ dominates the corner of Geary and Powell streets. Two blocks west on Geary from the St. Francis are **Geary Theater** ⑤ and the **Curran Theatre** ⑥.

For a deal on theater tickets, head back to Union Square, where **TIX Bay Area** ⑦ occupies a little booth on the east side of the square. Directly across from TIX Bay Area is **Maiden Lane** ⑧, a quaint two-block alley lined with boutiques, sidewalk cafés, and San Francisco's only Frank Lloyd Wright building. Looping back to Stockton Street, head south to O'Farrell Street to find the ultimate toy store, **F.A.O. Schwarz** ⑨. A couple blocks back north on Stockton, you'll find the Grand Hyatt hotel, in front of which sits **Ruth Asawa's Fantasy Fountain** ⑩ of San Francisco scenes. A half-block farther is Sutter Street; go right one block

PACIFIC OCEAN

Golden Gate Bridge

Fort Point

101

The Presidio

1

Land's End

Palace of the Legion of Honor

Phelan Beach

Baker Beach

Northern Waterfront

Lake St.

Lincoln Park

SEACLIFF

Point Lobos

Clement St.

8th Ave.

Arguello

Cliff House

43rd Ave.

34th Ave.

Geary Blvd.

25th Ave.

19th Ave.

Balboa St.

Blvd.

Turk

Golden Gate Park

RICHMOND

Fulton St.

Golden Gate Park

Kennedy Dr.

Middle Dr.

Stanyan

Lincoln Way

Judah St.

28th St.

Funston Ave.

7th Ave.

1

Lawton St.

Noriega St.

Ortega St.

SUNSET

19th Ave.

Clarendon Ave.

41st Ave.

Sunset Blvd.

Quintara St.

McCoppin Square

14th Ave.

Dewey Blvd.

Taraval St.

Vicente St.

Larsen Park

Dr.

Mt. Davidson

Stern Grove

Portola

Yerba Buena Ave.

Miramar

Great

Highway

San Francisco Zoo

Sloat Blvd.

STONESTOWN

Monterey

Blvd.

Ocean Ave.

Ave.

Juniper Serra Blvd.

Skyline Blvd.

Harding Park

Lake Merced

San Francisco State Univ.

Lake Merced Blvd.

Font Blvd.

Holloway Ave.

Garfield St.

Plymouth Ave

N

Brotherhood Way

0   1 mile

0   1 km

San Francisco Bay

Downtown San Francisco

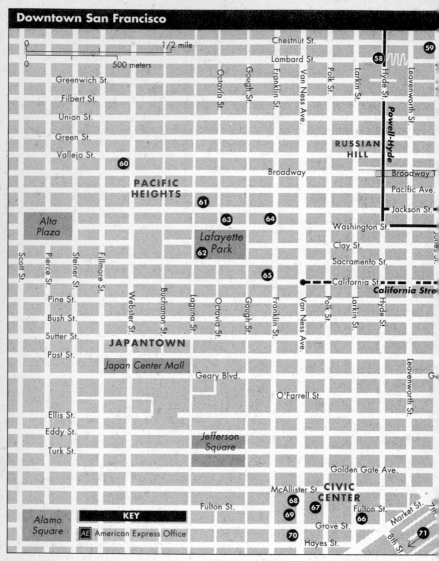

San Francisco Bay

TELEGRAPH HILL

NORTH BEACH

Powell-Mason

The Embarcadero

NOB HILL

CHINATOWN

FINANCIAL DISTRICT

UNION SQUARE

Maiden Ln.

YERBA BUENA

SOMA

Chestnut St.
Lombard St.
Greenwich St.
Filbert St.
Union St.
Green St.
Vallejo St.
Montgomery St.
Sansome St.
Battery St.
Davis St.
Front St.
Drumm St.
Clay St.
Halleck St.
Pine St.
Bush St.
Sutter St.
Post St.
Farrell St.
Ellis St.
Eddy St.
Turk St.
Howard St.
Market St.
Mission St.
Folsom St.
Howard St.
Harrison St.
Columbus Ave.
Mason St.
Powell St.
Taylor St.
Stockton St.
Grant Ave.
Kearny St.
Steuart St.
Spear St.
Main St.
Beale St.
Fremont St.
1st St.
2nd St.
3rd St.
4th St.
5th St.
6th St.
New Montgomery St.
Hawthorne St.
Davis St.
Front St.

to view the beaux arts–style **Hammersmith Building** ⑪, or left one block and check out art deco **450 Sutter Street** ⑫.

TIMING

Allow about two hours to see everything in Union Square. Stepping into the Macy's store on Union Square or browsing the other boutiques in the vicinity can eat up countless hours; if you're a shopper give yourself extra time here. The cable car ride from Powell and Market down to Fisherman's Wharf only takes about 20 minutes—but waiting in line can take twice as long.

Sights to See

👐 ❷ **Cable-car terminus.** This is the starting point for two of the three operating lines. The Powell-Mason line climbs up Nob Hill, then winds through North Beach to Fisherman's Wharf. The Powell-Hyde car also crosses Nob Hill, but then continues up Russian Hill and down Hyde Street to Victorian Park, across from the Buena Vista Cafe and near Ghirardelli Square. The cable-car system dates from 1873, when Andrew Hallidie demonstrated his first car on Clay Street; in 1964 the tramlike vehicles were designated national historic landmarks. In summertime there are often long lines to board any of the three systems; if possible, plan your cable-car ride for mid-morning or mid-afternoon during the week to avoid crowds. Buy your ticket ($2 one-way) on board, at nearby hotels, or at the police/information booth near the turnaround.

Note that although the area isn't dangerous the array of panhandlers, street preachers, and other regulars at this terminus can be daunting. An alternative is to stand in line instead at the Hyde Street end of the Powell-Hyde line, which affords views of the bay and Golden Gate Bridge while you wait. Better yet, if it's just the experience of riding a cable car you're after (rather than a trip to the wharf or Russian Hill), board the less-busy California line at Van Ness Avenue and ride it down to the Embarcadero. ⊠ *Powell and Market Sts.*

❻ **Curran Theatre.** This ornate space built in the 1920s showcases traveling companies of Broadway shows such as *The Phantom of the Opera.* ⊠ *445 Geary St.,* ☎ *415/474–3800.*

👐 ❾ **F.A.O. Schwarz.** It's worth stopping by this three-floor playland just to gawk at the 6-foot-tall stuffed animals, elaborate fairy-tale sculptures, and live toy soldiers. Among the wares are a large Barbie section, an astounding supply of lush and expensive stuffed animals (at up to $15,000), and just about every other toy imaginable. ⊠ *48 Stockton St.,* ☎ *415/394–8700.* ◷ *Mon.–Sat. 10–8, Sun. 11–6.*

⑫ **450 Sutter Street.** This 1928 terra-cotta skyscraper is an art deco masterpiece, with handsome Mayan-inspired designs covering both the exterior and interior surfaces. ⊠ *Between Stockton and Powell Sts.*

❺ **Geary Theater.** The home of the American Conservatory Theater has a serious neoclassical design lightened by colorful, carved terra-cotta columns depicting a cornucopia of fruits. After closing for earthquake-damage repairs, the theater, which was built in 1910, reopened in January 1996. ⊠ *415 Geary St.,* ☎ *415/749–2228.*

⑪ **Hammersmith Building.** Glass walls and a playful design distinguish this small, colorful 1907 beaux arts–style structure. The Foundation for Architectural Heritage once described the building as a "commercial jewel box"; appropriately, it was originally designed for use as a jewelry store. ⊠ *301 Sutter St.*

❽ **Maiden Lane.** Known as Morton Street in the Barbary Coast era, this red-light district reported at least one murder a week. After the 1906 fire destroyed the brothels, the street emerged as Maiden Lane, and it has since become a daytime pedestrian mall, with a patchwork of umbrella-shaded café tables, between Stockton and Kearny streets. The brick structure at 140 Maiden Lane is the only Frank Lloyd Wright building in San Francisco. With its circular interior ramp and skylights, it is said to have been a model for the Guggenheim Museum in New York. It now houses the Circle Gallery, which shows the limited-edition art jewelry (worth a look) of Erté. ⊠ *Between Stockton and Kearny Sts.*

⑩ Ruth Asawa's Fantasy Fountain. Ruth Asawa's sculpture honors the city's hills, bridges, and unusual architecture, plus a wonder-world of real and mythical creatures. Children and friends helped the artist shape the hundreds of tiny figures from baked clay, from which molds were made for the bronze casting. ⊠ *In front of Grand Hyatt at 345 Stockton St.*

❶ San Francisco Visitors Information Center. Conveniently located below the cable-car terminus, the center has a multilingual staff and maps, brochures, and information on daily events. Visitors can pick up coupons for substantial savings on tourist attractions, as well as pamphlets (and, depending on the season, discount vouchers) for most downtown hotels. ⊠ *Hallidie Plaza, lower level, Powell and Market Sts.*, ☎ *415/391–2000.* ⊙ *Weekdays 9–5:30, Sat. 9–3, Sun. 10–2.*

❼ TIX Bay Area. This service provides half-price day-of-performance tickets (cash or traveler's checks only) to performing-arts events, as well as regular full-price box-office services. Telephone reservations are not accepted for half-price tickets. Also available are $12.50 Golden Gate Park Explorer Passes, which provide entry to all the park's museums at a discount rate, and Muni Passports (short-term tourist passes for all city buses and cable cars). ⊠ *Stockton St. side of Union Sq.*, ☎ *415/433–7827.* ⊙ *Tues.–Thurs. 11–6, Fri.–Sat. 11–7.*

❸ Union Square. At center stage, the Victory Monument by Robert Ingersoll Aitken commemorates Commodore George Dewey's victory over the Spanish fleet at Manila in 1898. The 97-foot Corinthian column, topped by a bronze figure symbolizing naval conquest, was dedicated by Theodore Roosevelt in 1903 and withstood the 1906 earthquake. After the earthquake and fire of 1906, the square was dubbed "Little St. Francis" because of the temporary shelter erected for residents of the St. Francis Hotel. ⊠ *Between Powell, Stockton, Post, and Geary Sts.*

❹ Westin St. Francis Hotel. The second-oldest hotel in the city, originally built in 1904, was conceived by Charles Crocker and his associates as an elegant hostelry for their millionaire friends. The hotel's Turkish baths once had ocean water piped in. After the 1906 quake gutted the hotel, a larger, more luxurious residence was opened in 1907. The hotel has known its share of notoriety. Silent comedian Fatty Arbuckle's career plummeted faster than one of the St. Francis's glass-walled elevators after a wild 1921 party in one of the hotel's suites went awry. In 1975 Sara Jane Moore, standing among a crowd outside the hotel, attempted to shoot then-president Gerald Ford. As might be imagined, no plaques commemorate these events in the establishment's lobby. The ever-helpful staff will, however, gladly direct you to the traditional teatime ritual—or, if you prefer, to champagne and caviar—in the dramatic Art Deco Compass Rose lounge (☎ 415/774–0167), the only spot in town with a daily high tea (3–5 PM). Elaborate Chinese screens, secluded seating alcoves, and soothing background music make this an ideal rest stop after frantic shopping or sightseeing. Reservations are required. ⊠ *335 Powell at Geary St.*, ☎ *415/397–7000.*

South of Market (SoMa) and the Embarcadero

The vast tract of downtown land south of Market Street along the waterfront and west to the Mission District—also known by the acronym SoMa—has recently become the center of a burgeoning arts scene.

A Good Walk

Numbers in the text correspond to numbers in the margin and on the Downtown San Francisco map.

The showpiece of the South of Market area is the **San Francisco Museum of Modern Art** ⑬, housed in a modernist brick building and dominating a half-block of 3rd Street, between Howard and Mission streets. Across from the museum is the cluster of buildings known as Yerba Buena Center, between Folsom and Mission streets and 3rd and 4th streets. Within the project is the **Moscone Convention Center** ⑭, and **Yerba Buena Gardens** ⑮, a green expanse adjacent to the performance/gallery space known as **Center for the Arts** ⑯. If you're feeling scholarly, head one block east to the brand-new headquarters of the **California Historical Society;** then reverse your course and walk west to 4th Street, crossing over at Howard. South a half-block is the **Ansel Adams Center for Photography** ⑰. From Ansel Adams, head back north up 4th Street and cross Mission; walk a half-block west to the **Cartoon Art Museum** ⑱. Exiting the museum, cross 4th Street heading east to the **San Francisco Marriott** ⑲. East of the Marriott on the same block of Mission Street is dour-looking **St. Patrick's Catholic Church.**

Take 3rd Street north from and cross over Market Street to where it converges with 3rd, Kearny, and Geary. On this corner is dreary but historic **Lotta's Fountain.** Walk east on Market to New Montgomery and the **Palace Hotel** ⑳ and take a peek at the lobby-level glass-domed garden court. Continue east on Market Street, taking note of several "flatiron" buildings (including an older one at No. 540–548 and a newer one at No. 388) angling into the thoroughfare. Toward the end of Market is **Embarcadero Center** ㉑, a five-block retail-office complex that holds the **Hyatt Regency Hotel** ㉒. On the waterfront side of the hotel is outdoor **Justin Herman Plaza** ㉓.

Across the Embarcadero roadway from Justin Herman Plaza stands the **Ferry Building** ㉔. North of the Ferry Building at Pier 5 is one section of the 5-foot-wide, 2½-mile-long glass-and-concrete **Promenade Ribbon,** billed by the city as the "longest art form in the nation." At Embarcadero and Mission, you can't miss the ornate **Audiffred Building,** built in 1889 by a homesick gentleman as a reminder of his native France, and now housing the Boulevard restaurant. Heading west down Mission, turn south on Steuart Street; halfway down the block is the entrance to **Rincon Center** ㉕, which houses some famous murals. Across from Rincon Center on Steuart is the **Jewish Museum.**

TIMING

Because this walk contains several museums, set aside a whole afternoon. Plan on spending a couple of hours at SFMOMA. The Center for the Arts, Yerba Buena Gardens, and the Ansel Adams Center each merit an hour or more as well. For the walk down Market Street and along the waterfront, an hour should be sufficient unless you plan to browse in the Embarcadero Center's many shops.

Sights to See

⑰ Ansel Adams Center for Photography. Ansel Adams himself created this center in Carmel in 1967. In 1989 it moved to SoMa. The center showcases a variety of historical and contemporary photography, as well as changing exhibitions of Adams's work. ⊠ *250 4th St.,* ☎ *415/495–7000.* 🎟 *$4.* ⊙ *Tues.–Sun. 11–5, 1st Thurs. of month 11–8.*

California Historical Society. Founded in 1871, this vast repository of Californiania moved to its new home one block east of the Yerba Buena Gardens complex in late 1995. Its collection contains 500,000 photographs, 150,000 manuscripts, thousands of books, periodicals, prints, and paintings, as well as gold rush paraphernalia. The new building is an airy, sky-lit space with a central gallery, two adjacent galleries, a research library, and a storefront bookstore. ⊠ *678 Mission St.,* ☎ *415/357–1848,* 🎟 *$3.* ⊙ *Tues.–Sat. 11–5.*

⑱ **Cartoon Art Museum.** Krazy Kat, Zippy the Pinhead, Batman, and a whole crew of other colorful cartoon icons greet you as you walk in the door to the Cartoon Art Museum. Changing and permanent exhibits cover everything from the impact of underground comics to women cartoonists, the Peanuts' 40th anniversary, and African-American cartoonists. ⊠ *814 Mission St., Suite 200,* ☎ *415/546–3922.* 🎟 *$3.50.* ⊙ *Wed.–Fri. 11–5, Sat. 10–5, Sun. 1–5.*

⑯ **Center for the Arts.** The center showcases dance, music, performance, theater, visual arts, film, video, and installations—from the community-based to the international—with an emphasis on the cultural diversity of San Francisco. The complex includes two theaters, three visual-arts galleries, a film and video screening room, a gift shop, a café, and an outdoor performance stage, where there's midday music daily from April through October. ⊠ *701 Mission St.,* ☎ *415/978–2787.* 🎟 *Galleries $5; free 1st Thurs. of month 6–8 PM.* ⊙ *Galleries and box office: Tues.–Sun. 11–6.*

㉑ **Embarcadero Center.** A three-tier pedestrian mall connects the eight buildings that comprise the John Portman–designed complex of 100-plus shops, 40 restaurants, five cinemas, two hotels, and office space. Louise Nevelson's 54-foot-high black-steel sculpture, *Sky Tree*, stands guard over Building 3 and is among 20-plus works of art throughout the center. ⊠ *Sacramento St., between Battery St. and the Embarcadero.* ⊙ *Weekdays 10–7, Sat. 10–6, Sun. noon–6. Parking free on weekends with validation.*

㉔ **Ferry Building.** The beacon of the port area has a 230-foot clock tower modeled after the campanile of Seville's cathedral. On April 18, 1906, the four great clock faces on the tower, powered by the swinging of a 14-foot pendulum, stopped at 5:17 and stayed still for 12 months. The building has held its post since 1896 and is now the headquarters of the Port Commission and the World Trade Center's office. A waterfront promenade that extends from the piers north of here to the San Francisco–Oakland Bay Bridge is great for jogging, in-line skating, watching sailboats on the bay, or enjoying a picnic. Ferries from behind the Ferry Building sail to Sausalito, Larkspur, Tiburon, and the East Bay. ⊠ *The Embarcadero, between Mission and Vallejo Sts.*

㉒ **Hyatt Regency Hotel.** The hotel is noted for its spectacular lobby and 20-story hanging garden. The five glass elevators facing the lobby are fun to ride, but if you have vertigo, beware. ⊠ *Embarcadero 5.*

Jewish Museum. This small museum hosts exhibits on Jewish, art, history, and culture. Thankfully, curators here don't shy away from controversial programs, hosting exhibits such as *Art and the Rosenberg Era*, an in-depth look at freedom of expression, and *Bridges and Boundaries: African Americans and American Jews*. Plans are to move to Yerba Buena Center in 1998. ⊠ *Jewish Community Federation Build-*

ing, 121 Steuart St., ☎ *415/543–8880.* ✆ *$3; free 1st Mon. of month.* ☉ *Sun. 11–6, Mon.–Wed. noon–6, Thurs. noon–8.*

㉓ Justin Herman Plaza. On the waterfront side of the Hyatt Regency, Justin Herman Plaza plays host to arts-and-crafts shows, street musicians, skateboarders, and mimes on weekends year-round. On sunny days the plaza is a good spot to enjoy a snack from one of Embarcadero Center's dozen or so take-out shops. During the winter holidays an ice rink is set up here. ✉ *The Embarcadero just north of Steuart St.*

Lotta's Fountain. This quirky monument, now largely unnoticed by local passersby, was a gift to the city from singer Lotta Crabtree, a Madonna prototype. The fountain itself is unspectacular but Crabtree's history is interesting. Her "brash music-hall exploits" so enthralled San Francisco's early population of miners that they were known to shower her with gold nuggets and silver dollars after her performances. The buxom Ms. Crabtree is depicted in one of the Anton Refregier murals in Rincon Center. ✉ *Intersection of 3rd, Market, Kearny, and Geary Sts.*

⑭ Moscone Convention Center. The site of the 1984 Democratic convention is distinguished by a contemporary glass-and-girder lobby at street level (all convention exhibit space is underground) and a monolithic, column-free interior. ✉ *747 Howard St.*

⑳ Palace Hotel. The Palace, a Sheraton property, opened in 1875. The hotel has a storied past—President Warren Harding died here while still in office in 1923—some of which is recounted in glass cases off the main lobby. The original Palace was destroyed by fire following the 1906 earthquake, despite a 28,000-gallon reservoir fed by four artesian wells. The current building dates from 1909; late-1980s renovations included the restoration of the glass-domed Garden Court restaurant and the installation of original mosaic-tile floors in Oriental-rug designs. Maxfield Parrish's wall-size painting, *The Pied Piper,* dominates the hotel's Pied Piper Bar. The hotel conducts guided tours (☎ 415/546–5026) of its grand interior. ✉ *2 New Montgomery St.*

㉕ Rincon Center. A five-story rain column resembling a mini-rainstorm dominates the center's street-level mall area. In addition to the mall, there are two modern towers of offices and apartments. In front of all this is a former post office built in the Streamline Moderne style. In the post office's historic lobby is a series of murals by Anton Refregier. One of the largest WPA-era art projects, its 27 panels depict California life, from the days when Indians were the state's sole inhabitants through World War I. Completion of this significant work was interrupted by World War II and political infighting; the latter led to some alteration in Refregier's "radical" historical interpretations. A permanent exhibit below the murals contains interesting photographs and artifacts of life in the Rincon area in the 1800s. ✉ *Steuart and Mission Sts.*

⑲ San Francisco Marriott. You can't miss the Marriott: Its 40-story ziggurat construction topped with reflecting glass pinwheels has earned it comparisons with a jukebox, a high-rise parking meter, and a giant rectal thermometer. ✉ *4th and Mission Sts.*

★ ⑬ San Francisco Museum of Modern Art. SFMOMA took center stage in the SoMa arts scene in January 1995, winning immediate acclaim for its adventurous programming, which includes traveling exhibits and film/video series. Its strong permanent collection includes works by Matisse, Picasso, O'Keeffe, Frida Kahlo, Jackson Pollock, and Warhol, as well as a diverse photography section. The striking modernist structure, designed by Swiss architect Mario Botta, consists of a stepped-back, burnt-sienna brick facade and a central tower constructed of alternating bands of black and white stone. Inside, natural light from the tower floods the central atrium and some of the museum's galleries. SFMOMA's café, accessible from the street, provides a comfortable, reasonably priced refuge for drinks and light meals. ⊠ *151 3rd St.,* ☎ *415/357–4000.* ⌖ *$7; free 1st Tues. of each month.* ☉ *Tues.–Sun. 11– 6, Thurs. until 9 (½-price entry 6–9); closed major holidays.*

St. Patrick's Catholic Church. The brick, Gothic Revival building next to the Marriott was completed in 1872 and rebuilt after the 1906 earthquake and fire destroyed its interior. The murky, off-white interior has shadowy marble columns and dark stained-glass windows. ⊠ *756 Mission St.*

★ ⑮ **Yerba Buena Gardens.** A large expanse of green is surrounded by a circular walkway lined with benches and sculptures. The waterfall memorial to Martin Luther King, Jr., is the focal point of the gardens: Powerful streams of water surge over large, jagged stone columns, mirroring the enduring force of MLK's words that are carved on the stone walls and on glass blocks behind the waterfall. Above the memorial are two restaurants and an overhead walkway to Moscone Center's main entrance. ⊠ *Between 3rd, 4th, Mission, and Howard Sts.* ☉ *Sunrise–10 PM.*

The Financial District and Jackson Square

When San Francisco was a brawling, boozing, whoring, extravagant upstart of a town in the latter half of the 19th century, Jackson Square and the Financial District were at the heart of the action. It was on Montgomery Street that Sam Brannan proclaimed the historic gold discovery on the American River in 1848. Along with streams of prospectors came many other fortune-seekers: Saloon-keepers, gamblers, and prostitutes all flocked to the so-called Barbary Coast. Only one remnant of the gold-rush era remains: Along the former wharf-dominated streets below Montgomery, between California and Broadway, at least 100 ships abandoned by frantic crews and passengers caught up in gold fever now underlie many building foundations.

A Good Walk

Numbers in the text correspond to numbers in the margin and on the Downtown San Francisco map.

Starting at Montgomery and Market streets, go north one block to Sutter Street; heading west a half-block toward Kearny, you'll see the all-glass facade of the **Hallidie Building** ㉖. Head back to Montgomery and go north a block; just past Bush on the east side of the block is the **Mills Building and Tower** ㉗. Across the street is the Gothic "skyscraper" the **Russ Building** ㉘. Continue north to the end of the block and turn east at Pine Street. At the next corner (Sansome and Pine) is the **Pacific Stock Exchange** ㉙ and art deco Stock Exchange Tower. From here, go back west on Pine to see the granite-and-marble **Bank of America** ㉚. North of the BofA on Montgomery Street is the **Wells Fargo Bank History Museum** ㉛, which provides a good introduction to gold-rush history. The landmark **Transamerica Pyramid** ㉜ is north on Montgomery, at Clay Street. Walking through the small park on the east side of the pyramid, you'll exit on Washington Street; just to your left is Hotaling Place, a tiny, historic alley that is your entrée to **Jackson Square** ㉝, the heart of the Barbary Coast.

TIMING
The ground covered in this tour is fairly minimal; two hours should be enough time to see everything. The Wells Fargo museum deserves

a half hour. If you're interested in antiques, leave extra time for the shops in Jackson Square.

Sights to See

㉚ Bank of America. This 52-story polished red granite-and-marble building dominates nearly an entire downtown block. Inside, small exhibits of impressive original art are displayed. A massive, abstract black-granite sculpture designed by the Japanese artist Masayuki commands the corner of Kearny and California streets; it's been dubbed the "Banker's Heart" by local wags. Atop of the complex is the Carnelian Room (☎ 415/433–7500), a cocktail lounge and restaurant that offers elegant dining with a nighttime view of the city lights and the bay. This is an excellent spot for a drink at sunset; by day, the room is the private Banker's Club. ✉ *Between California, Pine, Montgomery, and Kearny Sts.*

㉖ Hallidie Building. Named for cable-car inventor Andrew Hallidie, this building is best viewed from across the street. Willis Polk's revolutionary all-glass curtain-wall—believed to be the world's first such structure, hangs a foot beyond the reinforced concrete of the frame. With its reflecting glass, decorative exterior fire escapes that appear to be metal balconies, and Venetian Gothic cornice, the unusual building dominates the block. Also notice the horizontal ornamental bands of birds at feeders. ✉ *130 Sutter St., between Kearny and Montgomery Sts.*

㉝ Jackson Square. Though most of San Francisco's first red-light district was destroyed in the 1906 fire, old brick buildings and narrow alleys recall the romance of rowdier days. Some of the city's earliest business buildings, survivors of the 1906 quake, still stand in Jackson Square, between Montgomery and Sansome streets. The tiny alley connecting Washington and Jackson streets is named for the head of the A.P. Hotaling and Company whiskey distillery, which was located at 451 Jackson, and had the largest liquor repository on the West Coast. A plaque on the side of the old Hotaling building repeats a famous query about its surviving the quake: "If, as they say, God spanked the town/for being over frisky,/Why did He burn the churches down/and save Hotaling's Whisky?" The Ghirardelli Chocolate Factory was once housed at 415 Jackson.

The Belli Building (✉ 722–728 Montgomery St.) was for years the headquarters of flamboyant attorney Melvin Belli. The structure is adorned with Victorian detailing and covered with ivy. The site was originally a warehouse and later the Melodeon Theater, where the immortal (just barely) Lotta Crabtree performed. It was also the "Birthplace of Freemasonry" (1849), as noted by a prominent plaque. Adjacent to the Belli Building is the Golden Era Building (✉ 732 Montgomery St.), where the city's most literary periodical was published during the 1850s and 1860s: Mark Twain and Bret Harte were two of its celebrated contributors. You'll have to conjure up your own tribute, as nothing commemorates the spot. ✉ *Between Washington, Broadway, Montgomery, and Sansome Sts.*

㉗ Mills Building and Tower. The circa-1891 Mills Building has been called the best remaining example of the first wave of steel-frame constructions built according to the Chicago School of architecture. The original Burnham and Root design called for white marble and brick, but the result was actually a 10-story all-steel construction with its own electric plant in the basement. Damage from the 1906 fire was slight; the building's walls were somewhat scorched but were easily refurbished. Two compatible additions east on Bush Street were added in 1914 and 1918 by Willis Polk, and in 1931 a 22-story tower completed the design. ✉ *220 Montgomery St.*

㉙ Pacific Stock Exchange. Ralph Stackpole's monumental 1930 granite sculptural groups, *Earth's Fruitfulness* and *Man's Inventive Genius*, flank this imposing structure, which dates from 1915. The Stock Exchange Tower around the corner at 155 Sansome Street, a 1930 modern classic by architects Miller and Pfleuger, has an art deco gold ceiling and a black marble-walled entry. ✉ *301 Pine St.; tower around corner at 155 Sansome St.*

㉘ Russ Building. The Russ Building was called "the skyscraper" when it was built in 1927. The Gothic design was modeled after the Chicago Tribune Tower, and until the 1960s it was San Francisco's tallest building—at just 31 stories. ✉ *235 Montgomery St.*

㉜ Transamerica Pyramid. The city's most-photographed high-rise is the 853-foot Transamerica Pyramid. Designed by William Pereira and Associates, the controversial symbol has become more acceptable to local purists over time. A fragrant redwood grove along the east side of the building, replete with benches and a cheerful fountain, is a nice place to unwind. ✉ *600 Montgomery St.*

㉛ Wells Fargo Bank History Museum. The showpiece here is the red, century-old Concord stagecoach that in the mid-1850s carried 18 passengers from St. Joseph, Missouri, to San Francisco in three weeks. The museum also displays nuggets and gold dust from mines, a mural-size map of the Mother Lode, original art by Western artists Charles Russell and Maynard Dixon, mementos of the poet bandit Black Bart, an old telegraph machine, and old bank drafts. ✉ *420 Montgomery St.,* ☎ *415/396–2619.* ▦ *Free.* ☽ *Banking days 9–5.*

Chinatown

Bordered roughly by Bush, Kearny, Powell, and Broadway, Chinatown is home to one of the largest Chinese communities outside Asia. In addition, recent immigrants from Southeast Asia are making their mark on the neighborhood. The two main drags are Grant Avenue, where most of the tourist shops reside, and Stockton Street, where the locals do business. Merely strolling through Chinatown and its many bazaars, restaurants, and curio shops yields endless pleasures, but you'll have a better chance of experiencing an authentic bit of one of the world's oldest cultures by venturing off the beaten track.

A Good Walk

Numbers in the text correspond to numbers in the margin and on the Downtown San Francisco map.

Visitors usually enter Chinatown through the green-tiled, dragon-flanked **Chinatown Gate** ㉞ at Bush Street and Grant Avenue. Two blocks farther at California is **Old St. Mary's Church** ㉟. Continue north on Grant Avenue and take a right on Commercial to the tiny but fascinating **Chinese Historical Society** ㊱ 1½ blocks down. Head back west to Kearny, and go north to the Holiday Inn. On the third floor is the **Chinese Culture Center** ㊲, which houses an art museum.

Take the suspended walkway over Kearny Street to **Portsmouth Square** ㊳. At Kearny and Washington is the unobtrusive **Buddha's Universal Church** ㊴. West on Washington is the **Old Chinese Telephone Exchange** ㊵. West past Grant Avenue on Washington is Waverly Place and **Tien Hou Temple** ㊶. Head south a block and turn right on Clay Street; a half-block up is the redbrick **Chinatown YWCA.** Return to Stockton and head south a half-block to the **Kong Chow Temple** ㊷. A small balcony overlooks the neighborhood. Next door is the elaborate **Chinese Six Companies** building.

TIMING

Allow at least two hours to see Chinatown. The museums deserve a half hour each, and both temples can be appreciated in a half hour.

Sights to See

39 **Buddha's Universal Church.** A five-story, hand-built temple, Buddha's Universal Church is decorated with murals and tile mosaics. The church is open the second and fourth Sunday of the month, except from January through March, when it presents a bilingual costume play Saturday and Sunday to celebrate the Chinese New Year. ✉ *720 Washington St.,* ☎ *415/982–6116.* ✉ *Play tickets $8–$10.*

34 **Chinatown Gate.** This pagoda-topped, green-tiled gate, flanked on either side of Grant Avenue by stone dragons, is an exotic introduction to one of San Francisco's most interesting and culturally cohesive neighborhoods. ✉ *Bush St. and Grant Ave.*

Chinatown YWCA. This handsome redbrick building was originally established as a meeting place and residence for Chinese women in need of social services. A large Chinese lantern welcomes those who enter through its arched doorway; inside, the lobby evokes early 20th-century Chinatown, with heavy, filigreed wood furniture and mirrors etched with delicate calligraphy. Julia Morgan, the architect of Hearst Castle, designed the building. ✉ *965 Clay St.*

37 **Chinese Culture Center.** This community organization displays the work of Chinese-American artists and exhibits relating to Chinese culture. Saturday afternoon (2 PM) walking tours ($15) of historic points in Chinatown can be arranged. ✉ *Holiday Inn, 750 Kearny St., 3rd floor,* ☎ *415/986–1822.* ✉ *Free.* ☉ *Tues.–Sat. 10–4, Sun. noon–4.*

36 **Chinese Historical Society.** This careworn but important museum documents the little-publicized history of Chinese immigrants and their descendants from the early 1800s to the present. ✉ *650 Commercial St., parallel to Clay St. off Kearny,* ☎ *415/391–1188.* ✉ *Free.* ☉ *Tues.–Sat. noon–4.*

Chinese Six Companies. Many fine examples of Chinese architecture line Stockton Street, but this is perhaps the most noteworthy. With its curved roof tiles and elaborate cornices, the imposing structure's oversize pagoda cheerfully dominates the block. ✉ *843 Stockton St.*

42 **Kong Chow Temple.** Amid the statuary, flowers, orange offerings, and richly colored altars (red signifies "virility," green "longevity," and gold "majesty") are a couple of plaques announcing that "Mrs. Harry S. Truman came to this temple's predecessor in June 1948 for a prediction on the outcome of the election. . . . This fortune came true." Place a dollar in the donation box as you enter. The air at Kong Chow Temple is often thick with incense, a bit ironic considering the Chinese Community Smoke-Free Project is two floors below. ✉ *855 Stockton St.*

40 **Old Chinese Telephone Exchange.** The original Chinatown burned down after the 1906 earthquake, and this was the first building to set the style for the new Chinatown. The intricate, three-tier pagoda, now the Bank of Canton, was built in 1909. The exchange's operators were renowned for their "tenacious memories"—they knew all their callers by name rather than number. ✉ *743 Washington St.*

NEED A BREAK?   Dim sum, a variety of pastries filled with meat, fish, and vegetables, is the Chinese version of a smorgasbord, delivered on stacked food-service carts from which customers make selections. At **New Asia** (✉ 772 Pacific Ave., ☎ 415/391–6666) dim sum is available daily from 8:30 AM to 3 PM.

③⑤ **Old St. Mary's Church.** This brick and granite building was dedicated in 1854 and served as the city's Catholic cathedral until 1891 (the current seat of the Catholic church in San Francisco, which replaced the successor to Old St. Mary's, is the ultramodern St. Mary's Cathedral at 1111 Gough Street). Old St. Mary's hosts a Noontime Concert series every Tuesday at 12:30. Across California Street is St. Mary's Park, a tranquil setting for local sculptor Beniamino (Benny) Bufano's *Sun Yat-Sen*. The 12-foot statue of the founder of the Republic of China was installed on the site of the leader's favorite reading spot during his years of exile in San Francisco. ⊠ *Grant Ave. and California St.*

③⑧ **Portsmouth Square.** This former potato patch that became the plaza for Yerba Buena (the Mexican settlement that was later renamed San Francisco) is also where Montgomery raised the American flag in 1846. Note the bronze galleon atop a 9-foot granite shaft; designed by Bruce Porter, the sculpture was erected in 1919 in memory of Robert Louis Stevenson, who often visited the site during his 1879–80 residence. Now dotted with pagoda-shaped structures, the park is a favorite spot for morning t'ai chi. By noon, dozens of men play a Chinese version of chess, engaged in not-always-legal competition that the police occasionally interrupt. A sand-covered children's playground sits below the main level of the square. ⊠ *Kearny St., between Washington and Clay Sts.*

④① **Tien Hou Temple.** Day Ju, one of the first three Chinese to arrive in San Francisco, dedicated this temple to the Queen of the Heavens and the Goddess of the Seven Seas in 1852. Climb three flights of stairs past two mah jongg parlors whose patrons hope the spirits above will favor them. In the entryway, elderly ladies can often be seen preparing "money" to be burned as offerings to various Buddhist gods. A (real) dollar placed in the donation box on their table will bring a smile (and is expected). Red-and-gold lanterns adorn the ceiling, and the dimly lit room is redolent with the scent of incense and oranges, placed everywhere as offerings. Notice the wood carving suspended from the ceiling, depicting a number of gods at play. ⊠ *125 Waverly Pl.* ☉ *Daily 10–4.*

North Beach and Telegraph Hill

Novelist and resident Herbert Gold calls North Beach "the longest-running, most glorious American bohemian operetta outside Greenwich Village." Indeed, to anyone who's spent some time in its eccentric old bars and cafés, or wandered its charming side streets and steep alleys, North Beach evokes everything from the wild Barbary Coast days to the no-less-sedate Beatnik era. You can still find family operettas performed at Caffè Trieste, Italian bakeries that appear frozen in time, and homages to Jack Kerouac and Allen Ginsberg. Like neighboring Chinatown, this is a section of the city where eating is unavoidable: The streets are packed with savory Italian delicatessens, bakeries, Chinese markets, coffeehouses, and ethnic restaurants.

A Good Walk

Numbers in the text correspond to numbers in the margin and on the Downtown San Francisco map.

Washington Square ④③ is at the intersection of Union Street and Columbus Avenue. Just north of the square is the double-turreted cathedral of **Saints Peter and Paul** ④④. Head south on Columbus to the corner of Vallejo and the **St. Francis of Assisi Church** ④⑤, a Victorian-era structure. From here you can slip down Columbus to a Beat-era landmark, the **City Lights bookstore** at No. 261, or walk east on Vallejo and north on **Grant Avenue** ④⑥, which is filled with eclectic shops and old-time bars and cafés. When you reach Union Street, you're just a block and a half north of Washington Square.

From the square, head up steep **Telegraph Hill** ㊼ to **Coit Tower** ㊽. Coit Tower can be reached by car (though parking is very tight) or public transportation—board the No. 39-Coit at Washington Square Park (Columbus Ave. and Union St.). To walk up to the tower, head east up Filbert Street; turn left at Grant and go one block north, then right at Greenwich and ascend the steps on your right. Cross the street at the top of the first set of stairs and continue up the curving stone steps to Coit Tower.

On the other side of Coit Tower, steps take you down the east side of Telegraph Hill. At Montgomery Street, perched on the side of the hill, is **Julius' Castle** ㊾, all royal spires and breathtaking views. A block to the right at 1360 Montgomery, where the Filbert steps intersect, is an art deco apartment building with etched-glass gazelle and palms counterpointing a silvered fresco of the heroic bridge worker. Descend the Filbert steps amid roses, fuchsias, irises, and trumpet flowers—courtesy of Grace Marchant, who labored for nearly 30 years to transform a dump into a treasure. The serene **Levi Strauss headquarters** ㊿ is at the foot of the hill.

TIMING

To visit Coit Tower, hike Telegraph Hill, and visit the sights mentioned here, set aside two to three hours. By its nature, though, North Beach is a place to linger.

Sights to See

★ ㊽ **Coit Tower.** The 180-foot tall Coit Tower stands as a monument to the city's volunteer firefighters. Early during the gold rush, Lillie Hitchcock Coit ("Miss Lil") was said to have deserted a wedding party and chased down the street after her favorite engine, Knickerbocker No. 5, clad in her bridesmaid finery. She was soon made an honorary member of the Knickerbocker Company, and after that always signed herself "Lillie Coit 5" in honor of her favorite fire engine. Lillie died in 1929 at the age of 86, leaving the city $125,000 to "expend in an appropriate manner . . . to the beauty of San Francisco." Inside the tower are 19 WPA-era murals depicting labor-union workers. Ride the elevator to the top of the tower to enjoy the panoramic view. ⊠ *Top of Telegraph Hill.* ▨ *$3.* ☉ *Daily 10–6.*

㊻ **Grant Avenue.** Originally called Calle de la Fundación, Grant Avenue is the oldest street in the city. Here you'll find dusty bars (like The Saloon, Grant & Green) that evoke the Wild West, odd curio shops and unusual import stores, atmospheric cafés, and authentic Italian delis.

NEED A
BREAK?

A Saturday afternoon must is **Caffè Trieste** (⊠ 601 Vallejo St., at corner of Grant Ave., ☎ 415/392–6739), where the Giotta family presents a weekly musical (patrons are encouraged to participate). Beginning at 1 PM, the program ranges from Italian pop and folk music to operas. A neighborhood favorite since 1956, this was once the headquarters of the area's beatnik poets, artists, and writers.

㊾ **Julius' Castle.** An official historic landmark (founder Julius Roz had his craftsmen use materials left from the 1915 Panama–Pacific Exposition), the Castle was recently refurbished using marbles and hardwoods. The dark-paneled Victorian interior fits the elegant setting, and the contemporary Italian food is worth the splurge. Ask for a table on the upper floor's outside terrace, where the views are especially dazzling. Reservations are essential. ⊠ *1541 Montgomery St.,* ☎ *415/392–2222.* ☉ *Daily 5–10 PM.*

㊿ Levi Strauss headquarters. This carefully landscaped complex appears so collegiate it is affectionately known as LSU (Levi Strauss University). Fountains and grassy knolls complement the redbrick buildings, providing a perfect environment for brown-bag lunches. ⊠ *Levi's Plaza, 1155 Battery St.*

㊺ St. Francis of Assisi Church. An 1860 Victorian Gothic building with a terra-cotta facade stands on the site of the frame parish church that served the Gold Rush Catholic community. ⊠ *610 Vallejo St.*

NEED A BREAK? To soak up brews and nighttime atmosphere, try funky **Specs' Museum Cafe** (⊠ 12 Adler Alley, ☎ 415/421–4112), in an alley across Columbus Avenue from City Lights bookstore. The café is cluttered with original memorabilia from the city's early seafaring days.

㊹ Saints Peter and Paul. This Romanesque cathedral was completed in 1924. Its twin-turreted towers are local landmarks. On the first Sunday of October, a mass followed by a parade to Fisherman's Wharf celebrate the annual Blessing of the Fleet. ⊠ *666 Filbert St., at Washington Square Park.*

㊼ Telegraph Hill. Telegraph Hill residents command some of the best views in the city, as well as the most difficult ascents to their aeries. (The charming, flower-lined steps sprinkling either side of the hill make the climbs more than tolerable for visitors, though.) The Hill rises from the east end of Lombard Street and is capped by Coit Tower.

㊸ Washington Square. This may well be the daytime social heart of what was once considered "Little Italy"—though in the early morning, the dominating sight is a hundred or more elderly Asians engaged in t'ai chi. By mid-morning groups of conservatively dressed elderly Italian men arrive. Nearby, kids toss Frisbees, jugglers juggle, and elderly Chinese matrons stare impassively at the passing parade. ⊠ *Between Columbus, Stockton, Filbert, and Union Sts.*

Nob Hill and Russian Hill

Once called the Hill of Golden Promise, the hill above Union Square was officially dubbed Nob Hill during the 1870s when "the Big Four"—Charles Crocker, Leland Stanford, Mark Hopkins, and Collis Huntington—built their hilltop estates. Nob Hill is still home to many of the city's elite, as well as several of San Francisco's finest hotels. Russian Hill has long been home to old San Francisco families and, during the 1890s, to a group of bohemian artists and writers that included Charles Norris, George Sterling, and Maynard Dixon.

A Good Walk

Numbers in the text correspond to numbers in the margin and on the Downtown San Francisco map.

Begin at California and Taylor streets at the **Masonic Auditorium** ㉛, an enormous, high-columned structure—the lobby mural is the highlight of a visit. Across California is **Grace Cathedral** ㉜. Go down California one block (toward Mason Street) to the striking **Pacific Union Club** ㉝, a brownstone whose shell survived the '06 quake. Just to the east across Mason Street is the **Fairmont Hotel** ㉞. Across California from the Fairmont is the **Mark Hopkins Inter-Continental Hotel** ㉟, famed for its Top of the Mark lounge. Head north three blocks on Mason Street to the **Cable Car Museum** ㊱, the "brain" of the cable-car network.

From the Cable Car Museum, continue four blocks north on Mason Street to Vallejo Street. Steep stairs lead to the multilevel **Ina Coolbrith Park** ⑤⑦ From here you can meander north on Mason Street to Union. Head west on Union and north on Hyde to the top of **Lombard Street** ⑤⑧, a.k.a. the "crookedest street in the world." Take the steps down to Leavenworth Street. A block north and a block east (on Chestnut) is the **San Francisco Art Institute** ⑤⑨, in a Spanish-style building.

TIMING

This tour covers a lot of ground, much of it steep. To do it all, including brief stops at Grace Cathedral and the Cable Car Museum, a person in reasonable shape will want to set aside 3½–4 hours.

Sights to See

⑤⑥ **Cable Car Museum.** On exhibit here are photographs, old cable cars, signposts, ticketing machines, and other memorabilia dating back to 1873. The four sets of massive powerhouse wheels that move the entire cable car system steal the show: The design is so simple it seems almost unreal. You can also go downstairs and check out the innards of the system. ⊠ *1201 Mason St., at Washington St.,* ☎ *415/474–1887.* ☑ *Free.* ۞ *Nov.–Mar., daily 10–5; Apr.–Oct., daily 10–6; closed some holidays.*

⑤④ **Fairmont Hotel.** The Fairmont's dazzling opening was delayed a year by the 1906 quake, but since then the marble palace has hosted presidents, royalty, movie stars (Valentino, Dietrich), and local nabobs. Things have changed since its early days: On the eve of World War I, you could get a room for as low as $2.50 per night, meals included. Nowadays, prices run as high as $6,000—this being for a night in the eight-room, Persian art–filled penthouse suite. The lobby is a warm blend of flamboyant rose-floral carpeting, lush red-velvet chairs, gold faux-marble columns, and gilt ceilings. The hotel's kitschy Tonga Room (☞ Nightlife, *below*) is a hoot. ⊠ *950 Mason St.,* ☎ *415/772–5000.*

⑤② **Grace Cathedral.** This soaring Gothic structure erected on the site of Charles Crocker's mansion took 53 years to build. The gilded bronze doors at the east entrance were taken from casts of Ghiberti's Gates of Paradise on the baptistery in Florence. Perhaps the most unique feature of Grace, the local seat of the Episcopal church, is its 35-foot-wide meditation labyrinth, a large, purplish rug that's a replica of the 13th-century stone labyrinth on the floor of the Chartres Cathedral. Outdoors is a terrazzo meditation labyrinth. Also noteworthy is an AIDS Memorial Chapel with a sculpture by the late artist Keith Haring. ⊠ *1051 Taylor St.,* ☎ *415/749–6300.* ۞ *Daily 7–6; gift shop Mon.–Sat. 10–5, Sun. 9:30–11 and 12:30–3:30.*

⑤⑦ **Ina Coolbrith Park.** This attractive park is composed of a series of terraces strung up a hill. An Oakland librarian and poet, Ina Coolbrith introduced both Jack London and Isadora Duncan to the world of books. In 1915 she was named poet laureate of California. The climb to the park is steep, so make use of the benches at various levels. ⊠ *Vallejo St., between Mason and Taylor Sts.*

⑤⑧ **Lombard Street.** San Francisco's "crookedest street" drops down the east face of Russian Hill in eight switchbacks. Few tourists with cars can resist the lure of the steep descent, but it's made less-than-scary by the very slow speed at which you must proceed. Pedestrians can make a quicker descent by taking the steps on either side of the street. ⊠ *Lombard St., between Hyde and Leavenworth Sts.*

⑤⑤ **Mark Hopkins Inter-Continental Hotel.** A combination of French château and Spanish Renaissance architecture (with terra-cotta detailing), this hotel has hosted statesmen, royalty, and Hollywood celebrities. The Top of the Mark cocktail lounge is remembered fondly by thousands of World War II veterans who jammed the lounge before leaving for overseas duty; wives and sweethearts watching the ships depart gave the northwest nook of the room its name—"Weepers' Corner." ⊠ *1 Nob Hill, corner of California and Mason Sts.,* ☎ *415/392–3434.*

51 **Masonic Auditorium.** Formally called the California Masonic Memorial Temple, this building was erected by Freemasons in 1957. The impressive lobby mosaic (done mainly in rich greens and yellows) depicts the Masonic fraternity's role in California history and industry. There's also an intricate model of King Solomon's Temple in the lobby. ⊠ *1111 California St.,* ☎ *415/776–4917.* ☉ *Lobby weekdays 8–5.*

53 **Pacific Union Club.** The quake and fire of 1906 knocked down all of Nob Hill's palatial mansions save one: the shell of the Flood brownstone. This broad-beamed structure was built by the Comstock silver baron in 1886. In 1909 the property was purchased by the Pacific Union Club, a bastion of the wealthy and powerful. Adjacent is a small park noted for its frequent art shows. ⊠ *1000 California St.*

59 **San Francisco Art Institute.** A Moorish-tiled fountain in a tree-shaded courtyard greets you as you enter the institute. The Spanish colonial-style building was erected on Russian Hill in 1926. Don't miss the impressive seven-section fresco painted in 1931 by Mexican master Diego Rivera, in the student gallery to the left as you enter the institute: It's one of only three Bay Area murals by Rivera. ⊠ *800 Chestnut St.,* ☎ *415/749–4588.* ▨ *Gallery free.* ☉ *McBean Gallery Tues.–Sat. 10–5 (Thurs. until 8), Sun. noon–5; student gallery daily 10–5.*

Pacific Heights

Some of the city's most expensive and dramatic real estate—including mansions and town houses priced at $1 million and up—is in Pacific Heights. Grand old face-lifted Victorians line the streets and offer magnificent vistas of the bay, although here and there glossy, glass-walled high-rise condos obstruct the view.

A Good Walk

Numbers in the text correspond to numbers in the margin and on the Downtown San Francisco map.

At Webster Street and Broadway are three notable **Broadway estates** ⑥⓪. South on Webster Street, is **Bourn Mansion.** Head east on Jackson Street to the red-sandstone **Whittier Mansion** ⑥①, at the corner of Laguna. One block south on Laguna is **Lafayette Park** ⑥②. Walking east on Washington along the edge of Lafayette Park, the most imposing residence is the formal French **Spreckels Mansion** ⑥③ at the corner of Octavia Street. Continue east to Franklin Street and turn left. Halfway down the block is the **Haas-Lilienthal House** ⑥④, open twice-weekly to the public. South on Franklin, stop to see several **Franklin Street buildings** ⑥⑤, and several more **noteworthy Victorians** nearby.

TIMING

Set aside about two hours to see all of the sights mentioned here. Unless you're in great shape, it'll be a slow walk up extremely steep Webster Street from the Union Street sights, and while most of the attractions are walk-bys, you'll be covering a good bit of pavement. Tours of the Haas-Lilienthal House take about one hour, and special guided tours of Pacific Heights from the house run two hours.

Sights to See

Bourn Mansion. This Georgian brick mansion was built in 1896 for William B. Bourn, who had inherited a Mother Lode gold mine. The architect, Willis Polk, was responsible for many of the most impressive commercial and private homes built from the pre-quake days until the early 1920s. Polk also designed Bourn's palatial Peninsula estate, Filoli. ✉ *2550 Webster St.*

(60) **Broadway estates.** Broadway uptown is home to several classic showplaces. The three-story Italian Renaissance palace at 2222 Broadway, with an intricately filigreed doorway, was built by Comstock mine heir James Flood and later donated to a religious order. The Convent of the Sacred Heart purchased the baroque brick Grant house at 2220 Broadway. These two buildings, along with a Flood property at 2120 Broadway are all used as school quarters. ✉ *Broadway St., between Fillmore and Buchanan Sts.*

(65) **Franklin Street buildings.** Don't be fooled by the neoclassical Golden Gate Church (✉ 1901 Franklin St.)—what at first looks like a stone facade is actually redwood painted white. At 1735 Franklin you'll find a stately brick Georgian built in the early 1900s for a coffee merchant. On the northeastern corner of Franklin and California streets is the "tapestry brick" Christian Science church; the Tuscan Revival building has noteworthy terra-cotta detailing. The Coleman House (✉ 1701 Franklin St.) is a twin-turreted Queen Anne mansion built for a gold-rush mining and lumber baron. Don't miss the large stained-glass window on the house's north side.

(64) **Haas-Lilienthal House.** This 1886 Queen Anne survived the 1906 earthquake and fire and is the only fully furnished Victorian open to the public. The carefully kept rooms offer an intriguing glimpse of turn-of-the-century taste and lifestyle. A small display of photographs on the bottom floor proves that this elaborate house was modest compared with some of the giants that fell to the fire. Volunteers conduct tours of the house two days a week, as well as an informative two-hour tour of the eastern portion of Pacific Heights on Sunday afternoon. ✉ *2007 Franklin St., near Washington St.,* ☎ *415/441–3004.* 🎫 *$5.* ⏲ *Wed. noon–4 (last tour at 3:15), Sun. 11–5 (last tour at 4:15); available for special tours with advance notice. Pacific Heights tours ($5) leave the house Sun. at 12:30* PM.

(62) **Lafayette Park.** Clusters of trees dot this four-block-square oasis for sunbathers and dog-and-Frisbee teams. During the 1860s, a tenacious squatter, Sam Holladay, built himself a big wooden house in the center of the park. Holladay even instructed city gardeners as if the land were his own, and defied all orders to leave. The house was finally torn down in 1936. ✉ *Between Laguna, Gough, Sacramento, and Washington Sts.*

Noteworthy Victorians. Two stunning Italianate Victorians (✉ 1818 and 1834 California St.) stand out on the 1800 block of California. A block farther is the Victorian-era Atherton House (✉ 1990 California St.), which combines Queen Anne, Stick-Eastlake, and other architectural elements. The Victorians on the east side of the 1800 block of Laguna Street cost only $2,000 to $2,600 when they were built during the 1870s. ✉ *California St., between Franklin and Octavia Sts.; Laguna St., between Pine and Bush Sts.*

(63) **Spreckels Mansion.** This formal French estate was built for sugar heir Adolph Spreckels and his wife, Alma. Mrs. Spreckels was so pleased with her house that she commissioned architect George Applegarth to design another building just like it: the city's European museum, the California Palace of the Legion of Honor in Lincoln Park. One of the

city's great iconoclasts, Alma Spreckels herself is the model for the bronze figure atop the Victory Monument in Union Square. ✉ *2080 Washington St., at Octavia St.*

61 **Whittier Mansion.** This red-sandstone structure was one of the most elegant 19th-century homes in the state. It has a Spanish-tiled roof and enormous scrolled bay windows on all four sides. An anomaly in a town that lost most of its grand mansions to the 1906 quake, the Whittier Mansion was built so solidly that only a chimney toppled over during the disaster. ✉ *2090 Jackson St., at Laguna St.*

OFF THE
BEATEN PATH

JAPANTOWN – Around 1860, a wave of Japanese-Americans arrived in San Francisco, which they named "Soko." After the 1906 fire destroyed wooden homes in other parts of the stricken city, many of these recent immigrants settled in the Western Addition. By the 1930s they had opened shops, markets, meeting halls, and restaurants and established Shinto and Buddhist temples. Japantown was virtually disbanded during World War II when many of its residents, including second- and third-generation Americans, were "relocated" in camps. Today Japantown, or "Nihonmachi," is centered on the slopes of Pacific Heights, north of Geary Boulevard, between Fillmore and Laguna streets; the Nihonmachi Cherry Blossom Festival is celebrated two weekends every April. The three-block-long Japan Center (✉ Post St., between Fillmore and Laguna Sts.) contains shops, restaurants, a cineplex, and the very fine Kabuki Hot Springs spa.

Civic Center and Mission Dolores

City Hall and the adjoining cultural institutions that make up San Francisco's Civic Center stand as one of the country's great governmental building complexes—a seeming realization of the visions put forth by turn-of-the-century proponents of the "City Beautiful." But illusion soon gives way to reality: On the streets and plazas of Civic Center, you'll find many of the city's most destitute residents eking out an existence, and much of the area is or has been undergoing seismic retrofitting in the wake of the 1989 Loma Prieta earthquake. The area will likely look better by the end of the century. It's a quick ride on the underground or a manageable walk to historic Mission Dolores from the Civic center.

A Good Tour
Numbers in the text correspond to numbers in the margin and on the Downtown San Francisco map.

Start your walk at the new **San Francisco Public Library** ⑥⑥ at Fulton and Larkin streets. Across from the library to the west are Civic Center Plaza and **City Hall** ⑥⑦. Across Van Ness Avenue from City Hall are—from north to south, each taking up most of a block—the **Veterans Building** ⑥⑧, the **War Memorial Opera House** ⑥⑨, and **Louise M. Davies Symphony Hall** ⑦⓪. The **Hayes Valley** strip of galleries, shops, and restaurants is a block south of Grove on Hayes Street, between Franklin and Laguna streets. Don't stray west past Laguna into the housing projects; east of Laguna is safe during the day. After you've explored Hayes Valley, backtrack to Gough and head south to Market. To visit **Mission Dolores** ⑦①, you have two options. The Van Ness Avenue Muni light-rail station is two blocks east; catch a J car, get off at 16th and Church streets, and walk one block east on 16th to Dolores Street. Or you can walk up Market Street to treelined Dolores Street (which runs into Market across from Safeway) and walk south to 16th Street. From the mission, you can easily proceed either to the **Mission District** or the **Castro** (☞ *below*).

TIMING

Walking the Civic Center area takes about 45 minutes, not counting tours of the library or Davies Hall, or shopping in Hayes Valley. Add 20 to 30 minutes to walk or train up to Mission Dolores, which can be explored in a half-hour.

Sights to See

67 **City Hall.** This French Renaissance Revival masterpiece of granite and marble was modeled after the Capitol building in Washington. Its dome, which is even higher than the Washington version, dominates the area. The palatial interior will be closed for seismic upgrading at least until 1998. ⊠ *Between Van Ness, Polk, Grove, and McAllister Sts.*

70 **Louise M. Davies Symphony Hall.** This 2,750-seat hall is the home of the San Francisco Symphony. The glass-encased wraparound lobby is visible from the street. Symphony conductor Michael Tilson-Thomas is the only U.S.-born conductor of a major American orchestra. ⊠ *201 Van Ness Ave.,* ☎ *415/552–8338.* 🎫 *Tours $3.* ⊙ *Tours of Davies Hall Wed. and Sat. by appointment, and of Davies and the Performing Arts Center Mon. every ½ hr 10–2.*

NEED A
BREAK?

For a cappuccino, a quick pizza, or a grilled chicken-breast sandwich, dash over to **Spuntino** (⊠ 524 Van Ness Ave., ☎ 415/861-7772). Depending on show times at the surrounding performing-arts spaces, this bustling bistro is sometimes open as late as midnight.

71 **Mission Dolores.** The adobe building housing the sixth of 21 California missions founded by Father Junípero Serra was originally known as Mission San Francisco de Assisi. Construction began in 1782 and ended in 1791. The mission's ceiling depicts original Costanoan Indian basket designs, executed in vegetable dyes. There is a small museum, and a cemetery (made famous by a scene in Alfred Hitchcock's *Vertigo*) with the graves of mid-19th-century European immigrants. ⊠ *Dolores and 16th Sts.,* ☎ *415/621–8203.* 🎫 *$2.* ⊙ *Daily 9–4.*

OFF THE
BEATEN PATH

MISSION DISTRICT – Home to lively Italian and Irish communities earlier in the century—you'll still find Italian restaurants and Irish pubs here, as well as Arabic bookstores, Vietnamese markets, and Filipino eateries—the Mission District has been heavily Latino since the late 1960s, when immigrants from Mexico and Central America began arriving. From the mission, you can head east on 16th Street to a "new bohemia" section of cafés and funky shops around 16th and Valencia streets, and then on into the heart of the Mission District—Valencia and Mission streets between 16th and 24th streets are the area's commercial core.

66 **San Francisco Public Library.** The new main library, which opened in April 1996, is a modernized version of the old beaux arts library that sits just across Fulton Street (that building is slated to become the new site of the Asian Art Museum in 1999). The new building contains several specialty rooms, including centers for the hearing and visually impaired, a gay-and-lesbian history center, African-American and Asian centers, and a rooftop garden and terrace. The new San Francisco History Room and Archives holds a wealth of historic photographs, maps, and other memorabilia. At the library's center is a five-story atrium with a skylight, a grand staircase, and murals painted by local artists. Across Hyde Street behind the library is brick-lined United Nations Plaza. ⊠ *Larkin St., between Grove and Fulton Sts.,* ☎ *415/557–4440 or 415/557–4567 (archives).* ⊙ *Mon. 10–6, Tues.–Thurs. 9–8, Fri. 11–5, Sat. 9–5, Sun. noon–5.*

⑥⑧ **Veterans Building.** The third and fourth floors of the Veterans Building formerly housed the San Francisco Museum of Modern Art. Herbst Theatre (☎ 415/392–4400), on the first floor, remains a popular venue for lectures and readings, classical ensembles, and dance performances. The San Francisco Arts Commission Gallery (☎ 415/554–6080), on the bottom floor at street level, displays the works of Bay Area artists. The mayor's office and other city departments are temporarily located in the Veterans Building during City Hall's renovation. ⊠ *401 Van Ness Ave.*

⑥⑨ **War Memorial Opera House.** The opera house is modeled after its European counterparts, with a vaulted and coffered ceiling, marble foyer, two balconies, and an unusual art deco chandelier, which resembles a huge silver sunburst. The San Francisco opera and ballet companies usually perform here, but the building is closed for seismic retrofitting and renovations that are scheduled for completion by September 1997. ⊠ *301 Van Ness Ave.,* ☎ *415/621–6600.*

OFF THE BEATEN PATH	**THE CASTRO –** Historians are still trying to discover what turned a sleepy working-class neighborhood east of the Civic Center into a mecca for lesbians and gay men. Some point to the San Francisco's libertarian traditions, and others note that as a huge military embarkation point during World War II, the city provided an anonymous haven. Whatever the cause, the area surrounding the intersection of Castro and Market streets became a social, cultural, and political center for gays. Especially on weekends, the streets of the Castro teem with a wide assortment of folks out shopping, pushing political causes, heading to art films, and lingering in bars and cafés. Cutting-edge clothing stores and unique gift shops predominate, as do pairs of pretty young things of all genders and sexual persuasions (even heterosexual) holding hands. The regal, 1,500-seat Castro Theatre (⊠ 429 Castro St.), which opened in 1922, is the neighborhood's landmark. The birthplace and workshop of the Names Project (⊠ 2362 Market St.), which manages the AIDS Memorial Quilt, is around the corner. Nurse a cappuccino at the Café Flore (⊠ 16th and Market St.) to overhear the latest Castro dish. From the Civic Center, take one of Market Street's above-ground antique trolleys.

The Northern Waterfront

For the sight, sound, and smell of the sea, hop the Powell-Hyde cable car from Union Square and take it to the end of the line. The views as you descend Hyde Street down to the bay are nothing short of breathtaking—tiny sailboats bob in the white caps, Alcatraz hovers ominously in the distance, and the Marin Headlands form a rugged backdrop to the fog-shrouded Golden Gate Bridge. Be sure to bring good walking shoes and a jacket or sweater for mid-afternoon breezes or foggy mists.

A Good Walk

Numbers in the text correspond to numbers in the margin and on the Northern Waterfront/Marina and the Presidio map.

Begin at the **National Maritime Museum** ① and, two blocks east, **Hyde Street Pier** ②. Across from the museum is redbrick **Ghirardelli Square** ③. A half-block east of the Hyde Street Pier on Beach Street lies the three-story **Cannery** ④, another attractive old brick complex whose restaurants and shops overlook an open-air courtyard. North of the Cannery on Jefferson Street is famous **Fisherman's Wharf** ⑤. Continue east for a couple more blocks and join the crowds at **Pier 39** ⑥, a playland and shopper's extravaganza.

Northern Waterfront/Marina and the Presidio

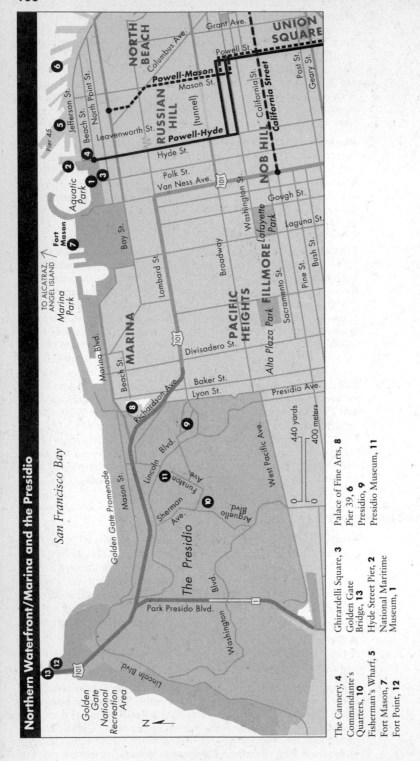

The Cannery, **4**
Commandante's Quarters, **10**
Fisherman's Wharf, **5**
Fort Mason, **7**
Fort Point, **12**

Ghirardelli Square, **3**
Golden Gate Bridge, **13**
Hyde Street Pier; **2**
National Maritime Museum, **1**

Palace of Fine Arts, **8**
Pier 39, **6**
Presidio, **9**
Presidio Museum, **11**

TIMING

For the entire Northern Waterfront circuit, set aside a half day, not including shopping or dining. Boat tours take from one to three hours or more.

Sights to See

Alcatraz Island. The boat ride to the island is brief (15 minutes), but affords beautiful views of the city, Marin County, and the East Bay. The audio tour, highly recommended, includes observations of guards and prisoners about life in one of America's most notorious penal colonies. A separate, ranger-led tour surveys the island's ecology. Plan your schedule to include at least three hours for the visit and boat rides combined. Advance reservations, even in the off-season, are strongly recommended. ⊠ *Pier 43½,* ☎ *415/546–2628.* ⊡ *$10 or $6.75 without audio; add $2 per ticket to charge by phone at 415/546–2700.* ⊙ *Daily, year-round.*

Angel Island. For an outdoorsy adventure, consider a day at Angel Island, just northwest of Alcatraz. Discovered by Spaniards in 1775 and declared a U.S. military reserve 75 years later, the island was used from 1910 until 1940 as a screening ground for Asian immigrants, who were often held for months, even years, before being granted entry. In 1963 the government deemed Angel Island a state park. Docent-led tours explain its history. A scenic path winds around the island's perimeter. ⊠ *Pier 43½,* ☎ *415/546–2628 or 415/435–1915 (info on island activities).* ⊡ *$9.* ⊙ *Late Oct.–early Mar., weekends only; early Mar.–late Oct., daily.*

❹ The Cannery. This three-story structure was built in 1894 to house what became the Del Monte Fruit and Vegetable Cannery. Among the shops and restaurants is the Museum of the City of San Francisco (☎ 415/928–0289), on the third floor and worth a brief visit. ⊠ *2801 Leavenworth St.,* ☎ *415/771–3112.* ⊙ *Mon.–Sat. 10–6, Sun. 11–6; until 8:30 Thurs.–Sat. in summer (restaurants open later).*

Ferries. Cruises are an exhilarating way to see the bay. Among the cruises offered by the Red and White Fleet (⊠ Pier 43½, ☎ 415/546–2628) are frequent one-hour swings under the Golden Gate Bridge and along the Northern Waterfront. More interesting—and just as scenic—are the tours to Sausalito, Angel Island, Alcatraz, Tiburon, Muir Woods, and the Napa Valley Wine Country. The Blue and Gold Fleet (⊠ Pier 39, ☎ 415/705–5555) conducts daily 1¼-hour tours under both the Bay and Golden Gate bridges, as well as Friday and Saturday night dinner-dance cruises (reservations required) from April until mid-December. Blue and Gold also runs ferries to Oakland, Alameda, and Vallejo (the latter includes trips on the Wine Train and to Marine World Africa USA). ⊠ *Fisherman's Wharf, between Piers 43½ and 39.*

❺ Fisherman's Wharf. The chaotic streets of the Wharf are home to numerous seafood restaurants—including sidewalk crab pots and counters that offer take-away shrimp and crab cocktails—and dozens of tourist magnets. T-shirts and sweats, gold chains galore, redwood furniture, and acres of artwork (some original) beckon visitors. Ferries to Alcatraz, Angel Island, and many other places also leave from here. The World War II submarine U.S.S. *Pampanito* (⊠ Pier 45, ☎ 415/441–5819) provides a fascinating (if claustrophobic) look at life down under during wartime. ⊠ *Jefferson St., between Leavenworth St. and Pier 39.*

NEED A
BREAK?
The swingin'est place on the wharf is the airy **Lou's Pier 47 Restaurant** and bar (✉ 300 Jefferson St., ☎ 415/771–0377). You won't be able to miss this joint: The sounds of live R&B, blues, and rock bands, many of them quite fine, flood the wharf.

❸ **Ghirardelli Square.** Across from the National Maritime Museum, this complex of 19th-century redbrick factory buildings—once the home of the aromatic Ghirardelli Chocolate Company—has been transformed into a network of specialty shops, cafés, restaurants, and galleries. (Don't worry, you can still find plenty of Ghirardelli chocolate here.) Two unusual shops in the Cocoa Building are Xanadu Gallery (☎ 415/441–5211) and Folk Art International (☎ 415/928–3340): Both display museum-quality tribal art from Asia, Africa, Oceania, and the Americas. ✉ *900 North Point,* ☎ *415/775–5500.* ☉ *Mon.–Sat. 10–9, Sun. 10–6.*

❷ **Hyde Street Pier.** The pier, one of the wharf area's best bargains, always bustles with activity. The highlight is the collection of historic ships: The *Balclutha,* an 1886 full-rigged, three-mast sailing vessel that sailed around Cape Horn 17 times; the *Eureka,* a side-wheel ferry; and the *C.A. Thayer,* a three-masted schooner. All three can be boarded. ✉ *End of Hyde St.,* ☎ *415/929–0202.* ✑ *$2; travelers with National Park Service Golden Eagle Pass enter pier free.* ☉ *Fall–spring, daily 10–5; summer, daily 10–6.*

❶ **National Maritime Museum.** You'll feel as if you're out to sea when you step inside this sturdy, rounded structure. Part of the San Francisco Maritime National Historical Park, which includes Hyde Street Pier, the museum exhibits ship models, photographs, maps, and other artifacts chronicling the development of San Francisco and the West Coast through maritime history. ✉ *Aquatic Park, at the foot of Polk St.,* ☎ *415/556–3002 or 415/929–0202.* ✑ *Free; donation suggested.* ☉ *Fall–spring, daily 9:30–5; summer, daily 10–6.*

❻ **Pier 39.** This shopping and entertainment complex is the most popular of San Francisco's waterfront attractions. Children will enjoy the brilliantly colored, double-decker Venetian Carousel. At the newly opened Underwater World, moving walkways transport visitors through a space surrounded on three sides by water filled with indigenous San Francisco Bay marine life. Above water, don't miss the hundreds of sea lions that bask and play on the docks on the pier's northwest side. Bring a camera. ✉ *Pier 39 off Jefferson St.*

The Marina and the Presidio

The Marina district was a coveted place to live until the 1989 earthquake, when the area's homes suffered the worst damage in the city due to the fact that the Marina is built on landfill. Though many homeowners and renters have left in search of more solid ground, it's still a popular place for young professionals. Especially on weekends, Chestnut and Union streets are filled with a fairly homogeneous, well-to-do crowd, and the Marina Safeway is known far and wide as a pickup joint for young singles (love among the broccoli bouquets).

Across from Safeway is the Fort Mason cultural complex. West of the Marina is the sprawling Presidio, a former military base that was recently turned over for civilian use. The current raging debate pits those who favor some private ownership of the Presidio against those who want it to be managed by the National Park Service for strictly public use. Whatever the outcome, the Presidio will still have some of the most stunning views and the best hiking and biking areas in San Francisco; a drive through can also be rewarding.

A Good Drive

*Numbers in the text correspond to numbers in the margin and on the
Northern Waterfront/Marina and the Presidio map.*

You can reach the Presidio by public transportation—Muni Bus 38 from
Union Square heads west to Fillmore Street (transfer to Bus 22 for Fort
Mason; walk three blocks west from the route's terminus) and to Park
Presidio Boulevard (transfer to Bus 28 to go through the Presidio—
but here is the place to use your car if you have one; you might even
consider renting one for a day to cover the area, as well as Lincoln Park,
Golden Gate Park, and the western shoreline.

Begin with a visit to **Fort Mason** ⑦. To get to the **Palace of Fine Arts** ⑧
by car, take Lombard Street west and stay in the right lane as it curves
toward Golden Gate Bridge; watch carefully for signs. Inside the Palace
is the **Exploratorium,** a hands-on science museum. The least confusing
way to get to the **Presidio** ⑨ from the Palace is to exit from the south
end of the Lyon Street parking lot and head east (left) on Bay Street.
Turn right (north) onto Baker Street, right onto Francisco and take it
across Richardson Avenue to Lyon Street. Make a left onto Lyon, a
right at Lombard Street, and proceed through the main gate to Presidio Avenue. Turn right onto Presidio, then take the first left, which
is still Presidio Avenue. Follow Presidio to Funston Avenue and take
a left, then turn right on Moraga Avenue. Just before Arguello Avenue
you'll find the old **Commandante's Quarters** ⑩ (now the Officers'
Club), a white adobe structure. From here, turn around and head a
half-block back up to Funston; follow it to its dead end at Lincoln Boulevard. On the left is the **Presidio Museum** ⑪, a 19th-century former hospital with exhibits on the history of the military in San Francisco. From
here it's four blocks west on Lincoln to the Presidio Visitors Information Center, on the corner of Lincoln and Montgomery Street.

Just before you get to the Visitors Information Center, you'll see a turnoff
on the right for **Fort Point** ⑫, a collection of military buildings sitting
in the shadow of the Golden Gate Bridge; the highlight is the redbrick
fortress directly underneath the bridge. To get there, follow Lincoln
Boulevard for a couple of miles, curving past a large cemetery and some
scenic turnoffs. Just before the bridge you'll see a parking lot marked
"Fort Point" on the right. Park and follow the signs leading to Fort
Point, walking downhill through a lightly wooded area; to the right is
the old mine depot and to the left is the Fort Point defense fortification, which is open for tours. To walk the short distance to the **Golden
Gate Bridge** ⑬, follow the signs from the Fort Point parking lot; to drive
across the bridge, continue a little ways past the parking lot, and
watch for the turnoff on the right. If you're going to walk across the
bridge, you'll want to park in the Fort Point lot.

TIMING

If you drive, plan to spend at least three hours, not including a walk
across the Golden Gate Bridge or hikes along the shoreline—each of
which will take a few hours. If you're coming with kids, you'll probably want to budget a little more time for the Exploratorium.

Sights to See

⑩ **Commandante's Quarters.** Built in 1776 and used during the Spanish
and Mexican regimes in California, this long, low, adobe structure may
be the oldest standing building in the city. When California came
under U.S. control, the Army continued to use it as a headquarters.
Now the Officers' Club, for members only, it was restored to its original form in 1934. Look for the plaque and old cannons in front near
the awning. ⊠ *Moraga Ave., between Funston and Arguello Aves.*

Exploratorium. This hands-on "museum of science, art, and human perception" is one of the best science museums in the world. The curious of all ages flock here to play with and learn from some of the 600 exhibits. Be sure to crawl through the dark, touchy-feely Tactile Dome. Regular science demonstrations (lasers, dissection of a cow's eye) begin around 10:30 each day. ⊠ *Near intersection of Baker and Beach Sts.,* ☎ *415/561–0360 for general information, 415/561–0362 for required reservations for Tactile Dome.* ⊡ *$9; free 1st Wed. of month.* ☉ *Tues.–Sun. 10–5 (Wed. until 9:30), legal Mon. holidays 10–5.*

❼ Fort Mason. Originally a depot for the shipment of supplies to the Pacific during World War II, Fort Mason was converted into a cultural center in 1977. It now houses nonprofit museums (including the Mexican, Italian-American, Craft and Folk Art, and African-American), theaters, galleries and some unusual shops. Most of the museums are closed Monday and some also aren't open on Tuesday. ⊠ *Buchanan St. and Marina Blvd.,* ☎ *415/979–3010 for event information.*

❿ Fort Point. Designed to mount 125 cannons with a range of up to 2 miles, Fort Point was constructed between 1853 and 1861 to protect San Francisco from sea attack in case of civil war—but it was never used for that purpose. It was, however, used as a coastal defense fortification post during World War II, when soldiers stood watch here. Standing under the shadow of the Golden Gate Bridge, the national historic site is now a museum filled with military memorabilia. Guided group tours and cannon drills are offered daily by National Park Rangers. The top floor affords a superb view of the bay. ⊠ *Off Lincoln Blvd., near Golden Gate Br.,* ☎ *415/556–1693.* ⊡ *Free.* ☉ *Wed.–Sun. 10–5.*

★ ⑬ Golden Gate Bridge. Connecting San Francisco with Marin County, the Golden Gate Bridge has long wowed sightseers with its unique rust-colored beauty and simple but powerful art deco design. At nearly 2 miles long, it is one of the longest bridges in the world—and also one of the strongest, made to withstand winds of over 100 miles per hour. Though frequently gusty and misty (walkers should wear warm clothing), the bridge offers unparalleled views of the Bay Area. A vista point on the Marin side affords a spectacular view of the city. ⊠ *Just off Lincoln Blvd., on Doyle Dr. above Ft. Point.*

★ ❽ Palace of Fine Arts. San Francisco's rosy rococo Palace of Fine Arts is at the very end of the Marina. The palace is the sole survivor of the many tinted plaster buildings (a temporary classical city of sorts) built for the 1915 Panama-Pacific International Exposition. Bernard Maybeck designed the classic beauty, which was reconstructed in concrete and reopened in 1967, thanks to legions of sentimental citizens and a huge private donation. The massive columns, great rotunda (dedicated to the glory of Greek culture), and swan-filled lagoon have been used in countless fashion layouts and recent films. ⊠ *Near intersection of Baker and Beach Sts.,* ☎ *415/563–7337 for palace tours.*

❾ Presidio. Currently part of the Golden Gate National Recreation Area, the Presidio was a military post for more than 200 years. Don Juan Bautista de Anza and a band of Spanish settlers first claimed the area in 1776. It became a Mexican garrison in 1822 when Mexico gained its independence from Spain, until U.S. troops forcibly occupied it in 1846. The U.S. Sixth Army was stationed here until October 1994, when the coveted space was finally transferred into civilian hands. The more than 1,400 acres of rolling hills, majestic woods, and redbrick army barracks present an air of serenity in the middle of the city. There are two beaches, a golf course, and picnic sites, and the views of the bay, Golden Gate Bridge, and Marin County are sublime. The Presidio Visitors Information Center (✉ Lincoln Blvd. and Montgomery St., ☎ 415/556–0865) offers maps, brochures, and schedules for guided walking and bicycle tours. It's open daily 10 to 5. ✉ *Between the Marina and Lincoln Park*.

⓫ **Presidio Museum.** Housed in a former military hospital built in 1863, the museum focuses on the role played by the military in San Francisco's development. Behind it are two cabins that housed refugees from the 1906 earthquake and fire. Photos on the wall of one depict rows and rows of temporary shelters at the Presidio and in Golden Gate Park following the disaster. ✉ *Lincoln Blvd. and Funston Ave.*, ☎ 415/556–0865. 🎟 *Free.* ◎ *Wed.–Sun. 10–4.*

Golden Gate Park

In 1887, Scotsman John McLaren transformed this desolate brush- and sand-covered expanse in the central-western part of San Francisco into a rolling, beautifully landscaped 1,000-acre oasis that stretches more than two miles and ends dramatically at the ocean. Because it is so large, the best way for many visitors to get from one end to the other is by car (though you'll want to do a lot of walking in between). Muni buses and streetcars provide service. From May through October, free guided walking tours of the park are offered every weekend by the Friends of Recreation and Parks (☎ 415/221–1311). If you plan to visit more than one attraction in the park, consider purchasing a Golden Gate Park Explorer Pass ($12.50), which grants admission to the de Young and Asian Art museums, plus the California Academy of Sciences, the Japanese Tea Garden, and (when it reopens) the Conservatory. The passes are good for up to six months (the length depends on which time of year you buy the pass), so you can visit the attractions at your leisure. The passes can be purchased at any of the above sights or at TIX Bay Area in Union Square. Be forewarned that the fog can sweep into the park with amazing speed; always bring a sweatshirt or jacket.

A Good Walk

Numbers in the text correspond to numbers in the margin and on the Golden Gate Park map.

If you're coming from downtown, board westbound Bus 5-Fulton or Bus 21-Hayes and continue to Arguello and Fulton streets, then walk south about 500 feet into the park to John F. Kennedy Drive. You can also take the N-Judah streetcar (underground part of the way) to many stops parallel to the park; from any stop past Arguello Boulevard, walk north a couple of blocks. Once in Golden Gate, a great place to start your tour is at the huge, glass **Conservatory** ① and surrounding gardens, on Conservatory Drive near Fulton Street. From there, walk west to the museums near 10th Avenue. Start at the **M.H. de Young Memorial Museum** ②, a repository for American art, and the **Asian Art Museum** ③, with its world-famous collection. Next to the museums is the **Japanese Tea Garden** ④, a beautifully landscaped Japanese garden with a tea pavilion.

Coming out of the tea garden, cut across the Music Concourse, where outdoor concerts are sometimes held, to the **California Academy of Sciences** ⑤: Along with one of the top five natural-history museums in the nation, this large structure also contains the Steinhart Aquarium and a planetarium. Coming out of the Academy of Sciences on its north side, stroll around to the west side of the building and find the small but charming Shakespeare Garden. From here walk west to the main road, turn left, and follow its curves to **Strybing Arboretum & Botanical Gardens** ⑥, green, rolling gardens with a multitude of plants and

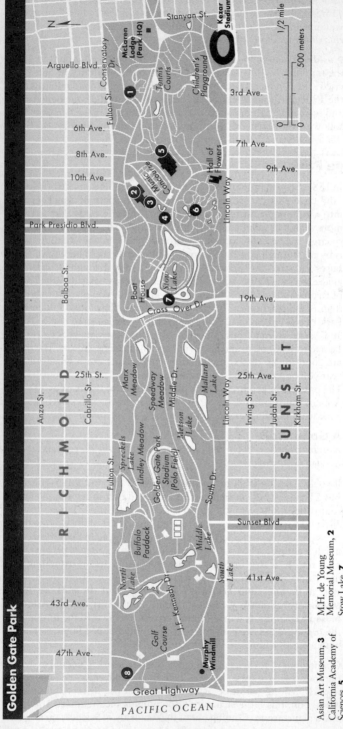

Golden Gate Park

Asian Art Museum, **3**
California Academy of
Sciences, **5**
Conservatory, **1**
Dutch Windmill, **8**
Japanese Tea
Garden, **4**

M.H. de Young
Memorial Museum, **2**
Stow Lake, **7**
Strybing Arboretum &
Botanical Gardens, **6**

trees from around the world. From Strybing walk west a short distance to **Stow Lake** ⑦, a peaceful pond encircling Strawberry Hill where you can rent boats or just loll on the shores. If you opt to walk the rest of the way out to the ocean, you'll pass by several meadows, a stadium, a buffalo paddock, and a few small lakes. Just past the park's golf course, and nearly at the ocean, you'll find the beautifully restored **Dutch Windmill** ⑧ and adjoining garden.

TIMING

You can easily spend a whole day in Golden Gate Park, with its multitude of museums, gardens, and other attractions, especially if you walk the whole distance (over 2 miles). Set aside at least an hour each for the Academy of Sciences, the Asian Art Museum, and the de Young Museum. Even if you plan to explore just the eastern end of the park (up to Stow Lake), allot at least four hours; this is where most of the human-made attractions are.

Sights to See

❸ **Asian Art Museum.** A world-famous collection of more than 12,000 sculptures, paintings, and ceramics from 40 countries, illustrating major periods of Asian art, is housed here. One standout permanent exhibit is the Leventritt collection of blue and white porcelains. On the second floor are treasures from Iran, Turkey, Syria, India, Tibet, Nepal, Pakistan, Korea, Japan, Afghanistan, and Southeast Asia. There are daily docent tours. In December 1999, the Asian Art Museum is scheduled to move to new quarters in the refurbished old main library building in the Civic Center. ⊠ *Tea Garden Dr., off John F. Kennedy Dr., near 10th Ave. and Fulton St.,* ☎ *415/668–8921.* ⊡ *$6 for both the Asian and de Young museums (additional $1 grants same-day admission to Legion of Honor Museum in Lincoln Park).* ⊙ *Wed.–Sun. 10–4:45, 1st Wed. of month 10–8:45.*

❺ **California Academy of Sciences.** One of the country's top five natural-history museums, the Academy houses an aquarium and a planetarium, plus numerous exhibits. **The Steinhart Aquarium,** with its 100,000-gallon Fish Roundabout, is home to 14,000 creatures, including a living coral reef with colorful fish, tropical sharks, and a rainbow of hard and soft corals. The "Touching Tide Pool" allows kids to cozy up to starfish, hermit crabs, and other sea creatures. Other exhibits include a floor that simulates various-level earthquakes; life-size elephant-seal models; and the **African Hall,** depicting animals (real but stuffed) specific to Africa in their native vegetation.

There is an additional charge (up to $2.50) for **Morrison Planetarium** shows (☎ 415/750–7141 for daily schedule). Laserium presents evening laser-light shows (☎ 415/750–7138 for schedule and fees) at Morrison Planetarium, accompanied by rock, classical, and other types of music; educational shows outline laser technology. Around the east corner of the building is the **Shakespeare Garden,** with 200 flowers mentioned by the Bard, as well as bronze-engraved panels with floral quotations. ⊠ *Music Concourse Dr., off South Dr., across from Asian Art and de Young museums,* ☎ *415/750–7145.* ⊡ *$7; $1 discount with Muni transfer; free 1st Wed. of month.* ⊙ *Memorial Day–Labor Day, daily 9–6; Labor Day–Memorial Day, daily 10–5.*

❶ **Conservatory.** The oldest building in the park (built in 1876) and the last remaining wood-frame Victorian conservatory in the country, the Conservatory is a copy of London's famous Kew Gardens. The building was severely damaged in a storm in late 1995; as of early 1996 it was unclear whether the Conservatory could be repaired, even at an exorbitant cost. ⊠ *Conservatory Dr., near Fulton St.*

❽ Dutch Windmill. At the very western end of the park is a restored 1902 windmill with wood-shingled arms and upper section and heavy cement bottom. The windmill overlooks the curvy, photogenic Queen Wilhelmina Tulip Garden, which blooms in early spring and late summer. ⊠ *Between 47th Ave. and the Great Hwy.*

❹ Japanese Tea Garden. This serene 4-acre landscape of small ponds, streams, waterfalls, stone bridges, Japanese sculptures, bonsai trees, miniature pagodas, and some nearly vertical wooden "humpback" bridges was created for the 1894 Mid-Winter Exposition. It's next to the Asian Art Museum. The Tea House is a popular spot for relaxing. Go in the spring if you can, when the cherry blossoms bloom. ⊠ *Tea Garden Dr., off John F. Kennedy Dr.,* ☎ *415/752–4227.* ☞ *$2.50.* ☉ *Daily 8:30–6:30 (closes earlier in winter).*

❷ M. H. de Young Memorial Museum. The de Young contains the best collection of American art on the West Coast, including paintings, sculpture, textiles, and decorative arts from colonial times through the 20th century. The John D. Rockefeller III Collection of American Paintings is especially noteworthy, with more than 200 paintings of American masters such as Copley, Eakins, Bingham, and Sargent. The de Young also has dramatic collections of African, Native American, and Meso-American art, including sculpture, baskets, textiles, and ceramics. The Cafe de Young has outdoor seating in the Oakes Garden. ⊠ *Tea Garden Dr., off John F. Kennedy Dr., near 10th Ave. and Fulton St.,* ☎ *415/863–3330 for 24-hr information.* ☞ *$6 for de Young and Asian museums (additional $1 grants same-day admission to Legion of Honor Museum in Lincoln Park); free 1st Wed. of month. (until 5).* ☉ *Wed.–Sun. 10–4:45 (1st Wed. of month until 8:45).*

❼ Stow Lake. This small, serene body of water surrounds Strawberry Hill; a couple of bridges allow you to cross over and ascend the hill. (The old 19th-century stone bridge on the southwest side of the lake is especially quaint.) A waterfall cascades down from the top of the hill, and panoramic views make it worth the short hike up here. Down below, rent a boat or bicycle (☎ 415/752–0347) or stroll around the perimeter. ⊠ *Just east of Cross Over Dr.*

❻ Strybing Arboretum & Botanical Gardens. The 70-acre arboretum specializes in plants from areas with climates similar to that of the Bay Area, such as the west coast of Australia, South Africa, and the Mediterranean; more than 8,000 plants and tree varieties bloom in gardens throughout the grounds. Group walks or children's walks can be arranged (☎ 415/661–3584), and Strybing regularly hosts classes, lectures, and plant sales. ⊠ *9th Ave., at Lincoln Way,* ☎ *415/661–1316.* ☞ *Free.* ☉ *Weekdays 8–4:30, weekends and holidays 10–5. Tours leave the bookstore weekdays at 1:30, weekends at 10:30 and 1:30.*

OFF THE BEATEN PATH   **THE HAIGHT –** East of Golden Gate Park is the neighborhood known as "the Haight." Despite the presence of a Gap store (on the legendary Haight-Ashbury corner, no less) and a growing number of upscale galleries and shops, this is still home to anarchist book collectives and shops selling incense and tie-dye T-shirts. Even a few "smoke shops" remain from the area's 1960s flower-power heyday. The Haight's famous political spirit—it was the first neighborhood in the United States to lead a freeway revolt, and it continues to host regular (sometimes successful) boycotts against chain stores—exists alongside some of the finest Victorian-lined streets in the city; more than 1,000 such houses occupy Golden Gate Park's "Panhandle" and the streets of Ashbury Heights. Haight Street itself is known for its vintage merchandise, including clothes, records, books, and a host of miscellany such as crystals, jewelry, and candles. At 710 Ashbury Street, just past Waller Street, was the '60s crash pad of Jerry Garcia and his Grateful Dead bandmates. ✉ *710 Ashbury St., just past Waller.*

Lincoln Park and the Western Shoreline

From Land's End in Lincoln Park are some of the best views of the Golden Gate (the name was originally given to the opening of San Francisco Bay long before the bridge was built) and the Marin Headlands. Ocean Beach and the Great Highway run along the western edge of the city from just below the historic Cliff House south to the sprawling San Francisco Zoo. The wind is often strong along the shoreline; summer fog can blanket the ocean beaches; and the water is cold and usually too rough for swimming.

A Good Drive

A car is very useful for exploring this stretch. There are plenty of hiking trails, and buses service most of the sights, but the distances between some are fairly great. Start at **Lincoln Park,** at 34th Avenue (the extension into the park is sometimes called Legion of Honor Drive) and Clement Street; those without a car can take the 38-Geary bus to get here. Within Lincoln Park is the **California Palace of the Legion of Honor.** From the museum, head back out on Legion of Honor Drive to Geary Boulevard and follow it west until it forks to the right (past 39th Avenue) and becomes Point Lobos Avenue. Just past 48th Avenue is parking for the **Cliff House.** (If you're coming by bus, go down to Geary and take the 38-Geary Limited to 48th Avenue and Point Lobos). Three-mile-long **Ocean Beach** begins just south of the Cliff House, flanked by the Great Highway. A couple of miles down, at the intersection of the Great Highway and Sloat Boulevard (turn left onto Sloat) is the **San Francisco Zoo,** which houses 1,000 species of birds and animals. If you're coming to the zoo from downtown, you can take the L-Taraval Muni streetcar directly.

TIMING

Given the distances between sights, you'll need at least three and a half hours here—more if you don't have a car. An hour can easily be spent in the Palace of the Legion of Honor, and an hour and a half at the zoo. Many linger at the Cliff House and Ocean Beach, soaking up the views.

Sights to See

★ **California Palace of the Legion of Honor.** The building itself—a ¾-scale adaptation of the 18th-century French original—is architecturally interesting and spectacularly situated on cliffs overlooking the ocean, the Golden Gate Bridge, and the Marin Headlands. The museum recently reopened after extensive renovations; a pyramidal glass skylight in the entrance court illuminates the new galleries on the expanded lower level. The 20-plus galleries on the upper level are devoted to the permanent collection of European art (paintings, sculpture, decorative arts, tapestries) from the 14th through the 20th centuries. The Rodin collection is noteworthy. (An original cast of Rodin's *The Thinker* welcomes you as you walk through the courtyard.) The lower level showcases prints and drawings, English and European porcelain, and ancient Assyrian, Greek, Roman, and Egyptian art; it also contains galleries for special exhibitions.

The Legion Café, on the lower level, has a garden terrace and a view of the Golden Gate Bridge. North of the museum (across El Camino del Mar) is George Segal's *The Holocaust* a sobering monument whose white-plaster figures lie sprawled and twisted on the ground, while one lone figure peers out from behind barbed wire. ⊠ *End of 34th Ave., off Clement St.,* ☎ *415/863–3330 for 24-hr information.* ▨ *$7 (allows same-day admission to de Young Museum in Golden Gate Park); free 2nd Wed. of month.* ☉ *Tues.–Sun. 10–5 (until 8:45 1st Sat. of month).*

The Cliff House. This San Francisco landmark has had three incarnations. The original, built in 1863, hosted several U.S. Presidents and wealthy locals who would drive their carriages out to Ocean Beach; it was destroyed by fire on Christmas day, 1894. The second and most beloved Cliff House was built in 1896; it rose eight stories with an observation tower 200 feet above sea level. It also succumbed to fire a year after surviving the 1906 quake. The present building, erected in 1909, has restaurants, a pub, and a gift shop. The dining areas overlook Seal Rock (the barking marine mammals sunning themselves are actually sea lions).

Just below the Cliff House is the Musée Mécanique (☎ 415/386–1170), a time-warped arcade with a collection of antique mechanical contrivances, including peep shows and nickelodeons. Also below the Cliff House is Golden Gate National Recreation Area Visitors' Center (☎ 415/556–8642), which contains historic photographs of the Cliff House and the glass-roofed Sutro Baths. The Sutro complex, which included six enormous baths, 500 dressing rooms, and several restaurants, covered 3 acres north of the Cliff House. The baths were closed in 1952 and burned in 1966. You can explore the ruins on your own or take ranger-led walks on weekends. ⊠ *1090 Point Lobos Ave.,* ☎ *415/386–3330.* ☉ *Weekdays 8 AM–10:30 PM, weekends 8 AM–11 PM; cocktails served nightly until 2 AM.*

Lincoln Park. At one time all the city's cemeteries were here, segregated by nationality. The cemeteries on this site have given way to an 18-hole golf course with large and well-formed Monterey cypresses lining the fairways. There are scenic walks throughout the 275-acre park, with postcard-perfect views from many spots, especially Land's End (the trail starts outside the Palace of the Legion of Honor, at the end of El Camino del Mar). The trails out to Land's End, however, are for skilled hikers only: Landslides are frequent, and danger lurks along the steep cliffs.

San Francisco Zoo. First established in 1889 in Golden Gate Park, the zoo now holds 1,000 species of birds and animals. Among the protected species here are the snow leopard, Sumatran tiger, jaguar, and Asian elephant. A favorite attraction is the greater one-horned rhino, next to the African elephants. Gorilla World is one of the largest and most natural gorilla habitats of any zoo in the world. The Primate Discovery Center houses 14 endangered species in atriumlike enclosures. The Feline Conservation Center, a larger, more naturalistic setting for rare cats, is designed to encourage breeding among endangered felines. Opening in spring 1997 is a 7-acre South American Gateway exhibit, which will re-create habitats replete with howler monkeys, tapirs, and a cloud forest. The children's zoo has a minipopulation of about 300 mammals, birds, and reptiles, plus an insect zoo, a baby-animal nursery, and a beautifully restored 1921 Dentzel Carousel. A ride astride one of the 52 hand-carved menagerie animals costs $1. ⊠ *Sloat Blvd. and the Great Hwy.,* ☎ *415/753–7083.* ▨ *$6.50; free 1st Wed. of month; children's zoo $1.* ☉ *Daily 10–5; children's zoo daily 11–4, Sat.–Sun. 10:30–4:30.*

DINING

By Jacqueline Killeen and Sharon Silva

San Francisco probably has more restaurants per capita than any other city in the United States, including New York. Practically every ethnic cuisine is represented. Since selecting recommended restaurants is a next-to-impossible task, we have chosen instead several restaurants to represent each popular style of dining in various price ranges, in most cases because of the superiority of the food, but in some instances because of the view or ambience.

Because we have covered those areas of town most frequented by visitors, this meant leaving out some great places in outlying districts such as the Mission, the Haight, Sunset, and Richmond. The outlying restaurants that are recommended were chosen because they offer a type of experience not available elsewhere. All listed restaurants serve dinner and are open for lunch unless otherwise specified; restaurants are not open for breakfast unless the morning meal is specifically mentioned. Parking accommodations are mentioned only when a restaurant has made special arrangements; otherwise you're on your own. There is usually a charge for valet parking and validated parking is not necessarily free and unlimited.

CATEGORY	COST*
$$$$	over $50
$$$	$30–$50
$$	$20–$30
$	under $20

per person for a three-course meal, excluding drinks, service, and 8½% sales tax

American

Castro

$$ ✕ **2223.** Dishes at John Cunin's hot spot (also known as the No-Name) include thin-crust pizza topped with pancetta and Teleme cheese, earthy portobello mushroom soup, chicken with garlic-mashed potatoes, and warm spinach salad with fingerling potatoes and apple-smoked bacon. For Sunday brunch, there might be banana soufflé pancakes or eggs Benedict built on a tasty herb scone. ✉ *2223 Market St.,* ☎ *415/431–0692. MC, V. No lunch Sat.*

Civic Center

$$$ ✕ **Stars.** Jeremiah Tower's dining room has a clublike ambience, and
★ the food ranges from grills to ragouts to sautés—some daringly creative and some classical. Dinners here are pricey, but those on a budget can order a hot dog at the bar. ✉ *150 Redwood Alley,* ☎ *415/861–7827. Reservations essential. AE, DC, MC, V. No lunch weekends. Valet parking at night.*

$$ ✕ **Carta.** There's a different menu from a different country or region every month, inspired by the travels of Carta's talented chefs to eclectic destinations—from Oaxaca, Turkey, and Russia to Provence, Morocco, and Greece. There are usually about 10 small plates, three main courses, and perhaps three desserts. ✉ *1772 Market St.,* ☎ *415/863–3516. AE, MC, V. Closed Mon. No lunch weekends.*

$$ ✕ **Stars Cafe.** At the Stars satellite, around the corner from the main restaurant, you can taste Jeremiah Tower's renowned cuisine at down-to-earth prices. Trademark items are pizzas from the wood-burning oven and luscious desserts. ✉ *500 Van Ness Ave.,* ☎ *415/861–4344. AE, DC, MC, V.*

Cow Hollow/Marina

$ ✕ **World Wrapps.** This hip place serves what are essentially global burritos: fillings range from Peking duck to Thai chicken, from roasted vegetables to couscous and cucumber. A wide selection of healthful smoothies—papaya, blackberry, and the like—matches up surprisingly well with the hearty wrapps. ⊠ *2257 Chestnut St.,* ☎ *415/563–9727. No credit cards.*

Embarcadero North

$$ ✕ **Fog City Diner.** The long, narrow dining room of Fog City emulates a luxurious railroad car. The menu is innovative, drawing its inspiration from regional cooking throughout the United States. ⊠ *1300 Battery St.,* ☎ *415/982–2000. D, DC, MC, V.*

$$ ✕ **MacArthur Park.** Year after year San Franciscans acclaim this as their favorite spot for ribs, but the oak-wood smoker and mesquite grill also turn out other all-American fare, from steaks and hamburgers to seafood. ⊠ *607 Front St.,* ☎ *415/398–5700. AE, DC, MC, V. No lunch weekends and most major holidays. Valet parking at night.*

Embarcadero South

$$–$$$ ✕ **Boulevard.** Nationally acclaimed chef Nancy Oakes's menu is seasonally in flux, but you will always find her signature juxtaposition of aristocratic fare—foie gras is a favorite—with homey comfort foods like pot roast and vanilla-cured pork loin. The weekday afternoon bar service is less formal and expensive than regular dining. ⊠ *1 Mission St.,* ☎ *415/543–6084. Reservations essential. AE, D, DC, MC, V. Closed major holidays. No lunch weekends. Valet parking.*

$$–$$$ ✕ **One Market.** The two-tiered, bustling brasserie of Bradley Ogden and Michael Dellar seats 170, and a large bar-café serves snacks from noon on. Ogden has a knack for integrating American and Italian cuisine—risotto and pasta might share the spotlight with Yankee pot roast and garlic mashed potatoes. ⊠ *1 Market St.,* ☎ *415/777–5577. Reservations essential for lunch. AE, DC, MC, V. No lunch Sat. Valet parking.*

Financial District

$$$ ✕ **Rubicon.** Sophisticated renditions of seafood and poultry and other fare are served on two floors to Hollywood big shots—the restaurant's investors list includes Robin Williams, Robert de Niro, and Francis Ford Coppola—and common folk, too. ⊠ *558 Sacramento St.,* ☎ *415/434–4100. AE, MC, V. Closed Sun. No lunch Sat. Valet parking at night.*

Nob Hill

$$–$$$ ✕ **Ritz-Carlton Restaurant and Dining Room.** The Ritz's Restaurant, a
★ cheerful, informal spot with a large garden patio for outdoor dining, serves breakfast, lunch, dinner, and a Sunday jazz brunch. The Dining Room, formal and elegant with a harpist playing, serves only two- to five-course dinners priced by the course, not by the item. Both rooms present a superb version of northern California cooking, based on local ingredients with Mediterranean and Asian overtones. ⊠ *600 Stockton St.,* ☎ *415/296–7465. AE, D, DC, MC, V. Dining Room closed Sun. Valet parking.*

South of Market

$$$ ✕ **Hawthorne Lane.** The large, high-ceiling bar at this popular SoMa
★ eatery serves irresistible small plates—Thai-style squid, tempura-battered green beans with mustard sauce, stylish pizzas. Patrons in the light-flooded dining room engage in more serious eating, from foie gras to grilled quail. ⊠ *22 Hawthorne St.,* ☎ *415/777–9779. Reservations essential for dining room. MC, V. No lunch weekends. Valet parking.*

Union Square

$$$–$$$$ **✕ Postrio.** Superchef Wolfgang Puck periodically commutes from Los
★ Angeles to make an appearance in his restaurant's open kitchen. A stun-
ning three-level bar and dining area is highlighted by palm trees and
museum-quality contemporary paintings. Attire is formal; food is
Puckish Californian with Mediterranean and Asian overtones, em-
phasizing pastas, grilled seafood, and house-baked breads. Substan-
tial breakfast and bar menus (with great pizza) can be found here as
well. ⊠ 545 Post St., ☎ 415/776–7825. Reservations essential. AE,
D, DC, MC, V. Valet parking.

$$$ **✕ Campton Place.** Chef Todd Humphries embellishes traditional Amer-
★ ican dishes with ethnic flavors from recent immigrations: You might
find cilantro and Szechuan peppers, for example, in his Nantucket Bay
scallops. Among Humphries's most popular contemporary American
dishes are such homespun fare as beef short ribs with potato puree,
and a hearty chicken pot pie. Breakfast and brunch are major events.
A bar menu offers samplings of appetizers, plus a caviar extravaganza.
⊠ 340 Stockton St., ☎ 415/955–5555. Reservations essential on
weekends. Jacket required. AE, D, DC, MC, V. Valet parking.

$$ **✕ Rumpus.** With Caesar salad, burgers, club sandwiches, and New York
steak at lunchtime, this casual bistro has a true American menu. But
there is also an utterly British bubble and squeak (cabbage and pota-
toes)—a taste of home for both of the partners and the head chef—
and a handful of pasta and risotto selections to keep Italophiles happy.
⊠ 1 Tillman Pl., ☎ 415/421–2300. AE, MC, V. Valet parking at night.

Chinese

Chinatown

$–$$ **✕ R&G Lounge.** Downstairs (entrance on Kearny Street) is a usually
packed, no-tablecloth dining room; the classier upstairs space (en-
trance on Commercial Street) serves exceptional Cantonese banquet
fare. A menu with photographs helps diners decide among the many
exotic dishes, from dried scallops with seasonal vegetables to steamed
bean curd with shrimp meat. ⊠ 631B Kearny St., ☎ 415/982–7877
or 415/982–3811. AE, DC, MC, V.

Embarcadero North

$$ **✕ Harbor Village.** Classic Cantonese cooking, dim-sum lunches, and
★ fresh seafood from the restaurant's own tanks are the hallmarks of this
400-seat branch of a Hong Kong establishment. The setting is opulent,
with Chinese antiques and teak furnishings. ⊠ 4 Embarcadero Cen-
ter, ☎ 415/781–8833. AE, DC, MC, V. Validated parking in Embar-
cadero Center Garage.

Embarcadero South

$$ **✕ Wu Kong.** Shanghai and Cantonese specialties at Wu Kong include
dim sum, braised yellow fish, and the incredible vegetarian goose—one
of Shanghai's famous mock dishes, created from paper-thin layers of
dried bean-curd sheets and mushrooms. ⊠ 101 Spear St., ☎ 415/957–
9300. AE, DC, MC, V. Validated parking at Rincon Center garage.

Financial District

$ **✕ Yank Sing.** This slightly classy two-level teahouse serves 70 varieties
of dim sum on a rotating basis. Alongside traditional offerings such
as pork buns, sticky rice and chicken wrapped inside lotus leaves, and
mini egg-custard pies are more inventive morsels employing basil and
other ingredients one doesn't readily associate with Cantonese cuisine.
⊠ 427 Battery St., ☎ 415/362–1640. AE, DC, MC, V. No dinner.

114

Downtown San Francisco Dining

Richmond District

$$ ✕ **Hong Kong Flower Lounge.** This outpost of a famous Asian restaurant is known in particular for its seafood—crabs, shrimp, catfish, lobsters, scallops—which is plucked straight from tanks and prepared in a variety of ways, from classic to contemporary. Good dim sum is offered at midday. ⊠ *5322 Geary Blvd.,* ☏ *415/668–8998. AE, D, DC, MC, V.*

$–$$ ✕ **Ton Kiang.** Regional Hakka specialties are served here, including salt-baked chicken, braised stuffed bean curd, and casseroles of meat and seafood cooked in clay pots, along with salt-and-pepper squid or shrimp, braised catfish, and stir-fried crab. Of the two branches on Geary Boulevard, the one at 5821 is more stylish, and serves excellent dim sum. ⊠ *3148 Geary Blvd.,* ☏ *415/752–4440;* ⊠ *5821 Geary Blvd.,* ☏ *415/387–8273. MC, V.*

French

Civic Center

$$–$$$ ✕ **California Culinary Academy.** Patrons watch the student chefs at work on a double-tier stage while dining on classic French cooking offered as a prix-fixe meal or a bountiful buffet. On the lower level is an informal, à la carte grill. ⊠ *625 Polk St.,* ☏ *415/771–3500. Reservations essential for Fri.-night buffet. AE, DC, MC, V. Closed weekends; hrs vary slightly with school programs.*

Embarcadero North

$$ ✕ **Pastis.** At lunchtime, the sunny cement bar and sleek wooden banquettes of chef-owner Gerald Hirigoyen's restaurant are crowded with workers from surrounding offices; they come to fuel up on steamed salmon with celery root, or vegetarian sandwiches layered with eggplant and asparagus. The evening menu may include seared scallops, duck confit, or chicken with dates. ⊠ *1015 Battery St.,* ☏ *415/391–2555. Reservations essential. No lunch weekends. AE, MC, V.*

Financial District

$$ ✕ **Le Central.** This is the quintessential bistro: noisy and crowded, with nothing subtle about the cooking. But the garlicky pâtés, leeks vinaigrette, steak with Roquefort sauce, cassoulet, and grilled blood sausage with crisp french fries keep the crowds coming. ⊠ *453 Bush St.,* ☏ *415/391–2233. AE, DC, MC, V. Closed Sun.*

$ ✕ **Café Claude.** With a zinc bar, old-fashioned banquettes, and cinema posters, this is one of the most atmospheric French cafés downtown. Order a croque monsieur, salade niçoise, or simple daube, and you'll soon be whistling the Marseillaise. ⊠ *7 Claude La.,* ☏ *415/392–3505. AE, DC, MC, V. Closed Sun.*

Japantown

$$$ ✕ **Yoyo Tsunami Bistro.** "Tsunami" here refers not to a wave but to the small plates, or tapas, the kitchen cleverly devises. Each night brings 20 choices on a rotating menu of 60 possibilities, and all blend French technique with Japanese ingredients. ⊠ *1611 Post St.,* ☏ *415/922–7788. AE, DC, MC, V. Valet parking.*

Lower Pacific Heights

$$$ ✕ **The Heights.** Customers work their way through a six-course tasting menu or choose from an à la carte one that changes regularly. A fricassee of wild mushrooms with sweetbreads and a vegetable pot-au-feu are tasty appetizers; lavender-scented roast duck atop braised pears and steelhead trout with lobster sauce may follow. The homemade ice creams and puff-pastry creations are sublime. ⊠ *3235 Sacramento St.,*

☎ *415/474–8890. AE, D, DC, MC, V. Closed Mon. No lunch. Valet parking.*

Midtown

$$$ ✕ **La Folie.** This pretty storefront café showcases the nouvelle cuisine of
★ Roland Passot. Much of the food is edible art—whimsical presentations
in the form of savory terrines, *galettes* (flat, round cakes), and napoleons—
or elegant accompaniments such as bone-marrow flan. ⊠ *2316 Polk St.,*
☎ *415/776–5577. AE, D, DC, MC, V. Closed Sun. No lunch.*

North Beach

$ ✕ **Des Alpes.** Basque dinners at rock-bottom prices are the big draw
here: Soup, salad, *two* entrées—sweetbreads on puff pastry and rare
roast beef are a typical pair—ice cream, and coffee are all included in
the budget price. Service is family-style. ⊠ *732 Broadway,* ☎ *415/788–
9900. D, DC, MC, V. Closed Mon. No lunch.*

Northern Waterfront

$$$ ✕ **Chez Michel.** The spare design of booths and blond wood is a fine
setting for gravlax with ginger vinaigrette, filet mignon with marrow
sauce, or duck breast with fresh figs. The menu changes seasonally, and
the dessert selections are consistently irresistible. ⊠ *804 Northpoint,*
☎ *415/775–7036. MC, V. Closed Mon. No lunch. Valet parking.*

Richmond District

$$–$$$ ✕ **Alain Rondelli.** Chef Rondelli adapts his background in classic-yet-
★ contemporary French cooking to the agricultural abundance and Asian-
Hispanic influences of California: a zap of jalapeño chili here, a bit of
star anise there. Two-part entrées are a Rondelli signature: a breast of
chicken followed with a confit of the leg in a custard tart, for example. ⊠ *126 Clement St.,* ☎ *415/387–0408. MC, V. Closed Mon.–Tues.*

South of Market

$$$ ✕ **Bistro M.** Michel Richard serves distinctive French cuisine—softened
with a strong California hand—for breakfast, lunch and dinner. At din-
ner, the Alsatian onion tart is a superb first course, followed by veal
shanks with garlic mashed potatoes or a perfectly cooked salmon fil-
let. Be sure to leave room for chef Richard's signature crunchy napoleon.
⊠ *Hotel Milano, 55 5th St.,* ☎ *415/543–5554. AE, D, DC, MC, V.
Valet parking.*

$$ ✕ **Fringale.** The bright-yellow paint on this dazzling bistro stands out
★ like a beacon on an otherwise bleak industrial street. Biarritz-born chef
Gerald Hirigoyen serves French Basque–inspired creations; his incredible crème brûlée is a hallmark. ⊠ *570 4th St.,* ☎ *415/543–0573.
Reservations essential. AE, MC, V. Closed Sun. No lunch Sat.*

Union Square

$$$$ ✕ **Fleur de Lys.** The menu changes constantly at this award-winning
restaurant; lobster soup with lemongrass, Maryland crab cakes, and
pork tenderloin with black beans bear witness to chef-partner Hubert
Keller's international scope. The intimate dining room, like a sheikh's
tent, is encased with hundreds of yards of paisley. ⊠ *777 Sutter St.,*
☎ *415/673–7779. Reservations essential. Jacket required. AE, DC,
MC, V. Closed Sun., most major holidays. No lunch. Valet parking.*

$$$$ ✕ **Masa's.** Presentation is as important as the food itself in this pretty,
★ flower-filled dining spot in the Vintage Court Hotel. Chef Julian Serrano
carries on the tradition of the late Masa Kobayashi. ⊠ *648 Bush St.,* ☎
*415/989–7154. Reservations essential. Jacket and tie. AE, D, DC, MC,
V. Closed Sun.–Mon. and 1st 2 wks of Jan. No lunch. Valet parking.*

German

Civic Center

$–$$ ✕ **Suppenkuche.** Bratwurst and braised red cabbage accompany a long list of German beers at this lively, hip outpost of German cuisine. The food—homemade soups, sauerbraten, smoked pork chops, schnitzel—is simple, tasty, and easy on the pocketbook. There's also a good Sunday brunch. ✉ *601 Hayes St.,* ☎ *415/252–9289. AE, MC, V. Closed Mon.*

Greek and Middle Eastern

Financial District

$$ ✕ **Faz.** Creamy *baba ghannooj* (eggplant spread), beef-and-rice-filled dolmas, and a Persian-inspired platter of feta cheese, pungent olives, and garden-fresh herbs are all great choices here. The signature house-smoked fish platter includes salmon, trout, and sometimes sturgeon. ✉ *161 Sutter St.,* ☎ *415/362–0404. AE, DC, MC, V. Valet parking at night. Closed Sun. No lunch Sat.*

North Beach

$$ ✕ **Maykadeh.** Lamb dishes with rice are the specialties in this authentic Persian restaurant, whose setting is so elegant that the modest check comes as a great surprise. ✉ *470 Green St.,* ☎ *415/362–8286. MC, V. Valet parking at night.*

$ ✕ **Helmand.** Authentic Afghani cooking, elegant surroundings with white napery and rich Afghan carpets, and amazingly low prices make Helmand worth a visit. Don't miss the *aushak* (leek-filled ravioli served with yogurt and ground beef). The lamb dishes are also exceptional. ✉ *430 Broadway,* ☎ *415/362–0641. AE, MC, V. No lunch weekends. Free validated parking at night at Helmand Parking, 468 Broadway.*

Indian

Northern Waterfront and Embarcadero

$$ ✕ **Gaylord's.** Mildly spiced northern Indian food is served here, along with meats and breads from the tandoori ovens and vegetarian dishes. The dining rooms are elegantly appointed, complete with Indian paintings and gleaming silver service. The Ghirardelli Square location has bay views. ✉ *Ghirardelli Sq.,* ☎ *415/771–8822;* ✉ *Embarcadero 1,* ☎ *415/397–7775. AE, D, DC, MC, V. No lunch Sun. at Embarcadero. Validated parking at Ghirardelli Sq. garage and Embarcadero Center garage.*

Italian

Civic Center

$$$ ✕ **Vivande Ristorante.** Owner-chef Carlo Middione's spacious restaurant features the rustic fare of southern Italy, from focaccia with grilled radicchio and fennel to pasta tossed with a tangle of mushrooms to grilled lamb chops. A late-supper menu attracts the Performing Arts Center crowd. ✉ *670 Golden Gate Ave.,* ☎ *415/673–9245. AE, DC, MC, V. Valet parking.*

Cow Hollow/Marina

$$ ✕ **Café Adriano.** House-made *strongozzi* (thick spaghetti) with a spicy
★ Umbrian tomato sauce, or *stracci* (pasta squares) with scallops are among the specialties at this neighborhood favorite. Roast leg of lamb with eggplant puree and simply cooked sea bass are main-course staples. ✉ *3347 Fillmore St.,* ☎ *415/474–4180. MC, V. Closed Mon. No lunch.*

$$ ✕ **Pane e Vino.** The Italian-born owner-chef here concentrates on spe-
★ cialties from Tuscany and the north. Roasted whole sea bass, creamy risotto, and pastas tossed with sprightly tomato sauces are among the

dishes regulars can't resist. ✉ *3011 Steiner St.,* ☎ *415/346–2111. MC, V. No lunch Sun.*

Embarcadero North

$$ ✕ **Il Fornaio.** This handsome tile-floored, wood-paneled complex combines a café, bakery, and upscale trattoria with outdoor seating. The Tuscan cooking features pizzas from a wood-burning oven, superb pastas and gnocchi, and grilled poultry and seafood. ✉ *Levi's Plaza, 1265 Battery St.,* ☎ *415/986–0100. AE, DC, MC, V. Valet parking.*

Financial District

$$ ✕ **Palio d'Asti.** Piedmontese specialties are showcased here; nearby Paninoteca Palio d'Asti (✉ 505 Montgomery)` prepares stylish take-out or eat-in lunchtime panini (sandwiches), served on housemade bread with fillings that range from grilled chicken to prosciutto to smoked salmon. ✉ *640 Sacramento St.,* ☎ *415/395–9800. AE, DC, MC, V. Closed Sun., some major holidays. No lunch Sat.*

Lower Pacific Heights

$$ ✕ **Oritalia.** The name says it all—the Orient and Italy. Chef Bruce Hill's fusion cuisine is delightful, with delicate gnocchi topped with tobiko caviar and rock shrimp, Korean beef studded with sesame seeds, and crispy shrimp and pork dumplings with cilantro-mint sauce among the offerings. ✉ *1915 Fillmore St.,* ☎ *415/346–1333. AE, DC, MC, V. Closed Mon. No lunch.*

North Beach

$$ ✕ **Rose Pistola.** The food at chef-owner Reed Hearon's eatery celebrates the neighborhood's cultural roots: pizzas from a wood-burning oven, pastas with traditional sauces, grilled fish and meats, hazelnut torte and creamy gelato. A large and inviting bar area opens onto the sidewalk. ✉ *532 Columbus Ave.,* ☎ *415/399–0499. Reservations essential. AE, DC, MC, V.*

$ ✕ **L'Osteria del Forno.** The northern Italian proprietors of this unpretentious restaurant prepare small plates of simply cooked vegetables, a few robust pastas, a roast of the day, creamy polenta, and wonderful thin-crust pizzas. ✉ *519 Columbus Ave.,* ☎ *415/982–1124. Reservations not accepted. No credit cards. Closed Tues.*

Russian Hill

$$ ✕ **Hyde Street Bistro.** The ambience says quintessential neighborhood bistro, but the food is part tavern, part trattoria, and closely in line with the Austro-Italian tradition of Italy's northeastern Friuli region. Strudels and spaetzles are served alongside pastas and polentas, potato dumplings are paired with Gorgonzola sauce, and the pastries belie the chef-owner's Austrian roots. ✉ *1521 Hyde St.,* ☎ *415/441–7778. AE, MC, V. Closed 3 days at Christmas. No lunch. Valet parking.*

Union Square

$$ ✕ **Kuleto's.** The contemporary cooking of northern Italy, the atmosphere of old San Francisco, and a terrific bar menu showcasing contemporary and traditional antipasti have made this spot off Union Square a hit. Grilled seafood dishes are among the specialties. Breakfast is also served. ✉ *221 Powell St.,* ☎ *415/397–7720. AE, D, DC, MC, V.*

Japanese

Financial District

$$–$$$ ✕ **Kyo-ya.** The range of this authentic Japanese restaurant is spectac-
★ ular, encompassing tempuras, one-pot dishes, deep-fried and grilled meats, and a choice of some three-dozen sushi selections. The lunch menu is more limited than dinner, but does include a sampler of four

classic dishes encased in a handsome lacquered box. ⊠ *Sheraton Palace Hotel, 2 New Montgomery St., at Market St.,* ☎ *415/546–5000. AE, MC, V. Closed Sun. No lunch Sat.*

Japantown

$ ✕ **Mifune.** Thin, brown *soba* (buckwheat) and thick, white *udon* (wheat) are the specialties at this North American outpost of an Osaka-based noodle empire. Seating is at wooden tables, where diners can be heard slurping down big bowls of such traditional Japanese combinations as fish cake–crowned udon and *tenzaru* (cold noodles and hot tempura served on lacquered trays with gingery dipping sauce). ⊠ *Japan Center, Kintetsu Building, 1737 Post St.,* ☎ *415/922–0337. Reservations not accepted. AE, D, DC, MC, V.*

$ ✕ **Sanppo.** This small place has an enormous selection of almost every type of Japanese food: yakis, nabemono dishes, donburi, udon, and soba, not to mention feather-light tempura, interesting side dishes, and sushi. ⊠ *1702 Post St.,* ☎ *415/346–3486. Reservations not accepted. MC, V. Closed Mon. No lunch Sun. Validated parking in Japan Center garage.*

Richmond District

$$ ✕ **Kabuto Sushi.** Behind a black-lacquered counter, master chef Sachio Kojima flashes his knives with the grace of a samurai warrior. In addition to exceptional sushi and sashimi, traditional Japanese dinners are served. ⊠ *5116 Geary Blvd.,* ☎ *415/752–5652. MC, V. Closed Mon. No lunch.*

Mediterranean

Civic Center

$$–$$$ ✕ **Zuni Café & Grill.** A spacious, window-filled balcony dining area over-
★   looks Zuni's large bar, where shellfish, one of the best oyster selections in town, and drinks are dispensed. A second dining room houses the giant pizza oven and grill. Even the hamburgers have an Italian accent—they're topped with Gorgonzola and served on herbed focaccia buns. ⊠ *1658 Market St.,* ☎ *415/552–2522. Reservations essential. AE, MC, V. Closed Mon., major holidays.*

Cow Hollow/Marina

$$–$$$ ✕ **PlumpJack Café.** The regularly changing menu at this clubby dining room spans the Mediterranean, with grilled figs and prosciutto and crispy duck confit among the possibilities. The racks that line the dining room hold some of the best-priced vintages in town. ⊠ *3201 Fillmore St.,* ☎ *415/346–9870. AE, MC, V. Closed Sun. No lunch Sat.*

Financial District

$$ ✕ **Vertigo.** The Transamerica Pyramid houses one of the city's most stunning restaurants, a three-tiered space with see-through ceilings, a parklike entrance, and inviting French and Italian cuisine with Asian accents. A seasonal menu combines the freshest possible ingredients—especially seafood—in creative combinations; a bar menu offers afternoon snacks. ⊠ *600 Montgomery St.,* ☎ *415/433–7250. AE, D, DC, MC, V. Valet parking. Closed Sun. No lunch Sat.*

North Beach

$$ ✕ **Moose's.** Local and national luminaries head for Moose's when they're
★   in town. A Mediterranean-inspired menu highlights innovative appetizers, pastas, seafood, and grills. The surroundings are classic and comfortable, with views of Washington Square and Russian Hill from a front café area and, in the rear, facing the open kitchen, counter seats for singles. There's live music at night and a fine Sunday brunch. ⊠

1652 Stockton St., ☎ *415/989–7800. Reservations essential on week-ends. AE, DC, MC, V. No lunch Mon. Valet parking.*

South of Market

$$ ✕ **LuLu.** Reed Hearon has brought a touch of the French-Italian Riv-
★ iera to a spacious San Francisco warehouse. Diners feast on a signa-
ture dish of sizzling mussels roasted in an iron skillet, plus pizzas and
pastas with inventive embellishments, and wood-roasted poultry, meats,
and shellfish; sharing dishes is the custom here. A café aside the restau-
rant serves food from morning until late at night. ✉ *816 Folsom St.,*
☎ *415/495–5775. Reservations essential. AE, DC, MC, V.*

Mexican/Latin American/Spanish

Cow Hollow/Marina

$$ ✕ **Café Marimba.** The regional specialties at chef Reed Hearon's colorful bistro include silken *mole negro* (sauce of chilies and chocolate)
from Oaxaca, served in tamales and other dishes; shrimp prepared with
roasted onions and tomatoes in the style of Zihuatanejo; and chicken
with a marinade from Yucatán, stuffed into one of the world's greatest tacos. ✉ *2317 Chestnut St.,* ☎ *415/776–1506. MC, V. No lunch
Mon. Valet parking.*

Russian Hill

$$ ✕ **Zarzuela.** This small, crowded storefront serves nearly 40 different
hot and cold tapas, plus a dozen main courses. There is a tapa to suit
every palate, from poached octopus atop new potatoes and hot, gar-
lic-flecked shrimp to slabs of Manchego cheese with paper-thin slices
of serrano ham. The paella of saffron-scented rice weighed down with
prawns, mussels, and clams is guaranteed to make the most unsenti-
mental Madrileño homesick. ✉ *2000 Hyde St.,* ☎ *415/346–0800. MC,
V. Closed Sun.*

South of Market

$ ✕ **Chevys.** This branch of a popular Mexican minichain is decked with
funky neon signs and "El Machino" turning out flour tortillas which
emphasize the freshest ingredients and sauces. Of note are the fajitas,
as well as the grilled quail and seafood. Another Chevys is in the Em-
barcadero Center. ✉ *4th and Howard Sts.,* ☎ *415/543–8060. AE, MC,
V. Validated parking at garage under building (enter from Minna St.).*

Russian

Richmond District

$–$$ ✕ **Katia's.** This bright Richmond District gem offers the food of Russia with considerable flair, at remarkably reasonable prices. The borscht,
a dollop of sour cream topping a mélange of beets, cabbage and other
vegetables, is sublime. ✉ *600 5th Ave.,* ☎ *415/668–9292. AE, DC,
MC, V. Closed Mon.*

Seafood

Civic Center

$$ ✕ **Hayes Street Grill.** Up to 15 different kinds of seafood are chalked
on the blackboard each night at this extremely popular restaurant. The
fish is simply grilled, accompanied by a choice of sauces ranging from
tartar to a spicy Szechuan peanut concoction. Appetizers are unusual,
and desserts are lavish. ✉ *320 Hayes St.,* ☎ *415/863–5545. Reserva-
tions essential. AE, D, DC, MC, V. Closed some holidays. No lunch
weekends.*

Financial District

$$$ ✕ **Aqua.** Chef-owner Michael Mina has a talent for creating contem-
★   porary versions of French, Italian, and American classics: Expect mus-
sel, crab, or lobster soufflés; lobster gnocchi with lobster sauce; and
ultra-rare *ahi* tuna paired with foie gras. Desserts are miniature mu-
seum pieces, and the wine list is superb. ⊠ *252 California St.,* ☏
*415/956–9662. Reservations essential. AE, DC, MC, V. Closed Sun.
No lunch Sat. Valet parking at night.*

Northern Waterfront

$$ ✕ **McCormick & Kuleto's.** This seafood emporium in Ghirardelli Square
has a fabulous view of the bay from every seat in the house, an old
San Francisco atmosphere, and dozens of varieties of fish and shell-
fish. The food has its ups and downs, but even on foggy days you can
count on the view. ⊠ *Ghirardelli Sq.,* ☏ *415/929–1730. AE, D, DC,
MC, V. Validated parking in Ghirardelli Sq. garage.*

Southeast Asian

Cow Hollow

$–$$ ✕ **Betelnut.** A pan-Asian menu and an adventurous drinks menu draw
a steady stream of diners. Not everything that comes from the kitchen
is wildly successful (but don't pass up a plate of the tasty stir-fried dried
anchovies, chilies, peanuts, garlic, and green onion), though with food
this intriguing it's hard to complain. ⊠ *2030 Union St.,* ☏ *415/929–
8855. MC, V.*

Richmond District

$–$$ ✕ **Le Soleil.** The food of Vietnam is the specialty of this pastel, light-
filled restaurant. Try the excellent raw-beef salad; crisp, flavorful
spring rolls; a simple stir-fry of chicken and aromatic fresh basil leaves;
or large prawns simmered in a clay pot. ⊠ *133 Clement St.,* ☏
415/668–4848. MC, V.

$–$$ ✕ **Straits Cafe.** This popular restaurant serves the unique fare of Sin-
gapore, a cuisine that combines the culinary traditions of China, India,
and the Malay archipelago. That exotic mix translates into complex
curries, rice cooked in coconut milk, sticks of fragrant *satay* (skewers
of chicken or beef), and seafood noodle soups. ⊠ *3300 Geary Blvd.,*
☏ *415/668–1783. AE, MC, V.*

South of Market

$ ✕ **Manora.** Crowds line up at both Manoras for the extensive selec-
tion of carefully prepared dishes. Good choices are the fish cakes and
curries. ⊠ *3226 Mission St.,* ☏ *415/550–0856;* ⊠ *1600 Folsom St.,*
☏ *415/861–6224. MC, V. Closed Mon. and no lunch at Mission St.;
no lunch weekends at Folsom St.*

Steak Houses

Marina

$$ ✕ **Izzy's Steak & Chop House.** Terrific steaks, chops, and seafood, plus
all the trimmings–such as cheesy scalloped potatoes and creamed
spinach—are served here. ⊠ *3345 Steiner St.,* ☏ *415/563–0487. AE,
DC, MC, V. No lunch. Validated parking at Lombard Garage.*

Midtown

$$$ ✕ **Harris'.** Ann Harris serves some of the best dry-aged steaks in town,
★   but don't overlook the grilled seafood or poultry. There is also an ex-
tensive bar menu and a first-rate pecan pie. ⊠ *2100 Van Ness Ave.,*
☏ *415/673–1888. AE, DC, MC, V. No lunch. Valet parking.*

Vegetarian

Civic Center

$$ ✕ **Millennium.** The kitchen here looks to the Mediterranean, with pastas, polenta, and grilled vegetables among its most successful dishes. For true believers, there is *seitan* (a whole-wheat meat substitute) steak in Marsala sauce, a chocolate mousse cake made from tofu, and organic wines and beers. A Continental breakfast is served weekdays, and brunch is served on Sunday. ⊠ *246 McAllister St.,* ☎ *415/487–9800. MC, V.*

Marina

$$ ✕ **Greens.** This beautiful restaurant with expansive bay views serves
★ an eclectic and creative spectrum of meatless cooking. The bread promises nirvana. Dinners are à la carte on weeknights, but only a five-course prix-fixe dinner is served on Saturday. ⊠ *Bldg. A, Fort Mason,* ☎ *415/771–6222. MC, V. No lunch Mon., no dinner Sun. Public parking at Fort Mason Center.*

LODGING

By Patrick
Hoctel

Few cities in the United States can rival San Francisco's variety in lodging. There are plush hotels ranked among the finest in the world, renovated older buildings with a European flair, bed-and-breakfasts in the city's Victorian "Painted Ladies," and popular chain hotels. One of the brightest spots in the lodging picture is the transformation of many handsome early 20th-century downtown high rises into small, distinctive hotels that offer personal service and European ambience. Another is the recent addition of ultradeluxe modern hotels such as the Miyako and the Mandarin Oriental, which specialize in attentive Asian-style hospitality. Reservations for all accommodations are advised, especially during the peak season, May through October.

The hotels listed below are on or close to public transportation lines. Some properties on Lombard Street and in the Civic Center area have free parking, but a car is more a hindrance than an asset in San Francisco. Average rates for double rooms downtown and at the wharf are in the $120 range. Adding to the expense are parking fees (up to $20 or more per day at some larger establishments) and the city's 12% hotel tax, which can significantly boost the cost of a lengthy stay. Check for special rates and packages when making reservations.

For those in search of true budget accommodations (under $50), try the Adelaide Inn (☞ Downtown/Union Square, *below*) or the YMCA Central Branch (⊠ 220 Golden Gate Ave., ☎ 415/885–0460).

An alternative to hotels and motels is staying in private homes and apartments, available through **American Family Inn/Bed & Breakfast San Francisco** (☎ 415/931–3083), **Bed & Breakfast International–San Francisco** (☎ 415/696–1690 or 800/872–4500), and **American Property Exchange** (☎ 415/863–8484 or 800/747–7784).

CATEGORY	COST*
$$$$	over $175
$$$	$120–$175
$$	$80–$120
$	under $80

All prices are for a standard double room, excluding 12% tax.

Downtown San Francisco Lodging

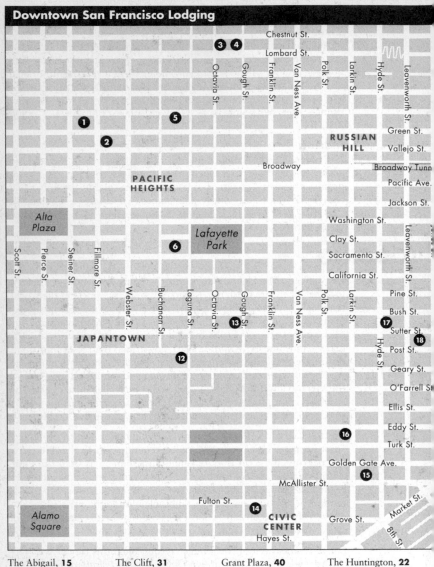

The Abigail, **15**
Adelaide Inn, **19**
Bed and Breakfast Inn, **5**
Campton Place, **38**
The Cartwright, **27**
Chancellor Hotel, **35**
Clarion Hotel, **47**

The Clift, **31**
Commodore International, **18**
Embassy Suites San Francisco Airport South Burlingame, **48**
Fairmont Hotel and Tower, **24**
Galleria Park, **45**

Grant Plaza, **40**
Harbor Court Hotel, **43**
Hotel Diva, **30**
Hotel Majestic, **13**
Hotel Monaco, **29**
Hotel Sofitel–San Francisco Bay, **49**
Hotel Triton, **37**

The Huntington, **22**
Hyatt-Fisherman's Wharf, **8**
Hyatt Regency, **42**
Inn at the Opera, **14**
Inn at Union Square, **34**
King George, **32**
La Quinta Motor Inn, **51**

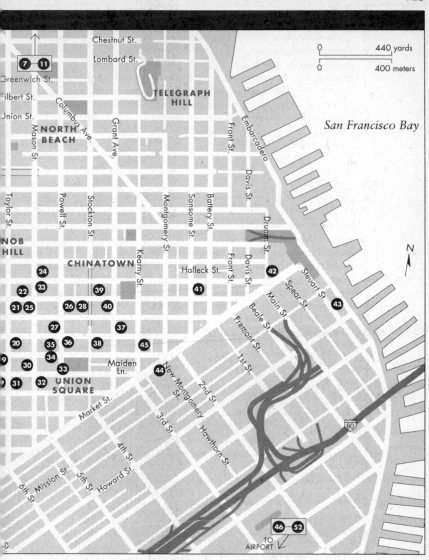

0 440 yards
0 400 meters

San Francisco Bay

Chestnut St.
Lombard St.
Greenwich St.
Filbert St.
Union St.
TELEGRAPH HILL
NORTH BEACH
Columbus Ave.
Grant Ave.
Mason St.
Powell St.
Stockton St.
Montgomery St.
Sansome St.
Battery St.
Front St.
Davis St.
Embarcadero
Taylor St.
NOB HILL
Kearny St.
Front St.
Davis St.
Drumm St.
Steuart St.
CHINATOWN
Halleck St.
Main St.
Spear St.
Beale St.
Fremont St.
1st St.
2nd St.
New Montgomery St.
Hawthorn St.
Maiden Ln.
UNION SQUARE
Market St.
3rd St.
4th St.
5th St.
Howard St.
Mission St.
6th St.
80
TO AIRPORT
N

Mandarin Oriental, **41**
The Mansions, **6**
Marina Inn, **3**
Mark Hopkins Inter–Continental, **23**
Marriott at Fisherman's Wharf, **7**
Nob Hill Lambourne, **28**

The Palace, **44**
Park Plaza, **52**
Petite Auberge, **21**
Phoenix Inn, **16**
Prescott Hotel, **20**
Radisson Miyako Hotel, **12**
Red Roof Inn, **46**
Ritz–Carlton, San Francisco, **39**
San Francisco Airport Hilton, **50**

San Remo, **11**
Sherman House, **2**
Sir Francis Drake, **36**
Town House Motel, **4**
Travelodge Hotel at Fisherman's Wharf, **10**
Tuscan Inn, **9**
Union Street Inn, **1**
Vintage Court, **26**
Westin St. Francis, **33**
White Swan Inn, **25**
York Hotel, **17**

Downtown/Union Square

$$$$ 🔲 **Campton Place.** Behind a simple brownstone facade, quiet reigns. Highly
★   attentive personal service begins the moment uniformed doormen greet
guests outside the marble-floored lobby. Rooms, small but well appointed, are decorated with Asian touches in subtle tones of gold and
brown, with double-pane windows, Chinese armoires, and good-size writing desks. From the ninth floor up, there are only four rooms to a floor.
They overlook an atrium, which lends a cozy, residential feel. The Campton Place Restaurant, listed prominently in *Condé Nast Traveler*'s "50
American Restaurants Worth the Journey," in 1995, is famed for its breakfasts. ✉ *340 Stockton St., 94108,* ☎ *415/781–5555 or 800/235–4300,*
FAX *415/955–5536. 117 rooms. Restaurant, bar. AE, DC, MC, V.*

$$$$ 🔲 **The Clift.** This Grand Heritage hotel towers over San Francisco's the-
★   ater district; its crisp, forest-green awnings and formal door service provide subtle hints of the elegance within. In the busy lobby, dark paneling
and four enormous chandeliers add a further note of grandeur. Rooms,
some rich with dark woods and burgundies, others refreshingly pastel, all have large writing desks, plants, and flowers. The Clift is noted
for its swift personalized service. Be sure to sample a cocktail in the
famous art deco Redwood Room lounge, complete with chandeliers
and a sweeping redwood bar. ✉ *495 Geary St., 94102,* ☎ *415/775–
4700 or 800/652–5438,* FAX *415/441–4621. 329 rooms. Restaurant,
bar, exercise room, meeting rooms. AE, DC, MC, V.*

$$$$ 🔲 **Westin St. Francis.** Host to the likes of Emperor Hirohito, Queen
Elizabeth II, and many presidents, the St. Francis, with its imposing
facade, black marble lobby, and gold-topped columns, looks more
like a great public building than a hotel. The effect is softened by the
columns and exquisite woodwork of the Compass Rose bar and restaurant; since its inception, this has been a retreat from the bustle of Union
Square, especially for those in a romantic frame of mind. An extensive
refurbishment of the entire hotel has gone on for several years, resulting
in improved guest rooms. The sandstone resurfacing of the exterior continues. Many of the rooms in the original building are small by modern standards, but all retain their original Victorian-style moldings and
light fixtures. Rooms in the modern tower are larger, with Oriental-
style lacquered furniture. ✉ *335 Powell St., 94102,* ☎ *415/397–7000
or 800/228–3000,* FAX *415/774–0124. 1,192 rooms. 3 restaurants, 3
bars, room service, exercise room, business services. AE, DC, MC, V.*

$$$ 🔲 **Galleria Park.** A few blocks east of Union Square, this hotel is close
★   to the Chinatown gate and the Crocker Galleria shopping area. The
comfortable rooms all have floral bedspreads, stylish striped wallpa-
per, and white furniture that includes a writing desk. Four floors are
no-smoking. ✉ *191 Sutter St., 94104,* ☎ *415/781–3060 or 800/792–
9639,* FAX *415/433–4409. 162 rooms, 15 suites. 2 restaurants, exer-
cise room. AE, D, DC, MC, V.*

$$$ 🔲 **Hotel Monaco.** Unquestionably the hottest new hotel in town, the
★   Hotel Monaco, with its yellow beaux-arts facade, stands in stark con-
trast to its more stately neighbor, the Clift. Inside, a faux steamer
trunk serves as a front desk, a dramatic staircase has bronze filigree
and gray-and-black marble steps, and a French inglenook fireplace climbs
two stories above the open lobby. Overhead, the three huge, hand-painted
domes of the vaulted ceiling are painted with hot-air balloons, World
War I-era planes and, seemingly, miles of blue sky. Behind champagne
white doors, rooms are an inviting blend of Chinese-inspired armoires,
bamboo writing desks, buttoned ottomans, and high-backed upholstered chairs. ✉ *501 Geary St., 94102,* ☎ *415/292–0100 or 800/214–
4220,* FAX *415/292–0111. 201 rooms. Restaurant, 2 bars, spa, health
club, parking (fee). AE, D, MC, V.*

$$$ 🗖 **Hotel Triton.** The Triton just may be the zaniest hostelry in town. Guests enter via a whimsical lobby of silk-taffeta furniture, star-patterned carpeting, and inverted gilt pillars—stylized spoofs of upside-down Roman columns. The hotel caters to fashion, entertainment, music, and film-industry types, who seem to appreciate the iridescent pink-and-gold-painted rooms with S-curved dervish chairs, curly-necked lamps, and oddball light fixtures. Attached to the hotel is the trendy newsstand, coffeehouse, and dining room, the Café de la Presse, which serves as a gathering place for foreign visitors. ⊠ *342 Grant Ave., 94108,* ☎ *415/394–0500 or 800/433–6611,* 𝔽𝔸𝕏 *415/394–0555. 133 rooms, 7 junior suites. Exercise room, laundry service, business services, meeting rooms. AE, D, MC, V.*

$$$ 🗖 **Inn at Union Square.** With its dark-timber double doors and its tiny but captivating lobby with trompe l'oeil bookshelves painted on the walls, this inn feels like someone's home. Comfortable, Georgian-style rooms promote indolence with sumptuous goose-down pillows; brass lion's-head door knockers are a unique touch. Complimentary Continental breakfast, afternoon tea, and evening wine and hors d'oeuvres are served in front of a fireplace in a sitting area on each floor. ⊠ *440 Post St., 94102,* ☎ *415/397–3510 or 800/288–4346,* 𝔽𝔸𝕏 *415/989– 0529. 30 rooms. No smoking. AE, DC, MC, V.*

$$$ 🗖 **Petite Auberge.** This inn's lobby, festooned with bears of all shapes, sizes, and costumes, sets the tone; the country kitchen and side garden create a pastoral atmosphere in the midst of downtown. Rooms are small, but each has bright flowered wallpaper, an old-fashioned writing desk, and a much-needed armoire—there's little or no closet space. The atmosphere borders on precious but doesn't stray past the mark. Next door, at 845 Bush Street, is a sister hotel, the 26-room White Swan Inn, similar in style but with an English-country flavor and larger rooms. ⊠ *863 Bush St., 94108,* ☎ *415/928–6000,* 𝔽𝔸𝕏 *415/775–5717. 26 rooms. Breakfast room. AE, MC, V.*

$$$ 🗖 **Prescott Hotel.** A gourmet's delight might be the best way to describe this plush hotel, thanks to its partnership with Wolfgang Puck's Postrio restaurant, which consistently hovers near the top of San Francisco's best-restaurant lists. Cuisine-conscious guests can order room service from Postrio and avoid trying to make a reservation. Thankfully, guests also have access to the health club next door at the Press Club. The Prescott's rooms, which vary only in size and shape, are traditional in style, with dark, rich color schemes. Each bed is backed by a partially mirrored wall and has a boldly patterned spread; bathrooms have marble-top sinks and gold fixtures. ⊠ *545 Post St., 94102,* ☎ *415/563– 0303 or 800/283–7322,* 𝔽𝔸𝕏 *415/563–6831. 165 rooms. Restaurant, bar. AE, D, DC, MC, V.*

$$$ 🗖 **Sir Francis Drake.** Although Beefeater-costumed doormen and dramatic red theater curtains still adorn the front of the Drake, the inside underwent a profound change a few years ago. The lobby is still opulent, with wrought-iron lion balustrades, chandeliers, and Italian marble, but guest rooms now have the flavor of a B&B, with California colonial-style furnishings and floral-print fabrics. The decor appeals to pleasure travelers, but business travelers will appreciate the modem hookups and voice mail. Party-giver extraordinaire Harry Denton runs the renowned Starlight Room on the top floor. ⊠ *450 Powell St., 94102,* ☎ *415/392–7755 or 800/227–5480,* 𝔽𝔸𝕏 *415/395–8599. 417 rooms. 2 restaurants, meeting room. AE, D, DC, MC, V.*

$$ 🗖 **The Cartwright.** This conveniently located hotel's motto is "It's like being at home." This is only true, however, if your home is filled with authentic European antiques, fluffy terry-cloth robes, and floral-print bedspreads and curtains, with English tea and wine from 5 to 6 every evening in the library. Guests may choose rooms with old-fashioned

carved-wood or brass beds. ⊠ *524 Sutter St., 94102,* ☎ *415/421–2865 or 800/227–3844,* FAX *415/398–6345. 114 rooms. Meeting rooms. AE, D, DC, MC, V.*

$$ 📟 **Chancellor Hotel.** This family-owned and -oriented hotel, although not as grand as some of its neighbors, more than lives up to its promise of comfort without extravagance—it's one of the best buys on Union Square. The moderate-sized, Edwardian-style rooms have high ceilings and peach, green, and rose color schemes; ceiling fans and deep bathtubs are a treat. Connecting rooms are available for couples with children. ⊠ *433 Powell St., 94102,* ☎ *415/362–2004 or 800/428–4748,* FAX *415/362–1403. 137 rooms. Restaurant, bar. AE, D, DC, MC, V.*

$$ 📟 **Commodore International.** Billing itself as an "urban adventure," the newly renovated Commodore provides a giddy alternative to its more stately competitors in the area. Entering the lobby of the hotel is like stepping onto the main deck of an ocean liner of yore: Neo deco chairs look like the backdrop for a film about transatlantic crossings. Steps away is the Titanic Cafe, where goldfish bowls and bathysphere-inspired lights add to the sea-cruise mood. The fairly large rooms with monster closets are painted in soft yellows and golds and all have themes such as the Historical Market Street Room and the Waterfront Room. ⊠ *825 Sutter St., 94109,* ☎ *415/923–6800 or 800/338–6848,* FAX *415/923–6804. 113 rooms. Restaurant, nightclub. AE, D, MC, V.*

$$ 📟 **Hotel Diva.** A gray awning and beaten-and-burnished silver facade give this hotel a slick, high-tech look that sets it apart from others in San Francisco. Although the Diva's proximity to the landmark Curran attracts theater folk and others of an artistic bent, it's also popular with tourists and business travelers. The black-and-silver color scheme with touches of gray extends to the nightclub-esque lobby and to the rooms, which vary in size and are comfortable but not fussy. Black-lacquered armoires, writing desks, and headboards complete the effect. ⊠ *440 Geary St., 94102,* ☎ *415/885–0200 or 800/553–1900,* FAX *415/346–6613. 110 rooms. Restaurant, exercise room, business services, meeting room. AE, D, DC, MC, V.*

$$ 📟 **King George.** Behind the George's white-and-green Victorian facade, rooms are compact but nicely furnished in classic English style, with walnut furniture and a muted rose color scheme. British and Japanese tourists and suburban couples seeking a weekend getaway frequent this adult-oriented hotel. ⊠ *334 Mason St., 94102,* ☎ *415/781–5050 or 800/288–6005,* FAX *415/391–6976. 140 rooms. AE, D, DC, MC, V.*

$$ 📟 **Vintage Court.** This bit of the Napa Valley just off Union Square has lavish rooms decorated in a Wine Country theme, and every afternoon complimentary wine is served in front of a crackling fire in the lobby. Continental breakfast is served each morning, and for fine food, guests need go no farther than the lobby to get to Masa's, the celebrated French restaurant. Guests have access to an affiliated health club one block away. ⊠ *650 Bush St., 94108,* ☎ *415/392–4666 or 800/654–1100,* FAX *415/433–4065. 107 rooms. Restaurant, bar. AE, D, DC, MC, V.*

$$ 📟 **York Hotel.** The peach-stone facade and ornate, high-ceiling lobby lend the York a touch of elegance. The moderate-size rooms are a tasteful mix of Mediterranean styles, with a terra-cotta, burgundy, and forest-green color scheme. ⊠ *940 Sutter St., 94109,* ☎ *415/885–6800 or 800/808–9675,* FAX *415/885–2115. 96 rooms. Bar, exercise room, nightclub. AE, D, DC, MC, V.*

$ 📟 **Adelaide Inn.** The bedspreads at this quiet retreat may not match the drapes or carpets, and the floors may creak, but the rooms are sunny, clean, and cheap: $42 to $48 for a double. Tucked away in an alley, this funky European-style pension hosts many guests from Germany, France, and Italy. ⊠ *5 Isadora Duncan Ct. (off Taylor between Geary* *and Post Sts.), 94102,* ☎ *415/441–2474 or 415/441–2261,* FAX *415/441–0161. 18 rooms share baths. Breakfast room, refrigerators. AE, MC, V.*

$ ☎ **Grant Plaza.** This bargain hotel in the shadow of the Chinatown gate has small but clean rooms from $39. The Grant stands midway between the shopping options of Union Square and the Italian cafés and restaurants of North Beach. ⊠ *465 Grant Ave., 94108,* ☎ *415/434–3883 or 800/472–6899,* FAX *415/434–3886. 72 rooms. AE, MC, V.*

Financial District

$$$$ ☎ **Hyatt Regency.** The gray concrete, bunkerlike exterior of the Hyatt Regency at the foot of Market Street is an unlikely introduction to the spectacular 17-story atrium lobby within. Rooms, some with bay-view balconies, are decorated in two styles: Both have cherry-wood furniture, but one strikes a decidedly more masculine tone with a black-and-brown color scheme, while the other has soft rose-and-plum combinations. ⊠ *5 Embarcadero Center, 94111,* ☎ *415/788–1234 or 800/233–1234,* FAX *415/398–2567. 803 rooms. 2 restaurants, lobby lounge. AE, D, DC, MC, V.*

$$$$ ☎ **Mandarin Oriental.** Since the Mandarin comprises the top 11 floors (38 to 48) of San Francisco's third-tallest building—the First Interstate Center—all rooms provide panoramic vistas of the city and beyond. As striking as the views are the glass-enclosed sky bridges that connect the front and back towers of the hotel. Rooms in the front tower fill up quickly because of their dramatic, sweeping view from the ocean all the way to the Golden Gate Bridge and beyond to Angel Island; the Mandarin Rooms in each tower are favorites because their bathtubs are flanked by windows. Rooms, all light, creamy yellow with black accents and wood tones, have a California–Asian flair. ⊠ *222 Sansome St., 94104,* ☎ *415/885–0999 or 800/622–0404,* FAX *415/433–0289. 154 rooms, 4 suites. Restaurant, lobby lounge. AE, D, DC, MC, V.*

$$$$ ☎ **The Palace.** One of the city's grand old hotels—with a guest list that has included Enrico Caruso, Woodrow Wilson, and Al Jolson—the Palace has an indoor lap pool with a skylight, a health club, and a business center. The Garden Court restaurant, with its leaded-glass, domed ceiling, is famous for lavish buffet breakfasts. With their 14-foot ceilings, rooms are splendid on a smaller scale. Modern amenities are carefully integrated into the classic decor, from the TV inside the mahogany armoire to the telephone in the marble bathroom. ⊠ *2 New Montgomery St., 94105,* ☎ *415/392–8600 or 800/325–3535,* FAX *415/543–0671. 550 rooms. 3 restaurants, 2 lounges, room service, health club. AE, D, DC, MC, V.*

$$$ ☎ **Harbor Court.** This cozy hotel, formerly a YMCA, is noted for the
★   exemplary service of its warm, friendly staff. The small rooms, some with bay views, have a sage-green color scheme and partial canopy beds resting on wood casements. The adult-oriented Harbor Court attracts corporate types (especially on weekdays) as well as the average traveler. Guests have free access to YMCA facilities (including a 150-foot heated indoor pool) on one side of the hotel, and Harry Denton's Bar and Grill on the other. ⊠ *165 Steuart St.,* ☎ *415/882–1300 or 800/346–0555,* FAX *415/882–1313. 131 rooms. Business services. AE, D, DC, MC, V.*

Nob Hill

$$$$ ☎ **Fairmont Hotel and Tower.** Perched atop Nob Hill, the Fairmont has the most awe-inspiring lobby in the city, with a soaring, vaulted ceiling; towering, hand-painted, faux-marble columns; gilt mirrors; red-velvet upholstered chairs; and a grand, wraparound staircase. The tower rooms, which have spectacular city and bay views, reflect a more modern style than their smaller Victorian counterparts in the older building. The Tonga Room, site of San Francisco's busiest happy hour, is a must-see. ⊠ *950 Mason St., 94108,* ☎ *415/772–5000 or 800/527– 4727,* ℻ *415/772–5013. 596 rooms. 5 restaurants, 5 bars, room service, spa, health club. AE, D, DC, MC, V.*

$$$$ 🏨 **The Huntington.** Attentive personal service is the hallmark of this hotel. Rooms and suites reflect the Huntington's traditional style, albeit with a '90s bent. Opulent materials such as raw silks and velvets are mixed and matched in a color scheme of cocoa, gold, and burgundy. ⊠ *1075 California St., 94108,* ☎ *415/474–5400 or 800/227–4683; in CA, 800/652–1539;* ℻ *415/474–6227. 140 rooms. Restaurant, bar. AE, D, DC, MC, V.*

$$$$ 🏨 **Mark Hopkins Inter-Continental.** The circular drive to this Nob Hill landmark across from the Fairmont leads to a lobby with floor-to-ceiling mirrors and marble floors. The rooms, with dramatic neoclassical furnishings of gray, silver, and khaki and bold leaf-print bedspreads, lead into bathrooms lined with Italian marble. Even-number rooms on high floors have views of the Golden Gate Bridge. No visit would be complete without a gander at the panoramic views from the Top of the Mark, *the* rooftop lounge in San Francisco since 1939. ⊠ *999 California St., 94108,* ☎ *415/392–3434 or 800/327–0200,* ℻ *415/421–3302. 392 rooms. Restaurant, 2 lounges, exercise room. AE, D, DC, MC, V.*

$$$$ 🏨 **Ritz-Carlton, San Francisco.** Consistently rated one of the top ho-
★   tels in the world by *Condé Nast Traveler,* the Ritz-Carlton is a stunning tribute to beauty, grandeur, and warm, attentive service. Beyond the neoclassical facade, crystal chandeliers and museum-quality 18th-century oil paintings adorn an opulent lobby. Rooms are elegant and spacious, and every bath is appointed with double sinks, hair dryers, and vanity tables. A maid service cleans twice a day, and guests staying on the butler level enjoy the added luxury of their own butler. The hotel's Dining Room, is a worthy destination in its own right. ⊠ *600 Stockton St., at California St., 94108,* ☎ *415/296–7465 or 800/241– 3333,* ℻ *415/291–0288. 336 rooms. 2 restaurants, 3 lounges, indoor pool, health club. AE, D, DC, MC, V.*

$$$ 🏨 **Nob Hill Lambourne.** This urban retreat designed with the traveling executive in mind takes pride in taking care of business while offering stress-reducing pleasures. Personal computers, fax machines, personalized voice mail, laser printers, and a fully equipped boardroom help guests maintain their edge, and the on-site spa, with massages, body scrubs, manicures, and pedicures, helps them take it off. Rooms have queen-size beds with double-padded, hand-sewn mattresses and contemporary furnishings in Mediterranean colors. A deluxe Continental breakfast and evening wine service are complimentary. ⊠ *725 Pine St., at Stockton, 94108,* ☎ *415/433–2287 or 800/274–8466,* ℻ *415/433–0975. 20 rooms. Spa, kitchenettes. AE, D, DC, MC, V.*

Fisherman's Wharf/North Beach

$$$$ 🏨 **Hyatt at Fisherman's Wharf.** Location is the key to this hotel's popularity with business travelers and families. The moderate-size guest rooms, a medley of greens and burgundies with dark woods and brass fixtures, have double-pane windows to keep out the often considerable street noise. Each floor has a laundry room. ⊠ *555 North Point St., 94133,* ☎ *415/563–1234 or 800/233–1234,* ℻ *415/563–2218. 313 rooms. Restaurant, sports bar, pool, outdoor hot tub, health club, coin laundry. AE, D, DC, MC, V.*

$$$ 🏨 **Marriott at Fisherman's Wharf.** Behind an unremarkable sand-color facade, the Marriott strikes a grand note in its lavish, low-ceiling lobby, with marble floors and English club-style furniture. With the Transamerica Pyramid downtown to its left and the Cannery nearby on its right, the hotel is well situated for business and pleasure. Rooms, all with turquoise, blue, and white color schemes, have dark natural wood, Asian art touches, and either a king-size bed or two double beds. ⊠ *1250 Columbus Ave., 94133, ☎ 415/775–7555 or 800/228–9290,* FAX *415/474–2099. 255 rooms. Restaurant, bar, health club. AE, D, DC, MC, V.*

$$$ ⊡ **Tuscan Inn.** The condolike exterior of the inn—reddish brick with white concrete—gives little indication of the charm of the relatively small, Italian-influenced guest rooms, with their white-pine furniture and floral bedspreads and curtains. Three floors are smoke-free. Room service is provided by Cafe Pescatore, the Italian seafood restaurant off the lobby. Morning coffee, tea, and biscotti are complimentary, and wine is served in the early evening. ⊠ *425 North Point St., 94133, ☎ 415/561–1100 or 800/648–4626,* FAX *415/561–1199. 220 rooms. Restaurant, meeting rooms, room service. AE, D, DC, MC, V.*

$$ ⊡ **Travelodge Hotel at Fisherman's Wharf.** Taking up an entire city block, the Travelodge is the only bayfront hotel at Fisherman's Wharf and is known for its reasonable rates. The higher-priced rooms on the third and fourth floors have balconies that provide unobstructed views of Alcatraz and overlook a landscaped courtyard and pool. Rooms have either a king-size bed or two double beds and are simply and brightly furnished. ⊠ *250 Beach St., 94133, ☎ 415/392–6700 or 800/578– 7878,* FAX *415/986–7853. 250 rooms. 3 restaurants, pool, free parking. AE, D, DC, MC, V.*

$ ⊡ **San Remo.** This three-story, blue-and-white Italianate Victorian has
★ reasonably priced rooms and a down-home ambience. The somewhat cramped rooms are crowded with furniture: vanities, rag rugs, pedestal sinks, ceiling fans, antique armoires, and brass, iron, or wooden beds. The rooms share six black-and-white tiled shower rooms, one bathtub chamber, and six scrupulously clean toilets with brass pull chains and oak tanks. Special rates are available for longer stays. ⊠ *2237 Mason St., 94133, ☎ 415/776–8688 or 800/352–7366,* FAX *415/776–2811. 62 rooms, 61 with shared baths. AE, DC, MC, V.*

Pacific Heights, Cow Hollow, and the Marina

$$$$ ⊡ **Sherman House.** This landmark mansion on a low hill in residen-
★ tial Pacific Heights is San Francisco's most luxurious small hotel. Rooms are individually decorated with Biedermeier, English Jacobean, or French Second Empire antiques. Tapestrylike canopies over four-poster beds, wood-burning fireplaces with marble mantels, and black-granite bathrooms with whirlpool baths complete the picture. The six romantic suites attract honeymooners from around the world, and the elegant in-house dining room serves superb French-inspired cuisine. ⊠ *2160 Green St., 94123, ☎ 415/563–3600 or 800/424–5777,* FAX *415/563–1882. 14 rooms. Dining room. AE, DC, MC, V.*

$$$ ⊡ **Bed and Breakfast Inn.** Hidden in an alleyway off Union Street, this ivy-covered, dark-green-and-white Victorian has English-country-style rooms, which are full of antiques, plants, and floral paintings. The Mayfair, a private flat above the main house, comes complete with a living room, kitchenette, latticed balcony, and spiral staircase leading to a sleeping loft. ⊠ *4 Charlton Ct., 94123, ☎ 415/921–9784. 5 rooms with bath, 4 rooms share baths, 2 flats. Breakfast room. No credit cards.*

$$$ ⊡ **Union Street Inn.** This ivy-draped Edwardian 1902 home affords a
★ cozy intimacy that has made it popular with honeymooners and other romantics. Of the six rooms, one standout is the Wildrose, with a garden view, whirlpool tub, and king-size brass bed. An elaborate com-

plimentary Continental breakfast is served to guests in the parlor, in the garden, or in their rooms. Special rates are available for longer stays, and off-season prices are considerably lower. ⊠ *2229 Union St., 94123,* ☎ *415/346–0424,* 𝖥𝖠𝖷 *415/922–8046. 6 rooms with bath. Breakfast room. AE, MC, V.*

$ 🖼 **Marina Inn.** This inn five blocks from the Marina offers B&B-style accommodations at motel prices. English-country-style rooms are sparsely appointed with a queen-size two-poster bed, private bath, small pine-wood writing desks, nightstands, and armoires; the wallpaper and bedspreads are aggressively floral. Complimentary Continental breakfast and afternoon sherry are served in the central sitting room. ⊠ *3110 Octavia St., 94123,* ☎ *415/928–1000 or 800/274–1420,* 𝖥𝖠𝖷 *415/928–5909. 40 rooms. Lounge, barbershop, beauty salon. AE, MC, V.*

$ 🖼 **Town House Motel.** What this family-oriented motel lacks in luxury it makes up for in value: The rooms are simply furnished and well kept. The motel is convenient to many sights of interest. The modest, medium-size rooms have a pastel, southwestern color scheme, lacquered-wood furnishings, and either a king-size bed or two doubles. Continental breakfast is complimentary. ⊠ *1650 Lombard St., 94123,* ☎ *415/885–5163 or 800/255–1516,* 𝖥𝖠𝖷 *415/771–9889. 24 rooms. Free parking. AE, D, DC, MC, V.*

Civic Center/Van Ness

$$$ 🖼 **Hotel Majestic.** One of San Francisco's original grand hotels, this
★   five-story yellow-and-white Edwardian with gingerbread and scrollwork looks like a wedding cake. Most rooms contain a fireplace and either a large, hand-painted, four-poster, canopied bed or two-poster bonnet twin beds, and most have a mix of French Empire and English antiques and custom furniture. The hotel's romantic Cafe Majestic evokes turn-of-the-century San Francisco. ⊠ *1500 Sutter St., 94109,* ☎ *415/441–1100 or 800/869–8966,* 𝖥𝖠𝖷 *415/673–7331. 57 rooms. Restaurant, bar. AE, DC, MC, V.*

$$$ 🖼 **Inn at the Opera.** This seven-story hotel a block or so from City
★   Hall, Davies Hall, and other major civic structures hosts the likes of Pavarotti and Baryshnikov, as well as lesser lights of the music, dance, and opera worlds. Behind the yellow faux-marble front and red carpet are rooms of various sizes, decorated with creamy pastels and dark wood furnishings. Even the smallest singles have queen-size beds. The bureau drawers are lined with sheet music, and every room is outfitted with terry-cloth robes, microwave ovens, minibars, fresh flowers, and a basket of apples. Those in the know say the back rooms are the quietest. ⊠ *333 Fulton St., 94102,* ☎ *415/863–8400 or 800/325–2708; in CA, 800/423–9610;* 𝖥𝖠𝖷 *415/861–0821. 48 rooms. Restaurant, lounge. AE, DC, MC, V.*

$$$ 🖼 **The Mansions.** This twin-turreted Queen Anne was built in 1887 and today houses one of the most unusual hotels in the city. Rooms, which contain an odd collection of furnishings, vary in theme from the tiny Tom Thumb Room to the opulent Josephine Suite, the favorite of such celebrities as Barbra Streisand. Owner Bob Pritikin's pig paintings and other "porkabilia" are scattered throughout the hotel. Other nice touches are the sculpture and flower gardens and the nightly concerts. Full breakfast is included. ⊠ *2220 Sacramento St., 94115,* ☎ *415/929–9444,* 𝖥𝖠𝖷 *415/567–9391. 21 rooms. Dining room, cabaret. AE, DC, MC, V.*

$$$ 🖼 **Radisson Miyako Hotel.** Next to the Japantown complex and near Fillmore Street, this pagoda-style hotel is frequented by Asian travelers and others with a taste for the East. Some guest rooms are in the tower building; others are in the garden wing, which has traditional seasonal gar-

dens. Japanese-style rooms have futon beds with tatami mats; Western rooms have traditional beds with mattresses. Both types of rooms feature Japanese touches such as shojis; most have their own soaking rooms with a bucket and stool and a Japanese tub (1 foot deeper than Western tubs). A chocolate is placed on a haiku by every guest's bed. ⊠ *1625 Post St., at Laguna St., 94115,* ☎ *415/922–3200 or 800/533–4567,* FAX *415/921–0417. 218 rooms. Restaurant, bar. AE, D, DC, MC, V.*

$$ ⊡ **Phoenix Inn.** This hideaway on the fringes of the Tenderloin district is a little bit south-of-the-equator and a little bit *Gilligan's Island.* Its bungalow-style rooms, decorated with casual, handmade bamboo furniture and original art by San Francisco artists, have white beamed ceilings, white wooden walls, and vivid tropical-print bedspreads. All rooms face a pool (with a mural by Francis Forlenza on its bottom). An in-house cable channel plays films made in San Francisco and films about bands on the road. Miss Pearl's Jam House restaurant and bar is a good place to hear reggae and indulge in Jamaican delights. ⊠ *601 Eddy St., 94109,* ☎ *415/776–1380, 415/861–1560, or 800/248–9466,* FAX *415/885–3109. 44 rooms. Restaurant, bar, pool, free parking. AE, D, DC, MC, V.*

$ ⊡ **The Abigail.** Faux-stone walls, a faux-marble front desk, and an old-fashioned telephone booth in the lobby make for an eclectic decor at this smallish hotel in a marginal neighborhood. Hissing steam radiators, sleigh beds, and antiques complete the mood. The new Millennium Restaurant, right off the lobby, has proven to be a hit with the gourmet organic crowd. ⊠ *246 McAllister St., 94102,* ☎ *415/861–9728 or 800/243–6510,* FAX *415/861–5848. 60 rooms. Restaurant. AE, D, DC, MC, V.*

The Airport

Because they cater primarily to midweek business travelers, the airport hotels often cut weekend prices drastically; be sure to inquire. A full complement of services and airport shuttle buses is provided by all of the following hotels.

$$$ **Embassy Suites San Francisco Airport South–Burlingame** (⊠ 150 Anza Blvd., Burlingame 94010, ☎ 415/342–4600 or 800/362–2779, FAX 415/343–8137). **Hotel Sofitel–San Francisco Bay** (⊠ 223 Twin Dolphin Dr., Redwood City 94065, ☎ 415/598–9000 or 800/763–4835, FAX 415/598–0459). **San Francisco Airport Hilton** (⊠ San Francisco International Airport, 94128, ☎ 415/589–0770 or 800/445–8667, FAX 415/589–4696).

$$ **Clarion Hotel** (⊠ 401 E. Millbrae Ave., Millbrae 94030, ☎ 415/692–6363 or 800/223–7111, FAX 415/697–8735). **Park Plaza** (⊠ 1177 Airport Blvd., Burlingame 94010, ☎ 415/342–9200 or 800/411-7275, FAX 415/342–1655).

$ **Red Roof Inn** (⊠ 777 Airport Blvd., Burlingame 94010, ☎ 415/342–7772 or 800/843–7663, FAX 415/342–2635). **La Quinta Motor Inn** (⊠ 20 Airport Blvd., South San Francisco 94080, ☎ 415/583–2223 or 800/531–5900, FAX 415/589–6770).

NIGHTLIFE AND THE ARTS

A spirit of playfulness has pervaded San Francisco's arts, entertainment, and nightlife scenes ever since its days as a rowdy sailors' port. Perhaps nothing is more purely San Franciscan than the Beach Blanket Babylon at Club Fugazi, a hysterical cabaret with no more noble purpose than to parody local moods and mores. In addition, the San Francisco Opera, the San Francisco Symphony, and the San Francisco Ballet are all nationally renowned, while dozens of alternative groups represent everything from gay and lesbian performance art to family circus and mime.

For information on who is performing where, check out the San Francisco *Chronicle*'s pink "Datebook" insert—or consult the *Bay Guardian,* free and available in racks around the city, listing neighborhood, avantgarde, and budget-priced events. *S.F. Weekly* is also free and packed with information on arts events around town. Another handy reference is *Key* magazine, offered free in most major hotel lobbies. For a phone update on sports and musical events, call the Convention and Visitors Bureau's *Events Hotline* (☎ 415/391–2001).

Nightlife

By Daniel Mangin

Updated by Dennis Harvey

Although San Francisco is a compact city, with the prevailing influences of some neighborhoods spilling into others, the following generalizations should help you find the kind of entertainment you're looking for. **Nob Hill** is noted for its plush piano bars and panoramic skyline lounges. **North Beach,** infamous for its topless and bottomless bistros, also maintains a sense of its beatnik past, and this legacy lives on in atmospheric bars and coffeehouses. **Fisherman's Wharf,** while touristy, is great for people-watching and attracts plenty of street performers. **Union Street** is home away from home for singles in search of company. South of Market—**SoMa,** for short—has become a hub of nightlife, with a bevy of highly popular nightclubs, bars, and lounges in renovated warehouses. Gay men and lesbians will find their scene in the **Castro** and **Mission districts** and on **Polk Street.** Twentysomethings and alternative types should check out the ever-funky **Mission** and **Haight Street** scenes.

Rock, Pop, Folk, and Blues

The **Blue Lamp** (⊠ 561 Geary St., ☎ 415/885–1464), a downtown hole in the wall showcasing blues performers, has an aura of faded opulence. **Bottom of the Hill** (⊠ 1233 17th St., at Texas St., ☎ 415/626–4455), in the Potrero Hill District, presents local alternative rock and blues. **DNA Lounge** (⊠ 375 11th St., near Harrison St., ☎ 415/626–1409), a longtime, two-floor SoMa haunt, hosts independent rock, funk, and rap. Live bands play most nights at 10; other nights the club is open for dancing to recorded music. **The Fillmore** (⊠ 1805 Geary Blvd., at Fillmore St., ☎ 415/346–6000), one of San Francisco's most famous rock music halls, serves up a varied menu of national and local acts: rock, reggae, grunge, jazz, comedy, folk, acid house, and more. **Freight and Salvage Coffee House** (⊠ 1111 Addison St., Berkeley, ☎ 510/548–1761), one of the finest folk houses in the country, is worth a trip across the bay. Folk, blues, Cajun, and bluegrass artists perform here, among them Taj Mahal, Iris DeMent, Laurie Lewis, and Greg Brown. **Great American Music Hall** (⊠ 859 O'Farrell St., between Polk and Larkin Sts., ☎ 415/885–0750) hosts top-drawer entertainment, running the gamut from the best in blues, folk, and jazz to alternative rock with a sprinkling of outstanding comedians. **Last Day Saloon** (⊠ 406 Clement St., between 5th and 6th Aves., ☎ 415/387–6343) presents a varied schedule of blues, Cajun, rock, and jazz. **Slim's** (⊠ 333 11th St., ☎ 415/522–0333) specializes in what it labels "American roots music"—blues, jazz, classic rock, and the like. The club has expanded its repertoire in recent years, with national touring acts playing alternative rock and roll and a series of "spoken word" concerts.

Jazz

Cafe du Nord (✉ 2170 Market St., at Sanchez St., ☎ 415/861–5016) hosts some of the liveliest jam sessions in town, fueled mainly by local talent.

Eleven (✉ 374 11th St., ☎ 415/431–3337), an Italian restaurant, dishes out funky, salsafied, and trad sounds that are called "Live Loft Jazz" because the stage is 12 feet off the ground.

Enrico's (✉ 504 Broadway Ave., ☎ 415/982–6223), a Beat Era tradition, is hep once again—the indoor/outdoor café has a high-life ambience, a fine menu (tapas and Italian), and mellow nightly jazz combos.

Heart and Soul (✉ 1695 Polk St., ☎ 415/673–6788), a sleek, plush "1940s big-city retro room," captures the ambience of another era with just a hint of lounge-revival irony. The kitchen serves excellent appetizers and meals while local and national combos and vocalists play jazz from the 1940s through the '60s.

Jazz at Pearl's (✉ 256 Columbus Ave., near Broadway, ☎ 415/291–8255) is a good bet—the talent level is remarkably high, especially considering that there is rarely a cover.

Kimball's East (✉ 5800 Shellmound St., Emeryville, ☎ 510/658–2555), in a shopping complex in Emeryville just off Highway 80 near Oakland, hosts such talents as David Benois, Herbie Hancock, Dr. John, and Nancy Wilson. With an elegant interior and fine food, it's one of the Bay Area's most luxurious supper clubs.

Orocco (✉ 3565 Geary St. at Arguello Blvd., ☎ 415/387–8788) is a newish addition to SF's wave of retro supper clubs. Malaysian chef Alexander Ong oversees sensational East-West hybrid dishes; the two-story room presents mellow live jazz most nights.

Up and Down Club (✉ 1151 Folsom St., ☎ 415/626–2388), a hip restaurant and club whose owners include supermodel Christy Turlington, books up-and-coming jazz artists downstairs and has dancing to a DJ upstairs, Monday through Saturday.

Yoshi's (☎ 510/652–9200), one of the Bay Area's best jazz venues, hosts jazz greats including Betty Carter, Kenny Burrell, Joshua Redman, and Cecil Taylor, along with blues and Latin performers. At press time, Yoshi's was planning a late-1996 move to a storefront below the Washington Street Parking Garage in Oakland's Jack London Square. Call the club for an update or check local papers.

Cabarets

Club Fugazi (✉ 678 Green St., ☎ 415/421–4222) presents the long-running (two decades-plus) *Beach Blanket Babylon,* a wacky musical revue send-up of San Francisco moods and mores. While the choreography is colorful, the singers brassy and the songs witty, the real stars of the show are the comically exotic costumes and famous ceiling-high "hats." Order tickets as far in advance as possible; the show has been sold out up to a month in advance. Those under 21 are admitted only to the Sunday matinee.

Coconut Grove (✉ 1415 Van Ness Ave., ☎ 415/776–1616) has a chic, '40s supper-club ambience, along with superb (if pricey) cocktails and nouvelle cuisine. Tom Jones, Connie Stevens, Diahann Carroll, Charo, and other pop icons are among the past headliners. There's dancing to live music on Thursday (Motown night), Friday (salsa), and Saturday (swing).

Eichelberger's (✉ 2742 17th St., ☎ 415/863–4177), named by its native New Yorker owners after the late Manhattan performance artist Ethyl Eichelberger, has a bar downstairs and a "classic supper club with a San Francisco twist"—the "twist" being its weekend schedule of cabaret acts, from drag chanteuses to veteran jazz stylists.

Finocchio's (✉ 506 Broadway, ☎ 415/982–9388), an amiable, world-famous club, has been generating confusion with its female impersonators since 1936. The scene at Finocchio's is decidedly retro, which for the most part only adds to its charm.

Josie's Cabaret and Juice Joint (✉ 3583 16th St., at Market St., ☎ 415/861–7933), a small café and cabaret in the Castro district, books performers who reflect the countercultural feel of the neighborhood—from stand-up comedians to drag queens to solo monologuists. National talents stopping through have included Lypsinka, lesbian comic Lea Delaria, and transsexual performance artist Kate Bornstein.

New Orleans Room (✉ Mason and California Sts., ☎ 415/772–5259), in the Fairmont Hotel, has a somewhat tacky 1960s hotel-bar ambience. Still, the talent on display is first-rate: Recent guests include comic Steve Allen, Latin band leader Pete Escovedo, and vocalists from soul diva Freyda Paine to Eartha Kitt and Broadway thrush Barbara Cook.

Comedy Clubs

Cobb's Comedy Club (✉ 2801 Leavenworth St., at the corner of Beach St., ☎ 415/928–4320), in the Cannery, books super stand-up comics such as Margaret Smith, Dana Gould, and Janeane Garofalo.

Punch Line (✉ 44-A Battery St., between Clay and Washington Sts., ☎ 415/397–7573), a launching pad for the likes of Jay Leno and Whoopi Goldberg, features some of the area's top talents. Buy tickets in advance at BASS outlets (☎ 510/762–2277) or from the club's charge line (☎ 415/397–4337). Only those 18 and over are admitted.

Dancing Emporiums

Cesar's Latin Palace (✉ 3140 Mission St., ☎ 415/648–6611), in the Mission district, lures all kinds of dancers with its salsa-style Latin music. Latin dance lessons from 9 to 10 PM are included in the price of admission Friday and Saturday nights. Sunday is Brazilian Night. Note: no alcohol is served here.

Metronome Ballroom (✉ 1830 17th St., ☎ 415/252–9000) is at its most lively on weekend nights, when ballroom dancers come for lessons and revelry. The ambience is lively but mellow at this smoke-and-alcohol-free spot.

Oz (✉ 335 Powell St., between Geary and Post Sts., ☎ 415/774–0116), on the top floor of the St. Francis Hotel—accessible via glass elevator—has marble floors and a splendid panorama of the city. Dancers can recharge on cushy sofas and bamboo chairs. The fine sound system belts out progressive house music and occasional hip-hop.

Sound Factory (✉ 525 Harrison St., between 1st St. and 2nd St., ☎ 415/543–1300) DJs play anything from grunge and deep house to '70s disco. Two "virtual reality pods" offer refuge; live bands perform at special events.

Piano Bars

Redwood Room (✉ Taylor and Geary Sts., ☎ 415/775–4700), in the Four Seasons Clift Hotel, is a classy art deco lounge with a low-key but sensuous ambience. Klimt reproductions cover the walls, and mellow sounds fill the air.

Ritz-Carlton Hotel (✉ 600 Stockton St., ☎ 415/296–7465) has a tastefully appointed lobby lounge where a harpist plays during high tea, daily from 2:30 to 5 PM. The lounge shifts to piano (with occasional vocal accompaniment) for cocktails until 11:30 weeknights and 1:30 AM weekends.

Washington Square Bar and Grill (✉ 1707 Powell St., ☎ 415/982–8123), affectionately known as the "Washbag" among San Francisco politicians and newspaper folk, hosts pianists performing jazz and popular standards.

Skyline Bars

Carnelian Room (✉ 555 California St., ☎ 415/433–7500), on the 52nd floor of the Bank of America Building, offers what is perhaps the loftiest view of San Francisco's magnificent skyline.

Crown Room (✉ California and Mason Sts., ☎ 415/772–5131), the aptly named lounge on the 24th floor of the Fairmont Hotel, is one of the most luxurious of the city's skyline bars. Just riding the glass-enclosed Skylift elevator is an experience in itself.

Harry Denton's Starlight Room (✉ Sir Francis Drake Hotel, 450 Powell St., ☎ 415/395–8595) has rose-velvet booths, romantic lighting, and staff clad in tuxes or full-length gowns, the better to re-create a 1950s high-life tenor. Whenever live combos aren't holding court over the small dance floor, taped Sinatra rules.

Top of the Mark (✉ Mark Hopkins Hotel, California and Mason Sts., ☎ 415/392–3434) hosts live music Wednesday through Saturday nights, and dancing to standards from the '20s, '30s, and '40s on Friday and Saturday. The view is superb seven nights a week.

Singles Bars

Harry Denton's (✉ 161 Steuart St., ☎ 415/882–1333), one of San Francisco's liveliest, most upscale saloons, is packed with well-dressed young professionals.

Holding Company (✉ 2 Embarcadero Center, ☎ 415/986–0797) is where scores of office workers gather after hours. The kitchen and bar are open Monday through Friday.

Johnny Love's (✉ 1500 Broadway, at Polk St., ☎ 415/931–8021) has been a hit ever since it was opened by the popular Mr. Love. Live music (heavy on the R&B) is offered most nights, along with DJ dancing slanted toward party-hearty '70s and '80s pop hits.

Perry's (✉ 1944 Union St., at Buchanan St., ☎ 415/922–9022), the most famous of San Francisco's singles bars, is usually jam-packed. You can dine here on great hamburgers as well as more substantial fare.

Longtime Favorites

Buena Vista (✉ 2765 Hyde St., ☎ 415/474–5044) the Wharf area's most popular bar, introduced Irish coffee to the New World—or so they say. Because it has a fine view of the waterfront, it's usually packed with tourists.

Cypress Club (✉ 500 Jackson St., ☎ 415/296–8555) is an eccentric restaurant-bar where sensual, '20s-style opulence clashes with Fellini/Dali frivolity. The decor alone makes it worth a visit, but it's also a fine spot for a before-dinner or after-theater chat. Raymond Chandler's *The Big Sleep* inspired the club's name.

Hard Rock Cafe (✉ 1699 Van Ness St., ☎ 415/885–1699), part of the famous chain of youth-oriented bars, is filled with a collection of rock-and-roll memorabilia that won't disappoint fans. It's not a favorite with San Franciscans, but tourists love the joint.

House of Shields (✉ 39 New Montgomery St., ☎ 415/392–7732), a saloon-style bar, attracts an older, Financial District crowd after work. Food is served weekdays until 8 PM, Saturday until 6.

Tonga Room (✉ 950 Mason St. at California St., ☎ 415/772–5278) is San Francisco's house of high kitsch. Fake palm trees and "grass huts," a "lake" (combos play pop standards on a floating barge), and sprinkler-system "rain" (complete with simulated thunder and lightning) create a tropical atmosphere that only grows more surreal as you quaff the selection of very fruity and very potent novelty cocktails.

Vesuvio Cafe (✉ 255 Columbus Ave., ☎ 415/362–3370), near the legendary City Lights Bookstore, is little altered since its heyday as a haven for the Beat poets.

Gay and Lesbian Nightlife

GAY MALE BARS

Alta Plaza Bar & Grill (✉ 2301 Fillmore St., ☎ 415/922–1444) is an upper Fillmore restaurant-bar that caters to nattily dressed guppies (gay yuppies) and their admirers. Live jazz is offered Sunday through Thursday nights; a DJ takes over on weekends.

Detour (✉ 2348 Market St., ☎ 415/861–6053) draws a crowd that's youngish and a bit surly. The music is loud but well selected; go-go dancers hold court on Saturday nights.

The Metro (✉ 3600 16th St., at Market St., ☎ 415/703–9750), more upscale than the nearby Detour, has a balcony that overlooks the intersection of Noe, 16th, and Market streets.

Midnight Sun (✉ 4067 18th St., ☎ 415/861–4186), one of the Castro's most popular bars, has riotously programmed giant video screens. Don't expect to hear yourself think.

N Touch (✉ 1548 Polk St., ☎ 415/441–8413), a tiny dance bar, has long been popular with Asian-Pacific Islander gay men. In addition to videos, there's karaoke Tuesday and Sunday nights, and go-go boys perform Thursday nights.

Pleasuredome (✉ Club Townsend, 177 Townsend St., ☎ 415/985–5256), a long-running, Sunday-only, gay-male-oriented dance event, shows no signs of slowing down.

LESBIAN BARS

Club Q (✉ 177 Townsend St., ☎ 415/647–8258), a monthly (first Friday of every month) dance party from Page Hodel's One Groove Productions, is geared to "women and their friends."

G-Spot (✉ Harrison and 9th Sts., ☎ 415/863–6623), at the Stud, is a hot spot on Saturday night, when a mostly lesbian crowd dances to pop with a bit of techno-beat.

Luna Sea (✉ 2940 16th St., No. 216C, at S. Van Ness Ave., ☎ 415/863–2989), a newcomer amid the burgeoning Mission district arts scene, is a women's gallery and theater space featuring an ever-changing lineup of visual-arts displays, performance art, and readings. Some events are for women only.

Red Dora's Bearded Lady Café and Cabaret (✉ 485 14th St., at Guerrero St., ☎ 415/626–2805), a neighborhood venue, serves a predominantly lesbian and gay clientele. It's also a gallery with mostly women's work, and a music outlet for local independent labels.

The Arts

By Robert Taylor

Updated by Dennis Harvey

Half-price, same-day tickets to many local and touring stage shows go on sale (cash only) at 11 AM, Tuesday through Saturday, at the **TIX Bay Area** booth on the Stockton Street side of Union Square, between Geary and Post streets. TIX is also a full-service ticket agency for theater and music events around the Bay Area (open until 6 PM Tues.–Thurs., 7 PM Fri.–Sat.). For recorded information about TIX tickets, call 415/433–7827. The city's charge-by-phone ticket service is **BASS** (☎ 510/762–2277 or 415/776–1999). **City Box Office** (✉ 153 Kearny St., Suite 402, ☎ 415/392–4400) has a downtown charge-by-phone service.

Through September 1997, the War Memorial Opera House will be closed for repairs; check local listings for alternative opera and ballet performance locations during this period.

Theater

Three major commercial theaters, operated by the Shorenstein-Nederlander organization, are the **Curran** (⊠ 455 Geary St., ☎ 415/474–3800), the **Golden Gate** (⊠ Golden Gate Ave., ☎ 415/474–3800), and **Orpheum** (⊠ 1192 Market St., ☎ 415/474–3800). **Marines Memorial Theatre** (⊠ Sutter and Mason Sts., ☎ 415/441–7444) presents touring shows plus some local performances. **Theatre on the Square** (⊠ 450 Post St., ☎ 415/433–9500) is a popular smaller venue.

The city's major nonprofit theater company is the **American Conservatory Theater (ACT),** which presents a season of approximately eight plays, from classics to contemporary works, in rotating repertory from October through late spring. ACT performs at the **Geary Theater** (⊠ 415 Geary St., ☎ 415/749–2228), a landmark 1910 building with superior acoustics that reopened in 1996 after extensive renovation.

The leading producer of new plays is the **Magic Theatre** (⊠ Bldg. D, Fort Mason Center, Laguna St. at Marina Blvd. ☎ 415/441–8822), which presents works by Octavio Solis, Jon Robin Baitz, Claire Chafee, and others. The **San Francisco Shakespeare Festival** performs free on summer weekends in Golden Gate Park (☎ 415/666–2222). The major avant-garde presenting organization is **Theater Artaud** (⊠ 450 Florida St., ☎ 415/621–7797). Some contemporary theater events, in addition to dance and music, are scheduled at **Center for the Arts at Yerba Buena Gardens** (⊠ 3rd and Howard Sts., ☎ 415/978–2787).

The **Lorraine Hansberry Theatre** (⊠ 620 Sutter St., ☎ 415/474–8800) specializes in plays by black writers. **Theatre Rhinoceros** (⊠ 2926 16th St., ☎ 415/861–5079) showcases gay and lesbian performers. **Brava!,** which fosters work by women playwrights and directors, has taken over the remodeled York Theatre (⊠ 2789 24th St., ☎ 415/641–7657).

Berkeley Repertory Theatre (⊠ 2025 Addison St., Berkeley, ☎ 510/845–4700) performs an adventurous mix of classics and new plays. **California Shakespeare Festival** (☎ 510/548–3422), the Bay Area's largest outdoor summer theater event, performs in an amphitheater east of Oakland, on Gateway Boulevard just off Highway 24.

Music

San Francisco Symphony (⊠ Davies Symphony Hall, 201 Van Ness Ave., ☎ 415/864–6000, for tickets 415/776–1999 or 510/762–2277) performs September through May under the direction of California-born Michael Tilson Thomas.

Cal Performances (⊠ Zellerbach Hall, Bancroft Way and Telegraph Ave., Berkeley, ☎ 510/642–9988) presents acclaimed artists in all disciplines, from classical soloists to the latest jazz, world music, theatre, and dance ensembles.

Old First Concerts (⊠ Old First Presbyterian Church, Van Ness Ave. at Sacramento St., ☎ 415/474–1608) is a well-respected Friday evening and Sunday afternoon series of chamber music, vocal soloists, new music, and jazz.

Stern Grove (⊠ Sloat Blvd. at 19th Ave., ☎ 415/252–6252) is the location of an annual free summer-music festival, 10 Sunday afternoons of symphony, opera, jazz, pop music, and dance. The amphitheater is in a eucalyptus grove below street level; summer in this area near the ocean can be cool.

Opera

San Francisco Opera (✉ 301 Van Ness Ave., ☎ 415/864–3330) performs a season of 10 operas from September to December. The Opera schedules occasional summer festivals. Seismic repairs of the War Memorial Opera House should be completed in time for the 1997 season, but call ahead to be sure.

Dance

San Francisco Ballet (☎ 415/865–2000), under the direction of Helgi Tomasson for more than a decade, has a primary season of classic and contemporary works that runs from February through May. Its annual December presentation of the *Nutcracker* is spectacular. The ballet will be performing in three Bay Area locations until the War Memorial Opera House reopens in late 1997.

OUTDOOR ACTIVITIES AND SPORTS

Beaches

By Casey
Tefertiller

Updated by
Dianne
Aaronson

Baker Beach

Baker Beach is not recommended for swimming—the water's fairly rough—but its north end is great for nude sunbathing (it's not legal but the law against it is seldom enforced.) The section where bathers are clothed is fine, too. The beach is in the southwest corner of the Presidio, beginning at the end of Gibson Road, which turns off Bowley Street. Weather is typical of the bay shoreline: summer fog, constant breeze, and occasional warmth. Picnic tables, grills, day-camp areas, and trails are available. The mile-long shoreline is ideal for jogging, fishing, and building sand castles.

China Beach

From April through October, China Beach, south of Baker Beach, has gentle waters. It's sometimes listed on maps as Phelan Beach.

Ocean Beach

South of the Cliff House, Ocean Beach stretches along the western (ocean) side of San Francisco. Wide and scenic, it's perfect for walking, running, or lying in the sun. The swimming's a bit rough, but surfers ride the waves.

Participant Sports

For information on participant sports, check the monthly issues of *City Sports* magazine, available free at sporting-goods stores, tennis centers, and other recreational sites. The most important running event of the year is the *Examiner* Bay-to-Breakers race on the third Sunday in May. For information on this race, call 415/512–5000, ext. 2222.

Bicycling

With its legendary hills, San Francisco provides countless cycling challenges—but also plenty of level ground. A completely flat route, the **Embarcadero** affords a clear view of open waters and the Bay Bridge on the pier side, and sleek high rises on the other. **Golden Gate Park** has paths throughout. Bike shops with rentals are strategically placed near favorite routes.

Boating and Sailing

Sailors take to San Francisco Bay year-round, but tricky currents make it hazardous for inexperienced navigators. Boat rentals and charters are available throughout the Bay Area and are listed under "Boat Rentals" in the Yellow Pages. **A Day on the Bay** (☎ 415/922–0227)

is in San Francisco's small craft marina, just minutes from the Golden
Gate Bridge and open waters. **Cass' Marina** (☎ 415/332–6789) in Sausalito has sailboat rentals and charters.

Stow Lake (☎ 415/752–0347) in Golden Gate Park has rowboat, pedal
boat, and electric boat rentals. The lake is open daily for boating, but
call for seasonal hours.

Fishing

Fishing boats leave from San Francisco, Sausalito, Berkeley, Emeryville,
and Point San Pablo. They go for salmon outside the bay or striped
bass and giant sturgeon within the bay. In San Francisco, lines can be
cast from San Francisco Municipal Pier, Fisherman's Wharf, or Aquatic
Park. Trout fishing is possible at Lake Merced. One-day licenses, good
for ocean fishing only, are available for $5.75 on the charters; sport-
ing-goods stores sell full-year state licenses. Most charters depart daily
from Fisherman's Wharf during the salmon-fishing season, March
through October.

Lovely Martha's Sportsfishing (✉ 156 Linden Ave., San Bruno 94066,
☎ 415/871–4445) has a "Little People Sportsfishing Program" for children. **Wacky Jacky** (✉ 473 Bella Vista Way, San Francisco 94127, ☎
415/586–9800) will take you salmon fishing in a sleek, fast, and comfortable 50-foot boat.

Fitness

The drop-in fee at **24-hour Nautilus** (✉ 2nd St. at Folsom, ☎ 415/543–
7808) is $15. The **Embarcadero YMCA** (✉ 169 Steuart St., ☎ 415/957–
9622), one of the finest facilities in San Francisco, has racquetball, an
indoor track, a swimming pool, and aerobics classes for $12. Those
who prefer a women-only atmosphere can work out at the **Women's
Training Center** (✉ 2164 Market St., ☎ 415/864–6835) for a $10 day
fee, which includes use of the sauna.

Golf

The **Presidio Golf Course** (✉ W. Pacific Ave. and Arguello Blvd., ☎
415/561–4653), an 18-holer managed by Arnold Palmer's company,
is by most accounts the city's best course. **Harding and Fleming Parks**
(✉ Lake Merced Blvd. and Skyline Blvd., ☎ 415/750–4653) are an
18-hole, par-72 course and a 9-hole executive course, respectively. **Lincoln Park** (✉ 34th Ave. and Clement St., ☎ 415/750–4653) is an 18-
hole, par 68 course. **Golden Gate Park** (✉ 47th Ave. at Fulton St., ☎
415/750–4653) is a "pitch and putt" 9-holer.

Tennis

The San Francisco Recreation and Park Department maintains 130 free
tennis courts throughout the city. At **Dolores Park** (✉ 18th and Dolores Sts.), six courts are available on a first-come, first-served basis.
There are 21 public courts in **Golden Gate Park** (☎ 415/753–7101).

Spectator Sports

3Com Park at Candlestick Point is the name of the stadium formerly
known as Candlestick Park. Though it has a new name, the stadium
is just as windy as ever—take along extra layers of clothing for day or
night games. City shuttles marked Ballpark Special leave from numerous
stops (☎ 415/673–6864). The best way get to the **Oakland Coliseum**
and **Oakland Coliseum–Arena** is on a BART train (☎ 415/992–2278)
to the Coliseum stop. To drive from San Francisco, take I–80 to I–580
to I–980 to I–880.

Baseball

The **San Francisco Giants** (☎ 415/467–8000) play at 3Com Park. Games rarely sell out. The **Oakland A's** play at the Oakland Coliseum (☎ 510/638–0500). Game-day tickets are usually available.

Basketball

The **Golden State Warriors** play NBA basketball at the Oakland Coliseum Arena. Tickets are available through BASS (☎ 510/762–2277).

Football

The **San Francisco 49ers** (☎ 415/468–2249) play at 3Com Park, but the games are almost always sold out far in advance. The brawling (on-field and off) **Oakland Raiders** play at the Oakland Coliseum. Except for high-profile games, tickets (☎ 510/639–7700 or 510/762–2277) are usually available.

Hockey

The **San Francisco Spiders** of the International Hockey League play at the Cow Palace (☎ 415/469–6065). Tickets are usually available on game day. The National Hockey League **San Jose Sharks** play at the San Jose Arena (☞ Sports *in* Side Trip to the Silicon Valley, *below*).

SHOPPING

By Alan Frutkin and Chris Borris

Where else in the world can you find mukluk slippers from Pakistan almost as easily as a Gap shirt? Multicultural San Francisco is the place for alternative shoppers for whom the word mall is repugnant. Its small, neighborhood stores purvey everything from gay and lesbian literature to New Age candles and Guatemalan baby slings. There are ginseng health potions in Chinatown, fine antiques and art in Jackson Square, vintage clothing and records in the Haight, handmade kites and kimonos in Japantown, and high-end boutiques on Union Street. And of course, there's always the Gap.

Major Shopping Districts

The Castro/Noe Valley

Often called the gay capital of the world, the Castro is filled with clothing boutiques, home accessory stores, and various specialty stores. **A Different Light Bookstore** (⌧ 489 Castro St., ☎ 415/431–0891) doubles as an unofficial community center. **Under One Roof** (⌧ 2362 Market St., ☎ 415/252–9430) donates the profits from its home and garden items, gourmet foods, bath products, books, and cards to northern California AIDS organizations.

Just south of Castro on 24th Street, Noe Valley is an enclave of gourmet food stores, used-record shops, and clothing boutiques. Much of Armistead Maupin's *Tales of the City* was filmed in this villagelike neighborhood, whose small shops and relaxed street life evoke a '70s mood.

Chinatown

Racks of Chinese silks, toy trinkets, colorful pottery, baskets, and carved figurines are displayed in racks on the sidewalks, alongside herb stores that specialize in ginseng and roots. Dominating all are the sights and smells of food: crates of bok choy, tanks of live crabs, and hanging whole chickens.

Embarcadero Center

Five modern towers of shops, restaurants, and offices plus the Hyatt Regency Hotel make up the Embarcadero Center, downtown at the end of Market Street. **The Nature Company,** with its clever gift items relating to the natural worlds of plants and animals, is in the complex.

Fisherman's Wharf
Pier 39 is one of the world's most visited sites, though the shops at Ghirardelli Square and the Cannery are more interesting. All three also have restaurants, plus musicians, mimes, magicians, and other entertainment.

The Haight
Haight Street is always an attraction for visitors, if only to see the sign at Haight and Ashbury streets. These days, in addition to renascent tie-dyed shirts, you'll find high-quality vintage clothing, funky jewelry, art from Mexico, and reproductions of art deco accessories.

Hayes Valley
Hayes Valley, just west of the Civic Center, is an up-and-coming shopping district. The **San Francisco Women Artists Gallery** (⊠ 370 Hayes St., ☎ 415/552–7392) is one of the area's biggest draws. **Worldware** (⊠ 336 Hayes St., ☎ 415/487–9030) sells environmentally conscious clothing and home furnishings.

Japantown
The three-block **Japan Center** (⊠ Laguna St. to Fillmore Sts., between Geary Blvd. and Post St.) includes an 800-car public garage and three shop-filled buildings. Especially worthwhile are the Kintetsu and Kinokuniya buildings, where shops and showrooms sell cameras, tapes and records, new and old porcelains, pearls, antique kimonos, tansu chests, paintings, and more.

The Marina District
Chestnut Street, one block north of Lombard Street and stretching from Fillmore Street to Broderick Street, caters to the shopping whims of Marina District residents. The **Red Rose Gallerie** (⊠ 2251 Chestnut St., ☎ 415/776–6871), specializes in "tools for personal growth," including body scents, exotic clothing, and audiotapes for rejuvenating the mind.

The Mission
Known as one of the city's sunniest neighborhoods, the Mission is also one of its most ethnically diverse, with a large Hispanic population and a sprinkling of everything else. In addition to those with a hunger for inexpensive Mexican food, the area draws bargain shoppers with its many used clothing, furniture, and alternative book stores. The main shopping streets are Mission and Valencia between 16th and 24th streets.

North Beach
Shopping here is clustered tightly around Washington Square and Columbus Avenue. Businesses here include clothing boutiques and antiques and vintage-wares shops. Once the center of the Beat movement, North Beach still has a bohemian spirit that's especially apparent at **City Lights Bookstore** (⊠ 261 Columbus Ave., ☎ 415/362–8193). **Juicey Lucy's & the Sample Store** (⊠ 703 Columbus Ave.) sells high-end samples at wholesale prices and serves shot glass–size tastes of unusual juices.

Pacific Heights
Pacific Heights residents head for Fillmore and Sacramento streets—Fillmore between Post Street and Pacific Avenue, and Sacramento Street between Lyon and Maple streets—where private residences alternate with good bookstores, fine clothing and gift shops, thrift stores, and art galleries. **Sue Fisher King Company** (⊠ 3067 Sacramento St., ☎ 415/922–7276) has an eclectic collection of home accessories.

South of Market
Dozens of discount outlets, most of them open seven days a week, have sprung up along the streets and alleyways bordered by 2nd, Townsend, Howard, and 10th streets. At the other end of the spectrum are the gift shops of the Museum of Modern Art (⊠ 151 3rd St.) and the Cen-

ter for the Arts at Yerba Buena Gardens (⊠ 3rd and Mission Sts.); both sell handmade jewelry and various other great gift items.

Union Square

Serious shoppers head straight to Union Square, San Francisco's main shopping artery and the site of major retailers, including Neiman Marcus, Macy's, F.A.O. Schwarz, the Virgin Megastore, the Disney Store, Borders Books and Music, Saks Fifth Avenue, and the boutiques of Hermès of Paris, Gucci, Celine of Paris, Alfred Dunhill, Louis Vuitton, and Cartier. Scheduled for a 1997 opening is a huge Nike Town store. Across from the cable-car turntable at Powell and Market streets is the San Francisco Shopping Centre (⊠ 865 Market St.), with the Nordstrom department store and three-dozen other businesses. The Crocker Galleria (⊠ 50 Post St.) is a complex of 40 to 50 shops and restaurants underneath a glass dome.

Union Street

Out-of-towners sometimes confuse Union Street with Union Square. Nestled at the foot of a hill between Pacific Heights and the Marina District, the street is lined with contemporary fashion and custom jewelry shops, along with a few antiques shops and art galleries.

SIDE TRIP TO MARIN COUNTY

Sausalito

By Robert Taylor and Sharron Wood

Like much of San Francisco, Sausalito had a raffish reputation before it went upscale. Discovered in 1775 by Spanish explorers and named Saucelito (Little Willow) for the trees growing around its springs, it was a port for whaling ships during the 19th century. In 1875 the railroad from the north connected with ferryboats to San Francisco and the town began attracting a fun-loving crowd. Even the chamber of commerce recalls the time when Sausalito had 25 saloons, gambling dens, and bordellos. Bootleggers flourished during Prohibition, and shipyard workers swelled the town's population during the 1940s, when tour guides divided the residents into "wharf rats" and "hill snobs."

Ensuing decades brought a bohemian element with the development of an artists' colony and a houseboat community. The town remains friendly and casual, although summer traffic jams can fray nerves. If possible, visit on a weekday—and take the ferry.

Bridgeway is Sausalito's main thoroughfare and prime destination, with the bay, yacht harbor, and waterfront restaurants on one side, and more restaurants, shops, hotels, and hillside homes. Stairs along the west side of Bridgeway climb the hill to Sausalito's wooded residential neighborhoods.

The **Village Fair** (⊠ 777 Bridgeway, ☎ 415/332–1902) is a four-story former warehouse that's been filled with potted plants and converted into a warren of clothing, craft, and gift boutiques. The Chart House restaurant perched on a pier jutting into the bay was built in 1893 as "Walhalla," later called **Valhalla.** Run for years by former San Francisco madam and Sausalito mayor Sally Stanford, it was one of the settings of the 1948 film *The Lady from Shanghai.*

The U.S. Army Corps of Engineers uses the **Bay Model,** a 400-square-foot replica of the entire San Francisco Bay and the San Joaquin–Sacramento River delta, to reproduce the rise and fall of tides, the flow of currents, and the other physical forces at work on the bay. Housed in a former World War II shipyard building, the Bay Model is next to a display of shipbuilding history. At the same site is the *Wapama*, a World War I–era steam freighter being restored by volunteers. Free tours of the ship are given on Saturdays at 11 AM. ⊠ *2100 Bridgeway, ☎ 415/332–3871.* ⊡ *Free.* ☉ *Tues.–Fri. 9–4, weekends 10–6; closed Sun. in winter.*

Some of the 400 **houseboats** that make up Sausalito's "floating homes community" line the shore of Richardson Bay. The sight of these colorful, quirky abodes is one of Marin County's most famous views—they range from rustic to eccentric to flamboyant. For a close-up view of the houseboats, park at the Bay Model and walk north.

The **Bay Area Discovery Museum** fills five former military buildings with entertaining and enlightening hands-on exhibits. Youngsters and their families can crew on a boat, explore in and under a house, and make multitrack recordings. From San Francisco take the Alexander Avenue exit from U.S. 101 and follow signs to East Fort Baker. ☎ *415/487–4398.* ⊡ *$7.* ☉ *Summer, Tues.–Sun. 10–5; fall–spring, Tues.–Thurs. 9–4 and Fri.–Sun. 10–5.*

Dining

$$$ ✕ **Mikayla at Casa Madrona.** Although the food at this longtime Sausalito hilltop dining room has followed a rocky course, the view has never been less than superb. The Californian menu, based on grilled fish and meats, is built around fresh local foods. Sunday brunch is popular. ⊠ *801 Bridgeway, ☎ 415/331–5888. Reservations essential on weekends. AE, D, DC, MC, V.*

$$ ✕ **Alta Mira.** This Sausalito landmark, in a Spanish-style hotel a block above Bridgeway, has spectacular views of the bay from a heated front terrace and a windowed dining room. It's a favored Bay location for Sunday brunch (try the famed eggs Benedict and Ramos Fizz), alfresco lunch, or cocktails at sunset. Though the California-Continental cuisine is inconsistent, the view never fails. ⊠ *125 Bulkley Ave., ☎ 415/332–1350. AE, DC, MC, V.*

$$ ✕ **Spinnaker.** Spectacular bay views, homemade pastas, and seafood specialties are the prime attractions in this contemporary building on a point beyond the harbor, near the yacht club. You may see a pelican perched on one of the pilings just outside. ⊠ *100 Spinnaker Dr., ☎ 415/332–1500. AE, DC, MC, V. Sun. brunch.*

$ ✕ **Lighthouse Coffee Shop.** This budget-priced coffee shop serves breakfast and lunch (omelets, sandwiches, and burgers) every day from 6:30 (7 on weekends). Most find the down-to-earth atmosphere and simple fare (including Danish meatballs, herring, and salmon open-faced sandwiches) a welcome break from tourist traps and seafood extravaganzas. ⊠ *1311 Bridgeway, ☎ 415/331–3034. Reservations not accepted. No credit cards. No alcohol.*

Tiburon

Located on a peninsula called Punta de Tiburon (Shark Point) by the Spanish explorers, this Marin County community maintains a villagelike atmosphere despite the ever-growing encroachment of commercial establishments concentrated in the downtown area. The harbor faces Angel Island across Raccoon Strait. San Francisco is directly south, 6 miles across the bay, which makes the view from the decks of restaurants on the harbor a major attraction. More low-key than Sausalito, Tiburon has always been a waterfront settlement, beginning in 1884 when ferryboats from San Francisco connected here with a railroad to San Rafael. Whenever the weather is pleasant, and particularly during the summer, the ferry is the most relaxing way to visit and avoid traffic and parking problems.

Tiburon's **Main Street** is lined on the bay side with restaurants that overlook the harbor and offer views of San Francisco from outdoor decks. On the other side of the narrow street are shops and galleries that sell casual clothing, gifts, jewelry, posters, and paintings.

During the 19th century the buildings along **Ark Row** were houseboats on the bay. Later they were beached and transformed into shops; now the tree-lined walk is lined with antiques and specialty stores.

On a hill above town is **Old St. Hilary's Historic Preserve,** a Victorian-era Carpenter Gothic church operated by the Landmarks Society as a historical and botanical museum. The surrounding wildflower preserve is especially spectacular in May and June, when the rare black jewel is in bloom. ⊠ *Esperanza and Alemany Sts.,* ☏ *415/435–1853.* ▱ *Free.* ◷ *Apr.–Oct., Wed. and Sun. 1–4.*

In a wildlife sanctuary on the route into Tiburon is the 1876 **Lyford House,** a Victorian fantasy that serves as the western headquarters for the National Audubon Society. House tours are conducted on Sunday from 1 to 4. ⊠ *Between Tiburon Blvd. and Richardson Bay,* ☏ *415/388–0717.*

Dining

$$ ✕ **Guaymas.** This large open kitchen churns out regional Mexican dishes such as *pato de granja* (roasted duck with pumpkin-seed sauce), *carnitas ropa* (slowly roasted pork with salsa and black beans), and *pollo en mole* (chicken with chocolate sauce, chilies, and 29 spices). The heated terrace bar has views of the bay. Sunday brunch is popular, so reserve in advance. ⊠ *5 Main St., at the ferry terminal,* ☏ *415/435–6300. DC, MC, V.*

$ ✕ **Sam's Anchor Cafe.** Perhaps the most well-known restaurant in Tiburon, Sam's is a major draw for tourists and old salts who flock to its outside deck for bay views and beer. A college hangout since 1921, the informal restaurant has mahogany wainscoting and old photos on the walls. Burgers, fresh seafood, sandwiches, soups, and salads are standards, but food pales next to atmosphere here. ⊠ *27 Main St.,* ☏ *415/435–4527. AE, D, DC, MC, V.*

Marin County A to Z

Arriving and Departing

BY BUS

Golden Gate Transit buses (☏ 415/332–6600) travel to Sausalito and Tiburon from 1st and Mission streets and other points in the city.

BY CAR

To get to Sausalito from San Francisco, cross the Golden Gate Bridge and head north on U.S. 101 to the Sausalito exit. Go south on Bridgeway to the municipal parking lot (bring plenty of change for the meters) near the center of town. The trip takes 20 to 45 minutes one-way. To get to Tiburon, take U.S. 101 to the Tiburon Boulevard exit.

BY FERRY

Golden Gate Ferry (☏ 415/332–6600) crosses the bay to Sausalito from the south wing of the Ferry Building at Market Street and the Embarcadero. The Red and White Fleet (☏ 415/546–2896) leaves from Pier 43½ at Fisherman's Wharf on trips to Sausalito and Tiburon. Red and White boats also sail from the Ferry Building to Tiburon. Note: Red and White has been purchased by the Blue and Gold Fleet, which may rename (and repaint) the ferries as part of the takeover.

SIDE TRIP TO THE EAST BAY

Oakland

By Robert
Taylor

Updated by
Sharron Wood

Originally the site of ranches, farms, a grove of redwood trees, and, of course, clusters of oaks, Oakland has long been a warm and spacious alternative to San Francisco. By the end of the 19th century, Mediterranean-style homes and gardens had been developed as summer estates. With swifter transportation, Oakland became a bedroom community for San Francisco; then it progressed to California's fastest-growing industrial city. In recent decades, Oakland has struggled to upgrade its image as a tourist destination. Art deco buildings in the downtown area around Broadway have been carefully refurbished, and the city is trying hard to attract visitors to the waterfront Jack London Square.

Oakland's major attractions, however, remain the same: the parks and civic buildings around Lake Merritt, which was created from a tidal basin in 1898; Jack London Square, where the author spent much of his time at the turn of the century; and the scenic roads and parks along the crest of the Oakland-Berkeley hills. Areas for shopping, browsing, or just relaxing at a café can be found on Lake Shore Avenue northeast of Lake Merritt, Piedmont Avenue near the Broadway exit from I–580, and College Avenue west of Broadway in North Oakland, which neighbors BART's Rockridge station. From the station, the local Bus 51 will take visitors to the University of California campus, about 1½ miles away in Berkeley.

Numbers in the margin correspond to points of interest on the Oakland map.

❶ The **Oakland Museum of California** is housed in landscaped buildings that display the state's art, history, and natural science. The Gallery of Natural Sciences surveys a typical stretch of California from the Pacific Ocean to the Nevada border, including plants and wildlife. A breathtaking film, *Fast Flight*, condenses the trip into five minutes. The museum's sprawling Cowell Hall of California History includes everything from Spanish-era artifacts and a gleaming fire engine that battled the flames in San Francisco in 1906 to souvenirs of the 1967 "summer of love." The museum's Gallery of California Art includes mystical landscapes painted by the state's pioneers, as well as contemporary paintings. ✉ *1000 Oak St., at 10th St.,* ☎ *510/238–3401.* ✦ *$4.* ☉ *Wed.–Sat. 10–5, Sun. noon–7.*

❷ **Lake Merritt** is a 155-acre oasis surrounded by parks, with several out-
❸ door attractions on the north side. The **Natural Science Center and Waterfowl Refuge** (☎ 510/238–3739) at the foot of Perkins Street is the nesting site of herons, egrets, geese, and ducks in the spring and summer. It's open daily 9–5.

The **Paramount Theater** (✉ 2025 Broadway, ☎ 510/465–6400) is perhaps the city's best example of the art deco style. It is a venue for concerts and performances of all kinds. For $1 you can take a two-hour tour of the building on the first and third Saturday of each month.

❹ **Preservation Parkway** is an idyllic little street lined with 14 restored Victorian homes and tidy, bright green lawns. You can enjoy the architecture from one of the benches next to the fountain or from the White House Café at 1233 Preservation Parkway; it is near the fountain and has outdoor seating.

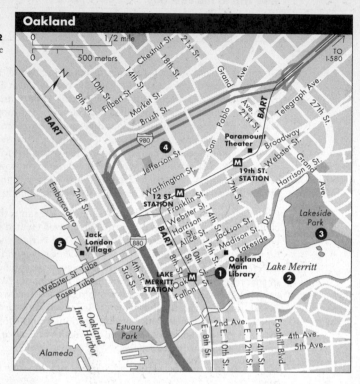

5 Jack London—adventurer, author of *The Call of the Wild, The Sea Wolf, Martin Eden,* and *The Cruise of the Snark,* and a former resident of Oakland—is commemorated with a bronze bust at **Jack London Square,** a collection of shops, restaurants, small museums, and historic sites. Community events such as boat and auto shows and a farmers' market take place here every Sunday. **Heinold's First and Last Chance Saloon** (⊠ 56 Jack London Sq., ☎ 510/839–6761), one of Jack London's hangouts, is intact.

Dining

$$ ✕ **Citron.** A smart, flower-filled dining room and a small but memorable Mediterranean menu have made this innovative restaurant one of Oakland's most celebrated dining establishments. The generously portioned selections might include fish fillets on a bed of lentils, beef daube laced with mushrooms, roast pork loin with cherry sauce, or seafood couscous. The place is small and popular, so reserve far in advance. ⊠ *5484 College Ave.,* ☎ *510/653–5484. Reservations essential on weekends. MC, V. No lunch.*

$–$$ ✕ **Oliveto Café & Restaurant.** In the formal dining room upstairs, gourmets indulge in chef Paul Bertolli's tagliatelle with smoked ham, ravioli with pumpkin, or chicken cooked under a brick. The café at street level is the place to sip wine or espresso, or snack on pizzas and pastries. ⊠ *5655 College Ave.,* ☎ *510/547–5356. Reservations essential on weekends. AE, DC, MC, V. No lunch weekends in restaurant.*

$–$$ ✕ **ZZA's Trattoria.** Pizzas, salads, house-smoked chicken, and homemade pasta, ravioli, and lasagna are served in this fun, family-oriented restaurant on the shore of Lake Merritt. ⊠ *552 Grand Ave.,* ☎ *510/839–9124. MC, V. No lunch Mon., Tues., weekends.*

$ ✕ **Rockridge Cafe.** This casual café is known for burgers, breakfasts, and mighty fine pie. ⊠ *5492 College Ave.,* ☎ *510/653–1567. MC, V. Sun. brunch.*

Berkeley

Although the University of California dominates Berkeley's heritage and contemporary life, the two are not synonymous: The city of 100,000 facing San Francisco across the bay has other interesting features for visitors. Surrounding the campus are no fewer than 55 cafés, without which the city might very well collapse. Students, faculty, and other Berkeley residents spend hours nursing coffee concoctions of various persuasions while they read, discuss, and debate—or eavesdrop on others doing the same.

Beyond the campus there are shops for browsing along Telegraph Avenue south from Bancroft Way (including some fine book and record stores); College Avenue near Ashby Avenue south of campus; and in the Walnut Square development at Shattuck and Vine streets northwest of campus. Shingled houses line the tree-shaded streets near College and Ashby avenues, and hillside homes with fine views rest on the winding roads near the intersection of Ashby and Claremont avenues. On the opposite side of the city, on 4th Street north of University Avenue, an industrial area has been converted into a pleasant shopping street with some stores selling handcrafted and eco-conscious goods, as well as a few popular eateries.

The **Phoebe Apperson Hearst Museum of Anthropology** has a collection of more than 4,000 artifacts. Items on display may cover the archaeology of ancient America or the crafts of Pacific Islanders. The museum also houses the collection of artifacts made by Ishi, the lone survivor of a California Indian tribe, who was brought to the Bay Area in 1911. ⊠ *UC Berkeley, Kroeber Hall,* ☎ *510/642–3681.* ☒ *$2.* ☉ *Wed.–Sun. 10–4:30, Thurs. until 9.*

The **University Art Museum** houses an impressive collection of works spanning five centuries, though the emphasis is on contemporary art. The museum's temporary and permanent exhibits are displayed in a low concrete building that appears earth-bound from the exterior, but gracefully airy from the interior, with its spiral of ramps and balcony galleries. The highlight is a series of vibrant paintings by the abstract expressionist Hans Hofmann. On the ground floor is the Pacific Film Archive, which presents daily programs of historic and contemporary films. ⊠ *2626 Bancroft Way,* ☎ *510/642–0808; for film-program information, 510/642–1124.* ☒ *Museum $6.* ☉ *Museum: Wed. and Fri.–Sun. 11–5, Thurs. 11–9.*

The 34-acre **Botanical Garden** contains approximately 13,500 species of plants from all over the world. Tours are given weekends at 1:30. The benches and shady picnic tables make this a relaxing stop. ⊠ *UC Berkeley, Centennial Dr.,* ☎ *510/642–3343.* ☒ *Free.* ☉ *Daily 9–4:45.*

☾ The fortresslike **Lawrence Hall of Science** is a laboratory, a science education center, and—most important to visitors—a dazzling repository of scientific knowledge and experiments. Changing hands-on displays allow children to look at insects under microscopes, play educational computer games, and enjoy other interactive exhibits. On weekends there are films, lectures, and demonstrations especially for children. ⊠ *UC Berkeley, Centennial Dr.,* ☎ *510/642–5132.* ☒ *$6.* ☉ *Daily 10–5.*

NEED A BREAK?   **Caffe Mediterraneum** (⊠ 2475 Telegraph Ave., ☎ 510/549–1128) is a relic of '60s-era Berkeley café culture, but far enough from campus to pull in a mostly nonstudent crowd. Allen Ginsberg wrote while imbibing here.

The 2,000-acre **Tilden Park** (☎ 510/562–7275), one of the 46 parks run by the East Bay Regional Park District, has swimming at Lake

Anza, a botanic garden, a golf course, a merry-go-round, an environmental education center, and miles of paths that wind up and down the Berkeley hills.

Dining

$$–$$$$ ✕ **Chez Panisse Café & Restaurant.** Alice Waters is still the mastermind behind the culinary wizardry at this legendary eatery, with Jean-Pierre Moullé lending hands-on talent as head chef. In the downstairs restaurant, where redwood paneling, a fireplace, and lavish floral arrangements create the ambience of a private home, dinners are prix fixe and pricey, but the cost is lower on weekdays. The daily-changing menu might include local rock cod with ginger sauce, chicken breast with chicken liver crostini, roast sirloin with red wine sauce, and roast truffled breast of guinea hen. Upstairs in the café the atmosphere is informal, the crowd livelier, the prices lower, and the menu more simple, with dishes such as calzone with goat cheese, mozzarella, prosciutto, and garlic. ⊠ *1517 Shattuck Ave., north of University Ave.,* ☎ *510/548–5525 for restaurant, 510/548–5049 for café. Reservations essential for restaurant, not accepted for café. AE, D, DC, MC, V. No lunch in restaurant, no dinner Mon.–Thurs. in café. Both closed Sun.*

$$ ✕ **Lalime's.** The Mediterranean menu here changes daily, with choices that might range from colorful Spanish paella to creamy Italian risotto to seared duck foie gras. The dining room, on two levels, is done in light colors, creating a cheerful ambience that makes this a sublime spot for any special occasion. ⊠ *1329 Gilman St.,* ☎ *415/527–9838. Reservations essential. MC, V. No lunch.*

$$ ✕ **Rivoli.** Husband and wife team Wendy Rucker and Roscoe Skipper use native California ingredients in French-and Italian-inspired dishes for a menu that changes weekly. Typical offerings include linguine with scallops, portobello mushroom fritters, ricotta tart, and rigatoni with eggplant, olives, and feta cheese. Desserts can range from a pear granita with gingersnaps and bittersweet chocolate *tiramisù* with espresso crème anglaise to a refreshing Meyer lemon tart. ⊠ *1539 Solano Ave.,* ☎ *510/526–2542. Reservations essential. AE, MC, V. No lunch.*

$$ ✕ **Venezia Caffe & Ristorante.** This family-friendly eatery was one of the first to serve fresh pasta in the Bay Area, and it continues to offer tasty selections (don't miss the house-made chicken sausage). The large dining room looks like a Venetian piazza, with a fountain in the middle, murals on the walls, and laundry hanging overhead. Children get their own menu, along with free antipasti and crayons. ⊠ *1799 University Ave.,* ☎ *510/849–4681. AE, DC, MC, V. No lunch weekends.*

$ ✕ **Bette's Oceanview Diner.** Buttermilk pancakes that you'll never forget are just one of the specialties at this 1930s-inspired diner, complete with checkered floors and burgundy booths. There are also huevos rancheros and lox and eggs for breakfast, and kosher East Coast franks, Chinese chicken salad, and a slew of sandwiches for lunch. The wait for a seat can be long; if you're starving, Bette's To Go, right next door, will press food into your hands in a hurry. ⊠ *1807 4th St.,* ☎ *415/644–3230. No credit cards. No dinner.*

The East Bay A to Z

Arriving and Departing

BY CAR

Take I–80 east across the Bay Bridge. To go to Oakland, take I–580 to the Grand Avenue exit for Lake Merritt. To reach downtown and the waterfront, take the I–980 exit from I–580. To get to Berkeley, stay on I–80 and take the University Avenue exit heading east to the campus. Both trips take 45 minutes one-way, longer during rush hour.

BART trains make two stops in Oakland. Use the Oakland City Center station for downtown or the Lake Merritt station for the lake and the Oakland Museum. Get off at BART's downtown Berkeley stop to visit the university, or at the Ashby or North Berkeley stations for other parts of town.

Visitor Information

Oakland Convention and Visitors Authority (⊠ 550 10th St., Suite 214, Oakland 94607, ☏ 510/839–9000). **UC Berkeley visitor center** (⊠ University Hall, Room 101, University Ave. and Oxford St., ☏ 510/642–5215).

SIDE TRIP TO THE PENINSULA

San Mateo County Coast

If your only experience of the towns south of San Francisco has been the high-tech metropolises of San Jose and Palo Alto, the coastal communities along the San Mateo Coast will come as a pleasant surprise. As you head toward Half Moon Bay along the winding, hilly Highway 92, past Christmas-tree farms and mom-and-pop stores, you'll soon realize that the pace of life is slower here than elsewhere in the Bay Area. The towns along the San Mateo Coast were founded around 1769, when Spanish explorer Gaspar de Portolá arrived. After the Mexican government gained control, the land was used for agriculture by ranchers who provided food to San Francisco's Mission Dolores. Soon lighthouses and ships were being built to facilitate the transport of goods to San Francisco.

Most of the towns that dot the coast from Pacifica in the north to Año Nuevo State Reserve in the south are no more than a few blocks long, providing just enough room for a bed-and-breakfast, a restaurant or two, and a few boutiques or galleries. Visitors come here mostly to be pampered in the area's many cozy bed-and-breakfasts, and to indulge in the many outdoor opportunities the coastal communities offer.

Half Moon Bay

The largest and most visited of the coastal communities, Half Moon Bay is nevertheless a tiny town with a population of less than 9,000. The town's hub, Main Street, is lined with five blocks of small crafts shops, art galleries, and outdoor cafés, many housed in renovated 19th-century structures.

Half Moon Bay comes to life on the third weekend in October, when 300,000 people gather for the **Half Moon Bay Art and Pumpkin Festival.** Arts, crafts, and all sorts of food (heavy on the pumpkin) are sold from booths up and down the street all weekend, and Saturday heralds in the Great Pumpkin Parade.

The 4-mile stretch of **Half Moon Bay State Beach** is perfect for long walks and kite flying, though the 50°F water and dangerous currents prevent most visitors from swimming.

The coastal communities can be easily explored on two wheels. **The Bicyclery** (⊠ 432 Main St., ☏ 415/726–6000) has bike rentals and will provide information on organized rides up and down the coast. If you prefer to go it alone, try the 3-mile bike trail that leads from Kelly Avenue in Half Moon Bay to Mirada Road in Miramar.

$$$$ ⊞ **Mill Rose Inn.** Probably the most decadent bed-and-breakfast in the entire Bay Area, the Mill Rose Inn pampers guests with in-room fireplaces, antique beds stacked high with down comforters, decanters of sherry and brandy on the tables, and almost any other amenity one could want. The wildly romantic rooms, most looking onto the lush gardens, are popular with honeymooners, as is the ultra-private gazebo spa. Room rates include a lavish champagne breakfast. ⊠ *615 Mill St.,* ☎ *415/726–9794,* ℻ *415/726–3031. 4 rooms, 2 suites. No-smoking rooms, refrigerators, in-room VCRs. AE, D, MC, V.*

$$–$$$ ⊞ **Old Thyme Inn.** Rooms in this Queen Anne Victorian house have been thoughtfully decorated, each with an herb motif. The more expensive rooms have fireplaces and whirlpool tubs. Antiques, fresh flowers, and a homemade breakfast make this a lovely place to spend a weekend. ⊠ *779 Main St.,* ☎ *415/726–1616,* ℻ *415/692–3802. 6 rooms, 1 suite. No-smoking rooms. MC, V.*

Pescadero

Walking down Stage Road, Pescadero's main street, it's hard to believe you're only 30 minutes from Silicon Valley. The few short blocks that comprise that downtown area could almost serve as the backdrop of a western movie, with Duarte's Tavern serving as the centerpiece. In fact, Pescadero was reportedly larger 100 years ago than it is today. This is a good place to stop for a bite or to browse for antiques housed in what looks like a converted barn. The town's real attraction, though, is its proximity to beaches and spectacular hiking.

At the **Pescadero Marsh Natural Reserve** (☎ 415/879–2170) hikers can spy on birds and other wildlife as they follow any of the trails that crisscross 500 acres of marshland. Early spring and fall are the best times to visit.

November through April you can look for mussels at **Pescadero State Beach,** where sandy expanses, tide pools, and rocky outcroppings form one of the coast's more scenic beaches. Barbecue pits and tables attract many picnicking families.

If you prefer mountain trails to sand dunes, head for **Pescadero Creek County Park,** a 7,500-acre expanse of shady, old-growth redwood forests, grasslands, and mountain streams. The park is actually composed of three smaller ones: Heritage Grove Redwood Preserve, Sam McDonald Park, and San Mateo Memorial County Park. The Pomponio Trail runs the length of the park.

$–$$ ✕ **Duarte's Tavern.** This 19th-century roadhouse serves simple American fare, with locally grown vegetables and fresh fish as standard items. Don't pass up the famed house artichoke soup, or old-fashioned berry pie à la mode. Breakfasts are hearty here—eggs, bacon, sausage, hotcakes—just as you might expect in such a farming community. ⊠ *202 Stage Rd, Pescadero,* ☎ *415/879–0464. MC, V.*

San Mateo County A to Z

By Bus: SamTrans (☎ 800/660–4287) buses travel to Half Moon Bay from the Daly City BART station. Another bus connects Half Moon Bay with Pescadero. Each trip takes approximately one hour. Call for schedules, since departures are infrequent.

By Car: To get to Half Moon Bay by car, take Highway 1, also known as the Coast Highway, south from San Francisco. A quicker route is via I–280, the Junípero Serra Freeway; follow it south as far as Highway 92, where you can turn west toward Half Moon Bay. To get to Pescadero, continue south on Highway 1 from Half Moon Bay.

VISITOR INFORMATION

California State Parks Bay Area District Office (⊠ 250 Executive Park Blvd., Suite 4900, San Francisco, ☎ 415/330–6300). **Half Moon Bay Chamber of Commerce** (⊠ 520 Kelly Ave., ☎ 415/726–8380).

Palo Alto and Woodside

Palo Alto's main attraction is the campus of the renowned Stanford University, whose 8,200 acres of grass-covered hills were once part of Leland Stanford's horse-breeding farm. Surrounding the campus are residential neighborhoods lined with cafés, bookstores, and music shops. Just to the west, Woodside is a rustic town where weekend warriors stock up on espresso and picnic fare before charging off on their mountain bikes.

Free one-hour walking tours of **Stanford University** leave daily at 11 AM and 3:15 PM from the Visitor Information Booth (☎ 415/723–2560 or 415/723–2053) at the front of the quadrangle. The main campus entrance, Palm Drive, is an extension of University Avenue from Palo Alto.

The **Stanford Art Gallery** presents visiting shows, some student works, and a selection of the university's historical artifacts. Through much of 1997, the gallery will display works from the Stanford Museum of Art, which is closed for renovations until 1998. ☎ 415/723–3469. ⊠ *Donation requested.* ☉ *Tues.–Fri. 10–5, weekends 1–5.*

The 2-mile-long **Stanford Linear Accelerator** is used for elementary-particle research. ⊠ *Sand Hill Rd., 2 mi west of main campus,* ☎ 415/926–2204 *for tour times and reservations.*

One of the few great country houses in California that remains intact in its original setting is **Filoli,** in Woodside. Built for wealthy San Franciscan William B. Bourn II, from 1915 to 1917, it was designed by Willis Polk in a Georgian Revival style, with redbrick walls and a tile roof. The name is not Italian but Bourn's acronym for "fight, love, live." As interesting to visitors as the house (which some may recall from the television series *Dynasty*) are the 16 acres of formal gardens. These were planned and developed over a period of more than 50 years and preserved for the public when the last private owner, Mrs. William P. Roth, deeded Filoli to the National Trust for Historic Preservation.

The gardens rise south from the mansion to take advantage of the natural surroundings of the 700-acre estate and its vistas. Among the designs are a sunken garden, walled garden, woodland garden, yew alley, and a rose garden developed by Mrs. Roth with more than 50 shrubs of all types and colors. In the middle of it all is a teahouse designed in the Italian Renaissance style. Spring is the most popular time to visit, but daffodils, narcissi, and rhododendrons are in bloom as early as February, and the gardens remain attractive in October and November. ⊠ *Cañada Rd., near Edgewood Rd., Woodside,* ☎ 415/364–2880. ⊠ *$10.* ☉ *Mid-Feb.–mid-Nov. for guided tours Tues.–Thurs. (reservations necessary), Fri.–Sat. for self-guided tours.*

Dining

$$–$$$ ✕ **Stars Palo Alto.** The glass walls of celebrity-chef Jeremiah Tower's dining room and bar disappear to offer alfresco seating on sunny days. The menu emphasizes the same fresh local ingredients, light cooking hand, and Mediterranean accent found at other Tower enterprises. ⊠ *365 Lytton Ave.,* ☎ 415/321–4466. *Reservations essential. AE, DC, MC, V.*

$$ ✕ **Evvia.** Oak floors, ceiling beams, a large fireplace, and hand-painted pottery create a stunning interior for this California–influenced Greek restaurant. Fried calamari and smelt, *spanakopita* (spinach-stuffed phyllo leaves), and white beans baked with tomato sauce and topped with feta are among the appetizers. Grilled striped bass served with a sprightly vinaigrette, classic moussaka, or lemony roast chicken will round out your meal. ✉ *420 Emerson St., Palo Alto,* ☎ *451/326–0983. AE, DC, MC, V. Closed Sun.*

$$ ✕ **Flea Street Cafe.** Specialties may include herb-roasted Cornish game hen with sage jalapeño gravy and red-onion cornbread stuffing, or fettuccine with duck sausage and pippin apples. Sunday brunch is a local institution. ✉ *Alameda de las Pulgas, Menlo Park (take Sand Hill Rd. west from the Stanford shopping center or east from I–280; turn right on Alameda),* ☎ *415/854–1226. MC, V. Closed Mon. No lunch Sat.*

$$ ✕ **Il Fornaio Cucina Italiana.** Buy gourmet fare to go, or stay here to sample superb antipasti, pizza, pasta, and calzone baked to perfection in a wood-burning oven. Italian breads and irresistible bread sticks, biscotti, cakes, and tortes are prime attractions. ✉ *520 Cowper St., Palo Alto,* ☎ *415/853–3888. AE, DC, MC, V. Weekend brunch.*

$$ ✕ **Village Pub.** In this pleasant restaurant near Filoli, patrons elbow up to a carved oak bar to sample the ale, or relax in the stylishly simple modern dining room to savor creative California-rustic fare. Duck, fresh seafood, steak, and pasta are regular offerings. ✉ *2967 Woodside Rd. (¾ mi from I–280W), Woodside,* ☎ *415/851–1294. AE, DC, MC, V. No lunch weekends.*

Palo Alto and Woodside A to Z

ARRIVING AND DEPARTING

By Car: The most pleasant direct route down the peninsula is I–280. For Stanford University, exit at Sand Hill Road and drive east to the Stanford Shopping Center. Turn right on Arboretum, then right again on Palm Drive, which leads to the center of campus. U.S. 101 along the bayshore is more direct but also more congested; from there take University Avenue or Embarcadero Road to Stanford.

By Train: CalTrain (☎ 800/660–4287) runs from 4th and Townsend streets in San Francisco to Palo Alto; from there take the shuttle bus to the Stanford campus.

SIDE TRIP TO SILICON VALLEY

Claudia
Gioseffi

Updated by
Sharron Wood

Silicon Valley, birthplace of America's computer industry, is a sprawling community of office parks, business-lined highways, shopping malls, and Spanish-style homes—their red-tiled roofs peeking through dense junipers and magnolias. El Camino Real, U.S. 101, and the more picturesque I–280 link the area's key towns: Sunnyvale, Cupertino, Santa Clara, and San Jose. The center of the Valley is San Jose, now the state's third largest city.

Santa Clara

In the center of Santa Clara University's campus is the **Mission Santa Clara de Assis,** the eighth of 21 California missions founded under the direction of Father Junípero Serra and the first to honor a woman. The mission's present site was the fifth chosen, after the first four were flooded by the Guadalupe River and destroyed by earthquakes. In 1926 the permanent mission chapel was destroyed by fire. Roof tiles of the current building, a replica of the original, were salvaged from earlier structures, which dated from the 1790s and 1820s. Early adobe walls and a garden remain as well. In the mid-1770s, Franciscan friars raised

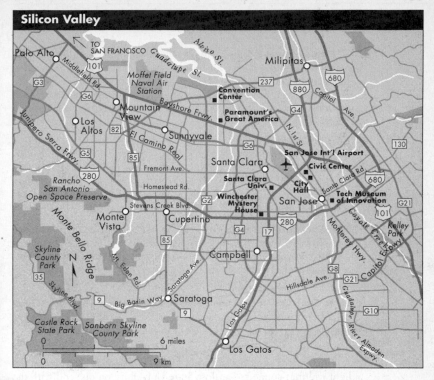

Silicon Valley

grapes here for sacramental wines; the olive and fig trees they planted at this time remain. Part of a wooden Memorial Cross from 1777 is set in front of the Santa Clara Mission church. ⊠ *500 El Camino Real,* ☎ *408/554–4023.* ☞ *Free.* ⊙ *Weekdays 8–6.*

Visitors to the **Intel Museum** can learn how computer chips are made and follow the development of Intel Corporation's microprocessor, memory, and systems product lines. Guided tours are available by reservation. ⊠ *Robert Noyce Bldg., 2200 Mission College Blvd. (off Mantague Expressway, just north of U.S. 101),* ☎ *408/765–0503.* ☞ *Free.* ⊙ *Weekdays 8–5.*

Skylights cast natural light for viewing the exhibitions in the **Triton Museum of Art,** across from Santa Clara's Civic Center. A permanent collection of 19th- and 20th-century sculpture by artists from the Bay Area is displayed in the garden, which you can see through a curved-glass wall at the rear of the building. Inside there are rotating exhibits of contemporary works in a variety of media and a permanent collection of 19th- and 20-century American artists, many from California. ⊠ *1505 Warburton Ave. (take Scott Blvd. north off El Camino Real),* ☎ *408/247–3754.* ☞ *Suggested donation $5.* ⊙ *Tues. 10–9, Wed.–Sun. 10–5.*

The tiny **Santa Clara Historic Museum** exhibits artifacts and photos that trace the history of the region. ⊠ *1509 Warburton Ave.,* ☎ *408/248–2787.* ☞ *Free.* ⊙ *Daily 1–4.*

Dining and Lodging

$$ ✕ **Birk's.** High-tech sensibilities will appreciate the modern open
★ kitchen and streamlined, multilevel dining area. The Birk's menu, though, is traditional, strong on grilled and smoked meat, fish, and fowl. Try the smoked prime rib, served with garlic mashed potatoes and creamed spinach, or rotisserie-grilled chicken or ribs. ⊠ *3955 Free-*

dom Circle at U.S. 101 and Great America Pkwy., ☎ *408/980–6400. AE, DC, MC, V. No lunch weekends.*

$$ ⊞ **Biltmore Hotel & Suites.** This hotel's central Silicon Valley location makes it a popular choice for business travelers. ⊠ *2151 Laurelwood Rd., Santa Clara 95054,* ☎ *408/988–8411 or 800/255–9925,* FAX *408/988–0225. 128 rooms, 132 suites. Restaurant, lounge, no-smoking rooms, pool, hot tub, fitness center, airport shuttle, free parking. AE, D, DC, MC, V.*

Santa Clara A to Z

ARRIVING AND DEPARTING

By Car: Take U.S. 101, I–280 (the Junipero Serra Freeway), or I–880 (Highway 17); all connect the Santa Clara and San Francisco Bay areas. The drive south from San Francisco to Santa Clara on I–280 takes 60 minutes depending on traffic, which can be heavy during rush hour.

By Train: CalTrain (☎ 800/660–4287) travels from San Francisco (4th and Townsend Sts.) to Santa Clara (Railroad and Franklin Sts., near the university) hourly, more often during commute hours. The trip takes approximately 1¼ hours.

VISITOR INFORMATION

Santa Clara Chamber of Commerce and Convention & Visitors Bureau (⊠ 2200 Laurelwood Rd., Santa Clara, 95054, ☎ 408/244–8244).

San Jose

A good way to explore California's third-largest city is to hop on the light rail that connects San Jose State University on one end with the Center for Performing Arts on the other; its route will give you a good overview of the city. The convention center stop is in the center of downtown, which you can explore on foot.

In collaboration with New York's Whitney Museum, the **San Jose Museum of Art** is exploring the development of 20th-century American art with exhibits of works from the permanent collections of both. ⊠ *110 S. Market St.,* ☎ *408/294–2787.* ⊠ *$6, free 1st Thurs. of month.* ☉ *Tues.–Wed. 10–5, Thurs. 10–8, Fri.–Sun. 10–5.*

The **Children's Discovery Museum,** near the convention center, exhibits interactive installations on space, technology, the humanities, and the arts. Children can dress up in period costumes, create jewelry from recycled materials, or play on a real fire truck. ⊠ *180 Woz Way, at Auzerais St.,* ☎ *408/298–5437.* ⊠ *$6.* ☉ *Tues.–Sat. 10–5, Sun. noon–5.*

The **Tech Museum of Innovation,** across from the convention center, presents high-tech information through hands-on lab exhibits that are fun and accessible, allowing visitors to discover and demystify disciplines such as interactive media, biotechnology, robotics, and space exploration. ⊠ *145 W. San Carlos St.,* ☎ *408/279–7150.* ⊠ *$6.* ☉ *Tues.–Sun. 10–5.*

Convinced that spirits would harm her if construction ever stopped, firearms-heiress Sarah Winchester constantly added to what is now called the **Winchester Mystery House.** For 38 years beginning in 1884, she kept hundreds of carpenters working around the clock, creating a bizarre, 160-room Victorian labyrinth with stairs going nowhere and doors that open into walls. ⊠ *525 S. Winchester Blvd., between Stevens Creek Blvd. and I–280,* ☎ *408/247–2101.* ⊠ *$12.95.* ☉ *9–5, later in summer and some weekends.*

The **Egyptian Museum and Planetarium** exhibits the West Coast's largest collection of Egyptian and Babylonian antiquities, including mummies and an underground replica of a pharaoh's tomb. The planetarium has programs such as the popular "Celestial Nile," which describes the significant role astrology played in ancient Egyptian myths and religions. ⊠ *1600 Park Ave., at Naglee Ave.,* ☎ *408/947–3636.* ⊠ *Museum $6, planetarium $4.* ⊙ *Daily 9–5; planetarium weekdays only.*

Occupying 25 acres of Kelley Park, the **San Jose Historical Museum** recreates San Jose in the 1880s. Its collection of original and replicate Victorian homes and shops, a firehouse, and a trolley line; the dusty Main Street recalls small-town America. ⊠ *1300 Senter Rd., at Keyes St.,* ☎ *408/287–2290.* ⊠ *$4.* ⊙ *Weekdays 10–4:30, weekends noon–4:30.*

OFF THE
BEATEN PATH

HAKONE GARDENS – Designed in 1918 by a man who had been an imperial gardener in Japan, these gardens in Saratoga, 10 miles west of San Jose, have been carefully maintained, with *koi* (carp) ponds and sculptured shrubs. ⊠ *21000 Big Basin Way,* ☎ *408/741–4994 for directions.* ⊠ *Free. Parking: $3 Mon. and Wed.–Fri., $5 weekends, free Tues.* ⊙ *Weekdays 10–5, weekends 11–5.*

Dining and Lodging

$$$ ✕ **Emile's.** Swiss chef and owner Emile Mooser's specialties include
★ house-cured gravlax, osso buco, and rack of lamb. The interior is distinguished by romantic lighting and unusual leaf sculpture on the ceiling. ⊠ *545 S. 2nd St.,* ☎ *408/289–1960. AE, MC, V. Closed Sun.–Mon. No lunch Tues.–Thurs. and Sat.*

$$$$ 🏨 **Fairmont Hotel.** Rooms here have every imaginable comfort, from down pillows and custom-designed comforters to oversize bath towels changed twice a day. ⊠ *170 S. Market St., at Fairmont Pl., San Jose 95113,* ☎ *408/998–1900 or 800/527–4727,* FAX *408/287–1648. 500 rooms, 41 suites. 4 restaurants, lounge, no-smoking floors, room service, in-room VCRs, health club, business services. AE, D, DC, MC, V.*

$$$ 🏨 **Hotel De Anza.** Business travelers will appreciate the many amenities at this lushly appointed art deco hotel, including computers, cellular phones, and personal voice-mail services. ⊠ *233 W. Santa Clara St., San Jose 95113,* ☎ *408/286–1000 or 800/843–3700,* FAX *408/286–0500. 100 rooms. Restaurant, nightclub, in-room modem lines, minibars, in-room VCRs, exercise room. AE, DC, MC, V.*

$$$ 🏨 **Inn at Saratoga.** All rooms at this five-story inn have secluded sitting alcoves overlooking a peaceful creek. A sun-dappled patio provides a quiet retreat. Modern business conveniences are available but discreetly hidden. ⊠ *20645 4th St., Saratoga 95070,* ☎ *408/867–5020 or 800/338–5020; in CA, 800/543–5020;* FAX *408/741–0981. 45 rooms. No-smoking rooms, business services, meeting room. AE, DC, MC, V.*

$$ 🏨 **Sundowner Inn.** This contemporary hotel provides voice mail, computer data ports, and remote-control televisions with ESPN, HBO, CNN, Nintendo, and VCRs, which you can use to play complimentary tapes. A complimentary breakfast buffet is served poolside. ⊠ *504 Ross Dr., Sunnyvale 94089,* ☎ *408/734–9900 or 800/223–9901,* FAX *408/747–0580. 97 rooms, 12 suites. Restaurant, no-smoking rooms, pool, sauna, exercise room, coin laundry, laundry service, meeting room. AE, D, DC, MC, V.*

Nightlife and the Arts

NIGHTLIFE

The **Plumed Horse** (⊠ 14555 Big Basin Way, Saratoga, ☎ 408/867–4711) is known for good jazz and blues. Try the **New West Melodrama** and **Comedy Vaudeville Show** (⊠ 157 W. San Fernando St., San Jose, ☎ 408/295–7469) for a fresh take on the Old West.

ARTS

If you're traveling in summer, try not to miss the **Mountain Winery Concert Series** (⊠ 14831 Pierce Rd., Box 1852, Saratoga 95070, ☎ 408/741–5181), where music is performed under the moon and stars on a stage surrounded by grapevines.

The **Center for Performing Arts** (⊠ 255 Almaden Blvd.) presents music, dance, and theater (☎ 408/277–3900 for events information). The well-regarded **San Jose Repertory Theatre** (⊠ 1 N. 1st St., Suite 1, ☎ 408/291–2255) performs at the Montgomery Theater (⊠ San Carlos and Market Sts.).

Sports

Home to the San Jose Sharks hockey team, the 20,000-seat **San Jose Arena,** completed in 1993, looks like a giant hothouse with its glass entrance and skylight ceiling. The venue also hosts tennis matches, basketball games, concerts, and other events. ⊠ *Santa Clara St. at Autumn St., San Jose,* ☎ *408/287–9200 or 408/998–2277 for tickets (BASS).* ⊙ *Ticket office weekdays 9:30–5:30, Sat. 9:30–1.*

San Jose A to Z

ARRIVING AND DEPARTING

By Car: The quickest route to San Jose from San Francisco is I–280. From there take the Guadalupe Parkway north, then the Santa Clara Street exit for the most direct route to downtown.

By Train: CalTrain (☎ 800/660–4287) runs from 4th and Townsend streets in San Francisco to San Jose's light-rail system (☎ 408/321–2300), which serves most major attractions, shopping malls, historic sites, and downtown.

VISITOR INFORMATION

San Jose Convention and Visitors Bureau (⊠ 150 W. San Carlos, ☎ 408/283–8833). **FYI Hotline** (☎ 408/295–2265).

SAN FRANCISCO A TO Z

Arriving and Departing

By Bus

Greyhound (☎ 800/231–2222) serves San Francisco from the Transbay Terminal at 1st and Mission streets.

By Car

Interstate 80 finishes its westward journey from New York's George Washington Bridge at the San Francisco–Oakland Bay Bridge. U.S. 101, running north–south through the entire state, enters the city across the Golden Gate Bridge and continues south down the peninsula, along the west side of the bay.

By Plane

The major gateway to San Francisco is the **San Francisco International Airport** (⊠ U.S. 101, south of San Francisco, ☎ 415/761–0800). **Oakland Airport** (⊠ 1 Airport Dr., off I–880, ☎ 510/577–4000) is across the bay but not much farther away from downtown San Francisco (take I–880 to I–980 to I–580 to I–80), although traffic on the Bay Bridge may at times make travel time longer.

Carriers serving San Francisco include **Alaska Air, American, Continental, Delta, Southwest, TWA, United,** and **USAir.** Carriers flying into Oakland include **American, Delta, Southwest,** and **United** (☞ Air Travel *in* Important Contacts A to Z for phone numbers).

SFO Airporter (☎ 415/495–8404) serves downtown hotels. **Supershuttle** (☎ 415/558–8500) will take you from the airport to anywhere within the city limits of San Francisco.

By Train

Amtrak (☎ 800/872–7245) trains—the *Zephyr,* from Chicago via Denver, and the *Coast Starlight,* traveling between Los Angeles and Seattle—stop in Emeryville (✉ 5885 Landregan St.) and Oakland (✉ 245 2nd St. in Jack London Sq.). Shuttle buses connect the Emeryville station and San Francisco's Ferry Building (✉ 30 Embarcadero at the foot of Market St.).

Getting Around

By Bus and Light Rail

San Francisco Municipal Railway System, or **Muni** (☎ 415/673–6864), includes buses and trolleys, surface streetcars, and below-surface streetcars, as well as cable cars. There is 24-hour service, the fare is $1. The exact fare is always required; dollar bills or change are accepted. Eighty-cent tokens can be purchased (in rolls of 10, 20, or 40) to reduce the cost.

A $6 pass good for unlimited travel all day on all routes can be purchased from ticket machines at cable-car terminals and at the Visitor Information Center in Hallidie Plaza.

You can use **Bay Area Rapid Transit** (**BART**) trains to reach Oakland, Berkeley, Concord, Richmond, Fremont, Colma, and Martinez; extensions are expected to open southeast to Castro Valley and Dublin. Trains also travel south from San Francisco as far as Daly City. Fares run from 90¢ to $3.45, and a $3 excursion ticket buys a three-county tour.

By Cable Cars

Cable cars are popular, crowded, and an experience to ride: Move toward one quickly as it pauses, wedge yourself into any available space, and hold on! The sensation of moving up and down some of San Francisco's steepest hills in a small, open-air, clanging conveyance is not to be missed.

The fare (for one direction) is $2. Exact change is preferred, but operators will make change. There are self-service ticket machines (which do make change) at a few major stops and at all the terminals. The one exception is the busy cable car terminal at Powell and Market streets; purchase tickets at the kiosk there. Be wary of street people attempting to "help" you buy a ticket.

The Powell-Mason line (No. 59) and the Powell-Hyde line (No. 60) begin at Powell and Market streets near Union Square and terminate at Fisherman's Wharf. The California Street line (No. 61) runs east and west from Market Street near the Embarcadero to Van Ness Avenue.

By Car

Driving in San Francisco can be a challenge because of the hills, the one-way streets, and the traffic. Take it easy, remember to curb your wheels when parking on hills, and use public transportation whenever possible. This is a great city for walking and a terrible city for parking. On certain streets, parking is forbidden during rush hours. Look for the warning signs; illegally parked cars are towed. Downtown parking lots are often full and always expensive. Finding a spot in North Beach at night, for instance, may be impossible.

Contacts and Resources

Doctors

Two hospitals with 24-hour emergency rooms are **San Francisco General Hospital** (⊠ 1001 Potrero Ave., ☏ 415/206–8000) and the **Medical Center at the University of California, San Francisco** (⊠ 500 Parnassus Ave., ☏ 415/476–1000).

Physician Access Medical Center (⊠ 26 California St., ☏ 415/397–2881) is a drop-in clinic in the Financial District, open weekdays 7:30 AM–5:30 PM. **Access Health Care** (☏ 415/565–6600) provides drop-in medical care at Davies Medical Center, Castro Street at Duboce Avenue, daily 8–8.

Emergencies

Ambulance (☏ 911). **Police** (☏ 911).

Guided Tours

ORIENTATION TOURS

Golden Gate Tours (☏ 415/788–5775) uses both vans and buses for its 3½-hour city tour ($25), offered mornings and afternoons. You can combine the tour with a bay cruise ($30). Customers are picked up at hotels and motels. Senior-citizen and group rates are available. Tours are daily; reserve a day ahead.

Gray Line (☏ 415/558–9400) operates tours of the city, the Bay Area, and northern California. The city tour ($26), on buses or double-decker buses, lasts 3½ hours and departs from the Transbay Terminal at 1st and Mission streets five to six times daily. Gray Line picks up at centrally located hotels. Make reservations the day before.

Gray Line-Cable Car Tours sends motorized cable cars on a one-hour loop from Union Square to Fisherman's Wharf ($15) and two-hour tours including the Presidio, Japantown, and the Golden Gate Bridge ($22). No reservations necessary.

The **Great Pacific Tour** (☏ 415/626–4499) uses 13-passenger vans for its daily 3½-hour city tour ($27). Bilingual guides may be requested, and they pick up at major San Francisco hotels. Tours are available to Monterey, the Wine Country, and Muir Woods.

Tower Tours (☏ 415/434–8687) uses 20-passenger vans for city tours and 25-passenger buses for trips outside San Francisco to Muir Woods and Sausalito, the Wine Country, Monterey and Carmel, and Yosemite. The city tour runs 3½ hours ($25). The Wine Country tour includes the historic Sonoma town square. Tours are daily; make reservations the day before.

SPECIAL-INTEREST TOURS

Near Escapes (☏ 415/386–8687) plans unusual activities in the city and around the Bay Area. Recent tours and activities included tours of a Hindu temple in the East Bay, the Lawrence Berkeley Laboratory, the aircraft maintenance facility at the San Francisco Airport, and the quicksilver mines south of San Jose. Send $1 and a self-addressed, stamped envelope for a schedule for the month you plan to visit San Francisco.

WALKING TOURS

Castro District: Trevor Hailey (☏ 415/550–8110) leads a 3½-hour tour focusing on the history and development of the city's gay and lesbian community, including restored Victorian homes, shops and cafés, and the NAMES Project, home of the AIDS memorial quilt. Tours depart at 10 AM Tuesday–Saturday from Castro and Market streets. Cost: $30, including brunch.

Chinatown with the "Wok Wiz": Cookbook author Shirley Fong-Torres (☎ 415/355–9657) leads a 3½-hour tour of Chinese markets, other businesses, and a fortune-cookie factory. Cost: $35 including lunch, $25 without lunch. Shorter tours start at $15.

Chinese Cultural Heritage Foundation (☎ 415/986–1822) conducts two walking tours of Chinatown. The Heritage Walk leaves Saturday at 2 PM and lasts about two hours; cost is $12. The Culinary Walk, a three-hour stroll through the markets and food shops, plus a dim sum lunch, is held every Wednesday at 10:30 AM: $25 adults, $10 children under 12.

City Guides (☎ 415/557–4266), a free service sponsored by Friends of the Library, tours Chinatown, North Beach, Coit Tower, Pacific Heights mansions, Japantown, the Haight-Ashbury, historic Market Street, the Palace Hotel, and downtown roof gardens and atriums. Schedules are available at the San Francisco Visitors Center at Powell and Market streets and at library branches.

Late-Night Pharmacies

Several **Walgreen Drug Stores** have 24-hour pharmacies, including stores at 500 Geary Street near Union Square (☎ 415/673–8413) and 3201 Divisadero Street at Lombard Street (☎ 415/931–6417).

Visitor Information

Redwood Empire Association Visitor Information Center (⊠ The Cannery, 2801 Leavenworth St., 2nd floor, 94133, ☎ 415/543–8334). **San Francisco Convention and Visitors Bureau** (⊠ 201 3rd St., Suite 900, 94103, ☎ 415/974–6900).

6 Sacramento and the Gold Country

Including Highway 49 from Nevada City to Mariposa

The gold-mining region of the Sierra Nevada foothills is a less expensive, if also less sophisticated, region of California but not without its pleasures, natural and man-made. Spring brings wildflowers, and in fall the hills are colored by bright-red berries and changing leaves. The hills are golden in the summer—and hot. Dining has improved remarkably in recent years, and many fine bed-and-breakfast inns have sprung up. The Gold Country has a mix of indoor and outdoor activities, one of the many reasons it's a great place to take the kids.

JAMES MARSHALL TURNED UP a gold nugget in the tailrace of a sawmill he was constructing along the American River and ushered in a whole new era for California. Before January 24, 1848, what became the Golden State had been a beautiful but sparsely populated land over which Mexico and the United States were still wrestling. With Marshall's discovery and its subsequent confirmation by President James Polk in his State of the Union speech on December 5, 1848, prospectors came to seek their fortunes in the Mother Lode.

By Bobbi Zane

As gold fever seized the nation, California's population of 15,000 swelled to 265,000 within three years—44,000 newcomers arrived by ship in San Francisco in the first 10 months alone, the majority of them men under 40, either unattached or with families back east. Most spent about two years in California before returning home, usually with empty pockets or having barely broken even. Historians have noted that the consequences of the gold rush were more than monetary: '49ers who remained in the state contributed to a freer culture that eschewed many of the constricting conventions and values of the eastern states.

Originally, the term Mother Lode denoted a gold-bearing quartz vein 120 miles long between Mariposa to the south and Auburn to the north. It ranged in width from 2 miles to only a few yards. By 1865 it had yielded more than $750 million in gold. As prospectors headed farther afield, the entire gold-rush region came to be known as the Mother Lode. Ironically, neither Marshall, nor John Sutter, on whose property Marshall discovered gold, got rich from the discovery.

The boom brought on by the gold rush lasted scarcely 20 years, but it changed California forever. It produced 546 mining towns, of which fewer than 250 remain. The hills were alive, not only with prospecting and mining but also with business, the arts, plenty of gambling, and a fair share of crime. Opera houses went up alongside brothels, and the California State Capitol in Sacramento was built with the gold dug out of the hills. Some of the nation's most treasured writers—Mark Twain and Bret Harte among them—began their careers writing about the mining camps. Gold-rush lore immortalized notorious bandits: Legend has it that Joaquin Murieta's crime spree—he robbed miners by day, then partied by night at local saloons—followed an assault on him and his family by Yankee prospectors. When the law finally caught up with the debonair Black Bart, who targeted Wells Fargo stagecoaches and left behind poems (signed "Black Bart—PO-8") at his crime scenes, he turned out to be a well-known San Franciscan.

The northern California cities of Sacramento, San Francisco, and Stockton grew quickly to meet the needs of the surrounding gold fields. Saloon keepers and canny merchants recognized that the real gold was to be made from the '49ers' pockets. Potatoes and onions sold for as much as $1 apiece, making entrepreneurs like storekeeper Samuel Brannan millionaires. Much important history was made in Sacramento, the key center of commerce during this period. Pony Express riders ended their nearly 2,000-mile journeys in the city in the 1860s. The Transcontinental Railroad, conceived here by the Big Four (Leland Stanford, Mark Hopkins, Collis P. Huntington, and Charles Crocker), was completed in 1869.

By the 1960s, the scars left on the Gold Country landscape by mining had largely healed. To promote tourism, townspeople began restoring vintage structures, historians developed museums, and the state established parks and recreation areas that preserved this extraordinary episode in American history. Today, visitors flock to Nevada City, Auburn, Coloma, Sutter Creek, and Columbia, not only to relive the past but also to explore museums and art galleries, experience traditional celebrations, and stay over at bed-and-breakfast inns.

Pleasures and Pastimes

Adventuring

Scenic and challenging Gold Country rivers, particularly the American and Tuolumne, lure whitewater enthusiasts each spring and summer. Early-morning balloon excursions take aeronauts above treetops in deep canyons of the American River. Throughout the region weekend prospectors pan for gold, turning up big nuggets frequently enough to inspire others to participate.

Dining

Given the small population of the Gold Country, the number of good restaurants is disproportionately large, especially in Nevada City. American, Italian, and Mexican fare is common, but Gold Country chefs also prepare ambitious Continental, French, and California cuisine. Away from Sacramento or the interstate highways, national fast-food chains are few and far between. It's not difficult, though, to find the makings for a good picnic in most Gold Country towns.

CATEGORY	COST*
$$$$	over $50
$$$	$30–$50
$$	$20–$30
$	under $20

*per person for a three-course meal, excluding drinks, service, and 7¼% tax

Lodging

Sacramento provides a complete range of lodgings: full-service hotels, budget motels, small inns, and even a fine hostel. The main accommodations in the larger towns along Highway 49—among them Placerville, Nevada City, Auburn, and Mariposa—are chain motels and bed-and-breakfast inns. Many Gold Country B&Bs occupy former mansions, miners' cabins, and other buildings that yield clues about life as it was lived 150 years ago.

CATEGORY	COST*
$$$$	over $175
$$$	$120–$175
$$	$80–$120
$	under $80

*All prices are for a standard double room, excluding 7¼% tax (12% in Sacramento).

Shopping

Shoppers visit the Gold Country in search of antiques, collectibles, art, quilts, toys, tools, decorative items, and furnishings. Handmade quilts and crafts can be found in Sutter Creek, Jackson, and Amador City; Auburn and Nevada City support a number of gift boutiques.

Exploring Sacramento and the Gold Country

Visiting Old Sacramento's museums is a good way to steep yourself in gold-rush history, but the Gold Country's heart lies along Highway 49, which winds the 325-mile north–south length of the historic mining area. The highway, often a twisty, hilly, two-lane road, begs for a convertible with the top down.

Great Itineraries

Numbers in the text correspond to numbers in the margin and on the Gold Country and Sacramento maps.

IF YOU HAVE 1 DAY

A tour of Auburn and Coloma, starting and ending in Sacramento, provides a survey of gold-rush history and geography. Drive east from Sacramento on I–80 to **Auburn** ⑯ for a tour of the landmark **Placer County Courthouse** and its museum, which documents the area's Native American, railroad, agricultural, and mining roots. Travel south on Highway 49 to the **Marshall Gold Discovery State Historic Park** ⑰ at Coloma. Head back to Sacramento for a cocktail or a soda at the bar on the *Delta King* and an evening stroll and dinner along the waterfront in **Old Sacramento.** The historical attractions will be closed, but you'll still get a feel for life here in the last half of the 19th century.

IF YOU HAVE 3 DAYS

In three days, you can make a larger loop from Sacramento. Begin your tour on Highway 49 north of I–80. Walk deep into the recesses of the **Empire Mine** ⑮ near **Grass Valley,** and then head 4 miles north on Highway 49 for a visit to the historic **Miners Foundry** in **Nevada City** ⑭. After lunch, travel the scenic, twisting highway south to ⊞ **Auburn** ⑯, where you can take in the **Placer County Courthouse** and museum, have dinner, and spend the night. Early the next morning, head south to tour the **Marshall Gold Discovery Site** ⑰ in Coloma. Continue south to ⊞ **Sutter Creek** ⑲, where you can spend the afternoon exploring the boutiques and antiques stores. If exploring a good vintage is more your game, take a detour to the **Shendandoah Valley** southeast of **Placerville** and taste some wine before continuing on to Sutter Creek. Either way, spend the night in one of the Sutter Creek's historic bed-and-breakfast inns. Return early to **Sacramento** the next day to visit the **California State Railroad Museum** ② and **Sutter's Fort** ⑫.

IF YOU HAVE 5 DAYS

Visit the **Empire Mine** ⑮, **Nevada City** ⑭, and ⊞ **Auburn** ⑯ on day one. See Coloma's **Marshall Gold Discovery Site** ⑰ on the second day, and then continue on to ⊞ **Sutter Creek** ⑲. On your third morning, visit the **Amador County Museum** in **Jackson** ⑳ before heading south on Highway 49 and east on Highway 4 for lunch in **Murphys** ㉒. Back on Highway 49 still southward is ⊞ **Columbia State Historic Park** ㉓. You can live a bit of history by dining and spending the night at the City Hotel. If you've been itching to pan for gold, do that in the morning in the state park, and then head back to ⊞ **Sacramento** (Highway 49 north to Highway 16 west) for a riverboat cruise. Visit the **California State Railroad Museum** ② and **Sutter's Fort** ⑫ on day five.

When to Tour the Gold Country

The Gold Country is the most pleasant in the spring, when the wildflowers are in bloom, and in the fall. Summers are beautiful, too, but also hot: temperatures in the 90s and even the 100s are common all summer long. Sacramento winters tend to be cold and foggy. Throughout the year Gold Country towns stage community and ethnic celebrations. In December, many towns deck themselves out for the Christmas holidays. Sacramento hosts the annual Jazz Jubilee in May and the California State Fair in August. Flowers bloom on Daffodil Hill in March. Nevada City hosts Music in the Mountains concerts in June and July.

The Gold Country

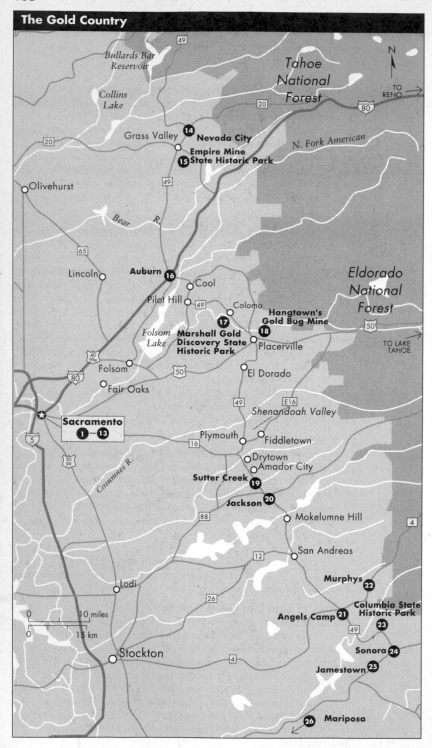

SACRAMENTO
Old Sacramento, Downtown, and Sutter's Fort

Old Sacramento, the State Capitol and park surrounding it, and Sutter's Fort lie on an east–west axis that begins at the Sacramento River. The walk from Old Sacramento to the State Capitol is easy, passing through the Downtown Plaza shopping mall and pedestrian-only K Street. This area takes on a festive atmosphere during a market held on Thursday evenings.

Downtown Sacramento, 87 miles northeast of San Francisco, is known for its tree-lined streets and many restored Victorian mansions. **Sacramento Heritage** (☎ 916/440–1355) supplies walking-tour maps of three historic areas—Capitol, Downtown, and Alkali Flat (the city's oldest residential district).

Old Sacramento and Downtown

Wood sidewalks and horse-drawn carriages on cobblestone streets lend a 19th-century feel to Old Sacramento, a 28-acre area along the Sacramento River waterfront. The museums at the north end of this district hold artifacts of state and national significance. Historic buildings house shops and restaurants. River cruises and train rides bring gold-rush history to life. Call the Event Hotline (☎ 916/558–3912) for information on living-history re-creations and merchant hours.

The centerpiece of Old Sacramento is the wharf area located at the foot of K Street, where the restored sternwheeler *Delta King* is permanently berthed. One can visualize the bustle of shipping activity that filled this area during the gold rush and in the years following. The ❶ **Visitor Information Center** (2nd and K Sts., ☎ 916/442–7644) here is open daily from 9 to 5.

★ ☝ ❷ What is now the **California State Railroad Museum** was once the terminus of the Transcontinental and Sacramento Valley railroads. Exhibits trace the history of the railroads and their role in the gold rush and later the westward expansion of the United States. The 100,000-square-foot museum is the largest of its kind in North America, with 21 locomotives and railroad cars on display and 46 exhibits. You can walk through a post-office car and peer into cubbyholes and canvas bags of mail, go through a sleeping car that simulates the swaying on the roadbed and the flashing lights of a passing town at night, or glimpse the elegance of the first-class dining car on the *Super Chief*, each of its tables set with a different china pattern. Allow at least a couple hours to experience the museum fully. ✉ *125 I St.*, ☎ *916/448–4466.* ☞ *$5.* ☺ *Daily 10–5.*

☝ ❸ The **Huntington, Hopkins & Co. Store** is a replica of the 1850 hardware store owned by partners Collis Huntington and Mark Hopkins, two of the Big Four businessmen who formed the Central Pacific Railroad. Displays show the picks, shovels, gold pans, and other paraphernalia miners used during the gold rush. ✉ *1104 Front St.*, ☎ *916/442–7644.* ☺ *Daily 11–5.*

☝ ❹ The building that holds the **Discovery Museum** is a replica of the 1854 City Hall and Waterworks. The museum presents a streamlined introduction to the history of Sacramento and its surroundings, complete with gold pans with which visitors can sift, an Indian thatched hut, memorabilia from the world wars, and a colorful stack of turn-of-the-century cans of local produce. Child-oriented, hands-on science exhibits rotate on a regular basis. ✉ *101 I St.*, ☎ *916/264–7057.* ☞ *$3.50.*

Sacramento

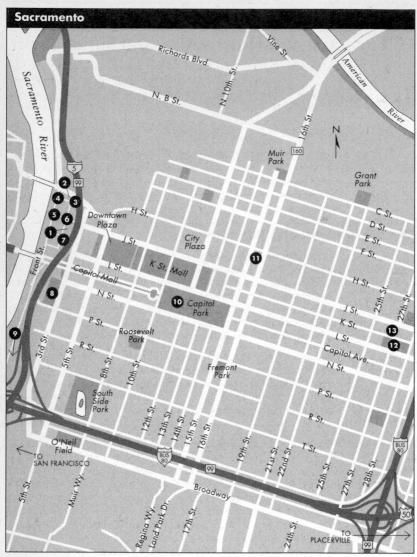

B.F. Hastings
Building, **6**
California Military
Museum, **7**
California State
Capitol, **10**
California State
Railroad Museum, **2**
Crocker Art
Museum, **8**
Discovery Museum, **4**
Eagle Theater, **5**
Governor's
Mansion, **11**
Huntington, Hopkins
& Co. Store, **3**
State Indian
Museum, **13**
Sutter's Fort, **12**
Towe Ford
Museum of
Automotive
History, **9**
Visitor Information
Center, **1**

🕙 *Tues.–Sun. 10–5 in summer; Tues.–Fri. noon–5, weekends 10–5 in winter.*

🖐 The **Central Pacific Passenger Depot** is a reconstructed 1876 station. There's rolling stock to admire, a typical waiting room, and a little café. Rides on a steam-powered train depart from the freight depot, just south of the passenger depot. The train makes a 40-minute loop along the Sacramento riverfront. ✉ *930 Front St., 🚂 $5 (free with same-day ticket from California State Railroad Museum, ☞ above); train ride, $5 additional, operates every weekend Apr.–Sept., 1st weekend of the month Oct.–Dec. 🕙 Depot daily 10–5.*

⑤ The **Eagle Theater** was the first building constructed as a theater in California. When it opened in 1848, the audience paid $3 and $5 in gold dust to sit on rough boards and watch professional actors. A replica was completed in 1976, and the theater remains in use today. ✉ *925 Front St., ☎ 916/323–6343.*

⑥ The **B. F. Hastings Building,** built in 1853, contains a reconstruction of the first chambers of the California State Supreme Court on its second floor. The first floor houses a Wells Fargo Bank and a small display of Wells Fargo memorabilia. ✉ *1000 2nd St. 🕙 Daily 10–5.*

⑦ The **California Military Museum** specializes in militia and military history from before statehood to modern times. Memorabilia on display in this storefront includes uniforms, documents, and flags. ✉ *1119 2nd St., ☎ 916/442–2883. 🎫 $2.25. 🕙 Tues.–Sun. 10–4:30.*

★ **⑧** The **Crocker Art Museum,** a few blocks from Old Sacramento, is the oldest art museum in the American West, with a collection of European, Asian, and California art, including *Sunday Morning in the Mines,* a large canvas depicting the mining industry of the 1850s. The museum's lobby and magnificent ballroom retain the original 1870s woodwork, plaster moldings, and imported tiles. ✉ *216 O St., ☎ 916/264–5423. 🎫 $4.50. 🕙 Wed. and Fri.–Sun. 10–5, Thurs. 10–9.*

🖐 **⑨** The **Towe Ford Museum of Automotive History** has a collection of more than 170 vintage cars, including most models manufactured by the Ford company between 1903 and 1950. Car clubs congregate here, and occasionally owners can be seen working on vehicles. A small gift shop sells vintage-car magazines. ✉ *2200 Front St., ☎ 916/442–6802. 🎫 $5. 🕙 Daily 10–6.*

⑩ The **California State Capitol** was built in 1869 and underwent extensive restoration in the late 1970s and early 1980s. The lacy plasterwork of the rotunda, 120 feet high, has the complexity and color of a Fabergé Easter egg. Underneath the gilded dome are marble floors, glittering chandeliers, monumental staircases, original artwork, replicas of 19th-century state offices, and legislative chambers decorated in the style of the 1890s. Guides conduct tours of the building and the 40-acre Capitol Park, dating to 1870 and one of the oldest gardens in the state. The park contains a rose garden, an impressive display of camellias (Sacramento's city flower), and the California Vietnam Veterans Memorial. ✉ *Capitol Mall and 10th St., ☎ 916/324–0333. 🎫 Free. 🕙 Daily 9–4; tours hourly.*

⑪ The **Governor's Mansion,** built in 1877 and used by the state's chief executives from the early 1900s until 1967, is a 15-room Victorian house with furnishings that reflect the tastes of its various residents over those years. ✉ *1526 H St., ☎ 916/323–3047. 🎫 $2. 🕙 Daily 10–4; tours hourly.*

★ ☘ ⑫ **Sutter's Fort,** Sacramento's earliest settlement, was founded by Swiss immigrant John Augustus Sutter in 1839. Self-guided tours with audio wands explain the exhibits, which include a blacksmith's shop, bakery, prison, living quarters, and livestock areas. Costumed docents sometimes reenact fort life, demonstrating crafts, food preparations, and firearm maintenance. ⊠ *2701 L St.,* ☎ *916/445–4422.* ▭ *$2.* ☉ *Daily 10–5.*

☘ ⑬ The **State Indian Museum** displays arts and crafts made by California's earliest inhabitants. Of interest is a display devoted to Ishi, the last Yahi Indian to emerge from the mountains (in 1911), who provided insight into the existence of this group of Native Americans. ⊠ *2601 K St.,* ☎ *916/324–0971.* ▭ *$2.* ☉ *Daily 10–5.*

Dining

CALIFORNIA

$$$ ✕ **Rio City Café.** Eclectic lunch and dinner menus and huge floor-to-ceiling windows with views of an Old Sacramento Wharf are the dual attractions of this bright restaurant. When the weather's good you can enjoy your meals at water's edge. Rio City serves both light and hearty fare: grilled vegetables on pasta, sautéed ahi with pomegranate sauce, and baked stuffed chicken breast. ⊠ *1110 Front St.,* ☎ *916/442–8226. AE, D, DC, MC, V.*

$$ ✕ **Capitol Grill.** This busy concept restaurant has a political theme, with campaign posters and other memorabilia tacked all over the walls. The moderate prices and casual atmosphere appeal to a young, after-work crowd. Contemporary California dishes on the menu often have Asian or Italian accents—sesame-crusted ahi, black-pepper fettuccine, Chinese noodle salad. ⊠ *2730 N St.,* ☎ *916/736–0744. AE, DC, MC, V. No lunch weekends.*

$$ ✕ **Paragary's Bar and Oven.** Pizza is the specialty at this casual, noisy restaurant, which is popular with the downtown state-worker crowd for lunch or dinner. You won't go hungry here—pasta, dessert, and even appetizer portions are enormous. ⊠ *1401 28th St.,* ☎ *916/457–5737. AE, D, DC, MC, V. No lunch weekends.*

CALIFORNIA–ITALIAN

$$ ✕ **Harlow's.** A popular spot for California-Italian cuisine, Harlow's has extraordinary seafood specials and wonderful cheesecake. Dining can be noisy and crowded, but the service is excellent, and people-watching is fun, especially at the bar. ⊠ *2708 J St.,* ☎ *916/441–4693. AE, D, DC, MC, V. Closed Sun.–Mon. No lunch weekends.*

CALIFORNIA/PACIFIC RIM

$$–$$$ ✕ **California Fats.** This is the better of two Old Sacramento restaurants carrying the Fats name. The extensive Pacific Rim–influenced menu is full of different flavors: seared ahi and glazed duck from a wood-fired oven, pizza, pastas with overtones of ginger and coriander, and venison in cashew crust, in addition to steaks and seafood. The restaurant's vibrant decor portrays the history of Chinese immigrants. ⊠ *1015 Front St.,* ☎ *916/441–7966. AE, MC, V.*

CHINESE

$$–$$$ ✕ **Frank Fat's.** Known as the "third house" of the California legislature where lawmakers and lobbyists have been making deals for more than 50 years, Frank Fat's is renowned more for its watering-hole atmosphere than its so-so Chinese food. The menu emphasizes Cantonese cuisine, but there are items from other regions of China. Signature dishes include brandy-fried chicken, stir-fried clams in black bean sauce, plus a couple of items from the American menu: New York steak and ba-

nana cream pie. ⊠ *806 L St.,* ☎ *916/442–7092. AE, MC, V. No lunch weekends.*

ITALIAN

$$$ ✕ **Biba.** Owner Biba Caggiano is an authority on Italian cuisine, au-
★ thor of several cookbooks, and star of a national TV show on cook-
ing. The Capitol crowd flocks here for her delicate pasta dishes, baked
spinach lasagna, and homemade tortellini. Caggiano also offers a great
osso buco, rabbit tenderloin, and grilled pork loin, as well as regional
specialties. ⊠ *2801 Capitol Ave.,* ☎ *916/455–2422. AE, MC, V.
Closed Sun. No lunch weekends.*

MEXICAN

$–$$ ✕ **Centro.** Its cuisine may not be as authentic as claimed, but Centro
deserves credit for conceiving dishes well outside the taco-burrito
realm. Unusual items include adobo marinated pork, black bean and
chipotle chili tamales, and salmon Veracruzana. ⊠ *2730 J St.,* ☎ *916/
442–2552. AE, DC, MC, V. No lunch weekends.*

Lodging

$$$–$$$$ 🏨 **Delta King.** This grand old riverboat, now permanently moored at
Old Sacramento's waterfront, once transported passengers between
Sacramento and San Francisco. Among many design elements of note
are its main staircase, mahogany paneling, and brass fittings. The best
of the 44 staterooms are on the river side toward the back of the boat.
The restaurant is locally popular, though the cuisine and service are
uneven. Rates include Continental breakfast. ⊠ *1000 Front St., 95814,*
☎ *916/444–5464 or 800/825–5464,* FAX *916/444–5314. 44 rooms.
Restaurant, bar, meeting rooms, parking (fee). AE, D, DC, MC, V.*

$$$–$$$$ 🏨 **Hyatt Regency at Capitol Park.** With its dramatic marble-and-glass
★ lobby and luxuriously appointed rooms, this hotel across the street from
the Capitol and adjacent to the convention center is arguably Sacra-
mento's finest. The service here is outstanding. The best rooms have
Capitol Park views. ⊠ *1209 L St., 95814,* ☎ *916/443–1234 or
800/233–1234,* FAX *916/321–6631. 500 rooms. 2 restaurants, lounge,
air-conditioning, pool, hot tub, exercise room, nightclub, meeting
rooms, car rental. AE, D, DC, MC, V.*

$$$–$$$$ 🏨 **Radisson Hotel Sacramento.** Mediterranean-style two-story build-
ings clustered around a large artificial lake on an 18-acre landscaped
site contain fairly large rooms, with art deco appointments and fur-
nishings. Many have patios or balconies. More a resort than other Sacra-
mento-area hotels, the Radisson presents summer jazz concerts in a
lakeside amphitheater and holds barbecues on warm evenings. ⊠ *500
Leisure La., 95815,* ☎ *916/922–2020 or 800/333–3333,* FAX *916/649–
9463. 314 rooms. 2 restaurants, air-conditioning, pool, exercise room,
boating, bicycles, meeting rooms. AE, D, DC, MC, V.*

$$–$$$$ 🏨 **Amber House Bed & Breakfast Inn.** Two artistic-themed residences
★ compose this bed-and-breakfast located in a historic district near the
Capitol. The original house, called the Poet's Refuge, is a Craftsman-
style home with five bedrooms decorated in literary themes. Next
door, a 1913 Mediterranean-style home has a French Impressionist motif.
Several rooms have bathrooms with double hot tubs, fireplaces, and
skylights. Service is excellent. Complimentary breakfast and beverages
are included. ⊠ *1315 22nd St., 95816,* ☎ *916/444–8085 or 800/755–
6526,* FAX *916/447–1548. 9 rooms. Air-conditioning, bicycles. AE, D,
DC, MC, V.*

$$–$$$ 🏨 **Abigail's Bed and Breakfast Inn.** This 1912 Colonial Revival man-
sion sits on a tree-shaded street near the Capitol. Two parlors flank a
grand staircase leading to comfortably furnished upstairs bedrooms with
pencil-post or canopied beds. One room has a hot tub. Room rates in-

clude full breakfast and afternoon refreshments. ⊠ *2120 G St., 95816,* ☎ *916/441–5007 or 800/858–1568,* FAX *916/441–0621. 5 rooms. Air-conditioning, outdoor hot tub. AE, D, DC, MC, V.*

\$\$–\$\$\$ ⊞ **Best Western Ponderosa.** Many consider this family-owned motel the best value downtown. Rooms are nicely appointed; many open to a courtyard surrounding the pool. Continental breakfast is included. ⊠ *1100 H St., 95814,* ☎ *916/441–1314; in CA, 800/830–1314;* FAX *916/441–5961. 98 rooms. Restaurant, lounge, pool, air-conditioning, laundry service, free parking. AE, D, DC, MC, V.*

\$\$–\$\$\$ ⊞ **Holiday Inn Capitol Plaza.** Despite its somewhat dreary ambience, this hotel has the best location for visiting Old Sacramento and the Downtown Plaza. It's also within walking distance of the Capitol. ⊠ *300 J St., 95814,* ☎ *916/446–0100 or 800/465–4329,* FAX *916/446–0100. 368 rooms. Restaurant, lounge, air-conditioning, pool, 2 saunas, convention center, free parking. AE, DC, MC, V.*

\$ ⊞ **Sacramento International Hostel.** This renovated landmark 1885 Victorian mansion has a grand mahogany staircase, stained-glass atrium, frescoed ceilings, and several carved and tiled fireplaces. Dormitory rooms and bedrooms suitable for singles, couples, and families are available, as is a shared kitchen. The hostel is within walking distance of most area attractions and the Amtrak and Greyhound stations. ⊠ *900 H St., 95814,* ☎ *916/443–1691 or 800/444–6111. 70 beds. MC, V.*

Nightlife and the Arts

BARS AND NIGHTCLUBS

Busby Berkeley's. DJs play music Tuesday through Saturday nights at this hotel nightclub with a view of the State Capitol and park. ⊠ *Hyatt Regency at Capitol Park, 1209 L St.,* ☎ *916/443–1234.*

Fox and Goose. A casual pub with live music in the evenings, the F&G has been rated the "best morning-after" spot by the *Sacramento Bee* for its breakfasts. ⊠ *1001 R St.,* ☎ *916/443–8825.*

Harlow's. The popular eatery (☞ Dining, *above*) draws a young crowd to its art deco bar–nightclub for DJ music after 9. ⊠ *1708 J St.,* ☎ *916/441–4693.*

CULTURAL EVENTS

Sacramento Community Center Theater is the home of the symphony, opera, ballet, and Music Circus, which presents professional musical theater in summer. ⊠ *13th and L Sts.,* ☎ *916/264–5291.*

SACTIX (⊠ Kiosk on south side of St. Rose of Lima Park, ☎ *916/442–2500*) has half-price, cash-only, day-of-the-event tickets for area arts and entertainment.

Outdoor Activities and Sports

BASKETBALL

The **Sacramento Kings** of the National Basketball Association play at the Arco Arena from October through April. ⊠ *1 Sports Pkwy.,* ☎ *916/928–6900.*

BICYCLING

Jedediah Smith Memorial Bicycle Trail runs for 23 scenic miles from Old Sacramento to Beals Point in Folsom, mostly along the American River.

FITNESS

Capitol Health Club has a workout area, aerobics classes, racquetball, handball, and basketball. ⊠ *1515 8th St.,* ☎ *916/442–3927.*

Shopping

MALLS

Downtown Plaza, comprising the K Street Mall along with many neighboring shops and restaurants, has shopping and entertainment; there's a Thursday-night market, and in winter an outdoor ice-skating rink is set up. **Arden Fair Mall,** northeast of downtown off I–80 in the North Area, is Sacramento's largest shopping center, anchored by a Nordstrom department store. **Pavilions Mall** (✉ Fair Oaks Blvd. and Howe Ave.) has many boutiques.

SPECIALTY SHOPS

Among the T-shirt and yogurt emporiums in Old Sacramento are some interesting art galleries and bookstores. The **Artists' Collaborative Gallery** (✉ 1007 2nd St., ☎ 916/444–3764) has ever-changing exhibits by top local artists and craftspeople. **Bookmine** (✉ 1015 2nd St., ☎ 916/441–4609) sells used and rare books. The **Elder Craftsman** (✉ 130 J St., ☎ 916/264–7762) specializes in items handcrafted by local senior citizens.

THE GOLD COUNTRY

Highway 49 from Nevada City to Mariposa

Highway 49 winds the length of the historic gold-mining area, linking the towns of Nevada City, Grass Valley, Auburn, Placerville, Sutter Creek, Sonora, and Mariposa. Most are gentrified versions of once-rowdy mining camps, vestiges of which remain in roadside museums, old mining structures, and historic inns.

Nevada City

⑭ *62 mi north of Sacramento, I–80 to Hwy. 49.*

Nevada City, once known as the Queen City of the Northern Mines, is the most appealing of the northern Mother Lode towns. The iron-shuttered brick buildings that line the narrow, winding downtown streets contain antiques shops, galleries, a winery, bookstores, boutiques, bed-and-breakfast inns, and many restaurants. Horse-drawn carriage tours add to the romance, as do gas-powered streetlights. At one point in the 1850s, Nevada City had a population of nearly 10,000, enough to support a lively cultural community, a tradition that continues to this day. The **Nevada City Chamber of Commerce** (✉ 132 Main St., ☎ 916/265–2692) has books about the area and a free walking-tour map of the most interesting old buildings.

With its gingerbread-trimmed bell tower, **Firehouse No. 1** is one of the Gold Country's most photographed buildings. Now a museum, it houses relics of the fateful Donner Party (victims of a severe Sierra Nevada snowstorm), gold-rush artifacts, and a Chinese Joss House. ✉ *214 Main St.,* ☎ *916/265–5468.* ☉ *Daily 11–4.*

The redbrick **Nevada Theatre,** built in 1865, is California's oldest theater in continuous use. Today it provides a stage for the Foothill Theater Company and other performing organizations. ✉ *401 Broad St.,* ☎ *916/265–6161.*

The **Miners Foundry,** erected in 1856, produced machines for gold mining and logging. The Pelton Water Wheel, a source of power for the mines, was invented here. A cavernous building, the foundry now serves as a cultural center that presents plays, concerts, a Victorian Christmas fair, a teddy-bear convention, antiques shows, themed period parties, and other events.✉ *325 Spring St.,* ☎ *916/265–5040.*

NEED A
BREAK?

Stop by the **Nevada City Winery** to taste wines produced from local grapes. ⊠ *Miners Foundry Garage, 321 Spring St., ☏ 916/265–9463. ☉ Tasting daily noon–5.*

Dining and Lodging

$$–$$$$ ✕ **Country Rose Cafe.** The lengthy French country menu at this antiques-laden café includes seafood, beef, lamb, chicken, and ratatouille. In the summer, there is outdoor service on a verdant patio. ⊠ *300 Commercial St., ☏ 916/265–6248. AE, MC, V. No lunch Sun.*

$$ ✕ **Friar Tuck's.** A guitar player performs nightly at this vaguely 1960s-retro gathering spot; sometimes patrons sing along. Hearty offerings include large portions of fondue, Iowa beef, Hawaiian fish specials, and Tuck's bouillabaisse. There's an extensive wine and beer list. ⊠ *111 N. Pine St., ☏ 916/265–9093. AE, MC, V. No lunch.*

$$ ✕ **Potager at Seleya's.** Fish, fowl, meat, and pasta dishes all come cre-
★ atively prepared at this sophisticated restaurant. Appetizers include wild mushrooms gratin and *potager* (soup). Beef Wellington, salmon roulade, and loin of lamb are signature entrées. Caesar salads are mixed at your table; breads and desserts are baked on the premises. The adjacent Potager to Go (☏ 916/265–0558) prepares gourmet-deli luncheon items. ⊠ *320 Broad St., ☏ 916/265–5697. AE, MC, V. Closed Mon. and major holidays. No lunch.*

$ ✕ **Cirino's.** American-Italian dishes—seafood, pasta, and veal—are served at this informal bar and grill. The restaurant's handsome Brunswick bar is of gold-rush vintage. ⊠ *309 Broad St., ☏ 916/265–2246. AE, D, MC, V.*

$–$$$ 🏠 **Flume's End.** This inn was built at the end of a historic flume that once brought water into Nevada City's mines. Rooms are on several levels, most with creek views. Two have hot tubs. The decor is eclectic Victorian, homey and casual, with romantic nooks. Room rates include a full breakfast. ⊠ *317 S. Pine St., 95959, ☏ 916/265–9665. 6 rooms. MC, V.*

$–$$$ 🏠 **Red Castle Inn.** A state landmark, this 1860 Gothic Revival mansion stands on a hillside overlooking Nevada City. Its brick exterior is trimmed with white icicle woodwork, and its porches and gardens add to the charm. The rooms, some of which overlook the town, have antique furnishings and are elaborately decorated. Room rates include full buffet breakfast. ⊠ *109 Prospect St., 95959, ☏ 916/265–5135. 7 rooms. MC, V.*

$–$$ 🏠 **Northern Queen Inn.** Most of the accommodations at this bright, creekside inn are typical motel units, but there are eight two-story chalets and eight rustic cottages with efficiency kitchens in a secluded, wooded area. ⊠ *400 Railroad Ave. (Sacramento St. exit off Hwy. 49), 95959, ☏ 916/265–5824, ᖴᗩᕼ 916/265–3720. 85 rooms. Restaurant, refrigerators, pool, spa, convention center. AE, DC, MC, V.*

Grass Valley

4 mi south of Nevada City on Hwy. 49.

More than half of California's total gold production was extracted from mines around Grass Valley. Unlike in neighboring Nevada City, urban sprawl surrounds Grass Valley's historic downtown, but the Empire Mine and the North Star Power House and Pelton Wheel Exhibit are among the Gold Country's most fascinating exhibits.

The **Grass Valley/Nevada County Chamber of Commerce** is housed in a reproduction of the home on this site owned by notorious dancer Lola Montez, who moved to Grass Valley in the early 1850s. Lola was no great talent—her popularity among miners derived from her suggestive "Spider Dance"—but her loves, which reportedly included composer Franz Liszt, were legendary. She had arrived in California not too long after, according to one account, being "permanently retired from her job as Bavarian king Ludwig's mistress," literary muse, and political adviser. Seems she pushed too hard for democracy, which contributed to his overthrow and her banishment as a witch! Or so the story went. The memory of licentious Lola lingers on in Grass Valley, as does her bathtub. ⊠ *248 Mill St.,* ☏ *916/273–4667.*

The landmark **Holbrooke Hotel,** built in 1851, hosted Lola Montez, Mark Twain, Ulysses S. Grant, and a stream of other U.S. presidents. Its saloon is one of the oldest still operating west of the Mississippi. ⊠ *212 W. Main St.,* ☏ *916/273–1353.*

★ ⑮ The **Empire Mine State Historic Park,** worked from 1850 right up to 1956, was one of California's richest quartz mines. An estimated 5.8 million ounces of gold were extracted from its 367 miles of underground passages. Tours allow visitors to peer into the mine's deep recesses and view the owner's "cottage," with its exquisite woodwork. The visitor center has mining exhibits and a picnic area. ⊠ *10791 E. Empire St. (Empire St. exit south from Hwy. 49),* ☏ *916/273–8522.* ☞ *$2.* ☉ *Daily 9–6 in summer, 10–5 in winter. Tours and lectures in summer on the hr 11–4; winter weekends only at 1 and 2.*

☾ The **North Star Power House and Pelton Wheel Exhibit** stars a 32-foot-high Pelton enclosed waterwheel, said to be the largest ever built. It was used to power mining operations and was a forerunner of the modern water turbines that generate hydroelectricity. There are hands-on displays for children and a picnic area. ⊠ *Empire and McCourtney Sts. (Empire St. exit north from Hwy. 49),* ☏ *916/273–4255.* ☞ *Donation requested.* ☉ *May–Oct., daily 10–5.*

Auburn

⑯ *24 mi south of Grass Valley on Hwy. 49, 34 mi northeast of Sacramento on I–80.*

Auburn is the Gold Country town most accessible to travelers on the interstate. An important transportation center during the gold rush, Auburn has a small old town with narrow climbing streets, cobblestones, wooden sidewalks, and many original buildings.

Auburn's standout structure is the **Placer County Courthouse.** The classic gold-domed building houses the Placer County Museum, which documents the area's history—Native American, railroad, agricultural, and mining—from the early 1700s to 1900. ⊠ *101 Maple St.,* ☏ *916/889–6500.* ☞ *Free.* ☉ *Tues.–Sun. 10–4.*

The **Bernhard Museum Complex,** whose centerpiece is the former Traveler's Rest Hotel, was built in 1851 and occupied by the Bernhard family from 1868 to 1957. The Bernhard Residence and adjacent winery buildings reflect family life in the late-Victorian era; a carriage house displays several period conveyances. ⊠ *291 Auburn-Folsom Rd.,* ☏ *916/889–4156.* ☞ *$1.* ☉ *Tues.–Fri. 11–3, weekends noon–4.*

A small, WPA-era building houses the **Gold Country Museum.** Worth a look, it surveys life in the mines and includes a walk-through mine tunnel, a gold-panning stream, and a replica saloon. ⊠ *1273 High St., off Auburn-Folsom Rd.,* ☏ *916/889–4134.* ☞ *$1.* ☉ *Tues.–Fri. 10–3:30, weekends 11–4.*

Dining and Lodging

$$–$$$ ✕ **Latitudes.** An 1870 Victorian is the setting for delicious, light mul-
★   ticultural cuisine. The restaurant serves no red-meat dishes, but the varied menu (which changes monthly) includes seafood, chicken, and
turkey entrées prepared with Mexican spices, curries, cheese, or teriyaki
sauce. The beer and wine list is as extensive and eclectic as the menu.
Sunday brunch here is deservedly popular. ⌧ *130 Maple St.,* ☎
916/885–9535. AE, MC, V. No lunch Sat., no dinner Mon.–Tues.

$ ✕ **Awful Annie's.** In good weather, patrons sit outside and take in the
view of old-town Auburn at this popular spot for breakfast (a specialty:
omelets with chili) or lunch. ⌧ *160 Sacramento Way,* ☎ *916/888–
9857. AE, MC, V. No dinner.*

$–$$$ 🏨 **Powers Mansion Inn.** This inn hints at the opulence the gold-rush
gentry enjoyed. Two light-filled parlors have gleaming oak floors,
Asian antiques, and ornate Victorian chairs and settees. Photos on the
walls relate the story of the gold fortune that built the mansion. A sec-
ond-floor maze of narrow corridors leads to the guest rooms, which
have brass and pencil-post beds with handmade quilts. Breakfast is in-
cluded in the room rate. ⌧ *164 Cleveland Ave., 95603,* ☎ *916/885–
1166,* FAX *916/885–1386. 11 rooms. AE, MC, V.*

$$ 🏨 **Holiday Inn.** Perched on a hill above the freeway across from Old
Auburn, the city's newest hotel has an imposing columned entrance
and welcoming lobby. Rooms are chain-standard, but attractively furnished; all have work areas, computer-data ports, and coffeemakers.
⌧ *120 Grass Valley Hwy.,* ☎ *916/8887–8787 or 800/814–8787,* FAX
*916/887–9824. 96 rooms. Restaurant, lounge, pool, spa, business
services, convention center. AE, D, DC, MC, V.*

$ 🏨 **Auburn Inn.** The decor at this well-maintained inn is contemporary,
in teal and pastel colors. There are king- and queen-size beds, suites,
and no-smoking rooms. Though a short distance from the freeway, the
inn is fairly quiet. Continental breakfast is included in the price. ⌧ *1875
Auburn Ravine Rd., Foresthill exit north from I–80, 95603,* ☎
916/885–1800 or 800/272–1444, FAX *916/888–6424. 81 rooms. Pool,
spa, coin laundry. AE, D, DC, MC, V.*

Coloma

25 mi south of Auburn on Hwy. 49.

The California gold rush started in Coloma. "My eye was caught with
the glimpse of something shining in the bottom of the ditch," James
Marshall recalled later. Unfortunately, Marshall himself never found
any more "color," as gold came to be called.

★ ⑰   Most of Coloma lies within **Marshall Gold Discovery State Historic Park.**
Though it is often crowded with tourists in summer, Coloma hardly resembles the mob scene it was in 1848 when 2,000 prospectors had
staked out claims along the streambed. Its population swelled rapidly
to 10,000, supporting 13 hotels, three banks, and many stores and businesses. But when reserves of the precious metal dwindled, prospectors
left as quickly as they had come. The park contains a number of buildings dating back to the gold rush, a working replica of John Sutter's mill,
about 100 yards from where James Marshall first saw gold, and a self-
guided trail leading to a monument marking his discovery. The museum
here is not as interesting as the outdoor exhibits. ⌧ *Hwy. 49,* ☎
916/622–3470. ⌧ *$5 per vehicle (day use).* ☉ *Park daily 8 AM–sunset.
Museum summer, daily 10–5; Labor Day–Memorial Day, daily 10–4:30.*

Dining and Lodging

$$–$$$ ✕⊞ **Vineyard House.** The site of an early, prize-winning winery, this
★ 1878 country inn became an important hotel and the social center of
the Coloma area. Said to be haunted by Robert Chalmers, a state sen-
ator in the 1880s who owned the home (or perhaps by his destitute
widow, Louisa), the inn has seven rooms, furnished with antiques and
late-19th-century artworks. The cellar bar, once used as a jail, is especially busy. The restaurant (usually closed Mon.–Wed.) is popular
for its traditional American food—chicken, beef, seafood, and pasta.
Room rates include breakfast. ⊠ *530 Cold Springs Rd., off Hwy. 49,
95613,* ☎ *916/622–2217,* FAX *209/622–5379. 7 rooms, 6 with shared
bath. Restaurant, bar. AE, MC, V.*

$$–$$$ ⊞ **Coloma Country Inn.** A restored 1852 Victorian set on 5 acres of state
parkland is now a fine bed-and-breakfast inn. Five rooms are in the main
house, with two suites in a carriage house. Appointments include antique double beds, private sitting areas, handmade quilts, stenciled
friezes, and fresh flowers. Balloon and whitewater-rafting packages are
available. Room rates include full country breakfast. ⊠ *345 High St.,
95613,* ☎ *916/622–6919. 7 rooms, 2 with shared bath. No credit cards.*

Placerville

*10 mi south of Coloma on Hwy. 49, 44 mi east of Sacramento on
U.S. 50.*

It's hard to imagine now, but in 1849 4,000 miners had staked out every
gully and hillside in Placerville, turning the town into a rip-roaring camp
of log cabins, tents, and clapboard houses. The area was then was known
as Hangtown, a graphic allusion to the summary nature of frontier justice. It took on the name Placerville in 1854 and became an important
supply center for the miners, where several American industrialists—
Mark Hopkins, Philip Armour, and John Studebaker—got their start.

★ ⑱ **Hangtown's Gold Bug Mine,** owned by the city of Placerville, has a fully
lighted shaft and is open for touring. A shaded stream runs through
the park, and there are picnic facilities. ⊠ *1 mi off U.S. 50, north on
Bedford Ave.,* ☎ *916/642–5238.* ⊠ *$1.* ☉ *May–Sept., daily 10–4;
late Mar.–Apr. and late Sept.–Oct., weekends 10–4.*

OFF THE **APPLE HILL** – Roadside stands sell fresh produce in this area filled with or-
BEATEN PATH chards and vineyards. During the fall harvest season members of the
Apple Hill Growers Association (⊠ 4103 Carson Rd., Camino, ☎ 916/
644-7692) open their orchards for apple picking, picnicking, and wine
and cider tasting. Many sell baked items and picnic food. ⊠ About 5 mi
east of Hwy. 49; take Camino exit from U.S. 50.

Dining and Lodging

$$$ ✕ **Zachary Jacques.** It's not easy to locate, but call for directions—
★ this country-French restaurant is worth the effort. A seasonally chang-
ing menu focuses on fresh fish and vegetables. Appetizers may include
escargots or mushrooms prepared in several ways, roasted garlic with
olive oil served on tapenade toast, or spicy lamb sausage. Entrées such
as roast rack of lamb, *daube Provençale* (beef stew), scallops and
prawns in lime butter, and chateaubriand garni receive traditional
preparation. ⊠ *1821 Pleasant Valley Rd.,* ☎ *916/626–8045. AE,
MC, V. Closed Mon. No lunch.*

$$ ✕ **Cafe Luna.** Tucked into the back of the Creekside Place shopping
complex is a small restaurant with about 30 seats indoors, plus tables
outdoors overlooking a creek. An extensive wine selection complements

such heart-healthy entrées as grilled chicken breast with blueberry and pasilla salsa as well as linguine with chicken breast. ✉ *451 Main St.,* ☎ *916/642–8669. AE, MC, V. Closed Sun. No dinner Mon.–Tues.*

$ ✕ **Lil' Mama D. Carlo's Italian Kitchen.** This comfortable Italian restaurant with a pleasant wait staff serves enormous portions of pasta, chicken, and some vegetarian dishes, heavy on the garlic, often in a red sauce. The wine list features local vintages. ✉ *482 Main St.,* ☎ *916/626–1612. MC, V. No lunch weekends.*

$$ ⊡ **Best Western Placerville Inn.** This motel's serviceable rooms are done in the chain's trademark pastels; the pool comes in handy during the hot summer months. There is a coffee shop–restaurant on the premises. ✉ *6850 Greenleaf Dr. near U.S. 50's Missouri Flats exit, 95667,* ☎ *916/622–9100 or 800/528–1234,* 🖷 *916/622–9376. 105 rooms. Restaurant, pool, hot tub. AE, D, DC, MC, V.*

Shenandoah Valley

16 mi south of Placerville on Shenandoah Road, east of Hwy. 49.

The most concentrated Gold Country wine-touring area lies in the rolling hills of the Shenandoah Valley, just east of Plymouth. This section of Amador County contains 17 wineries, mostly family-run operations on scenic back roads. Robust zinfandel is the primary grape grown here, but wineries also produce chardonnay and cabernet sauvignon. Most are open weekend afternoons; several have shady picnic areas, gift shops, and galleries or museums. Maps are available from the **Amador County County Chamber of Commerce** (☞ Contacts and Resources *in* Sacramento and the Gold Country A to Z, *below*).

Sobon Estate (✉ 14430 Shenandoah Rd., ☎ 209/245–6554) operates the Shenandoah Valley Museum, illustrating pioneer life and wine making in the valley. It's open daily 10–5. **Charles Spinetta Winery** (✉ 12557 Steiner Rd., ☎ 209/245–3384), which has a wildlife gallery, is open Tuesday through Sunday 10–5.

Lodging

$$ ⊡ **Amador Harvest Inn.** This bed-and-breakfast adjacent to Deaver Vineyards occupies a bucolic lakeside spot in the Shenandoah Valley. A contemporary Cape Cod–style structure has homey guest rooms with private baths. Public areas include a spacious living room with fireplace and a music room with a view of the lake. Room rates include full breakfast. ✉ *12455 Steiner Rd., 95669,* ☎ *209/245–5512. 5 rooms. MC, V.*

Amador City

6 mi south of Plymouth on Hwy. 49.

The history of tiny Amador City mirrors the boom-to-bust-to-boom cycle of many Gold Country towns. With an output of $42 million in gold, its Keystone Mine was one of the most productive in the Mother Lode. After all the gold was extracted, the miners cleared out and the area suffered, but Amador City now derives its wealth from tourists, who come to browse through its antiques and specialty shops and see historic landmarks.

Dining and Lodging

$$–$$$ ✕⊡ **Imperial Hotel.** The whimsically decorated rooms at this 1879
★   hotel mock Victorian excesses in a 20th-century way. Antique furnishings include iron and brass beds, gingerbread flourishes, and, in one room, art deco appointments. The two front rooms, which can be noisy, have

balconies. The hotel's fine restaurant serves meals in a bright dining room and on the patio outdoors. The menu changes quarterly; the cuisine ranges from vegetarian to country-hearty to trendy. Breakfast is included in the lodging rates; there is a two-night minimum weekends. ⊠ *Box 195, Hwy. 49, 95601,* ☎ *209/267–9172 or 800/242–5594,* ℻ *209/267– 9249. 6 rooms. Restaurant, bar. AE, D, DC, MC, V.*

Sutter Creek

★ ⑲ *2 mi south of Amador City on Hwy. 49.*

Sutter Creek is a charming conglomeration of balconied buildings, Victorian homes, and neo–New England structures. The stores along Highway 49 (called Main Street in the town proper) are worth visiting to hunt for works by the many local artists and craftspeople.

Dining and Lodging

$–$$ ✕ **Ron and Nancy's Palace.** This unpretentious restaurant serves Continental cuisine, with daily specials such as chicken marsala and veal piccata. The hearty lunch menu has a varied sandwich selection and some of the entrées available for dinner. ⊠ *76 Main St.,* ☎ *209/267– 1355. AE, D, DC, MC, V.*

$ ✕ **Somewhere in Time.** Sip a cup of tea, sample a sinful dessert, or lunch on sandwiches and salad before or after browsing through the antiques shops in this very Victorian boutique–dining complex. The building, erected in 1860, was originally a miners' saloon run by Chinese immigrants. ⊠ *34 Main St.,* ☎ *209/267–5789. D, MC, V. No dinner.*

$$–$$$ ⛉ **Foxes Bed & Breakfast.** The rooms in this white clapboard house,
★   built in 1857, are handsome, with high ceilings, antique beds, and lofty armoires topped with floral arrangements. All rooms have queen-size beds; four have wood-burning fireplaces and/or cable TV. A menu allows guests to select a full breakfast (included in room rate) cooked to order and delivered on a silver service to their rooms or to the gazebo in the garden. ⊠ *Box 159, 77 Main St., 95685,* ☎ *209/267–5882,* ℻ *209/267–0712. 7 rooms. D, MC, V.*

$$–$$$ ⛉ **Gold Quartz Inn.** Soft pastels, floral wallpaper, ruffled curtains, and period furnishings decorate the spacious rooms at this inn at the edge of Sutter Creek. All have king-size beds, many have additional beds and large porches, and two are equipped for people with disabilities. Breakfast is served in the dining room and afternoon tea in the butler's pantry; both are included in the room rate. ⊠ *15 Bryson Dr., 95685,* ☎ *209/267–9155 or 800/752–8738,* ℻ *209/267–9170. 24 rooms. Air-conditioning, laundry, meeting rooms. AE, MC, V.*

$$ ⛉ **Picture Rock Inn.** Original redwood paneling, wainscoting, beams, and cabinets lend the Picture Rock a cozy feel, as do leaded- and stained-glass windows. Eclectic furnishings span several eras from Victorian to art deco—a 1920s carousel horse is suspended mid-leap in the front room. Most rooms have views; all have private baths. Room rates include full breakfast. ⊠ *55 Eureka St., 95685,* ☎ *209/267–5500. 6 rooms. Air-conditioning. AE, D, MC, V.*

$ ⛉ **Aparicio's Hotel.** Budget-minded travelers will appreciate this clean hotel. Large rooms contain two queen beds; they're decorated with antique reproductions. ⊠ *271 Hanford St., Box 1839, 95685,* ☎ *209/267– 9177,* ℻ *209/267–5303. 52 rooms. Restaurant, lounge, meeting rooms. AE, D, MC, V.*

OFF THE   **DAFFODIL HILL –** Each spring a 4-acre hillside east of Sutter Creek erupts
BEATEN PATH   in a riot of yellow and gold as 300,000 daffodils emerge and burst into bloom. The garden is the work of members of the McLaughlin family,

which has owned this site since 1887. Daffodil plantings began in the 1930s and continue each winter. Timing of the display depends upon weather but usually takes place between mid-March and mid-April. ⊠ *Shake Ridge Rd., about 13 mi east of Sutter Creek,* ☎ *209/223-0350,* ⊠ *Free.* ⊙ *Daily in season 9–5.*

Jackson

② *8 mi south of Sutter Creek on Hwy. 49.*

Jackson once had the world's deepest and richest mines, the Kennedy and Argonaut, which together produced $70 million in gold. These were deep rock mines, tunnels for which extended as much as a mile underground. Most of the miners who worked the lode here were of Serbian or Italian origin; they gave the town a European character that persists to this day. Churches, cemeteries, and festivals carry Serbian or Italian names. Jackson has a number of aboveground pioneer cemeteries in which the headstones tell the stories of local Serbian and Italian families. The terraced cemetery on the grounds of the handsome **St. Sava Serbian Orthodox Church** (⊠ 724 N. Main St.) is the most impressive.

Jackson wasn't the Gold Country's rowdiest town, but the party lasted longer here than most anywhere else: "Girls' dormitories" and nickel slots flourished until the mid-1950s. Now the heart of Jackson's historic section is the **National Hotel** (⊠ 2 Water St.), which operates an old-time saloon in the lobby; the hotel is especially active on weekends, when people come from miles around to participate in the Saturday-night sing-alongs.

The **Amador County Museum,** built in the late 1850s as a private home, provides a colorful take on gold-rush life. Many original furnishings are on display: a kitchen with wood stove, a bathroom, the Amador County bicentennial quilt, furnishings, and a classroom. A time line recounts the county's checkered past. The museum also conducts hourly tours of large-scale working models of the nearby Kennedy Mine. ⊠ *225 Church St.,* ☎ *209/223–6386.* ⊠ *Museum free; building with mine $1.* ⊙ *Wed.–Sun. 10–4.*

Dining and Lodging

$–$$ ✕ **Upstairs Restaurant.** Chef Layne McCollum takes a creative approach to contemporary American cuisine—gourmet fowl, fresh seafood, and meat—in this intimate (12 tables) restaurant with fresh flowers, white table linens, and soft music. The baked-brie and roast-garlic appetizer and homemade soups are specialties; local wines are reasonably priced. Downstairs there's a casual lunch spot and wine bar and lounge area. ⊠ *164 Main St., 95642,* ☎ *209/223–3342. AE, D, DC, MC, V. Closed Mon.*

$ ✕ **Rosebud's Cafe.** Art deco decor and music from the 1930s and 1940s set the mood at this casual, homey café. Among the classic American menu items are hot roast beef, turkey, and meat loaf with mashed potatoes smothered in gravy. Charbroiled burgers, freshly baked pies, and espresso or gourmet coffees round out the menu. ⊠ *26 Main St., 95641,* ☎ *209/223–1035. MC, V. No dinner.*

$$–$$$ ▥ **Court Street Inn.** This Victorian has tin ceilings and a redwood staircase. The cozy first-floor Muldoon Room has a fireplace; Blair Room has a large whirlpool and a Wedgwood stove. The Indian House, a two-bedroom guest cottage, has a large bathroom. Room rates include a full breakfast and evening refreshments. ⊠ *215 Court St., 95642,*

☎ 209/223–0416 or 800/200–0416. 7 rooms. Outdoor hot tub. AE, MC, V.

$ 🏨 **Best Western Amador Inn.** Convenience and price are the main attractions of this sprawling two-story motel right on the highway. Rooms are nicely decorated; many have fireplaces. ⊠ 200 S. Hwy. 49, Box 758, 95642, ☎ 209/223–0211 or 800/543–5221, FAX 209/223–4836. 118 rooms. Restaurant, pool, laundry service. AE, D, DC, MC, V.

Angels Camp

㉑ 20 mi south of Jackson on Hwy. 49.

Angels Camp is famed chiefly for its jumping-frog contest held each May, based on Mark Twain's "The Jumping Frog of Calaveras County." The writer reputedly heard the story of the jumping frog from Ross Coon, proprietor of Angels Hotel, which has been operating since 1856.

Angels Camp Museum holds a granny's attic of gold-rush relics—historic photos, rocks, petrified wood, and old mining equipment. The huge Pelton Water Wheel exhibit explains how the apparatus was used to supply water power to the mines. ⊠ 753 S. Main St., ☎ 209/736–2963. 🎫 $1. ☉ Mar.–Labor Day, daily 10–3; Labor Day–Mar., Wed.–Sun. 10–3.

OFF THE BEATEN PATH
MOANING CAVERN – Visitors reach a vast underground chamber housing ancient crystalline rock formations—including a stalactite several yards long and numerous stalagmites—and an archaeological site via a 235-step spiral staircase. The cavern is 2 miles south of the town of Vallecito, which is east of Angels Camp off Highway 4. ⊠ Parrots Ferry Rd., ☎ 209/736–2708. 🎫 $6.75. ☉ Summer, daily 9–6; winter, daily 10–5.

Murphys

㉒ 10 mi east of Angels Camp on Hwy. 4.

Murphys is a well-preserved town of white picket fences, Victorian houses, and interesting shops. In **Murphys Historic Hotel and Lodge,** the guest register records the visits of Horatio Alger and Ulysses S. Grant, who joined the 19th-century swarms visiting the giant sequoia groves in nearby Calaveras Big Trees State Park, on Highway 4, 15 miles east of Murphys.

The **Kautz Ironstone Winery and Caverns** is worth a visit even if you don't like wine; tours take visitors into aging underground tunnels cooled by a waterfall from a natural spring. The winery schedules entertainment, concerts, art shows, and other events on weekends. ⊠ Six Mile Rd., 95247, ☎ 209/728–1251. ☉ Daily 11–5.

Dining and Lodging

$ ✕ **Grounds.** Light Italian entrées, grilled fresh vegetables, chicken breast, seafood, and steak are the specialties at this storefront deli and coffee shop. Lunches—sandwiches, homemade soups and salads—are fresh and presented well. The atmosphere here is friendly and the service attentive. ⊠ 402 Main St., ☎ 209/728–8663. MC, V. Closed Tues. No dinner Wed.

$$–$$$$ 🏨 **Dunbar House 1880.** The oversize rooms in this elaborate Italianate-style home, decorated with an eclectic selection of antiques, have brass beds, down comforters, wood-burning stoves, and claw-foot tubs. Broad wraparound verandas encourage lounging, as do colorful gardens and shady elm trees. The Cedar room's sunporch has a two-

person whirlpool tub and a view of a white-flowering almond tree; in Sequoia you can gaze at the garden while soaking in a bubble bath. Breakfast (included) is an elegant affair. ⊠ *271 Jones St., Box 1375, 95247,* ☎ *209/728–2897 or 800/225–3764, ext. 321;* ℻ *209/728–1451. 4 rooms. Refrigerators, in-room VCRs. AE, MC, V.*

$–$$ 🍴 **Murphys Historic Hotel and Lodge.** This 1855 stone hotel figured in Bret Harte's story "A Night at Wingdam." The register contains signatures of Mark Twain and bandit Black Bart. Accommodations are in the historic hotel and a modern motel-style addition. The older rooms are furnished with antiques, many of them large, heavy, and hand-carved. The hotel has a friendly old-time saloon. Continental breakfast is included in the room rate. ⊠ *457 Main St., 95247,* ☎ *209/728–3444 or 800/532–7684,* ℻ *209/728–1590. 29 rooms (9 historic rooms share baths). Restaurant, bar, meeting rooms. AE, D, DC, MC, V.*

Columbia State Historic Park

★ 🍴 ㉓ *14 mi south of Angels Camp, Hwy. 49 to Parrots Ferry Rd.*

Columbia State Historic Park, known as the Gem of the Southern Mines, comes as close to a gold-rush town in its heyday as you can get. Visitors ride stagecoaches, pan for gold, or watch a blacksmith working at his anvil. Street musicians give lively performances in summer. Restored or reconstructed buildings include a Wells Fargo Express office, a Masonic temple, stores, saloons, two hotels, a firehouse, churches, a school, and a newspaper office. All are staffed to simulate a working 1850s town. ☎ *209/532–4301.* 🎫 *Free.* ⊗ *Park daily 8:30–5; museum daily 9–4:30; closed Thanksgiving and Dec. 25.*

Dining and Lodging

$–$$ ✕🍴 **City Hotel.** The rooms in this restored 1856 hostelry are furnished with period antiques. Two have balconies overlooking Main Street, and six parlor rooms open onto a second-floor sitting room. All the accommodations have private half baths with showers nearby; robes and slippers are provided. The restaurant (closed Mon.), one of the Gold Country's best, serves French-accented California cuisine complemented by a huge selection of California wines. The What Cheer Saloon is right out of a western movie. Room rates include breakfast. ⊠ *Main St., Box 1870, Columbia 95310,* ☎ *209/532–1479,* ℻ *209/532–7027. 10 rooms with ½ bath. Restaurant, bar. AE, D, MC, V.*

$–$$ 🍴 **Fallon Hotel.** The state of California restored this 1857 hotel. All rooms have antiques and a private half bath; there are separate men's and women's showers. Continental breakfast is served; if you occupy one of the five balcony rooms, you can sit outside with your coffee and watch the town wake up. ⊠ *Washington St., Box 1870, Columbia 95310,* ☎ *209/532–1470. 14 rooms with ½ bath. AE, D, MC, V.*

Nightlife and the Arts

Columbia Actors' Repertory, a local professional company, presents a full season of plays, comedies, and musicals at the Historic Fallon House Theater. The City Hotel (☞ *above*) offers combined lodging, dinner, and theater packages. ⊠ *Box 1079, 95310,* ☎ *209/532–4644.*

Sonora

㉔ *4 mi south of Columbia, Parrotts Ferry Rd. to Hwy. 49.*

Miners from Mexico founded Sonora and made it the biggest town in the Mother Lode. Following a period of racial and ethnic strife, the Mexicans moved on, leaving Americans to build the city based on commerce that is visible today. Sonora's downtown historic section sits atop the

Big Bonanza Mine, one of the richest in the state. Another mine, on the site of nearby Sonora High School, yielded a 28-pound nugget and produced 990 pounds of gold in a single week in 1879. Reminders of the gold rush are everywhere in Sonora, in prim Victorian houses, typical Sierra stone storefronts, and awning-shaded sidewalks. Reality intrudes beyond the town's historic heart with strip malls, shopping centers, and modern motels. If the countryside surrounding Sonora seems familiar, that's because much of it has appeared in western and other movies over the years. Scenes from *High Noon, For Whom the Bell Tolls, The Virginian, Back to the Future III,* and *The Unforgiven* were filmed here.

The **Tuolumne County Museum and History Center** occupies a building that served as a jail until 1951. It's been restored to an earlier period and houses a jail museum, historic exhibits, a case with gold nuggets, an extensive collection of vintage firearms and paraphernalia, and the libraries of a historical society and a genealogical society. ⊠ *158 W. Bradford St.,* ☎ *209/532–1317.* ⊡ *Free.* ☉ *Sun., Mon., and Wed. 9–4; Tues., Thurs., and Fri. 10–4; Sat. 10–3:30.*

Dining and Lodging

$$ ✕ **Josephine's California Trattoria.** This restaurant with indoor and outdoor dining serves contemporary California and traditional Tuscan cuisine. Seared ahi, roasted red peppers, duckling with polenta, Delta crayfish risotto, and angel hair pasta with fresh seafood are among the seasonal dishes one might find on the menu. Single-portion pizzas are a staple. The extensive, reasonably priced wine list showcases Sierra foothill and Italian vintages. ⊠ *Gunn House Hotel, 286 S. Washington,* ☎ *209/533–4111. AE, D, MC, V. No lunch.*

$ ✕ **Coyote Creek Cafe & Grill.** The fare here is multinational—lunch might include pasta Castroville (with artichoke-hearts marinara), Zuni black-bean plate, and Szechuan chicken. Spanish tapas and grilled steak are among the dinner entrées. The low-key, friendly café presents live music on Monday and Wednesday. ⊠ *177 S. Washington St.,* ☎ *209/532–9115. Reservations not accepted. D, MC, V.*

$$–$$$ 🛏 **Ryan House Bed and Breakfast Inn.** One of the oldest houses in Sonora, this 1850s farmhouse is just steps from town. Attentive innkeepers make a homey place to stay, but there's more privacy than might be expected at such a small inn. Guest rooms are furnished with antiques; everyone has access to the three parlors and the sunny kitchen. A garden suite in the attic has a large sitting area set into the gables, a pink and burgundy bathroom with double soaking tub, and a brass-and-iron bed. Room rates include full breakfast (including the best scones in California). Lodging-and-theater packages are available. ⊠ *153 S. Shepherd St., 95370,* ☎ *209/533–3445 or 800/831–4897. 4 rooms. Air-conditioning. AE, MC, V.*

$ 🛏 **Sonora Oaks Motor Hotel.** Standard motel-issue rooms here are clean and fairly spacious. Larger ones have outside sitting areas; four have fireplaces, whirlpool tubs, and tranquil hillside views. Because the motel is right off Highway 108, front rooms can be noisy. ⊠ *19551 Hess Ave., 95370, 100 rooms.* ☎ *209/533–4400 or 800/532–1944,* ℻ *209/532–1964. Restaurant, lounge, pool, meeting rooms. AE, D, DC, MC, V.*

Jamestown

㉕ *4 mi south of Sonora on Hwy. 49.*

Compact Jamestown supplies a touristy, superficial view of gold rush–era life. Shops filling brightly colored buildings along Main Street sell antiques and gift items.

Dining and Lodging

$ ✕⊞ **National Hotel.** The decor at this hotel, in business since 1859, is simple—brass beds, patchwork quilts, and lace curtains. Not all rooms have phones or private baths; those without baths have antique washbasins. The saloon, with its original 19th-century redwood bar, is a great place to linger. The popular restaurant (reservations required) serves mountain-size portions: hamburgers and fries, salads, Italian entrées. Room rates include breakfast. ⊠ *77 Main St., Box 502, 95327,* ☎ *209/984–3446; in CA, 800/894–3446;* ℻ *209/984–5620. 11 rooms, 6 with shared bath. Restaurant. AE, D, DC, MC, V.*

Mariposa

㉖ *31 mi south of Jamestown on Hwy. 49.*

Mariposa marks the southern end of the Mother Lode. Much of the land in this area was part of a 44,000-acre land grant Col. John C. Fremont acquired from Mexico before gold was discovered and California became a state.

At the **California State Mining and Mineral Museum,** a glittering, 22-pound chunk of ore makes it clear what the gold rush was about. Displays include a replica of a typical tunnel dug by hard-rock miners, a miniature stamp mill, and a panning and sluicing exhibit. ⊠ *Mariposa County Fairgrounds, Hwy. 49,* ☎ *209/742–7625.* ⊡ *$3.50.* ☉ *May–Sept., Wed.–Sun. 10–6; Oct.–Apr., Wed.–Sun. 10–4.*

Dining and Lodging

$ ✕ **Castillo's Mexican Food.** Tasty tacos, enchiladas, chili rellenos, and burrito combinations, plus chimichangas, fajitas, steak, and seafood, are served in a casual storefront setting. ⊠ *4995 5th St.,* ☎ *209/742–4413. MC, V.*

$$ ⊞ **Little Valley Inn.** Pine paneling, historical photos, and old mining tools recall Mariposa's heritage at this modern bed-and-breakfast inn with three rooms in a building separate from the main house. The large grounds include a creek where guests can pan for gold (a helpful dog stirs the creekbed). Room rates include a full breakfast. ⊠ *3483 Brooks Rd., off Hwy. 49,* ☎ *209/742–6204 or 800/889–5444,* ℻ *209/742–5099. 3 rooms. Refrigerators, in-room VCRs, horseshoes. AE, MC, V.*

$ ⊞ **Comfort Inn of Yosemite.** Formerly the Gold Rush Inn, this dramatic white three-story building with a broad veranda sits on a hill above Mariposa. Some of the spacious, comfortable rooms have sitting areas. Room rates include Continental breakfast. ⊠ *4994 Bouillon St., Mariposa 95338,* ☎ *209/966–4344 or 800/221–2222,* ℻ *209/966–4655. 62 rooms. Pool, outdoor hot tub.*

SACRAMENTO AND THE GOLD COUNTRY A TO Z

Arriving and Departing

By Bus

Greyhound (☎ 800/231–2222) serves Sacramento, Auburn, and Placerville. It's a two-hour trip from San Francisco's Transbay Terminal at 1st and Mission streets to the Sacramento station at 7th and L streets.

By Car

Sacramento lies at the junction of I–5 and I–80, just under 90 miles northeast of San Francisco. It's about an eight-hour drive north on I–5 from Los Angeles. I–80 continues northeast through the Gold Country toward Reno, about three hours from Sacramento; Lake Tahoe is two hours east of Sacramento via U.S. 50 or I–80.

By Plane

Sacramento Metro Airport (☎ 916/648–0700), 12 miles northwest of downtown Sacramento on I–5, is served by **Alaska, America West, American, Delta, Northwest, Southwest,** and **United** (☞ Air Travel *in* Important Contacts A to Z for phone numbers).

San Francisco International Airport and **Oakland International Airport** are about two hours from Sacramento.

By Train

Amtrak (☎ 800/872–7245) runs trains to Sacramento frequently from Oakland's Jack London Square station (⊠ 245 2nd St.). Trains making this three-hour trip stop in Emeryville, Richmond, Martinez, and Davis; some stop at Berkeley and Suisin-Fairfield as well. Shuttle buses connect the Emeryville station (⊠ 5885 Landregan St.) and San Francisco's Ferry Building (⊠ 30 Embarcadero, at the foot of Market St.).

Getting Around

By Bus

Sacramento Regional Transit (☎ 916/321–2877) buses and light-rail trains transport passengers in Sacramento. Buses run 5 AM–10 PM, trains 4:30 AM–12:30 AM.

By Car

Traveling by car is the most convenient way to see the Gold Country, since most of the area's towns are too small to provide a base for public transportation. From Sacramento, three highways fan out toward the east, all intersecting with Highway 49: I–80 heads 30 miles northeast to Auburn; U.S. 50 goes east 40 miles to Placerville; and Highway 16 angles southeast 45 miles to Plymouth. Highway 49 is an excellent two-lane road that winds and climbs through the foothills and valleys, linking the principal Gold Country towns.

Contacts and Resources

Emergencies

Ambulance (☎ 911). **Police** (☎ 911).

Mercy Hospital of Sacramento Promptcare (⊠ 4001 J St., ☎ 916/453–4424). **Sutter General Hospital** (⊠ 2801 L St., ☎ 916/733–8900). **Sutter Memorial Hospital** (⊠ 52nd and F Sts., ☎ 916/733–1000).

Guided Tours

Capital City Cruises (⊠ 1401 Garden Hwy., Suite 125, Sacramento 95833, ☎ 916/921–1111) runs year-round, two-hour narrated cruises, as well as brunch, dinner-dance, and murder-mystery cruises, on the Sacramento River. **Channel Star Excursions** (⊠ 110 L St., Sacramento 95814, ☎ 916/552–2933 or 800/433–0263) operates the *Spirit of Sacramento,* a paddlewheel riverboat, which takes passengers on happy-hour, dinner, luncheon, and champagne brunch cruises in addition to one-hour narrated river tours. **Coloma Country Inn** (⊠ Box 502, Coloma 95613, ☎ 916/622–6919) operates ballooning and rafting packages on the American River in conjunction with bed-and-breakfast accommodations. **Gold Prospecting Expeditions** (⊠ 18170 Main St., Jamestown 95327, ☎ 209/984–4653 or 800/596–0009, FAX 209/984–0711) arranges one-hour to two-week excursions. **Outdoor Adventure River Specialists (O.A.R.S.)** (⊠ Box 67, Angels Camp 95222, ☎ 209/736–4677 or 800/346–6277, FAX 209/736–2902) operates whitewater rafting trips on the Stanislaus, American, Merced, and Tuolumne rivers from late March through early October.

Hop Around (✉ 2600 North Ave., Sacramento 95838, ☎ 916/927–2877 or 800/356–9838), a $12 shopping and narrated sightseeing shuttle operated by Gray Line/Frontier Tours, covers most downtown tourist attractions. Buses pick up passengers at major hotels.

A Taste of Murphys (✉ Big Trees Carriage Co., ☎ 209/728–2602) conducts an interesting half-day tour of Murphys-area wineries and historic spots in a horse-drawn wagon. The fee ($40) includes wine tasting and a picnic lunch.

Visitor Information

Amador County Chamber of Commerce (✉ 125 Peek St., Jackson 95642, ☎ 209/223–0350). **El Dorado County Chamber of Commerce** (✉ 542 Main St., Placerville 95667, ☎ 916/621–5885 or 800/457–6279). **Grass Valley/Nevada County Chamber of Commerce** (✉ 248 Mill St., Grass Valley 95945, ☎ 916/273–4667 or 800/655–4667). **Mariposa County Visitor's Bureau** (✉ 5158 Hwy. 140, Mariposa 95338, ☎ 209/966–2456 or 800/208–2434). **Placer County Tourism Authority** (✉ 13464 Lincoln Way, Auburn, 95603, ☎ 916/887–2111 or 800/427–6463). **Sacramento Convention and Visitors Bureau** (✉ 1421 K St., Sacramento 95814, ☎ 916/264–7777). **Sacramento Heritage** (✉ 630 I St., Sacramento 95814, ☎ 916/440–1355). **Tuolumne County Visitors Bureau** (✉ Box 4020, 55 W. Stockton St., Sonora 95370, ☎ 209/533–4420 or 800/446–1333).

7 Lake Tahoe

*The California
and Nevada Shores*

*The largest alpine lake in North
America is famous for its clarity, deep
blue water, and snowcapped peaks.
Though Lake Tahoe possesses
abundant natural beauty and accessible
wilderness, nearby towns are highly
developed and the roads around it
often congested. Summertime is
generally cooler here than in the
foothills, and the clean mountain air
bracingly crisp. When it gets hot, the
plentiful beaches and brisk water are
only minutes away.*

Updated by
Deke
Castleman

LAKE TAHOE lies 6,225 feet above sea level in the Sierra Nevada mountain range, straddling the state line between California and Nevada. The border gives this popular resort region a split personality. About half the visitors here arrive intent on low-key sightseeing, hiking, fishing, camping, and boating. The rest head directly for the Nevada side of the lake, where bargain dining and big-name entertainment draw customers into the glittering casinos. Tahoe is also a popular wedding and honeymoon destination: couples can get married with no waiting period or blood tests at chapels all around the lake. On Valentine's Day the chapels become veritable factories—four times as many ceremonies take place that day than any other. Incidentally, the legal marrying age in California and Nevada is 18 years, but one must be 21 to gamble or drink.

Summer's cool temperatures provide respite from the heat in the surrounding deserts and valleys. Although swimming in Lake Tahoe is always brisk—68°F is about as warm as it gets—the lake's beaches are generally crowded in summer. Those who prefer solitude can escape to the many state parks, national forests, and protected tracts of wilderness that ring the 22-mile-long, 12-mile-wide lake. From mid-autumn to late spring, multitudes of skiers and winter-sports enthusiasts are attracted to Tahoe's 15 downhill skiing resorts and 11 cross-country centers—North America's largest concentration of skiing facilities. Ski resorts try to open by Thanksgiving, if only with machine-made snow, and operate through May or even later. Most accommodations, restaurants, and some parks are open year-round.

The first white man to find this spectacular region was Capt. John C. Fremont in 1844, guided by famous scout Kit Carson. Not long afterward, silver was discovered in Nevada's Comstock Lode at Virginia City, and as the bonanza hit, the Tahoe Basin's forests were leveled to provide lumber for mine-tunnel supports. By the turn of the century, wealthy Californians were building lakeside estates here, some of which survive. Improved roads brought the less affluent in the 1920s and 1930s, when modest bungalows began to fill the shoreline, where the woods had grown back. The first casinos opened in the 1940s. Ski resorts brought another development boom as the lake became a year-round destination.

Lake Tahoe's water is 99.7% pure, cleaner than drinking water in most U.S. cities. The water is so clear that you can see as deep as 75 feet. Over the last few decades, however, road construction and other building projects have washed soil and minerals into the lake, leading to a growth of algae that threatens its fabled clarity. After the environmental movement gained strength in the 1970s, a moratorium on new shoreline construction was declared and a master plan was instituted to control development.

During some summer weekends it seems that absolutely every tourist—100,000 at peak periods—is in a car on the one main road that circles the 72-mile shoreline. The crowds and congestion increase as the day wears on. At a vantage point overlooking Emerald Bay early in the morning, on a trail in the national forests that ring the basin, or on a sunset cruise on the lake itself, one can forget the nearby glitz and commercial development and absorb the grandeur.

Pleasures and Pastimes

Camping

Campgrounds abound in the Tahoe area, run by the state park service, the U.S. Forest Service, city utility districts, and private operators. Sites range from primitive and rustic to upscale and luxurious. Make summer reservations far in advance, as spaces are almost always in high demand (☞ Contacts and Resources *in* Lake Tahoe A to Z, *below*).

Dining

Restaurants at Lake Tahoe range from rock-and-wood decor to elegant French, with stops along the way for Swiss chalet and spare modern. The food, too, is varied and may include delicate Continental or nouvelle-Californian sauces, mesquite- and olive-wood-grilled specialties, and wild game in season. On weekends and in high season, expect a long wait to be seated in the more popular restaurants. During slower periods, some places may close temporarily or limit their hours, so call ahead to verify.

Casinos use their restaurants to attract gaming customers. Their marquees often tout "$5.99 prime rib dinners" or "$1.39 breakfast specials." Some of these meal deals may not be top quality; they're generally found in the coffee shops and buffets. But the finer restaurants in casinos generally deliver good food, service, and atmosphere.

Unless otherwise noted, even the most expensive Tahoe eating places welcome customers in casual clothes—not surprising in this year-round vacation mecca—but don't expect to be served in most restaurants if you're barefoot, shirtless, or wearing a skimpy bathing suit.

CATEGORY	COST*
$$$$	over $50
$$$	$30–$50
$$	$20–$30
$	under $20

per person for a three-course meal, excluding drinks, service, and 7%–7¼% tax

Gambling

Nevada's major casinos are also full-service hotels and resorts. They make discounted lodging packages available throughout the year. The casinos share an atmosphere of garish neon and noise, but conditioned air and no-smoking areas eliminate the smoky pall of the past. Six are clustered on a strip of U.S. 50 in Stateline—Caesars, Harrah's, Harvey's, Horizon, and Lakeside, plus Bill's, a lower-stakes "junior" casino (no lodging) that appeals to less-experienced players. Four others stand on the north shore: the Hyatt Regency, Cal-Neva, Tahoe Biltmore, and Crystal Bay Club. Open 24 hours a day, 365 days a year, these casinos have table games (craps, blackjack, roulette, baccarat, poker, keno, pai gow, bingo, and big six), race and sports books, and thousands of slot machines—1,750, for instance, at Harrah's. There is no charge to enter and there is no dress code.

The hotels attract potential players into their high-profit casinos with shows, celebrity entertainers, and restaurants and lounges that are open around the clock. All gamblers are offered complimentary beverages; higher-stakes players can qualify for complimentary meals, rooms, room service, golf, even private yacht parties. Parking is plentiful in enclosed garages and open lots; valet parking is technically free, but a $1–$2 tip is customary.

Golf

The Tahoe area is nearly as popular with golfers as it is with skiers. Half a dozen superb courses dot the mountains around the lake, with magnificent views, fresh cool air, lush fairways and greens, and thick pines shading it all. Encountering wildlife is not uncommon if you have to search for your ball out-of-bounds.

Hiking

There are five U.S. National Forests in the Tahoe Basin and a half-dozen state parks. The main areas for hiking include the Tahoe Rim Trail, a 150-mile trail along the ridgelines above the lake; Desolation Wilderness, a vast 63,473-acre preserve of granite peaks, glacial valleys, sub-alpine forests, the Rubicon River, and more than 50 lakes; and the trail systems near Lake Tahoe Visitor Center and D. L. Bliss, Emerald Bay, Sugar Pine Point, and Lake Tahoe-Nevada state parks.

Lodging

Quiet inns on the water, motel rooms in the heart of the casino area, rooms at the casinos themselves, and lodges close to ski runs are among the Tahoe options. During summer and ski season the lake is crowded; reserve space as far ahead as possible. Spring and fall give you a little more leeway and lower—sometimes significantly lower—rates. Price categories listed below reflect high-season rates.

CATEGORY	COST*
$$$$	over $175
$$$	$120–$175
$$	$80–$120
$	under $80

All prices are for a standard double room, excluding 9%–10% tax.

Skiing

Lake Tahoe area is a Nordic skier's paradise. You can even cross-country ski on fresh snow right on the lakeshore beaches. Skinny skiing (slang for cross-country) at the resorts can be costly, but you get the benefits of machine grooming and trail preparation. If it's bargain Nordic you're after, take advantage of thousands of acres of public forest and parkland trails.

The mountains around Lake Tahoe are bombarded by blizzards throughout the winter (and sometimes the fall and spring); 10- to 12-foot bases are not uncommon. The profusion of downhill resorts guarantees a nearly infinite variety of terrains, conditions, and challenges. To save money, look for packages offered by lodges and resorts; some include interchangeable lift tickets that allow you to try different slopes. Midweek packages are usually lower in price, and most resorts offer family discounts. Free shuttle-bus service is available between most ski resorts and lodgings.

Sno-Park Areas

There are five public Sno-Park areas in the vicinity, some for snowmobiling and cross-country skiing, as well as sledding. All are maintained by the Department of Parks and Recreation (☞ Contacts and Resources *in* Lake Tahoe A to Z, *below*), and to use them you need to obtain a permit in advance.

Swimming

Thirty-six public beaches line Lake Tahoe. Lifeguards stand duty at some of the swimming beaches, and yellow buoys mark safe areas where motorboats are not permitted. Opening and closing dates for beaches vary with the climate and available park-service personnel.

Exploring Lake Tahoe

The most common way to explore the Lake Tahoe area is to drive the 72-mile road that follows the shore, through wooded flatlands and past beaches, climbing to vistas on the rugged west side of the lake and descending to the busiest commercial developments and casinos. Undeveloped Lake Tahoe-Nevada State Park occupies well more than half of the Nevada side of Lake Tahoe, stretching between the glitzy border towns of Crystal Bay and Stateline. The California side, particularly South Lake Tahoe, is more fully developed, though much wilderness remains.

Great Itineraries

Although, or perhaps because, the distance around Lake Tahoe is relatively short, the desire to experience the whole area can be overwhelming. It takes only one day "to see it"—drive around the lake, stretch your legs at a few overlooks, take a nature walk, and wander among the casinos at Stateline. If you have more time, you can laze on a beach and swim, venture onto the lake or into the mountains, and sample Tahoe's finer restaurants. If you have five days, you can write a guidebook! But be careful—you may become so attached to Tahoe that you begin visiting realtors and researching the job market.

Numbers in the text correspond to numbers in the margin and on the Lake Tahoe map.

IF YOU HAVE 3 DAYS

On your first day, stop in **South Lake Tahoe** ① and pick up provisions for a picnic lunch. Start with some morning beach fun at the **Pope-Baldwin Recreation Area** ③ and check out the area's **Tallac Historic Site.** Head west on Highway 89, stopping at the **Lake Tahoe Visitor Center** ④ and the **Emerald Bay** ⑤ lookout. Have lunch at the lookout, or hike down— be forewarned: the hike back up is steep—to **Vikingsholm,** a Viking castle replica. In the late afternoon, explore the trails and mansions at **Sugar Pine Point State Park** ⑦, then backtrack on Highway 89 and U.S. 50 for dinner in South Lake Tahoe. On your second day, cruise on the *Tahoe Queen* glass-bottom sternwheeler out of South Lake Tahoe or the MS *Dixie II* sternwheeler out of **Zephyr Cove** ⑰ in the morning, and then ride the **Heavenly Tram** ② at Heavenly Ski Resort. Have lunch high above the lake and (except in snow season) take a walk on one of Heavenly's nature trails. If you're itching to try your luck at the casinos, **Stateline** ⑱ is only moments away from the tram base; visit one before having dinner in the area. Start your third day by heading north on U.S. 50, stopping at **Cave Rock** ⑯ and (after turning north on Highway 28) at **Sand Harbor Beach** ⑮. If *Bonanza* looms large in your memory, drop by **Ponderosa Ranch** ⑭, or continue on to **Crystal Bay** ⑫ to hike the Stateline Lookout Trail above Crystal Bay. If you have the time, drive to **Tahoe City** ⑧ to see its Gatekeeper's Log Cabin Museum.

IF YOU HAVE 5 DAYS

Pick up a picnic on your first day and visit **Pope-Baldwin Recreation Area** ③. Then head west to **Lake Tahoe Visitor Center** ④ and the **Emerald Bay** ⑤ lookout. Hike to **Vikingsholm** or, if that seems too strenuous, proceed directly to **Sugar Pine Point State Park** ⑦. Have dinner in **Tahoe City** ⑧ or South Lake Tahoe. On your second day, cruise on the *Tahoe Queen* or MS *Dixie II* in the morning, then ride the **Heavenly Tram** ② and have lunch and possibly a hike. Spend the late afternoon or early evening at one of the **Stateline** ⑱ casinos. On the third day, visit **Cave Rock** ⑯ and the **Ponderosa Ranch** ⑭, and hike the Stateline Lookout Trail above **Crystal Bay** ⑫. Have lunch in Crystal Bay and spend

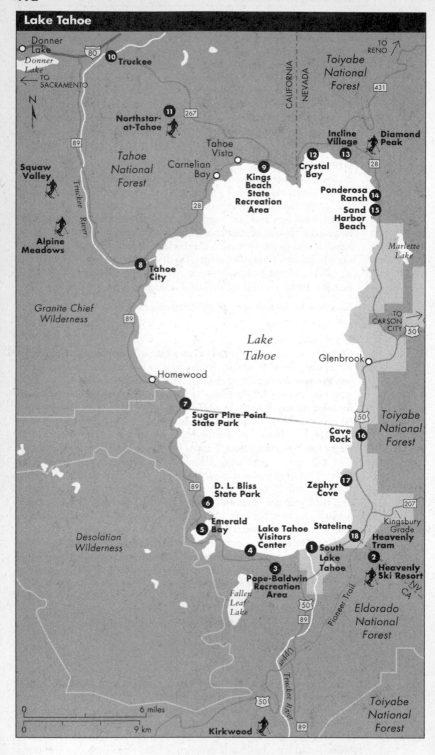

the afternoon at the nearby **Kings Beach State Recreation Area** ⑨. On the fourth day, hang out at **Sand Harbor Beach** ⑮ or, if it's winter, on the ski slopes. On day five, rent a bike and ride from **D. L. Bliss State Park** ⑥ to **Tahoe City** ⑧ and explore the Gatekeeper's Log Cabin Museum.

When To Tour Lake Tahoe

Except to ski bunnies, Tahoe is the most fun during the summer. The best strategy for avoiding crowds is to do as much as you can as early as you can to avoid the crowds, which can build to monumental proportions by mid-afternoon. The parking lots for the Lake Tahoe Visitor Center, Vikingsholm castle hike, and Gatekeeper's Log Cabin Museum can be jammed at any time. Weekends are most congested, but weekdays are busy as well.

If you can swing it, September and October, when the throngs have dissipated but the weather is still pleasant, are among the most satisfying months to visit Lake Tahoe. During the winter ski season, Tahoe's populations swells on the weekends—if you're able to come mid-week you'll almost have the resorts and neighboring towns to yourself. The visitor centers, mansions, state parks, and beaches are mostly closed between November and May.

THE CALIFORNIA SIDE

South Lake Tahoe to Carnelian Bay

Lake Tahoe lends itself to a geopolitical division between the two states that share it. The California side is the more developed, both with commercial enterprises—restaurants, motels, lodges, resorts, residential subdivisions, and the like—and public-access facilities, such as historic sites, parks, and campgrounds, and beaches.

South Lake Tahoe

❶ *50 mi south of Reno on Hwy. 431, 198 mi northeast of San Francisco on I–80 to U.S. 50.*

South Lake Tahoe's raison d'être is tourism: The lake region's largest community feeds the casinos at Stateline; the ski slopes at Heavenly Valley; the swimmers, boaters, cyclists, and campers of the south shore; and the hikers and backpackers of Eldorado National Forest and Desolation Wilderness. U.S. 50 heading northeast into town is lined with motels, lodges, and restaurants, but as you head northwest on Highway 89, which straddles the lakefront, commercial development gives way to more wooded national-forest lands.

★ ☞ ❷ Whether you're a skier or not, you'll want to ride 2,000 feet up the slopes of Heavenly Ski Resort on the 50-passenger **Heavenly Tram,** which runs part way up the mountain, to 8,200 feet. There you'll find a memorable view of Lake Tahoe and the Nevada desert. When the weather's fine you can take one of three (successively more difficult) hikes around the mountaintop. ⊠ *North on Ski Run Blvd. off U.S. 50 and follow signs to parking lot,* ☎ *702/586–7000.* ⊠ *Tram $10.50.* ☉ *Tram runs June–Sept., daily 10–9; Nov.–May, daily 9–4.*

NEED A BREAK?   At the top of the Heavenly Tram, **Monument Peak Cafe** (☎ 702/586-7000, ext. 6347), open daily during tram hours, serves basic American food cafeteria style—lunch, dinner, and Sunday brunch in summer and lunch only in winter.

The 500-passenger *Tahoe Queen* (⊠ Ski Run Marina, off U.S. 50, ☎ 916/541–3364 or 800/238–2463), a glass-bottom paddlewheeler, makes 2¼-hour lake cruises year-round during the day from South Lake Tahoe and operates sunset and dinner cruises. Fares are $14–$18. In winter, the boat shuttles skiers to north-shore ski areas on weekdays for $18 round-trip.

Dining and Lodging

$$–$$$ ✕ **Nepheles.** A rough-pine chalet on the road to Heavenly Ski Resort houses this cozy restaurant serving creative California cuisine. Entrées range from aged-beef-and-prawns stir fry and pecan-encrusted chicken breast to broiled elk with black-currant merlot sauce and *ahi* tuna in a pineapple vinaigrette. Appetizers include a Thai-chicken-and-smoked-ham taco, escargots, and swordfish egg rolls. ⊠ *1169 Ski Run Blvd.,* ☎ *916/544–8130. AE, D, DC, MC, V. No lunch.*

$$–$$$ ✕ **Swiss Chalet.** Swiss decor is carried out with great consistency at this Tahoe institution. The Continental menu includes schnitzel, sauerbraten, fondue, steaks, fresh seafood, and homemade pastries. ⊠ *2544 U.S. 50,* ☎ *916/544–3304. AE, MC, V. Closed Nov. 25–Dec. 5. No lunch.*

$$ ✕ **Scusa!** This intimate Italian restaurant on the road to the Heavenly Ski Resort has a smart, modern decor. Cappelini, linguine, fettuccine, penne, ravioli, and lasagna are on the menu, along with hearty calzones, exotic pizzas, steak, chicken, and fresh fish entrées. The panfried calamari with red peppers and capers are a treat, and don't pass up the rosemary-flavored flat bread, baked fresh daily. ⊠ *1142 Ski Run Blvd.,* ☎ *916/542–0100. AE, MC, V. No lunch.*

$ ✕ **Red Hut Waffle Shop.** A vintage Tahoe diner, all chrome and red plastic, the Red Hut is a tiny place with a dozen counter stools and a dozen booths. It's a traditional breakfast spot for locals and visitors in the know, who appreciate the huge omelets, the banana, pecan, and coconut waffles, and other good food. ⊠ *2749 U.S. 50,* ☎ *916/541–9024. Reservations not accepted. No credit cards. No dinner.*

$$–$$$ ✕⌂ **Christiania Inn.** An antiques-filled bed-and-breakfast across the street from the base of the Heavenly Tram, the Christiania is a local favorite. The American-Continental menu emphasizes fresh seafood, prime beef, and veal. Midday buffets are served on holidays, and appetizers, soups, and salads are available in the lounge daily after 1:30, winter only. Upstairs at the inn ($$–$$$$), two rooms and four suites come with king- or queen-size beds and private baths. Three of the suites are two-story affairs with wood-burning fireplaces and wet bars; two have saunas and one has a whirlpool tub. A complimentary Continental breakfast is delivered to the door each morning. ⊠ *3819 Saddle Rd., 96151,* ☎ *916/544–7337 or 916/541–5210,* ℻ *916/541–5342. 6 rooms. Restaurant, bar. MC, V.*

$$$–$$$$ ⌂ **Embassy Suites.** In this opulent all-suite hotel, decorated Sierra-lodge
★   style, fountains and waterwheels splash in the soaring, nine-story atriums, where complimentary full breakfasts and evening cocktails are served daily. Glass elevators rise to guest suites, each with a living room, dining area, and separate bedroom. ⊠ *4130 Lake Tahoe Blvd., 96150,* ☎ *916/544–5400 or 800/362–2779,* ℻ *916/544–4900. 400 suites. 3 restaurants, indoor pool, spa, exercise room, nightclub. AE, D, DC, MC, V.*

$$$ ⌂ **Forest Inn Suites.** The location is excellent—5½ acres bordering a pine forest, a half block from Harrah's and Harvey's, and adjacent to a supermarket, cinema, and shops. Rooms are modern and pleasant. Ski rentals are available, and a free shuttle to Heavenly Valley ski area is provided. ⊠ *1101 Park Ave., 96150,* ☎ *916/541–6655; in CA, 800/822–5950;* FAX *916/544–3135. 124 units. Kitchens, 2 pools, 2 hot tubs, putting green, exercise room, health club, volleyball, boating, bicycles, coin laundry. AE, D, DC, MC, V.*

$$–$$$ ⊞ **Best Western Station House Inn.** This pleasant inn has won design
★ awards for its exterior and interior. The rooms have king- and queen-size beds and double-vanity bathrooms. The location is good, near a private beach yet close to the casinos. American breakfast is complimentary October–May. ⊠ *901 Park Ave., 96150,* ☎ *916/542–1101 or 800/822–5953,* FAX *916/542–1714. 102 rooms. Restaurant, lounge, pool, hot tub. AE, D, DC, MC, V.*

$$–$$$ ⊞ **Inn by the Lake.** This luxury motel across the road from the beach
★ is far from the flashy casinos but connected to them by free shuttle bus. The rooms and bathrooms are spacious and comfortable, furnished in contemporary style (blond oak and pale peach). All have balconies; some have lake views, wet bars, and in-room kitchens. Room rates include Continental breakfast. ⊠ *3300 Lake Tahoe Blvd., 96150,* ☎ *916/542–0330 or 800/877–1466,* FAX *916/541–6596. 99 rooms. Pool, sauna, spa, bicycles, coin laundry. AE, D, DC, MC, V.*

$–$$$ ⊞ **Best Western Lake Tahoe Inn.** This large motel near Harrah's sits on 6 acres, with gardens and the Heavenly Ski Resort directly behind. Rooms are modern and decorated in soothing colors. ⊠ *4110 Lake Tahoe Blvd., 96150,* ☎ *916/541–2010 or 800/528–1234,* FAX *916/542–1428. 400 rooms. Restaurant, lounge, 2 pools, hot tub. AE, D, DC, MC, V.*

$$ ⊞ **Lakeland Village Beach and Ski Resort.** This complex on 1,000 feet of private beach has a wide range of accommodations: studios, suites, and town houses, all with kitchens and fireplaces. ⊠ *3535 Lake Tahoe Blvd., 96150,* ☎ *916/544–1685 or 800/822–5969,* FAX *916/544–0193. 208 units. Kitchens, 2 pools, wading pool, hot tub, 2 saunas, tennis courts, beach, boating, fishing, coin laundry. AE, MC, V.*

$$ ⊞ **Royal Valhalla Motor Lodge.** Two- and three-bedroom suites with complete kitchens make this motel at Stateline Avenue attractive to families. Some rooms have private balconies; decor is simple, modern. Continental breakfast is complimentary. ⊠ *4104 Lakeshore Blvd., 96157,* ☎ *916/544–2233 or 800/999–4104,* FAX *916/544–1436. 100 rooms. Pool, hot tub, coin laundry. AE, DC, MC, V.*

$$ ⊞ **Tahoe Seasons Resort.** Most rooms at this resort, which is set among pine trees on a mountain across from the Heavenly Ski Resort, are outfitted with a fireplace. Every room has a whirlpool and minikitchen. The decor is contemporary, heavy on the teal. ⊠ *3901 Saddle Rd., 96157,* ☎ *916/541–6700, 916/541–6010, or 800/540–4874;* FAX *916/541–0653. 183 suites. Restaurant, lounge, refrigerators, pool, hot tub, tennis courts, volleyball, parking, airport shuttle. AE, DC, MC, V.*

$–$$ ⊞ **Best Tahoe West Inn.** A long-established motel proud of its repeat business, the Tahoe West is three blocks from the beach and downtown casinos. The exterior is rustic, rooms are neatly furnished, and beds are queen size. Twelve rooms have kitchenette. Free shuttle to casinos and ski areas is provided. ⊠ *4107 Pine Blvd., 96150,* ☎ *916/544–6455 or 800/522–1021; in CA, 800/700–8246;* FAX *916/544–0508. 60 rooms. Pool, hot tub, sauna, beach. AE, D, DC, MC, V.*

$–$$ ⊞ **Travelodge.** There are two members of the national chain in South Lake Tahoe; both are convenient to casinos, shopping, and recreation and have some no-smoking rooms. Free local calls, HBO, and in-room coffee add to the budget appeal. ⊠ *3489 U.S. 50 at Bijou Center, 96150,* ☎ *916/544–5266 or 800/982–1466,* FAX *916/544–6985; 59 rooms.* ⊠ *4003 U.S. 50, South Lake Tahoe 96150,* ☎ *916/541–5000 or 800/982–2466,* FAX *916/544–6910; 66 rooms. Pool at each; Bijou Center has restaurant. AE, D, DC, MC, V.*

Outdoor Activities and Sports

CROSS-COUNTRY SKIING

For the ultimate in groomed conditions, head to America's largest cross-country ski resort, **Royal Gorge** (⊠ Box 1100, Soda Springs, CA 95728, ☎ 916/426–3871), which has 197 miles of 18-foot-wide track for all abilities, 88 trails on 9,172 acres, two ski schools, and 10 warming huts. Four cafés, two hotels, and a hot tub and sauna are also on-site. **Kirkwood Ski Resort** (☞ Downhill Skiing, *below*) has 50 miles of groomed-track skiing, with skating lanes, instruction, and rentals.

DOWNHILL SKIING

Heavenly Ski Resort gives skiers plenty of choices. Go up the Heavenly Tram on the California side to ski the imposing face of Gunbarrel or the gentler runs at the top, or ride the Sky Express high-speed quad chair to the summit and choose wide cruising runs or steep tree skiing. Or drive over the Kingsbury Grade to the Boulder or Stagecoach lodges and stay on the Nevada-side runs, which are usually less crowded. Snowmaking covers both sides, top to bottom, for generally good conditions. The ski school, like everything else at Heavenly, is large and has a program for everyone, beginner to expert. ⊠ *Ski Run Blvd., Box 2180, Stateline, NV 89449,* ☎ *916/541–1330 or 800/243–2836; snow information, 916/541–7544;* FAX *916/541–2643. 4,800 acres, rated 20% beginner, 45% intermediate, 35% expert. Longest run 5½ mi, base 6,540', summit 10,040'. Lifts: 24 total, including 3 high-speed quads.*

Kirkwood Ski Resort lies 36 miles south of Lake Tahoe in an alpine-village setting. Most of the runs off the top are rated expert only, but intermediate and beginning skiers have their own vast bowl, where they can ski through trees or wide-open spaces. This is a destination resort, with 120 condominiums, several shops and restaurants in the base village, overnight RV parking, and a shuttle bus to Lake Tahoe. There is snowboarding on all runs, and lessons, rentals, and sales are available. (For Nordic skiing, ☞ Cross-Country Skiing, *above*.) ⊠ *Hwy. 88, Box 1, Kirkwood, CA 95646,* ☎ *209/258–6000; lodging information, 209/258–7000; snow information, 209/258–3000;* FAX *209/258–8899. 2,000 acres, rated 15% beginner, 50% intermediate, 35% advanced. Longest run 2½ mi, base 7,800', summit 9,800'. Lifts: 10 chairs, 1 surface.*

Shopping

There's some good shopping south of town at the "Y" intersection of U.S. 50 and Highway 89 at the **Factory Outlet Stores.**

Pope-Baldwin Recreation Area

❸ *5 mi west of South Lake Tahoe on Hwy. 89.*

At the Pope-Baldwin Recreation Area's **Tallac Historic Site,** a museum and three magnificently restored estates allow visitors a glimpse of the lifestyles of the 1920s wealthy. Cultural events take place from June to September. The Valhalla Renaissance Festival (☎ 916/542–4166), which re-creates the arts, culture, and entertainments of the 15th and 16th centuries, is held at Camp Richardson in June. Guided tours of the Pope House and a museum at the Baldwin Estate are available in summer. ☑ *Tallac Historic Site free, Pope House tour $2 (hrs vary, reservations necessary,* ☎ *916/541–5227).* ☉ *Tallac Historic Site year-round dawn–dusk. Recreation Area late May–Oct., dawn–dusk. Museum June–Labor Day, daily 10–4; Labor Day–Sept., daily 10–3.*

❹ The U.S. Forest Service operates the **Lake Tahoe Visitors Center** on Taylor Creek. You can visit the site of a Washoe Indian settlement; walk self-guided trails through meadow, marsh, and forest; and inspect the

Stream Profile Chamber, an underground, underwater display with windows letting visitors look right into Taylor Creek (in the fall you may see spawning salmon digging their nests). In summer, forest service naturalists organize discovery walks and nighttime campfires, with singing and marshmallow roasts. The center has a free cassette player and a self-guided audio tour of the lake. ☎ 916/573–2674 (in season only). ☉ June–Sept. daily and Oct. weekends 8–5:30.

Emerald Bay State Park

★ ❺ *4 mi west of Pope-Baldwin Recreation Area on Hwy. 89.*

Emerald Bay, a 3-mile-long and 1-mile-wide fjord-like bay, was carved by massive glaciers millions of years ago. Famed for its jewel-like shape and colors, it surrounds Fannette, Tahoe's only island. Highway 89 is high above the lake at the centerpiece of Emerald Bay State Park; from the **Emerald Bay lookout** you can survey the whole scene.

A steep, mile-long trail from the lookout leads down to **Vikingsholm,** a 38-room estate completed in 1929. The owner, Lora Knight, had this precise replica of a 1,200-year-old Viking castle built out of materials native to the area, without disturbing the existing trees. She furnished it with Scandinavian antiques and hired artisans to custom-build period reproductions. The sod roof sprouts wildflowers each spring. There are picnic tables nearby and a gray-sand beach for strolling. The hike back up is a major huff (especially for those not used to the elevation), but there are a number of benches and stone culverts to rest on. At the 150-foot-high peak of Fannette Island are the remnants of a stone structure known as the Tea House, built in 1928 so that guests of Lora Knight might motorboat to the island and have a place to enjoy afternoon refreshments. The island is off-limits February through June to protect nesting Canada geese; the rest of the year, it's open for day use only. *Vikingsholm:* ☎ 916/525–7277. ▨ $2. ☉ Memorial Day–Labor Day, daily 10–4.

D. L. Bliss State Park

❻ *3 mi north of Emerald Bay State Park on Hwy. 89.*

D. L. Bliss State Park takes its name from Duane LeRoy Bliss, a 19th-century lumber magnate. At one time Bliss owned nearly 75% of Tahoe's lakefront, along with local steamboats, railroads, and banks. The Bliss family donated these 1,200 acres to the state in the 1930s; the park now shares 6 miles of shoreline with Emerald Bay State Park. At the north end of Bliss is **Rubicon Point,** which overlooks one of the lake's deepest spots. Short trails lead to an old lighthouse and Balancing Rock, which weighs in at 250,000 pounds and balances on a fist of granite. Hikes also take you to remote beaches and all the way to Vikingsholm in Emerald Bay State Park. ☎ 916/525–7277. ▨ $5 per vehicle (day use). ☉ Spring–fall.

Camping

⛺ **D. L. Bliss State Park Campground.** A wooded, hilly, quiet setting makes for blissful family camping near the lake. Reserve sites as far in advance as possible. ▨ Off Hwy. 89, ☎ 800/444–7275 for reservations. 168 sites. ▨ $14–$19.

Sugar Pine Point State Park

★ ❼ *8 mi north of D. L. Bliss State Park on Hwy. 89.*

The main attraction at Sugar Pine Point State Park is **Ehrman Mansion,** a stone-and-shingle 1903 summer home, furnished in period style, that manifests the rustic aspirations of the era's wealthy residents. Also in the park are a log trapper's cabin from the mid-19th century, a nature preserve with wildlife exhibits, a lighthouse, the start of the 10-mile-long biking trail to Tahoe City, and an extensive system of hiking and cross-country trails. ☎ *916/525–7232 year-round or 916/525–7982 in season.* ⊠ *Free. State park $5 per vehicle (day use).* ⊙ *Memorial Day–Labor Day, daily 11–4.*

Camping

⚠ **General Creek Campground.** This woodsy, homey campground on the mountain side of Highway 89 is one of the few public campgrounds to remain open year-round, primarily for cross-country skiers. ⊠ *Hwy. 89,* ☎ *800/444–7275 for reservations. 175 sites.* ⊠ *$14.*

Tahoe City

8 *10 mi north of Sugar Pine Point State Park on Hwy. 89, 14 mi south of Truckee on Hwy. 89.*

Tahoe City holds many stores and restaurants within a compact area. Here, Highway 89 turns north from the lake to Squaw Valley, Donner Lake, and Truckee, while Highway 28 continues northeast around the lake toward Kings Beach and Nevada. The Outlet Gates control the surface level of Lake Tahoe and the amount of water spilled into the Truckee River, the lake's only outlet. Before the severe drought of the late 1980s and early 1990s, one could look down and see the river's giant trout from Fanny Bridge, so called because one could usually see the backsides of rows of visitors leaning over the railing.

★ The **Gatekeeper's Log Cabin Museum** in Tahoe City preserves one of the best records of the area's past, displaying Washoe and Paiute artifacts as well as late-19th- to early-20th-century settlers' memorabilia. ⊠ *130 W. Lake Blvd.,* ☎ *916/583–1762.* ⊠ *Free.* ⊙ *May 15–Oct. 1, daily 11–5.*

The **Watson Cabin Living Museum,** a 1909 log cabin built by Robert M. Watson and his son and filled with turn-of-the-century furnishings, is in the middle of Tahoe City. Costumed docents act out the daily life of a typical pioneer family. ⊠ *560 N. Lake Blvd.,* ☎ *916/583–8717 or 916/583–1762.* ⊠ *Free.* ⊙ *June 15–Labor Day, daily noon–4.*

Dining and Lodging

$$$ ✕ **Christy Hill.** Panoramic lake views and fireside dining distinguish this restaurant, which serves California cuisine—fresh seafood (such as mahi with ginger and pepper crust in a cabernet demi sauce) and game (including broiled New Zealand venison)—prepared by the owner-chef. ⊠ *115 Grove St., Lakehouse Mall,* ☎ *916/583–8551. MC, V. Closed Sun. (spring and fall) and Mon. No lunch.*

$$–$$$ ✕ **Grazie! Ristorante & Bar.** The smell of garlic warms you as soon as you enter this northern Italian restaurant, as does the wide, double-sided fireplace. There are a half-dozen hearty pasta dishes and six pizza choices, but the stars are the antipasti and pasta salads. Chicken is cooked on a wood-burning rotisserie and rack of lamb on the grill; both are served with homemade sauces. ⊠ *Roundhouse Mall, 700 N. Lake Blvd.,* ☎ *916/583–0233. AE, D, DC, MC, V.*

$$–$$$ ✕ **Wolfdale's.** An intimate restaurant occupying a remodeled 100-
★ year-old house, Wolfdale's serves a popular mix of Japanese-California cuisine and elegant service. The menu, which changes weekly, showcases several imaginative entrées, such as grilled Southwest-style chicken with celery-root potatoes and brazed lamb shank with tomatoes, rosemary, and parsnip puree. ⊠ *640 N. Lake Blvd.,* ☎ *916/583–5700. MC, V. Closed Tues. No lunch.*

$-$$$ ✕ **Jake's on the Lake.** Handsome, spacious rooms of oak and glass
★ provide a suitably classy setting for Continental food on the water. The
seafood bar here is extensive; a varied dinner menu includes meat and
poultry but emphasizes fresh fish. ⊠ *Boatworks Mall, 780 N. Lake
Blvd.,* ☎ *916/583–0188. AE, MC, V. No lunch in winter, except during holiday season.*

$$$$ ✕⊞ **Resort at Squaw Creek.** Nearly half the guest rooms are suites at
this complex, composed of a main lodge, an outdoor arcade of shops
and boutiques, and a 405-room hotel. Some units have a fireplace and
full kitchen, and all have original art, custom furnishings, and good
views. Outdoors, just a few feet from the hotel entrance, you can
board a triple chairlift to Squaw Valley's slopes. Restaurant options
range from haute cuisine to a pastry-and-coffee shop. ⊠ *400 Squaw
Creek Rd., 96146,* ☎ *916/583–6300,* ℻ *916/581–6632. 405 rooms.
4 restaurants, bar, 3 pools, 4 hot tubs, sauna, 18-hole golf course, tennis center, exercise room, ice-skating. AE, D, DC, MC, V.*

$$$-$$$$ ✕⊞ **Sunnyside Restaurant and Lodge.** Only the river-rock fireplace and
★ a mounted buffalo head remain from the early-1900s lodge that originally stood on this site. Its impressive, sunny replacement, built in the
mid-1980s, has a marina and an expansive lakefront deck with steps
down to a narrow gravel beach. Rooms are decorated in a crisp, nautical style, with prints of boats hanging on the pinstripe wall coverings
and sea chests as coffee tables. Each room has its own deck, with lake
and mountain views. Continental breakfast is included in the rate, but
this is not a full-service hotel. Seafood is the specialty of the very fine
Continental restaurant ($$–$$$). ⊠ *1850 W. Lake Blvd.,* ☎ *916/583–
7200; in CA, 800/822–2754;* ℻ *916/583–2551. 23 rooms. Restaurant, lounge, beach. AE, MC, V.*

$$$-$$$$ ⊞ **Chinquapin Resort.** A deluxe development on 95 acres of forested
★ land 3 miles northeast of Tahoe City contains roomy one- to four-bedroom town houses and condos with spectacular views of the lake and
the mountains. Each unit has a fireplace, a fully equipped kitchen, and
laundry facilities. ⊠ *3600 N. Lake Blvd., 96145,* ☎ *916/583–6991
or 800/732–6721,* ℻ *916/583–0937. 172 town houses and condos.
Pool, saunas, 7 tennis courts, hiking, horseshoes. MC, V. 1-wk minimum stay July–Aug., 2-night minimum stay in winter.*

$-$$ ⊞ **Rodeway Inn.** This skinny, seven-story tower is within easy walking distance of the beaches, marina, shops, and restaurants of Tahoe
City. Rooms are clean and comfortable, if not luxurious, and have great
lake views. ⊠ *645 N. Lake Blvd., 96145,* ☎ *916/583–3711 or
800/228–2000,* ℻ *916/583–6938. 51 rooms. Pool, hot tub, laundry.
AE, D, DC, MC, V.*

Outdoor Activities and Sports

DOWNHILL SKIING

Alpine Meadows Ski Area is a ski-cruiser's paradise, with skiing from
two peaks—Ward, a great open bowl, and Scott, for tree-lined runs. Alpine
has some of Tahoe's most reliable conditions and a fine snowmaking system; it's usually the first in the area to open each November and the last
to close, in May or even June. The base lodge has rentals, a cafeteria,
restaurant-lounge, bar, bakery, sports shop, ski schools for adults and
children of all skill levels and for skiers with disabilities. There's also an
area for overnight RV parking. Ski from every lift; there are no "transportation" lifts and snowboarding is prohibited. ⊠ *6 mi northwest of
Tahoe City off Hwy. 89, 13 mi south of I-80, Box 5279, Tahoe City,
CA 96145,* ☎ *916/583–4232; snow phone, 916/581–8374; information, 800/441–4423;* ℻ *916/583–0963. 2,000 acres, rated 25% easier,*

40% more difficult, 35% most difficult. Longest run 2½ mi, base 6,835', summit 8,637'. Lifts: 2 high-speed quads, 2 triples, 7 doubles, 1 surface.

Squaw Valley USA was the site of the 1960 Olympics. The immense resort has changed significantly since then, but the skiing is still first-class, with steep chutes and cornices on six Sierra peaks. Beginners delight in riding the tram to the top, where there is a huge plateau of gentle runs. At the top of the tram, you'll find the High Camp Bath and Tennis Club in the lodge, which has impressive views from its restaurants, bars, and outdoor ice-skating pavilion. Base facilities are clustered around the Village Mall, with shops, dining, condos, hotels, and lodges. The valley golf course doubles as a cross-country ski facility. On the other side of the golf course is the Resort at Squaw Creek, with its own run and quad chairlift that runs to Squaw's ski terrain. ⊠ *Hwy. 89, 5 mi northwest of Tahoe City, Squaw Valley USA, CA 96146,* ☎ *916/583–6985; reservations, 800/545–4350; snow information, 916/583–6955;* FAX *916/581– 7106. 4,000 acres, rated 25% beginner, 45% intermediate, 30% advanced. Longest run 3 mi, base 6,200', summit 9,050'. Lifts: 6-passenger gondola, cable car, 3 quads, 8 triples, 15 doubles, 5 surface.*

GOLF

Resort at Squaw Creek Golf Course (⊠ 400 Squaw Creek Rd., Olympic Valley, ☎ 916/583–6300), an 18-hole championship course, was designed by Robert Trent Jones Jr. Golfers use pull carts at the nine-hole **Tahoe City Golf Course** (⊠ Hwy. 28, Tahoe City, ☎ 916/583–1516).

Carnelian Bay to Kings Beach

5 to 10 mi northeast of Tahoe City on Hwy. 28.

The small lakeside commercial districts of Carnelian Bay and Tahoe Vista service the thousand or so locals who live here year-round and the thousands more who have summer residences or launch their boats here. Kings Beach, the last town heading east on Highway 28 before the Nevada border, is to Crystal Bay what South Lake Tahoe is to Stateline: a bustling California village full of motels and rental condos, restaurants and shops, used by the hordes of hopefuls who pass through on their way to the "luck" machines and gaming tables in Nevada.

❾ The 28-acre **Kings Beach State Recreation Area,** one of the largest such areas on the lake, is open year-round. Its more than half-mile-long beach becomes crowded with people swimming, sunbathing, jet skiing, riding in paddle boats, and playing volleyball and Frisbee. There's a good playground for kids here. ⊠ *North Lake Blvd., Kings Beach,* ☎ *916/546–7248.* ☞ *Free day use, parking $4.*

Dining

$$–$$$ ✕ **Captain Jon's.** The dining room is small and cozy, with linen cloths and fresh flowers on the tables. On chilly evenings a fireplace with a raised brick heath warms diners. The lengthy dinner menu is old-style country French, with two dozen daily specials; the emphasis is on fish and hearty salads. The restaurant's lounge, which serves light meals, is in a separate building on the water, with a pier where guests can tie up their boats. ⊠ *7220 N. Lake Blvd., Tahoe Vista,* ☎ *916/546–4819. AE, DC, MC, V. Closed Mon. No lunch in winter (usually Nov.–May).*

$–$$$ ✕ **Gar Woods Grill and Pier.** This stylish but casual lakeside restaurant recalls the area's past, with light-pine paneling, floor-to-ceiling picture windows overlooking the lake, a river-rock fireplace, and boating photographs. The menu includes such eclectic dishes as Thai chicken salad, grilled-salmon salad, stir-fry, seafood sauté, and pastas. There's an extensive wine list, and Sunday brunch is served. ⊠ *5000 N. Lake Blvd., Carnelian Bay,* ☎ *916/546–3366. AE, MC, V.*

$ ✕ **Log Cabin Caffe.** Almost always hopping, this Kings Beach eatery specializes in healthy, hearty breakfast and lunch entrées—pancakes, waffles, freshly baked pastries, health-food sandwiches, and ice cream. It's a good place on the north shore for an espresso or cappuccino. Get here early on weekends; this is a popular spot for brunch. ⊠ *8692 N. Lake Blvd.,* ☎ *916/546–7109. MC, V.*

Outdoor Activities and Sports

GOLF

Old Brockway Golf Course (⊠ Hwys. 267 and 28, Kings Beach, ☎ 916/546–9909) is a nine-hole, par-35 course.

SNOWMOBILING

Snowmobiling Unlimited (⊠ Box 460, Carnelian Bay 96140, ☎ 916/583–5858) conducts guided tours, rents equipment, and operates a track to zoom around on.

SWIMMING

The **North Tahoe Beach Center** has a 26-foot hot tub and a beach with an enclosed swim area and four sand volleyball courts. The popular spot has a barbecue and picnic area, a fitness center, windsurfing and nonmotorized boat rentals, a snack bar, and a clubhouse with games. ⊠ *7860 N. Lake Blvd., Kings Beach,* ☎ *916/546–2566.* 🎟 *$7.*

Truckee

🔟 *13 mi northwest of Kings Beach on Hwy. 267, 14 mi north of Tahoe City on Hwy. 89.*

Old West facades line the main street of Truckee, a favorite stopover for people traveling from the Bay Area to the north shore of Lake Tahoe. Galleries and boutiques are plentiful, but you will also find low-key diners, discount skiwear, and an old-fashioned five-and-dime store. Stop by the information booth in the Amtrak depot (⊠ Railroad St. at Commercial Rd.) for a walking-tour map of historic Truckee.

Donner Memorial State Park commemorates the Donner Party, a group of 89 westward-bound pioneers who were trapped in the Sierras in the winter of 1846–47 in snow 22 feet deep. Only 47 survived, some by cannibalism and others by eating animal hides. The Immigrant Museum's hourly slide show details the Donner Party's plight. Other displays relate the history of other settlers and of railroad development through the Sierras. ⊠ *Off I–80, 2 mi west of Truckee,* ☎ *916/582–7892.* 🎟 *$2.* ☉ *Sept.–May, daily 10–4; June–Aug., daily 10–5; closed Thanksgiving, Dec. 25.*

Northstar-at-Tahoe

⓫ *6 mi south of Truckee on Hwy. 267, 15 mi north of Tahoe City on Hwy. 28 to Hwy. 267.*

Dining and Lodging

$$$$ ✕🏨 **Northstar-at-Tahoe Resort.** This is the Sierras' most complete destination resort. The center of action is the Village Mall, a concentration of restaurants, shops, recreation facilities, and accommodations—hotel rooms, condos, and private houses. The resort is popular with families because of its many sports activities. Summer rates are lower than winter rates. ⊠ *Off Hwy. 267, Box 129, 96160,* ☎ *916/562–1010 or 800/533–6787,* 📠 *916/562–2215. 230 units. 3 restaurants, deli, 18-hole golf course, 10 tennis courts, horseback riding, bicycles, skiing, sleigh rides, snowmobiling, recreation room, baby-sitting. AE, D, MC, V.*

Outdoor Activities and Sports

CROSS-COUNTRY AND DOWNHILL SKIING

Northstar-at-Tahoe Resort. Two northeast-facing, wind-protected bowls provide some of the best powder skiing in the Lake Tahoe area, including steep chutes and long cruising runs. Top-to-bottom snowmaking and intense grooming assure good conditions. Northstar-at-Tahoe also gives cross-country skiers access to alpine ski slopes for telemarking and provides 40 miles of groomed, tracked trails with a wide skating lane. There's a ski shop, rentals, and instruction. ⊠ *Hwy. 267 between Truckee and Kings Beach, Box 129, Truckee, 96160; snow information,* ☎ *916/562–1330,* FAX *916/562–2215. 1,800 acres, rated 25% beginner, 50% intermediate, 25% advanced. Longest run 2.9 mi, base 6,400', summit 8,600'. Lifts: 6-passenger express gondola, 3 doubles, 3 triples, 2 tows, 4 high-speed quads.*

NEVADA SIDE

From Crystal Bay to Stateline

You don't need a roadside marker to know when you've crossed from California into Nevada. The lake's water and the pine trees may be identical, but the flashing lights and elaborate marquees of casinos announce legal gambling in garish hues.

Crystal Bay

⑫ *1 mi east of Kings Beach on Hwy. 28., 30 mi north of South Lake Tahoe on U.S. 50 to Hwy. 28.*

Right at the Nevada border, Crystal Bay holds a cluster of casinos; one, the **Cal-Neva Lodge** (☞ Dining and Lodging, *below*), is bisected by the state line. This joint opened in 1927 and has weathered nearly as many scandals—the largest involving Frank Sinatra—as it has blizzards. The **Tahoe Biltmore** has a popular $1.39 breakfast special served 24 hours a day. **Jim Kelley's Nugget** closes during the winter months.

Dining and Lodging

$–$$ ✕ **Soule Domain.** A romantic, 1927 pine-log cabin with a stone fireplace is the setting for some of Lake Tahoe's most creative and delicious dinners. Chef-owner Charles Edward Soule IV's specialties include grilled tuna with papaya-mango salsa, and filet mignon with shiitake mushrooms, Gorgonzola, and brandy. ⊠ *Cove St., across from Tahoe Biltmore,* ☎ *916/546–7529. Reservations essential on weekends. AE, DC, MC, V. No lunch.*

$$–$$$ ✕🏨 **Cal-Neva Lodge.** All the rooms in this hotel on Highway 28 at Crystal Bay have views of Lake Tahoe and the mountains. There is an arcade with video games for children, cabaret entertainment, and, in addition to rooms in the main hotel, 12 cabins with living rooms and seven two-bedroom chalets. ⊠ *2 Stateline Rd., Box 368, 89402,* ☎ *702/832–4000 or 800/225–6382,* FAX *702/831–9007. 220 rooms. Restaurant, coffee shop, pool, hot tub, sauna, tennis courts, casino, 3 chapels. AE, D, DC, MC, V.*

Incline Village

⑬ *3 mi east of Crystal Bay on Hwy. 28.*

Incline Village, one of Nevada's few master-planned communities, dates back to the early 1960s; it's still privately owned. Check out **Lakeshore Drive** to see some of the most expensive real estate in Nevada. Incline is the only town on Lake Tahoe without a central commercial district, planned this way to prevent congestion and to preserve a natural feel.

There are plenty of recreational diversions—hiking and biking trails, the area's greatest concentration of tennis courts, and a **Recreation Center** (✉ 980 Incline Way, ☎ 702/832–1300) with an eight-lane swimming pool, a cardiovascular-fitness area, a basketball court, a game room, and a snack bar.

OFF THE BEATEN PATH **MT. ROSE –** If you want to ski the absolute highest slopes in the Lake Tahoe region, Highway 431 leads north out of Incline Village to Mt. Rose. Reno is another 30 miles farther.

⑭ The popular 1960s television western *Bonanza* inspired the **Ponderosa Ranch** theme park. Attractions include the Cartwrights' ranch house, a western town, and a saloon. There's also a self-guided nature trail, free pony rides for children, and, if you're here from 8 to 9:30 in the morning, a breakfast hayride. ✉ *Hwy. 28, 2 mi south of Incline Village,* ☎ *702/831–0691.* 🎟 *$8.50, hayride $2.* ☉ *Mid-Apr.–Oct., daily 9:30–5.*

Dining and Lodging

$$ ✗ **Stanley's Restaurant and Lounge.** With its intimate bar and pleasant dining room, this casual local favorite is a good bet any time for straightforward American fare on the hearty side (barbecued pork ribs, beef Stroganoff). Lighter bites, such as seafood Cobb salad, are also available, along with ample breakfasts; try the eggs Benedict or a chili-cheese omelet. There's a deck for outdoor dining in summer and live music on Friday night. ✉ *941 Tahoe Blvd.,* ☎ *702/831–9944. Reservations not accepted. AE, MC, V.*

$ ✗ **Azzara's.** A typical Italian trattoria with light, inviting decor, Azzara's serves a dozen pasta dishes and many pizzas, as well as chicken, lamb, veal, and shrimp—but no beef. Dinners include soup or salad, vegetable, pasta, and garlic bread. This is a no-smoking restaurant. ✉ *Incline Center Mall, 930 Tahoe Blvd.,* ☎ *702/831–0346. MC, V. Closed Mon.*

$$$–$$$$ ✗🏨 **Hyatt Lake Tahoe Resort Hotel/Casino.** Some of the rooms in this luxurious hotel on the lake have fireplaces, but all the accommodations here are top-notch. A children's program and rental bicycles are available. The restaurants are Lone Eagle Grille (fairly good Continental, with steak, seafood, pasta, and rotisserie dishes), Ciao Mein Trattoria (Asian-Italian), and Sierra Cafe (open 24 hours). ✉ *Lakeshore and Country Club Drs., 89450,* ☎ *702/831–1111 or 800/233–1234,* 🆔 *702/831–7508. 460 rooms. 2 restaurants, coffee shop, lounge, room service, pool, spa, 2 saunas, tennis courts, health club, casino, laundry service. AE, D, DC, MC, V.*

Outdoor Activities and Sports

BOAT CRUISE
The **Sierra Cloud** (☎ 702/831–1111), a trimaran with a big trampoline lounging surface, cruises the north-shore area mornings and afternoons from the Hyatt Regency Hotel in Incline Village May–October. Fares run from $25–$35.

CROSS-COUNTRY AND DOWNHILL SKIING
Diamond Peak has a fun, family atmosphere with many special programs and affordable rates. A learn-to-ski package, with rentals, lesson, and lift ticket, is $29; a parent-child ski package is $38, with each additional child's lift ticket $5. There is a half-pipe run just for snowboarding. Snowmaking covers 80% of the mountain, and runs are well groomed nightly. The ride up the mile-long Crystal chair rewards you with the best views of the lake from any ski area. Diamond Peak is less crowded than some

of the larger areas, and has free shuttles to lodging in nearby Incline Village. Diamond Peak Cross-Country (✉ off Hwy. 431, ☎ 702/832–1177) has 22 miles of groomed track with skating lanes. The trail system goes from 7,400 feet to 9,100 feet with endless wilderness to explore. ✉ *1210 Ski Way, Incline Village, NV 89450, off Hwy. 28 to Country Club Dr., ☎ 702/832–1177 or 800/468–2463, FAX 702/832–1281. 655 acres, rated 18% beginner, 49% intermediate, 33% advanced. Longest run 2½ mi, base 6,700', summit 8,540'. Lifts: 6 doubles, 1 quad.*

GOLF

Incline Championship (✉ 955 Fairway Blvd., ☎ 702/832–1144) is an 18-hole, par-72 course with a driving range. Carts are mandatory. **Incline Executive** (✉ 690 Wilson Way, ☎ 702/832–1150) is an easy 18 holer; par is 58. Carts are mandatory.

OFF THE BEATEN PATH

CARSON CITY AND VIRGINIA CITY – Nevada's capital, Carson City, is less than an hour away from Lake Tahoe. At Spooner Junction, where Highway 28 meets U.S. 50, head east on U.S. 50, away from the lake. In 10 miles you reach U.S. 395, where you turn left and go 1 mile north to Carson City. Most of its historic buildings and other attractions are along U.S. 395, the main street through town. At the south end of town, is the Carson City Chamber of Commerce (✉ 1900 S. Carson St., ☎ 702/882–1565), which has visitor information. About a 30-minute drive northeast of Carson City on Highway 342 off U.S. 50 is the fabled mining town of Virginia City, which has sites and activities of historical interest amid touristy diversions.

Sand Harbor Beach

★ ⑮ *4 mi south of Incline Village on Hwy. 28, 22 mi north of South Lake Tahoe on U.S. 50 to Hwy. 28.*

Sand Harbor Beach, within the Lake Tahoe-Nevada State Park, has a popular beach that is sometimes filled to capacity by 11 AM on summer weekends. A pop-music festival (☎ 702/832–1606 or 800/468–2463) is held here in July and a Shakespeare festival every August.

U.S. 50 from Spooner Junction to Zephyr Cove

13 mi south of Sand Harbor Beach (to Cave Rock) on Hwy. 28 to U.S. 50.

★ ⑯ **Cave Rock,** 25 yards of solid stone at the southern end of Lake Tahoe-Nevada State Park, is sacred to the Washoe Indians, who used it as a burial site. The tunnel through rock is one of only three drive-throughs in all of Nevada. Tahoe Tessie, the lake's version of the Loch Ness monster, is reputed to live in a cavern below the impressive outcrop, which is the throat of an extinct volcano. Cave Rock towers over a parking lot, lakefront picnic ground and boat launch; the rest area provides the best vantage point of this spectacular cliff. ✉ *U.S. 50, 3 mi south of Glenbrook.*

⑰ The largest settlement between Incline Village and Stateline is **Zephyr Cove,** which is still only a tiny resort. It has a beach, marina, campground, picnic area, coffee shop in a historic log lodge, rustic cabins for rent, and nearby riding stables. The 550-passenger **MS Dixie II** (☎ 702/588–3508), a sternwheeler, sails year-round from Zephyr Cove Marina to Emerald Bay on lunch and dinner cruises. Fares are $14–$35. The **Woodwind** (☎ 702/588–3000), a glass-bottom trimaran, sails on regular and champagne April–October cruises from Zephyr Cove Resort. Fares are $14–$20.

OFF THE
BEATEN PATH

KINGSBURY GRADE – This road, also known as Route 207, is one of three roads that access Tahoe from the east. Originally a toll road used by wagon trains to get over the Sierras' crest, it leads to spectacular views of the Carson Valley. Off Route 206, which intersects 207, is Genoa, the oldest settlement in Nevada. Along Main Street are small museums and the state's longest-standing saloon.

Stateline

⑱ *5 mi south of Zephyr Cove on U.S. 50.*

Stateline is a great border town in the Nevada tradition. Its four high-rise casinos are as vertical and contained as the commercial district of South Lake Tahoe on the California side is horizontal and sprawling. And Stateline is as relentlessly indoors as the rest of the lake is undeniably outdoors. This strip is where you'll find the most concentrated action at the lake: restaurants (including the typically Nevada buffets), showrooms with famous headliners and razzle-dazzle revues, luxury rooms and suites, and, of course, 24-hour gambling.

Dining and Lodging

$$–$$$$
★
✕ **Llewellyn's Restaurant.** Elegantly decorated in blond wood and pastels, the restaurant atop Harvey's casino merits special mention. Almost every table has superb views of Lake Tahoe. Dinner entrées—seafood, meat, and poultry—are served with unusual accompaniments, such as sturgeon in potato crust with saffron sauce or veal with polenta, herbs, and pancetta. Lunches are reasonably priced, with gourmet selections as well as hamburgers. The adjacent bar (with the same view) is comfortable. ⊠ *Harvey's Resort, U.S. 50,* ☎ *702/588–2411 or 800/553–1022. AE, D, DC, MC, V.*

$$–$$$
✕ **Chart House.** It's worth the drive up the steep grade to see the view from here—try to arrive for sunset. The American menu of steak and seafood is complemented by an abundant salad bar. There is a children's menu. ⊠ *329 Kingsbury Grade,* ☎ *702/588–6276. AE, D, DC, MC, V. No lunch.*

$$$–$$$$
✕⌂ **Harrah's Tahoe Hotel/Casino.** Luxurious guest rooms here have private bars and two full bathrooms, each with a television and telephone. All rooms have views of the lake and the mountains, but the least-obstructed views are from the higher floors. There is an enclosed children's arcade on the lower level. Top-name entertainment is presented in the South Shore Room. Among the restaurants, the romantic 16th-floor Summit (jacket and tie) is a standout. The menu changes nightly and includes creatively presented salads; lamb, venison, or seafood entrées with delicate sauces; and sensuous desserts. Other restaurants serve Italian, Pacific Rim, deli, and traditional meat-and-potatoes cuisine. There's also a 24-hour café and an ice-cream parlor. ⊠ *U.S. 50, Box 8, 89449,* ☎ *702/588–6611 or 800/648–3773,* ℻ *702/788–3274. 534 rooms. 7 restaurants, room service, indoor pool, hot tubs, barbershop, beauty salon, health club, casino, video games, laundry service, kennel. AE, D, DC, MC, V.*

$$–$$$$
★
✕⌂ **Harvey's Resort Hotel/Casino.** Owner Harvey Gross played an important role in persuading the state to keep U.S. 50 open year-round, making Tahoe accessible in winter. His namesake hotel, which started as a cabin in 1944, is now the largest resort in Tahoe. Any description of the place runs to superlatives, from the 40-foot-tall crystal chandelier in the lobby to the 88,000-square-foot casino. Rooms have custom furnishings, oversize marble baths, and minibars. The health club, spa, and pool are free to guests, a rarity for this area. Among its restau-

rants, Llewellyn's (☞ *above*) is outstanding. Also noteworthy is the Sage Room Steak House, which serves prime beef, veal, and seafood, as well as Continental dishes such as braised pheasant and escargots. ⊠ *U.S. 50, Box 128, 89449,* ☎ *702/588–2411 or 800/648–3361,* ℻ *702/782–4889. 741 rooms. 8 restaurants, wading pool, barbershop, beauty salon, health club, casino, chapel. AE, D, DC, MC, V.*

$$–$$$$ 🏨 **Caesars Tahoe.** Most of the rooms and suites at this opulent 16-story hotel-casino have oversize Roman tubs, king-size beds, two telephones, and a view of Lake Tahoe or the encircling mountains. The lavish casino encompasses 40,000 square feet. Top-name entertainers perform in the 1,600-seat Circus Maximus. The local Planet Hollywood is here, plus Chinese, Italian, and American restaurants, a 24-hour coffee shop, and a yogurt emporium. ⊠ *55 U.S. 50, Box 5800, 89449,* ☎ *702/588–3515, reservations and show information, 800/648–3353;* ℻ *702/586–2068. 440 rooms. 7 restaurants, coffee shop, indoor pool, hot tub, saunas, tennis, health club, parking. AE, D, DC, MC, V.*

$$–$$$ 🏨 **Horizon Casino Resort.** Many of the guest rooms at this small complex have lake views. The casino has a Beaux Arts decor, brightened by pale molded wood and mirrors. The Grande Lake Theatre, Golden Cabaret, and Aspen Lounge present shows and name and up-and-coming entertainers. Le Grande Buffet has a nightly prime-rib special. ⊠ *U.S. 50, Box C, 89449,* ☎ *702/588–6211 or 800/322–7723,* ℻ *702/588–1344. 539 rooms. 3 restaurants, pool, wading pool, 3 hot tubs, exercise room, meeting rooms. AE, D, DC, MC, V.*

$$–$$$ 🏨 **Lakeside Inn and Casino.** The smallest of the Stateline casinos, and not nearly as glitzy as the big four, Lakeside has a rustic look. Guest rooms are in lodges, away from the casino area. ⊠ *U.S. 50 at Kingsbury Grade, Box 5640, 89449,* ☎ *702/588–7777 or 800/624–7980,* ℻ *702/588–4092. 123 rooms. Restaurant. AE, D, DC, MC, V.*

Nightlife

Major entertainment is found at the larger casinos. The top venues are the Circus Maximus at Caesars Tahoe, the Emerald Theater at Harvey's, the South Shore Room at Harrah's, and Horizon's Grand Lake Theatre. Each theater is as large as a Broadway house. Typical headliners are Jay Leno, David Copperfield, Kenny Rogers, and Johnny Mathis. For Las Vegas–style production shows—fast-paced dancing, singing, and novelty acts—try Harrah's or the Horizon. The big showrooms also occasionally present performances of Broadway musicals by touring Broadway companies or by casts assembled for the casino. Reservations are almost always required for superstar shows. Depending on the act, cocktail shows usually cost $12–$40, including Nevada's sales and entertainment taxes. Smaller casino cabarets sometimes have a cover charge or drink minimum.

Bars around the lake present pop and country-music singers and musicians, and in winter the ski resorts do the same. Summer alternatives are outdoor music events, from chamber quartets to jazz bands and rock performers, at Sand Harbor and the Lake Tahoe Visitors Center amphitheater.

Outdoor Activities and Sports

GOLF

Edgewood Tahoe (⊠ U.S. 50 and Lake Pkwy., behind Horizon Casino, Stateline, ☎ 702/588–3566) is an 18-hole, par-72 course with a driving range. Green fees include cart; the course is open 7–3. **Lake Tahoe Golf Course** (⊠ U.S. 50, between Lake Tahoe Airport and Meyers, ☎ 916/577–0788) has 18 holes, par 70, and a driving range. **Tahoe Par-**

adise Golf Course (⊠ U.S. 50, near Meyers, South Lake Tahoe, ☎ 916/577–2121) has 18 holes, par 66.

SCUBA DIVING

Diving Edge (⊠ 176 Shady La., Stateline, ☎ 702/588–5262) is a full-service PADI dive center with rentals and instruction.

LAKE TAHOE A TO Z

Arriving and Departing

By Bus

Greyhound Lines (☎ 800/231–2222) stops in Sacramento, Truckee, and Reno, Nevada.

By Car

Lake Tahoe is 198 miles northeast of San Francisco, a drive of just under four hours when traffic and the weather cooperate. Avoid the heavy traffic leaving the San Francisco area for Tahoe on Friday afternoon and returning on Sunday afternoon. The major route is I–80, which cuts through the Sierra Nevada about 14 miles north of the lake; from there state highways 89 and 267 reach the north shore. U.S. 50 is the more direct highway to the south shore, taking about 2½ hours from Sacramento. From Reno, you can get to the north shore by heading west on Highway 431 off U.S. 395, 8 miles south of town (a total of 35 miles). For the south shore, continue south on U.S. 395 through Carson City, and then head west on U.S. 50 (55 miles total).

By Plane

Reno–Tahoe International Airport (☎ 702/328–6400), 35 miles northeast of the closest point on the lake, is served by airlines that include **American, America West, Continental, Delta, Northwest, Reno Air, Sky West, Southwest,** and **United** (☞ Air Travel *in* Important Contacts A to Z for phone numbers). **Tahoe Casino Express** (☎ 702/785–2424 or 800/446–6128) has daily scheduled transportation from Reno to South Lake Tahoe, starting at 6:15 AM, then hourly from 8:15 to 3:15 PM, then 5:30, then every two hours until 12:30 AM.

Lake Tahoe Airport (☎ 916/542–6180) on U.S. 50, 3 miles south of the lake's shore, is served by no commercial airliners.

Getting Around

By Bus

South Tahoe Area Ground Express (STAGE, ☎ 916/573–2080) runs 24 hours along U.S. 50 and through the neighborhoods of South Lake Tahoe. **Tahoe Area Regional Transit** (TART, ☎ 916/581–6365 or 800/736–6365) operates buses along Lake Tahoe's northern and westerns shores between Tahoma (from Meeks Bay in summer) and Incline Village daily 6:30–6:30. Free shuttle buses run among the casinos, major ski resorts, and motels of South Lake Tahoe.

By Car

The scenic 72-mile highway around the lake is marked Highway 89 on the southwest and west, Highway 28 on the north and northeast shores, and U.S. 50 on the east and southeast. It takes about three hours to drive, but allow plenty of extra time—heavy traffic on busy holiday weekends can prolong the trip, and there are frequent road repairs in summer. During winter, sections of Highway 89 may be closed, making it impossible to complete the circular drive—call 800/427–7623 to check road conditions. I–80, U.S. 50, and U.S. 395 are all-weather highways, but there may be delays as snow is cleared during major storms. Carry tire chains from October to May (car-rental agencies provide them with their vehicles).

By Taxi

Yellow Cab (☎ 916/588–5555) serves all of Tahoe Basin. **Sierra Taxi** (☎ 916/577–8888) serves Tahoe's south shore. On the north shore, try **Tahoe-Truckee Taxi** (☎ 916/583–8294).

Contacts and Resources

Emergencies

Ambulance (☎ 911). **California Highway Patrol** (☎ 916/587–3510). **Nevada Highway Patrol** (☎ 702/687–5300). **Police** (☎ 911).

Guided Tours

BY BOAT

The *Tahoe Queen* (☞ South Lake Tahoe, *above*), the *Sierra Cloud* (☞ Incline Village, *above*), and MS *Dixie II* and *Woodwind* (☞ Zephyr Cove, *above*) all provide guided boat tours.

BY BUS OR CAR

Gray Line (☎ 916/541–7223 or 800/822–6009) runs daily tours to South Lake Tahoe, Carson City, and Virginia City. **Luxury Limousines of Tahoe** (☎ 916/544–3333 or 800/458–9743) also provides tours of area attractions.

High Mountain Outback Adventures (✉ 2286 Utah Ave., South Lake Tahoe 96150, ☎ 916/541–5875) operates a trek skirting the Desolation Wilderness in four-wheel-drive all-terrain vehicles (ATVs).

BY HOT-AIR BALLOON

Lake Tahoe Balloons (☎ 916/544–1221) conducts year-round excursions (champagne brunch included) over the lake or over the Carson Valley.

BY PLANE

CalVada Seaplanes Inc. (☎ 916/525–7143) provides rides over the lake for $45–$81 per person, depending on the length of the trip. **High Country Soaring** (☎ 702/782–4944) glider rides over the lake and valley depart from the Douglas County Airport, Gardnerville.

Reservations Agencies

Destinet (☎ 800/444–7275); campgrounds in state parks. **Lake Tahoe Visitors Authority** (☎ 800/288–2463); south-shore lodging. **Tahoe North Visitors and Convention Bureau** (☎ 800/824–6348); north-shore lodging.

Road Conditions

California roads in Tahoe area (☎ 916/445–7623). **California roads approaching Tahoe** (☎ 800/427–7623). **Nevada roads** (☎ 702/793–1313).

Visitor Information

California State Department of Parks and Recreation (☎ 916/653–8569). **Lake Tahoe Hotline** (☎ 916/542–4636 for south-shore events, ☎ 916/546–5253 for north-shore events, ☎ 702/831–6677 for Nevada events). **Lake Tahoe Visitors Authority** (✉ 1156 Ski Run Blvd., South Lake Tahoe, CA 96150, ☎ 916/544–5050 or 800/288–2463). **Tahoe North Visitors and Convention Bureau** (✉ Box 5578, Tahoe City, CA 96145, ☎ 916/583–3494 or 800/824–6348, FAX 916/581–4081). **Ski Phone** (☎ 415/864–6440). **U.S. Forest Service** (☎ 916/587–2158).

8 The Sierra National Parks

Yosemite, Kings Canyon and Sequioa

The highlight for many California travelers is a visit to one of the national parks in the Sierra Nevada mountain range. Yosemite is the state's most famous park and every bit as sublime as one expects. Its Yosemite-type or U-shape valleys were formed by the action of glaciers during recent ice ages. Other examples are found in Kings Canyon and Sequoia national parks, which are adjacent to each other and usually visited together. All the Sierra National Parks contain fine, tall groves of Sequoiadendron gigantea trees.

Updated by
Claudia
Gioseffi

YOSEMITE, KINGS CANYON, AND SEQUOIA national parks are famous throughout the world for their unique sights and experiences. Yosemite, especially, should be on your "don't miss" list. Unfortunately, it's on everyone else's as well (the park hosts approximately 4 million visitors annually), so advance reservations are essential. A week's stay at all three parks costs $5 per car, $3 per person if you don't arrive in a car. During a week's stay, you can exit and reenter the parks as frequently as you wish by showing your pass.

Pleasures and Pastimes

Camping

One highlight of a camping trip to the Sierra national parks is opening your eyes in the morning to nearby meadows and streams, then suddenly seeing the unforgettable landscape of giant granite in the distance, as if for the first time. Another is looking up at an awe-inspiring number of stars and spying one falling quickly through the night sky.

Destinet (☞ Contacts and Resources *in* Sierra National Parks A to Z, *below*) handles reservations for all Yosemite campgrounds. You can reserve campsites no sooner than eight weeks in advance. If space is available, you can also make reservations in person at the Campground Reservations Office in Yosemite Valley, but this is a chancy strategy. The campgrounds outside the valley that are not on the reservation system are first-come, first-served.

Campgrounds near each of the major tourist centers in Kings Canyon and Sequoia parks are equipped with tables, grills, drinking water, garbage cans, and either flush or pit toilets. The one campground that takes reservations, which can be made through Destinet from one day up to five months in advance, is Lodgepole in Sequoia. All others assign sites on a first-come, first-served basis; on weekends in July and August they are often filled by Friday afternoon.

Dining

Snack bars, coffee shops, and cafeterias in the parks are not expensive, but you may not want to waste precious time hunting about for food, especially during the day; instead, stop at a grocery store and fill your ice chest with the makings of a picnic to enjoy under the umbrellas of giant trees. The three fanciest accommodations within Yosemite National Park are also the prime dining spots. Especially in the off-season it's easy to zip out of the park to dine at the restaurants in the border towns (☞ Outside Yosemite National Park, *below*). With few exceptions (all noted), dress is casual at the restaurants listed below.

CATEGORY	COST*
$$$$	over $50
$$$	$30-$50
$$	$20-$30
$	under $20

per person for a three-course meal, excluding drinks, service, and 7¼% tax

Hiking

Hiking is the primary outdoor sport in the Sierra national parks. A good mix of spectacular views and levels of strenuousness might include Bridalveil Fall and Glacier Point hikes. Trails to upper and lower Yosemite Falls and Mirror Lake are favorites because of their beauty, moderate duration, and reasonable difficulty. The parks' visitor centers have trail maps.

Lodging

Most accommodations inside Yosemite, Kings Canyon, and Sequoia can best be described as "no frills." Many have no electricity or plumbing. Other than the Ahwahnee and Wawona hotels in Yosemite, lodging is geared toward those who prefer basic motels, rustic cabins, and campgrounds in natural, forest settings to full service and luxury. Except during the off-peak season, November to March, rates in Yosemite are pricey given the general quality of the lodging because of limited availability. Reservations (☞ Contacts and Resources for each park *in* Sierra National Parks A to Z, *below*) should be made well in advance, especially in summer.

Reservations are recommended for visits to Kings Canyon and Sequoia at any time of the year because it's a long way out if they're full. All the parks' lodges and cabins are open during the summer months, but in winter only some in Grant Grove remain open. From November through April, excluding holiday periods, low-season rates are in effect, resulting in savings of 20%–30%. The town of Three Rivers on Highway 198 southwest of Sequoia has a few more lodges and restaurants from which to choose.

CATEGORY	COST*
$$$$	over $175
$$$	$120–$175
$$	$80–$120
$	under $80

All prices are based on the cost of a room for two people, or a standard double room, excluding 9%–10% tax.

Nature Lore

In Yosemite from early May to late September and during some holiday periods, actor Lee Stetson portrays noted naturalist John Muir, bringing to life Muir's wit, wisdom, and storytelling skill. Stetson's programs—"Conversation with a Tramp" and "The Spirit of John Muir"—are two of the park's best-loved shows. Locations and times are listed in the *Yosemite Guide,* the newspaper handed to visitors upon entering the park. Stetson, as John Muir, also leads free interpretive walks twice a week; the walks start at the visitor center.

Exploring the Sierra National Parks

The Sierra national parks encompass two basic geographical regions. The most famous is Yosemite Valley. Its granite peaks and domes, such as El Capitan and Half Dome, rise more than 3,000 feet above the valley floor; two of the five waterfalls that cascade over the valley's rim are among the world's 10 highest; and the Merced River, placid here, runs through the valley. Such extravagant praise has been written of this valley (John Muir described it as "a revelation in landscape affairs that enriches one's life forever") and so many beautiful photographs taken (by Ansel Adams and others) that you may wonder if the reality can possibly measure up. For almost everyone, it does; Yosemite is a reminder of what "breathtaking" and "marvelous" really mean.

The other two Sierra national parks, Kings Canyon and Sequoia, are usually spoken of together. These adjacent parks share their administration and a main highway. Although you may want to concentrate on either Kings Canyon or Sequoia, most people visit both parks in one trip.

Great Itineraries

We recommend allowing several days to explore the parks, but if your time is limited, a one-day guided tour of one of the parks will at least allow you a glimpse of their wonders. We also recommend that you make your plans far enough in advance so you can stay in the parks themselves, not in one of the "gateway cities" in the foothills or Central Valley. You'll probably be adjusting to a higher altitude, dealing with traffic, and exercising a fair amount, so save your energy for exploring, not driving to and from the parks.

Yosemite Valley is the primary destination for many visitors, especially those who won't be making backpack or pack-animal trips. Because the valley is only 7 miles long and averages less than a mile in width, you can visit sites in whatever order you choose and return to your favorites at different times of the day. Famous for their hiking trails and giant sequoia trees, Kings Canyon and Sequoia provide a true wilderness experience, less interrupted by civilization and crowds.

Numbers in the text correspond to numbers in the margin and on the Yosemite and Kings Canyon and Sequoia National Parks maps.

IF YOU HAVE 3 DAYS

Exploring only Yosemite National Park is the best strategy for those whose time is limited. Enter the park via the Big Oak Flat Entrance. The sign for misty **Bridalveil Fall** ③ will be on your right shortly after traffic is diverted onto a one-way road heading east into Yosemite Valley. Continue east, following the signs to Yosemite Valley's **visitor center** ①, which has information and a store with picnic supplies. Loop back west for a picnic near **Yosemite Falls** ②, the highest waterfall in North America. Continue west for a valley view of famous **El Capitan** ⑦ peak. You can also picnic at this spot. Take Wawona Road south to Glacier Point Road for the bird's-eye view from **Glacier Point** ⑨ of Yosemite Valley, El Capitan, **Half Dome** ⑧, **Vernal Fall** ⑤, and **Nevada Fall** ⑥. If you want to avoid the busloads at Glacier Point, stop at **Sentinel Dome** ⑩ instead—after a mildly strenuous 1-mile hike you get a view similar to the one from the Glacier Point except for the peek into the valley. Continue on Highway 41 to the Wawona Hotel, where you can have a relaxing drink on the veranda in good weather or in the cozy lobby bar.

On day two, spend the morning and early afternoon walking through the **Mariposa Grove of Big Trees** ⑫ (take the Big Trees Tram if you don't want to walk as much). Return to Wawona and visit the **Pioneer Yosemite History Center** ⑪, where a living-history program re-creates Yosemite's past. Head back to Yosemite Valley on Wawona Road for an early-evening beverage at the Ahwahnee Hotel's bar (enjoy the patio view in good weather) and explore the hotel's lobby and other public areas. Have dinner at the Ahwahnee or one of the other valley eateries. On the third morning, have breakfast near the visitor center before hiking to **Vernal Fall** ⑤ or **Nevada Fall** ⑥ and exit the park upon your return to the visitor center.

IF YOU HAVE 5 DAYS

Spend your first two days exploring the **Yosemite Valley area** ①–⑩ and Wawona's **Mariposa Grove of Big Trees** ⑫ and **Pioneer Yosemite History Center** ⑪. On the third day, pack plenty of food and drive to **Hetch Hetchy Reservoir** ⑬ via Big Oak Flat Road and Highway 120. Then continue east on Tioga Pass Road—also called Highway 120, it's open only in summer—to **Tuolumne Meadows** ⑭, the largest subalpine meadow in the Sierra. (If Tioga Pass Road is closed, on day three you can take a hike to **Vernal Fall** ⑤ or **Nevada Fall** ⑥ instead.) On the fourth day leave early from Tuolumne Meadows and head southward to Kings Canyon National Park, entering on Highway 180 at the Big Stump Entrance. Stop at **Grant Grove** ⑮ and walk along the 1-mile Big Stump

Trail. If you're camping you'll need to get situated before sunset; if you're staying at one of the park's lodges, settle and then have dinner. On the fifth day, pass briefly through **Lodgepole** ⑳ and pick up tickets to the Crystal Cave. First, though, visit the **Giant Forest** ㉒, known for its numerous and varied trails through a series of sequoia groves. Then stop at the **Crystal Cave** ㉓, decorated with stalactites and stalagmites, before returning home.

When to Tour the Sierra National Parks

Summer is the most crowded season for all the parks, though the population density at Kings Canyon and Sequioa is much less than at Yosemite. During extremely busy periods—when snow closes high country roads in late spring or on crowded summer weekends—Yosemite Valley may be closed to all vehicles unless their drivers have overnight reservations, though this rarely happens. Because the parks are accessible year-round, it is possible to avoid these conditions. From mid-April to Memorial Day and from Labor Day to mid-October, the weather is usually warm, calm, and hospitable, and the parks less bustling.

The falls at Yosemite are at their most spectacular in May and June. By the end of the summer, however, some may have dried up. They begin flowing again in late fall with the first storms, and during the winter they may be dramatically hung with ice. Because the Yosemite valley floor is only 4,000 feet high, snow there is never very deep, and it is possible to camp even in the winter (January highs are in the mid-40s, lows in the mid-20s). Tioga Pass Road is closed in winter (roughly late October–May), so you can't see Tuolumne Meadows then. The road to Glacier Point beyond the turnoff for Badger Pass is also not cleared in winter, but it is groomed for cross-country skiing. In parts of Kings Canyon and Sequoia snow may remain on the ground into June; the flowers in the Giant Forest meadows hit their peak in July.

YOSEMITE NATIONAL PARK

Yosemite Valley, Wawona, Tuolumne Meadows, Mono Lake

Yosemite, with 1,170 square miles of parkland, is 94½% undeveloped wilderness, accessible only to backpackers and horseback riders, many sights can be explored by the more than 1,000 miles of roads, hiking trails, and bicycle trails. Most visitor facilities are located in Yosemite Village. Yosemite is so large it functions as five parks. Yosemite Valley is open all year. Hetch Hetchy and Wawona are both open all year, though Hetch Hetchy sometimes closes during severe weather. Mariposa Grove of Big Trees is open spring to fall. The high country, Tuolumne Meadows, is open for summer hiking. Badger Pass Ski Area is open in winter only. Christmas is a very busy time, with lodging reservations best made up to a year in advance. The western boundary dips as low as 2,000 feet in the chaparral-covered foothills; the eastern boundary rises to 13,000 feet at points along the Sierra crest.

Yosemite Valley Area

184 mi southeast of San Francisco on I–80 to I–580 to I–205 to Hwy. 120, 313 mi northeast of Los Angeles on I–5 to Hwy. 140.

Yosemite National Park's headquarters is near the east end of the Yosemite Valley, where there are also restaurants, stores, a gas station, ❶ the Ahwahnee Hotel, Yosemite Lodge, a medical clinic, and a **visitor**

center, where park rangers provide information and wilderness permits (necessary for overnight backpacking). There are exhibits on natural and human history as well as an adjacent Indian Cultural Museum and a re-created Ahwahneechee village. ⊠ *Off Northside Dr.,* ☎ *209/372–0264.* ☉ *Daily 9–5; extended hrs in summer.*

★ ❷ **Yosemite Falls** is the highest waterfall in North America and the fifth-highest in the world. The upper falls (1,430 feet), the middle cascades (675 feet), and the lower falls (320 feet) combine for a total of 2,425 feet and, when viewed from the valley, appear as a single waterfall. From the parking lot there is a ¼-mile trail to the base of the falls. If you elect to make the trek, the Yosemite Falls Trail is a strenuous 3½-mile climb rising 2,700 feet, taking you above the top of the falls. It starts from Sunnyside Campground.

★ ❸ **Bridalveil Fall,** a filmy fall of 620 feet that is often diverted as much as 20 feet one way or the other by the breeze, is the first view of Yosemite Valley for those who arrive via the Wawona Road. Native Americans called the fall Pohono ("puffing wind"). There is a very short (¼-mile) trail from a parking lot on the Wawona Road to its base.

❹ At 1,612 feet, **Ribbon Fall** is the highest single fall in the valley but also the first one to dry up in the summer because the snow and rain that fall upon the rock's flat surface evaporate quickly at this height.

❺ **Vernal Fall** (317 feet) is bordered by fern-covered black rocks, and rainbows play in the spray at the base. The hike on a paved trail from the Happy Isles nature area to the bridge at the base of Vernal Fall is only moderately strenuous and less than 1 mile long. It's another steep ¾-mile along Yosemite's Mist Trail, open only in the warmer months, up to the top of Vernal Fall.

❻ **Nevada Fall** (594 feet) in Yosemite Valley is the first major fall as the Merced River comes out of the high country. It's an additional, not very strenuous 2 miles along the Mist Trail from Vernal Fall (☞ *above*) to the top of Nevada Fall.

Vernal and Nevada falls are on the Merced River at the east end of Yosemite Valley. The roads here are closed to private cars, but a free shuttle bus runs frequently from the village. Both falls can also be viewed from Glacier Point (☞ *below*). From late June through early September, the Happy Isles nature area is open daily 9–5 and has exhibits on ecology.

★ ❼ **El Capitan** is the largest exposed granite monolith in the world, almost twice the height of the Rock of Gibraltar. It rises 3,593 feet above the valley, with an apparently vertical front thrust out from the valley's rim.

★ ❽ **Half Dome** is the most distinctive rock in Yosemite: The west side of the dome is fractured vertically and cut away to form a 2,000-foot cliff. Its top, which rises 4,733 feet from the valley floor, is 8,842 feet above sea level.

★ ❾ **Glacier Point** yields what may be the most spectacular view of the valley and the High Sierra that you can get without hiking. The Glacier Point Road leaves Highway 41 about 23 miles southwest of the valley; then it's a 16-mile drive, with fine views into higher country. From the parking area, walk a few hundred yards and you'll be able to see Nevada, Vernal, and Yosemite falls as well as Half Dome and other peaks. This road is closed beyond the turnoff for Badger Pass Ski Area in the winter.

❿ A hike to **Sentinel Dome** yields most of the Glacier Point view—El Capitan, Half Dome, and several falls—minus the peek into the floor of Yosemite Valley. A 1.1-mile path begins at a parking lot on Glacier Point Road a few miles below the point. The trail is just long and strenuous enough to keep the crowds and tour buses away, but it's by no means rugged (though the last few hundred feet on the rock itself are a bit steep).

Dining and Lodging

$$–$$$ ✕ **Mountain Room Broiler.** The food becomes secondary when you see Yosemite Falls through this dining room's window-wall. Best bets are steaks, chops, roast duck, and a fresh herb-basted roast chicken. ✉ *Yosemite Lodge, off Northside Dr.,* ☎ *209/372–1281. D, DC, MC, V. No lunch.*

$$$$ ✕▦ **Ahwahnee Hotel & Restaurant.** This grand, 1920s-style mountain
★ lodge is constructed of rocks and sugar-pine logs, with exposed timbers. The decorative style of the Grand Lounge and Solarium is a tribute to the local Miwoks and Paiutes; the motifs continue in the room decor. The Ahwahnee Restaurant ($$$–$$$$) with its 34-foot-tall trestle-beamed ceiling, full-length windows, and twinkling chandeliers, is the most impressive and romantic in Yosemite. Classic American specialties focus on steak, trout, and prime rib, all competently prepared. Generations of Californians have made a ritual of spending Christmas and New Year's here, so make plans well in advance; reservation lotteries are conducted for both periods. Another busy season is during January and February, when the Ahwahnee hosts its annual Chef's Holiday, featuring cooking instructions and banquets by leading chefs from all over the United States. ✉ *Ahwahnee Rd. in Yosemite Village,* ☎ *209/372–1488 or 209/372–1489. 123 rooms. Restaurant, lounge, pool, tennis. D, DC, MC, V.* 209/252(4848 Reserve

$–$$ ✕▦ **Yosemite Lodge.** The rooms in this lodge vary from functional motel-style units with two double beds to downright spartan cabins with no baths but within walking distance of Yosemite Falls. The lodge's Four Seasons Restaurant ($–$$) has high-finish natural wood tables and many potted representatives of the local greenery and flora. Breakfast is hearty and all-American. The dinner menu covers the full beef, chicken, and fish spectrum, plus vegetarian fare. ✉ *Off Northside Dr.,* ☎ *209/372–1269. 495 rooms. Restaurant, lounge, pool. D, DC, MC, V.*

$ ▦ **Curry Village.** These are plain accommodations: cabins with bath and without, and tent cabins with rough wood frames and canvas walls and roofs. It's a step up from camping (linens, blankets, and maid service are provided), but food and cooking are not allowed because of the animals. If you stay in a cabin without bath, showers and toilets are centrally located, as they would be in a campground. ✉ *180 cabins, 426 tent cabins, 8 hotel rooms. Cafeteria, pool, ice-skating. D, DC, MC, V.*

$ ⛺ **Housekeeping Camp.** These rustic tent cabins set along the Merced River are usually rented for several weeks at a time and are difficult to get; reserving at least 366 days in advance is advised. You can cook here on gas stoves rented from the front desk. ✉ *Along Southside Dr. 282 tent cabins with no bath (maximum 4 per cabin). Toilet and shower in central shower house. D, DC, MC, V.*

Outdoor Activities and Sports

BICYCLING

Yosemite Lodge and **Curry Village** have bicycle rentals, $5.25 per hour or $20 per day, from April–November.

Yosemite National Park

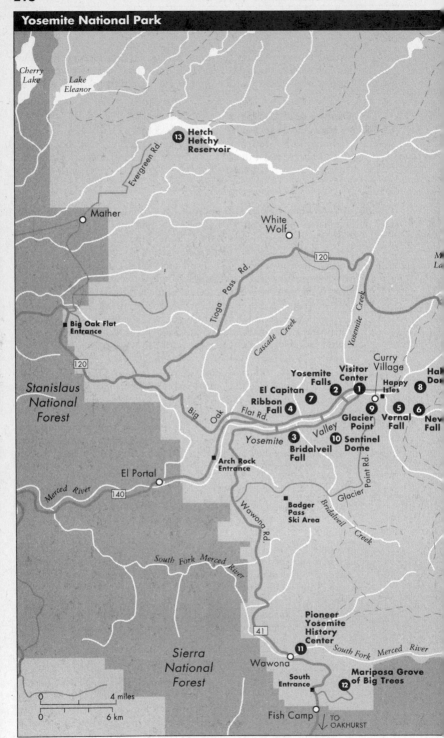

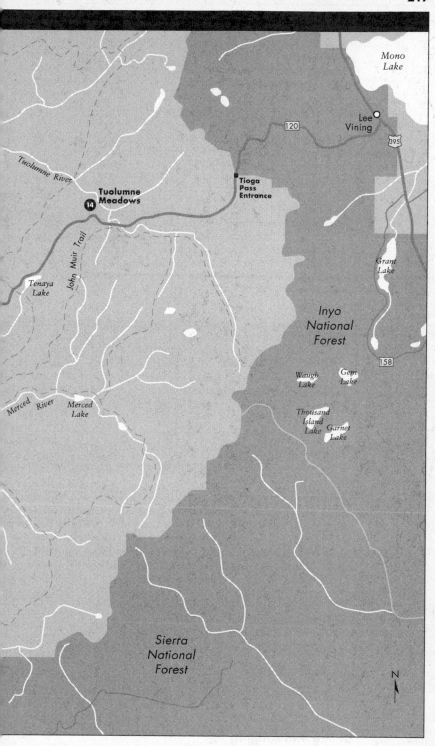

CAMPING

Thousands enjoy camping in Yosemite every year, but there are a few things to remember. Use the metal food-storage boxes found at every site. Park regulations mandate that visitors store food properly to prevent bears from getting it. Move all food, coolers, and items with a scent from your car to the storage box. Canisters for backpackers may be rented for $3 per day in most park stores. Keep an eye peeled for rattlesnakes below 7,000 feet. Though rarely fatal, bites require a doctor's attention. Marmots, small members of the squirrel family, enjoy getting under a vehicle and chewing on radiator hoses and car wiring. Always check under the hood before driving away. Finally, don't drink the water directly from streams and lakes, as intestinal disorder may result. Destinet (☞ Contacts and Resources *in* Sierra National Parks A to Z, *below*) handles reservations.

ROCK CLIMBING

Yosemite Mountaineering (☎ 209/372–1244 Sept.–May or 209/372–1335 June–Aug.) conducts beginner through intermediate rock-climbing and backpacking classes. A one-day session includes a hands-on introduction to climbing. Classes are held April–September, weather permitting. In winter it operates cross-country ski instruction and snow-camping trips.

WINTER SPORTS

Badger Pass Ski Area (☎ 209/372–1000), off Yosemite National Park's Glacier Point Road, has nine runs serviced by one triple and three double chairlifts, and an excellent ski school. Gentle slopes make this an ideal beginners area. The cross-country center has a groomed and tracked 21-mile loop from Badger Pass to Glacier Point, where, with reservations, you can overnight in a hut and eat prepared meals. Snowshoeing is also available. Curry Village in Yosemite Valley has an outdoor skating rink.

Wawona

25 mi south of Yosemite Valley on Hwy. 41; 16 mi north of Fish Camp on Hwy. 41.

⑪ The historic buildings in **Pioneer Yosemite History Center** were moved to Wawona from their original sites. A living-history program in summer re-creates Yosemite's past. The program runs from late June to early September, Wednesday through Sunday 9 AM to 1 PM and 2 to 5 PM. However, the center is open year-round. Nearby are a post office, gift shop and small store, and service station. ⊠ *On Hwy. 41, Wawona,* ☎ *209/375–6551.* ☉ *Hrs vary; call ahead.*

⑫ **Mariposa Grove of Big Trees,** a fine grove of naturally fire-resistant *Sequoiadendron gigantea* can be visited on foot or on the one-hour tram rides in summer. Admission is $7; the grove is open daily 9–6. The Grizzly Giant is the oldest tree here; its age is estimated to be 2,700 years. The tree's base diameter is 30.7 feet; its circumference is 96½ feet; and its height is 210 feet. The road to the grove closes when Yosemite is crowded; park in Wawona and take the free shuttle, which operates late spring through early fall, 9 to 5. It picks up passengers near the Wawona service station. ⊠ *Off Hwy. 41 near the Fish Camp entrance to Yosemite National Park.*

Dining and Lodging

$–$$ ✕🏨 **Wawona Hotel and Dining Room.** The Wawona Hotel, an 1879 National Historic Landmark, sits at the southern end of Yosemite National Park, near the Mariposa Grove of Big Trees. It's an old-fashioned Victorian estate of whitewashed buildings with wraparound verandas. Most rooms are small but pleasant; half do not have private bath. You can watch deer graze on the meadow while dining in the Wawona's romantic, candlelit dining room (reservations essential; $–$$$), which dates back to the late 1800s. The menu emphasizes home-grown California ingredients, such as grilled trout coated with corn meal, braised pork chops stuffed with apples and roasted almonds on a bed of wild rice, and rib-eye steak with onions and red potatoes. A traditional Sunday brunch is served from 7:30 to 1:30. ✉ *Hwy. 41, Wawona 95389,* ☎ *209/375–6556 (front desk), 209/375–6556 (dining room). 105 rooms. Restaurant, lounge, outdoor pool, tennis, 9-hole golf course, horseback riding. D, DC, MC, V.*

Hetch Hetchy, Tuolumne, and Mono Lake

⑬ The **Hetch Hetchy Reservoir** is located about 40 miles from Yosemite Valley, via Big Oak Flat Road and Highway 120. The reservoir supplies water and power to San Francisco. Some say John Muir died of heartbreak when this beautiful valley was dammed and buried beneath 300 feet of water in 1913.

Tioga Pass Road (Highway 120), open only in summer, is a scenic route
⑭ to **Tuolumne Meadows,** the largest subalpine meadow in the Sierra. It's 55 miles from Yosemite Valley. There are campgrounds, a gas station, a store (with a very limited and expensive choice of provisions), stables, a lodge, and a visitor center, which is open from late June until Labor Day from 8 AM until 7:30 PM. Since this area is the trailhead for many backpack trips into the High Sierra, it is a perfect spot from which to embark on a two-day hike. It will take about that amount of time to get acclimated to the altitude: 8,575 feet.

Highway 120 meets U.S. 395 at the town of Lee Vining. North on U.S. 395 is impressive **Mono Lake,** renowned for its striking "tufa towers" and nesting grounds for migratory birds. The tufa's visibility comes "courtesy" of the City of Los Angeles, which since the '40s (and not without great controversy) has been diverting water from streams that feed the lake, resulting in a lowering of its level.

Mono Basin Visitors Center (✉ Hwy. 395, ☎ 619/647–3044 for brochures or information) in Lee Vining provides ranger- and naturalist-led tours of Mono Lake's tufa and other wildlife, daily in the summer, weekends only (sometimes on cross-country skis) in winter.

OUTSIDE YOSEMITE NATIONAL PARK

Bass Lake, El Portal, Fish Camp, and Oakhurst

Several towns surrounding Yosemite National Park, all within an hour's drive of Yosemite Village, provide additional dining and lodging options.

Bass Lake

18 mi south of Yosemite National Park's South Entrance, Hwy. 41 to Bass Valley Rd.

Dining

$–$$$ ✕ **Ducey's on the Lake.** This lodge-style resort overlooking scenic Bass Lake attracts a lively crowd of boaters, locals, and tourists. The high-ceilinged, exposed-beam dining room serves tournedos of beef, steak, lobster, and pasta dishes. Burgers, sandwiches, and salads are the fare at the upstairs Bar & Grill. There is dancing and entertainment Friday and Saturday. Overnight guests can book lakefront suites at the nearby Pines Resort. ✉ *54432 Rd. 432, Bass Lake,* ☎ *209/642–3131. Reservations essential for Sun. brunch. D, DC, MC, V.*

Outdoor Activities and Sports
Pines Marina (✉ Bass Lake Reservoir, ☎ 209/642–3565), open April–October, rents ski boats, house- and fishing boats, Jet Skis, and funabouts.

El Portal

8 mi west of Yosemite National Park's Arch Rock Entrance on Hwy. 140.

Dining and Lodging

$$–$$$ ✕🏨 **Yosemite View Lodge.** This complex at the Yosemite National Park boundary should be nearly complete by the beginning of 1997. The back building, perched on the Merced River, has rooms with balconies overlooking the bolder-strewn river, majestic pines, and a picnic patio with hot tubs and heated pools. Rooms are large and pleasant with king beds, and most have fireplaces and kitchenettes; all have refrigerators and microwaves. Open all year, the lodge is on the public bus route to the park and near fishing and river rafting. The fare at the on-site Parkline ($–$$) restaurant includes burgers, steak, and chicken dishes prepared simply. ✉ *11136 Hwy. 140, 95318,* ☎ *209/379–2681 or 800/321–5261,* FAX *209/379–2704. 300 rooms. Restaurant, bar, 2 pools, 3 hot tubs, exercise room, game room. MC, V.*

$$ ✕🏨 **Cedar Lodge.** The lobby of this complex, nestled among tall pines, is heavy on plaid and teddy bears. Rooms range from suites with kitchenettes to family units to more romantic accommodations with spa tubs for two. The uncomplicated menu at the restaurant ($–$$) includes steaks, burgers, and a somewhat passé notion of exotica: chicken marsala, calamari, steak Doré, and other dishes smothered in accent marks. Things go further retro—to the *Happy Days* era—at Oldies 'N' Goodies ($). ✉ *9966 Hwy. 140, El Portal 95318,* ☎ *209/379–2612 or 800/321–5261,* FAX *209/379–2712. 206 rooms. 2 restaurants, pools, hot tubs, spas, business center. AE, MC, V.*

Fish Camp

37 mi south of Yosemite Valley floor, 10 mi south of Yosemite National Park's South Entrance on Hwy. 41.

The small town of Fish Camp has service stations and convenience stores, some fast food, and the **Yosemite Mountain–Sugar Pine Railroad,** a 4-mile scenic, historic steam-train ride through the forest. A Saturday-evening Moonlight Special excursion includes dinner and old-fashioned entertainment. ✉ *56001 Hwy. 41,* ☎ *209/683–7273.* 🎫 *$9.75.* ☉ *Daily Mar.–Oct. and on limited basis in winter.*

Dining and Lodging

$$$$ ✕🏨 **Tenaya Lodge at Yosemite.** One of the region's largest hotels, this is for people who enjoy hiking in the wilderness but prefer coming home to luxury. A southwestern motif prevails in the ample rooms, which are decorated in mauve, green, and rust. ✉ *1122 Hwy. 41, Box 159, 93623,* ☎ *209/683–6555 or 800/635–5807,* FAX *209/683–8684. 242 rooms. 2 restaurants, 2 lounges, room service, indoor-outdoor pools, health club, laundry service and dry cleaning, meeting room. AE, D, DC, MC, V.*

$$–$$$ ✕🏨 **Narrow Gauge Inn.** This motel-style property is comfortably furnished, with old-fashioned decor and railroad memorabilia. The inn's lodge-like restaurant ($$–$$$), which serves straightforward California and ranchero-inspired cuisine, is festooned with moose, bison, and other wildlife trophies. ✉ *48571 Hwy. 41, 93623,* ☎ *209/683–7720,* FAX *209/683–2139. 26 rooms. Restaurant, bar, pool, hot tub. D, MC, V. Closed late Oct.–weekend before Easter.*

Oakhurst

50 mi south of Yosemite Valley, 23 mi south of Yosemite National Park's South Entrance on Hwy. 41.

Dining and Lodging

$$$$ ✕ **Erna's Elderberry House.** This restaurant, operated by Vienna-born
★ Erna Kubin, owner of Château du Sureau (☞ *below*), is another expression of her passion for beauty, charm, and impeccable service. White walls and dark beams accent the dining room's high ceilings, and arched windows reflect the glow of many candles. A six-course, prix-fixe dinner in rhythm with the seasons is elegantly paced and accompanied by superb wines (let your waiter choose them for you). This is a dining experience to remember. Sunday brunch is also served. ✉ *48688 Victoria La., Oakhurst,* ☎ *209/683–6800. MC, V. Closed 1st 3 wks of Jan. No lunch Sat.–Tues., no dinner Tues.*

$$$$ 🏨 **Château du Sureau.** This romantic, beautiful inn is a fairy tale. From
★ the moment regal gates magically open and you step out of your car (think mice-driven coach), and a lady in waiting takes your coat and bags, you will not lift a finger. A winding staircase seems to carry you up to your room; you'll fall asleep in the glow of a crackling fire amid goosedown pillows and a comforter that rivals Cloud Nine. Château du Sureau is enveloped in an alluring serenity that greets you when you raise the curtains next morning and breathe in the fragrant gardens and cool air from the mist shrouded pines. Take in a hearty, European breakfast in the dining room downstairs, and plan your Sierra stay in the piano room, with its exquisite ceiling mural. ✉ *48688 Victoria La., Box 577, 93644,* ☎ *209/683–6860,* FAX *209/683–0800. 9 rooms. Restaurant, outdoor pool. MC, V.*

$$–$$$ 🏨 **Yosemite Country Inn.** One of the newest in Oakhurst, this inn seems to be sunwashed at all times of the day and year, thanks to high ceilings and skylights. Beamed ceilings in the private rooms and rugged stone accent walls in the common rooms complement the surrounding mountain landscape. The inn is within walking distance of restaurants, shopping, golf, and Bass Lake. ✉ *40489 Hwy. 41, 93644,* ☎ *209/683–8282,* FAX *209/658–7030. 120 rooms, 3 suites. Refrigerators, pool, hot tub. AE, D, DC, MC, V. Closed whenever roads are impassable.*

KINGS CANYON AND SEQUOIA NATIONAL PARKS

Grant Grove, Cedar Grove, and Lodgepole

General Grant and Sequoia national parks were established in 1890, along with Yosemite. Additions to General Grant National Park over the years included the Redwood Canyon area and the drainages of the south and middle forks of the Kings River. The whole region was eventually renamed Kings Canyon National Park.

The major attractions of the parks are the big trees (*Sequoiadendron gigantea*—the most extensive groves and the most impressive specimens are found here) and the stunning alpine scenery. They are not as tall as the coast redwoods (*Sequoia sempervirens*), but they are older and more massive. The exhibits at the visitor centers explain the special relationship between these trees and fire (their thick, fibrous bark helps protect them from fire and insects) and their ability to live so long and grow so big.

The parks encompass land from only 1,200 feet above sea level to more than 14,000 feet. Mt. Whitney, on the eastern side of Sequoia, is the highest mountain (14,494 feet) in the contiguous United States. The greatest portion of both parks is accessible only on foot or with a pack animal. The Generals Highway (46 miles from Highway 180 in Kings Canyon National Park to the Ash Mountain Entrance in Sequoia National Park) links two major groves in the two parks and is open year-round (except during severe weather).

The two parks possess sublime camping areas. You have to be able to live without water and power hookups, though: there are none. Potwisha, Grant Grove, Lodgepole, Dorst, and Cedar Grove campgrounds are the only areas where trailers and RVs are permitted (space for them even here is scarce). The length limit for RVs is 40 feet, for trailers 35 feet. Disposal stations are available in most of the main camping areas. Lodgepole, Potwisha, and Azalea campsites stay open all year, but Lodgepole is not plowed and camping is limited to recreational vehicles in plowed parking lots or snow tenting. Other campgrounds are open when the snow melts until late September or October. Campers should be aware that the nights, and even the days, can be chilly into early June.

Horseback riding is available at Grant Grove, Cedar Grove, Wolverton (between Lodgepole and Giant Forest), and Mineral King. Ask at the visitor centers for specifics. In the winter there is cross-country skiing and snowshoeing. Networks of marked trails are found at Grant Grove and Giant Forest. Rangers lead snowshoe walks ($1 snowshoe rental or bring your own) through Grant Grove and Giant Forest on winter weekends.

Grant Grove and Cedar Grove

100 mi southeast of Oakhurst, Hwy. 41 to Hwy. 180.

⓯ Grant Grove is the grove (or what remains of a larger grove decimated by logging) that was designated as General Grant National Park in 1890. It is now Kings Canyon's most highly developed area. A walk along the 1-mile Big Stump Trail, starting near the park entrance, graphically demonstrates the effects of heavy logging on these groves. Another, ⅓-mile paved trail is fairly accessible to travelers with disabilities. The most famous tree in this area is the approximately 2,000-year-old General Grant. The Gamlin Cabin is a pioneer cabin. The Centennial Stump, the remains of a large sequoia cut for display at the 1876 Philadelphia Centennial Exhibition, can also be viewed here. ⊠ *Kings Canyon Hwy. (Hwy. 180), 1 mi from Big Stump Entrance.*

Grant Grove Village has a visitor center, gas station, grocery store, campgrounds, coffee shop, overnight lodging, trail maps, and horse rentals. The visitor center has exhibits on the *Sequoiadendron giganteum* and the area. ⊠ *Kings Canyon Hwy.*

⓰ Hume Lake, a reservoir built early this century by loggers, is now the site of many Christian camps and a public campground. This small, pretty lake, just outside Kings Canyon's borders, has views of high mountains in the distance. ⊠ *Hwy. 180 northeast 8 mi from Grant Grove, off Hume Lake Rd. (also accessible off side road from Generals Hwy.).*

★ **⓱** The **Cedar Grove** area is a valley that snakes along the south fork of the Kings River. A spectacular drive along Kings Canyon Highway takes one hour from Grant Grove to the end of the road, where you turn

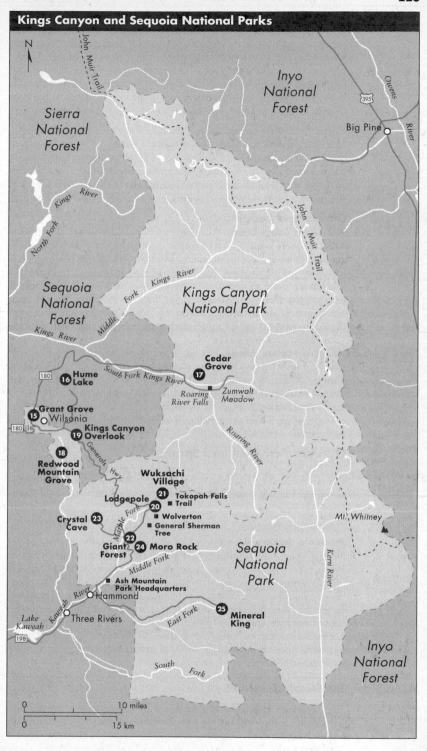

Kings Canyon and Sequoia National Parks

around for the ride back. Built by convict labor in the 1930s, the road (usually closed November through April) clings to some dramatic cliffs along the way, so you should watch out for falling rocks. The highway passes the scars where large groves of big trees were logged at the beginning of the century. It runs along the south fork and through dry foothills covered with yuccas that bloom in the summer. There are amazing views down into the deepest gorge in the United States, at the confluence of the two forks, and up the canyons to the High Sierra.

Cedar Grove was named for the incense cedars that grow in the area. Horses can be rented here, a good way to continue your explorations; there are also campgrounds, lodgings, a small ranger station, a snack bar, a convenience market, and a gas station. Short trails circle Zumwalt Meadow and lead to the base of Roaring River Falls; Cedar Grove is the trailhead for many backpackers.

Dining and Lodging

$ ✕⛺ **Cedar Grove Lodge.** Although accommodations are close to the road and there is quite a bit of traffic through here, Cedar Grove manages to retain a quiet atmosphere. Book way in advance—the motel-lodge has only 18 rooms. Each room is air-conditioned and carpeted and has a private shower and two queen-size beds. A self-serve restaurant has top sirloin, hamburgers, hot dogs, and sandwiches for lunch and dinner. Breakfast is eggs, bacon, and toast. You can take food from the restaurant to picnic tables along the river's edge. *AE, MC, V. Closed mid-Oct.–mid-May.*

$ ✕⛺ **Grant Grove Village.** The nicest accommodations here are the carpeted cabins with private baths, electric wall heaters, and double beds. Simpler cabins, heated by woodstoves and lit by kerosene lamps, are near a central rest room and shower facility. A family-style coffee shop serves American standards for breakfast, lunch, and dinner: eggs, burgers, and steak. There are also chef's salads, fruit platters, and seasonal fish specials. *AE, MC, V.*

Outdoor Activities and Sports

WINTER SPORTS

Rentals (including snowshoes), lessons, and tours are offered by **Sequoia Ski Touring Center** (☎ 209/565–3435 at Wolverton and Grant Grove).

YEAR-ROUND SPORTS

Montecito Sequoia Resort provides year-round family-oriented recreation. Depending on the season, lodging rates include all meals or just breakfast and dinner. Winter activities include cross-country skiing and lessons. Summer activities, offered in a six-night Club Med–like package, include canoeing, sailing, waterskiing, horseback riding, a preschool program, volleyball, horseshoes, tennis, archery, nature hikes, and a heated pool. In spring and fall, most of the summer activities occur, but guests are able to book shorter stays. ⊠ *Generals Hwy., 4 mi south of Hume Lake,* ☎ *800/227–9900 for brochures and information,* FAX *415/967–0540.*

Along the Generals Highway

The **Generals Highway** begins south of Grant Grove, continuing through the lower portion of Kings Canyon National Park and through a grand section of the Sequoia National Forest before entering Sequoia National Park.

★ ⑱ The **Redwood Mountain Grove** is the largest grove of big trees in the world. There are several paved turnouts off the Generals Highway from which you can look out over the grove (and into the smog of the Central Valley), but the grove itself is accessible only on foot or horseback.

⑲ Kings Canyon Overlook, a large turnout on the north side of the Generals Highway less than 2 miles from Redwood Mountain Grove, affords vistas across the canyon of the backcountry and mountain peaks. If you drive east on Highway 180 to Cedar Grove along the south fork, you will see these canyons at much closer range.

Lodgepole

⑳ *26 mi south of Grant Grove on the Generals Hwy.*

Lodgepole sits in a canyon on the Marble Fork of the Kaweah River. Lodgepole pines, rather than sequoias, grow here because the U-shape canyon conducts air down from the high country that is too cold for the big trees but is just right for lodgepoles. This developed area has a campground, gas station, store, public laundry, gift shop, and post office. An ice cream parlor and public showers are open in the summer only.

★ ☽ The **Lodgepole Visitor Center** has the best exhibits in Sequoia or Kings Canyon, a small theater that shows films about the parks, and the Walter Fry Nature Center (open in the summer), which has hands-on exhibits and activities that are geared toward children. You can buy tickets for the Crystal Cave (☞ *below*) at the visitor center. A very short marked nature trail leads from behind the visitor center down to the river. Except when the river is flowing fast (be cautious), this is a good place to rinse one's feet in cool water, because the trail runs past a "beach" of small rocks along the river. ☏ 209/565–3782. ☉ *Daily 8–6 in summer, 9–5 in winter.*

The **Tokopah Falls Trail** is a strenuous yet rewarding 2-mile hike up the river from the Lodgepole Campground (pick up a map at the Lodgepole visitor center; (☞ *above*), but it is the closest you can get to the high country without taking a long hike. Remember to bring insect repellent during the summer, when the mosquitoes can be ferocious.

㉑ Wuksachi Village will replace the dining, lodging, and other facilities that have been housed for years in Giant Forest Village. At press time (mid-1996) bidding on the concession was still in process and the precise plans for Wuksachi and for the phasing out of Giant Forest Village (some or none of which may be open in 1997) had not been finalized. Some parts of Wuksachi could be up and running by summer 1997. Call the park service (☏ 209/565–3134) for an update.

Giant Forest

㉒ *4 mi south of Lodgepole on the Generals Hwy.*

The Giant Forest is known for its numerous and varied trails through a series of sequoia groves. Well-constructed trails range in length from ⅓ mile to as far as one cares to walk. They are not paved, crowded, or lined with barricades, so one quickly gets the feeling of being alone in the woods, surrounded by rows of impressive trees.

Be sure to visit one of the meadows here. You can get the best views of the big trees from them, and in July the flowers are in full bloom. Round Meadow is the most easily accessible, with its ⅓-mile, wheelchair-accessible "Trail for All People." Crescent and Log Meadows are accessible but slightly longer trails than Round Meadow. Tharp's Log, at Log Meadow, is a pioneer cabin built in a fallen sequoia. There is also a log cabin at Huckleberry Meadow that children will enjoy exploring.

The most famous tree at Huckleberry Meadow is the **General Sherman Tree.** In summer there is usually a ranger nearby to answer questions, and there are benches so you can sit and contemplate the tree's immensity: It is 274.9 feet tall and 102.6 feet around at its base, but what's also extraordinary is that it is so wide for such a long way up—the first major branch is 130 feet above the ground.

The Congress Trail starts at the General Sherman Tree and travels past a series of large trees and younger sequoias. This is probably the most popular trail in the area, and it also has the most detailed booklet, so it is a good way to learn about the ecology of the groves. The booklet costs 50¢ and is available in summer from a vending machine near the General Sherman Tree.

A 2½-mile spur road takes off from the Generals Highway that leads to other points of interest in the Giant Forest area as well as to the trails to Crescent and Log meadows. The road actually goes through the Tunnel Log (there is a bypass for RVs that are too tall—7 feet, 9 inches and more—to fit). Auto Log is a fallen tree onto which you can drive your car for a photograph.

★ ㉓ **Crystal Cave** is the best known of Sequoia's many caves. Its interior was formed from limestone that metamorphosed into marble and is decorated with stalactites and stalagmites. To visit the cave, you must first stop at the Lodgepole Visitor Center (☞ *above*) or the Foothills Visitor Center at Ash Mountain (on the Generals Highway 1 mile inside Sequoia National Park) to buy a ticket—they're not sold at the cave. Then, drive to the end of a narrow, twisting, 7-mile road off the Generals Highway, 2.2 miles south of Giant Forest Village. From the parking area it is a 15-minute hike down a steep path to the cave's entrance. There are 45-minute guided tours daily on the half hour between 10 AM and 3 PM from mid-June through Labor Day and hourly Friday through Monday from mid-May to mid-June and after Labor Day through September. ☎ *209/565–3758 or 209/565–3134.* ✍ *$4.*

★ ㉔ **Moro Rock,** a granite monolith 6,725 feet high, rises from the edge of the Giant Forest. During the depression, the Civilian Conservation Corps built a staircase to the top. There are 400 steps, and the trail often climbs along narrow ledges over steep drops. The view from the top is striking. Southwest you look down the Kaweah River to Three Rivers, Lake Kaweah, and—on clear days—the Central Valley and the Coast Range. Northeast you look up into the High Sierra. Below, you look down thousands of feet to the middle fork of the Kaweah River.

Mineral King

㉕ *52 mi south of Lodgepole, on the Generals Hwy. and Mineral King Rd.*

The Mineral King area was incorporated into Sequoia National Park in 1978 after residents and conservationists in the 1960s derailed plans for a winter-sports resort. It is accessible in summer only by a narrow, twisty, and steep road (trailers and RVs not recommended) that takes off from Highway 198 several miles outside the park entrance. This is a tough but exciting 25-mile drive (budget 90 minutes each way) to a beautiful high valley. There are two campgrounds and a ranger station here; facilities are very limited, but some supplies are available. Many backpackers use this as a trailhead; fine day-hiking trails lead from here as well.

SIERRA NATIONAL PARKS A TO Z

Yosemite National Park

Arriving and Departing

BY BUS

Yosemite VIA (✉ 300 Grogan Ave, Merced, ☎ 209/384–2576 or 800/369–7275) runs three daily buses from Merced to Yosemite Valley. There are **Greyhound** (☎ 800/231–2222) and **Amtrak** (☎ 800/872–7245) connections with Yosemite VIA in Merced. The 2½-hour trip costs $33 per person, round-trip, which includes admission to the park.

BY CAR

Yosemite is a four- to five-hour drive from San Francisco (take I–580 to I–205 to Highway 120) and a six-hour drive from Los Angeles (take I–5 north to Fresno and Highway 41 north to Yosemite). From the west, Highways 41, 120, and 140 all intersect with Highway 99, which runs north–south through the Central Valley.

Via Highway 41: As you come from the south, Highway 41 through Madera County is the most direct path to Yosemite from Fresno. Highway 41 (called Wawona Road inside the park) provides the most dramatic entrance, via the Wawona Tunnel, into Yosemite Valley. Sixty-four miles from Fresno (or 60 from Madera; connect with Highway 41 via Highway 145), Highway 41 leaves the San Joaquin Valley floor to climb through oak-studded hills before descending to the town of Oakhurst, the southern terminus of Highway 49, which links the Gold Country towns for 300-plus miles to the north. Highway 41 continues to the north past the Bass Lake turnoff into Fish Camp and on through the park's South Entrance.

Via Highway 140: Arch Rock Entrance is 75 miles northeast of Merced via Highway 140, the least mountainous road.

Via Highway 120: Highway 120 is the northernmost route—the one that travels farthest and slowest through the foothills. You'll arrive at the park's Big Oak Flat Entrance, 88 miles east of Manteca. If you are coming from the east, you could cross the Sierra from Lee Vining on Highway 120 (Tioga Pass). This route takes you over the Sierra crest, past Tuolumne Meadows, and down the west slope of the range. It's scenic, but the mountain driving may be stressful for some, and it's open only in the summer.

BY PLANE

Fresno Air Terminal (✉ 5175 Clinton Way, ☎ 209/498–4095) is the nearest major airport. It is served by (☞ Air Travel *in* Important Contacts A to Z for phone numbers) **Delta, American, USAir,** and several regional carriers. **United Express** serves Merced Airport (✉ 20 Macready Dr., ☎ 209/385–6873).

Getting Around

BY BUS

Thanks to the free shuttle bus that runs around the eastern end of Yosemite Valley (7:30 AM–10 PM in the summer and early fall, 10–10 the rest of the year), it is possible to visit the park without your own car. From 9 to 5 in the summer, another free shuttle runs from Wawona to the Mariposa Grove of Big Trees.

BY CAR

Auto traffic in Yosemite National Park is sometimes restricted during peak periods. Check conditions before driving in. Large RVs and trailers are not allowed on some roads. You should have tire chains when you drive in these mountains from November through April; the eastern entrance to the park at Tioga Pass is at nearly 10,000 feet.

BY FOOT

If you are hiking up any of the steep trails, remember to stay on the trail. Also consider the effect of the altitude on your endurance. Talk to the rangers at the visitor centers about which trails they recommend to get you acclimated to the altitude (more than 6,000 feet at Giant Forest) before you can exert yourself fully. If you plan to backpack overnight, you'll need a wilderness permit (free), available at visitor centers or ranger stations.

Contacts and Resources

GUIDED TOURS

California Parlor Car Tours (✉ Cathedral Hill Hotel, 1101 Van Ness Ave., San Francisco 94109, ☎ 415/474–7500 or 800/227–4250) runs several California tours that include Yosemite. Lodging and some meals are included; you can choose to stay in either Yosemite Lodge or the Ahwahnee (there's a difference in price, of course).

Yosemite Concession Services (☎ 209/252–4848 for reservations) conducts daily guided bus tours of Glacier Point, the Yosemite Valley floor, and the Mariposa Grove of Big Trees, along with tram rides and trips on horseback. The Grand Tour covers the park highlights. Fees run from $5 for a one-way Glacier Point excursion to $65 for a full-day horseback ride.

RESERVATIONS

Camping: Destinet (✉ Box 85705, San Diego 92186, ☎ 619/452–8787; in the U.S. and Canada; 800/365–2267; TTY 800/284–7275).

Lodging: Yosemite Concession Services Corporation (✉ Central Reservations, 5410 E. Home, Fresno 93727, ☎ 209/252–4848).

ROAD CONDITIONS

Yosemite Area Road and Weather Conditions (☎ 209/372–0200).

VISITOR INFORMATION

Southern Yosemite Visitors Bureau (✉ Box 1404, Oakhurst 93644, ☎ 209/683–4636). **Yosemite National Park** (✉ National Park Service, Information Office, Box 577, Yosemite National Park 95389, ☎ 209/372–0200 for 24-hr information or 209/372–0264).

Sequioa and Kings Canyon National Parks

Arriving and Departing

BY BUS

Greyhound (☎ 800/231–2222) serves Fresno and Visalia. **Amtrak** (☎ 800/872–7245) serves Fresno.

BY CAR

Under average conditions, it takes about six hours to reach Kings Canyon and Sequoia national parks from San Francisco and about five hours to do so from Los Angeles. Two major routes, Highways 180 and 198, intersect with Highway 99, which runs north–south through the Central Valley.

From the north, enter Kings Canyon National Park via Highway 180, 53 miles east of Fresno. From the south, enter Sequoia National Park via Highway 198, 36 miles from Visalia. If you are driving up from Los Angeles, take Highway 65 north from Bakersfield to Highway 198 east of Visalia.

BY PLANE

Fresno Air Terminal (⊠ 5175 Clinton Way, ☎ 209/498–4095) is the nearest major airport to Kings Canyon and Sequoia national parks.

Getting Around

BY BUS

Sequoia Guest Services (☎ 209/565–3381) runs a shuttle bus between major points in the Giant Forest and Lodgepole. One-time fares are $1 per person and $3 for a family of five or fewer; all-day passes are $3 per person and $6 for a family of five or fewer.

BY CAR

Most people take Highway 180 to Kings Canyon–Sequoia, coming into Kings Canyon National Park at the Big Stump Entrance. Highways 180 and 198 are connected through the parks by the Generals Highway, a paved two-lane road that is open year-round but may be closed for weeks at a time during heavy snowstorms (carry chains in winter). Drivers of RVs and drivers who are not comfortable on mountain roads should probably avoid the southern stretch between the Potwisha Campground and Giant Forest Village. These very twisty 16 miles of narrow road rise almost 5,000 feet and are not advised for vehicles over 22 feet long. Few roads up the west slope of the Sierra rise so quickly through the foothills and offer such spectacular views of the high country. The rest of the Generals Highway is a well-graded, two-lane road and a pleasure to drive.

Highway 180 (called Kings Canyon Highway inside the park) beyond Grant Grove to Cedar Grove and the road to Mineral King are open only in summer. Both roads, especially the latter, which is very steep and unpaved in sections, may present a challenge to inexperienced drivers. Large vehicles are discouraged. Campers and RVs are not advised on the Mineral King road. Trailers are not allowed in Mineral King campgrounds.

Contacts and Resources

EMERGENCIES

Ambulance (☎ 911). **Police** (☎ 911).

GUIDED TOURS

Sequoia Guest Services (☎ 209/565–3381) conducts an all-day van tour of Kings Canyon. Admission is $$22, mid-May–mid-October.

RESERVATIONS

Camping: Destinet (⊠ Box 85705, San Diego 92186, ☎ 619/452–8787; in the U.S. and Canada, 800/365–2267, TTY 800/284–7275), for Lodgepole only.

Lodging: Sequoia Guest Services (⊠ Box 789, Three Rivers 93271, ☎ 209/561–3314, FAX 209/561–3135).

ROAD CONDITIONS

Sequoia/Kings Canyon Road and Weather Information (☎ 209/565–3351).

Northern California Road Conditions. (☎ 800/427–7623).

VISITOR INFORMATION

National Park Service, Fort Mason (⊠ Bldg. 201, San Francisco 94123, ☎ 415/556–0560). **Sequoia and Kings Canyon National Parks** (⊠ Three Rivers 93271, ☎ 209/565–3134).

9 Monterey Bay

*From Santa Cruz
to Carmel Valley*

*The Monterey Peninsula is steeped in
history. The town of Monterey was
California's first capital, the Carmel
Mission headquarters for California's
entire 18th-century mission system.
The peninsula also has a rich literary
past. John Steinbeck's novels
immortalize the area, and Robert
Lewis Stevenson strolled its streets for
inspiration for* Treasure Island. *The
present is equally illustrious. Blessed
with a natural splendor undiminished
by time or commerce, the peninsula is
home to visionary marine habitats and
luxurious resorts and golf courses.*

By Claudia
Gioseffi

N 1542, **MONTEREY BAY'S** white sand beaches, pine forests, and rugged coastline captivated European explorer Juan Rodríguez Cabrillo, who claimed it for Spain. Spanish missionaries, Mexican rulers, and land developers would come and go, all of them instinctively knowing enough not to destroy the peninsula's God-given assets or historical sites. The area has never relied solely on its looks, however. Certainly you can't ignore its deep green forests of Monterey cypress—oddly gnarled trees that grow nowhere else—its aquamarine waters, or the dance of cloud shadows upon its rolling emerald hills and winsome meadows. Yet there are industrial, a bit messy, claims to fame—whaling for one, sardines for another. And its meticulously preserved adobe houses and missions, layers of a Spanish and Mexican past left remarkably undisturbed, create a terra-cotta skyline that testifies to the Monterey Peninsula's singular place in California history.

With the arrival of Father Junípero Serra and Commander Don Gaspar de Portola from Spain in 1770, Monterey became both the military and ecclesiastical capital of Alta California. Portola established the first of California's four Spanish presidios; Serra founded the second of 21 Franciscan missions, later moving it from Monterey to its current site in Carmel.

When Mexico revolted against Spain in 1822, Monterey remained the capital of California under Mexican rule. The town grew into a lively seaport, drawing Yankee sea traders who added their own cultural and political influence. Then, on July 7, 1846, Commodore John Sloat arrived in Monterey and raised the American flag over the Custom House, claiming California for the United States.

Although Monterey's whaling industry boomed at this time, and would continue to thrive until the early 1900s, the city's political importance in the new territory was short-lived. The state constitution was framed in Colton Hall, but Monterey was all but forgotten once gold was discovered at Sutter's Mill near Sacramento. After the gold rush, the state capital moved from Monterey and the town became a sleepy backwater.

At the turn of the century, the Monterey Peninsula began to draw tourists with the opening of the Del Monte Hotel, the most palatial resort the West Coast had ever seen. It was then that writers and artists such as John Steinbeck, Henry Miller, Robinson Jeffers, Francis McComas, and Ansel Adams also discovered the peninsula, adding their legacy to the region while capturing its magic on canvas, paper, and film. And in the 1920s and 1930s, Cannery Row's now-extinct sardine industry took off. In 1995 in nearby Salinas, sardines were packed again for the first time since the 1950s and visitors can buy them in Cannery Row, where activity has returned in the form of renovated buildings that house specialty shops, boutiques, and restaurants.

All aspects of the peninsula's diverse cultural and maritime heritage can be felt today, from Monterey's Path of History to its lively harbor and wharf. Modern-day attractions include the Monterey Jazz Festival and the Monterey Bay National Marine Sanctuary—the nation's largest undersea canyon, larger and deeper than the Grand Canyon. The sanctuary supports a rich brew of marine life, from fat, barking sea lions to tiny plantlike anemones. Carmel Valley, the "Sunbelt" of the Monterey Peninsula, averages 283 sunny days a year and, seemingly, that many resorts; the fertile Salinas Valley has become the "Salad Bowl of the Nation." Pacific Grove's century-old Victorians have redefined the bed-and-breakfast trade for the 1990s, and Pebble Beach's championship golf courses are the scene of many a prestigious tournament. A variety of special annual events pay tribute to old traditions; ethnic and religious festivals and fiestas, such as Pacific Grove's Butterfly Parade, the Carmel Shakespeare Festival, and the Santa Rosalia Festival, link the past with the present every September.

Pleasures and Pastimes

Dining

Monterey is the richest area for dining along the coast between San Francisco and Los Angeles. The surrounding waters abound with fish, wild game roams the foothills, and the inland valleys are the vegetable basket of California; nearby Castroville dubs itself the Artichoke Capital of the World. The region also takes pride in producing better and better wines. When it comes to dress, San Francisco's conservatism extends this far south. Except at beachside stands and the inexpensive eateries listed below, casual but attractive resort wear is the norm. The few places where more formal attire is required are noted.

CATEGORY	COST*
$$$$	over $50
$$$	$30–$50
$$	$20–$30
$	under $20

per person for a three-course meal, excluding drinks, service, and 6½%–8¼% tax

Golf

Beginning with the opening of the Del Monte Golf Course in 1897, golf has been an integral part of the Monterey Peninsula's social and recreational scene. Greens fees for 18 holes run from $15 to $225, depending on the time and course. Many hotels will help with golf reservations or have golf packages; inquire when you make lodging reservations.

Lodging

Monterey-area accommodations range from no-frills motels and historic hotels to upscale establishments that are a bit impersonal and clearly designed for conventions. Others pamper the individual traveler in grand style, especially some of the small inns and bed-and-breakfasts in Carmel. Pacific Grove has quietly turned itself into the region's B&B capital. Carmel and Carmel Valley also have fine B&Bs; other lodgings vary from beachside motels to luxury complexes. Even more luxurious are the resorts in exclusive Pebble Beach. The rates below are for two people in the high season, April to October. Keep in mind that winter rates, especially at the larger hotels, drop by as much as 50% and that lodgings booked through Monterey's 800/555–9283 number include an informational brochure, two tickets to the Monterey Bay Aquarium, and discount coupons good at restaurants and shops.

CATEGORY	COST*
$$$$	over $175
$$$	$120–$175
$$	$80–$120
$	under $80

All prices are for a standard double room, excluding 10½% tax.

Whale Watching

On their annual migration between the Bering Sea and Baja California, 45-foot gray whales can be spotted not far off the Monterey coast. They sometimes can be seen with binoculars from shore, but a whale-watching cruise is the best way to view these magnificent mammals

up close. The migration south takes place between December and
March—late January is prime viewing time. The migration north is from
March to June. Two thousand blue whales and 600 humpbacks come
north from Mexico to spend the summer feeding; they're easily spotted late summer and early fall. Rarer minke whales, orcas, sperm
whales, and fin whales have been sighted in mid-August. Even if no
whales surface, bay cruises nearly always encounter some unforgettable
marine life.

Exploring Monterey Bay

The population centers here are towns, not cities, and their individual
charms complement Monterey Bay's natural beauty. Santa Cruz sits
at the top of the curve, and the Monterey Peninsula, including Monterey, Pacific Grove, and Carmel, occupies the lower end. In between,
Highway 1 cruises along the coastline, passing windswept beaches piled
high with sand dunes. Along the route are fields of artichoke plants,
the towns of Watsonville and Castroville, and Fort Ord, which recently
shed its army fatigues for civilian clothes. Different times of day and
season bring out the various moods: Walking at the edge of the ocean
on a stark winter morning, seabirds in loud commotion overhead; spotting a rainbow on the horizon after an afternoon squall; sipping a cool
chardonnay in the warm glow of an outdoor fireplace as the sun slips
into the Pacific.

Great Itineraries

Despite its compact size, the Monterey Peninsula is packed with diversions—it would take more than a weekend to get beyond the surface. If you have an interest in California history and historic preservation,
the place to start is Monterey, with its adobe buildings along the downtown Path of History. Fans of Victorian architecture will want to explore the many fine examples in Pacific Grove. In Carmel you can shop
till you drop, and when summer and weekend hordes overwhelm the
town's boutiques, art galleries, housewares outlets, and gift shops, you
can slip off to enjoy the coast.

*Numbers in the text correspond to numbers in the margin and on the
Monterey Bay, Monterey and Pacific Grove, and Carmel and 17-Mile
Drive maps.*

IF YOU HAVE 3 DAYS
Visit 🏛 **Monterey** ②–⑲, a seaside town with a vibrant history. Walk
along the streets of Cannery Row and stop at **Steinbeck's Spirit of Monterey Wax Museum** ⑯ or the **Old General Store** ⑰, and then have
lunch before heading to the **Monterey Bay Aquarium** ⑲, at the south
end of the Row, for the rest of the afternoon. After your aquarium visit,
head on foot via oceanfront Recreation Trail to **Fisherman's Wharf** ⑬
to enjoy the sights and catch the sunset. If you're not up to the hub-
bub along the wharf, slip into the serene bar at the Monterey Plaza
Hotel. The following day, visit the **Larkin House** ⑥, **Cooper–Molera
Adobe** ⑦, and (Robert Louis) **Stevenson House** ⑧, stopping for lunch
when the need hits. Then pick up some juice and late-afternoon snacks
to take on **17-Mile Drive** ㉕–㉙. Don't miss **Bird Rock** ㉕, the **Lone Cypress** ㉗, or **Pebble Beach Golf Links** ㉙. Catch the sunset along 17-Mile
Drive or at nearby **Point Lobos State Reserve** ㉞. On the third day, drive
a short distance south to **Carmel** ㉚–㉞. Visit the **Carmel Mission** ㉛ and
have lunch while browsing through the **Ocean Avenue** shopping area
before stopping at **Tor House** ㉜, the residence of poet Robinson Jeffers. No matter what time of year you're visiting Monterey Bay, stroll
over to Scenic Road and spend time on Carmel Beach before leaving
the area.

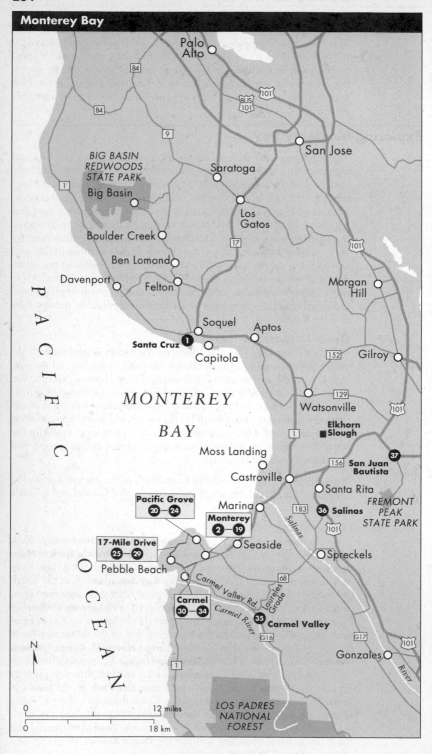

IF YOU HAVE 5 DAYS

On your first three days, visit **Monterey** ②–⑲, stopping at the **Custom House** ②, **Larkin House** ⑥, **Cooper-Molera Adobe** ⑦, **Stevenson House** ⑧, and **Colton Hall** ⑨ on day one. On your second morning, get a visceral feel for Monterey Bay marine life with a **whale-watching or other cruise,** have lunch upon your return to dry land, and then visit **Steinbeck's Spirit of Monterey Wax Museum** ⑯, the **Old General Store** ⑰, and **Fisherman's Wharf** ⑬. On the morning of day three, head to **Monterey Bay Aquarium** ⑲, have lunch along Cannery Row upon exiting, and then spend the rest of the afternoon either tasting wine at **Ventana Vineyards** on the Monterey–Salinas Highway or enjoying the Monterey waterfront. On your fourth day, visit **Carmel Mission** ㉛ and **Tor House** ㉜ and have lunch while exploring the shops along **Ocean Avenue** in Carmel. Pick up some juice and late-afternoon snacks to take on **17-Mile Drive** ㉕–㉙. Catch the sunset along 17-Mile Drive or at nearby **Point Lobos State Reserve** ㉞. On day five explore the shoreline and Victorian houses of **Pacific Grove** ⑳–㉔ in the morning and lunch there. If you have time, visit **San Juan Bautista** ㊲, a classic mission village, before departing.

IF YOU HAVE 7 DAYS

On days one through three, explore **Monterey** ②–⑲. Spend day four in **Carmel** ㉚–㉞ and along **17-Mile Drive** ㉕–㉙. On day five, stop in **Pacific Grove** ⑳–㉔, including the oldest continuously operating lighthouse on the West Coast, **Point Piños Light Station** ㉒. Visit **Asilomar State Beach,** a sanctuary of dunes, tidal pools, and pocket-size beaches on day six. On your last day in the area, drive inland to **San Juan Bautista** ㊲.

When to Tour Monterey Bay

Summer is peak season with crowds everywhere and generally has mild weather. A sweater or windbreaker is nearly always necessary along the coast, where a cool breeze usually blows and fog is on the way in or out. Inland, temperatures in Salinas or Carmel Valley can be a good 15 or 20 degrees warmer than those in Carmel and Monterey. Off-season, from November to April, fewer people visit and the mood is more introspective. The rains come in January and February. Most of the historic sights in Monterey are open daily, though hours vary between peak and nonpeak season; call ahead to be sure.

MONTEREY BAY

Santa Cruz to Carmel Valley

Set along 90 miles of arc-shape coastline, like jewels in a tiara, the towns of Monterey Bay—halfway between northern and southern California—combine the somewhat funky, beachcomber aspects of the state's culture with more glamorous, refined tendencies. Past and present merge gracefully here. As preservationist and the city of Monterey's first mayor, Carmel Martin, described it early in this century: "Monterey Bay is the one place where people can live without being disturbed by manufacturing and big factories. I am certain that the day is coming when this will be the most desirable place in the whole state of California."

Santa Cruz

❶ *74 mi south of San Francisco, I–280 to Hwy. 17 to Hwy. 1; 48 mi north of Monterey on Hwy. 1.*

The beach town of Santa Cruz is sheltered by the surrounding mountains from the coastal fog to the north and south and from the smoggy skies of the San Francisco Bay area. The climate here is mild, and it is usually warmer and sunnier than elsewhere along the coast this far north. Something of a haven for those opting out of the rat race, and a bastion of '60s-style counterculture values, Santa Cruz has been at the forefront of such very Californian trends as health food, recycling, and environmentalism. It is less manicured than its upmarket neighbors to the south (it's been looking downright scruffy of late, say some) but more urban than the agricultural towns between it and the Monterey Peninsula. Nearby Capitola, Soquel, and Aptos are home to some quality restaurants and small inns.

The town gets something of its youthful ambience from the nearby **University of California at Santa Cruz.** The school's harmonious redwood buildings are perched on the forested hills above the town, and the campus is tailor-made for the contemplative life, with a juxtaposition of sylvan settings and sweeping vistas over open meadows onto the bay. The humanities faculty offers a major in the "History of Consciousness," and this does seem to be the perfect spot for it.

The earthquake of 1989 laid low much of **Pacific Garden Mall,** in the historic downtown section. The epicenter of the quake was only a few miles away, in the Santa Cruz mountains, and the unreinforced masonry of the town's older buildings proved extremely vulnerable. Rebuilding has been a long process, especially along Pacific Avenue, in the heart of the downtown area.

NEED A
BREAK?

Caffè Pergolesi (✉ 418 Cedar St., ☎ 408/426–1775), a Victorian residence not far from the downtown area, has become a humming coffeehouse with a very European flair. You can read the newspaper and enjoy a pastry at one of the veranda tables or have a light meal inside, surrounded by local artists' works.

★ ♻ Santa Cruz has been a seaside resort since the mid-19th century, and the merry-go-round and Giant Dipper roller-coaster at the **Santa Cruz Beach Boardwalk** roller-coaster date back to the early 1900s. Elsewhere along the boardwalk the Casino Arcade has its share of video-game technology, as does Neptune's Kingdom, which features a state-of-the-art miniature golf course with robotic and fiber-optic special effects, but this is still primarily a place of good old-fashioned fun. The colonnades of the turn-of-the-century Cocoanut Grove (☎ 408/423–2053), now a convention center and banquet hall, host a lavish Sunday brunch beneath the glass dome of its Sun Room. ✉ *Boardwalk: along Beach St. west from the San Lorenzo River,* ☎ *408/423–5590 or 408/426–7433.* 🎟 *17.95 (day pass for unlimited rides).* ☉ *Memorial Day–Labor Day 11 AM–9 PM; rest of yr, weekends and holidays 11 AM–9 PM, later in summer.*

The **Santa Cruz Municipal Wharf** is lined with restaurants and is enlivened from below by the barking and baying of the sea lions that lounge in communal heaps under the wharf's pilings and shamelessly accept any seafood offerings tossed their way. Down the West Cliff Drive promontory at **Seal Rock,** pinnipeds hang out, sunbathe, and occasionally frolic.

The **Lighthouse** (a.k.a. the Mark Abbott Memorial Lighthouse) has a surfing museum with artifacts that include the remains of a board a shark munched on. ✉ *W. Cliff Dr.,* ☎ *408/429–3429.* ☉ *Museum: summer, Mon. and Wed.–Fri. noon–4, weekends noon–5; rest of yr, Mon., Thurs., and Fri. noon–4, weekends noon–5.*

♻ **Natural Bridges State Park** has tidal pools and a colony of monarch butterflies. ✉ *2531 W. Cliff Dr.,* ☎ *408/423–4609.* 🎟 *$6 parking fee.* ☉ *Park 8 AM–sunset, visitor center 10–4.*

Dining and Lodging

$$ ★ ✕ **Chez Renee.** The husband-and-wife team that owns this retreat serves French-inspired cuisine. Specialties include sweetbreads with two sauces (Madeira and mustard), duck and home-preserved brandied cherries, and deep-sea scallops garnished with smoked salmon and dill. Save room for the excellent dessert soufflés. ✉ *9051 Soquel Dr., Aptos,* ☎ *408/688–5566. MC, V. No lunch Sat.*

$$ ✕ **El Palomar.** The spacious restaurant of the Palomar Hotel, with vaulted ceilings and wood beams, serves California Mexican cuisine with an emphasis on seafood. Homemade tamales, seviche, and chili verde are among the best dishes. ✉ *1336 Pacific Ave.,* ☎ *408/425–7575. Reservations not accepted. AE, D, MC, V.*

$–$$ ✕ **O Mei Sichuan Chinese Restaurant.** Not your run-of-the-mill chop-suey joint, this sophisticated place serves some unusual dishes: *gan pung* (boneless chicken crisp-fried and served with a spicy garlic sauce), *gan bian* (dried sautéed beef with hot pepper and ginger on crispy rice noodles), and rock cod prepared Taiwan style (filleted and breaded, with chili-vinegar sauce). ✉ *2316 Mission St. (Hwy. 1),* ☎ *408/425–8458. AE, MC, V. No lunch weekends.*

$ ✕ **Scontriano's Dolphin Restaurant.** Occupying a scenic site at the end of the Municipal Wharf, this small, casual restaurant serves up standard breakfasts—hotcakes, French toast, omelets, cereals—plus seafood lunches and dinners. ✉ *At the end of Santa Cruz Municipal Wharf,* ☎ *408/426–5830. MC, V.*

$$$–$$$$ ⊡ **Dream Inn.** Within a short stroll of the Beach Boardwalk and wharf, this beachfront resort opens right onto Cowell Beach. If it's too cold to swim in the ocean, you can head for the heated swimming pool and tub. Rooms have balconies or patios, plus refrigerators and VCRs. Children under 12 stay free with parents. ✉ *175 W. Cliff Dr., 95060,* ☎ *408/426–4330 or 800/662–3838,* ℻ *408/427–2025. 164 rooms. 2 restaurants, pool, sauna, hot tub. AE, D, DC, MC, V.*

$$$–$$$$ ⊡ **Inn at Depot Hill.** This inventively designed hotel in a former rail depot has taken the *Orient Express* as its theme. Each double room or suite, complete with fireplace and feather beds, is inspired by a different European destination—Delft, the Netherlands; Portofino, Italy; Sissinghurst, England; the Côte d'Azur, France. One is decorated like a Pullman car for a railroad baron. Some accommodations have balconies with private hot tubs. Full breakfast is included, as well as wine and hors d'oeuvres. ✉ *250 Monterey Ave., Capitola-by-the-Sea 95010,* ☎ *408/462–3376 or 800/572–2632,* ℻ *408/462–3697. 8 rooms. AE, MC, V.*

$$–$$$$ ★ ⊡ **Darling House Bed and Breakfast by the Sea.** A superb 1910 mansion on the promontory overlooking the Pacific was built as a summer house for a rich Colorado family by William Weeks, architect of Santa Cruz's Cocoanut Grove. Modern plumbing and electricity are among the few concessions made to the 1990s; in all other ways, the house retains a turn-of-the-century atmosphere. Room rates include Continental breakfast. No pets are allowed; smoking is permitted outdoors only. ✉ *314 W. Cliff Dr., 95060,* ☎ *408/458–1958 or 800/458–1958. 8 rooms, 6 with shared bath. Hot tub. AE, D, MC, V.*

Nightlife and the Arts

The **Cabrillo Music Festival** in Santa Cruz (☎ 408/426–6966 or 408/429–3444), one of the longest-running new music festivals, showcases American and other composers for two weeks in early August.

Shakespeare Santa Cruz (✉ Performing Arts Complex, University of California at Santa Cruz, ☎ 408/459–2121) puts on a six-week Shakespeare festival in July and August that also includes 20th-century works. Some performances are outdoors in the striking Redwood Glen.

Outdoor Activities and Sports

BEACHES

Surfers in Santa Cruz gather for the spectacular waves and sunsets at **Pleasure Point** (⊠ East Cliff Dr. and Pleasure Point Dr.). The surf at **New Brighton State Beach** (⊠ 1500 State Park Dr., Capitola) is challenging; campsites are available. South of Santa Cruz, **Manresa State Beach** (⊠ Manresa Dr., La Selva Beach, ☎ 408/761–1795) has premium surfing conditions, but the water here is treacherous, so the beach is recommended only for sunbathing.

BICYCLING

Bikes can be rented from **Surf City Rentals** (⊠ 46 Front St., Santa Cruz, ☎ 408/423–9050).

BOATS AND CHARTERS

Stagnaro Fishing Trips (⊠ Center of Santa Cruz Municipal Wharf, ☎ 408/427–2334) operates salmon and rock-cod fishing expeditions; the $39 fee includes bait. The company also operates $18 whale-watching cruises December through April.

Monterey

48 mi south of Santa Cruz on Hwy. 1; 122 mi south of San Francisco on I–280 to Hwy. 17 to Hwy. 1; 334 mi north of Los Angeles on U.S. 101 to Hwy. 68 west from Salinas.

★ ♺ Monterey was California's first capital. A good deal of the city's early history can be gleaned from the well-preserved adobe buildings of **Monterey State Historic Park** (☎ 408/649–7118). Far from being a hermetic period museum, the park facilities are an integral part of the day-to-day business life of the town—some of the buildings still serve as government offices and include a store and a restaurant. A 2-mile self-guided walking tour of the park is outlined in the brochure "Path of History," available at the Chamber of Commerce or at many of the landmark buildings contained in the park. A $5 ticket offered by the park gains visitors entrance to Casa Soberanes, the Cooper-Molera Adobe, the Larkin House, and the Stevenson House (☞ *below*) and includes a guided walking tour of the area.

❷ The **Custom House,** built by the Mexican government in 1827 and considered the oldest government building west of the Rockies, was the first stop for sea traders whose goods were subject to duty. An upper story was later added to the adobe structure. At the beginning of the Mexican-American War in 1846, Commodore John Sloat raised the American flag over the building and claimed California for the United States. Now the lower floor displays examples of a typical cargo from a 19th-century trading ship. ⊠ *1 Custom House Plaza across from Fisherman's Wharf,* ☎ *408/649–2909.* ☞ *Free.* ☼ *Sept.–May, daily 10–4; June–Aug., daily 10–5.*

❸ The **Monterey Maritime Museum** includes the private collection of maritime artifacts of a former Carmel mayor, Allen Knight. Among the exhibits of ship models, scrimshaw items, and nautical prints, the highlight is the enormous multifaceted Fresnel lens from the Point Sur Lighthouse. ⊠ *5 Custom House Plaza,* ☎ *408/375–2553.* ☞ *$5.* ☼ *Daily 10–5.*

❹ The **Pacific House,** a former hotel and saloon, is now a museum of early California life. There are Native American artifacts, gold-rush relics, historic photographs of old Monterey, and a costume gallery displaying various period fashions. ⊠ *10 Custom House Plaza,* ☎ *408/649–2907.* ☞ *Free.* ☼ *Sept.–May, daily 10–4; June–Aug., daily 10–5.*

Monterey and Pacific Grove

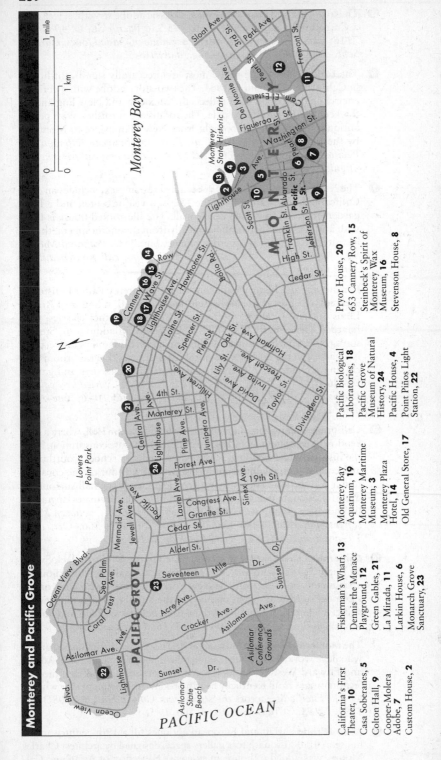

Monterey Bay

PACIFIC OCEAN

California's First Theater, **10**
Casa Soberanes, **5**
Colton Hall, **9**
Cooper-Molera Adobe, **7**
Custom House, **2**

Fisherman's Wharf, **13**
Dennis the Menace Playground, **12**
Green Gables, **21**
La Mirada, **11**
Larkin House, **6**
Monarch Grove Sanctuary, **23**

Monterey Bay Aquarium, **19**
Monterey Maritime Museum, **3**
Monterey Plaza Hotel, **14**
Old General Store, **17**

Pacific Biological Laboratories, **18**
Pacific Grove Museum of Natural History, **24**
Pacific House, **4**
Point Piños Light Station, **22**

Pryor House, **20**
653 Cannery Row, **15**
Steinbeck's Spirit of Monterey Wax Museum, **16**
Stevenson House, **8**

⑤ The low-ceilinged **Casa Soberanes,** a classic adobe structure, was once a Custom House guard's residence. ✉ *336 Pacific St.,* ☎ *408/649–7118.* ⌨ *$2.* ⊙ *Varied hrs; call for schedule of guided tours. Gardens Sept.–May, daily 10–4; June–Aug., daily 10–5.*

⑥ The **Larkin House,** one of the most architecturally significant homes in California, was built in 1835. The two-story adobe with a veranda encircling the second floor reflects the Mexican and New England influences on the Monterey style. The rooms are furnished with period antiques, many of them brought from New Hampshire to Monterey by the Larkin family. ✉ *510 Calle Principal, between Jefferson and Pacific Sts.,* ☎ *408/649–7118.* ⌨ *$2.* ⊙ *Varied hrs; call for schedule of guided tours.*

⑦ The restored **Cooper-Molera Adobe,** a 2-acre complex, includes an early California house dating from the 1820s, a visitor center, and a large garden enclosed by a high adobe wall. The tile-roofed house is filled with antiques and memorabilia, mostly from the Victorian era, that illustrate the life of a prosperous pioneer family. ✉ *Polk and Munras Sts.,* ☎ *408/649–7118.* ⌨ *$2.* ⊙ *Varied hrs; call for schedule of guided tours.*

⑧ For literary and history buffs, one of the Monterey Path of History's greatest treasures is the **Stevenson House,** named in honor of Robert Louis Stevenson, author of *Treasure Island* and other classics, who boarded there briefly in a tiny upstairs room. In addition to Stevenson's room, which is furnished with items from his family's estate, there is a gallery of the author's memorabilia and several period rooms, including a children's nursery stocked with Victorian toys and games. ✉ *530 Houston St.,* ☎ *408/649–7118.* ⌨ *$2.* ⊙ *Varied hrs; call for schedule of guided tours. Gardens Sept.–May, daily 10–6; June–Aug., daily 10–5.*

⑨ California's equivalent of Independence Hall is **Colton Hall,** where a convention of delegates met in 1849 to draft the first state constitution. Now the historic white building, which has served as a school, courthouse, and county seat, is a museum furnished as it was during the constitutional convention. The extensive grounds outside the hall surround a more notorious building, the Old Monterey Jail, where inmates languished behind thick granite walls. ✉ *500 block of Pacific St., between Madison and Jefferson Sts.,* ☎ *408/646–5640.* ⌨ *Free.* ⊙ *Mar.–Oct., daily 10–noon and 1–5; Nov.–Feb., 10–noon and 1–4.*

⑩ **California's First Theater** was constructed in the 1840s by Jack Swan, an English sailor who settled in Monterey, as a saloon with adjoining apartments. Soldiers from the New York Volunteers who were on assignment in Monterey put on plays in the building. Performances are still given here (☞ *Nightlife and the Arts, below*). ✉ *Scott and Pacific Sts.,* ☎ *408/649–7118 or 408/375–4916; docent schedule varies.*

The **Monterey Peninsula Museum of Art** showcases distinguished artists who have worked in the area, among them photographers Ansel Adams and Edward Weston. Another focus is international folk art; the collection ranges from Kentucky hearth brooms to Tibetan prayer wheels. ✉ *559 Pacific St., across the street from Colton Hall,* ☎ *408/372–7591.* ⌨ *$3.* ⊙ *Tues.–Sat. 10–5, Sun. 1–5.*

⑪ At **La Mirada,** Asian and European antiques fill a 19th-century adobe house. A 10,000-square-foot gallery space, designed by architect Charles Moore, was added to house an extensive collection of Asian and Californian regional art. The permanent collection includes works by Armin Carl Hansen, as well as a large netsuke collection. Outdoors are magnificent rose and rhododendron gardens. ⊠ *720 Via Mirada, at Fremont St.,* ☎ *408/372–3689.* ▣ *$3.* ☉ *Tues.–Sat. 10–4, Sun. 1–4.*

★ ◔ ⓬ **Dennis the Menace Playground** (⊠ Fremont St. and Camino El Estero, Monterey), in Lake El Estero Park, is an imaginative play area whose name pays tribute to the cartoon creation of longtime local resident Hank Ketcham. The equipment is on a grand scale and made for daredevils; there's a dizzyingly high rotating platform, a clanking suspension bridge, and a real Southern Pacific steam locomotive. Rowboats and paddleboats can be rented on U-shape Lake El Estero, home to a varied assortment of ducks, mud hens, and geese.

Inevitably, visitors are drawn to Monterey's waterfront, if only because the mournful barking of sea lions that can be heard throughout the town makes its presence impossible to ignore. The whiskered marine ◔ ⓭ mammals are best enjoyed while walking along **Fisherman's Wharf,** an aging pier crowded with souvenir shops, fish markets, seafood restaurants, and popcorn stands. Although tacky and touristy to the utmost, the wharf is a good place to visit with children.

Cannery Row has undergone several transformations since it was immortalized in John Steinbeck's 1945 novel of the same name. The street that Steinbeck described was crowded with sardine canneries processing, at their peak, nearly 200,000 tons of the smelly silver fish a year. During the mid-1940s, however, the sardines mysteriously disappeared from the bay, eventually causing the canneries to close. Over the years the old tin-roof canneries have been converted to restaurants, art galleries, and minimalls with shops selling T-shirts, fudge, and plastic otters. Recent tourist development along the row has been more tasteful, however, including several stylish inns and hotels.

⓮ The historic **Monterey Plaza Hotel** (⊠ 400 Cannery Row) sits on the site of an estate built by Hugh Tevis for his bride, who died on their honeymoon. It's a good place to relax over a drink and watch for otters.

Although John Steinbeck would have trouble recognizing Cannery Row today, there are still some historical and architectural features from ⓯ its colorful past. One building to notice is **653 Cannery Row,** with its tiled Chinese dragon roof, which dates from 1929.

⓰ Characters from the novel *Cannery Row* are depicted in wax at **Steinbeck's Spirit of Monterey Wax Museum,** which also features a 25-minute description of the history of the area over the past 400 years, with a recorded narration by the novelist himself. ⊠ *700 Cannery Row,* ☎ *408/375–3770,* ▣ *$4.95.* ☉ *Daily 9–9.*

⓱ The building now called the **Old General Store** (⊠ 835 Cannery Row) is the former Wing Chong Market that Steinbeck called Lee Chong's Heavenly Flower Grocery in *Cannery Row.* A weathered wooden ⓲ building at 800 Cannery Row was the **Pacific Biological Laboratories** where Edward F. Ricketts, the inspiration for Doc in *Cannery Row,* did much of his marine research.

★ ◔ ⓳ Science, conservationism, and theater meet at the spectacular **Monterey Bay Aquarium.** The Outer Bay wing, which opened in March 1996, is devoted to the mysteries of the open ocean and completes the aquarium's picture of Monterey Bay, the nation's largest marine sanctuary. Its million-gallon indoor ocean—highlighted by the largest window on earth—innovatively re-creates the sunlit blue water where Monterey Bay meets the open sea. In this habitat, blue and soupfin sharks, barracuda, pelagic stingrays, ocean sunfish (which can weigh a ton or more), green sea turtles, and schools of fast-moving tuna swim together. Some of these sea creatures are on exhibit for the first time. The Outer Bay wing also houses the country's largest collection of jellyfish, graceful oceanic drifters whose other-worldly ballet attracts record-breaking numbers of visitors. Since it opened in 1984, the entire aquarium, winner of the 1995 "Academy Award" of urban development, the Urban Land Institute's Award for Excellence, has been extremely popular. Expect long lines and sizable crowds on weekends, especially during the summer. Braving the crowds is worth it, however, especially to see the original wing's three-story Kelp Forest exhibit, the only one of its kind in the world, and another display of the sea creatures and vegetation found in the inner Monterey Bay. Among other standouts are a bat-ray petting pool, where the flat velvetlike creatures can be touched as they swim by; a 55,000-gallon sea-otter tank; and an enormous outdoor artificial tidal pool that supports anemones, crabs, sea stars, and other colorful creatures. ⊠ *886 Cannery Row,* ☎ *408/648–4888 or 800/756–3737 in CA for advance tickets.* ⊡ *$13.75.* ⊘ *Daily 10–6, 9–6 on holidays and in summer. Box office closes at 5:30.*

OFF THE BEATEN PATH	**VENTANA VINEYARDS –** A five-minute drive from downtown Monterey leads to one of the peninsula's most highly regarded wineries, particularly for chardonnays and Johannisberg Rieslings. Ventana's knowledgeable and hospitable owners, Doug and LuAnn Meador, invite guests to bring lunch to eat while tasting wines on a patio and deck. ⊠ *2999 Monterey–Salinas Hwy. (Hwy. 68),* ☎ *408/372-7415.* ⊘ *Daily 11–5.*

Dining and Lodging

$$$ ✕ **Duck Club.** The elegant dining room of the Monterey Plaza Hotel (☞ *below*) is built over the waterfront on Cannery Row, overlooking the bay. The view and automated piano music make for a romantic setting. The California menu strongly emphasizes duck but also includes seafood, meat, and pasta. ⊠ *400 Cannery Row,* ☎ *408/646–1700. AE, D, DC, MC, V.*

$$$ ✕ **Fresh Cream.** Local residents recommend this outstanding restaurant in Heritage Harbor, with its beautiful views over the bay. The cuisine is French, with light, imaginative California accents. Some favorites on the seasonal menu are the rack of lamb Dijonnaise and the roast boned duck in black-currant sauce. Fresh Cream presents live chamber music on Wednesday nights. ⊠ *99 Pacific St., Suite 100C,* ☎ *408/375–9798. AE, D, DC, MC, V. No lunch Sat.–Thurs.*

$$–$$$ ✕ **Whaling Station Inn.** A pleasing mixture of rough-hewn wood and
★   sparkling white linen makes this restaurant a festive yet comfortable place in which to enjoy some of the best mesquite-grilled fish and meats in town. There are excellent artichoke appetizers and fresh salads. ⊠ *763 Wave St.,* ☎ *408/373–3778. AE, D, DC, MC, V. No lunch.*

$$ ✕ **Bradley's Harbor Front Restaurant.** This restaurant—with possibly the best location on the harbor—is so far out on a pier that it's almost seaworthy. Though the exterior is salty, windblown, and surrounded by dry-docked boats, the atmosphere inside recalls a 1920s European bistro. Regional American fare with various ethnic influences includes avocado pancakes with salsa and fresh fish specials. The desserts are rich and delicious. ⊠ *32 Cannery Row at the Coast Guard Pier,* ☎ *408/655–6799. Reservations essential on weekends. AE, D, DC, MC, V.*

$$ ✕ **Cafe Fina.** Italian seafood dishes are the specialty of this understated wharf restaurant. Highlights include mesquite-grilled fish dishes and pasta Fina, a linguine in clam sauce with baby shrimp and tomatoes. The wine list is extensive. ⊠ *47 Fisherman's Wharf,* ☎ *408/372–5200. AE, D, DC, MC, V.*

$$ ✕ **Domenico's.** Under the same ownership as the Whaling Station Inn and nearby Abalonetti, Domenico's serves Italian seafood preparations, mesquite-grilled meats, and homemade pastas. The blue-and-white

nautical decor keeps the place comfortably casual; white drapery lends an air of elegance lacking in most restaurants on the wharf. ⊠ *50 Fisherman's Wharf,* ☎ *408/372–3655. AE, D, DC, MC, V.*

$$ ✕ **Ferrante's.** Gorgeous views of both the town and the bay can be seen from this California-Italian restaurant atop the 10-story Monterey Marriott. The chicken cashew fettuccine with sun-dried tomatoes is especially good. Brunch is served Sunday. ⊠ *350 Calle Principal,* ☎ *408/649–4234. AE, D, DC, MC, V. No lunch.*

$$ ✕ **Montrio.** In November 1995 *Esquire* named the then eight-month-
★ old Montrio its Restaurant of the Year, declaring that it "sums up in every way what is best about California restaurants." The publication also singled out Montrio's chef, Brian Whitmer, as one of America's finest. If your appetite for hearty cooking and clean, strong flavors has been stimulated by a day of bracing Monterey Bay breezes, this European-inspired American bistro is the place to go. Grilled Portobello mushroom "steak" with ragout of vegetables—the most requested dish—and risotto with artichokes are just two of the menu highlights. Housed in a landmark building that served as Monterey's firehouse from 1890 to 1910, the restaurant has an interior that is a montage of brick, rawhide, and wrought iron. Whimsical paintings, crayons on every table, and unusual sound mufflers on the ceiling (they're supposed to be clouds) keep the mood lighthearted. ⊠ *414 Calle Principal,* ☎ *408/648–8880. Reservations essential on weekends. AE, D, MC, V.*

$–$$ ✕ **Abalonetti.** From a squid lover's point of view, wharfside Abalonetti is the best place in town, serving all kinds of squid dishes: deep-fried, sautéed with wine and garlic, or baked with eggplant. Abalone is another specialty, and the fresh fish is broiled or blackened and served with beurre blanc or pesto. Seafood pasta and wood-fired pizza are also on the menu. ⊠ *57 Fisherman's Wharf,* ☎ *408/373–1851. AE, D, DC, MC, V.*

$–$$ ✕ **Paradiso Trattoria.** Follow the aroma of marinating olives, roasted garlic, and platters of focaccia to this bright Cannery Row establishment where California and Mediterranean specialties and pizzas from a wood-burning oven are the luncheon fare. Seafood is a good choice for dinner, which is served in a formal dining room that overlooks a lighted beachfront and lapping surf. Every table has an ocean view. ⊠ *654 Cannery Row,* ☎ *408/375–4155. AE, D, DC, MC, V.*

$–$$ ✕ **Tarpy's Roadhouse.** Fun, dressed-down roadhouse lunch and dinner are served in a renovated farmhouse built in the early 1900s by the Ryans, legendary local folk. The kitchen cooks everything Mom used to make, only better. ⊠ *2999 Monterey–Salinas Hwy. (Hwy. 68), at Canyon Del Rey Rd.,* ☎ *408/647–1444. MC, V.*

$ ✕ **Old Monterey Cafe.** Breakfast here, which is served until early afternoon, can include fresh-baked muffins and eggs Benedict. This is also a good place to relax with a cappuccino or coffee made from freshly ground beans. ⊠ *489 Alvarado St.,* ☎ *408/646–1021. Reservations not accepted. DC, MC, V.*

$$$$ ▦ **Old Monterey Inn.** Perhaps no other inn conjures up the past and
★ beauty of the Monterey Peninsula or provides such a complete escape so close to everything the area has to offer. The three-story English Tudor country manor that became the Old Monterey Inn in 1978 was completed in 1929, replete with hand-carved window frames, balustrades, Gothic archways, and ceiling panels. Loving restoration by proprietors Gene and Ann Swett included a rose garden now surrounded by giant holly trees, 100-year-old gnarled oaks, pines, fragrant eucalyptus, and majestic redwoods. The couple's thoroughness and thoughtfulness extend to their hospitality—a well-stocked medicine cabinet, the book placed on your bed at night, a sumptuous featherbed and down com-

forter. ⊠ *500 Martin St., 93940,* ☎ *408/375–8284 or 800/350–2344,* FAX *408/375–6730. 10 rooms. Concierge. MC, V.*

$$$$ 🏨 **Spindrift Inn.** This small hotel on Cannery Row has the street's only
★ private beach; a rooftop garden overlooks Monterey Bay. Spacious rooms
with sitting areas, Oriental rugs, fireplaces, canopied beds, and down
comforters are among the indoor pleasures. Continental breakfast,
brought to the room on a silver tray, and afternoon tea are also included.
⊠ *652 Cannery Row, 93940,* ☎ *408/646–8900 or 800/841–1879,*
FAX *408/646–5342. 41 rooms. AE, D, DC, MC, V.*

$$$–$$$$ 🏨 **Hotel Pacific.** Other, newer hotels in downtown Monterey clash with
the early California architecture and small-town ambience, but the adobe-
style Hotel Pacific fits right in. All rooms are suites, handsomely ap-
pointed with four-poster feather beds, hardwood floors, Indian rugs,
fireplaces, honor bars, and balconies or patios. Room rates include Con-
tinental breakfast and afternoon tea. ⊠ *300 Pacific St., 93940,* ☎
408/373–5700; in CA, 800/554–5542; FAX *408/373–6921. 105 rooms.*
2 hot tubs. AE, D, DC, MC, V.

$$$–$$$$ 🏨 **Hyatt Regency Monterey.** Although its rooms and atmosphere are
less glamorous than at some other resorts in the region, the facilities
here are excellent. ⊠ *1 Old Golf Course Rd., 93940,* ☎ *408/372–1234*
or 800/233–1234; in CA, 800/824–2196; FAX *408/375–3960. 575*
rooms. 2 restaurants, lounge, sports bar, 2 pools, 2 hot tubs, tennis
court, exercise room. AE, D, DC, MC, V.

$$$–$$$$ 🏨 **Monterey Bay Inn.** This hotel, anchoring Cannery Row, is under the
same ownership as the Spindrift Inn and demonstrates the same attention
to detail. Spacious rooms, decorated in peach and green tones, have
private balconies, VCR, honor bar, terry-cloth robes, and binoculars
for viewing marine life; most rooms have breathtaking bay views. In-
room Continental breakfast is included. ⊠ *242 Cannery Row, 93940,*
☎ *408/373–6242 or 800/424–6242,* FAX *408/373–7603. 47 rooms.*
2 hot tubs, sauna, exercise room. AE, D, DC, MC, V.

$$$–$$$$ 🏨 **Monterey Plaza Hotel.** This sophisticated full-service hotel commands
★ a superb waterfront location on Cannery Row, where frolicking sea
otters can be observed from the wide outdoor patio and from many
of the room balconies. The architecture and decor blend early Cali-
fornia and Mediterranean styles and retain a little of the old cannery
design. ⊠ *400 Cannery Row, 93940,* ☎ *408/646–1700 or 800/631–*
1339; in CA, 800/334–3999; FAX *408/646–0285. 285 rooms. Restau-*
rant, bar, exercise room. AE, D, DC, MC, V.

$$–$$$$ 🏨 **Best Western Monterey Beach Hotel.** Rooms here may be nondescript, but this hotel has a great waterfront location about 2 miles north
of town, with panoramic views of the bay and the Monterey skyline.
Grounds are pleasantly landscaped, and the hotel has a large pool with
a sunbathing area. ⊠ *2600 Sand Dunes Dr., 93940,* ☎ *408/394–3321*
or 800/242–8627, FAX *408/393–1912. 196 rooms. Restaurant, lounge,*
pool, hot tub. AE, D, DC, MC, V.

$$–$$$$ 🏨 **Cannery Row Inn.** This is a modern, small hotel on a street above
Cannery Row with bay views from the private balconies of some rooms.
Gas fireplaces and complimentary Continental breakfast are among the
amenities. ⊠ *200 Foam St., 93940,* ☎ *408/649–8580 or 800/876–8580,*
FAX *408/649–2566. 32 rooms. Hot tub. AE, D, MC, V.*

$$–$$$ 🏨 **Monterey Hotel.** Standard rooms in this 1904 structure, which was
restored in the late 1980s, are small but well appointed with reproduction
antique furniture; master suites have fireplaces and sunken baths. Room
rates include complimentary Continental breakfast and afternoon tea.
⊠ *406 Alvarado St., 93940,* ☎ *408/375–3184 or 800/727–0960,* FAX
408/373–2894. 44 rooms. Parking (fee). AE, D, DC, MC, V.

$–$$ 🏨 **Arbor Inn.** This stylish motel has a friendly, country-inn atmosphere. Continental breakfast is served in a pine-paneled lobby with a

tile fireplace. Rooms are light and airy, some with fireplaces and some with accessibility for visitors with disabilities. ⊠ *1058 Munras Ave., 93940,* ☎ *408/372–3381,* FAX *408/372–4687. 55 rooms. Hot tub. AE, D, DC, MC, V.*

$–$$ 🖭 **Monterey Motor Lodge.** A pleasant location on the edge of Mon-
★ terey's El Estero Park gives this motel an edge over its many competi-
tors along Munras Avenue. Indoor plants and a large, secluded courtyard with pool are other pluses. ⊠ *55 Aguajito Rd., 93940,* ☎ *408/372–8057 or 800/558–1900,* FAX *408/655–2933. 45 rooms. Restaurant, pool. AE, D, DC, MC, V.*

Nightlife and the Arts

BARS, CLUBS

Doc Ricketts' Lab (⊠ 95 Prescott St., ☎ 408/649–4241) hosts live bands nightly one block above Cannery Row. The varied program includes rock, blues, jazz, reggae, and folk.

Kalisa's (⊠ 851 Cannery Row, ☎ 408/372–3621) is a long-established, freewheeling café in a Cannery Row landmark building. It presents a potpourri of entertainment that can include belly dancing, flamenco, jazz, folk dancing, and magic.

Planet Gemini (⊠ 625 Cannery Row, ☎ 408/373–1449) presents comedy shows most nights, followed by dancing to live rock music. There is country-and-western music and dancing Wednesday nights.

Safari Club (⊠ Bay Park Hotel, 1425 Munras Ave., ☎ 408/649–1020) holds karaoke nights Thursday through Saturday.

Sly McFlys (⊠ 700 Cannery Row, ☎ 408/649–8050), a popular watering hole, has a publike atmosphere.

Virgo's (⊠ 2200 N. Fremont St., ☎ 408/375–6116) is Monterey's outpost for country-and-western music.

MUSIC FESTIVALS

Dixieland Monterey (⊠ 177 Webster St., Suite A-206, Monterey 93940, ☎ 408/443–5260), held on the first full weekend of March, presents Dixieland jazz bands in cabarets, restaurants, and hotel lounges on the Monterey waterfront.

Monterey Jazz Festival (⊠ Box JAZZ, Monterey 93942, ☎ 408/373–3366) attracts jazz and blues greats from around the world to the Monterey Fairgrounds on the third full weekend of September.

Monterey Bay Blues Festival (⊠ Box 1400, Seaside 93955, ☎ 408/394–2652) brings out blues fans in June to the Monterey Fairgrounds.

THEATER

California's First Theater (⊠ Scott and Pacific Sts., ☎ 408/375–4916) is home to the Troupers of the Gold Coast, who perform 19th-century melodramas.

Monterey Bay Theatrefest (☎ 408/622–0700) presents free, outdoor performances at Custom House Plaza on weekend afternoons and evenings during most of the summer.

Wharf Theater (⊠ Fisherman's Wharf, ☎ 408/649–2332) focuses on the American musical past and present.

Outdoor Activities and Sports

BEACHES

Around Monterey, the local waters are generally too cold and turbu-
lent for swimming. **Monterey Municipal Beach,** east of Wharf No. 2, has shallow waters that are warm and calm enough for wading.

BICYCLING

For bicycle rentals try **Bay Bikes** (⊠ 640 Wave St., ☎ 408/646–9090). **Adventures by the Sea Inc.** (⊠ 299 Cannery Row, ☎ 408/372–1807) rents bikes, kayaks, roller skates, and Rollerblades. Mopeds, motorcycles, and bikes can be rented from **Monterey Moped Adventures** (⊠ 1250 Del Monte Ave., ☎ 408/373–2696); a driver's license is required.

CAR RACING

Four major races take place each year on the 2.2-mile, 11-turn **Laguna Seca Raceway** (⊠ 1021 Monterey–Salinas Hwy., ☎ 408/648–5100 or 800/327–7322; in CA, 800/367–9939). They range from Indianapolis 500–style races to a historic car race with more than 300 restored race cars from earlier eras.

FISHING

Half- and full-day fishing trips can be arranged by **Monterey Sport Fishing** (⊠ 96 Fisherman's Wharf, ☎ 408/372–2203 or 800/200–2203), **Randy's Fishing Trips** (⊠ 66 Fisherman's Wharf, ☎ 408/372–7440), and **Sam's Fishing Fleet** (⊠ 84 Fisherman's Wharf, ☎ 408/372–0577).

GOLF

Laguna Seca Golf Club (⊠ 10520 York Rd., off Hwy. 68, ☎ 408/373–3701), a course with an 18-hole layout updated by Robert Trent Jones Jr., has a $55 greens fee (cart rental $25) for nonmembers.

Old Del Monte Golf Course (⊠ 1300 Sylvan Rd., ☎ 408/373–2436) has the most reasonable greens fees in the area: $50 per player plus $15 cart rental, with an $18 twilight special after 2:30 in winter and 4:30 in summer.

KAYAKING

Monterey Bay Kayaks (⊠ 693 Del Monte Ave., ☎ 408/373–5357 or 800/649–5357 in CA) has rentals, classes, and guided natural-history tours.

ROLLER SKATING

Del Monte Gardens (⊠ 2020 Del Monte Ave., ☎ 408/375–3202), an old-fashioned rink, rents skates.

SCUBA DIVING

Aquarius Dive Shops (⊠ 2040 Del Monte Ave., ☎ 408/375–1933; 32 Cannery Row, Suite 4, ☎ 408/375–6605) gives diving lessons, rents equipment, and operates guided dive tours. Call ☎ 408/657–1020 for **local scuba-diving conditions.**

TENNIS

Monterey Tennis Center (☎ 408/372–0172) has details about facilities.

WHALE WATCHING

Monterey Sport Fishing (⊠ 96 Fisherman's Wharf, ☎ 408/372–2203 or 800/200–2203), **Randy's Fishing Trips** (⊠ 66 Fisherman's Wharf, ☎ 408/372–7440), and **Sam's Fishing Fleet** (⊠ 84 Fisherman's Wharf, ☎ 408/372–0577) operate whale-watching expeditions.

Shopping

John Riley Golf (⊠ 601 Wave St., ☎ 408/373–8855) carries custom-made golf clubs. **Loes Hinse** (⊠ 542 Lighthouse Ave., ☎ 408/373–7553) is the well-kept secret of locals who prefer to wear original designs. **Old Monterey Book Co.** (⊠ 136 Bonifacio Pl. off Alvarado St., ☎ 408/372–3111) specializes in rare old books and prints. **Sea Fantasies** (⊠ 400 Cannery Row, ☎ 408/375–5033) owner Lee Austin collects rare pearls, precious coral, and ancient marine fossils on adventures to Fiji, India, and West Africa. He designs furniture, sculpture, and jewelry with his finds.

Pacific Grove

3 mi south of Monterey on Hwy. 1 to Hwy. 68; from Cannery Row, Wave St. becomes Ocean View Blvd. at Monterey–Pacific Grove border.

If not for the dramatic strip of coastline in its backyard, Pacific Grove could easily pass for a typical small town in the Heartland. Beginning as a summer retreat for church groups more than a century ago, the town recalls its prim and proper Victorian heritage in the host of tiny board-and-batten cottages and stately mansions lining its streets.

Even before the church groups migrated here, however, Pacific Grove had been receiving thousands of annual guests in the form of bright orange-and-black monarch butterflies. Known as Butterfly Town USA, Pacific Grove is the winter home of monarchs that migrate south from Canada and the Pacific Northwest to take residence in the pine and eucalyptus groves between October and March. The sight of a mass of butterflies hanging from the branches like a long, fluttering veil is unforgettable.

A prime way to enjoy Pacific Grove is to walk or bicycle along its 3 miles of city-owned shoreline, a cliff-top area following Ocean View Boulevard that is landscaped with succulents and native plants and has plenty of park benches on which to sit and gaze at the sea. A variety of marine and bird life can be spotted here, including colonies of cormorants drawn to the massive rocks rising out of the surf.

20 21 The **Pryor House** (⊠ 429 Ocean View Blvd.) is a massive shingled structure with a leaded- and beveled-glass doorway. **Green Gables** (⊠ 5th St. and Ocean View Blvd.), a romantic Swiss Gothic–style mansion with steeply peaked gables and stained-glass windows, is now a bed-and-breakfast inn.

Lovers Point Park, on Ocean View Boulevard midway along the waterfront, has a grassy area with a gorgeous coastal view. A sheltered beach there has a children's pool and picnic area. Glass-bottom boat rides, which permit viewing of the plant and sea life below, are available in summer.

★ ☺ 22 At **Point Piños Light Station,** the oldest continuously operating lighthouse on the West Coast, visitors can learn about the lighting and foghorn operations and wander through a small museum containing historical memorabilia from the U.S. Coast Guard. ⊠ *Asilomar Ave. between Ocean View Blvd. and Lighthouse Ave.,* ☎ *408/648–3116.* ⊡ *Free.* ☺ *Weekends 1–4.*

23 Although many of their original nesting grounds have vanished, the **Monarch Grove Sanctuary** (⊠ 1073 Lighthouse Ave.), is still a good spot for viewing butterflies. It is adjacent to the Butterfly Grove Inn.

☺ 24 If you are in Pacific Grove when the monarch butterflies aren't, an approximation of this annual miracle is on exhibit at the **Pacific Grove Museum of Natural History.** In addition to a finely crafted butterfly-tree exhibit, the museum displays a collection of 400 mounted birds native to Monterey County and screens a film about the monarch butterfly. ⊠ *165 Forest Ave.,* ☎ *408/648–3116.* ⊡ *Free.* ☺ *Tues.–Sun. 10–5.*

★ A beautiful coastal area in Pacific Grove is **Asilomar State Beach,** on Sunset Drive between Point Piños and the Del Monte Forest. The 100 acres of dunes, tidal pools, and pocket-size beaches form one of the region's richest areas for marine life.

Dining and Lodging

$$$ ✕ **Melac's.** Complementing Pacific Grove's quiet charm, this warm country restaurant is as friendly as its food is delicious. French-born Jacques

Melac greets his guests personally and enjoys helping them pair wines with wife Janet's menu. The couple met in Paris when she attended the Cordon Bleu School, where she graduated first in her class. At Melac's she cooks each generously portioned dish to order, optimizing on seasonal local ingredients. Request the grilled quail with roasted garlic and Oregon chanterelles, seafood cassoulet, or roasted duckling with port and fresh figs, if they're on the menu, and settle in for the evening. ✉ *663 Lighthouse Ave.,* ☎ *408/375–1743. AE, DC, MC. V. Closed Sun.–Mon. No lunch Sat.*

$$$ ✕ **Old Bath House.** A romantic, nostalgic atmosphere permeates this
★   converted bathhouse overlooking the water at Lovers Point. The Continental menu here makes the most of local seafood and produce. When they're available, the salmon and Monterey Bay prawns are particularly worth ordering. The restaurant has a less expensive menu for late-afternoon diners. ✉ *620 Ocean View Blvd.,* ☎ *408/375–5195. AE, D, DC, MC, V. No lunch.*

$$ ✕ **Fandango.** With its stone walls and country furniture, this restaurant has the earthy feel of a southern European farmhouse. Complementing the ambience are the robust flavors of the cuisine, which ranges from southern France, Italy, Spain, and Greece to North Africa, from couscous and paella to cannelloni. ✉ *223 17th St.,* ☎ *408/372–3456. AE, D, DC, MC, V.*

$$ ✕ **The Tinnery.** This family-oriented restaurant serves pancakes and omelets for breakfast, burgers and other sandwiches for lunch. Broiled salmon with fresh Hollandaise sauce, mesquite-grilled meats, and English fish-and-chips are dinner-menu highlights. ✉ *631 Ocean View Blvd., at 17th St.,* ☎ *408/646–1040. Reservations not accepted. AE, D, DC, MC, V.*

$–$$ ✕ **Consuelo's.** Meals here start with complimentary quesadillas, presented on a huge platter, then move into fare such as fajitas, tostadas, enchiladas, marinated chicken, and flautas. There's a children's menu as well. If the weather's nice you can sit outside under the shade of a huge Indian pine tree. ✉ *361 Lighthouse Ave.,* ☎ *408/372–8211. AE, MC, V.*

$–$$ ✕ **El Cocodrilo.** No, El Cocodrilo Rotisserie and Seafood Grill doesn't serve crocodile, but it does serve alligator—in nuggets with sauce or in a small tureen called Gator Gumbo. The restaurant's main draws are its fun environment—overrun with wooden crocodiles, ant eaters, and toucans—and adventurous Latin American concoctions. Amazon catfish and bayou brochette are especially tasty, as are the *pupusas* (fancy quesadillas) and *tostaditas* (tortillas topped with green cashew salsa). If you can't decide what to order, try the Jamaican curry crabcakes and Bahamian chowder. The wine bar opens at 4 PM, and there's live jazz early on Thursday evenings. ✉ *701 Lighthouse Ave.,* ☎ *408/655–3311. AE, D, MC, V. Closed Tues.*

$–$$ ✕ **Gernot's.** The ornate Victorian-era Hart Mansion is a delightful setting in which to dine on seafood and game served with light sauces. Continental specialties include wild boar bourguignonne, roast venison, and veal medallions. ✉ *649 Lighthouse Ave.,* ☎ *408/646–1477. AE, MC, V. Closed Mon. No lunch.*

$ ✕ **Fishwife.** Good fresh fish with a Mexican twist makes this the locals' choice for lunch or a casual dinner. ✉ *Corner of Sunset Ave. and Asilomar Blvd. at the end of Hwy. 68,* ☎ *408/375–7107. Reservations essential on weekends. AE, D, DC, MC, V.*

$ ✕ **Peppers.** This cheerful white-walled café serves fresh seafood and traditional dishes from Mexico and Latin America. The red and green salsas are excellent. ✉ *170 Forest Ave.,* ☎ *408/373–6892. AE, D, DC, MC, V. Closed Tues. No dinner Mon.–Sat.*

$$$–$$$$ ⊡ **Martine Inn.** Most bed-and-breakfasts in Pacific Grove are Victo-
★   rian houses; this one is a pink stucco Mediterranean-style villa over-
looking the water. Its owners have assembled one of the most extensive
antiques collections of any California B&B, including a mahogany suite
exhibited at the 1893 Chicago World's Fair, movie costume designer
Edith Head's bedroom suite, and an 1860 Chippendale Revival four-
poster bed. A glassed-in parlor affords a stunning ocean view. Room
rates include full breakfast, wine, and hors d'oeuvres. ⊠ *255 Ocean
View Blvd., 93950,* ☎ *408/373–3388 or 800/852–5588,* FAX *408/373–
3896. 20 rooms. AE, MC, V.*

$$$–$$$$ ⊡ **Seven Gables Inn.** Four yellow-gabled clapboard buildings share a
corner lot and a breathtaking view of the ocean. The main house was
built in 1886, the other three between 1910 and 1940. Various-period
European antiques—gold-leaf mirrors, crystal chandeliers, inlaid wood
furnishings, and marble statues—create a formal atmosphere. The gra-
cious innkeeper, Susan Flatley, grew up in the house and shares her knowl-
edge about it and the area. Room rates include a full breakfast and
afternoon tea. ⊠ *555 Ocean View Blvd., 93950,* ☎ *408/372–4341.
14 rooms. Refrigerators. MC, V. No smoking indoors. 2-night mini-
mum weekends, 3-night minimum holiday weekends.*

$$–$$$$ ⊡ **The Centrella.** This handsome century-old Victorian mansion and
★   garden cottages two blocks from Lovers Point Beach has an attractive
garden, claw-foot bathtubs, and wicker and brass furnishings. Depending
on the time of day, a sideboard in the large parlor is laden with breakfast treats, cookies and fruit, sherry and wine, or hors d'oeuvres. ⊠
612 Central Ave., 93950, ☎ *408/372–3372 or 800/233–3372,* FAX
408/372–2036. 26 rooms, 2 with shared bath. AE, MC, V.

$$–$$$ ⊡ **Gosby House Inn.** Most of the rooms in this yellow Victorian bed-
and-breakfast in the town center have a private bath, and some have
fireplaces. The inn has an informal, country air; its innkeepers are knowledgeable and can supply tourism or restaurant suggestions. Room
rates include full breakfast, plus afternoon hors d'oeuvres served in a
sunny parlor or by the fireplace in the living room. ⊠ *643 Lighthouse
Ave., 93950,* ☎ *408/375–1287 or 800/527–8828,* FAX *408/655–9621.
22 rooms, 2 with shared bath. AE, MC, V.*

$$–$$$ ⊡ **Green Gables Inn.** Stained-glass windows framing an ornate fire-
★   place and other interior detail work compete with the spectacular bay
views at this century-old house built by a sea captain to house his mistress. Guest·rooms in a carriage house, perched on a hill out back, are
larger, have ocean views and more modern amenities, and afford more
privacy, though the rooms in the main house have more charm. The
breakfast buffet is tempting, but breakfast in bed is also an option; afternoon hors d'oeuvres are served with wine, sherry, or tea. ⊠ *104 5th
St., 93950,* ☎ *408/375–2095 or 800/722–1776,* FAX *408/375–5437.
11 rooms, 4 with shared bath. AE, MC, V.*

$$ ⊡ **Asilomar Conference Center.** A summer camp–like atmosphere per-
vades this assortment of 28 rustic but comfortable lodges in the mid-
dle of a 105-acre state park across from the beach. Breakfast is included.
⊠ *800 Asilomar Blvd., Box 537, 93950,* ☎ *408/372–8016,* FAX
408/372–7227. 314 rooms. Cafeteria, pool. MC, V.

Outdoor Activities and Sports

GOLF

Pacific Grove Municipal Golf Course (⊠ 77 Asilomar Blvd., ☎ 408/648–
3177) has greens fees—$24 to $28; cart rental $23—at only a fraction
of those in nearby Pebble Beach. The course has spectacular ocean views
on its back nine—and ice-plant-covered sand dunes that make keep-
ing on the fairway a must. Tee times may be reserved up to seven days
in advance.

TENNIS

Pacific Grove Municipal Courts (☎ 408/648–3129) has information about the town's public tennis courts.

Shopping

American Tin Cannery Outlet Center (✉ 125 Ocean View Blvd., ☎ 408/372–1442) carries leading designer clothing, jewelry and accessories, along with home decorating items, at 25%–65% discounts. **Wooden Nickel** (✉ Central and Fountain Aves., ☎ 408/646–8050) sells country-French accent pieces for the home.

17-Mile Drive and Pebble Beach

Off Sunset Dr. in Pacific Grove, or Hwy. 1 at North San Antonio Rd. in Carmel.

Some sightseers balk at the $6.50-per-car fee, but most agree that it is
★ well worth the price to explore **17-Mile Drive,** an 8,400-acre microcosm of the Monterey coastal landscape. Once inside, you see primordial nature preserved in quiet harmony with palatial estates. All along 17-Mile Drive are rare Monterey cypress, trees so gnarled and twisted that Robert Louis Stevenson once described them as "ghosts fleeing before the wind."

㉕ **Bird Rock,** the largest of several islands at the southern end of the Monterey Country Club's golf course teems with harbor seals, sea lions,
㉖ cormorants, and pelicans. Sea creatures and birds also make use of **Seal Rock,** the larger of a group of islands just south of Bird Rock. The most
㉗ photographed tree is the **Lone Cypress,** a weather-sculpted tree growing out of a precipitous, rocky outcropping above the waves. A parking area makes it possible to stop for a view of the Lone Cypress, but walking out to it is no longer allowed.

Many of the stately homes along 17-Mile Drive reflect the classic Monterey or Spanish Mission style typical of the region. A standout
㉘ is the **Crocker Marble Palace,** a waterfront estate designed after a Byzantine castle. This baroque mansion is easily identifiable by its dozens of marble arches. Underground pipes heat water in the estate's beach.

Perhaps no more famous concentration of celebrated golf courses exists
㉙ ists anywhere in the world. Most notable is the **Pebble Beach Golf Links,** with its famous 18th hole, around which the ocean plays a major role. Even if you're not a golfer, views of impeccable greens can be enjoyed over a drink or lunch at the Lodge at Pebble Beach or the Inn at Spanish Bay, the two resorts located along the drive.

Dining and Lodging

$$$$ ✕🖫 **Inn at Spanish Bay.** This 270-room resort sprawls across a breathtaking stretch of shoreline along 17-Mile Drive. Under the same management as the Lodge at Pebble Beach (☞ *below*), the inn has a slightly more casual feel, though its 600-square-foot rooms are no less luxurious. The inn has its own tennis courts and golf course, but guests also have privileges at all the Lodge facilities. For dinner, the excellent Bay Club restaurant, which serves haute Italian cuisine, overlooks the coastline and the golf links, or try Roy's Restaurant for more casual and innovative Euro-Asian fare. ✉ *Box 1589, 2700 17-Mile Dr., 93953,* ☎ *408/647–7500 or 800/654–9300,* 🆁🅰🆇 *408/647–7443. 270 rooms. 3 restaurants, pool, tennis, health club. AE, DC, MC, V.*

$$$$ ✕🖫 **Lodge at Pebble Beach.** Quietly luxurious rooms with fireplaces
★ and wonderful views set the tone at this renowned resort, built in 1919. The golf course, tennis club, and equestrian center are also highly regarded. Guests of the lodge have privileges at the Inn at Spanish Bay.

Carmel and 17-Mile Drive

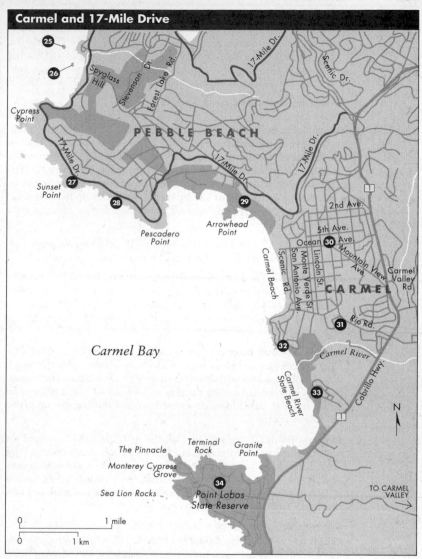

Bird Rock, **25**
Carmel Mission, **31**
Carmel Plaza, **30**
Carmel River State Park, **33**
Crocker Marble Palace, **28**
Lone Cypress, **27**
Pebble Beach Golf Links, **29**
Point Lobos State Reserve, **34**
Seal Rock, **26**
Tor House, **32**

Overlooking the 18th green, the very fine Club XIX restaurant is an intimate, café-style spot serving classic French preparations of veal, lamb, and duck, as well as foie gras and caviar. ⊠ *Box 1418, 17-Mile Dr., 93953,* ☎ *408/624–3811 or 800/654–9300,* FAX *408/625–8598. 161 rooms. 3 restaurants, coffee shop, lounge, pool, massage, sauna, golf, tennis, health club, horseback riding, beach, bicycles. AE, DC, MC, V.*

Outdoor Activities and Sports

GOLF

Pebble Beach Golf Links (⊠ 17-Mile Dr., ☎ 408/625–8518) takes center stage each winter during the AT&T Pro-Am (known for years as the "Crosby"), where show-business celebrities and pros team up for what is perhaps the nation's most glamorous golf tournament. Golfers from around the world make this course one of the busiest in the region, despite greens fees of $225 plus $20 for a cart. Individual reservations for nonguests can only be made one day in advance on a space-available basis.

Peter Hay (⊠ 17-Mile Dr., ☎ 408/624–3811), a nine-hole pitch-and-putt course, charges $10 per person, no reservations necessary.

Poppy Hills (⊠ 17-Mile Dr., ☎ 408/625–2035), designed in 1986 by Robert Trent Jones Jr., was named by *Golf Digest* as one of the world's top 20 courses. Greens fees for the general public are $105, cart $30 additional. Individuals may reserve up to one month in advance, groups up to a year.

Spanish Bay Golf Links (⊠ North end of 17-Mile Dr., ☎ 408/624–3811), which hugs a choice stretch of shoreline, is designed in the rugged manner of a traditional Scottish course with sand dunes and coastal marshes interspersed among the greens. Fees are $135 per player plus $20 cart rental; individuals are advised to make reservations up to two months in advance.

Spyglass Hill (⊠ Spyglass Hill Rd., ☎ 408/624–3811), where the holes are long and unforgiving, is a famous Pebble Beach course. With the first five holes bordering on the Pacific, and the rest reaching deep into the Del Monte Forest, the views offer some consolation. Greens fees run $175 plus $20 for a cart; reservations are essential and may be made up to one month in advance.

HORSEBACK RIDING

Pebble Beach Equestrian Center (⊠ Portola Rd. and Alva La., ☎ 408/624–2756) rents horses, a great way to enjoy the Del Monte Forest, which has 26 miles of bridle trails.

Carmel

5 mi south of Monterey on Hwy. 1 (or via 17-Mile Drive's Carmel Gate).

Although the community has grown quickly over the years and its population quadruples with tourists on weekends and during the summer, Carmel retains its identity as a quaint village; buildings still have no street numbers, and live music is banned in the local watering holes. You can wander the side streets at your own pace, poking into hidden courtyards and stopping at Hansel-and-Gretel-like cafés for tea and crumpets.

Downtown Carmel's chief lure is shopping. Its main street, **Ocean Avenue,** is a charming (except to architectural purists) mishmash of ersatz English Tudor, Mediterranean, and other styles. **Carmel Plaza,** in the east end of the village proper, is one of several newer malls. It has more than 50 shops, restaurants, and small branches of major department stores.

It helps to be pushy in airports.

Introducing the revolutionary new TransPorter™ from American Tourister.® It's the first suitcase you can push around without a fight. TransPorter's™ exclusive four-wheel design lets you push it in front of you with almost no effort–the wheels take the weight. Or pull it on two wheels if you choose. You can even stack on other bags and use it like a luggage cart.

Stable 4-wheel design.

TransPorter™ is designed like a dresser, with built-in shelves to organize your belongings. Or collapse the shelves and pack it like a traditional suitcase. Inside, there's a suiter feature to help keep suits and dresses from wrinkling. When push comes to shove, you can't beat a TransPorter™ For more information on how you can be this pushy, call 1-800-542-1300.

Shelves collapse on command.

American Tourister®

Making travel less primitive.®

Use your MCI Card® for the easy way to call when traveling.

MCI ★ Calling Card

415 555 1234 2244
J.D. SMITH

Convenience on the road

- Your MCI Card® number is your home number, guaranteed.
- Pre-programmed to speed dial to your home.
- Call from any phone in the U.S.

1 - 8 0 0 - 7 5 4 - 8 9 4 1

http://www.mci.com

Before it became an art colony in the early 20th century and long before it became a shopping and browsing mecca, Carmel was an important religious center in the early days of Spanish California. That heritage is preserved in the Mission San Carlos Borromeo del Rio

★ ③ Carmelo, more commonly known as the **Carmel Mission.** Founded in 1770, it served as headquarters for the mission system in California under Father Junípero Serra. Adjoining the stone church is a tranquil garden planted with California poppies and a series of museum rooms that include an early kitchen, Father Serra's spartan sleeping quarters, and the oldest college library in California. ⊠ *Rio Rd. and Lasuen Dr.,* ☎ *408/624–3600.* ⚲ *$2.* ☉ *Sept.–May, Mon.–Sat. 9:30–4:30, Sun. 10:30–4:30; June–Aug., Mon.–Sat. 9:30–7:30, Sun. 10:30–7:30.*

Scattered throughout the pines in Carmel are the houses and cottages that were built for the steady stream of writers, artists, and photographers who discovered the area decades ago. Among the most impressive

③ dwellings is **Tor House,** a stone cottage built by the poet Robinson Jeffers in 1919 on a craggy knoll overlooking the sea. The low-ceilinged rooms are filled with portraits, books, and unusual art objects, including a white stone from the Great Pyramid in Egypt. The highlight of the small estate is Hawk Tower, a detached edifice set with stones from the Carmel coastline, as well as one from the Great Wall of China. Within the tower is a Gothic-style room, which served as a retreat for the poet's wife, Una, an accomplished musician. The docents who lead tours are well informed about the poet's work and life. ⊠ *26304 Ocean View Ave.,* ☎ *408/624–1813 or 408/624–1840.* ⚲ *$5. No children under 12.* ☉ *Tours Fri. and Sat. 10–3; reservations suggested.*

Carmel's greatest beauty is its rugged coastline, with pine and cypress

③ forests and countless inlets. **Carmel River State Park** stretches for 106 acres along Carmel Bay. On sunny days the waters appear nearly as turquoise as those of the Caribbean. The park has a sugar-white beach with high dunes and a nature preserve that provides excellent bird-watching for pelicans, kingfishers, hawks, and sandpipers. ⊠ *Off Scenic Rd., south of Carmel Beach,* ☎ *408/626–4909.* ☉ *Daily 9 AM–sunset.*

③ **Point Lobos State Reserve,** a 456-acre headland, lies just south of Carmel. There are few roads, and the best way to explore is to walk along one of the many hiking trails. The Cypress Grove Trail leads through a forest of rare Monterey cypress (one of only two natural groves remaining), clinging to the rocks above an emerald-green cove. Sea Lion Point Trail is a good place to observe sea lions. From the other trails you can spot otters, harbor seals, and (during certain times of the year) migrating whales. Part of the reserve is an undersea marine park open to qualified scuba divers. If you have a dog, note that state law prohibits dogs within the reserve. ⊠ *Hwy. 1,* ☎ *408/624–4909, or 800/444–7275 to reserve for scuba diving.* ⚲ *$6 per vehicle.* ☉ *May–Sept., daily 9–6:30; Oct.–Apr., daily 9–4:30.*

Dining and Lodging

$$$ ✗ **Anton and Michel.** Superb Continental cuisine is served at this elegant restaurant in Carmel's shopping district. The tender lamb dishes are fantastic and well complemented by the extensive wine list. The real treats, however, are the flaming desserts. Outdoor dining is available in the courtyard. ⊠ *Ocean and 7th Aves.,* ☎ *408/624–2406. AE, D, DC, MC, V.*

$$$ ✗ **Cafe Gringo.** Maybe it's not 100% Mexican, but Gringo has its own style—something the chef calls New Wave Mexican cuisine. It means dishes such as fresh tamales with artichokes and mushrooms tossed in for a more exotic taste, or quesadilla with Monterey Jack and manchego cheeses, bacon, and roasted *pasilla* chili topped with a mango salsa.

The full bar serves Mexican beers; South American, Chilean, and local wines; and, of course, margaritas. Service is first class. ⊠ *Paseo San Carlos Courtyard, San Carlos Ave. between Ocean and 7th Aves.,* ☏ *408/626–8226. AE, MC, V.*

$$$ ✕ **Crème Carmel.** This bright and airy small restaurant has a California-French menu that changes according to season. Specialties include charbroiled Muscovy duck with celery-root puree and green peppercorn, and beef tenderloin prepared with cabernet. ⊠ *San Carlos St., near 7th Ave.,* ☏ *408/624–0444. AE, DC, MC, V. No lunch.*

$$$ ✕ **French Poodle.** Specialties on the traditional French menu at this intimate restaurant include duck breast in port and an excellent abalone; for dessert, the "floating island" is delicious. ⊠ *Junipero and 5th Aves.,* ☏ *408/624–8643. AE, DC, MC, V. Closed Sun., Wed. No lunch.*

$$–$$$ ✕ **Casanova.** Southern French and northern Italian cuisine come together in one of the most romantic restaurants in Carmel. A heated outdoor garden and extensive list of more than 1,000 domestic and imported wines enhance the dining experience. Specialties include housemade pasta and desserts. ⊠ *5th Ave. between San Carlos and Mission,* ☏ *408/625–0501. AE, D, DC, MC, V.*

$$ ✕ **Flaherty's Seafood Grill & Oyster Bar.** This bright blue-and-white-tiled fish house cranks out steaming bowls of mussels, clams, cioppino, and crab chowder. Seafood pastas and daily fresh fish selections are also available. ⊠ *6th Ave. and San Carlos St.,* ☏ *408/624–0311. AE, MC, V.*

$$ ✕ **Hog's Breath Inn.** Although it is resting somewhat on its Hollywood laurels, the eatery co-owned by actor and former Carmel mayor Clint Eastwood has a convivial publike atmosphere with roaring fireplaces and rustic decor. The food is no-nonsense: meat and seafood entrées with sautéed vegetables. Many items—Dirty Harry Burger, Sudden Impact (Polish sausage) sandwich, etcetera—are named after Eastwood movies. ⊠ *San Carlos St. and 5th Ave.,* ☏ *408/625–1044. Reservations not accepted. AE, DC, MC, V.*

$$ ✕ **Kincaid's Bistro on the Boulevard.** Robert Kincaid's namesake bistro
★ reflects his culinary roots at Monterey's ever-popular Fresh Cream. With Kincaid's, he takes French bistro cuisine farther into the country. Cassoulet made with white beans, duck confit, rabbit sausage, and garlic prawns is always on the stove and best enjoyed with a rustic red wine. Dried sage and lavender hanging from exposed ceiling beams, rag-painted floors, and ochre-washed walls make you feel as if you've stepped into an old farmhouse in Provence. Be sure to leave room for dessert, particularly the soufflé with lemon and orange zest or the chocolate bag with chocolate shake. ⊠ *Crossroads Center, 217 Crossroads Blvd.,* ☏ *408/624–9626. AE, D, MC, V. Closed Sun. No lunch Sat.*

$$ ✕ **La Bohème.** This campy, offbeat restaurant offers a one-selection, fixed-price menu, which includes soup and salad. You may be bumping elbows with your neighbor in the cozy, faux-European-village courtyard, but the predominantly French cuisine is delicious, and the atmosphere is friendly. ⊠ *Dolores St. and 7th Ave.,* ☏ *408/624–7500. Reservations not accepted. MC, V. No lunch.*

$$ ✕ **Lugano Swiss Bistro.** Geography is destiny, and good Swiss cooking derives its singular character from a blend of French, Italian, and German cuisines. At Lugano, fondue is the centerpiece. The house specialty is an original version made with Gruyère, Emmentaler, and Appenzeller—custom has it that if a lady loses her dipping cube in the fondue she pays with a kiss; if a man loses one, he buys a bottle of wine. Rosemary chicken, plum-basted duck, and fennel pork loin rotate on the rotisserie to the sound of accordion music. Call ahead for a table in the back room, with its hand-painted street scene of the chef's native Lugano. ⊠ *The Barnyard, Hwy. 1 and Carmel Valley Rd.,* ☏ *408/626–3779. AE, MC, V. Closed Mon.*

$$ ✕ **Pine Inn.** An old favorite of locals, this Victorian-style restaurant serves traditional American fare. Outdoor dining is also available at tables set up around the gazebo. ⊠ *Ocean Ave. and Monte Verde St.,* ☎ *408/624–3851. AE, D, DC, MC, V.*

$$ ✕ **Raffaello.** Sparkling, elegant Raffaello serves excellent northern Italian cuisine, superb pasta, Monterey Bay prawns with garlic butter, local sole poached in champagne, and the specialty of the house, veal Piemontese. ⊠ *Mission St., between Ocean and 7th Aves.,* ☎ *408/624– 1541. AE, DC, MC, V. Closed Tues. and 1st wk in Jan. No lunch.*

$$ ✕ **Simpson's.** Not the newest or most creative place in town, this dependable restaurant has warm service and a good wine list. Family run— a daughter brings you to your table, one son is in the kitchen, another tends bar, and Mom manages the room—it maintains a comforting, old-fashioned American ambience. A large, open dining room, tables with white tablecloths, lots of flowers, and kitschy dinner Muzak set the mood for steak and potatoes, rice and seafood. ⊠ *San Carlos St. and 5th Ave.,* ☎ *408/624–5755. AE, MC, V. No lunch. Closed Sun.*

$–$$ ✕ **Rio Grill.** The best bets in this Santa Fe–style setting are the meat
★ and seafood (such as fresh tuna or salmon) cooked over an oakwood grill. ⊠ *101 Crossroads Blvd., Hwy. 1 and Rio Rd.,* ☎ *408/625–5436. AE, MC, V.*

$ ✕ **Friar Tuck's.** This busy, wood-paneled coffee shop serves huge omelets at breakfast and at lunch dishes up 16 varieties of hamburgers. ⊠ *5th Ave. and Dolores St.,* ☎ *408/624–4274. Reservations not accepted. No credit cards. No dinner Sept.–June.*

$ ✕ **Thunderbird Bookstore and Restaurant.** At this well-stocked bookstore, you can also enjoy a light lunch or dinner, or order a cappuccino and a pastry and browse among the books. A hearty beef soup, sandwiches, popovers, and cheesecake are the best-sellers. ⊠ *3600 The Barnyard, Hwy. 1 and Carmel Valley Rd.,* ☎ *408/624–9414. AE, MC, V.*

$$$$ ✕🖾 **Highlands Inn.** An unparalleled location on high cliffs above the
★ Pacific just south of Carmel gives the Highlands views that stand out even in a region famous for them. Accommodations are in plush spa suites and condominium-style units with wood-burning fireplaces and ocean-view decks; some have full kitchens. The specialties on the contemporary French menu at the inn's Pacific's Edge restaurant include fillet of beef with blue-cheese potato gratin, roasted shallots, and a Portobello mushroom sauce; grilled Atlantic salmon wrapped in pancetta with local baby artichokes; and a succulent honey-roasted breast of duck. ⊠ *Hwy. 1, Box 1700, 93921,* ☎ *408/624–3801 or 800/538–9525; in CA, 800/682–4811; restaurant 408/624–0471;* 🖹🖹 *408/626–1574. 142 rooms. 2 restaurants, lounges, pool, hot tub. AE, D, DC, MC, V.*

$$$$ 🖾 **Carriage House Inn.** This small inn with a wood-shingled exterior has rooms with open-beam ceilings, fireplaces, down comforters, and sunken baths. Continental breakfast, wine, and hors d'oeuvres are included in the room rates. ⊠ *Junipero Ave., between 7th and 8th Aves., Box 1900, 93921,* ☎ *408/625–2585 or 800/422–4732,* 🖹🖹 *408/624– 2967. 13 rooms. AE, D, DC, MC, V.*

$$$–$$$$ 🖾 **La Playa Hotel.** Now a pink, Mediterranean-style villa, the hotel was originally built in 1902 by Norwegian artist Christopher Jorgensen for his bride, a member of the famous Ghirardelli chocolate clan. The Terrace Grill and central garden, riotous with color, provide wonderful views of Carmel's magnificent coastline. All rooms are done in rose, beige, and blue tones, with hand-carved furniture. Some accommodations have ocean views. You can also opt for a cottage; all have full kitchens and a patio or terrace, and some have wood-burning fireplaces. ⊠ *Camino Real at*

8th Ave., Box 900, 93921, ☎ 408/624–6476 or 800/582–8900, ℻ 408/624–7966. 80 rooms. Restaurant, pool. AE, DC, MC, V.

$$$–$$$$ 🏨 **Tickle Pink Motor Inn.** This inn perched on a towering cliff has spec-
★ tacular vistas of the Big Sur coastline, which you can contemplate from your private balcony. Fall asleep to the sound of surf crashing below and wake up to Continental breakfast and the morning paper in bed. If you prefer the company of fellow travelers, breakfast is also served buffet-style in the lounge, as are complimentary wine and cheese in the afternoon. Many rooms have wood-burning fireplaces, and there are four luxurious spa suites. The staff is friendly and ready to please. ⊠ *155 Highlands Dr., Carmel 93923, ☎ 408/624–1244 or 800/635–4774, ℻ 408/626–9516. 34 rooms. Outdoor hot tub. AE, MC, V.*

$$–$$$$ 🏨 **Lobos Lodge.** Pleasant white stucco units set amid cypresses, oaks, and pines on the edge of the business district have fireplaces. Some have private brick patios. Continental breakfast is included. ⊠ *Monte Verde St. and Ocean Ave., Box L–1, 93921, ☎ 408/624–3874, ℻ 408/624–0135. 30 rooms. AE, MC, V.*

$$–$$$$ 🏨 **Mission Ranch.** Clint Eastwood rescued this venerable inn, originally built in the 1850s. The main farmhouse, set in pastureland next to the ocean, where sheep still graze, has six rooms around a Victorian par-
lor; other options include cottages, a hayloft, and a bunkhouse. Hand-made quilts, princess-and-the-pea stuffed mattresses, and carved wooden beds round out the country ambience. ⊠ *26270 Dolores St., 93923, ☎ 408/624–6436 or 800/538–8221, ℻ 408/626–4163. 31 rooms. Restaurant, piano bar, tennis courts, exercise room, pro shop. AE, D, DC, MC, V.*

$$–$$$$ 🏨 **Pine Inn.** A traditional favorite of generations of Carmel visitors has
★ Victorian-style decor complete with grandfather clock, padded fabric panels, antique tapestries, and marble-topped furnishings. Only four blocks from the beach, the inn has its own brick courtyard of specialty shops. ⊠ *Ocean Ave. and Lincoln St., Box 250, 93921, ☎ 408/624–3851 or 800/228–3851, ℻ 408/624–3030. 49 rooms. Dining room. AE, D, DC, MC, V.*

$$$ 🏨 **Cobblestone Inn.** Quilts and country antiques, stone fireplaces in
★ guest rooms and the sitting-room area, and a complimentary gourmet breakfast buffet and afternoon tea contribute to the homey feel at this English-style inn. ⊠ *8th and Junipero Aves., Box 3185, 93921, ☎ 408/625–5222, ℻ 408/625–0478. 24 rooms. AE, DC, MC, V. No smoking.*

$$$ 🏨 **Tally Ho Inn.** This is one of the few inns in Carmel's center that have good views out over the ocean. There are penthouse units with fire-places and a pretty English garden courtyard. Continental breakfast and after-dinner brandy are included. ⊠ *Monte Verde St. and 6th Ave., Box 3726, 93921, ☎ 408/624–2232 or 800/624–2290, ℻ 408/624–2661. 14 rooms. AE, D, MC, V.*

$$–$$$ 🏨 **Best Western Carmel Mission Inn.** This modern inn on the edge of Carmel Valley has a lushly landscaped pool and hot tub area and is close to the Barnyard and Crossroads shopping centers. Rooms are large, some with spacious decks. ⊠ *3665 Rio Rd., at Hwy. 1, 92923, ☎ 408/624–1841 or 800/348–9090, ℻ 408/624–8684. 165 rooms. Restaurant, bar, pool, hot tub. AE, D, DC, MC, V.*

$$–$$$ 🏨 **Cypress Inn.** For more than 60 years, this inn has been known for its bright white Moorish Mediterranean facade with Spanish tile roof. When Doris Day became part owner in 1988, she added her own touches. Posters from her many movies and a couple of gold albums grace the walls of the cocktail lounge; photo albums of her favorite canines top the coffee table in the "living-room" lobby. Although a gen-erous breakfast is served in a sunny breakfast room, choose to enjoy your morning meal in the garden courtyard surrounded by bougainvillea, a turquoise sky, and a blue jay or two at the next table. ✉ *Lincoln St. and 7th Ave., 93921,* ☎ *408/624–3871 or 800/443–7443,* FAX *408/624–8216. 34 rooms. AE, MC. V.*

Nightlife and the Arts

MUSIC

Carmel Bach Festival (☎ 408/624–2046 or 800/513–2224) has presented the work of Johann Sebastian Bach and his contemporaries in concerts and recitals for more than 50 years.

Chamber Music Society of the Monterey Peninsula (☎ 408/625–2212) presents well-known chamber groups in concert and holds an annual chamber-music contest for young musicians.

Monterey County Symphony (☎ 408/624–8511) performs a series of classical to pop concerts October through May in Salinas and Carmel.

THEATER

Contemporary Carmel Theatre Festival (☎ 408/655–3200) presents the work of modern playwrights and boundary-breaking performance ensembles.

Pacific Repertory Theater (☎ 408/622–0700) specializes in contemporary comedy and drama.

Sunset Community Cultural Center (✉ San Carlos St. between 8th and 10th Aves., ☎ 408/624–3996), which presents concerts, lectures, and headline performers throughout the year, is the Monterey Bay area's top venue for the performing arts.

Shopping

ART GALLERIES

Carmel Art Association (✉ Dolores St. between 5th and 6th Aves., ☎ 408/624–6176) exhibits the paintings, sculpture, and prints of local artists.

Cottage Gallery (✉ Mission St. and 6th Ave., ☎ 408/624–7888) focuses on traditional impressionism and classical realism.

Fireside Gallery (✉ Dolores St. between 5th and 6th Aves. in Pantiles Court, ☎ 408/624–1416) represents internationally known artists.

Highlands Sculpture Gallery (✉ Dolores St. between 5th and 6th Aves., ☎ 408/624–0535) is devoted to indoor and outdoor sculpture, primarily work done in stone, bronze, wood, and metal.

LaRue Gallery (✉ Dolores St. between 5th and 6th Aves., ☎ 408/625–5636) shows impressionism, western realism, and some folk art.

Masterpiece Gallery (✉ Dolores St. and 6th Ave., ☎ 408/624–2163) exhibits early California impressionists and Bay Area figurative art.

Photography West Gallery (✉ Ocean Ave. and Dolores St., ☎ 408/625–1587) exhibits 20th-century photography by artists such as Ansel Adams, who lived and worked in the region for many years.

BOOKS

Blake's Bookshop (✉ The Crossroads, Hwy. 1 and Rio Rd., ☎ 408/626–1010) is a cozy hideaway where you can browse through a full range of fiction, nonfiction, and children's books by a fireplace in an Old English-style library.

CHILDREN

Mischievous Rabbit (✉ Lincoln Ave. between 7th and Ocean Aves., ☎ 408/624–6854) sells toys, nursery bedding, books, music boxes, party supplies, china, and hand-painted and handmade clothing embellished with characters from *Winnie the Pooh* tales.

CLOTHING AND ACCESSORIES

Madrigal (⊠ Carmel Plaza and San Carlos Ave., ☎ 408/624–3477) specializes in sportswear, sweaters, and accessories for women and men.

Pat Areias (⊠ Lincoln Ave. south of Ocean Ave., ☎ 408/626–8668) puts a respectfully modern spin on the Mexican tradition of great silversmithing—one that acknowledges the trade's Spanish and Indian roots—with a line of sterling silver buckles, belts, and jewelry.

GARDEN

Shop in the Garden (⊠ Lincoln Ave. near Ocean Ave., ☎ 408/624–6047) is a secret garden, hidden in a courtyard behind shops. You'll hear the babble of its outdoor fountains and tinkle of its wind chimes before you see it.

MEMORABILIA

Golf Arts and Imports (⊠ Dolores St. and 6th Ave., ☎ 408/625–4488) carries antique golf prints and clubs, rare golf books, and other golfing memorabilia.

Carmel Valley

35 *5–10 mi east of Carmel, Hwy. 1 to Carmel Valley Rd.*

Carmel Valley Road, which turns inland at Highway 1 just south of Carmel, is the main thoroughfare through this secluded enclave of horse ranchers and other well-heeled residents who prefer the valley's perpetually dry, sunny climate to the fog and wind on the coast. You can spend a pleasant couple of hours rambling up the road and back. In tiny Carmel Valley village are several crafts shops and art galleries. **Garland Ranch Regional Park** (⊠ Carmel Valley Rd., 10 mi east of Carmel, ☎ 408/659–4488) has hiking trails and picnic facilities.

The beautiful **Château Julien** winery, recognized internationally for its chardonnay and merlot, gives tours weekdays at 10:30 AM and 2:30 PM by appointment. The tasting room is open daily. ⊠ *8940 Carmel Valley Rd.,* ☎ *408/624–2600.* ⊘ *Weekdays 8–5, weekends 11–5.*

Dining and Lodging

$$$$ ✕🏨 **Quail Lodge.** Guests at this highly regarded resort on the grounds of a private country club have access to golf, tennis, and 853 acres of wildlife preserve, including 11 lakes, frequented by deer and migratory fowl. Spacious, modern rooms with European decor are clustered in several low-rise buildings. The Covey at Quail Lodge (jacket required; no lunch) serves European cuisine in a romantic lakeside setting. Specialties include rack of lamb, mustard-crested salmon with shrimp capellini, abalone, and mousseline of sole. ⊠ *8205 Valley Greens Dr., 93923,* ☎ *408/624–1581 or 800/538–9516,* 🅵🅰🆇 *408/624–3726. 100 rooms. 2 restaurants, 2 lounges, piano bar, 2 pools, hot tub, golf, putting green, tennis courts. AE, DC, MC, V.*

$$$$ 🏨 **Carmel Valley Ranch Resort.** This all-suite resort, well off Carmel
★ Valley Road on a hill overlooking the valley, is a stunning piece of contemporary California architecture. Down-home touches include handmade quilts, wood-burning fireplaces, and watercolors by local artists. Rooms have cathedral ceilings, oversize decks, and fully stocked wet bars. ⊠ *1 Old Ranch Rd., 93923,* ☎ *408/625–9500 or 800/422–7635,* 🅵🅰🆇 *408/624–2858. 100 suites. Restaurant, pool, hot tub, saunas, golf, tennis courts. AE, DC, MC, V.*

$$$$ 🎌 **Stonepine Estate Resort.** The former estate of the Crocker banking family has been converted to an ultradeluxe (and ultraexpensive) inn nestled in 330 pastoral acres with riding trails and an equestrian center. The main house, richly paneled and furnished with antiques, holds eight individually decorated suites and a private dining room for guests only. Less formal but still luxurious rooms are also available in the ranch-style Paddock House. ⊠ *150 E. Carmel Valley Rd., Box 1543, 93924,* ☎ *408/659–2245,* FAX *408/659–5160. 14 rooms. Dining room, pool, tennis, archery, exercise room, horseback riding, mountain bikes. AE, MC, V.*

$$–$$$$ 🎌 **Valley Lodge.** In this small, pleasant inn, there are rooms surrounding a garden patio and separate one- and two-bedroom cottages with fireplaces and full kitchens. Continental breakfast and morning paper are included. ⊠ *Carmel Valley Rd. at Ford Rd., Box 93, 93924,* ☎ *408/659–2261 or 800/641–4646,* FAX *408/659–4558. 31 rooms. Pool, hot tub, sauna, exercise room. AE, MC, V.*

Outdoor Activities and Sports

GOLF

Carmel Valley Ranch Resort (⊠ 1 Old Ranch Rd., ☎ 408/626–2510), designed by Pete Dye, has a front nine that runs along the Carmel River and back nine that reaches well up into the mountains. Guests at the resort have access to the course; the $97 greens fee includes cart rental.

Golf Club at Quail Lodge (⊠ 8000 Valley Greens Dr., ☎ 408/624–2770) incorporates several lakes into its course. Although private, the course is open to guests at the adjoining Quail Lodge and by reciprocation with other private clubs. The $90 greens fee ($115 for nonguests) includes cart rental.

Rancho Cañada Golf Club (⊠ Carmel Valley Rd., ☎ 408/624–0111) has 36 holes, some of them overlooking the Carmel River. Fees range from $15 to $70 plus $25 cart rental, depending on course and tee time selected.

TENNIS

Carmel Valley Inn Swim and Tennis Club (⊠ Carmel Valley Rd. and Laureles Grade, Carmel Valley, ☎ 408/659–3131) allows nonmembers to play on its courts for a small fee.

Shopping

Bighorn Gallery (⊠ 26390 Carmel Rancho La., ☎ 408/625–2288) exhibits artworks on western, wildlife, marine, aviation, and African themes.

Tancredi & Morgen (⊠ Valley Hills Center, Carmel Valley Rd., ☎ 408/625–4477), a country store, sells ornate birdcages, sweet-smelling herbal garlands, antique toys, and hand-embroidered children's clothing.

Maison Val du Soleil (⊠ 8 El Caminito Rd., Carmel Valley Village, ☎ 408/659–5757) contains two floors of country-French antiques and contemporary paintings. Southwest landscapes by American artists and street scenes by French watercolorist Jack Lestrade are noteworthy.

Salinas

③⑥ *17 mi east of the Monterey Peninsula on Hwy. 68; from Carmel Valley Rd, take Laureles Grade north to Hwy. 68.*

Salinas is the population center of a rich agricultural valley where fertile soil, an ideal climate, and a good underground water supply produce optimum growing conditions for crops such as lettuce, broccoli, tomatoes, strawberries, flowers, and wine grapes. This unpretentious town may lack the sophistication and scenic splendors of the coast, but it will interest literary and architectural buffs. Turn-of-the-century buildings have been the focus of ongoing renovation, much of it centered on the original downtown area of South Main Street, with its handsome stone storefronts. The memory and literary legacy of Salinas native (and winner of the Pulitzer and Nobel prizes) John Steinbeck are well honored here.

The **Steinbeck Center Foundation** has information about John Steinbeck exhibits, tours of area landmarks mentioned in his novels, and a schedule of events for the annual Steinbeck festival. ⊠ *371 Main St.,* ☎ *408/753–6411.* ⊘ *Weekdays 9–4 and Sat. (May–Sept.) 10–2.*

★ John Steinbeck did much of his research for *East of Eden,* a novel partially drawn from his Salinas boyhood, at what is now called the **Steinbeck Library.** The library contains tapes of interviews with people who knew Steinbeck and a display of photos, first editions, letters, original manuscripts, and other items pertaining to the novelist. Entrance to the archives, which contain original manuscripts and first editions, is by appointment only. ⊠ *350 Lincoln Ave.,* ☎ *408/758–7311.* ▨ *Free.* ⊘ *Mon.–Wed. 10–9, Thurs.–Sat. 10–6.*

Harvey-Baker House, a preserved redwood home built in 1868 for Salinas's first mayor, is one of the finest private residences built in the town during the 19th century. ⊠ *238 E. Romie La.,* ☎ *408/757–8085.* ▨ *Free.* ⊘ *1st Sun. of month 1–4, weekdays by appointment.*

The meadows above the Alisal Slough hold the **Jose Eusebio Boronda Adobe,** the last unaltered adobe home from Mexican California. The house contains furniture and period artifacts. ⊠ *333 Boronda Rd.,* ☎ *408/757–8085.* ▨ *Free.* ⊘ *Weekdays 10–2, Sun. 1–4, Sat. by appointment.*

Dining

$ ✕ **Steinbeck House.** John Steinbeck's birthplace, a Victorian frame house, has been converted to a lunch-only restaurant, run by the volunteer Valley Guild. The restaurant contains some Steinbeck memorabilia and presents a menu focusing on locally grown produce. ⊠ *132 Central Ave.,* ☎ *408/424–2735.* ⊘ *Weekdays for 2 sittings at 11:45 AM and 1:15 PM.*

Outdoor Activities and Sports

One of the oldest and most famous rodeos in the West is the annual **California Rodeo** (☎ 408/757–2951) in Salinas, which takes place during a week of festivities starting in mid-July.

San Juan Bautista

③⑦ *18 mi north of Salinas on U.S. 101.*

★ Sleepy San Juan Bautista, protected from development since 1933, when much of it became **San Juan Bautista State Historic Park,** is about as close to early-19th-century California as you can get. On the first Saturday of each month, on Living History Day, costumed volunteers entertain visitors with period events—quilting bees, tortilla making, and butter churning. ⊠ *Hwy. 156,* ☎ *408/623–4881.* ▨ *$2.* ⊘ *Daily 10–4:30.*

The centerpiece for the village is a wide green plaza, ringed by historic buildings: a restored blacksmith shop, a stable, a pioneer cabin, and a jailhouse. Running along one side of the square is **Mission San Juan Bautista,** a long, low colonnaded structure founded by Father Lasuen in 1797. A poignant spot adjoining it is Mission Cemetery, where more than 4,300 Native Americans who converted to Christianity are buried in unmarked graves. ⊠ *408 S. 2nd St.,* ☎ *408/623–2127.* 🖾 *$1.* ⊙ *Mar.–Oct., daily 9:30–5:30; Nov.–Feb., daily 9:30–4:30.*

After the mission era, San Juan Bautista became an important crossroads for stagecoach travel. The principal stop in town was the **Plaza Hotel,** a collection of adobe buildings with furnishings from the 1860s. The **Castro-Breen Adobe,** once owned by survivors from the Donner Party and furnished with Spanish colonial antiques, presents a view of domestic life in the village. It is next door to the Plaza Hotel.

Shopping

Small antiques shops and art galleries line San Juan Bautista's side streets.

OFF THE
BEATEN PATH

ELKHORN SLOUGH – A few miles north of Monterey, east of the tiny harbor town of Moss Landing, is one of only two federal research reserves in California, the Elkhorn Slough at the National Estuarine Research Reserve. Its 1,400 acres of tidal flats and salt marshes form a complex environment supporting more than 200 species of birds. A walk along the meandering waterways and wetlands can reveal hawks, white-tailed kites, owls, herons, and egrets. Sharks may be observed in the summer months. You can wander at leisure or, on weekends, take a guided walk (10 AM and 1 PM) to the heron rookery. ⊠ *1700 Elkhorn Rd., Watsonville,* ☎ *408/728–2822 for directions.* 🖾 *$2.50; free with any California hunting or fishing license.* ⊙ *Wed.–Sun. 9–5.*

MONTEREY BAY A TO Z

Arriving and Departing

By Bus

Greyhound Lines (☎ 800/231–2222) serves Monterey from San Francisco three times daily; the trip takes from three to five hours, depending on the number of stops.

By Car

The drive south from San Francisco to Monterey can be made comfortably in three hours or less. The most scenic way is to follow Highway 1 down the coast past flower, pumpkin, and artichoke fields and the seaside communities of Pacifica, Half Moon Bay, and Santa Cruz. Unless the drive is made on sunny weekends when locals are heading for the beach, the two-lane coast highway takes no longer than the freeway.

Of the freeways from San Francisco, a fast but enjoyable route is I–280 south to Highway 17, just south of San Jose. Highway 17 crosses the redwood-filled Santa Cruz mountains between San Jose and Santa Cruz, where it intersects with Highway 1. Another option is to follow U.S. 101 south through San Jose to Salinas and then take Highway 68 west to Monterey.

From Los Angeles, the drive to Monterey can be made in less than a day by heading north on U.S. 101 to Salinas and then heading west on Highway 68. The spectacular but slow alternative is to take U.S. 101 to San Luis Obispo and then follow the hairpin turns of Highway 1 up the coast. Allow at least three extra hours if you do.

By Plane

Monterey Peninsula Airport (⊠ 200 Fred Kane Dr., ☎ 408/648–7000) is 3 miles from downtown Monterey—on Highway 68 to Olmsted Road—and is served by **American Eagle, United Airlines** and **United Express,** and **USAir** (☞ Air Travel *in* Important Contacts A to Z for phone numbers).

By Train

Amtrak (☎ 800/872–7245) runs the *Coast Starlight* between Los Angeles and Seattle, making a stop in Salinas (✉ 11 Station Pl.).

Getting Around

By Bus

Monterey–Salinas Transit (☎ 408/424–7695) provides frequent service between towns and many major sightseeing spots and shopping areas for $1.25 per ride, with an additional $1.25 for each zone you travel into, or $3.75 to $7.50 for a day pass, according to zone.

By Car

Highway 1 runs north–south, linking the towns of Santa Cruz, Monterey, and Carmel. Highway 68 runs northeast from Pacific Grove toward Salinas, which U.S. 101 bisects. North of Salinas, U.S. 101 links up with Highway 156 to San Juan Bautista. Parking is especially difficult in Carmel and in the vicinity of the Monterey Bay Aquarium on Cannery Row.

Contacts and Resources

Doctors

Community Hospital of Monterey Peninsula (✉ 23625 Holman Hwy., Monterey, ☎ 408/624–5311). **Monterey County Medical Society** (☎ 408/373–4197).

Emergencies

Ambulance (☎ 911). **Police** (☎ 911).

Guided Tours

California Parlor Car Tours (☎ 415/474–7500 or 800/227–4250) operates motor-coach tours of northern California departing from San Francisco that include the Monterey Peninsula.

Chardonnay II (☎ 408/423–1213) accommodates 49 passengers for cruises on Monterey Bay, leaving from the yacht harbor in Santa Cruz.

Rider's Guide (✉ 484 Lake Park Ave., Ste. 255, Oakland 94610, ☎ 510/653–2553) produces a self-guided audiotape tour detailing the history, landmarks, and attractions of the Monterey peninsula and Big Sur for $12.95, or $15.95 in vinyl binder, plus $2 postage.

Pharmacies

Surf 'n' Sand (✉ 6th and Junipero Sts., Carmel, ☎ 408/624–1543) has a pharmacy open weekdays 9–6:30, Saturday and holidays 9–2.

Visitor Information

Monterey Peninsula Visitors and Convention Bureau (✉ 380 Alvarado St., Monterey 93942, ☎ 408/649–1770). **Monterey Wine Country Associates** (☎ 408/375–9400). **Salinas Chamber of Commerce** (✉ 119 E. Alisal St., Salinas 93902, ☎ 408/424–7611). **Santa Cruz County Conference and Visitors Council** (✉ 701 Front St., Santa Cruz 95060, ☎ 408/425–1234 or 800/833–3494). **Santa Cruz Winegrowers** (☎ 408/479–9463).

10 The Central Coast

*From Big Sur
to Santa Barbara*

Highway 1 between Big Sur and Santa Barbara is a spectacular stretch of terrain, requiring concentration and nerve to drive. The road demands an unhurried pace, but even if it didn't, you'd find yourself stopping often to take in the scenery. Don't expect much in the way of dining, lodging, or even history until you arrive at Hearst Castle, publisher William Randolph Hearst's testament to his own fabulousness. Sunny, well-scrubbed Santa Barbara's Spanish-Mexican heritage is reflected in the architectural style of its courthouse and mission.

THE COASTLINE BETWEEN CARMEL and Santa Barbara, a distance of just over 200 miles, is one of the most popular drives in California. Except for a few small-

Updated by
Colleen Dunn
Bates

ish cities—Ventura and Santa Barbara in the south and San Luis Obispo in the north—the area is sparsely populated. Between settlements, whose inhabitants relish their isolation at the sharp edge of land and sea. Grazing cattle dot the landscape, and in the springtime wildflowers cover the hillsides. Around Big Sur, the Santa Lucia mountains drop down to the Pacific with dizzying grandeur, but as you move south, the shoreline gradually flattens into the long, sandy beaches of Santa Barbara and Ventura.

Throughout the region are bed-and-breakfast inns and pleasant little towns, such as Cambria and Ojai, where resident artists create and sell their work. The wineries of the Santa Ynez Valley are steadily building reputations for their quality vintages. The Danish town of Solvang is an amusing stopover for hearty Scandinavian fare and an architectural change of pace.

Santa Barbara is your introduction to the sand, surf, sun, and the unhurried hospitality and easy living of southern California. Only 95 miles north of Los Angeles, Santa Barbara works hard to maintain its relaxed atmosphere and cozy scale. Wedged between the Pacific and the Santa Ynez Mountains, it's never had much room for expansion. The city's setting, climate, and architecture combine to produce a Mediterranean feel that permeates not only its look but its pace.

Pleasures and Pastimes

Dining

The Central Coast from Big Sur to Solvang is far enough off the interstate to ensure that nearly every restaurant or café has its own personality—from chic to down-home and funky. There aren't many restaurants from Big Sur until you reach Hearst Castle. Cambria's cooks, true to the town's British-Welsh origins, serve up English fare complete with peas and Yorkshire pudding but also California and Continental cuisine. In Solvang, count on traditional Danish smorgasbord and sausages.

The dishes of Santa Barbara's chefs rival those of their counterparts in the state's larger centers. Fresh seafood is plentiful, prepared old-style American in longtime wharfside hangouts or with more trendy accents at newer eateries. If you're after good, cheap food with an international flavor, follow the locals to Milpas Avenue on the east edge of Santa Barbara's downtown. Dining attire on the Central Coast is generally casual, though slightly dressy casual wear is the custom at the expensive to very expensive restaurants listed below.

CATEGORY	COST*
$$$$	over $50
$$$	$30–$50
$$	$20–$30
$	under $20

*per person for a three-course meal, excluding drinks, service, and
7¼%–7¾% sales tax

Lodging

Big Sur has only a few places to stay, but even its budget accommodations have character. From San Simeon to San Luis Obispo there are many moderately priced hotels and motels—some nicer than others, but mostly just basic lodgings. Wherever you stay, make your reservations well ahead of time in the summer, particularly in Santa Barbara, where bargain lodging is hard to come by.

CATEGORY	COST*
$$$$	over $175
$$$	$120–$175
$$	$80–$120
$	under $80

All prices are for a standard double room, excluding 9%–10% tax.

Missions

Three important California missions are within the Central Coast region. La Purisima is the most fully restored, Santa Barbara's is perhaps the most beautiful of the state's 21 missions, and Mission San Luis Obispo de Tolosa has a fine museum with many Chumash Indian artifacts.

Wineries

Centered in the Solvang area and spreading north toward San Luis Obispo and south toward Santa Barbara is a winemaking region with much of the variety but none of the glitz or crowds of northern California's Napa Valley. Many wineries are in the rolling hills of the Santa Maria or Santa Ynez valleys. They tend to be fairly small, but most have tasting rooms (some have tours) and you'll often meet the winemakers themselves. There are maps and brochures at visitor centers in Solvang, San Luis Obispo, and Santa Barbara, or you can contact the wine associations of Paso Robles and Santa Barbara (☞ Contacts and Resources *in* Central Coast A to Z, *below*).

Exploring the Central Coast

Driving is the only way to experience the Central Coast. The entire distance from Big Sur to Santa Barbara could be tackled in one long day, but that would defeat the purpose of taking the slower, scenic coastal highway. Even a brief trip would allow the luxury of winding down Highway 1 to take in the rugged coastline from Monterey through Big Sur to San Luis Obispo. A better option is to plan on taking several days, allowing time to savor Big Sur, Hearst Castle, the beaches, and Santa Barbara.

Great Itineraries

The three-day itinerary below is arranged as a loop from either San Francisco or Los Angeles. The seven-day trip is organized from north to south.

Numbers in the text correspond to numbers in the margin and on the Central Coast and Santa Barbara maps.

IF YOU HAVE 3 DAYS

Especially in the summertime, make reservations for a visit to Hearst Castle well before you depart for the coast. Maximize your time by taking U.S. 101 from San Francisco or Los Angeles directly to **San Luis Obispo** ⑩. Just north of town, stop by the kitschy, wonderful **Madonna Inn.** Continue on to **Mission San Luis Obispo de Tolosa,** overlooking the San Luis Creek. Drive west on Highway 46 and north on Highway 1 and overnight in 🏨 **Cambria.** Take a morning tour of **Hearst Castle** ⑦, spend some time viewing the exhibits at the visitor center, and then head south on U.S. 101 to 🏨 **Santa Barbara** ⑬–㉘. Spend the late afternoon at **Stearns Wharf** ⑬ or along **Cabrillo Boulevard.** In the morning, visit the **Santa Barbara County Courthouse** ㉑ and **Mission Santa Barbara** ㉖ before continuing to your next destination.

The Central Coast

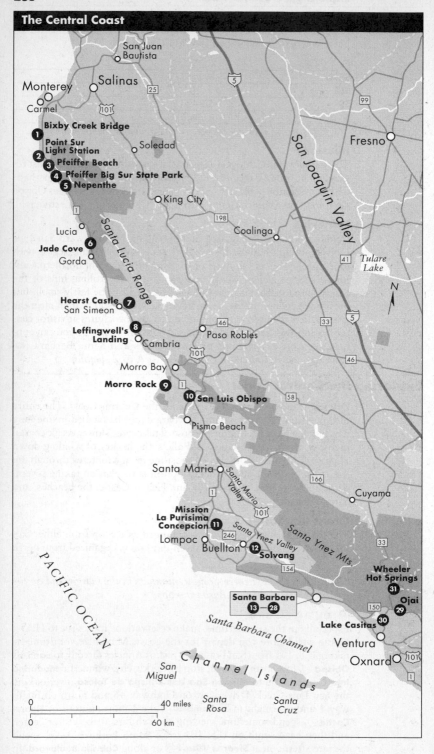

Monterey
Carmel

Salinas

San Juan
Bautista

Soledad

1 Bixby Creek Bridge
2 Point Sur
Light Station
3 Pfeiffer Beach
4 Pfeiffer Big Sur State Park
5 Nepenthe

King City

Lucia

Santa Lucia Range

6 Jade Cove
Gorda

7 Hearst Castle
San Simeon

8 Leffingwell's
Landing
Cambria

Paso Robles

Morro Bay

9 Morro Rock

10 San Luis Obispo

Pismo Beach

Santa Maria

Santa Maria Valley

11 Mission
La Purisima
Concepcion
Lompoc

12 Solvang
Buellton

Santa Ynez Valley

Santa Ynez Mts

Santa Barbara
13 — 28

Santa Barbara Channel

PACIFIC OCEAN

San
Miguel

Santa
Rosa

Santa
Cruz

Channel Islands

San Joaquin Valley

Fresno

Coalinga

Tulare
Lake

N

Cuyama

Wheeler
Hot Springs
31

Ojai
29

30
Lake Casitas

Ventura

Oxnard

0   40 miles
0   60 km

IF YOU HAVE 7 DAYS

Make ⛰ **Big Sur** your destination for the first day and most of the second. If you're in the area on a weekend, take a tour of **Point Sur Light Station** ②, which has stood for a century on its sandstone cliff. Watch the waves break on **Pfeiffer Beach** ③, one of the few places where you may actually set foot on the shore. Observe the glories of **Los Padres National Forest** up close by hiking one of the many trails in the **Ventana Wilderness,** or stay along the shore and hunt for jade at **Jade Cove** ⑥. Plan to reach ⛰ **Cambria** by the evening of day two. Have dinner and explore the town's shops. On day three, take a morning tour of **Hearst Castle** ⑦ (make those reservations ahead of time), have lunch, and take the quicker of two possible routes—U.S. 101 south to Highway 246 east—to **Mission La Purisima Concepcion** ⑪, the most fully restored mission in the state. Loop back on 246 to U.S. 101 heading south to ⛰ **Santa Barbara** ⑬–㉘. On day four, visit **Stearns Wharf** ⑬ and walk or bike to sandy **East Beach** ⑰ and the **Andree Clark Bird Refuge** ⑱. Have dinner on **State Street** and check out the area's shops and clubs. On your fifth day, get a feel for the city's architecture and history at the **Santa Barbara County Courthouse** ㉑ and **Mission Santa Barbara** ㉖. North of the mission, the paths along the 65-acre **Santa Barbara Botanic Garden** ㉘ wind through an impressive cross-section of local vegetation. Have dinner in **Montecito** and explore the Coast Village Road shopping district. It's a short walk from here to the shore to catch the sunset. On your sixth day, experience the area's marine life on a half-day cruise of the **Channel Islands.** On day seven, drive east along the coast on U.S. 101 and then on Highway 150 inland to ⛰ **Ojai** ㉙. Set in a jewel-like valley, Ojai is famous as the location for Frank Capra's film *Lost Horizon* and for the spa at **Wheeler Hot Springs** ㉛. Sample the therapeutic services at the spa and, reinvigorated, wander Ojai in the afternoon or proceed directly to your next destination.

When to Tour the Central Coast

The Central Coast is hospitable most of the year. Fog often rolls in north of Pismo Beach during the summer; you'll need a jacket, especially after sunset, close to the shore. The rains usually come December through March. Santa Barbara is pleasant year-round. Hotel rooms fill up in the summer, but from April to early June and in the early fall the weather is almost as fine and it's less hectic. Most of the Central Coast's major sights are open daily year-round. One exception is the Point Sur Light Station, which is available for touring only on weekends and, April to October, Wednesdays.

HIGHWAY 1 TO SOLVANG

Big Sur, San Simeon, and San Luis Obispo

Big Sur

152 mi south of San Francisco, I–280 to U.S. 101 to Hwy. 68 west to Hwy. 1 south; 27 mi south of Monterey on Hwy. 1.

Startling views and hairpin turns alternate in quick succession on Highway 1 along the Central Coast. Long a retreat of artists and writers, Big Sur has managed to preserve its ancient forests and rugged coast from the onslaught of development, serving as a reminder of California's impressive geological history. Much of the area lies within several state parks and the more than 165,000-acre **Ventana Wilderness,** itself part of the Los Padres National Forest. The counterculture spirit of Big Sur is evident today in tie-dyed clothing upon some locals and the presence of the Esalen Institute, a mecca of the human growth-potential movement. Originally established as a home to curative baths in 1910, Esalen exploded in the 1960s as a place to explore consciousness, environmental issues, and nude bathing.

❶ The graceful arc of **Bixby Creek Bridge** is a photographer's dream. There is a small parking area on the north side from which to take a photo or begin a walk across the 550-foot span. ⊠ *Hwy. 1, 13 mi south of Carmel.*

★ ❷ **Point Sur Light Station,** a century-old beacon, stands watch from atop a sandstone cliff. Four lighthouse keepers lived here with their families. Their homes and working spaces are open to the public on 2½-to 3-hour, ranger-led tours. Considerable walking is involved. ⊠ *Point Sur State Historical Park, Hwy. 1, 19 mi south of Carmel,* ☎ *408/625–4419.* ⊠ *$5.* ⊙ *Tours Sat. 10 AM and 2 PM, Sun. 10 AM, plus Apr.–Oct., Wed. 10 and 2.*

❸ A hole in one of the big, sea-washed rocks at **Pfeiffer Beach** lets you watch the waves break first on the sea side and then again on the beach side. ⊠ *Off Hwy. 1; the 2-mi road to beach is immediately past the Big Sur Ranger Station.* ⊠ *$5 per vehicle.*

❹ A short hiking trail at **Pfeiffer Big Sur State Park** leads up a small, redwood-filled valley to a waterfall. You can go back the same (easier) way or continue on the trail and take a loop that leads you along the valley wall, with views of the tops of the redwood trees you were just walking among. ⊠ *Hwy. 1,* ☎ *408/667–2315.*

❺ **Nepenthe** overlooks lush meadows to the ocean below. The house was once owned by Orson Welles and Rita Hayworth, though his biographer says they spent little time there. Downstairs from the on-site restaurant and café is a crafts and gift shop, displaying, among other items, the work of Kaffe Fassett, the famous fabric designer who grew up at Nepenthe. ⊠ *Hwy. 1, 2½ mi south of Big Sur Ranger Station.*

❻ **Jade Cove** is a well-known jade-hunting spot along the coast. Rock hunting is allowed on the beach, but you may not remove anything from the walls of the cliffs. ⊠ *Hwy. 1, 10 mi south of Lucia.*

Dining and Lodging

$–$$ **✕ Nepenthe.** You'll not find a grander coastal view between San Fran-
★ cisco and Los Angeles than the one from here. The food is average—from roast chicken with sage to sandwiches and hamburgers—so it is the location, in magnificent Big Sur, that rates the star. Nepenthe serves lunch and dinner; the outdoor Café Kevah serves breakfast and lunch. ⊠ *Hwy. 1, south end of town,* ☎ *408/667–2345. AE, MC, V.*

$$$$ **✕▦ Post Ranch Inn.** This luxurious retreat is the ultimate in environ-
★ mentally conscious architecture. Visitors leave their cars at the gate and are bused up onto the cliff 1,200 feet above the ocean to the redwood guest houses, all with dizzyingly splendid views of either the Pacific or the mountains. Each unit has its own spa tub, stereo system, private deck, and massage table, and because there are no televisions, there is every incentive to explore the glorious surrounding hiking country. Continental breakfast is included. ⊠ *Hwy. 1, Box 219, 93920,* ☎ *408/667–2200 or 800/527–2200,* ℻ *408/667–2824. 30 units. Restaurant, bar, 2 pools, spa, exercise room, library. AE, MC, V.*

$$$$ **✕▦ Ventana Inn.** Rooms at this quintessential California getaway are in buildings that are scattered in clusters on a hillside above the Pacific, done in natural woods with cool tile floors. Activities here are purposely limited to sunning at poolside—there is a clothing-optional deck—and walks in the hills nearby. The hotel's stone and wood Ventana Restaurant serves California cuisine with Continental influences. For a real event, come here for weekend brunch on the terrace, with spectacular views over golden hills down to the ocean. Room rates include Continental breakfast and complimentary afternoon wine and cheese buffet. ⊠ *Hwy. 1, 93920,* ☎ *408/667–2331 or 800/628–6500,* FAX *408/667–2419. 62 rooms. Restaurant, 2 lap pools, 2 Japanese baths, sauna, exercise room. 2-night minimum stay on weekends and holidays. AE, D, DC, MC, V.*

$–$$$ ✕⊡ **Deetjen's Big Sur Inn.** This inn has a certain rustic charm, at least for travelers not too attached to creature comforts. There are no locks on the doors (except from the inside), the heating is by wood-burning stove in half of the rooms, and your neighbor can often be heard through the walls. Still, it's a special place, set among redwood trees with each room individually decorated and given a name like Château Fiasco. The restaurant (reservations essential), which consists of four intimate dining rooms in the main house, serves stylish fare that includes roasted half duck, filet mignon, and lamb chops for dinner, wonderfully light and flavorful pancakes for breakfast (but no lunch). ⊠ *Hwy. 1, south end of town, 93920,* ☎ *408/667–2377, restaurant 408/667–2378. 20 rooms, 14 with bath. Restaurant. MC, V.*

$$–$$$ ⊡ **Big Sur Lodge.** The motel-style cottages of this Pfeiffer Big Sur State Park property make it the best bet in Big Sur for families. The lodging area sits in a meadow surrounded by redwood and oak trees. Some accommodations have fireplaces, some kitchens. None have TV or phone. ⊠ *Hwy. 1, Box 190, 93920,* ☎ *408/667–2171 or 800/424–4787,* FAX *408/667–3110. 61 rooms. Restaurant, pool. AE, MC, V.*

Outdoor Activities and Sports

CAMPING

There are many campsites along Highway 1, but they can fill up early anytime but winter. In Big Sur, campsites are at Pfeiffer Big Sur and Julia Pfeiffer Burns state parks. Near Hearst Castle, camping is available at several smaller state parks (San Simeon, Atascadero, Morro Bay, Montana de Oro, Avila Beach, and Pismo Beach). Most of the sites require reservations from Destinet (☎ 800/444–7275).

San Simeon

57 mi south of Big Sur on Hwy. 1.

Whalers founded San Simeon in the 1850s but had virtually abandoned the town by the time Senator George Hearst reestablished it 20 years later. Hearst bought up most of the surrounding ranch land, built a 1,000-foot wharf, and turned San Simeon into a bustling port. His son, William Randolph, further developed the area during the construction of Hearst Castle. Today, San Simeon is basically a row of gift shops, restaurants, and motels—the closest to the castle—along Highway 1.

★ ❼ **Hearst Castle,** known officially as the Hearst San Simeon State Historical Monument, sits in solitary splendor atop La Cuesta Encantada (the Enchanted Hill). Its buildings and gardens are spread over the 127 acres that were the heart of newspaper magnate William Randolph Hearst's 250,000-acre ranch.

Buses from the visitor center at the bottom of the hill take visitors to the neoclassical extravaganza above. Hearst devoted nearly 30 years and some $10 million to building this elaborate estate. He commissioned renowned architect Julia Morgan—who was also responsible for buildings at U.C. Berkeley—but was very much involved with the final product, a pastiche of Italian, Spanish, Moorish, and French styles. The art-filled main building and three guest "cottages" are connected by terraces and staircases and surrounded by reflecting pools, gardens, and statuary at every turn. In its heyday, this place was a playground for Hearst, Hollywood celebrities, and the rich and powerful from around the world.

Although construction began in 1919, the project was never officially completed. Work was halted in 1947 when Hearst had to leave San Simeon due to failing health. The Hearst family presented the property to the state of California in 1958.

Guides conduct four different daytime tours and one evening tour of various parts of the main house and grounds. Daytime tours take just under two hours. Docents dress in period costume as Hearst's guests and staff for the slightly longer evening tour, which begins at sunset. All tours include a half-mile walk and 150–400 stairs. An interesting free exhibit at the visitor center examines the life of this master of yellow journalism and inspiration for Orson Welles's film *Citizen Kane*—something about which Hearst was none too pleased. Reservations for the tours, which can be made up to eight weeks in advance, are a virtual necessity. ⊠ *San Simeon State Park, 750 Hearst Castle Rd.,* ☎ *805/927–2020 or 800/444–4445.* ☞ *Day tour $14, evening tour (spring and fall) $25.* ☉ *Tours daily 8:20 AM–3 PM (later in summer) and most Fri. and Sat. evenings Mar.–May and Sept.–Dec. AE, D, MC, V.*

Dining and Lodging

$–$$ ✕ **San Simeon Restaurant.** This ocean-view restaurant makes the most of its proximity to Hearst Castle with a mind-boggling decor of imitation Greek columns, statues, and tapestries. The menu is standard American; prime rib is the big draw. ⊠ *Hwy. 1 (east side),* ☎ *805/927–4604. AE, DC, MC, V.*

$ ✕ **Europa.** The menu here includes dishes from Germany, Hungary, and Italy—spätzle, egg dumplings and paprika, and homemade pasta. Steaks and fresh fish are also served. Crisp linen tablecloths brighten the small dining room. ⊠ *9240 Castillo Dr. (Hwy. 1),* ☎ *805/927–3087. MC, V. Closed Sun. No lunch.*

$–$$ 🏨 **San Simeon Lodge.** This unpretentious motel sits right across from the ocean. Many of its quite serviceable rooms have sea views. ⊠ *9520 Castillo Dr. (Hwy. 1), 93452,* ☎ *805/927–4601,* 🖷 *805/927–2374. 63 rooms. Restaurant, bar, lounge, pool. AE, D, MC, V.*

$ 🏨 **Motel 6.** This is a two-story motel with comfortable, if standard, rooms decorated in blue and rust, opening onto an interior corridor. ⊠ *9070 Castillo Dr. (Hwy. 1), 93452,* ☎ *805/927–8691,* 🖷 *805/927–5341. 100 rooms. Pool. AE, D, DC, MC, V.*

Cambria

9 mi south of San Simeon on Hwy. 1.

Cambria, an artists' colony full of turn-of-the-century homes, is divided into the newer West Village and the original East Village. Each has its own personality and B&Bs, restaurants, art galleries, and shops selling unusual wares. You can still detect traces of the Welsh miners who settled here in the 1890s. Moonstone Beach Drive, which runs along ❽ the coast, is lined with motels. **Leffingwell's Landing,** a state picnic ground at its northern end, is a good place for examining tidal pools and watching otters as they frolic in the surf. Walkers will love the maze of footpaths along the beach side of Moonstone Beach Drive.

Dining and Lodging

$–$$ ✕ **Hamlet at Moonstone Gardens.** Set in the middle of 3 acres of lux-
★ uriant gardens, this restaurant has an enchanting patio that's perfect
for lunch. The upstairs dining room looks over the Pacific or the gardens. Fish of the day comes poached in white wine; other entrées range
from hamburgers to rack of lamb. Downstairs at the Pacific Wine Works,
you can taste wines from more than 50 wineries. ✉ *Hwy. 1 at Moonstone Beach Dr.,* ☎ *805/927–3535. MC, V. Closed Dec. 18–25.*

$–$$ ✕ **Robin's.** "Multiethnic" only begins to describe the dining possibil-
ities here. Tandoori prawns, quesadillas, fettuccine dishes with chow
mein overtones, a Thai red curry, an array of salads (more for lunch
than dinner), quite a few vegetarian entrées, hamburgers for the kids,
and some truly fine desserts (house specialty: French apple pie with fresh
whipped cream) are all on Robin's menu. ✉ *4095 Burton Dr.,* ☎
805/927–5007. MC, V. No lunch Sun.

$$$ 🏨 **Fog Catcher Inn.** Its landscaped gardens and 10 thatched-roof dbuild-
ings lend the Fog Catcher the feel of an English country village. Most
rooms (among them 10 minisuites) have ocean views. All have fireplaces
and are done in floral chintz with light wood furniture. Room rates
include breakfast. ✉ *6400 Moonstone Dr., 93428,* ☎ *805/927–1400
or 800/425–4121. 60 rooms. Pool, hot tub. AE, D, DC, MC, V.*

$$$ 🏨 **Squibb House.** The newest of several fine B&Bs in Cambria is
housed in a Gothic Revival Italianate structure restored by its owner,
Bruce Black, whose craftsmen built many of the pine furnishings in the
100-year-old carpentry shop next door. The carpentry shop has been
transformed into a gift shop offering a fine selection of antiques, local
crafts, and housewares. Room rates include Continental breakfast. ✉
4063 Burton Dr., 93428, ☎ *805/927–9600. 5 rooms. Fireplaces in
rooms. MC, V.*

$$–$$$ 🏨 **Best Western Fireside Inn.** This modern motel has spacious rooms,
with sofas, upholstered lounge chairs, refrigerators, and coffeemakers.
Some rooms have whirlpools or ocean views, and all have fireplaces.
Continental breakfast is served in a room adjacent to the pool. The
inn is just across from the beach, with fishing nearby. ✉ *6700 Moonstone Beach Dr., 93428,* ☎ *805/927–8661 or 800/528–1234,* FAX
805/927–8584. 46 rooms. Pool, hot tub. AE, D, DC, MC, V.

$–$$$ 🏨 **Bluebird Motel.** Rooms at this garden motel near Cambria's East
Village range from simply furnished doubles to nicer creekside suites
with fireplace and refrigerator. ✉ *1880 Main St., 93428,* ☎ *805/927–
4634 or 800/552–5434,* FAX *805/927–5215. 37 rooms. AE, D, DC,
MC, V.*

$$ 🏨 **San Simeon Pines Resort.** Set amid 9 acres of pines and cypresses,
★ this motel-style resort has its own golf course and is directly across from
Leffingwell's Landing, a state picnic area on the rocky beach. The accommodations include cottages with their own landscaped backyards.
Areas are set aside for adults and families. As this is a wildlife preserve,
pets are not allowed. ✉ *7200 Moonstone Beach Dr. (mailing address:
Box 117, San Simeon 93452),* ☎ *805/927–4648. 58 rooms. Pool, 9-
hole golf course, croquet, shuffleboard, playground. AE, MC, V.*

Morro Bay

20 mi south of Cambria on Hwy. 1.

★ **9** Morro Bay is separated from the ocean by a 4½-mile sandpit and a cause-
way, built in the 1930s, that leads to the huge monolith of **Morro Rock.**
A short walk around the base of the rock—actually an extinct volcano—
leads to a breakwater, with the calm, sheltered harbor (home of a large
fishing fleet) on one side and the crashing waves of the Pacific on the

other. Morro Bay is also a wildlife preserve, protecting the nesting areas of endangered peregrine falcons; one doesn't need to get too close to divine that the rock is alive with birds. The town is dominated by the tall smokestacks of the PG&E plant just behind the waterfront, which can be seen from anywhere in the bay. Also in town is a huge chessboard with human-size pieces.

Dining and Lodging

$–$$ ✕ **Dorn's.** This very pleasant seafood café, open for breakfast, lunch, and dinner, overlooks the harbor. It looks like a Cape Cod cottage, with gray walls, mahogany wainscoting, awnings, and bay windows. Excellent fish and native abalone are on the dinner menu. ⊠ *801 Market St.,* ☎ *805/772–4415. AE, MC, V.*

$ ✕ **Margie's Diner.** This mom-and-pop diner-café serves generous por-
★   tions of all-American favorites: ham or steak and eggs, three-egg omelets, chili, hot and cold sandwiches, chicken fried steak, deep-dish apple pie—you name it, and don't forget the milk shakes (or the 10 kinds of burger). ⊠ *1698 N. Main St.,* ☎ *805/772–2510. Reservations not accepted. No credit cards.*

$–$$ 🏠 **Sea Air Inn.** Rooms in this modern, well-kept motel, a block from the waterfront, are clean and comfortable. Some have ocean views, some have refrigerators, and all have coffeemakers. Location is the main drawing card. Room rates include Continental breakfast. ⊠ *845 Morro Ave., 93442,* ☎ *805/772–4437,* 𝖥𝖠𝖷 *805/772–8860. 25 rooms. AE, D, MC, V.*

Outdoor Activities and Sports

FISHING

There is access to freshwater- and surf-fishing spots all along the coast. **Virg's Sport Fishing** (⊠ Morro Bay embarcadero, ☎ 805/772–1222) and **Bob's Sportfishing** (⊠ Morro Bay embarcadero, ☎ 805/772–3340) operate deep-sea trips.

San Luis Obispo

⑩ *14 mi south of Morro Bay on Hwy. 1, 230 mi south of San Francisco on I–280 to U.S. 101, 112 mi north of Santa Barbara on U.S. 101.*

San Luis Obispo, about halfway between San Francisco and Los Angeles, is home to two decidedly different institutions: California Polytechnic State University, known as Cal Poly, and the exuberantly goofy, garish Madonna Inn. The town has several restored Victorian-era homes; the Chamber of Commerce (☞ Contacts and Resources *in* Central Coast A to Z, *below*) has a list of self-guided historic walks. On Thursday from 6 to 9 PM, a four-block-long evening farmers' market takes place on Higuera Street. The still-in-business Ah Louis Store at 800 Palm Street was started in 1884 to serve the Chinese laborers building the Pacific Coast and Southern Pacific railroads.

★   **Mission San Luis Obispo de Tolosa,** established in 1772, overlooks San Luis Obispo Creek. The mission's museum exhibits artifacts of the Chumash Indians and early Spanish settlers. ⊠ *782 Monterey St.,* ☎ *805/543–6850.* ◻ *Free.* ☺ *Memorial Day weekend–Dec. 31, daily 9–5; Jan.–late May, daily 9–4.*

Dining and Lodging

$$–$$$ ✕ **Cafe Roma.** Authentic northern Italian rustic cuisine is the specialty of this warm, elegant restaurant located on Railroad Square. Under a large mural of sunny Tuscany, you can dine on squash-filled ravioli with sage and butter sauce or filet mignon glistening with port and gorgonzola.

✉ *1819 Osos St.,* ☎ *805/541–6800. AE, D, DC, MC, V. Closed Mon. No lunch weekends.*

$$ ✕ **Buona Tavola.** Locals favor this northern Italian restaurant, whose menu highlights include homemade agnolotti filled with scampi in a creamy saffron sauce and braised lamb shank with grilled polenta. Outdoor dining is available on a flower-filled patio. ✉ *1037 Monterey St.,* ☎ *805/545–8000. D, MC, V.*

$ ✕ **Big Sky.** Charles Myers, owner of this spacious, comfortable restaurant, aims to provide what he calls "world beat" cuisine, using local ingredients: organic fruits and vegetables, hormone-free chicken, pork and chicken sausages produced in San Luis Obispo. This results in an eclectic menu that encompasses dishes from the Mediterranean, the Sun Belt, North Africa, and the Southwest. Fish caught nearby is prepared in three different styles: Oriental, Cajun, and Southwest. ✉ *1121 Broad St.,* ☎ *805/545–5401. MC, V. No dinner Sun.*

$$–$$$$ ✕▥ **Apple Farm.** Decorated to the hilt with floral bedspreads and wall-
★ paper, and with watercolors by local artists, each room in this country-style hotel has a gas fireplace; some have canopy beds and cozy window seats. The adjoining restaurant serves such hearty country fare as chicken with dumplings and smoked ribs, and the breakfasts are copious. ✉ *2015 Monterey St., 93401,* ☎ *805/544–2040; in CA, 800/255–2040 in CA;* 𝔽𝔸𝕏 *805/546–9495. 101 rooms. Restaurant, pool, hot tub. AE, D, MC, V.*

$$–$$$$ ✕▥ **Madonna Inn.** A designer's imagination run amok, this place is
★ as much a tourist attraction as a place to stay. It is the ultimate in kitsch, from its rococo bathrooms to its pink-on-pink, froufrou dining areas. Each room is unique, to say the least: Rock Bottom is all stone, even the bathroom; the Safari Room is decked out in animal skins; Old Mill features a waterwheel that powers cuckoo-clock-like figurines. Even if you don't stay overnight, try a meal at the restaurant, where the food is perfectly adequate, with decor-matching desserts. ✉ *100 Madonna Rd., 93405,* ☎ *805/543–3000 or 800/543–9666,* 𝔽𝔸𝕏 *805/543–1800. 109 rooms. Coffee shop, bar, dining room. MC, V.*

$–$$ ▥ **Adobe Inn.** This clean, well-run inn serves excellent full breakfasts, with fresh muffins and such daily specials as blueberry crepes or waffles topped with strawberries. ✉ *1473 Monterey St., 93401,* ☎ *805/549–0321 or 800/676–1588. 15 rooms. AE, D, MC, V.*

Nightlife and the Arts

MUSIC

The **San Luis Obispo Mozart Festival** (☎ 805/781–3008) takes place in late July and early August. Settings include the Mission San Luis Obispo de Tolosa and the Cal Poly Theater. Not all the music is Mozart; you'll hear Haydn and other composers. The Festival Fringe presents free concerts outdoors.

En Route Highway 1 and U.S. 101 become one road for a short stretch just south of San Luis Obispo. San Luis Bay Drive loops off the highway to Avila Beach, a usually quiet town that comes alive on weekends, when Cal Poly students take over. As you continue south, 20 miles of sandy, southern California-style shoreline begins at the town of Pismo Beach, where the action centers on the shops and arcades near the pier. From here there are **two routes to Solvang.** The direct route is U.S. 101, past Arroyo Grande, Santa Maria, and rural countryside that is becoming increasingly less rural. At Buellton, head east on Highway 246 to Solvang. The other option is to take Highway 1, which twists along the coast (and inland a bit at times) past Guadalupe, Vandenberg Air Force Base, and Lompoc. Along the roads near Lompoc, also known as the

Flower-Seed Capital of the World, vast fields of brightly colored flowers bloom from May through August. At Lompoc, Highway 246 travels east from Highway 1, past Mission La Purisima Concepcion through Buellton to Solvang. Highway 1 continues south and east until it rejoins U.S. 101 at Las Cruces, 9 miles below Buellton.

Mission La Purisima Concepcion

★ ⓫ *58 mi south of San Luis Obispo, Hwy. 1 to Hwy. 246 east or U.S. 101 to Hwy. 246 west.*

This mission, the most fully restored in the state, was founded in 1787. Its stark and still-remote setting powerfully evokes the life of the early Spanish settlers in California. Once a month from March through September, costumed docents demonstrate crafts; every day, displays illustrate the secular as well as religious life of the mission. A corral near the parking area holds several farm animals, including sheep that are descendants of the original mission stock. ⊠ *2295 Purisima Rd. off Mission Gate Rd.,* ☎ *805/733–3713 or 805/733–1303 to schedule a tour.* ▨ *$5.* ☉ *Daily 9–5; closed Thanksgiving, Dec. 25, Jan. 1.*

Solvang

⓬ *23 mi east of Mission La Purisima Concepcion, 3 mi east of U.S. 101, on Hwy. 246.*

You'll know when you've reached the Danish town of Solvang: The architecture suddenly turns to half-timbered buildings, windmills, and flags galore. Although it's aimed squarely at tourists, there is a genuine Danish heritage here—more than two-thirds of the town is of Danish descent. The 300 or so shops selling Danish goods and an array of knickknacks and specialty gift items are all within easy walking distance, many along Copenhagen Drive and Alisal Road. Solvang Bakery, at 460 Alisal Road, is one of a half-dozen aroma-filled bakeries in town. If Solvang seems too serene and orderly to be true, find a copy of William Castle's 1961 film, *Homicidal,* which used the town as the backdrop for gender-bending murder and mayhem.

Dining and Lodging

$–$$ ✕ **Royal Scandia Restaurant.** The main dining room here is decorated
★ like an old Danish cottage, with vaulted ceilings, rafters, and lots of brass and frosted glass. The menu caters to traditional American tastes but includes a Danish smorgasbord every evening. Champagne brunch is served on Sunday. ⊠ *400 Alisal Rd.,* ☎ *805/688–8000. AE, D, DC, MC, V.*

$ ✕ **Restaurant Molle-Kroen.** A busy upstairs dining room serves smorgasbord and other Danish specialties. It has a cheerful, light setting, with flowers on the tables and booths. The local folks come here when they want a good meal at a good price. ⊠ *435 Alisal Rd.,* ☎ *805/688–4555. AE, D, DC, MC, V.*

$$–$$$$ ☷ **Chimney Sweep Inn.** The larger (and more expensive) cottages here, built in a half-timbered style, were inspired by the C. S. Lewis children's books, *The Chronicles of Narnia.* The cottages have kitchens and fireplaces; some have private hot tubs. Room rates include Continental breakfast. ⊠ *1554 Copenhagen Dr., 93463,* ☎ *805/688–2111 or 800/824–6444,* 𝔽𝔸𝕏 *805/688–8824. 28 rooms. Hot tub. AE, D, MC, V.*

$$–$$$ ☷ **Solvang Royal Scandinavian Inn.** Rooms here—Scandinavian modern style, of course—have nice touches, like hand-painted furniture. The large, brick-walled, dark-timbered lobby has a fireplace and over-

stuffed chairs. ✉ *400 Alisal Rd., 93464,* ☎ *805/688–8000 or 800/624–5572,* 𝔽𝔸𝕏 *805/688–0761. 133 rooms. Restaurant, lounge, pool, hot tub. AE, D, DC, MC, V.*

$–$$$ 🏨 **Best Western Kronborg Inn.** Rooms at this comfortable motel three blocks from the center of town are spacious; most have balconies overlooking the pool. Continental breakfast is included. ✉ *1440 Mission Dr., 93463,* ☎ *805/688–2383,* 𝔽𝔸𝕏 *805/688–1821. 39 rooms. Pool, hot tub. AE, D, DC, MC, V.*

Nightlife and the Arts

Pacific Conservatory of the Performing Arts (☎ 805/922–8313 or 800/549–7272 in CA) presents a full spectrum of theatrical events, from classical to contemporary, with a few musicals thrown in, in different theaters in Solvang and Santa Maria. Summer events in Solvang are held in the open-air Festival Theatre, on 2nd Street off Copenhagen Drive.

Outdoor Activities and Sports

Cachuma Lake (✉ Hwy. 154, ☎ 805/688–4658), a jewel of an artificial lake 12 miles east of Solvang, has hiking, fishing, horseback riding, boating, and interpretive nature programs.

BICYCLING

Quadricycles, four-wheel carriages, and other types of bikes are available at **Surrey Cycle Rental** (✉ 475 1st St.) and **Breezy's Carriages** (✉ 414 1st St.), both in Solvang at ☎ 805/688–0091.

GLIDER RIDES

Windhaven Glider (✉ Santa Ynez Airport, Hwy. 246 east of Solvang, ☎ 805/688–2517) takes passengers on scenic rides of 15–20 or 35–40 minutes.

OFF THE BEATEN PATH | **SAN MARCOS PASS –** Highway 154 winds its spectacular way south from Solvang (drive east on Highway 246 to 154) through the Los Padres National Forest. This former stagecoach route rejoins U.S. 101 just north of Santa Barbara. The lively Cold Spring Tavern (☞ Santa Barbara Dining and Lodging, *below*) has been serving travelers since the stagecoach days.

SANTA BARBARA AND OJAI

Santa Barbara and Ojai have long been oases for Los Angeles residents in need of rest and recuperation, but they are no mere outposts. Santa Barbara combines the best attributes of a resort town and a sophisticated city, and visitors to Ojai find that it's a hub of artistic creativity.

Santa Barbara

45 mi south of Solvang on U.S. 101.

The attractions in Santa Barbara begin with the ocean and end in the foothills of the Santa Ynez Mountains. In the few miles between the beaches and the hills are downtown, then the old mission, and, a little higher up, the botanic gardens. A few miles farther up the coast, but still very much a part of Santa Barbara, is the exclusive residential district of Hope Ranch. To the east is the district called Montecito, whose informal but classy Coast Village Road has shops and restaurants. Montecito also holds the exclusive San Ysidro Ranch resort.

Santa Barbara is on a jog in the coastline, so the ocean is actually to the south. Directions can be confusing. "Up" the coast is west, "down" toward Los Angeles is actually east, and the mountains are north. A car is handy, but not essential, if you're planning on staying pretty much in town. The beaches and downtown are easily explored by bicycle or on foot, and the Santa Barbara Trolley takes visitors to most major hotels and sights, which can also be reached on the local buses.

The **visitor information center** (⊠ 1 Santa Barbara St., at Cabrillo Blvd., ☎ 805/965–3021) distributes a free guide to a scenic drive that circles the town with a detour into the downtown. It passes the harbor, beaches, Hope Ranch, and the old mission, yields fine views on the way to Montecito, then returns you to the beaches. You can pick up the drive, marked with blue SCENIC DRIVE signs, anywhere along the loop. A free guide to the downtown, the "Red Tile Walking Tour," is also available free from the visitor centers. It hits historical spots in a 12-block area.

⑬ Stearns Wharf extends the length of three city blocks into the Pacific. The view from here back toward the city gives you a sense of Santa Barbara's size and general layout. Although it's a nice walk from the Cabrillo Boulevard parking areas, you can drive out and park (for a fee) on the pier, then wander through the shops or stop for a meal at one of the wharf's restaurants or at the snack bar. ⊠ *Cabrillo Blvd. at the foot of State St.*

🐾 **⑭ Sea Center,** a branch of the Museum of Natural History that specializes in exhibits of marine life, is a major attraction on Stearns Wharf. Exhibits—aquariums, life-size models of whales and dolphins, undersea dioramas, interactive computer-video displays, and the remains of shipwrecks—depict marine life from the Santa Barbara coastline to the Channel Islands. Visitors to the Touch Tank handle marine invertebrates, fish, and marine plants collected from nearby waters. ⊠ *211 Stearns Wharf,* ☎ *805/962–0885.* 🎟 *$2.* ☉ *Sea Center daily 10–5 (call weekday mornings Oct.–May to make sure school field trips haven't closed center to public), Touch Tank daily noon–4.*

⑮ A paved, man-made breakwater protects the **Santa Barbara Yacht Harbor.** You can take a ½-mile walk along the breakwater, check out the tackle and bait shops, or hire a boat. ⊠ *West end of Cabrillo Blvd.*

⑯ The **Moreton Bay Fig Tree,** which was planted in 1877, is so huge it reputedly can provide shade for 10,000 people. In recent years it has become a gathering place for homeless people. ⊠ *Chapala St. between U.S. 101 and Cabrillo Blvd.*

⑰ East Beach, a wide swath of sand at the east end of Cabrillo Boulevard, is a great spot for people-watching. An inordinate number of sunbathers here look as if they ought to be fashion models. Sand volleyball courts, summertime lifeguard and sports competitions, and arts-and-crafts shows on Sundays and holidays make for an often-lively experience. Showers (no towels), lockers, and beach rentals—also a weight room—are provided at Cabrillo Pavilion Bathhouse (⊠ 1118 Cabrillo Blvd., ☎ 805/965–0509). For children who quickly tire of the beach, there's an elaborate jungle-gym play area next to the bathhouse.

⑱ The **Andree Clark Bird Refuge,** a peaceful lagoon and gardens, sits just north of East Beach. Bike trails and footpaths, punctuated by signs identifying both native and migratory birds, skirt the lagoon. ⊠ *1400 E. Cabrillo Blvd.* 🎟 *Free.*

🐾 **⑲** The natural settings of the **Santa Barbara Zoo** shelter elephants, exotic birds, and big-game cats, such as the rare amur leopard, a thick-furred, high-altitude dweller from Asia. Youngsters enjoy the scenic railroad and barnyard petting zoo. A gorilla habitat that opened in 1996

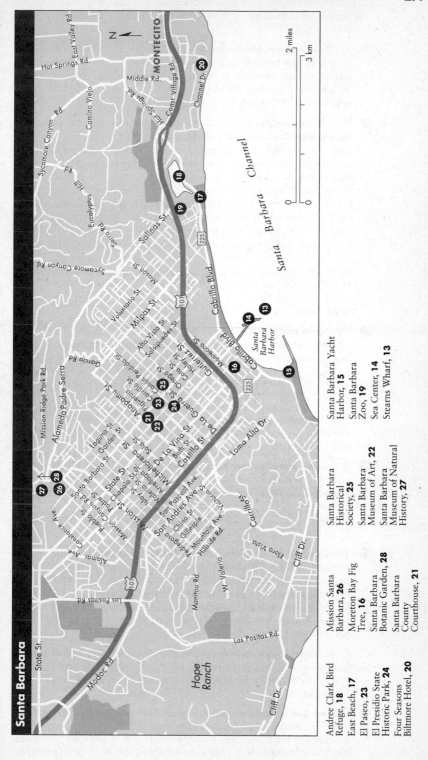

Santa Barbara

Andree Clark Bird
Refuge, **18**
East Beach, **17**
El Paseo, **23**
El Presidio State
Historic Park, **24**
Four Seasons
Biltmore Hotel, **20**

Mission Santa
Barbara, **26**
Moreton Bay Fig
Tree, **16**
Santa Barbara
Botanic Garden, **28**
Santa Barbara
County
Courthouse, **21**

Santa Barbara
Historical
Society, **25**
Santa Barbara
Museum of Art, **22**
Santa Barbara
Museum of Natural
History, **27**

Santa Barbara Yacht
Harbor, **15**
Santa Barbara
Zoo, **19**
Sea Center, **14**
Stearns Wharf, **13**

became an instant hit. ⊠ *500 Niños Dr.,* ☏ *805/962–6310.* ☑ *$5.* ⊙ *Daily 10–5.*

⑳ The **Four Seasons Biltmore Hotel** (☞ Dining and Lodging, *below*) has long been the favored spot for Santa Barbara's high society and the visiting rich and famous to indulge in quiet California-style elegance. Its lobby and gardens are always perfectly manicured. ⊠ *120 Channel Dr. east of Cabrillo Blvd.*

★ **㉑** With its brilliant, hand-painted tiles and spiral staircase, the **Santa Barbara County Courthouse** has all the grandeur of a Moorish palace. This magnificent building was completed in 1929, part of a rebuilding process after a 1925 earthquake destroyed many downtown structures. At the time Santa Barbara was also in the midst of a cultural awakening, and the trend was toward an architecture appropriate to the area's climate and history. The result is the harmonious Mediterranean-Spanish look of much of the downtown area, especially municipal buildings. An elevator takes visitors to an arched observation area in the courthouse tower that has a panoramic view of the city. The murals in the supervisors' ceremonial chambers on the courthouse's second floor were painted by an artist who did backdrops for some of Cecil B. DeMille's silent films. ⊠ *1100 block of Anacapa St.,* ☏ *805/962–6464.* ⊙ *Weekdays 8:30–4:30, weekends 10–5. Free 1-hr guided tours Mon.–Sat. 2 PM, Wed. and Fri. 10:30 AM and 2 PM.*

㉒ The **Santa Barbara Museum of Art** houses a fine permanent collection of ancient sculpture, Asian art, a collection of French Impressionist paintings, and a sampling of American artists, such as Grandma Moses. ⊠ *1130 State St.,* ☏ *805/963–4364.* ☑ *$4; free Thurs. and 1st Sun. of month.* ⊙ *Tues.–Sat. 11–5 (until 9 PM Thurs.), Sun. noon–5. Guided tours Tues.–Sun. 1 PM, Wed., Thurs. and Sat. noon.*

㉓ The **El Paseo** shopping arcade was built around an old adobe home. There are several newer arcades nearby and also many small art galleries (☞ Shopping, *below*). ⊠ *800 block of State St.*

㉔ **El Presidio State Historic Park** was founded in 1782 as the Presidio—one of four military strongholds established by the Spanish along the coast of California. The guardhouse, El Cuartel, is one of the two original adobe buildings that remain of the complex and is the oldest building owned by the state. ⊠ *123 E. Cañon Perdido St.,* ☏ *805/966–9719.* ☑ *Free.* ⊙ *Daily 10:30–4:30.*

㉕ The museum of the **Santa Barbara Historical Society** exhibits decorative and fine arts, furniture, costumes, and documents from the town's past. Adjacent is the Gledhill Library, a collection of books, photographs, maps, and manuscripts about the area. ⊠ *136 E. De La Guerra St.,* ☏ *805/966–1601.* ☑ *Museum $3, library $2 per hr up to $5.* ⊙ *Museum Tues.–Sat. 10–5, Sun. noon–5; library Tues.–Fri. 10–4, 1st Sat. of month 1–4.*

☾ Children and adults will enjoy the elaborate **Kids' World public playground,** a complex maze of fantasy climbing structures, turrets, slides, and tunnels built by Santa Barbara parents. ⊠ *Santa Barbara St. near Micheltorena St.*

★ **㉖** **Mission Santa Barbara,** established in 1786, sits north of downtown at the base of the Santa Ynez foothills. Its architecture and layout evolved from adobe-brick buildings with thatched roofs to more permanent edifices as the mission's population burgeoned during its early years. An earthquake in 1812 destroyed the third church built on the site; its replacement, the present structure, still active as a Catholic church, became a boys' school and a seminary in the post–Mission era. A garden with cacti, palm trees, and other succulents makes for a pleasant stroll. ⊠ *2201 Laguna St.,* ☎ *805/682–4149.* ☜ *$3.* ☉ *Daily 9–5.*

☺ ㉗ The full-size skeleton of a blue whale at the entrance serves as a land-mark for **Santa Barbara Museum of Natural History.** The highlights of the complex are the planetarium and E. L. Wiegand Space Lab; a room of dioramas illustrating Chumash Indian history and culture; and the bird diversity room, filled with startlingly lifelike taxidermized specimens, complete with nests and eggs. Many of the exhibits have interactive components. ⊠ *2559 Puesta del Sol Rd.,* ☎ *805/682–4711.* ☜ *$5.* ☉ *Mon.–Sat. 9–5, Sun. and holidays 10–5.*

★ ㉘ Five-plus miles of trails meander through the 65 acres of native plants in the **Santa Barbara Botanic Garden.** The Mission Dam, built in 1806, stands just beyond the redwood grove and above the partially uncovered aqueduct that once carried water to Mission Santa Barbara. An ethnobotanical display exhibits replicas of the plants used by the Chumash Indians. ⊠ *1212 Mission Canyon Rd.,* ☎ *805/682–4726.* ☜ *$3.* ☉ *Mar.–Oct. weekdays 9–5, weekends 9–6; Nov.–Feb., weekdays 9–4, weekends 9–5. Guided tours daily at 2 PM; additional tour at 10:30 AM Thurs., Sat., and Sun.*

OFF THE BEATEN PATH **CHANNEL ISLANDS NATIONAL PARK AND NATIONAL MARINE SANCTUARY –** Hearty travelers should consider a day visit or overnight camping trip to one of the five Channel Islands that often appear in a haze off the Santa Barbara horizon. The most popular is Anacapa Island, 11 miles off the coast. The islands' remoteness and unpredictable seas protected them from development and now provide a nature enthusiast's paradise—both underwater and on land. On a good day, you'll be able to view seals, sea lions, and much bird life. From December through March, migrating whales can be seen close up. On land, tide pools are often accessible. Underwater, divers can view fish, giant squid, and coral. Frenchy's Cove, on the west end of the island, has a swimming beach and fine snorkeling. The waters of the channel are often rough and can make for a rugged trip out to the islands (☞ Boats and Charters *in* Outdoor Activities and Sports, *below,* for information about group outings).

Dining and Lodging

$$$–$$$$ ✕ **The Stonehouse.** This atmospheric restaurant in a turn-of-the-century granite farmhouse is part of the San Ysidro Ranch resort. The contemporary southern American menu offers such treats as dry-aged New York steak with smoked tomato-horseradish sauce and clam hash, seared rare *ahi* tuna in an herb crust with sun-dried-tomato couscous, and an excellent four-course vegetarian menu. Even better than the generally wonderful food is the pastoral setting. Be sure to have lunch—salads, pastas, and sandwiches—on the tree-house-like outdoor patio. At night, the candlelit interior becomes seriously romantic. ⊠ *900 San Ysidro La., Montecito,* ☎ *805/969–4100. Reservations essential. AE, MC, V.*

$$$ ✕ **Citronelle.** The offspring of Michel Richard's famed Citrus in Los ★ Angeles has brought Santa Barbarans some of the best California-French cuisine they've ever had this close to home. The accent is on Riviera-style dishes: light and delicate but loaded with intriguing good tastes. The desserts are unmatched anywhere in southern California. There are splendid, sweeping views of the harbor from the dining room's picture windows—make sure to arrive before sunset. ⊠ *901 E. Cabrillo Blvd.,* ☎ *805/963–0111. Reservations essential. AE, D, DC, MC, V.*

\$\$–\$\$\$ ✕ **Palace Café.** The Palace has won acclaim for its Cajun and Creole dishes, such as blackened redfish and jambalaya with dirty rice. Caribbean fare here includes delicious coconut shrimp. Just in case the dishes aren't spicy enough for you, each table has a bottle of hot sauce. Be prepared for a wait of up to 45 minutes on weekends. ⊠ *8 E. Cota St.,* ☏ *805/966–3133. AE, MC, V. No lunch.*

\$\$ ✕ **Café Buenos Aires.** The always busy Buenos Aires serves salads, sandwiches, pastas, and traditional Argentine empanadas (small turnovers filled with chicken, beef, or vegetables) for lunch. Dinner can be fashioned out of potato omelets, Spanish red sausage in beer sauce, octopus stewed with tomato and onion, and other tapas. Argentine specialties—grilled short ribs or grilled rib-eye steak sautéed in sweet butter, both served with homemade french fries (with or without garlic and parsley)—pastas, and larger empanadas are among the main entrées. ⊠ *37 E. Victoria St.,* ☏ *805/963–0242. Reservations essential for dinner. AE, DC, MC, V.*

\$\$ ✕ **Cold Spring Tavern.** Well worth the drive out of town, this century-old roadhouse is on the former stagecoach route through the San Marcos Pass. It's part Harley-biker hangout, part romantic country hideaway, a mix that works surprisingly well. Game dishes—rabbit, venison, quail—are the specialty, along with such American standards as ribs, steak, and a great chili. It's a one-of-a-kind spot. ⊠ *5995 Stagecoach Rd., San Marcos Pass,* ☏ *805/967–0066. AE, MC, V.*

\$\$ ✕ **Pane & Vino.** This tiny trattoria, and its equally small sidewalk dining terrace, sits in a tree-shaded, flower-decked shopping center in Montecito, just east of Santa Barbara. The cold antipasto is very good, as are grilled meats and fish, pastas, and salads. ⊠ *1482 E. Valley Rd., Montecito,* ☏ *805/969–9274. Reservations essential. AE, MC, V. No lunch Sun.*

\$–\$\$ ✕ **Arigato Sushi.** Sushi fans will appreciate the excellent, fresh seafood served in this small, atmospheric Japanese restaurant and sushi bar. Innovation reigns here, with creations such as sushi pizza on seaweed and Hawaiian sashimi salad. ⊠ *11 W. Victoria St.,* ☏ *805/965–6074. Reservations not accepted. AE, MC, V. No lunch.*

\$–\$\$ ✕ **Brigitte's.** This lively State Street café serves quintessential Californian cuisine and local wines at relatively low prices to a handsome crowd of locals and tourists. The individual pizzas are always worth trying, as are the pastas (such as basil fettuccine with prawns and roasted peppers in pesto), grilled fresh fish, and roast lamb. ⊠ *1327 State St.,* ☏ *805/966–9676. Reservations not accepted. MC, V. No lunch Sun.*

\$–\$\$ ✕ **Harbor Restaurant.** This sparkling spot on the pier is where locals like to take out-of-town guests for great views and average American food. The casual, nautical bar and grill upstairs serves sandwiches, large salads, and a huge variety of appetizers; the outdoor terrace is a glorious spot for a sandwich or a beer on a sunny day. Downstairs you'll find healthy portions of fresh seafood, prime rib, and steaks. Every seat has a harbor view. ⊠ *210 Stearns Wharf,* ☏ *805/963–3311. AE, MC, V.*

\$–\$\$ ✕ **Montecito Café.** The ambience is upscale yet casual at this pleasant restaurant serving contemporary California-American cuisine—fresh fish, grilled chicken, steak, and pasta. The salads and lamb dishes are particularly inventive. ⊠ *1295 Coast Village Rd.,* ☏ *805/969–3392. AE, MC, V.*

\$ ✕ **Castagnola Seafood Restaurant.** This unassuming spot just two blocks from the beach serves good, fresh broiled fish. The homemade clam chowder is excellent. ⊠ *205 Santa Barbara St.,* ☏ *805/962–8053. Reservations not accepted. AE, D, MC, V.*

$ ✕ **La Super-Rica.** A favorite of Julia Child's, this food stand with patio
★ serves the best and hottest Mexican dishes between Los Angeles and
San Francisco. Fans drive for miles to fill up on the soft tacos and incredible beans. ✉ *622 N. Milpas St., at Alphonse St.,* ☎ *805/963–*
4940. No credit cards.

$ ✕ **Roy.** Voted best new restaurant and best dinner under $10 by local
papers, this downtown storefront is a real bargain. Owner-chef Leroy
Gandy serves a $10 fixed-price dinner that includes a small salad, fresh
soup, and a tempting roster of Cal-Mediterranean main courses: shrimp
ravioli, marinated leg of lamb with eggplant ratatouille, grilled salmon
with pineapple-orange-mango chutney and a mint-butter sauce. Expect
a wait on weekends. ✉ *7 W. Carrillo St.,* ☎ *805/966–5636. Reser-*
vations not accepted. AE, MC, V. Closed Mon.

$ ✕ **Your Place.** Tasty seafood, curries, and vegetarian dishes keep this
small restaurant packed for lunch and dinner. The sea scallops garnished
with crispy basil are alone worth a trip. Your Place has consistently
been named best Thai restaurant by local periodicals. ✉ *22 Milpas St.,*
☎ *805/966–5151. AE, DC, MC, V. Closed Mon.*

$$$$ ✕⬚ **Four Seasons Biltmore Hotel.** This is Santa Barbara's grande dame.
★ Muted pastels and bleached woods give the cabanas behind the main
building a light, airy touch without sacrificing the hotel's reputation
for understated elegance. Surrounded by lush gardens and palm trees,
the Biltmore is a bit more formal than other properties in town. Dining is indoors and formal at the hotel's highly regarded La Marina Restaurant—the California–Continental menu changes monthly—and outdoors
and more casual at The Patio. ✉ *1260 Channel Dr., Montecito 93108,*
☎ *805/969–2261 or 800/332–3442,* ⅉ *805/969–4682. 234 rooms.*
2 restaurants, bar, 2 pools, hot tub, putting green, tennis courts, cro-
quet, health club, shuffleboard. AE, DC, MC, V.

$$$$ ✕⬚ **San Ysidro Ranch.** At this luxury "ranch" you can feel at home
★ in jeans and cowboy boots, but be prepared to dress for dinner. A hideout for the Hollywood set, this romantic place hosted John and Jackie
Kennedy on their honeymoon. Guest cottages, all with down comforters
and wood-burning stoves or fireplaces, are scattered among 14 acres
of orange trees and flower beds; hiking trails crisscross 500 acres of
open space surrounding the property. The Stonehouse Restaurant (☞
above) is a Santa Barbara institution. The hotel, which welcomes children and pets, provides personal beauty services and 24-hour room service. ✉ *900 San Ysidro La., Montecito 93108,* ☎ *805/969–5046 or*
800/368–6788, ⅉ *805/565–1995. 43 rooms. Restaurant, pool, mas-*
sage, spa, tennis courts, boccie, exercise room, horseback riding, horse-
shoes. Two-day minimum stay on weekends, 3 days on holidays. AE,
MC, V.

$$$–$$$$ ⬚ **Santa Barbara Inn.** Directly across the street from East Beach, this
three-story gussied-up motel has an interior decor featuring light
woods, teal accents, and subdued tones. The location—many of the
rooms have ocean views—and the excellent restaurant, Citronelle, are
the real draws, not the inn itself. ✉ *901 E. Cabrillo Blvd., 93103,* ☎
805/966–2285 or 800/231–0431, ⅉ *805/966–6584. 71 rooms.*
Restaurant, pool, hot tub. AE, D, DC, MC, V.

$$$–$$$$ ⬚ **Simpson House Inn.** Traditional B&B fans will enjoy the beautifully
★ appointed Victorian main house of this inn, set on a quiet acre in the
heart of town. Those seeking total privacy and sybaritic comfort should
choose one of the exceptional new cottages or century-old barn suites,
each complete with wood-burning fireplace, luxurious bedding, state-
of-the-art electronics, and whirlpool-equipped bath. Room rates include
full breakfast. ✉ *121 E. Arrellaga St., 93101,* ☎ *805/963–7067 or*

800/676–1280, FAX *805/564–4811. 14 rooms. 2-night minimum stay on weekends. AE, D, MC, V.*

$$$–$$$$ 🏨 **The Upham.** This handsomely restored Victorian hotel on an acre of gardens in the historic downtown area was established in 1871. Period furnishings and antiques adorn the rooms and cottages, some of which have fireplaces and private patios. Room size varies from small to quite spacious. Continental breakfast and afternoon wine and cheese are served in the lobby and on the garden veranda. ⊠ *1404 De La Vina St., 93101,* ☎ *805/962–0058 or 800/727–0876,* FAX *805/963–2825. 50 rooms. AE, D, DC, MC, V.*

$$–$$$$ 🏨 **Villa Rosa.** The rooms and intimate lobby of this Spanish-style stucco-and-wood hotel one block from the beach are decorated in an informal southwestern style. Rates include Continental breakfast, wine and cheese in the afternoon, and port and sherry in the evening. ⊠ *15 Chapala St., 93101,* ☎ *805/966–0851,* FAX *805/962–7159. 18 rooms. Pool, hot tub. AE, MC, V.*

$$–$$$ 🏨 **Ambassador by the Sea.** The wrought-iron trim and mosaic tiling on this Spanish-style building near the harbor and Stearns Wharf give it the feel of a typical California beach motel. The rooms have verandas, and sundecks overlook the ocean and a bike path. ⊠ *202 W. Cabrillo Blvd., 93101,* ☎ *805/965–4577,* FAX *805/965–9937. 32 rooms. Pool. AE, D, DC, MC, V.*

$$–$$$ 🏨 **Old Yacht Club Inn.** Built in 1912 as a private home in the California Craftsman style, this inn near the beach was one of Santa Barbara's first bed-and-breakfasts. The rooms have turn-of-the-century furnishings and Oriental rugs. The adjacent Hitchcock House holds four rooms with private entrances. Guests receive complimentary full breakfast and evening wine, along with the use of bikes and beach chairs. There is no smoking. ⊠ *431 Corona del Mar Dr., 93103,* ☎ *805/962–1277 or 800/676–1676; in CA, 800/549–1676;* FAX *805/962–3989. 9 rooms. Dining room. AE, D, MC, V.*

$ 🏨 **Motel 6.** The low price and location near the beach are the pluses for this no-frills place. Reserve well in advance all year. ⊠ *443 Corona del Mar Dr., 93103,* ☎ *805/564–1392. 51 units. Pool. AE, D, DC, MC, V.*

Nightlife and the Arts

Most major hotels present nightly entertainment during the summer season and live weekend entertainment all year. State Street has a good jazz scene. Santa Barbara supports a professional symphony and chamber orchestra and an impressive art museum. The proximity to the University of California at Santa Barbara assures an endless stream of visiting artists and performers. To see what's scheduled around town pick up a copy of the free weekly *Santa Barbara Independent* newspaper.

BARS AND CLUBS

Joe's Cafe (⊠ 536 State St., Santa Barbara, ☎ 805/966–4638), where steins of beer accompany hearty bar food, makes for a rowdy, collegiate outing.

Plow & Angel (⊠ San Ysidro Ranch, 900 San Ysidro La., Montecito, ☎ 805/969–5046) has live jazz on Thursdays and Fridays; then and at other times it's perfect for those seeking quieter conversation, an early California feeling, perhaps even romance.

Soho (⊠ 1221 State St., ☎ 805/962–7776), a hip restaurant and hangout, presents weeknight jazz music; on weekends, the mood livens with good blues and rock.

State & A (⊠ 1201 State St., ☎ 805/966–1010), a very popular bar and grill, is for people-watchers and fans of easygoing California rock music.

Zelo (✉ 630 State St., ☎ 805/966–5792), a high-energy restaurant, doubles as a progressive rock and punk dance club with offbeat videos and innovative lighting.

Performing Arts

Arlington Theater (✉ 1317 State St.), an enormous Moorish-style former movie palace, is home to the Santa Barbara Symphony.

Center Stage Theatre (✉ Paseo Nuevo, 700 block of State St., 2nd floor) presents plays and readings.

Granada Theatre (✉ 1216 State St.), a peculiarly "restored" movie palace, is the headquarters of the Santa Barbara Civic Light Opera.

The Lobero (✉ 33 E. Cañon Perdido St.), a state landmark, hosts community theater groups and touring professionals.

Outdoor Activities and Sports

BEACHES

Santa Barbara's beaches don't have the big surf of the shoreline farther south, but they also don't have the crowds. A short walk from the parking lot can usually find you a solitary spot. Be aware that fog often hugs the coast until about noon in May and June.

The usually gentle surf at **Arroyo Burro County Beach** (✉ Cliff Dr. at Las Positas Rd.) makes it ideal for families with young children. **Goleta Beach Park** (✉ Ward Memorial Hwy.) is a favorite with the college students from the nearby University of California campus. Successively west of Santa Barbara off U.S. 101 are El Capitan, Refugio, and Gaviota state beaches, each with campsites, picnic tables, and fire pits. East of the city is the sheltered, sunny, often crowded state beach at Carpinteria.

BICYCLING

The level, two-lane, 3-mile Cabrillo Bike Lane passes the Santa Barbara Zoo, Andree Clark Bird Refuge, beaches, and the harbor. There are restaurants along the way, or you can stop for a picnic along the palm-lined path looking out on the Pacific.

Beach Rentals (✉ 22 State St., ☎ 805/966–6733) has bikes, quadricycles, and skates.

Cycles 4 Rent (✉ Fess Parker's Red Lion Resort, 633 E. Cabrillo, ☎ 805/564–4333, ext. 444) has bikes and quadricycles.

BOATS AND CHARTERS

Island Packers (✉ 1867 Spinnaker Dr., Ventura, ☎ 805/642–1393) conducts day trips and camping excursions to the five Channel Islands. Boats link up with national-park naturalists for hikes and nature programs. A limited number of visitors are allowed on each island, and unpredictable weather can limit island landings. Reservations are essential in the summer.

Santa Barbara Sailing Center (✉ Santa Barbara Yacht Harbor launching ramp, ☎ 805/962–2826 or 800/350–9090) provides sailing instruction, rents and charters sailboats, and organizes dinner and sunset-champagne cruises, island excursions, and whale-watching expeditions.

SEA Landing (✉ Cabrillo Blvd. at Bath and breakwater, ☎ 805/963–3564) operates fully equipped surface and deep-sea fishing charters year-round, plus dinner cruises and island and whale-watching excursions.

GOLF

Santa Barbara Golf Club (✉ Las Positas Rd. and McCaw Ave., ☎ 805/687–7087) has an 18-hole course.

Sandpiper Golf Course (✉ 7925 Hollister Ave., Goleta, ☎ 805/968–1541), a challenging 18-hole course, is a former stop on the women's professional tour.

HORSEBACK RIDING

The Circle Bar B Guest Ranch (✉ 1800 Refugio Rd., Goleta, ☎ 805/968–3901) operates trail rides—minimum 1½ hour—for parties of 1 to 26; one four-hour excursion includes a picnic lunch.

POLO

Santa Barbara Polo & Racquet Club (✉ Via Real off Santa Claus La., Carpinteria, ☎ 805/684–6683) invites the public to watch Sunday matches April through October. Admission is $5.

TENNIS

Many Santa Barbara hotels have their own courts, but there are also excellent public facilities. Day permits, for $3, are available at these courts (☎ 805/564–5517): **Las Positas Municipal Courts** (✉ 1002 Las Positas Rd.), **Municipal Courts** (✉ Near Salinas St. and U.S. 101), and **Pershing Park** (✉ Castillo St. and Cabrillo Blvd.).

VOLLEYBALL

The east end of Santa Barbara's East Beach has more than a dozen sand-lots. There are some casual pickup games, but if you get into one, be prepared—these folks play serious volleyball.

Shopping

State Street, the commercial hub of Santa Barbara, is a joy to shop. Thrift shops, elegant women's wear, bookstores, sporting goods, shopping centers, quirky storefronts—it's all here, and it's all accessible on foot or on the 25¢ battery-powered trolley that runs between the waterfront and the 1300 block. A swank collection of boutiques lines Montecito's **Coast Village Road,** where the landed gentry pick up truffle oil, picture frames, and designer sweats.

SHOPPING AREAS

In all, 32 shops, art galleries, and studios share the courtyard and gardens of **El Paseo** (✉ Cañon Perdido St., between State and Anacapa Sts.), a shopping arcade rich in history. Lunch on the outdoor patio is a nice break from a downtown tour. Open-air **Paseo Nuevo** (✉ 700 and 800 blocks of State St.) is home to upscale chains such as the Eddie Bauer Home Store, Nordstrom, and the California Pizza Kitchen but is more notable for such cherished local institutions as Stampa Barbara (rubber-stamp paradise) and children's clothier This Little Piggy.

In Santa Barbara a dozen **antiques and gift shops** are clustered in restored Victorian buildings on Brinkerhoff Avenue, two blocks west of State Street at West Cota Street. Serious antiques hunters head a few miles south of Santa Barbara to the beach town of Summerland, which is rife with shops and markets. Wanda Livernois publishes a map and guide to Santa Barbara antiques dealers, available at 533 Brinkerhoff Avenue (or ☎ 805/962–4247 to have one mailed).

BOOKS

Chaucer's Bookstore (✉ 3321 State St., ☎ 805/682–6787) is a well-stocked independent.
Earthling Book Shop and Café (✉ 1137 State St., ☎ 805/965–0926) is arguably Santa Barbara's cultural and intellectual center. Rambling yet homey, the Earthling holds book signings, poetry readings, a children's story time, and many other events. The book and magazine selection is terrific.

CLOTHING

Pacific Leisure (✉ 929 State St., Santa Barbara, ☎ 805/962–8828) stocks the latest in California casual and beach wear, shoes, and beach towels.

In case you want to be welcomed there.

We're here to see that you're always welcomed at establishments everywhere. That's why millions of people carry the American Express® Card – for peace of mind, confidence, and security, around the world or just around the corner.

do more

AMERICAN EXPRESS

Cards

In case you're running low.

We're here to help with more than 118,000 Express Cash locations around the world. In order to enroll, just call American Express before you start your vacation.

do more

Express Cash

And just in case.

We're here with American Express® Travelers Cheques
and Cheques *for Two*.® They're the safest way to carry
money on your vacation and the surest way to get a
refund, practically anywhere, anytime.
Another way we help you...

do more ®

**Travelers
Cheques**

Swept Away (✉ 732 State St., ☎ 805/962–8291) is a great place to shop for the quintessential casual southern California look—sophisticated but beachy cotton women's clothing.

Territory Ahead (✉ 515 State St., ☎ 805/962–5558), a high-quality, outdoorsy catalog company whose only showroom is in Santa Barbara, sells fashionably rugged clothing for men and women.

Wendy Foster (✉ Paseo Nuevo, ☎ 805/965–2634), a local clothier, captures the fluid California style of women's wear.

Yellowstone Clothing (✉ 527 State St., ☎ 805/963–9609) has a wide selection of high-quality used and vintage clothing.

KITCHEN

Jordano's (✉ 614 Chapala St., ☎ 805/965–3031) attracts cooks and kitchen junkies from Los Angeles and beyond. Part professional restaurant supply, part gourmet store, part cooking school, this sprawling shop stocks everything from seafood forks to espresso machines, flavored oils to herb pots.

Ojai

🟢 *40 mi southeast of Santa Barbara, U.S. 101 to Hwy. 150 to Hwy. 33.*

In and around rural Ojai acres of orange and avocado groves look like the picture-postcard images of agricultural southern California from decades ago. Recent years have seen an influx of showbiz types and other Angelenos who have opted for a life out of the fast lane. Moviemaker Frank Capra used the Ojai Valley as a backdrop for his 1936 classic, *Lost Horizon.* The compact town can be easily explored on foot, or hop on a new trolley that takes riders on a 45-minute loop daily from 8:30 to 5:30. If you tell the driver you're a visitor, you'll get an informal guided tour. If you want to walk, the **Ojai Visitor Center** (✉ 338 E. Ojai Ave.) has information. Be aware that the valley sizzles in the summer, when temperatures routinely reach 90°F.

The works of local artists can be seen in the Spanish-style shopping arcade along the main street. **The Art Center** (✉ 113 S. Montgomery, ☎ 805/646–0117) exhibits artworks and presents theater and dance. **The Ojai Valley Museum** (✉ 109 S. Montgomery, ☎ 805/646–2290) documents the valley's history and displays Native American artifacts. It's open Wednesday through Monday from 1 to 4.

A stroll around town should include a stop at **Bart's Books** (✉ 302 W. Matilija, ☎ 805/646–3755), an outdoor store sheltered by native oaks and overflowing with used books. **Local Hero** (✉ 254 E. Ojai Ave., ☎ 805/646–3165) sells books and hosts music, readings, and booksignings on weekend evenings. There's also a café here. On Sunday, local organic and specialty growers sell their produce from 10 to 2 at the **Farmers Market** (✉ On the plaza behind the arcade). On Wednesday evenings in summer, the free all-American music played by the Ojai Band draws upward of 2,000 listeners to **Libbey Park** in the heart of town.

A hiker's paradise, Ojai is home of the 9-mile **Ojai Valley Trail** and many more miles of trails in the surrounding hills. The Ojai Chamber of Commerce (☞ Contacts and Resources *in* Central Coast A to Z, *below*)
🟢 publishes a regional trail map. Nearby **Lake Casitas** on Highway 150, which has boating, fishing, and camping, was the venue for the 1984 Summer Olympic rowing events.

One of the attractions in Ojai is a hot spring that makes use of natu-
🟢 ral mineral water from nearby hills. The spa at **Wheeler Hot Springs** emerges like an oasis 7 miles north of town on Highway 33. Its tall

palms and herb gardens are fed by an adjacent stream, and natural mineral waters fill the four redwood hot tubs and a large pool. Massage and skin-care services are also available. The well-kept spa's restaurant is a major draw (☞ Dining and Lodging, *below*). ⊠ *16825 Maricopa Hwy.,* ☎ *805/646–8131 or 800/994–3353.* ⊘ *Mon.–Thurs. 9–9, Fri.–Sun. 9 AM–10 PM. Reservations advised at least a wk in advance for weekends, especially for spa.*

Dining and Lodging

$$$ ✕ **L'Auberge.** Tasty country-French–Belgian food is paired with a terrific country setting here. When the weather's fine, those in the know reserve an early table on the patio so they can accompany their rack of lamb with a glorious sunset. ⊠ *314 El Paseo Rd.,* ☎ *805/646–2288. AE, MC, V. No lunch weekdays.*

$$–$$$ ✕ **Wheeler Hot Springs Restaurant.** The menu, California-Mediterranean in spirit, changes seasonally but always showcases herbs and vegetables grown in the spa's garden. The restaurant presents live entertainment Thursday through Sunday. Packages are available that include Saturday or Sunday brunch, massage, and hot tub. ⊠ 16825 Maricopa Hwy., ☎ 805/646–8131 or 800/994–3353. ⊠ *Reservations essential. AE, MC, V. Closed Mon.–Wed. No dinner Sun.*

$$$$ ✕▥ **Oaks at Ojai.** This well-known, comfortable but not luxurious
   ★   health spa has a solid fitness program that includes lodging, three nutritionally balanced, surprisingly good low-calorie meals, complete use of spa facilities, and 16 optional fitness classes. ⊠ *122 E. Ojai Ave., 93023,* ☎ *805/646–5573 or 800/753–6257,* ℻ *805/640–1504. 46 rooms. Dining room, pool, hot tubs, sauna, exercise room. 2-day minimum stay. D, MC, V.*

$$$$ ✕▥ **Ojai Valley Inn & Spa.** This outdoorsy, golf-oriented resort is set in landscaped grounds lush with flowers. The peaceful setting comes with hillside views in nearly all directions; nearby is the inn's 800-acre ranch, where guests can hike, mountain bike, ride horses, and birdwatch. Some of the nicer rooms are in the original adobe building and preserve such luxurious features as huge bathrooms and the original tiles. Families make use of popular Camp Ojai, held in summer and on holidays for kids 4–12, and the remarkable collection of miniature animals in the petting farm. Scheduled for completion in early 1997 is a spa with 21 massage and treatment rooms, cardiovascular floor, beauty salon, quiet rooms, and three penthouse guest rooms. The two restaurants tout "Ojai regional cuisine," using locally grown produce and locally made foods. ⊠ *Country Club Rd., 93023,* ☎ *805/646– 5511 or 800/422–6524,* ℻ *805/646–7969. 207 units. 2 restaurants, bar, 2 pools, spa, 18-hole golf course, tennis courts, hiking, horseback riding, mountain bikes. AE, D, DC, MC, V.*

$$–$$$ ▥ **Best Western Casa Ojai.** This spacious, modern hotel sits on Ojai's main street, across from Soule Park Golf Course. Rooms are simple and clean. Continental breakfast is included. ⊠ *1302 E. Ojai Ave., 93023,* ☎ *805/646–8175 or 800/255–8175,* ℻ *805/640–8247. 45 units. Pool, hot tub. AE, D, DC, MC, V.*

The Arts

For more than five decades, the **Ojai Festival** (☎ 805/646–2094) has attracted internationally known progressive and traditional musicians for concerts the weekend after Memorial Day.

CENTRAL COAST A TO Z

Arriving and Departing

By Bus
Greyhound Lines (☎ 800/231–2222) provides service from San Francisco and Los Angeles to San Luis Obispo and Santa Barbara.

By Car
The only way to see the most dramatic section of the Central Coast, the 70 miles between Big Sur and San Simeon, is by car. Heading south on Highway 1, you'll be on the ocean side of the road and will get the best views. Don't expect to make good time along here. The road is narrow and twisting with a single lane in each direction, making it difficult to pass slower traffic or the many lumbering RVs. In fog or rain, the drive can be downright nerve-racking. I–280 from San Francisco linking to U.S. 101 to San Luis Obispo is the quicker, easier alternative, but it misses the coast entirely.

By Plane
American/American Eagle, Skywest/Delta, United/United Express, and **USAir Express** (☞ Air Travel *in* Important Contacts A to Z for phone numbers) fly into **Santa Barbara Municipal Airport** (⊠ 500 Fowler Rd., ☎ 805/683–4011), 8 miles from downtown.

Santa Barbara Airbus (☎ 805/964–7759 or 800/733–6354) shuttles travelers between Santa Barbara and Los Angeles Airport. **Aero Airport Limousine** (☎ 805/965–2412) serves Los Angeles Airport (by reservation only). The **Santa Barbara Metropolitan Transit District** (☎ 805/683–3702) Bus 11 runs from the airport to the downtown transit center.

By Train
Amtrak (☎ 800/872–7245) runs the *Coast Starlight* from Los Angeles along the coast from Santa Barbara to San Luis Obispo. From there it heads inland for the rest of the route to the San Francisco Bay Area and Seattle. Local numbers are, in Santa Barbara, ☎ 805/963–1015; in San Luis Obispo, ☎ 805/541–0505.

Getting Around

By Bus
From Monterey and Carmel, **Monterey–Salinas Transit** (☎ 408/899–2555) operates buses to Big Sur May–September . From San Luis Obispo, **Central Coast Transit** (☎ 805/541–2228) runs buses around the town and out to the coast. **Santa Barbara Metropolitan Transit District** (☎ 805/683–3702) provides local service. The **State Street** and **Waterfront shuttles** cover their respective territories during the day.

By Car
Highway 1 and U.S. 101 run more or less parallel, with Highway 1 hugging the coast and 101 remaining a few to a few-dozen miles inland. Along some stretches the two roads join and run together for a while. Plan on three to four hours' driving time for the 90 miles from Big Sur to Morro Bay on Highway 1—this is not a freeway, and you'll probably want to stop at some of the 300 scenic turnouts along this way. Once you start south from Carmel, there is no route off until Highway 46 heads inland from Cambria to connect with U.S. 101. At Morro Bay, Highway 1 moves inland for 13 miles and connects with U.S. 101 at San Luis Obispo. From here, south to Pismo Beach, the two highways run concurrently. U.S. 101 is the quicker route to Santa Barbara; Highway 1 rejoins it just north of town at Las Cruces.

Contacts and Resources

Doctors

St. Francis Hospital (✉ 601 E. Micheltorena St., Santa Barbara, ☏ 805/962–7661).

Emergencies

Ambulance (☏ 911). **Police** (☏ 911).

Guided Tours

California Parlour Car Tours (✉ Cathedral Hill Hotel, 1101 Van Ness Ave., San Francisco 94109, ☏ 415/474–7500 or 800/227–4250) operates 3- to 10-day San Francisco–Los Angeles (or vice versa) bus tours that travel along the Central Coast, visiting Hearst Castle, Santa Barbara, and Monterey.

Santa Barbara Trolley Co. (☏ 805/965–0353) has five daily, regularly scheduled runs from 10 AM to 4 PM in Santa Barbara. Motorized San Francisco–style cable cars deliver visitors to major hotels, shopping areas, and attractions. Stop or not, as you wish, and pick up another trolley when you're ready to move on. All depart from and return to Stearns Wharf. The fare is $4.

Road Conditions

Caltrans (☏ 800/427–7623).

Visitor Information

Big Sur Chamber of Commerce (✉ Box 87, 93920, ☏ 408/667–2100). **California Dept. of Parks and Recreation (Big Sur)** (☏ 408/667–2315). **Cambria Chamber of Commerce** (✉ 767 Main St., 93428, ☏ 805/927–3624). **Ojai Chamber of Commerce** (✉ Box 1134, 93024, ☏ 805/646–8126). **Paso Robles Wine Country** (✉ 1940 Spring St., Paso Robles 93446, ☏ 805/239–8463). **San Luis Obispo Chamber of Commerce** (✉ 1039 Chorro St., 93401, ☏ 805/781–2777 or 800/756–5056). **San Simeon Chamber of Commerce** (✉ Box 1, 9255 Hearst Dr., 93452, ☏ 805/927–3500 or 800/342–5613). **Santa Barbara Conference and Visitors Bureau** (✉ 12 E. Carrillo St., 93101, ☏ 805/966–9222 or 800/927–4688). **Santa Barbara County Vintners' Association** (✉ Box 1558, Santa Ynez 93460, ☏ 805/688–0881). **Santa Barbara Visitor Centers** (✉ 1 Santa Barbara St., at Cabrillo Blvd., ☏ 805/965–3021). **Solvang Conference and Visitors Bureau** (✉ Box 70, 1511A Mission Dr., 93464, ☏ 805/688–6144 or 800/468–6765).

11 Los Angeles

*Downtown, Hollywood,
Beverly Hills, and the Coast*

*In certain lights Los Angeles displays
its Spanish heritage, but much more
evident is its cultural vibrancy as a
20th-century center on the Pacific Rim.
Hollywood, the beaches, and
Disneyland are all within an hour's
drive. Also here are Beverly Hills,
noted for its shops and mansions;
important examples of 20th-century
domestic architecture; and freeways.
Everything about Los Angeles is
grand—even overdone—which is part
of the city's charm: It's all for show,
but the show's usually a good one.*

YOU'RE PREPARING FOR YOUR TRIP to Los Angeles. You're psyching up with Beach Boys CDs and Hollywood epics. You've pulled out your Hawaiian shirts and tennis shorts. You've studied the menu at Taco Bell. You've even labored on a Stairmaster and gone to a tanning salon, just so you won't look too much like a tourist when you hit the Coast.

Well, relax. *Everybody's* a tourist in LaLa Land. Even the stars are starstruck (just look at all the celebrities watching other celebrities at Spago and Eclipse). Los Angeles is a city of ephemerals, of transience, and above all, of illusion. Nothing here is quite real, and that's the reality of it all. That air of anything-can-happen—and it often does—is what motivates thousands to move to and millions to visit this promised land each year and visitors don't come just from the East or Midwest, mind you, but from the Far East, Down Under, Europe, and South America as well.

No matter how fast-forward Los Angeles seems to spin, the heart of the city—or at least its stomach—is still deep in the 1950s. Sure, no one here will be ridiculed as a "health-food nut" for preferring a more nutritious diet, but nothing is more Californian than a steak at Morton's or greasy chili dogs and fries at any of a hundred dives.

None of this was imagined when Spanish settlers founded Pueblo de la Reina de Los Angeles in 1781. In fact, no one predicted a golden future for desert-dry southern California until well after San Francisco and northern California had a head start with their own gold rush. The dusty outpost of Los Angeles eventually had oil and orange groves, but the golden key to its success came on the silver screen: the movies. The same sunshine that draws today's visitors beckoned Cecil B. DeMille and Jesse Lasky in 1913; the two show-biz pioneers were the first to shoot a feature-length movie here. It took another 14 years to break through the cinematic sound barrier, but meanwhile the silent-film era made Hollywood synonymous with fantasy and glamour.

Outrageous partying, extravagant homes, eccentric clothing, and money, money, money have been symbols of life in Los Angeles ever since. Even the more conservative oil, aerospace, computer, banking, and import/export industries on the booming Pacific Rim have enjoyed the prosperity that inevitably leads to fun living.

For some, this place is built on personal enhancements—the body beautiful, a big fat bank account, and the hottest hot rod—while others try to right global wrongs through the arts, politics, or spiritual exploration. For some it is enough just to surf and sun. Set off from the rest of the continent by mountains and desert, and from the rest of the world by an ocean, this corner of creation has evolved a unique identity that engenders envy, fascination, ridicule, and scorn—often all at once. Don't count on observing and absorbing it all in a day, a week, or even two. Indeed, this second largest American city gives you too many choices between its canyons and its coast; odds are you'll be exhausted far faster than you can anticipate in this far-flung, far-out metropolis.

EXPLORING LOS ANGELES

By Jane E. Lasky and William P. Brown

It's best to view Los Angeles as a collection of destinations, each to be explored separately. Don't jump willy-nilly from place to place. We've divided the major sightseeing areas of Los Angeles into eight major tours:

Downtown holds many skyscrapers, Little Tokyo, Chinatown, and world-class museums.

Hollywood is filled with famous sights, wacky museums, and historic buildings.

Wilshire Boulevard, a major thoroughfare, slices through a fascinating cross-section of the city.

Westside neighborhoods, including West Hollywood and Beverly Hills, are posh and trendy, with plenty of shopping and sightseeing opportunities.

Santa Monica, Venice, Pacific Palisades, and Malibu are seaside towns with quintessential southern California beaches and numerous attractions.

Palos Verdes, San Pedro, and Long Beach also edge the Pacific; the popular *Queen Mary* is berthed in Long Beach.

Highland Park, Pasadena, and **San Marino** are well-to-do inland suburbs; the famed Huntington Library is in San Marino.

The San Fernando Valley is home to Universal Studios, Burbank, and of course, many malls.

Orientation

Before trying to take on Los Angeles, a brief orientation lesson, using LAX (Los Angeles International Airport) as a starting point, will be helpful. Head north from LAX and, barring bad traffic, you'll soon reach the coastal area of Santa Monica, from which two major thoroughfares run due east into downtown. Sunset Boulevard winds around the upscale residential areas of Bel-Air and Beverly Hills before hitting the commercial stretch known as the Sunset Strip. Sunset then passes through Hollywood and ends downtown near Chinatown and Dodger Stadium. The other major street, south of Sunset, is Wilshire Boulevard, which takes you from Santa Monica through Westwood, past Beverly Hills, through the financial Wilshire district, and into the city center.

For a good overall view of Los Angeles, head up to the Griffith Park Observatory, just east of Hollywood proper. Standing on the terraces there (where James Dean, Natalie Wood, and Sal Mineo stood in the movie *Rebel Without a Cause*), you're well above this massive city, so the various parts should start to make sense. To the south are Long Beach and Orange County. To the left, a few miles southeast, is downtown, and below to the right is Hollywood (look for the whimsical Capitol Records Building, which resembles a stack of old 45s). About six miles southwest of that, you'll notice ABC's twin executive towers, marking Century City, and on a clear day you can see the Pacific Ocean in the distance. Directly to your right, the Hollywood Hills run west past the HOLLYWOOD sign through Beverly Hills, Bel-Air, and on to the coastline, where the hills become the Santa Monica Mountains, rising above the ritzy shoreline community of Malibu. Over the hill behind Griffith Park lies the San Fernando Valley and, to the east of that, the San Gabriel Valley.

Downtown

All those jokes about Los Angeles being a city without a center are simply not true anymore. A few decades ago Angelenos ruthlessly turned their backs on downtown and hightailed it to the suburbs—but there was and still is a downtown. And now the city core is enjoying a resurgence of attention from urban planners, real-estate developers, and down-

Exploring Los Angeles *(Boxes Refer to Detail Maps)*

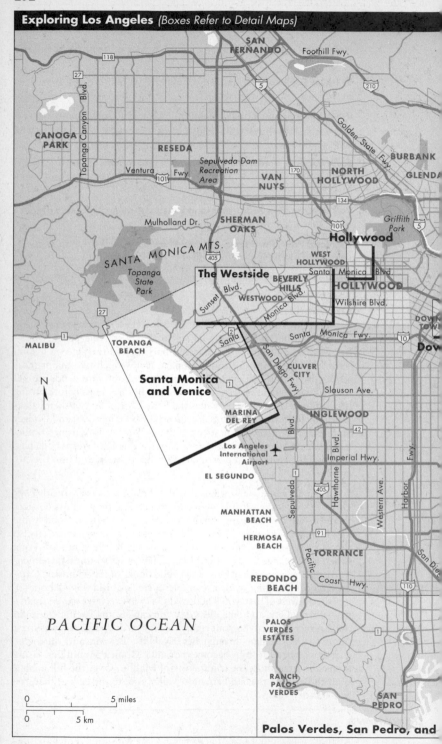

SAN FERNANDO

Foothill Fwy.

118

27

BURBANK

Golden State Fwy.

CANOGA PARK

RESEDA

Ventura 101 Fwy

Sepulveda Dam Recreation Area

VAN NUYS

170

NORTH HOLLYWOOD

GLENDA

134

Mulholland Dr.

SHERMAN OAKS

101

Griffith Park

Hollywood

SANTA MONICA MTS.

Topanga State Park

405

WEST HOLLYWOOD

The Westside

BEVERLY HILLS

Santa Monica Blvd.

HOLLYWOOD

WESTWOOD

Monica Blvd.

Wilshire Blvd.

27

Sunset Blvd.

2

Santa

Santa Monica Fwy.

10

DOWN TOWN

MALIBU

1

TOPANGA BEACH

San Diego Fwy.

CULVER CITY

Dow

Santa Monica and Venice

1

Slauson Ave.

N

MARINA DEL REY

INGLEWOOD

42

Los Angeles International Airport

Imperial Hwy.

Sepulveda Blvd.

Hawthorne Blvd.

Western Ave.

Harbor Fwy.

San Die

EL SEGUNDO

1

405

MANHATTAN BEACH

HERMOSA BEACH

91

Pacific

TORRANCE

REDONDO BEACH

Coast Hwy.

110

PACIFIC OCEAN

PALOS VERDES ESTATES

1

0		5 miles
0	5 km	

RANCH PALOS VERDES

SAN PEDRO

Palos Verdes, San Pedro, and

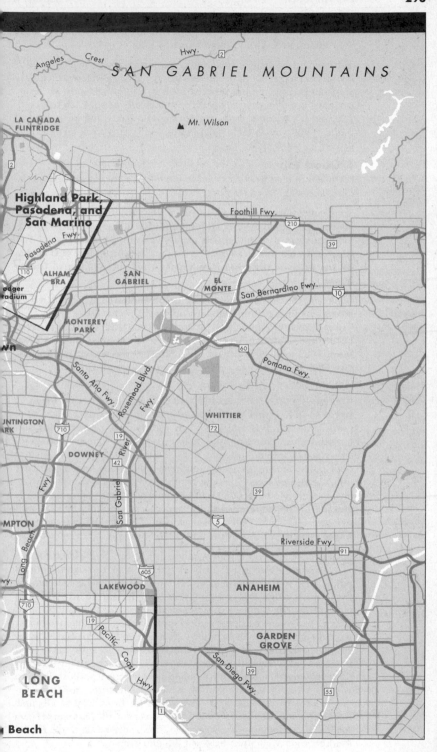

town office workers who have discovered the advantages of living close to work. During the day, downtown is relatively safe (though be on your guard, just as you should be in any major city).

The tour below assumes that you're exploring downtown by car, but if you want to get out of the driver's seat, try DASH—Downtown Area Short Hop. This minibus service travels in a loop past most of the attractions listed here, stopping every two blocks or so. Each ride costs 25¢, but it's worth it since you can travel quickly and be assured of finding your way. DASH (☎ 213/626–4455) runs weekdays and Saturdays 5 AM–10 PM.

A Good Tour

Numbers in the text correspond to numbers in the margin and on the Downtown Los Angeles map.

Start your tour about a mile north of downtown's skyline in **Chinatown** ①, on the west side of North Broadway, where you'll see Pagoda-like structures in an outdoor arcade. Drive south a few blocks to Cesar Chavez Avenue and head east to visit the city's birthplace at **El Pueblo de Los Angeles Historical Monument,** which houses festive **Olvera Street** ②.

Walk across Alameda Street to tour **Union Station** ③, which often doubled as a film set during Hollywood's golden era. Drive south from Union Station along Main Street until you reach Temple, the northern border of downtown. Across Temple is the **Los Angeles Children's Museum** ④. One block south on Main Street is the rear of **Los Angeles City Hall** ⑤, downtown's original skyscraper and a movie and TV landmark for decades.

Continue south to 2nd street and head east two blocks to **Little Tokyo** ⑥, where sushi bars and noodle stands line San Pedro Street. Head back north along San Pedro to 1st Street, and then west several blocks to Grand Avenue. North of 1st, you'll see two large square buildings on either side of a round structure. They're surrounded by a moat; an outdoor public area holds a large fountain. This is Los Angeles's theater hub, the **Music Center** ⑦, a sight familiar to Academy Awards viewers. Head south two blocks on Grand Avenue and park your car near the **Museum of Contemporary Art** ⑧, a modern, red sandstone building with pyramidal skylights. Walk across California Plaza to Hill Street to board **Angel's Flight** ⑨, L.A.'s petite answer to San Francisco's cable cars.

Back on Grand Avenue, walk south to 5th Street. To the left is the historic **Biltmore Hotel** ⑩, a 1923 brick palace. Walk through the hotel's public areas to the opposite side to Pershing Square, where trees shade the business crowd and concrete walls tantalize graffiti artists. Across Grand from the Biltmore is the **Central Library** ⑪, the nation's third largest; its 1½-acre garden is a good spot to relax. Walking two blocks west along 5th Street and a half-block north on Figueroa Street brings you to the **Westin Bonaventure Hotel and Suites** ⑫, easily recognized by its bevy of cylindrical, mirrored towers. Loop back east on 4th Street to **Broadway.** The **Bradbury Building** ⑬ warrants a walk-through to witness its skylit Victorian lobby, which was featured in *Blade Runner.* Return to your car and drive south on Broadway to Olympic Boulevard, and then head west to Hope Street and the **Museum of Neon Art** ⑭. For a blooming-big downtown finale, drive east to the **Flower Market** ⑮, on Wall Street between 7th and 8th streets.

TIMING

A downtown visit involves parking stops, so be prepared with plenty of quarters for meters—and make sure you read street-sign restrictions

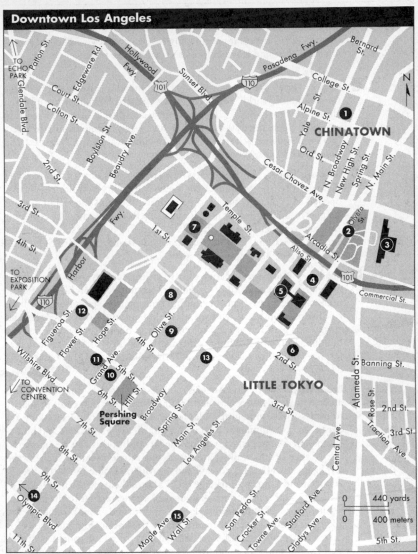

Downtown Los Angeles

CHINATOWN

LITTLE TOKYO

Pershing Square

TO ECHO PARK

TO EXPOSITION PARK

TO CONVENTION CENTER

440 yards

400 meters

N

Angel's Flight, **9**

Biltmore Hotel, **10**

Bradbury Building, **13**

Central Library, **11**

Chinatown, **1**

Flower Market, **15**

Little Tokyo, **6**

Los Angeles Children's Museum, **4**

Los Angeles City Hall, **5**

Museum of Contemporary Art, **8**

Museum of Neon Art, **14**

Music Center, **7**

Olvera Street, **2**

Union Station, **3**

Westin Bonaventure Hotel and Suites, **12**

to avoid fines and towing. This day-long tour (more if you stop in the museums) is more easily done on weekends, when hordes of office-workers aren't in evidence. If you go midweek, time your visit after the morning rush hour and leave before the evening one begins.

Sights to See

Angel's Flight. The turn-of-the-century funicular railway dubbed "the shortest in the world" began operating again in 1996 after having been closed for nearly 30 years. Two orange-and-black wooden Victorian cars take riders on a 70-second ride up a steep incline from Hill Street (between 3rd and 4th) to the fountain-filled California Plaza. ⊠ *25¢ one-way.* ⊙ *Daily 6 AM–10 PM.*

Biltmore Hotel. The beaux-arts Biltmore, a creation of Shultze and Weaver, also the architects for New York City's Waldorf-Astoria, opened in 1923. The hotel's outstanding lobby has the feel of a Spanish palace, and its indoor pool looks like a Roman baths. The Academy Awards were held here in the 1930s, and this hotel has also been the site of many films, from *Chinatown* and *Altered States* to *Splash!* ⊠ *506 S. Grand Ave.*

★ **Bradbury Building.** The site of turn-of-the-century sweatshops, this marvelous specimen of Victorian-era commercial architecture now houses genteel law firms beyond its pink marble staircases. The interior atrium courtyard, with its glass skylight and open balconies and elevator, is picture perfect and, naturally, a popular movie locale. The building is only open Monday through Saturday 9 to 5; its owners prefer that you not wander too far past the lobby. ⊠ *304 S. Broadway,* ☎ *213/626–1893.*

Broadway. One of Los Angeles's busiest streets has dozens of shops and sidewalk vendors between 1st and 9th streets that cater primarily to brides-to-be, immigration lawyers, and smart shoppers looking for cheap stereo equipment. Be on your guard, as pickpockets and homeless people can approach you on the street, but this can be an exhilarating slice-of-life walk, past florid old movie theaters such as the **Orpheum** (⊠ 842 S. Broadway) and the **Million Dollar** (⊠ 310 S. Broadway). **Grand Central Market** (⊠ 317 S. Broadway, ☎ 213/624–2378) is the city's largest food market, as well as a testament to the city's diversity. The block-long marketplace of colorful and exotic produce, herbs, and meat draws a faithful clientele from the Latino community, senior citizens on a budget, and Westside matrons for whom money is no object. Even if you don't plan to buy anything, this a delightful place to browse: The butcher shops display everything from lambs' heads to bulls' testicles to pigs' tails; the produce stalls are piled high with locally grown avocados and very ripe, very red tomatoes. Herb stalls promise remedies for all your ills.

★ **Central Library.** Major fires in the 1980s closed the library for six years. Today, at twice its former size, it's the third-largest public library in the nation. The original Goodhue building still stands, completely restored to its 1926 condition, with shimmering Egyptian-style bas-reliefs around its roofline. Enter through wooden doors that recall an old Spanish-era mission to see Dean Cornwell's murals depicting the history of California. A 1½-acre outdoor garden within the library complex has a restaurant. ⊠ *630 W. 5th St.,* ☎ *213/228–7000.* ⊠ *Free.* ⊙ *Mon. and Thurs.–Sat. 10–5:30, Tues.–Wed. noon–8, Sun. 1–5.*

Chinatown. Though hardly as vibrant as San Francisco's version, this sector still offers (beyond the usual tourist hokum) an authentic slice of Southeast Asian life. The main drag is North Broadway, where giant dragons snake down the center of the pavement during Chinese

New Year celebrations. More than 15,000 Chinese and Southeast Asians live in the Chinatown area, but many thousands more regularly frequent its markets and restaurants (dim-sum parlors are the most popular). Bilingual signs indicate street names in Chinese and English. ⊠ *Between Yale, Bernard, Ord, and Alameda Sts.*

OFF THE BEATEN PATH **CARROLL AVENUE –** (⊠ 1300 block of Carroll Ave., Angelino Heights), now designated a historical monument in one of Los Angeles's oldest neighborhoods, has the city's densest concentration of Victorian homes, including the **Sessions House** (⊠ 1330 Carroll) and the **Haunted House** (⊠ 1345 Carroll), the latter seen in Michael Jackson's *Thriller* video.

⑮ Flower Market. Stores and stalls here open up in the middle of the night to sell wholesale flowers and houseplants to the city's florists. Many of the sellers stay open until late morning, peddling leftovers at bargain prices to anyone who comes along. The public is officially welcome after 9 AM. ⊠ *700 block of Wall St.*

❻ Little Tokyo. The original neighborhood of Los Angeles's Japanese community, this area has been deserted by most of those immigrants, who moved on to suburbia. Still, Little Tokyo remains a cultural focal point. Nisei Week ("Nisei" is the name for second-generation Japanese) is celebrated here every August with traditional drums, dancing, a carnival, and a huge parade. Little Tokyo has dozens of sushi bars, tempura restaurants, and trinket shops. The Japanese American Cultural and Community Center (⊠ 244 S. San Pedro St., ☎ 213/628–2725) presents such events as Kabuki theater straight from Japan. ⊠ *Between 1st, San Pedro, 3rd, and Los Angeles Sts.*

☚ ❹ Los Angeles Children's Museum. The first of several strictly-for-kids museums now open in the city, this one has all hands-on exhibits. At Sticky City, kids pillow fight with abandon in a huge room. They put on their own news shows in a TV studio, and witness seemingly real hologram dinosaurs in the Cave. ⊠ *310 N. Main St.,* ☎ *213/687–8800.* ⊡ *$5.* ☼ *Weekends 10–5, also Tues.–Fri. 11:30–5 during summer vacation.*

❺ Los Angeles City Hall. The often-filmed, very recognizable City Hall has made appeared on *Superman, Dragnet,* and other popular television shows. Opened in 1928, the 27-story building remained the only building to break the 13-story height limit (earthquakes, you know) until 1957. You can ride an elevator to the observation deck. ⊠ *200 N. Spring St.*

★ ❽ Museum of Contemporary Art. The permanent collection here represents art from 1940 to the present, including works by Mark Rothko, Franz Kline, and Susan Rothenberg. The red sandstone building was designed by Japanese architect Arata Isozaki and opened in 1986. Pyramidal skylights add a striking geometry to the seven-level, 98,000-square-foot building. Don't miss the gift shop or the lively café. ⊠ *250 S. Grand Ave.,* ☎ *213/626–6222.* ⊡ *$6, Thurs. 5–8 free.* ☼ *Tues.–Wed. and Fri.–Sun. 11–5, Thurs. 11–8.*

⑭ Museum of Neon Art. This museum pays tribute to a form of lighting that evolved from an advertising tool into a fine art in less than half a century. In spring and summer, MONA schedules nighttime bus tours to historic and contemporary neon signs throughout the city. ⊠ *Renaissance Tower, 501 W. Olympic Blvd.,* ☎ *213/489–9918.* ⊡ *$3.50.* ☼ *Tues.–Sun. 11–6, until 8 on Thurs.*

❼ Music Center. The cultural center for Los Angeles since its opening in 1969, this multiuse venue often hosts the Academy Awards. Limousines arrive for the event at the Hope Street drive-through, and celebrities are whisked through the crowds to the largest and grandest of the three theaters, the Dorothy Chandler Pavilion. It is named after the widow of the *Los Angeles Times* publisher—she was instrumental in raising the money to build the complex. The round building in the middle, the Mark Taper Forum, is a smaller theater that often presents works of an experimental nature and others on a pre-Broadway run. The Ahmanson, at the north end, is the venue for many musical comedies. The vast complex's cement plaza has a fountain and Jacques Lipchitz sculpture. ⊠ *1st St. and Grand Ave.,* ☎ *213/972–7211.* ▭ *Tour free.* ☉ *45-min tour Tues.–Sat. 10–1:30; schedule subject to change; call 213/972–7483 for reservations.*

❷ Olvera Street. One of the most historic tourist sites in Los Angeles, this lively one-block showcase tantalizes with tile walkways, piñatas, mariachis, and authentic Mexican food. Olvera Street should not be dismissed as merely some gringo approximation of the real thing; after all, this is the symbol of the city's beginnings as an outpost for early Latin settlers. On weekends, the restaurants are packed, and there is usually music in the plaza and along the street. Two Mexican holidays, Cinco de Mayo (May 5) and Independence Day (September 16), also draw huge crowds. To see Olvera Street at its quietest, visit on a late weekday afternoon. The long shadows heighten the romantic feel of the street.

Avila Adobe (⊠ E–10 Olvera St.), completed in 1818, is considered the oldest building still standing in Los Angeles. The graceful, simple adobe with a traditional interior courtyard is furnished in the style of the 1840s. It's open Monday–Saturday, 10–3.

Olvera Street Visitors Center is housed in Sepulveda House (⊠ 622 N. Main St., ☎ 213/628–1274), a Victorian built in 1887 as a hotel and boardinghouse. The center is open Monday–Saturday 10–3. **Pelanconi House** (⊠ 17 Olvera St.), built in 1855, was the first brick building in Los Angeles and has been home to La Golondrina restaurant for 60 years. During the 1930s, famed Mexican muralist David Alfaro Siqueiros was commissioned to paint a mural on the south wall of **Italian Hall** (⊠ 650 N. Main St.). The patrons were not prepared for—and certainly not pleased by—an anti-imperialist mural depicting the oppressed workers of Latin America held in check by a menacing American eagle. It was promptly whitewashed into oblivion, and remains under the paint to this day.

At the beginning of Olvera Street, the Mexican-style **Plaza** is shaded by a huge Moreton Bay fig tree. On weekends mariachis and folkloric dance groups often perform here. Two annual events worth seeing if you're in town for them are the Blessing of the Animals and Los Posadas. The blessing takes place at 2 on the Saturday before Easter. Residents bring their pets (not just dogs and cats but horses, pigs, cows, birds, hamsters) to be blessed by a priest. For Las Posadas (every night between December 16 and 24), merchants and visitors parade up and down the street, led by children dressed as angels, to commemorate Mary and Joseph's search for shelter on Christmas Eve.

The **Old Firehouse** (☎ 213/628–1274), an 1884 building on the south side of the Plaza, contains early fire-fighting equipment and old photographs. Buildings seen on tours that start here include the Merced Theater, Masonic Temple, Pico House, and Garnier Block—all ornate examples of the late 19th-century style.

NEED A   The dining choices on Olvera Street range from fast-food stands to com-
BREAK?   fortable, sit-down restaurants. The most authentic Mexican food is at **La**

Luz del Dia (✉ 107 Paseo de la Plaza, ☎ 213/628–7495), which serves traditional favorites such as *chile rellenos* and pickled cactus, as well as handmade tortillas patted out in a practiced rhythm by the women behind the counter. **La Golondrina** (☎ 213/628–4349) and **El Paseo** (☎ 213/626–1361) restaurants, across from each other in the middle of Olvera Street, have delightful patios and extensive menus.

★ **❸ Union Station.** This building is among those that have defined Los Angeles to moviegoers the world over. It was built in 1939 in a Spanish-mission style that subtly combines Streamline Moderne and Moorish design elements. The waiting room alone is worth a look, its majestic scale so evocative of movies past that you'll half expect to see Carole Lombard or Barbara Stanwyck step off a train and sashay through. ✉ *800 N. Alameda St.*

⓬ Westin Bonaventure Hotel and Suites. John Portman designed these five shimmering cylinders in the sky without a 90° angle. Sheathed in mirrored glass, the building looks like science-fiction fantasy. Nonguests can use only one elevator, which rises through the roof of the lobby to soar on the outside to the revolving restaurant and bar on the 35th floor. ✉ *404 S. Figueroa St.,* ☎ *213/624–1000.*

OFF THE
BEATEN PATH

EXPOSITION PARK AND U.S.C. – Much of the impressive architecture of Exposition Park, the site of the 1932 Olympics, still stands. The park includes two major museums, the California Museum of Science and Industry and the Natural History Museum, and also Memorial Coliseum, the major venue for the 1932 and 1984 Olympics. The coliseum was rebuilt after suffering severe damage in the 1994 earthquake. The University of Southern California adjoins the park.

California Museum of Science and Industry (✉ 700 State Dr., ☎ 213/744–7400) is especially intriguing to children because there are many "hands-on" exhibits meant to be punched, twisted, or turned. The Aerospace Complex has planes, rockets, and satellites, plus an IMAX theater. The Hall of Health reveals the inner workings of the body, with side displays on AIDS awareness, substance abuse, and Health for Life. The Urban Environment exhibit looks at recycling, reusing, and reducing waste. Exciting Beginnings shows how chicks, frogs, and humans develop from eggs. Open daily from 10–5, the museum charges no admission fee.

The Natural History Museum of Los Angeles County (✉ 900 Exposition Blvd., ☎ 213/744–3414) has three dozen halls and galleries. The main building is a 1913 Spanish Renaissance structure with travertine columns, walls, and domes, and inlaid marble floors. The museum has a rich collection of prehistoric fossils, an extensive bird- and marine-life exhibit, and a display of insect life. A brilliant display of stones can be seen in the Hall of Gems and Minerals, and there's an elaborate taxidermy exhibit of North American and African mammals set in detailed replicas of their natural habitats. Other exhibits include pre-Columbian artifacts and crafts from the South Pacific. The Times-Mirror Hall of Native American Cultures delves into the Indian history of Los Angeles. The Ralph M. Parsons Discovery Center has many hands-on science-oriented exhibits. The museum is open Tuesday–Sunday 10–5; admission is $6 (free on the first Tuesday of the month).

The University of Southern California (☎ 213/740–2300), known as U.S.C., is the oldest major private university on the West Coast. Free one-hour campus tours take place weekdays, passing by the more notable of the institution's 191 buildings, such as the Romanesque Doheny Memorial Library; Widney Hall, a two-story clapboard building dating to 1880; and Mudd Memorial Hall of Philosophy, which contains a rare-book collection dating back to the Middle Ages. ✉ *Exposition Park and University: Figueroa St., at Exposition Blvd.*

Hollywood

Once a glamour center, Hollywood was where most big motion picture studios were headquartered and where movies premiered with such tremendous fanfare that they became the talk of the globe. Now Paramount is the only original major studio still physically in Hollywood, and the occasional film debut doesn't come close to its former grandeur. Today the core of the famous town is actually somewhat seedy. So why visit? Because its legacy is forever in the air, an eternal tribute to American film's hold on the world's imagination, a hold so strong that most visitors are able to look past the junky shops and campy museums and sense the town's glittering past. Though Hollywood is no longer "Hollywood," no visit to Los Angeles would be complete without at least a brief peek.

A Good Tour

Numbers in the text correspond to numbers in the margin and on the Hollywood map.

To get a good glimpse of the heart of Hollywood, for part of your visit you'll want to go it on foot—an anomaly in this vehicle-driven metropolis. To be assured that your car will be safe, it's best to park in a pay-lot next to **Mann's Chinese Theater** ①, where the cream of Hollywood's royalty cemented (literally) its immortality. Across the street from Mann's is the exuberant art deco facade of El Capitan Theater. As you walk east on Hollywood Boulevard, the main attraction is at your feet. Between Gower Street and Sycamore Avenue are the hundreds of star-studded dedications that form the **Hollywood Walk of Fame** ②. The first block east of Highland Avenue contains the world's glitziest McDonald's and the even kitschier **Hollywood Wax Museum** ③.

Back on Hollywood Boulevard, walk east a few blocks to the sedate art deco masterpiece that houses **Fredrick's of Hollywood** ④. Continue east to the legendary corner of **Hollywood and Vine** ⑤. From here, you can spot two major points of interest, the 13-story **Capitol Records Building** ⑥, and the art deco **Pantages Theater** ⑦.

Return to your car and drive north on Highland Avenue and then east on Franklin Avenue, past the giant **HOLLYWOOD sign** ⑧ crowning the Hollywood Hills on the left. Continue east to the vast confines of **Griffith Park** ⑨. Head north on Vermont Avenue into the park. Within the 4,000-acre wilderness refuge are many attractions, most notably the **Griffith Park Observatory** and the **Los Angeles Zoo.** South of Griffith Park's main gate, at Hollywood Boulevard and Vermont Avenue, is Frank Lloyd Wright's **Hollyhock House** ⑩, part of Barnsdall Park.

From Hollyhock, take Vermont Avenue south to Franklin Avenue, head west to Highland Avenue, and turn north. On the left is the famed **Hollywood Bowl** ⑪, a tiered outdoor amphitheater. Across Highland in a parking lot is a converted barn called the **Hollywood Studio Museum** ⑫. The museum is in Tinseltown's first movie studio, which later became Paramount Pictures. To tour the current version of **Paramount Studios** ⑬, take Highland south to Melrose Avenue and head east. You won't be able to miss the studio's famous main gate. From Paramount, head back north on Gower Street to Santa Monica Boulevard and **Hollywood Memorial Park Cemetery** ⑭, where Rudolph Valentino and many other legends are buried in style.

Hollywood

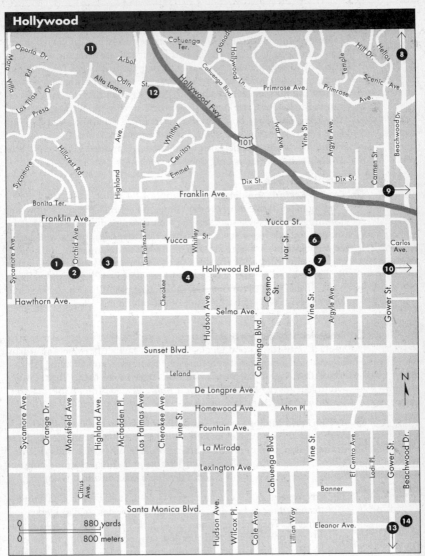

0   880 yards
0   800 meters

Capitol Records
Building, **6**
Frederick's of
Hollywood, **4**
Griffith Park, **9**
Hollyhock House, **10**
Hollywood
Bowl, **11**
Hollywood
Memorial Park
Cemetery, **14**
HOLLYWOOD sign, **8**
Hollywood Studio
Museum, **12**

Hollywood and
Vine, **5**
Hollywood Walk
of Fame, **2**
Hollywood Wax
Museum, **3**
Mann's Chinese
Theater, **1**
Pantages
Theater, **7**
Paramount
Studios, **13**

TIMING

Your best bet for a safe walk down Hollywood Boulevard along the Walk of Fame is during daylight hours, leisurely accomplished in an-hour-and-a-half. Plan around half an hour for any attraction at which you stop along this way. Motoring through Griffith Park takes half an hour, but allow an extra hour or so each for the Griffith Park Obser-vatory and the Gene Autry Museum. Keep in mind that the park is over-run with locals on weekends, so get there during the week if possible. Weekday-only Paramount Studios tours take two hours. All the sights listed below are open daily except for the Gene Autry Museum and Hollyhock House, which are closed Monday, and the Hollywood Stu-dio Museum, which is only open on weekends.

Sights to See

❻ **Capitol Records Building.** This symbol of '50s chic came to be when two big musical talents of the day (singer Nat King Cole and songwriter Johnny Mercer) suggested that the record company's headquarters be shaped to look like a stack of 45 rpm records. Although a weird con-cept back then, compared to much of what's gone up since, this build-ing doesn't seem all that odd. On its south wall, look at L.A. artist Richard Wyatt's mural *Hollywood Jazz, 1945–1972*, immortalizing musical greats Duke Ellington, Billie Holiday, Ella Fitzgerald, and Miles Davis. The lights at the top of the building spell out Hollywood in Morse Code. ✉ *1756 N. Vine St.*

❹ **Frederick's of Hollywood.** Be sure to look inside this popular tourist spot, if only for a good giggle. There are racks of risqué and trashy lingerie and a museum that features the undergarments of living (Shirley MacLaine, Cybill Shepherd) and no-longer-living (Mae West) Holly-wood legends. ✉ *6608 Hollywood Blvd.,* ☎ *213/466–8506.* ➣ *Free.* ☾ *Mon.–Sat. 10–6, Sun. noon–5.*

★ ☙ ❾ **Griffith Park.** Mining tycoon Griffith J. Griffith donated these 4,000 acres to the city of Los Angeles in 1896. Griffith Park has many picnic areas; hiking, biking, and horseback riding trails; a miniature, kids-oriented village; the Los Angeles Zoo; two 18-hole golf courses, a nine-hole ex-ecutive course, a pro shop, and a driving range; and tennis courts.

The **Los Angeles Zoo** (✉ Ventura and Golden State Fwys., ☎ 213/666–4090)is noted for its breeding of endangered species such as koalas and white tigers. The 113-acre compound holds more than 2,000 mam-mals, birds, amphibians, and reptiles, grouped according to the geo-graphic areas where they are naturally found—Africa, Australia, Eurasia, North America, and South America. A tram stops at various points along the way. The zoo is open daily from 10–5; admission is $8.25, plus $3 for Safari Shuttle Tour.

On a clear night, head for the **Griffith Park Observatory and Plane-tarium** (✉ Los Feliz Blvd. and Vermont Ave. entrance, ☎ 213/664–1191), an art-deco landmark immortalized in the James Dean film *Rebel Without a Cause*. Climb the observatory stairs (admission is free) to take a look through the giant telescope. There are also laserium ($7) and planetarium ($4) shows. Observatory hours are Tuesday–Friday 2:30–10, weekends 12:30–10; call to confirm schedule.

Gene Autry Western Heritage Museum (✉ 4700 W. Heritage Way, ☎ 213/667–2000) celebrates the American West—both the movie and real-life versions—with memorabilia, art, and artifacts. The collection includes Teddy Roosevelt's Colt revolver, Buffalo Bill Cody's saddle, and Annie Oakley's gold-plated Smith and Wesson guns. Video screens show clips from old Westerns. Admission is $7.50; the museum is open Tuesday–Sunday 10–5.

OFF THE
BEATEN PATH

FOREST LAWN MEMORIAL PARK – East of Griffith Park in the town of
Glendale, this cemetery is more than just a place where loved ones are
laid to rest: It holds 300 landscaped acres and includes a major collec-
tion of marble statuary and art treasures, among them a replica of
Leonardo da Vinci's *The Last Supper* done entirely in stained glass.
Among the famous people buried here are Walt Disney, Errol Flynn, Nat
King Cole, Clara Bow, Gracie Allen and George Burns, Alan Ladd,
Clark Gable, Carole Lombard, Theda Bara, and Jean Harlow. ⊠ *1712
S. Glendale Ave., Glendale,* ☎ *213/254–3131.* ⊙ *Daily 8–5.*

⑩ **Hollyhock House.** The first of several houses Frank Lloyd Wright designed in Los Angeles, this 1921 manse was commissioned by heiress
Aline Barnsdall. A perfect example of the pre-Columbian style of
which Wright was so fond at that time, the house features a stylized
hollyhock flower, which appears in a broad band around its exterior
and even on the dining room chairs. Hollyhock House has been restored and furnished to include original furniture designed by Wright.
⊠ *4800 Hollywood Blvd.,* ☎ *213/662–7272.* ⊠ *$2.* ⊙ *Tour Tues.–Sun.
at noon, 1, 2, and 3.*

⑪ **Hollywood Bowl.** Summer-evening concerts have been a tradition since
1922 at this amphitheater cradled in the Hollywood Hills. Musical fare
runs from pop to jazz to classical. The 17,000-plus seating capacity
ranges from boxes (where fancy alfresco preconcert meals are catered)
to concrete bleachers in the rear. Some prefer the back rows for their
romantic appeal. ⊠ *2301 N. Highland Ave.,* ☎ *213/850–2000.* ⊙
Grounds daily sunrise–sunset; call for schedule.

⑭ **Hollywood Memorial Park Cemetery.** Many Hollywood stars rest in
this serene spot. Walk through the entrance to the lake area and you'll
find the crypt of Cecil B. DeMille and the graves of Nelson Eddy and
Douglas Fairbanks, Sr. Inside the Cathedral Mausoleum is Rudolph
Valentino's crypt (where fans and the press turn up every August 23,
the anniversary of his death). Other stars interred in this section are
Peter Lorre and Eleanor Powell. In the Abbey of Palms Mausoleum,
Norma Talmadge and Clifton Webb are buried. ⊠ *6000 Santa Monica Blvd.,* ☎ *213/469–1181.* ⊙ *Daily 8–5.*

★ ⑧ **HOLLYWOOD sign.** Even on the smoggiest of days, this town's trademark
sign can be spotted from miles away. The 50-foot-tall letters, which
originally spelled out "Hollywoodland," were erected in 1923 to promote a real-estate development scheme. In 1949 the "land" portion
of the insignia was taken down. In the past, pranksters have altered it
to spell out sayings like Hollyweed (in the 1970s, to commemorate le-
nient marijuana laws) and Perotwood (during the 1992 presidential
election). In 1995 a fence was erected around the sign to deter intruders.

⑫ **Hollywood Studio Museum.** The place where the first feature-length film,
The Squaw Man, was produced in 1913, this unusual landmark became
Paramount Pictures. The museum contains a re-creation of Cecil B. De-
Mille's original office, early movie artifacts, and a screening room
showing vintage films about Hollywood and its legends. ⊠ *2100 N.
Highland Ave.,* ☎ *213/874–2276.* ⊠ *$4.* ⊙ *Sat. 10–4, Sun. noon–4.*

⑤ **Hollywood and Vine.** The mere mention of this intersection inspires images of a street corner bustling with stars, starlets, and moguls passing
by, on foot or in snazzy convertibles. But these days, Hollywood and
Vine is far from the action, and pedestrian traffic is, alas, pedestrian. No
stars, no starlets, no moguls. The famed Brown Derby restaurant that
once stood near the southeast corner is long gone, and the intersection
these days is little more than a place for visitors to get their bearings.

★ **②** **Hollywood Walk of Fame.** All along this mile-long stretch of Hollywood Boulevard sidewalk, entertainment legends' names are embossed in brass, each at the center of a pink star embedded in a dark gray terrazzo circle. The first eight stars were unveiled in 1960 at the northwest corner of Highland Avenue and Hollywood Boulevard: Olive Borden, Ronald Colman, Louise Fazenda, Preston Foster, Burt Lancaster, Edward Sedgwick, Ernest Torrence, and Joanne Woodward (some of these names have stood the test of time better than others). Since then, more than 2,000 others have been immortalized, though that honor doesn't come cheap—the personality in question (or more likely his or her movie studio or record company) must pay $5,000 for the privilege. Walk a few blocks and you'll quickly find that all the names are not familiar. To aid in the identification, celebrities are classified by one of five logos: a motion picture camera, a radio microphone, a television set, a record, and a theatrical mask. Here's a guide to a few of the more famous celebs' stars: Marlon Brando at 1765 Vine, Charlie Chaplin at 6751 Hollywood, W. C. Fields at 7004 Hollywood, Clark Gable at 1608 Vine, Marilyn Monroe at 6774 Hollywood, Rudolph Valentino at 6164 Hollywood, Michael Jackson at 6927 Hollywood, and John Wayne at 1541 Vine.

🖐 **③** **Hollywood Wax Museum.** Visitors make celebrity sightings that real life can no longer provide (Mary Pickford, Elvis Presley, and Clark Gable) and one or two that real life never did (*The Mask*). Living legends on display include the *Baywatch* cast and actresses Sharon Stone and Roseanne. ⊠ *6767 Hollywood Blvd.,* ☎ *213/462–8860.* ⌑ *$8.95.* ☾ *Sun.–Thurs. 10 AM–midnight, Fri. and Sat. 10 AM–2 AM.*

NEED A   **Me & Me** (⊠ 6687 Hollywood Blvd., ☎ 213/464-8448) is a fun place
BREAK?   to munch on what may be the city's best falafel, made right in front of you. Don't expect table service or anything fancy from this hole-in-the-wall.

★ **①** **Mann's Chinese Theater.** The former "Grauman's Chinese," a fantasy of Chinese pagodas and temples, is a place only Hollywood could have turned out. You have to buy a movie ticket to appreciate the interior trappings, but the courtyard is open for browsing. Here you'll see those oh-so-famous cement hand- and footprints. This tradition is said to have begun at the theater's opening in 1927, with the premiere of Cecil B. DeMille's *King of Kings,* when actress Norma Talmadge accidentally stepped into the wet cement. Now more than 160 celebrities have contributed. Oddball imprints include one of Jimmy Durante's nose. ⊠ *6925 Hollywood Blvd.,* ☎ *213/464–8111.*

❼ **Pantages Theater.** Opened in 1930 as the very pinnacle of movie-theater opulence, this legitimate venue hosted the Academy Awards from 1949 to 1959. Today it mostly presents large-scale Broadway musicals. ⊠ *6233 Hollywood Blvd.*

⓭ **Paramount Studios.** The only original major movie studio still in Hollywood has produced more than 3,000 films. Stars, such as Mae West, Mary Pickford, and John Barrymore, were under contract here. The studio occupies two large city blocks, and its three arched entrances are familiar landmarks from films such as the 1950 classic *Sunset Boulevard* (which showed the entrance at Marathon and Bronson avenues). You can explore the lot on two-hour guided walking tours or by joining the audience for tapings of TV shows. Children under 10 are not admitted. ⊠ *5555 Melrose Ave.; for tours or tapings check in at 860 N. Gower St.,* ☎ *213/956–5575.* ⌑ *$15.* ☾ *2-hr tour weekdays on the hr 9–2.*

Wilshire Boulevard

Wilshire Boulevard begins in downtown Los Angeles and runs west, through Beverly Hills and Santa Monica, ending at the cliffs above the Pacific Ocean. Along the way are many of Los Angeles's top architectural sites, museums, and shops. The east-west thoroughfare may be the most historic tour in Los Angeles, as certain sights literally date back to prehistoric times.

A Good Drive

Start your tour west of downtown at the former **Bullocks Wilshire** store (now occupied by Southwestern University of Law), an art deco wonder. The next area you'll pass is **Koreatown.** Farther west, just past Vermont Avenue, is the **Ambassador Hotel.** At Western Avenue is the still-operational **Wiltern Theater,** an art deco palace. **Hancock Park** is the grandiose neighborhood just west of Western Avenue. The **Getty House** on Irving Boulevard was once the estate of the wealthy oil family.

Starting at La Brea heading west on Wilshire is the **Miracle Mile,** in the 1930s *the* place to shop in Los Angeles. The few blocks leading up to Fairfax Avenue are known as Museum Row. Starting at Curson Avenue is a grassy park called Hancock Park (a real park, not to be confused with the residential neighborhood of the same name). Here are the **La Brea Tar Pits,** which contain fossils preserved in the sticky natural substance. Also in Hancock Park is the **Los Angeles County Museum of Art** (LACMA) the city's largest museum. Across the street is the **Craft and Folk Art Museum.** On the next block is the **Carole & Barry Kaye Museum of Miniatures;** at Fairfax Avenue is the **Petersen Automotive Museum.** On the north side of Wilshire at Fairfax, the **May Company** building has been taken over by LACMA. Take a right here and you'll come across **Farmers Market,** one of Los Angeles's most enduring attractions.

TIMING
All these sights are on Wilshire or within a few blocks north or south. Until you reach Museum Row, Wilshire Boulevard is best viewed through your car window. Traffic moves slowly, so you can cruise easily without pulling over. This tour is best done at midday or on weekends. Try not to drive during rush hour—or on a bright day just before sunset, when the sun can be blinding. The drive from MacArthur Park to the museums (all of which are closed Monday) will probably take less than half an hour. Devote a half hour to an hour to the smaller museums; you could easily spend a half day exploring the Los Angeles County Museum of Art.

Sights to See

The Ambassador. This grand hotel opened in 1921. It housed the famed Coconut Grove nightclub, where everyone who was anyone went to dance in a fantasy Tahitian-island setting. The Ambassador's Grand Ballroom hosted several Academy Awards presentations during the 1930s and 1940s and was used as a set for film versions of *A Star is Born.* On a sadder note, the ballroom is where presidential candidate Robert F. Kennedy was gunned down in June 1968. ⊠ *Wilshire Blvd. at Vermont Ave.*

Bullocks Wilshire. The copper-trimmed Moderne exterior of this former department store has often been a background for films. The building is now used by the Southwestern University of Law for its library, offices, and classrooms. The behind-the-store parking lot was quite an innovation in 1929—it was the first such facility constructed by a large Los Angeles store to accommodate the automobile. On the ceiling of the porte cochere, a mural depicts the history of transportation, strangely without giving a nod to the one Los Angeles necessity—the car. ⊠ *3050 Wilshire Blvd.*

Carole & Barry Kaye Museum of Miniatures. A world of pint-size exhibits can be found here, including sized-down local landmarks such as the Hollywood Bowl. An original Greene and Greene Craftsman house is displayed in ½th scale. There's also a tribute to America's First Ladies (as far back as Martha Washington), dolled up in their inaugural ball gowns. ⊠ *5900 Wilshire Blvd.,* ☎ *213/937–6464.* ⊠ *$7.50.* ☉ *Tues.–Sat. 10–5, Sun. 11–5.*

Craft and Folk Art Museum. This museum consistently offers fascinating exhibits of antique and contemporary works from around the world, everything from jewelry and pottery to sunglasses and architecture. The museum's collections include Japanese, Mexican, American, and East Indian folk art, textiles, and masks. ⊠ *5800 Wilshire Blvd.,* ☎ *213/937–5544.* ⊠ *$4.* ☉ *Tues.–Sun. 11–5.*

★ ☾ **Farmers Market.** A favorite L.A. attraction since the 1930s, what once really was only a farmers market now holds 120 shops, salons, stores, and produce stalls. Thirty restaurants (many offering alfresco dining under umbrellas) serve international and domestic fare. The market is next to CBS Television Studios, so you may even run into a celebrity. ⊠ *6333 W. 3rd St., at Fairfax Ave.,* ☎ *213/933–9211.* ☉ *Mon.–Sat. 9–6:30, Sun. 10–5 (later in summer).*

NEED A | **Kokomo** (⊠ 3rd St. side of Farmers Market, ☎ 213/933–0773) serves
BREAK? | some of the best diner food anywhere in L.A. The reasonable prices almost always include lively, entertaining service.

Getty House. In the past, the mayor of Los Angeles called this white-brick, half-timber edifice home. Its previous occupants, the Getty family, donated the estate to the city. ⊠ *605 S. Irving Blvd.*

Hancock Park. This area is not an actual park, but rather one of the city's most genteel neighborhoods, remaining in vogue since its development in the 1920s. Old-money families built English Tudor homes with East Coast landscaping schemes that defy the local climate and history.

Koreatown. Beginning in the 1970s, large numbers of Koreans settled in the area south of Wilshire Boulevard, along Olympic Boulevard between Vermont and Western avenues. Many street signs are in Korean only, and the typical offerings of Korean shops are available in the large Koreatown Plaza mall, on the corner of Western and San Marino avenues.

★ ☾ **La Brea Tar Pits.** The city's world-famous fossil source is in **Hancock Park,** an actual park not to be confused with the same-named residential neighborhood. About 35,000 years ago, deposits of oil rose to the Earth's surface, collected in shallow pools, and coagulated into sticky asphalt. In the early 20th century, geologists discovered that the sticky goo contained the largest collection of Pleistocene fossils ever found at one location: more than 200 varieties of birds, mammals, plants, reptiles, and insects. More than 100 tons of fossil bones have been removed during more than 70 years of excavations. Statues of mammoths in the big pit near the corner of Wilshire Boulevard and Curson Avenue depict the way in which many of them were entombed: Edging down to a pond of water to drink, animals were caught in the tar and unable to extricate themselves. There are several oozing pits scattered around Hancock Park; construction in the area has often had to accommodate them, and in nearby streets and along sidewalks, little bits of tar occasionally ooze up, unstoppable.

A satellite of the Natural History Museum of Los Angeles County, the **George C. Page Museum of La Brea Discoveries** holds more than one million Ice Age fossils. A bas-relief around four sides depicts life in the Pleistocene era. The glass-enclosed Paleontological Laboratory permits observation of the ongoing cleaning, identification, and cataloging of fossils excavated from the nearby asphalt deposits. *The La Brea Story* and *A Whopping Small Dinosaur* are short documentary films shown every 15–30 minutes. A hologram magically puts flesh on "La Brea Woman," and an interactive mechanism shows visitors just how hard it would be to free oneself from the tar. ⊠ *5801 Wilshire Blvd.,* ☎ *213/936–2230.* ☜ *$6, free 1st Tues. of month.* ☉ *Tues.–Sun. 10–5.*

★ **Los Angeles County Museum of Art.** The largest museum complex in Los Angeles is composed of five buildings surrounding the grand Times Mirror Central Court. The **Ahmanson Building,** built around a central atrium, houses the museum's collection of paintings, sculpture, costumes and textiles, and decorative arts. Highlights include a unique assemblage of glass from Roman times to the 19th century, the renowned Gilbert collection of mosaics and monumental silver, and an Indian and Southeast Asian art collection considered to be one of the most comprehensive in the world.

The **Hammer Building** presents major traveling exhibitions, as well as prints, drawings, and photographs. The **Anderson Building** shows 20th-century painting and sculpture. The museum's Japanese sculpture, paintings, ceramics, lacquerware, and impressive collection of netsuke are on view in the **Japanese Pavilion.** The **Contemporary Sculpture Garden** holds nine large-scale outdoor sculptures. The **B. Gerald Cantor Sculpture Garden** has bronzes by Auguste Rodin, Émile-Antoine Bourdelle, and George Kolbe. ⊠ *5905 Wilshire Blvd.,* ☎ *213/857–6000; ticket information, 213/857–6010.* ☜ *$6, free 2nd Wed. of month.* ☉ *Tues.–Thurs. 10–5, Fri. 10–9, weekends 11–6.*

May Company. The futuristic gold-tile, bowed facade of this former department store, acquired in mid-1996 by the Los Angeles County Museum of Art, brightens up its Wilshire neighborhood. The design exemplifies late art deco architectural styling. ⊠ *Wilshire Blvd. at Fairfax Ave. (northeast corner).*

Miracle Mile. Wilshire Boulevard between La Brea and Fairfax avenues was given this dubious title in the 1930s as a promotional gimmick to attract shoppers. The area went into decline in the '50s and '60s, but is now enjoying a comeback as Los Angeles's art deco heritage has come to be appreciated and restored. Exemplary architecture includes the El Rey Theater at 5519 Wilshire, now a nightclub.

★ ☾ **Petersen Automotive Museum.** Cars of the stars are among the popular vehicles on display here, along with such movie creations as Fred's rockmobile from *The Flintstones.* A history of the automobile is also among the permanent collection, which includes rare French luxury cars from the '30s and '40s on view and race cars built in southern California. An entire gallery surveys the development of the motorcycle. There's a great gift shop for the automotive enthusiast, and a research library. ⊠ *6060 Wilshire Blvd.,* ☎ *213/930–2277.* ☜ *$7.* ☉ *Tues.–Sun. 10–6.*

★ **Wiltern Theater.** At the southeast corner of Wilshire Boulevard and Western Avenue sits this magnificent example of all-out art deco design, inside and out. Originally a movie theater, the Wiltern is now a multiuse arts complex. ⊠ *3780 Wilshire Blvd.*

The Westside

The Westside of Los Angeles is where the rents and real-estate prices are the most expensive, the restaurants (and the restaurateurs) the most famous, and the shops the most chic. It's the best of the good life, southern-California style. Short on traditional tourist attractions, it more than makes up for this with great shopping districts and outdoor cafés and a lively nightlife.

Trendy **West Hollywood** includes the Sunset Strip. Once an almost forgotten parcel of county land surrounded by the city of L.A. and Beverly Hills, West Hollywood became an official city in 1984.

At the abrupt Doheny Drive end of the strip, Sunset Boulevard enters glamorous **Beverly Hills.** Suddenly, effervescent street life gives way to expansive, perfectly manicured lawns and palatial homes. It is on this stretch of Sunset, especially during the day, that you'll see hawkers peddling maps to stars' homes. Are the maps reliable? Well, that's a matter of debate. Stars do move around, so it's difficult to keep any map up to date. But the fun is in looking at some of these magnificent homes, regardless of whether or not they're owned by a star at the moment. Incorporated into L.A. early in the century, Beverly Hills has been thriving ever since. As a vibrant high-echelon enclave within the larger city, it has retained and enhanced its reputation for wealth and luxury, an assessment with which you will surely agree as you drive along any of its main thoroughfares; Sunset or Wilshire boulevards or Santa Monica Boulevard (which is actually two parallel streets at this point: "Santa Monica" is the northern one; "Little Santa Monica," the southern).

Westwood, directly south of the UCLA campus, was once a quiet college town, but it's now one of the busiest places in the city on weekend evenings—so busy that during the summer, many streets are closed to car traffic and visitors must park at the Federal Building at Wilshire Boulevard and Veteran Avenue and shuttle over. However you arrive, Westwood is a delightful village filled with clever boutiques, trendy restaurants, movie theaters, and colorful street life.

A Good Tour

Numbers in the text correspond to numbers in the margin and on the Westside map.

When locals refer to the Westside, they don't mean the coast, but rather the inland portion of Los Angeles west of downtown and Hollywood. Start along **Melrose Avenue** ① between La Brea and Fairfax avenues. Park anywhere along this mile-long strip and join in the parade of colorful folks, many clad in way-out clothes and wild hair styles, walking past the many one-of-a-kind shops. Continue west on Melrose to San Vicente Boulevard. You can't miss the colbalt-color **Pacific Design Center** ②, which houses prestigious interior-design showrooms. Head south on San Vicente to Beverly Boulevard and L.A.'s trendiest mall, the **Beverly Center** ③. After your credit cards stop sizzling, backtrack north to Santa Monica Boulevard, in the heart of West Hollywood. A few blocks farther north you'll hit the **Sunset Strip** ④. Head east on the strip (keep your eyes on the road, not those giant billboards) for a while, perhaps stopping if a section captures your fancy, then loop back west on Sunset to just past Doheny Drive. Residential Beverly Hills begins here. North of Sunset on Loma Vista Drive is historic **Greystone Mansion** ⑤, often used as a movie locale. Farther west on Sunset at Rodeo Drive is the pink **Beverly Hills Hotel & Bungalows** ⑥.

Motor south along **Rodeo Drive** ⑦. Between Santa Monica and Wilshire boulevards is some of the most expensive commercial real estate in the world. The regal **Regent Beverly Wilshire Hotel** ⑧ serves as a temporary residence for the rich, famous, and cultured.

From Wilshire, continue south on Beverly Drive to Pico Boulevard and head west to the **Museum of Tolerance** ⑨. Continue west on Pico and north on Westwood Boulevard to reach **Westwood Memorial Park** ⑩. After paying your respects to the Hollywood legends buried here, drive north on Westwood Boulevard to Wilshire Boulevard. Westwood is home to **UCLA** ⑪ and the **Armand Hammer Museum of Art and Cultural Center** ⑫. This area is good for a stroll.

TIMING

Midday is a good time visit the Westside. Walking Melrose can take an hour or more, depending on how much of a shopper you are. Metered parking along Melrose is difficult, and parking on side streets is sometimes limited, so read signs. One hint: Go for lunch and valet park, and then tour the area before picking up your vehicle. The sights west of Melrose can be appreciated from your car. Be sure to walk a bit of Rodeo Drive, though. The Museum of Tolerance (closed Saturday) requires up to three hours. Westwood can be walked or cruised, and visiting the Armand Hammer Museum (closed Monday) takes about an hour.

Sights To See

⑫ **Armand Hammer Museum of Art and Cultural Center.** The permanent collection here includes thousands of works by Honoré Daumier. The Hammer regularly presents special blockbuster exhibits. ✉ *10899 Wilshire Blvd.,* ☎ *310/443–7000.* ✑ *$4.50, free Thurs. 6–9; parking $2.75.* ☉ *Tues., Wed., Fri., and Sat. 11–7, Thurs. 11–9, Sun. 11–5.*

③ **Beverly Center.** The hulking monolith dominating the corner of La Cienega and Beverly boulevards was designed as an all-in-one stop for shopping, dining, and movies (☞ *Shopping, below*). Don't be surprised if you see a movie star, minus make-up, out on a spree here. ✉ *8500 Beverly Blvd.,* ☎ *310/854–0070.*

★ ⑥ **Beverly Hills Hotel.** Greta Garbo, Howard Hughes, and other guests kept a low profile when staying at this landmark hotel, also known as the Pink Palace, while other film luminaries—Cecil B. DeMille, for instance—cut very visible deals in the Polo Lounge. ✉ *9641 Sunset Blvd.*

⑤ **Greystone Mansion.** Doheny Drive is named for oilman Edward Doheny, the original occupant of this 1927 Tudor mansion. Now owned by the city of Beverly Hills, it sits on 18½ landscaped acres and has been used in such films as *The Witches of Eastwick* and *Indecent Proposal*. The gardens are open for self-guided tours, and peeking (only) through the windows is permitted. Occasionally, concerts are held in the mansion's courtyard on summer afternoons. ✉ *905 Loma Vista Dr.,* ☎ *310/550–4796.* ✑ *Free.* ☉ *Fall and winter, daily 9–5; spring and summer, daily 9–6.*

★ ① **Melrose Avenue.** Panache meets paparazzi and Beverly Hills chic contends with post-punk Hollywood hip along the stretch of Melrose between Fairfax and La Brea avenues. Here you'll find one-of-a-kind boutiques, some great vintage clothing and collectibles shops, and small, trendy restaurants.

★ ⑨ **Museum of Tolerance.** A sobering experience in the midst of Westside glamour, this important museum is adjacent to the Simon Weisenthal Center. Using state-of-the-art interactive technology, the museum challenges visitors to confront bigotry and racism. One of the most affecting sections covers the Holocaust—each visitor is issued a "passport" bearing the name of a child whose life was dramatically changed by the German Nazi rule and by World War II. Later, the museumgoer

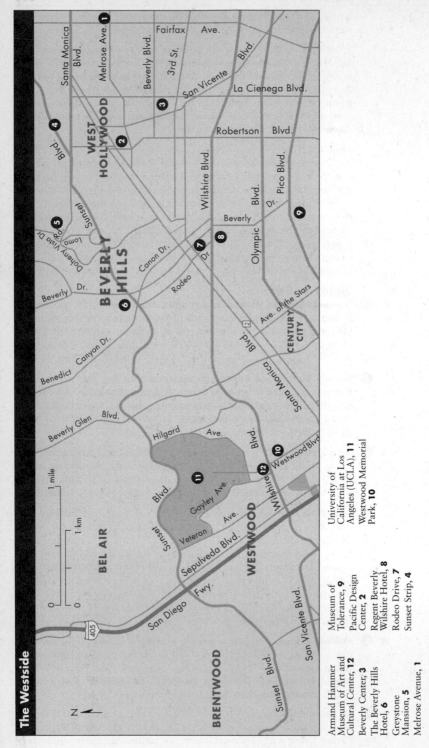

The Westside

N

Santa Monica Blvd.
Melrose Ave.
Fairfax Ave.
Beverly Blvd.
3rd St.
San Vicente
La Cienega Blvd.
Blvd.
WEST HOLLYWOOD
Robertson Blvd.
Wilshire Blvd.
Sunset
Doheny Dr.
Lomo Vista Dr.
BEVERLY HILLS
Canon Dr.
Rodeo
Beverly Dr.
Pico Blvd.
Beverly
Olympic Blvd.
Dr.
Ave. of the Stars
CENTURY CITY
Benedict Canyon Dr.
Beverly Glen Blvd.
Santa Monica Blvd.
Hilgard Ave.
Blvd.
BEL AIR
Sunset
Gayley Ave.
Ave.
Veteran
Sepulveda Blvd.
WESTWOOD
Westwood Blvd.
San Diego Fwy.
405
BRENTWOOD
San Vicente Blvd.
Sunset Blvd.

1 mile
1 km
0

Armand Hammer
Museum of Art and
Cultural Center, **12**
Beverly Center, **3**
The Beverly Hills
Hotel, **6**
Greystone
Mansion, **5**
Melrose Avenue, **1**

Museum of
Tolerance, **9**
Pacific Design
Center, **2**
Regent Beverly
Wilshire Hotel, **8**
Rodeo Drive, **7**
Sunset Strip, **4**

University of
California at Los
Angeles (UCLA), **11**
Westwood Memorial
Park, **10**

learns the fate of that child. Anne Frank artifacts are part of the museum's permanent collection. Museum reservations are advised. ⊠ *9786 W. Pico Blvd.,* ☎ *310/553–8403.* ☜ *$8.* ☉ *Sun. 10:30–5, Mon.–Thurs. 10–4, Fri. 10–1.*

② **Pacific Design Center.** At the center of Los Angeles's thriving interior decorating business, these two glass buildings are known as the "Blue Whale" and the "Green Whale." Cesar Pelli designed the blue structure in the mid-1970s; the center added the green one, also by Pelli, in 1988. The buildings are open to the public weekdays 9–5; you can browse in many of the more than 200 showrooms or opt for a free group tour at 10 AM. Note: Purchases can be made only through design professionals (a referral system is available). The **Murray Feldman Gallery** (⊠ 8687 Melrose Ave., ☎ 310/657–0800), which presents art, design, and cultural exhibitions, sits on the adjacent 2-acre public plaza. The gallery is open Tuesday–Saturday noon–6. ⊠ *Melrose Ave. at San Vicente Blvd.*

⑧ **Regent Beverly Wilshire Hotel.** Anchoring the south end of Rodeo Drive since opening in 1928, the hotel often hosts visiting royalty and celebrities. The lobby is small for a hotel of this size and offers little opportunity to meander; you might stop for a drink or meal in one of the hotel's restaurants. ⊠ *9500 Wilshire Blvd.*

★ **⑦** **Rodeo Drive.** Strolling this famed, boutique-lined street can make for a fun afternoon. Here you can find a $200 pair of socks wrapped in gold leaf and stores that take customers only by appointment. Some of the Rodeo (pronounced ro-*day*-o) shops may be familiar because they supply clothing for network television shows and their names often appear among the credits. Others, such as Gucci, have worldwide reputations. Several nearby restaurants have outside patios where you can sit and sip a drink while watching the fashionable shoppers saunter by. At the southern end of this thoroughfare is Via Rodeo, a curvy cobblestone street that somewhat emulates the picture-perfect layout of Disneyland's main drag, though the boutiques that thrive here are definitely for adults—with money. ⊠ *Between Santa Monica and Wilshire Blvds.*

★ **④** **Sunset Strip.** The Strip was famous in the '50s because of the TV show *77 Sunset Strip,* but it was popular as far back as the 1930s, when nightclubs like Ciro's and Mocambo were going strong. Drive the length of the Strip first—to absorb its hustle and bustle, vanity billboards touting new movies and records and stars, and dazzling shops—and then pick a section to explore on foot. The outdoor cafés of the Sunset Plaza area (including the nouvelle Chinese favorite, Chin Chin) are packed for lunch and on warm evenings. At Horn Street are a monster Tower Records complex, the fine literary establishment Book Soup, and Wolfgang Puck's famous Spago restaurant.

⑪ **University of California at Los Angeles.** Some of the architecture on this campus, such as the Romanesque library, is spectacular, and the Franklin Murphy Sculpture Garden contains works by Henry Moore and Gaston Lachaise. The Mildred Mathias Botanic Garden is accessible from Tiverton Avenue on the southeast side of the campus. Maps and information are available at drive-by kiosks at major entrances, and the UCLA Campus Visits Program conducts free one-hour walking tours (☎ 310/206–0616) on weekdays 10:30 AM and 2:30 PM. Reservations essential. ⊠ *Le Conte Ave., Sunset Blvd., and Hilgard Ave. border the campus.*

⑩ **Westwood Memorial Park.** The Westwood stretch of Wilshire Boulevard is a corridor of cheek-by-jowl office buildings of varying, often jarring architectural styles. Tucked behind one of these behemoths is

1218 Glendon Avenue. In this very unlikely place for a cemetery is the simply marked wall crypt of Marilyn Monroe. Also buried here is Natalie Wood.

Santa Monica, Venice, Pacific Palisades, and Malibu

The towns that hug the coastline of Santa Monica Bay reflect the economic diversity of Los Angeles, from rich-as-can-be Malibu to yuppie-seedy Venice.

Santa Monica is a tidy little city, about 8.3 miles square, where expatriate Brits tend to settle (there's an English music hall and several pubs here), attracted perhaps by the cool, foggy climate. The sense of order is reflected in the economic-geographic stratification: The most northern section has broad streets lined with superb, older homes. As you drive south, real estate prices drop $50,000 or so every block or two.

Indeed, Venice was a turn-of-the-century fantasy that never quite came true. Abbot Kinney, a wealthy Los Angeles businessman, envisioned this little piece of real estate, which then seemed so far from downtown, as a romantic replica of Venice, Italy. He developed an incredible 16 miles of canals, floated gondolas on them, and built scaled-down versions of the Doge's Palace and other Venetian landmarks. Some canals were rebuilt in 1996, but don't reflect the Old World connection quite as well as they could. Figures. Ever since Kinney first planned his project, it was plagued by ongoing engineering problems and disasters and drifted into disrepair. Three small canals and bridges do remain and can best be viewed by walking along Dell Avenue, from Washington Street to Venice Boulevard.

By the late 1960s, however, actors, artists, musicians, hippies, and anyone who wanted to live near the beach but couldn't afford to, were attracted by the low rents in Venice, and the place quickly became SoHo-by-the-Sea. The trade-off was that the area was pretty rundown, and the remaining canals were stagnant and fairly smelly, but as the area's appeal grew and a more upscale crowd started moving in, these drawbacks were rectified. Venice's locals today are a grudgingly thrown-together mix of aging hippies, yuppies with the disposable income to spend on inflated rents, senior citizens who have lived here for decades, and the homeless.

Just south of Venice is a quick shift of values: the popular singles enclave of Marina del Rey is the largest man-made boat harbor in the world, with a commercial area catering to the whims of boat owners and boat groupies. The stretch between Admiralty Way and Mindinao Way has some of the area's best restaurants—expensive but worth it. Most of the better hotel chains, such as the Ritz-Carlton, also have properties here.

North of Santa Monica, Malibu has a worldwide reputation for its swank beach houses, television- and film-star residents, and mud slides. Pacific Palisades, connecting Santa Monica to Malibu, is a pleasant drive in daytime or evening. The narrow-but-expensive Malibu beachfront houses were home to movie stars back in the 1930s and are preferred by many of their modern-day successors, who enjoy the get-away-from-it-all feeling this coastline area of Los Angeles provides.

A Good Tour

Numbers in the text correspond to numbers in the margin and on the Santa Monica and Venice map.

Look for the arched neon sign at the entrance to the **Santa Monica Pier** ①, the city's number-one landmark, built in 1909. Park your car in one of the area lots. Nearby **Pacific Park** ② is an exciting state-of-the-art amusement center. The first street east of Pacific Coast Highway is Ocean Avenue, where **Palisades Park** ③, a strip of lawn and palms perched above the cliffs, provides panoramic ocean views. East a few more blocks is the **Third Street Promenade** ④, an active shopping and dining and entertainment mall. Head south on Third and west on Pico Boulevard to Main Street, on which you'll find the **Santa Monica Museum of Art** ⑤ and the **California Heritage Museum** ⑥. Next stop is Venice. Drive along Main Street through the stylish shopping district until you hit Rose Avenue, and then turn west toward the sea. The main attraction of this dead end is the **Venice Boardwalk** ⑦, home to a classic California beach scene.

South of Venice in Marina del Rey's **Burton Chace Park** ⑧, you can watch the wind carry colorful sailboats from the marina out to sea. Loop back north past Santa Monica on Highway 1 to Pacific Palisades, where **Will Rogers State Historic Park** ⑨, the famed humorist and cowboy's former estate, is a fine picnicking spot. A couple of miles north, just inside the city limits of Malibu, is the **J. Paul Getty Museum** ⑩, built by its namesake to house his extensive art collection. Farther down on the beach side of the highway, the Spanish-Moorish **Adamson House** ⑪ is tiled to the hilt. Next door, **Malibu Lagoon State Beach** ⑫ has extensive paths that take you through a reserve with many native birds.

TIMING

You would do well to visit the area in two excursions: Santa Monica to Venice in one day and Pacific Palisades to Malibu in another. The museums in Santa Monica (both closed Monday and Tuesday) are small—you need no more than an hour for each of them. You could easily spend half a day at Venice Boardwalk, but don't stay after dark, when the crowd becomes unsavory. It's safer (they do have break-ins in this area) and easier to park in a pay lot in lieu of busy street parking. You can drive through Marina del Rey, or get out at Burton Chace Park for a longer look. If you drive toward Malibu during rush hour, expect to proceed at a snail's pace. Will Rogers State Historic Park and Malibu Lagoon State Beach make for good walks; plan at least a half an hour at each. The Getty Museum (closed Monday) deserves two hours, but the Adamson House (closed Monday and Tuesday) requires only a brief walk-through. Try to be outdoors come sunset.

Sights to See

★ ⑪ **Adamson House.** The Rindge family, which owned much of the Malibu Rancho in the early part of the 20th century, built this Moorish-Spanish home in 1928. Malibu was quite isolated then, with all visitors and supplies arriving by boat at the nearby Malibu Pier. The Rindges led an enviable Malibu lifestyle, decades before it was trendy. The house is right on the beach (high chain-link fences keep out curious beachgoers). The family operated the Malibu Tile Company; their home is predictably encrusted with magnificent tile work in rich blues, greens, yellows, and oranges. Even an outside dog shower, near the servants' door, is a tiled delight. Docent-led tours help visitors to envision family life here and to learn about the history of Malibu and its real estate (you can't have one without the other). ✉ *23200 Pacific Coast Hwy.,* ☏ *310/456–8432.* ▱ *$2; fee parking.* ☉ *Wed.–Sat. 11–3.*

⑧ **Burton Chace Park.** At the tip of a jetty and surrounded on three sides by water and moored boats, this 6-acre patch of green provides a cool and breezy spot from which to watch sea vessels move in and out of the channel. It's also great for a picnic. *Mindinao Way, off Lincoln Blvd.*

314

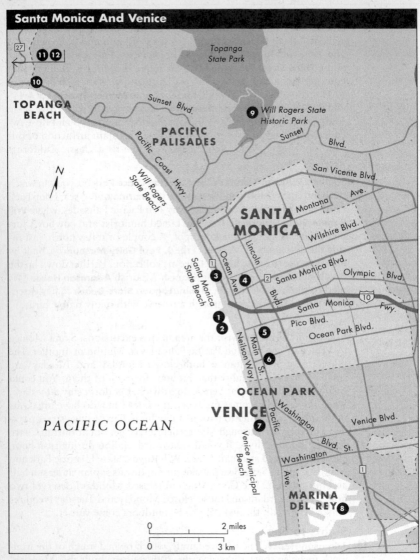

Adamson House, **11**
Burton Chace Park, **8**
California Heritage
Museum, **6**
J. Paul Getty
Museum, **10**
Malibu Lagoon State
Beach, **12**
Pacific Park, **2**

Palisades Park, **3**
Santa Monica
Museum of Art, **5**
Santa Monica Pier, **1**
Third Street
Promenade, **4**
Venice Boardwalk, **7**
Will Rogers State
Historic Park, **9**

⑥ California Heritage Museum. Housed in an 1894-vintage, late-Victorian home once owned by the founder of Santa Monica, this museum was moved to its present site in the late 1970s. Three rooms have been fully restored: the dining room in the style of 1890 to 1910; the living room, 1910–1920; and the kitchen, 1920–1930. The second-floor galleries contain photography and historical exhibits, as well as shows by contemporary California artists. ⊠ *2612 Main St.,* ☎ *310/392–8537.* ⊠ *$2.* ⊙ *Wed.–Sat. 11–4, Sun. noon–4.*

★ ⑩ J. Paul Getty Museum. You'll want to plan in advance to visit this famous museum, which contains one of the country's finest collections of Greek and Roman antiquities. The oil millionaire began collecting art in the 1930s, concentrating on three distinct areas: Greek and Roman antiquities, Baroque and Renaissance paintings, and 18th-century decorative arts. In 1946 he purchased a large Spanish-style home on 65 acres in a canyon just north of Santa Monica to house the collection. By the late 1960s, the museum could no longer accommodate the rapidly expanding collection, and Getty decided to build this new building, which was completed in 1974. It's a a re-creation of the Villa dei Papiri, a luxurious 1st-century Roman house that stood on the slopes of Mt. Vesuvius, overlooking the Bay of Naples, prior to the volcano's eruption in AD 79. The two-level, 38-gallery building and its extensive gardens provide an appropriate and harmonious setting for Getty's artworks. Note that in late 1997, all the art except the antiquities will be moved to a new J. Paul Getty Center in Brentwood. The catch in visiting the Malibu Getty is that parking is limited and reservations are necessary; they should be made one week in advance. The only other way in if you're not on a tour—handy if you've arrived too late to reserve a parking slot—is to take MTA Bus 434 from Santa Monica. If you ask, the driver will give you an entrance pass. ⊠ *17985 Pacific Coast Hwy.,* ☎ *310/458–2003.* ⊠ *Free.* ⊙ *Tues.–Sun. 10–5.*

NEED A BREAK? Try **PierView** (⊠ 22718 Pacific Coast Hwy., ☎ 310/456–6962), just south of the Malibu Pier at the edge of the ocean, for sandwiches, pizzas, and Mexican fare including shark fajitas.

⑫ Malibu Lagoon State Beach. Visitors to this haven for native and migratory birds are asked to stay on the boardwalks so that the egrets, blue herons, avocets, and gulls can enjoy the marshy area. The signs that give opening and closing hours refer only to the parking lot; the lagoon itself is open 24 hours and is enjoyable in the early morning and at sunset. Luckily, street-side parking is available then (but not at midday). ⊠ *Pacific Coast Hwy., adjacent to Adamson House.*

⑫ ❷ Pacific Park. California's only oceanfront amusement facility is on two acres of the Santa Monica Pier. The 11 rides include a roller coaster, a giant Ferris wheel, a flying submarine, and the Rock and Roll, a spinning experience with a light show and rousing music. ⊠ *380 Santa Monica Pier, Santa Monica,* ☎ *310/260–8747.* ⊠ *Rides $1–$3.* ⊙ *Summer, daily 10 AM–midnight; winter hrs vary.*

❸ Palisades Park. The ribbon of green that runs along the top of the cliffs from Colorado Avenue to just north of San Vicente Boulevard has flat walkways, usually filled with casual strollers as well as joggers who like to work out with a spectacular view of the Pacific.

❺ Santa Monica Museum of Art. Designed by architect Frank Gehry, a Santa Monica resident, this highly regarded museum presents painting, sculpture, video, and performance art. ⊠ *2437 Main St.,* ☎ *310/399–0433.* ⊠ *$4.* ⊙ *Wed.–Sun. 11–6, Fri. 11–10.*

★ ☝ ❶ **Santa Monica Pier.** Cafés, gift shops, a psychic adviser, and arcades are
all on the pier, along with a recently added amusement park. The
trademark 46-horse carousel, built in 1922, has appeared in many films,
including *The Sting.* ✉ *Colorado Ave., west of Ocean Ave.,* ☎ *310/458–
8900.* ✆ *Rides 50¢.* ☉ *Carousel summer, Tues.–Sun. 10–9; winter,
weekends 10–5.*

☝ ❹ **Third Street Promenade.** Only foot traffic is allowed along a three-block
stretch of Third Street. Outdoor cafés, clever boutiques, street vendors,
several multiplexes, and a rich nightlife (the mix of folks down here is
great, from grannies out for a bite to skateboarders and street musicians) have made this one of Santa Monica's main gathering spots. ✉
3rd St., between Wilshire Blvd. and Broadway.

★ ☝ ❼ **Venice Boardwalk.** Also known as Ocean Front Walk, the boardwalk
delivers year-round action. Bikini-clad skaters put on impromptu
demonstrations, vying for attention with the unusual breeds of dogs
promenading with the locals. A bodybuilding club works out on the
adjacent beach, and it's nearly impossible not to stop and ogle the strong-
men's pecs. Bicycles and skates can be rented at the south end of the
boardwalk, along Washington Street near the Venice Pier.

NEED A
BREAK?
The boardwalk is lined with fast-food stands, and food can then be carried a few feet to the beach for a picnic. From a patio table at the **Sidewalk Cafe** (✉ 1401 Ocean Front Walk, ☎ 310/399–5547), you can
watch the free spirits on parade.

★ ❾ **Will Rogers State Historic Park.** The two-story ranch house on the 187-
acre estate of the late humorist and cowboy is a folksy blend of Navajo
rugs and Mission-style furniture. Rogers's only extravagance was raising the roof several feet (he waited till his wife was in Europe to do it)
so he could practice his lasso technique indoors. The nearby museum
features Rogers memorabilia. Rogers was a polo enthusiast, and in the
1930s, his front-yard polo field attracted such friends as Douglas Fairbanks for weekend games. The tradition continues, with free games
scheduled from late spring to early fall when the weather's good. The
park's broad lawns are excellent for picnicking, and there's hiking on
miles of eucalyptus-lined trails. ✉ *1501 Will Rogers State Park Rd.,
Pacific Palisades,* ☎ *310/454–8212.* ✆ *Free, parking $5.* ☉ *Park 8–6,
later in summer. House daily 10–5.*

Palos Verdes, San Pedro, and Long Beach

The hilly Palos Verdes Peninsula is home to horse lovers and other gentrified folk, many of them East Coast executive transplants. The real
estate in these small peninsula towns, ranging from expensive to very
expensive, is zoned for stables, and you'll often see riders along the
streets (they have the right of way).

Neat 1920s-era white clapboards, and dozens of boats of all sizes, epit-
omize San Pedro (locals steadfastly ignore the correct Spanish pronunciation—it's "San Peedro" to them), an old seaport community with
a strong Mediterranean and Eastern European flavor. There are enticing
Greek and Yugoslavian markets and restaurants throughout the town.

Long Beach began as a seaside resort in the 19th century, and during
the early part of the 20th century it was a popular destination for Mid-
westerners and Dust Bowlers in search of a better life. They built street
after street of modest wood homes. To preserve transportation and shipping interests for the city of Los Angeles, Wilmington was annexed in

the late 19th century. A narrow strip of land, mostly less than ½ mile wide, it follows the Harbor Freeway from downtown south to the port.

A Good Drive

Numbers in the text correspond to numbers in the margin and on the Palos Verdes, San Pedro, and Long Beach map.

Begin at **South Coast Botanic Garden** ①, on Palos Verdes Drive North, off of Highway 1. This former dump has been transformed into a version of Eden. From the gardens, head toward the coast on Hawthorne Boulevard to Palos Verdes Drive West and turn left. Less than a mile farther on your right you'll see **Point Vicente Lighthouse,** and, another 2½ miles away, on your left, you'll see an all-glass structure surrounded by fern gardens. This modern masterpiece, **Wayfarers Chapel** ②, designed by Lloyd Wright, Frank's talented son, brings outdoors inside with transparent walls. Continue south on Palos Verdes Drive. A stark white building houses **Cabrillo Marine Aquarium** ③, where kids are encouraged to touch the creatures that thrive in the museum's tide pool. From here, take Pacific Avenue north to 6th Street and turn right, leading you harborside to the **Ports O' Call Village** ④, several small fishermen's retreats, all of them connected by cobblestone walkways.

Follow the Harbor Freeway north, exiting at Pacific Coast Highway, to reach the **Banning Residence Museum and Park** ⑤. Take Pacific Coast Highway toward Long Beach, and follow the sign leading to the **Queen Mary** ⑥. Climb aboard one of the finest art deco ships still afloat. Then take Panorama Drive across Queensway Bay to Shoreline Drive and **Shoreline Village** ⑦, a waterfront outdoor shopping district. Wind down in adjacent **Shoreline Aquatic Park** ⑧ for the best view of the harbor and the Long Beach skyline. Take Ocean Boulevard west to Long Beach Boulevard and head north (or right) to San Antonio Drive. Turn left here to Virginia Road and then right, past a golf course, to the historic adobe two-story **Rancho Los Cerritos** ⑨. Then drive north to the 405 freeway, and go southeast and exit at Palo Verde Avenue. Turn right (south) onto Palo Verde, which will dead end at Bixby Hills Estate, a gated community. Tell the guard at the entrance that you'd like to visit **Rancho Los Alamitos** ⑩, and you'll be sent up the hill to the historic dwelling. After that, take the Pacific Coast Highway south to a southern California version of Venice, inaptly called **Naples** ⑪, on Los Alamitos Bay, where—no surprise—the ancient art of gondola riding is all the rage.

TIMING

Plan on spending an hour or more at the South Coast Botanic Garden; Wayfarers Chapel is worth another half hour. If you bring kids to the Cabrillo Marine Aquarium (closed Monday), expect to stay a couple of hours. The Banning Residence Museum and Park (closed Monday) takes an hour to appreciate fully. You'll probably want to spend two or three hours exploring the *Queen Mary,* Shoreline Village, and Shoreline Aquatic Park. Ranchos Los Cerritos and Los Amigos take an hour to visit, as does Naples.

Sights to See

⑤ Banning Residence Museum and Park. General Phineas Banning, an early Los Angeles entrepreneur, is credited with developing the San Pedro harbor into a viable economic entity and naming the area Wilmington (he was from Delaware). Part of his estate has been preserved in a 20-acre park that offers excellent picnicking possibilities. A 100-year-old wisteria, near the arbor, blooms in the spring. The interior of the house can be seen on docent-led tours. ✉ *401 E. M St., Wilmington,* ☎

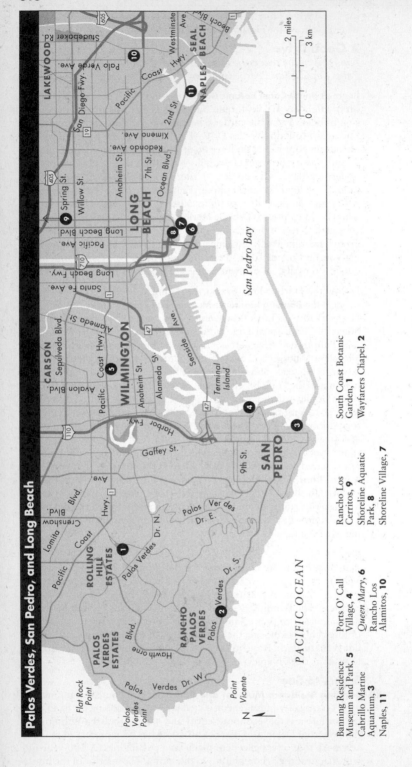

Palos Verdes, San Pedro, and Long Beach

Banning Residence
Museum and Park, **5**
Cabrillo Marine
Aquarium, **3**
Naples, **11**

Ports O' Call
Village, **4**
Queen Mary, **6**
Rancho Los
Alamitos, **10**

Rancho Los
Cerritos, **9**
Shoreline Aquatic
Park, **8**
Shoreline Village, **7**

South Coast Botanic
Garden, **1**
Wayfarers Chapel, **2**

PACIFIC OCEAN

San Pedro Bay

310/548–7777. ✉ House $2. ⊙ House tour Tues.–Thurs. 12:30–2:30 and weekends 12:30–3:30 on ½ hr.

☝ ❸ **Cabrillo Marine Aquarium.** This gem of a small museum is dedicated to the marine life that flourishes off the southern California coast, particularly near San Pedro. Set in a modern Frank Gehry–designed building right on the beach, the museum is popular with school groups. The 35 saltwater aquariums include a shark tank, and a see-through tidal tank gives visitors a chance to see the long view of a wave. On the back patio, docents supervise as visitors reach into a shallow tank to touch starfish and sea anemones. ✉ *3720 Stephen White Dr., San Pedro,* ☎ *310/548–7562.* ✉ *Free, parking $6.50.* ⊙ *Tues.–Fri. noon–5, weekends 10–5.*

⓫ **Naples.** Actually three small islands in man-made Alamitos Bay, Naples is best experienced on foot—park near Bayshore Drive and 2nd Street and walk across the bridge, where you can meander through Italian-named streets. This well-restored area has eclectic architecture: vintage Victorians, Craftsman bungalows, and Mission Revivals. You may spy a real gondola or two on the neighborhood's well-maintained canals. (The developer who came up with the Naples canal idea learned from the mistakes and bad luck that did in those in Venice, just up the coast, and built the canals to take full advantage of the tidal flow that would keep them clean.) You can hire a gondola for a ride, but not on the spur of the moment. Gondola Getaway conducts one-hour rides. ✉ *5437 E. Ocean Blvd., east from Long Beach pier,* ☎ *310/433–9595.* ✉ *Rides $55 per couple, $10 each additional person.* ⊙ *Cruises noon–midnight.*

❹ **Ports O'Call Village.** Not far from Cabrillo Marine Aquarium, this is a commercial rendition of shipping villages from different places around the globe, with shops, restaurants, and fast-food windows. Two companies run year-round 1- to 1½-hour harbor cruises and January–April whale-watching cruises. Call 310/831–1073 for schedules. ✉ *Between Harbor Blvd. and 6th St., San Pedro,* ☎ *310/831–0287.*

★ ❻ ***Queen Mary.*** The largest passenger ship ever built now sits snugly in Long Beach Harbor. What seemed like sure folly when Long Beach officials bought the boat in 1964 put the city on the proverbial map. The 50,000-ton *Queen Mary* was launched in 1934, a floating treasure of art deco splendor. It took a crew of 1,100 to minister to the needs of its 1,900 demanding passengers. As you explore this most luxurious of luxury liners, you'll admire the extensive wood paneling, the gleaming nickel- and silver-plated handrails, and the hand-cut glass. Tours of the ship are available, and guests are invited to browse the 12 decks and witness close up the bridge, staterooms, officers' quarters, and engine rooms. There are several restaurants and shops on board. ✉ *Pier J, Long Beach,* ☎ *310/435–3511.* ✉ *$10, guided 1-hr tour $3 extra.* ⊙ *Daily 10–4:30, later in summer.*

❿ **Rancho Los Alamitos.** Said to be the country's oldest one-story domestic building still standing, this landmark was built in 1806, when the Spanish flag still flew over California. There's a blacksmith shop in the barn. ✉ *6400 E. Bixby Hill Rd.,* ☎ *310/431–3541.* ✉ *Free.* ⊙ *Wed.–Sun. 1–5, free 90-min tour every ½ hr 1–4.*

❾ **Rancho Los Cerritos.** The former home (built in 1884) of the Don Juan Temple family has two features associated with Monterey-style adobes: It has two stories and a narrow balcony across the front. It's easy to imagine Zorro, that swashbuckling fictional hero of the rancho era, jumping from the balcony onto a waiting horse and making his escape. The 10 rooms have been furnished in the style of the period and are open for viewing. The gardens here were designed in the 1930s by well-known landscape architect Ralph Cornell. ⊠ *4600 Virginia Rd.,* ☎ *310/570–1755.* ☒ *Donations accepted.* ☉ *Wed.–Sun. 1–5, free self-guided tour weekdays, free 50-min guided tour weekends hourly 1–4.*

❽ Shoreline Aquatic Park. Set literally in the middle of Long Beach Harbor is this much-sought-after resting place for RVers. Kite flyers love the winds here. On a short walk, the modern skyline, Shoreline Village, the *Queen Mary,* and the ocean all vie for attention. Long Beach Water Sports (⊠ 730 E. 4th St., ☎ 310/432–0187) rents aquacycles and kayaks during the summer months, but the park's lagoon is off-limits for swimming. ⊠ *205 Marina Dr.*

❼ Shoreline Village. The most successful of the pseudo–New England or British harbors lies between downtown Long Beach and the *Queen Mary.* In addition to gift shops and restaurants, there's a 1906 carousel with bobbing giraffes, camels, and horses. ⊠ *Shoreline Dr. and Pine Ave.,* ☎ *310/435–2668.* ☒ *Carousel $1.* ☉ *May–Sept., daily 10 AM–11 PM; Oct.–Apr., daily 10–9.*

★ ❶ South Coast Botanic Garden. This Rancho Palos Verdes botanical garden began life ignominiously—as a garbage dump-cum-landfill. It's hard to believe that as recently as 1960, truckloads of waste (3½ million tons) were being deposited here. With the intensive ministerings of the experts from the L.A. County Arboreta Department, the dump soon sprouted lush gardens, with plants from every continent except Antarctica eventually organized into color groups. Self-guided walking tours take visitors past flower and herb gardens, rare cacti, and a lake with ducks. ⊠ *26300 S. Crenshaw Blvd., Rancho Palos Verdes,* ☎ *310/544–6815.* ☒ *$5.* ☉ *Daily 9–5.*

❷ Wayfarers Chapel. Architect Lloyd Wright, son of Frank Lloyd Wright, designed this modern glass church in 1949 to blend in with an encircling redwood forest. The redwoods are gone, but another forest has taken their place, lush with ferns and azaleas, adding up to a breathtaking combination of ocean, vegetation, and an architectural wonder. This "natural church" is a popular wedding site, so avoid visiting on weekends. ⊠ *5755 Palos Verdes Dr. S, Rancho Palos Verdes,* ☎ *310/377–1650.*

Highland Park, Pasadena, and San Marino

The suburbs north of downtown Los Angeles have a rich architectural heritage and are home to several fine museums. Highland Park, midway between downtown Los Angeles and Pasadena, was a genteel suburb in the late 1800s whose Anglo population tried to keep an Eastern feeling alive in their civic and private architecture despite the decidedly Western landscape. Although now fully absorbed into the general Los Angeles sprawl, Pasadena was once a separate and distinctly defined—and very refined—city. Its varied buildings, augmented by lush landscaping, are among the most spectacular in southern California. San Marino, Pasadena's prestigious neighbor, is a residential retreat where each mansion seems to outdo the next.

A Good Drive

Numbers in the text correspond to numbers in the margin and on the Highland Park, Pasadena, San Marino map.

Take the Pasadena Freeway (110) north to the Avenue 43 exit. Be sure to slow down, as the exit ramp is extremely short. On the east side of the freeway, you'll notice **Heritage Square** ①, a collection of Victorians preserved and moved from different parts of the city. On the other side of the freeway, on Avenue 43, is **El Alisal** ②, a two-story house made out of boulders. The next signal north on Avenue 43 is Figueroa Avenue. Turn right and follow posted signs to the **Southwest Museum** ③, a repository of Native American artifacts. Turn left at Orange Grove Boulevard and take it to Westmoreland Place (off the 300 block of Orange Grove), on the edge of Brookside Park (home to the **Rose Bowl** ④). Turn onto Westmoreland to reach the **Gamble House** ⑤, a pristine example of the Craftsman movement in architecture that appeared in the film *Back to the Future*.

Backtrack on Orange Grove Boulevard to the corner of Walnut Street, where you'll discover a beaux-arts estate, the Fenyes Mansion, home to the **Pasadena Historical Society** ⑥. Continue south on Orange Grove Boulevard to Colorado Boulevard, and turn left. This is Pasadena's main drag and the route for the New Year's Day Rose Parade. On the first block to your left you'll see a round, contemporary building often televised during the parade, the **Norton Simon Museum** ⑦.

Continue east down Colorado Boulevard to **Old Town Pasadena** ⑧, which has few Little Old Ladies but plenty of hidden alleyways and restored buildings dating back to the late 1800s. You'll want to walk around this happening section of Pasadena, heading east. On your right a few blocks, the **Pasadena Civic Center** looks like a domed Italian church. Los Robles Avenue crosses Colorado Boulevard near here. Walk one-half block north on Los Robles to the **Pacific Asia Museum** ⑨. Its Chinese courtyard garden is surrounded by Eastern treasures. If you've got kids, head east three blocks on Colorado Boulevard to El Molino Avenue. Turn right and go three blocks to **Kidspace** ⑩. Continue south on El Molino to California Boulevard and turn left. Follow signs to the world-renowned **Huntington Library, Art Collections, and Botanical Gardens** ⑪.

TIMING

Only on Thursday and weekends are all or most of the sights below open. Heritage Square and El Alisal have afternoon hours, so schedule the Highland Park part of this tour after lunch. Perusing Pasadena could take a full day, more if you want to savor its museums (the Norton Simon is open afternoons only). Both the Gamble House and Fenyes Mansion can be appreciated in an hour or less, as can Heritage Square and El Alisal, but expect to spend two or three hours at the Norton Simon and a few hours exploring Old Town. Set aside at least a half day for the Huntington Library, Art Collections and Botanical Gardens. But be sure the sun is shining—you'll want to explore outdoors as well as indoors at the Huntington.

Sights to See

❷ **El Alisal.** This was once the home of eccentric Easterner-turned-Westerner Charles Lummis. The Harvard graduate was captivated by Native American culture (he founded the Southwest Museum), often living the lifestyle of the natives, much to the shock of his more staid Angeleno contemporaries. His home, built from 1898 to 1910, is constructed of boulders from the arroyo itself, a romantic notion until recent earthquakes made the safety of such homes questionable. The art nouveau fireplace was designed by Gutzon Borglum, the sculptor of Mt. Rushmore. ✉ *200 E. Ave. 43, entrance on Carlotta Blvd.,* ☏ *213/222–0546.* ▧ *Free.* ☉ *Fri.–Sun. noon–4.*

❺ **Gamble House.** Built by Charles and Henry Greene in 1908, this is a spectacular example of Craftsman-style bungalow architecture. The term "bungalow" can be misleading, since the Gamble House is a huge two-story home. To wealthy Easterners such as the Gambles, this type of

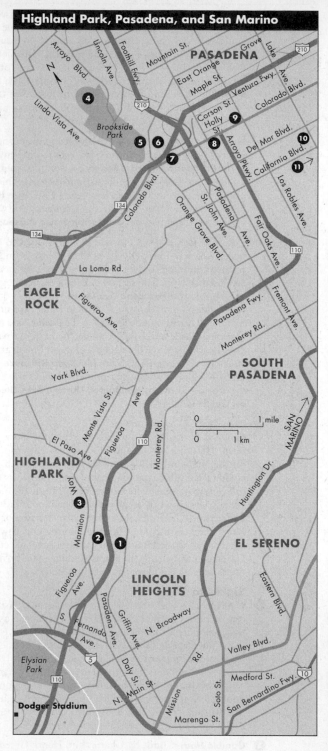

Highland Park, Pasadena, and San Marino

vacation home seemed informal compared to their accustomed mansions. What makes visitors swoon here is the craftsmanship: the hand-shaped teak interiors, the Greene-designed furniture, the Louis Tiffany glass door. The house is on a private road that's not well marked; take Orange Grove Boulevard to the 300 block to find Westmoreland Place. ⊠ *4 Westmoreland Pl.,* ☎ *818/793–3334.* ⊡ *$5.* ⊙ *Thurs.–Sun. noon–3, 1-hr tour every 15–20 mins.*

❶ Heritage Square. In an ambitious attempt to save some of the city's architectural gems from the wrecking ball, Los Angeles Cultural Heritage Board moved four residences and a depot, a church, and a carriage barn to this small park. The most breathtaking building is the 1885 **Hale House.** The almost-garish colors of both the interior and exterior are not the whim of some hippie painter, but rather a faithful re-creation of the palette that was in fashion in the late 1800s. The **Palms Depot,** built in 1886, was moved to the site from the Westside of L.A. The night the building was moved, down city streets and up freeways, is documented in photomurals on the depot's walls. Docents dress in period costume. ⊠ *3800 Homer St., off Ave. 43 exit,* ☎ *818/449–0193.* ⊡ *$5, free Fri. 10–3.* ⊙ *Weekends and most holidays noon–4, tours every hr.*

★ ⓫ Huntington Library, Art Collections, and Botanical Gardens. If you only have time for one stop in the Pasadena area, it should be San Marino, where railroad tycoon Henry E. Huntington built his hilltop home in the early 1900s; since then it has established a reputation as one of the most extraordinary cultural complexes in the world. The library contains 6 million items, including such treasures as a Gutenberg Bible, the earliest known edition of Chaucer's *Canterbury Tales,* George Washington's genealogy in his own handwriting, and first editions by Ben Franklin and Shakespeare. The art gallery, devoted to British art from the 18th and 19th centuries, contains the original *Blue Boy* by Gainsborough, *Pinkie,* a companion piece by Lawrence, and the monumental *Sarah Siddons as the Tragic Muse* by Reynolds. Visitors to this vast property have several options, including a 12-minute slide show introducing the Huntington; a 1¼-hour guided tour of the gardens; a 45-minute audiotape about the art gallery (which can be rented for a nominal fee); a 15-minute introductory talk about the library; and inexpensive, self-guided tour leaflets.

An awesome 130-acre garden, formerly the grounds of the estate, the **Huntington Gardens** include a 12-acre Desert Garden with the largest group of mature cacti and other succulents in the world, all arranged by continent. The Japanese Garden holds traditional Japanese plants, stone ornaments, a moon bridge, a Japanese house, a bonsai court, and a Zen rock garden. Besides these gardens, there are collections of azaleas and 1,500 varieties of camellia. The 1,000-variety rose garden is displayed chronologically, so the development leading to today's strains of roses can be observed. There are also herb, palm, and jungle gardens, plus a Shakespeare garden, where plants mentioned in the playwright's works are grown.

The **Huntington Pavilion,** built in 1980, has views of the surrounding mountains and valleys, plus a bookstore, displays, and information kiosks. Both the east and west wings of the pavilion display paintings. The Ralph M. Parsons Botanical Center at the pavilion includes a botanical library, a herbarium, and a laboratory for research on plants. ⊠ *1151 Oxford Rd.,* ☎ *818/405–2100.* ⊡ *$7.50; tours available.* ⊙ *Tues.–Fri. 1–4:30, weekends 11–4:30.*

MISSION SAN GABRIEL ARCHANGEL – More than 200 years ago Father Junípero Serra dedicated this mission to the great archangel and messenger from God, St. Gabriel. As the founders approached the mission site, they were confronted by "savage" Native Americans. In the heat of battle, one of the padres produced the canvas painting *Our Lady of Sorrows,* which so impressed the Indians that they laid down their bows and arrows. Within the next 50 years, the San Gabriel Archangel became the wealthiest of all California missions. In 1833 the Mexican government confiscated the mission and it began to decline; in 1855 the U.S. government returned the mission to the church, but by this time the Franciscans had departed. In 1908 the Claretian Fathers took charge. Mission San Gabriel Archangel's adobe walls preserve an era of history, and the magnificent cemetery stands witness to the many people who lived here, although you can only gaze at the structure because the 1994 earthquake left it unsafe to enter. ✉ *537 W. Mission Dr., San Gabriel,* ☎ *818/457–3048.* ✉ *Donations accepted.* ⊘ *Daily 9:30–4:15.*

🖑 ❿ **Kidspace.** At this children's museum housed in an elementary-school gymnasium, kids can talk to a robot; direct a television or radio station; and dress up in the real uniforms of a firefighter, an astronaut, and a football player. "Critter Caverns" beckons with its large tree house and secret tunnels for exploring insect life up close (don't worry, the bugs are fake). ✉ *390 S. El Molino Ave.,* ☎ *818/449–9143.* ✉ *$5.* ⊘ *Sept.–May, Wed. 2–5, weekends 12:30–5; school vacations, weekdays 1–5, weekends 12:30–5; June–Aug., Tues.–Fri. 1–5.*

★ ❼ **Norton Simon Museum.** Like the more famous Getty Museum, the Norton Simon is a tribute to the art acumen of an extremely wealthy businessman. In 1974, Simon reorganized the failing Pasadena Museum of Modern Art and assembled one of the world's finest collections—richest in its Rembrandts, Goyas, Degas, and Picassos. Rembrandt's development can be traced in three oils—*The Bearded Man in the Wide Brimmed Hat, Self Portrait,* and *Titus.* The most dramatic Goyas are two oils—*St. Jerome* and the portrait of *Dona Francisca Vicenta Chollet y Caballero.* Picasso's renowned *Woman with Book* is one of the highlights of a comprehensive collection of his paintings, drawings, and sculptures. The museum's Impressionist and Cubist holdings are extensive. Southeast Asian artworks date from 100 BC, and the museum also has bronze, stone, and ivory sculptures from India, Cambodia, Thailand, and Nepal. Early Renaissance, Baroque, and Rococo artworks are also well represented. A magical Tiepolo ceiling highlights the Rococo period. ✉ *411 W. Colorado Blvd.,* ☎ *818/449–6840.* ✉ *$4.* ⊘ *Thurs.–Sun. noon–6.*

❽ **Old Town Pasadena.** Once the victim of decay, Pasadena's rejuvenated downtown includes bistros, elegant restaurants, and boutiques. On Raymond Street the former Hotel Green, now the Castle Apartments, is a faded Moorish fantasy of domes, turrets, and balconies. It's reminiscent of the Alhambra but with a greenish tint. Holly Street, between Fair Oaks and Arroyo, has shops with vintage '50s objects, jewelry, and clothes; it's an area that's best explored on foot. Old Town is bisected by Colorado Boulevard, which, west of Old Town, rises onto the Colorado Street Bridge, a section of roadway on graceful arches that was built in 1912 and restored in 1993. On New Year's Day throngs line Colorado Boulevard to watch the Rose Parade.

If browsing Pasadena's many vintage shops leaves you hungry, walk down to Fair Oaks Avenue to the **Market City Cafe** (✉ 33 S. Fair Oaks Ave., ☎ 818/568–0203), which you'll recognize by the life-size black-and-white cow in the window.

⑨ Pacific Asia Museum. Designed in the style of a northern Chinese imperial palace with a central courtyard, this gaudy building is devoted entirely to the arts and crafts of Asia and the Pacific Islands. Most objects are on loan from private collections and other museums. Changing special exhibits focus on the objects of a single country. ⊠ *46 N. Los Robles Ave.,* ☎ *818/449–2742.* ☜ *$4, free 3rd Sat. of month.* ☉ *Wed.–Sun. 10–5.*

⑥ Pasadena Historical Society. The 1905 Fenyes Mansion, the society's headquarters, still has its original furniture and paintings on the main and second floors. In the basement are exhibits on Pasadena's history. There are also 4 acres of well-landscaped gardens. ⊠ *470 W. Walnut St.,* ☎ *818/577–1660.* ☜ *$4.* ☉ *Thurs.–Sun. 1–4, 1-hr docent-led tour.*

④ Rose Bowl. Set at the bottom of a wide area of the arroyo in an older wealthy neighborhood that must endure the periodic onslaught of thousands of cars and party-minded football fans, the stadium is closed except for games and special events such as the monthly Rose Bowl Swap Meet. Held the second Sunday of the month, it is considered the granddaddy of West Coast flea markets. ⊠ *Arroyo Blvd.*

③ Southwest Museum. Readily spotted from the freeway, this Mission Revival building stands erect halfway up Mt. Washington. Inside is an extensive collection of Native American art and artifacts, with special emphasis on the people of the Plains, Northwest Coast, Southwest United States, and Northern Mexico. The basket collection is outstanding. ⊠ *234 Museum Dr., off Ave. 43 exit,* ☎ *213/221–2163.* ☜ *$5.* ☉ *Tues.–Sun. 11–5.*

NEED A BREAK?	**Señor Fish** (⊠ 5111 Figueroa Ave., ☎ 213/257–2498), not too far from the Southwest Museum, looks like a taco stand, but don't pass it up. Its intriguing selections include octopus tostada, scallop burritos, and refreshing seviche.

The San Fernando Valley

Although there are other valleys in the Los Angeles area, this is the one that people refer to simply as "the Valley." City people still see it as a mere collection of bedroom communities, not worth serious thought. But the Valley has come a long way since the early 20th century when it was mainly orange groves and small ranches. Now home to more than 1 million people, this large portion of Los Angeles (with its own monthly magazine) is an area of neat bungalows and ranch-style homes situated on tidy parcels of land, with shopping centers never too far away. Fine restaurants and several major movie and television studios are an integral part of this community.

A Good Drive

Three studios in the Valley offer tours. Take the Hollywood Freeway (U.S. 101) north to Universal City and **Universal Studios Hollywood** and **CityWalk.** Exit Universal on Barham Boulevard and turn left toward Burbank. After driving about a mile, the street curves to the right, where you'll see **Warner Bros. Studios,** with billboards of current films and television shows made there decorating the outside wall. After the curve you will be on West Olive Avenue, which leads to Hollywood Way and Gate No. 4, the entrance for tours (reserve in advance).

The next stop is **NBC Television Studios,** which has tours and offers admittance to some productions. Just a minute away at the second big intersection, West Olive and Alameda avenues, is the main entrance. Continue east, and **Disney Studios,** a very colorful bit of architecture, is on the next block to your right. Continue east on Alameda two miles to the Golden State Freeway (I–5). Drive north about seven miles to San Fernando Mission Road, exit, and follow the road west a quarter of a mile. On your left you'll spot **Mission San Fernando Rey de España,** a historical landmark that doubles as a movie set. Continue on San Fernando Mission Boulevard to Sepulveda Boulevard and turn left on Sepulveda, looking for signs to Highway 118. Enter the on-ramp heading east, and travel about two miles to the Foothill Freeway (I–210) east. Follow about five miles along the base of the San Gabriel Mountains and take Angeles Crest Highway, and then follow signs to **Descanso Gardens.** A cool spot on a warm day, these picturesque gardens are sheltered by giant oak trees.

TIMING

One or two of these Valley attractions will make for a good half- or full-day trip. Rush-hour traffic jams on the San Diego and Hollywood freeways can be brutal, so avoid these thoroughfares at these times.

Sights To See

★ **Descanso Gardens.** Once part of the vast Spanish Rancho San Rafael that covered more than 30,000 acres, these gardens encompass 165 acres of chaparral–covered slopes. A forest of California live oak trees furnishes a dramatic backdrop for thousands of camellias and azaleas, and a breathtaking 4-acre rose garden. Descanso's Tea House has pools, waterfalls, a Zen garden, and a gift shop. It's a relaxing spot reflection. Trams traverse the grounds, but be sure to spend some time strolling on your own to absorb this beautiful place fully. ✉ *1418 Descanso Dr., La Canada,* ☎ *818/952–4400.* 💲 *$5, $2.50 3rd Tues. of month.* ⊙ *Daily 9–4:30.*

Disney Studios. Although tours are not offered of this state-of-the-art animation studio, the view from West Olive Avenue proves that Disney's innovations encompass architecture as well as cinema. There's a water tower with Mickey Mouse climbing the side and Snow White's Seven Dwarfs just beyond the main gate. Almost entirely made of glass, the Michael Graves–designed building looks like the hull of an enormous ocean liner. ✉ *500 S. Buena Vista St., at Alameda Ave.*

Mission San Fernando Rey de España. This mission was established in 1797 and named in honor of King Ferdinand III of Spain. Fifty-six Native Americans joined the mission to make it a self-supporting community, but in the mid-1830s it began to decline after changes made under Mexican rule prompted the Native Americans to leave. The mission deteriorated further until 1923, when a restoration program was initiated. The church's interior is decorated with Native American designs and artifacts of Spanish craftsmanship depicting the mission's 18th-century culture. The structure has been used in countless film and TV productions. ✉ *15151 San Fernando Mission Blvd.,* ☎ *818/361–0186.* 💲 *$4.* ⊙ *Daily 9–5.*

NBC Television Studios. This major network's headquarters is in Burbank. For those who wish to be part of a live studio audience, free tickets are made available for tapings of the various NBC shows, and studio tours are offered daily. ✉ *3000 W. Alameda Ave., Burbank,* ☎ *818/840–3537.* 💲 *$6.* ⊙ *Tour daily 1–3.*

★ **Universal Studios Hollywood.** The five- to seven-hour Universal tour is an enlightening and amusing (if a bit sensational) day at the world's largest television and movie studio. The complex stretches across more than 420 acres, many of which are traversed during the course of the tour by trams featuring usually witty running commentary by enthusiastic guides. You can experience the parting of the Red Sea, an avalanche, and a flood;

meet a 30-foot-tall version of King Kong; live through an encounter with a runaway train; and endure a confrontation with aliens armed with death rays—all without ever leaving the safety of the tram. You can also experience the perils of The Big One—an all-too-real simulation of an 8.3 earthquake, complete with collapsing earth, deafening train wrecks, floods, and other life-threatening amusements. If you missed Kevin Costner's epic film, *Waterworld*, Universal delivers a facsimile in the form of a sea-war extravaganza. At *Lucy: A Tribute to Lucille Ball*, a 2,200-square-foot heart-shape museum contains a re-creation of the *I Love Lucy* set, plus other artifacts from the hit 1950s program. At the Entertainment Center, the longest and last stop of the day, you can stroll around to enjoy various shows. In one, theater animals beguile you with their tricks; in another, you can pose for a photo session with the Incredible Hulk; and at the Star Trek Theater, you can have yourself filmed and inserted as an extra in a scene from a galactic adventure. ⊠ *100 Universal City Pl.,* ☎ *818/508–9600.* 🎟 *$33.* ⊙ *Box office daily 9–7.*

Warner Bros. Studios. Two-hour tours at this major studio center more on actual filmmaking than the one at Universal. They vary from day to day to take advantage of goings-on at the lot, but most tours see the back-lot sets, the prop-construction department, and the sound complex. Reservations are essential one week in advance; children under 10 are not admitted. The tour involves much walking, so you should dress comfortably. ⊠ *4000 Warner Blvd.,* ☎ *818/954–1744.* 🎟 *$29.* ⊙ *Tours weekdays 9–4 every ½ hr.*

OFF THE BEATEN PATH	**MULHOLLAND DRIVE –** The dividing line between the San Fernando Valley and Los Angeles proper, this is one of the most famous thoroughfares in this vast metropolis. Driving the length of the hillside road is slow and can be treacherous, but the rewards are sensational views of valley and city on each side and expensive homes along the way through the Hollywood Hills almost to the Pacific Ocean.

DINING

Updated by Jane E. Lasky and William P. Brown

Los Angeles was once known only for its chopped Cobb salad, Green Goddess dressing, drive-in hamburger stands, and outdoor barbecues. Today it is home to many of the best French and northern Italian restaurants in the United States, and fierce competition among upscale restaurateurs has made it one of the least expensive big cities—here or abroad—in which to eat well. Reservations are essential at the best restaurants, and at almost all restaurants on weekend evenings. The city's no-smoking ordinance applies to all restaurants. If you do want to smoke, choose a restaurant with an outdoor area (smoking is allowed outdoors) or one that incorporates a full-scale bar.

CATEGORY	COST*
$$$$	over $50
$$$	$30–$50
$$	$20–$30
$	under $20

per person for a three-course meal, excluding drinks, service, and 8¼% tax

American

BEVERLY HILLS

$$$ ✕ **Grill on the Alley.** A popular place for power lunching, The Grill is known for great steaks, fresh seafood, chicken pot pies, and crab cakes. Repeat customers like the restaurant's creamy Cobb salad and homemade rice pudding. ⊠ *9560 Dayton Way,* ☎ *310/276–0615.*

Downtown Los Angeles Dining and Lodging

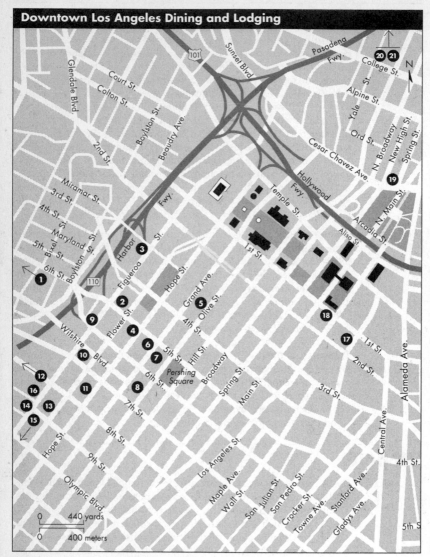

Dining

Cafe Pinot, **4**

Clearwater Cafe, **21**

Mon Kee's Seafood
Restaurant, **19**

Nicola, **9**

Pacific Dining Car, **1**

Restaurant
Horikawa, **17**

Rex Il Ristorante, **8**

Yujean Kang's
Gourmet Chinese
Cuisine, **20**

Lodging

Biltmore Hotel, **7**

Figueroa Hotel, **14**

Holiday Inn L.A.
Downtown, **12**

Hotel
Inter-Continental
Los Angeles, **5**

Hyatt Regency Los
Angeles, **11**

The Inn at 657, **15**

The InnTowne, **16**

New Otani Hotel
and Garden, **18**

Omni Los Angeles,
Hotel and Centre, **10**

Orchid Hotel, **13**

Sheraton Grande
Hotel, **3**

Westin Bonaventure
Hotel and Suites, **2**

Wyndham Checkers
Hotel, **6**

Reservations essential. AE, DC, MC, V. Closed Sun. Valet parking in evening.

$ ✕ **Ed Debevic's.** Go to this fun eatery if you're feeling nostalgic or want to entertain the kids. Old Coca-Cola signs, a blaring jukebox, gum-chewing waitresses in bobby socks, and meat loaf and mashed potatoes recall diners of yore. ⊠ *134 N. La Cienega,* ☎ *310/659–1952. AE, D, DC, MC, V. Valet parking.*

$ ✕ **RJ's the Rib Joint.** This place has an outstanding salad bar with dozens of fresh choices and return privileges. Portions of everything—ribs, chili, barbecued chicken, mile-high layer cakes—are gigantic and top-quality, at reasonable prices. ⊠ *252 N. Beverly Dr.,* ☎ *310/274–7427. AE, D, DC, MC, V. Valet parking in evening.*

CENTURY CITY (BEVERLY HILLS AND HOLLYWOOD MAP)

$ ✕ **Dive!** When you walk in here, you'll feel as though you've just climbed down the hatch of a submarine. The sandwiches are nautical miles ahead of what you might find at a traditional deli, with such specialties as a Chinese chicken salad sub, and a brick oven–baked Tuscan steak sub. For dessert, try the s'mores, or a lemon-bar concoction with white chocolate and raspberry sauce. ⊠ *10250 Santa Monica Blvd.,* ☎ *310/788–3483. Reservations not accepted. AE, D, DC, MC, V. Valet parking or free self-park.*

DOWNTOWN

$$$–$$$$ ✕ **Pacific Dining Car.** This 70-year-old restaurant, one of L.A.'s oldest, is open around the clock. Best known for well-aged steaks, rack of lamb, and an extensive California wine list, it's a favorite haunt of politicians and lawyers around City Hall and of sports fans after Dodgers games. High tea is served every day from 3 to 5:30 PM. ⊠ *1310 W. 6th St.,* ☎ *213/483–6000. AE, DC, MC, V. Valet parking.*

$$$ ✕ **Nicola.** Celebrity chef Larry Nicola's restaurant provides a contrast
★ in moods: One room is intimate, the other more open and airy; both see many business deals sealed over lunch and dinner. The largely American menu has international overtones: Consider broiled Chilean sea bass with caramelized orange and ginger potatoes, roasted prime rib of pork with tomatillo sauce and corn succotash, and Mediterranean range chicken with tabbouleh and Lebanese fried potatoes. The wine list is very impressive, with plenty of California favorites. A kiosk in the courtyard operated by Nicola is popular with area workers looking for a quick (but tasty) bite. ⊠ *Sanwa Bank Bldg., 601 S. Figueroa St.,* ☎ *213/485–0927. AE, D, DC, MC, V. Closed Sun. No lunch Sat. Valet parking.*

LOS FELIZ (BEVERLY HILLS AND HOLLYWOOD MAP)

$$–$$$ ✕ **Vida.** Chef-owner Fred Eric's quirky cuisine includes Cajun Okra Winfrey Creole gumbo and the spicy Cobb salad, almost predictably called Ty Cobb. Heavy on bamboo, skylights, and shoji screens, the decor is tranquil yet compelling. Book a booth in the airy front room if you're seeking privacy. Be brave in your menu selections, as progressive Vida is all about taking culinary chances. ⊠ *1930 N. Hillhurst Ave.,* ☎ *213/660–4446. AE, DC, MC, V. No lunch. Valet parking.*

MID-WILSHIRE (BEVERLY HILLS AND HOLLYWOOD MAP)

$$$ ✕ **Campanile.** Portofino meets Hollywood head on in this massive restau-
★ rant, once Charlie Chaplin's office complex. Spago proteges Mark Peel and Nancy Silverton (she's also the force behind the adjacent La Brea Bakery) serve up lamb dishes (including one marinated in eggplant, roasted onions, and artichokes), aromatic breads (the rosemary's the best), and rewarding desserts (especially the inventive rice flan with lime caramel and brandy snaps). Dine in their enclosed courtyard for more intimacy, especially nice at breakfast, an ideal time to try out this au

Beverly Hills and Hollywood Dining and Lodging

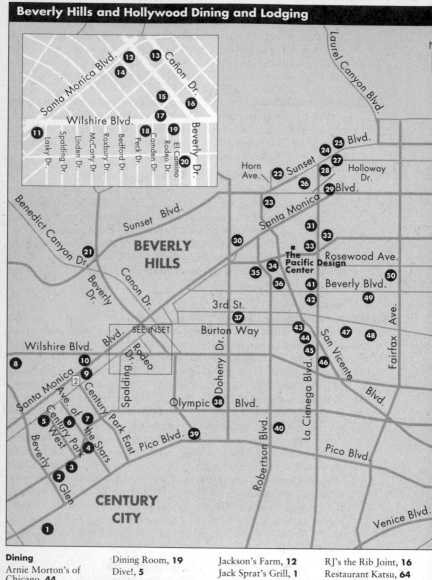

Dining

Arnie Morton's of Chicago, **44**

Barney Greengrass, **18**

Ca'Brea, **57**

California Pizza Kitchen, **20**

Campanile, **58**

Canter's, **50**

Cava, **47**

Cha Cha Cha, **66**

Chan Dara, **62**

Citrus, **56**

Dining Room, **19**

Dive!, **5**

Drai's **32**

Eclipse, **35**

Ed Debevic's, **46**

El Cholo, **63**

Fenix, **27**

Grill on the Alley, **17**

Hard Rock Cafe, **42**

Harry's Bar & American Grill, **7**

Il Fornaio Cucina Italiana, **15**

Jackson's Farm, **12**

Jack Sprat's Grill, **1**

Le Colonial, **36**

Le Dôme, **26**

L'Orangerie, **31**

The Mandarin, **14**

Matsuhisa, **45**

Morton's, **34**

Nate 'n' Al's, **13**

The Palm, **30**

Patina, **59**

Picante Grill, **38**

Pinot Hollywood, **61**

RJ's the Rib Joint, **16**

Restaurant Katsu, **64**

Roscoe's House of Chicken 'n' Waffles, **60**

Sofi, **48**

Spago, **22**

Swingers, **49**

Tavola Calda, **51**

Tommy Tang's, **52**

Vida, **65**

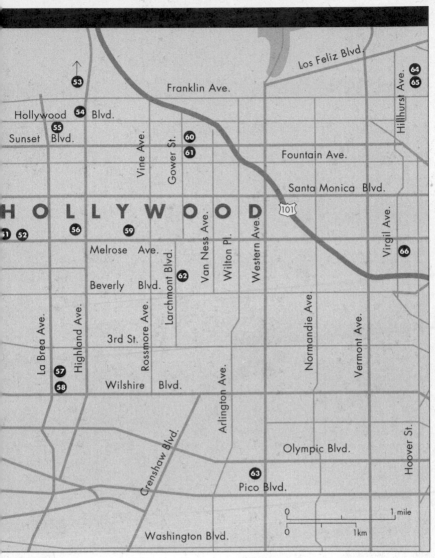

Lodging

The Argyle, **27**

Banana Bungalow Hotel and International Hostel, **53**

The Beverly Hills Hotel and Bungalows, **21**

Beverly Hills Plaza Hotel, **8**

Beverly Prescott Hotel, **39**

Carlyle Inn, **40**

Century City Courtyard by Marriott, **3**

Century Plaza Hotel and Tower, **6**

Chateau Marmont Hotel, **25**

Clarion Hotel Hollywood Roosevelt, **55**

Four Seasons Los Angeles, **37**

Holiday Inn Express, **2**

Hollywood Holiday Inn, **54**

Hotel Nikko, **43**

Hotel Sofitel Los Angeles, **41**

Hyatt on Sunset, **24**

Le Parc Hotel, **33**

Merv Griffin's Beverly Hilton, **10**

Mondrian Hotel, **28**

Park Hyatt, **4**

Peninsula Beverly Hills, **11**

Regent Beverly Wilshire, **19**

Summerfield Suites Hotel, **29**

Wyndham Bel Age Hotel, **23**

332

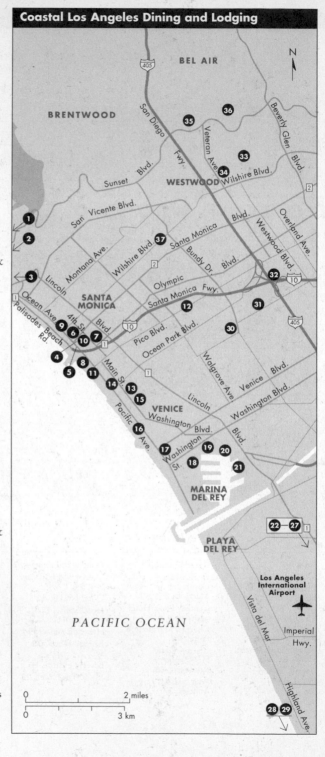

Coastal Los Angeles Dining and Lodging

courant brasserie without making much of a monetary commitment. Star-gazing is an ancillary pleasure at this trendy, yet not overly pretentious, eatery. ⊠ *624 S. La Brea Ave.,* ☎ *213/938–1447. Reservations essential. AE, D, DC, MC, V. No lunch weekends; no dinner Sun. Valet parking.*

PACIFIC PALISADES (COASTAL LOS ANGELES MAP)

$ ✕ **Gladstone's 4 Fish.** This is perhaps the most popular restaurant along the southern California coast. The food is not the world's greatest, but familiar seashore fare is prepared adequately and in large portions, and the prices are certainly right. Best bets: crab chowder, steamed clams, three-egg omelets, hamburgers, barbecued ribs, and chili. ⊠ *17300 Pacific Coast Hwy., Pacific Palisades,* ☎ *310/454–3474. AE, D, DC, MC, V. Valet parking.*

PASADENA (DOWNTOWN LOS ANGELES MAP)

$–$$ ✕ **Clearwater Cafe.** Dishes here cater to low-fat, low-sodium palates, but that doesn't mean a loss in taste—the spicy catfish has a certain bite and the mixed vegetable grill with creamy polenta satisfies even the most discerning vegetarian. ⊠ *168 W. Colorado Blvd.,* ☎ *818/356–0959. AE, D, MC, V. Valet parking.*

SAN FERNANDO VALLEY

$ ✕ **Paty's.** Near NBC, Warner Brothers, and the Disney Studio, Paty's is a good place for star-gazing without having to mortgage your home to pay for the meal. Breakfast omelets are plump, and the biscuits are homemade and served with high-quality jam. Lunches and dinners include Swiss steak and a hearty beef stew that is served in a hollowed-out loaf of home-baked bread. Roast turkey is served with dressing and a moist, sweet loaf of home-baked nut or raisin bread. All desserts are worth saving room for: New Orleans bread pudding with a hot brandy sauce is popular, and the Danishes are gigantic. If you're in a hurry, call ahead with your order and the restaurant will deliver directly to your car. ⊠ *10001 Riverside Dr., Toluca Lake,* ☎ *818/761–9126. Reservations not accepted on weekends. AE, MC, V.*

SANTA MONICA (COASTAL LOS ANGELES DINING MAP)

$$ ✕ **Gilliland's.** Gerri Gilliland was teaching cooking in her native Ireland, took a vacation in southern California, and never went back. Instead, she stayed and created this restaurant, which offers the best of both culinary worlds and showcases her fascination for Mediterranean dishes. The soda bread, Irish stew, and corned beef and cabbage are wonderful, as are the Louisiana crab cakes served with fresh corn, herbs, onions, tomatillo sauce, and sour cream. Hand-colored lithographs cover the walls, and the bar is made of mahogany. The garden setting comes with retractable awnings and heat lamps for chilly nights. ⊠ *2424 Main St.,* ☎ *310/392–3901. AE, D, DC, MC, V.*

$$ ✕ **Ocean Avenue.** This cavernous restaurant, operating since 1946, isn't right on the water, but the Pacific is just across the street, so ask for a table by the window. Daily specials are always a good choice, but when in doubt order the cioppino, a fish stew made with Dungeness crab, clams, mussels, and prawns, or the Maine lobster, boiled or steamed. ⊠ *1401 Ocean Ave., Santa Monica,* ☎ *310/394–5669. AE, DC, MC, V. Valet parking.*

$–$$ ✕ **Broadway Deli.** The name is misleading, so don't come here expecting hot corned beef and pastrami sandwiches. This joint venture of Michel Richard and Bruce Marder is a cross between a European brasserie and an upscale diner. Whatever you feel like eating, you will probably find it on the menu, from a platter of assorted smoked fish or Caesar salad to shepherd's pie, carpaccio, steak, and broiled salmon with creamed spinach. There are also excellent side dishes (such as corn muffins, mashed

potatoes with mushroom gravy, and potato pancakes), desserts, and
freshly baked breads. ⊠ *1457 3rd St. Promenade,* ☎ *310/451–0616.
Reservations not accepted. AE, MC, V. Valet parking weekends and
evenings.*

VENICE (COASTAL LOS ANGELES DINING MAP)

$$–$$$ ✕ **West Beach Cafe.** Best bets at Bruce Marder's restaurant are Cae-
★   sar salad, rack of lamb, ravioli with port and radicchio, fisherman's
soup, and what many consider the best hamburger and fries in all of
Los Angeles. ⊠ *60 N. Venice Blvd.,* ☎ *310/823–5396. AE, DC, MC,
V. Closed Mon. Valet parking.*

WEST HOLLYWOOD

$$$–$$$$ ✕ **Arnie Morton's of Chicago.** The West Coast addition to this ever-
expanding national chain brought joy and cholesterol to the hearts of
Los Angeles meat lovers, many of whom claim that Morton's serves
the best steaks in town. In addition to a 24-ounce porterhouse, a New
York strip, and a double-cut filet mignon, there are giant veal and lamb
chops, thick cuts of prime rib, and imported lobsters. ⊠ *435 S. La
Cienega Blvd.,* ☎ *310/246–1501. AE, DC, MC, V. No lunch.*

$$$–$$$$ ✕ **Fenix.** Anticipate abundant art-deco splendor from the Argyle hotel's
★   culinary wonderland. Beyond the back glass wall, a sensuous swim-
ming pool's stylized plaster palm trees set the tone. Inside, nostalgia
continues with plush banquettes and a grand piano. Chef Ken Frank
is renowned for his potato pancakes filled with golden caviar. Other
signature dishes include spinach soup with Maine lobster, Atlantic
salmon grilled with lemon zest and caviar, and filet mignon with red
wine, shallots, and bone marrow. Some Franco-California items such
as honey duck salad with mango and seared foie gras evince an Asian
influence. ⊠ *8358 Sunset Blvd.,* ☎ *213/848–6677. Reservations es-
sential. AE, DC, D, MC, V. Valet parking.*

$$$ ✕ **Morton's.** When Arnie Morton's son and daughter decided to open
this upscale clubhouse for the music and entertainment industry, it was
only natural that choice steaks should be the cornerstone of their
menu. Good broiled fish and chicken dishes, as well as pasta, veal, and
pizza, are also prepared. ⊠ *8764 Melrose Ave.,* ☎ *310/276–5205. Reservations essential. Jacket required. AE, D, DC, MC, V. Closed Sun. Valet
parking.*

$$$ ✕ **The Palm.** A West Coast replay of the famous Manhattan steak
house—down to the New York–style waiters rushing you through
your Bronx cheesecake—this is where you'll find the biggest and best
lobster, good steaks and chops, great french-fried onion rings, and paper-
thin potato slices. The big deal for dinner, though, is the prime rib. ⊠
9001 Santa Monica Blvd., ☎ *310/550–8811. AE, DC, MC, V. No lunch
weekends. Valet parking.*

$$ ✕ **Hard Rock Cafe.** Big burgers, rich milk shakes, banana splits, BLTs,
and other anti-nouvelle food delights, along with loud music and
plenty of rock-and-roll memorabilia, have made this barn the favorite
of teenagers from around the globe. ⊠ *8500 Beverly Blvd.,* ☎ *310/276–
7605. Reservations not accepted. AE, DC, MC, V. Valet parking in Beverly Center.*

$ ✕ **Roscoe's House of Chicken 'n' Waffles.** Come here for real down-
home southern cooking: fried chicken, waffles, grits, and potatoes, at
bargain prices. ⊠ *1514 N. Gower St.,* ☎ *213/466–9329. Reservations
not accepted. AE, D, DC, MC, V.*

$ ✕ **Swingers.** Droves of poseurs wearing Doc Martens and grungy
garb take to this all-day, late-night coffee shop gone hyper-hip—so be
prepared for a wait (and loud music). Eat and schmooze at curbside
tables or inside. Top-quality dogs and burgers as well as chicken breast
sandwiches on fresh rosemary bread are mainstays of the hangout's

frugal menu. ⊠ *8020 Beverly Blvd.,* ☏ *213/653–5858. AE, D, MC, V. Street parking.*

Cajun

$$–$$$ ✕ **Orleans.** The jambalaya and gumbo dishes are hot—in more ways than one–at this tiled French Quarter–style eatery whose cuisine was created with the help of New Orleans celebrity-chef Paul Prudhomme. The blackened salmon is probably the best catch. Most menu items are available in low-sodium, low-fat versions. ⊠ *11705 National Blvd.,* ☏ *310/479–4187. AE, DC, MC, V. Valet parking.*

California Cuisine

$$$ ✕ **Hotel Bel-Air.** You couldn't ask for a lovelier setting, in a romantic
★ country garden, and the California-Continental cooking is very good indeed. Seasonal dishes use fresh fare in a fanciful way, for instance, tuna and monkfish medallions with chive mashed potatoes; lobster risotto with fava beans and chanterelles; and grilled fillet of Great Lakes whitefish with saffron couscous. ⊠ *701 Stone Canyon Rd.,* ☏ *310/472–1211. Reservations essential. Jacket and tie. AE, DC, MC, V. Valet parking.*

$$$ ✕ **Dining Room.** This elegant, European-style salon offers wonderful
★ California cuisine (try the loin of Colorado lamb accompanied by eggplant and sweet-pepper lasagna), plus splendid service. Adjoining the Dining Room is a sophisticated cocktail lounge, with romantic lighting and a pianist playing show tunes. ⊠ *Regent Beverly Wilshire Hotel, 9500 Wilshire Blvd.,* ☏ *310/275–5200. Jacket and tie. AE, D, DC, MC, V. Valet parking.*

$$$ ✕ **Jackson's Farm.** Looking more like a French farmhouse—recycled
★ brick, ceiling fans—than an uptown eatery, this place has some of L.A.'s best down-home cooking. The menu includes white-corn soup, crab cakes with lemon-caper tartar sauce, and rotisserie chicken with garlic mashed potatoes and spinach. ⊠ *439 N. Beverly Dr.,* ☏ *310/273–5578. AE, DC, MC, V. Parking across from restaurant.*

$ ✕ **California Pizza Kitchen.** You'll find good wood-fired pizza at a fair price here, without the usual pizza-parlor surroundings. The tandoori pie is made without cheese. The pastas are equally interesting and carefully prepared. ⊠ *207 S. Beverly Dr.,* ☏ *310/275–1101. Reservations not accepted. AE, D, DC, MC, V.*

$$ ✕ **Cafe Pinot.** Fancy eating in a glass house? Try Joachim Splichal's latest effort, right next to L.A.'s main library. You can gaze out at the skyline if your conversation comes to a standstill, a likely occurrence as the noise level is often high. The fine Continental-California bistro fare, including five-mustard roasted chicken, makes up for it, though. ⊠ *700 W. 5th St.,* ☏ *213/239–6500. Reservations essential. AE, DC, MC, V. No lunch Fri.–Sat. Self and valet parking.*

$$$$ ✕ **Patina.** Not far from Paramount Studios, proprietor-chef Joachim
★ Splichal does wonders with game, fish, and potato dishes in his time-honored shrine to Franco-California cuisine. Top-quality food and Asian-style service have made this one of Los Angeles's most prestigious dining arenas. Sample Santa Barbara shrimp accompanied by fried leeks and mashed potatoes, lasagna filled with potatoes, or partridge baked to perfection. Desserts include a lemon parfait tart with raspberries and kumquat lime sauce, a work of art that's a slice of heaven.

⊠ *5955 Melrose Ave.,* ☎ *213/467–1108. AE, DC, D, MC, V. No lunch Wed.–Mon. Valet parking.*

$$$ ✕ **Pinot Hollywood.** Joachim Splichal strikes again, this time in the heart of studio row. John Dory and ahi tuna are cooked over an oak-wood grill, and gnocchi mixed with brioche croutons and salty ham hocks satisfy hearty appetites. A spacious outdoor patio affords an alternative, more casual venue for sandwiches and salads. ⊠ *1448 N. Gower St.,* ☎ *213/461–8800. Reservations essential. AE, D, DC, MC, V. Valet parking.*

$$–$$$ ✕ **Citrus.** One of L.A.'s most prominent chefs, Michel Richard, cre-
★   ates superb dishes by blending French and American cuisines. You can't miss with the tuna burger, the impossibly thin angel-hair pasta—or the deep-fried potatoes, sautéed foie gras, rare duck, or carpaccio salad. Get your doctor's permission before even looking at Richard's irresistible desserts. ⊠ *6703 Melrose Ave.,* ☎ *213/857–0034. Jacket required. AE, MC, V. Closed Sun. Valet parking.*

MALIBU (COASTAL LOS ANGELES MAP)

$$–$$$ ✕ **Granita.** Wolfgang Puck's Granita has such stunning interior details as handmade tiles embedded with seashells, blown-glass lighting fixtures, and etched-glass panels with wavy edges. And it's as close as you can come to the beach without getting sand in your shoes. The menu favors seafood items, such as grilled John Dory with stir-fried vegetables and curry lime sauce and grilled Atlantic salmon in lemongrass broth with seared carrots and wild mushrooms, but includes some Puck staples: spicy shrimp pizza with sun-dried tomatoes and herb pesto, roasted Chinese duck with dried-fruit chutney, seared foie gras with caramelized walnuts and blood-orange port-wine glaze, and Caesar salad with oven-baked bruschetta. ⊠ *23725 W. Malibu Rd.,* ☎ *310/456–0488. Reservations essential. D, DC, MC, V. No lunch Mon.–Tues.*

WEST HOLLYWOOD

$$–$$$ ✕ **Eclipse.** Celebs and anybody else who can snag a reservation frequent
★   this happening restaurant. An active bar encourages sipping, nibbling, and fraternizing sessions, but the experience doesn't stop there. Chef Serge Falesitch injects just a hint of Provençal magic into his California-Mediterranean fare in dishes such as salmon in parchment with fresh herbs. Fresh seafood is another highlight, flash grilled or roasted in fruitwood-burning ovens. Who wouldn't want to savor at least one meal in this light and airy in-spot (created by Lambert Monet, Claude's ultra-artsy grandson), with its high-beamed ceilings and picture-perfect patio-garden setting? ⊠ *8800 Melrose Ave.,* ☎ *310/724–5959. Reservations essential. AE, D, DC, MC, V. No lunch. Valet parking.*

$$–$$$ ✕ **Spago.** This is the restaurant that propelled owner/chef Wolfgang
★   Puck into the culinary spotlight. The proof is in the tasting: roasted cumin lamb on lentil salad with fresh coriander and yogurt chutney, fresh oysters with green chili and black pepper mignonette, grilled free-range chickens, and grilled Alaskan baby salmon. The biggest seller is not on the menu, so ask. It's known as the Jewish pizza, with cream cheese and smoked salmon as toppings. Be safe: Make reservations at least two weeks in advance. ⊠ *1114 Horn Ave.,* ☎ *310/652–4025. Reservations essential. Jacket required. D, DC, MC, V. No lunch. Valet parking.*

Caribbean

HOLLYWOOD

$–$$ ✕ **Cha Cha Cha.** Off the beaten path near Silver Lake, this small, hip
★   yet not pretentious restaurant attracts a discerning, eclectic crowd. Sit indoors or on the enclosed patio, very tropical in its decor, à la a Carmen Miranda flick. There's Jamaican jerk chicken, swordfish bro-

chette, fried plantain chips, and assorted flans. If you're in the mood
for pizza, try this shack's Caribbean versions. ⊠ *656 N. Virgil Ave.,
Hollywood,* ☎ *213/664–7723. AE, D, DC, MC, V. Valet parking.*

Chinese

BEVERLY HILLS

$–$$ ✕ **The Mandarin.** A good-looking restaurant with the best crystal and
★ linens, the Mandarin serves Szechuan and Chinese country cuisine.
Minced chicken in lettuce-leaf tacos, Peking duck (order ahead of
time), a superb beggar's chicken, scallion pancakes, and any of the noodle dishes are recommended. ⊠ *430 N. Camden Dr.,* ☎ *310/859–0926.
Reservations essential. AE, DC, MC, V. No lunch weekends. Valet parking evenings.*

DOWNTOWN

$–$$ ✕ **Mon Kee's Seafood Restaurant.** The fish here are morning-fresh, the
garlic crab is addictive, and the steamed catfish is a masterpiece of gentle flavors. In fact, almost everything on the menu is excellent. This is
a crowded, frantic place; be prepared to wait for a table. ⊠ *679 N.
Spring St.,* ☎ *213/628–6717. Reservations not accepted. AE, DC, MC,
V. Pay parking lot.*

PASADENA (DOWNTOWN LOS ANGELES MAP)

$$–$$$ ✕ **Yujean Kang's Gourmet Chinese Cuisine.** Mr. Kang is one of the finest
★ nouvelle-Chinese chefs in the nation. Forget any and all preconceived
notions of what Chinese food should look and taste like. Start with
the tender slices of veal on a bed of enoki and black mushrooms,
topped with a tangle of quick-fried shoestring yams, or the sea bass
with kumquats and a passion-fruit sauce, and finish with poached plums,
or watermelon ice under a mantle of white chocolate. ⊠ *67 N. Raymond Ave.,* ☎ *818/585–0855. AE, D, DC, MC, V.*

Continental

SANTA MONICA (COASTAL LOS ANGELES MAP)

$$ ✕ **Schatzi on Main.** Owner Arnold Schwarzenegger has seen to it that
the chef's dishes include his Austrian homeland favorites such as Wiener
schnitzel, bratwurst, and smoked pork chops. Other choices range from
Peking roast duck and pasta with shrimp to seared swordfish medallions
and New York–style pizza. There's an indoor area and a patio. ⊠ *3110
Main St.,* ☎ *310/399–4800. AE, D, DC, MC, V. Valet parking.*

WESTWOOD (COASTAL LOS ANGELES MAP)

$$$ ✕ **Dynasty Room.** This peaceful dining room in the Westwood Mar-
quis Hotel's lobby evokes European elegance with a contemporary flair
and tables set far enough apart for privacy or romance. The well-han-
dled Continental fare includes roasted rack of lamb with grilled leeks,
asparagus, and artichokes. ⊠ *930 Hilgard Ave.,* ☎ *310/208–8765.
Reservations essential. AE, D, DC, MC, V. No lunch. Valet parking.*

Deli

BEVERLY HILLS

$$ ✕ **Barney Greengrass.** Diners at this eatery on the fifth floor of the
★ Barneys New York store munch on high-concept deli fare such as por-
tobello mushrooms, roasted peppers, and arugula on sourdough. Ex-
pect lots of smoked salmon, sturgeon, and cod—with or without bagels
flown in fresh from the Big Apple. ⊠ *9570 Wilshire Blvd.,* ☎ *310/777–
5877. AE, MC, V. Valet parking.*

$ ✕ **Nate 'n' Al's.** A famous gathering place for Hollywood comedians,
gag writers, and their agents, Nate 'n' Al's serves first-rate matzo-ball
soup, lox and scrambled eggs, cheese blintzes, potato pancakes, and
deli sandwiches. ⊠ *414 N. Beverly Dr.,* ☎ *310/274–0101. Reserva-
tions not accepted. AE, MC, V. Free parking.*

$ ✗ **Art's Delicatessen.** One of the best Jewish-style delicatessens in the
★ city serves mammoth corned beef, pastrami, and other sandwiches,
named after celebrities. ⊠ *12224 Ventura Blvd., Studio City,* ☎
818/762–1221. Reservations not accepted. AE, D, DC, MC, V.

WEST HOLLYWOOD

$ ✗ **Canter's.** Ex-New Yorkers claim that this granddaddy of deli-
★ catessens (it opened in 1928) is the closest in atmosphere, smell, and
menu to a Big Apple corned-beef and pastrami hangout. It's open 24-
hours-a-day (attracting an eclectic late-night crowd) and has a yummy
in-house bakery. ⊠ *419 N. Fairfax Ave.,* ☎ *213/651–2030. MC, V.
Valet parking.*

French

SAN FERNANDO VALLEY

$$–$$$ ✗ **Pinot Bistro.** Joachim Splichal, owner-chef of top-rated Patina,
★ opened this perfectly designed synthesis of Parisian bistros. One can
smell the fumes of seasoned escargots and the aroma of skillfully
brewed espressos. Dishes are authentic: fresh oysters, country pâtés,
bouillabaisse, braised tongue and spinach, pot-au-feu, and steak with
french fries. The pastry chef specializes in chocolate desserts. ⊠ *12969
Ventura Blvd., Studio City,* ☎ *818/990–0500. AE, D, DC, MC, V. No
lunch weekends. Valet parking.*

$$ ✗ **Cafe Bizou.** This cozy restaurant is so popular that at times it's booked
★ months in advance. If you can manage a reservation (not impossible,
especially on the weekend), look forward to fine French bistro fare at
bargain prices. Soups are creamy (like the luscious potato-leek) and
appetizers range from homemade ravioli stuffed with lobster and
salmon puree to black tagliatini pasta tossed with shrimp. Fish dishes
are prominent, like sesame-seed-coated salmon on potato pancake tri-
angles. For dessert, try the tasty tarte tartin. ⊠ *14016 Ventura Blvd.,
Sherman Oaks,* ☎ *818/788–3536. Reservations essential. AE, MC,
V. No lunch weekends. Valet parking.*

SANTA MONICA (COASTAL LOS ANGELES MAP)

$$–$$$ ✗ **Chinois on Main.** Both the look of this place and Wolfgang Puck's
★ merging of Asian and French cuisines are great fun. Specialties include
grilled Mongolian lamb chops with cilantro vinaigrette and wok-fried
vegetables, Shanghai lobster with spicy ginger-curry sauce, and rare duck
with a wondrous plum sauce. The best desserts are three differently
flavored crème brûlées. This is one of L.A.'s most crowded spots—and
one of its noisiest. ⊠ *2709 Main St.,* ☎ *310/392–9025. Reservations
essential. AE, D, DC, MC, V. No lunch Sat.–Tues. Valet parking.*

WEST HOLLYWOOD

$$$–$$$$ ✗ **Drai's.** Rolls Royce and Range Rover owners frequent this see-and-
be-seen restaurant, where French chef Claude Segal's fare undergoes
diligent preparation. Owner Victor Drai's spiffy restaurant is big on
bistro fare such as osso buco, pot-au-feu, and beef bourguignonne. An-
ticipate lots of attitude from the fashionable crowd—and more from
the staff, which tends to hurry you through your meal by suggesting
a move to the bar before you've had time to breathe, let alone digest
the pleasurable French feast. ⊠ *730 N. La Cienega Blvd., West Hol-
lywood,* ☎ *310/358–8585. Valet parking.*

$$$–$$$$ ✗ **L'Orangerie.** For sheer elegance and classic good taste, it would be
★ hard to find a match for L'Orangerie in this country. And the cuisine,
albeit nouvelle-light, is as French as its namesake in Versailles. Specialties
include coddled eggs served in the shell and topped with caviar, duck
with foie gras, John Dory with roasted figs, rack of lamb for two, and
an unbeatable apple tart served with a jug of double cream. ⊠ *903 N.*

La Cienega Blvd., ☎ *310/652–9770. Reservations essential. Jacket and tie. AE, D, DC, MC, V. Closed Mon. No lunch. Valet parking.*

$$$ ✕ **Le Dôme.** Hordes of show- and music-biz celebrities keep this brasserie humming. The food is honest, down-to-earth French: cockles in white wine and shallots; veal ragout; veal tortellini with prosciutto, sun-dried tomatoes, peas, and Parmesan sauce; and a genuine, stick-to-the-ribs cassoulet. ⊠ *8720 Sunset Blvd.,* ☎ *310/659–6919. Reservations essential. AE, DC, MC, V. Closed Sun. No lunch Sat. Valet parking.*

Greek

MID-WILSHIRE (BEVERLY HILLS AND HOLLYWOOD MAP)

$ ✕ **Sofi.** Hidden down a narrow passageway is this friendly little taverna that makes you feel like you've been transported straight to Mykonos. The food is authentic Greek: *dolmades* (stuffed grape leaves), lamb gyros, a sampling of traditional salads, phyllo pies, spanakopita, and souvlaki. ⊠ *8030¼ W. 3rd St.,* ☎ *213/651–0346. AE, D, DC, MC, V. No lunch Sun.*

Health Food

WESTSIDE (BEVERLY HILLS AND HOLLYWOOD MAP)

$$ ✕ **Jack Sprat's Grill.** Virtue tastes like vice, as sassy salsas and inventive, light sauces accompany mostly grilled entrées. Boneless, skinless chicken breasts are perked up with mango-kiwi-mint salsa and grilled vegetables go well with Dijon mustard sauce. Other pluses are chef and co-owner Mark Brown's dynamite salads, guilt-free air fries, and a to-die-for flourless chocolate cake. Should you hanker for high-caloric fare, don't fret. The menu, which includes big, juicy New York steaks, doesn't discriminate. ⊠ *10668 W. Pico Blvd.,* ☎ *310/837–6662. AE, MC, V. Self parking.*

Italian

BEVERLY HILLS

$–$$ ✕ **Il Fornaio Cucina Italiana.** What was once a bakery-café has been transformed into one of the best-looking contemporary trattorias in California, and the food is more than worthy of the setting. From the huge brass-and-stainless-steel rotisserie come crispy roasted duck, herb-basted chickens, and juicy rabbit. Nearby, cooks paddle a tasty variety of pizzas and calzones in and out of the oakwood-burning oven. Sunday brunch is terrific. ⊠ *301 N. Beverly Dr.,* ☎ *310/550–8330. AE, DC, MC, V. Valet parking.*

CENTURY CITY (BEVERLY HILLS AND HOLLYWOOD MAP)

$$–$$$ ✕ **Harry's Bar & American Grill.** The decor and selection of dishes are acknowledged copies of Harry's Bar in Florence. But for first-rate food—paper-thin carpaccio, grilled fish and steaks, and excellent pastas (ravioli filled with artichokes or tortellini with Maine lobster and shiitake sauce)—the check will be far lower than it would be in Italy. ⊠ *2020 Ave. of the Stars,* ☎ *310/277–2333. Reservations essential. AE, DC, MC, V. No lunch weekends. Valet parking.*

DOWNTOWN

$$$$ ✕ **Rex Il Ristorante.** Owner Mauro Vincenti remodeled two ground
★ floors of a historic art deco building to resemble the main dining salon of the circa-1930 Italian luxury liner *Rex.* His cuisine, the lightest of *nuova cucina,* is equally special. Be prepared for small and costly portions of such delights as herb-breaded lamb chops with spinach or calamari with black squid-ink pasta. ⊠ *617 S. Olive St.,* ☎ *213/627–2300. Reservations essential. Jacket and tie. AE, DC, MC, V. Closed Sun. No lunch Sat.–Wed. Valet parking.*

$–$$ ✕ **Tra di Noi.** The name means "between us," and Malibu natives are trying to keep this charming, simple *ristorante* just that—a local secret. It's run by a mama (who does the cooking), son, and daughter-in-law. Regular customers, film celebrities and non-show-biz folk alike, love the unpretentious atmosphere here and bring their kids. Nothing fancy or *nuovo* on the menu, just great lasagna, freshly made pasta, mushroom and veal dishes, and crisp fresh salads. ✉ *3835 Cross Creek Rd.,* ☎ *310/456–0169. AE, MC, V. No lunch Sun.*

$$
★   ✕ **Ca'Brea.** There isn't a pizza to be found on the menu, but you won't care, what with the roast leg of lamb with black truffle and mustard sauce, whole boneless chicken marinated and grilled with herbs, and the ever-popular osso buco. ✉ *346 S. La Brea Ave.,* ☎ *213/938–2863. AE, D, DC, MC, V. Closed Sun. No lunch weekends.*

$ ✕ **Tavola Calda.** This low-tech Italian nirvana draws a crowd attracted to inexpensive entrées, all under $10. Best bets on the limited menu are the gourmet pizzas and the risotto. ✉ *7371 Melrose Ave.,* ☎ *213/658–6340. Reservations not accepted. AE, DC, MC, V. Valet parking.*

$$
★   ✕ **Ca'del Sol.** Start with fresh rock shrimp sautéed in a spicy garlic and tomato sauce or citrus-marinated chicken wings and follow with a radicchio and arugula salad with a creamy Venetian dressing. Then go on to a pleasurable plate of linguine covered in Manila clams and scallops and doused in a generous olive oil, garlic, and white wine mixture. Finish up with a giant hunk of Italian-styled cheesecake covered in marinated strawberries. ✉ *4100 Cahuenga Blvd., North Hollywood,* ☎ *818/985–4669. Reservations essential. AE, DC, MC, V. No lunch Sat. Valet parking.*

$$$–$$$$
★   ✕ **Valentino.** Rated among the nation's best Italian restaurants, Valentino is generally considered to have the best wine list outside Western Europe. Owner Piero Selvaggio introduced Los Angeles to a style of light, modern Italian cuisine. He serves superb prosciutto, fried calamari, lobster cannelloni, fresh broiled porcini mushrooms, and osso buco. He continues to reinvent this culinary palace, which is currently decorated to effect a Tuscan feel, with glazed walls integrated with gold leaf and comfortable yet elegant furniture that doesn't upstage the gorgeous food presentation. ✉ *3115 Pico Blvd.,* ☎ *310/829–4313. Reservations essential. AE, DC, MC, V. Closed Sun. Valet parking.*

$$$
★   ✕ **Drago.** Authentic Sicilian fare is hard to come by in the City of Angels, but Celestino Drago's fine home-styled fare is perfectly prepared and attentively served in stark designer surroundings. Sample Drago's unforgettable pappardelle with pheasant and morel mushroom ragout or ostrich breast with cherry sauce. Savory pumpkin soup is accompanied by chestnut gnocchi. ✉ *2628 Wilshire Blvd.,* ☎ *310/828–1585. AE, DC, MC, V. Valet parking.*

$$ ✕ **Remi.** It's not easy to find authentic Venetian cuisine in southern California, but here is one place you can. Order the linguine with scallops, mussels, shrimp, and fresh chopped tomatoes; the whole wheat crepes with ricotta and spinach, topped with a tomato, carrot, and celery sauce; or the roasted pork chop stuffed with smoked mozzarella and prosciutto, served with roast potatoes and fennel. ✉ *1451 3rd St. Promenade,* ☎ *310/393–6545. Reservations essential. AE, DC, MC, V. Parking in nearby multistory mall parking lots.*

Japanese

BEVERLY HILLS

$$$$
★   ✕ **Matsuhisa.** This high-profile eatery is an upmarket pleasure palace. Pacific Rim cuisine is pushed to new limits by chef Nobu Matsuhisa, who has introduced ideas he picked up while journeying through Peru. His signature caviar-capped sea scallops are stuffed with black truffles and sea urchin wrapped in a shiso leaf. Tempuras are lighter than usual here, and the sushi is top-notch, fresh and authentic. ✉ *129 N. La Cienega Blvd.,* ☎ *310/659–9639. Reservations essential. AE, DC, MC, V. Valet parking.*

DOWNTOWN

$$–$$$ ✕ **Restaurant Horikawa.** This menu at this department store of Japanese cuisines includes sushi, teppan steak, tempura, sashimi, shabu-shabu, teriyaki, and a $75-per-person seven-course dinner. All are good or excellent, but the sushi bar is the best. The decor is traditional Japanese, with private dining rooms accommodating two to 24, where guests sit on tatami floor mats. ✉ *Sumitomo Bank Bldg., 111 S. San Pedro St.,* ☎ *213/680–9355. AE, MC, V. No lunch Sat. Valet parking.*

LOS FELIZ (BEVERLY HILLS AND HOLLYWOOD MAP)

$$$
★   ✕ **Restaurant Katsu.** A stark, simple, perfectly designed sushi bar with a small table area serves exquisite and delicious Japanese delicacies. You can't go wrong when ordering—whether it's the seafood shabu-shabu or the *yadokari nabe* (an assortment of seafood in an abalone shell). Definitely a treat for both the eye and the palate, Katzu sets high standards for sushi, in both presentation and quality. ✉ *1972 N. Hillhurst Ave.,* ☎ *213/665–1891. Reservations essential. AE, DC, MC, V. No lunch weekends. Valet parking.*

Mexican

BEVERLY HILLS

$ ✕ **Picante Grill.** Authentic Mexican fare meets health-conscious Californian cuisine in this cozy, tile-floored taqueria. Lean chicken, pork, and steak tacos—made with all fresh ingredients and a secret marinade containing no fat—have diners lining up around the block. Special favorites are those served in Picante's signature mild green chili- or jalepeño-flavored tortillas. Spice up your order with homemade salsas of varying heats. ✉ *9111 W. Olympic Blvd.,* ☎ *310/276–3899. MC, V.*

HOLLYWOOD

$
★   ✕ **El Cholo.** The progenitor of the upscale chain, this place has been packing them in since the '20s. It serves good-size margaritas and a zesty assortment of tacos (including some you make yourself). It's friendly and fun, with large portions for a reasonable number of pesos. ✉ *1121 S. Western Ave.,* ☎ *213/734–2773. AE, DC, MC, V. Valet and metered parking.*

SANTA MONICA (COASTAL LOS ANGELES MAP)

$–$$
★   ✕ **Border Grill.** This very trendy, very loud eating hall is owned by talented Mary Sue Milliken and Susan Feniger, whose tastes are among the most eclectic in town. Grilled tandoori skirt steak marinated in garlic and cilantro, Yucatán seafood tacos, vinegar-and-pepper-grilled turkey, and spicy baby-back ribs are all on their menu. ✉ *1445 4th St.,* ☎ *310/451–1655. AE, D, DC, MC, V. No lunch.*

Pacific Rim

SANTA MONICA (COASTAL LOS ANGELES MAP)

$$
★   ✕ **Typhoon.** Owner Brian Vidor's menu roams Asia—*Goi Cuon* (cold Vietnamese spring roll), Philippine lightly fried squid, and Taiwanese stir-fried eggplant, all of which are outstanding. The pièce de résistance, however, is the crispy-skinned whole catfish in a subtly spicy-sweet black

bean sauce. The decor is smart—a high-tech, minimalist blend of mahogany and cement, bordered by an arc of plate-glass windows overlooking the tarmac at Santa Monica's small-craft airport, a landing strip favored by the rich and famous. Take a cool drink up to the outside patio and see who's boarding the Warner Bros. jet. ⊠ *3221 Donald Douglas Loop S, Santa Monica,* ☎ *310/390–6565. AE, DC, MC, V. No lunch Sun.*

WEST HOLLYWOOD

$$ ✕ **Tommy Tang's.** A lot of people watching goes on at this grazing ground for yuppies and celebs. Although portions are on the small side, they are decidedly innovative—crisp duck marinated in ginger and plum sauce, crab spring rolls with tangy yogurt sauce, blackened sea scallops, and a low-calorie spinach and grilled chicken salad. There is also a happening sushi bar overlooking the upbeat restaurant's garden patio. ⊠ *7313 Melrose Ave.,* ☎ *213/937–5733. AE, DC, MC, V. Valet parking.*

Spanish

MID-WILSHIRE [BEVERLY HILLS AND HOLLYWOOD MAP]

$$–$$$ ✕ **Cava.** You can graze on tapas—the baked artichoke topped with bread crumbs and tomato or a fluffy potato omelet served with crème fraîche—or feast on bigger entrées such as paella and *zarzuela* (lightly baked shrimp, scallops, clams, mussels, and fresh fish in a hearty tomato wine sauce). ⊠ *8384 W. 3rd St.,* ☎ *213/658–8898. AE, D, DC, MC, V. Valet parking.*

Thai

HOLLYWOOD

$–$$ ✕ **Chan Dara.** Try any of the noodle dishes, especially those with crab and shrimp. Also tops on the extensive menu are *satay* (appetizers on skewers) and barbecued chicken and catfish. Dine alfresco on the patio or just have dessert there. Recommended: Mango tart and crème brûlée. ⊠ *310 N. Larchmont Blvd.,* ☎ *213/467–1052. AE, DC, MC, V. No lunch weekends.*

Vietnamese

WEST HOLLYWOOD

$$–$$$ ✕ **Le Colonial.** A bright blue neon sign beckons hungry gourmands to
★ this restaurant right out of pre-War Saigon, complete with whirling fans hanging from a burgundy pressed-tin ceiling. Authentic dishes include chili-flavored sea bass wrapped in banana leaves; roasted chicken with lemongrass; fried spring rolls packed with pork, mushrooms, and shrimp; and shredded chicken and cabbage doused in lime juice. The carefully chosen wine list complements this exotic cuisine, and variations on Vietnamese desserts include ginger crème brûlée served with sweet strawberries. All you need is some sultry weather, and you'll have made the leap from Los Angeles to Saigon in a single meal. ⊠ *8783 Beverly Blvd.,* ☎ *310/289–0660. AE, DC, MC, V. No lunch weekends. Valet parking.*

LODGING

By Jane E.
Lasky

Because Los Angeles is so spread out it's good to select lodgings not only for ambience, amenities, and price but also for a location that is convenient to where you plan to spend most of your time. After you decide which area of the city is best suited to your needs, reserve a room. Many hotels offer tickets to amusement parks or plays as well as special prices for weekend visits. Hotels listed below are organized according to their location, then by price category, following this scale:

CATEGORY	COST*
$$$$	over $175
$$$	$120–$175
$$	$80–$120
$	under $80

All prices are for a standard double room, excluding 14% occupancy tax.

Downtown

$$$$ ⊞ **Biltmore Hotel.** The lobby ceiling of this 1923 historic landmark was painted by Italian artist Giovanni Smeraldi; imported Italian marble and plum velvet upholstery grace the bar. Such luminaries as Mary Pickford, J. Paul Getty, and Britain's Princess Margaret have stayed at the Biltmore. The guest rooms are done in pastels, with traditional French furniture and armoires. Bernard's, one of L.A.'s most celebrated Continental restaurants, is on the premises, as is a Roman-style health club. On the 9th and 11th floors, designated as the Executive floors, desks are specially equipped for business travelers. The 10th floor comes complete with a concierge and a lounge that offers afternoon tea, Continental breakfast, board games, a fax machine, and big-screen TV. ⊠ *506 S. Grand Ave., 90071,* ☎ *213/624–1011 or 800/245–8673,* ℻ *213/612–1545. 683 rooms. Restaurants, lounge, no-smoking floors, room service, health club. AE, DC, MC, V.*

$$$$ ⊞ **Hotel Inter-Continental Los Angeles.** Part of California Plaza and within walking distance of the Music Center, the sleek high rise offers floor-to-ceiling views. Guest rooms are decorated in contemporary style with California casual and Asian overtones. In each are glass-topped tables and desks, in color schemes of either ivory and peach or celadon and brown. The sculpture *Yellow Fin*, by Richard Serra, dominates an expansive lobby, and other important artworks are on view throughout, on loan from the nearby Museum of Contemporary Art. The Grand Cafe serves California cuisine in a stylish atmosphere. ⊠ *251 S. Olive St., 90012,* ☎ *213/617–3300 or 800/442–5251,* ℻ *213/617–3399. 415 rooms, 18 suites. Restaurant, no-smoking floors, room service, pool, health club, business services. AE, D, DC, MC, V.*

$$$$ ⊞ **Hyatt Regency Los Angeles.** In the heart of the downtown financial district, minutes away from the Convention Center, Dodger Stadium, and the Music Center, this high-rise hotel has traditionally furnished rooms with rich mahogany and cherry woods and marble baths. A wall of windows in every accommodation offers city views. Security is high at this upscale hotel, with well-lighted hallways and no blind corners. The hotel is part of Broadway Plaza, a mall containing 35 shops. ⊠ *711 S. Hope St., 90017,* ☎ *213/683–1234 or 800/233–1234,* ℻ *213/629–3230. 485 rooms, 41 suites. Restaurant, coffee shop, lounges, no-smoking floors, health club, parking. AE, D, DC, MC, V.*

$$$$ ⊞ **Omni Los Angeles Hotel and Centre.** Wedged in among the other high rises at the start of Wilshire Boulevard, the Omni is convenient to Dodger Stadium, museums, Chinatown, and the Music Center. The sparse-looking contemporary decor of the guest rooms is in beige, blue, and green. ⊠ *930 Wilshire Blvd., 90017,* ☎ *213/629–4321 or 800/445–8667,* ℻ *213/612–3977. 900 rooms. 4 restaurants, coffee shop, lounge, exercise room, parking (fee). AE, D, DC, MC, V.*

$$$$ ★   ⊞ **Sheraton Grande Hotel.** This 14-story hotel, with its reflecting glass facade, is near Dodger Stadium, the Music Center, and downtown's Bunker Hill District. Guest rooms—oversized, with wall-to-wall windows and awesome city views—have dark wood furniture, sofas, and minibars; colors are mauve, peach, and gray; baths are marble. Butler service comes with every room. There are complimentary privileges at a local state-of-the-art YMCA, and there's a lovely landscaped pool

on the premises. ⊠ *333 S. Figueroa St., 90071,* ☎ *213/617–1133 or 800/524–7263,* ℻ *213/613–0291. 469 rooms. Restaurants, bar, no-smoking floors, room service, pool, cinemas. AE, D, DC, MC, V.*

$$$$ 🏨 **Westin Bonaventure Hotel and Suites.** This is architect John Portman's striking contribution to downtown Los Angeles: a 35-story, five-tower, mirrored-glass high-rise in the center of downtown. Rooms—a number of which are on the small side—have a wall of glass, streamlined pale furnishings, and comfortable appointments. One tower is endowed with oversize suites, 94 in all. The outside elevators provide stunning city views; there are also 5 acres of ponds, and waterfalls in the lobby, which was renovated in 1994. ⊠ *404 S. Figueroa St., 90071,* ☎ *213/624–1000 or 800/228–3000,* ℻ *213/612–4894. 1,274 rooms, 94 suites. Restaurants, lounge, no-smoking floors, pool, parking (fee). AE, D, DC, MC, V.*

$$$$ 🏨 **Wyndham Checkers Hotel.** Set in one of this neighborhood's few
★ remaining historical buildings—it opened as the Mayflower Hotel in the '20s—this hotel offers the sophistication and luxury of the Biltmore across the street, but on a smaller scale. Guest rooms are furnished with oversize beds, upholstered easy chairs, and writing tables, and they have marble baths. A library is available for small meetings or tea. ⊠ *535 S. Grand Ave., 90071,* ☎ *213/624–0000,* ℻ *213/626–9906. 188 rooms. Restaurant, no-smoking floors, lap pool, spa, exercise room, valet parking (fee). AE, D, DC, MC, V.*

$$$–$$$$ 🏨 **New Otani Hotel and Garden.** This 21-story, ultramodern hotel has
★ a ½-acre rooftop Japanese-style garden. Inside, the decor is a serene blend of Westernized luxury and Eastern simplicity. Each room has a phone in the bathroom, a refrigerator, an alarm clock, and a color TV; most rooms have a *yukata* (cotton robe). If you're so inclined, book a Japanese suite, where you'll sleep on a futon on the floor. ⊠ *120 S. Los Angeles St., 90012,* ☎ *213/629–1200 or 800/273–2294,* ℻ *213/622-0989. 434 rooms, 20 suites. Restaurants, lounges, room service, massage, sauna, parking (fee). AE, D, DC, MC, V.*

$$ 🏨 **Figueroa Hotel.** This 12-story hotel, built in 1926, has managed to keep its charming Spanish style intact. Terra-cotta-color rooms carry out the Spanish look, with hand-painted furniture and, in many rooms, ceiling fans. ⊠ *939 S. Figueroa St., 90015,* ☎ *213/627–8971 or 800/421–9092,* ℻ *213/689–0305. 285 rooms. Restaurants, coffee shop, lounge, pool, free parking. AE, DC, MC, V.*

$$ 🏨 **Holiday Inn L.A. Downtown.** This six-floor hotel offers Holiday Inn's usual services and standard no-frills room decor. The rooms—large, by downtown standards—are decorated in a peach color scheme. The hotel is convenient, close to the Museum of Contemporary Art, convention center, and Los Angeles Sports Arena. Guests can work out for free at the nearby Bally's Total Fitness Center at ARCO Plaza. ⊠ *750 Garland Ave., 90017,* ☎ *213/628–5242 or 800/628–5240,* ℻ *213/628–1201. 205 rooms. Restaurant, lounge, no-smoking floors, pool, free parking. AE, D, DC, MC, V.*

$$ 🏨 **The InnTowne.** This contemporary three-story hotel with large beige-and-white rooms is 1½ blocks from the convention center. The swimming pool is surrounded by palm trees and a small garden. ⊠ *913 S. Figueroa St., 90015,* ☎ *213/628–2222 or 800/457–8520,* ℻ *213/687–0566. 170 rooms. Coffee shop, lounge, pool, free parking. AE, D, DC, MC, V.*

$ 🏨 **Inn at 657.** This unassuming inn, run by retired attorney Patsy
★ Carter, is reminiscent of a tiny European-style hotel. Suites are roomy and tastefully decorated and have stocked kitchens containing coffee, tea, and soft drinks, all included in the price. The rate also includes a hearty breakfast, local telephone calls, gratuities, taxes, and parking.

The inn's location is convenient, close to the convention center and the University of Southern California campus. ⊠ *657 W. 23rd St., 90027,* ☎ *213/741–2200 or 800/347–7512. 6 suites. No-smoking rooms, outdoor hot tub. No credit cards.*

$ 🏨 **Orchid Hotel.** One of the smaller downtown hotels, this 1920s vintage property is very reasonably priced. There are no frills, but the standard rooms are clean, with Western/Oriental decor in pastel tones. Note that there is no parking at the hotel, but public lots are close by. If you're staying at least a week, ask about lower weekly rates. ⊠ *819 S. Flower St., 90017,* ☎ *213/624–5855 or 800/874–5855,* FAX *213/624–8740. 62 rooms, 2 suites. Coin laundry. AE, DC, MC, V.*

Hollywood and West Hollywood

$$$$ 🏨 **The Argyle.** Staying at this early Art Deco hotel is like checking into
★ an exclusive private club—many a star called this address home, among them Marilyn Monroe, John Wayne, Clark Gable, and Errol Flynn. Ask for a city or mountain view. Both are great (although the rooms are a bit small by Los Angeles standards), but the city-side accommodations are more expensive. ⊠ *8358 Sunset Blvd., West Hollywood 90069,* ☎ *213/654–7100 or 800/225–2637,* FAX *213/654–1004. 64 rooms, 43 suites. Restaurant, pool, sauna, health club, business services, meeting rooms. AE, D, DC, MC, V.*

$$$$ 🏨 **Le Parc Hotel.** A boutique hotel housed in a modern low-rise building, the four-story Le Parc is in a lovely residential area. Suites, decorated in earth tones and shades of wine and rust, have sunken living rooms, balconies, fireplaces, VCRs, and kitchenettes. The hotel is near Farmers Market, CBS Television City, and the Los Angeles County Museum of Art. Cafe Le Parc is a private dining room for hotel guests only. ⊠ *733 N. West Knoll Dr., West Hollywood 90069,* ☎ *310/855–8888 or 800/578–4837,* FAX *310/659–5230. 154 suites. Restaurant, pool, tennis court, health club, parking (fee). AE, DC, MC, V.*

$$$$ 🏨 **Mondrian Hotel.** The exterior of the 12-story hotel is actually a giant
★ surrealistic mural; inside are fine artworks. Accommodations are spacious, with futuristic furniture by Le Starck. Ask for south-corner suites; they tend to be quieter than the rest. The hotel is convenient to major recording, film, and TV studios and is a favorite resting place for big-time rock-and-roll artists. ⊠ *8440 Sunset Blvd., West Hollywood 90069,* ☎ *213/650–8999 or 800/525–8029,* FAX *213/650–5215. 224 suites. Restaurant, room service, pool, health club, parking (fee). AE, D, DC, MC, V.*

$$$$ 🏨 **Summerfield Suites Hotel.** Accommodations at this four-story, all-suite luxury hotel are decorated in a modern style in shades of blue and pink. All have private balconies, fireplaces, and kitchens. Great for business travelers—it's near "Restaurant Row on La Cienega"—it's not as expensive as other hotels in this price category, and rates even include breakfast. ⊠ *1000 Westmont Dr., West Hollywood 90069,* ☎ *310/657–7400 or 800/833–4353,* FAX *310/854–6744. 109 suites. Bar, pool, sauna, health club, parking (fee). AE, D, DC, MC, V.*

$$$$ 🏨 **Wyndham Bel Age Hotel.** This European-style all-suite hotel just off
★ the Sunset Strip has a soothing, residential feel. The understated country-French decor is in dark woods and rose and mauve color schemes with detailed wrought iron furniture; the suites are spacious, with large living rooms. South-facing rooms have private terraces that look out over the Los Angeles skyline as far as the Pacific. Some touches are downright extravagant, such as original art, private terraces, and a daily newspaper. The hotel has a distinctive restaurant that serves fine Russian meals with a French flair. ⊠ *1020 N. San Vicente Blvd., West Hollywood 90069,* ☎ *310/854–1111 or 800/424–4443,* FAX

310/854–0926. 200 *suites. Restaurants, lounge, room service, pool, health club, concierge, parking (fee). AE, D, DC, MC, V.*

$$$ ☶ **Chateau Marmont Hotel.** Although planted on the Sunset Strip amid
★   giant billboards and much sun-bleached Hollywood glitz, this castle
of Old World charm and French Normandy design still promises its
guests a secluded hideaway close to Hollywood's hot spots. A haunt
for many reclusive show-biz personalities and discriminating world trav-
elers since it opened in 1929, this is the ultimate in privacy. ⊠ *8221
Sunset Blvd., Hollywood 90046,* ☎ *213/656–1010 or 800/242–8328,*
FAX *213/655–5311. 10 rooms, 53 suites. Dining room, room service,
pool, exercise room, concierge, free parking. AE, DC, MC, V.*

$$$ ☶ **Clarion Hotel Hollywood Roosevelt.** The site of the first Academy
Awards ceremony, this hotel across from Mann's Chinese Theatre has
an Art Deco lobby and a pool decorated by artist David Hockney. Most
rooms have pastel decor with pine furniture; for a treat, try one of the
40 Hollywood-theme suites, such as the Gable/Lombard Suite or the
Shirley Temple Suite. ⊠ *7000 Hollywood Blvd., Hollywood 90028,*
☎ *213/466–7000 or 800/252–7466,* FAX *213/466–9376. 320 rooms,
39 suites. 3 restaurants, lounge, no-smoking floor, pool, car rental, parking (fee). AE, D, DC, MC, V.*

$$$ ☶ **Hyatt on Sunset.** In the heart of the Sunset Strip, this Hyatt is a fa-
vorite of music-biz execs and rock stars who appreciate the two-line
phones and voice mail available here. There are penthouse suites, and
all rooms facing the boulevard have private patios. The contemporary
rooms are decorated in pastels and have modern furniture; some have
aquariums. ⊠ *8401 Sunset Blvd., West Hollywood 90069,* ☎ *213/656–
1234 or 800/233–1234,* FAX *213/650–7024. 262 rooms, 20 suites.
Restaurant, lounge, no-smoking floors, pool, parking (fee). AE, D, DC,
MC, V.*

$$ ☶ **Hollywood Holiday Inn.** You can't miss this hotel, one of Hollywood's
tallest buildings. The rooms are decorated in floral prints and pastels
in standard-issue Holiday Inn fashion. There is a safekeeping box in
each room. The hotel is only minutes from Hollywood attractions. ⊠
1755 N. Highland Ave., Hollywood 90028, ☎ *213/462–7181,* FAX
*213/466–9072. 470 rooms. Restaurant, coffee shop, pool, coin laun-
dry, parking (fee). AE, D, DC, MC, V.*

$ ☶ **Banana Bungalow Hotel and International Hostel.** Mostly hostel-
style rooms are offered here, with four to six beds in each; you'll be
sharing a room with unknown people, unless you book one of the 12
double-occupancy rooms—be sure to specify what you want when booking. Checkout is early, by 10:30 AM. ⊠ *2775 Cahuenga Blvd. W, Hollywood 90068,* ☎ *213/851–6236 or 800/446–7835,* FAX *213/851–1569.
45 rooms. Pool, exercise room, billiards, recreation room, theater, airport shuttle, free parking. MC, V.*

Beverly Hills

$$$$ ☶ **The Beverly Hills Hotel and Bungalows.** Spruced up and reopened in
★   1995 after $100 million in renovations, this California landmark is known
affectionately as the "Pink Palace." Set on 12 acres, with private walkways meandering through vibrant tropical plants, coconut palms, ole-
anders, and a citrus garden, the hotel has hosted many a Hollywood
legend (among them Howard Hughes and Elizabeth Taylor). Renovations included a refurbished lobby with two fireplaces and alcoved
conversation areas and rooms nearly double their former size, decorated
with Ralph Lauren linens, state-of-the-art soundproofing, marble and
granite bathrooms, stereos with CD players, and plain paper facsimile
machines. Chilled towels are provided to cool off guests sitting aside
the Olympic-sized pool, and sun-dried cherry scones among the edibles

at California-style high tea in the new Tea Lounge. The rooms are individually decorated, some with tufted stools at the foot of canopied beds and many with patios. In the 21 bungalows are wood-burning fireplaces, one-of-a-kind furnishings, and yards of marble. Some rooms even contain pianos, treadmills, and silk bathrobes. Of particular note is the four-bedroom bungalow 5 with its own lap pool, specifically designed to meet financier (and frequent guest) Walter Annenberg's needs. The famous Polo Lounge with its banana leaf wallpaper is still a meeting place for Hollywood moguls; it serves Sunday brunch with a mariachi band as accompaniment. ⊠ *9641 Sunset Blvd., 90210,* ☎ *310/276–2251,* FAX *310/281–2905. 194 rooms, 21 bungalows. Restaurants, lounge, room service, pool, private cabanas, tennis courts, jogging trails, exercise room, concierge, valet parking (fee). AE, DC, MC, V.*

$$$$ ★ 🏨 **Four Seasons Los Angeles.** Some say this property resembles a French château with the refinement of a European manor house. Rooms are eclectic, some done in pastels, others in a black-and-beige scheme. All suites have French doors and balconies. An outstanding restaurant on the premises serves California cuisine. ⊠ *300 S. Doheny Dr., Los Angeles 90048,* ☎ *310/273–2222,* FAX *310/274–3891. 179 rooms, 106 suites. Restaurant, lounge, room service, pool, exercise room, free parking and fee parking. AE, DC, MC, V.*

$$$$ 🏨 **Hotel Nikko.** Distinctive Japanese accents distinguish this contemporary hotel near Restaurant Row. Large guest rooms done in traditional pastels cater to business travelers. Traditional Japanese soaking tubs dominate luxurious bathrooms, and a bedside remote-control conveniently operates in-room lighting, temperature, TV, VCRs, and CD players. Pangaea, the hotel restaurant, serves Pacific Rim cuisine. ⊠ *465 S. La Cienega Blvd., Los Angeles 90048,* ☎ *310/247–0400,* FAX *310/247–0315. 297 rooms, 10 suites. Restaurant, lounge, room service, pool, health club, business services, parking. AE, D, DC, MC, V.*

$$$$ 🏨 **Hotel Sofitel Los Angeles.** This hotel provides first-class service and the sort of intimacy you usually expect in small European-style hotels. The country-French guest rooms are done in terra-cotta and navy, with lots of pine. The back of the property faces a brick wall, so request a southern view. ⊠ *8555 Beverly Blvd., Los Angeles 90048,* ☎ *310/278–5444 or 800/521–7772,* FAX *310/657–2816. 298 rooms, 13 suites. Restaurant, pool, sauna, health club, parking (fee). AE, DC, MC, V.*

$$$$ 🏨 **Merv Griffin's Beverly Hilton.** This large hotel complex with many shops and restaurants may seem nondescript, but in fact it's a popular place for big spenders and Hollywood bigwigs. The large lobby is a favorite meeting place; sitting areas are upholstered with tropical-style fabrics, while other areas look more upscale, with leather furniture surrounded by plenty of marble. Most rooms, decorated in warm tones, have balconies overlooking Beverly Hills or downtown. On the premises is Trader Vic's, but you're also within walking distance of Century City and downtown Beverly Hills eateries. ⊠ *9876 Wilshire Blvd., 90210,* ☎ *310/274–7777,* FAX *310/285–1313. 581 rooms. 3 restaurants, refrigerators, pool, wading pool, exercise room, parking (fee). AE, D, DC, MC, V.*

$$$$ ★ 🏨 **Peninsula Beverly Hills.** A circular motor court surrounded by flowered hedges, poplar trees, and philodendrons, greets guests in rare style. The hotel's design is classic French Renaissance with contemporary overtones. Rooms are decorated like luxury homes, with antiques, rich fabrics, and marble floors. ⊠ *9882 Little Santa Monica Blvd., 90212,* ☎ *310/551–2888 or 800/462–7899,* FAX *310/788–2319. 195 rooms. Restaurants, bar, lap pool, health club, concierge, business services, parking. AE, D, DC, MC, V.*

$$$$ 🏨 **Regent Beverly Wilshire.** This 12-story landmark property has Ital-
★   ian Renaissance–style architecture with a French neoclassic influence;
the guest rooms have appropriate period furnishings in subtle hues of
soft beige and cream, wheat, peach, rose, and celery, and glorious
marble bathrooms. The multilingual staff provides personal service (including private butlers) and many other extras, such as the fresh strawberries and cream and designer water that are delivered to your room
upon arrival. Pet amenities include a bowl of Evian and biscuits served
on a silver tray. ⊠ *9500 Wilshire Blvd., 90212,* ☎ *310/275–5200; in
CA, 800/427–4354;* FAX *310/274–2851. 279 rooms, 69 suites. Restaurants, bar, lounge, no-smoking floors, pool, spa, concierge, business
services, parking (fee). AE, D, DC, MC, V.*

$$$ 🏨 **Beverly Hills Plaza Hotel.** There's a very family-style European feel
★   at this all-suite hotel; the friendly staff will get to know you by name,
given half the chance. The cozy black-and-white lobby has overstuffed
sofas and lots of plants. All the suites are off the pool. Furnishings are
smart and contemporary; all accommodations have a kitchen/living
room, one bedroom, and bath. ⊠ *10300 Wilshire Blvd., 90024,* ☎
310/275–5575, FAX *310/278–3325. 116 suites. Restaurant, pool, ex-
ercise room, parking (fee). AE, D, DC, MC, V.*

$$$ 🏨 **Beverly Prescott Hotel.** This small, 12-story luxury hotel is perched
on a hill overlooking Beverly Hills, Century City, and the mighty Pa-
cific. The open-air architecture is enhanced by soothing rooms decorated in warm salmon and caramel tones. Furnishings are stylish, and
the rooms are spacious, with private balconies. Six suites are equipped
with Jacuzzis. ⊠ *1224 S. Beverwil Dr., 90035,* ☎ *310/277–2800 or
800/421–3212,* FAX *310/203–9537. 139 rooms, 18 suites. Restaurant,
room service, pool, health club, business services, parking (fee). AE,
D, DC, MC, V.*

$$$ 🏨 **Carlyle Inn.** Service is the byword of this intimate, small hostelry in
the city's design district. The four-story, contemporary hotel gives
guests several extras: a buffet breakfast in the morning and a glass of
wine in the late afternoon. Modern rooms are done in peach with light-
pine furniture and black accents. ⊠ *1119 S. Robertson Blvd., 90035,*
☎ *310/275–4445 or 800/322–7595,* FAX *310/859–0496. 32 rooms.
Restaurant, exercise room, parking (fee). AE, D, DC, MC, V.*

Century City

(BEVERLY HILLS AND HOLLYWOOD DINING AND LODGING MAP)

$$$$ 🏨 **Century Plaza Hotel and Tower.** Beside the 20-story hotel on 10
acres—with tropical plants and reflecting pools—a 30-story tower is
lavishly decorated with fine art and antiques. Rooms in both are fur-
nished like a mansion, with a mix of classic and contemporary ap-
pointments. Each room has a refrigerator and balcony with an ocean
or a city view. ⊠ *2025 Ave. of the Stars, 90067,* ☎ *310/277–2000,*
FAX *310/551–3355. 998 rooms, 74 suites. 2 restaurants, pools, health
club, parking. AE, D, DC, MC, V.*

$$$$ 🏨 **Park Hyatt.** This hotel has elegant, modern rooms decorated in soft
pastels and equipped with minibars, lavish marble baths, and facili-
ties for travelers with disabilities. ⊠ *2151 Ave. of the Stars, 90067,* ☎
310/277–2777, FAX *310/785–9240. 367 rooms. Restaurant, indoor and
outdoor pools, health club. AE, D, DC, MC, V.*

$$$ 🏨 **Century City Courtyard by Marriott.** Near the Century City business
complex, this more-than-comfortable hotel mixes California archi-
tecture with traditional fabrics and furnishings in soft hues. ⊠ *10320
W. Olympic Blvd., Los Angeles 90064,* ☎ *310/556–2777 or 800/321–
2211,* FAX *310/203–0563. 133 rooms. Restaurant, exercise room, free
parking. AE, D, DC, MC, V.*

$$ ▦ **Holiday Inn Express.** This hotel is small but designed for comfort. Baths have whirlpool tubs and a phone. Complimentary Continental breakfast is served. ⊠ *10330 W. Olympic Blvd., Los Angeles 90064,* ☎ *310/553–1000,* FAX *310/277–1633. 47 rooms. Parking (fee). AE, D, DC, MC, V.*

Bel-Air, Westwood, and West Los Angeles

(COASTAL LOS ANGELES DINING AND LODGING MAP)

$$$$ ▦ **Hotel Bel-Air.** This charming, secluded hotel—a celebrity mecca—
★ is one of Los Angeles's and America's best. Extensive exotic gardens and a creek complete with swans give it the ambience of a top-rated resort. The rooms and suites are impeccably decorated in peach and earth tones. All are villa–bungalow style, with Mediterranean decor creating the feel of a fine home. For the quietest accommodations, ask for a room near the former stable area. ⊠ *701 Stone Canyon Rd., Bel-Air 90077,* ☎ *310/472–1211,* FAX *310/476–5890. 92 rooms. Restaurant, lounge, pool, health club, parking (fee). AE, DC, MC, V.*

$$$$ ▦ **Westwood Marquis Hotel and Gardens.** This hotel near UCLA is a favorite of corporate and entertainment types. Each individualized suite in its 15 stories has a view of Bel-Air, the Pacific Ocean, or Century City. South-facing suites overlooking the pool have expansive views of city and sea. ⊠ *930 Hilgard Ave., Los Angeles 90024,* ☎ *310/208–8765,* FAX *310/824–0355. 257 suites. 2 restaurants, lounge, room service, no-smoking floor, pools, health club, parking (fee). AE, D, DC, MC, V.*

$$$ ▦ **Summit Hotel Bel-Air.** This two-story hotel feels very southern California, with patios and terraces overlooking lush tropical greenery. Despite lots of marble, the lobby is comfortable and fairly intimate and is dominated by a huge tropical flower arrangement. Guest rooms are decorated in muted tones of cream and gray, with furniture in sleek, modern shapes and art deco–style fixtures. ⊠ *11461 Sunset Blvd., Los Angeles 90049,* ☎ *310/476–6571 or 800/333–3333. 161 rooms, 8 suites. Restaurant, lounge, no-smoking rooms, pool, tennis courts, health club, concierge, business services, parking (fee). AE, D, DC, MC, V.*

$$–$$$ ▦ **Century Wilshire Hotel.** Most units in this three-story European-style hotel are suites with kitchenettes and tiled baths, and all are decorated in homey, English-style pastels. Within walking distance of UCLA and Westwood Village, this simple hotel has views of Wilshire and the courtyard. The clientele here is mostly European. ⊠ *10776 Wilshire Blvd., West Los Angeles 90024,* ☎ *310/474–4506,* FAX *310/474–2535. 99 rooms. Pool, free parking. AE, DC, MC, V.*

$ ▦ **Best Western Royal Palace Inn & Suites.** This small hotel just off the San Diego Freeway is decorated with modern touches, lots of wood, and mirrors. Guest rooms are done in rich greens and browns, with contrasting soft peach and rose tones. All rooms are suites, with cooking facilities—including microwaves and refrigerators—and a queen sleeper sofa in addition to the two queen-size beds in each unit. ⊠ *2528 S. Sepulveda Blvd., West Los Angeles 90064,* ☎ *310/477–9066 or 800/251–3888,* FAX *310/478–4133. 23 rooms, 32 suites. Pool, exercise room, billiards, laundry service, free parking. AE, D, DC, MC, V.*

Santa Monica

(COASTAL LOS ANGELES DINING AND LODGING MAP)

$$$$ ▦ **Loews Santa Monica Beach Hotel.** The centerpiece of this seaside property two blocks south of the Santa Monica Pier is a five-story glass atrium with views of the Pacific. Rooms are casual with rattan and wicker furniture and quilted bedspreads, in mauve, peach, coral, and sky-blue color schemes. Most have ocean views and private balconies, and all guests have direct access to the beach and pier. ⊠ *1700 Ocean Ave., 90401,* ☎ *310/458–6700,* FAX *310/458–6761. 350 rooms, 31 suites. Restaurant, café, no-smoking floors, indoor-outdoor pool, health club, concierge, business services, parking (fee). AE, D, DC, MC, V.*

$$$$ ⊞ **Miramar Sheraton.** Across the street from Pacific Palisades Park on a bluff, this hotel is close to area beaches, deluxe shopping areas, and many eateries. Divided into three buildings, the hotel includes the Palisades, done in traditional furnishings and dark woods; the Tower, which has contemporary decor in soft pastels; and the Bungalows, small cottages in a garden setting. Many rooms have balconies overlooking the ocean; some have bidets. ⊠ *101 Wilshire Blvd., 90401,* ☎ *310/576–7777 or 800/325–3535,* FAX *310/458–7912. 240 rooms, 62 suites, 32 bungalows. Restaurants, lounge, pool, health club, parking (fee). AE, D, DC, MC, V.*

$$$$ ⊞ **Shutters on the Beach.** Three separate buildings—just yards from
  ★   the Pacific—are linked by trellises, balconies, and awnings, like resorts and cottages of the 1920s. Contemporary rooms are on the small side but tidily decorated. In the marble bathroom you'll find an oversize Jacuzzi tub, some with a glass window that opens to look across the room to the outdoors. This is Los Angeles's only hotel sitting directly on the sand in full view of the Pacific. ⊠ *1 Pico Blvd., Santa Monica 90405,* ☎ *310/458–0030,* FAX *310/458–4589. 198 rooms. Restaurants, in-room safes, no-smoking floors, pool, health club, concierge, parking (fee). AE, D, DC, MC, V.*

$ ⊞ **Carmel Hotel By The Sea.** This Old World four-story hotel, built in 1925, is one block from the beach and Santa Monica Place, as well as from movie theaters and many fine restaurants. The art deco–style lobby is appealing, and electric ceiling fans and plenty of space add spice to the simple if tattered room decor done in wine, hunter green, and beige tones. ⊠ *201 Broadway, 90401,* ☎ *310/451–2469 or 800/445–8695,* FAX *310/393–4180. 102 rooms, 8 suites. Restaurant, parking (fee). AE, D, DC, MC, V.*

Marina del Rey

[COASTAL LOS ANGELES DINING AND LODGING MAP]

$$$$ ⊞ **Marina Beach Airport Marriott.** This luxurious, nine-story high-rise
  ★   property has a high-tech design softened by pastel tones accented with brass and marble. Ask for upper-floor rooms that face the marina. A gazebo in the patio and rooms with water views are among the other nice touches at this Mediterranean-style hotel. ⊠ *4100 Admiralty Way, 90292,* ☎ *310/301–3000,* FAX *310/448–4870. 375 rooms. Restaurant, lounges, pool, health club, business services, airport shuttle, parking (fee). AE, D, DC, MC, V.*

$$$$ ⊞ **Marina del Rey Hotel.** This waterfront hotel equipped with private slips is on the marina's main channel, making cruises and charters easily accessible. Guest rooms (contemporary, with a nautical feel) have balconies and patios, and many have harbor views. The hotel is within walking distance of shopping and only a bike ride away from Fisherman's Village. There are meeting rooms, a gazebo area, and complimentary access to a nearby fitness club. ⊠ *13534 Bali Way, 90292,* ☎ *310/301–1000,* FAX *310/301–8167. 158 rooms. Restaurant, lounge, pool, putting green, airport shuttle, free parking. AE, DC, MC, V.*

$$$–$$$$ ⊞ **Marina International Hotel.** This hotel is across from a sandy beach within the marina. Each of the very private rooms has a balcony or patio that faces the garden or the courtyard. Ask for one of the bungalows— they're huge if not terribly inspiring. Boat charters are available for up to 200 people. ⊠ *4200 Admiralty Way, 90292,* ☎ *310/301–2000,* FAX

310/301–6687. *110 rooms, 25 bungalows. Restaurant, lounge, pool, health club, airport shuttle, free parking. AE, DC, MC, V.*

$$$–$$$$ ⚑ **Ritz-Carlton, Marina del Rey.** The European-style Ritz sits on some
★ prime real estate at the northern end of a basin with a panoramic view of the Pacific. The well-appointed, blue-and-green traditional rooms have French doors, marble baths, honor bars, and plenty of amenities— from plush terry robes to maid service twice a day. ✉ *4375 Admiralty Way, 90292,* ☎ *310/823–1700,* ℻ *310/823–2403. 306 rooms. Restaurants, pool, tennis courts, fitness center, business services, parking (fee). AE, D, DC, MC, V.*

$$ ⚑ **Marina Pacific Hotel & Suites.** This hotel faces the Pacific and one of the world's most vibrant boardwalks; it's nestled among Venice's art galleries, shops, and elegant, offbeat restaurants. Amenities include conference facilities and a delightful sidewalk café. For active travelers, there are ocean swimming, roller skating along the strand, racquetball, and tennis nearby. ✉ *1697 Pacific Ave., Venice 90291,* ☎ *310/399–7770 or 800/421–8151,* ℻ *310/452–5479. 57 rooms, 35 suites, 1-bedroom apartments. Restaurant, laundry service, free parking. AE, D, DC, MC, V.*

South Bay Beach Cities

[COASTAL LOS ANGELES DINING AND LODGING MAP]

$$$–$$$$ ⚑ **Crowne Plaza Redondo Beach & Marina Hotel.** Across the street from the King Harbor Marina, this swank five-story hotel overlooks the Pacific. The magnificent lobby has a 2,200-gallon saltwater aquarium as the focal point, and there are plenty of amenities and special touches throughout, including indoor and outdoor dining, a nightclub, and the famous Gold's Gym. Rooms are done in a tropical seaside theme with wicker furniture and soft colors. ✉ *300 N. Harbor Dr., Redondo Beach 90277,* ☎ *310/318–8888 or 800/368–9760,* ℻ *310/376– 1930. 339 rooms, 5 suites. Restaurant, lounge, pool, sauna, tennis courts, exercise room, business services, parking (fee). AE, D, DC, MC, V.*

$$ ⚑ **Barnabey's Hotel.** Modeled after a 19th-century English inn, with
★ four-poster beds, lace curtains, and antique European furnishings, Barnabey's also has an enclosed greenhouse pool. The London Pub resembles a cozy English hangout, with entertainment nightly; Barnabey's Restaurant serves Continental cuisine and has private, curtained booths. A complimentary English buffet breakfast is served. ✉ *3501 Sepulveda Blvd. (at Rosecrans), Manhattan Beach 90266,* ☎ *310/545–8466 or 800/552–5285,* ℻ *310/545–8621. 122 rooms, 2 suites. Restaurants, lounge, no-smoking floor, pool, airport shuttle, free parking. AE, D, DC, MC, V.*

Airport

$$$–$$$$ ⚑ **Sheraton Gateway Hotel at LAX.** This luxurious 14-story hotel suits business and leisure travelers alike. The contemporary rooms are decorated in plums and aquas, with light woods and contemporary furnishings. Forty-eight rooms were designed especially for people with disabilities. ✉ *6101 W. Century Blvd., Los Angeles 90045,* ☎ *310/642–1111 or 800/325–3535,* ℻ *310/410–1852. 804 rooms, 91 suites. Restaurants, lounges, pool, exercise room, concierge. AE, D, DC, MC, V.*

$$$ ⚑ **Doubletree Hotel LAX.** This three-wing hotel is a good place to stay
★ if you want to be pampered but also need to be close to the airport. Rooms and suites are decorated in muted earth tones of creams and tans to complement the contemporary decor; many suites have private outdoor hot tubs. The expansive, luxurious lobby is decorated in marble and brass. ✉ *5400 W. Century Blvd., Los Angeles 90045,* ☎ *310/216–5858,* ℻ *310/670–1948. 720 rooms, 42 suites. Restau-*

rants, lounge, pool, sauna, health club, business services, parking (fee). AE, D, DC, MC, V.

$$$ 🏨 **Wyndham Hotel at Los Angeles Airport.** This contemporary 12-story hotel is close to LAX, Hollywood Park, the Forum, and Marina del Rey. Rooms are small (250 square feet) and done in greens and yellows. Ask for a room with a view facing north. The Wyndham keeps business travelers in mind, providing in-room fax machines, computer hookups, and voice mail, plus large meeting rooms with ample banquet space. ⊠ *6225 W. Century Blvd., Los Angeles 90045,* ☎ *310/670–9000,* FAX *310/670–7852. 591 rooms, 12 suites. Restaurants, lounge, no-smoking floors, pool, health club, parking (fee). AE, D, DC, MC, V.*

$$ 🏨 **Airport Marina Resort Hotel & Tower.** In a quiet, residential area, convenient to jogging paths, tennis, and golf, this contemporary hotel is composed of four separate buildings, the main one a 12-story high rise. The rooms are warm, with lots of wood; all have views of either the pool, ocean, or airport. A shuttle service goes to LAX, Marina del Rey, and Fox Hills Mall. ⊠ *8601 Lincoln Blvd., Los Angeles 90045,* ☎ *310/670–8111,* FAX *310/337–1883. 570 rooms, 12 suites. Restaurant, pool, airport shuttle. AE, D, DC, MC, V.*

$ 🏨 **Holiday Inn–LAX.** This international-style hotel appeals to families as well as business types, with standard Holiday Inn rooms decorated in earth tones—beige, burgundy, orange, and green. Amenities include a California-cuisine restaurant and cocktail lounge and multilingual telephone operators. ⊠ *9901 La Cienega Blvd., Los Angeles 90045,* ☎ *310/649–5151,* FAX *310/670–3619. 403 rooms. Restaurant, pool, exercise room, airport shuttle, parking (fee). AE, D, DC, MC, V.*

$ 🏨 **Red Lion Los Angeles Airport.** Just three miles north of LAX and a few minutes from Marina del Rey, this deluxe hotel is convenient for business travelers. The oversize guest rooms on 12 floors have a '90s version of art deco–style decor. Extra special is the California Suite, with beautiful furnishings and its own hot tub. ⊠ *6161 Centinela Ave., Culver City 90231,* ☎ *310/649–1776,* FAX *310/649–4411. 368 rooms. Restaurants, lounge, no-smoking floors, pool, sauna, health club, free parking. AE, D, DC, MC, V.*

Pasadena

$$$–$$$$ 🏨 **Ritz-Carlton Huntington Hotel.** The main building of this landmark
★　　　hotel, a Mediterranean-style structure in warm-color stucco, fits perfectly with the lavish houses of the surrounding San Marino neighborhood, Pasadena's upscale neighbor. Walk through the intimate lobby into the central courtyard, dotted with tiny ponds and lush plantings, to the wood-paneled grand lounge, where you can have afternoon tea while enjoying a sweeping view of Los Angeles in the distance. Guest rooms are traditionally furnished and handsome, although a bit small for the price; the large marble-fitted bathrooms also look old-fashioned. The landscaped grounds are quite fine, with their Japanese and horseshoe gardens and the historic Picture Bridge, with murals depicting scenes of California along its 20 gables. ⊠ *1401 S. Oak Knoll Ave., Pasadena 91106,* ☎ *818/568–3900 or 800/241–3333,* FAX *818/568–1842. 383 rooms, 22 suites. Restaurants, no-smoking floors, pool, tennis courts, health club, parking (fee). AE, D, DC, MC, V.*

San Fernando Valley

$$$$ 🏨 **Universal City Hilton and Towers.** This 24-story glass tower blends contemporary luxury with the charm of an Old World European hotel. The pleasant rooms are decorated in warm tones of burgundy and hunter green, and the bathrooms have wall-to-wall marble. Breathtaking views of the San Fernando Valley and hills can be enjoyed through floor-to-ceiling windows. A popular place for TV location filming, the hotel is close to Universal Amphitheater, Universal Studios Tour, CityWalk, and the Hollywood Bowl. ⊠ *555 Universal Terrace Pkwy., Universal City 91608,* ☎ *818/506–2500,* FAX *818/509–2058. 446 rooms. Restaurants, 2 lounges, no-smoking floors, pool, health club, parking (fee). AE, D, DC, MC, V.*

$$$ ⚏ **Burbank Airport Hilton.** This contemporary Hilton is geared to business meetings—there's a state-of-the-art convention center on the premises. The mauve-and-pink lobby is large; rooms have standard-issue hotel decor. In other words, don't expect anything snazzy. Ask for a room with a mountain view. ⊠ *2500 Hollywood Way, Burbank 91505,* ☎ *818/843–6000,* FAX *818/842–9720. 487 rooms, 77 suites. Restaurant, in-room VCRs, pool, spa, parking (fee). AE, D, DC, MC, V.*

$$ ⚏ **Sportsman's Lodge Hotel.** An English country–style building with a resort atmosphere, this hotel features beautiful grounds with waterfalls, a swan-filled lagoon, and a bright white gazebo. Guest rooms are large, and are decorated in soft colors like mauve and blue. Studio suites with private patios are available, and there's an Olympic-size swimming pool. The hotel is close to the Universal Studios Tour and Universal Amphitheater. ⊠ *12825 Ventura Blvd., North Hollywood 91604,* ☎ *818/769–4700 or 800/821–8511,* FAX *213/877–3898. 193 rooms. Restaurants, pool, health club, free parking. AE, D, DC, MC, V.*

$ ⚏ **Safari Inn.** Often used for location filming, this motel-like property two miles from Warner Bros. and Universal studios is made up of two buildings. A neighborhood feel is achieved through homey decor, done in antique white and gold and rattan-and-bamboo furniture. A fine Italian restaurant called Jane's Cucina is on the premises. ⊠ *1911 W. Olive, Burbank 91506,* ☎ *818/845–8586 or 800/782–4373,* FAX *818/845–0054. 110 rooms. Restaurant, lounge, refrigerators, pool, free parking. AE, DC, MC, V.*

NIGHTLIFE AND THE ARTS

For the most complete listing of arts and entertainment events, get the current issue of *Los Angeles* magazine. The Calendar section of the *Los Angeles Times* also covers this beat, as do the more irreverent free publications, the *L.A. Weekly* and the *L.A. Reader.* For a telephone report on current music, theater, dance, film, and special events, plus a discount ticket source, call 213/688–2787. Most tickets can be purchased by phone (with a credit card) from Ticketmaster (☎ 213/365–3500), TeleCharge (☎ 800/762–7666), Good Time Tickets (☎ 213/464–7383), Tickets L.A. (☎ 213/660–8587), or Murray's Tickets (☎ 213/234–0123).

Nightlife

Los Angeles nightclubs aren't known for keeping their doors open until the wee hours. This is still an early-to-bed city, and it's safe to say that by 2 AM, most venues have closed for the night. The accent is on trendy rock clubs, smooth country-and-western establishments, intimate jazz spots, and comedy clubs.

The Sunset Strip offers an assortment of nighttime diversions. Comedy clubs, restaurants with piano bars, cocktail lounges, and hard-rock clubs proliferate. Westwood's beer bars attract college students. Downtown has the Music Center for concerts and theater, some smaller theaters, and a few trendy clubs. Some of Los Angeles's best jazz clubs, discos, and comedy clubs are scattered throughout the San Fernando and San Gabriel valleys.

Dress codes vary. Jackets are expected at cabarets and hotels. Discos are generally casual, although some will turn away the denim-clad. The rule of thumb is to phone ahead and check the dress code, but on the whole, Los Angeles is oriented toward casual wear.

Jazz

Atlas Bar & Grill (✉ 3760 Wilshire Blvd., ☎ 213/380–8400). The eclectic entertainment at this snazzy supper club inside the historic Wiltern building includes torch singers as well as a jazz band.

Baked Potato (✉ 3787 Cahuenga Blvd. W, North Hollywood, ☎ 818/980–1615). In this tiny club they pack you in like sardines to hear a powerhouse of jazz and blues. The featured item on the menu is, of course, the baked potato: they're jumbo and stuffed with everything from steak to vegetables.

House of Blues (✉ 8430 Sunset Blvd., Hollywood, ☎ 213/650–1451). The most happening nightclub on the Sunset Strip, this house has an impressive following, with three bars surrounding the large dance floor. Past performers have included Etta James, Lou Rawls, Joe Cocker, and the Commodores.

Jax (✉ 339 N. Brand Blvd., Glendale, ☎ 818/500–1604). This intimate club serves a wide variety of food, from ribs to pasta; live music is an added draw.

Jazz Bakery (✉ 3221 Hutchison, Culver City, ☎ 310/271–9039). On weekends Jim Britt opens his photography studio, adjacent to the Helms Bakery Building, to serve coffee, desserts, and a nice selection of world-class jazz, enhanced by great acoustics and a smoke-free environment. The $17–$20 admission (no credit cards) includes refreshments.

Marla's Jazz Supper Club (✉ 2323 W. Martin Luther King Jr. Blvd., Los Angeles, ☎ 213/294–8430). Owned by comedy star Marla Gibbs of *The Jeffersons* and *227,* the room pops with blues, jazz, and easy listening. James Ingram plays here from time to time.

Folk, Pop, and Rock

Blue Saloon (✉ 4657 Lankershim Blvd., North Hollywood, ☎ 818/766–4644). For rock and roll (and blues), this is the place to go. (You'll also catch a smattering of country at times.)

Club Lingerie (✉ 6507 Sunset Blvd., Hollywood, ☎ 213/466–8557). One local describes this place as "clean enough for the timid, yet seasoned quite nicely for the tenured scenester."

Ghengis Cohen Cantina (✉ 740 N. Fairfax Ave., West Hollywood, ☎ 213/653–0640). At this longtime music industry hangout, you can hear up-and-coming talent, usually in a refreshingly mellow format like MTV's "Unplugged" performances. A plus is the restaurant's updated Chinese cuisine.

Kingston 12 (✉ 814 Broadway, Santa Monica, ☎ 310/451–4423). This Santa Monica club is known for its rap music, although reggae is also on tap, as is a menu of fine Jamaican food.

McCabe's Guitar Shop (✉ 3101 Pico Blvd., Santa Monica, ☎ 310/828–4497; concert information, 310/828–4403). This is retro-central: Arlo Guthrie sings here on occasion and Alan Ginsberg spouts poetic rhetoric sometimes, too. Folk, acoustic rock, bluegrass, and soul concerts are featured in this guitar store on weekend nights.

Pier 52 (✉ 52 Pier Ave., Hermosa Beach, ☎ 310/376–1629). Monday through Saturday nights dance bands play pure rock and roll. Sunday, however, is designated the day of blues.

The Palace (⊠ 1735 N. Vine St., Hollywood, ☎ 213/462–3000). The "in" spot for the upwardly mobile, this plush multilevel art deco palace speaks of postwar excess: A huge space with lively entertainment, a fabulous sound system, laser lights, two dance floors, four bars, a comfortable balcony, and a full bar and dining room on the top-level patio. The patrons here dress to kill.

The Roxy (⊠ 9009 Sunset Blvd., West Hollywood, ☎ 310/276–2222). Los Angeles's highest profile rock club, classy and comfortable, offers performance art as well as theatrical productions.

The Strand (⊠ 1700 S. Pacific Coast Hwy., Redondo Beach, ☎ 310/316–1700). This major concert venue covers a lot of ground, hosting hot new acts or such old favorites as Asleep at the Wheel, blues man Albert King, rock vet Robin Trower, and Billy Vera.

The Troubadour (⊠ 9081 Santa Monica Blvd., West Hollywood, ☎ 310/276–6168). In the early '70s this was one of the hottest clubs in town for major talent and it's rolling again.

Viper Room (⊠ 8852 Sunset Blvd., West Hollywood, ☎ 310/358–1880). This musicians' hangout, part-owned by actor Johnny Depp, devotes itself to music and dance in the pop, rock, blues, and jazz/fusion genres. Downstairs is a cozy basement room for gabbing and smoking.

Whisky A Go Go (⊠ 8901 Sunset Blvd., West Hollywood, ☎ 310/652–4202). This, the most famous rock-and-roll club on the Sunset Strip, presents up-and-coming alternative, very hard rock, and punk bands. Mondays launch L.A.'s cutting-edge acts.

Cabaret

L.A. Cabaret (⊠ 17271 Ventura Blvd., Encino, ☎ 818/501–3737). This two-room club features a variety of comedy acts as well as karaoke. Famous entertainers often make surprise appearances. Light fare such as chicken and fish dishes are served.

LunaPark (⊠ 665 Robertson Blvd., West Hollywood, ☎ 310/652–0611). A self-described "club in progress," this very hip New York–style cabaret features an eclectic mix of music, with three stages and two bars. Locally famous drag queens strut their stuff here.

Queen Mary (⊠ 12449 Ventura Blvd., Sherman Oaks, ☎ 818/506–5619). Female impersonators vamp it up as Diana Ross, Barbra Streisand, and Bette Midler in this small club where every seat is a good one.

Dance Clubs

Circus Disco and Arena (⊠ 6655 Santa Monica Blvd., Hollywood, ☎ 213/462–1291 or 213/462–1742). An ethnically mixed gay and straight crowd flocks to these two huge side-by-side discos, which feature techno and rock music.

Coconut Teaszer (⊠ 8117 Sunset Blvd., Los Angeles, ☎ 213/654–4773). Dancing to live music—raw-rock at its best—in two separate rooms, a great barbecue menu, and killer drinks make for lively fun. Pool tables are always crowded.

Crush Bar (⊠ 1743 Cahuenga Ave., Hollywood, ☎ 213/463–7685). If the 1960s is a decade that appeals to you, stop by this happening dance club, open Friday and Saturday evenings.

Florentine Gardens (⊠ 5951 Hollywood Blvd., Hollywood, ☎ 213/464–0706). Here's one of Los Angeles's largest dance areas (with spectacular lighting), big on Latin/fusion. It's open Friday, Saturday, and Sunday.

Moonlight Tango Cafe (⊠ 13730 Ventura Blvd., Sherman Oaks, ☎ 818/788–2000). This high-energy club-restaurant, big on the swing era, really gets moving in the wee hours, when a conga line inevitably takes shape on the dance floor.

Sunset Room (✉ 9229 Sunset Blvd., Beverly Hills, ☎ 310/271–8355). This hot, hip place on the ground floor of an office building is a great place for posing, power-staring, and dancing.

Country Music

In Cahoots (✉ 223 N. Glendale Ave., Glendale, ☎ 818/500–1665). At this raucous dance hall you can learn the two-step or the West Coast swing during lessons offered twice each night. All week long there's live music.

Comedy and Magic

Comedy and Magic Club (✉ 1018 Hermosa Ave., Hermosa Beach, ☎ 310/372–1193). This beachfront club features many magicians and comedians seen on TV and in Las Vegas.

Comedy Store (✉ 8433 Sunset Blvd., Hollywood, ☎ 213/656–6225). Los Angeles's premier comedy showcase has been going strong for over a decade. Famous comedians occasionally make unannounced appearances.

Groundlings Theater (✉ 7307 Melrose Ave., Hollywood, ☎ 213/934–9700). The entertainment here consists of original skits, music, and improv, with each player contributing his/her own flavor to the usually hilarious performance.

Ice House Comedy Club and Restaurant (✉ 24 N. Mentor Ave., Pasadena, ☎ 818/577–1894). Three-act shows here feature comedians, celebrity impressionists, ventriloquists, and magicians from Las Vegas, as well as from television shows.

Igby's Comedy Cabaret (✉ 11637 W. Pico Blvd., Los Angeles, ☎ 310/477–3553). You'll see familiar television faces, as well as up-and-coming comedians, Wednesday through Sunday at this friendly club. Reservations are required.

The Improvisation (✉ 8162 Melrose Ave., West Hollywood, ☎ 213/651–2583). The Improv is a transplanted New York establishment showcasing comedians and some vocalists. This place was the proving ground for Liza Minnelli and Richard Pryor, among others. Reservations are recommended.

Bars

BEVERLY HILLS

La Scala (✉ 410 N. Canon, ☎ 310/275–0579). A quaint bar with an immense wine selection, La Scala is honeycombed with celebrities nightly.

CENTURY CITY

Harper's Bar and Grill (✉ 2040 Ave. of the Stars, ☎ 310/553–1855). A central place to meet friends for cocktails before a show at the Shubert Theater, it offers warm decor and generous drinks.

DOWNTOWN

Grand Avenue Sports Bar (✉ 506 S. Grand St., ☎ 213/612–1595). This sleek bar in the Biltmore Hotel serves until 2 AM. Bring lots of money.

Little Joe's (✉ 900 N. Broadway, ☎ 213/489–4900). A must for sports buffs. The prices are low and the big-screen TV is always tuned to the hottest game. W.C. Fields frequented the bar in the '30s.

Pacific Dining Car (✉ 1310 W. 6th St., ☎ 213/483–6000). A Los Angeles landmark, this large bar is open 24 hours and serves gourmet hors d'oeuvres nightly at no charge.

Rex (✉ 617 S. Olive St., ☎ 213/627–2300). This piano bar on the ground floor of the historic Oviatt Building radiates the Art Deco ambience of a 1930s cruise liner.

The Tower (⊠ 1150 S. Olive St., ☎ 213/746–1554). This bar and restaurant atop the 32-story Transamerica Building provides a terrific view and an elegant cocktail environment.

HOLLYWOOD

Dresden Room (⊠ 1760 N. Vermont Ave., ☎ 213/665–4294). Everything old is new again in L.A., as evidenced by this unassuming '40s-style bar that has been rediscovered by a happening '90s crowd.

El Coyote (⊠ 7312 Beverly Blvd., ☎ 213/939–7766). For a pick-me-up margarita, stop by this kitschy restaurant/bar and get a glass of the best—and cheapest—in town.

Hollywood Athletic Club (⊠ 6525 Sunset Blvd., ☎ 213/962–6600). A hip place to hang out is this old billiard parlor attracting a rowdy pool crowd.

Musso & Franks Grill (⊠ 6667 Hollywood Blvd., ☎ 213/467–5123). Film-studio moguls and movie extras alike flock to this long-running hit, where the Rob Roys are just as smooth and the clientele just as eclectic as ever. If the restaurant is too packed, or if you're there alone, you'll be encouraged to dine at the New York–style bar.

Tiki Ti (⊠ 4427 W. Sunset Blvd., ☎ 213/669–9381). This small cocktail lounge is big with the singles crowd. The building, housing some of the city's best tropical rum drinks, emulates a Tahitian hut.

Yamashiro's (⊠ 1999 N. Sycamore Ave., ☎ 213/466–5125). A lovely tradition is to meet at this Japanese restaurant/bar at sunset for cocktails on the terrace.

MARINA DEL REY/VENICE

The Warehouse (⊠ 4499 Admiralty Way, ☎ 310/823–5451). Ex-cinematographer Burt Hixon collected tropical drink recipes on his South Seas forays and whips up one of the most sinfully rich piña coladas this side of Samoa. The bar is popular, so get here early.

MID-WILSHIRE

Tom Bergin's (⊠ 840 S. Fairfax Ave., ☎ 213/936–7151). One of L.A.'s most frequented Irish pubs, it's plastered with Day-Glo shamrocks bearing the names of the masses of regular patrons who have passed through its door.

PASADENA

Beckham Place (⊠ 77 W. Walnut, ☎ 818/796–3399). A rather fancy "Olde English" pub, it's known for its huge drinks, free roast beef sandwiches at Happy Hour, and wing chairs placed near a roaring fire.

SANTA MONICA AND THE BEACHES

Oar House (⊠ 2941 Main St., ☎ 310/396–4725). Something old has been glued or nailed to every square inch of this place, from motorcycles to carriages. Drinks are downright cheap here, and it's also a popular place to dance.

WEST HOLLYWOOD

Le Dôme (⊠ 8720 W. Sunset Blvd., ☎ 310/659–6919). The circular bar here draws a stars and lesser folk. The best time to visit is after 11 PM, when this upmarket hangout really starts to jump.

WEST LOS ANGELES

Q's (⊠ 11835 Wilshire Blvd., West Los Angeles, ☎ 310/477–7550). This upscale pool hall with a dozen tables and a bar serves a yuppified clientele and neighborhood brat-packers.

Gay and Lesbian Nightlife

The greatest concentration of clubs is on or around Santa Monica Boulevard in West Hollywood, but there are options elsewhere and the usually straight Circus and Coconut Teaszer (☞ Dance Clubs, *above*) attract a gay and lesbian crowd some nights.

Axis/Love Lounge (✉ Axis: 652 N. La Peer Dr., ☎ 310/659–0471; ✉ Love Lounge: 657 N. Robertson Blvd., ☎ 310/659–0472). These two clubs on one site have different entrances and schedule different events. Some nights are for lesbians and some are for gay men, and there are frequent theme parties. The music runs the gamut: new wave, hi-NRG, tribal, rock, and Latin house.

Girl Bar (☎ 213/460–2531). L.A.'s more glamorous lesbians show up for Girl Bar parties, which are thrown at several places; call the information line for locations. In recent years, Girl Bar has been held on Friday at Axis and on Saturday at the Love Lounge (☞ *above*). Occasional parties are held at West Hollywood hotels such as the Mondrian.

The Palms (✉ 8572 Santa Monica Blvd., ☎ 310/652–6188). A friendly publike lesbian bar in the heart of West Hollywood, the Palms has DJ dancing some nights, live bands and jukebox selections on others. There's a pool table. Wednesday's a hot night, as is Sunday's beer blast.

Rage (✉ 8911 Santa Monica Blvd., ☎ 310/652–7055). This midsize dance club has been around for years; it remains a favorite of the "gym boy" set. There's also a video lounge.

Revolver (✉ 8851 Santa Monica Blvd., ☎ 310/659–8851). A youngish crowd patronizes this bar, where a half dozen video screens play campy film and music clips.

The Arts

Theater

MAJOR THEATERS

Geffen Playhouse (✉ 10886 Le Conte Ave., Westwood, ☎ 310/208–6500 or 310/208–5454). An acoustically superior theater with great sight lines, the 498-seat playhouse showcases new plays in the summer, primarily musicals and comedies. Many of the productions here are on their way to or from Broadway. This is also where Jason Robards and Nick Nolte got their starts (when the theater was called the Westwood Playhouse).

James A. Doolittle Theater (✉ 1615 N. Vine St., Hollywood, ☎ 213/462–6666; Ticketmaster, 213/365–3500). In the heart of Hollywood, this house has an intimate feel despite its 1,038-seat capacity. New plays, dramas, comedies, and musicals are presented here year-round.

John Anson Ford Ampitheater (✉ 2580 Cahuenga Blvd., Hollywood, ☎ 213/974–1343). This 1,300-seat outdoor house in the Hollywood Hills is best known for its free summer jazz, dance, and cabaret concerts.

Music Center (✉ 135 N. Grand Ave., ☎ 213/972–7211). This big downtown complex includes three theaters. The Ahmanson Theater, which has a variable seating capacity, presents classics and new plays. The 3,200-seat Dorothy Chandler Pavilion presents some plays in between performances of the L.A. Philharmonic, L.A. Master Chorale, and L.A. Opera. The 760-seat Mark Taper Forum (☎ 213/972–7353), under the direction of Gordon Davidson, presents new works that often go on to Broadway, such as *Angels in America* and *Master Class*.

Pantages (✉ 6233 Hollywood Blvd., Hollywood, ☎ 213/468–1700; Ticketmaster, 213/365–3500). Once the home of the Academy Awards telecast and Hollywood premieres, this 2,600-seat house is a splendid example of Hollywood art deco, although the acoustics could use some updating. Large-scale musicals from Broadway are usually presented here.

Wilshire Theater (✉ 8440 Wilshire Blvd., Beverly Hills, ☎ 213/468–1716 or 213/468–1799; Ticketmaster, 213/365–3500). The interior of this 1,900-seat house is art deco; musicals from Broadway are the usual fare.

SMALLER THEATERS

Actors' Gang Theatre (✉ 6209 Santa Monica Blvd., Hollywood, ☎ 213/465–0566). This theater, whose founders include film actor-director Tim Robbins, is the hottest of L.A.'s fringe presenters; the fare runs from Moliere to Eric Bogosian to international works by traveling companies.

Cast Theater (✉ 804 N. El Centro, Hollywood, ☎ 213/462–0265). Musicals, revivals, and avant-garde improv pieces are done here.

Coast Playhouse (✉ 8325 Santa Monica Blvd., West Hollywood, ☎ 213/650–8507). The specialty of this 99-seat house is excellent original musicals and new dramas.

Fountain Theater (✉ 5060 Fountain Ave., Hollywood, ☎ 213/663–1525). This theater, which seats 80, presents original American dramas and stages flamenco dance concerts. Marian Mercer and Rob Reiner got their starts here.

Japan America Theater (✉ 244 S. San Pedro St., downtown, ☎ 213/680–3700). This community-oriented 880-seat theater at the Japan Cultural Arts Center is home to local theater, dance troupes, and the L.A. Chamber Orchestra, plus numerous children's theater groups.

Santa Monica Playhouse (✉ 1211 4th St., Santa Monica, ☎ 310/394–9779). With 99 seats, this house is worth visiting for its cozy, library-like atmosphere; the good comedies, dramas, and children's programs presented here are a further incentive.

Skylight Theater (✉ 1816½ N. Vermont Ave., Los Feliz, ☎ 213/666–2202). Many highly inventive productions have been hosted in this 99-seat theater.

Theatre/Theater (✉ 1713 Cahuenga Blvd., Hollywood, ☎ 213/871–0210). Angelenos crowd into this 70-seat house to view original works by local authors as well as international playwrights.

Concerts

Dorothy Chandler Pavilion (✉ 135 N. Grand Ave., ☎ 213/972–7211). Part of the Los Angeles Music Center and—with the Hollywood Bowl—the center of L.A.'s classical music scene, the 3,200-seat Pavilion is the home of the Los Angeles Philharmonic. The L.A. Opera presents classics from September through June.

Greek Theater (✉ 2700 N. Vermont Ave., ☎ 213/665–1927). This open-air auditorium near Griffith Park has some classical performances on its mainly pop/rock/jazz schedule from June through October.

Hollywood Bowl (✉ 2301 Highland Ave., ☎ 213/850–2000). A fixture of the local music scene since 1920, the Bowl is one of the world's largest outdoor amphitheaters, in a park surrounded by mountains, trees, and gardens. The Bowl's season runs early July–mid-September; the L.A. Philharmonic spends its summer season here. There are performances daily except Mondays (and some Sundays); the program ranges from jazz to pop to classical. Concertgoers usually arrive early, bringing or buying picnic suppers. There are plenty of picnic tables, and box-seat subscribers can reserve a table right in their own box. Restaurant dining is available on the grounds (☎ 213/851–3588); reserve ahead. The seats are wood, so you might bring or rent a cushion—and bring a sweater; it gets chilly here in the evening. A convenient way to enjoy the Hollywood Bowl experience without the hassle of parking is to take one of the Park-and-Ride buses, which leave from various locations around town; call the Bowl for information.

Shrine Auditorium (✉ 665 W. Jefferson Blvd., ☎ 213/749–5123). Built in 1926 by the Al Malaikah Temple, the auditorium's decor could be called Baghdad and Beyond. Touring companies from all over the world, along with assorted gospel and choral groups, appear in this one-of-a-kind, 6,200-seat theater, as do the higher profile televised awards shows such as The American Music Awards and The Grammys.

Wilshire Ebell Theater (✉ 4401 W. 8th St., ☎ 213/939–1128). The Los Angeles Opera Theatre comes to this Spanish-style building, erected in 1924, as do a broad spectrum of other musical performers.

Wiltern Theater (✉ Wilshire Blvd. and Western Ave., ☎ 213/380–5005 or 213/388–1400). The home of the Los Angeles Opera Theater was constructed in 1930 and is listed in the National Register of Historic Places. The Wiltern also schedules pop, rock, and dance performances.

Dance
Bella Lewistsky Dance Co. (☎ 213/580–6338). One of L.A.'s major resident companies schedules modern dance performances regularly around town.

Cal State L.A.'s Dance Department (✉ 5151 State University Dr., ☎ 213/343–5124). The department presents several prominent dance events each year—including the Dance Fair in March and Dance Kaleidoscope in July—at their state-of-the-art Luckman Theater.

Shrine Auditorium (✉ 665 W. Jefferson Blvd., ☎ 213/749–5123). Touring dance companies, such as the Kirov, the Bolshoi, and the American Ballet Theater (ABT) perform here.

UCLA Center for the Arts (✉ 405 N. Hilgard Ave., ☎ 310/825–2101). Visiting companies, such as Martha Graham, Paul Taylor, and Hubbard Street Dance Company, are apt to show up here.

Movie Palaces
Mann's Chinese Theater (✉ 6925 Hollywood Blvd., Hollywood, ☎ 213/464–8111). Perhaps the world's best-known theater houses three movie screens, and it still hosts many gala premieres.

Pacific Cinerama Dome (✉ 6360 Sunset Blvd., Hollywood, ☎ 213/466–3401). This futuristic, geodesic structure was the first theater designed specifically for Cinerama in the United States. The gigantic screen and multitrack sound system create an unparalleled cinematic experience.

Pacific's El Capitan (✉ 6838 Hollywood Blvd., Hollywood, ☎ 213/467–7674). Restored to its original Art Deco splendor, this classic movie palace reopened across the street from Mann's Chinese in 1991. First-run movies are on the bill, as are Disney animation debuts.

Silent Movie (✉ 611 N. Fairfax Ave., ☎ 213/653–2389). Though not a movie palace itself, this theater revives classics like Charlie Chaplin's *The Gold Rush* and the portfolio of Buster Keaton films. Open Wednesday, Friday, and Saturday evenings, it's known as the only silent movie house in the world, complete with a vintage organ.

Vista Theater (✉ 4473 Sunset Dr., Los Feliz, ☎ 213/660–6639). At the intersection of Hollywood and Sunset boulevards, this 70-year-old cinema was once Bard's Hollywood Theater, where both moving pictures and vaudeville played. A Spanish-style facade leads to an ornate Egyptian interior.

Television

Audiences Unlimited (✉ 100 Universal City Plaza, Bldg. 153, Universal City 91608, ☎ 818/506–0043) is a nifty organization that helps fill seats for television programs (and sometimes theater events, as well). There's no charge, but the tickets are distributed on a first-come, first-served basis. Tickets can be picked up at Fox Television Center (✉ 5746 Sunset Blvd., Van Ness Ave. entrance), which is open weekdays 8:30–6, or at the Glendale Galleria Information Desk between 10 and 9 daily. Note: You must be 16 or older to attend a television taping. For a schedule, send a self-addressed envelope to Audiences Unlimited a few weeks prior to your visit.

OUTDOOR ACTIVITIES AND SPORTS

Beaches

From downtown, the easiest way to hit the coast is by taking the Santa Monica Freeway (I–10) due west. Once you reach the end of the freeway, I–10 turns into the famous Highway 1, better known as the Pacific Coast Highway, or PCH, and continues up to Oregon. Other basic routes from the downtown area include Pico, Olympic, Santa Monica, Sunset, or Wilshire boulevards. The MTA bus line runs every 20 minutes to and from the beaches along each of these streets.

Los Angeles County beaches (and state beaches operated by the county) have lifeguards. Public parking (for a fee) is available at most. The following beaches are listed in north–south order. Some are excellent for swimming, some for surfing (check with lifeguards for current conditions), and others are better for exploring.

Leo Carillo State Beach. This beach along a rough and mountainous stretch of coastline is the most fun at low tide, when spectacular tide pools blossom. Rock formations on the beach have created secret coves for picnickers looking for solitude. There are hiking trails, sea caves, and tunnels. Whales, dolphins, and sea lions are often seen swimming in the offshore kelp beds. The waters here are rocky and best for experienced surfers and scuba divers; the fishing is good. Picturesque campgrounds are set back from the beach. Camping is $17–18 per night. ✉ *35000 block of PCH, Malibu,* ☎ *818/880–0350 or 800/444–7275. Parking, lifeguard, rest rooms, showers, fire pits.*

Zuma Beach County Park. This is Malibu's largest and sandiest beach, and a favorite spot of surfers. ✉ *30050 PCH, Malibu,* ☎ *310/457–9891. Parking, lifeguard, rest rooms, showers, food, playground, volleyball.*

Westward Beach/Point Dume State Beach. A favorite spot for surfing, this ½-mile-long sandy beach has tide pools and sandstone cliffs. ✉ *South end of Westward Beach Rd., Malibu,* ☎ *310/457–9891. Parking, lifeguard, rest rooms, food.*

Paradise Cove. With its pier and equipment rentals, this sandy beach is a mecca for sportfishing boats. Though swimming is allowed, there are lifeguards during the summer only. ✉ *28128 PCH, Malibu,* ☎ *310/457–9891. Parking, rest rooms, showers, food (concessions open summer only).*

Malibu Lagoon State Beach/Surfrider Beach. The steady 3- to 5-foot waves make this beach, just north of Malibu Pier, great for long-board surfing. The International Surfing Contest is held here in September. Water runoff from Malibu Canyon forms a natural lagoon, which is a sanctuary for many birds. There are also nature trails perfect for romantic sunset strolls. ✉ *23200 block of PCH, Malibu,* ☎ *818/880–0350. Parking, lifeguard, rest rooms, picnicking, visitor center.*

Las Tunas State Beach. Las Tunas is small (1,300 feet long, covering a total of only 2 acres), narrow, and sandy, with some rocky areas, and set beneath a bluff. Surf fishing is the biggest attraction here. There is no lifeguard, and swimming is not encouraged because of steel groins set offshore to prevent erosion. ✉ *19400 block of PCH, Malibu,* ☎ *310/457–9891. Parking, rest rooms.*

Topanga Canyon State Beach. This rocky beach stretches from the mouth of the Topanga Canyon down to Coastline Drive. Catamarans dance in these waves and skid onto the sands, where dolphins sometimes come close enough to shore to startle sunbathers. The area near the canyon is a great surfing spot. ✉ *18700 block of PCH, Malibu,* ☎ *310/394–3266. Parking, lifeguard, rest rooms, food.*

Will Rogers State Beach. This wide, sandy beach is several miles long and has even surf. Parking in the lot here is limited, but there is plenty of beach, volleyball, and bodysurfing, attracting a predominantly gay crowd. ✉ *15800 PCH, Pacific Palisades,* ☎ *310/394–3266. Parking, lifeguard, rest rooms.*

Santa Monica Beach. In addition to the active pier and promenade, a man-made breakwater just offshore has caused the sand to collect and form the widest stretch of beach on the entire Pacific coast. If you're up for some sightseeing on land, this is one of the more popular gathering places for L.A.'s young, toned, and bronzed. The beach has bike paths, facilities for people with disabilities, playgrounds, and volleyball. In summer, free rock and jazz concerts are held at the pier on Thursday nights. ✉ *West of PCH, Santa Monica,* ☎ *310/394–3266. Parking, lifeguard, rest rooms, showers.*

Venice Municipal Beach. The surf and sands of Venice are fine, but the main attraction here is the boardwalk scene. Venice combines the beefcake of some of L.A.'s most serious bodybuilders with the productions of lively crafts merchants and street musicians. There are roller skaters, comedians, and rappers to entertain you, and cafés to feed you. ✉ *1531 Ocean Front Walk, Venice,* ☎ *310/394–3266. Parking, rest rooms, showers, food, picnicking.*

Playa del Rey. One of the more attractive features of this beach is an area called Del Rey Lagoon, a grassy oasis in the heart of Playa del Rey. A pond is inhabited by dozens of ducks, and barbecue pits and tables are available to picnickers. ✉ *6660 Esplanade, Playa del Rey.* ☎ *310/322–7036. Parking, lifeguard, rest rooms, food.*

Manhattan State Beach. Here are 44 acres of sandy beach for swimming, diving, surfing, and fishing. Polliwog Park is a grassy landscape a few yards back from the beach that parents with young children may appreciate for its duck pond. ✉ *West of Strand, Manhattan Beach,* ☎ *310/372–2166. Volleyball, parking, lifeguard, rest rooms, showers, food.*

Redondo State Beach. The beach is wide, sandy, and usually packed in summer, and parking is limited. Rock and jazz concerts are held at the pier during the summer. ✉ *Foot of Torrance Blvd., Redondo Beach,* ☎ *310/372–2166. Volleyball, parking, lifeguard, rest rooms, showers, food.*

Participant Sports

For information about tennis courts, hiking and biking trails, and anything else sports-related, call the **City of Los Angeles Recreation and Parks**

Department (⊠ 200 N. Main St., Suite 1380, City Hall East, 90012, ☎ 213/485–5515). Also helpful is the **Los Angeles County Parks and Recreation Department** (⊠ 433 S. Vermont Ave., 90020, ☎ 213/738–2961).

Bicycling

Perhaps the most famous bike path in the city, and definitely the most beautiful, can be found on the Pacific Ocean beach, from Temescal Canyon down to Redondo Beach. San Vicente Boulevard in Santa Monica has a wide cycling lane next to the sidewalk that runs for about 5 miles. Another haven for two-wheelers is the marked path for cyclers that traverses Griffith Park.

Fishing

Shore fishing and surf casting are excellent on many of the beaches. Pier fishing is another popular method of hooking your dinner. The Malibu, Santa Monica, and Redondo Beach piers all have nearby bait-and-tackle shops.

If you want to break away from the piers, **Marina del Rey Sport Fishing** (⊠ Dock 2, Fiji Way, Marina del Rey, ☎ 310/822–3625) operates boat excursions for $20 per half day. **Redondo Sport Fishing Company** (⊠ 233 N. Harbor Dr., Redondo Beach, ☎ 310/372–2111) has half-day charters that start at $20 per person. You can rent a pole for $7, and you'll need a license, which will cost $6.30. Sea bass, halibut, bonita, yellowtail, and barracuda are the usual catch.

Skipper's Twenty Second Street Landing (⊠ 141 W. 22nd St., San Pedro, ☎ 310/832–8304) operates an overnight charter. These boats, complete with bunk beds and full galley, leave around 10 PM and dock between 5 PM and 9 PM the next night. Per-person price is $60. Day charters are available as well, at $28–$40, with 11-hour excursions on weekends for $32.

The most popular and unquestionably the most unusual form of fishing in the L.A. area involves no hooks, bait, or poles. The great **grunion runs,** which take place March–August, are a natural phenomenon in which hundreds of thousands of small silver fish, called grunion, wash up on southern California beaches to spawn and lay their eggs in the sand. The Cabrillo Marine Aquarium (☎ 310/548–7562) in San Pedro has entertaining and educational programs about grunion throughout most of their spawning season. During certain months it is prohibited to touch the grunion, so please check with the Fish and Game Department (☎ 310/590–5132) before going to see them wash ashore.

Golf

Rancho Park Golf Course (⊠ 10460 W. Pico Blvd., ☎ 310/838–7373) is a beautifully designed course, but the towering pines will make those who slice or hook regret that they ever took up golf. There's a two-level driving range, a nine-hole pitch 'n' putt, a snack bar, and a pro shop where you can rent clubs. Perhaps the most concentrated area of golf courses in the city can be found in Griffith Park. **Harding Golf Course and Wilson Golf Course** (⊠ 4730 Crystal Springs Dr., ☎ 213/663–2555) are about 1½ miles inside the park entrance at Riverside Drive and Los Feliz Boulevard. Bridle paths surround the outer fairways, and the San Gabriel Mountains make a scenic background. The nine-hole **Roosevelt Course** (⊠ 2650 N. Vermont Ave., ☎ 213/665–2011) can be reached through the park's Hillhurst Avenue entrance.

There's usually no waiting at the nine-hole **Los Feliz Pitch 'n' Putt** (⊠ 3207 Los Feliz Blvd., ☎ 213/663–7758). **Holmby Hills** (⊠ 601 Club View Dr., Beverly Hills, ☎ 310/276–1604) is a nine-hole pitch-and-putt course.

Health Clubs

There are dozens of health-club chains in the city including the most popular local chain, **Bally Total Fitness Club and Sports Connection** (⊠ 1628 El Centro, ☎ 213/461–0227), between Hollywood and Sunset boulevards. This is the flagship operation; to find the Bally club nearest you, call 800/695–8111. **Gold's Gym** (⊠ 360 Hampton Dr., Venice, ☎ 310/392–6004; ⊠ 1016 N. Cole Ave., Hollywood, ☎ 213/462–7012) charges $15 a day or $50 a week to use its weights and Nautilus machines. The fee to use **Easton Gym** (⊠ 8053 Beverly Blvd., West Hollywood, ☎ 213/651–3636) is $10 per day, or $40 per week.

DANCE AND WORKOUT STUDIOS

A popular place to reconfigure your figure is the trendy **Voight Fitness Center** (⊠ 980 N. La Cienega Blvd., West Hollywood, ☎ 310/854–0741). Downtown, visit **Studio A Dance** (⊠ 2306 Hyperion Ave., Silverlake, ☎ 213/661–8311), where user-friendly aerobics, jazz, and ballet classes are taught by supportive instructors.

Hiking

Will Rogers Historic State Park has a splendid nature trail. Other parks in the L.A. area that also have hiking trails include Brookside Park, Elysian Park, and Griffith Park. In the Malibu area, Leo Carillo State Beach and the top of Corral Canyon have incredible rock formations and caves that can be explored on foot. For further information on hiking locations and scheduled outings in Los Angeles, contact the Sierra Club (☎ 213/387–4287).

Ice-Skating

In the Valley, there's the **Pickwick Ice Center** (⊠ 1001 Riverside Dr., Burbank, ☎ 818/846–0032). In Pasadena, try the **Ice Skating Center** (⊠ 310 E. Green St., ☎ 818/578–0800). In Rolling Hills, try the **Culver City Ice Arena** (⊠ 4545 Sepulveda Blvd., ☎ 310/398–5718).

In-Line and Roller Skating

Moonlight Rollerway (⊠ 5110 San Fernando Rd., Glendale, ☎ 818/241–3630) and **Skateland** (⊠ 18140 Parthenia St., Northridge, ☎ 818/885–1491) are two of the more popular rinks in Los Angeles.

Jogging

A popular scenic course can be found at **Exposition Park.** Circling the Coliseum and Sports Arena is a jogging-workout trail with pull-up bars and other simple equipment placed every several hundred yards. **San Vicente Boulevard** in Santa Monica has a wide grassy median that splits the street for several picturesque miles. The **Hollywood Reservoir,** just east of Cahuenga Boulevard in the Hollywood Hills, is encircled by a 3.2-mile asphalt path and has a view of the Hollywood sign. Within hilly **Griffith Park** are many miles of paths and challenging terrain, but Crystal Springs Drive from the main entrance at Los Feliz to the zoo is a relatively flat 5 miles. Circle Drive, around the perimeter of **UCLA** in Westwood, provides a 2½-mile run through academia.

Racquetball and Handball

The **Racquet Center** (⊠ 10933 Ventura Blvd., Studio City, ☎ 818/760–2303) in the San Fernando Valley offers court time for $10–$14. There's another Racquet Center in South Pasadena (⊠ 920 Lohman La., ☎ 213/258–4178).

Tennis

Many public parks (☎ 213/485–5515) have courts that charge an hourly fee. Lincoln Park (⊠ Lincoln and Wilshire Blvd., Santa Monica), Griffith Park (⊠ Riverside Dr. and Los Feliz Blvd.), and Barrington Park

(✉ Barrington, south of Sunset Blvd.) all have well-maintained courts with lights.

Water Sports

Action Water Sports (✉ 4144 Lincoln Blvd., Marina del Rey, ☎ 310/306–9539) rents kayaks for $35 per day during the summer. Dive shops, such as **New England Divers** (✉ 4148 Viking Way, Long Beach, ☎ 310/421–8939) and **Dive & Surf** (✉ 504 N. Broadway, Redondo Beach, ☎ 310/372–8423), will provide you with everything you need (the diving's particularly good off Leo Carillo State Beach and Catalina Island). The signature water sport in L.A. is surfing (☞ Beaches, *above*). Good windsurfing can be found all along the coast, and there are a number of places from which certified windsurfers can rent equipment, such as **Malibu Ocean Sports** (✉ 22935 Pacific Coast Hwy., Malibu, ☎ 310/486–6302).

Spectator Sports

Some of the major sports venues in the area are **Anaheim Stadium** (✉ 2000 Gene Autry Way, ☎ 714/254–3100), the **Great Western Forum** (✉ 3900 W. Manchester Blvd., Inglewood, ☎ 310/673–1773), the **L.A. Sports Arena** (✉ 3939 S. Figueroa St., downtown, ☎ 213/748–6131), and the **L.A. Coliseum** (✉ 3911 S. Figueroa St., downtown, ☎ 213/748–6131).

Baseball

The **Dodgers** play at Dodger Stadium (✉ 1000 Elysian Park Ave., exit off I–110, Pasadena Fwy.). For ticket information, call 213/224–1400. For **California Angels** ticket information, contact Anaheim Stadium (☎ 714/937–7200).

Basketball

The **Los Angeles Lakers'** home court is the Forum; for ticket information, call 310/419–3182. L.A.'s "other" team, the **Clippers** make their home at the L.A. Sports Arena; for ticket information, call 213/748–8000. The **University of Southern California** (☎ 213/740–2311) plays at the L.A. Sports Arena. The **Bruins of the University of California** at Los Angeles (☎ 310/825–2101) play at Pauley Pavilion on the UCLA campus.

Football

The NFL Rams and Raiders deserted Los Angeles, but college teams bring out fans in droves. The **USC Trojans'** (☎ 213/740–2311) home turf is the Coliseum. The **UCLA Bruins** (☎ 310/825–2101) pack 'em in at the Rose Bowl in Pasadena.

Hockey

The **L.A. Kings** (☎ 310/673–6003) put their show on ice at the Forum. Disney's **Mighty Ducks** (☎ 714/704–2500) push the puck at The Pond in Anaheim.

Horse Racing

Santa Anita Race Track (✉ Huntington Dr. and Colorado Pl., Arcadia, ☎ 818/574–7223) is still the dominant site for exciting thoroughbred racing. **Hollywood Park** (✉ Century Blvd. and Ave. of the Champions, Inglewood, ☎ 310/419–1500) is another favorite racing venue. For harness racing, **Los Alamitos** (✉ 4961 Katella Ave., Anaheim, ☎ 714/995–1234) has both day and night racing.

SHOPPING

By Jane E.
Lasky

When asked where they want to shop, visitors to Los Angeles inevitably answer, "Rodeo Drive." But this famous thoroughfare is only one of many enticing shopping streets in this world-class city. There are also plenty of malls, the modern-day Angeleno's equivalent of a main street, town square, back fence, malt shop, and county fair, all rolled into one. Distances between shopping spots can be vast, however, so don't try to hit too many different areas in one day—if you do, you'll spend more time driving than spending. Most Los Angeles shops are open from 10 to 6, although many remain open until 9 or later, particularly at the shopping centers, on Melrose Avenue, and in Westwood Village during summer. Check the *Los Angeles Times* for sales.

Shopping Districts

Beverly Center and Environs

The **Beverly Center** (✉ 8500 Beverly Blvd., at La Cienega Blvd., ☎ 310/854–0070) covers more than 7 acres and has 200 stores. **MAC** (☎ 310/659–6201) in the center has a line of professional makeup at reasonable prices, and the knowledgeable staff provides hints on how to apply your makeup. **Shauna Stein** (☎ 310/652–5511) sells interesting women's clothes by such designers as Gaultier. **Traffic** (☎ 310/659–4313) and **Traffic Studio** (☎ 310/659–3438) sell contemporary men's and women's clothing.

The **Beverly Connection** (✉ 100 N. La Cienega Blvd., at Beverly Blvd., ☎ 213/651–3611), directly across the street from the Beverly Center, on the east side of La Cienega between Beverly Boulevard and 3rd Street, is a multilevel mall. **Book Star** (☎ 310/289–1734) in the mall is a giant warehouse-style store selling every conceivable kind of reading material. In the immediate neighborhood are some one-of-a-kind shops. **Freehand** (✉ 8413 W. 3rd St., ☎ 213/655–2607) is an eye-catching gallery of contemporary American crafts, clothing, and jewelry, mostly by California artists. **Trashy Lingerie** (✉ 402 N. La Cienega, ☎ 310/652–4543) is just what its name suggests.

Beverly Hills

Barneys New York (✉ 9570 Wilshire Blvd., ☎ 310/276–4400) is especially popular with Gen-Xers, who come for the cutting-edge designer clothing, including threads by Comme des Garçons, Giorgio Armani, Donna Karan, and Azzedine Alaia. The store's second-floor Chelsea Passage department has a pristine collection of home furnishings.

Along the half-dozen blocks of **Rodeo Drive** between Wilshire and Santa Monica boulevards, you'll find an abundance of big-name retailers. Don't ignore the streets that surround illustrious Rodeo Drive, as there are plenty of treasures to be purchased among them as well.

The **Rodeo Collection** (✉ 421 N. Rodeo Dr., ☎ 310/276–9600) is one of several Beverly Hills–style shopping centers—but don't dare call them malls. Many famous upscale European designers operate behind glitzy doors in this piazza-like area of marble and brass, among them Fila (☎ 310/276–1732), Mondi (☎ 310/274–8380), and Gianni Versace (☎ 310/276–6799).

Two Rodeo Drive (✉ Rodeo Dr. and Wilshire Blvd., ☎ 310/247–7040), a.k.a. Via Rodeo, houses glossy retail shops on a private cobblestone street that somewhat resembles a Hollywood back lot. Amid the outdoor cafés and sculpted fountains of the Italianate piazza are two-dozen boutiques, including Christian Dior and Gianfranco Ferre.

Some of the many other enterprises in Beverly Hills include **Emporio Armani Boutique** (✉ 9533 Brighton Way, ☎ 310/271–7790), **Polo/Ralph Lauren** (✉ 444 N. Rodeo Dr., ☎ 310/281–7200), **Cartier** (✉ 370 N. Rodeo Dr., ☎ 310/275–4272), **Van Cleef and Arpels** (✉ 300 N. Rodeo Dr., ☎ 310/276–1161), **Tiffany & Co.** (✉ 210 N. Rodeo Dr., ☎ 310/273–8880), and **Saks Fifth Avenue** (✉ 9600 Wilshire Blvd., ☎ 310/275–4211).

Men's fashions can be found at **Alfred Dunhill of London** (✉ 201 N. Rodeo Dr., ☎ 310/274–5351), **Battaglia** (✉ 306 N. Rodeo Dr., ☎ 310/276–7184), **Bernini** (✉ 362 N. Rodeo Dr., ☎ 310/278–6287), **Carroll and Co.** (✉ 466 N. Rodeo Dr., ☎ 310/273–9060) and **Bijan** (✉ 420 N. Rodeo Dr., ☎ 310/273–6544).

For women's fashions, try **Celine** (✉ 460 N. Rodeo Dr., ☎ 310/273–1243), **Chanel** (✉ 400 N. Rodeo Dr., ☎ 310/278–5500), **Fred Hayman** (✉ 273 N. Rodeo Dr., ☎ 310/271–3000), **Harari** (✉ 390 N. Bedford Dr., ☎ 310/859–1131), and **Theodore** (✉ 453 N. Rodeo Dr., ☎ 310/276–9691).

Department Stores

Macy's (✉ 8500 Beverly Blvd., ☎ 310/854–6655), at the Beverly Center and elsewhere, carries an extensive collection of clothing for men and women, as well as housewares and cosmetics.

Neiman Marcus (✉ 9700 Wilshire Blvd., Beverly Hills, ☎ 310/550–5900), the high-end, Texas-based chain, carries a spectacular selection of women's fashions and accessories—especially the shoes.

Nordstrom (✉ ✉ 10830 W. Pico Blvd., West Los Angeles, ☎ 310/470–6155), at Westside Pavilion and elsewhere, has clothing for men and women and a reputation for fine customer service.

Robinsons-May (✉ 9900 Wilshire Blvd., ☎ 310/275–5464, and elsewhere) has many women's selections, some for men, and a good housewares department.

Century City

Century City Shopping Center & Marketplace (✉ 10250 Santa Monica Blvd., ☎ 310/277–3898), set among gleaming, tall office buildings on what used to be the Twentieth Century-Fox film studios back lot, is an open-air mall with an excellent roster of shops, restaurants, and department stores. The center's **Wild Pair** (☎ 310/203–8769) is *the* place to go for trendy shoes and bags.

Downtown

The **Cooper Building** (✉ 860 S. Los Angeles St., ☎ 213/622–1139) is a bargain hunter's heaven: Eight floors of small clothing and shoe shops (mostly for women) offer fantastic discounts. Grab a free map in the lobby. Nearby are myriad discount outlets selling everything from shoes and suits to linens and lingerie.

Seventh Street Marketplace (✉ 735 S. Figueroa St., ☎ 213/955–7150), is an indoor/outdoor multilevel shopping center with an extensive courtyard. Stores surrounding the courtyard include G. B. Harb (☎ 213/624–4785), a fine shop for fashion.

Melrose Avenue

West Hollywood, especially the 1½ miles of **Melrose Avenue** from La Brea Avenue to a few blocks west of Crescent Heights, is definitely one of Los Angeles's trendiest shopping areas, with loads of intriguing shops and bistros. La Cienega Boulevard between Santa Monica and Beverly boulevards is lined with antiques dealers selling everything from Chinese to French to Viennese collectibles. Nearby lies L.A.'s poshest antiquarian niche: the 8400 block of Melrose Place.

Betsey Johnson (⊠ 7311 Melrose Ave., ☎ 213/931–4490) holds frequent—and often dramatic—sales on the American designer's vivid, hip women's fashions. **Comme des Fous** (⊠ 7384 Melrose Ave., ☎ 213/653–5330) is an avant-garde clothing shop packed with innovative European designs for women. **Off the Wall** (⊠ 7325 Melrose Ave., ☎ 213/930–1185) specializes in "antiques and weird stuff": rare Bakelite radios, vintage vending machines, art deco furniture, and the like. **Wacko** (⊠ 7402 Melrose Ave., ☎ 213/651–3811) is a wild space crammed with all manner of wacky blow-up toys, cards, and other semi-useless items that make good Los Angeles keepsakes. **Wasteland** (⊠ 7428 Melrose Ave., ☎ 213/653–3028) carries an extensive collection of retro clothing, both used and new, all reasonably priced. It's a fun place to shop for '50s bowling shirts, '40s rayon dresses, funky ties, worn jeans, and leather jackets. **Wound and Wound** (⊠ 7374 Melrose Ave., ☎ 213/653–6703) has an impressive collection of windup toys and music boxes.

Santa Monica and Venice

Third Street Promenade (☎ 310/393–8355) is a pedestrian-only street lined with boutiques, movie theaters, clubs, pubs, and restaurants. It's as busy at night as it is during the day, with street performers to entertain as you mosey along.

Montana Avenue from 7th to 17th streets has many exclusive clothing, antiques, and housewares boutiques. **ABS Clothing** (⊠ 1533 Montana Ave., ☎ 310/393–8770) sells contemporary sportswear designed in Los Angeles. **Brenda Cain** (⊠ 1211 Montana Ave., ☎ 310/395–1559) showcases antique jewelry and home accessories, but the hot ticket here is the amazing array of Arts and Crafts pottery by such makers as Roseville and Weller. **Weathervane II** (⊠ 1209 Montana Ave., ☎ 310/393–5344) one of the street's larger shops, has classic and offbeat fashions.

Main Street leading from Santa Monica to Venice (Pico Blvd. to Rose Ave.) has good restaurants and unusual shops and galleries. **Malina** (⊠ 2654C Main St., ☎ 310/392–2611) sells French fashions like Le Petit Bateau for children and Kenzo for women, as well as the store's own line.

The **Psychic Eye Bookstore** (⊠ 218 Main St., ☎ 310/396–0110) is a spiritual haven selling wind chimes, incense, and crystal jewelry, as well as books on sorcery and other occult subjects. It's worth a look, even for skeptics. The artsy **Abbot Kinney Boulevard** area has galleries, cafés, boutiques, and antiques shops.

West Los Angeles

The **Westside Pavilion** (☎ 310/474–6255) is a postmodern mall on Pico and Overland boulevards. The three levels of shops and restaurants run the gamut from high-fashion boutiques for men and women to toy stores and housewares shops.

SIDE TRIPS

Big Bear Lake and Lake Arrowhead

By William P.
Brown

Local legend has it that in 1845, Don Benito Wilson—General George Patton's grandfather—and his men charged up along the San Bernardino River in pursuit of a troublesome band of Native Americans. As Wilson entered a clearing, he discovered a meadow teeming with bears. The rest, of course, is history: Wilson later became mayor of Los Angeles, and the

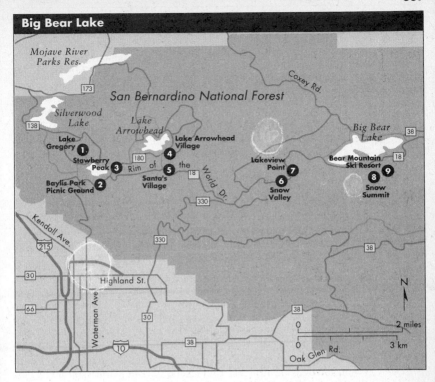

Big Bear Lake

area he'd stumbled upon was developed into a delightful mountain playground, centered around the man-made lakes of Arrowhead and Big Bear.

Visitors come in winter for downhill and cross-country skiing, and in summer to breathe cool mountain air, hike in the woods, sniff the daffodils, and play in the water. Spring and fall bring clear, sweeping views of the San Bernardino Valley, one of southern California's most awesome panoramas.

Take I–10 east from Los Angeles to Highway 330, which connects with Highway 18—the Rim of the World Scenic Byway—at Running Springs. This is approximately the midpoint of the scenic drive, which hugs the mountainside from Big Bear Lake to Cajon Pass. The trip should take about 90 minutes to Lake Arrowhead, and two hours to Big Bear. Highway 38, the back way into Big Bear, is actually longer, but it can be faster when the traffic on the more direct route is heavy.

Numbers in the margin correspond to points of interest on the Big Bear map.

1 **Lake Gregory,** at the ridge of Crestline, was formed by a dam constructed in 1938. Because the water temperature in summer is seldom extremely cold—as it can be in the other lakes at this altitude—this is the best swimming lake in the mountains, but it's open in summer only, and there's a minimum charge to swim. You can rent rowboats at Lake Gregory Village.

2 If you're up for a barbecue in a wooded setting, visit **Baylis Park Picnic Ground,** which has plenty of good spots for eating alfresco.

3 Just past the town of Rim Forest is the fire lookout tower at **Strawberry Peak.** Visitors who brave the steep stairway to the tower are treated to a magnificent view and a lesson on fire spotting by the staff.

❹ For some, **Lake Arrowhead Village** is a quaint alpine community with shops and eateries; for others, it has all the ambience of a shopping mall. Lake Arrowhead, on the other hand, is decidedly a gem, although it can become crowded with speedboats and waterskiers in summer. The *Arrowhead Queen,* operated daily by LeRoy Sports (☎ 909/336–6992) provides 50-minute cruises around the lake, leaving from the waterfront marina. Reservations are essential in summer. The cost varies, but the maximum is $9.50. **Lake Arrowhead Children's Museum** (☎ 909/336–3093), on the village's lower level, has hands-on exhibits, a climbing maze, and a puppet stage. Admission is $3.50.

❺ **Santa's Village,** a favorite with children, has a petting zoo, rides, riding stables, and bakery filled with goodies. ✉ *Hwy. 18, Skyforest,* ☎ *909/337–2484.* 🎟 *$11, includes 12 rides.* ⏲ *Hrs vary seasonally; call ahead.*

❻ **Snow Valley,** one of the major ski areas in the San Bernardino Mountains, has snowmaking capabilities and a dozen lifts. Summer visitors will also find hiking trails, horseback riding, and fishing here. ✉ *Rim Dr., 5 miles east of Running Springs,* ☎ *909/867–5151.*

❼ **Lakeview Point** looks into deep Bear Creek Canyon; Big Bear Lake is usually visible in the distance. A 15½-mile drive will take you completely around the lake. Big Bear Lake Village is on the south shore. The town is a pleasant combination of alpine and Western-mountain style, with the occasional chaletlike building. The paddle wheeler *Big Bear Queen* (☎ 909/866–3218) departs daily, May through October, from Big Bear Marina for 90-minute, $9.50 tours of the lake. Fishing-boat and equipment rentals are available from several lakeside marinas, including Pine Knot Landing (☎ 909/866–2628).

❽ **Snow Summit** (☎ 909/866–4621) is a top ski resort just southeast of Big Bear Village. It has a 8,200-foot peak and is equipped with a high-speed quad chair, 12 chairlifts, and 20 miles of runs at all levels.

❾ **Bear Mountain Ski Resort** (☎ 909/585–2519) also to the southeast of Big Bear Village, has 11 chairlifts and 35 trails, from beginner to expert. On busy winter weekends and holidays, your best bet is to reserve your tickets before you head for the mountain.

Dining and Lodging

For price charts, *see* Los Angeles Dining and Los Angeles Lodging, *above.*

$ ✕ **Blue Ox Bar and Grill.** This casual restaurant serves oversize steaks, ribs, burgers, and chicken—all cooked simply but well. The bar is great for meeting and greeting. ✉ *441 W. Big Bear Blvd., Big Bear City,* ☎ *909/585–7886. AE, DC, MC, V.*

$ ✕ **George and Sigi's Knusperhauschen.** Don't let the campy gingerbread-house look fool you: This restaurant offers wonderful Eastern European fare. The schnitzel and sauerbraten are a delight. ✉ *829 W. Big Bear Blvd., Big Bear City,* ☎ *909/585–8640. MC, V. Closed Mon. and Tues. No lunch.*

$ ✕ **Iron Squirrel.** Hearty French cooking with American influences is presented in a country-French setting. The veal Normandie comes highly recommended, and other traditional dishes, such as rack of lamb with garlic, are nicely prepared. ✉ *646 Pineknot Blvd., Big Bear Lake,* ☎ *909/866–9121. AE, MC, V.*

$$$–$$$$ 🏨 **Apples Bed and Breakfast Inn.** Surrounded by an acre of pine trees, this inn has individually decorated rooms (four are equipped with their own Jacuzzis), plus a large gathering room with a wood-burning stove, baby grand piano, game table, and library loft. Breakfast and

after-dinner dessert are included in the rates. ✉ *Box 7172, Big Bear Lake 92315,* ☎ *909/866–0903. 12 rooms all with private baths. Outdoor hot tub. AE, D, MC, V.*

$$$–$$$$ 🏨 **Lake Arrowhead Resort.** The design and Old World graciousness of the lodge are reminiscent of the Alps. In addition to the lakeside luxury, guests receive membership privileges at the attached Village Bay Club and Spa (fee is $5). ✉ *27984 Hwy. 189, Arrowhead Village 92352,* ☎ *909/336–1511 or 800/800–6792. 261 rooms. Restaurant, coffee shop, lounge, pool, tennis courts, health club, beach. AE, D, DC, MC, V.*

$$–$$$$ 🏨 **Big Bear Inn.** This château-like inn's rooms are furnished with brass beds and antiques and other bric-a-brac from all over Europe. ✉ *Box 1814, Big Bear Lake 92315,* ☎ *909/866–3471 or, in CA, 800/232–7466. 80 rooms, 6 suites. Restaurant, lounge, pool, hot tub, meeting rooms. AE, D, DC, MC, V.*

$$–$$$ 🏨 **Gold Mountain Manor.** A restored mansion made of logs and dating back to the 1930s, the manor now serves as a historic bed-and-breakfast inn. It earned its fame when Clark Gable and Carole Lombard honeymooned in what is now the Clark Gable Room. The rooms are furnished with quilts and antiques. Rates include breakfast. There's no smoking. ✉ *Box 2027, Big Bear City 92314,* ☎ *909/585–6997. 7 rooms; 4 with private baths. AE, DC, MC, V.*

$$–$$$ 🏨 **Robinhood Inn and Lodge.** Near Snow Summit, this property has reasonably priced rooms (with or without kitchens) and condos. Each room (some with fireplaces and/or hot tubs) is decorated with simple country furniture and bright colors. All accommodations face a courtyard with an outdoor whirlpool spa. ✉ *Box 1881, Big Bear Lake 92315,* ☎ *909/866–4643. 21 rooms all with private bath. Restaurant, spa. AE, MC, V.*

Big Bear/Lake Arrowhead A to Z

VISITOR INFORMATION

Arrowhead Chamber of Commerce (☎ 909/337–3715). **Bear Lake Resort Association** (☎ 909/866–7000).

Catalina Island

When you approach Catalina Island through the typical early morning ocean fog, it's easy to wonder if perhaps there has been some mistake. What is a Mediterranean island doing 22 miles off the coast of California? Don't worry, you haven't left the Pacific—you've simply arrived at one of the Los Angeles area's most popular resorts.

Though lacking the sophistication of some European pleasure islands, Catalina does offer virtually unspoiled mountains, canyons, coves, and beaches. In fine weather, it draws thousands of southern California boaters, who tie up their vessels at moorings spotted in coves along the coast. The exceptionally clear water surrounding the island lures divers and snorkelers. Although there's not much sandy beach, sunbathing and water sports are also popular. The main town, Avalon, is a charming, old-fashioned beach community, where palm trees rim the main street and yachts bob in the crescent-shape bay.

Cruise ships sail into Avalon twice a week. The Catalina Island Company, which has a near-monopoly on sightseeing tours on the island beyond Avalon, has excellent service.

Discovered by Juan Rodriguez Cabrillo in 1542, the island has sheltered many dubious characters, from Russian fur trappers (seeking sea-otter skins), slave traders, pirates, and gold miners to bootleggers, filmmakers, and movie stars. In 1919, William Wrigley Jr., the chew-

Catalina Island

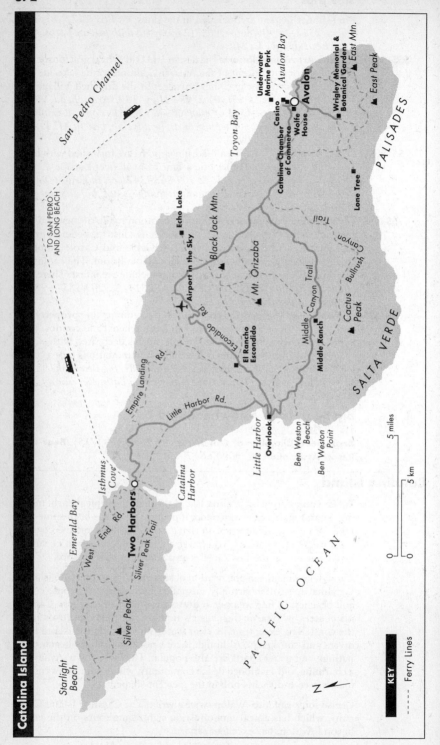

San Pedro Channel

TO SAN PEDRO
AND LONG BEACH

Underwater
Marine Park

Avalon Bay

Avalon

Wrigley Memorial &
Botanical Gardens

East Mtn.

Casino

East Peak

Catalina Chamber
of Commerce

Wolfe
House

Toyon Bay

PALISADES

Echo Lake

Black Jack Mtn.

Lone Tree

Airport in the Sky

Canyon Trail

Mt. Orizaba

Escondido Rd.

Middle Canyon Trail

Bullrush

Cactus
Peak

El Rancho
Escondido

Middle Ranch

SALTA VERDE

Empire Landing Rd.

Little Harbor Rd.

Little Harbor
Overlook

Ben Weston Beach

Isthmus Cove

Emerald Bay

Ben Weston Point

West End Rd.

Two Harbors

Catalina Harbor

Little Harbor

Silver Peak Trail

PACIFIC OCEAN

Silver Peak

Starlight Beach

5 miles

5 km

N

KEY

----- Ferry Lines

ing-gum magnate, purchased a controlling interest in the company developing the island. Wrigley had the island's most famous landmark, the Casino, built in 1929, and he made Catalina the site of spring training for his Chicago Cubs baseball team.

In 1975, the Santa Catalina Island Conservancy, a nonprofit foundation, acquired about 86 percent of the island to help preserve the natural resources here. Although Catalina can certainly be seen in a day, there are several inviting hotels that make it worth extending your stay for one or more nights. Between Memorial Day and Labor Day, be sure to make reservations *before* heading here. After Labor Day, rooms are much easier to find on shorter notice, rates drop dramatically, and a number of hotels offer packages that include transportation from the mainland and/or sightseeing tours.

Everyone walks in Avalon, where private autos are restricted. But taxis, trams, and shuttles can take you to hotels, attractions, and restaurants. If you are determined to have a set of wheels, you can rent a bicycle (about $6 per hour) or a golf cart ($35 per hour, cash only) along Crescent Avenue as you walk in from the dock. To hike into the interior of the island you will need a permit, available free from Doug Bombard Enterprises (⊠ Island Plaza, Avalon, ☎ 310/510–7265).

The **Catalina Island Company Visitors Center** (☎ 310/510–1520) is on the corner of Crescent and Catalina avenues, across from Green Pier. On the northwest point of Crescent Bay is the **Casino,** Avalon's most prominent landmark. The circular structure, considered one of the finest examples of art deco architecture anywhere, has many Spanish-influenced details. Its floors and murals show off brilliant blue and green Catalina tiles. "Casino" is the Italian word for "gathering place," and has nothing to do with gambling here. The **Catalina Island Museum,** on the lower level of the Casino, displays the history of the island (admission is $1). The **Avalon Theater** (☎ 310/510–0179) has a classic 1929 theater pipe organ.

Wolfe House was built in 1928 by noted architect Rudolph Schindler. Its terraced frame is carefully set into a steep site, affording extraordinary views. The house is a private residence, rarely open for public tours, but you can get a good view of it from the path below it and from the street. ⊠ *124 Chimes Tower Rd.*

The **Wrigley Memorial and Botanical Garden,** 2 miles south of Avalon via Avalon Canyon Road, displays only plants native to southern California, including several that grow only on Catalina Island: Catalina ironwood, wild tomato, and rare Catalina mahogany. The Wrigley family commissioned the garden as well as the monument, which has a grand staircase and a Spanish mausoleum that's decorated with colorful Catalina tile. Although the mausoleum was never used by the Wrigleys, who are instead buried in Los Angeles, the structure—and the view from it—are worth a look. ⊡ *Mausoleum $1.* ⊗ *Tram service from Avalon daily 8–5.*

The fairly primitive **Two Harbors** resort at Catalina's west end has long been a summer boating destination. Once inhabited by pirates and smugglers and later a movie location, it recalls the days before tourism was the island's major industry. Popular activities here include swimming, diving, boating, hiking, and beachcombing. **Catalina Safari Shuttle Bus** (☎ 310/510–2800) has regular bus service between Avalon and Two Harbors. **Catalina Express Coastal Shuttle** (☎ 310/519–1212) takes visitors on a 45-minute cruise from Avalon to Two Harbors.

Dining and Lodging

For price charts, *see* Dining *and* Lodging, *above.*

$–$$ ✕ **Cafe Prego.** This waterfront restaurant specializes in pasta, seafood, and steak. ✉ *603 Crescent Ave.,* ☎ *310/510–1218. AE, D, DC, MC, V.*

$ ✕ **Sand Trap.** Basically an expanded taco stand on the way to the Wrigley Memorial, the Sand Trap specializes in omelets, burritos, *tortas* (layered tortilla casseroles), and quesadillas. There's a shaded patio dining area and a tranquil golf-course view. ✉ *Falls Canyon,* ☎ *310/510–1349. No credit cards. No dinner.*

$$$$ 🏨 **Inn on Mt. Ada.** Occupying the former Wrigley Mansion, the island's most exclusive hotel affords all the comforts of a millionaire's mansion—and at millionaire's prices, beginning at $320 a night during the summer season. The six bedrooms are elegantly decorated, some with canopy beds and all with traditional furniture, and overstuffed chairs. The views across the water to the mainland are spectacular, and the service is discreet. All meals, beverages, snacks, and the use of a golf cart are complimentary. ✉ *Box 2560, Avalon 90704,* ☎ *310/510–2030. 6 rooms all with private bath. MC, V.*

$$$–$$$$ 🏨 **Hotel Vista del Mar.** This friendly hotel has bright rooms that open onto a central atrium. There are fireplaces, hot tubs, wet bars, contemporary rattan decor, and abundant greenery. Two suites have ocean views. Rates include Continental breakfast. ✉ *417 Crescent Ave., Avalon 90704,* ☎ *310/510–1452. 15 rooms all with private bath. AE, D, MC, V.*

$$$ 🏨 **Hotel Metropole and Marketplace.** This romantic hotel has a French Quarter ambience: It overlooks a flower-filled courtyard of restaurants and shops. Some guest rooms have balconies, ocean views, fireplaces, and hot tubs. Continental breakfast is served. A sundeck on the roof is popular. ✉ *225 Crescent Ave., Avalon 90704,* ☎ *310/510–1884 or 800/541–8528. 48 rooms all with private bath. AE, MC, V.*

$$–$$$ 🏨 **Pavilion Lodge.** Across the street from the beach, this motel has simply furnished but spacious rooms. There's a large, attractively appointed grassy courtyard in the center of the complex. Rates include Continental breakfast. ✉ *Box 737, Avalon 90704,* ☎ *800/851–0217. 72 rooms. AE, D, DC, MC, V.*

Catalina Island A to Z

ARRIVING AND DEPARTING

By Boat: Catalina Express (☎ 310/519–1212 or 800/995–4386) makes the hour-long run from Long Beach or San Pedro to Avalon and Two Harbors; round-trip fare from Long Beach and San Pedro is $35.

Service is also available from Newport Beach through **Catalina Passenger Service** (☎ 714/673–5245), which leaves from Balboa Pavilion at 9 AM, takes 75 minutes to reach the island, and costs $33. The return boat leaves Catalina at 4:30 PM. You can make arrangements to boat in one direction and fly in the other, but you must make reservations separately. Reservations are advised.

By Plane: Island Express (☎ 310/436–2012) flies hourly from San Pedro and Long Beach. The trip takes about 15 minutes and costs $60 one-way, $121 round-trip.

GUIDED TOURS

Santa Catalina Island Company (☎ 310/510–2000 or 800/428–2566) tours include a coastal cruise to Seal Rocks (summer only), the *Flying Fish* boat trip (evenings, summer only), the inland motor tour, the Skyline Drive, the Casino tour, the Avalon scenic tour, and a submerged glass-bottom-boat tour, where the vessel sinks 5 feet under. Reservations are highly recommended for the inland tours; the others are offered several times daily. Tours cost $7.50–$34.50. Docents of the **Catalina Conservancy** (☎ 310/510–1421) conduct walks of the area.

LOS ANGELES A TO Z

Arriving and Departing

By Bus
Greyhound Lines (✉ 208 E. 6th St., ☎ 800/231–2222).

By Car
Los Angeles is at the western terminus of I–10, a major east–west interstate highway that runs all the way east to Florida. I–15, angling down from Las Vegas, swings through the eastern communities around San Bernardino before heading on down to San Diego. I–5, which runs north–south through California, leads up to San Francisco and down to San Diego.

By Plane
The major gateways to Los Angeles are:

Los Angeles International Airport, commonly called LAX (☎ 310/646–5252) is serviced by over 85 major airlines, including **Air Canada, America West, American, British Airways, Continental, Delta, Japan Air Lines, Northwest, Skywest, Southwest, TWA, United,** and **USAir** (☞ Air Travel *in* Important Contacts A to Z for phone numbers). Departures are from the upper level and arrivals on the lower level.

Long Beach Airport (☎ 310/570–2600), at the southern tip of Los Angeles County, is served by Alaska, America West, Presidential Air, and Sunjet International airlines.

Burbank/Glendale/Pasadena Airport (☎ 818/840–8847) serves the San Fernando Valley with commuter, and some longer, flights. Alaska Airlines, American, America West, Skywest, Southwest, and United Airlines are represented.

For information about **John Wayne Orange County Airport** (☎ 714/252–5006) and **Ontario International Airport** (☎ 909/988–2700), *see* Orange County A to Z *in* Chapter 12.

BETWEEN THE AIRPORT AND DOWNTOWN
A taxi ride to downtown from LAX can take 30 minutes—if there is no traffic. But in Los Angeles, that's a big if. Visitors should request the flat fee ($30 at press time) to downtown or choose from the several ground transportation companies that offer set rates.

SuperShuttle (☎ 310/782–6600 or 213/775–6600) offers direct service between the airport and hotels. The trip to or from downtown hotels costs about $12. The seven-passenger vans operate 24 hours a day. In the airport, call 310/782–6600 or use the SuperShuttle courtesy phone in the luggage area; the van should arrive within 15 minutes. **Shuttle One** (✉ 9100 S. Sepulveda Blvd., No. 128, ☎ 310/670–6666) features door-to-door service and low rates ($10 per person from LAX to hotels in the Disneyland/Anaheim area). **Airport Coach** (☎ 714/938–8900 or 800/772–5299) provides regular service between LAX and the Pasadena and Anaheim areas.

The following limo companies charge a flat rate for airport service, ranging from $65 to $95: **Jackson Limousine** (☎ 213/734–9955), **A-1**

Los Angeles Freeways

West Coast Limousine (☎ 213/756–5466), and **Dav-El Livery** (☎ 310/550–0070).

Flyaway Service (☎ 818/994–5554) offers transportation between LAX and the central San Fernando Valley for $3.50. For the western San Fernando Valley and Ventura area, contact the **Great American Stage Lines** (☎ 800/287–8659). They charge $11–$21 one way.

MTA (☎ 213/626-4455) also offers limited airport service to all areas of greater LA; bus lines depart from bus docks directly across the street from airport parking lot C. Prices vary from $1.35 to $3.10; some routes require transfers. The best line to take to downtown is the direct express line 439, which costs $1.85 and takes 45–50 minutes.

By Train
Los Angeles can be reached by **Amtrak** (☎ 800/872–7245). The *Coast Starlight* travels from Seattle–Portland and Oakland–San Francisco down to Los Angeles. The *Sunset Limited* goes to Los Angeles from New Orleans, the *Texas Eagle* from San Antonio, and the *Southwest Chief* and the *Desert Wind* from Chicago. Trains terminate at **Union Station** (✉ 800 N. Alameda St.) in downtown Los Angeles.

Getting Around

By Bus
A bus ride on the **Metropolitan Transit Authority (MTA)** (☎ 213/626–4455) costs $1.35, with 25¢ for each transfer.

DASH (Downtown Area Short Hop) minibuses travel around the downtown area, stopping every two blocks or so. There are five different routes with pickups at five-minute intervals. You pay 25¢ every time you get on, no matter how far you go. DASH (☎ 213/626–4455) runs weekdays 6:30 AM–6 PM, Saturday 10 AM–5 PM.

By Car
In Los Angeles, it's not a question of whether wheels are a hindrance or a convenience: They're a necessity. If you plan to drive extensively, consider buying a *Thomas Guide,* which contains detailed maps of the entire county. Despite what you've heard, traffic is not always a major problem, especially if you avoid rush hours (7–9 AM and 3–7 PM). Seat belts must be worn by all passengers at all times.

More than 35 major companies and dozens of local rental companies serve a steady demand for cars at Los Angeles International Airport and various city locations. For a list of the major car-rental companies, *see* Car Rentals *in* Important Contacts A to Z.

If expense is no object, **Luxury Line** (✉ 300 S. La Cienega Blvd., West Hollywood, ☎ 310/657–2800) can rent you everything from sub compacts to Rolls-Royces, Jaguars, and Ferraris. The Marina del Rey branch of **Budget** (✉ 9775 Airport Blvd., ☎ 310/645–4500) rents upscale vehicles—Jaguars, Mercedes, BMWs, and Miata or Corvette convertibles.

By Limousine
Limousines come equipped with everything from a full bar and telephone to a hot tub and a double bed. Reputable companies include **Dav-El Livery** (☎ 310/550–0070), **First Class** (☎ 310/476–1960), and **World Limousine** (☎ 310/474–6622 or 818/887–7878).

By Subway
The **Metro Red Line** runs 4½ miles through downtown, from Union Station to MacArthur Park, making five stops. The fare is $1.35.

By Taxi

You probably won't be able to hail a cab on the street in Los Angeles. Instead, you should phone one of the many taxi companies. The metered rate is $1.60 per mile. Two of the more reputable companies are **Independent Cab Co.** (☎ 213/385–8294) and **United Independent Taxi** (☎ 213/653–5050).

By Train

The **Metrorail Blue Line** runs daily, 5 AM–10 PM, from downtown Los Angeles (✉ Flower and 7th Sts.) to Long Beach (✉ 1st St. and Long Beach Ave.), with 18 stops en route, most of them in Long Beach. The fare is $1.35 one way.

Contacts and Resources

Doctors

The **Los Angeles Medical Association Physicians Referral Service** (☎ 213/483–6122) is open weekdays 8:45–4:45. Most larger hospitals in Los Angeles have 24-hour emergency rooms. Two are **Cedar-Sinai Medical Center** (✉ 8700 Beverly Blvd., ☎ 310/855–5000) and **Queen of Angels Hollywood Presbyterian Medical Center** (✉ 1300 N. Vermont Ave., ☎ 213/413–3000).

Emergencies

Ambulance (☎ 911). **Police** (☎ 911).

Guided Tours

ORIENTATION TOURS

Los Angeles is so spread out and has such a wealth of sightseeing possibilities that an orientation bus tour may prove useful. The cost is between $25 and $40. All tours are fully narrated by a driver-guide. Reservations must be made in advance. Many hotels can book them for you.

L.A. Tours and Sightseeing (✉ 6333 W. 3rd St., at the Farmers' Market, ☎ 213/937–3361 or 800/286–8752) has a $38 tour covering various parts of the city, including downtown, Hollywood, and Beverly Hills. The company also operates tours to Disneyland, Universal Studios, Magic Mountain, beaches, and stars' homes.

Starline Tours of Hollywood (✉ 6541 Hollywood Blvd., Hollywood 90028, ☎ 800/959–3131 or 213/463–3333) picks up passengers from area hotels as well as around the corner from Mann's Chinese Theater (✉ 6925 Hollywood Blvd.). Universal Studios, Sea World, Knott's Berry Farm, stars' homes, Disneyland, and other attractions are on this company's agenda. Price range is from $26 to $68.

A more personalized look at the city can be had by planning a tour with **Casablanca Tours** (✉ Clarion Hollywood Roosevelt Hotel, 7000 Hollywood Blvd., Cabana 4, Hollywood 90028, ☎ 213/461–0156), which offers a four-hour insider's look at Hollywood and Beverly Hills. Tours are in minibuses with a maximum of 14 people, and prices are equivalent to the large bus tours—$35 to $68.

PERSONAL GUIDES

Elegant Tours for the Discriminating (☎ 310/472–4090) is a personalized sightseeing and shopping service for the Beverly Hills area. Joan Mansfield offers her extensive knowledge of Rodeo Drive to one, two, or three people at a time. Lunch is included.

L.A. Nighthawks (☎ 310/392–1500) will arrange your nightlife for you. For a rather hefty price, you'll get a limousine, a guide, and immediate entry into L.A.'s hottest nightspots.

SPECIAL-INTEREST TOURS

Advantage Tours and Charters (☎ 310/823–0321 or 213/933–1475) specializes in touring area museums, both large and small.

Grave Line Tours (☎ 213/469–4149) is a clever, off-the-beaten-track tour that digs up the dirt on notorious suicides and visits the scenes of various murders, scandals, and other crimes via a luxuriously renovated hearse. Tours, which begin daily at 9:30 AM and last 2½ hours (a 12:30 tour will be scheduled if the morning one is full, and sometimes a 3:30 PM tour leaves as well), are offered Tuesday–Sunday and cost $40 per person.

Trolleywood Tours (✉ 6715 Hollywood Blvd., Suite 103, Hollywood 90028, ☎ 213/469–8184 or 800/782–7287) has daily tours that takes you through downtown Hollywood and by the Hollywood Sign, past star's homes and through historical parts of town. Cost is $9–$27 per person, depending on the tour.

Visitors who want something dramatically different should check with Marlene Gordon of **The Next Stage** (✉ Box 35269, Los Angeles 90035, ☎ 213/939–2688). This innovative tour company takes 4–46 people, on buses or vans, in search of ethnic L.A., Victorian L.A., Underground L.A. (in which all the places visited are underground), as well as the Insomniac's Tour and Wacky L.A.

LA Today Custom Tours (✉ 14964 Camarosa Dr., Pacific Palisades 90272, ☎ 310/454–5730) has a wide selection of offbeat tours, some of which tie in with seasonal and cultural events, such as theater, museum exhibits, and the Rose Bowl. Groups range from 8 to 800, and prices are from $6 to $85.

WALKING TOURS

Walking is something that Angelenos don't do much of, except perhaps in Westwood and Beverly Hills and in parks throughout the city. But there is no better way to see things close up.

A self-guided walking tour of **Palisades Park** is detailed in a brochure available at the park's Visitors Center (✉ 1400 Ocean Blvd., Santa Monica).

The **Los Angeles Conservancy** (☎ 213/623–CITY) offers low-cost walking tours of the downtown area. Each Saturday at 10 AM one of six different tours leaves from the Olive Street entrance of the Biltmore Hotel. Cost is $5 per person. Make reservations because group size is limited.

Late-Night Pharmacies

The **Kaiser Bellflower Pharmacy** (✉ 9400 E. Rosecrans Ave., Bellflower, ☎ 310/461–4213) is open around the clock. The **Horton and Converse** pharmacies (✉ 6625 Van Nuys Blvd., Van Nuys, ☎ 818/782–6251; 11600 Wilshire Blvd., W. Los Angeles, ☎ 310/478–0801) are open until 2 AM.

Visitor Information

Los Angeles Convention and Visitors Bureau (✉ 633 W. 5th St., Suite 6000, 90071, ☎ 213/624–7300). **California Visitor Information Center** (✉ 685 S. Figueroa St., ☎ 213/689–8822).

12 Orange County

Including Disneyland, Newport Beach, Laguna, and Dana Point

Orange County is one of California's top tourist destinations, and once you've arrived here it doesn't take long to see why. The county has made tourism its number one industry, attracting nearly 40 million visitors annually. Two theme parks, Disneyland and Knott's Berry Farm, entice millions on their own. But Orange County is more than just Anaheim: It also has lively beaches, upscale shopping, some fine museums, and San Juan Capistrano, home of the annual swallow migration.

ORANGE COUNTY IS SUCH A MAGNET for conventioneers and tourists that it's easy to forget that people actually live here, too—many of

Updated by
Bonnie Steele

them in high-priced Mediterranean-style suburbs along the 24-mile-long coastline. Orange County residents shop in the classy malls that lure visitors as well. Like visitors, locals can be found at the beach sunning themselves or waiting for the next big wave. Locals even dine and stay at the luxurious oceanfront resorts that perch on the edge of the Pacific. Served by convenient airports and only an hour's drive from Los Angeles, Orange County is both a destination on its own and a very popular excursion from Los Angeles.

Pleasures and Pastimes

Dining

Orange County has long been a fast-food haven, but you can also find fancy French, inspired Italian, and, as elsewhere in California, plenty of fresh seafood.

CATEGORY	COST*
$$$$	over $35
$$$	$25–$35
$$	$15–$25
$	under $15

per person for a three-course meal, excluding drinks, service, and 7¼% tax

Lodging

The Ritz-Carlton Laguna Niguel, one of the world's top-rated hotels, is Orange County's headline property. Anaheim has some stellar hostelries, and a general upgrading of the area surrounding Disneyland has increased the number of reliable inexpensive and moderately priced chain motels. Prices listed here are based on summer rates. Winter rates, especially near Disneyland, tend to be somewhat less. It pays to shop around for promotional and weekend rates.

CATEGORY	COST*
$$$$	over $100
$$$	$75–$100
$$	$50–$75
$	under $50

All prices are for a double room; local hotel taxes vary.

Scenic Drives

Driving the seaside edge of Orange County on the Pacific Coast Highway is an eye-opening experience. Here the incongruities of southern California are revealed—the powerful, healing ocean vistas and the scars of commercial exploitation; the simple beach life and the tacky bric-a-brac of the tourist trail. Oil rigs line the road from Long Beach south to Huntington Beach, and then suddenly give way to pristine stretches of water and dramatic hillsides, many untouched because the land is owned by the government. For a mountain tour, drive the Santiago Canyon Road, which winds through the Cleveland National Forest in the Santa Ana Mountains. Tucked away in these mountains are Modjeska Canyon, Irvine Lake, and Silverado Canyon, of silver-mining lore. In addition to the beautiful scenery, this route has views of some of the most spectacular homes in Orange County.

Surfing

There are 50 surf breaks along the Orange County coastline, with wave action ranging from beginner to expert. If you are not an expert, you can get a sense of the action on a boogie board at one of the beginners' beaches. Surfing is permitted at most beaches year-round, except at Huntington State Beach, Salt Creek Beach Park, Aliso County Beach, Capistrano Beach, Sunset Beach, and Newport Beach, where it is permitted only in summer. "The Wedge" at Newport Beach, one of the most famous surfing spots in the world, is known for its steep, punishing shore break. Don't miss the spectacle of surfers, who appear tiny in the midst of the waves, flying through this treacherous place.

Exploring Orange County

Before visiting Orange County, select a primary attraction and then plan excursions to other sights. If Disneyland is the highlight, you'll probably want to organize your activities around the tourist attractions that fill the central county and take excursions to selected coastal spots. The reverse is true if you're planning to hang out on the beach. In that case, select a coastal headquarters and make forays to the Magic Kingdom. If you're traveling with children, you could easily devote several days to the theme parks: a day or two for Disneyland, a day for Knott's Berry Farm, and perhaps a day driving to some of the area's lesser-known attractions.

Great Itineraries
Numbers in the text and in the margin correspond to numbers on the Orange County map.

IF YOU HAVE 1 DAY
You're going to **Disneyland** ①!

IF YOU HAVE 3 DAYS
You're still going to **Disneyland** ①, but on day two, head to the coast and explore **Newport Harbor.** Have lunch at Ruby's then take a 90-minute harbor cruise. On day three, visit **Laguna Beach** and **Dana Point,** then either hang out on the beach or head back north to Costa Mesa, where you can browse through **South Coast Plaza** ⑫, one of the world's largest shopping centers, have dinner in the mall, and then enjoy an evening show at the nearby South Coast Repertory Theater or the Orange County Performing Arts Center.

When to Tour Orange County
Orange County is a year-round destination, but you can beat the crowds and the heat by coming during spring and fall, which are in many ways more pleasant. Smart parents give kids their Disney fix during this period.

INLAND ORANGE COUNTY

Anaheim

26 mi east of Los Angeles on I–5.

Orange County's largest city has Disneyland, the West's capital of family entertainment, as its centerpiece. The Anaheim Convention Center lures almost as many conventioneers as Disneyland attracts children, and for many visitors, a trip to the Magic Kingdom may be the bonus of an Anaheim meeting.

★ When Disney carved **Disneyland** out of the orange groves in 1955, it consisted of four lands and fewer than 20 major attractions radiating from his idealized American Main Street. Much has changed in the intervening years, including the expansion of the park to include four more lands and 40 more attractions. But Main Street retains its turn-of-the-century charm, and it's in ever-sharper contrast with the world just outside the park gates.

Each of Disney's lands has its own theme rides. Stepping through the doors of Sleeping Beauty's castle into **Fantasyland** can be a dream come true for children. Mickey Mouse may even be there to greet them. Once inside, they can join Peter Pan's Flight; go down the rabbit hole with Alice in Wonderland; take an aerial spin with Dumbo the Flying Elephant; take Mr. Toad's Wild Ride; spin around in giant cups at the Mad Tea Party; swoosh through the Matterhorn; or visit It's a Small World, where figures of children from 100 countries worldwide sing of unity and peace.

Visitors to **Frontierland** can take a cruise on the steamboat *Mark Twain* or the sailing ship *Columbia* and experience the sights and sounds of the spectacular Rivers of America. Kids of every age enjoy rafting to Tom Sawyer's Island for an hour or so of climbing and exploring. Some visitors to **Adventureland** have taken the Jungle Cruise so many times that they know the patter offered up by the operators by heart. Also here is Indiana Jones Adventure and the chance to explore the ruins of an ancient excavation site to look for the lost Temple of the Forbidden Eye.

The twisting streets of **New Orleans Square** offer interesting browsing and shopping, strolling Dixieland musicians, and the ever-popular Pirates of the Caribbean ride. The Haunted Mansion, populated by 999 holographic ghosts, is nearby. Theme shops purvey hats, perfume, Mardi Gras merchandise, and gourmet items. The gallery here has original Disney art.

The animated bears in **Critter Country** may charm kids of all ages, but it's **Splash Mountain,** the steepest, wettest Disney adventure, that keeps them coming back for more.

In late 1997, Disneyland plans to close down **Tomorrowland,** including Submarine Voyage, Space Mountain, and Star Tours, to rebuild a bigger and better futuristic play area.

Mickey's Toontown is a pint-size playground. Kids can climb up a rope ladder on the *Miss Daisy,* Donald's Boat, talk to a mailbox, and walk through Mickey's House and meet Mickey, all the while feeling that they're inside a cartoon. Bring your camera; there are photo opportunities everywhere. The Roger Rabbit Car Toon Spin, the largest and most unusual black-light ride in Disneyland history, always packs them in.

A stroll along **Main Street** evokes a small-town America, circa 1900, that never existed except in the popular imagination and fiction and films. Interconnected shops and restaurants line both sides of the street. The Emporium, the largest and most comprehensive of the shops, sells Disney products and magic tricks, hobby and sports memorabilia, clothing, and photo supplies.

Disneyland is big and, during the summer season, crowded. Planning a strategy for your visit will help you get the most out of it. If you can, pick a rainy midweek day; most Disney attractions are indoors. Arrive early; the box office opens a half hour before the park's scheduled opening time. Go immediately to the most popular attractions: Pirates of the Caribbean, Haunted Mansion, It's a Small World, and Splash Mountain. Mickey's Toontown tends to be most crowded in the mornings. Lines for rides will also be shorter during the evening Fantasmic! show, parades, and fireworks display (usually around 9:30), as well as near opening or closing times. Just the same, even on a slow day expect to wait in line for 15 minutes or so.

384

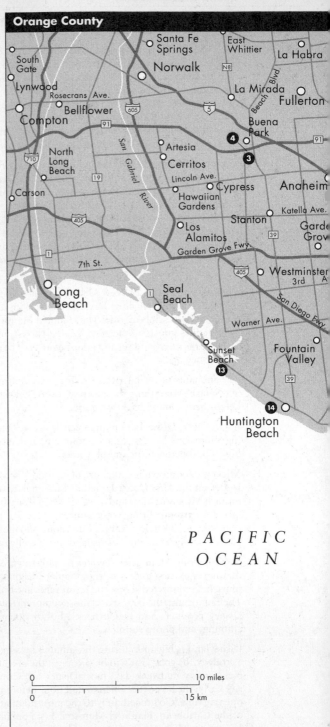

Orange County

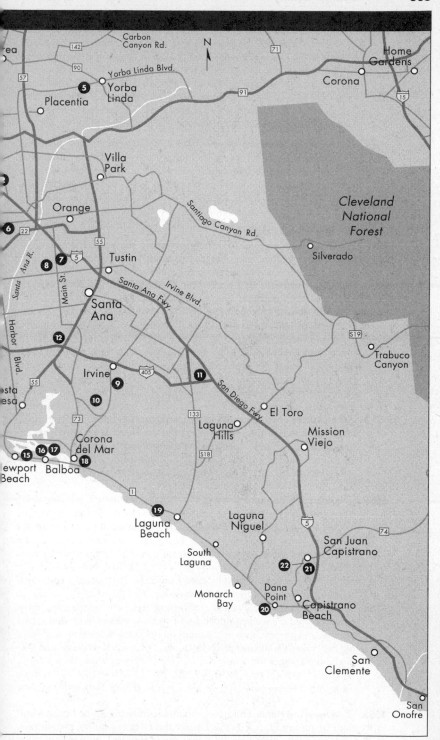

Fast-food spots abound, but you can also get healthier fare, such as fruit, pasta, and frozen yogurt. When shopping, remember that there are lockers just off Main Street in which you can store purchases and thereby avoid lugging bundles around all day. If your feet get tired, you can move from one area of the park to another on the train or monorail or even in a horse-drawn carriage. ✉ *1313 Harbor Blvd.,* ☎ *714/999–4565.* ✇ *$33.* ◷ *June–mid-Sept., Sun.–Fri. 9 AM–midnight, Sat. 9 AM–1 AM; mid-Sept.–May, weekdays 10–6, Sat. 9 AM–midnight, Sun. 9 AM–10 PM. Hrs and prices subject to change.*

❷ The **Anaheim Museum,** housed in a 1908 Carnegie Library building, documents the city's history, including the original wine-producing colony. Changing exhibits include painting, sculpture, women's history, and hobbies. A hands-on children's gallery keeps the kids entertained. ✉ *241 S. Anaheim Blvd.,* ☎ *714/778–3301.* ✇ *$1.50.* ◷ *Wed.–Fri. 10–4, Sat. noon–4; closed holidays.*

Dining and Lodging

$$$$ ✕ **JW's.** This is an elegant French surprise in the heart of convention-
★ busy Anaheim. The menu changes frequently to spotlight fresh seafood, game, and produce. The extensive wine list is priced reasonably. ✉ *Anaheim Marriott, 700 W. Convention Way,* ☎ *714/750–8000. AE, D, DC, MC, V. Closed Sun. No lunch. Valet parking.*

$$$–$$$$ ✕ **White House.** This mansion, built in 1909, bears a striking resemblance to its namesake. Several small dining rooms have crisp linens, candles, flowers, and in some cases, fireplaces. The northern Italian menu (with French influences) includes pastas, scaloppine, and a large seafood selection. Vegetarian entrées are also prepared. A four-course prix-fixe menu is available until 6:30 for $27.50 per person. ✉ *887 S. Anaheim Blvd.,* ☎ *714/772–1381. AE, DC, MC, V. No lunch weekends.*

$$–$$$ ✕ **The Catch.** This very reliable restaurant across the street from Anaheim Stadium is popular with sports fans, who enjoy its sports-bar atmosphere and friendly service. The menu features hearty portions of steak, seafood, and salads. ✉ *1929 S. State College Blvd., Anaheim,* ☎ *714/634–1829. AE, DC, MC, V. No lunch weekends.*

$$$$ 🛏 **Anaheim Hilton and Towers.** This hotel is virtually a self-contained city—complete with its own post office. The lobby is dominated by a bright, airy atrium, and guest rooms are decorated in pinks and greens with light-wood furniture. Because it caters to conventioneers, it can be busy and noisy, with long lines at restaurants. ✉ *777 Convention Way, 92802,* ☎ *714/750–4321 or 800/222–9923,* ℻ *714/740–4460. 1,576 rooms. 4 restaurants, 3 lounges, pool, health club ($10 charge), concierge, business services, children's programs. AE, D, DC, MC, V.*

$$$$ 🛏 **Anaheim Marriott.** Rooms at this busy hotel are compact but have balconies and are well equipped for business travelers, with desks, two phones, and modem hookups. Rooms on the north side have good views of Disneyland's summer fireworks shows. Discounted weekend and Disneyland packages are available. ✉ *700 W. Convention Way, 92802,* ☎ *714/750–8000 or 800/228–9290,* ℻ *714/750–9100. 979 rooms, 54 suites. 3 restaurants, 2 lounges, 2 pools, health club, video games, concierge. AE, D, DC, MC, V.*

$$$$ 🛏 **Disneyland Hotel.** This hotel, which is connected to the Magic King-
★ dom by monorail, carries the Disney theme in the lobby, restaurants, entertainment, shops, and spacious guest rooms. Consisting of three towers surrounding lakes, streams, tumbling waterfalls, and lush landscaping, the hotel gleams with brass and marble. On most days, guests staying at the hotel receive early admission to the park. In Goofy's

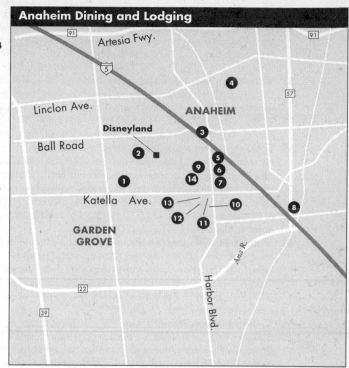
Anaheim Dining and Lodging

Kitchen, kids can breakfast with their favorite Disney characters. There are marina and park views, and rooms in the Bonita tower overlook the Fantasy Waters, a nighttime Disney-theme lighted fountain and music display. ⊠ *1150 W. Cerritos Ave., 92802,* ☎ *714/778–6600,* FAX *714/956–6597. 1,136 rooms. 6 restaurants, 5 lounges, 3 pools, spa, health club, beach, concierge floor, business services. AE, DC, MC, V.*

$$$ ⊞ **Holiday Inn Maingate.** This establishment is one block south of Disneyland. Kids under 20 stay free when accompanied by their parents. Children under 13 eat free in the hotel restaurant when dining with a parent. ⊠ *1850 S. Harbor Blvd., 92802,* ☎ *714/750–2801 or 800/624–6855,* FAX *714/971–4754. 310 rooms, 3 suites. Dining room, lounge, pool, video games. AE, D, DC, MC, V.*

$$$ ⊞ **Holiday Inn at the Park.** This salmon-colored, Mediterranean-style building at the edge of Disneyland was designed for families visiting the Magic Kingdom. It has pleasant, if functional, rooms with southwestern decor, some including separate sitting areas. Shuttle service is available to nearby attractions, including Knott's Berry Farm, Movieland Wax Museum, and Medieval Times. Children stay free with their parents. ⊠ *1221 S. Harbor Blvd., 92805,* ☎ *714/758–0900 or 800/545–7275,* FAX *714/533–1804. 252 rooms, 2 suites. Restaurant, lounge, pool, sauna, spa, video games. AE, D, DC, MC, V.*

$$$ ⊞ **Inn at the Park Hotel.** This hotel, a longtime favorite of conventioneers, has spacious rooms. All have balconies, and those in the tower have good views of Disneyland's summer fireworks shows. The hotel also has one of the most attractive pool areas around. The refreshingly bright lobby is inviting, with a tropical feel. ⊠ *1855 S. Harbor Blvd., 92802,* ☎ *714/750–1811 or 800/421–6662,* FAX *714/971–3626. 500 rooms. Restaurant, coffee shop, lounge, pool, spa, exercise room, video games. AE, D, DC, MC, V.*

$$ **Candy Cane Inn.** This very attractive motel has lush landscaping and spacious, clean rooms, just steps from the entrance to Disneyland's parking lot. Minirefrigerators and microwaves are available; Continental breakfast is included. ⊠ *1747 S. Harbor Blvd., 92803,* ☎ *714/774–5284 or 800/345–7057,* FAX *714/772–5462. 172 rooms. Pool. AE, D, MC, V.*

$$ **Castle Inn and Suites.** This colorful, cutesy motel across the street from Disneyland has been done up to resemble a castle, with faux stone trim, turrets, and towers. Children under 18 stay free. ⊠ *1734 S. Harbor Blvd., 92802,* ☎ *714/774–8111 or 800/521–5653,* FAX *714/956–4736. 197 rooms. Refrigerators, pool, wading pool. AE, D, DC, MC, V.*

$$ **Quality Hotel Maingate.** A large, open, red-tile lobby is filled with mirrors, plants, and flowers. Minisuites, which are larger than the basic rooms and include a sofa with a pull-out bed and a refrigerator, are ideal for families on a budget. The hotel is close to Disneyland and the Convention Center. ⊠ *616 Convention Way, 92802,* ☎ *714/750–3131 or 800/231–6215,* FAX *714/750–9027. 186 rooms, 98 suites. 2 restaurants, lounge, pool. AE, D, DC, MC, V.*

$$ **Ramada Maingate/Anaheim.** Clean and reliable, this chain hotel has guest rooms done in tones of mauve, and room service from McDonald's. The property is across the street from Disneyland and provides free shuttle service to the park. ⊠ *1460 S. Harbor Blvd., 92802,* ☎ *714/772–6777 or 800/447–4048,* FAX *714/999–1727. 465 rooms. Restaurant, pool. AE, D, DC, MC, V.*

$–$$ **Best Western Stovall's Inn.** Very well-kept, this motel stacks up well against area hotels in a similar price range. Nice touches include the topiary gardens, room decor in soft desert colors, and a friendly staff. Nintendo rentals are available. Ask about discounts if you're staying several nights. ⊠ *1110 W. Katella Ave. 92802,* ☎ *714/778–1880 or 800/854–8175,* FAX *714/778–3805. 290 rooms. Restaurant, lounge, 2 pools. D, MC, V.*

$–$$ **Desert Palm Inn and Suites.** This budget hotel midway between Disneyland and the Convention Center has large suites (some with balconies) that can accommodate as many as eight people, and every room has a microwave and a refrigerator. The brightly colored decor is attractive, if functional, and the staff is friendly. Book well in advance. ⊠ *631 W. Katella Ave., 92802,* ☎ *714/535–1133 or 800/635–5423,* FAX *714/491–7409. 103 rooms and suites. Pool, sauna, exercise room, laundry service. D, MC, V.*

Nightlife and the Arts

BARS AND NIGHTCLUBS

Cowboy Boogie Co. (⊠ 1721 S. Manchester, ☎ 714/956–1410) has three dance floors and four bars; a country band plays on Sunday night, and music is piped in the rest of the week. Wednesday nights, when the club includes more than country music on its playlist, the place is packed. Country line-dancing lessons are offered during the week.

Outdoor Activities and Sports

Anaheim Hills Public Country Club (⊠ 6501 Nohl Ranch Rd., Anaheim Hills, ☎ 714/748–8900) is an 18-hole, 71 par course. **H.G. Dad Miller** (⊠ 430 N. Gilbert Rd., Anaheim, ☎ 714/774–8055) is an 18-hole, 71 par course. For information about other public golf courses in Anaheim, phone the **Southern California Public Links Golf Association** (☎ 714/994–4747). Anaheim has 50 public tennis courts; phone the Parks and Recreation Department for information (☎ 714/254–5191).

Buena Park

5 mi north of Anaheim on I–5.

★ ⓒ ❸ **Knott's Berry Farm** doesn't match Disneyland's high-tech brand of fantasy, but rather offers a dose of reality. The farm has been rooted in the community since 1934, when Cordelia Knott began serving chicken dinners on her wedding china to supplement the family's income. The dinners and the boysenberry pies proved more profitable than husband Walter's berry farm, so the family moved first into the restaurant business and then into the entertainment business. The park, with its Old West theme, is now a 150-acre complex with 100-plus rides and attractions, 60 eating places, and 60 shops.

Many of the buildings in **Ghost Town** were relocated here from their original mining-town sites. You can stroll down the street, stop and chat with the blacksmith, pan for gold, crack open a geode, ride in an authentic 1880s passenger train, or take the Gold Mine ride and descend into a replica of a working gold mine. A real treasure here is the antique Dentzel carousel, with a menagerie of animals. **Camp Snoopy** is a kid-size High Sierra wonderland where Snoopy and his Peanuts-gang friends hang out. Tall trees frame **Wild Water Wilderness,** where you can ride white water in an inner tube in Big Foot Rapids and commune with the native peoples of the Northwest coast in the spooky Mystery Lodge.

Thrill rides are placed throughout the park: the **Boomerang** roller coaster; **X-K-1,** a living version of a video game; **Kingdom of the Dinosaurs;** and **Montezooma's Revenge,** a roller coaster that goes from 0 to 55 mph in less than five seconds. The park's **Jaguar!, The Streaking Big Cat of Roller Coasters,** simulates the motions of a cat stalking its prey, twisting, spiraling, speeding up and slowing down as it takes guests on its stomach-dropping course.

Knott's also has entertainment throughout the day, with shows scheduled in Ghost Town, the Bird Cage Theater, and the Good Time Theater; occasionally stars appear here. ⊠ *8039 Beach Blvd.,* ☎ *714/220–5200.* ☞ *$28.50.* ☉ *June–mid-Sept., daily 9 AM–midnight; mid-Sept.–May, weekdays 10–6, Sat. 10–10, Sun. 10–7; park closes during inclement weather.*

❹ **Movieland Wax Museum.** Visitors will find more than 70 years of movie magic immortalized in 400 wax sculptures of Hollywood's greatest stars including Michael Jackson, John Wayne, Marilyn Monroe, Geena Davis, Bruce and Brandon Lee, and George Burns. Figures are displayed in a maze of realistic sets from movies such as *Gone with the Wind, Star Trek, The Wizard of Oz,* and *Home Alone.* The Chamber of Horrors is designed to scare the daylights out of you. You can buy a combination ticket ($16.90) that also allows you admission to Ripley's Believe It or Not, the somewhat schlocky chain attraction across the street. ⊠ *7711 Beach Blvd.,* ☎ *714/522–1155.* ☞ *$12.95.* ☉ *Daily 9–7.*

Dining and Lodging

$ ✕ **Mrs. Knott's Chicken Dinner Restaurant.** Mrs. Knott's fried-chicken dinners and boysenberry pies are what made Knott's Berry Farm famous. Her restaurant serves breakfast, lunch, and dinner. ⊠ *Knott's California MarketPlace, 8039 Beach Blvd., Buena Park,* ☎ *827-1776. AE, D, DC, MC, V.*

$$–$$$ 🏨 **Buena Park Hotel and Convention Center.** Rooms at this hotel adjacent to Knott's Berry Farm are done in earthtones, with modern, light-oak furniture. The hotel provides complimentary shuttle service to Disneyland. A special Family Value Vacation package is offered. ⊠ *7675*

Crescent Ave., 90620, ☎ *714/995–1111 or 800/854–8792,* FAX *714/828–8590. 314 rooms, 36 suites. 2 restaurants, lounge, pool, Club floor. AE, DC, MC, V.*

Nightlife and the Arts

La Mirada Theater for the Performing Arts (✉ 14900 La Mirada Blvd., ☎ 714/994–6310), a few miles northwest of Buena Park in La Mirada, presents Broadway shows, concerts, and film series.

Ⓒ **Medieval Times Dinner and Tournament** (✉ 7662 Beach Blvd., ☎ 714/521–4740 or 800/899–6600) takes guests back to the days of knights and ladies. Knights on horseback compete in medieval games, sword fighting, and jousting. Dinner, all of which is eaten with your hands, includes appetizers, whole roasted chicken or spareribs, soup, pastry, and beverages such as mead.

Ⓒ **Wild Bill's Wild West Extravaganza** (✉ 7600 Beach Blvd., ☎ 714/522–6414) is a two-hour action-packed Old West show featuring foot-stomping musical numbers, cowboys, Indians, can-can dancers, trick-rope artists, knife throwers, and audience participation in sing-alongs. An all-you-can-eat dinner, which includes homestyle country biscuits, soup, salad, chicken and ribs, baked potatoes, and apple pie with ice cream, is served during the show.

Fullerton

8 mi north of Buena Park on I–5 to Hwy. 72.

Fullerton is the educational center of Orange County, with Cal State Fullerton, Southwestern University of Law and two other houses of higher learning. It's an old railroading and citrus-processing town.

Dining

$$$$ ✕ **The Cellar.** The name tells the story here: an intimate subterranean dining room with a beamed ceiling and stone walls, wine racks, and casks. Appropriately, the list of wines from Europe and California is among the best in the West. The bill of fare is classic French cuisine that has been lightened for the California palate. In addition to serving fine cuisine, the elegant restaurant is noted for its excellent service. ✉ *305 N. Harbor Blvd.,* ☎ *714/525–5682. Reservations essential. AE, DC, MC, V. Closed Sun.–Mon. No lunch.*

$$ ✕ **Mulberry Street Ristorante.** The movers and shakers in north Orange County gather regularly at this friendly, noisy, watering hole designed to resemble a turn-of-the-century New York eatery. The kitchen serves up northern Italian fare—prodigious portions of pasta, seafood, chicken, and veal. ✉ *114 W. Wilshire Ave.,* ☎ *714/525–1056. AE, DC, MC, V. No lunch Sun.*

$ ✕ **Angelo's & Vinci's Cafe Ristorante.** The show's the thing at this funky Italian eatery created by actor-choreographer Steven Peck. Entertaining surroundings include giant knights in shining armor, tableaux of Italian street scenes, an altar with old family photos and cherubs from Sicily, and a pair of aerialist puppets and a tightrope walker overhead. Locally popular for huge portions of Sicilian-style pasta and pizza, this is a busy, noisy place. ✉ *550 N. Harbor Blvd.,* ☎ *714/879–4022. AE, MC, V.*

Yorba Linda and Brea

7 mi north of Anaheim, Hwy. 57 to Yorba Linda exit.

❺ The **Richard Nixon Presidential Library and Birthplace** is the final resting place of the 37th president and his wife Pat. Displays illustrate the checkered career of Nixon, the only president forced to resign from office. Visitors can listen to Nixon's Checkers speech or to the so-called smoking-gun tape from the Watergate days, among other recorded material. Within the main building is a small but interesting gift shop that contains presidential souvenir items. ⊠ *18001 Yorba Linda Blvd.,* ☎ *714/993–3393.* ⚑ *$5.95.* ☉ *Mon.–Sat. 10–5, Sun. 11–5.*

Dining

$$$$ ✕ **La Vie en Rose.** A reproduction of a Norman farmhouse with a large
★ turret, this restaurant across from the Brea Mall serves French food—seafood, lamb, veal, and melt-in-your-mouth pastries. ⊠ *240 S. State College Blvd. (take Hwy. 90 west from Yorba Linda and head north on State College Blvd.), Brea,* ☎ *714/529–8333. AE, DC, MC, V. Closed Sun.*

Garden Grove and Orange

South of Anaheim, I–5 to Hwy. 22.

❻ The **Crystal Cathedral** is the domain of television evangelist Robert Schuller. The sparkling glass structure resembles a four-pointed star, with more than 10,000 panes of glass covering a weblike steel truss to form translucent walls. ⊠ *12141 Lewis St., Garden Grove,* ☎ *714/971–4013; reservations for Christmas and Easter productions, 714/544–5679.* ⚑ *Donation requested.* ☉ *Guided tours Mon.–Sat. 9–3:30; call for schedule.*

Dining and Lodging

$$ ✕ **La Brasserie.** It doesn't *look* like a typical brasserie, but the varied French cuisine befits the name over the door. One dining room in the multilevel house is done as an attractive, cozy library. There's also an inviting bar-lounge. The specialty here is veal chops. ⊠ *202 S. Main St., Orange,* ☎ *714/978–6161. AE, MC, V. Closed Sun. No lunch Sat.*

$$$–$$$$ ▦ **Doubletree Hotel Orange County.** This contemporary, 20-story hotel has a dramatic lobby of marble and granite with waterfalls cascading down the walls. Guest rooms are large and come equipped with a small conference table. The hotel is near the shopping center called The City, UCI Medical Center, Anaheim Stadium, Arrowhead Pond, and the Anaheim Convention Center. Discount rates are available for summer weekends. The hotel's restaurant ($–$$) specializes in steak and seafood.⊠ *100 The City Dr., Orange, 92668,* ☎ *714/634–4500 or 800/222–8733,* ℻ *714/978–3839. 435 rooms, 19 suites. 2 restaurants, lounge, pool, 2 tennis courts, health club, concierge. AE, D, DC, MC, V.*

Santa Ana

12 mi south of Anaheim, I–5 to Hwy. 55.

The Orange County seat is undergoing a dramatic restoration of its downtown area. Gleaming new government buildings meld with turn-of-the-century structures to give a sense of where the county came from and where it is going.

❼ The **Bowers Museum of Cultural Art,** once a small cultural-arts gallery, is now the largest museum in Orange County, having tripled in size after a $12 million expansion and restoration of its original 1936 Spanish-style buildings. Permanent galleries display sculpture, costumes, and artifacts from Oceania; sculpture from west and central Africa; Pacific Northwest wood carvings; dazzling beadwork of the Plains cultures; and California basketry. Adjacent to the museum, Bowers Kidseum provides children with a hands-on version of the main museum, with interactive exhibits geared toward kids ages 6–12, as well as classes, storytelling, and arts and crafts workshops. The Topaz Cafe prepares

an ethnically eclectic menu. ⊠ *2002 N. Main St.,* ☎ *714/567–3600.*
⌨ *$4.50.* ☉ *Tues.–Sun. 10–4, Thurs. 10–9.*

⑧ The **Fiesta Marketplace** in downtown Santa Ana affords a glimpse into
contemporary Hispanic culture. The best time to visit is on the weekend, when the place takes on a lively fiesta atmosphere. You'll find bargain Western wear, imports from Mexico and Guatemala, and authentic
tacos and quesadillas.

Dining

$$ ✕ **National Sports Bar.** Appetizers, burgers, pasta, and chicken highlight
the menu at this casual sports bar and restaurant. After dinner, wander
into the bar area to watch a game, play a round of pool, or enjoy an icy
glass of beer from the wide selection of domestic and imported brews
on tap. ⊠ *101 Sand Pointe,* ☎ *714/979–0900. AE, D, DC, MC, V.*

Shopping

Main Place. (⊠ 2800 North Main St., ☎ 714/547–7800) has Robin-
sons-May, Macy's, and Nordstrom as its anchors. Although many of
the 190 shops are upscale, the warehouse-style mall is busy and noisy.

Irvine

6 mi from Santa Ana, south on I–5 to east on I–405.

⑨ The **Irvine Museum** displays a collection of California impressionist paint-
ings, dated 1890 to 1930, that give viewers an idea of the pristine land-
scape that preceded housing developments and freeways. The collection
was assembled by Joan Irvine Smith, granddaughter of James Irvine,
who once owned one-quarter of what is now Orange County. ⊠ *Tower
17, 18881 Von Karman Ave., 12th floor,* ☎ *714/476–2565.* ⌨ *Free.*
☉ *Tues.–Sat. 11–5.*

⑩ The **University of California at Irvine** was established on 1,000 acres of
rolling ranch land donated by the Irvine family in the mid-1950s. The
Bren Events Center Fine Art Gallery (☎ 714/824–6610) on campus,
free and open Tuesday–Friday 1–5, sponsors exhibitions of 20th-cen-
tury art. Tree lovers will be enthralled by the campus; it's an arbore-
tum with more than 11,000 trees from all over the world. ⊠ *San Diego
Fwy. (I–405) to Jamboree Rd., west to Campus Dr. S.*

⑪ The **Entertainment Center at Irvine Spectrum,** one of Orange County's
newest attractions, is a 32-acre complex anchored by the 21-screen Ed-
wards Cinema, which has an IMAX 3-D theater. Other highlights in-
clude Sega City's virtual reality arcade, Out-Takes digital photo studio,
shops, and several restaurants. Parking is a nightmare here, so be pre-
pared to search for a spot. ⊠ *At intersection of San Diego Fwy. (I–405),
Santa Ana Fwy. (I–5), and Laguna Fwy. (I–133).*

Dining and Lodging

$$$ ✕ **Chanteclair.** This Franco-Italian country house is a tasteful retreat
amid an island of modern high-rise office buildings. French Riv-
iera–type cuisine is served, and the chateaubriand for two and rack of
lamb are recommended. ⊠ *18912 MacArthur Blvd.,* ☎ *714/752–8001.
Jacket required. AE, D, DC, MC, V. No lunch Sat.*

$$ ✕ **Mitsuba.** Excellent Chinese food and sushi are offered buffet-style
in what resembles a formal eating hall in Taiwan. There's organiza-
tion amid the chaos as everyone gets served in short order. ⊠ *14110
Culver Dr.,* ☎ *714/551–1688. MC, V.*

$$ ✕ **Prego.** An attractive approximation of a Tuscan villa, with an outdoor patio, this Prego does best with spit-roasted meats and charcoal-
grilled fresh fish. California and Italian wines are reasonably priced.

✉ *18420 Von Karman Ave.,* ☎ *714/553–1333. AE, DC, MC, V. No lunch weekends. Valet parking.*

$$$$ 🏨 **Hyatt Regency Irvine.** Offering all the amenities of a first-class resort, this hotel is elegantly decorated in contemporary colors, and the marble lobby is flanked by glass-enclosed elevators. Soft cottons make guest furnishings comfortable and appealing. Special golf packages at nearby Tustin Ranch and Pelican Hills are available. There is a complimentary shuttle to local shopping centers. The lower weekend rates are a great deal. ✉ *17900 Jamboree Rd., 92714,* ☎ *714/975–1234 or 800/233–1234,* FAX *714/852–1574. 526 rooms, 10 suites. 2 restaurants, 2 lounges, pool, 4 tennis courts, health club, bicycles, concierge, business services. AE, D, DC, MC, V.*

$$$ 🏨 **Atrium Hotel.** This hotel, reminiscent of one you'd discover along the Mediterranean, is across the street from John Wayne airport and convenient to most area offices. The staff caters to business travelers, with rooms that have large work areas, coffeemakers, and two phones. All rooms have private balcony, some overlooking the pool and others looking out at the gardens. Special rates are available for weekend guests. ✉ *18700 MacArthur Blvd., 92715,* ☎ *714/833–2770,* FAX *714/757–1228. 209 rooms. 2 restaurants, lounge, pool, health club. AE, D, DC, MC, V.*

$$$ 🏨 **Irvine Marriott.** This contemporary hotel towers over Koll Business Center, making it convenient for business travelers. Despite its size, the hotel has an intimate feel. Oriental-style rooms all have small balconies. Weekend discounts and packages are usually available. ✉ *1800 Von Karman Ave., 92715,* ☎ *714/553–0100,* FAX *714/261–7059. 489 rooms, 24 suites. 2 restaurants, sports bar, indoor-outdoor pool, massage, spa, 4 tennis courts, health club, concierge, business services. AE, D, DC, MC, V.*

Nightlife and the Arts

NIGHTCLUB

Metropolis (✉ 4255 Campus Dr., ☎ 714/725–0300) is the hottest ticket in Orange County, with iron-and-gilt decor, pool tables, a sushi bar, restaurant, entertainment, dancing, and theme nights throughout the week; admission is $5.

PERFORMING ARTS

The **Irvine Meadows Amphitheater** (✉ 8808 Irvine Center Dr., ☎ 714/855–4515 or 714/855–6111) is a 15,000-seat open-air venue that presents musical events from May through October. Both reserved and lawn seating are available.

Costa Mesa

5 mi from Irvine on I–405 west to Hwy. 55 south.

⑫ **South Coast Plaza** is the most amazing of all the Orange County malls, and the largest. It's actually two enclosed shopping centers, complete with greenery and waterfalls, plus South Coast Village, an open-air collection of boutiques and restaurants, with a movie house that shows art and foreign films. The three shopping areas are connected by a free tram. Of the two enclosed malls, the older, larger section, anchored by Nordstrom and Macy's, has an old-fashioned merry-go-round and more uspcale shops, such as Rizzoli Bookstore, Gucci, J. Crew, Calvin Klein, Gianni Versace, Burberry's, Armani, F.A.O. Schwarz, Saks Fifth Avenue, and Mark Cross. Kids will want to browse through the Disney and Sesame Street stores. The newer and less popular Crystal Court has a Robinsons-May department store as its main attraction. ✉ *3333 Bristol St.,* ☎ *714/435–2000.*

NEED A
BREAK?

Planet Hollywood (✉ 1641 W. Sunflower St., ☎ 714/434–7827), across the street from South Coast Plaza, recalls the 1930s and '40s with changing displays of movie memorabilia, giant TV screens showing clips of old movies, and loud rock music. The fare here has a '50s diner flair, with hamburgers topping the menu.

Dining and Lodging

$$–$$$ ✕ **Bangkok IV.** Despite its shopping-mall location—it occupies an indoor
  ★ patio on the third floor of the Crystal Court—this restaurant serves artistically prepared Thai cuisine. The decor is dramatic, with stylish flower arrangements and black-and-white appointments. Menu items designated as hot can be prepared with milder spices upon request. ✉ *3333 Bear St.,* ☎ *714/540–7661. Reservations essential. AE, DC, MC, V.*

$$ ✕ **Mandarin Gourmet.** Owner Michael Chang provides what the critics and locals consider the best Chinese cuisine in the area. His specialties include a crisp-yet-juicy Peking duck, cashew chicken, and, seemingly everyone's favorite, mu-shu pork. ✉ *1500 Adams Ave.,* ☎ *714/540–1937. AE, DC, MC, V.*

$ ✕ **Wolfgang Puck Cafe.** The famous chef has tried here to create an institutional-style café, complete with high noise level. The menu lists Puck's famous pizzas, chicken salad, and pastas; the most popular item may be the half chicken with huge portions of garlic mashed potatoes. ✉ *South Coast Plaza, 3333 Bristol St.,* ☎ *714/546–9653. Reservations not accepted. MC, V.*

$$$$ ▥ **Westin South Coast Plaza.** Rooms at this modern high-rise hotel in the heart of Orange County's shopping-entertainment complex are done in soft colors, mostly cream and beige, and the public areas are bright and pleasant. Fitness fans will enjoy the health club in the vicinity. The hotel is a short walk from 60 restaurants, theaters, and (across the Unity Bridge) the South Coast Plaza shopping mall. Discounts are sometimes available on weekends. ✉ *686 Anton Blvd., 92626,* ☎ *714/540–2500 or 800/228–3000,* ℻ *714/662–6695. 373 rooms, 17 suites. Restaurant, lounge, pool, 2 tennis courts, shuffleboard, volleyball, concierge floor. AE, D, DC, MC, V.*

$$–$$$ ▥ **Country Side Inn and Suites.** A taste of Europe can be found in these hotel rooms surrounding a flower-filled cobblestone courtyard. The accommodations here provide a good lodging value in this high-priced area. Rooms and lobbies are nicely decorated in Queen Anne–style furnishings with floral wall coverings. Breakfast and evening cocktails and hors d'oeuvres are included in rates. Ask about discounts on room rates, which can reduce the price to well below this category. ✉ *325 S. Bristol St., 92626,* ☎ *714/549–0300 or 800/322–9992,* ℻ *714/662–0828. 150 rooms and 150 suites. Restaurant, lounge, 2 pools, exercise room. DC, MC, V.*

Nightlife and the Arts

PERFORMING ARTS

Orange County Performing Arts Center (✉ 600 Town Center Dr., ☎ 714/556–2787) contains a dramatic 3,000-seat facility for opera, ballet, and symphony, hosting such notables as the Los Angeles Philharmonic, the Pacific Symphony, and the New York City Opera.

South Coast Repertory Theater (✉ 655 Town Center Dr., Costa Mesa, ☎ 714/957–4033) is an acclaimed regional theater complex with two stages that present both traditional and new works. A resident group of actors forms the nucleus of this facility's innovative productions. The California Scenario, a 1.6-acre sculpture garden designed by Isamu Noguchi, is a block from the theater complex.

THE COAST

Coastal Orange County is dotted with small beach towns and world-class resorts. You can catch a monster wave with the bronzed local kids, get a glimpse of some rich-and-famous lifestyles, and take a walk through the shoreline's natural treasures. Although there is bus service along the coast road, it's best to explore the area by car.

Scenic Pacific Coast Highway (Highway 1) runs along Orange County's coast. Wherever you pull over, a public beach is actually only steps away. At the north end of the county are Huntington Beach followed by Newport, Balboa, Laguna, and Dana Point. Laguna, one of the most popular stops, feels almost like the Mediterranean with its sandy cliffside beaches and community of artists.

Huntington Beach

4 mi west of Costa Mesa, Hwy. 55 to Hwy. 1 north.

For years Huntington Beach was little more than a string of tacky surf shops, T-shirt emporiums, and hot-dog stands across Pacific Coast Highway from the beach. In the early '90s, however, a face-lift began, aimed at transforming the funky surf town into a shining resort area. The city's three beaches—Bolsa Chica State Beach, Huntington City Beach, and Huntington State Beach—stretch across nine miles of Pacific coastline, some of it containing the hippest surfing in southern California. The 8½-mile **Beach Trail**—used by bicyclers, joggers, walkers, and rollerbladers—meanders from Huntington Beach to Newport Beach.

★ ⑬ **Bolsa Chica Ecological Reserve** (☎ 714/897–7003), just east of the Bolsa Chica State Beach, is a great place if you're interested in wildlife. A walk-through will reward you with a chance to see a restored 300-acre salt marsh that is home to 315 species of birds, plus other animals and plants. You can see many of them along the 1½-mile loop trail that meanders through the reserve. The walk is especially delightful in winter, when you're likely to see great blue herons, snowy and great egrets, common loons, and other migrating birds.

⑭ The very long (1,853 feet) **Huntington Pier** is the centerpiece of Huntington City Beach. The Pierside Pavilion, across Pacific Coast Highway from the pier, contains shops, a restaurant, a nightclub, and a theater complex. The **International Surfing Museum** (⊠ 411 Olive Ave., ☎ 714/960–3483) open from Wednesday through Sunday, noon to 5 (admission $2), has an extensive collection of surfing memorabilia.

Lodging

$$$$ 🏨 **Waterfront Hilton.** This oceanfront hotel rises 12 stories above the surf. The Mediterranean-style resort is decorated in soft mauves, beiges, and greens and offers a panoramic view from many rooms. Ocean-view suites have balconies and wet bars. ⊠ *21100 Pacific Coast Hwy., 92648,* ☎ *714/960–7873 or 800/822–8773,* FAX *714/960–2642. 270 rooms, 24 suites. 2 restaurants, lounge, pool, 2 tennis courts, health club, bike and beach-equipment rentals, concierge, children's programs. AE, DC, MC, V.*

Outside Activities and Sports

RUNNING

The **Santa Ana Riverbed Trail** hugs the Santa Ana River for 20.6 miles between the Pacific Coast Highway at Huntington State Beach and Imperial Highway in Yorba Linda; there are entrances, as well as rest rooms and drinking fountains, at all crossings.

TENNIS

Edison Community Center (✉ 21377 Magnolia St., ☎ 714/960–8870) has four courts available on a first-come, first-served basis in the daytime. **Murdy Community Center** (✉ 7000 Norma Dr., ☎ 714/960–8895) has four courts, also available first-come, first-served during the day. Both facilities accept reservations for play after 5 PM; both charge $2 an hour.

Newport Beach

South of Huntington Beach on Hwy. 1.

Newport Beach has a dual personality: It's best known as an upscale beach town, with its island-dotted yacht harbor and a history of such illustrious residents as John Wayne, author Joseph Wambaugh, and Watergate scandal figure Bob Haldeman. And then there's inland Newport Beach, just southwest of John Wayne airport, a business and commercial hub with a major shopping center and a clutch of high-rise office buildings and hotels.

Set within the Newport Beach harbor are eight small islands, including Balboa and Lido. The homes lining the shore may seem modest, but this is some of the most expensive real estate in the world.

★ ⑮ **Newport Harbor,** which shelters nearly 10,000 small boats, will seduce even those who don't own a yacht or qualify as seaside high society. You can explore the charming avenues and surrounding alleys. To see Newport Harbor from the water, take a one-hour gondola cruise operated by Gondola Company of Newport (✉ 3404 Via Oporto, #201, ☎ 714/675–1212).

Newport Pier, which juts out into the ocean near 20th Street, is the focal point of Newport's beach community. Street parking is difficult here, so grab the first space you find and be prepared to walk. A stroll along Ocean Front reveals much of the character of this place. On weekday mornings head for the beach near the pier, where you're likely to encounter the dory fishermen hawking their predawn catches, as they've done for generations. On weekends the walk is alive with kids (of all ages) on skates, skateboards, and bikes weaving among the strolling pedestrians and whizzing past fast-food joints, swimsuit shops, and bars.

⑯ The Balboa Pavilion, perched on the bay side of the **Balboa Peninsula,** is a historic Victorian. Built in 1905 as a bath- and boathouse, it hosted big-band dances in the 1940s. Today it houses a restaurant and shops and is a departure point for harbor and whale-watching cruises. Adjacent to the pavilion is the three-car ferry, which connects the peninsula to Balboa Island. Several blocks surrounding the pavilion support restaurants, beachside shops, and a small Fun Zone—a local hangout with a Ferris wheel, video games, rides, and arcades.

NEED A
BREAK?

Take a stroll to the end of the Balboa Pier and grab a burger and shake at **Ruby's** (☎ 714/675–7829). You can eat indoors at this '50s-style diner or order your meal at the take-out window and enjoy your food outside on a bench overlooking the ocean. Be warned, however, that seagulls tend to swoop down in search of leftover fries.

⑰ The **Newport Harbor Art Museum** is recognized for its impressive collection of abstract expressionist works and cutting-edge contemporary works by California artists. ✉ *850 San Clemente Dr.,* ☎ *714/759–1122.* ⊞ *$4.* ⊙ *Tues.–Sat. 10–5, Sun. noon–5.*

LIDO ISLE – An island in Newport Harbor, the location of many elegant homes, provides some insight into the upper-crust Orange County mindset. A number of grassy areas offer great harbor views; each is marked "Private Community Park." ⊠ *Hwy. 55 to PCH in Newport Beach, turn left at signal on Via Lido and follow onto island.*

Dining and Lodging

$$$$ ✕ **Antoine.** This candlelit dining room is made for romance and quiet
★ conversation. It serves the best French cuisine of any hotel in southern California; the fare is nouvelle, but is neither skimpy nor gimmicky. ⊠ *Sutton Place Hotel, 4500 MacArthur Blvd.,* ☎ *714/476–2001. Jacket and tie. AE, DC, MC, V. Closed Sun.–Mon. No lunch.*

$$$$ ✕ **Pascal.** Although it's in a shopping center, you'll think that you're
★ in St-Tropez once you step inside this bright and cheerful bistro. And, after one taste of Pascal Olhat's light Provençale cuisine, you'll swear you're in the south of France. Try the sea bass with thyme, the rack of lamb, and the lemon tart. ⊠ *1000 N. Bristol St.,* ☎ *714/752–0107. AE, DC, V. Closed Sun.*

$$$$ ✕ **The Ritz.** This is one of the most comfortable southern California restaurants—the bar area has red leather booths, etched-glass mirrors, and polished brass trim. Don't pass up the smorgasbord appetizer, the roast Bavarian duck, or the rack of lamb from the spit. ⊠ *880 Newport Center Dr.,* ☎ *714/720–1800. AE, DC, MC, V. No lunch weekends.*

$$ ✕ **The Cannery.** The building once was a cannery, and it has wonderful wharf-side views. The seafood entrées are good, and the sandwiches at lunch are satisfying, but the location and lazy atmosphere are the real draw. ⊠ *3010 Lafayette Ave.,* ☎ *714/675–5777. AE, D, DC, MC, V.*

$$ ✕ **Le Biarritz.** Newport Beach natives have a deep affection for this restaurant, with its country-French decor, hanging greenery, and garden room. There's food to match the mood: a veal-and-pheasant pâté, seafood crepes, boned duckling and wild rice, sautéed pheasant with raspberries, and warm apple tart for dessert. ⊠ *414 N. Old Newport Blvd.,* ☎ *714/645–6700. AE, D, DC, MC, V. Closed Sun. No lunch Sat.*

$$ ✕ **Marrakesh.** In a Casbah setting straight out of a Hope-and-Crosby road movie, diners become part of the scene—you eat with your fingers while sitting on the floor or lolling on a hassock. Chicken *b'stilla* (traditional chicken dish served over rice), rabbit couscous, and skewered pieces of marinated lamb are the best of the Moroccan dishes. It's fun. ⊠ *1100 Pacific Coast Hwy.,* ☎ *714/645–8384. AE, DC, MC, V. No lunch.*

$ ✕ **Crab Cooker.** If you don't mind waiting in line, this shanty of a place serves fresh fish grilled over mesquite at low-low prices. The clam chowder, crusty Fisherman's bread, and coleslaw are good, too. A fresh fish take-out market attracts locals. ⊠ *2200 Newport Blvd.,* ☎ *714/673–0100. Reservations not accepted. No credit cards.*

$ ✕ **El Torito Grill.** Southwestern cooking incorporating south-of-the-bor-
★ der specialties is the attraction here. The just-baked tortillas with a green-pepper salsa, the turkey molé enchilada, and the miniature blue-corn duck tamales are good choices. The bar serves hand-shaken margaritas and 20 brands of tequila. ⊠ *Fashion Island, 941 Newport Center Dr.,* ☎ *714/640–2875. AE, D, DC, MC, V.*

$ ✕ **Hard Rock Cafe Newport Beach.** You can pick up your official Hard Rock Cafe T-shirt here after munching a hamburger or a sandwich. ⊠ *451 Newport Center Dr.,* ☎ *714/640–8844. Reservations not accepted. AE, DC, MC, V.*

$$$$ 🏨 **Four Seasons Hotel.** This 20-story hotel lives up to its chain's repu-
★   tation. Marble and antiques fill the airy lobby; all rooms—decorated with
beiges, peaches, and southwestern touches—have spectacular views, private bars, and original art on the walls. Children are given special attention, with kid-friendly amenities including balloons, cookies and
milk, and a small game book. ⊠ *690 Newport Center Dr., 92660,* ☎
714/759–0808 or 800/332–3442, 𝖥𝖠𝖷 *714/759–0568. 285 rooms. 2 restaurants, lounge, pool, massage, sauna, steam room, 2 tennis courts, health
club, mountain bikes, concierge, business center. AE, D, DC, MC, V.*

$$$$ 🏨 **Sutton Place Hotel.** The eye-catching ziggurat design is the trademark of this ultramodern hotel in Koll Center. The decor is southern
Californian, with striking pastel accents. Luxuriously appointed rooms
have minibars and built-in hair dryers. This is also the home of Antoine, one of the best restaurants in Orange County. Special weekend
theater and Pageant of the Masters packages are available. There is a
complimentary shuttle to the airport and local shopping malls. ⊠
4500 MacArthur Blvd., 92660, ☎ *714/476–2001 or 800/243–4141,*
𝖥𝖠𝖷 *714/476–0153. 435 rooms. 2 restaurants, lounge, pool, 2 tennis
courts, health club, concierge, business services. AE, D, DC, MC, V.*

$$$ 🏨 **Newport Beach Marriott Hotel and Tennis Club.** Overlooking New-
port Harbor, this Mediterranean-style hotel attracts a large foreign clien-
tele. Arriving guests' first view of the hotel's interior is the distinctive
fountain surrounded by a high, plant-filled atrium. Rooms, done in laven-
der, cream, and teal, are housed in two towers. They each have bal-
conies or patios, and overlook lush gardens or the Pacific. The hotel
is across the street from Fashion Island shopping center. ⊠ *900 New-
port Center Dr., 92660,* ☎ *714/640–4000 or 800/228–9290,* 𝖥𝖠𝖷
*714/640–5055. 570 rooms, 8 suites. 2 restaurants, lounge, 2 pools,
sauna, golf, 8 tennis courts, health club, concierge, business services.
AE, D, DC, MC, V.*

$$$ 🏨 **Sheraton Newport Beach.** Bamboo trees and palms decorate the lobby
in this southern California beach-style hotel. Vibrant teals, mauves, and
peaches make up the color scheme. The hotel is convenient to John Wayne
airport. ⊠ *4545 MacArthur Blvd., 92660,* ☎ *714/833–0570,* 𝖥𝖠𝖷
*714/833–3927. 335 rooms. Restaurant, lounge, pool, 2 tennis courts,
health club. AE, D, DC, MC, V.*

Nightlife

The Cannery (⊠ 3010 Lafayette Ave., ☎ 714/675–5777) has live entertainment (☞ Dining, *above*). **Studio Cafe** (⊠ 100 Main St., Balboa
Peninsula, ☎ 714/675–7760) presents jazz musicians every night and
is famous for its potent blue drinks. **Tibbie's Music Hall** (⊠ 4647
MacArthur Blvd., ☎ 714/252–0834) serves up comedy shows along
with prime rib, fish, and chicken Thursday through Sunday.

Outdoor Activities and Sports

BOAT RENTALS

Balboa Boat Rentals (☎ 714/673–7200) has sailboats ($25 an hour)
and small motorboats ($30). You must have a driver's license, and some
knowledge of boating is helpful; rented boats are not allowed out of
the bay. Ocean boats are available for hire at $65 an hour.

BOAT TOURS

The Cannery restaurant (☎ 714/675–5777) operates weekend brunch
cruises of Newport Harbor for $31 for adults, $22 for children. Cruises
last two hours and depart at 10 AM and 1:30 PM.

Catalina Passenger Service (☎ 714/673–5245) at the Balboa Pavilion conducts a full selection of sightseeing tours and fishing excursions
to Catalina and around Newport Harbor. The 45-minute narrated tour

of Newport Harbor, at $6, is the least expensive. A 90-minute tour is $8. Whale-watching cruises (Dec.–Mar.) are especially enjoyable.

Hornblower Dining Yachts (☎ 714/646–0155) operates Saturday dinner harbor cruises with dancing for $56.95; Sunday brunch cruises are $39.45. Reservations are required.

FISHING

Davey's Locker (☎ 714/673–1434) in the Balboa Pavilion is known for sportfishing. The cost is $35 per person per day; a half-day costs $22. Or, for $35 a half-day you can rent a small motorboat to fish in the harbor. Full-day fishing trips, which run from 11–5, are $55. A complete tackle shop is also available.

Shopping

Fashion Island is an upscale shopping mall anchored by department stores such as Robinsons–May, Neiman Marcus, and Macy's. Atrium Court, an enclosed Mediterranean-style section, has a gourmet food court with exotic coffee drinks, a tropical fruit-juice bar, and more along these lines. ⊠ *Newport Center Dr., between Jamboree and MacArthur Blvds., off Pacific Coast Hwy.,* ☎ *714/721–2022.*

Corona del Mar

South of Newport Beach on Hwy. 1.

Corona del Mar is a small jewel of a town with an exceptional beach—actually, two beaches, Little Corona and Big Corona, which are separated by a cliff. You can walk clear out onto the bay on a rough-and-tumble rock jetty; there are also tide pools and caves to explore. The town itself stretches only a few blocks along Pacific Coast Highway, but some of the fanciest stores in the county are here. Beach facilities include fire pits, volleyball courts, food, rest rooms, and parking.

⑱ **Sherman Library and Gardens,** a botanical garden and library specializing in Southwest flora and fauna, offers a diversion from sun and sand. You can wander among cactus gardens, rose gardens, a wheelchair-height touch-and-smell garden, and a tropical conservatory. ⊠ *2647 E. Coast Hwy., Corona del Mar,* ☎ *714/673–2261.* ⊡ *$2, free Mon.* ☉ *Gardens daily 10:30–4.*

En Route **Crystal Cove State Park** (☎ 714/494–3539), midway between Corona del Mar and Laguna, is a hidden treasure: 3½ miles of unspoiled beach with some of the best tide pooling in southern California. Here you can see starfish, crabs, and other live sealife on the rocks. On the inland side of PCH are 2,400 acres of backcountry, perfect for hiking and mountain biking. Docents conduct nature walks on Saturday morning. Parking costs $6 per car.

Laguna Beach

South of Newport Beach on Hwy. 1.

Laguna Beach has been called SoHo by the Sea, which is at least partly right. It is an artists' colony that, during the 1950s and '60s, attracted the beat, hip, and far-out, but it is also a colony of conservative wealth. The two camps coexist in relative harmony, with Art prevailing in the congested village, and Wealth entrenched in the canyons and on the hillsides surrounding the town.

A **statue of Eiler Larsen,** Laguna's town greeter, who for years stood at the edge of town saying hello and goodbye to visitors, serves as a source for local nostalgia. In recent years a man who calls himself Number One Archer has assumed the role of greeter, waving to tourists from a spot at the corner of Pacific Coast Highway and Forest Avenue.

Walk along the town's main street, Pacific Coast Highway, or along side streets, such as Forest or Ocean, and you'll pass gallery after gallery with art ranging from billowy seascapes to neon sculpture and kinetic structures. In addition, you'll find crafts, high-fashion, beachwear, and jewelry shops.

The **Pageant of the Masters** (☎ 714/494–1147 or 800/487–3378) is Laguna's most impressive event, a blending of life and art. Live models and carefully orchestrated backgrounds are arranged in striking mimicry of famous paintings.

⑲ The **Laguna Art Museum** has historical and contemporary California art. Special exhibits change quarterly.⊠ *307 Cliff Dr.,* ☎ *714/494–6531.* ⌚ *$5.* ☉ *Tues.–Sun. 11–5.*

Dining and Lodging

$$$–$$$$ ✕ **Five Feet.** The first of a number of Chinese-European restaurants in
★ Orange County, Five Feet continues to delight diners with its innovative culinary approaches. You'll find delicate pot stickers, wontons stuffed with goat cheese, and a salad featuring sashimi, plus steak and fresh fish. The decor showcases the work of local artists. ⊠ *328 Gleneyre St.,* ☎ *714/497–4955. AE, D, DC, MC, V. No lunch Sat.–Thurs.*

$$ ✕ **Beach House.** A Laguna tradition, the Beach House has a water view from every table. Fresh fish, lobster, and steamed clams are the drawing cards. It's open for breakfast, lunch, and dinner. ⊠ *619 Sleepy Hollow La.,* ☎ *714/494–9707. AE, MC, V.*

$$ ✕ **Kachina.** The creation of chef David Wilhelm, this tiny restaurant housed beneath an art gallery draws locals and visitors with contemporary southwestern-style cuisine and a boisterous atmosphere. Even hearty eaters can make a meal by selecting several items from the appetizer portion of the menu. Kachina is a good place for weekend brunch. ⊠ *222 Forest Ave.,* ☎ *714/497–5546. AE, DC, MC, V.*

$ ✕ **Tortilla Flats.** This hacienda-style restaurant specializes in first-rate chile rellenos, carne Tampiquena, soft-shell tacos, and beef or chicken fajitas. There's also a wide selection of Mexican tequilas and beers. Sunday brunch is served. ⊠ *1740 S. Coast Hwy.,* ☎ *714/494–6588. AE, MC, V.*

$$$$ 🏨 **Surf and Sand Hotel.** Laguna's largest hotel is right on the beach. The rooms are decorated in soft sand colors and bleached wood and have wooden shutters and private balconies. The popular lounge on the top floor is a great place to end your evening, with a piano bar and a welcoming fireplace. Weekend packages are available. ⊠ *1555 S. Coast Hwy., 92651,* ☎ *714/497–4477 or 800/524–8621,* ℻ *714/494–2897. 153 rooms, 4 suites. 2 restaurants, 2 lounges, pool, beach, concierge. AE, DC, MC, V.*

$$$–$$$$ 🏨 **Inn at Laguna Beach.** This oceanfront Mediterranean-style inn is close
★ to Main Beach yet far enough away to be secluded. Set on a bluff overlooking the ocean, the inn has luxurious amenities and many rooms with views. ⊠ *211 N. Coast Hwy., 92651,* ☎ *714/497–9722 or 800/544–4479,* ℻ *714/497–9972. 70 rooms. Pool, free parking. AE, D, DC, MC, V.*

$$$ 🏨 **Eiler's Inn.** A light-filled courtyard is the focal point of this European-style B&B. Rooms are on the small side, but each is unique and decorated with antiques, which are constantly being updated by the owners. Breakfast is served outdoors, and in the afternoon wine and cheese are laid out, often accompanied by live music. A sundeck in back has an ocean view. ⊠ *741 S. Coast Hwy., 92651,* ☎ *714/494–3004,* ℻ *714/497–2215. 12 rooms all with private baths. AE, MC, V.*

$$$ ⛌ **Hotel Laguna.** This downtown landmark is the oldest hotel in Laguna. Lobby windows look out onto manicured gardens, and a patio restaurant overlooks the ocean and the hotel's own private beach. Complimentary wine and cheese are offered to guests in the afternoon. ⊠ *425 S. Coast Hwy., 92651, ☎ 714/494–1151 or 800/524–2927,* FAX *714/497–2163. 63 rooms. 2 restaurants, lounge. AE, D, DC, MC, V.*

Nightlife and the Arts

BARS AND NIGHTCLUBS

The **Sandpiper** (⊠ 1183 S. Pacific Coast Hwy., ☎ 714/494–4694) is a tiny hole-in-the-wall dancing joint that attracts an eclectic crowd. The **White House** (⊠ 340 S. Pacific Coast Hwy., ☎ 714/494–8088), a two-story neighborhood club on the main strip, has nightly entertainment that runs the gamut from rock to Motown, reggae to pop.

Outdoor Activities and Sports

BEACHES

Laguna Beach's **Main Beach Park,** at the end of Broadway at Pacific Coast Highway, has sand volleyball, two half-basketball courts, children's play equipment, picnic areas, rest rooms, showers, and road parking. **Woods Cove** (⊠ Pacific Coast Hwy., at Diamond St.) is especially quiet during the week. Big rock formations hide lurking crabs. As you climb the steps to leave, you'll see a stunning English-style mansion that was once the home of Bette Davis. In South Laguna, **Aliso County Park** (☎ 714/661–7013) is a recreation area with a pier for fishing, barbecue pits, parking, food, and rest rooms.

EQUIPMENT

To rent a bicycle, try **Rainbow Bicycles** (☎ 714/494–5806). **Hobie Sports** (☎ 714/497–3304) rents surfboards and boogie boards.

TENNIS

Six metered courts can be found at Laguna Beach High School. Six courts are available at Alta Laguna Park on a first-come, first-served basis. For directions, call 714/497–0716.

Shopping

If you can look past the inflatable palm trees, unimaginative T-shirts, and other tourist novelties, you'll discover some good browsing in Laguna Beach's art galleries, antiques shops, one-of-a-kind craft boutiques, and custom jewelry stores. Arty Forest Avenue and nearby thoroughfares are good starting points. **Georgeo's Art Glass and Jewelry** (⊠ 269 Forest Ave., ☎ 714/497–0907) contains a large selection of etched and blown-glass bowls, vases, glassware, and jewelry. **Art Center Gallery** (⊠ 266 Forest Ave., ☎ 714/376–7596) features works of local artists. **Susan Drake Gallery** (⊠ 220 Forest Ave., ☎ 714/494–3610) specializes in southwestern art.

Dana Point

South of Laguna Beach on Hwy. 1.

Dana Point is Orange County's newest aquatic playground, a small-boat marina tucked into a dramatic natural harbor surrounded by high bluffs.

Dana Point Harbor was first described more than 100 years ago by its namesake Richard Henry Dana in his book *Two Years Before the Mast.* The marina has docks for small boats and marine-oriented shops and restaurants. Recent development includes a hillside park with bike and walking trails, hotels, small shopping centers, and a collection of eateries. Dana Wharf Sportfishing (☎ 714/496–5794) has charters year-round and runs whale-watching excursions in winter, and the community sponsors an annual whale festival in late February.

☙ ❷⓪ Programs and excursions of the **Orange County Marine Institute** are designed to entertain and educate participants about the ocean. Two tanks contain touchable sea creatures, and there is a complete skeleton of a gray whale on view. Anchored near the institute is *The Pilgrim,* a full-size replica of the square-rigged vessel on which Richard Henry Dana sailed. Tours of *The Pilgrim* are given Sunday from 11 to 2:30. *Sea Explorer* provides public cruises on weekends. ⊠ *24200 Dana Point Harbor Dr.,* ☎ *714/496–2274.* ☉ *Daily 10–4:30.*

OFF THE
BEATEN PATH

THE NAUTICAL HERITAGE MUSEUM – Here you'll find a very fine collection of ship models, paintings, 18th- and 19th-century seafaring documents, and navigation instruments. ⊠ *24532 Del Prado Ave., Dana Point,* ☎ *714/661-1001.* ☜ *Free.* ☉ *Weekdays 10–4.*

Dining and Lodging

$$$ ✗ **Dining Room.** Long considered one of the best restaurants in Orange County, the Dining Room offers an innovative and very flexible prix-fixe menu featuring contemporary Mediterranean specialties: lobster risotto, grilled tuna chop, veal shank Oslo bubo, almond soufflé. You can choose two to five courses; the price depends on the number of courses. This is an elegant room with subdued lighting, crystal chandeliers, original paintings, and antiques. ⊠ *Ritz-Carlton, Laguna Niguel Hotel, 1 Ritz-Carlton Dr., Dana Point,* ☎ *714/240–2000. Reservations essential. Jacket required. AE, D, DC, MC, V. No lunch.*

$$–$$$ ✗ **Watercolors.** This cheerful dining room provides a cliff-top view of the harbor and an equally enjoyable Continental/California menu that includes low-calorie choices. Try the baked breast of pheasant, roast rabbit, grilled swordfish, and either the Caesar or poached spinach salad. ⊠ *Marriott's Laguna Cliffs Resort, 25135 Park Lantern,* ☎ *714/661–5000. AE, D, DC, MC, V. Valet parking.*

$$ ✗ **Delaney's Restaurant.** Fresh seafood from nearby San Diego's fishing fleet is what this place is all about. Your choice is prepared as simply as possible. If you have to wait for a table, pass the time at the popular oyster bar, which is staffed only on the weekends. The bar area attracts an older crowd, thick with divorcées in search of new spouses. ⊠ *25001 Dana Dr.,* ☎ *714/496–6195. AE, D, DC, MC, V.*

$$ ✗ **Luciana's.** This intimate Italian restaurant is a real find, especially for couples seeking a romantic evening. Dining rooms are small, dressed with crisp white linens and warmed by fireplaces. The well-prepared food is served with care. ⊠ *24312 Del Prado Ave.,* ☎ *714/661–6500. AE, DC, MC, V. No lunch.*

$$$$ 🛏 **Blue Lantern Inn.** Perched atop the bluffs, this Contemporary Cape Cod–style bed-and-breakfast has stunning harbor and ocean views. Rooms are decorated with period furnishings, fireplaces, stocked refrigerators, and jetted baths. Breakfast and afternoon refreshments are included in the price. ⊠ *34343 St. of the Blue Lantern, 92629,* ☎ *714/661–1304,* 🅵🅰🆇 *714/496–1483. 29 rooms all with private bath. Health club, library, concierge. AE, MC, V.*

$$$$ 🛏 **Marriott's Laguna Cliffs Resort.** Formerly known as the Dana Point
★   Resort, this Cape Cod–style hillside property is decorated in shades of sea-foam green and peach. The lobby is filled with large palm trees and original artwork, and most rooms have ocean views. Since being purchased by Marriott, the hotel has been upgrading its restaurant and guest rooms. In summer, the Capistrano Valley Symphony performs on the resort's attractively landscaped grounds. ⊠ *25135 Park Lantern,*

92629, ☎ 714/661–5000 or 800/533–9748, FAX 714/661–5358. *350 rooms. Restaurant, 2 lounges, 2 pools, 3 spas, health club, basketball, croquet, volleyball, children's programs. AE, D, DC, MC, V.*

$$$$ ⊞ **Ritz-Carlton Laguna Niguel.** This acclaimed hotel has earned world-
★ class status for its gorgeous setting right on the edge of the Pacific, its sumptuous Mediterranean architecture and decor, and its reputation for flawless service. With colorful landscaping outside and an impos-ing marble-column entry, it feels like an Italian country villa. Every pos-sible amenity is available to guests. Rooms have traditional furnishings, sumptuous fabrics, marble bathrooms, and private balconies with ocean or garden views. ⊠ *1 Ritz-Carlton Dr., 92629,* ☎ *714/240–2000 or 800/241–3333,* FAX *714/240–0829. 362 rooms, 31 suites. 3 restau-rants, lounge, 2 pools, beauty salon, golf privileges, 4 tennis courts, health club, concierge. AE, D, DC, MC, V.*

$$ ⊞ **Best Western Marina Inn.** Set right in the marina, this fairly basic
★ motel is convenient to docks, restaurants, and shops. Rooms vary in size from two doubles and a bath to family units with kitchens and fireplaces. Many rooms in this three-level motel have balconies and har-bor views. ⊠ *24800 Dana Point Harbor Dr., 92629,* ☎ *714/496–1203 or 800/255–6843,* FAX *714/248–0360. 136 rooms, 10 suites. Pool, health club. AE, D, DC, MC, V.*

Outdoor Activities and Sports

BEACHES

Doheny State Park (☎ 714/496–6171), at the south end of Dana Point, one of the best surfing spots in southern California, has an in-terpretive center devoted to the wildlife of the Doheny Marine Refuge, and there are food stands and shops nearby. Camping is permitted here, though there are no hook-ups, and there are picnic facilities and a pier for fishing. **Swim Beach,** inside Dana Point Harbor, also has a fishing pier, barbecues, food, parking, rest rooms, and a shower.

San Juan Capistrano

5 mi north of Dana Point on Hwy. 74.

This town is best known for its mission and for the swallows that mi-grate here each year from their winter haven in Argentina. The arrival of the birds and St. Joseph's Day, March 19, launches a week of fes-tivities. After summering in the arches of the old stone church, the swal-lows head home around St. John's Day, October 23.

★ ㉑ **Mission San Juan Capistrano,** founded in 1776 by Father Junípero Serra, was the major Roman Catholic outpost between Los Angeles and San Diego. A main draw is a chance to see the original Great Stone Church, which is permanently supported by scaffolding. Many of the mission's adobe buildings have been preserved to illustrate mission life, with ex-hibits of an olive millstone, tallow ovens, tanning vats, metalworking furnaces, and padres' living quarters. The bougainvillea-covered Serra Chapel is believed to be the oldest building still in use in California. Mass is still held at the mission. ⊠ *Camino Capistrano and Ortega Hwy.,* ☎ *714/248–2048.* 💲 *$4.* ☉ *Daily 8:30–5; spontaneous do-cent tours available.*

㉒ The **San Juan Capistrano Library,** a postmodern structure erected in 1983, is near Mission San Juan Capistrano. Architect Michael Graves mixed classical design with the style of the mission to striking effect. Its courtyard has secluded places for reading, as well as a water foun-tain. ⊠ *31495 El Camino Real,* ☎ *714/493–1752.* ☉ *Mon.–Thurs. 10–9, Fri. and Sat. 10–5.*

Dining

$$ ✕ **El Adobe.** This early California–style eatery serves enormous por-
tions of mildly seasoned Mexican food. Mariachi bands play Friday
and Saturday nights and for Sunday brunch. ✉ *31891 Camino Capis-
trano,* ☎ *714/830–8620. AE, D, DC, MC, V.*

$$ ✕ **L'Hirondelle.** Duckling is the specialty at this Belgian inn, and it is
★ prepared three different ways. ✉ *31631 Camino Capistrano,* ☎
*714/661–0425. Reservations essential. AE, MC, V. Closed Mon. No
lunch.*

Nightlife

Coach House (✉ 33157 Camino Capistrano, San Juan Capistrano, ☎
714/496–8930) draws big local crowds for jazz and rock headliners.

ORANGE COUNTY A TO Z

Arriving and Departing

By Bus

The **Los Angeles MTA** has limited service to Orange County. You can
take the No. 460 to Anaheim from downtown; it goes to Knott's Berry
Farm and Disneyland. **Greyhound** (☎ 714/999–1256) has scheduled
bus service to Orange County.

By Car

Two major freeways, I–405 (San Diego Freeway) and I–5 (Santa Ana
Freeway), run north and south through Orange County. South of Laguna they merge into I–5. Avoid these during rush hours (6–9 AM and
3:30–6 PM), when they slow to a crawl and back up for miles.

By Plane

John Wayne Orange County Airport (☎ 714/252–5252) in Santa Ana
is the county's main facility. It is serviced by **Alaska Airlines, America
West Airlines, American, Continental, Delta, Northwest, Reno Air,
Southwest, TWA, United** (☞ Air Travel *in* Important Contacts A to Z
for phone numbers), and several commuter airlines. **Ontario International Airport** (☎ 909/988–2700) is 30 miles north of Anaheim. The
airlines that fly into John Wayne airport also fly to Ontario, along with
SkyWest, United Express, and USAir Express.

BETWEEN THE AIRPORTS AND HOTELS

Airport Bus (☎ 800/772–5299), a shuttle service, carries passengers
from John Wayne airport and LAX to Anaheim, Buena Park, and
Newport Beach. Fare from John Wayne to Anaheim is $10, from LAX
to Anaheim $14.

Prime Time Airport Shuttle (☎ 800/262–7433) offers door-to-door service to LAX and John Wayne airports, hotels near John Wayne, and
the San Pedro cruise terminal. The fare is $11 from Anaheim hotels to
John Wayne and $12 from Anaheim hotels to LAX. Children under
two ride free (but must have a car seat).

Super Shuttle (☎ 714/517–6600) provides 24-hour door-to-door service from all the airports to all points in Orange County. The fare to
the Disneyland area is $10 from John Wayne, $34 from Ontario, $13
from LAX. Phone for other fares and reservations.

By Train

Amtrak (☎ 800/872–7245) makes several stops in Orange County:
Fullerton, Anaheim, Santa Ana, San Juan Capistrano, and San Clemente.
There are 11 departures daily, nine on weekends.

Getting Around

By Bus

The **Orange County Transportation Authority** (OCTA, ☎ 714/636–7433) will take you virtually anywhere in the county, but it will take time; OCTA buses go from Knott's Berry Farm and Disneyland to Huntington and Newport beaches. Bus 1 travels along the coast.

By Car

Highways 22, 55, and 91 go west to the ocean and east to the mountains: Take Highway 91 or Highway 22 to inland points (Buena Park, Anaheim) and take Highway 55 to Newport Beach. To help alleviate traffic, Highway 91 recently opened a toll lane called the Fast Track. Caution: Orange County freeways are undergoing major construction; expect delays at odd times. Pacific Coast Highway (Highway 1; also known locally as PCH and in parts as Coast Highway) allows easy access to beach communities, and is the most scenic route. It follows the entire Orange County coast, from Huntington Beach to San Clemente.

Contacts and Resources

Doctors

Anaheim Memorial Hospital (✉ 1111 W. La Palma, ☎ 714/774–1450). **Western Medical Center** (✉ 1025 S. Anaheim Blvd., Anaheim, ☎ 714/533–6220). **Hoag Memorial Presbyterian Hospital** (✉ 301 Newport Blvd., Newport Beach, ☎ 714/645–8600). **South Coast Medical Center** (✉ 31872 Pacific Coast Hwy., South Laguna, ☎ 714/499–1311).

Emergencies

Ambulance (☎ 911). **Police** (☎ 911).

Guided Tours

Pacific Coast Gray Line Tours (☎ 714/978–8855) provides guided tours from Orange County hotels to Disneyland, Knott's Berry Farm, Universal Studios Hollywood, Six Flags Magic Mountain, and the San Diego Zoo.

Visitor Information

Anaheim/Orange County Visitor and Convention Bureau (✉ 800 W. Katella Ave., 92802, ☎ 714/999–8999). **Buena Park Convention & Visitors Office** (✉ 6280 Manchester Blvd., Suite 103, 90621, ☎ 714/562–3560). **Dana Point Chamber of Commerce** (✉ 24681 La Plaza, Suite 120, 92629, ☎ 714/496–1555). **Huntington Beach Conference and Visitors Bureau** (✉ 101 Main St., Suite 2A, 92648, ☎ 800/729–6232). **Laguna Beach Visitors Bureau and Chamber of Commerce** (✉ 252 Broadway, 92651, ☎ 714/494–1018). **Newport Beach Conference and Visitors Bureau** (✉ 3300 W. Coast Hwy., 92663, ☎ 800/942–6278). **Orange County Visitor Information Hot Line** (☎ 714/635–8900). **San Juan Capistrano Chamber of Commerce and Visitors Center** (✉ 31931 Camino Capistrano, Suite D, 92693, ☎ 714/493–4700).

13 San Diego

To visitors, the city and county of San Diego may seem like a conglomeration of theme parks: Old Town and the Gaslamp Quarter historically oriented ones, the wharf area a maritime-heritage playground, La Jolla a genteel throwback to southern California elegance, Balboa Park a convergence of the town's cerebral and action-oriented personae. There are, of course, real theme parks—Sea World and the zoo and Wild Animal Park—but the great outdoors, in the form of forests, landscaped urban areas, and a string of sandy beaches, forms the biggest of them all.

SAN DIEGO COUNTY is the nation's sixth largest—larger than nearly a dozen U.S. states—with a population of more than 2.5 million. It sprawls east from the Pacific Ocean through dense urban neighborhoods to outlying suburban communities that seem to sprout on canyons and cliffs overnight. Its eastern boundaries are the Cleveland National Forest, where the pines and manzanita are covered with snow in the winter, and the Anza-Borrego Desert, where delicate pink and yellow cactus blooms herald the coming of spring. San Diegans visit these vast wildernesses for their annual doses of seasonal splendors, then return to the city, where flowers blossom year-round and the streets are dry and clean. One of the busiest international borders in the United States marks the county's southern line, where approximately 60 million people a year legally cross between Mexico's Baja California peninsula and San Diego. To the north, the marines at Camp Pendleton practice land, sea, and air maneuvers in southern California's largest coastal greenbelt, marking the demarcation zone between the congestion of Orange and Los Angeles counties and the more relaxed expansiveness of San Diego.

EXPLORING SAN DIEGO

By Edie Jarolim   San Diego is more a chain of separate communities than a cohesive city. Many of the major attractions are at least 5 miles away from one another. The streets are fun for getting an up-close look at how San Diegans live, but true southern Californians use the freeways, which crisscross the county in a sensible fashion. If you are going to drive around San Diego, study your maps before you hit the road. The freeways are convenient and fast most of the time, but if you miss your turnoff or get caught in commuter traffic, you'll experience a none-too-pleasurable hallmark of southern California living—freeway madness.

If you stick with public transportation, plan on taking your time. San Diego's trolley line has expanded into Old Town; a new light rail line called the *Coaster* runs from Oceanside into downtown; and the bus system covers almost all the county—but making the connections necessary to see the various sights is time consuming. Fashion Valley Shopping Center in Mission Valley is one of the two major bus transfer points—downtown is the other. Some buses have bicycle racks in the back, and a bike is a great mode of transportation here. The bike-path system, although never perfect, is extensive and well marked. With the large distances between sights, taxis can be expensive and are best used for getting around once you're in a given area.

Balboa Park

Balboa Park is set on 1,400 beautifully landscaped acres. Hosting the majority of San Diego's museums and a world-famous zoo, the park serves as the cultural center of the city, as well as a recreational paradise. Many of the park's Spanish-Moorish buildings originally housed exhibits for the Panama–California International Exposition of 1915, which celebrated the opening of the Panama Canal. The Spanish theme first instituted in the early 1900s was in part carried through in new buildings designed for the California Pacific International Exposition of 1935–36.

If you're driving in via the Laurel Street Bridge, the first parking area you'll come to is off El Prado to the left, going toward Pan American Plaza; you'll see more lots as you continue down along the same road.

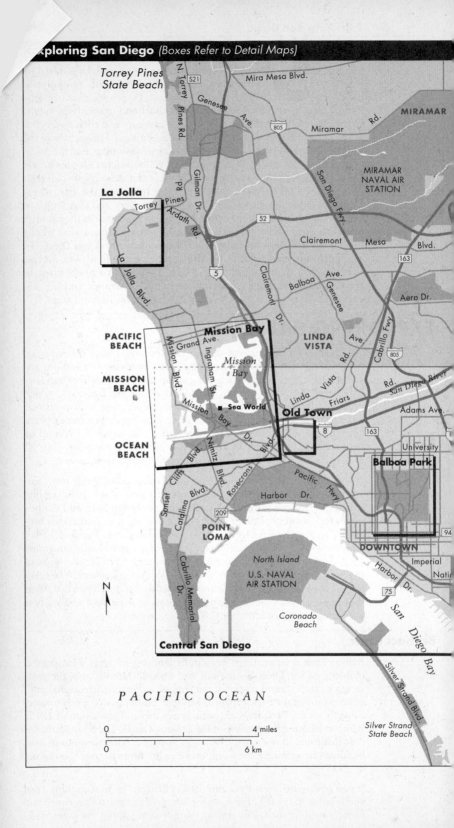

Torrey Pines
State Beach

S21

Mira Mesa Blvd.

Genesee Ave.

805

Miramar

Rd.

MIRAMAR

N. Torrey Pines Rd.

Gilman Dr.

MIRAMAR
NAVAL AIR
STATION

San Diego Fwy.

La Jolla

Torrey Pines Rd.

Ardath Rd.

52

Clairemont Mesa Blvd.

163

La Jolla Blvd.

Balboa Ave.

Genesee Ave.

Aero Dr.

5

Clairemont Dr.

Cabrillo Fwy

805

**PACIFIC
BEACH**

Mission Bay

Grand Ave.

Mission Blvd.

Ingraham St.

Mission
Bay

**LINDA
VISTA**

Linda Vista Rd.

Friars Rd.

San Diego River

**MISSION
BEACH**

■ Sea World

Mission Bay Dr.

Old Town

8

Adams Ave.

163

E

University

**OCEAN
BEACH**

Nimitz Blvd.

Rosecrans Blvd.

Pacific Hwy

Balboa Park

Sunset Cliffs Blvd.

Catalina Blvd.

209

Harbor Dr.

**POINT
LOMA**

94

DOWNTOWN

Imperial

Cabrillo Memorial Dr.

North Island
U.S. NAVAL
AIR STATION

Harbor Dr.

Natio

75

San Diego Bay

N

Coronado
Beach

Silver Strand Blvd.

Central San Diego

PACIFIC OCEAN

0   4 miles

0   6 km

Silver Strand
State Beach

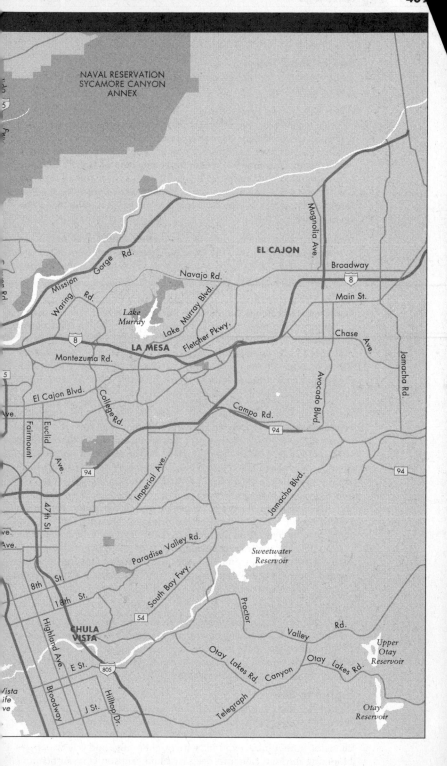

NAVAL RESERVATION
SYCAMORE CANYON
ANNEX

5

EL CAJON

Magnolia Ave.

Broadway

8

Navajo Rd.

Mission Gorge Rd.

Waring Rd.

Lake Murray Blvd.

Lake Murray

Main St.

Fletcher Pkwy.

Chase Ave.

Jamacha Rd.

8

LA MESA

Montezuma Rd.

Avocado Blvd.

5

El Cajon Blvd.

College Rd.

Campo Rd.

94

Ave.

Fairmount Ave.

Euclid Ave.

94

Imperial Ave.

Jamacha Blvd.

94

47th St.

Paradise Valley Rd.

Sweetwater Reservoir

ve.
Ave.

8th St.

South Bay Fwy.

Proctor

18th St.

54

Valley Rd.

Upper Otay Reservoir

CHULA VISTA

Highland Ave.

E St.

805

Otay Lakes Rd. Canyon

Otay Lakes Rd.

Vista
ife
ve

Broadway

J St.

Hilltop Dr.

Telegraph

Otay Reservoir

From April through October, trams run throughout the park from 9:30–5:30, approximately every 8–12 minutes; the rest of the year, service is 11–5 and frequency is 12–24 minutes.

Some Good Tours

Numbers in the text correspond to numbers in the margin and on the Balboa Park map.

Enter via Cabrillo Bridge through the West Gate, which depicts the Panama Canal's linkage of the Atlantic and Pacific oceans, and park just south of the **Alcazar Garden** ⑪. It's a short stretch north across El Prado to the landmark California Building, modeled on a cathedral in Mexico and now home to the **San Diego Museum of Man** ⑩. Look up to see a pantheon of celebrated busts and statues of heroes of the early days of the state. Next door is the **Simon Edison Centre for the Performing Arts,** which adjoins the sculpture garden of the **San Diego Museum of Art** ⑨.

Continuing east, you'll come to the **Timken Museum of Art** ⑧, the **Botanical Building** ⑦, and the **Casa del Prado,** which was gutted and rebuilt in its 1915 Spanish colonial style in 1971. At the end of the row is the **San Diego Natural History Museum** ④.

Return to the history museum and cross Plaza de Balboa to reach the **Reuben H. Fleet Space Theater and Science Center** ③. You're now on the opposite side of the Prado and heading west. You'll next pass **Casa de Balboa** ②, home to history, photography, model-railroad, and sports museums. To the west are the temporary quarters of the **Balboa Park Visitors Center** ①, and if you continue west on El Prado, you'll reach the **Mingei International Museum** ⑫ of folk art. Your starting point, the Alcazar Garden, is just west of the Mingei.

Another option is to walk south from the Plaza de Panama. The **Japanese Friendship Garden** ⑭ is the first place on your left. If you continue along, you'll come to the **Spreckels Organ Pavilion** ⑬. The road forks here; veer to the right to reach the **House of Pacific Relations** ⑮. Inside the Balboa Park Club, which you'll pass next, is a huge WPA mural. Continue on beyond the Palisades Building to reach the **San Diego Automotive Museum** ⑯. The road loops back at the space ship–like **San Diego Aerospace Museum and International Aerospace Hall of Fame** ⑰. As you head north again, you'll notice the Starlight Bowl on your right. A bit beyond is perhaps the most impressive structure on this tour, the **Federal Building,** used for indoor sports these days. Its main entrance was modeled after the Palace of Governors in the ancient Maya city of Uxmal, Mexico. You'll be back at the Spreckels Organ Pavilion after this.

TIMING

You'll want to devote an entire day to the zoo. Most park museums are open daily 10–4; during the summer, a number have extended hours. On Tuesdays, the museums have free admission on a rotating basis. There are free Sunday concerts at the Spreckels Organ Pavilion. Christmas on El Prado is not to be missed.

Sights to See

⓫ **Alcazar Garden.** The gardens surrounding the Alcazar Castle in Seville were the model for the landscaping here; you'll feel like royalty resting on the benches by the tiled fountains. The flower beds are ever-changing horticultural exhibits, with bright orange and yellow poppies blooming in the spring and deep rust and crimson chrysanthemums appearing in the fall. It's off El Prado, next to the Mingei International Museum and across from the Museum of Man.

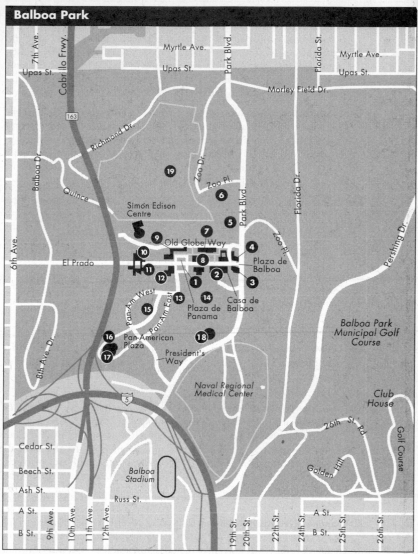

Balboa Park

Alcazar Garden, **11**

Balboa Park Visitors Center, **1**

Botanical Building, **7**

Carousel, **5**

Casa de Balboa, **2**

Centro Cultural de la Raza, **18**

House of Pacific Relations, **15**

Japanese Friendship Garden, **14**

Mingei International Museum, **12**

Miniature Railroad, **6**

Museum of Photographic Arts, **2**

Museum of San Diego History, **2**

Reuben H. Fleet Space Theater and Science Center, **3**

San Diego Aerospace Museum and International Aerospace Hall of Fame, **17**

San Diego Automotive Museum, **16**

San Diego Hall of Champions–Sports Museum, **2**

San Diego Model Railroad Museum, **2**

San Diego Museum of Art, **9**

San Diego Museum of Man, **10**

San Diego Natural History Museum, **4**

San Diego Zoo, **19**

Spreckels Organ Pavilion, **13**

Timken Museum of Art, **8**

❶ Balboa Park Visitors Center. The office sells the Passport to Balboa Park, which affords entry to nine museums for $18. Also available here is a schedule and route map for the free trams that operate around the park. Restoration of the center's usual home, the House of Hospitality, began in 1995 and should be completed by June 1997. For the time being, the information facility is set up on the Plaza de Panama, adjacent to its old site. ☎ 619/239–0512. ⊙ *Daily 9–4.*

❼ Botanical Building. The graceful, redwood-lathed structure built for the 1915 exposition houses more than 500 types of tropical and subtropical plants. Ceiling-high tree ferns shade tiny, fragile orchids and feathery bamboo. The Lily Pond, filled with giant koi fish and blooming water lilies, is popular with photographers. ⊠ *1550 El Prado,* ☎ *619/235–1116.* ▨ *Free.* ⊙ *Fri.–Wed. 10–4.*

❺ Carousel. Beyond the Spanish Village and just behind the zoo parking lot, riders on an antique merry-go-round stretch from their seats to grab the brass rings suspended an arm's-length away and earn a free ride. ⊠ *1889 Zoo Pl.,* ▨ *$1.25.* ⊙ *Daily 11:30–5:30 during the extended summer vacation; during the school year, open only on school holidays and weekends.*

❷ Casa de Balboa. This structure on the east side of El Prado houses (☞ *below*) the Museum of Photographic Arts, the Museum of San Diego History, the San Diego Model Railroad Museum, and the San Diego Hall of Champions–Sports Museum.

⑱ Centro Cultural de la Raza. An old water tower was converted into a cultural center that focuses on Mexican, Native American, and Chicano arts. ⊠ *2004 Park Blvd.,* ☎ *619/235–6135.* ▨ *Free.* ⊙ *Wed.–Sun. noon–5.*

⑮ House of Pacific Relations. This is not really a house but a cluster of red tile–roof, stucco cottages representing more than 25 foreign countries. And the word "pacific" refers not to the ocean—most of the nations represented are European, not Asian—but to the goal of maintaining peace. The cottages, decorated with crafts and pictures, hold open houses each Sunday. ⊠ *2160 Pan American Rd. W,* ☎ *619/234–0739.* ▨ *Free.* ⊙ *Sun. 12:30–4:30; hrs may vary with the seasons.*

⑭ Japanese Friendship Garden. The rocks and trees are arranged to inspire contemplation in the park's Eastern-style garden, which is still being developed. It currently includes an exhibit house, a traditional sand-and-stone garden, a picnic area with a view of the canyon below, a snack bar, and a small gift shop. A $2 million expansion was undertaken in 1995–96 to landscape an additional 11 acres. By the time you read this, a tea pavilion may have been completed. ⊠ *2215 Pan American Rd. E,* ☎ *619/232–2780.* ▨ *$2.* ⊙ *Fri.–Sun. and Tues. 10–4.*

⑫ Mingei International Museum. One of only a handful of facilities in the world devoted to the subject of folk art, the Mingei, which moved to Balboa Park in 1996, mounts colorful and creative exhibits of toys, pottery, textiles, costumes, and gadgets from all over the globe. ⊠ *1439 El Prado,* ☎ *619/239–0003.* ▨ *$5.* ⊙ *Tues.–Sun. 10–4:30.*

❻ Miniature Railroad. Adjacent to the zoo parking lot, a pint-size 48-passenger train runs a half-mile loop through eucalyptus groves. The engine is a small-scale version of the General Motors F-3 locomotive. ⊠ *2885 Zoo Pl.,* ☎ *619/239–4748.* ▨ *$1.25.* ⊙ *Daily 11–4:30.*

❷ Museum of Photographic Arts. World-renowned photographers, such as Ansel Adams, Imogen Cunningham, Henri Cartier-Bresson, and

Edward Weston, are represented in the museum's collection, along with lesser-known contemporary artists. ⊠ *Casa de Balboa, 1649 El Prado,* ☎ *619/239–5262.* ☞ *$3.* ⊙ *Daily 10–5; closed national holidays and for installations.*

❷ Museum of San Diego History. The San Diego Historical Society maintains its research library in the Casa de Balboa's basement and organizes shows on the first floor. Permanent and rotating exhibits focus on local urban history after 1850, when California became part of the United States. ⊠ *Casa de Balboa, 1649 El Prado,* ☎ *619/232–6203.* ☞ *$4.* ⊙ *Wed.–Sun. 10–4:30.*

★ ☝ **❸ Reuben H. Fleet Space Theater and Science Center.** Children and adults alike enjoy the clever interactive exhibits that teach scientific principles. The IMAX Dome Theater screens exhilarating nature and science films. At night, the Laserium presents laser shows set to rock music (mostly heavy metal). In addition, there are sometimes planetarium shows under the Space Theater dome. ⊠ *1875 El Prado,* ☎ *619/238–1233 or 619/232–6866 for advance tickets.* ☞ *Science Center $2.50, or included with price of theater ticket; Space Theater tickets $6; laser shows $7; planetarium show $3.* ⊙ *Mon.–Tues. 9:30–6; Sun., Wed.–Thurs. 9:30–9; Fri.–Sat. 9:30 AM–10 PM (hrs change seasonally; call ahead).*

⑰ San Diego Aerospace Museum and International Aerospace Hall of Fame. Every available inch of space in the rotunda of this streamlined edifice is filled with exhibits about aviation and aerospace pioneers, including examples of enemy planes during the world wars. A collection of real and replicated aircraft fills the central courtyard. ⊠ *2001 Pan American Plaza,* ☎ *619/234–8291.* ☞ *$5, active military personnel free.* ⊙ *Daily 10–4:30.*

⑯ San Diego Automotive Museum. Even if you don't know a choke from a chassis, you're bound to admire the sleek designs you'll see here. The museum maintains a core collection of vintage motorcycles and cars, ranging from an 1886 Benz to a De Lorean, as well as a series of rotating exhibits from collections around the world. ⊠ *2080 Pan American Plaza,* ☎ *619/231–2886.* ☞ *$6.* ⊙ *Daily 10–4:30.*

❷ San Diego Hall of Champions–Sports Museum. Celebrate local jock heroes via a vast collection of memorabilia, uniforms, paintings, photographs, and computer and video displays. An amusing bloopers film is screened at the Sports Theater. ⊠ *Casa de Balboa, 1649 El Prado,* ☎ *619/234–2544.* ☞ *$3.* ⊙ *Daily 10–4:30.*

☝ **❷ San Diego Model Railroad Museum.** When the six model-train exhibits are in operation, you'll hear the sounds of chugging engines, screeching brakes, and shrill whistles. ⊠ *Casa de Balboa, 1649 El Prado,* ☎ *619/696–0199.* ☞ *$3.* ⊙ *Tues.–Fri. 11–4, weekends 11–5.*

★ **❾ San Diego Museum of Art.** Known primarily for its Spanish Baroque and Renaissance paintings, including works by El Greco, Goya, Rubens, and Van Ruisdale, San Diego's most comprehensive art museum also has strong holdings of Southeast Asian art, Indian miniatures, and contemporary California paintings. If traveling shows from other cities come to San Diego, you can expect to see them here. An outdoor Sculpture Garden exhibits both traditional and modern pieces in a striking natural setting. IMAGE, the Interactive Multimedia Art Gallery Explorer, allows visitors to locate the highlights of the museum's holdings on screen and custom-design a tour. ⊠ *Casa de Balboa, 1450 El Prado,* ☎ *619/232–7931.* ☞ *$7 Tues.–Thurs., $8 Fri.–Sun.* ⊙ *Tues.–Sun. 10–4:30.*

Take a respite from museum-hopping with a cup of coffee or a glass of California chardonnay in the San Diego Museum of Art's **Sculpture Garden Café** (☎ 619/232–7931), which also has a small selection of tasty—if somewhat costly—gourmet lunches from 11:30 AM to 2 PM Tuesday–Sunday.

⑩ San Diego Museum of Man. Housing an extensive collection first assembled for the 1915 exposition and amplified over the years, this is one of the best-respected anthropological museums in the country. Exhibits focus on southwestern, Mexican, and South American cultures. ⌧ *1350 El Prado,* ☎ *619/239–2001.* ◲ *$4.* ☉ *Daily 10–4:30.*

❹ San Diego Natural History Museum. The museum focuses on the plants and animals of southern California and Mexico; it frequently schedules free guided nature walks on the weekends, as well as films and lectures throughout the week. Look for an $18 million expansion of the museum starting in 1997. ⌧ *1788 El Prado,* ☎ *619/232–3821.* ◲ *$6.* ☉ *Fri.–Wed. 9:30–4:30, Thurs. 9:30–6:30.*

★ ☾ **⑲ San Diego Zoo.** Balboa Park's—and perhaps the city's—most famous attraction is its 100-acre zoo. Nearly 4,000 animals of some 800 diverse species roam in expertly crafted habitats that spread down into, around, and above the natural canyons. The zoo's charm and fame come from its tradition of creating hospitable environments that replicate natural habitats as closely as possible: The flora and the fauna in the zoo, including many rare species, are even more costly than the animals.

Exploring the zoo fully requires the stamina of a healthy hiker, but open-air trams that run throughout the day allow visitors to see 80% of the exhibits on their 3-mile tour. The Kangaroo bus tours include the same informed and amusing narrations as the others—one of the guides on both is a professional comedian—but for a few dollars more they let you get on and off as you like at eight different stops. The Skyfari ride, which soars 170 feet above ground, gives a good overview of the zoo's layout and, on clear days, a panorama of the park, downtown San Diego, the bay, and the ocean, far past the Coronado Bridge.

Still, the zoo is at its best when you wander the paths that climb through the huge, enclosed **Scripps Aviary,** where brightly colored tropical birds swoop between branches just inches from your face. **Gorilla Tropics,** beside the aviary, is among the zoo's latest ventures into bioclimatic zone exhibits, where animals live in enclosed environments modeled on their native habitats.

The zoo's simulated Asian rain forest, **Tiger River,** brings together 10 exhibits with more than 35 species of animals. The mist-shrouded trails winding down a canyon into Tiger River pass by fragrant jasmine, ginger lilies, and orchids, giving the visitor the feeling of descending into a South American jungle. In **Sun Bear Forest,** playful cubs constantly claw apart the trees and shrubs. At **Hippo Canyon**—a 2-acre African rain forest at the base of Tiger River—you can watch the huge but surprisingly graceful beasts frolicking underwater. A 1996 exhibit lets you look at polar bears plunging into a chilly pool. Delayed for many months by red tape has been the arrival of Shi Shi and Bay Yun, a pair of giant pandas from China; at press time there was no word on when they might finally appear.

Goats and sheep at the **Children's Zoo** beg to be petted and are particularly adept at snatching bag lunches; bunnies and guinea pigs seem willing to be fondled endlessly. In the nursery windows, you can see baby lemurs and spider monkeys playing with Cabbage Patch kids, looking much like the human babies peering from strollers through the glass.

The exhibits are designed in size and style for four-year-olds, but that doesn't deter children of all ages from having fun.

The **Wedgeforth Bowl,** a 3,000-seat amphitheater, holds various animal shows throughout the day. Behind-the-scenes tours, walking tours, tours in Spanish, and tours for the hearing or sight impaired are available; inquire at the entrance. ✉ *2920 Zoo Dr.,* ☎ *619/234–3153.* ✏ *$15 includes zoo, Children's Zoo, and animal shows; $21 includes above, plus 35-min guided bus tour and Skyfari ride; Kangaroo bus tour $8 additional; zoo free to children under 12 during Oct. and to all on Founder's Day, Oct. 3.* ☉ *Fall–spring, daily 9–4 (visitors may remain until 5); summer, daily 9–9 (visitors may remain until 10). Children's Zoo and Skyfari ride close earlier.*

⑬ Spreckels Organ Pavilion. Dedicated in 1915 by sugar magnates John D. and Adolph B. Spreckels, the 2,000-seat pavilion holds the 4,445-pipe Spreckels Organ, believed to be the largest outdoor pipe organ in the world. You can hear this impressive instrument at one of the year-round, 2 PM Sunday-afternoon concerts. On summer evenings, local military bands, gospel groups, and barbershop quartets hold concerts, and at Christmas, the park's Christmas tree and life-size nativity display turn the pavilion into a seasonal wonderland. ✉ *2211 Pan American Rd. E,* ☎ *619/226–0819.*

⑧ Timken Museum of Art. This modern structure is made of travertine marble imported from Italy. The small museum houses a selection of minor works by major European and American artists as well as a superb collection of Russian icons. ✉ *1500 El Prado,* ☎ *619/239– 5548.* ✏ *Free.* ☉ *Oct.–Aug., Tues.–Sat. 10–4:30, Sun. 1:30–4:30.*

OFF THE BEATEN PATH	**HILLCREST** - Northwest of Balboa Park, Hillcrest is San Diego's Castro Street, the center for the gay community and artists of all types. University, 4th, and 5th avenues are filled with cafés, boutiques, and excellent bookstores. Like most of San Diego, Hillcrest has been undergoing redevelopment. The largest project is the Uptown District, on University Avenue at 8th Avenue. This self-contained residential-commercial center was built to resemble an inner-city neighborhood, with shops and restaurants within easy walking distance of high-priced town houses. To the northeast, Adams Avenue, reached via Park Boulevard heading north off Washington Street, is San Diego's Antiques Row.

Downtown

Downtown's natural attributes were easily evident to its original booster, Alonzo Horton, who arrived in San Diego in 1867. Horton looked at the bay and the acres of flatland surrounded by hills and canyons and knew he had found San Diego's heart. Though Old Town, under the Spanish fort at the Presidio, had been settled for years, Horton understood that it was too far away from the water to take hold as the commercial center of San Diego. He bought 960 acres along the bay at 27½¢ per acre and gave away the land to those who would develop it or build houses. Within months, he had sold or given away 226 city blocks; settlers camped on their land in tents as their houses and businesses rose.

As downtown grew into San Diego's transportation and commercial hub, residential neighborhoods blossomed along the beaches and inland valleys. The business district gradually moved farther away from the original heart of downtown, at 5th Avenue and Market Street, past Broadway, up toward Balboa Park. Downtown's waterfront fell into bad times during World War I, when sailors, gamblers, and prostitutes were drawn to one another and the waterfront bars.

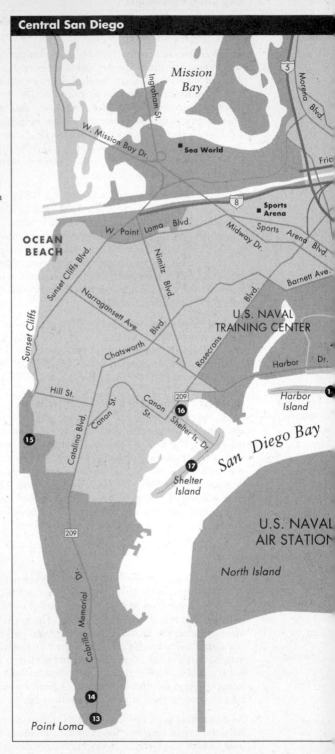

Central San Diego

Mission Bay

Ingraham St.

W. Mission Bay Dr.

Sea World

Morena Blvd.

Fri...

Sports Arena

Sports Arena Blvd.

W. Point Loma Blvd.

Midway Dr.

OCEAN BEACH

Sunset Cliffs Blvd.

Nimitz Blvd.

Barnett Ave.

Narragansett Ave.

Blvd.

U.S. NAVAL
TRAINING CENTER

Sunset Cliffs

Chatsworth

Rosecrans

Harbor   Dr.

Hill St.

Canon St.

Canon St.

209

16

Harbor
Island

1

15

Catalina Blvd.

Shelter Is. Dr.

San Diego Bay

17

Shelter
Island

209

U.S. NAVAL
AIR STATION

Cabrillo Memorial Dr.

North Island

14

13

Point Loma

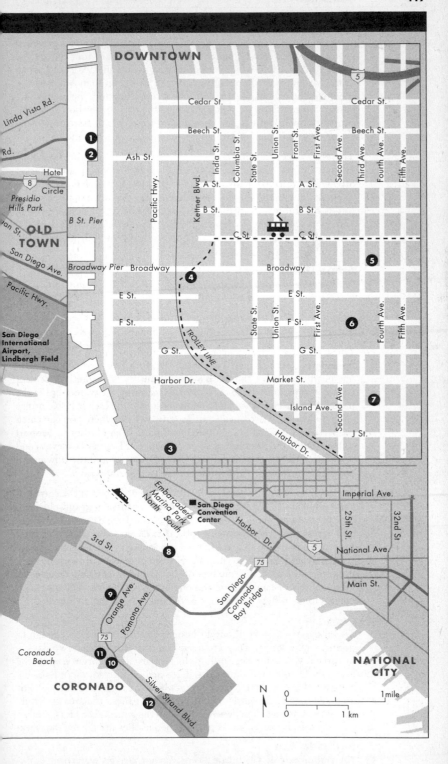

DOWNTOWN

Linda Vista Rd.

Rd.

Hotel
Circle

Presidio
Hills Park

OLD
TOWN

San Diego Ave.

Pacific Hwy.

San Diego
International
Airport,
Lindbergh Field

Cedar St.

Beech St.

Ash St.

Pacific Hwy.

Kettner Blvd.

India St.

Columbia St.

State St.

Union St.

Front St.

First Ave.

Second Ave.

Third Ave.

Fourth Ave.

Fifth Ave.

Cedar St.

Beech St.

A St.

B St.

C St.

A St.

B St.

C St.

B St. Pier

Broadway Pier

Broadway

Broadway

E St.

F St.

G St.

Harbor Dr.

State St.

Union St.

First Ave.

Second Ave.

Fourth Ave.

Fifth Ave.

E St.

F St.

G St.

Market St.

Island Ave.

J St.

TROLLEY LINE

Harbor Dr.

Embarcadero
Marina Park
North South

San Diego
Convention
Center

Harbor Dr.

Imperial Ave.

25th St.

32nd St

National Ave.

Main St.

3rd St.

Orange Ave.

Pomona Ave.

San Diego-
Coronado
Bay Bridge

Coronado
Beach

CORONADO

Silver Strand Blvd.

NATIONAL
CITY

N

0   1mile

0   1 km

But Alonzo Horton's modern-day followers, city leaders intent on prospering while preserving San Diego's natural beauty, have reclaimed the downtown area. Replacing old shipyards and canneries are hotel towers and waterfront parks. The 760,000-square-foot San Diego Convention Center, which hosted its first events in 1990, is thriving; as the forum for the Republican National Convention in August 1996 it enjoyed heavy media attention. A few blocks inland, the hugely successful Horton Plaza shopping center led the way for the hotels, restaurants, shopping centers, and housing developments that are now rising on every square inch of available space in downtown San Diego.

There are large, reasonably priced ($3–$7 per day) parking lots along Harbor Drive, Pacific Highway, and lower Broadway and Market Street. The price of many downtown parking meters has gone up to $1 an hour, with the length of permissible stay extended to three hours; unless you know for sure that your stay in the area will be short, you're better off with a lot. If you're planning to tour the Embarcadero, the lot on the Cruise Ship pier, which costs only $1 an hour with a maximum of $3 a day, is a bargain.

Some Good Tours

Numbers in the text correspond to numbers in the margin and on the Central San Diego map.

Most people do a lot of parking-lot hopping when visiting downtown, but for the energetic, two distinct areas may be explored on foot.

Those who want to stay near the water might start a walk of the **Embarcadero** ① at the foot of Ash Street on Harbor Drive, where the *Berkeley*, headquarters of the **Maritime Museum** ②, is moored. A cement pathway runs south from the *Star of India* along the waterfront to the pastel B Street Pier. Another two blocks south on Harbor Drive brings you to the foot of Broadway and Broadway Pier, where you can catch the ferry to Coronado. Continue south past Tuna Harbor to **Seaport Village** ③. Six blocks north of Seaport Village at Kettner Boulevard and Broadway are the mosaic-domed Santa Fe Depot and the downtown annex of the **Museum of Contemporary Art, San Diego** ④.

A tour of the working heart of downtown might begin at the corner of 1st Avenue and Broadway, near Spreckels Theatre, a grand old stage that presents pop concerts and touring plays these days. A block east and across the street sits the historic **U.S. Grant Hotel** ⑤. If you cross Broadway, you'll be able to enter **Horton Plaza** ⑥, San Diego's favorite retail playland. Fourth Avenue, the eastern boundary of Horton Plaza, doubles as the western boundary of the 16-block **Gaslamp Quarter** ⑦. Head south to Island Avenue and one block east to the William Heath Davis House, where you can get a touring map of the district.

TIMING

The above walks take about an hour each, though there's enough to do in downtown San Diego to keep you busy for at least two days— or three if you really like to shop. In January and February, when the gray whales migrate from the Pacific Northwest to southern Baja, it's a must to book a whale-watching excursion at the Broadway pier. For a guided tour of the Gaslamp Quarter, plan to visit the area on Saturday, when parking is also less restricted on the streets. The Horton Plaza parking lots, however, are as packed then as they are during the week.

Sights to See

❶ The Embarcadero. The bustle along Harbor Drive's waterfront walkway comes less these days from the activities of tuna and other fishing folk, but it remains the nautical soul of San Diego. People here still make a living from the sea: restaurants line the piers, as do sea vessels of every variety—cruise ships, ferries, tour boats, houseboats, and naval destroyers. Many boats along the Embarcadero have been converted into floating gift shops, and others are awaiting restoration.

On the north end of the Embarcadero, at Ash Street, you'll find the Maritime Museum (☞ *below*). Just south of it, the pastel **B Street Pier** is used by ships from major cruise lines as both a port of call and a departure point. The cavernous pier building has a cruise-information center and a small, cool bar and gift shop. Day-trippers getting ready to set sail gather at the **Broadway Pier,** also known as the excursion pier. Tickets for harbor tours and whale-watching trips are sold here.

The navy's Eleventh Naval District has control of the next few waterfront blocks to the south. A steady stream of joggers, bicyclists, and serious walkers on the Embarcadero pathway picks up speed at **Tuna Harbor,** the former hub of one of San Diego's earliest and most successful industries, commercial tuna fishing. These days, you'll see only a few boats that continue in this trade tied up at the docks. The **San Diego Convention Center** was designed by Arthur Erickson; the blue sky and sea complement the building's nautical lines. The center often holds trade shows that are open to the public, and tours of the building are available.

NEED A BREAK?	Those waiting for their boats at the Broadway Pier can enjoy some New England–style clam chowder in an edible sourdough bowl at the **Bay Cafe** (✉ 1050 N. Harbor Dr., ☎ 619/595–1083).

❼ Gaslamp Quarter. The 16-block National Historic District centered on 5th and 4th avenues from Broadway to Market Street contains most of San Diego's Victorian-style commercial buildings from the late 1800s. In the latter part of the 19th century, businesses thrived in this area, but at the turn of the century downtown's commercial district moved farther west toward Broadway, and many of San Diego's first buildings fell into disrepair. During the early 1900s, the quarter became known as the Stingaree district. Prostitutes picked up sailors in lively area taverns, and dance halls and crime flourished here.

In 1974, history buffs, developers, architects, and artists formed the Gaslamp Quarter Council. Bent on preserving the district, they gathered funds from the government and private benefactors and began cleaning up the quarter, restoring the finest old buildings, and attracting businesses and the public back to the heart of New Town. Two decades later, their efforts have paid off.

At the farthest end of the redeveloped quarter, the **William Heath Davis House** (✉ 410 Island Ave., at 3rd Ave., ☎ 619/233–4692), one of the first residences in town, now serves as the information center for the Gaslamp Quarter. Davis was a San Franciscan whose ill-fated attempt to develop the waterfront area preceded the more successful one of Alonzo Horton. In 1850, Davis had this prefab saltbox-style house shipped around Cape Horn and assembled in San Diego. During museum hours—weekdays 10–2, Sat. 10–5, Sun. noon–4—docents are available to show you around the house; the admission is $1. Two-hour walking tours of the historic district leave from the Davis House on Saturday at 11; the cost for these or a self-guided audio tour (phone ahead to reserve a headset) is $5. The museum also has a detailed map of the district.

Across the street from the William Heath Davis House stands the **Horton Grand Hotel** (✉ 311 Island Ave.). In the mid-1980s, this quintessentially Victorian hostelry was created by joining together two historic hotels, the Kahle Saddlery and the Grand Hotel, built in the boom days of the 1880s; Wyatt Earp stayed at the Kahle Saddlery—then called the Brooklyn Hotel—while he was in town speculating on real estate ventures and opening gambling halls. The two hotels were dismantled and reconstructed on a new site, about four blocks from their original locations. A small Chinese Museum serves as a tribute to the surrounding Chinatown district, a collection of modest homes that once housed Chinese laborers and their families.

Many of the quarter's landmark buildings are on 4th and 5th avenues, between Island Avenue and Broadway. Among the nicest are the Backesto Building, the Louis Bank of Commerce, and the Mercantile Building, all on 5th Avenue, and the Keating Building on F Street. Johnny M's 801, at the corner of 4th Avenue and F Street, is a restored turn-of-the-century tavern with a 12-foot mahogany bar and a spectacular stained-glass domed ceiling.

The section of G Street between 6th and 9th avenues has become a haven for galleries; stop in any one of them to pick up a map of the downtown arts district. For information about openings and other current events in the district, call the **Gaslamp Quarter Hot Line** (☎ 619/233–4691).

NEED A
BREAK?

Fifth Avenue between F and G streets is lined with restaurants, a number of them with outdoor patios. **Trattoria La Strada** (✉ 702 5th Ave., ☎ 619/239–3400) is a good place to sit out on a fine afternoon with a glass of wine and an antipasto. Many hip coffeehouses have also sprung up in the Gaslamp Quarter; you can nurse a double espresso at **Café LuLu** (✉ 419 F St., ☎ 619/238–0114) for hours.

★ ❻ **Horton Plaza.** Downtown's centerpiece is the shopping, dining, and entertainment mall that fronts Broadway and G Street from 1st to 4th avenues and covers more than six city blocks. Designed by Jon Jerde and completed in 1985, Horton Plaza is far from what one would imagine a shopping center—or city center—to be. A collage of pastels with elaborate, colorful tile work on benches and stairways, cloth banners waving in the air, and modern sculptures marking the entrances, Horton Plaza rises in uneven, staggered levels to six floors; great views of downtown from the harbor to Balboa Park and beyond can be had here. The complex's innovative architecture has strongly affected the rest of downtown's development, and new apartment and condominium complexes along G and Market streets mimic its brightly colored towers and cupolas.

Horton Plaza has a large, multilevel parking garage; the long lines of cars in search of a place to land show just how successful the complex has become. The first three hours of parking are free with validation; after that, it's $1 for every half hour. If you use this garage, be sure to remember where you leave your car. The lot is notoriously confusing, and the various levels, coded by fruits and vegetables, don't quite match up with the levels the shops are on.

Robinsons-May, Nordstrom, and Mervyn's department stores anchor the shopping sections, with an eclectic assortment of nearly 150 clothing, sporting-goods, jewelry, book, and gift shops flanking them. Other attractions include a Sam Goody's megastore and a Hard Rock Cafe. A movie complex, restaurants, and a long row of take-out ethnic food shops and dining patios line the uppermost tier. On the lowest level, facing 1st Avenue, is the Farmers Market, an upscale grocery with fresh gourmet meats, seafood, and produce. The San Diego Repertory Theatre, one of the longest-burning and brightest lights in San Diego's burgeoning theater scene, has two stages below ground level. The **International Visitor Information Center,** at street level on the corner of 1st Avenue and F Street, is a good resource.

② **The Maritime Museum.** Three restored ships that may be toured for one admission price afford a glimpse into San Diego's heyday as a commercial seaport. The *Berkeley,* an 1898 riverboat moored at the foot of Ash Street doubles as museum headquarters. The boat's carved-wood paneling, stained-glass windows, and plate-glass mirrors have been restored, and its main deck serves as a floating museum, with exhibits on oceanography, naval history, and the America's Cup Race. Anchored next to the *Berkeley,* the small Scottish steam yacht *Medea,* launched in 1904, may be boarded but has no interpretive displays. The most interesting of the three ships is the *Star of India,* a windjammer built in 1863 and docked at the foot of Grape Street. The ship's high wooden masts and white sails flapping in the wind have been a harbor landmark since 1926. Built at Ramsey on the Isle of Man, the *Star of India* made 21 trips around the world in the late 1800s, when it traveled the East Indian trade route, shuttled immigrants from England to Australia, and served the Alaskan salmon trade. ⌧ *1306 N. Harbor Dr.,* ☎ *619/234–9153.* ⌨ *$6.* ☉ *Ships daily 9–8.*

④ **Museum of Contemporary Art, San Diego.** The downtown annex of the city's modern art museum, which opened in 1993 while the main facility in La Jolla was undergoing renovation, has taken on its own personality. The two-story building has four small galleries that host rotating shows. It's fronted by a Sculpture Plaza that is dominated by a huge work by artist Jonathan Borofsky. ⌧ *1001 Kettner Blvd.,* ☎ *619/234–1172 or 619/454–3541 (recorded exhibition information).* ⌨ *$4; 1st Tues. of month free.* ☉ *Tues. and Thurs.–Sat. 10–5, Wed. 10–8, Sun. noon–5.*

★ **③** **Seaport Village.** Three shopping plazas reflect the architectural styles of early California, especially New England clapboard and Spanish Mission. A ¼-mile wooden boardwalk that runs along the bay, as well as 4 miles of simulated dirt-road and cobblestone paths, leads to a bustling array of specialty shops, snack bars, and restaurants—more than 75 in all. The Broadway Flying Horses Carousel, created by I. D. Looff in Coney Island in 1890, was moved from its next home, Salisbury Beach in Massachusetts, and faithfully restored for Seaport Village's West Plaza; tickets are $1. The Time Out entertainment center near the carousel has video games. ☎ *619/235–4013 or 619/235–4014.*

NEED A BREAK? In the Central Plaza, **Upstart Crow & Co.** (☎ 619/232–4855), a combination bookstore and coffeehouse, serves cappuccino, espresso, and great pastries and cakes.

⑤ **U.S. Grant Hotel.** Far more formal than most other hotels in San Diego, the doyenne of downtown lodgings has a marble lobby, gleaming chandeliers, white-gloved doormen, and other touches that hark back to the more gracious era when it was built (1910). Over the years, it became noted for its famous guests—U.S. presidents from Woodrow Wilson to George Bush have stayed here—but it got a different kind of press in 1969, when the old-boy's-clubby Grant's Grill became the site of a sit-in by eight local women who objected to its policy of allowing males only before 3 PM. ⌧ *326 Broadway.*

En Route San Diego's Mexican-American community is centered in Barrio Logan, under the Coronado Bridge on the downtown side, and **Chicano Park,** spread along National Avenue from Dewey to Crosby streets, is the barrio's recreational hub. If you're headed for Coronado, it's worth taking a short detour to see the huge murals of Mexican history painted on the bridge supports at National Avenue and Dewey Street; they're among the best examples of folk art in the city.

Coronado

The streets of Coronado are wide, quiet, and friendly, with lots of neighborhood parks where young families mingle with the area's many senior citizens. Grand old homes face the waterfront and the Coronado Municipal Golf Course, with its setting under the bridge, at the north end of Glorietta Bay; it's the site of the annual Fourth of July fireworks. Community celebrations and live-band concerts take place in Spreckels Park on Orange Avenue.

Coronado is visible from downtown and Point Loma and accessible via the arching blue 2.2-mile-long San Diego–Coronado Bridge, a landmark just beyond downtown's skyline. There is a $1 toll for crossing the bridge into Coronado, but cars carrying two or more passengers may enter through the free car-pool lane.

You can board the ferry, operated by San Diego Harbor Excursion (☎ 619/234–4111; in CA, 800/442–7847), at downtown San Diego's Embarcadero from the Broadway Pier, at Broadway and Harbor Drive; you'll arrive at the Ferry Landing Marketplace. Not long ago, San Diego Harbor Excursion (☎ 619/235–8294 for reservations and schedules) instituted water-taxi service from Seaport Village to Ferry Landing Marketplace, Le Meridien Resort, and the Hotel Del Coronado.

A Good Tour

Numbers in the text correspond to numbers in the margin and on the Central San Diego map.

Coronado is easy to navigate without a car. When you depart the ferry, you can explore the shops at the **Ferry Landing Marketplace** ⑧ and, from there, catch a trolley-like tour bus—the fare is 50¢—that runs down **Orange Avenue** ⑨, Coronado's main tourist drag. The **Hotel Del Coronado** ⑩ is at the end of Orange Avenue. A bit northwest of the hotel is the **Coronado Beach Historical Museum** ⑪. If you've brought your swimsuit, you might continue on to **Silver Strand Beach State Park** ⑫.

TIMING

A leisurely stroll through Coronado takes an hour or so, more if you shop or walk along the beach. If you're a history buff, you might want to visit on Thursday or Saturday, when you can combine the 1½-hour walking tour of Coronado's historic homes with a visit to the Coronado Beach Historical Museum, open Wednesday through Sunday afternoons. The tour departs at 11 AM from the Glorietta Bay Inn, another of the island's outstanding early structures, across from the Hotel Del. Whenever you come, if you're not staying on the island, remember to get back to the dock in time to catch the final ferry out. The last trolley to the Ferry Landing Marketplace leaves from Silver Strand State Park at about 6:15.

Sights to See

⑪ **Coronado Beach Historical Museum.** A restored Cape Cod–style cottage contains a museum that celebrates the island's history with photographs and displays of its formative events and major sites: the Hotel Del Coronado, including an original chamber pot from one of the rooms; Tent City, a summer resort just south of the Del developed by John Spreckels at the turn of the century; the early ferry boats; and the North Island Naval Air Station. ⊠ *1126 Loma Ave.,* ☎ *619/435–7242.* 🖼 *Free; donations accepted.* ☉ *Wed.–Sat. 10–4, Sun. noon–4.*

8 **Ferry Landing Marketplace.** The aptly named point of disembarkation for the ferry, this collection of shops is actually a new development on an old site. Its buildings resemble the gingerbread domes of the Hotel Del Coronado, long the area's main attraction. ⊠ *1st St. and B Ave.,* ☎ *619/435–8895.*

★ **10** **Hotel Del Coronado.** The island's most prominent landmark, selected as a National Historic Site, the Del, as natives call it, has a colorful history, integrally connected with that of Coronado itself. The hotel was completed in 1888, and Thomas Edison himself threw the switch as the Del became the world's first electrically lighted hotel. A red carpet leads up the front stairs to the main lobby, with its grand oak pillars and ceiling, and out to the central courtyard and gazebo. To the right is the Crown Room, a cavernous room with an arched ceiling made of notched sugar pine and constructed without nails. The Grand Ballroom overlooks the ocean and the hotel's long white beach. The patio surrounding the sky-blue swimming pool is a great place for sitting back and imagining what the bathers looked like during the '20s, when the hotel rocked with the good times. ⊠ *1500 Orange Ave.,* ☎ *619/435–6611.* ☜ *$10 for 1-hr guided tour from lobby Thurs.–Sat. 10 and 11 AM, $5 for headsets for self-guided tour.*

9 **Orange Avenue.** It's easy to imagine you're on a street in Cape Cod when you stroll along this thoroughfare, Coronado's version of a downtown: The clapboard houses, small restaurants, and boutiques—many of them selling nautical paraphernalia—are in some ways more characteristic of New England than they are of California. But the East Coast illusion tends to dissipate as quickly as a winter fog here when you catch sight of one of the avenue's many citrus trees—or realize it's February and the sun is warming your face.

12 **Silver Strand Beach State Park.** The stretch of sand that runs along Silver Strand Boulevard from the Hotel Del Coronado to Imperial Beach dispels the illusion that Coronado is an island. The clean beach is a perfect family gathering spot, with rest rooms and lifeguards.

Harbor Island, Point Loma, and Shelter Island

Point Loma curves around the San Diego Bay west of downtown and the airport, protecting the center city from the Pacific's tides and waves. Its bayside shores front huge estates, with sailboats and yachts packed tightly in private marinas. Harbor Island and Shelter Island were constructed out of detritus from San Diego Bay.

A Good Tour

Numbers in the text correspond to numbers in the margin and on the Central San Diego map.

Take Catalina Drive all the way south to the tip of Point Loma to reach **Cabrillo National Monument** ⑬; you'll be retracing the steps of the earliest European explorers if you use this as a jumping-off point for a tour. Just north of the monument are the white headstones of **Fort Rosecrans National Cemetery** ⑭. Continue north on Catalina Boulevard to Hill Street and turn left to reach the dramatic **Sunset Cliffs** ⑮, at the western side of Point Loma near Ocean Beach. Return to Catalina Boulevard and backtrack south for a few blocks to find Canon Street, which leads toward the peninsula's eastern (bay) side. Almost at the shore, you'll see **Scott Street** ⑯, the main commercial drag of Point Loma. Scott Street is bisected by Shelter Island Drive, which leads to two areas formed of landfill, **Shelter Island** ⑰ and (via Rosecrans Street and North Harbor Drive) **Harbor Island** ⑱.

TIMING

If you're interested in seeing the tidal pools at Cabrillo National Monument, you'll need to call ahead to find out when low tide will occur. Scott Street, with its Point Loma Seafoods, is a good place to find yourself at lunchtime, and Sunset Cliffs Park is where you might want to be when the daylight starts to wane. This drive takes about an hour if you stop briefly at each sight.

Sights to See

★ ⓭ **Cabrillo National Monument.** This 144-acre preserve marks the site of the first European visit to San Diego, made by Portuguese explorer Juan Rodríguez Cabrillo, who had earlier gone on voyages with Hernán Cortés, came to this spot, which he called San Miguel, in 1542. Government grounds were set aside to commemorate his discovery in 1913 and today the monument, with its rugged cliffs and shores and outstanding overlooks, is one of the most frequently visited of all National Park Service sites. The **visitor center** presents films and lectures about Cabrillo's voyage, the sea-level tidal pools, and the gray whales migrating offshore. Exploring the grounds consumes time and calories; bring a picnic and rest on a bench overlooking the sailboats headed to sea.

Interpretive stations with recorded information in six languages—including, appropriately enough, Portuguese—have been installed along the walkways that edge the cliffs. Signs explain the views and posters depict the various navy, fishing, and pleasure craft that sail into and fly over the bay.

A **statue of Cabrillo** overlooks downtown from the next windy promontory, where visitors gather to admire the stunning panorama over the bay, from the snowcapped San Bernardino Mountains, 130 miles north, to the hills surrounding Tijuana to the south. The stone figure standing on the bluff looks rugged and dashing, but he is a creation of an artist's imagination—no portraits of Cabrillo are known to exist.

The moderately steep 2-mile **Bayside Trail** winds through coastal sage scrub, curving under the clifftop lookouts and bringing you ever closer to the bayfront scenery. The oil lamp of the **Old Point Loma Lighthouse** was first lit in 1855. The lighthouse is open to visitors.

The western and southern cliffs of Cabrillo Monument are prime whale-watching territory. More accessible sea creatures can be seen in the **tidal pools** at the foot of the monument's western cliffs. Drive north from the visitor center to the first road on the left, which winds down to the coast guard station and the shore. When the tide is low, you can walk on the rocks around saltwater pools filled with starfish, crabs, anemones, octopuses, and hundreds of other sea creatures and plants. ⊠ *1800 Cabrillo Memorial Dr.,* ☎ *619/557–5450.* ▨ *$4 per car, $2 per person entering on foot or by bicycle; free for Golden Age Passport holders, people with disabilities, and children under 17.* ⊙ *Park daily 9–5:15, Old Lighthouse 9–5, Bayside Trail 9–4, tidal-pool areas 9–4:30 in winter; in summer, park is open until sunset and other areas have extended hrs.*

⓮ **Fort Rosecrans National Cemetery.** Many of the 65,000 laid to rest here were killed in battles that predate California's statehood. Perhaps the most impressive structure in the cemetery is the 75-foot granite obelisk called the Bennington Monument, which commemorates the 66 crew members who died from a boiler explosion and fire on board the U.S.S. *Bennington* in 1905. ☎ *619/553–2084.* ⊙ *Daily 8–5, 8–7 on Memorial Day.*

⓲ **Harbor Island.** In 1961, a 1½-mile-long peninsula was created out of 12 million cubic yards of sand and mud dredged from San Diego Bay.

Restaurants and high-rise hotels line the inner shores of Harbor Island. Across from the western end of Harbor Island, at the mainland's Spanish Landing Park, a bronze plaque marks the arrival in 1769 of a party of Spaniards who headed north from San Diego to conquer California.

16 **Scott Street.** Running along Point Loma's waterfront from Shelter Island to the Marine Corps Recruiting Center on Harbor Drive, this thoroughfare is lined with deep-sea fishing charters and whale-watching boats. It's a good spot from which to watch fishermen (and women) haul marlin, tuna, and puny mackerel off their boats.

NEED A BREAK?

The freshest and tastiest fish to be found along Point Loma's shores comes from **Point Loma Sea Foods** (⊠ 2805 Emerson St., ☎ 619/223–1109), off Scott Street behind the Vagabond Inn. There are a couple of places to sit outside, but most people squeeze into the small dining area behind the store.

17 **Shelter Island.** Actually a peninsula, the island is the center of San Diego's yacht-building industry. A long sidewalk runs from the landscaped lawns of the **San Diego Yacht Club** (tucked down Anchorage Street off Shelter Island Drive), past boat brokerages to hotels and marinas, which line the inner shore, facing Point Loma. There are picnic tables, fire rings, and permanent barbecue grills along the grass. The huge Friendship Bell was given to San Diegans by the people of Yokohama.

15 **Sunset Cliffs.** As their name suggests, the 60-foot-high bluffs on the western side of Point Loma just south of Ocean Beach are a perfect place to watch the sun descend over the sea. To view the tidal pools along the shore, you can descend a staircase on Sunset Cliffs Boulevard at the foot of Laredo Street. Small coves and beaches dot the coastline and are popular with surfers drawn to the pounding waves. Needle's Eye is considered especially challenging; it's said that the chain-link fence surrounding a space between the rock is there because a surfer rode his board into it.

La Jolla

La Jollans have long considered their village to be the Monte Carlo of California, and with good cause. Its coastline curves into natural coves backed by verdant hillsides and covered with homes worth millions. Though La Jolla is considered part of San Diego, it has its own postal zone and a coveted sense of class; old-monied residents mingle here with visiting film stars and royalty who frequent established hotels and private clubs. If development and construction have radically altered the once-serene and private character of the village, it has gained a cosmopolitan air that makes it a popular vacation resort.

The Native Americans called the site La Hoya, meaning "the cave," referring to the grottos dotting the shoreline. The Spaniards changed the name to La Jolla, meaning "the jewel," and its residents have cherished the name and its allusions ever since.

To reach La Jolla from I–5, take the Ardath Road exit if you're traveling north and drive slowly down Prospect Street so you can appreciate the breathtaking view. If you're heading south, get off at the La Jolla Village Drive exit, which will lead into Torrey Pines Road. Prospect Street and Girard Avenue, La Jolla's main drags, are lined with expensive shops and office buildings. The La Jolla nightlife scene is an active one, with jazz clubs, piano bars, and watering holes for the elite younger set coming and going with the trends.

La Jolla

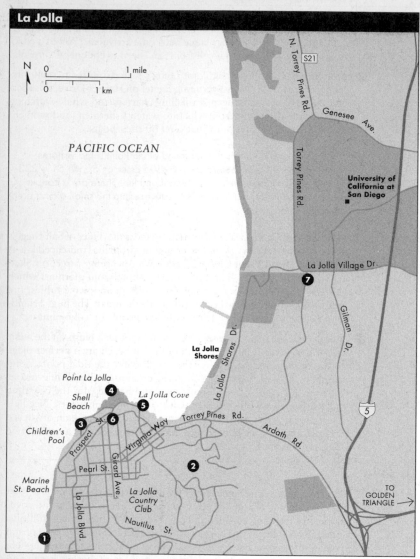

N

0   1 mile

0   1 km

PACIFIC OCEAN

S21

N. Torrey Pines Rd.

Genesee Ave.

Torrey Pines Rd.

University of
California at
San Diego ■

La Jolla Village Dr.

7

Gilman Dr.

La Jolla Shores Dr.

**La Jolla
Shores**

5

Point La Jolla

Shell
Beach

4

La Jolla Cove

5

Prospect St.

3   **6**

Virginia Way

Torrey Pines Rd.

Ardath Rd.

Children's
Pool

Girard Ave.

Pearl St.

2

TO
GOLDEN
TRIANGLE →

Marine
St. Beach

La Jolla Blvd.

La Jolla
Country
Club

Nautilus St.

1

La Jolla Caves, **5**

La Jolla Cove, **4**

La Valencia Hotel, **6**

Mount Soledad, **2**

Museum of
Contemporary Art,
San Diego, **3**

Stephen Birch
Aquarium-
Museum, **7**

Windansea Beach, **1**

A Good Tour

Numbers in the text correspond to numbers in the margin and on the La Jolla map.

At the intersection of La Jolla Boulevard and Nautilus Street, turn toward the sea to reach **Windansea Beach** ①, one of the best surfing spots in town. **Mount Soledad** ②, east on Nautilus Street, is La Jolla's highest spot. The town's remodeled cultural center, the **Museum of Contemporary Art, San Diego** ③, lies on the less trafficked southern end of Prospect. Continue north on Prospect and turn west onto Coast Boulevard to reach the village's great natural attraction, **La Jolla Cove** ④. Just past the far northern point of the cove, in front of the La Jolla Cave and Shell Shop, a trail leads down to **La Jolla Caves** ⑤. One block inland from the cove is Prospect Street. At the intersection of Prospect and Girard Avenue sits the pretty-in-pink **La Valencia Hotel** ⑥. The La Jolla Shores Drive beaches are some of the finest in San Diego. Inland a bit is the **Stephen Birch Aquarium-Museum** ⑦.

TIMING

This tour makes for a leisurely day, though it can be driven in a couple of hours, including stops to take in the views and explore La Jolla Village. The Museum of Contemporary Art is closed Monday.

Sights to See

⑤ **La Jolla Caves.** It's 133 steps down to Sunny Jim Cave, the largest of the grottoes in La Jolla Cove; they may be entered behind the La Jolla Cave and Shell Shop. Claustrophobic types can stay behind and look at the photos of the caves in the shop, and browse a good selection of shells and coral jewelry. ⊠ *1325 Coast Blvd.,* ☎ *619/454–6080.* ☞ *$1.50.* ◷ *Mon.–Sat. 10–5, Sun. 11–5, sometimes later in summer.*

★ ④ **La Jolla Cove.** The wooded spread that looks out over a shimmering blue inlet is what first attracted everyone from the Native Americans to the glitterati to La Jolla. You'll find it beyond where Girard Avenue deadends into Coast Boulevard, marked by towering palms that line the sidewalk. The **Children's Pool,** at the south end of the park, is aptly named for its curving beach and shallow waters, protected by a sea wall from strong currents and waves. Walk through **Ellen Browning Scripps Park,** past the groves of twisted junipers to the cliff's edge.

⑥ **La Valencia Hotel.** The Art Deco–style La Valencia, which has operated as a luxury hotel since 1928, has long been a gathering spot for Hollywood celebrities. The hotel's grand lobby, with floor-to-ceiling windows overlooking La Jolla Cove, is a popular wedding spot, and the Whaling Bar is still a favorite meeting place for La Jolla's power brokers. ⊠ *1132 Prospect St.,* ☎ *619/454–0771.*

② **Mount Soledad.** The top of this mountain, on which there's a large white cross, is an excellent vantage point from which to get a sense of San Diego's geography: Looking down from here, you can see the coast from the county's northern border to the south far beyond downtown— barring smog and haze.

③ **Museum of Contemporary Art, San Diego.** After a two-year expansion and remodeling project, the main facility of San Diego's modern art museum reopened in March 1996. The light-filled Axlined Court serves as the new entrance to the museum; it does triple duty as reception area, exhibition hall, and forum for special events. A patterned terrazzo floor subtly leads visitors in the directions of the galleries where the museum's permanent collection is on display. The museum's downtown facility hosts most of the rotating exhibits now. The artworks get major competition from the striking redesign and from

the museum's setting: You can look out from the top of a grand stairway onto a garden that contains rare 100-year-old California plant specimens and, beyond that, to the Pacific Ocean. The permanent collection
of post-1950s art has a strong representation of California artists but
also includes examples of every major art movement of the past half
century, plus important pieces by San Diego and Tijuana artists. An
expanded bookstore and refurbished Sherwood Auditorium both have
separate outside entrances now, so you don't have to enter the museum
to browse the excellent collection of modern-art volumes and gifts or
attend the museum's nighttime programs. ⊠ *700 Prospect St.,* ☎
619/454–3541. ☉ *Tues. and Thurs.–Sat. 10–5, Wed. 10–8, Sun.
noon–5.* ⊡ *$4; free first Tues. of the month.*

❼ Stephen Birch Aquarium-Museum. The largest oceanographic exhibit
in the United States, operated under the aegis of the Scripps Institute
of Oceanography, sits at the end of a signed drive leading off North
Torrey Pines Road just south of La Jolla Village Drive. More than 30
huge tanks are filled with colorful saltwater fish, and a spectacular
70,000-gallon tank simulates a La Jolla kelp forest. Next to the fish
themselves, the most interesting attraction is the 12-minute simulated
submarine ride. ⊠ *2300 Expedition Way,* ☎ *619/534–3474.* ⊡ *$6.50,
active military free; parking $3.* ☉ *Daily 9–5; closed Thanksgiving,
Dec. 25.*

❶ Windansea Beach. Fans of pop satirist Tom Wolfe may recall *The
Pump House Gang,* which pokes fun at the So-Cal surfing culture. Wolfe
drew many of his barbs from observations he made at Windansea, the
surfing beach just west of La Jolla Boulevard near Nautilus Street. The
wave action here is said to be as good as that in Hawaii.

Mission Bay

The 4,600-acre Mission Bay aquatic park is San Diego's monument
to sports and fitness. Admission to its 27 miles of bayshore beaches
and 17 miles of ocean frontage is free. A 5-mile-long pathway runs
through this section of the bay from a trailer park and miniature golf
course, south past the high-rise Hilton Hotel to Sea World Drive. Playgrounds and picnic areas abound on the beach and low grassy hills of
the park. On weekday evenings, joggers, bikers, and skaters line the
path. In the daytime, swimmers, water-skiers, fishers, and boaters—
some in single-person kayaks, others in crowded powerboats—vie for
space in the water. One Mission Bay caveat: Swimmers should note
signs warning about water pollution; certain areas of the bay are
chronically polluted, and bathing is strongly discouraged.

A Good Tour

*Numbers in the text correspond to numbers in the margin and on the
Mission Bay map.*

If you're coming from I–5, the **Visitor Information Center** ① is just about
at the end of the Clairemont Drive–East Mission Bay Drive exit (you'll
see the prominent sign). Where East Mission Bay Drive turns into Sea
World Drive you can detour left to **Fiesta Island** ② or continue around
the curve to the west for the turnoff sign for **Sea World** ③. You'll next
come to Ingraham Street, the central north–south drag through the bay.
If you take it north, you'll soon see Vacation Road, which leads into
the focal point of this part of the bay, the waterskiing mecca of **Vacation Isle** ④. At Ingraham, Sea World Drive turns into Sunset Cliffs Boulevard and intersects with West Mission Bay Drive. Almost immediately
south of where West Mission Bay Drive turns into Mission Boulevard
is the resurrected **Belmont Park** ⑤.

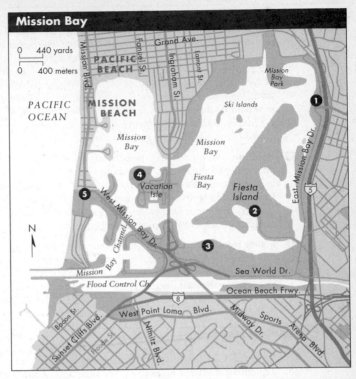

Mission Bay

0   440 yards
0   400 meters

PACIFIC
OCEAN

PACIFIC
BEACH

MISSION
BEACH

Grand Ave.

Mission
Bay
Park

Ski Islands

Mission
Bay

Mission
Bay

Fiesta
Bay

Vacation
Isle

Fiesta
Island

West Mission Bay Dr.

Mission Bay Channel

Mission Bay
Flood Control Ch.

Sea World Dr.

Ocean Beach Frwy.

West Point Loma Blvd.

Sunset Cliffs Blvd.

Bacon St.

Nimitz Blvd.

Froude St.

Midway Dr.

Sports   Arena   Blvd.

East Mission Bay Dr.

Fanuel St.

Ingraham St.

Lamont St.

Mission Blvd.

N

TIMING

It would take less than an hour to drive through Mission Bay. You may
not find a visit to Sea World fulfilling unless you spend at least a half
day. The park is open daily, but not all its attractions operate year-round.

Sights to See

5 Belmont Park. The once-abandoned amusement park between the bay
and Mission Beach boardwalk is now a shopping, dining, and recreation area. Twinkling lights outline the refurbished **roller coaster,** created as the Giant Dipper in 1925. There's also an antique carousel.
The Plunge, an indoor swimming pool, opened in 1925 as the largest—
60 by 125 feet—salt-water pool in the world. It's had fresh water since
1951. ⊠ *3146 Mission Blvd.,* ☎ *619/488–0668 (park), 619/488–1549
(roller coaster), 619/488–3110 (pool).*

2 Fiesta Island. The most undeveloped area of Mission Bay Park is popular with dog-owners—it's the only place in the park where their pets
can run free—as well as with jetskiers and speedboat racers. At Christmas, it provides an excellent vantage point for viewing for the bay's
Parade of Lights. In July, the annual Over-the-Line Tournament, a competition involving a local variety of softball, attracts thousands of
players and oglers, drawn by the teams' raunchy names and outrageous
behavior.

3 Sea World. One of the world's largest marine-life amusement parks is
spread over 100 tropically landscaped bayfront acres, where a cool breeze
always seems to rise from the water. The traditional favorite exhibit
at Sea World is the **Shamu show,** with giant killer whales entertaining
the crowds, but performing dolphins, sea lions, and otters at other shows
also delight audiences. **Shamu Backstage** is a behind-the-scenes look
at the exhibit. **Baywatch at Sea World,** features waterski stunts and
beachfront antics similar to those seen on the syndicated TV show. Other

exhibits include the **Penguin Encounter**, the **Shark Encounter**, the hands-on **California Tide Pool**, and **Mission: Bermuda Triangle**, which replicates the thrills of a submersible dive to the ocean bottom. Many hotels offer Sea World specials, worth seeking out as the children's fee ($22.95) is quite hefty. ✉ *1720 South Shores Rd., near the west end of I–8,* ☎ *619/226–3815 or 619/226–3901 for recorded information.* ✍ *$30.95; parking $5 cars, $2 motorcycles, $7 RVs and campers; 90-min behind-the-scenes walking tours $6 additional. MC, V.* ☺ *Daily 10–dusk; extended hrs during summer. Call ahead to inquire about park hrs for the day you intend to visit.*

❹ Vacation Isle. Ingraham Street bisects this Mission Bay island, which provides two distinct experiences to visitors. The west side is taken up by the Princess Resort, but you don't have to be a guest to enjoy the hotel's lushly landscaped grounds and bayfront restaurants. Waterski clubs congregate at Ski Beach on the east side of the island, where there's a parking lot as well as picnic and restroom facilities.

❶ Visitor Information Center. On a glassed-in patio overlooking the bay, you can peruse a free map while enjoying a cold drink from the snack bar. The center is a gathering spot for the runners, walkers, and exercisers who take part in group activities in the area. There's also a small gift shop. ✉ *2688 E. Mission Bay Dr.,* ☎ *619/276–8200.* ☺ *Mon.–Sat. 9–5 (until 6 or 7 in summer), Sun. 9:30–4:30 (until 5:30 in summer).*

Old Town

Although Old Town is often credited as being the first European settlement in southern California, the true beginnings took place overlooking Old Town from atop Presidio Park. There, Father Junípero Serra established the first of California's missions, San Diego de Alcalá, in 1769. In 1774, the hilltop was declared a Royal Presidio, or fortress, and the mission was moved to its current location along the San Diego River, 6 miles west of the original. Native Americans, responding to the loss of their land as the mission expanded along the riverbed, attacked and burned it in 1775. A later assault on the presidio was less successful, and their revolt was short-lived.

The pioneers living within the presidio's walls were mostly Spanish soldiers, poor Mexicans, and mestizos of Spanish and Native American ancestry, many of whom were unaccustomed to farming San Diego's arid land. They existed marginally until 1821, when Mexico gained independence from Spain, claimed its lands in California, and flew the Mexican flag over the presidio. In 1846, during the war between Mexico and the United States, a detachment of marines raised the U.S. flag over the plaza on a pole said to have been a mainmast. The flag was torn down once or twice, but by early 1848, Mexico had surrendered California, and the U.S. flag remained. In 1850, San Diego became an incorporated city, with Old Town as its center.

Old Town's boundaries and reputation as a historic attraction and shopping-dining center have spread in the past few years. On San Diego Avenue, the district's main drag, art galleries and expensive gift shops are interspersed with curio shops, restaurants, and open-air stands selling inexpensive Mexican pottery, jewelry, and blankets. The best of an ever-changing array of shopping plazas constructed in mock Mexican-plaza style is the Old Town Esplanade, between Harney and Conde streets. Juan and Congress streets are also lined with shops and restaurants.

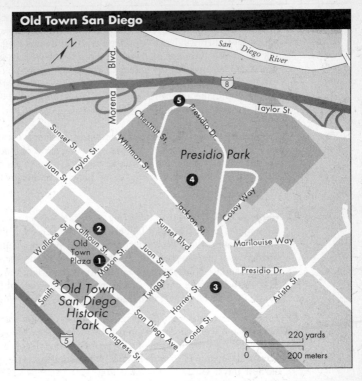

A Good Tour

Numbers in the text correspond to numbers in the margin and on the Old Town San Diego map.

It's possible to trek around Old Town and see all its sights in one day, but unless you regularly hike the Himalayas, we recommend making this a walking-driving combination. Visit the information center at Wallace Street and San Diego Avenue in Old Town Plaza to orientate yourself to the various sights in **Old Town San Diego State Historic Park** ①. Cross north on the west side of the plaza to **Bazaar del Mundo** ②, where you can shop or enjoy some nachos on the terrace of a Mexican restaurant. **Heritage Park** ③ is perched on a hill off Juan Street, three blocks east of the bazaar. Heading west on Juan Street and north on Taylor Street takes you to Presidio Drive, which leads up the hill on which **Presidio Park** ④ and the **Junípero Serra Museum** ⑤ sit.

TIMING

Try to time your visit to coincide with the free daily tours of Old Town given at 2 PM by costumed volunteers at the Robinson-Rose House; they vary depending on the guide, but they're always interesting. If possible, avoid coming here on the weekends as the parking lots are even fuller than usual when San Diegans are off work. Another way to visit old town is on the San Diego Trolley. It takes about two hours to walk through Old Town. If you drive to the Presidio, allot another hour to explore the grounds and museum.

Sights to See

❷ **Bazaar del Mundo.** North of San Diego's Old Town Plaza lies the unofficial center of Old Town, a shopping and dining enclave built to represent a colonial Mexican square. The central courtyard is always in blossom, with magenta bougainvillea, scarlet hibiscus, and irises, poppies, and petunias in season. Ballet Folklorico and flamenco dancers perform on weekend afternoons, and the bazaar frequently holds arts-and-crafts exhibits and Mexican festivals in the courtyard. Colorful shops specializing in Latin American crafts and unusual gift items border the square. Although many of the shops here have high-quality wares, prices can be considerably higher than those at shops on the other side of Old Town plaza; it's a good idea to do some comparative shopping before you make any purchases. ⊠ *2754 Calhoun St.,* ☎ *619/296–3161.* ☉ *Shops daily 10–9.*

NEED A BREAK?
La Panadería bakery (⊠ Bazaar del Mundo, southeast corner, ☎ 619/291-7662) sells fresh, hot *churros*—long sticks of fried dough coated with cinnamon and powdered sugar. Get some hot chocolate to go along and then sit out on one of the benches and enjoy the sugar rush.

❸ **Heritage Park.** The most interesting of the six former residences in this park might be the Sherman Gilbert House, which has a widow's walk and intricate carving on its decorative trim. Bronze plaques detail the history of all the houses, some of which may seem surprisingly colorful; they are in fact accurate representations of the bright tones of the era. The climb up to the park is a little steep, but the view of the harbor is great. ⊠ *2455 Heritage Park Row (park office),* ☎ *619/694–3049.*

❺ **Junípero Serra Museum.** The original Spanish presidio and California's first mission were perched atop the 160-foot hill overlooking Mission Valley; it's now the domain of a museum devoted to cofounders Father Serra and Captain Gaspar de Portola. It houses artifacts from San Diego's earliest days. ⊠ *2727 Presidio Dr.,* ☎ *619/297–3258.* ⚏ *$3.* ☉ *Tues.–Sat. 10–4:30, Sun. noon–4:30.*

★ ❶ **Old Town San Diego State Historic Park.** The six square blocks on the site of San Diego's original pueblo are the heart of Old Town. Most of the 20 historic buildings preserved or recreated by the park cluster around **Old Town Plaza,** bounded by Wallace Street on the west, Calhoun Street on the north, Mason Street on the east, and San Diego Avenue on the south.

The tour map available at the Robinson-Rose House gives details on all of the historic houses on the plaza and in its vicinity; a few of the more interesting ones are noted below. All the houses are open to visitors daily 10–5; currently none charges admission though donations are appreciated.

The **Robinson-Rose House** (⊠ 4002 Wallace St., ☎ 619/220–5422), on the west end of Old Town Plaza, serves as the park office. This was the original commercial center of old San Diego, housing railroad offices, law offices, and the first newspaper press. One room has been restored and outfitted with period furnishings; park rangers show films and distribute information from the living room. An excellent free walking tour of the park leaves from here daily at 2 PM, weather permitting. From 10 to 1 every Wednesday and the first Saturday of the month, park staff and volunteers in period costume give cooking and crafts demonstrations at the Machado y Stewart adobe; adjacent to the Bandini House near Juan Street, you can watch a blacksmith hammering away at his anvil, starting at 10 every Wednesday and Saturday.

On San Diego Avenue, beside the state park headquarters, **Dodson's Corner** is a modern retailer in a mid-19th-century setting; two of the shops in the complex, which sells everything from quilts and western clothing to pottery and jewelry, are reconstructions of homes that stood on the spot in 1848.

On Mason Street, at the corner of Calhoun Street, **La Casa de Bandini** is one of the prettiest haciendas in San Diego. Built in 1829 by a Peruvian, Juan Bandini, the house served as Old Town's social center during Mexican rule. Albert Seeley, a stagecoach entrepreneur, purchased the home in 1869, built a second story, and turned it into the Cosmopolitan Hotel, a comfortable way station for travelers on the day-long trip south from Los Angeles. These days, Casa Bandini's colorful gardens and main-floor dining rooms house a popular Mexican restaurant.

Seeley Stable, next door to La Casa de Bandini on Calhoun Street, became San Diego's stagecoach stop in 1867 and was the transportation hub of Old Town until near the turn of the century, when the Southern Pacific Railroad became the favored mode of travel. The stable now houses a collection of horse-drawn vehicles and western memorabilia, including an exhibit on the California *vaquero,* the original American cowboy, and an array of Native American artifacts.

La Casa de Estudillo was built on Mason Street in 1827 by the commander of the San Diego Presidio, Jose Maria Estudillo. The largest and most elaborate of the original adobe homes, it was occupied by members of the Estudillo family until 1887. After being left to deteriorate for some time, it was purchased and restored in 1910 by sugar magnate and developer John D. Spreckels, who advertised it in bold lettering on the side as "Ramona's Marriage Place." The small chapel in the house was believed to be the setting for the wedding in Helen Hunt Jackson's popular novel.

The **San Diego Union Newspaper Historical Museum** (⊠ Twigg St. and San Diego Ave.) is in the Casa de Altamirano, a New England–style wood-frame house prefabricated in Maine and shipped around Cape Horn in 1851. The building has been restored to replicate the newspaper's offices of 1868, when the first edition of the *San Diego Union* was printed.

❹ Presidio Park. The rolling hillsides of the 40-acre green space overlooking Old Town from the north end of Taylor Street are popular with picnickers, and many couples have taken their wedding vows on the park's long stretches of lawn, some of the greenest in San Diego. It's a nice walk to the summit from Old Town if you're in good shape and wearing the right shoes—it should take about half an hour. At the end of Mason Street, a footpath on the left leads up to the Presidio Ruins, where adobe walls and a bastion have been built above the foundations of the original fortress and chapel.

DINING

By Kathryn Shevelow

In the recent past, a "good San Diego restaurant" usually resembled the bland Chamber of Commerce eatery humorist Calvin Trillin dubs "La Maison de la Casa House," but these days good new restaurants appear on the scene with dizzying rapidity. A stroll down 5th Avenue will give ample evidence of San Diego's love affair with Italian cuisine, echoed in other parts of the city, but the cooking of Spain and France, as well as the various cuisines of Latin America, Asia, the Middle East—and even the United States—are well represented. Of course, San Diego has numerous palaces of innovative California cuisine, which borrows from all these culinary traditions. Another hybrid is Pacific Rim cuisine, a mélange of North American, Latin American, and Asian influences and ingredients.

In addition to downtown, other areas of San Diego share in the new sense of energy, undoubtedly fueled by a collective "caffeine high" thanks to the coffeehouses springing up everywhere from the Gaslamp Quarter to the gas station on the corner. The "Uptown" neighborhood of Hillcrest reminds everyone of San Francisco, partly because of its large gay population, partly because of its urban—and culinary—sophistication. It's no accident that the best new restaurant to open in San Diego in recent memory, Laurel, is on the border of Hillcrest and downtown. And La Jolla, once a sleepy, if wealthy, beach community, is now bursting with restaurants. On weekends, it pulsates with activity until the wee hours.

The guide that follows introduces the visitor to some of San Diego's most accomplished restaurants. One cluster of important culinary traditions, Asian cooking—including the cuisines of China and, especially, Vietnam—is not well represented because its finest practitioners tend to fall outside of the areas of the city commonly visited by tourists. **Phuong Trang** (E 4170 Convoy St., P 619/565-6750) and **Pho Hoa** (E 6921 Linda Vista Rd., P 619/492-9108) are two of several fine Vietnamese establishments. Deserving a special mention is the Chinese restaurant widely considered to be the best in the city: **Emerald Chinese Seafood Restaurant** (E 3709 Convoy St., P 619/565-6888). Come here for a memorable (but not inexpensive) Hong Kong–style dinner or for the unsurpassed dim sum, served daily.

San Diego is an informal city. The advised attire at most of the restaurants listed below is casual. Only one of these restaurants requires men to wear ties. Restaurants are grouped first by type of cuisine, then by neighborhood.

CATEGORY	COST*
$$$$	over $50
$$$	$30–$50
$$	$20–$30
$	under $20

per person for a three-course meal, excluding drinks, service, and 7¼% sales tax

American

Beaches

$$$ ✕ **The Mission Cafe and Coffeehouse.** Breakfast dishes are the strong suit at this slightly shabby Mission Beach café. Portions are large, and they are served "any time." Try the French toast (slices of homemade cinnamon bread artfully arranged over a drizzle of blackberry puree), the tamales with eggs and green chili salsa, or the Mission Rosemary, a mélange of roasted rosemary potatoes, scrambled eggs, tomatoes, and grilled rosemary bread. Dinner entrées include "Chino-Latino" fusion dishes, such as the Pacific Rim risotto, with corn, water chestnuts, and zucchini. The Mission serves good beer on tap, a variety of specialty coffee drinks, and shakes and smoothies. ⊠ *3795 Mission Blvd.*, ☎ *619/488–9060. No credit cards.*

Downtown

$$$ ✕ **Rainwater's.** This tony restaurant is as well known for the size of
★   its portions as for the high quality of its cuisine. The menu includes meat and fish dishes, but this is really the place to come if you crave a perfectly done, thick and tender steak. All the entrées are accompanied by such tasty side dishes as shoestring potatoes, onion rings, and creamed corn. ⊠ *1202 Kettner Blvd., 2nd floor*, ☎ *619/233–5757. AE, DC, MC, V. No lunch weekends.*

La Jolla

$–$$ ╳ **Brockton Villa Restaurant.** This informal restaurant in a restored beach cottage overlooks La Jolla Cove and the ocean. Breakfast and lunch (or weekend brunch) allow you the full advantage of the fabulous day-time view, but don't overlook dinner, whether you're in the mood for a turkey burger or a rack of lamb. The Brockton serves a good range of coffee drinks. You'll have to fight the crowds on sunny weekends. ✉ *1235 Coast Blvd.,* ☎ *619/454–7393. AE, D, MC, V.*

$ ╳ **Choices.** This small cafeteria in the Sports and Health Center at the Scripps Clinic complex serves tasty, low-fat, low-cholesterol food. There's an all-you-can-eat salad bar and a daily selection of healthy sandwiches and entrées. ✉ *10820 N. Torrey Pines Rd.,* ☎ *619/554–3663. Reservations not accepted. No credit cards. Closed weekends. No dinner except Fri. on occasion.*

$ ╳ **Hard Rock Cafe.** The high-energy shrine to rock-and-roll and American food cranks its music up to ear-shattering decibels and hangs rock memorabilia on every available inch of wall space. It's is not a place to come for intimate—or audible—conversation, but the burgers are fine. ✉ *909 Prospect St.,* ☎ *619/454–5101. Reservations not accepted. AE, DC, MC, V.*

Uptown

$$ ╳ **Montanas American Grill.** One of Hillcrest's most popular restaurants, sleek, trendy Montanas serves hearty California-American food. Stick with the least complicated dishes: pastas, barbecued meats, chicken, and salmon, or try the venison chili accompanied by jalapeño cornbread. The appetizer duck cakes are tasty and rich. Wash down your barbecue with one of the microbrewery beers on tap. ✉ *1421 University Ave.,* ☎ *619/297–0722. Reservations essential on weekends. AE, DC, MC, V. No lunch weekends.*

$ ╳ **Crest Cafe.** Often jammed with loyal regulars, this Hillcrest institution specializes in good renditions of basic American café food. You can't go wrong with the old favorites, such as pancakes, burgers, onion rings, salads, and the homemade desserts. ✉ *425 Robinson Ave.,* ☎ *619/295–2510. MC, V.*

$ ╳ **Hob Nob Hill.** This comforting restaurant is still under the same ownership and management as it was when it started in 1944; with its dark wood booths and patterned carpets, Hob Nob Hill seems suspended in the 1950s. But you don't need to be a nostalgia buff to appreciate the bargain-price American home cooking—dishes such as pot roast, fried chicken, and corned beef like your mother never really made. Reservations are suggested for Sunday's copious breakfasts. ✉ *2271 1st Ave.,* ☎ *619/239–8176. AE, D, MC, V.*

Belgian

Beaches

$$–$$$ ╳ **Belgian Lion.** Among the signature dishes here is the cassoulet, a wonderful rich stew of white beans, lamb, pork, sausage, and duck that makes you feel protected from the elements (even in San Diego, where you don't need protection). Lighter meals include braised sea scallops with leeks or poached salmon with fresh vegetables. An impressive selection of wines complements the food. ✉ *2265 Bacon St., Ocean Beach,* ☎ *619/223–2700. Reservations essential. AE, D, DC, MC, V. Closed Sun.–Wed. No lunch.*

436

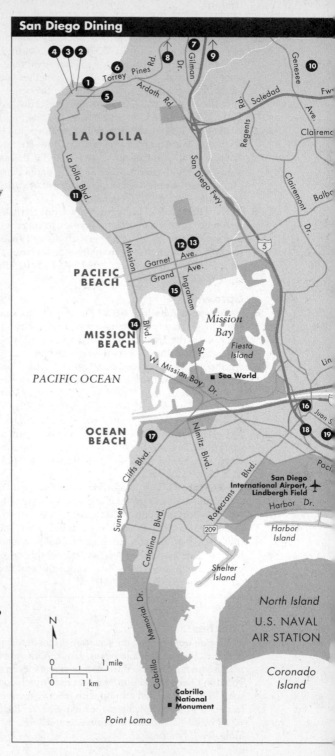

San Diego Dining

LA JOLLA

PACIFIC
BEACH

MISSION
BEACH

PACIFIC OCEAN

OCEAN
BEACH

Mission
Bay

Fiesta
Island

■ Sea World

San Diego
International Airport,
Lindbergh Field ✈

Harbor
Island

Shelter
Island

North Island

U.S. NAVAL
AIR STATION

Coronado
Island

Cabrillo
National
Monument

Point Loma

Torrey Pines Rd.

Ardath Rd.

La Jolla Blvd.

San Diego Fwy.

Regents Rd.

Soledad

Genesee

Claireme

Clairemont

Balbo

Dr.

Gilman

Dr.

Fw

Mission

Garnet Ave.

Grand Ave.

Ingraham St.

Blvd.

W. Mission Bay Dr.

Nimitz Blvd.

Blvd.

Rosecrans

Harbor Dr.

Paci

Juan S.

Lin

209

Sunset

Cliffs Blvd.

Catalina Blvd.

Memorial Dr.

Cabrillo

N

0   1 mile

0   1 km

Cajun and Creole

Downtown

$–$$ ✕ **Bayou Bar and Grill.** Lazily revolving ceiling fans, dark-green wainscoting, and light-pink walls help create a New Orleans atmosphere for the spicy Cajun and Creole specialties served here. You might start with a bowl of superb seafood gumbo and then move on to the sausage, red beans, and rice, the duck esplanade, or any of the fresh Louisiana Gulf seafood dishes. Rich Louisiana desserts include bread pudding, praline cheesecake, and Creole pecan pie. ⊠ *329 Market St.,* ☎ *619/696–8747. AE, D, DC, MC, V.*

California

Uptown

$$ ✕ **California Cuisine.** The menu at this minimalist-chic dining room—
★   gray carpet, stark white walls, and changing displays of locally created artworks—is consistently innovative. Daily selections may include grilled fresh venison served with wild mushrooms and mashed potatoes; the tasty warm chicken salad entrée is a regular feature. You can count on whatever you order to be carefully prepared and elegantly presented. Heat lamps make the back patio a romantic year-round option. ⊠ *1027 University Ave.,* ☎ *619/543–0790. AE, D, DC, MC, V. Closed Mon. No lunch weekends.*

Chinese

Downtown

$–$$ ✕ **Panda Inn.** Even if you're allergic to shopping, the Panda Inn is rea-
★   son enough to come to Horton Plaza. One of the best Chinese restaurants in town, this dining room at the top of Horton Plaza serves subtly seasoned Mandarin and Szechuan dishes in an elegant setting that feels far removed from the rush of commerce below. The fresh seafood dishes are noteworthy, as are the Peking duck, spicy Szechuan bean curd, and twice-cooked pork. Indeed, it's hard to find anything on this menu that's not outstanding. ⊠ *506 Horton Plaza,* ☎ *619/233–7800. AE, D, DC, MC, V.*

Continental

Downtown

$$–$$$ ✕ **Dobson's.** At lunchtime, local politicos and media types rub elbows
★   at the long, polished bar of this highly regarded restaurant; evening patrons include many theatergoers. Although the small two-tier building is suggestive of an earlier era—the lower level looks like a men's club and the upper level has a wrought-iron balcony, elegant woodwork, and gilt cornices—there's nothing outdated about the cuisine. Among the carefully prepared entrées, which change daily, may be roasted quail with fig sauce or chicken risotto. Dobson's signature dish, a superb mussel bisque, comes topped with a crown of puff pastry. The wine list is excellent. ⊠ *956 Broadway Circle,* ☎ *619/231–6771. Reservations essential on weekends. AE, DC, MC, V. Closed Sun. No lunch Sat.*

La Jolla

$$$ ✕ **Top O' the Cove.** Although the reliable but rather stolid menu of this La Jolla institution has been surpassed by glitzier newcomers, year after year San Diego diners give high marks for romance to this cozy, intimate spot with an ocean view. The filet mignon and roasted rack of lamb are reliable choices, as are the boneless chicken breast sautéed with shrimp and shellfish and the sliced duck breast with Armagnac

walnut sauce. ✉ *1216 Prospect St.,* ☎ *619/454–7779. Reservations essential on weekends. AE, DC, MC, V.*

$$–$$$ ✕ **Triangles.** This bar and grill strives for variety. The California-inspired menu, which changes daily, may include fresh fish (try the grilled *ahi* tuna in soy madeira sauce) or rack of lamb. Along with rich dishes, you'll also find some lighter and vegetarian preparations. A small patio, surrounded by lush landscaping, is pleasant at lunch. ✉ *4370 La Jolla Village Dr., in the Northern Trust Bldg.,* ☎ *619/453–6650. AE, DC, MC, V. Closed Sun. No lunch Sat.*

Deli

La Jolla

$ ✕ **SamSon's.** As close as you'll come to a real Jewish deli in San Diego, SamSon's has dill pickles set out on the tables; the menu and portions are enormous. If you're having trouble deciding, go for one of the daily soup-and-sandwich specials, especially the whitefish when it's available. And you can't go wrong with a lox plate for breakfast or a corned beef sandwich for lunch. ✉ *8861 Villa La Jolla Dr.,* ☎ *619/455–1462. AE, D, DC, MC, V.*

French

Coronado

$$$–$$$$ ✕ **Marius.** Le Meridien hotel's highly touted restaurant is the kind of place where on any given evening half the clientele seems to be celebrating a birthday. But even if it's not a special occasion, you will appreciate the refined, high-ceilinged dining room and the impressive menu of French dishes ranging from Paris haute cuisine to Provençale country cooking. The food and presentation are top-notch, the service attentive and professional. ✉ *2000 2nd St.,* ☎ *619/435–3000. Reservations essential on weekends. AE, D, DC, MC, V. Closed Sun.–Mon. No lunch.*

La Jolla

$$–$$$$ ✕ **Cindy Black's.** La Jolla abounds with overpriced and underachieving restaurants, but this one offers true value: subtle, stylishly presented dishes, often with a Mediterranean touch. The menu changes seasonally, but possibilities include arugula and red pepper salad, a hearty spaghetti with white beans in a Chianti sauce, tender grilled salmon on caramelized onions, and some seductive desserts: a house soufflé and a beyond-decadent Belgian-chocolate "brownie" with homemade caramel ice cream. Reasonable prix-fixe menus are served all Sunday evening and during the early-bird hours on weeknights. ✉ *5721 La Jolla Blvd.,* ☎ *619/456–6299. AE, D, DC, MC, V.*

French Caribbean

Downtown

$$ ✕ **Alizé.** Comfortable Alizé showcases the cooking of the French West
★ Indies, a savory mixture of Caribbean and Continental traditions. The moderate prices cover a four-course dinner, a great bargain for a meal this satisfying. As you would expect, seafood reigns supreme (although red meat does appear on the menu, including a signature rack of lamb); the most interesting preparations include the *zouritte*, with calamari, ginger, and coconut milk, and the seabass *arachides*, baked with spices in a corn husk. The menu achieves a good balance between the exotic and the more familiar. Lunch includes a variety of salads, sandwiches, and light entrées. ✉ *The Paladion, 777 Front St., Suite 430,* ☎ *619/234–0411. No lunch Sun. AE, D, DC, MC, V.*

French and Mediterranean

Uptown

$$$ ✕ **Laurel.** Long a San Diego culinary star, chef Douglas Organ has out-
★ done himself this time. Below street level in a room that combines com-
fort with sophistication, Laurel spotlights the cooking of southern
France and the Mediterranean. Its culinary philosophy is straightfor-
ward: the best fresh ingredients prepared simply, *con gusto*. The menu
changes daily, but many favorite dishes appear regularly. For starters,
try the red pepper and seafood soup or the lightly smoked trout served
with warm potato salad. Among the entrées, the risotto is always a good
choice, especially when it's made with wild mushrooms. The grilled
boar is lean and flavorful, the roasted guinea hen succulent. Desserts
include a fine *pot au chocolat* and delicious fruit crumbles and tarts.
⊠ *505 Laurel St., at 5th Ave.,* ☎ *619/239–2222. Reservations essential.
AE, D, DC, MC, V. No lunch weekends.*

Greek

Downtown

$ ✕ **Athens Market.** As in many Greek restaurants, the appetizers here—
such as *taramousalata* (fish roe dip) and stuffed grape leaves—can be
superior to the heavier traditional beef and lamb entrées. Greek music
and belly dancers add to the festive atmosphere on weekend evenings.
The adjacent Victorian-style coffeehouse, under the same ownership,
is open from early morning until mid-afternoon. ⊠ *109 W. F St.,* ☎
619/234–1955. AE, D, DC, MC, V.

Indian

La Jolla

$$ ✕ **Star of India.** Signature dishes here include chicken *tikka masala*,
prepared tandoori style in a cream and tomato curry, and *saag gosht*,
lamb in a spinach curry. Seafood entrées are generally the least successful. The nan bread, baked on the tandoor oven, comes either plain
or stuffed with a variety of fillings. An all-you-can-eat buffet lunch,
available daily, is a good way to satisfy your curiosity about a variety
of dishes. A second Star of India is downtown on F Street. ⊠ *1000
Prospect St.,* ☎ *619/459–3355; 423 F St.,* ☎ *619/544–9891. AE, D,
DC, MC, V.*

Mission Valley

$ ✕ **KC's Tandoor.** True, this is a fast-food restaurant, in one of the city's
ubiquitous minimalls, but the tandoori chicken is flavorful, the nan bread
is rich and chewy, and the many curries are truly impressive. Hearty
appetites will find a bargain in the all-you-can-eat buffet brunch on
Sundays. A second KC's is northeast of the University of California
off I-805. ⊠ *Frias Mission Center, 5608 Mission Center Rd.,* ☎
619/497–0751; 9450 Scranton Rd., ☎ *619/535–1941. MC, V.*

Italian

Beaches

$ ✕ **Tosca's.** With its fluorescent lighting and red-checkered vinyl table-
cloths, this Pacific Beach eatery is typical of pizza restaurants everywhere. But you are, after all, in California, which means you can opt
for wheat or semolina crusts for your individually sized pizzas or cal-
zones; choose toppings or fillings from an array of exotic ingredients,
including artichokes, pesto, and feta cheese; and wash it all down with
a microbrew from Sierra Nevada (on tap, yet). ⊠ *3780 Ingraham St.,*
☎ *619/274–2408. AE, D, DC, MC, V.*

Downtown

$$–$$$ ✕ **Bella Luna.** Small yet stylish, Bella Luna has developed a loyal following. The menu includes dishes from all over Italy: Try the stuffed mozzarella appetizer or the calamari in tomato sauce. Pastas are particularly recommended, especially linguine with clams, fettuccine with salmon, and black squid-ink linguine served with a spicy seafood sauce; if you still have room for an entrée, consider the rack of lamb. ⊠ *748 5th Ave.,* ☎ *619/239–3222. Reservations essential on weekends. AE, DC, MC, V.*

$$–$$$ ✕ **Trattoria La Strada.** Tuscan cuisine is the specialty here, prepared so well that your taste buds will be convinced they've died and gone to Italy. Try the *antipasto di mare,* with tender shrimp and shellfish, or the *insalata Patrizia,* a salad with arugula, avocado, hearts of palm, and mozzarella. Pasta is always a good bet. ⊠ *702 5th Ave.,* ☎ *619/239–3400. Reservations essential on weekends. AE, D, DC, MC, V.*

$$–$$$ ✕ **Trattoria Mamma Anna.** A few examples of the owners' native Si-
★ cilian cuisine show up on the menu, such as the tasty *fagottini di melanzane* appetizer, eggplant stuffed with breadcrumbs, peppers, pine nuts and raisins. But the fare here ventures into the rest of Italy as well: the ravioli *con salsa di funghi* (spinach and ricotta ravioli with cream and mushroom sauce) is exquisite, as is the deceptively simple fettuccine *montanari* (homemade pasta with garlic, tomatoes, and wild mushrooms). Be forewarned: portions are generous. If you can get as far as the second courses, try the *pollo campagnola* (chicken breast with vegetables and olives) or the simple grilled swordfish served with lemon. ⊠ *644 5th Ave.,* ☎ *619/235–8144. Reservations essential on weekends. AE, D, MC, V.*

$$ ✕ **Fio's.** Glitzy young singles mingle with staid business-suit types in this lively, popular place. Contemporary variations on traditional Italian cuisine are served in a high-ceilinged, brick-and-wood dining room overlooking the 5th Avenue street scene. The menu includes pizzas baked in the wood-fire oven and classic Italian dishes. ⊠ *801 5th Ave.,* ☎ *619/234–3467. Reservations essential on weekends. AE, D, DC, MC, V. No lunch weekends.*

La Jolla

$$ ✕ **Piatti Ristorante.** On weekends, this trattoria-style restaurant is
★ filled to overflowing with a lively mix of singles and local families, who keep returning for the country-style Italian food. A wood-burning oven turns out excellent pizzas, and imaginative pastas include the *pappardelle fantasia* (wide saffron noodles with shrimp, fresh tomatoes, and arugula) and a wonderfully garlicky spaghetti *alle vongole* (served with clams in the shell). Among the *secondi* are good versions of roast chicken and Italian sausage with polenta. A fountain splashes softly on the tree-shaded patio, where heat lamps allow diners to sit out even on chilly evenings. ⊠ *2182 Avenida de la Playa,* ☎ *619/454–1589. Reservations essential. AE, MC, V.*

Latin American

Old Town

$ ✕ **Berta's Latin American Restaurant.** The food here, which manages to be tasty and health-conscious at the same time, ranges all over the map. Try the Brazilian seafood *vatapa* (shrimp, scallops, and fish served in a sauce flavored with ginger, coconut, and chilis) or the Peruvian *pollo a la huancaina* (chicken with chilis and a feta cheese sauce). The simple dining room is small, but there's also a patio. ⊠ *3928 Twiggs St.,* ☎ *619/295–2343. AE, MC, V.*

Mexican

Beaches

$–$$ ✕ **Palenque.** A welcome alternative to the standard Sonoran-style
★   café, this family-run restaurant in Pacific Beach serves regional Mexican dishes. Recommendations include the chicken with mole, in the
regular chocolate-based or green-chili version, and the mouthwatering *camarones en chipotle*, large shrimp cooked in a chili and tequila
cream sauce (an old family recipe of the proprietor). Palenque is a bit
hard to spot from the street and service is often slow, but the food is
worth your vigilance and patience. ✉ *1653 Garnet Ave., Pacific Beach,*
☎ *619/272–7816. AE, D, DC, MC, V. No lunch Mon.*

Mission Valley

$ ✕ **El Tecolote.** You'll find the usual taco-burrito fare at El Tecolote, but
come also to sample Mexican regional specialties, such as the enchiladas in mole sauce, the fish fillet Ensenada style, or the decadent
Aztec layered cake (tortillas stacked with cheese, chilis, enchilada
sauce, guacamole, and sour cream). ✉ *6110 Friars Rd. W,* ☎ *619/295–
2087. AE, DC, D, MC, V. No lunch Sun.*

Old Town

$ ✕ **Old Town Mexican Café.** You'll find all the Mexican standards here,
as well as specialties such as *carnitas*, chunks of roast pork served with
fresh tortillas and condiments. The enchiladas with spicy ranchero or
green chili sauce are nice variations on an old theme. You can watch
the corn tortillas being handmade on the premises and pick up a dozen
to take home with you. ✉ *2489 San Diego Ave.,* ☎ *619/297–4330.*
AE, D, MC, V.

Uptown

$ ✕ **Chilango's Mexico City Grill.** A tiny but cheerful storefront restau-
rant, Chilango's has one of the most interesting menus in town. The
burritos and tortas (sandwiches) are like no others in the city; daily
specials might include enchiladas in *mole verde* (green chili sauce), moist
vegetarian tamales, and a fabulous chicken *mole poblano* (a sauce made
with chilis and bittersweet chocolate). A mouthwatering array of
breakfast dishes is served until 1 PM. This highly regarded restaurant
quickly fills to overflowing, so consider coming in off-hours or ordering
takeout. ✉ *142 University Ave.,* ☎ *619/294–8646. No credit cards.*

$ ✕ **El Indio Shop.** El Indio has been serving some of the city's best Mex-
ican fast food since 1940. The menu is extensive; try the large burritos, the *tacquitos* (fried rolled tacos) with guacamole, or the giant
quesadillas. You can eat at one of the indoor tables or on the patio
across the street; El Indio is also perfect for beach-bound takeout. ✉
3695 India St. (from downtown, take I–5 to Washington St. exit), ☎
619/299–0333. D, MC, V.

Pacific Rim

La Jolla

$$$ ✕ **Cafe Japengo.** The cuisine here is Asian-inspired, with many North
and South American touches. There's a selection of grilled, wood-
roasted, and wok-fried entrées for dinner; try the shrimp and scallops
with dragon noodles or the grilled swordfish with red-bean miso stew.
The curry fried calamari and the Japengo potstickers appetizers are guar-
anteed to stimulate your taste buds. You can also order fine sushi from
your table or from a seat at the sushi bar. Unfortunately, the quality
of the service doesn't match that of the food. ✉ *8960 University Cen-
ter La.,* ☎ *619/450–3355. Reservations essential on weekends. AE,*
D, DC, MC, V. No lunch weekends.

Seafood

Downtown

$$$ ✕ **Anthony's Star of the Sea Room.** The Anthony's chain of local seafood restaurants, a venerable San Diego institution, has long been serving up adequately prepared seafood dishes to tourists and residents alike. The flagship of the Anthony's fleet, the Star of the Sea Room, is much more formal and expensive than the others. The enormous selection of fresh fish from around the world, the always meticulous cuisine, and the magnificent harbor view guarantee a loyal clientele. ✉ *1360 N. Harbor Dr.,* ☎ *619/232–7408. Reservations essential. Jacket required. AE, D, DC, MC, V. No lunch.*

$$$ ✕ **Sally's.** Chef Fabrice Poigin has a delicate touch: order the light, greaseless crab cakes and bite into chunks of fresh crab. The seafood salad is likewise fresh and lightly dressed. Recommended entrées include seafood paella, studded with pieces of fish and shellfish, a rich bouillabaisse, and unusually moist and tender grilled swordfish. The three-course prix-fixe daily special at dinner is often irresistible. ✉ *Hyatt Regency San Diego, 1 Market Pl.,* ☎ *619/687–6080. Reservations essential on weekends. AE, D, DC, MC, V.*

$–$$$ ✕ **The Fish Market.** Diners at this bustling, informal restaurant choose from a large variety of extremely fresh fish, mesquite grilled and served with lemon and tartar sauce. Also good are shellfish dishes, such as steamed clams or mussels, and the sushi. Most of what is served here has lived in the water, but even dedicated fish-avoiders may think it worth their while to trade selection for the stunning view: Enormous plate-glass windows look directly out onto the harbor. A more formal restaurant upstairs, the Top of the Market, has a distinctive menu of exquisitely prepared seafood. It's expensive but worth the splurge. ✉ *750 N. Harbor Dr.,* ☎ *619/232–3474 for the Fish Market,* ☎ *619/234–4867 for the Top of the Market. AE, D, DC, MC, V.*

La Jolla

$$$ ✕ **George's at the Cove.** At most restaurants you get either good food
★ or good views; at George's, you don't have to choose. The elegant main dining room, with a wall-length window overlooking La Jolla Cove, is renowned for its daily fresh seafood specials; the menu also includes several good chicken and meat dishes. The smoked chicken, broccoli, and black bean soup, and the salmon-and-shrimp sausage make fine starters; the fresh pasta entrées are also highly recommended. Desserts are uniformly excellent. For more informal dining, try the Cafe ($–$$) on the second floor. The Ocean Terrace ($–$$), on the top floor, affords a sweeping view of the coast; wonderful for breakfast, lunch, or brunch on a fine day, the Ocean Terrace (like the Cafe) does not take reservations, so you may have a wait. ✉ *1250 Prospect St.,* ☎ *619/454–4244. Reservations essential for main dining room on weekends. AE, D, DC, MC, V.*

Old Town

$$–$$$ ✕ **Cafe Pacifica.** Imaginative appetizers, salads, pastas, and entrées are
★ among the highlights on the menu at Cafe Pacifica; there is also a crème brûlée worth blowing any diet for. The emphasis here is on Mediterranean-style seafood, and this restaurant serves some of the best in town. You can't go wrong with any of the fresh fish preparations grilled or lightly sautéed. Other good bets include the tasty pan-fried catfish; yummy, greaseless fish tacos; and superb crab cakes. ✉ *2414 San Diego Ave.,* ☎ *619/291–6666. Reservations essential. AE, D, DC, MC, V. No lunch Sat.–Mon.*

Thai

Uptown

$–$$ ✕ **Thai Chada.** This is one of the best Thai restaurants in town; the
★ large windows and comfortable booths provide a low-key setting for
consistently well prepared food. Try any of the noodle dishes, especially the *pad thai*, rice noodles fried with fresh shrimp, egg, bean sprouts,
scallions, and ground peanuts; the Tom Ka Kai chicken soup, with coconut milk, lemongrass, lime juice, and scallions; or the roast duck curry.
A sister restaurant, Thai Chada 2, is in Pacific Beach. ✉ *142 University Ave.,* ☎ *619/297–9548; Thai Chada 2, 1749 Garnet Ave.,* ☎
*619/270–1888. AE, D, DC, MC, V. Sat. lunch at Thai Chada 2 only;
both restaurants no lunch Sun.*

$ ✕ **Saffron Chicken.** Saffron specializes in chicken spit-roasted over a
wood fire, accompanied by appealing side dishes. The chicken is wonderfully moist and comes with a choice of sauces: try the peanut or
chili. Among the accompaniments, the Cambodian salad is particularly
fresh and crunchy. There's limited outdoor seating, but this is an ideal
place to pick up lunch or dinner to take to Mission Bay or the beach.
✉ *3731B India St. (from downtown, take I–5 to Washington St. exit),*
☎ *619/574–0177. Reservations not accepted. MC, V.*

Vegetarian

Uptown

$ ✕ **Monsoon.** Vegans and vacationers suffering with "tourist tummy"
from too many burgers and fries should make a pilgrimage to this café,
which serves vegetarian dishes from around the world. The fresh, colorful food looks and tastes good, though some dishes are a trifle bland.
There is an ample selection of soups and (large) salads, along with more
substantial fare, such as spinach pie, curries, and veggie burgers. ✉
Hillcrest Center, 3975 5th Ave., ☎ *619/298–3155. MC, V.*

LODGING

Updated by
Alan Frutkin

San Diego is spread out, so the first thing to consider when selecting
lodgings here is location. If you plan to do a lot of sightseeing, take
into account a hotel's proximity to the attractions you most want to
visit. Even the most expensive areas offer some reasonably priced
rooms. Those wishing to find bed-and-breakfast accommodations in
town can contact the **Bed & Breakfast Guild of San Diego** (☎ 619/523–
1300), which lists a number of high-quality member inns, or **Bed &
Breakfast Directory for San Diego** (✉ Box 3292, 92163, ☎ 619/297–
3130 or 800/619–7666), which covers San Diego County.

CATEGORY	COST*
$$$$	over $175
$$$	$120–$175
$$	$80–$120
$	under $80

*All prices are for a double room in high (summer) season, excluding 10½%
San Diego room tax.*

Coronado

$$$$ ⊞ **Le Meridien San Diego at Coronado.** Flamingos greet you at the en-
★ trance of this 16-acre, lushly landscaped resort. Its low-slung, Cape
Cod–style buildings perfectly capture Coronado's understated old-
money ambience. The large rooms and suites are done in a cheerful,
California–country French fashion, with colorful Impressionist prints;

all rooms have separate showers and tubs and come with plush robes and Limoges bath accessories. (Watch out for what looks like a gift basket on the vanity, though—it's an extension of the minibar.) The spa facilities are top-notch, as is the award-winning Marius restaurant, which serves innovative French Provençale cuisine. ⊠ *2000 2nd St., 92118,* ☎ *619/435–3000 or 800/543–4300 (central reservations),* FAX *619/435–4183. 300 rooms, including 7 suites and a 28-unit villa complex. 2 restaurants, 3 pools, massage, sauna, spa, steam room, 6 tennis courts, aerobics, exercise room. AE, D, DC, MC, V.*

$$$$ ⊞ **Loews Coronado Bay Resort.** You can park your boat at the 80-slip marina of this resort, set on a secluded 15-acre private peninsula on the Silver Strand. Didn't bring it along this time? Never mind. You can rent one here. Rooms are formally but tastefully decorated, with pale yellows, pinks, and greens, and flowered bedspreads. All have furnished balconies with views of water—either bay, ocean, or marina. ⊠ *4000 Coronado Bay Rd., 92118,* ☎ *619/424–4000,* FAX *619/424–4400 or 800/235–6397. 438 rooms, 25 suites. 3 restaurants, deli, 3 pools, 2 spas, 5 tennis courts, fitness center, windsurfing, boating, jet skiing, bicycles, children's programs. AE, D, DC, MC, V.*

$$$–$$$$ ⊞ **Hotel Del Coronado.** Built in 1888, "the Del" is a historic and social landmark. The rooms and suites in the original, ornate Victorian building are charmingly quirky. Some have sleeping areas that seem smaller than the baths. Others are downright palatial; two are even said to come with a resident ghost. The public areas are grand, if perhaps a bit dark for modern tastes; a lower-level shopping arcade lined with historic photographs is fascinating, but tear yourself away to stroll around the hotel's manicured grounds. More standardized accommodations are available in the newer high rise. Service can be a bit chaotic; there's often a long line at the front desk. ⊠ *1500 Orange Ave., 92118,* ☎ *619/435–6611 (hotel), 619/522–8000 or 800/468–3533 (reservations),* FAX *619/522–8262. 692 rooms. 3 restaurants, deli, pool, sauna, steam room, 8 tennis courts, croquet, beach, bicycles. AE, D, DC, MC, V.*

$$–$$$ ⊞ **Glorietta Bay Inn.** The main building of this property was built in 1908 for sugar baron John D. Spreckels, who once owned most of downtown San Diego. Rooms here and in the newer motel-style buildings are attractively furnished, with flowered bedspreads and green rugs; all have refrigerators. Tours ($5) of the island's historical buildings depart from the inn's lobby three mornings a week. ⊠ *1630 Glorietta Blvd., 92118,* ☎ *619/435–3101 or 800/283–9383,* FAX *619/435–6182. 98 rooms. Pool, bicycles. AE, D, DC, MC, V.*

Downtown

$$$$ ⊞ **Hyatt Regency San Diego.** This high rise adjacent to Seaport Vil-
★ lage successfully combines Old World opulence with California airiness and space. Palm trees pose next to ornate tapestry couches in the high-ceiling, light-filled lobby, and all of the British Regency–style guest rooms—complete with tasteful window treatments and furniture of red mahogany and pecan—have views of the water. The hotel's proximity to the convention center attracts a large business trade. The "Business Plan" includes access to an area with desks and other basic office supplies; each room on the special business floor has a fax machine. But the Regency also provides well-heeled leisure travelers a superb location and facilities. ⊠ *One Market Pl., 92101,* ☎ *619/232–1234 or 800/233–1234 (central reservations),* FAX *619/233–6464. 875 rooms, including 55 suites and Regency Club rooms. 2 restaurants, lobby lounge, piano bar, pool, 4 tennis courts, health club, boating. AE, D, DC, MC, V.*

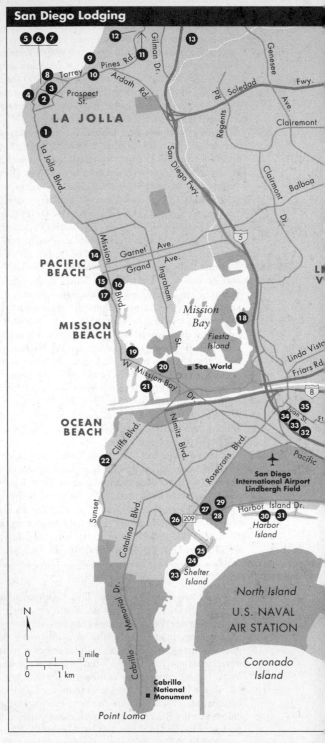

San Diego Lodging

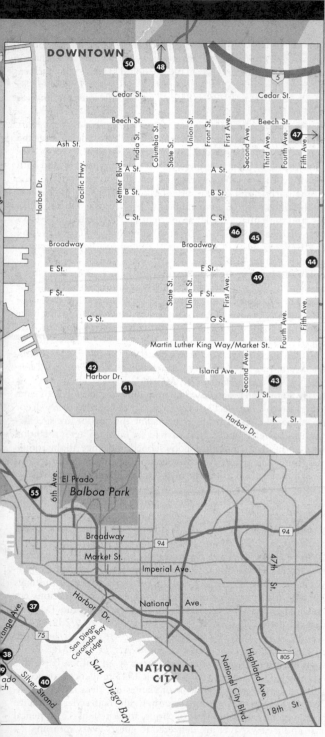

DOWNTOWN

Cedar St.
Beech St.
Ash St.
A St.
B St.
C St.
Broadway
E St.
F St.
G St.
Harbor Dr.

Pacific Hwy.
Kettner Blvd.
India St.
Columbia St.
State St.
Union St.
Front St.
First Ave.
Second Ave.
Third Ave.
Fourth Ave.
Fifth Ave.

Cedar St.
Beech St.
A St.
B St.
C St.
Broadway
E St.
F St.
G St.

Martin Luther King Way/Market St.
Island Ave.
Harbor Dr.
J St.
K St.

El Prado
Balboa Park
6th Ave.
Broadway
Market St.
Imperial Ave.
National Ave.
Harbor Dr.
94
47th St.
Highland Ave.
National City Blvd.
805
18th St.

San Diego-
Coronado Bay
Bridge
75
Orange Ave.
Silver Strand
San Diego Bay

NATIONAL
CITY

$$$–$$$$ 🏨 **Horton Grand Hotel.** A Victorian confection in the heart of the historic Gaslamp District, the Horton Grand comprises two 1880s hotels moved brick by brick from nearby locations. Its delightfully retro rooms are furnished with period antiques, ceiling fans, and gas-burning fireplaces. The choicest rooms overlook a garden courtyard. There's high tea in the afternoon and jazz in the evening. The place is a charmer, but service can be erratic. ⊠ *311 Island Ave., 92101,* ☎ *619/544–1886 or 800/542–1886,* FAX *619/239–3823. 132 rooms. Restaurant, lounge. AE, D, DC, MC, V.*

$$$–$$$$ 🏨 **Westgate Hotel.** A nondescript modern high-rise hides what must be the most opulent hotel in San Diego: The lobby, modeled after the anteroom at Versailles, has hand-cut Baccarat chandeliers; rooms are individually furnished with antiques, Italian marble counters, and bath fixtures with 24-karat-gold overlays. From the ninth floor up, the views of the harbor and city are breathtaking. Afternoon high tea is served in the lobby to the accompaniment of piano music. Horton Plaza is nearby, and the Tijuana trolley stops right outside the door. ⊠ *1055 2nd Ave., 92101,* ☎ *619/238–1818, 800/221–3802, or 800/522–1564 in CA;* FAX *619/557–3737. 223 rooms. 3 restaurants, lounge, barbershop, exercise room. AE, D, DC, MC, V.*

$$$ 🏨 **Doubletree Hotel at Horton Plaza.** Although it is fronted by a startling lighted blue obelisk, this high rise is all understated marble and brass. The spacious rooms were recently redesigned in pastels of coral blue and pale orange. With its prime downtown location, the hotel attracts many business travelers and provides fax, photocopy, and room service. ⊠ *910 Broadway Circle, 92101,* ☎ *619/239–2200 or 800/528–0444 (central reservations),* FAX *619/239–0509. 450 rooms, 14 suites. Restaurant, lobby lounge, sports bar, pool, sauna, spa, 2 tennis courts, health club. AE, D, DC, MC, V.*

$$$ 🏨 **Embassy Suites San Diego Bay.** The front door of each spacious suite opens out onto this hotel's 12-story atrium. The contemporary decor is pleasant, and the views from rooms facing the harbor are spectacular. Business travelers will find it easy to set up shop here; the hotel provides a 24-hour fax and photocopy service, and since all the rooms are suites, the work space in each is separate from the sleeping area. Families can make good use of the in-room refrigerators, microwaves, and separate sleeping areas. A cooked-to-order breakfast and afternoon cocktails are complimentary, as are airport transfers. ⊠ *601 Pacific Hwy., 92101,* ☎ *619/239–2400 or 800/362–2779 (central reservations),* FAX *619/239–1520. 337 suites. Restaurant, sports bar, pool, sauna, exercise room. AE, D, DC, MC, V.*

$$$ 🏨 **U.S. Grant Hotel.** This San Diego classic, built in 1910, sits across
★   the street from Horton Plaza. Crystal chandeliers and polished marble floors in the lobby as well as Queen Anne–style mahogany furnishings in the stately and spacious rooms hark back to a more gracious era when such dignitaries as Charles Lindbergh and Franklin D. Roosevelt stayed here. ⊠ *326 Broadway, 92101,* ☎ *619/232–3121, 800/237–5029, or 800/437–4824;* FAX *619/232–3626. 220 rooms, 60 suites. Restaurant, piano bar, exercise room. AE, D, DC, MC, V.*

$$–$$$ 🏨 **Balboa Park Inn.** Directly across the street from Balboa Park, this B&B is housed in four Spanish colonial–style 1915 residences connected by courtyards. One- and two-bedroom suites are decorated in contemporary Italian, French, Spanish, or early-Californian style; some have fireplaces, wet bars, whirlpool tubs, patios, and kitchens. Continental breakfast and a newspaper are delivered to guests every morning. ⊠ *3402 Park Blvd., 92103,* ☎ *619/298–0823 or 800/938–8181,* FAX *619/294–8070. 26 suites. Bar. AE, D, DC, MC, V.*

$$ 🏨 **Harbor Hill Guest House.** This three-story home, within walking distance of the harbor and Balboa Park, has comfortable rooms, with a private entryway and full kitchen on each level. Not fancy or antiques-filled, this is a cheerful, friendly place that's excellent for families as well as for couples or singles. Continental breakfast is included. ✉ *2330 Albatross St., 92101,* ☎ *619/233–0638. 6 rooms. MC, V.*

$–$$ 🏨 **Gaslamp Plaza Suites.** Accommodations in San Diego's 11-story first
★   "skyscraper" are done in shades of burgundy and pink in a European style, with contemporary dark wood furniture. Guests can enjoy the view and a complimentary Continental breakfast on the rooftop terrace. Many of the rooms rent as vacation ownerships; book ahead if you're visiting in high season. ✉ *520 E St., 92101,* ☎ *619/232–9500,* FAX *619/238–9945. 60 suites. Restaurant, airport and Amtrak shuttle. AE, D, DC, MC, V.*

$–$$ 🏨 **Rodeway Inn.** This property is clean, comfortable, and nicely decorated. Continental breakfast is included in the room rate. ✉ *833 Ash St., 92101,* ☎ *619/239–2285, 800/228–2000 (central reservations), or 800/522–1528 in CA;* FAX *619/235–6951. 45 rooms. Sauna. AE, D, DC, MC, V.*

$ 🏨 **La Pensione.** Rooms are modern, with good working areas and kitchenettes. The hotel is convenient to the restaurants of the city's version of Little Italy. ✉ *1700 India St., 92101,* ☎ *619/236–8000 or 800/232–4638,* FAX *619/236–8088. 81 rooms. Café, kitchenettes, laundry. AE, MC, V.*

$ 🏨 **Super 8 Bayview.** This motel's location is less noisy than those of other low-cost establishments. The accommodations are nondescript but clean, and there are rooms for nonsmokers, and some with refrigerators. Continental breakfast is included in the room rate. ✉ *1835 Columbia St., 92101,* ☎ *619/544–0164 or 800/537–9902,* FAX *619/237–9940. 101 rooms. Laundry, airport and Amtrak shuttle. AE, DC, MC, V.*

Harbor Island, Shelter Island, and Point Loma

$$$$ 🏨 **Sheraton Harbor Island Resort.** A shuttle bus connects this resort's two high-rise buildings. The East Tower has the better sports facilities. The smaller, more intimate West Tower has larger rooms with a separate area suitable for business entertaining. Rooms throughout are California-style spiffy. Views from the upper floors of both sections are superb, but because the West Tower is closest to the water, it affords fine outlooks from the lower floors, too. ✉ *1380 Harbor Island Dr., 92101,* ☎ *619/291–2900 or 800/325–3535 (central reservations),* FAX *619/692–2337. 1,050 rooms. 3 restaurants, 2 bars, deli, 2 pools, massage, sauna, spa, 4 tennis courts, exercise room, jogging, boating, airport shuttle. AE, D, DC, MC, V.*

$$$ 🏨 **Bay Club Hotel & Marina.** Rooms in this appealing low-rise Shelter Island property are large, light, and furnished with rattan tables and chairs and Polynesian tapestries; all have refrigerators and views of either the bay or the marina from outside terraces. A buffet breakfast and limo service to the airport or Amtrak are included in the room rate. ✉ *2131 Shelter Island Dr., 92106,* ☎ *619/224–8888 or 800/672–0800, 800/833–6565 in CA;* FAX *619/225–1604. 105 rooms. Restaurant, pool, spa, exercise room, bicycles. AE, D, DC, MC, V.*

$$$ 🏨 **Travelodge Hotel–Harbor Island.** This more upscale Travelodge provides visitors the views and amenities of more expensive hotels, plus such perks as in-room coffeemakers and complimentary parking, airport shuttle, and local phone calls. The Waterfront Cafe & Club overlooks the marina, and (Gen-Xers take note) singer Florence Henderson has been known to pull her boat into a slip here and join in the karaoke evenings on Friday and Saturday nights. ⌧ *1960 Harbor Island Dr., 92101,* ☎ *619/291–6700 or 800/578–7878 (central reservations),* 𝖥𝖠𝖷 *619/293–0694. 207 rooms. Restaurant, bar, pool, exercise room, jogging, car rental. AE, D, DC, MC, V.*

$$–$$$ 🏨 **Kona Kai Plaza Las Glorias Resort and Marina.** Though the Kona Kai's name may suggest a Polynesian theme, this 11-acre property was recently refurbished in a mixture of Mexican and Mediterranean styles. The spacious and light-filled lobby, with its Maya sculptures and terracotta tiles, opens onto a lush green esplanade that overlooks the hotel's marina. The rooms are well appointed, if a bit small, and most look out onto either the marina or the San Diego Bay. ⌧ *1551 Shelter Island Dr., 92106,* ☎ *619/221–8000 or 800/566–2524,* 𝖥𝖠𝖷 *619/221–5953. 207 rooms. Restaurant, 2 pools, sauna, spa, 2 tennis courts, jogging, volleyball, beach, airport and Amtrak shuttle, free parking. AE, D, DC, MC, V.*

$$ 🏨 **Best Western Posada Inn.** One of the more upscale members of the Best Western chain, the Posada Inn is not on Harbor Island but on one of the neighboring thoroughfares adjacent to Point Loma. Many of the rooms, which are clean, comfortable, and nicely furnished, have wonderful views of the harbor. ⌧ *5005 N. Harbor Dr., 92106,* ☎ *619/224–3254 or 800/231–3811,* 𝖥𝖠𝖷 *619/224–2186. 112 rooms. Restaurant, bar, pool, spa, exercise room, airport shuttle. AE, D, DC, MC, V.*

$$ 🏨 **Best Western Shelter Island Marina Inn.** This waterfront inn, with an airy, skylit lobby, is a good choice if you have a boat to dock; the adjacent marina has guest slips. Both harbor- and marina-view rooms are available. Standard accommodations are fairly small; if you're traveling with family or more than one friend, the two-bedroom suite with an eat-in kitchen is a good deal. ⌧ *2051 Shelter Island Dr., 92106,* ☎ *619/222–0561 or 800/922–2336,* 𝖥𝖠𝖷 *619/222–9760. 68 rooms, 29 suites. Restaurant, bar, pool, spa, free parking. AE, D, DC, MC, V.*

$ 🏨 **Outrigger Motel.** A good bet for those traveling as a family, this motel, adjacent to the two resort peninsulas, is less expensive than its offshore counterparts. Rooms are large and have eat-in kitchens. It's a short, scenic walk along the bay from here to Harbor Island. Although some rooms show signs of wear and tear (such as water stains on the bathroom wallpaper), its operators have embarked on a gradual upgrade of the premises, installing new carpeting and replacing bedspreads and kitchen appliances. ⌧ *1370 Scott St., 92106,* ☎ *619/223–7105. 37 rooms with kitchen. Pool, laundry. AE, D, DC, MC, V.*

$ 🏨 **Travelodge Point Loma.** For far less money, you'll get the same view here as at the higher-priced hotels. Of course, there are fewer amenities and the neighborhood (near the navy base) isn't as serene, but the rooms, all with coffeemakers, are adequate and clean. ⌧ *5102 N. Harbor Dr., 92106,* ☎ *619/223–8171 or 800/578–7878 (central reservations),* 𝖥𝖠𝖷 *619/222–7330. 45 rooms. Pool. AE, D, DC, MC, V.*

Hotel Circle, Mission Valley, and Old Town

$$–$$$$ 🏨 **Heritage Park Bed & Breakfast Inn.** One of the beautifully restored
★ mansions in Old Town's Heritage Park, this romantic 1889 Queen Anne has eight guest rooms and a suite decorated with period antiques. Breakfast and afternoon refreshments are included in the room rate. ⌧ *2470 Heritage Park Row, 92110,* ☎ *619/295–7088 or 800/995–2470. 6 rooms with bath, 2 with shared bath, 1 2-bedroom suite. AE, MC, V.*

$$$ 🏨 **Best Western Hacienda Hotel Old Town.** This pretty white hotel, with balconies and Spanish tile roofs, is in a quiet part of Old Town, away from the freeway and the main retail bustle. Accommodations are not really large enough to earn the "suite" label the hotel gives them, but they're decorated in tasteful southwestern style and equipped with microwaves, coffeemakers, minifridges, clock radios, and VCRs. ⊠ *4041 Harney St., 92110,* ☎ *619/298–4707 or 800/888–1991,* FAX *619/298–4771. 150 suites. Restaurant, pool, free parking. AE, D, DC, MC, V.*

$$$ 🏨 **San Diego Marriott Mission Valley.** This high-rise hotel is well
★ equipped for business travelers—the front desk provides 24-hour fax and photocopy services, and all rooms come with desks, computer modem hook-ups, and private voice mail—but the Marriott also caters to vacationers, with comfortable rooms, a friendly staff, and free transportation to the malls. ⊠ *8757 Rio San Diego Dr., 92108,* ☎ *619/692–3800 or 800/228–9290 (central reservations),* FAX *619/692–0769. 356 rooms. Restaurant, bar, pool, sauna, tennis court, exercise room, free parking. AE, D, DC, MC, V.*

$$–$$$ 🏨 **Ramada Inn Old Town.** The hacienda-style Ramada has Spanish colonial–style fountains, courtyards, and painted tiles, and southwestern decor in the rooms. Breakfast, cocktail reception, and transfers to the airport, bus, and Amtrak are all complimentary. ⊠ *2435 Jefferson St., 92110,* ☎ *619/260–8500 or 800/272–6232 (central reservations),* FAX *619/297–2078. 152 rooms. Restaurant, pool, airport and Amtrak shuttle. AE, D, DC, MC, V.*

$$–$$$ 🏨 **San Diego Mission Valley Hilton.** Directly fronting I–8, this property has soundproof rooms decorated in a colorful, contemporary style. When you're indoors, the modern accommodations, along with the stylish public areas and lush greenery in the back, make you forget this hotel's proximity to the freeway. Although geared toward business travelers—the hotel has a business center and guests are allowed complimentary use of an IBM personal computer—children stay free, and small pets are accepted ($25). ⊠ *901 Camino del Rio S, 92108,* ☎ *619/543–9000, 800/733–2332, or 800/445–8667;* FAX *619/543–9358. 350 rooms. Restaurant, bar, sports bar, pool, spa, fitness center, airport shuttle, free parking. AE, D, DC, MC, V.*

$$ 🏨 **Best Western Hanalei Hotel.** A two-story complex has poolside rooms, and a high-rise building surrounds a Hawaiian-style garden. Rooms are decorated in tropical prints in shades of emerald and rose; some have tile floors, and others have wall-to-wall carpeting. Guests have access to an adjacent golf course, and free transport is provided to local malls and Old Town. The hotel is virtually surrounded by heavy traffic, which can make for a noisy stay. ⊠ *2270 Hotel Circle N, 92108,* ☎ *619/297–1101 or 800/882–0858,* FAX *619/297–6049. 412 rooms. 2 restaurants, bar, pool, spa, free parking. AE, D, DC, MC, V.*

$–$$ 🏨 **Vacation Inn.** Already an excellent value for Old Town, this cheer-
★ ful new property further pleases its guests by throwing in such perks as Continental breakfast and afternoon snacks, garage parking, and airport shuttle. You'll find all of today's conveniences—coffeemakers, microwave ovens, and refrigerators—but rustic colors and reproduction furnishings lend rooms an old-country-inn feel. Families and tourists will appreciate the walking distance to Old Town attractions and the sundeck and heated pool off the shaded courtyard. ⊠ *3900 Old Town Ave.,* ☎ *619/299–1619 or 800/451–9846,* FAX *619/299–1619. 119 rooms, 6 suites. Bar, pool, spa. AE, D, DC, MC, V.*

$ 🏨 **Days Inn Hotel Circle.** Rooms in this large complex are par for a chain motel but have the perk of minifridges; some units also have stoves. ⊠ *543 Hotel Circle S, 92108,* ☎ *619/297–8800, 800/227–4743 (weekdays 8–4:30), 800/325–2525 (central reservations);* FAX *619/298–6029. 280 rooms. Restaurant, pool, beauty salon, spa, laundry. AE, D, DC, MC, V.*

La Jolla

$$$$ ⊡ **Sheraton Grande Torrey Pines.** The view of the Pacific from this low-
★ rise, high-class property atop the Torrey Pines cliffs is superb. Amenities include complimentary butler service—just pick up the phone in the
morning, and a carafe of Starbucks coffee and a newspaper will be delivered to your room, gratis. The oversize accommodations, tastefully
decorated in muted tones, are simple but elegant; most have balconies
or terraces. In addition to easy access to one of the best public golf courses
in town, guests also have privileges at the fine health club–sports center next door ($7.50). ⊠ *10950 N. Torrey Pines Rd., 92037,* ☎
619/558–1500 or 800/325–3535 (central reservations), 𝔽𝔸𝕏 *619/450–
4584. 400 rooms, including 17 suites. Restaurant, bar, in-room safes,
pool, 3 tennis courts, exercise room, bicycles. AE, D, DC, MC, V.*

$$$–$$$$ ⊡ **La Valencia.** A La Jolla landmark, this pink Art Deco confection drew
★ film stars down from Hollywood in the 1930s and '40s for its setting
and views of La Jolla Cove. Many rooms have a genteel European look,
with antique pieces and plush, richly colored rugs. The restaurants are
top-notch, the Whaling Bar is a popular gathering spot, and the hotel
is ideally located near the shops and restaurants of La Jolla village and
what is arguably the prettiest beach in San Diego. Rates are lower if
you're willing to look out on the village, but on a clear, sunny day, the
ocean views may be worth every extra penny. ⊠ *1132 Prospect St.,
92037,* ☎ *619/454–0771 or 800/451–0772,* 𝔽𝔸𝕏 *619/456–3921. 100
rooms. 3 restaurants, bar, pool, exercise room. AE, D, DC, MC, V.*

$$$–$$$$ ⊡ **Sea Lodge.** This low-lying compound on La Jolla Shores beach has
a definite Spanish flavor to it, with its palm trees, fountains, red-tile
roofs, and Mexican tile work. Rooms have rattan furniture and flo-
ral-print bedspreads; all have hair dryers, coffeemakers, refrigerators,
and irons, as well as wooden balconies that overlook lush landscap-
ing and the sea. Early reservations are a must; families will find plenty
of room and distractions for both kids and parents. ⊠ *8110 Camino
del Oro, 92037,* ☎ *619/459–8271 or 800/237–5211,* 𝔽𝔸𝕏 *619/456–
9346. 128 rooms, 19 with kitchenette. Restaurant, bar, pool, hot tub,
sauna, 2 tennis courts, Ping-Pong, beach. AE, D, DC, MC, V.*

$$–$$$$ ⊡ **Prospect Park Inn.** This European-style inn sits in a prime spot in La
★ Jolla Village, one block from the beach and near some of the best shops
and restaurants. Many rooms have sweeping ocean views from their
balconies. Continental breakfast is included in the reasonable room rates,
and parking is free. There is no smoking on the premises. ⊠ *1110 Prospect
St., 92037,* ☎ *619/454–0133 or 800/433–1609,* 𝔽𝔸𝕏 *619/454–2056.
24 rooms, including 2 suites. Bar, kitchenettes. AE, D, DC, MC, V.*

$$$ ⊡ **Colonial Inn.** A tastefully restored Victorian-era building, this is the
oldest hotel in La Jolla. The feel in the Colonial's public spaces is of
turn-of-the-century elegance; in keeping with the period, rooms are for-
mal and a bit staid. Ocean views cost more than village views. The inn
is on one of La Jolla's main thoroughfares, near boutiques, restaurants,
and La Jolla Cove. ⊠ *910 Prospect St., 92037,* ☎ *619/454–2181,
800/832–5525, or 800/826–1278 in CA;* 𝔽𝔸𝕏 *619/454–5679. 75 rooms.
Restaurant, bar, pool. AE, DC, MC, V.*

$$$ ⊡ **Hyatt Regency La Jolla.** The Hyatt is the cornerstone of the Aven-
tine complex in La Jolla's Golden Triangle, about 10 minutes from the
beach and the village. The postmodern design elements of the striking
lobby continue in the spacious, comfortable rooms, where warm
cherry-wood furnishings contrast with austere gray closets (their stainless-steel handles make them look like large wall safes). The hotel's four
trendy restaurants include the Cafe Japengo (☞ *Dining, above*); you
can work off some of the calories at one of the best health clubs in the
city. Rates are lower on the weekends at this business-oriented hotel.

✉ *3777 La Jolla Village Dr., 92122,* ☎ *619/552–1234 or 800/233–1234 (central reservations),* FAX *619/552–6066. 400 rooms and suites. 4 restaurants, bar, pool, spa, 2 tennis courts, health club, jogging, basketball. AE, D, DC, MC, V.*

$$$ 🔂 **Scripps Inn.** You'd be wise to make reservations well in advance for this small, quiet inn tucked away on Coast Boulevard; its popularity with repeat visitors ensures that it is booked year-round. Kitchen facilities and lower weekly and monthly rates (not available in summer) make it attractive to long-term guests. Some rooms could use a bit more upkeep (and decor that includes plastic shower curtains doubling as closet doors isn't terribly stylish), but all accommodations have ocean views, and two have fireplaces. Continental breakfast is served in the lobby each morning. ✉ *555 Coast Blvd. S, 92037,* ☎ *619/454–3391. 13 rooms. Kitchenettes. AE, D, MC, V.*

$$–$$$ 🔂 **Best Western Inn by the Sea.** In a quiet section of La Jolla Village, within five blocks of the beach, the five-story Inn by the Sea has all the modern amenities at reasonable rates for La Jolla. Rooms are done in cheerful pastel tones and have private balconies with views of either the sea or the village. Continental breakfast, newspaper, and local phone calls are on the house. ✉ *7830 Fay Ave., 92037,* ☎ *619/459–4461 or 800/462–9732,* FAX *619/456–2578. 132 rooms. Pool, free parking. AE, D, DC, MC, V.*

$$–$$$ 🔂 **La Jolla Bed & Breakfast Inn.** Built in 1913 by Irving Gill, this B&B in a quiet section of La Jolla is just down the street from the Museum of Contemporary Art. Rooms are of various sizes and styles—some are done in Laura Ashley prints, others have wicker or rattan furnishings—but all are pretty and come with fresh fruit, sherry, and terry robes. The gardens in the back were planned by Kate Sessions, who was instrumental in landscaping Balboa Park. ✉ *7753 Draper Ave., 92037,* ☎ *619/456–2066,* FAX *619/456–1510. 16 rooms, 15 with private bath. Library. MC, V.*

$$–$$$ 🔂 **La Jolla Cove Motel.** This motel with studios and suites, some with spacious oceanfront balconies, overlooks the famous La Jolla Cove beach. If it doesn't have the charm of some of the older properties of this exclusive area, this motel gives its guests the same first-class views at much lower rates. A complimentary Continental breakfast is included in the room rate. ✉ *1155 S. Coast Blvd., 92037,* ☎ *619/459–2621 or 800/248–2683. 117 rooms. Kitchenettes, pool, spa, putting green, coin laundry. AE, D, DC, MC, V.*

$$ 🔂 **Holiday Inn Express.** Formerly the La Jolla Palms Inn, this modest property is in the southern section of La Jolla, near beaches, shops, and restaurants. Many rooms are remarkably large, with huge closets; some have kitchenettes, and three suites have separate eat-in kitchens. The rooms are nothing to write home about, but this is a good value for families who want to stay in this tony area and still have a few dollars left over for shopping and dining. Complimentary Continental breakfast is included in the room rates. ✉ *6705 La Jolla Blvd., 92037,* ☎ *619/454–7101 or 800/451–0358,* FAX *619/454–6957. 61 rooms. Pool, spa, billiards, laundry. AE, D, DC, MC, V.*

$$ 🔂 **The Lodge at Torrey Pines.** On a bluff between La Jolla and Del Mar, ★ the lodge (formerly the Torrey Pines Inn) commands a view of miles and miles of coastline. The public Torrey Pines Golf Course is adjacent, and scenic Torrey Pines State Beach and nature reserve are close by; the village of La Jolla is a 10-minute drive away. Most rooms have been renovated with dark wood furnishings and contemporary fabrics. One drawback: the building is quite old; walls between units are thin, and the plumbing can be noisy. Still, the service here is excellent and the lodge is a good value, especially for golfers. ✉ *11480 N. Torrey Pines Rd., 92037,* ☎ *619/453–4420 or 800/995–4507,* FAX *619/453–*

0691. 74 rooms. Restaurant, 2 bars, coffee shop, pool. AE, D, DC, MC, V.

$$ ⊞ **Summer House Inn.** Don't expect an idyllic hideaway: Summer House stands at the intersection of two of the busiest roads in La Jolla. Still, this pleasant, modern high-rise is five minutes from the village, a few blocks from the beach, convenient to freeway entrances, and reasonably priced. Rooms on the north side, away from Torrey Pines Road, are quietest. The ones on the highest floors have the best views (and are, accordingly, more expensive). ⊠ *7955 La Jolla Shores Dr., 92037,* ☎ *619/459–0261 or 800/666–0261,* FAX *619/459–7649. 90 rooms. Restaurant, kitchenettes, pool, beauty salon, massage, spa. AE, D, DC, MC, V.*

Mission Bay and Beaches

$$$–$$$$ ⊞ **Catamaran Resort Hotel.** Tiki torches light the way for guests stay-
★   ing at one of the six two-story buildings or the 14-story high rise (the view from the upper floors of the latter is spectacular). The room decor—dark wicker furniture and tropical prints—echoes the hotel's Polynesian theme. The popular Cannibal Bar hosts Top 40 and rock-and-roll groups, while a classical or jazz pianist tickles the ivories at the Moray Bar; Catamaran guests can also take advantage of the entertainment facilities at the sister Bahia Hotel. Although it's more couples-oriented than the Bahia, children 18 or under stay free. ⊠ *3999 Mission Blvd., 92109,* ☎ *619/488–1081, 800/288–0770, or 800/233–8172 in Canada;* FAX *619/488–1387 (reservations), 619/488–1619 (front desk). 312 rooms. Restaurant, bar, coffee shop, piano bar, pool, spa, exercise room, nightclub. AE, D, DC, MC, V.*

$$$–$$$$ ⊞ **Crystal Pier Motel.** You can drive your car onto the Crystal Pier and park in front of one of this classic motel's blue-and-white cottages, equipped with kitchenettes and patios overlooking the sea. A landmark since the 1930s, this place is no longer the bargain it once was, nor does it have the amenities of the other properties in its price category; you're paying for character and proximity to the ocean. The more people you come with, the more reasonable this place is: The cottages sleep up to four but cost the same no matter what the occupancy. ⊠ *4500 Ocean Blvd.,* ☎ *619/483–6983 or 800/748–5894,* FAX *619/483–6811. 26 cottages. Kitchenettes. 3-night minimum stay June 15–Sept. 15, 2-night minimum rest of yr. D, MC, V.*

$$$–$$$$ ⊞ **San Diego Hilton Beach and Tennis Resort.** Spread out on the picturesque grounds of this deluxe resort, low-level bungalows are surrounded by trees, Japanese bridges, and ponds; a high-rise building has accommodations with views of Mission Bay Park. The well-appointed rooms are decorated in rose and teal, and most have wet bars, spacious bathrooms, and patios or terraces. ⊠ *1775 E. Mission Bay Dr., 92109,* ☎ *619/276–4010 or 800/445–8667 (central reservations),* FAX *619/275–7991. 357 rooms. Restaurant, bar, coffee shop, pool, putting greens, 5 tennis courts, exercise room, boating, marina, bicycles, playground, car rental, children's programs. AE, D, DC, MC, V.*

$$$ ⊞ **Bahia Hotel.** This huge complex, on a 14-acre peninsula in Mission Bay Park, has furnished studios and suites with kitchens; many have wood-beamed ceilings and tropical decor. The hotel's *Bahia Belle* cruises Mission Bay at sunset, and guests can return for yuks at the on-premises Comedy Isle club. Rates are reasonable for a place so well located—within walking distance of the ocean—and with so many amenities, including use of the facilities at the Catamaran Hotel. ⊠ *998 W. Mission Bay Dr., 92109,* ☎ *619/488–0551, 800/288–0770, or 800/233–8172 in Canada;* FAX *619/488–1387 (reservations) or 619/488–7055. 321 rooms. Restaurant, bar, piano bar, pool, spa, 2* *tennis courts, watersport rentals and lessons, bicycles, rollerblading. AE, D, DC, MC, V.*

$$$ 🏨 **Hyatt Islandia.** Its location in appealing Mission Bay Park is one of the many pluses of this property, which has rooms in several low-level, lanai-style units, as well as marina suites and rooms in a high-rise building. Many rooms overlook the hotel's gardens and fish pond; others have dramatic views of the bay area. This hotel is famous for its lavish Sunday champagne brunch. ✉ *1441 Quivira Rd., 92109,* ☎ *619/224–1234 or 800/233–1234 (central reservations),* FAX *619/224–0348. 422 rooms. 2 restaurants, pool, spa, exercise room, marina, boating. AE, D, DC, MC, V.*

$$–$$$ 🏨 **Dana Inn & Marina.** This hotel, which has an adjoining marina, is a bargain in the Mission Bay area. If accommodations are not as grand as those in the nearby hotels, they're more than adequate. High ceilings in the second-floor rooms give a welcome sense of space, and some even have a view of the inn's marina. There are many on-premises sports facilities, and the Dana Inn is within walking distance of Sea World, the beach, and a pleasant park. ✉ *1710 W. Mission Bay Dr., 92109,* ☎ *619/222–6440, 800/326–2466,* FAX *619/222–5916. 196 rooms. Restaurant, pool, spa, 2 tennis courts, Ping-Pong, shuffleboard, boating. AE, D, DC, MC, V.*

$$ 🏨 **Surfer Motor Lodge.** This four-story building is right on the beach and directly behind a shopping center with many restaurants and boutiques. Rooms are plain, but those on the upper floors have good views. ✉ *711 Pacific Beach Dr., 92109,* ☎ *619/483–7070 or 800/787–3373,* FAX *619/274–1670. 52 rooms. Restaurant, bar, pool, bicycles. AE, DC, MC, V.*

$–$$ 🏨 **Ocean Manor Apartment Hotel.** Some folks have been returning for ★ 20 years to this well-priced Ocean Beach hotel, which rents units by the day (three-day minimum for those with kitchens), week, or month in winter; you'll need to reserve months in advance. The comfortable studios and one- and two-bedroom suites are furnished plainly in the style of the 1950s. There is no maid service, but fresh towels are always provided. ✉ *1370 Sunset Cliffs Blvd., 92107,* ☎ *619/222–7901 or 619/224–1379 (guest calls). 22 units. Pool, Ping-Pong, shuffleboard. MC, V.*

$ 🏨 **Mission Bay Motel.** A half-block from the beach and right on the local main street, this motel has modest units, some with kitchenettes. Great restaurants and nightlife are within walking distance, but you may find the area a bit noisy. ✉ *4221 Mission Blvd., 92109,* ☎ *619/483–6440. 50 rooms. Pool. MC, V.*

Hostels

Banana Bungalow San Diego (✉ 707 Reed Ave., Mission Beach 92109, ☎ 619/273–3060 or 800/546–7835).

HI–Hostel on Broadway (✉ 500 W. Broadway, San Diego 92101, ☎ 619/525–1531).

NIGHTLIFE AND THE ARTS

By Dan Janeck

Updated by Albert M. Columbo

San Diego is renowned for its unbeatable variety of sun-and-surf recreational activities, but most visitors are delighted by the momentum the city gains after dark. Current nightclub and cultural listings can be found in the *Reader,* a free weekly; *San Diego* magazine; and the *San Diego Union-Tribune.* Those "in the know" rely on San Diego's many community micromags found in most coffeehouses in La Jolla, Pacific Beach, downtown, and Hillcrest.

Nightlife

Rock, Pop, Folk, Reggae, and Blues

Belly Up Tavern. This eclectic live-concert venue hosts critically acclaimed artists who play everything from reggae, rock, new wave, Motown, and other music. Sunday nights are usually free and spotlight local R&B artists. ⊠ *143 S. Cedros Ave., Solana Beach,* ☎ *619/481–9022.* ⊘ *Daily 11 AM–1:30 AM; call for entertainment schedule. MC, V.*

Bodie's. This bar hosts the best rock and blues bands in San Diego and some from out of town. ⊠ *528 F St., Gaslamp Quarter,* ☎ *619/236–8988.* ⊘ *Daily 6 AM–2 AM. No credit cards.*

Brick by Brick. San Diego's top alternative and experimental rock groups play this club. ⊠ *1130 Buenos Ave., Bay Park, near Mission Bay,* ☎ *619/276–3993.* ⊘ *Nightly 8 PM–1 AM. MC, V.*

Casbah. You might hear rock, reggae, funk, and every other kind of band—except Top 40—at this small club. ⊠ *2501 Kettner Blvd., near the airport,* ☎ *619/232–4355.* ⊘ *Live bands nightly at 9:30. No credit cards.*

Livewire. This underground twentysomething hole-in-the-wall hangout has more character than most other places; there are also more tattoos and pierced body parts than there are people. ⊠ *2103 El Cajon Blvd., North Park,* ☎ *619/291–7450,* ⊘ *Daily 5 PM–2 AM. No credit cards.*

Patrick's II. A downtown pub with definite Irish tendencies, Patrick's is a prime place to hear live New Orleans–style jazz, blues, and rock. ⊠ *428 F St., downtown,* ☎ *619/233–3077.* ⊘ *Entertainment nightly 9–2. No credit cards.*

Winston's Beach Club. Local bands, reggae groups, and, occasionally, '60s rock bands play this bowling alley turned rock club. The crowd here can get rowdy. ⊠ *1921 Bacon St., Ocean Beach,* ☎ *619/222–6822.* ⊘ *Live bands nightly 9 PM–2 AM. MC, V.*

Jazz

Croce's. The intimate jazz cave of restaurateur Ingrid Croce (singer-songwriter Jim Croce's widow) hosts superb acoustic-jazz musicians. Next door, Croce's Top Hat puts on live R&B nightly from 9 until 2. ⊠ *802 5th Ave., Gaslamp Quarter,* ☎ *619/233–4355.* ⊘ *Nightly 7:30 PM–2 AM. AE, D, DC, MC, V.*

Elario's. This club, on the top floor of the Summer House Inn, has an ocean view and an incomparable lineup of internationally acclaimed jazz musicians. ⊠ *7955 La Jolla Shores Dr., La Jolla,* ☎ *619/459–0541.* ⊘ *Shows Thurs.–Sat. 8 PM–midnight. AE, DC, MC, V.*

Humphrey's by the Bay. This is the premier promoter of the city's best jazz, folk, and light-rock summer concert series, held out on the grass. The rest of the year the music moves indoors to Humphrey's Lounge. ⊠ *2241 Shelter Island Dr.,* ☎ *619/523–1010 for taped concert information.* ⊘ *Entertainment hours vary. AE, D, DC, MC, V.*

Country-Western

In Cahootz. A great sound system, a large dance floor, and occasional big-name performers make this lively spot a choice destination for cowgirls and -boys and city slickers alike. ⊠ *5373 Mission Center Rd., Mission Valley,* ☎ *619/291–8635.* ⊘ *Weeknights 5 PM–2 AM, weekends 5:30 PM–2 AM. AE, D, MC, V.*

Zoo Country. Enjoy live music Friday through Sunday or a DJ seven nights a week at this hangout for line-dancin', two-steppin' cowpersons. ⊠ *1340 Broadway, El Cajon,* ☎ *619/442–9900.* ⊘ *Daily noon–2 AM. AE, D, MC, V.*

Dance Clubs

Club Emerald City. Alternative dance music and an uninhibited clientele keep this spot unpredictable—and worth a visit for the adventurous. ⊠ *945 Garnet Ave., Pacific Beach,* ☎ *619/483–9920.* ☉ *Tues.–Sun. 8:30 PM–2 AM. No credit cards.*

Club Hedonism. Listed in *Details* magazine as one of the best nights out in America, this is still a favorite of local club kids "serving" hi-tech fashion. San Diego's celebrated DJ Jon Bishop spins the latest in underground club music, and video screens play continuous loops of enigmatic clips. ⊠ *1051 University Ave., Hillcrest,* ☎ *619/497–4588.* ☉ *Thurs. 9 PM–2AM. No credit cards.*

Club Metro. DJs spin techno, house, hip hop, and acid jazz for a fun crowd at this newish night spot. ⊠ *504 4th Ave., Gaslamp Quarter,* ☎ *619/239–6334* ☉ *Wed.–Sun. 8 PM–2 AM. AE, D, MC, V.*

Johnny M's. Get down to '70s and '80s dance music at this huge disco. A blues room is open Wednesday, Friday, and Saturday from 10 PM to 1:30 AM, and the DJ plays from 8 PM until 1:30 AM. ⊠ *801 4th St., Gaslamp Quarter,* ☎ *619/233–1131.* ☉ *Tues.–Sat. 8 PM–2 AM; restaurant open daily 11 AM–2 AM. AE, D, MC, V.*

World Beat Center. The ever-changing format at this lively place for those 18 and up revolves around music and culture. Music genres include, but aren't limited to, ska, alternative rock, techno, and cultural dance. ⊠ *1845 Hancock St., Middletown,* ☎ *619/296–9334.* ☉ *Hours vary; call for schedule of events.*

Bars and Nightclubs

Blue Tattoo. This place is a popular destination for San Diego's young professionals. There's a dress code (no jeans, T-shirts, hats, sweat shirts, or tennis shoes) on Friday and Saturday nights. Entertainment varies nightly. ⊠ *835 5th Ave., Gaslamp Quarter,* ☎ *619/238–7191.* ☉ *Wed.–Sun. 8 PM–2 AM. AE, D, DC, MC, V.*

Club Bocca. This multilevel dance club is frequented by famous live R&B, Old School, and rock performers, such as the Ohio Players, Morris Day and the Time, Mary Jane Girls, and Blue Oyster Cult. There's also an Italian restaurant here, a sports bar, and DJ dancing on weekends. ⊠ *2828 Camino del Rio S, Mission Valley,* ☎ *619/299–3059.* ☉ *Weekdays 11 AM–2 AM, Sat. 4 PM–2 AM, Sun. 10 AM–2 AM. AE, D, DC, MC, V.*

Club 66. Located under the restaurant Dakota's, this impressive club with stainless-steel decor and gas-station memorabilia is modeled after Route 66. You'll have fun dancing to disco, high energy, and Top 40 while taking it all in. ⊠ *901 5th Ave., downtown,* ☎ *619/234–4166.* ☉ *Wed.–Sat. 8 PM–2 AM. AE, D, MC, V.*

E Street Alley. Off the street down a short alley, this club is a marvel for the senses. The Blue Room is a plush lounge with live jazz on Thursday and blues the rest of the week. Club E is a smartly designed, spacious dance club with a DJ spinning Top 40 tunes. Chino's is an exquisite restaurant featuring American cuisine with a Southeast Asian flair. ⊠ *919 4th Ave. (on E St. between 4th and 5th), downtown,* ☎ *619/231–9200.* ☉ *Tues.–Thurs. 10 PM–2 AM, Fri. and Sat. 8 PM–2 AM. Restaurant hours: 11:30 AM–2:30 PM and 5:30 PM–11 PM. AE, D, DC, MC, V.*

Moose McGillycuddy's. Fun music powers the dance floor here, and the staff serves up drinks and Mexican food. This spot has a positive energy about it. ⊠ *1165 Garnet Ave., Pacific Beach,* ☎ *619/274–2323,* ☉ *Daily 4 PM–2 AM. AE, D, MC, V.*

Piano Bars/Mellow

Hotel Del Coronado. The fairy-tale hostelry has piano music in its Crown Room and Palm Court. The Ocean Terrace Lounge has live bands nightly from 9 PM to 1 AM. ⊠ *1500 Orange Ave., Coronado,* ☎ *619/435–6611.* ☉ *Daily 10:30 AM–1:30 AM. AE, D, DC, MC, V.*

Top O' the Cove. Show tunes and standards from the '40s to the '80s are the typical piano fare at this magnificent Continental restaurant in La Jolla. ☒ *1216 Prospect St.,* ☎ *619/454–7779.* ☉ *Entertainment Wed.–Sun.; hours vary. AE, DC, MC, V.*

Westgate Hotel. One of the most elegant settings in San Diego has piano music in the Plaza Bar. ☒ *1055 2nd Ave., downtown,* ☎ *619/238– 1818.* ☉ *Daily 11 AM–2 AM, entertainment Mon.–Sat. 8:30 PM–closing. AE, D, DC, MC, V.*

Comedy and Cabaret

Comedy Isle. This club inside the Bahia Hotel serves up the latest in local and national talent. ☒ *998 W. Mission Bay Dr., Mission Bay,* ☎ *619/488–6872.* ☉ *Shows Thurs. 8:30 PM, Fri. and Sat. 8:30 and 10:30 PM. Reservations accepted. AE, DC, MC, V.*

The Comedy Store. In the same tradition as the Comedy Store in West Hollywood, San Diego's version hosts some of the best national touring and local talent. ☒ *916 Pearl St., La Jolla,* ☎ *619/454–9176.* ☉ *Shows Sun.–Thurs. 8 PM, Fri. and Sat. 8 and 10:30 PM. AE, MC, V.*

Tidbits. The best of southern California's female impersonators appear in hilarious nightly cabaret and comedy "tidbits," with charity benefit shows on Sundays. ☒ *3838 5th Ave., Hillcrest,* ☎ *619/543–0300.* ☉ *6 PM–1:30 AM; shows usually begin around 9, but times vary.*

Singles Bars

Dick's Last Resort. On weekends, fun-loving party people line up to get into this enormous barnlike restaurant and bar. ☒ *345 4th Ave., downtown,* ☎ *619/231–9100.* ☉ *Daily 10 AM–2 AM. AE, MC, V.*

El Torito. Notable happy hours and the central location attract yuppies and students to this Mexican restaurant. ☒ *445 Camino del Rio S, Mission Valley,* ☎ *619/296–6154.* ☉ *Daily 11 AM–midnight. AE, D, DC, MC, V.*

Old Bonita Store & Bonita Beach Club. This South Bay hangout with a DJ who spins retro house music attracts singles 25–35. ☒ *4014 Bonita Rd., Bonita,* ☎ *619/479–3537.* ☉ *Daily 11 AM–2 AM. AE, D, MC, V.*

U. S. Grant Hotel. The classiest spot in town for meeting fellow travelers—while relaxing with a scotch or martini at the mahogany bar— presents best local Latin, jazz, and blues bands alternate appearances. ☒ *326 Broadway, downtown,* ☎ *619/232–3121.* ☉ *Daily 11:30 AM–1:30 AM. AE, D, DC, MC, V.*

Gay and Lesbian Nightlife

Bourbon Street. This piano bar with relaxing surroundings and a courtyard out back resembles those in New Orleans. There's live entertainment nightly. ☒ *4612 Park Blvd., University Heights,* ☎ *619/291–0173.* ☉ *Weekdays noon–2 AM, Sat. 11 AM–2 AM, Sun. 9 AM–2 AM. D, MC, V.*

Club Bombay. A lesbian dance club with occasional live entertainment, Club Bombay has Sunday barbecues and nightly drink specials. ☒ *3175 India St., Middletown,* ☎ *619/296–6789.* ☉ *Mon.–Thurs. 4 PM–2 AM, Fri.–Sat. 2 PM–2 AM, Sun. 1 PM–2 AM. No credit cards.*

The Flame. This friendly dance club caters to lesbians most of the week. On Tuesday, the DJ spins for the popular Boys' Night. ☒ *3780 Park Blvd., Hillcrest,* ☎ *619/295–4163.* ☉ *Daily 5 PM–2 AM. No credit cards.*

Flicks. This video bar has music and comedy on four big screens. Drink specials and video formats vary each night. ☒ *1017 University Ave., Hillcrest,* ☎ *619/297–2056.* ☉ *Daily 2 PM–2 AM. No credit cards.*

Rich's San Diego. Muscular go-go boys dance to house music for a lively crowd at this popular dance club. ☒ *1051 University Ave., Hillcrest,* ☎ *619/497–4588.* ☉ *Thurs.–Sat. 9 PM–2 AM, Sun. 7 PM–2 AM. No credit cards.*

The Arts

By Marael
Johnson

Updated by
Albert M.
Columbo

Half-price tickets to most theater, music, and dance events can be
bought on the day of performance at the **TIMES ARTS TIX Ticket Center** (Horton Plaza, ☎ 619/497–5000). Only cash is accepted. ARTS
TIX also sells advance full-price tickets. Visa and MasterCard holders
may buy tickets for many scheduled performances through **Ticket-
Master** (☎ 619/220–8497).

Theater

Diversionary Theatre (⊠ 4545 Park Blvd., University Heights, ☎
619/220–0097) is a gay and lesbian theater that stages comedies and
dramas on gay themes.

Gaslamp Quarter Theatre Company (⊠ Hahn Cosmopolitan Theatre,
444 4th Ave., downtown, ☎ 619/234–9583) stages comedies, dramas,
mysteries, and musicals at a 250-seat venue.

La Jolla Playhouse (⊠ Mandell Weiss Center for the Performing Arts,
University of California at San Diego, 2910 La Jolla Village Dr., ☎
619/550–1010) presents exciting and innovative productions, May to
November, under the artistic direction of Michael Greif.

Lawrence Welk Resort Theatre (⊠ 8860 Lawrence Welk Dr., Escondido, ☎ 619/749–3448 or 800/932–9355) puts on polished Broad-
way-style productions.

Old Globe Theatre (⊠ Simon Edison Centre for the Performing Arts,
Balboa Park, 1363 Old Globe Way, ☎ 619/239–2255) is the oldest
professional theater in California, performing classics, contemporary
dramas, and experimental works.

San Diego Repertory Theatre (⊠ Lyceum, 79 Horton Plaza, ☎ 619/235–
8025), San Diego's first resident acting company, performs contemporary
works year-round.

Sledgehammer Theatre (⊠ 1620 6th Ave., ☎ 619/544–1484), one of
San Diego's cutting-edge theaters, stages avant-garde pieces in St. Ce-
cilia's church.

The Theater in Old Town (⊠ 4040 Twiggs St., Old Town, ☎ 619/688–
2494) presents punchy revues and occasional classics. Shows like *Forbidden Broadway, Ruthless, Gilligan's Island,* and *Forbidden Hollywood*
have made this a popular place.

Concerts

Copley Symphony Hall (⊠ 750 B St., downtown, ☎ 619/699–4200)
has been home to the San Diego Symphony Orchestra. At press time,
the symphony was experiencing financial difficulties and its future was
uncertain. In past years, its performance season ran October–May, with
a series of outdoor pop concerts held near Seaport Village during the
summer.

La Jolla Chamber Music Society (☎ 619/459–3724) presents internationally acclaimed chamber ensembles, orchestras, and soloists at Sherwood Auditorium and the Civic Theatre.

Open-Air Theatre (⊠ San Diego State University, ☎ 619/594–6947)
presents top-name rock, reggae, and popular artists in summer concerts under the stars.

Sherwood Auditorium (⊠ 700 Prospect St., La Jolla, ☎ 619/454–2594),
a 550-seat venue in the Museum of Contemporary Art, San Diego, hosts
classical and jazz events.

Spreckels Theatre (⊠ 121 Broadway, ☎ 619/235–9500), a desig-
nated-landmark theater erected more than 80 years ago, hosts musical events—everything from Mostly Mozart to small rock concerts.
Ballets and theatrical productions are also held here.

Opera

San Diego Opera (✉ Civic Theatre, 202 C St., downtown, ☎ 619/232–7636 or 619/236–6510) draws international artists and has developed an impeccable reputation. The season of five operas runs January–April in the 3,000-seat, state-of-the-art Civic Theatre.

Dance

California Ballet Company (☎ 619/560–5676 or 619/560–6741) performs high-quality contemporary and traditional works, from story ballets to Balanchine, September to May, along with an annual *Nutcracker.*

OUTDOOR ACTIVITIES AND SPORTS

At least one stereotype of San Diego is true—it is an active, outdoors-oriented community. People recreate here more than they spectate. As a visitor, it's hard not to join in. As you would expect, the emphasis is on fun in the sun and surf—sailing, swimming, surfing, diving, and fishing head the list. Here is a sampling of favorite activities and the best places to enjoy them: scuba diving off La Jolla Cove, surfing at almost any of the beaches, golfing at Torrey Pines, roller skating at Mission Bay, jogging along the Embarcadero, playing volleyball on Ocean Beach, windsurfing on Mission Bay, and jet-skiing at the Snug Harbor Marina.

Beaches

Updated by
Albert M.
Columbo

The 70 miles of coastline in and around San Diego are dotted with some of the best beaches on the West Coast. Some are wide and sandy, others narrow and rocky; some are almost always crowded with athletes and sun-worshipers, others seem created for solitary beachcombers and romantic pairs. Among the standouts are Imperial Beach in South Beach, a classic southern California beach favored by surfers, swimmers, and Frisbee maniacs; Silver Strand State Beach, a relatively calm, family-friendly beach on the isthmus of Coronado; La Jolla Cove, where tidal pools and cliff coves provide exciting diversions for explorers; and Torrey Pines State Beach in Del Mar, one of the easiest and most comfortable beaches to visit in the area.

San Diego is a destination for surfers; the variety of breaks and their exposure to ocean swells make the surf off this portion of the Pacific coast remarkably consistent and fun. For a surf and weather report, call 619/221-8884.

Overnight camping is not allowed on any San Diego city beaches, but there are campgrounds at some state beaches throughout the county (☎ 800/444–7275 for reservations). Lifeguards are stationed at city beaches (from Sunset Cliffs to Black's Beach) in the summertime, but coverage in winter is provided by roving patrols only. Dogs are not permitted at most beaches in San Diego, and tickets for breaking the law can be expensive. Dog Beach at Ocean Beach is the only one within San Diego where dogs are allowed to run unleashed. Rivermouth in Del Mar is the only beach in the North County that permits the same. It is rarely a problem, however, to bring your pet to isolated beaches during the winter.

Pay attention to all signs listing illegal activities; undercover police often patrol the beaches, carrying their ticket books in coolers. Glass is prohibited on all beaches, and fires are allowed only in fire rings or barbecues. Alcoholic beverages—including beer—are completely banned on some city beaches; others allow you to partake between 8 AM and 8 PM only. Check out the signs posted at the parking lots and lifeguard towers before you hit the shore with a six-pack or some wine coolers.

Imbibing in beach parking lots, on boardwalks, and in landscaped areas is always illegal; where drinking is permitted, stay on the sand.

The beaches below are listed from south to north, starting just above the Mexican border.

South Bay

Border Field State Beach. This marshy area with wide chaparrals and wildflowers is a favorite among horse riders and hikers. However, frequent sewage contamination from Tijuana makes the water dangerous for swimming. For this reason, the beach is often closed, especially during the rainy season. There is ample parking, and there are rest rooms. ⊠ *Exit I–5 at Dairy Mart Rd. and head west along Monument Rd.*

South Beach. One of the few beaches where dogs are free to romp, this is a good spot for long, isolated walks. The rocky beach and the chance of sewage contamination from Tijuana tend to discourage crowds. Rest rooms and other facilities are scarce. ⊠ *At the end of Seacoast Dr. Take I–5 to Coronado Ave. and head west on Imperial Beach Ave. Turn left onto Seacoast Dr.*

Imperial Beach. In July, this classic southern California beach is the site of one of the nation's largest annual sand-castle competitions. Surfers and swimmers flock here to enjoy the water, waves, and beach, which is an ideal playing field for the Frisbee games of the predominantly young crowd. There are lifeguards on duty during the summer, parking lots, food vendors nearby, and rest rooms. Note: Although the surf here can be excellent, this is another spot at which to be careful of sewage contamination. ⊠ *Take Palm Ave. west from I–5 until it hits water.*

Coronado

Silver Strand State Beach. This area on the isthmus of Coronado (commonly mislabeled an island) was set aside as a state beach in 1932. The name is derived from the tiny silver seashells found in abundance near the water. The water is relatively calm, making this beach ideal for families; lifeguards and rangers are on duty year round. There is abundant parking available. There is also a campground ($14–$16 per night) and facilities but no hook-ups; spots are available on a first-come, first-served basis and stays are limited to one night. ⊠ *From San Diego–Coronado Bay Bridge, turn left onto Orange Ave., which becomes Hwy. 75, and follow signs,* ☎ *619/435–5184.* ⊞ *Parking $4.*

Coronado Beach. This beach is surprisingly uncrowded on most days, since the locals go to the less touristy areas in the south or north. It's perfect for sunbathing or games of Frisbee and Smash Ball (played with paddles and a small ball). Parking can be a little difficult on the busiest days, but there are plenty of rest rooms and service facilities, as well as fire rings. ⊠ *From the bridge turn left on Orange Ave. and follow signs.*

Point Loma

Sunset Cliffs. Beneath the jagged cliffs on the west side of the Point Loma peninsula is one of the more secluded beaches in the area, popular primarily with surfers and locals. The tide goes out each day to reveal tidal pools teeming with life at the south end of the peninsula, near Cabrillo Point. Farther north, the often-large waves attract surfers and the lonely coves attract sunbathers. Stairs are available at the foot of Bermuda and Santa Cruz avenues, but much of the access is limited to treacherous cliff trails. There are no facilities. Your visit here will be much more enjoyable at low tide; check the local newspaper for tide schedules. ⊠ *Take I–8 west to Sunset Cliffs Blvd. and head south.*

San Diego

Ocean Beach. The north end of this beach, past the second jetty, is known as Dog Beach because it's the only one within the San Diego city limits that allows canines to romp around without a leash. The south end of Ocean Beach, near the pier, is a hangout for surfers and transients. Much of the area, though, is a haven for local hippies, volleyball players, sunbathers, and swimmers. You'll find food vendors and fire rings here; limited parking is available. ⊠ *Take I–8 west to Sunset Cliffs Blvd. and head south. Turn right on Voltaire St., West Point Loma Blvd., or Newport Ave.*

Mission Beach. The boardwalk stretching along Mission Beach is popular with strollers, roller skaters, and bicyclists cruising at the posted 15-mph speed limit. Surfers, swimmers, and volleyball players congregate at the south end, which tends to get extremely crowded, especially on hot summer days. Parking can be a challenge, but there are plenty of rest rooms and restaurants in the area. ⊠ *Exit I–5 at Garnet Ave. and head west to Mission Blvd. Turn south and look for parking.*

Pacific Beach. The boardwalk turns into a sidewalk here, but there are still bike paths and picnic tables running along the beachfront. The beach is a favorite for families, teens, and surfers alike. Parking can be a problem, although there is a small lot at the foot of Ventura Place. ⊠ *Exit I–5 at Garnet Ave. and head west to Mission Blvd. Turn north and look for parking.*

La Jolla

The beaches of La Jolla combine unusual beauty with good fishing, exciting scuba diving, and fine surf. On the down side, they are crowded and have limited parking facilities. Don't even think about bringing your pet—dogs are not even allowed on the sidewalks above some La Jolla beaches.

Tourmaline Surfing Park. This is one of La Jolla's top surfing beaches. Parking here is easier than at nearby Windansea Beach. ⊠ *Take Mission Blvd. north (it turns into La Jolla Blvd.) and turn west on Tourmaline St.*

Windansea Beach. The surf at Windansea—whose habitués were lampooned in Tom Wolfe's *The Pump House Gang*—is world-class. ⊠ *Take Mission Blvd. north (it turns into La Jolla Blvd.) and turn west on Nautilus St.*

Marine Street Beach. This is an ideal stretch of sand for sunbathing and beach games. ⊠ *Accessible from Marine St. off La Jolla Blvd.*

Children's Pool. For the tykes, a circular seawall preserves this shallow lagoon. Small waves and no riptide provides a safe, if crowded, haven. ⊠ *Follow La Jolla Blvd. north. When it forks, take the left, Coast Blvd.*

Shell Beach. Just north of the Children's Pool is a small cove, accessible by stairs, with a relatively secluded beach. The exposed rocks just off the coast here have been designated a protected habitat for seals; you can watch them sun themselves and frolic in the water. ⊠ *Continue along Coast Blvd. north from the Children's Pool.*

La Jolla Cove. This one of the prettiest spots in the world. A palm-tree-lined park sits on top of cliffs formed by the incessant pounding of the waves. At low tide the tidal pools and cliff caves provide an exciting destination for explorers. Divers explore the underwater delights of the San Diego–La Jolla Underwater Park, an ecological reserve. The cove is also a favorite of rough-water swimmers, for whom buoys mark distances. ⊠ *Follow Coast Blvd. north to signs, or take the La Jolla Village Dr. exit from I–5, head west to Torrey Pines Rd., turn left, and drive down hill to Girard Ave. Turn right and follow signs.*

La Jolla Shores. This is one of the most popular and overcrowded beaches in the county. On summer holidays, all access routes are usually closed. The lures are a wide sandy beach; fun surf for boogie-boarders, body-surfers, and regular surfers; and a concrete boardwalk paralleling the beach. Go early to get a parking spot. ⊠ *From I–5 take La Jolla Village Dr. west and turn left onto La Jolla Shores Dr. Head west to Camino del Oro or Vallecitos St. Turn right and look for parking.*

Black's Beach. The late-1970s prohibition against public nudity doesn't stop nudists from frequenting this isolated beach, officially called Torrey Pines City Park Beach. Storms have weakened the cliffs over the past few years; they're dangerous to climb and should be avoided. Access along the shore coincides with low tides. The powerful waves attract surfers, and secluded trails attract nudist nature lovers. There are no lifeguards on duty, and strong ebb tides are common: only experienced swimmers should take the plunge. ⊠ *Take Genesee Ave. west from I–5 and follow signs to glider port; easier access, via a paved path, is available on La Jolla Farms Rd., but parking there is limited to 2 hrs.*

Del Mar

Torrey Pines State Beach. This is one of the easiest and most comfortable beaches to visit. The large parking lot is rarely full. Lifeguards are on duty weekends (weather permitting) from Easter until Memorial Day, daily from then until Labor Day, and again on weekends through September. Torrey Pines tends to get crowded during the summer, but more isolated spots under the cliffs are within a short walk in either direction. Exotic trails up into the hillside park make for fine hiking. ⊠ *Take the Carmel Valley Rd. exit west from I–5,* ☎ *619/755–2063.* 🖃 *Parking $4.* ☉ *Daily 8–sunset.*

Del Mar Beach. The numbered streets of Del Mar, from 15th to 29th, end at a wide, sandy beach, popular with volleyball players, surfers, and sunbathers. Although parking can be a problem on nice summer days, access is relatively easy, and the beach and water are both extremely comfortable. The portions of Del Mar south of 15th Street are lined with beautiful cliffs and are rarely crowded. ⊠ *Take the Via de la Valle exit from I–5 west to Old Hwy. 101 (also known as Camino del Mar in Del Mar) and turn left.*

Participant Sports

Bicycling

On any given summer day, Old Highway 101, from La Jolla to Oceanside, looks like a freeway for cyclists. Never straying more than a quarter mile from the beach, it is easily the most popular and scenic bike route around. Although the roads are narrow and winding, experienced cyclists like to follow Lomas Santa Fe Drive in Solana Beach east into Rancho Santa Fe, perhaps even continuing east on Del Dios Highway, past Lake Hodges, to Escondido. For more leisurely rides, Mission Bay, San Diego Harbor, and the Mission Beach boardwalk are all flat and scenic. For those who like to race on a track, San Diego even has a velodrome (☎ 619/296–3345) in Balboa Park.

Bikes can be rented at any number of places, including **Bicycle Barn** in Pacific Beach (⊠ 746 Emerald St., ☎ 619/581–3665) and **Hamel's Action Sports Center** in Mission Beach (⊠ 704 Ventura Pl., ☎ 619/488–5050). A free comprehensive map of all county bike paths is available from the local office of the **California Department of Transportation** (⊠ 2829 Juan St., Old Town, ☎ 619/688–6699).

Diving

At La Jolla Cove, you'll find the **San Diego–La Jolla Underwater Park,** an ecological preserve. Farther north, off the south end of Black's Beach, the rim of **Scripps Canyon** lies in about 60 feet of water. The canyon plummets to more than 900 feet in some sections. Another popular diving spot is Sunset Cliffs in Point Loma, where sea life is relatively close to shore. Strong rip currents make it an area best enjoyed by experienced divers. Diving equipment and boat trips can be arranged through **San Diego Divers Supply** (⌧ 4004 Sports Arena Blvd., ☎ 619/224–3439). **Diving Locker** (⌧ 1020 Girard Ave., Pacific Beach, ☎ 619/272–1120) has locations throughout the area. For general diving information, contact the San Diego City Lifeguards' Office (☎ 619/221–8884).

Fishing

The Pacific Ocean is full of corbina, croaker, and halibut just itching to be your dinner. No license is required to fish from a public pier, such as the Ocean Beach pier. A fishing license from the state Department of Fish and Game (☎ 619/525–4215), available at most bait-and-tackle stores, is required for fishing from the shoreline, although children under 15 won't need one.

Fisherman's Landing (⌧ 2838 Garrison St., Point Loma, ☎ 619/221–8500), **H&M Landing** (⌧ 2803 Emerson St., Point Loma, ☎ 619/222–1144), and **Seaforth Boat Rental** (⌧ 1641 Quivira Rd., West Mission Bay, ☎ 619/223–1681) operate from half-day to multiday fishing excursions out of San Diego. **Helgren's Sportfishing** (☎ 619/722–2133) has charters from Oceanside Harbor.

Fitness

Several hotels have exercise rooms or full-scale health clubs (☞ Lodging, *above*). The dozen **Family Fitness Centers** in the area (including centers in Mission Valley, ☎ 619/281–5543; and the Sports Arena–Point Loma area, ☎ 619/224–2902) allow nonmembers to use the facilities for a small fee.

Golf

Most public courses in the area provide an inexpensive current list of fees and charges for all San Diego courses. The **Southern California Golf Association** (☎ 818/980–3630 or 213/877–0901) publishes an annual directory with detailed and valuable information on all clubs. Another good resource for golfers is the **Southern California Public Links Golf Association** (☎ 714/994–4747). The following are a few of the better places to play in the area.

PUBLIC COURSES

Coronado Golf Course (⌧ 2000 Visalia Row, Coronado, ☎ 619/435–3121) has 18 holes, a driving range, equipment rentals, and a clubhouse. Views of San Diego Bay and the Coronado Bridge from the back 9 holes on this good walking course make it popular—and rather difficult to get on.

Eastlake Country Club (⌧ 2375 Clubhouse Dr., Chula Vista, ☎ 619/482–5757), a newer facility, has 18 holes, a driving range, equipment rentals, and a snack bar. A fun course for golfers of almost all levels of expertise, it's not overly difficult, though features such as water hazards provide a challenge.

Mission Bay Golf Center (⌧ 2702 N. Mission Bay Dr., San Diego, ☎ 619/490–3370) has 18 holes, a driving range, equipment rentals, and a restaurant. A not-very-challenging executive (par 3 and 4) course, Mission Bay is lit for night play.

Torrey Pines Municipal Golf Course (⌧ 11480 N. Torrey Pines Rd., La Jolla, ☎ 619/452–3226) has 36 holes, a driving range, and equipment rentals. Torrey Pines has views of the Pacific from every hole and is sufficiently challenging to host the Buick Invitational in February. It's not easy to get a good tee time at this justly popular course; out-of-towners are better off booking the instructional Golf Playing Package, which includes cart, fees, and a golf-pro escort for the first three holes.

RESORTS

La Costa Resort and Spa (⊠ Costa del Mar Rd., Carlsbad, ☏ 619/438–9111 or 800/854–5000) has 36 holes, a driving range, a clubhouse, equipment rentals, and a pro shop. One of the premier golf resorts in southern California, La Costa hosts the Mercedes Championships (formerly the Tournament of Champions) in January.

Rancho Bernardo Inn and Country Club (⊠ 17550 Bernardo Oaks Dr., Rancho Bernardo, ☏ 800/542–6096 in CA or 800/854–1065) has 108 holes (on five courses), a driving range, equipment rentals, and a restaurant. The golf's fine here, and Rancho Bernardo Inn lays out one of the best Sunday brunches in the county.

Horseback Riding

Holidays on Horseback (☏ 619/445–3997), in the East County town of Descanso, leads rides ranging from one to nine hours in the Cuyamaca Mountains. It rents special, easy-to-ride fox trotters to beginners. South of Imperial Beach, near the Mexican border, **Sandi's Rental Stables** (⊠ 2060 Hollister St., Imperial Beach, ☏ 619/424–3124) leads rides through Border Field State Park.

Jogging

From downtown, the most popular run is along the Embarcadero, which stretches around the bay. Trails snake through the canyons of Balboa Park. Mission Bay, renowned for its wide sidewalks and basically flat landscape, may be the most popular jogging spot in San Diego. Trails head west around Fiesta Island from Mission Bay, providing distance as well as a scenic route. Del Mar has the finest running trails along the bluff; park your car near 15th Street and run south along the cliffs for a gorgeous view of the ocean. Some tips: Don't run in bike lanes, and check the local newspaper's tide charts before heading to the beach.

Organized runs occur almost every weekend. They're listed in *Competitor* magazine (☏ 619/793–2711), available free at bike and running shops, or call the **San Diego Track Club** (☏ 800/450–7382). **The Sports Authority** (⊠ 8550 Rio Vista Shopping Center, Mission Valley, ☏ 619/295–1682) has supplies and information.

Surfing

Beginners should paddle out at Mission, Pacific, Tourmaline, La Jolla Shores, Del Mar, or Oceanside Beach. Experienced surfers should hit Sunset Cliffs, the La Jolla reef breaks, Black's Beach, or Swami's, on Cliff Roadside Park in Encinitas. Most public beaches have separate areas for surfers. Many local surf shops rent boards, including **Star Surfing Company** (☏ 619/273–7827) in Pacific Beach and **La Jolla Surf Systems** (☏ 619/456–2777) and **Hansen's** (☏ 619/753–6595) in Encinitas.

Swimming

The most spectacular pool in town is Belmont Park's the **Plunge** (⊠ 3115 Ocean Front Walk, Mission Bay, ☏ 619/488–3110). The **Downtown YMCA** (⊠ 500 W. Broadway Ave., ☏ 619/232–7451) is centrally located.

Tennis

Many hotels (☞ Lodging, *above*) have tennis courts. Public facilities in San Diego include the **Balboa Tennis Club at Morley Field** (☏ 619/295–9278), in Balboa Park, which has 25 courts, 19 of which are lighted. Nonmembers can make reservations after paying a $4 fee. The **La Jolla Tennis Club** (☏ 619/454–4434) has 9 free public courts near downtown La Jolla, 5 of them lighted. The 12 lighted courts at the privately owned **Peninsula Tennis Club** (☏ 619/226–3407) in Ocean Beach are available to the public for a $3 day-use fee.

Water Sports

Mission Bay is one of the most popular waterskiing areas in southern California. Boats and equipment can be rented from **Seaforth Boat Rentals** (⊠ 1641 Quivera Rd., near Mission Bay, ☎ 619/223–1681). Sailboats can be rented from **Harbor Sailboats** (⊠ Harbor Island Dr., ☎ 619/291–9570). Windsurfing rentals and instruction are available at the **Bahia Hotel** (⊠ 998 W. Mission Bay Dr., ☎ 619/488–0551) and other resorts in the Mission Bay area. **California Water Sports** (☎ 619/434–3089) has information about Jet Ski rentals and purchases.

Spectator Sports

For information on tickets to any event, contact **Teleseat** (☎ 619/452–7328). **San Diego Jack Murphy Stadium** (⊠ 9449 Friars Rd., ☎ 619/525–8282) is at the intersection of I–8 and I–805. To get to the **San Diego Sports Arena** (⊠ 3500 Sports Arena Blvd., ☎ 619/224–4171), take the Rosecrans exit off I–5 and turn right onto Sports Arena Boulevard.

Baseball

The National League **San Diego Padres** (☎ 619/283–4494) play from April into October at San Diego Jack Murphy Stadium. Tickets range from $5 to $13 and are usually readily available.

Football

Hometown heroes the NFL **San Diego Chargers** (☎ 619/280–2111) fill San Diego Jack Murphy Stadium August through December. The San Diego State University Aztecs compete in the exciting Western Athletic Conference, with home games also at Jack Murphy.

Horse Racing

The annual summer meeting of the **Del Mar Thoroughbred Club** (☎ 619/755–1141) on the Del Mar Fairgrounds attracts hordes of Beautiful People, along with the best horses and jockeys in the country. Racing begins in July and continues through early September, every day except Tuesday. There's also a satellite wagering facility (☎ 619/755–1167). Take I–5 north to the Via de la Valle exit.

Ice Hockey

The **San Diego Gulls** (☎ 619/224–4625) play their games from late October to March at the San Diego Sports Arena (☎ 619/224–4171). Ticket prices range from 8 to $12.

Soccer

San Diego Sockers (☎ 619/224–4625) games are raucous, since San Diegans love to support their Sockers, a very successful Continental Indoor Soccer League team. The season runs June–September at the San Diego Sports Arena (☎ 619/224–4171). Tickets range from $6 to $12.50.

SHOPPING

Shopping Districts

Coronado

By Marael Johnson

Updated by Albert M. Columbo

Orange Avenue, in the center of town, has six blocks of ritzy boutiques and galleries. The elegant Hotel Del Coronado (⊠ 1500 Orange Ave.) houses exclusive specialty shops. **Ferry Landing Marketplace** (⊠ 1201 1st St. at B Ave.) has many boutiques and shops.

Downtown

Horton Plaza, bordered by Broadway, 1st Avenue, G Street, and 4th Avenue in the heart of center city, is a shopper's Disneyland—visually exciting, multilevel department stores; one-of-a-kind shops; fast-food counters; classy restaurants; a farmers' market; live theater; and cinemas. Victorian buildings and renovated warehouses in the historic Gaslamp Quarter along 4th and 5th avenues house art galleries, antiques, and specialty shops.

The Paladion (✉ 777 Front St.) is San Diego's answer to Rodeo Drive. This posh complex hosts a collection of upscale boutiques—including Cartier, Tiffany, Alfred Dunhill, Gianni Versace, and Salvatore Ferragamo.

Golden Triangle

San Diego's Golden Triangle area, several miles east of coastal La Jolla, is served by **University Towne Centre** (✉ La Jolla Village Dr., between I–5 and I–805). This megamall has the usual range of department stores, specialty shops, sportswear chains, restaurants, and cinemas. The **Costa Verde Shopping Center,** on the corner of Genesee Avenue and La Jolla Village Drive, is an enormous strip mall of convenience stores and inexpensive eateries.

Hotel Circle

The Hotel Circle area, northeast of downtown near I–8 and Freeway 163, has four major shopping centers. **Fashion Valley** (✉ 452 Fashion Valley), **Hazard Center** (✉ 7676 Hazard Center Dr.), **Mission Valley Center** (✉ 1640 Camino del Rio N), and **Rio Vista Shopping Center,** (Rio San Diego Drive, Stadium Way exit off I–8) contain hundreds of shops, as well as restaurants, cinemas, and branches of almost every San Diego department store.

Kensington, Hillcrest, and North Park

Three of San Diego's older, established neighborhoods, a few miles north and northeast of downtown, have numerous specialty shops. **Adams Avenue,** in Kensington, is Antiques Row. More than 20 dealers sell everything from postcards and kitchen utensils to cut glass and porcelain . **University Avenue** at 5th Avenue (near the neon Hillcrest sign) has book, music, and gift shops. You'll find International Male, the Gap, and clothing boutiques, among them California Man, Gamma, and London Underground. Don't miss Babette Schwartz, a zany pop-culture store. **Uptown District,** a shopping center on University Avenue, has several furniture, gift, and specialty shops like Obelisk and Laguna Trends. Retro rules in North Park. **Park Boulevard** and **University Avenue at 30th Street** host many "nostalgia" shops, featuring clothing, accessories, furnishings, wigs, and thrift stores with bric-a-brac of the 1920s–60s.

La Jolla

La Jolla, about 15 miles northwest of downtown on the coast, is an ultra-chic, ultra-exclusive resort community. High-end and trendy boutiques line Girard Avenue and Prospect Street. Coast Walk, nestled along the cliffside of Prospect Street, has several levels of sophisticated shops, galleries, and restaurants, as well as a spectacular ocean view.

Old Town

North of downtown, off I–5, the popular Old Town historic district is reminiscent of a colorful Mexican marketplace. Adobe architecture, flower-filled plazas, fountains, and courtyards highlight the shopping areas of **Bazaar del Mundo, La Esplanade,** and **Old Town Mercado,** where you will find international goods, toys, souvenirs, and arts and crafts.

Seaport Village

On the waterfront, a few minutes from downtown, **Seaport Village** contains theme shops, restaurants, arts-and-crafts galleries, and commanding views of Coronado, the bridge, and passing ships.

SIDE TRIP TO THE SAN DIEGO NORTH COAST

By Kevin Brass

Updated by
Bobbi Zane

An explosion of development throughout the 1980s turned the north coast into an extension of San Diego. Beyond the freeways, though, though, the communities have maintained their charm. Some of the finest restaurants and beaches in San Diego County can be found in the area, along with such natural and historical attractions as San Diego Wild Animal Park and Mission San Luis Rey. The mission is a well-preserved remnant of California's first European settlers. Please note that the area code for most of the region north and east of Del Mar and Rancho Bernardo will change to 760 during 1997. Calls dialed with the old 619 code (listed with all numbers below) will go through for most of the year; after the "grace period" ends, callers will hear a reminder of the new 760 code. For meal and accommodation price categories, see the separate charts in San Diego Dining and Lodging, *above*.

Numbers in the margin correspond to points of interest on the San Diego North County map.

Del Mar

★ ❶ *23 mi north of downtown San Diego on I–5, 9 mi north of La Jolla on S21.*

Del Mar is best known for its race track, chic shopping strip, celebrity visitors, and wide beaches. **Del Mar Plaza** (☒ 15th St., at S21—a.k.a. Camino del Mar), contains restaurants with great ocean views. The center's boutiques are excellent barometers of the latest in southern California style. **Seagrove Park** (☒ 15th St., west end) in Del Mar is a small stretch of grass overlooking the ocean; concerts are performed here on summer evenings. Access to Del Mar's beaches is from the streets that run east–west off Coast Boulevard.

❷ The **Del Mar Fairgrounds** is home to the **Del Mar Thoroughbred Club** (☒ 2260 Jimmy Durante Blvd., ☎ 619/755–1141), which goes by the slogan "Where the Turf Meets the Surf." Crooner Bing Crosby and his Hollywood buddies—Pat O'Brien, Gary Cooper, and Oliver Hardy, among others—organized the club in the '30s, primarily because Crosby thought it would be fun to have a track near his Rancho Santa Fe home. Even now the racing season here (usually July–September, post time Wednesday through Monday at 2 PM) is one of the most fashionable in California. There is also a satellite wagering facility here. Del Mar Fairgrounds hosts more than 100 different events each year, from a cat show to an auto race. ☒ *Fairgrounds: Via de la Valle Rd. exit west from I–5,* ☎ *619/755–1161.*

☾ **Freeflight,** a small exotic-bird training facility adjacent to the Del Mar Fairgrounds, is open to the public. Visitors are allowed to handle the birds—a guaranteed child pleaser. ☒ *2132 Jimmy Durante Blvd.,* ☎ *619/481–3148.* ☜ *$1.* ☉ *Daily 10–4.*

Dining and Lodging

$$ ✕ **Cilantro's.** Shark fajitas and spit-roasted chicken with a mild chili sauce are among the subtly spiced, gourmet Mexican and Southwest-style dishes served at this Del Mar restaurant. The inexpensive tapas menu, with such delicacies as crab tostadas and three-cheese quesadillas, is a little easier on the wallet. ☒ *3602 Via de la Valle,* ☎ *619/259–8777. AE, DC, MC, V.*

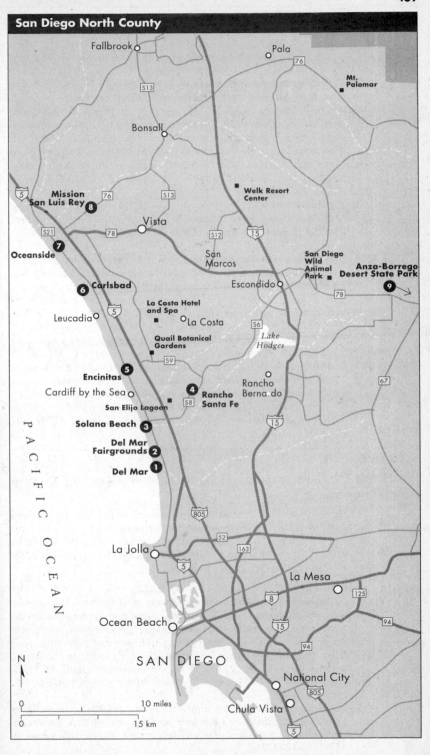

San Diego North County

Fallbrook

Pala

76

Mt. Palomar

S13

Bonsall

Welk Resort Center

5

Mission San Luis Rey 8

76

S13

Vista

S21

78

15

7 **Oceanside**

San Marcos

S12

San Diego Wild Animal Park

Anza-Borrego Desert State Park 9

6 **Carlsbad**

Escondido

78

67

Leucadia

La Costa Hotel and Spa

La Costa

5

Quail Botanical Gardens

S6

Lake Hodges

S9

5 **Encinitas**

Cardiff by the Sea

San Elijo Lagoon

4 **Rancho Santa Fe**

S8

Rancho Berna.do

3 **Solana Beach**

Del Mar Fairgrounds 2

1 **Del Mar**

15

805

La Jolla

52

163

La Mesa

5

125

8

Ocean Beach

15

94

SAN DIEGO

94

N

National City

805

Chula Vista

5

PACIFIC OCEAN

0   10 miles
0   15 km

$$ ✕ **Il Fornaio.** Del Mar's talk-of-the-town *ristorante* serves northern Italian cuisine—fresh seafood, homemade pastas, and crispy pizzas. Il Fornaio also operates a wine bar in the adjacent outdoor piazza, where diners can sit under an umbrella and enjoy the ocean view. ⌧ *1555 Camino del Mar, Suite 301,* ☎ *619/755–8876. AE, DC, MC, V.*

$$ ✕ **Pacifica Del Mar.** The ocean view alone would be enough to lure
★   crowds to this contemporary restaurant, which emphasizes an imaginative California cuisine of fresh ingredients prepared with Southwest, Cajun, Italian, and Pacific Rim touches. But the cuisine consistently gets top ratings from San Diego restaurant reviewers as well. Start with the smoked corn, chicken, and black-bean chowder, and then go on to the grilled prawn salad, blackened catfish, or one of the free-range chicken dishes. ⌧ *1555 Camino del Mar, Suite 321,* ☎ *619/792–0476. AE, D, DC, MC, V.*

$ ✕ **Johnny Rockets.** This '50s-style malt-and-burger joint, on the Del Mar Plaza's lower level, dishes up juicy burgers, thick malts, and fries. ⌧ *1555 Camino del Mar, Suite 102,* ☎ *619/755–1954. MC, V.*

$$$–$$$$ ⊡ **L'Auberge Del Mar Resort and Spa.** L'Auberge is filled with darkwood antiques, and all its spacious rooms have wet bars; many have fireplaces, full marble baths, and private balconies with garden and coastal views. The spa specializes in aromatherapy and European herbal wraps and treatments. ⌧ *1540 Camino del Mar, Del Mar 92014,* ☎ *619/259–1515 or 800/553–1336,* ⨎ *619/755–4940. 120 rooms. 2 restaurants, bar, 2 pools, outdoor hot tub, beauty salon, spa, 2 tennis courts, health club, meeting rooms. AE, D, DC, MC, V.*

$$–$$$ ⊡ **Stratford Inn.** Rooms at this pleasant inn, three blocks from the ocean, are large, with ample closet space and dressing areas; some have ocean views. Suites with kitchenettes are available. Continental breakfast is complimentary. ⌧ *710 Camino del Mar, 92014,* ☎ *619/755–1501 or 800/446–7229,* ⨎ *619/755–4704. 93 rooms. 2 pools. AE, D, DC, MC, V.*

Solana Beach

❸   *1 mi north of Del Mar on S21, 25 mi north of downtown San Diego on I–5 to Lomas Santa Fe Dr. west.*

Solana Beach is a quiet community just north of Del Mar. Early Solana settlers used dynamite to blast the town's **Fletcher Cove** (⌧ Lomas Santa Fe Dr., west end) out of the overhanging cliffs. Called Pill Box by locals because of a bunkerlike lifeguard station that overlooks it, the Fletcher Cove beach is easy to reach.

Dining

$ ✕ **California Pizza Kitchen.** Bright, noisy, and cheerful, this popular restaurant in Solana Beach's Beachwalk shopping center produces designer pizzas in its wood-fired oven, ranging from the conventional to the outlandish: moo-shu-chicken calzone, mixed-grill vegetarian, rosemary chicken potato, roasted garlic chicken, and five-cheese and tomato. Pastas are good, too, as are the enormous salads. ⌧ *437 S. Hwy. 101,* ☎ *619/793–0999. Reservations not accepted. AE, D, DC, MC, V.*

$ ✕ **Fidel's.** Rich in North County tradition, Fidel's serves well-prepared Mexican dishes in a low-key, pleasant atmosphere. The restaurant's outdoor patio area draws a lively crowd. ⌧ *607 Valley Ave.,* ☎ *619/755–5292. MC, V.*

Rancho Santa Fe

④ *4 mi east Solana Beach on S8 (Lomas Santa Fe Dr.), 29 mi north of downtown San Diego on I–5 to S8 east.*

Groves of huge, drooping eucalyptus trees cover the hills and valleys of Rancho Santa Fe, hiding the exclusive community's posh estates. The little village of Rancho has some elegant and expensive shops and restaurants, but it is no accident that there is little else to see or do here; the residents guard their privacy religiously.

Dining and Lodging

$$$$ ✕ **Mille Fleurs.** This gem of a French auberge is a most romantic hide-
★ away, with contemporary Gallic cuisine to enhance the mood. It's a mile from Chino's, the county's most famous vegetable farm, where the chef shops daily. ⊠ *6009 Paseo Delicias,* ☎ *619/756–3085. Reservations essential. AE, DC, MC, V. No lunch weekends.*

$$$$ ✕⌧ **Rancho Valencia Resort.** One of southern California's hidden trea-
★ sures, this luxurious resort has accommodations in Spanish-style casitas scattered among landscaped grounds. Gardens yield a year-round profusion of flowers: crimson bougainvillea, fragrant orange blossoms, and roses. Many of the spacious suites are split level, with sunken living rooms, each with a corner fireplace that can be seen from the bed. Each suite also has a private patio and wet bar. Rancho Valencia is adjacent to three well-designed golf courses and is one of the top tennis resorts in the country; a full tennis program includes group or private instruction. The inn's first-rate restaurant has earned raves for its California cuisine. ⊠ *5921 Valencia Circle, 92067,* ☎ *619/756– 1123 or 800/548–3664,* ⅮⅩ *619/756 -0165. 43 suites. Restaurant, bar, 2 pools, 2 outdoor hot tubs, 18 tennis courts, health club, hiking, croquet, bicycles. AE, DC, MC, V.*

$$–$$$$ ✕⌧ **Inn at Rancho Santa Fe.** Most accommodations here are in red-tile-roofed cottages scattered about the property's park-like 20 acres. Some have two bedrooms, private patios, fireplaces, and hot tubs. The inn also maintains a beach house at Del Mar for guest use and has membership at the exclusive Rancho Santa Fe Golf Club. ⊠ *5951 Linea del Cielo, 92067,* ☎ *619/756–1131 or 800/654–2928,* ⅮⅩ *619/759– 1604. 90 rooms. 3 dining rooms, bar, swimming pool, 3 tennis courts, exercise room, croquet, meeting rooms. AE, DC, M, V.*

Encinitas

⑤ *6 mi north of Solana Beach on S21, 7 mi west of Rancho Santa Fe on S9, 28 mi north of downtown San Diego on I–5.*

Encinitas is best known as the flower capital of the world, and although the flower industry is not as prevalent as it once was, the city is still home to Paul Ecke Poinsettias, the largest producer of the popular Christmas blossom. During the spring bloom season, commercial nurseries on both sides of I–5 are open to the public. The palm trees of Sea Cliff Roadside Park and the golden domes of the Self-Realization Fellowship at 939 2nd Street mark the entrance to downtown Encinitas.

One example of the Encinitas area's dedication to horticulture can be found at the **Quail Botanical Gardens,** home to thousands of different varieties of plants, especially drought-tolerant species. Individual displays include Central American, Himalayan, Australian, and African tropical gardens; a California native plant display; a typical old-fashioned demonstration garden; and plantings of subtropical fruit. ⊠ *230 Quail Gardens Dr.,* ☎ *619/436–3036.* ▱ *$3.* ☉ *Daily 9–5.*

Dining and Lodging

$ ✕ **Rico's Taco Shop.** Short on frills but long on great eats, this Mexican fast-food café serves chicken taquitos, carne asada burritos, and the best fish burritos and tacos in town. The owners are friendly and health conscious, too: no lard is used in the recipes. ⊠ *Target Shopping Center, 165-L S. El Camino Real,* ☎ *619/944–7689. D, MC, V.*

$ ✕ **Vigilucci's.** This Italian trattoria has a cozy atmosphere, knowledgeable Italian waiters, and a stylish menu. Try the pastas—spaghetti *al funghetto,* with a fresh mushroom sauce, or the *tagliatelle alla bolognese,* with ground duck, chicken, and veal in a tomato sauce. ⊠ *505 1st St. (Hwy. 101),* ☎ *619/942–7332. AE, D, DC, MC, V. No lunch weekends.*

$$ 🏨 **Moonlight Beach Motel.** Folksy and laid-back, this motel is the closest to the beach at Encinitas. Rooms are basic but spacious and clean; all have kitchenettes. Some have ocean views. Weekly rates are available. ⊠ *233 2nd St., 92024,* ☎ *619/753–0623 or 800/323–1259,* FAX *619/944–9827. 24 rooms. AE, DC, MC, V.*

$$ 🏨 **Radisson Inn Encinitas.** This low rise blends nicely into an Encinitas hillside just east of Old Highway 101. Rooms have plush, richly colored rugs and comfy upholstered chairs; some have kitchenettes and/or ocean views. Continental breakfast is complimentary. ⊠ *85 Encinitas Blvd., 92024,* ☎ *619/942–7455 or 800/333–3333,* FAX *619/632–9481. 90 rooms. Restaurant, bar, pool, outdoor hot tub. AE, D, DC, MC, V.*

$ 🏨 **Budget Motels of America.** Shag carpeting and kitschy murals decorate the rooms at this motel, but the place is clean, low-priced, and convenient to the beach and freeway. Continental breakfast is included in the room rate. ⊠ *133 Encinitas Blvd., 92024,* ☎ *619/944–0260 or 800/795–6044,* FAX *619/944–2803. 122 rooms. AE, D, DC, MC, V.*

Carlsbad

❻ *6 mi from Encinitas on S21, 36 mi north of downtown San Diego on I–5.*

The Carlsbad area was originally settled by wealthy Mexicans, but the coastal town owes its name and Bavarian look to John Frazier, who lured people to the area a century ago with talk of the healing powers of mineral water bubbling from a coastal well. The water was found to have the same properties as water from the German mineral wells of Karlsbad—hence the name of the new community. Remnants from this era, including the original well and a monument to Frazier, are found at the **Alt Karlsbad Haus** (⊠ 2802A Carlsbad Blvd).

Dining and Lodging

$$$$ ✕🏨 **La Costa Hotel and Spa.** Don't expect glitz and glamour at this famous resort; it's surprisingly low-key, with low-slung buildings and vaguely Southwest contemporary–style rooms decorated in neutral tones. Although many guests come for La Costa's tranquil setting, the resort has one of the most comprehensive sports programs in the area. The spa is world-famous, with services ranging from massages to nutritional counseling; spa cuisine is available in three restaurants. One-day spa packages are available to nonguests. ⊠ *2100 Costa del Mar Rd., 92009,* ☎ *619/438–9111 or 800/854–5000,* FAX *619/438–9007. 480 rooms. 5 restaurants, 2 lounges, pool, beauty salon, spa, golf, 21 tennis courts, health club, hiking and jogging trails, bicycles, conference center, car rental. AE, D, DC, MC, V.*

$$$–$$$$ ⊞ **Carlsbad Inn.** The palm trees seem a bit out of place on the mani-
cured lawn of this sprawling European-style inn and time-share con-
dominium complex, with its gabled roofs and stone supports—but this
is Carlsbad, after all, where *alte* Germany meets southern California.
The public areas and rooms are decorated in appealing Old World style;
all the accommodations have VCRs, many have kitchenettes, and some
have fireplaces, private spas, and views. ⊠ *3075 Carlsbad Blvd.,
92008,* ☎ *619/434–7020 or 800/235–3939,* ⅢX *619/729–4853. 60
rooms. Pool, outdoor hot tub, health club. AE, D, DC, MC, V.*

$$–$$$ ⊞ **Best Western Beach View Lodge.** Reservations are essential at this
reasonably priced, Mediterranean-style low-rise near the beach. De-
spite the name, few rooms have a beach view. Functional rooms have
light-wood or whitewashed furnishings; some have fireplaces and bal-
conies. Complimentary Continental breakfast is included in the rates.
The Best Western Beach Terrace Inn on the water—better views, higher
prices—is under the same ownership. ⊠ *3180 Carlsbad Blvd., 92008,*
☎ *619/729–1151 or 800/433–5415,* ⅢX *619/729–1151. 41 rooms.
Kitchens or kitchenettes, pool, outdoor hot tub. AE, D, DC, MC, V.*

Oceanside

❼ *8 mi north of Carlsbad on S21, 37 mi north of downtown San Diego
on I–5.*

With 900 slips, **Oceanside Harbor** (☎ 619/966–4570) is the north coast's
center for fishing, sailing, and ocean-water sports. Oceanside Pier, the
longest on the West Coast, has shops and restaurants.

Lodging
$ ⊞ **Oceanside Travelodge.** This basic chain motel is near the beach and
centrally located. ⊠ *1401 N. Coast Hwy., 92054,* ☎ *619/722–1244
or 800/578–7878,* ⅢX *619/722–3228. 28 rooms. Laundry. AE, D, DC,
MC, V.*

Mission San Luis Rey

★ ❽ *4 mi northeast of Oceanside on Hwy. 76, 37 mi north of downtown
San Diego on I–5 to Hwy. 76 east.*

Mission San Luis Rey was built by Franciscan friars in 1798 under the
direction of Father Fermin Lasuen to help educate and convert local
Native Americans. The well-preserved San Luis Rey was the 18th and
largest of the California missions. Displays illuminate early mission life:
the sala (parlor), friars bedroom, weaving room, kitchen, and a col-
lection of religious art. Retreats are still held here, but a picnic area,
gift shop, and museum (which has the most extensive collection of old
Spanish vestments in the United States) are also on the grounds today.
Self-guided tours are available. ⊠ *4050 Mission Ave., San Luis Rey,*
☎ *619/757–3651.* Ⅲ *$3.* ⊙ *Mon.–Sat. 10–4:30, Sun. noon–4:30.*

OFF THE   **SAN DIEGO WILD ANIMAL PARK –** This 2,200-acre preserve in the San
BEATEN PATH Pascal Valley is an extension of the San Diego Zoo designed to protect
endangered species of animals from around the world. Five exhibit areas
have been carved out of the dry, dusty canyons and mesas to represent
the animals' natural habitats in North Africa, South Africa, East Africa,
Asian swamps, and Asian plains. The best way to see these preserves is
on the 50-minute, 5-mile Wgasa Bushline Monorail ride (included in the
price of admission). More than 3,000 animals of 450 species roam or fly
through the expansive grounds. Photographers with zoom lenses can get
spectacular shots of zebras, gazelles, rhinos, and other animals (a seat
on the right-hand side of the monorail is best for viewing the majority of

the animals). The park is as much a botanical garden as a zoo, and botanists collect rare and endangered plants for preservation. The 5-foot-tall desert cypress found here is native to the Sahara; only 16 such trees are still in existence there. ⊠ *Take I–15 north to Via Rancho Pkwy. and follow signs (6 mi),* ☎ *619/234–6541 or 619/480–0100.* ◪ *$18.95, includes all shows and monorail tour; a combination pass ($28.50) grants entry, within 5 days of purchase, to both the San Diego Zoo and the San Diego Wild Animal Park. Parking $3. AE, D, MC, V.* ☉ *Daily 9 AM; call ahead for closing hrs, which vary with season.*

San Diego North Coast A to Z

Arriving and Departing

BY BUS

The San Diego Transit District (☎ 619/233–3004) covers the city of San Diego up to Del Mar. The **North County Transit District** (☎ 619/743–6283) serves San Diego County from Del Mar north.

Greyhound (☎ 800/231–2222) has regular routes connecting San Diego to points north, with stops in Del Mar, Solana Beach, Encinitas, Escondido, Vista, and Oceanside.

BY CAR

Interstate 5, the main freeway artery connecting San Diego to Los Angeles, follows the coastline. To the west, running parallel to it, is S21 (known locally, but not signed, as Old Highway 101), which never strays more than a quarter-mile from the ocean. Watch the signs, because the road has a different name as it passes through each community.

BY PLANE

Palomar Airport (⊠ 2198 Palomar Airport Rd., Carlsbad, ☎ 619/431–4646) is a general aviation airport run by the county of San Diego and open to the public. Commuter airlines sometimes have flights from Palomar to Orange County and Los Angeles.

BY TAXI

Several companies are based in the North County, including **Bill's Cab Co.** (☎ 619/755–6737).

BY TRAIN

Amtrak (☎ 619/722–4622 in Oceanside, or 800/872–7245) operates trains daily between Los Angeles, Orange County, and San Diego, with stops in Solana Beach and Oceanside. **Coaster** (Coast Express Regional Rail Service, ☎ 800/262–7837 or 619/722–6283) operates commuter rail service between San Diego and Oceanside with weekday-only service to San Diego, Old Town, Sorrento Valley, Solana Beach, Encinitas, Carlsbad Poinsettia Station, Carlsbad Village Station, and Oceanside.

Contacts and Resources

GUIDED TOURS

Civic Helicopters (⊠ 2192 Palomar Airport Rd., ☎ 619/438–8424) gives whirlybird tours of the area. The tours run about $70 per person per half hour and go along the beaches to the Del Mar racetrack.

VISITOR INFORMATION

San Diego North County Convention and Visitors Bureau (⊠ 720 N. Broadway, Escondido 92025, ☎ 619/745-4741.)

SIDE TRIP TO THE DESERT

The Anza-Borrego Desert State Park encompasses more than 600,000 acres of desert, most of it wilderness. Springtime, when the wildflowers are in full bloom, is a good season to visit the park. There are year-round springs, and sandstone canyons where you can walk in the footsteps of prehistoric camels, zebras, and giant ground sloths.

Anza-Borrego Desert State Park

9 *88 mi from downtown San Diego (to park border due west of Borrego Springs), east on I–8, north on Hwy. 67, east on S4 and Hwy.78, north on Hwy. 79, and east on S2 and S22.*

Anza-Borrego Desert State Park is too vast even to consider exploring in its entirety. Hiking, nature study, and bicycling are popular activities. Rangers and displays at an excellent underground **Visitor Information Center** (⊠ 200 Palm Canyon Dr., Borrego Springs, ☎ 619/767–4205) can point you in the right direction.

One of the most popular camping and hiking areas is **Borrego Palm Canyon,** just a few minutes west of the Anza-Borrego Visitor Information Center. A 1½-mile trail leads to a small oasis with a waterfall and palm trees. The Borrego Palm Canyon campground is one of only two developed campgrounds with flush toilets and showers in the park. (The other is Tamarisk Grove Campground at the intersection of Route 78 and Yaqui Pass Road.)

Geology students from all over the world visit the Fish Creek area of Anza-Borrego to explore a famous canyon known as **Split Mountain** (⊠ Split Mountain Rd., south from Hwy. 78 at Ocotillo Wells), a narrow gorge with 600-foot perpendicular walls that was formed by an ancestral stream. Fossils in this area have led geologists to think that a sea covered the desert floor at one time. A 2-mile nature trail just west of Split Mountain rewards a hiker with a good view of shallow caves created by erosion.

Another trail in the Split Mountain area leads to one of two stands of **elephant trees** (10 feet tall, with swollen branches and small leaves) in Anza-Borrego Desert State Park.

Many of the Anza-Borrego Desert's sites can be seen from paved roads, but some require driving on dirt roads. Rangers recommend using four-wheel-drive vehicles when traversing dirt roads. Carry the appropriate supplies: shovel and other tools, flares, blankets, and plenty of water. Canyons are susceptible to flash flooding; inquire about weather conditions before entering. ⊠ *Park headquarters 200 Palm Canyon Dr., 92004,* ☎ *619/767–5311.* ☞ *$5 (day use) Oct.–May.* ⊙ *Park 24 hrs year-round, visitor center Oct.–May daily 9–5, June–Sept. weekends and holidays 9–5.*

Borrego Springs

31 mi from Julian, east on Hwy. 78 and north on S3.

For visitors who are uninterested in communing with the desert without a shower and pool nearby, this oasis that Anza-Borrego Desert State Park surrounds has several hotels and restaurants.

Dining and Lodging

$$–$$$$ ✕☲ **La Casa del Zorro.** You need walk only a few hundred yards from this low-key resort to be alone under the sky, and you may well see roadrunners crossing the highway. There are 17 different types of accommodations, set in comfortable one- to three-bedroom ranch-style houses complete with living rooms and kitchens; some three-bedroom suites have private pools. The elegant Continental restaurant puts on a good Sunday brunch. ⊠ *3845 Yaqui Pass Rd., 92004,* ☎ *619/767–*

5323 or 800/824–1884, FAX 619/767–4782. 77 rooms, including 42 suites and 19 casitas. Restaurant, lounge, 3 pools, beauty salon, 6 tennis courts, health club, bicycles, children's programs, meeting rooms. AE, D, DC, MC, V.

$–$$$ ✕🏨 **Palm Canyon Resort.** One of the largest properties around Anza-Borrego Desert State Park, this resort includes a hotel (¼ mile from the visitor center), an RV park, a restaurant, and recreational facilities. More upscale rooms have wet bars, refrigerators, ceiling fans, and balconies or patios. ⊠ *221 Palm Canyon Dr., 92004,* ☎ *619/767–5341 or 800/242–0044,* FAX *619/767–4073. 60 rooms. Restaurant, 2 pools, coin laundry, convention center. AE, D, DC, MC, V.*

Salton Sea

85 mi (to park headquarters) from Borrego Springs, Hwy. 78E to Hwy. 111N.

The Salton Sea, due east of Anza-Borrego Desert State Park, was created in 1905–07, when the Colorado River flooded north through canals meant to irrigate the Imperial Valley. The water is extremely salty, even saltier than the Pacific Ocean, and it is primarily a draw for fishermen seeking corbina, croaker, and tilapia. Some boaters and swimmers also use the lake. The state runs a park, **Salton Sea State Recreation Area** (⊠ Hwy. 111N, at northeast edge of Salton Sea, ☎ 619/393–3059) with sites for day camping, recreational vehicles, and primitive camping.

Birdwatchers will love the **Salton Sea National Wildlife Refuge.** A hiking trail and observation tower make it easy to spot the dozens of varieties of migratory birds stopping at Salton Sea. ⊠ *Off Hwy. 86, south end of Salton Sea,* ☎ *619/348–5278.*

Anza-Borrego Desert A to Z

Arriving and Departing

BY BUS

The **Northeast Rural Bus System** (NERBS, ☎ 619/765–0145) connects Julian, Borrego Springs, Oak Grove, Ocotillo Wells, Agua Caliente, Ramona, and many of the other small communities with El Cajon, 15 miles east of downtown San Diego, and the East County line of the San Diego trolley, with stops at Grossmont shopping center and North County Fair. Service is by reservation, and buses do not run on Sundays or on some holidays.

BY CAR

From downtown San Diego, take I–8 east to Highway 67 north, to State Road 4 and Highway 78 east, to Highway 79 north, to State Road 2 and State Road 22 east.

Visitor Information

Anza-Borrego Desert State Park (⊠ Box 299, Borrego Springs 92004, ☎ 619/767–5311). **Borrego Springs Chamber of Commerce** (⊠ 622 Palm Canyon Dr., Box 66, Borrego Springs 92004, ☎ 619/767–5555). **Destinet** (☎ 800/444–7275), for campsite reservations. **Wildflower hotline** (☎ 619/767–4684), during spring blooming season only.

SAN DIEGO A TO Z

Arriving and Departing

By Bus

Greyhound (☎ 619/239–8082 or 800/231–2222) operates 26 buses a day between the downtown terminal at 120 West Broadway and Los

Angeles, connecting with buses to all major U.S. cities. Many buses are express or nonstop; others make stops at coastal towns en route.

By Car

Interstate 5 stretches from Canada to the Mexican border and bisects San Diego. Interstate 8 provides access from Yuma, Arizona, and points east. Drivers coming from Nevada and the mountain regions beyond can reach San Diego on I–15.

By Plane

San Diego is served by **San Diego International Airport, Lindbergh Field** (☎ 619/231–2100). Flying time is 5 hours from New York, 3½ hours from Chicago, and ¾ hour from Los Angeles. The airport is a five-minute drive from downtown.

Carriers serving San Diego include **Aeromexico, Alaska Airlines, America West, American, Continental, Delta, Midwest Express, Northwest, Reno Air, Sky West, Southwest, TWA, United,** and **USAir** (☞ Air Travel *in* Important Contacts A to Z for phone numbers).

BETWEEN THE AIRPORT AND DOWNTOWN

San Diego Transit (☎ 619/233–3004) Route 2 buses leave every 10 to 15 minutes Monday through Friday and every 15 to 20 minutes Saturday and Sunday from about 5:30 AM–1 AM. Buses depart from the front of East Terminal's USAir section and travel along Broadway, downtown. The fare is $1.50 per person, 75¢ for senior citizens.

Cloud 9 Shuttle (☎ 619/278–8877; in San Diego, 800/974–8885) and **Public Shuttle** (☎ 619/990–8770) operate van shuttles that take you directly to your destination, often for less than a cab would cost.

If you have rented a car at the airport, you can take Harbor Drive, at the perimeter of the airport, to downtown, only about 3 miles away.

The taxi fare from the airport to downtown hotels runs $7–$9.

By Train

Amtrak trains (☎ 800/872–7245) from Los Angeles arrive at Santa Fe Depot (✉ 1050 Kettner Blvd., corner of Broadway, near the heart of downtown, ☎ 619/239–9021). There are additional stations in Solana Beach (☎ 619/259–2697) and Oceanside (☎ 619/722–4622), both in north San Diego County.

Getting Around

By Bus

The **San Diego Transit Information Line** (☎ 619/233–3004, TTY/TDD 619/234–5005; open daily 5:30 AM–8:30 PM) can provide details on getting to and from any location.

The **Day Tripper Transit Pass** is good for unlimited trips on the same day on San Diego Transit buses and on the trolley and the ferry for $5; there's also a four-day pass for $15. Both passes are available at the **Transit Store** (✉ 102 Broadway, ☎ 619/234–1060); one-day passes can be purchased at UCSD, the ferry landing, and at trolley stations.

Regional bus companies that service areas outside the city include **ATC Van Co.** (☎ 619/427–5660), for Coronado, the Silver Strand, and Imperial Beach; **Chula Vista Transit** (☎ 619/233–3004), for Bonita and Chula Vista; **National City Transit** (☎ 619/474–7505), for National City; **North County Transit District** (☎ 619/722–6283), for the area bound by the ocean, east to Escondido, north to Camp Pendleton, and south to Del Mar; and **Northeast Rural Bus System** (☎ 619/765–0145) or

Southeast Rural Bus System (☎ 619/478–5875), for access to rural county towns.

By Car

A car is essential for San Diego's sprawling freeway system. Avoid the freeways during rush hour when possible. All the major car-rental companies are represented in San Diego. For a list, *see* Car Rentals *in* Important Contacts A to Z.

Limousine companies operate airport shuttles and customized tours. Rates vary and are per hour, per mile, or both, with some minimums established. Companies that provide service include **Advantage Limousine Service** (☎ 619/563–1651), **La Jolla Limousines** (☎ 619/459–5891), **Limousines by Linda** (☎ 619/234–9145), and **Olde English Livery** (☎ 619/232–6533).

By Ferry

The **San Diego-Coronado Ferry** (☎ 619/234–4111) leaves from the Broadway Pier daily, every hour on the hour, 9 AM–10 PM Sunday–Thursday, until 10 PM Friday and Saturday. The fare is $2 each way and 50¢ for each bicycle.

By Taxi

Taxi fares are regulated at the airport—all companies charge the same rate (generally $1.80 for the first mile, $1.20 for each additional mile). Fares vary among companies on other routes, however, including the ride back to the airport. If you call ahead and ask for the flat rate ($7) you'll get it, otherwise you'll be charged by the mile (which works out to $9 or so).

Cab companies that serve most areas of the city are **Co-op Silver Cabs** (☎ 619/280–5555), **Coronado Cab** (☎ 619/435–6211), **La Jolla Cab** (☎ 619/453–4222), **Orange Cab** (☎ 619/291–3333), and **Yellow Cab** (☎ 619/234–6161).

By Trolley

The **San Diego Trolley** (☎ 619/233–3004) travels from downtown to within 100 feet of the U.S.–Mexican border, stopping at 21 suburban stations en route. The basic fare is $1.75 one way, 75¢ for senior citizens. The trolley also travels from downtown to Encanto, Lemon Grove, La Mesa, El Cajon, and Santee in East County. Tickets must be purchased just before boarding. Ticket-vending machines are located at each station. Trolleys operate daily, approximately every 15 minutes, 5 AM–9 PM, then every 30 minutes until 1 AM. The Bayside line serves the Convention Center and Seaport Village. A line to Old Town opened in summer 1996; one to Mission Valley is slated to begin operating in 1998.

Contacts and Resources

Doctors and Dentists

Hospital emergency rooms, with physicians on duty, are open 24 hours. Major hospitals are **Mercy Hospital and Medical Center** (✉ 4077 5th Ave., ☎ 619/294–8111), **Scripps Memorial Hospital** (✉ 9888 Genesee Ave., La Jolla, ☎ 619/457–4123), **Veterans Administration Hospital** (✉ 3350 La Jolla Village Dr., La Jolla, ☎ 619/552–8585), and **UCSD Medical Center** (✉ 200 W. Arbor Dr., Hillcrest, ☎ 619/543–6222).

Hotel Doctors (☎ 619/275–2663) provides 24-hour medical service to guests at San Diego hotels.

The **San Diego County Dental Society** (☎ 619/275−0244) can provide referrals Monday through Friday to those with dental emergencies. Hotel Doctors (☞ *above*) provides dental emergency referrals.

Emergencies
Ambulance (☎ 911). **Police** (☎ 911).

Guided Tours
ORIENTATION TOURS
Gray Line Tours (☎ 619/491−0011; outside CA, 800/331−5077) and **San Diego Mini Tours** (☎ 619/477−8687) have two daily sightseeing excursions for about $25.

Old Town Trolley (☎ 619/298−8687) travels to almost every attraction and shopping area on open-air trackless trolleys. Drivers double as tour guides. You can take the full two-hour, narrated city tour or get on and off as you please at any of the nine stops. An all-day pass costs $17. The trolley, which leaves every 30 minutes, operates daily 9−5 in summer, 9−4 in winter.

Free two-hour trolley tours of the downtown redevelopment area, including the Gaslamp Quarter, are hosted by **Centre City Development Corporation's Downtown Information Center** (☎ 619/235−2222). Groups of 35 passengers leave from 225 Broadway, Suite 160, downtown, the first and third Saturday of each month at 10 AM. Reservations are necessary. The tour may be canceled if there aren't enough passengers.

San Diego Harbor Excursion (☎ 619/234−4111) operates narrated cruises of the San Diego Harbor, departing from Broadway Pier. **Hornblower Invader Cruises** (☎ 619/234−8687) of San Diego Harbor also depart from Broadway Pier sail on narrated cruises of San Diego Harbor, departing from Broadway Pier. **Classic Sailing Adventures** (☎ 619/224−0800) has morning and afternoon tours of the harbor and San Diego Bay and nighttime in summer cruises.

SPECIAL-INTEREST TOURS
The Gaslamp Quarter Foundation (☎ 619/233−4692) leads two-hour, historical tours ($5) of the restored downtown historic district on Saturday at 11 AM.

Six-passenger hot-air balloons lift off from San Diego's North Country. Most flights are at sunrise or sunset and are followed by a champagne celebration. Companies with daily service, weather permitting, are **Pacific Horizon** (☎ 619/756−1790 or 800/244−1790) and **Skysurfer** (☎ 619/481−6800; in CA, 800/660−6809). Balloon flights average $145 per person.

Civic Helicopters (☎ 619/438−8424 or 800/438−4354) has helicopter tours starting at $69 per person per half hour.

On weekends, the State Park Department (☎ 619/220−5422) gives free walking tours of **Old Town.** Groups leave from 4002 Wallace Street at 2 PM daily, weather permitting.

Walkabout (☎ 619/231−7463) conducts several different free walking tours throughout the city each week.

Gray whales migrate south to Mexico and back north from mid-December to mid-March. As many as 200 whales pass the San Diego coast each day, coming within yards of tour boats. During whale-watching season, *The Apollo* (☎ 619/221−8500), a luxury motor yacht, operates narrated tours on Saturday and Sunday. **Classic Sailing Adventures** (☎ 619/224−0800) tailors whale-watching expeditions for up to six people. **H&M Landing** (☎ 619/222–1144) and **Seaforth Sportfishing** (☎ 619/224–3383) have daily whale-watching trips in large party boats.

Visitor Information

International Visitor Information Center (✉ 11 Horton Plaza, at 1st Ave. and F St., ☎ 619/236–1212). **San Diego Convention & Visitors Bureau** (✉ 401 B St., Suite 1400, San Diego 92101, ☎ 619/232–3101). **Visitor Information Center** (✉ 2688 E. Mission Bay Dr., San Diego 92109, ☎ 619/276–8200).

14 Palm Springs

*The Desert Resorts
and Joshua Tree*

*Palm Springs and its neighbors—Palm
Desert, Rancho Mirage, Indian Wells—
are among the fastest-growing and
wealthiest communities in the nation.
The desert lures visitors and residents
for the same reasons: striking scenery
and the therapeutic benefits of a warm,
arid climate. Resort hotel complexes
contain championship golf courses,
tennis stadiums, and sparkling
swimming pools—lushly landscaped
oases, towering palms, natural
waterfalls, and hot mineral springs
round out the picture.*

THE DESERT AROUND PALM SPRINGS hasn't always been a haven for luxury resorts, but various settlers over the years have recognized the region's rich nat-

By Bobbi Zane

ural attributes. The Agua Caliente Band of Indians discovered the hot springs in the Coachella Valley—the valley in which the entire desert-resorts area lies—and made use of their healing properties. In the last half of the 19th century, at the southern end of the valley, farmers established a date-growing industry. By 1900, word had spread about the manifold health benefits of the area's dry climate, inspiring wealthy folk from the northern United States to winter under the warm desert sun.

By the time of the Great Depression, the region had caught Hollywood's eye. It was an ideal hideaway: Clark Gable, Ginger Rogers, Humphrey Bogart, and other celebrities could slip into town, play a few sets of tennis, lounge around the pool, attend a party or two, and, unless things got out of hand—like they did between Ava Gardner and Frank Sinatra the time Lana Turner dropped by—remain safely beyond the reach of gossip columnists.

Growth hit the desert in the 1970s, as developers began to construct the world-class golf courses, country clubs, and residential communities, which now draw not only pop celebrities but tycoons and politicians. Privacy is still the watchword, however; many communities, particularly in Rancho Mirage and Indian Wells, are walled and gate-guarded. There has been a downside to the region's growth: urban sprawl and overbuilding—of sometimes less than stellar structures.

Palm Springs lost a bit of its luster as the wealthy moved on to newer, more glamorous communities—Palm Desert, Rancho Mirage, Indian Wells—during this period. The city, once the unrivaled hub of desert society and commerce, is reinventing itself. Once-exclusive Palm Canyon Drive is a lively avenue punctuated by coffeehouses, a brew pub, outdoor cafés and bars, and frequent special events. There's also an active lesbian and gay community in Palm Springs. Always a discreet mecca, Palm Springs is now a well-advertised destination, with many dining and lodging spots either hospitable to or completely oriented toward gay travelers.

You'll still find celebrities in the desert, where streets are named for Bob Hope, Gerald Ford, Dinah Shore, and Frank Sinatra. Hollywood stars, sports personalities, politicians, and other high-profile folk can be spotted at charity events, in restaurants, or on the golf course. Roseanne, Jay Leno, Leslie Nielsen, and even Dr. Ruth have relaxed at the Westin Mission Hills Resort, and Goldie Hawn and Kurt Russell have been spotted poolside at the Ingleside Inn, where Greta Garbo once hung out. Sylvester Stallone has been known to escape the crowds at La Quinta Resort. The prospect of a brush with glamour, along with the desert's natural beauty, heightens the area's appeal for tourists, who, despite leveling off in recent years, continue to come in significant numbers.

Pleasures and Pastimes

Desert Wildlife

Visitors who want to learn about the natural history of the desert and see some spectacular scenery can get an overall view at the top of the Palm Springs Aerial Tramway or explore the terrain at ground level at the Living Desert Wildlife and Botanical Park and Joshua Tree National Park. Exhibits in the Palm Springs Desert Museum describe it all.

Dining

Once considered a culinary wasteland, the desert now supports many trendy restaurants. But diligent diners can also get a good meal at storefront restaurants and diners. Those who are careful about fat and cholesterol will find that many desert restaurant menus include heart-healthy items. Dining is casual; except where noted, reservations are not needed.

CATEGORY	COST*
$$$$	over $50
$$$	$30–$50
$$	$20–$30
$	under $20

per person for a three-course meal, excluding drinks, service, and 7¼% tax

Golf

Frequently called the Golf Capital of the World, the Palm Springs area has more than 85 golf courses, many of which are familiar to golf fans as the sites of championship tournaments. Visitors can tee off where the pros play at PGA West, Mission Hills North, and La Quinta, or improve their swings by taking instruction at one of the clubs.

Lodging

Accommodations in Palm Springs run the full gamut: resorts, inns, clubs, spas, lodges, and condos from small and private to big and bustling. Chains such as Motel 6, Holiday Inn, Ramada, and TraveLodge have opened facilities. Visitors can stay here for as low as $40 per night to $1,600—or even higher; rates vary widely from summer (low) to winter (high) season. Budget lodgings are most easily found in Palm Springs proper; discounts are sometimes given for extended stays. Condos, apartments, and individual houses may be rented by the day, week, month, or for longer periods. Some hotels, including Marriott's Desert Springs Resort and Spa, have villas for rent.

CATEGORY	COST*
$$$$	over $175
$$$	$120–$175
$$	$80–$120
$	under $80

All prices are for a standard double room, excluding 9%–11% tax.

Nightlife and the Arts

The Fabulous Palm Springs Follies—a vaudeville-style revue starring retired professional performers—is a must-see for most visitors. Arts festivals occur on a regular basis, especially during the winter and spring. Nightlife options include a good jazz bar and hotel entertainment; this is a popular getaway for L.A. and other gay folk, who can choose from a number of welcoming clubs and cafés. The "Desert Guide" from *Palm Springs Life* magazine, available at most hotels and visitor information centers, has nightlife listings; the gay scene is covered in the *Bottom Line* newspaper.

Outdoor Sports and Activities

With approximately 30,000 pools in the desert region, swimming (or at least hanging out poolside) is a daily ritual. Several hundred courts make playing or watching tennis a serious pursuit. More than 35 miles of bike trails crisscross the Palm Springs area; the terrain here is mostly flat. Indian Canyons, Mt. San Jacinto State Park and Wilderness, Living Desert Wildlife and Botanical Park, Joshua Tree National Park, and Big Morongo Canyon Preserve have hiking trails. Golf (☞ *above*) is another popular option. In the desert, it's wise to avoid outdoor activities midday, take precautions against the sun, and wear a hat any time of the year. Always drink plenty of water to prevent dehydration.

Shopping

Shopping is a serious pursuit in the Palm Springs area: well over half of the respondents to a recent visitor survey ranked shopping as the "recreation" they enjoyed most. Boutiques, art galleries, and an ever-growing collection of consignment, estate-sale, and antiques shops make for a diverse browsing. El Paseo in Palm Desert has upscale galleries and shops.

Exploring Palm Springs

Some visitors' idea of "exploring" Palm Springs is to navigate the distance from their hotel room to the pool or spa—this has, after all, always been a place for indulging oneself. Most social, sports, shopping, and entertainment scenes revolve around Palm Springs and Palm Desert. Cathedral City and Rancho Mirage are west of Palm Desert (and east of Palm Springs) on Highway 111. Indian Wells, La Quinta, and Indio are all east of Palm Desert on the highway. North of Palm Springs is Desert Hot Springs. As for the region's natural wonders, Joshua Tree National Park and other attractions are easily visited as day trips from any of the resort towns.

Great Itineraries

Numbers in the text correspond to numbers in the margin and on the Palm Springs Desert Resorts map.

IF YOU HAVE 1 DAY

If you've just slipped into town on a quick visit from Los Angeles or elsewhere, focus your activities around Palm Springs, where two generations of Hollywood stars lived and played. Get an early-morning scenic overview by taking the **Palm Springs Aerial Tramway** ① to the top of Mt. San Jacinto. In the afternoon, head for **Palm Canyon Drive** ② in Palm Springs, have lunch alfresco at the trendy Blue Coyote Cafe, take in the **Show Biz Museum** at the Plaza Theater, and poke around for Hollywood memorabilia at Heritage Galleries and Antique District on **North Palm Canyon Drive.**

IF YOU HAVE 3 DAYS

On your first day, take the **Palm Springs Aerial Tramway** ① and visit **Palm Canyon Drive** ②. On day two, head to **Palm Desert,** the trendiest of the desert cities, where a walk through the canyons and hillsides of the **Living Desert Wildlife and Botanical Park** ⑨ will reward you with wildlife sightings, sweeping vistas, and, in spring, carpets of colorful flowers. Work off lunch in Palm Desert by browsing through the entire length of the chic **El Paseo** shopping area. If you're not into shopping and it's not the height of summer, slip over to the **Indian Canyons** ⑥ in Palm Springs and view the remnants of early Agua Caliente Indian life. On the third morning, take in the **Palm Springs Desert Museum** ④, which has a first-class art gallery and a sculpture garden. In the afternoon pamper yourself by partaking of the **Spa Experience** at the Spa Hotel. Then, appropriately relaxed, head for the Plaza Theater and a performance of the **Fabulous Palm Springs Follies.**

IF YOU HAVE 5 DAYS

Ride the **Palm Springs Aerial Tramway** ① and cruise **Palm Canyon Drive** ② on the first day. Explore the **Living Desert** ⑨ and grab lunch while checking out the shops at **El Paseo** on the second or visit the **Indian Canyons** ⑥. The third day, visit the **Palm Springs Desert Museum** ④, have lunch, and then spend the afternoon lounging poolside at your hotel or touring **Moorten Botanical Garden** ⑤. Spend the entire fourth day touring **Joshua Tree National Park** ⑩, making a circular excursion that begins and ends at the Cottonwood Visitor Center. Following all this activity, you'll be ready for a fifth **day of total relaxation**—including a massage, aromatherapy, herbal wraps, and other regimens—at Marriott's Desert Springs Resort and Spa. If you're more exercise-oriented, play a round of golf at an area course.

When to Tour Palm Springs

During the "season" (January through April), the desert weather is at its best, with daytime temperatures ranging between 70° and 90°F. This is the time when you're most likely to see a colorful display of wildflowers and when most of the world-class golf and tennis tournaments take place. Prices soar and accommodations can be difficult to secure without advance reservations at this time. The fall months are nearly as lovely, less crowded, and less expensive. During the summer months, daytime temperatures rise to 110°F or higher, though evenings cool to the mid-70s. Some attractions close during this period. Hotel prices frequently average 50% less in summer than in winter and early spring.

THE DESERT RESORTS AND JOSHUA TREE NATIONAL PARK

The Agua Caliente Band of Cahuilla Indians settled in and around what is now the Palm Springs Desert Resorts area about 1,000 years ago. They considered the mineral springs to be sacred, with great curative and restorative powers. The springs became a tourist attraction in 1871 when the tribe built a bathhouse on the site to serve passengers on a pioneer stage route. The Agua Caliente still own about 32,000 acres of Palm Springs desert, 6,700 of which lie within the city limits of Palm Springs. The Indians, while dedicated to preserving their historic homeland, will doubtless account for the next "boom" in the desert. Following the lead of nearby tribes, which operate profitable bingo parlors in Indio and Cabazon, the Agua Caliente have opened a casino in the Spa Hotel in downtown Palm Springs.

The desert became a Hollywood hideout in the 1920s, when La Quinta Hotel opened the Coachella Valley's first golf course. But it took a pair of tennis-playing celebrities to put Palm Springs on the map in the 1930s; actors Charlie Farrell and Ralph Bellamy bought 200 acres of land for $30 an acre and opened the Palm Springs Racquet Club, which soon listed Ginger Rogers, Humphrey Bogart, and Clark Gable among its members. Farrell served as the town's mayor in the '50s.

Joshua Tree, upgraded from "monument" status in the mid-1990s, is just beginning to bloom as a national park. Major projects and facilities are still in the future, but it will only be a matter of time before development around the park occurs. In the meantime, nature, particularly in the form of spring wildflowers, continues to bloom with spectacular regularity. The Cottonwood Springs area is one of the desert's best for wildflower viewing. During the spring, carpets of white, yellow, purple, and red flowers stretch as far as the eye can see on the hillsides east of the freeway.

Exploring the Desert

★ ☺ ❶ A trip on the **Palm Springs Aerial Tramway** yields a stunning overview of the desert. The 2½-mile ascent brings you to an elevation of 8,516 feet in less than 20 minutes. On clear days, which are common, the view stretches 75 miles from the peak of Mt. San Gorgonio to the north to the Salton Sea in the southeast. At the top you'll find several diver-

Palm Springs Desert Resorts

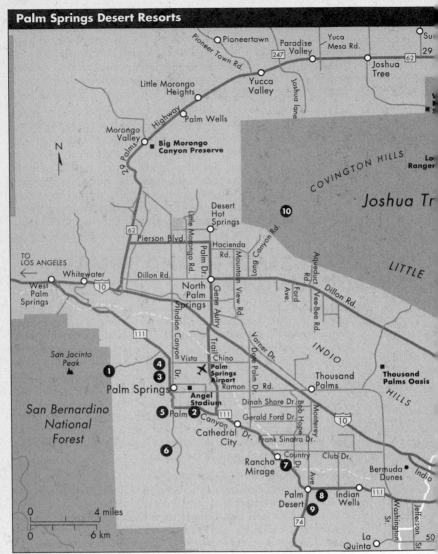

El Paseo, **8**

Indian Canyons, **6**

Joshua Tree
National Park, **10**

Living Desert Wildlife
and Botanical Park, **9**

Moorten Botanical
Garden, **5**

Palm Canyon Drive, **2**

Palm Springs Aerial
Tramway, **1**

Palm Springs Desert
Museum, **4**

Rancho Mirage, **7**

Village Green
Heritage Center, **3**

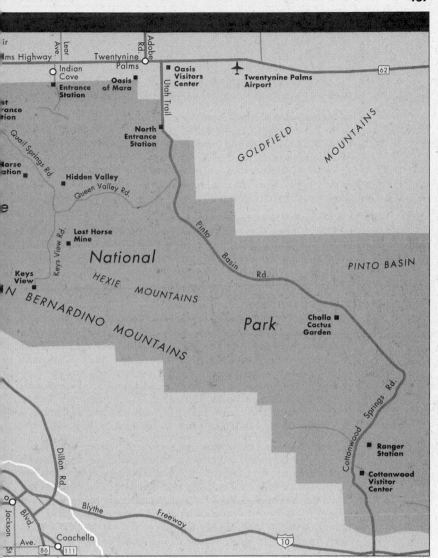

ir

Lear Ave.

ms Highway

Twentynine Palms

Adobe Rd.

○ Indian Cove

■ Entrance Station

Oasis of Mara ■

■ Oasis Visitors Center

✈ Twentynine Palms Airport

62

GOLDFIELD

MOUNTAINS

st rance tion

Quail Springs Rd.

Utah Trail

North Entrance Station

orse ation ■

Hidden Valley ■

Queen Valley Rd.

Keys View Rd.

Lost Horse Mine ■

National

Keys View ■

HEXIE *MOUNTAINS*

Pinto Basin Rd.

PINTO BASIN

N BERNARDINO MOUNTAINS

Park

Cholla Cactus Garden ■

Cottonwood Springs Rd.

Dillon Rd.

■ Ranger Station

■ Cottonwood Vistitor Center

○

Jackson St.

Blvd.

Blythe

Freeway

Jackson St.

Ave.

86

Coachella

111

10

sions. Mountain Station has an alpine buffet restaurant, cocktail lounge, apparel and gift shops, a theater screening a 22-minute film on the history of the tramway, and picnic facilities. The tram is a popular attraction; lines can be long. ⊠ *One Tramway Rd.,* ☎ *619/325–1391.* ☞ *$16.95.* ☉ *Tram cars depart at least every 30 mins from 10 AM weekdays and 8 AM weekends; last car up leaves at 8 PM, last one down 9:45 PM. Closed Aug. for maintenance.*

Mt. San Jacinto Wilderness State Park, accessible only by hiking or taking the Palm Springs Aerial Tramway (☞ *above*), has 54 miles of hiking trails, and camping and picnic areas; guided wilderness mule rides are available here during snow-free months. During winter the Nordic Ski Center has cross-country ski equipment for rent. ☎ *909/659–2607 for park information.* ☞ *Free; permits (also free) required for day or overnight wilderness hiking.*

② A stroll down **Palm Canyon Drive,** which is lined with shops, includes the Palm Springs Starwalk, stars imbedded in the sidewalk (à la the Hollywood Walk of Fame) honoring celebrities. The tiny but illuminating Showbiz Museum is adjacent to the Plaza Theater. On Thurs-★ day nights the **Village Fest** fills the section between Tahquitz Canyon Way and Baristo Road with street musicians, a farmers' market, and stalls with food, crafts, art, and antiques.

③ Three spaces at the **Village Green Heritage Center** illustrate pioneer life in Palm Springs. The McCallum Adobe, dating back to 1885, holds the collections of the Palm Springs Historical Society and McCallum family, early settlers in the desert. Miss Cornelia White's House, built in 1894, holds another pioneer family's memorabilia. Ruddy's General Store Museum surveys the commercial output of a later pioneer era, the 1930s and 1940s. ⊠ *221 and 223 S. Palm Canyon Dr.,* ☎ *619/323–8297.* ☞ *50¢ (each site).* ☉ *House Wed. and Sun. noon–3, Thurs.–Sat. 10–4; store Thurs.–Sun. 10–4; summer hrs flexible.*

④ The **Palm Springs Desert Museum** focuses on western and Native American art. The display on the natural history of the desert is itself worth a visit, and the grounds hold several striking sculpture gardens. An expansion and renovation project, scheduled for completion by late 1996, added six new galleries for modern and contemporary art. The Annenberg Theater presents plays, concerts, lectures, operas, and other cultural events. ⊠ *101 Museum Dr.,* ☎ *619/325–0189.* ☞ *$4; free 1st Fri. of month.* ☉ *Tues.–Thurs. and weekends 10–4, Fri. 10–8.*

The **Palm Springs Air Museum,** a showcase for World War II fighter planes, was scheduled to open in late 1996. ⊠ *745 N. Gene Autry Trail,* ☎ *619/778–6262.* ☞ *$7.50.* ☉ *Wed.–Mon. 10–5.*

⑤ Four-acre **Moorten Botanical Garden** nurtures more than 3,000 plant varieties in settings that simulate their original environments. Indian artifacts and rock, crystal, and wood forms are exhibited. ⊠ *1701 S. Palm Canyon Dr.,* ☎ *619/327–6555.* ☞ *$2.* ☉ *Mon.–Sat. 9–4:30, Sun. 10–4.*

⑥ The **Indian Canyons** are the ancestral home of the Agua Caliente Band of Indians, who selected these canyons for their lush oases, abundant water, and wildlife. Visitors can see remnants of this life: rock art, house pits and foundations, irrigation ditches, bedrock mortars, pictographs, and stone houses and shelters built atop high cliff walls. Three canyons are open: Palm Canyon, noted for its lush stand of Washingtonia palms; Murray, home of Peninsula bighorn sheep and a herd of wild ponies; and Andreas, where a stand of fan palms contrasts with sharp rock formations. The trading post in Palm Canyon has hiking maps, refreshments,

Indian art, jewelry, and weavings. ✉ 38-500 S. Palm Canyon Dr., ☎ 619/325–5673. 🎫 $5. ☉ Daily 8–5, summer 8–6.

NEED A BREAK?

The Spa Experience is a sampling of services available at the **Spa Hotel and Casino.** Sink into a tub filled with naturally hot mineral water from the original Agua Caliente spring, rest in the cool white relaxation room, swim in the outdoor mineral pool, or let the sauna warm your spirits. Use of fitness facilities is included. Massages, skin care, and beauty and body therapies are also available. ✉ 100 N. Indian Canyon Dr., ☎ 619/325–1461. 🎫 Spa Experience $17.25, massages $69–$92. ☉ Sun.–Thurs. 9–6, Fri.–Sat. 9–7.

7 Elegant resorts, fine dining, world-class golf and tennis tournaments, and celebrity residents come together in **Rancho Mirage.** The city holds the famed Eisenhower Medical Center and Betty Ford Center as well as numerous celebrity estates.

At the Heart Institute of the Desert's **Heartland Museum,** a walk through the huge heart-valve portal leads to interactive exhibits, such as the 14-foot-tall "Plaque Attack" walk-in replica of a coronary artery. Visitors can grab a healthful bite at the Heart Beat Cafe. ✉ 39-600 Bob Hope Dr., Rancho Mirage, ☎ 619/324–3278. 🎫 $2.50. ☉ Weekdays 7–6:30, Sat. 8–noon.

8 Some of the best desert people-watching, shopping, and dining can be found along trendy **El Paseo,** a 2-mile-long avenue just west of Highway 111 in Palm Desert (☞ Shopping, below).

★ **9** Come eyeball to eyeball with coyotes, mountain lions, bighorn sheep, golden eagles, and owls at the **Living Desert Wildlife and Botanical Park,** which recently added a habitat for endangered cheetahs. Easy to challenging trails traverse desert gardens populated with plants of the Mojave, Colorado, and Sonoran deserts. One exhibit pinpoints the San Andreas earthquake fault across the valley. During the holidays, the park presents Wildlights, an evening light show. Shuttle service, interpretive tours, wildlife shows (daily in Tennity Amphitheater), strollers, and wheelchairs are available. ✉ 47-900 Portola Ave., ☎ 619/346–5694. 🎫 $7. ☉ Sept.–July, daily 9–5.

The **Jude E. Poynter Golf Museum,** at the Victor J. LoBue Institute of Golf College at the College of the Desert, exhibits golf memorabilia, artwork, photos, and golf clubs. ✉ Fred Waring Dr. at San Pablo Ave., Palm Desert, ☎ 619/341–0994. 🎫 Free. ☉ Daily 7 AM–10 PM.

OFF THE BEATEN PATH

BIG MORONGO CANYON PRESERVE – Once an Indian village and later a cattle ranch, this serene natural oasis contains a year-round stream and waterfalls that support a variety of plants, birds (birders love this area), and animals. A shaded meadow makes for enjoyable picnics, and hiking options include several choice trails. No pets are permitted at the preserve. ✉ East Dr.; take I–10 or Indian Canyon Dr. to Hwy. 62 east, ☎ 619/363–7190. 🎫 Free. ☉ Daily 7:30 am–sunset.

★ **10** **Joshua Tree National Park** comprises 794,000 acres of complex, ruggedly beautiful scenery. Its mountains of jagged rock, natural cactus gardens, and lush oases shaded by tall fan palms mark the meeting place of the Mojave (high) and Colorado (low) deserts. This is prime hiking, rock-climbing and exploring country, where coyotes, desert pack rats, and exotic plants, such as the creamy white yucca, red-tipped ocotillo, and cholla cactus, reside. Extensive stands of Joshua trees give the park its name. The trees were named by early white settlers who felt their unusual forms resembled the biblical Joshua raising his arms toward heaven.

Portions of the park can be seen in a half-day excursion from desert-resort cities. A full day's driving tour would reveal highlights and allow time for a nature walk or two and stops at many of the 50 wayside exhibits, which provide insight into Joshua Tree's geology and rich vegetation. Some of the park is above 4,000 feet; it can be chilly in winter. There are few services within the park and little water; visitors are advised to carry an ample supply.

Those planning a half-day visit to Joshua Tree National Park should enter from the south on Cottonwood Springs Road, off I–10 east of Mecca. The Cottonwood Visitor Center has a small museum, picnic tables, water, and a 1-mile interpretive trail to the **Cottonwood Spring Oasis.** Those planning to spend a full day in Joshua Tree can come in from the south and drive north to the sights near the Oasis Visitor Center (☞ *below*) or enter from the north or west off Highway 62.

At the **Cholla Cactus Gardens,** a huge stand of the legendary "jumping cactus," a short trail interprets the wildlife and plants typical of the Colorado Desert.

Geology Tour Road, recommended for four-wheel-drive vehicles, is a self-guided 18-mile dirt road that winds through some of the park's most fascinating landscape.

Keys View is the most scenic overlook in Joshua Tree National Park. At elevation 5,185 feet, the view extends across the desert to Mt. San Jacinto and on clear days as far south as the Salton Sea. Sunrise and sunset are magical times, when the light throws rocks and trees into high relief before (or after) bathing the hills in brilliant shades of red, orange, and gold.

A crawl through the big boulders that block **Hidden Valley,** once a cattle rustlers' hangout, reveals a bit of the wild and woolly human history of Joshua Tree. The 1.1-mile loop trail from Hidden Valley to **Barker Dam** goes past petroglyphs (painted over by a film crew) on the way to a dam built by early ranchers and miners; today the dam collects rainwater and is used by wildlife.

The **Oasis Visitor Center** has an excellent selection of free and low-cost brochures, books, posters, and maps as well as several educational exhibits. Rangers are on hand to answer questions. **Oasis of Mara** (a half-mile walk from the visitor center), inhabited first by Indians and later by prospectors and homesteaders, now provides a home for birds, small mammals, and other wildlife. ✉ *Park mailing address: 74-485 National Park Dr., Twentynine Palms 92277,* ☎ *619/367–7511.* ✉ *$5 per car.* ☉ *Visitor centers daily 8–5, park 24 hrs.*

Dining

CATHEDRAL CITY

$ ✕ **Red Bird Diner.** Hosts Art and Gayla Morris serve '50s-style food at their diner, which is decorated with life-size murals of the decade's icons: James Dean, Ed Sullivan, and a bright-red T-Bird. Lamb is the Red Bird's specialty, but Art also cooks country-fried steak, liver and onions, and chicken and dumplings. ✉ *35-955 Date Palm Dr.,* ☎ *619/324–7707. AE, D, DC, MC, V.*

LA QUINTA

$–$$ ✕ **La Quinta Cliffhouse.** Sweeping mountain views at sunset and the
★   early-California ambience of a western movie set draw patrons to this "concept" restaurant perched halfway up a hillside. The eclectic menu

roams the globe: grilled shrimp Provençale, Caesar salad with chicken, ahi tuna Szechuan style, and *tiramisù*. Sunday brunch is always crowded. ⊠ *78-250 Hwy. 111,* ☎ *619/360–5991. AE, DC, MC, V.*

PALM DESERT

$$$–$$$$ ★ ✕ **Cuistot.** Chef-owner Bernard Dervieux trained with French culinary star Paul Bocuse, but he's taken a more worldly approach at his own restaurant, tucked into the back of an El Paseo courtyard. Signature dishes include spinach linguine with shrimp, Chinese-style duck, and rack of lamb with rosemary. Well-prepared food and attentive service have kept Cuistot popular for more than a decade. ⊠ *73-111 El Paseo,* ☎ *619/340–1000. AE, D, MC, V. Closed Mon. No lunch Sun.*

$$–$$$ ✕ **Ristorante Mamma Gina.** The son of the original Mamma Gina in Florence opened this simply furnished trattoria, which ranks among the best Italian restaurants in the Palm Springs area. The Tuscan chef prepares deep-fried artichokes, fettuccine with porcini mushrooms, prawns with artichokes and zucchini, robust soups, and other specialties in an open kitchen. ⊠ *73-705 El Paseo,* ☎ *619/568–9898. Reservations essential. AE, DC, MC, V.*

$$ ✕ **Palomino Euro Bistro.** One of the hot spots in the desert, this restaurant specializes in grilled and roasted entrées: spit-roasted garlic chicken, oak-fired thin-crust pizza, and oven-roasted prawns. It's an interesting, if noisy, setting, with huge reproductions of famous French Impressionist paintings filling the walls. ⊠ *73-101 Hwy. 111,* ☎ *619/773–9091. AE, D, DC, MC, V. No lunch.*

$–$$ ✕ **Café des Beaux Arts.** This desert version of a sidewalk café has good garlicky French food and a trendy ambience, particularly at lunchtime, when the place is very busy. ⊠ *73-640 El Paseo,* ☎ *619/346–0669. AE, MC, V. No dinner Tues.*

$ ✕ **Daily Grill.** The smell of cookies baking might make you more hungry than you thought you were. Good thing, because portions—such as a dinner-plate-size chicken pot pie—are huge at this bustling deli–coffee shop. Best buys are the blue-plate specials, which include soup or salad and turkey meat loaf, a beef-dip sandwich, or turkey steak plus unlimited, thirst-quenching lemonade. ⊠ *73-061 El Paseo,* ☎ *619/779–9911. AE, DC, MC, V.*

$ ✕ **La Donne Cucina Italiana.** Families like this busy restaurant-deli and its large portions of homemade pasta, risotto, chicken, and other dishes. ⊠ *72-624 El Paseo,* ☎ *619/773–9441. Reservations essential. D, MC, V. Closed Sun. No lunch.*

$ ✕ **Le Peep.** This casual coffeehouse serves breakfast and lunch. Deep-skillet entrées—down-home sausage, eggs Benedict, omelets, and frittatas—anchor the huge breakfast menu. ⊠ *73-725 El Paseo,* ☎ *619/773–1004. AE, DC, MC, V. No dinner.*

PALM SPRINGS

$$–$$$ ✕ **Blue Coyote Grill.** Diners sit under blue umbrellas and munch on burritos, tacos, fajitas (or more unusual items, such as Yucatan lamb or orange chicken) at this casual restaurant with several flower-decked patios in addition to inside dining rooms. Two busy cantinas serve up tasty margaritas to a youngish crowd. ⊠ *445. N. Palm Canyon Dr.,* ☎ *619/327–1196. AE, DC, MC, V.*

$$–$$$ ✕ **Otani Garden Restaurant.** Sushi, tempura, and teppan (grilled) specialties are served in a serene garden setting at Otani. An always-fresh Sunday brunch buffet includes tempura, stir-fried entrées, salads, sushi, and desserts. ⊠ *266 Avenida Caballeros,* ☎ *619/327–6700. AE, DC, MC, V. No lunch Sat.*

$$ ✕ **Las Casuelas Original.** A longtime favorite, this restaurant serves great (in size and taste) margaritas and average Mexican dishes: crab enchilada,

carne asada, lobster Ensenada. It gets very crowded during the winter. ⊠ *368 N. Palm Canyon Dr.,* ☎ *619/325–3213. AE, DC, MC, V.*

$ ✕ **Louise's Pantry.** A local landmark near the downtown Plaza Theater, this 1940s-style diner—bright yellow decor, with booths and a long counter—serves down-home cooking, such as chicken and dumplings and short ribs of beef. There's usually a line to get in. Breakfast is served all day. ⊠ *124 S. Palm Canyon Dr.,* ☎ *619/325–5124. MC, V.*

RANCHO MIRAGE

$$$$ ✕ **Morton's of Chicago.** The desert version of this national steak-house chain lures in the meat-and-potatoes crowd with its selection of prime beef and seafood, contemporary hors d'oeuvres, and traditional desserts. Huge LeRoy Neiman serigraphs hang in the bustling dining room. The bar is quiet and clubby. ⊠ *74-880 Country Club Dr.,* ☎ *619/340–6865,* FAX *619/340–2645. AE, DC, MC, V. No lunch.*

$$ ✕ **Bankok V.** Dedicated spicy-food fans gather at this well-decorated
★ restaurant to savor artistically prepared traditional Thai cuisine. The spring rolls are crisp and fresh. When you order be sure to tell them how hot you want your food. ⊠ *69-930 Hwy. 111,* ☎ *619/770–9508. AE, DC, MC, V. No lunch.*

$$ ✕ **Shame on the Moon.** This contemporary bistro serves American and Continental cuisine; specialties include pasta, fresh fish, and filet mignon. ⊠ *69-950 Frank Sinatra Dr.,* ☎ *619/324–5515. Reservations essential. AE, MC, V. No lunch.*

Lodging

INDIAN WELLS

$$$$ 🏨 **Hyatt Grand Champions Resort.** This stark white resort on 34 acres of natural desert hosts the *Newsweek* Champions/Evert Cup Women's Professional Tennis Tournament, which is played in the largest stadium in the West. Rooms are suite-style and are either split-level, one-, or two-bedroom garden villas or penthouses. All have balconies or terraces, living areas, and minibars. Some have fireplaces and private butler service. ⊠ *44-600 Indian Wells La., 92210,* ☎ *619/341–1000 or 800/233–1234,* FAX *619/568–2236. 336 units. 3 restaurants, lounge, 4 pools, hot tubs, driving range, 2 golf courses, putting green, 12 tennis courts, health club, pro shop. AE, D, DC, MC, V.*

$$$$ 🏨 **Stouffer Renaissance Esmeralda Resort.** The centerpiece of this luxurious Mediterranean-style resort is an eight-story atrium lobby with a fountain, surrounded by a dual grand staircase, which flows through a rivulet in the lobby floor to cascading pools and outside to lakes surrounding the property. Given its size, the hotel has a surprisingly intimate ambience. Spacious guest rooms are decorated in light wood with green and blue accents; they have sitting areas, balconies, refreshment centers, two TV sets, and travertine-marble vanities in bathrooms. One pool has a sandy beach. Golf and tennis instruction are available. ⊠ *44-400 Indian Wells La., 92210,* ☎ *619/773–4444 or 800/552–4386,* FAX *619/773–9250. 560 rooms, 44 suites. 2 restaurants, lounge, 3 pools, 2 outdoor hot tubs, 2 golf courses, 7 tennis courts, health club. AE, D, DC, MC, V.*

LA QUINTA

$$$$ 🏨 **La Quinta Resort and Club.** The desert's oldest resort, which opened
★ in 1926, is a lush green oasis. Rooms are in historic adobe casitas separated by broad expanses of lawn and in newer, two-story units surrounding individual swimming pools and brilliant gardens. Fireplaces, robes, stocked refrigerators, and fruit-laden orange trees contribute to a discreet and sparely luxurious atmosphere. A premium is placed on privacy, which accounts for La Quinta's continuing lure for the brightest Hollywood stars. Frank Capra, for example, lived here for many

years, and it's said that Greta Garbo roamed the grounds bumming cigarettes from guests. Contemporary stars such as Michael Jackson and Clint Eastwood have sought tranquillity here. Now managed jointly with PGA West, La Quinta arranges access to some of the most celebrated golf courses in the area; golf packages include accommodations, breakfast, and rounds of golf. Pros John and Tracy Austin direct the Tennis Center, which provides clinics, private lessons, junior programs, and competitions. ⊠ *49-499 Eisenhower Dr., 92253,* ☎ *619/564–4111 or 800/854–1271,* FAX *619/564–7656. 640 rooms, including 22 suites. 5 restaurants, wine bar, lounge, 25 pools, 35 outdoor hot tubs, beauty salon, 4 golf courses, 30 tennis courts, health club, children's programs. AE, D, DC, MC, V.*

PALM DESERT

$$$$ 🏨 **Marriott's Desert Springs Resort and Spa.** This sprawling hotel is the most spectacular-looking resort in the desert. It's a U-shape building with arms wrapped around the largest private lake in the desert, with 3 miles of shoreline. The centerpiece is an indoor, stair-stepped waterfall that flows into the lake. From the base of the fall, guests and visitors can board boats for a 10-minute tour of the grounds or a cruise to one of the hotel's restaurants. Rooms have lake or mountain views, balconies, oversize bathrooms, and minibars. There are long walks from the lobby to rooms; if driving, request one close to the parking lot. Because the resort hosts business groups and conventions, guests will find it busier and dressier than most other desert hotels, with group activities often occupying pool and lawn areas. ⊠ *74-855 Country Club Dr., 92260,* ☎ *619/341–2211 or 800/228–9290,* FAX *619/341–1730. 891 rooms, 51 suites. 5 restaurants, 2 lounges, 3 pools, hot tubs, spa, 2 golf courses, putting green, 21 tennis courts, badminton, croquet, health club, jogging, volleyball, convention center. AE, D, DC, MC, V.*

$$–$$$ 🏨 **Tres Palmas Bed and Breakfast.** This contemporary B&B just a few steps from El Paseo is also near the Living Desert. Enormous windows, high open-beamed ceilings, whitewashed wood, and textured peach tile floors lend the inn a bright and spacious feel. Southwest decor in common areas and guest rooms (which are functional rather than luxurious) incorporates some fine old Navajo rugs from the innkeepers' collection. Room rates include breakfast. ⊠ *73-135 Tumbleweed La.,* ☎ *619/773–9858. 5 rooms with private baths. Pool, outdoor hot tub. MC, V.*

PALM SPRINGS

$$$$ 🏨 **Sundance Villas.** Two- and three-bedroom duplex homes in this complex are all available for rental. Units are decorated in soft desert colors and have full kitchens, bathrooms with huge sunken tubs, outdoor pools and spas, and laundry facilities. The villas are away from most desert attractions in a secluded residential area at the north end of Palm Springs. Rates, though high, are for up to six people. ⊠ *303 W. Cabrillo Rd., 92262,* ☎ *619/325–3888 or 800/455–3888,* FAX *619/323–3029. 19 villas. Kitchens, pool, hot tub, tennis court. AE, D, DC, MC, V.*

$$$–$$$$ 🏨 **Abbey West.** This historic property in a quiet residential neighborhood at the north end of town is a knockout, with deep-green and white decor reflecting the art deco style of 1930s Hollywood. Large rooms have private entrances and patios, galley kitchens, and VCRs. There are several tree-shaded patios, a clothing-optional sunbathing area, and an outdoor exercise facility. Room rates include breakfast and lunch served buffet style. The inn, which caters to a gay clientele, is part of the Harlow Club Hotels group. ⊠ *772 Prescott Circle, 92262,* ☎ *619/325–0229 or 800/223–4073,* FAX *619/322–8534. 17 rooms. Pool, outdoor hot tub. AE, D, DC, MC, V.*

$$$–$$$$ ⊞ **Harlow El Alameda.** A historic resort now catering to a gay clientele, this is ideal for those seeking secluded accommodations in a lush garden setting. Smallish rooms are located in hacienda-style buildings surrounding a pool; many have fireplaces, private patios, and unusually large bathrooms. Crimson bougainvillea cascades from the rooftops; 10 varieties of date palms grow on the property, as do fruit-laden orange, tangerine, and grapefruit trees. There's a secluded clothing-optional sunbathing area. Room rates include breakfast and lunch. ⊠ *175 E. El Alameda, 92262,* ☎ *619/323–3977 or 800/223–4073,* 𝖥𝖠𝖷 *619/320–1218. 15 rooms. Pool, outdoor hot tub, exercise room. AE, D, DC, MC, V.*

$$$–$$$$ ⊞ **Hyatt Regency Suites.** This hotel's striking six-story asymmetrical atrium lobby holds a fountain and an enormous metal sculpture suspended from the ceiling. One- and two-bedroom suites have private balconies. Ask for the ones in the back of the hotel; they have pool and mountain views. Guests here have golf privileges at Rancho Mirage Country Club. ⊠ *285 N. Palm Canyon Dr., 92262,* ☎ *619/322–9000 or 800/233–1234,* 𝖥𝖠𝖷 *619/322–4027. 194 suites. 2 restaurants, lounge, pool, beauty salon, outdoor hot tub, health club. AE, D, DC, MC, V.*

$$$–$$$$ ⊞ **Inn at the Racquet Club.** Built by actors Charlie Farrell and Ralph Bellamy in the 1930s, this legendary resort (formerly the Palm Springs Racquet Club) brought the movie stars to the Springs. The once-private club became known for Hollywood high jinks and the "discovery" of Marilyn Monroe. Recently renovated, original red-roof cottages have fireplaces and private patios. ⊠ *2743 N. Indian Canyon Dr., 92262,* ☎ *619/325–1281 or 800/367–0946,* 𝖥𝖠𝖷 *619/325–3429. 72 rooms. Restaurant, lounge (weekends only), 3 pools, 3 hot tubs, sauna, exercise room, 10 tennis courts, meeting rooms. AE, DC, MC, V.*

$$$–$$$$ ⊞ **Palm Springs Hilton Resort and Racquet Club.** The cool, white marble elegance of this plant-filled resort hotel, just off Palm Canyon Drive, make it a popular choice, as do its two superb restaurants. Rooms have private balconies and refrigerators. ⊠ *400 E. Tahquitz Canyon Way, 92262,* ☎ *619/320–6868 or 800/522–6900,* 𝖥𝖠𝖷 *619/323–2755. 260 rooms. 2 restaurants, pool, hot tub, 6 tennis courts, health club, pro shop. AE, D, DC, MC, V.*

$$$–$$$$ ⊞ **Spa Hotel and Casino.** With its brilliant pink facade, you can't miss the Spa as you drive through the Springs. This hotel has had its ups and downs since it was built in 1963 over the original Agua Caliente springs. Its rooms are decorated in soft desert pinks and blues and lightwood furniture. Not trendy or splashy, the Spa, which is now owned by the Agua Caliente tribe, appeals to an older crowd that appreciates its soothing waters and downtown location. ⊠ *100 N. Indian Canyon Dr., 92262,* ☎ *619/778–1507 or 800/854–1279,* 𝖥𝖠𝖷 *619/325–3344. 230 rooms. Restaurant, 2 lounges, pool, outdoor hot tubs, spa, exercise room, casino. AE, D, DC, MC, V.*

$$–$$$$ ⊞ **Casa Cody.** This clean, western-style bed-and-breakfast is just a few steps from the Palm Springs Desert Museum. Spacious studios and one- and two-bedroom suites are furnished simply. Service is personal and gracious; room rates include Continental breakfast. ⊠ *175 S. Cahuilla Rd., 92262,* ☎ *619/320–9346 or 800/231–2639,* 𝖥𝖠𝖷 *619/325–8610. 24 units. Kitchens, 2 pools, outdoor hot tub. AE, D, DC, MC, V.*

$$–$$$$ ⊞ **Ingleside Inn.** Like many other desert lodgings, this hacienda-style inn attracts its share of Hollywood personalities, who appreciate good service and relative seclusion. Many rooms have antiques, fireplaces, whirlpool tubs and steam showers, stocked refrigerators, and private patios. Those in the main building are dark and cool, even in summer. The adjacent Melvyn's Restaurant is locally popular. ⊠ *200 W. Ramon Rd., 92264,* ☎ *619/325–0046 or 800/772–6655,* 𝖥𝖠𝖷 *619/325–0710. 29 rooms. Restaurant, bar, pool, hot tub. AE, D, DC, MC, V.*

$$–$$$$ 🖫 **La Mancha Private Pool Villas and Court Club.** Only four blocks from
★ downtown Palm Springs, this Spanish-Moroccan Hollywood-style re-
treat blocks out the rest of the world with plenty of panache. Opulent
villas surrounded by landscaped gardens have kitchens, fireplaces, and
private pools; four have private tennis courts. Convertibles for local
transportation are available for rental. ⊠ *444 N. Avenida Caballeros,
92262,* ☎ *619/323–1773 or 800/647–7482,* 🕾 *619/323–5928. 65
villas. Restaurant, pool, putting greens, 7 tennis courts, croquet, health
club, paddle tennis, bicycles, airport shuttle. AE, DC, MC, V.*

$$–$$$$ 🖫 **Villa Royale.** Each room in this bed-and-breakfast is decorated on
a European theme. Some have private hot tubs, fireplaces, and kitchens.
The grounds include lush gardens. ⊠ *1620 Indian Trail, 92264,* ☎
619/327–2314 or 800/245–2314, 🕾 *619/322–3794. 34 rooms.
Restaurant, lounge, 2 pools, hot tub. AE, D, MC, V.*

$$–$$$$ 🖫 **Wyndham Palm Springs.** The main appeal of this hotel is its loca-
tion adjacent to the Palm Springs Convention Center. The terra-cotta
Spanish-colonial building surrounds the largest swimming pool in
Palm Springs. Rooms are well equipped with hair dryers, "on-command
TV," and huge walk-through bathrooms in the suites. Because the ma-
jority of the Wyndham's customers are on business, the atmosphere
here is more serious than at most desert establishments. ⊠ *888 Tahquitz
Canyon Way, 92262,* ☎ *619/322–6000 or 800/996–3426,* 🕾 *619/322–
5551. 410 rooms, including 158 suites. 2 restaurants, lounge, pool, wad-
ing pool, beauty salon, 2 outdoor hot tubs, exercise room, bicycles,
video games, business services. AE, D, DC, MC, V.*

$$–$$$ 🖫 **Korakia Pensione.** This historic Moorish-style home, built in the 1920s
by Scottish artist Gordon Coutts, has long been a haven for the cre-
ative set. Winston Churchill came here to paint; more recently pho-
tographer Annie Leibovitz has enjoyed the home's scenic mountain view.
Inside, rooms are furnished with antiques, handmade furniture, and
Oriental rugs; some have fireplaces, and most have kitchens. The pen-
sione has gotten a fair amount of press in recent years; the homey am-
bience of days past has given way to a brusquer style. Room rates include
Continental breakfast. ⊠ *257 S. Patencio Rd., 92262,* ☎ *619/864–
6411. 18 rooms. Pool. No credit cards.*

$–$$ 🖫 **Bee Charmer Inn.** This Southwest-style inn with a red-tile roof and
terra-cotta tile floors caters exclusively to women. Spacious rooms sur-
round a pool and tropical courtyard; comfortably but not lavishly decorated in soft pastel colors, they come with refrigerators and microwaves.
Three rooms have wet bars, and one has a whirlpool bath. Owner Judy
Nelson occasionally has barbecues and afternoon entertainment. Rates
include Continental breakfast. ⊠ *1600 E. Palm Canyon Dr., 92264,*
☎ *619/778–5883. 14 rooms. Pool. AE, D, MC, V.*

$–$$ 🖫 **Howard Johnson Lodge.** This typical motel-style property is popu-
lar with tour groups. Ask for special discounts. ⊠ *701 E. Palm Canyon
Dr., 92264,* ☎ *619/320–2700 or 800/854–4345,* 🕾 *619/320–1591.
206 rooms. Coffee shop, lounge, 2 pools, outdoor hot tub, coin laundry. AE, D, DC, MC, V.*

$–$$ 🖫 **Vagabond Inn.** Rooms are smallish at this centrally located motel
but clean and comfortable. The Vagabond gives good value for budget prices. ⊠ *1699 S. Palm Canyon Dr., 92264,* ☎ *619/325–7211 or
800/522–1555,* 🕾 *619/322–9269. 120 rooms. Coffee shop, pool, outdoor hot tub, 2 saunas. AE, D, DC, MC, V.*

RANCHO MIRAGE

$$$$ 🖫 **Marriott's Rancho Las Palmas.** The atmosphere is luxuriously laid-
★ back at this family-oriented resort on 240 landscaped acres. An early
California-Spanish theme prevails throughout the public areas and
guest accommodations. Rooms in a series of two-story buildings are

unusually large; all have sitting areas and views of colorful gardens or well-manicured fairways and greens. ⊠ *41-000 Bob Hope Dr., 92270,* ☎ *619/568–2727 or 800/458–8786,* FAX *619/568–5845. 450 rooms. 2 restaurants, bar, 2 snack bars, 2 pools, 2 outdoor hot tubs, barbershop, beauty salon, 27-hole golf course, putting green, 25 tennis courts, health club, jogging, children's programs, playground, business services, convention center. AE, D, DC, MC, V.*

$$$$ ★ 🏨 **Ritz-Carlton Rancho Mirage.** This hotel is tucked into a hillside in the Santa Rosa Mountains with sweeping views of the valley below. Sheep from the surrounding bighorn preserve frequently visit the grounds. The surroundings are elegant, with gleaming marble and brass, original artwork, deep plush carpeting, and remarkable comfort. All rooms are spacious and meticulously appointed with antiques, fabric wall coverings, marble bathrooms, and often two phones and two TVs. Service is impeccable. ⊠ *68-900 Frank Sinatra Dr., 92270,* ☎ *619/321–8282 or 800/241–3333,* FAX *619/321–6928. 221 rooms, 19 suites. 3 restaurants, bar, outdoor hot tub, spa, 10 tennis courts, 9-hole pitch-and-putt golf, basketball, health club, croquet, hiking, volleyball, children's programs, business services. AE, D, DC, MC, V.*

$$$$ 🏨 **Westin Mission Hills Resort.** A sprawling Moroccan-style resort on 360 acres, adjacent to the annual Nabisco Dinah Shore LPGA Classic, the Westin is surrounded by fairways and putting greens. Rooms are in two-story buildings enveloping patios and fountains scattered throughout the property. The rooms have soft desert colors, terra-cotta tile floors, shuttered windows, and private patios or balconies; amenities include double sinks, in-room coffeemakers, and refrigerators. Paths and creeks meander through the complex, encircling a lagoon-style swimming pool with a 60-foot water slide. It's a place to spot the famous (and used-to-be-famous): Jay Leno, Walter Cronkite, Carol Burnett, Sargent Shriver, Beverly Sills, Chad Everett, Terry Bradshaw, and Magic Johnson have all graced these premises. ⊠ *71-333 Dinah Shore Dr., 92270,* ☎ *619/328–5955 or 800/228–3000,* FAX *619/321–2955. 512 rooms. 7 restaurants, lounge, 3 pools, outdoor hot tubs, 2 18-hole golf courses, 7 tennis courts, health club, children's programs. AE, D, DC, MC, V.*

Nightlife and the Arts

CLUBS

Cecil's on Sunrise (⊠ 1775 E. Palm Canyon Dr., Palm Springs, ☎ 619/320–4202) is a Top 40 disco dance club with retro memorabilia.

Cactus Corral (⊠ 67-501 E. Palm Canyon Dr., Cathedral City, ☎ 619/321–8558) attracts the country-music set with live music and dancing.

C. C. Construction Company (⊠ 68-449 Perez Rd., Cathedral City, ☎ 619/324–4241) is the largest gay nightclub in the Palm Springs desert region, catering to a mixed crowd with dancing nightly.

Costas (⊠ Marriott's Desert Springs Resort and Spa, 74-855 Country Club Dr., Palm Desert, ☎ 619/341–1795) has live bands for dancing in a lakeside setting.

Peabody's Jazz Studio and Coffee Bar (⊠ 134 S. Palm Canyon Dr., Palm Springs, ☎ 619/322–1877) presents jazz in a warm atmosphere on weekends.

Zelda's (⊠ 169 N. Indian Canyon Dr., Palm Springs, ☎ 619/325–2375) has two rooms, one with a beachy atmosphere featuring techno jazz and another featuring Top 40 dance music and a Male Dance Revue.

Of the many desert arts festivals, **La Quinta Arts Festival** (☎ 619/564–1244), normally held the third weekend in March, displays the best work and has the classiest entertainment, food, and celebrities.

FILM

Nortel Palm Springs International Film Festival (☎ 619/322–2930), held in mid-January, brings more than 150 feature films from 25 countries, plus panel discussions, short films and documentaries, to Palm Desert's McCallum Theatre.

THEATER

Annenberg Theater (✉ Palm Springs Desert Museum, 101 Museum Dr., ☎ 619/325–4490) hosts Broadway shows, opera, lectures, Sunday-afternoon chamber concerts, and other events.
Fabulous Palm Springs Follies (✉ Plaza Theater, 128 S. Palm Canyon Dr., ☎ 916/864–6514), the hottest ticket in the desert, presents 10 sell-out performances each week. The vaudeville-style revue stars extravagantly costumed retired (but very much in shape) showgirls, singers, and dancers. Admission is $24.50–$39.
McCallum Theatre (✉ 73-000 Fred Waring Dr., Palm Desert, ☎ 619/340–2787), the principal cultural venue in the desert, presents film, classical and popular music, opera, ballet, and theater.

Outdoor Activities and Sports

BICYCLING

Big Horn Bicycles (✉ 302 N. Palm Canyon, Palm Springs, ☎ 619/325–3367) operates tours to celebrity homes and Indian Canyons and rents bikes. **Mac's Bicycle Rental** (✉ 70-053 Hwy. 111, Rancho Mirage, ☎ 619/321–9444) will deliver mountain, three-speed, and tandem bikes to area hotels. **Palm Springs Recreation Department** (✉ 401 S. Pavilion Way, ☎ 619/323–8272) has maps of some city trails and information about bike-rental shops.

FITNESS

Marriott's Desert Springs Resort and Spa has the most luxurious hotel health club, with a 30-station gym, Lifecycles, fitness classes, personal training, and sauna and steam rooms. ✉ 74-855 Country Club Dr., Palm Desert 92260, ☎ 619/341–1856. ☞ $24. ☉ Daily 6:30 AM–7:30 PM.

GOLF

Mission Hills Resort Golf Club (✉ 71-501 Dinah Shore Dr., Rancho Mirage, ☎ 619/328–3198), a challenging Pete Dye–designed course, hosts major tournaments and well-known politicians and movie stars.
PGA West (✉ 56–150 PGA Blvd., La Quinta, ☎ 619/564–7177) has three championship courses open to the public. PGA West also provides instruction and golf clinics.
Tahquitz Creek Palm Springs Golf Resort (✉ 1885 Golf Club Dr., Palm Springs, ☎ 619/328–1005) has 36 holes and a 50-space driving range.
Tommy Jacobs' Bel-Aire Greens Country Club (✉ 1001 S. El Cielo Rd., Palm Springs, ☎ 619/322–6062) is a nine-hole executive course.

The **Bob Hope Desert Classic** takes place January–February. **Dinah Shore LPGA Championship** is a March or April event. Palm Springs hosts more than 100 golf tournaments annually. The Palm Springs Desert Resorts Convention and Visitors Bureau **Events Hotline** (☎ 619/770–1992) lists dates and locations.

POLO

The **Eldorado Polo Club** (✉ 50-950 Madison St., Indio, ☎ 619/342–2223), known as the Winter Polo Capital of the West, is home to world-class polo events. You can pack a picnic and watch practice matches free during the week; there's a $6 per person charge on weekends.

TENNIS

The combined **Newsweek Champions/Evert Cup Women's Professional Tennis Tournament** (☎ 619/341–2757) is held at the Hyatt Grand Champions Resort in Indian Wells for 10 days in March; it attracts top-ranked players on the international grand-slam circuit.

Demuth Park (✉ 4375 Mesquite Ave., no phone) has four lighted courts. **Palm Springs Tennis Center** (✉ 1300 Baristo Rd., ☎ 619/320–0020) has nine lighted courts—fees run $12–$14—and can make arrangements for partners to play at area hotels. **Ruth Hardy Park** (✉ Tamarisk and Caballeros, no phone) has eight lighted courts.

Shopping

SHOPPING DISTRICTS

Palm Desert's **El Paseo,** a 2-mile Mediterranean-style avenue with fountains and courtyards, contains French and Italian fashion boutiques, shoe salons, jewelry designers, children's shops, nearly 30 galleries, and restaurants.

Palm Canyon Drive is Palm Springs' main shopping destination. Its commercial core extends from Alejo Road on the north to Ramon Road on the south. Anchoring the center of the drive is the Desert Fashion Plaza, a functional more than fashionable mall. Village Fest, held here on Thursday nights, brings out craftspeople, antiques sellers, a farmers' market, and entertainment.

Palm Desert Town Center is the largest enclosed mall in the desert, with more than 140 specialty shops, major department stores, movie theaters, an ice-skating rink, and restaurants.

ANTIQUES AND COLLECTIBLES

Many of the items for sale in the **Heritage Gallery and Antique District,** a collection of consignment and second-hand shops along North Palm Canyon Drive in Palm Springs, come from the homes of celebrities and other wealthy residents.

Classic Consignment Co. (✉ 73–847 El Paseo, Palm Desert, ☎ 619/568–4948) shows full sets of Rosenthal china and Baccarat crystal, barely used contemporary glass and Lucite furnishings, accessories, fine art, and jewelry. Prices match the shop's trendy location.
Consignment Sale (✉ 817 N. Palm Canyon, ☎ 619/323–2335) has home furnishings, fine china and crystal, accessories, and art.
Desert Liquidators (✉ 798 N. Palm Canyon, ☎ 619/323–2411) carries furnishings, jewelry, and movie posters from the '30s and '40s.
Estate Sale Co. (✉ 4185 E. Palm Canyon, Palm Springs, ☎ 619/321–7628) is the biggest consignment store in the desert, with a warehouse of furniture, fine art, china and crystal, accessories, jewelry, movie memorabilia, and exercise equipment. Prices are set to keep merchandise moving out the door.
The Village Attic (✉ 849 N. Palm Canyon, ☎ 619/320–6165) specializes in '50s furniture and accessories.

DRIED FRUIT

Hadley's Fruit Orchards (✉ 48-980 Seminole Rd., Cabazon, ☎ 909/849–5255) sells dried fruit, nuts, date shakes, and wines.

Oasis Date Gardens (✉ 59-111 Hwy. 111, Thermal, ☎ 619/399–5665) conducts twice-a-day tours that show how dates are pollinated, grown, sorted, stored, and packed for shipping. Included are an educational video and a free shake with promotional coupon (widely available in the Palm Springs area).

Shields Date Gardens (⊠ 80-225 Hwy. 111, Indio, ☎ 619/347–0996) presents a continuous slide program on the history of the date and sells shakes.

FACTORY OUTLETS

Desert Hills Factory Stores (⊠ 48-650 Seminole Rd., Cabazon, ☎ 909/849–6641) is an outlet center with more than 150 name-brand fashion shops selling at a discount. **Spa Gear** here sells fashionable spa attire at a fraction of what you'd pay at hotel boutiques.

VINTAGE CLOTHING

Patsy's Clothes Closet (⊠ 4121 E. Palm Canyon Dr., Palm Springs, ☎ 619/324–8825) specializes in high-fashion and designer clothing for women and men, "much of it hardly worn," the owners claim.

PALM SPRINGS A TO Z

Arriving and Departing

By Bus
Greyhound (☎ 800/231–2222) provides service to the Palm Springs Depot (⊠ 311 N. Indian Canyon Dr., ☎ 619/325–2053) from Los Angeles, San Diego, and elsewhere.

By Car
Palm Springs is about a two-hour drive east of Los Angeles and a three-hour drive northeast of San Diego. Highway 111 brings you right onto Palm Canyon Drive, the main thoroughfare in Palm Springs and connecting route to other desert communities. From Los Angeles take the San Bernardino Freeway (I–10E) to Highway 111. From San Diego, I–15N connects with the Pomona Freeway (Highway 60), leading to the San Bernardino Freeway (I–10E) east. An alternative, more scenic route from San Diego begins east on I–8. Then take Highways 67, 78, and 79 north to Aguanga, where Highway 371 heads east to Highway 74, which joins Highway 111 between Palm Desert and Indian Wells. Desert exits are clearly marked: Highway 111 for Palm Springs, Monterey for Palm Desert, Washington for La Quinta. If you're coming from the Riverside area, you can also take Highway 74 east.

By Plane
Major airlines serving **Palm Springs Regional Airport** include **Alaska American/American Eagle, America West Express, Reno Air, SkyWest, United/United Express,** and **US Air Express** (☞ Air Travel *in* Important Contacts A to Z for phone numbers). The airport is about 2 miles east of the city's main downtown intersection; most hotels provide service to and from the airport.

By Train
Amtrak (☎ 800/872–7245) passenger trains serve the Indio area, 20 miles east of Palm Springs. From Indio, Greyhound Lines bus service is available to Palm Springs.

Getting Around

By Bus
SunBus, operated by the Sunline Transit Agency (☎ 619/343–3451), serves the entire Coachella Valley from Desert Hot Springs to Mecca.

By Car

The desert-resort communities occupy a stretch of about 20 miles between I–10 in the east and Palm Canyon Drive in the west. Although some areas such as Palm Canyon Drive in Palm Springs and El Paseo are walkable, having a car is the best way to get around.

By Taxi

Checker Cab (☎ 619/325–2868) and **Valley Cabousine** (☎ 619/340–5845) serve the Palm Springs Desert Resorts area.

Contacts and Resources

Car Rentals

Most major car-rental companies are represented in the Palm Springs area (☞ Car Rental *in* Important Contacts A to Z).

Emergencies

Ambulance (☎ 911). **Police** (☎ 911).

Desert Hospital (☎ 619/323–6511).

Gregory Yates, D.D.S. (☎ 619/327–8448).

Guided Tours

AERIAL TOURS

Fantasy Balloon Flights (☎ 619/398–6322) organizes trips in the Coachella Valley. **Sunrise Balloons** (☎ 800/548–9912) has balloon excursions and helicopter tours.

CELEBRITY TOURS

Gray Line Tours (☎ 619/325–0974) conducts a 1½-hour tour of Palm Springs proper that covers its history, points of interest, and celebrity residences. The cost is $12. Buses leave at 10 AM. **Palm Springs Celebrity Tours** (☎ 619/770–2700) has hour-long and 2½-hour tours that cover Palm Springs area history, points of interest, and celebrity homes. Prices range from $11 to $16.

DESERT TOURS

Covered Wagon Tours (☎ 619/347–2161) takes visitors on an old-time, two-hour exploration of the desert with a cookout at the end of the journey. **Desert Adventures** (☎ 619/864–6530) takes to the wilds with Jeep tours of Indian canyons, off-road in the Santa Rosa Mountains, into a mystery canyon, and to Joshua Tree National Park.

Telephone Service

Beginning on March 22, 1997, the Palm Springs Desert Resorts area code will change from 619 to 760. Calls to the new code will continue to go through using either code until September 27, 1997, after which callers will be instructed to use the 760 code.

Vacation Rentals

Rental Connection (✉ Box 8567, Palm Springs 92263, ☎ 619/320–7336 or 800/462–7256). **Sunrise Co.** (✉ 76-300 Country Club Dr., Palm Desert 92211, ☎ 800/869–1130).

Visitor Information

Palm Springs Desert Resorts (✉ 69-930 Hwy. 111, Suite 201, Rancho Mirage 92270, ☎ 619/770–9000 or 800/967–3767; Activities Hotline ☎ 619/770–1992). **Palm Springs Visitor Information Center** (✉ 2781 N. Palm Canyon Dr., Palm Springs 92262, ☎ 800/347–7746).

15 The Mojave Desert and Death Valley

When most people assemble their "must-see" list of California attractions, the desert isn't often among the top contenders. What with its heat and vast, sparsely populated tracts of land, the desert is no Disneyland. But that's precisely why it deserves a closer look. The natural riches here are overwhelming: rolling waves of sand dunes, black cinder cones thrusting up hundreds of feet into the air from a blistered desert floor, riotous sheets of wildflowers, bizarrely shaped Joshua trees basking in the orange glow of a sunset, and an abundant silence that is both dramatic and startling.

By Aaron
Sugarman and
Dianne
Aaronson

THE MOJAVE DESERT begins just north of the San Bernardino Mountains, along the northern edge of Los Angeles, and extends north 150 miles into the Eureka Valley and east 200 miles to the Colorado River. Death Valley lies north and east of the Mojave, jutting into Nevada near Beatty. The Mojave, with elevations ranging from 3,000 to 5,000 feet above sea level, is known as the High Desert; Death Valley, the Low Desert, with points at almost 300 feet below sea level, is the lowest spot in the United States.

Because of the vast size of California's deserts, an area about as big as Ohio, and the frequently extreme weather, careful planning is essential for an enjoyable desert adventure. Conveniences, facilities, trails, gas stations, and supermarkets do not lurk just around the corner from many desert sights. Be sure to fill your tank before entering Death Valley—fuel is cheaper on the interstates and you'll avoid running out. Also, check your vehicle's oil and its water and tire pressure. It is advisable on the steeper grades to shut off your air-conditioning to avoid engine overheating. Different regions of the desert can be easily handled in day trips, but more extensive exploring will require overnight stays. Reliable maps are a must, as signage is limited and, in some places, nonexistent. Other important accessories include a compass, a cellular phone, extra food and water (three gallons per person per day is recommended, plus additional radiator water), sunglasses, extra clothes (for wind or cool nights), and a hat (if you're going to do any walking around in the sun). Bring along sufficient clothing to block the sun's rays. A pair of binoculars can come in handy, and don't forget your camera: you're likely to see things you've never seen before.

Pleasures and Pastimes

Camping
Because vegetation in the desert is sparse, campers are truly one with the elements, including the hot sun. Most campsites are primitive, but the scenic rewards are many, and some campgrounds are so inexpensive they're actually free. Be sure to bring equipment that can handle extreme temperatures.

Dining
The Fred Harvey–operated restaurants in Death Valley range from a cafeteria to an upscale Continental restaurant. There are fast-food and chain establishments in Ridgecrest, Victorville, and Barstow. Experienced desert travelers carry an ice chest well stocked with food and beverages. Replenish your food stash at the larger towns of Ridgecrest and Barstow, where you'll find a better selection and non-tourist prices at the various supermarkets.

CATEGORY	COST*
$$$$	over $50
$$$	$30–$50
$$	$20–$30
$	under $20

per person for a three-course meal, excluding drinks, service, and tax

Hiking
Hiking trails are abundant throughout the desert and meander toward sights that would be missed from the road. Plan your walks before or after the noonday sun, bring protective clothing, and be wary of tarantulas, snakes, and other potentially hazardous creatures. Paths through canyons are sometimes partially protected from the heat, so if your time is limited, save these for midday.

Lodging

Larger towns such as Barstow seem to have a motel on every corner, but there are only three in all of Death Valley, the cheapest in Stovepipe Wells Village. Those preferring quiet nights and an unfettered view of the desert sky and Mosaic Canyon will enjoy Stovepipe. The lack of phone and TV adds to the rustic atmosphere. Families with children may prefer the Furnace Creek end of Death Valley, with easy access to the visitor center and various sights.

CATEGORY	COST*
$$$$	over $175
$$$	$120–$175
$$	$80–$120
$	under $80

All prices are for a standard double room, excluding tax.

Exploring the Desert

The Mojave Desert is a sprawling space, but many of its visitable attractions are conveniently situated on a north–south axis along U.S. 395 and Highway 178. This Western Mojave region has Ridgecrest as its major northern hub and Victorville as its southern one. The Eastern Mojave runs along an east–west axis alongside the parallel routes of I–15 and I–40, with Barstow as the western hub, moving east toward Needles. If you plan to stop overnight en route to Death Valley, both Lone Pine and Ridgecrest on U.S. 395 have tourist services and accommodations, as do Barstow and Baker on I–15.

Great Itineraries

Though you can move quickly from sight to sight within the Mojave and Death Valley on the well-maintained interstate and state highways, allow yourself to linger. Once within this environment, where there is always enough space and time, you may regret packing too much into a short stay. In three days you could visit Ridgecrest and Death Valley but would have to move briskly from point to point. If you have five days, you can still visit the most interesting sights, but will have less time to linger. Seven days would allow for leisurely hikes through the canyons, a full-day tour of the Petroglyph Canyons, off-road adventures, and a thorough perusal of old mining towns and museums.

Numbers in the text correspond to numbers in the margin and on the Mojave Desert and Death Valley maps.

IF YOU HAVE 3 DAYS
Randsburg, a well-preserved, still-vibrant gold town in the **Rand Mining District** ②, is a good starting point from either San Francisco or Los Angeles. Pack a picnic lunch and drive through colorful **Red Rock Canyon State Park** ③ and take a walk among the volcanic rock formations of **Fossil Falls** ④ before moving on to 🔯 **Ridgecrest** ⑤ for a stop at the Maturango Museum, which also serves as a tourist information center. Have dinner and spend the night in Ridgecrest. The following day, see the surreal **Trona Pinnacles** ⑥, and then continue on to the 🔯 **Furnace Creek** ⑩ visitor center before catching awe-inspiring perspectives of the Death Valley region from **Artists Palette** ⑬, **Zabriskie Point** ⑭, and **Dante's View** ⑮. Return home on the third day after stopping at the **Harmony Borax Works** ⑨, where the famed 20-mule teams once toiled, and hiking through **Golden Canyon** ⑪.

IF YOU HAVE 7 DAYS
Leave from Los Angeles, driving over the **San Andreas Fault** ①, with stops at the **Rand Mining District** ②, **Red Rock Canyon** ③, and **Fossil**

Falls ④ before stopping in 🖼 **Ridgecrest** ⑤ to dine and lodge. Or, from San Francisco, visit Fossil Falls and then stop briefly at the Maturango Museum in Ridgecrest before driving to Red Rock Canyon and the Rand Mining District. Take a full-day tour of the Petroglyph Canyons (spring and fall weekends only), or visit the **Bureau of Land Management Regional Wild Horse and Burro Corrals** on the way to the **Trona Pinnacles** ⑥ and 🖼 **Stovepipe Wells Village** ⑦ in Death Valley. (If you've toured Petroglyph when the days are long, you should be able to see some of the pinnacles before nightfall.) On the third day, take a morning stroll through **Mosaic Canyon** before driving north for a full day at **Scotty's Castle** ⑧—have lunch there or pack a picnic and eat along the roadside—and then loop back toward 🖼 **Furnace Creek** ⑩. If you're in the area on a performance day, zip down to Death Valley Junction to see the 8:15 PM show at **Marta Becket's Amargosa Opera House** ⑯. Drop in at the Furnace Creek visitor center on day four, hike through **Golden Canyon** ⑪, and drive to **Badwater** ⑫, the lowest point in the Northern Hemisphere, before returning via **Artists Palette** ⑬. Visit the lookout at **Zabriskie Point** ⑭ and walk along **Dante's View** ⑮ before driving south to 🖼 **Baker** ⑰. Use Baker as your fifth-day base. Drive along Kelbaker Road to the **Kelso Dunes** ⑱ and visit the **Mitchell Caverns** in **Providence Mountains State Recreation Area** ⑲. If time permits, drive through **Afton Canyon** ⑳ before overnighting in 🖼 **Barstow** ㉑. On day six, hike around the **Rainbow Basin National Natural Landmark** ㉒ and tour the **Calico Early Man Archeological Site** ㉔ (Wednesday through Sunday; the last tour starts at 3:30 PM). On day seven, especially if you have kids, visit **Calico Ghost Town** ㉓ before leaving the desert.

When to Tour the Mojave Desert and Death Valley

The early morning is the best time to visit sights and avoid an excess of tourists, but museums and visitor information centers often do not open until 10 AM; some antiques shops in Randsburg are closed until noon. If you can schedule your town arrivals for late afternoon, visit the information centers just before closing hours to line up an itinerary for the next day. Plan indoor activities for midday during hot months. Keep in mind that because fewer people visit the desert, its attractions are only open at select times: Petroglyph Canyon tours are given weekends only; the Calico Early Man Archeological Site does not offer tours Mondays and Tuesdays; and so on.

THE WESTERN MOJAVE
Rand Mining District and Ridgecrest

The prime Western Mojave attractions are along or near U.S. 395 or Highways 14 and 178. The key sights after the San Andreas Fault are listed clockwise, heading north and west from Randsburg, looping around eastward to the Trona Pinnacles.

Numbers in the margin correspond to points of interest on the Mojave Desert map.

❶ The infamous **San Andreas Fault** traverses the desert near Cajon Pass, a few miles south of I-15's U.S. 395 exit. If you're driving from Los Angeles, it's an apocalyptic way to start a desert trip.

Rand Mining District

❷ *137 mi northeast of Los Angeles, I–10 to I–15 to U.S. 395; 360 mi from San Francisco, I–80 to I–580 to I–5 to Hwy. 178 to Hwy. 14 to U.S. 395.*

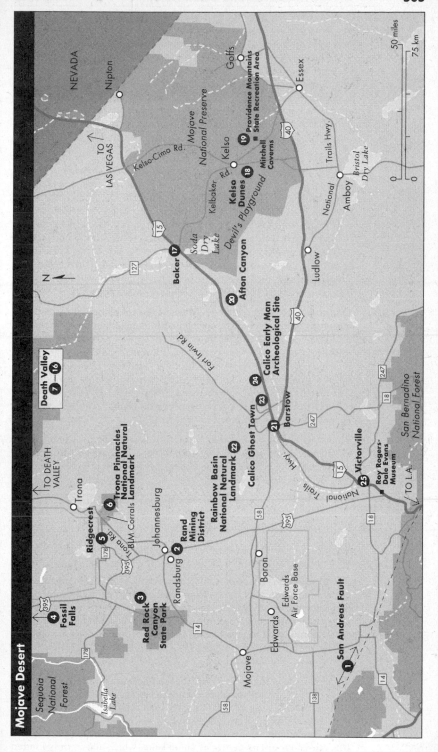

The towns of Randsburg, Red Mountain, and Johannesburg make up the Rand Mining District. **Randsburg** is among the few authentic gold-mining communities not to have become a ghost town. It first boomed with the discovery of gold in the Rand Mountains in 1895 and, along with the neighboring settlements, grew to support the successful Yellow Aster Mine. Rich tungsten ore was discovered during World War I, and silver was found in 1919. Randsburg still has some original gold-rush buildings, plus a few antiques shops, a general store, and the city jail. ⊠ *U.S. 395, 70 mi north of its intersection with I–15, 21 mi east of Hwy. 14 on Red Rock–Randsburg Rd.*

❸ **Red Rock Canyon State Park** is a feast for the eyes with its layers of pink, white, red, rust, and brown rocks. Entering the park from the south, you pass through a steep-walled gorge and enter a wide bowl tinted pink by what was once hot volcanic ash. The human history of this area goes back some 20,000 years to the canyon dwellers known only as the Old People. Mojave Indians roamed the land for several hundred years until gold-rush fever hit the region in the mid- to late 1800s; remains of mining operations dot the countryside. The canyon was later invaded by filmmakers and has starred in westerns. The ranger station is northwest on Abbott Drive off Highway 14. ⊠ *Hwy. 14, 17 mi west of U.S. 395 via Red Rock–Randsburg Rd.*

En Route   On the way to Fossil Falls you'll pass **Little Lake,** a good place to see migrating waterfowl in the spring and fall, including several varieties of ducks and geese and perhaps pelicans as well. The area just north of the lake is often covered with wildflowers. As you pass the lake, a red cinder cone known as Red Hill comes into view ahead of you. The hill is a small volcano that was once active and is now being mined. Approaching the falls, you cross a large volcanic field; the falls themselves drop an impressive distance along the channel cut by the Owens River through the hardened lava flows 20,000 years ago.

❹ The roughly hewn, stark black rocks of **Fossil Falls,** the direct result of volcanic eruptions in the Western Mojave area, are a study in shape and texture. ⊠ *20 mi north on U.S. 395 from Hwy. 14, then ½ mi east on Cinder Cone Rd.*

Ridgecrest

❺ *35 mi north of Randsburg, U.S. 395 to Hwy. 178.*

Ridgecrest, with its range of stores, dining, and lodging options, is a good hub for exploration of the northwestern Mojave.

The **Maturango Museum,** which also serves as a visitor information center, is worth a stop. Here you will find in-depth pamphlets and books regarding the northern Mojave and Death Valley—its sights, history, flora, and fauna. Small but informative exhibits detail the natural and cultural history of the northern Mojave. ⊠ *100 E. Las Flores Ave., at China Lake Blvd., 93555,* ☎ *619/375–6900,* 𝐅𝐀𝐗 *619/375–0479.* ☞ *$2.* ⊙ *Wed.–Sun. 10–5.*

★ On weekends in the spring and fall, the Maturango Museum arranges the only tours to the **Petroglyph Canyons,** among the desert's most amazing spectacles. (Call ahead, ☎ 619/375–6900; space is limited on these full-day excursions.) The two canyons, commonly called Big and Little Petroglyph, are in the Coso mountain range on the million-acre **U.S. Naval Weapons Center at China Lake,** which allows only limited access. Each of the canyons holds a superlative concentration of rock art, the largest of its kind in the Northern Hemisphere. Thousands of images are scratched or pecked into the shiny desert varnish—oxidized minerals—that coats the canyon's dark basaltic rocks. Some of the figures are animals and people, but some seem more abstract, and it isn't clear to historians whether they're mythology of an ancient people or hunting records. Even the age of these glyphs remains a matter of debate. All are exceptionally preserved and protected; the feeling of living history is incredible here. 🖼 *$20, children under 6 not admitted; $40 for less regular "extended trips" for photographers and others who want to see sunrise and sunset in the Little Petroglyph Canyon.* ☉ *Tours Mar.–1st weekend in July and Sept.–1st weekend in Dec.*

OFF THE BEATEN PATH	**BUREAU OF LAND MANAGEMENT REGIONAL WILD HORSE AND BURRO CORRALS** – Animals gathered from public lands throughout the Southwest are fed and prepared for adoption here. Unlike at urban zoos, it's okay to feed the animals, so bring along an apple or a carrot to share with the horses (the burros are usually too wild to approach). ☒ *Hwy. 178, 3 mi east of Ridgecrest,* ☎ *619/446–6064 to arrange tours.* 🖼 *Free.* ☉ *Weekdays 7:30 AM–4 PM.*

❻ **Trona Pinnacles National Natural Landmark** is not easy to reach—the best road to the area changes with the weather and can be impassable after a rain. But it's worth the effort, especially to sci-fi buffs, who will recognize the pinnacles as *Star Trek*'s Final Frontier. These fantasy formations of calcium carbonate, known as tufa, were formed underwater along cracks in the lake bed—first as hollow tubes, then mounds, and finally as the spires visible today. A ½-mile trail winds around this surreal landscape. Wear sturdy shoes—tufa cuts like coral. ☒ *From the Trona–Red Mountain Rd., take Hwy. 178 east for 8 mi. Or, from its junction with U.S. 395, take Hwy. 178 for 29 mi to dirt intersection; turn southeast and go ½ mi to a fork. Continue south via right fork, cross railroad tracks, and drive onward 5 mi to pinnacles.*

Dining and Lodging

$$ ✕ **Farris' Garden Grill.** The fare is American to the core—steaks, seafood, and prime rib—at this classy but casual restaurant. ☒ *1050 N. Norma St.,* ☎ *619/446–6543, AE, D, DC, MC, V.*

$$ 🏨 **Heritage Inn.** This hotel has pleasantly appointed rooms, all with king- or queen-size beds. The facility is geared toward commercial travelers, but the inn's staff is equally attentive to tourists' concerns. Room rates include complimentary breakfast. A sister property nearby is an all-suites hotel. ☒ *1050 N. Norma St.,* ☎ *619/446–6543 or 800/843–1586,* 📠 *619/446–2884. 124 rooms. 2 restaurants, bar, pool, hot tub, coin laundry, business services, meeting rooms. AE, D, DC, MC, V.*

⛺ **Red Rock Canyon State Park.** The park's campground is in the colorful cliff region of the southern El Paso Mountains, which present many hiking opportunities. The 50 sites include firepits, pit toilets, and water but no hookups. ☒ *Off Hwy. 14, 30 mi southwest of Ridgecrest,* ☎ *805/942–0662 for reservations.* 🖼 *$7 per evening, $1 additional for dogs.* ☉ *Visitor center weekends.*

DEATH VALLEY

Stovepipe Wells Village and Furnace Creek

With more than 3.3 million acres, **Death Valley National Park** is the largest national park outside Alaska. Distances are deceiving here: Some sights appear in clusters, but others require extensive travel. Visitors need to plan excursions carefully. The trip to Scotty's Castle, for example, can take a half day. Fees of $5 per vehicle, collected at the park's entrance stations and at the Visitor Center at Furnace Creek (☞ below), are valid for seven days.

Numbers in the margin correspond to points of interest on the Death Valley map.

The topography of Death Valley is a minilesson in geology. Two hundred million years ago, seas covered the area, depositing layers of sediment and fossils. Between 35 million and 5 million years ago, faults in the earth's crust and volcanic activity pushed and folded the ground, causing mountain ranges to rise and the valley floor to drop. The valley was then filled periodically by lakes, which eroded the surrounding rocks into fantastic formations and deposited the salts that now cover the floor of the basin. Today, the area has 14 square miles of sand dunes, 200 square miles of crusty salt flats, 11,000-foot mountains, hills, and canyons of many colors. There are more than 1,000 species of plants and trees—21 of which are unique to the valley, like the yellow Panamint daisy and the blue-flowered Death Valley sage.

Stovepipe Wells Village

❼ *102 mi northeast of Ridgecrest, Hwy. 178 to Hwy. 190.*

Stovepipe Wells Village was the first resort in Death Valley. The tiny town, which dates back to 1926, takes its name from the stovepipe that marked a nearby well. There's a motel, a restaurant, a grocery store, a landing strip, and campgrounds here.

The polished, multicolored, partly marble walls of **Mosaic Canyon** are extremely narrow in spots. A reasonably easy ¾-mile hike yields the flavor of the area, or you can continue farther into the canyon for a few more miles. ⊠ *Off Hwy. 190, on 3 mi gravel immediately southwest of Stovepipe Wells Village.*

Dining and Lodging

$$ ✕ **Toll Road Restaurant.** This comfortable Old West–style restaurant adjoins the Badwater Saloon. Salad lovers can make a whole meal at the salad bar. ⊠ *Hwy. 190, Stovepipe Wells Village,* ☎ *619/786–2604, AE, D, MC, V.*

$ ▥ **Stovepipe Wells Village.** A landing strip for light aircraft is an unusual touch for a motel, as is a heated mineral pool, but the rest is pretty basic. The property includes a dining room (open only for breakfast and dinner) and a grocery store. ⊠ *Hwy. 190, Death Valley National Park 92328,* ☎ *619/786–2387,* ℻ *619/786–2389. 82 rooms. Restaurant, bar, pool. AE, D, MC, V.*

▲ **Mahogany Flat.** The campground here has 10 well-shaded tent spaces—plus tables and pit toilets, but no water—in a forest of juniper and piñon pine. ⊠ *Off Wildrose Rd., just south of Charcoal Kilns.* ▥ *Free.* ☉ *Mar.–Nov.*

▲ **Wildrose.** This canyon has 39 tent or RV sites, none shaded, and stoves or fireplaces, tables, and pit toilets. No water is available in winter. ⊠ *Off Wildrose Rd., adjacent to Wildrose Ranger Station.* ▥ *Free.* ☉ *Year-round.*

En Route Visible from Highway 190 heading east past Stovepipe Wells are **sand dunes** that cover a 14-square-mile field. The sand that forms the hills is actually minute pieces of quartz and other rock.

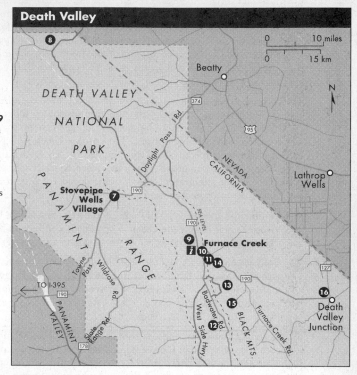

Death Valley

Scotty's Castle

8 *44 mi north of Stovepipe Wells Village; head east on Hwy. 190, then north at signs for castle.*

Scotty's Castle is an odd apparition rising out of a canyon. This $2.5 million Moorish mansion, begun in 1924 and never completed, takes its name from Walter Scott, better known as Death Valley Scotty. An ex-cowboy, prospector, and performer in Buffalo Bill's Wild West Show, Scotty always told people the castle was his, financed by gold from a secret mine. That secret mine was, in fact, a Chicago millionaire named Albert Johnson, who was advised by doctors to spend time in a warm, dry climate. The house contains works of art, imported carpets, handmade European furniture, and a tremendous pipe organ. Costumed rangers portray life at the castle in 1939. Tours are conducted frequently, but waits of up to two hours are possible. ☎ *619/786–2392.* ☒ *$8.* ⊙ *Daily 8–7; tours 9–5.*

Camping
⚠ **Mesquite Springs.** There are 60 tent or RV spaces here, some shaded, with stoves or fireplaces, tables, flush toilets, and water. ☒ *2 mi south of Scotty's Castle.* ☒ *$10.* ⊙ *Year-round.*

Furnace Creek Area

54 mi south of Scotty's Castle, 25 mi southeast of Stovepipe Wells Village on Hwy. 190.

9 The renowned mule teams hauled borax from the **Harmony Borax Works** to the railroad town of Mojave. Those teams were a sight to behold: 20 mules hitched up to a single massive wagon, carrying a load of 10 tons of borax through burning desert to a town 165 miles away. The teams plied the route between 1884 and 1907, when the railroad finally arrived in Zabriskie. The Borax Museum, 2 miles farther south, houses original mining machinery and historical displays in a building that used to serve as a boardinghouse for miners; the adjacent structure is the original mule-team barn. ⊠ *Harmony Borax Works Rd., west off Hwy. 190.*

⑩ **Furnace Creek** is a bustling center of activity amid the sprawling quiet of Death Valley. Covered with tropical landscaping, it has jogging and bicycle paths, golf, tennis, horseback riding, a general store, and, rare for these parts, dining options. The Furnace Creek Ranch (☞ *below*) operates most of the above, plus guided carriage rides and hay rides for guests and nonguests. The rides traverse trails with views of the surrounding mountains, where multicolored volcanic rock and alluvial fans form a background for date-palm trees and other vegetation.

Exhibits on the desert, trail maps, and brochures can be found at the **Visitor Center at Furnace Creek.** The rangers conduct guided walks of the area. ⊠ *Hwy. 190,* ☎ *619/786–2331.* ☉ *Daily 8–7.*

⑪ **Golden Canyon** is named for the glowing color of its walls. A mild hike into this spacious landform affords some spectacular views of yellow and orange rock. Farther up the canyon, you'll encounter a colorful formation called Red Cathedral. ⊠ *Badwater Rd., 3 mi south from Furnace Creek; turn left into parking lot.*

⑫ Reaching **Badwater,** one sees a shallow pool, containing mostly sodium chloride, saltier than the sea, lying lifeless against an expanse of desolate salt flats—a sharp contrast to the expansive canyons and elevation not too far away. Here's the legend: one of the early surveyors saw that his mule wouldn't drink from the pool and noted "badwater" on his map. Badwater is one of the lowest spots in North America—280 feet below sea level—and also one of the hottest. ⊠ *Badwater Rd., 19 mi south of Visitor Center at Furnace Creek.*

★ ⑬ The **Artists Palette** is one of the most magnificent sights in Death Valley. Artists Drive, the approach to the area, is one-way heading north off Badwater Road, so if you're visiting Badwater it's more efficient to come here on the way back. The drive winds through foothills composed of colorful sedimentary and volcanic rocks. ⊠ *8 mi north of Badwater, Badwater Rd. to Artists Dr.; 10 mi south of Furnace Creek, Hwy. 190 to Badwater Rd. to Artists Dr.*

⑭ **Zabriskie Point** is one of Death Valley National Park's most scenic spots. Not particularly high—only about 710 feet—it overlooks a striking badlands panorama with wrinkled, multicolored hills. Film buffs of a certain vintage may recognize it—or at least its name—from the film *Zabriskie Point* by the Italian director Michelangelo Antonioni. ⊠ *Hwy. 190, 5 mi south of Furnace Creek.*

OFF THE BEATEN PATH
TWENTY MULE TEAM CANYON – The thrills in this colorful canyon are more than just natural. At times on the loop road off Highway 190, the soft rock walls reach high on both sides, making it seem like you're on an amusement-park ride. Remains of prospectors tunnels are visible here, along with some brilliant rock formations. ⊠ *Twenty Mule Team Rd., off Hwy. 190, 1½ mi south of Zabriskie Point. Trailers not permitted.*

★ ⑮ **Dante's View** is more than 5,000 feet up in the Black Mountains. In the dry desert air, you can see most of the 110 miles the valley stretches across. The oasis of Furnace Creek is a green spot to the north. The view up and down is equally astounding: the tiny blackish patch far below is Badwater, the lowest point in the country, at 280 feet below sea level; on the western horizon is Mt. Whitney, the highest spot in the continental United States, at 14,494 feet. Those in great shape may want to try the 14-mile hike up to Telescope Peak. The view, not surprisingly, is breathtaking—as is the 3,000-foot elevation gain of the hike. ⊠ *Dante's View Rd. off Hwy. 190, 21 mi south of Zabriskie Point.*

Dining and Lodging

$$$ ✕ **Inn Dining Room.** Adobe walls, lace tablecloths, two fireplaces, and many windows with views of the Panamint Mountains make for a visual and culinary mirage at this Furnace Creek Inn restaurant. Its six-course, fixed-price menu shows a Continental influence: escargots and breast of duck are among the usual appetizers. Seasonally changing main courses might include gulf shrimp in a shallot and garlic beurre blanc or charbroiled French-cut lamb chops with minted pear; a few vegetarian entrées are usually available as well. The wine list is extensive. ⊠ *Furnace Creek Inn Resort, Hwy. 190,* ☎ *619/786–2345, ext. 120. Jacket required. AE, D, MC, V. Closed mid-May–mid-Oct.*

$$$$ ▦ **Furnace Creek Inn.** This historic, rambling stone structure tumbling down the side of a hill is something of a desert oasis; the creek meanders through its beautifully landscaped gardens. The pool here is spring-fed. All the rooms have views; just fewer than half have balconies. One of the inn's restaurants serves Italian cuisine and has live music and dancing except Monday nights. Continental dishes are prepared at the other. ⊠ *Hwy. 190, Box 1, Death Valley National Park 92328,* ☎ *619/786–2361,* ℻ *619/786–2514. 2 restaurants, bar, pool, 2 tennis courts, meeting rooms. AE, DC, MC, V. Closed mid-May–mid-Oct.*

$–$$ ▦ **Furnace Creek Ranch.** This was originally crew headquarters for a borax company, the activities of which the on-site Borax Museum details. Four two-story buildings adjacent to the golf course have motel-type rooms that are good for families. The general store on the ranch sells supplies and gifts. ⊠ *Hwy. 190, Box 1, Death Valley National Park 92328,* ☎ *619/786–2345,* ℻ *619/786–2514. 224 rooms. Restaurant, bar, coffee shop, pool, 18-hole golf course, 4 tennis courts, horseback riding, meeting rooms. AE, DC, MC, V.*

⚕ **Furnace Creek.** This campground has 135 RV and tent sites (some shaded), tables, fireplaces, flush and pit toilets, water, and a dump station. Pay showers, a laundry, and a swimming pool are available at Furnace Creek Ranch (☞ *above*). ⊠ *Adjacent to Visitor Center at Furnace Creek,* ☎ *800/365–2267 (Destinet).* ▤ *$16.* ☉ *Year-round.*

Death Valley Junction

30 mi south of Furnace Creek, 25 mi south of Zabriskie Point on Hwy. 190.

⑯ **Marta Becket's Amargosa Opera House** is an unexpected pleasure in an unlikely place. Marta Becket is an artist and dancer from New York who first saw the town of Amargosa while on tour in 1964. Three years later she came back, had a flat tire in the same place, and on impulse decided to buy a boarded-up theater amid a complex of run-down Spanish colonial buildings. Today, the population is still in single digits (cats outnumber people here), but it swells when cars, motor homes, and buses roll in to catch the show she has been presenting for more than two dozen years. To compensate for the sparse crowds her show attracted in the early days, Becket painted herself an audience, turning the walls and ceiling of the theater into a trompe l'oeil masterpiece. Now she often performs her blend of classical ballet, mime, and 19th-century melodrama to sell-out crowds. After the show, you can meet her in the adjacent art gallery, where she sells her paintings and autographs her posters and books. ✉ *Hwy. 127,* ☎ *619/852–4441,* FAX *619/852–4138. Call ahead for reservations.* ✏ *$8. Performances Nov., Feb., Mar., and Apr., Sat. and Mon. 8:15 PM; Oct., Dec., Jan., and May (through Mother's Day weekend) Sat. only.*

THE EASTERN MOJAVE
Mojave National Preserve to Victorville

The Eastern Mojave is a sharp contrast to Death Valley, with welcome sights of vegetation and somewhat cooler temperatures. Much of this land is untended, so precautions are necessary when driving the many back roads, where towns and services are often few and far between. In many cases, cellular phones are beyond their operating range.

Numbers in the margin correspond to points of interest on the Mojave Desert map.

Baker

⑰ *84 mi south of Death Valley Junction on Hwy. 127.*

Baker, population 500, lies between the East and West Mojave areas and Death Valley National Park. You can't miss the city's 134-foot thermometer, the height of which commemorates the U.S. temperature record, which was set in Death Valley on July 10, 1913. The thermometer is also a landmark for the National Park Service's **Mojave Desert Information Center** (☎ 619/733–4040). For a "hub," Baker offers only minimal provisions. There are a few lackluster grocery stores, some fast food, and several gas stations.

Dining and Lodging

$ ✕▣ **Bun Boy Motel and Restaurant.** The no-frills Bun Boy is conveniently located at the intersection of two highways. It's small but pleasant. The large diner adjacent to the motel, one of Baker's few dining options, serves surprisingly tasty American food. ✉ *I–15 at State Rd. 177, Box 130, Baker 92309,* ☎ *619/733–4363. 20 rooms. Restaurant. AE, D, DC, MC, V.*

Mojave National Preserve

Kelbaker Rd., south from Baker.

⑱ Although a broad range of terrain qualifies, nothing says "desert" quite like graceful, wind-blown sand dunes. And the white-sand **Kelso Dunes** are perfect, pristine desert dunes. They cover 70 square miles, often at heights of 500–600 feet, and can be reached in an easy half-mile walk from where you leave your car. When you reach the top of one of the dunes, kick a little bit of sand down the lee side and find out why they say the sand "sings." In the town of Kelso, a Mission Revival depot dating from 1925 is one of the very few of its kind still standing. ✉ *Kelbaker Rd., 42 mi south of Baker (7 mi past town of Kelso).*

⑲ At an elevation of 4,300 feet, the visitor center at the **Providence Mountains State Recreation Area** has spectacular views of mountain peaks, dunes, buttes, rocky crags, and desert valleys. At the nearby **Mitchell Caverns Natural Preserve** is the rare opportunity to see all three types of cave formations—dripstone, flowstone, and erratics—in one place. The year-round 65°F temperature is also a nice break from the heat. ✉ *Essex Rd., 16 mi north of I–40,* ☎ *805/942–0662.* ✏ *$4.* ☺

Guided tours of caves conducted Sept.–June, weekdays 1:30, weekends and holidays 1:30 and 3; July and Aug., weekends only. Tours gather at visitor center.

Afton Canyon

⓴ *27 mi southwest of Baker, I–15 to Afton Canyon Rd.*

Because of its colorful, steep walls, Afton Canyon is often called the Grand Canyon of the Mojave. Afton was carved out over many thousands of years by the rushing waters of the Mojave River, which makes another of its rare aboveground appearances here. And where you find water in the desert, you'll find trees, grasses, and wildlife. The canyon has been popular for a long time; Indians and later white settlers following the Mojave Trail from the Colorado River to the Pacific coast often set up camp here, near the welcome presence of water. ⊠ *Take the Afton turnoff and follow dirt road about 3 mi southwest.*

Camping

🏕 **Afton Canyon Campground.** The 22 sites here are 1,408 feet up in a wildlife area where the Mojave River surfaces. The area is surrounded by high-desert scenic cliffs and a mesquite thicket. ⊠ *Afton Canyon Rd. off I–15.* 🎫 *$4.* ☉ *Year-round.*

Barstow Area

㉑ *63 mi southwest of Baker on I–15.*

Barstow was established in 1886 when a subsidiary of the Atchison, Topeka, and Santa Fe Railroad began construction of a depot and hotel at this junction of its tracks and the 35th-parallel transcontinental lines. Midway between Las Vegas and Los Angeles, Barstow is home to a wide variety of hotel and restaurant chains and factory outlets. The **Desert Information Center** (⊠ 831 Barstow Rd., ☎ 619/255–8760) has exhibits about desert ecology, wildflowers, wildlife, and other features of the desert environment. Radio information for travelers is provided at 1610 AM.

㉒ **Rainbow Basin National Natural Landmark** looks as if it could be on Mars, perhaps because so many sci-fi movies depicting the red planet have been filmed here. There is a tremendous sense of upheaval; huge slabs of red, orange, white, and green stone tilt at crazy angles like ships about to capsize. At points along the spectacularly scenic 6-mile drive, it is easy to imagine you are alone in the world, hidden among the colorful badlands that give the basin its name. Hike the many washes and you are likely to see the fossilized remains of creatures that roamed the basin 12 million to 16 million years ago: mastodons, large and small camels, rhinos, dog-bears, birds, and insects. Leave any fossils you find where they are—they are protected by federal law. ⊠ *8 mi north of Barstow; take Fort Irwin Rd. 5 mi north to Fossil Bed Rd., a graded dirt road, and head west 3 mi. Call the Desert Information Center in Barstow (☎ 619/255–8760) for more information.*

㉓ **Calico Ghost Town** became a wild—and rich—mining town after a rich deposit of silver was found around 1881. In 1886, after more than $85 million worth of silver, gold, and other precious metals were harvested from the multicolored "calico" hills, the price of silver fell and the town slipped into decline. Frank "Borax" Smith helped revive the town in 1889 when he started mining the unglamorous but profitable mineral borax, but that boom busted by the turn of the century. The effort to restore the ghost town was started by Walter Knott of Knott's Berry Farm fame in 1960. Knott handed the land over to San Bernardino

County in 1966, and it became a regional park. Today, the 1880s come back to life as you stroll the wooden sidewalks of Main Street, browse through several western shops, roam the tunnels of Maggie's Mine, and take a ride on the Calico–Odessa Railroad. Special festivals in March, May, October, and November add to Calico's Old West flavor. ⊠ *Ghost Town Rd., 3 mi north of I–15,* ☎ *619/254–2122.* 🖅 *$5.* ⊙ *Daily 9–5.*

★ ㉔ If you're at all curious about life 200,000 years ago, the **Calico Early Man Archaeological Site** is a must-see. Nearly 12,000 tools—scrapers, cutting tools, choppers, hand picks, stone saws, and the like—have been excavated from the site since 1964. Prior to finding the site, many archaeologists believed the first humans came to North America "only" 10,000 to 20,000 years ago. Dr. Louis Leakey, the noted archaeologist, was so impressed with the findings that he became the Calico Project director from 1963 to his death in 1972; his old camp is now a visitor center and museum. The Calico excavations provide an opportunity to see artifacts, buried in the walls and floors of the excavated pits, fashioned by the earliest known Americans. The only way in is by guided tour, and visitors are required to wear hard hats. ⊠ *15 mi northeast of Barstow, I–15 to Minneola Rd. north for 3 mi,* ☎ *619/256–8313.* ⊙ *Guided tours of the dig Wed. 1:30 and 3:30, Thurs.–Sun. 9:30, 11:30, 1:30, and 3:30.*

Dining and Lodging

$ ✕ **Carlos & Toto's.** If your palate has tired of chain restaurants and food from your cooler, you will thoroughly enjoy this touch of Mexico. Locally famous for its fajitas, the restaurant is open seven days a week and has a Sunday buffet brunch from 9:30 AM to 2 PM. ⊠ *901 W. Main St.,* ☎ *619/256–7413, AE, D, MC, V.*

$ 🏨 **Holiday Inn.** This large facility has king- and queen-size suites in addition to comfortable standard-size rooms. It's convenient to restaurants and shops, sights, and the Desert Information Center. ⊠ *1511 E. Main St., Barstow,* ☎ *619/256–5673,* 🆁🆇 *619/256–5917. 245 rooms. Restaurant, pool, hot tub, laundry service, meeting rooms. AE, D, MC, V.*

⚠ **Calico Ghost Town Regional Park.** There are 250 sites here, plus cabin and bunkhouse accommodations. ⊠ *Ghost Town Rd., 3 mi north of I–15, east from Barstow,* ☎ *619/254–2122 or 800/862–2442 for reservations.* 🖅 *$15 per night for tent camping, $19 for full RV hook-ups; 2-night minimum (includes Ghost Town admission).* ⊙ *Year-round.*

Victorville

㉕ *34 mi southwest of Barstow on I–15.*

At the southwest corner of the Mojave is the quiet and sprawling town of **Victorville,** home of the Roy Rogers–Dale Evans Museum (☞ *below*).

Mojave Narrows Regional Park makes use of one of the few spots where the Mojave River flows aboveground. The park has 87 camping units, hot showers, secluded picnic areas, and two lakes, surrounded by cottonwoods and cattails, where there is fishing, rowboat rentals, a bait shop, equestrian paths, and a trail for visitors with disabilities. ⊠ *Mojave Narrows Regional Park, 18000 Yates Rd.,* ☎ *619/245–2226.* 🖅 *$4 per vehicle weekdays, $5 weekends; dry camping $10 a night, camping with utilities $15 a night.* ⊙ *Wed.–Mon. 7:30–sunset.*

The **Roy Rogers–Dale Evans Museum** exhibits the personal and professional memorabilia of the famous stars, along with NRA testimonials and safari trophies—stuffed exotic cats and other animals "taken" by Roy and sometimes Dale. Even Trigger and Bullet have been preserved, though they apparently died of natural causes. ⊠ *15650 Seneca Rd. (take Roy Rogers Dr. exit off I–15),* ☎ *619/243–4547.* ⌨ *$5.* ☯ *Daily 9–5; closed Thanksgiving, Dec. 25.*

Dining and Lodging

$$ ✕ **Crown N Sword.** Old English prime ribs of beef are a mainstay at this hotel restaurant. Luncheons include a buffet every day but Saturday. ⊠ *Green Tree Inn, 14173 Green Tree Blvd.,* ☎ *619/245–3461. AE, D, DC, MC, V.*

$ ⊞ **Best Western Green Tree Inn.** This member of the chain and its welcome, shaded lawn sit right off I–15, a few blocks from the Roy Rogers–Dale Evans Museum. Many of the rooms are suite-size and have refrigerators and microwaves, making the inn a good choice for families. The decor is no-nonsense but clean. ⊠ *14173 Green Tree Blvd., 92392,* ☎ *619/245–3461 or 800/528–1234. 168 rooms. Restaurant, coffee shop, bar, pool, hot tub, shuffleboard, meeting rooms. AE, D, DC, MC, V.*

⚟ **Mojave Narrows Regional Park.** (☞ *above*).

THE MOJAVE DESERT AND DEATH VALLEY A TO Z

Getting Around

By Car

The Mojave is shaped like a giant *L*, with one leg north and the other east. To travel north through the Mojave, take I–10 east out of Los Angeles to I–15 north. Just through Cajon Pass, pick up U.S. 395, which runs north through Victor Valley, Boron, the Rand Mining District, and China Lake. To travel east, continue on I–15 to Barstow. From Barstow there are two routes: I–40, which passes through the mountainous areas of San Bernardino County, whisks by the Providence mountains, and enters Arizona at Needles; or the more northerly I–15, which passes south of Calico, near Devil's Playground and the Kelso Sand Dunes, and then veers northeast toward Las Vegas.

Some travelers may wish to avoid Cajon Pass, elevation 4,250 feet. To do this, take I–210 north of Los Angeles to Highway 14 north. Head east 67 miles on Highway 58 to the town of Barstow and pick up I–15 there. Continue east on I–15 to Highway 127, a very scenic route north through the Mojave to Death Valley.

Death Valley can be entered from the southeast or the west. From the southeast, take Highway 127 north from I–15 and then link up with either Highway 178, which travels west into the valley and then cuts north toward Badwater before meeting up with Highway 190 at Furnace Creek. To enter from the west, exit U.S. 395 at either Highway 190 or 178.

Much of the desert can be seen from the comfort of an air-conditioned car. Don't despair if you are without air-conditioning—just avoid the middle of the day and the middle of the summer, good advice for all desert travel. Believe everything you've ever heard about desert heat; it can be brutal. But during mornings and evenings, particularly in the spring and fall, the temperature ranges from cool and crisp to pleasantly warm and dry: perfect for hiking and driving.

Camping

The Mojave Desert and Death Valley have about two dozen campgrounds in a variety of desert settings. For further information the following booklets are useful (*see* Visitor Information, *below,* for addresses and phone numbers): *High Desert Recreation Resource Guide,* from the Mojave Chamber of Commerce; *San Bernardino County Regional Parks,* from the Regional Parks Department; and *California Desert Camping,* from the Bureau of Land Management.

Telephone Service

Beginning March 22, 1997, the area code for the regions covered in this chapter will change from 619 to 760. Calls to the new code will continue to go through using either code until September. 27, 1997, after which time callers will be instructed to use the 760 code.

Contacts and Resources

Emergencies
Ambulance (☎ 911). **Police** (☎ 911).

BLM Rangers (☎ 619/255–8700). **Community Hospital** (Barstow, ☎ 619/256–1761). **San Bernardino County Sheriff** (☎ 619/256–1796 for Barstow, ☎ 619/733–4448 for Baker).

Guided Tours
Audubon Society (✉ Western Regional Office, 555 Audubon Pl., Sacramento 95825, ☎ 916/481–5332). **California Native Plant Society** (✉ 1722 J St., No. 17, Sacramento 95814, ☎ 916/447–2677). **Furnace Creek Inn** (☎ 619/786–2345, ext. 222). **Nature Conservancy** (✉ 201 Mission St., 4th floor, San Francisco 94105, ☎ 415/777–0487). **Sierra Club** (✉ 730 Polk St., San Francisco 94109, ☎ 415/776–2211).

Visitor Information
Bureau of Land Management (✉ California Desert District Office, 6221 Box Springs Blvd., Riverside 92507, ☎ 714/697–5200). **Baker Chamber of Commerce** (✉ Box 131, Baker 92309, ☎ 619/733–4469). **Barstow Area Chamber of Commerce** (✉ 222 E. Main St., Suite 216, Barstow 92311, ☎ 619/256–8617). **California Desert Information Center** (✉ 831 Barstow Rd., Barstow 92311, ☎ 619/255–8760). **Death Valley Chamber of Commerce** (✉ Box 157, Shoshone 92384, ☎ 619/852–4524). **Mojave Chamber of Commerce** (✉ 15836 Sierra Hwy., Mojave 93591, ☎ 805/824–2481). **National Park Service** (✉ Visitor Center at Furnace Creek, 92328, ☎ 619/786–2331). **Ridgecrest Area Convention and Visitors Bureau** (✉ 100 W. California Ave., Ridgecrest 93555, ☎ 619/375–8202). **San Bernardino County Regional Parks Department** (✉ 825 E. 3rd St., San Bernardino 92415, ☎ 909/387–2594).

16 Portraits of California

BOHEMIA BY THE BAY

I **LIVE ON RUSSIAN HILL,** which seeps downward into Chinatown, the Barbary Coast, the International Settlement, and the traditional Italian-fisherman settlement of North Beach. Vines cling to the wall opposite my house, there's a fig tree bearing inedible, fog-stunted figs, but the dappled sun and green make it resemble a wall and fig trees I remember in Fiesole. Sometimes the street outside smells like the harbor of Port-au-Prince—the drains have been clogged during my 35 years here—but most often the sweet sea fog and currents of wind keep the air crisply laundered.

A few days after I arrived to settle forever, at least temporarily, taking my dinner one night at the "lonely table" of the New Pisa Restaurant—seven courses plus wine, $1.75—I was startled at the end of my meal, apple with a slice of Monterey jack, coffee poured into the wine glass, when an entire Japanese opera troupe arose to do honor to the cook. In 1960 we still imported courtesy, not Hondas, from Japan. They sang, in Japanese, every verse of "Oh! Susanna."

I realized I had fumbled my way into a very important corner of the universe.

I was not the first to make this discovery. San Francisco's street ambling, its site as a hilly port, its speculative fervor, its early prosperity, its newness and oldness, have always given it unique advantages. This city has studied hard how to entertain itself and others. Mark Twain came for the gold rush; Ambrose Bierce, Joaquin Miller, Bret Harte, Isadora Duncan, and the Emperor Norton were famous beatniks and hippies before the words. The Emperor Norton wore flowers, dressed like a burning bush, printed his own currency; now street poets hawk their wares in North Beach and at the Café Macondo in the Mission—still living off the yearning for distraction a Mediterranean, forever-springtime climate helps to nurture.

Naughtiness has always had a central position in San Francisco, in keeping with the city's tradition of taking its frivolity seriously. The Barbary Coast and the International Settlement, archaeological remnants of which can still be found in the bidets and outdoor erotic murals not yet extirpated on the Jackson Square area, specialized in drink, sex, and the genial spending of money. This was a port, after all.

Besides the ever-popular sex adventurers, chafing at the limits, there are San Francisco's Bohemian stockbrokers, lawyers, physicians (Dr. Flash Gordon, the motorcycle specialist, for example), even real estate speculators. A Zen Center musician from Green Gulch Farm leaned on my shoulder, crossing Upper Grant, muttering, "The punk monk is drunk." Part-time, many try for Bohemianism, and the nice thing is, all can succeed. Why not? The rules are generous in San Francisco, unlike the rules for major-league baseball, where you have to be tall.

In the shadow of AIDS, the ever-popular earthquake threat, and our general mortality, San Francisco treasures the moment. That's a tendency of all port cities (we may set sail tomorrow). On a walk a few days ago I saw Jesus Christ Satan with his cape and his frisky small animals, striding down Polk Street as if he had someplace to go in order to carry out a curse, perform an exorcism, or consult his veterinarian. The Sisters of Perpetual Indulgence, an order of male nuns, were gathered for an action meeting at the California Culinary Academy (a sort of barber college for future chefs). Warren Hinckle, the eye-patched saloon journalist and career scamp, was arguing that his beloved basset hound should be allowed to dine with him at Moose's on Washington Square because it's a seeing-eye animal, pointing out dangerous martinis. (The smell of the hound was the main argument against his proposal). A compromise was reached: the lunch would last no more than three hours.

I used to bet starchy journalists sent out from the East Coast to staff the *Wall Street Journal, Time,* and *Newsweek* bureaus that they would be wearing leather jackets and boots within six weeks. I always won. It's immoral to bet, but this wasn't gambling—it was a sure thing. What smog is to Los Angeles, the loosening of armor is to San Francisco. Spirit gets to the folks.

My personal doctor is one of the world's great collectors of Alice in Wonderland books and memorabilia, delivering scholarly papers along with flu shots. In my native town of Cleveland, the Paris of Northeastern Ohio, there were terrific medical practitioners, but very few Alice in Wonderland specialists.

The beatnik, hippie, anarchist, punk, gay activist, legalize-marijuana, heavy metal youthquakes all pass through San Francisco, and even when they fade away, they don't fade away. There are still members of the IWW, the Wobblies, agitating to organize guitar shops and coffee houses.

WHERE OTHER TOWNS have been malled, San Francisco has been north-beached; counterculture has become dominant. Take the Mission, which now has 35 bookstores within a 120-minute walk of its minicapitol at Valencia and 16th; Russian Hill, where art students from the San Francisco Institute of Art, the oldest school of the fine arts west of Hoboken (with some of the oldest permanent floating art students, too), mingle with raffish biotech millionaires and writers who have managed the long trek up the slope from North Beach; Potrero Hill, where Farley's plays host to filmmakers, Mime Troupe revolutionaries, and folks who just like to take their lattes in the company of such characters while they do their laundry.

This city makes it easy for Bohemians to set down their lightly packaged roots. When I found San Francisco, I found home. I found Left Bank Paris and Greenwich Village in a permanent laboratory condition, wrapped in a convoluted time warp of past and future within the instant present tense of California. Oddly enough for a committed wanderer in this land of loose nuts, I have dwelled in the same flat on Russian Hill 35 years now. The more things change, the more they become different. But this is *communitas*. These sticky things are roots.

Bohemian culture has elaborated an urgent hundred-year-long operetta for the entertainment of San Francisco and the world. While this corner of America seemed at first to have the same connection with real life that *The Mikado* has with Japan, I gradually came to realize that "North Beach," "Bohemian," "beatnik," "hippie," "New Wave," are not substitutes for real life but metaphors of reality. San Francisco is not *really* an operetta: three of my children were conceived here; there are schools, strikes, and churches; people get rich and go bankrupt; my beard turns gray, and the wrinkles of my face grow more wrinkly. I see a neighbor who used to ride a bicycle now hobbling with an aluminum walker. The crowded hills and flatlands are not inhabited by stand-ins and chorus; those are genuine Italians, Chinese, Australians, castaways, alcoholics and non-alcoholics (some of the latter, like me, the worst kind), dropouts from the Midwest, remittance persons from Texas and New York and Boston, Californicaters—all the men and women in funny clothes who give flesh to the metaphor—plus genuine residential neighborhoods, shops, and houses and flats, filled with people who pass the time by working and looking out for themselves as sensibly as possible. Bohemian America is Middle America turned peculiar. But here, even the Middle Americans seem to have curlicues at their edges. Thanks to the audience climbing onto the scenery, thanks to the players climbing back into the audience, San Francisco remains a stage for ongoing rehearsal of that urgent Bohemian operetta. They are not just singing arias, opening their mouths like the birds and letting it peep out; they are doing the work of the world.

Thank you, creators of sourdough bread, Monterey jack cheese, red wine, and getting there on foot.

Thank you, whichever unknown geniuses deep in human history invented the soulful metaphor and goofing around. San Francisco almost makes you think that it could have been the same person.

— Herbert Gold

LIVING WITH THE CERTAINTY OF A SHAKY FUTURE

THERE'S NEVER BEEN any question whether or not there will be another earthquake in San Francisco. The question is how soon. Even the kids here grow up understanding that it's just a matter of time, and from grade school on, earthquake safety drills become routine. At the first rumble, duck under your desk or table or stand in a doorway, they are instructed. Get away from windows to avoid broken glass. When the shaking stops, walk—don't run—outdoors, as far away from buildings as possible.

Sure as there are hurricanes along the Gulf of Mexico and blizzards in Maine, San Francisco's earthquakes are inevitable. Nobody here is surprised when the rolling and tumbling begins—it happens all the time. Just in the six months following the jarring 1989 earthquake, for instance, seismologists reported hundreds of aftershocks, ranging from the scarcely perceptible to those strong enough to bring down buildings weakened by October's jolt.

The Bay Area itself was created in upheaval such as this. Eons ago, a restless geology of shifting plates deep in the earth gave birth to the Sierra Mountains and the Pacific Coast Range. Every spring when the snows melted, the runoff rushed down from the mile-high Sierra peaks westward across what would eventually be known as California. Here, the runoff ran up against the coastal range, and a vast inland lake was formed.

The rampaging waters from the yearly thaw eventually crashed through the quake-shattered Coast Range to meet the Pacific Ocean, creating the gap now spanned by the Golden Gate Bridge. This breakthrough created San Francisco Bay, one of the world's great natural harbors, its fertile delta larger than that of the Mississippi River. What a fabulous setting for the city-to-be—surrounded on three sides by water, set off by dramatic mountainscapes to the north and south, and blessed by cool ocean breezes.

All this and gold, too. The twisting and rolling of so-called terra firma exposed rich veins of gold at and near ground level that otherwise would have remained hidden deep underground. The great upheaval pushed the Mother Lode to the surface and set the scene for the gold rush. But before the '49 miners came the Europeans. In the late 15th century, the Spanish writer Garci Ordonez de Montalvo penned a fictional description of a place he called California, a faraway land ruled by Queen Califia, where gold and precious stones were so plentiful the streets were lined with them. Montalvo's vision of wealth without limit helped fuel the voyages of the great 15th- and 16th-century European explorers in the new world. They never did hit pay dirt here, but the name California stuck nevertheless.

Northern California was eventually settled, and in 1848, the population of San Francisco was 832. The discovery of gold in the California hills brought sudden and unprecedented wealth to this coastal trading outpost and her population exploded; by the turn of the century San Francisco was home to 343,000 people.

En route to its destiny as a premier city of the West, San Francisco was visited by innumerable quakes. Yet while the city's very foundations shook, residents found that each new rattler helped to strengthen San Francisco's self-image of adaptability. Robert Louis Stevenson wrote of the quakes' alarming frequency: "The fear of them grows yearly in a resident; he begins with indifference and ends in sheer panic." The big shaker of 1865 inspired humorist Mark Twain to look at the quakes in a different light by writing an earthquake "almanac" for the following year, which advised:

Oct. 23—Mild, balmy earthquakes.
Oct. 26—About this time expect more earthquakes; but do not look for them . . .
Oct. 27—Universal despondency, indicative of approaching disaster. Abstain from smiling or indulgence in humorous conversation . . .
Oct. 29—Beware!
Oct. 31—Go slow!
Nov. 1—Terrific earthquake. This is the great earthquake month. More stars fall

and more worlds are slathered around carelessly and destroyed in November than in any month of the twelve.
Nov. 2—Spasmodic but exhilarating earthquakes, accompanied by occasional showers of rain and churches and things.
Nov. 3—Make your will.
Nov. 4—Sell out.

ON THE WHOLE, those who settled in San Francisco were more inclined toward Twain's devil-may-care attitude—those who succumbed to Stevenson's panic didn't stick around for long. Certainly the multitude of vices that saturated the metropolis were sufficient to distract many men from their fears; throughout Chinatown and the infamous Barbary Coast, opium dens, gin mills, and bordellos operated day and night.

Money flowed. Money tempted. Money corrupted. The city was built on graft, and city hall became synonymous with corruption under the influence of political crooks like Blind Chris Buckley and Boss Ruef. The very building itself was a scandal. Planned for completion in six months at a cost of half a million dollars, the city hall ultimately took 29 years to build at a graft-inflated cost of $8 million, an astronomical sum at the dawning of the 20th century. When the San Andreas Fault set loose the 1906 earthquake, the most devastating ever to hit an American city, city hall was one of the first buildings to come crashing down. Its ruins exposed the shoddiest of building materials, an ironic symbol of the city's crime-ridden past.

The 1906 earthquake and fire has come to define San Francisco both for itself and the outside world. In the immediate aftermath of the catastrophe, San Franciscans wondered whether they ought to believe the preachers and reformers who declared that this terrible devastation had been wrought upon their wicked city by the avenging hand of God. San Franciscans asked themselves whether, somehow, they had earned it.

But the city was quick to prove its character. Fifty years earlier, six separate fires had destroyed most of San Francisco—yet each time it was rebuilt by a citizenry not ready to give up on either the gold or the city that gold had built. Now, in 1906, heroic

firefighters dynamited one of the city's main thoroughfares to prevent the inferno from spreading all the way to the Pacific. The mood of San Franciscans was almost eerily calm, their neighborliness both heartwarming and jaunty. "Eat, drink, and be merry," proclaimed signs about town, "for tomorrow we may have to go to Oakland." No sooner had the flames died than rebuilding began—true to San Francisco tradition. Forty thousand construction workers poured into town to assist the proud, amazingly resilient residents.

The 1906 earthquake provided a chance to rethink the hodgepodge, get-rich-quick cityscape that had risen in the heat of gold-rush frenzy. City fathers imported the revered urban planner Daniel Burnham, architect of the magnificent 1893 Chicago World's Fair, to reinvent San Francisco. "Make no little plans," Burnham intoned. "They have no power to stir men's souls."

The city's new Civic Center, built under Burnham's direction, was raised to celebrate the city's comeback and is regarded as one of America's most stately works of civic architecture. Its city hall stands as a monument to the city's will to prevail—from its colonnaded granite exterior to its exuberant interior, once described by Tom Wolfe as resembling "some Central American opera house. Marble arches, domes, acanthus leaves . . . quirks and galleries and gilt filigrees . . . a veritable angels' choir of gold." The inscription found over the mayor's office seems to sum it all up: "San Francisco, O glorious city of our hearts that has been tried and not found wanting, go thou with like spirit to make the future thine."

In 1915 San Francisco dazzled the world with its Panama–Pacific International Exposition, designed to prove not only that it was back, but that it was back bigger and better and badder than ever before. An architectural wonderland, the Expo was built on 70 acres of marshy landfill, which later became the residential neighborhood called the Marina District. When the October 1989 earthquake struck, this neighborhood was badly damaged, and became a focus as the entire nation tuned in to see how San Francisco and her people would fare this time around.

Like the gold that surfaced in the Mother Lode, the 1989 quake once again brought out the best in this region's people. Out at Candlestick Park, 62,000 fans were waiting for the start of the World Series between the San Francisco Giants and the Oakland A's when everything started shaking. They cut loose with a big cheer after the temblor subsided. One San Francisco fan quickly hand-lettered a sign and held it aloft: "That was Nothing—Wait Til the Giants Bat." When it became apparent that there would be no ball played that night, the fans departed from the ballpark, just like in a grade school earthquake safety drill, quietly and in good order.

This was what millions of TV viewers across the nation first saw of the local response to this major (7.1) earthquake and, by and large, the combination of good humor and relative calm they observed was an accurate reflection of the prevailing mood around the city. San Franciscans were not about to panic. Minutes after the quake struck, a San Francisco couple spread a lace tablecloth over the hood of their BMW and, sitting in the driveway of their splintered home, toasted passersby with champagne. Simultaneously, across San Francisco Bay, courageous volunteers and rescue workers set to work digging through the pancaked rubble of an Oakland freeway in the search for survivors, heedless that they, too, could easily be crushed in an aftershock. Throughout the Bay Area, hundreds volunteered to fight the fires, clear away the mess, assist survivors, and donate food, money, and clothing.

San Francisco's city seal features the image of a phoenix rising from the flames of catastrophe, celebrating the city's fiery past and promising courage in the face of certain future calamity. The 1989 shake possessed only about one-fortieth the force of the legendary 1906 quake, and all projections point to the inevitability of another Big One, someday, on at least the scale of '06. Often people from other, more stable, parts of the world have trouble understanding how it is possible to live with such a certainty.

The *San Francisco Bay Guardian,* shortly after the 1989 quake, spoke for many Bay Area residents: "We live in earthquake country. Everybody knows that. It's a choice we've all made, a risk we're all more or less willing to accept as part of our lives. We're gambling against fate, and last week our luck ran out. It was inevitable—as the infamous bumper sticker says, 'Mother Nature bats last.' "

Former San Francisco Mayor Dianne Feinstein explained it this way: "Californians seem undaunted. We will never be a match for Mother Nature. But the principal thing that seems to arise from the ash and rubble of a quake is the strong resolve to rebuild and get on with life."

— John Burks

THERE MUST BE A THERE HERE SOMEWHERE

"Hollywood is a town that has to be seen to be disbelieved."

— Walter Winchell

WHILE HOSTING a British broadcaster-friend on his first trip to Los Angeles, I reluctantly took him to the corner of Hollywood and Vine. Driving toward the renowned street-corner, I explained (again) that this part of town isn't the "real" Hollywood. But he wasn't listening. He was on a pilgrimage and too filled with the anticipation of coming upon a sacred place to hear my warning. When we reached the intersection, his reaction was written all over his face: He was, as he later said, "gobsmacked."

As we pulled up to the light, a bedraggled hooker crossed Hollywood Boulevard. Otherwise, nothing was happening. Worse, this looked like someplace where nothing noteworthy or memorable ever had, would, or could happen. The area has been called squalid, but that gives it too much credit for being interesting. All there was to see were a few small and struggling businesses, the hulk of a long-defunct department store, and a couple of unremarkable office buildings.

To rescue the moment from disaster, I went into my standard routine: I pointed out that the northeast corner is where the Brown Derby restaurant once stood. I hoped this would conjure a strong enough image of movie stars dining in a giant hat to blot out the sun-bleached desolation before our eyes. I then recounted historian Richard Alleman's theory about how this unprepossessing street-corner got so famous. Alleman, who wrote *The Movie Lover's Guide to Hollywood,* believes that, because the radio networks, which maintained studios in the vicinity during the 1930s and 1940s, began their broadcasts with the words "brought to you from the corner of Hollywood and Vine . . ." the intersection became glamorous by association—at least to radio listeners who'd never seen it.

Any first-time visitor to Tinseltown is bound for some initial disappointment because, like a matinee idol, the place looks somehow smaller in person. Between the world-famous landmarks and the stars' names embedded in the sidewalks are long stretches of tawdriness that have resisted more than a decade of cleanup and restoration and look all the worse under the vivid glare of the southern California sun. Even the best of Hollywood looks a little wan and sheepish in broad daylight, as if caught in the act of intruding upon a reality in which it does not belong.

Pressed to show my British friend the "real" Hollywood, I took him on a tour of the more outstanding architecture along Hollywood Boulevard. He was duly captivated by the lunatic exuberance of Hollywood's art deco movie palaces, exemplified in the zigzaggy Moderne contours of the Pantages, and by the flamboyant absurdity of such thematically designed theaters as Mann's Chinese, the Egyptian, the baroque El Capitan, and other architectural treasures in and around Hollywood that have nothing directly to do with movies yet are spiritual cousins. Among these are the Tail O' the Pup hotdog stand; the Capitol Records building, looking— deliberately, mind you—like a stack of 45s; and an assortment of mock Mayan, Mission, Moorish, Moderne, and made-up-style structures housing video stores, fast-food franchises, and offices.

Yet despite the grand movie houses, the famous names underfoot, and the impressively zany architecture, my friend still felt he'd missed the enchantment, the excitement . . . the movies.

It's hard to fault the intrepid visitor for expecting a more dynamic, glitzier dream capital. Even seasoned locals, who understand that Hollywood is a state of mind more than a geographical location, can only just manage to intellectualize the concept, and still secretly hunger for evidence that all the magic and glamour come from an appropriately magical and glamorous place. But, except for the occasional gala premiere, you're not likely to see any movie stars in Hollywood. The workaday world of filmmaking and the off-duty hangouts of the movie crowd have largely moved elsewhere. There is only one movie studio—Paramount—still operating within Hollywood's city limits. Universal Studios, Disney, and the Warner Bros. Studios are in the San Fernando Valley, across the hills to the north, as are most network-television studios. And, although firmly rooted in the spirit of Hollywood, Disneyland is a world away in Anaheim.

Even a cursory glance at Hollywood's history raises serious doubts that the town was ever as glamorous as we insist it no longer is, and pinning down exactly when its star-studded golden era was is a slippery business. Most people point to the 1930s and 1940s, and the images evoked by those days are irresistible: tan, handsome leading men posed, grinning, with one foot on the running board of a snazzy convertible; heartbreakingly beautiful actresses clad in slinky silk gowns and mink, stepping from long black limousines into the pop of photographers' flash bulbs. Hollywood was an industry—an entire city—whose purpose was to entertain and that further dazzled us with its glittering style of life. The view from ground zero, naturally, was a bit different: long hours; the tedium of the filmmaking process; the rarity of achieving and maintaining a successful career, much less stardom; and, for those who did achieve it, the precarious tightrope walk balancing publicity and privacy. Both sides of the equation are well known and much documented. Indeed, for a place so enamored of its own appeal, Hollywood has never been shy about depicting itself in an unflattering light. Some of the most memorable films ever are rather grim portrayals of the movie business: *A Star Is Born, Sunset Boulevard,* and, most recently, *The Player.* That there is a very seamy side to the movie business is very old news and is as much a part of the legend as are fame and fortune. Scandal is a long-running subplot in Hollywood's epic history and has often proved as much a box-office draw as a liability.

THE TRICK to seeing Hollywood is knowing *how* to look at it, as well as where to look for it. The magic of movies is that reality, at least on film, can be made to look any way the filmmakers want it to look. The problem with visiting Hollywood is that your own field of vision isn't as selective as a movie camera's lens, and you're working without a script. It may be helpful to think of Hollywood the town as something of a relic, a symbol of past grandeur (both real and imagined), an open-air museum of artifacts and monuments, but hardly the whole story. Tennessee Williams said, "Ravaged radiance is even better than earnest maintenance," and, as regards Hollywood, I couldn't agree more. It helps a bit to visit in the evening, when the neon, theater marquees, and orchestrated lighting show off the extravagant buildings' shapes to advantage.

It may be that in order to fully experience Hollywood, you have to go outside it.

Only after we'd driven through the canyons, Beverly Hills, and Bel Air and were rounding the last corner of Sunset that leads to the Pacific Coast Highway and out to Malibu did my British visitor feel truly satisfied. "Yes, well," he said finally, "this is really much more like it, then," and seemed almost physically relieved to have found someplace that matched his expectations of luxurious living. And these are physically lovely places, fitting backdrops for a Hollywood lifestyle, and, in fact, where successful movie people live.

The variety of fun and fanciful buildings you'll see throughout Los Angeles reveals, I think, the essence of Hollywood. How else to explain the incongruous jumble of architectural styles sitting side by side in almost any neighborhood? A '50s futuristic house next door to a Queen Anne Victorian, a Craftsman bungalow abutting a French château, a redbrick Georgian across the street from a tile-roof Spanish revival—all on the same block—can be viewed as an extrapolation of a movie-studio back lot, on which a New York street is steps from a Parisian sidewalk café, and both are just a stone's throw from an antebellum plantation house.

If it's celebrity sightings you want, you'll have to take your chances. Many Angelenos live long, happy, and productive lives without ever personally sighting a movie star, but, for the visitor, not seeing one can be a bigger letdown than a rainy week at the beach. Here are a few things you can do to greatly improve the odds of seeing somebody famous: Book a table (weeks in advance) at Spago, Wolfgang Puck's star-studded hot spot off Sunset; dine at Musso & Frank's, Hollywood's oldest restaurant and a favorite celebrity hangout for more than 60 years; wander Rodeo Drive on a sunny afternoon; stroll Melrose Avenue between La Brea and Fairfax during the dinner hour; stop by Tower Records on Sunset, especially if some blockbuster CD has just been released.

Although it's almost become an amusement-park thrill ride, Universal Studio's tour does give a good in-person approximation of the excitement you get from the movies, and, in the bargain, offers a fun look behind the scenes of filmmaking. Universal Studios aside, the business of Hollywood is making movies and getting people into theaters, not drumming up tourism for the town where it all started. And, besides, there are limits to what even movie magicians can do, especially in broad daylight. Given that the original appeal of Hollywood to moviemakers was the perpetual sunshine that allowed them to shoot outdoors on virtually any day of the year (and thereby make more movies and, therefore, more money) and the ready access to dozens of different landscapes, it is no small irony that over the years the most compelling reason to shoot a movie in Hollywood has become the ready access to soundstages in which the world (this one and others) can be re-created and the weather made to perform on cue. Hollywood has never hesitated to substitute reality with a more convenient or photogenic stand-in. This is an industry whose stock-in-trade is sleight of hand. Along with romance, car chases, and happy endings.

Whatever Hollywood is or isn't, I like the place just the way it is: flawed, scarred, energetic, and full of mysteries and contradictions. Living nearby and seeing it often haven't harmed my love of movies or taken any of the enchantment from the experience of sitting in a darkened theater and giving myself over to the doings on screen. After all, that's where to find the real Hollywood.

— Jane E. Lasky

IDYLLING IN SAN DIEGO

I'**VE NEVER BEEN TO** Sea World; performing fish give me the willies. And during the two years I lived within striking distance of Balboa Park, I had to take visiting friends to the zoo so many times I began having nightmares about koalas. But if I came to dislike various theme-park aspects of the city, I nevertheless loved San Diego. At first sight.

A typical easterner, I went out to San Diego in the late 1970s expecting to find a smaller version of Los Angeles. The freeways were there, along with a fair share of traffic congestion, but so was an oceanscape of surprisingly pristine beauty. The first drive I took from the University of California, where I was doing graduate research, knocked me for a loop: I rounded a curve on La Jolla Shores Drive to confront a coastline that could match any on the French Riviera.

I was also taken by the distinctiveness of the many shoreline communities. For one thing, the beaches tend to get funkier as you head south from the old-money enclave of La Jolla: Pacific Beach, with its Crystal Pier, is an aging Victorian resort taken over by teenagers while transients and surfers share the turf at Ocean Beach. To the north, Del Mar has a strip of shops that rival those of Rodeo Drive, and Carlsbad and Oceanside show the democratizing influence of nearby Camp Pendleton.

Unlike Los Angeles, San Diego is still strongly defined by its relationship to the ocean—to some degree by default. During the latter half of the 19th century, the town was banking on a rail link to the east. A building boom in the 1880s was largely based on the assumption that San Diego would become the western terminus of the Santa Fe Railroad line; the city hoped to compete with Los Angeles, which was already connected by rail to San Francisco and thus to the national railroad network. The link was completed in 1885, but it proved unsuccessful for a variety of reasons, including the placement of the line through Temecula Canyon, where 30 miles of track were washed out repeatedly in winter rainstorms. The Santa Fe soon moved its West Coast offices to San Bernardino and Los Angeles, and to this day there is no direct rail service from San Diego to the eastern part of the United States.

Instead, San Diego's future was sealed in 1908, when President Theodore Roosevelt's Great White Fleet stopped here on a world tour to demonstrate U.S. naval strength. The navy, impressed during that visit by the city's excellent harbor and temperate climate, decided to build a destroyer base on San Diego Bay in the 1920s; the newly developing aircraft industry soon followed (Charles Lindbergh's plane *Spirit of St. Louis* was built here). Over the years San Diego's economy became largely dependent on the military and its attendant enterprises, which provided jobs as well as a demand for local goods and services by those stationed here.

San Diego's character—conservative where Los Angeles's is cutting edge—was formed in large part by the presence of its military installations, which now occupy more than 165,000 acres of land in the area. And the city conducts most of its financial business in a single neighborhood, the district fronting San Diego Bay, in this way resembling New York more than its economic rival up the coast. San Diego has set some of its most prestigious scientific facilities on the water—Scripps Institute of Oceanography, naturally, but also Salk Institute. Jonas Salk didn't need the Pacific marine environment for his research, but his regular morning runs along Torrey Pines Beach no doubt cleared his head.

San Diego also has the ocean to thank for its near-perfect weather. A high-pressure system from the north Pacific is responsible for the city's sunshine and dry air; moderating breezes off the sea (caused by the water warming and cooling more slowly than the land) keep the summers relatively cool and the winters warm and help clear the air of pollution. In the late spring and early summer the difference between the earth and water temperatures generates coastal fogs. This phenomenon was another of San Diego's delightful surprises: I never tired of watching the mist roll in at night, wonderfully romantic, as thick as any I'd ever seen in London and easier to enjoy in the balmy air.

If I loved San Diego from the start, I had a hard time believing in its existence. It was difficult to imagine that a functioning American city could be so attractive, that people lived and worked in such a place every day. Although I'd never considered myself a Puritan, I quickly came to realize that I'd always assumed work and leisure environments had to be separate, that one was supposed to toil in unpleasant surroundings in order to earn the time spent in idyllic settings.

I found that I could get used to working on sunny days but that it was impossible to remain unaffected by the city's physical presence. Rampant nature conspires in a variety of ways to force you to let your guard down here. In northern East Coast cities, plants are generally orderly and prim: shrubs trimmed, roses demurely draped around railings, tulips set in proper rows. Even the famed cherry blossoms of Washington, D.C., are profuse in neat columns. In San Diego, the flora, whimsical at best, sometimes border on obscenity. The ubiquitous palms come in comedic pairs: short, squat trees that look like overgrown pineapples play Mutt to the Jeff of the tall, skinny variety. The aptly named bottle-brush bushes vie for attention with bright red flame trees, beaky orange birds-of-paradise, and rich purple bougainvillea spilling out over lush green lawns. Only in Hawaii had I previously encountered anthurium, a waxy red plant with a protruding white center that seems to be sticking its tongue out at you. "We're still on the mainland," I felt like telling them all on some days: "Behave yourselves."

RONICALLY, it was the Victorians who were largely responsible for this indecorous natural profusion. Difficult as it is to imagine now, it's the sparse brown vegetation of San Diego's undeveloped mesas that accurately reflects the climate of the region, technically a semiarid steppe. When Spanish explorer Juan Rodríguez Cabrillo sailed into San Diego Bay in 1542, looking for a shortcut to China, he and his crew encountered a barren, desolate landscape that did not inspire them to settle here, or even stop for very long.

It wasn't until the late 19th century, when the Mediterranean in general and Italy in particular were all the rage among wealthy residents, that the vegetation now considered characteristic of southern California was introduced to San Diego. In 1889, money raised by the Ladies Annex to the Chamber of Commerce was used to plant trees in Balboa Park, and between 1892 and 1903 a wide variety of exotic foliage was brought into the city: eucalyptus, cork oak, and rubber trees, to name a few. As homeowners in the area can attest, most of the landscaped local vegetation couldn't survive if it were not watered regularly.

No doubt both the natural setting and the relentlessly fine weather help contribute to the clash of cultures that exists here. The conservative traditionalism of the military presence in town is posed against the liberal hedonism of visiting sun seekers, as well as a large local student population. Nude bathing is popular at Black's Beach in La Jolla, a spot that's reasonably private because it's fairly inaccessible. You have to hike down steep cliffs in order to get to the water. Rumor has it that every year a few navy men are killed when they lose their footing on the cliffs, so intent are they at peering through their binoculars.

But I suspect it's the rare person of any political persuasion who can confront the southern California attitude toward nudity with equanimity. I hadn't wanted to believe all the stereotypes, but the first time I went to a dinner party in town, the host asked the group if we wanted to adjourn to the hot tub after we ate. I hadn't brought my bathing suit, so I declined.

The next day, I consulted a local expert about whirlpool etiquette. "What does one do?" I asked. "Undress in front of a group of relative strangers and jump into the water with them? Does one rip off one's clothes with abandon? Fold them carefully afterward? Or go into another room and come out in the raw?" "All that's up to the individual," she answered. "Do whatever you feel comfortable with." "None of it," I asserted. "Where I come from, when people of different genders take their clothes off together, they tend to have sex." "That's optional, too," she said.

Nods to certain So-Cal conventions notwithstanding, San Diego has never come close to approaching the much-touted libertinism of Los Angeles. It has the porno theaters and sleazy clubs you'd expect in a liberty port, but little entertainment of a more sophisticated nature. Celebrities who came down from Hollywood in the 1920s and '30s sought out suites at the La Valencia Hotel and other chic La Jolla locales for the privacy, not the nightlife; the gambling they did at Del Mar racetrack to the north was of the genteel sort. Those who sought thrills—and booze during Prohibition—headed farther south, to Mexico. Raymond Chandler, who spent most of his last 13 years in La Jolla and died there in 1959, wrote a friend that the town was "a nice place . . . for old people and their parents."

FOR ALL ITS conservatism, the one thing San Diego didn't conserve was its past—in some cases because there was little to save. When Father Junípero Serra arrived in 1769 to establish the first of the California missions, he did not find the complex dwellings that characterized so many of the Native American settlements he had encountered in Mexico. Nor did his fellow Spaniards improve much upon the site during their stay; the town that the Mexicans took over in 1822 was rudimentary, consisting mostly of rough adobe huts. The mission church had been moved to a new site in 1774, and the original Spanish presidio, abandoned in the 1830s, was in ruins by the next decade; some grass-covered mounds and a giant cross built in 1913 on Presidio Hill, incorporating the tiles of the original structure, are all that's left of it.

Though a romanticized version of the city during the Mexican period (1822–49), today's Old Town district gives a rough idea of San Diego's layout at that time, when somewhat more impressive structures, such as Casa Estudillo and the Bandini House, were built. San Diego didn't really begin to flourish, however, until 1850, the year that California became a state. At that point the dominant architectural influence came from the East Coast; their enthusiasm for becoming American caused San Diegans to reject their Spanish and Mexican roots as inappropriately "foreign." Thus the first brick structure in the state, the Whaley House (1856), was built in typical New England nautical style. Most of the original Old Town was destroyed by fire in 1872, and a good deal of what was left fell victim to the construction of I–5.

During the Victorian era (1880–1905), the site of the city's development moved south; entrepreneur Alonzo Horton may have miscalculated the success of the rail link to the East Coast, but when he bought up a huge lot of land in 1867 for his "Addition," he knew the city's future lay on the harbor. It was in this area, now the city's financial district, that many of the neo-Gothic structures characteristic of the period were built. Perhaps it's perversely fitting that a number of the Victorian relics in downtown San Diego were removed in conjunction with the 15-block Horton Redevelopment Project, of which the huge Horton Plaza shopping complex is the center.

San Diego finally began to reject the East Coast architectural style at the turn of the century, and at the Panama–California International Exposition of 1915 the city celebrated its Spanish roots—as well as a Moroccan and Italian past it never had—with a vengeance. The beautiful Spanish-style structures built for the occasion fit right into the Mediterranean landscape that had been cultivated in Balboa Park during the Victorian era; today these buildings house most of the city's museums. San Diego became even more thoroughly Hispanicized during the 1920s and '30s as Spanish colonial–style homes became popular in new suburbs, such as Mission Hills and Kensington, as well as in the beach communities that were developing. Downtown buildings began looking like Italian palaces and Moorish towers.

San Diego's landscape of ravines and hills is partly responsible for the city's sprawling development in the 20th century, and the popularization of the automobile in the 1930s helped ensure its continuing growth in an outward direction. The physical barriers have been overcome by an ever-expanding highway system—though not by a viable public transportation network—but the discrete, individual neighborhoods created by them remain, if their populations sometimes shift. For example, Kearny Mesa, formerly a middle-class suburban neighborhood, is now one of the many Southeast Asian communities in the city.

In some ways, as residents and visitors alike have long feared, San Diego is coming to look more like Los Angeles. Faceless developments are cropping up all over once-deserted canyons and mesas, and the huge, castlelike Mormon temple built along I–5 north of La Jolla wouldn't look out of place in Disneyland. But in the years since I lived there, San Diego has also become more like a city—that is, what easterners know to be the city in its divinely ordained form.

As recently as the early 1980s, virtually no one went downtown unless required to. It was a desolate place after dark, and people who worked there during the day never stayed around in the evening to play. Gentrification of sorts began in the mid-1970s, as the low rents attracted artists and real-estate speculators. At about the same time the city designated the formerly rough Stingaree neighborhood as the Gaslamp Quarter, but revitalization, in the form of street-level shops and art galleries, didn't really take until Horton Plaza was completed in 1985. For many years the newly installed gaslights illuminated only the homeless.

The poor and disenfranchised are still here—indeed, many lost their homes to various redevelopment projects—but now there's a concentration of good restaurants, and a serious art and theater scene is developing in the district, too. The area is also a terminus for the San Diego Trolley. This inexpensive transportation link to Mexico has, among other things, allowed Mexican artists to bring their works to a wider market and fostered a cultural as well as a touristic exchange with Tijuana, which has cleaned up its own act considerably in recent years.

I like the infusion of life into downtown San Diego, and I even like Horton Plaza, which, with its odd angles and colorful banners, looks like it was designed by Alice in Wonderland's Red Queen. But maybe I miss that spot of unadulterated blight that once helped me to believe in San Diego's reality.

Reality seems to be setting in on a large scale these days. San Diego's bad neighborhoods still don't look like slums as I know them, but gang-related crime is on the increase in the southeast part of the city. In recent years, sewage spills have closed a number of southern beaches, and the problem is likely to grow, since neither San Diego nor Tijuana has enacted any large-scale programs for effective waste disposal. Friends tell me that even the weather is changing for the worse, a fact they attribute to global warming.

Would I move back to San Diego? In a minute. Like many other temporary residents, I left the city vowing to return; unlike many others, I've never managed to do more than visit. I used to think that if I had the chance I'd live in Hillcrest, a close-knit inland community with lots of ethnic restaurants and theaters that show foreign films, but I've come to realize that would only be transplanting my East Coast life into the sun. Now I think I'll wait until I'm rich and can afford to move to La Jolla; no doubt I'll be old enough by then to fit in, so I'll fully enjoy that suite in the La Valencia Hotel overlooking the cove.

— Edie Jarolim

BOOKS AND VIDEOS

San Francisco

BOOKS> Many novels are set in San Francisco, but none come better than *The Maltese Falcon,* by Dashiell Hammett, the founder of the hard-boiled school of detective fiction. *The Barbary Coast: An Informal History of San the Francisco Underworld,* published in 1933 and still in print, is Herbert Asbury's searing look at life in what really was a wicked city before the turn of the century. Another standout is Vikram Seth's *Golden Gate,* a novel in verse about life in San Francisco and Marin County in the early '80s. Others are John Gregory Dunne's recent *The Red White and Blue,* and Alice Adams's *Rich Rewards.*

Two books that are filled with interesting background information on the city are Richard H. Dillon's *San Francisco: Adventurers and Visionaries* and *San Francisco: As It Is, As It Was,* by Paul C. Johnson and Richard Reinhardt.

Armistead Maupin's soap-opera-style *Tales of the City* stories are set in San Francisco; they were made into a successful 1993 PBS series.

VIDEOS➤ *San Francisco*, starring Clark Gable and Jeanette MacDonald, re-creates the 1906 earthquake with outstanding special effects. In *Escape from Alcatraz*, Clint Eastwood plays the prisoner who allegedly escaped from the famous jail on a rock in the San Francisco Bay. *The Times of Harvey Milk*, about San Francisco's first openly gay elected official, won the Academy Award for best documentary feature in 1984. Alfred Hitchcock immortalized Mission Dolores and the Golden Gate Bridge in *Vertigo*, the eerie story of a detective with a fear of heights, starring Jimmy Stewart and Kim Novak. A few other noteworthy films shot in San Francisco are *Dark Passage*, with Humphrey Bogart; the 1978 remake of *Invasion of the Body Snatchers*; and the 1993 comedy *Mrs. Doubtfire*, starring Robin Williams.

Los Angeles

BOOKS➤ *Los Angeles: The Enormous Village, 1781–1981*, by John D. Weaver, and *Los Angeles: Biography of a City*, by John and LaRee Caughey, will give you a fine background in how it came to be the city it is today. The unique social and cultural life of the whole southern California area is explored in *Southern California: An Island on the Land*, by Carey McWilliams.

One of the most outstanding features of Los Angeles is its architecture. *Los Angeles: The Architecture of Four Ecologies*, by Reyner Banham, relates the physical environment to the architecture. *Architecture in Los Angeles: A Compleat Guide*, by David Gebhard and Robert Winter, is exactly what the title promises and is very useful.

Many novels have been written with Los Angeles as the setting. One of the very best, Nathanael West's *Day of the Locust*, was first published in 1939, but still rings true. Budd Schulberg's *What Makes Sammy Run?*, Evelyn Waugh's *The Loved One*, and Joan Didion's *Play It As It Lays* are unforgettable. Other novels that give a sense of contemporary life in Los Angeles are *Sex and Rage*, by Eve Babitz, and *Less Than Zero*, by Bret Easton Ellis. Raymond Chandler and Ross Macdonald have written many suspense novels with a Los Angeles background.

VIDEOS AND TV➤ *Day of the Locust* and *Play It As It Lays* were made into two of the grimmer cinematic portraits of life in Los Angeles. Billy Wilder's *Sunset Boulevard* is a classic portrait of a faded star and her attempt to recapture past glory. Roman Polanski's *Chinatown*, arguably one of the best American films ever made, is a fictional account of the wheeling and dealing that helped make L.A. what it is today. Southern California's varied urban and rural landscapes are used to great effect (as is an all-star cast that includes Ethel Merman and Spencer Tracy) in Stanley Kramer's manic *It's a Mad, Mad, Mad, Mad World*.

San Diego

BOOKS➤ There is no better way to establish the mood for your visit to Old Town San Diego than by reading Helen Hunt Jackson's 105-year-old romantic novel, *Ramona*, a best-seller for more than 50 years and still readily available. The Casa de Estudillo in Old Town has been known for many years as Ramona's Marriage Place because of its close resemblance to the house described in the novel. Richard Henry Dana Jr.'s *Two Years Before the Mast* (1869), based on the author's experiences as a merchant sailor, provides a masculine perspective on early San Diego history.

Other novels with a San Diego setting include Raymond Chandler's mystery about the waterfront, *Playback;* Wade Miller's mystery, *On Easy Street;* Eric Higgs's gothic thriller, *A Happy Man;* Tom Wolfe's satire of the La Jolla surfing scene, *The Pump House Gang;* and David Zielinski's modern-day story, *A Genuine Monster*.

VIDEOS AND TV➤ Filmmakers have taken advantage of San Diego's diverse and amiable climate since the dawn of cinema. Westerns, comedy-westerns, and tales of the sea were early staples: *Cupid in Chaps, The Sagebrush Phrenologist* (how's that for a title?), the 1914 version of *The Virginian*, and Lon Chaney's *Tell It to the Marines* were among the silent films shot in the area. Easy-to-capture outdoor locales have lured many productions south from Hollywood over the years, including the following military-oriented talkies, all or part of which were shot in San Diego: James Cagney's *Here Comes the Navy* (1934), Errol Flynn's *Dive Bomber* (1941), John Wayne's *The Sands of Iwo Jima* (1949), Ronald Reagan's *Hellcats of the Navy* (1956, costarring Nancy Davis, the future First Lady), Rock Hudson's *Ice Station Zebra* (1967), Tom Cruise's *Top Gun*

(1986), Sean Connery's *Hunt for Red October* and Charlie Sheen's *Navy Seals* (1990), and Danny Glover's *Flight of the Intruder* (1991). Rob Lowe did not make his infamous home videos here, but he did shoot some of *Desert Shield* (1991).

In a lighter military vein, the famous talking mule hit the high seas in *Francis Joins the Navy* (1955), in which a very young Clint Eastwood has a bit part. The Tom Hanks–Darryl Hannah hit *Splash* (1984), *Spaceballs* (1987), *Hot Shots* (1991), *Wayne's World II* (1993), and Ellen Degeneres's *Mr. Wrong* (1996) are more recent comedies with scenes filmed here. The city has a cameo role in the minihit *Flirting with Disaster* (1996), and one of the best comedies ever made, director Billy Wilder's *Some Like It Hot*—starring Marilyn Monroe, Jack Lemmon, and Tony Curtis—takes place at the famous Hotel Del Coronado (standing in for a Miami resort).

The amusingly low-budget *Attack of the Killer Tomatoes* (1976) makes good use of local scenery—and the infamous San Diego Chicken. The producers must have liked what they found in town as they returned for three sequels: *Return of the Killer Tomatoes* (1988), *Killer Tomatoes Strike Back* (1990), and—proving just how versatile the region is as a film location—*Killer Tomatoes Go to France* (1991). Unlike many films in which San Diego itself doesn't figure in the plot, the screen version of Helen Hunt Jackson's novel *Ramona* (1936) starring Loretta Young as the title character, incorporated historical settings (or replicas).

Television producers zip south for series and made-for-TV movies all the time. The alteration of San Diego's skyline in the 1980s was partially documented on the hit show *Simon & Simon*. San Diego is virtually awash in syndicated productions: *Silk Stalkings, Baywatch, High Tide,* and *Renegade* all shoot here. Reality and cop shows love the area, too: *Unsolved Mysteries,* *Rescue 911, America's Missing Children, Totally Hidden Video, America's Most Wanted,* and *America's Funniest People* have all taped in San Diego, making it one of the most-seen—yet often uncredited—locales in movie- and videoland.

Around the State

BOOKS➤ John Steinbeck immortalized the Monterey-Salinas area in numerous books, including *Cannery Row* and *East of Eden*. Joan Didion captured the heat—solar, political, and otherwise—of the Sacramento Delta area in *Run River*. Mark Twain's *Roughing It* and Bret Harte's *The Luck of Roaring Camp* evoke life during the Gold Rush.

VIDEOS AND TV➤ Steinbeck's *East of Eden* was a hit film starring James Dean and later a television movie; both are on video now. Buster Keaton's masterpiece *Steamboat Bill, Jr.* was shot in Sacramento. The cult favorite *Harold and Maude* takes place in the San Francisco Bay Area. The exteriors in Alfred Hitchcock's *Shadow of a Doubt* were shot in Santa Rosa, and his ultracreepy *The Birds* was shot in Bodega Bay, along the North Coast. *Shack Out on 101* is a loopy 1950s beware-the-Commies caper also set on the California coast.

Erich von Stroheim used a number of northern California locations for his films: *Greed* takes place in San Francisco but includes excursions to Oakland and other points in the East Bay. Carmel is one of the locations for his *Foolish Wives*. As we note in the Mojave Desert chapter, the various *Star Trek* movies and Michelangelo Antonioni's *Zabriskie Point* are among the features that have made use of the eastern desert region. Initial footage of Sam Peckinpah's western *Ride the High Country* was shot in the Sierra Nevada mountains before his studio yanked him back to southern California, where he blended the original shots with ones of the Santa Monica Mountains and the Hollywood Hills.

INDEX

NOTES

NOTES

NOTES

NOTES

NOTES

NOTES

NOTES

What's hot, where it's hot!

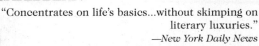

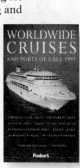

Escape to ancient cities and exotic

islands  *with CNN Travel Guide, a*

wealth of valuable advice. Host Valerie Voss will take you

to all of your favorite destinations,

including those off the beaten path.

Tune into your passport to the world.

CNN TRAVEL GUIDE
SATURDAY 12:30 PM ET   SUNDAY 4:30 PM ET

CNN✈
Airport Network

Your
Window
To The
World
While You're
On The
Road

Keep in touch when you're traveling. Before you take off, tune in to CNN Airport Network. Now available in major airports across America, CNN Airport Network provides nonstop news, sports, business, weather and lifestyle programming. Both domestic and international. All piloted by the top-flight global resources of CNN. All up-to-the minute reporting. And just for travelers, CNN Airport Network features two daily Fodor's specials. "Travel Fact" provides enlightening, useful travel trivia, while "What's Happening" covers upcoming events in major cities worldwide. So why be bored waiting to board? TIME FLIES WHEN YOU'RE WATCHING THE WORLD THROUGH THE WINDOW OF CNN AIRPORT NETWORK!

Fodor's Travel Publications

Available at bookstores everywhere, or call 1–800–533–6478, 24 hours a day.

Gold Guides

U.S.

Alaska

Arizona

Boston

California

Cape Cod, Martha's Vineyard, Nantucket

The Carolinas & the Georgia Coast

Chicago

Colorado

Florida

Hawai'i

Las Vegas, Reno, Tahoe

Los Angeles

Maine, Vermont, New Hampshire

Maui & Lāna'i

Miami & the Keys

New England

New Orleans

New York City

Pacific North Coast

Philadelphia & the Pennsylvania Dutch Country

The Rockies

San Diego

San Francisco

Santa Fe, Taos, Albuquerque

Seattle & Vancouver

The South

U.S. & British Virgin Islands

USA

Virginia & Maryland

Washington, D.C.

Foreign

Australia

Austria

The Bahamas

Belize & Guatemala

Bermuda

Canada

Cancún, Cozumel, Yucatán Peninsula

Caribbean

China

Costa Rica

Cuba

The Czech Republic & Slovakia

Eastern & Central Europe

Europe

Florence, Tuscany & Umbria

France

Germany

Great Britain

Greece

Hong Kong

India

Ireland

Israel

Italy

Japan

London

Madrid & Barcelona

Mexico

Montréal & Québec City

Moscow, St. Petersburg, Kiev

The Netherlands, Belgium & Luxembourg

New Zealand

Norway

Nova Scotia, New Brunswick, Prince Edward Island

Paris

Portugal

Provence & the Riviera

Scandinavia

Scotland

Singapore

South Africa

South America

Southeast Asia

Spain

Sweden

Switzerland

Thailand

Tokyo

Toronto

Turkey

Vienna & the Danube

Fodor's Special-Interest Guides

Caribbean Ports of Call

The Complete Guide to America's National Parks

Family Adventures

Gay Guide to the USA

Halliday's New England Food Explorer

Halliday's New Orleans Food Explorer

Healthy Escapes

Kodak Guide to Shooting Great Travel Pictures

Net Travel

Nights to Imagine

Rock & Roll Traveler USA

Sunday in New York

Sunday in San Francisco

Walt Disney World, Universal Studios and Orlando

Walt Disney World for Adults

Where Should We Take the Kids? California

Where Should We Take the Kids? Northeast

Worldwide Cruises and Ports of Call

Fodor's
Special Series

Affordables

Caribbean

Europe

Florida

France

Germany

Great Britain

Italy

London

Paris

**Fodor's Bed &
Breakfasts and
Country Inns**

America

California

The Mid-Atlantic

New England

The Pacific
Northwest

The South

The Southwest

The Upper Great
Lakes

The Berkeley Guides

California

Central America

Eastern Europe

Europe

France

Germany & Austria

Great Britain
& Ireland

Italy

London

Mexico

New York City

Pacific Northwest
& Alaska

Paris

San Francisco

**Compass American
Guides**

Arizona

Canada

Chicago

Colorado

Hawaii

Idaho

Hollywood

Las Vegas

Maine

Manhattan

Montana

New Mexico

New Orleans

Oregon

San Francisco

Santa Fe

South Carolina

South Dakota

Southwest

Texas

Utah

Virginia

Washington

Wine Country

Wisconsin

Wyoming

Fodor's Citypacks

Atlanta

Hong Kong

London

New York City

Paris

Rome

San Francisco

Washington, D.C.

Fodor's Español

California

Caribe Occidental

Caribe Oriental

Gran Bretaña

Londres

Mexico

Nueva York

Paris

**Fodor's Exploring
Guides**

Australia

Boston &
New England

Britain

California

Caribbean

China

Egypt

Florence & Tuscany

Florida

France

Germany

Ireland

Israel

Italy

Japan

London

Mexico

Moscow & St.
Petersburg

New York City

Paris

Prague

Provence

Rome

San Francisco

Scotland

Singapore & Malaysia

Spain

Thailand

Turkey

Venice

Fodor's Flashmaps

Boston

New York

San Francisco

Washington, D.C.

**Fodor's Pocket
Guides**

Acapulco

Atlanta

Barbados

Jamaica

London

New York City

Paris

Prague

Puerto Rico

Rome

San Francisco

Washington, D.C.

Mobil Travel Guides

America's Best
Hotels & Restaurants

California & the West

Frequent Traveler's
Guide to Major Cities

Great Lakes

Mid-Atlantic

Northeast

Northwest & Great
Plains

Southeast

Southwest & South
Central

Rivages Guides

Bed and Breakfasts
of Character and
Charm in France

Hotels and Country
Inns of Character and
Charm in France

Hotels and Country
Inns of Character and
Charm in Italy

Hotels and Country
Inns of Character and
Charm in Paris

Hotels and Country
Inns of Character and
Charm in Portugal

Hotels and Country
Inns of Character and
Charm in Spain

Short Escapes

Britain

France

New England

Near New York City

Fodor's Sports

Golf Digest's Best
Places to Play

Skiing USA

USA Today
The Complete Four
Sport Stadium Guide

**Fodor's Vacation
Planners**

Great American
Learning Vacations

Great American
Sports & Adventure
Vacations

Great American
Vacations

Great American
Vacations for
Travelers with
Disabilities

National Parks and
Seashores of the East

National Parks of
the West

WHEREVER YOU TRAVEL, *H*ELP IS NEVER FAR AWAY.

From planning your trip to

providing travel assistance along

the way, American Express®

Travel Service Offices are

always there to help.

For the office nearest you in California, call
1-800-YES-AMEX.